biztantra
Management for the Flat World!

HOUGHTON MIFFLIN

A Note for the Reader

Introducing the "GLOCAL" TEXT *Editions from Biztantra, the next level of adaptation publishing for the student community*

India has been a beacon of progress and foreign investment in the recent years. We have been growing at a rate of over 8% annually in our GDP estimates. With almost all of the Fortune 500 companies setting up operations in our country, the need and demand for management students is reaching an all-time high. In order to meet this growing need, all leading management institutes are instilling the approach of "Glocal" education – i.e. Global + Local perspectives.

In 2004, Biztantra and Houghton Mifflin (HMCo) published India's first ever adaptation program covering the entire spectrum of management education. It is a matter of pride that over 100,000 management students have embraced our product line since its launch. It is also gratifying to know that the Indian Institutes of Management have also adopted these adaptations.

We have been researching the need for Indian content in foreign textbooks for over four years. We believe that Indian students are now much more sophisticated, globally aware, and cognizant of the global brands and companies, compared to just a few years ago. Equally important, these students are aware of the Indian companies which are making rapid strides on the global scene.

To meet the needs of these students, we at Biztantra and HMCo are now pleased to introduce the first ever *Glocal Texts* range in India. This is another testament to Biztantra's innovative team and its strong partnership with Boston-based Houghton Mifflin Co. HMCo is a leader in academic publishing in the US with revenues of over $1.3 US billion. The *Glocal Texts* are Indian adaptations of these HMCo textbooks with the right blend of both Indian and International case studies. The *Glocal Texts* give Indian students the right mix of what needs to be learnt from Indian companies as well as imbibing the wisdom of global corporations. Hence, it will be a textbook range with a "Glocal Perspective".

It is a matter of pleasure that the works of world's leading academicians and celebrated authors such as A Parasuraman, Ricky Griffin, Charles Hill, Gareth Jones will be published under the *Glocal Texts* range.

These titles will be adapted by a team of highly capable Indian professors taken from IIM Bangalore, Indian Institute of Foreign Trade and International Management Institute to name a few. At the same time we have also recruited young and budding academicians who are from a select group of private MBA institutes in order to bridge the gap between the top 10 and the upcoming institutions of tomorrow.

The first set of books will cover the areas of Strategic Management, Financial Accounting, Marketing Research, OB, Consumer Behavior, Microeconomics, Global Marketing and International Management. Other areas too will shortly follow.

We sincerely hope that the *Glocal Texts* will touch a chord with Indian students and might redefine management learning. We would be happy to receive your comments and suggestions and ideas at rahul@dreamtechbt.com.

Best regards,

Rahul Gupta
CEO, Biztantra

Timothy J. Cullen
Manager (Rights & International Business)
Houghton Mifflin Company

Tools to Enhance the Learning Experience . . .

Chapter Opening Cases

Each chapter begins with a case scenario about an actual company, product, or situation that illustrates key concepts discussed in the chapter.

Ch. 1 Bajaj: Truly Hamara Bajaj
Ch. 2 Exploring the Indian Affluent
Ch. 3 Hyundai Santro: The Sun(rise)shine Car
Ch. 4 Product Placement Grows More Prominent
Ch. 5 Making the Apple iPod Iconic
Ch. 6 Cadbury's Dairy Milk Pass Ho Gaya
Ch. 7 The Indian Whisky Market: Make it Large
Ch. 8 McDonald's Pricing Reminisces Memory
Ch. 9 Mouthshut.com: Compare and Contrast
Ch. 10 Housing Boom in India
Ch. 11 Food Retail in India gets organised
Ch. 12 ICICI Bank: Hum Hai Naa
Ch. 13 McDonald's India: I am loving it
Ch. 14 The Rising Indian Middle Class
Ch. 15 Surf Excel: Never have stains been so welcome
Ch. 16 Hum Tum: Creating Buzz through Hum and Tum
Ch. 17 The Telecom Boom takes over India
Ch. 18 Ka-ching! Consumers Buy (and Sell) Special Somethings on eBay
Ch. 19 There is a Pesticide in my Cola
Ch. 20 Is Your Personal Data Private? Is It Safe?

Marketing Implications Sections

For every major concept discussed, Marketing Implications sections show how consumer behavior applies to the practice of marketing, including such basic marketing functions as market segmentation, target market selection, positioning, market research, promotion, price, product, and place decisions.

Emphasis on Globalization and E-Commerce

Interwoven throughout the text are many cross-cultural examples as well as information on how the Internet has impacted consumer behavior. The wealth of these examples throughout the text emphasizes the text's practical and contemporary orientation.

Current and Cutting Edge Coverage

In addition to providing a balanced perspective, including both psychological (micro) and sociological (macro) topics on the field of consumer behavior, the text provides the most up-to-date research possible. This includes several novel chapters that often do not appear in other textbooks: "Symbolic Consumer Behavior," "Knowledge and Understanding," and "The Dark Side of Consumer Behavior and Marketing."

Conceptual Model Provides the "Big Picture"

Students learn best when they see the "big picture"—when they understand what the concepts mean and how they relate to each other. The conceptual model used in Hoyer and MacInnis's ***Consumer Behavior,*** Fourth Edition, allows students to see how the chapters and the topics in the book are interrelated and interdependent. This organizing scheme makes the chapters more integrative and helps students see how the many different aspects of consumer behavior "fit together."

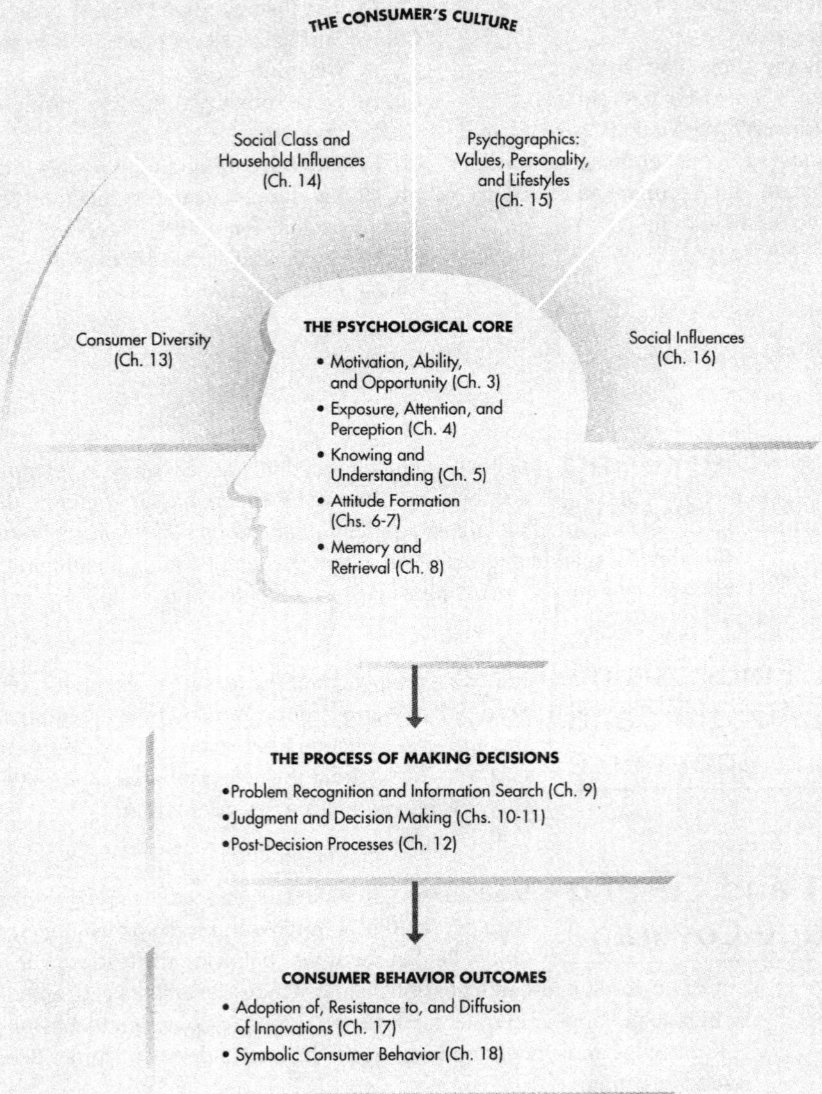

Consumer Behavior

About the Authors

Wayne D. Hoyer

Wayne D. Hoyer is the James L. Bayless/William S. Farrish Fund Chair for Free Enterprise, Chairman of the Department of Marketing, and Director of the Center for Customer Insight in the McCombs School of Business at the University of Texas at Austin. He received his Ph.D. in Consumer Psychology from Purdue University in 1980. Wayne has published over 60 articles in various publications including the *Journal of Consumer Research, Journal of Marketing, Journal of Marketing Research, Journal of Advertising Research*, and *Journal of Retailing.* A 1998 article in the *Journal of Marketing Research* (with Susan Broniarczyk and Leigh McAlister) won the O'Dell Award in 2003 for the article that had the most impact in the marketing field over that five year period. In addition to *Consumer Behavior*, he has co-authored two books on the topic of advertising miscomprehension. Dr. Hoyer's research interests include consumer information processing and decision making (especially low-involvement decision making), customer relationship management, and advertising effects (particularly miscomprehension and the impact of humor). He is a former associate editor for the *Journal of Consumer Research* and serves on the editorial review boards of the *Journal of Marketing, Journal of Consumer Research, International Journal of Research in Marketing*, and the *Journal of Public Policy and Marketing.* Dr. Hoyer is a member of the American Psychological Association, the Association for Consumer Research, and the American Marketing Association. His major areas of teaching include consumer behavior, customer strategy, and marketing communications.

Deborah J. MacInnis

Debbie MacInnis is Chairperson and Professor of Marketing at the University of Southern California in Los Angeles, CA. She received her Ph.D. in marketing from the University of Pittsburgh in 1986. She also holds a B.S. degree in psychology from Smith College. Debbie has published papers in the *Journal of Consumer Research, Journal of Marketing Research, Journal of Marketing, Marketing Science, Journal of Advertising, Journal of Advertising Research, and Journal of Personality and Social Psychology* in the areas of marketing communications, information processing, imagery, emotions, and brand images. She has served as Associate Editor of the *Journal of Consumer Research* and the *Journal of Consumer Psychology.* She has also served as a member of the editorial review boards of the *Journal of Consumer Research, Journal of Marketing Research, Journal of Marketing, Journal of the Academy of Marketing Sciences, International Journal of Internet Marketing and Advertising, Journal of Market Focused Management*, and the *Journal of Consumer Behaviour.* She has won Outstanding Reviewer Awards for her reviewing efforts on behalf of the *Journal of Marketing, Journal of Marketing Research, Journal of Consumer Research* and the *Journal of the Academy of Marketing Sciences.* She has served as President of the Association for Consumer Research, and has served that organization as Treasurer and conference co-chair. She has also served as Vice President of Conferences and Research for the Academic Council of the American Marketing Association and is a member of the AMA Knowledge Development Coalition. Debbie is a recipient of the Alpha Kappa Psi award, an honor awarded to the best paper published in the *Journal of Marketing.* Her research has also been selected as a finalist for the Practice Prize Competition, which is awarded to a paper that significantly contributes to the practice of marketing by virtue of its rigor and relevance. She has received the Teaching Innovation Award from the Marshall School of Business and has been named as a Faculty Fellow at USC's Center for Excellence in Teaching. Her classes have won national awards through the SAA National Advertising Competition. Debbie's major areas of teaching include consumer behavior, integrated marketing communications, and marketing management. Debbie lives in Los Angeles with her husband, two children, and three pets.

About the Indian Adaptor

Pinaki Dasgupta

Dr. Pinaki Dasgupta is Associate Professor at the Indian Institute of Foreign Trade (IIFT). Before his current stint at IIFT he was in the corporate sector and worked for seven years in the advertising industry for Rediffusion DY & R and Mudra Group. During his industry tenure, Dr Dasgupta had the opportunity to work closely with brands like Airtel, Canon, U.P. Tourism, The Taj group and Andrew Yule (Tea Division). With over seven years of academic experience now, moving from the corporate sector in 1998, Dr Dasgupta specializes in Consumer Behavior and Strategic Brand Management. At IIFT he is involved in teaching, training and consultancy. He has been working on Brand Maruti for the last four years, largely in the area of brand and product related issues. Dr. Dasgupta is also associated with several other institutions in development of course work and pedagogical activities. His teaching assignments involve both domestic and international assignments, which is mainly an outcome of IIFT's academic collaborations with IFM- Tanzania. IIFT's association with the government and it's origin being Ministry of Commerce, Dr. Dasgupta has completed a large number of trade and marketing related sponsored research, for the Ministry of Textiles, Ministry of Commerce, Ministry of External Affairs, India Trade Promotion Organization (ITPO) and Indian Ocean Rim (IOR). Dr. Dasgupta has been a regular panel speaker in the vernacular MDP programmes of the Institute also.

Consumer Behavior

4TH EDITION (Glocal Text)

Wayne D. Hoyer
University of Texas at Austin

Deborah J. MacInnis
University of Southern California

Indian Adaptor

Pinaki Dasgupta
Indian Institute of Foreign Trade (IIFT), New Delhi

biztantra
Management for the Flat World!
19-A, Ansari Road, Daryaganj, Delhi-110002

Houghton Mifflin Company   Boston   New York

This edition has been published by arrangement with the **Houghton Mifflin Co., USA** and published in India by **Biztantra, An Imprint of Dreamtech Press, 19-A, Ansari Road, Daryaganj, New Delhi-110002.**

ISBN (10): 81-7722-754-8
(13): 978-81-7722-754-3

Edition : 2008

Printed at : Himal Impressions, 168, Raja Garden, New Delhi.

Brief Contents

Contents

PART 1 An Introduction to Consumer Behavior

PART 2 The Psychological Core

PART 3 The Process of Making Decisions

11 Judgement and Decision Making Based on Low Consumer Effort 261

12 Post-Decision Processes 287

PART 4 The Consumer's Culture

PART 5 Consumer Behavior Outcomes

PART 6 Consumer Welfare

Preface to the Original Edition

At just about every moment of our lives, we engage in some form of consumer behavior. When we watch an ad on TV, talk to friends about a movie we just saw, brush our teeth, go to a ball game, buy a new CD, or even throw away an old pair of shoes, we are behaving as a consumer. In fact, being a consumer reaches into every part of our lives.

Given its omnipresence, the study of consumer behavior has critical implications for areas such as marketing, public policy, and ethics. It also helps us learn about ourselves—why we buy certain things, why we use them in a certain way, and how we get rid of them.

In this book we explore the fascinating world of consumer behavior, looking at a number of interesting and exciting topics. Some of these are quickly identified with our typical image of consumer behavior. Others may be surprising. We hope you will see why we became stimulated and drawn to this topic from the very moment we had our first consumer behavior course as students. We hope you will also appreciate why we choose to make this field our life's work, and why we developed and continue to remain committed to the writing of this textbook.

Why the New Edition of This Book?

There are a number of consumer behavior books in the market. An important question concerns what this book has to offer and what distinguishes it from other texts? As active researchers in the field of consumer behavior, our overriding goal is to continue providing a treatment of the field that is up-to-date and cutting edge. There has been an explosion of research on a variety of consumer behavior topics over the last twenty years. Our primary aim is to provide a useful summary of this material for students of marketing. However, in drawing on cutting edge research, we wanted to be careful to not become too "academic." Instead, our objective is to present cutting edge topics in a manner that is accessible and easy for students to understand.

The fourth edition of the text includes these changes and improvements:

- The text has been made shorter and more streamlined so that the material is easier for students to process.
- The conceptual model that guides our book is a strong feature that differentiates our book from others on the market. In this edition we have made it more visually prominent to more clearly show how the various topics of consumer behavior relate to one another. It also serves as a strong organizing feature of the book, helping students see exactly where the current chapter fits into a larger set of topics.
- New to this edition is a set of learning objectives that preview each chapter. These learning objectives indicate the key content areas of each chapter and will help guide students' conceptual orientation.
- New opening cases focus on Swatch, P&G, ING Direct, iPod, George Foreman, Ford, Shopping.com, McDonald's, eBay, KFC, Southwest Airlines, beer advertising, product placement, consumer behavior in China, consumer behavior in Thailand, consumer behavior in Korea, buzz marketing, and identity theft.
- The Marketing Implications sections clearly demonstrate how theory meets the real world in practical terms. These sections appear more prominently in this

edition and have been expanded and updated to show students how chapter concepts apply to the strategy and practice of marketing.

- In this edition, we restructured the key topical areas relating to macro-level issues into two streamlined chapters: "Consumer Diversity," which examines how age, gender, sexual orientation, region, ethnicity, and religion impact on consumer behavior and "Social Class and Household Influences," which examines these influences on acquisition, consumption, and disposition decisions.
- Coverage of Internet-related consumer behavior issues has been expanded, and new web addresses have been added to help students understand key examples and illustrations of concepts.
- Coverage of the latest research from the academic field of consumer behavior has been added to every chapter. We have included the new AMA definition of marketing, new information related to environmental issues (such as recycling), the latest research on the effects of memory and retrieval, the values that characterize Western culture, and the effect of specific personality characteristics on consumer behavior. In addition, we have added information on the latest VALS segments and other applied online psychographic research, as well as new content on word of mouth communication and innovation diffusion.
- Special new research and behavioral topics include the emotions, post-decision regret, decision framing, privacy (including identity theft), gambling, and obesity.
- An extensively revised, student-friendly writing style and headings make the text even more accessible.
- Numerous new advertisements offer concrete illustrations of consumer behavior concepts in action.
- Numerous new examples highlight how all kinds of organizations use consumer behavior in their marketing efforts.

Textbook Features

As award-winning teachers, we have tried to translate our instructional abilities and experience into the writing of this text. The following features have been a natural outgrowth of these experiences.

Conceptual Model. First, we believe that students can learn best when they see the big picture—when they understand what concepts mean, how they are used in business practice, and how they relate to one another. In our opinion, consumer behavior is too often presented as a set of discrete topics with little or no relationship to one another. We have therefore developed an overall conceptual model that helps students grasp the big picture and see how the chapters and topics are themselves interrelated. Further, the overall model guides the organization of the book, making the chapters far more *integrative* than most other books.

Practical Orientation, with an Emphasis on Globalization and E-commerce. Another common complaint of some treatments of consumer behavior is that they reflect general psychological or sociological principles and theories, but provide very little indication of how these principles and theories relate to business practice. Given our notion that students enjoy seeing how the concepts in consumer behavior can apply to business practice, a second objective of the book was to provide a very practical orientation. We include a wealth of contemporary real-world examples to illustrate key topics. We also try to broaden students' horizons by providing a number of international examples. Given the importance of consumer behavior to electronic commerce, we also provide a number of examples of consumer behavior in an e-commerce context. The abundance of global and e-commerce examples make our book *more global* and *e-commerce based* than other texts on the market.

Current and Cutting Edge Coverage. Third, we provide coverage of the field of consumer behavior that is as current and up-to-date as possible (including many of the recent research advances). This includes several *novel chapters* that often do not appear in other textbooks: "Symbolic Consumer Behavior," "Knowing and Understanding," and "The Dark Side of Consumer Behavior and Marketing." These topics are at the cutting edge of consumer behavior research and are likely to be of considerable interest to students.

Balanced Treatment of Micro and Macro Topics. Fourth, our book tries to provide a balanced perspective on the field of consumer behavior. Specifically, we give treatment to both psychological (micro) consumer behavior topics (e.g., attitudes, decision making) and sociological (macro) consumer behavior topics (e.g., subculture, gender, social class influences). Also, although we typically teach consumer behavior by starting with the more micro topics and then moving up to more macro topics, we realize that some instructors prefer the reverse sequence. The Instructor's Resource Manual therefore provides a revised table of contents and model that shows how the book can be taught for those who prefer a macro first, micro second approach.

Broad Conceptualization of the Subject. Fifth, we present a broad conceptualization of the topic of consumer behavior. While many books focus on what products or services consumers buy, consumer behavior scholars have recognized that the topic of consumer behavior is actually much broader. Specifically, rather than studying buying per se, we recognize that consumer behavior includes a *set* of decisions (what, whether, when, where, why, how, how often, how much, and how long) about *acquisition* (including, but not limited to buying), *usage,* and *disposition* decisions. Focusing on more than what products or services consumers buy provides a rich set of theoretical and practical implications for both our understanding of consumer behavior and the practice of marketing.

Finally, we consider the relevance of consumer behavior to *many constituents,* not just marketers. Chapter 1 indicates that consumer behavior is important to marketers, public policy makers, ethicists and consumer advocacy groups, and consumers themselves (including students' own lives). Some chapters focus exclusively on the implications of consumer behavior for public policy makers, ethicists, and consumer advocacy groups. Other chapters consider these issues as well, though in less detail.

Content and Organization of the Book

One can currently identify two main approaches to the study of consumer behavior: a "micro" orientation, which focuses on the individual psychological processes that consumers use to make acquisition, consumption, and disposition decisions, and a "macro" orientation, which focuses on group behaviors and the symbolic nature of consumer behavior. This latter orientation draws heavily from such fields as sociology and anthropology. The current book and overall model have been structured around a "micro to macro" organization based on the way we teach this course and the feedback that we have received from reviewers. (As mentioned previously, for those who prefer a "macro to micro" structure, we provide in the Instructor's Resource Manual an alternative Table of Contents that reflects how the book could be easily adapted to this perspective).

Chapter 1 presents an introduction to consumer behavior and provides students with an understanding of the breadth of the field, and its importance to marketers, advocacy groups, public policy makers, and consumers themselves. It also presents the overall model that guides the organization of the text. Chapter 2 focuses on the groups who conduct research on consumers and how that research is both collected and used by different constituents.

Part Two, "The Psychological Core" focuses on the inner psychological processes that affect consumer behavior. We see that consumers' acquisition, usage, and disposition behaviors and decisions are greatly affected by the amount of effort they put into engaging in behaviors and making decisions. Chapter 3 describes three critical factors that affect effort: the (1) *motivation* or desire, (2) *ability* (knowledge and information), and (3) *opportunity* to engage in behaviors and make decisions. In Chapter 4, we then examine how information in consumers' environments (i.e., ads, prices, product features, word of mouth communications, and so on) is internally processed by consumers—how they come in contact with these stimuli (*exposure*), notice them (*attention*), and *perceive* them. Chapter 5 continues by discussing how we compare new stimuli to our knowledge of existing stimuli, a process called *categorization*, and how we attempt to understand or *comprehend* them on a deeper level. In Chapters 6 and 7, we see how attitudes are formed and changed depending on whether the amount of effort consumers devote to forming an attitude is high or low. Finally, because consumers often must recall the information they have previously stored in order to make decisions, Chapter 8 looks at the important topic of consumer *memory*.

Whereas Part Two examines some of the internal factors that influence consumers' decisions, a critical domain of consumer behavior involves understanding how consumers make acquisition, consumption, and disposition decisions. Thus in Part Three we examine the sequential steps of the consumer decision-making process. In Chapter 9, we examine the initial steps of this process—*problem recognition* and *information search*. Similar to the attitude change processes described earlier, we next examine the consumer decision-making process, both when *effort is high* (Chapter 10) and when it is *low* (Chapter 11). Finally, the process does not end after a decision has been made: in Chapter 12 we see how consumers determine whether they are *satisfied* or *dissatisfied* with their decisions and how they *learn* from choosing and consuming products/services.

Part Four reflects a "macro" view of consumer behavior that examines how various aspects of *culture* affect consumer behavior. First, we see how consumer diversity (in terms of age, gender, sexual orientation, region, ethnicity, and religion) can affect consumer behavior (Chapter 13). Chapter 14 then examines how *social class* and households are classified and how these factors affect acquisition, usage, and disposition behaviors. Chapter 15 examines how these external influences affect our personality, lifestyle, and values, as well as consumer behavior. Chapter 16 considers how, when, and why the specific *reference groups* (friends, work group, clubs) to which we belong can influence acquisition, usage, and disposition decisions and behaviors.

Part Five, "Consumer Behavior Outcomes" examines the effects of the numerous influences and decision processes discussed in Parts Two, Three, and Four. Chapter 17 builds on the topics of internal decision-making and group behavior by examining how consumers adopt new offerings, and how their *adoption* decisions affect the spread or *diffusion* of an offering through a market. Because products and services often reflect deeply felt and significant meanings (e.g., our favorite song or restaurant), Chapter 18 focuses on the interesting topic of *symbolic consumer behavior.*

Part Six, "Consumer Welfare" covers two topics that have been of great interest to consumer researchers in recent years. Chapter 19 directs our attention to *consumerism and public policy* issues. Chapter 20 examines the "*dark side of consumer behavior*" and focuses on some negative outcomes of consumer-related behaviors (compulsive buying and gambling, prostitution, etc.) as well as marketing practices that have been the focus of social commentary in recent years.

Pedagogical Features

Based on our extensive teaching experience, we have incorporated a number of features that should help students learn about consumer behavior.

Chapter Opening Cases. Each chapter begins with a case scenario about an actual company or situation that illustrates key concepts discussed in the chapter and their importance to marketers. This will help students grasp the "big picture" and understand the relevance of the topics from the start of the chapter.

Chapter Opening Model. Each chapter also begins with a conceptual model that shows the organization of the chapter, the topics discussed, and how they relate to both one another and to other chapters. Each model reflects an expanded picture of one or more of the elements presented in the overall conceptual model for the book (described in Chapter 1).

Marketing Implications. Numerous *Marketing Implications* sections are interspersed throughout each chapter. These sections illustrate how various consumer behavior concepts can be applied to the practice of marketing, including such basic marketing functions as market segmentation, target market selection, positioning, market research, promotion, price, product, and place decisions. An abundance of marketing examples (from both the U.S. and abroad) provide concrete applications and implementations of the concepts to marketing practice.

Abundant Use of Exhibits. Each chapter contains a number of illustrated examples, including photos, advertisements, charts, and graphs. These illustrations help to make important topics personally relevant and engaging, help students remember the material, and make the book more accessible and aesthetically pleasing, thereby increasing students' motivation to learn. Each model, graph, ad, and photo also has an accompanying caption that provides a simple description and explanation of how the exhibit relates to the topic it is designed to illustrate.

End of Chapter Summaries. The end of each chapter provides students with a simple and concise summary of topics. These summaries are a good review tool to use with the conceptual model to help students get the big picture.

End of Chapter Questions and Exercises. Each chapter includes a set of discussion and review questions and application exercises designed to involve students on a more experiential and interactive level. Exercises include experiential exercises (e.g., watching and analyzing consumers and ads), mini-research projects, or thought-provoking questions.

Glossary. Every chapter contains a set of key terms that are both highlighted in the text and defined in the glossary at the end of the text. These terms and their definitions should help students identify and remember the central concepts described in the chapter.

Instructor's Resource Manual

Instructor's Resource Manual (with Power Point slides). The Instructor's Resource Manual, prepared by Professor Russell Casey, has been completely revised and updated to provide a thorough review of material in the text as well as supplementary materials that can be used to expand upon the text and enhance classroom presentations. An alternate table of contents and consumer behavior model for presenting the text in a "macro to micro" approach has been provided as well as different sample syllabi. Included for each chapter are a chapter summary, learning objectives, a comprehensive chapter outline, a list of useful websites (with descriptions of how they might assist the instructor in preparing for or teaching a class session), and several suggested classroom activities. Classroom activities include questions for each chapter that stimulate group discussion, suggestions for bringing additional examples (videos, readings, etc.) into the classroom, and special experiential activities created by Professor Sheri Bridges, with detailed guidelines for facilitation.

Acknowledgments

Special recognition is extended to Marian Wood, whose assistance was instrumental to the completion of this project. Her tireless work on this project is greatly appreciated. We have also been extremely fortunate to work with a wonderful team of dedicated professionals from Houghton Mifflin. We are very grateful to Joanne Dauksewicz, Shelley Dickerson, and Susan Holtz, whose enormous energy and enthusiasm spurred our progress on this Fourth Edition. We also appreciate the efforts of Sheri Bridges at Wake Forest University for her work on the Experiential Exercises and Russell Casey of Clayton State University for his work on the Instructor's Resource Manual and Test Bank. The quality of this book and its ancillary package has been helped immensely by the insightful and rich comments of a set of researchers and instructors who served as reviewers. Their thoughtful and helpful comments had real impact in shaping the final product. In particular, we wish to thank:

Larry Anderson
Long Island University
Mike Ballif
University of Utah
Sharon Beatty
University of Alabama
Russell Belk
University of Utah
Joseph Bonnice
Manhattan College
Carol Bruneau
University of Montana
Margaret L. Burk
Muskingum College
Carol Calder
Loyola Marymount University
Paul Chao
Eastern Michigan University
Dennis Clayson
University of Northern Iowa
Joel Cohen
University of Florida
Sally Dibb
University of Warwick
Richard W. Easley
Baylor University
Richard Elliott
Warwick Business School
Abdi Eshghi
Bentley College
Frank W. Fisher
Stonehill College
Ronald Fullerton
Lake Erie College
Philip Garton
Leicester Business School
Peter L. Gillett
University of Central Florida
Debbora Heflin
Cal Poly - Pomona
Elizabeth Hirschman
Rutgers University
Raj G. Javalgi
Cleveland State University
Harold Kassarjian
UCLA
Patricia Kennedy
University of Nebraska - Lincoln
Robert E. Kleine
Ohio Northern University
Scott Koslow
University of Waikato
Robert Lawson
William Patterson University
Phillip Lewis
Rowan College of New Jersey
Kenneth R. Lord
Mercer University
Bart Macchiette
Plymouth State College
Michael Mallin
Kent State University
Lawrence Marks
Kent State University
David Marshall
University of Edinburgh
Anil Mathur
Hofstra University
Matt Meuter
California State University, Chico
Martin Meyers
University of Wisconsin - Stevens Point
Vince Mitchell
Cass School of Business, City of London
Lois Mohr
Georgia State University
James R. Ogden
Kutztown University
Thomas O'Guinn
University of Illinois
Judith Powell
Virginia Union University
Marco Protano
Bilkent University
Michael Reilly
Montana State University
Gregory M. Rose
University of Washington–Tacoma
Mary Mercurio Scheip
Eckerd College
Marilyn Scrizzi
Stonehill College
John Shaw
Providence College
C. David Shepherd
Kennesaw State University
Robert E. Smith
Indiana University
Eric Richard Spangenberg
Washington State University
Bruce Stern
Portland State University
Barbara Stewart
University of Houston
Jane Boyd Thomas
Winthrop University
Phil Titus
Bowling Green State University
Rajiv Vaidyanathan
University of Minnesota, Duluth
Stuart Van Auken
Florida Gulf Coast University
Janet Wagner
University of Maryland
Tommy E. Whittler
University of Kentucky

Adaptor's Note

The Indian Consumer of today has moved on from being a Mrs. Sharma to Anita or Sunita, where the identity of the individual is more important than probably his or her lineage. The women of today, the youth of today, the "seniors" population of the society or even the men of the house do not seem to carry the conventional image of the past. The woman is known as herself, the youth is more defined, evolved and perhaps recluse, the seniors of the society are not the dependant lot but probably believe in; "Sir Utha Ke Jiyo" syndrome. The men have become more responsible and are not just the bread earner but bread-maker (read home-maker) too. More and more men (even women) are leaving conventional jobs and kickstarting their own entrepreneurial ventures and that could be anything from adventure tourist guide or yoga instructor or for that matter a chef too as a career option. What is however, of our concern is the impact on the buyer behavior trends. Three aspects that have impacted the buyer behavior trends of today are:

1. The changing economic scenario
2. The impact of cable and satellite television
3. The changing social dynamics of the society

The economic liberalization of 1991 has had a deep impact in the way India today approaches the world and how India is looked at by the world. The upward trends noticeable from 2003-04 onwards are more noteworthy and the adage of knowledge economy has impacted livelihoods within the country. The BPO boom, the surge in the IT and ITES sector, the core sector's transition to a dominant position and the impact of the services economy have all been significant achievements. The cable and satellite entry in 1991 has been a landmark for the country and since then, viewing contents and more recently viewing format has undergone changes. Our thought process, lifestyles and even personality have seen transformation. Finally, the intrinsic changes within the consumers of today also affect consumer behavior trends too. Break up of joint families and the rise of the nuclear families, changing mindsets and willingness to experiment and risk seeking traits or even the present-day youth's individualism are all fallouts of the changing dynamics of the society. A movie like "Life in a Metro" released in May 2007 is a true representation of the changing lifestyles in urban metropolis. This however is in sharp contrast to the rural and suburban lifestyles which may have undergone very little changes. The population migration still remains a dominant trend and the agrarian sector remains the key source of income. The contrasting milieu on two sides of the continuum presents an India which is extreme, highly heterogeneous and divided. The north-south divide and the differences in tastes, cultures and lifestyles have long been proverbial aspects discussed, but the dichotomy is increasing.

This Indian Adaptation of the book explores three important perspectives of the Indian consumer psyche. The first aspect is about the intrinsic traits of the Indian consumer, which makes him so different from the rest of the world—the tastes, lifestyle, food habits, cultural and multi-cultural traits that are firmly embedded in the consumer. The second significant aspect is about the changing consumer behavioral trends in the country. From the deeply entrenched values and beliefs to the new face of India is a long journey that the Indian population has taken. The last part is more of social class issues pertaining to age, occupation and educational profiling that are unique to the country. With a young population today where the median age is about twenty one, the imperatives for the marketers are very different as compared to markets of North America, Europe or Japan. The three facets have been kept into consideration while planning for the Indian adaptation.

Most chapters resonate with the thought process as indicated in the above paragraph, either in a description through a visible trend or through a mere watermark representation in an illustrative case or happening. The chapter starts with an opening case helping in emphasizing the concepts and principles to be discussed in the ensuing pages. The case helps explain the point better and relate concepts to practical situations more clearly. The cases range from product specific instances to trends and events that have at some point in time encashed upon behavioral traits. Movies, websites, product and service brands and even issues in consumer rights have also been showcased through the opening cases. Movies like Dhoom 2 and Hum Tum are cases in point, wherein merchandise promotions, in-film product placements to buzz marketing have all been employed. Ideas which are not uncommon but have been brought to notice from the subtlety that existed. The pesticide problem of Coke-Pepsi and subsequent efforts made by the two brands to shed the image of "cobra" to a cola and its effects on consumer buying have all been showcased.

After the opening case the chapter discussions through the various concepts and principles have also been reinforced through examples, instances and practical realms of life. The chapters of Social Class, Family, Group and Reference Groups have been completely overhauled to bring in a larger and specific perspective from the Indian scenario. Particularly in the chapter on social class and population which extensively delves into the population evolution in India, the author has made efforts to size the population into distinct homogenous groups. An attempt which is pioneering and novel in its own way, since most population discussions have focused on the US divide of Baby-Boomers, Seniors, Gen-X and Y.

We do hope the adaptation is found of interest and of need in the course on Consumer Behavior and the usual problems of grappling with trying to relate to Indian context and situations gets largely reduced. The opening cases, we do hope, help instructors relate the concepts and principles to the students and make learning more interesting and lucid.

Pinaki Dasgupta
Faculty, Indian Institute of
Foreign Trade (IIFT),
New Delhi

PART

1

An Introduction to Consumer Behavior

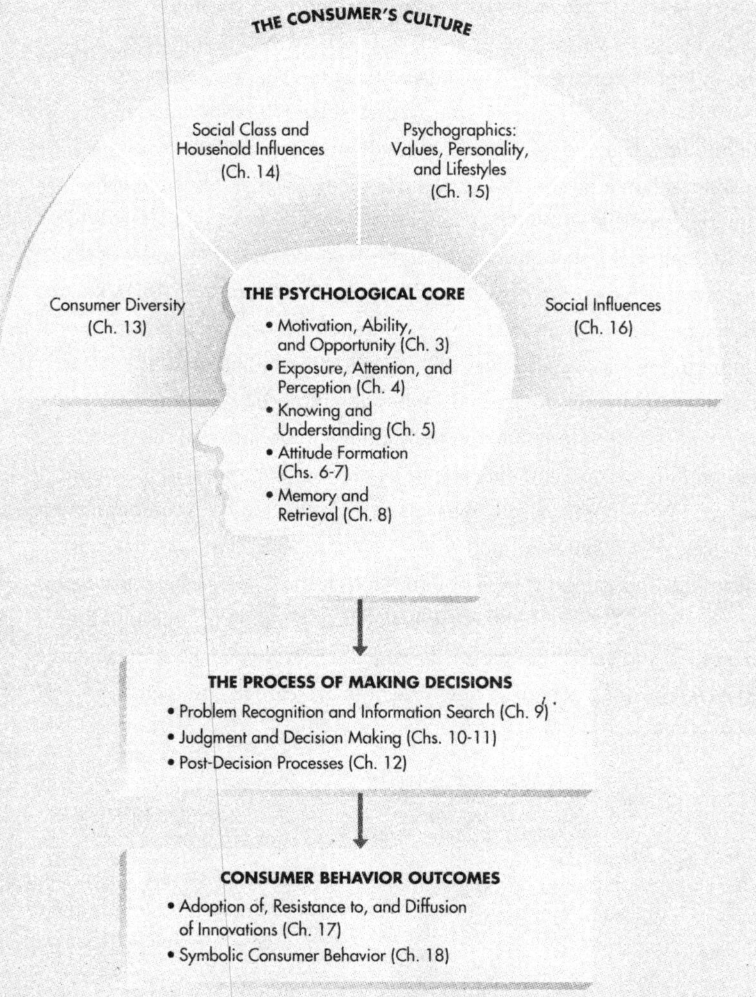

Part One introduces the subject of consumer behavior and provides an overview of the various topics it encompasses. You will learn that consumer behavior involves much more than purchasing products. In addition, you will find out that marketers are always studying consumer behavior for clues to who buys, uses, and disposes of what products, as well as when, where, and why.

Chapter 1 defines consumer behavior and examines its importance to marketers, advocacy groups, public policy makers, and consumers themselves. It also presents and explains the overall model that guides the organization of this text. As this model indicates, consumer behavior covers four basic domains: (1) the psychological core (2) the process of making decisions, (3) the consumer's culture, and (4) the outcomes of consumer behavior.

Chapter 2 focuses on the critical importance of consumer behavior research and its special implications for marketers. You will learn about various research methods, types of data, and ethical issues related to consumer research. With this background, you will be able to understand how consumer research helps marketers develop more effective strategies and tactics for reaching and satisfying customers.

chapter 1 Understanding Consumer Behavior

LEARNING OBJECTIVES

After studying this chapter you will be able to:

- Define consumer behavior and explain its elements.
- Identify the four domains of consumer behavior.
- Discuss the benefits of studying consumer behavior.

INTRODUCTION

Bajaj: Truly Hamara Bajaj

A company with over 70+ years of existence in the Indian market that started off as a typical family run business. The founder Shri. Jamnalal Bajaj had strong Gandhian leanings and was actively associated with the Indian freedom movement. In fact, his son, Shri. Kamalnayan Bajaj too was associated with the freedom struggle very closely. Bajaj group's diversified interests included a wide range of industries, spanning automobiles (two-wheelers and three-wheelers), home appliances, lighting, iron and steel, insurance, travel and finance. After Rahul Bajaj took over the business in 1965, the company went into a fast track mode and for over four decades was, under his leadership, the turnover of the Bajaj Auto, the flagship company went up from Rs.72 million to Rs.46.16 billion (USD 936 million). Through the 60's, 70's and the 80's Bajaj scooters was almost a generic brand to the scooter category. It dominated the Indian market and had a near monopoly situation. In the mid 80's when the motorbike segment started developing, Bajaj was not far behind in realizing the importance of the growing market. Rising fuel costs, changing consumer mindset and rapid urbanization meant that motorbike as a category was gradually replacing the scooter segment. Hero Honda one of the early entrants in the 100cc bike segment had the first mover advantage and gained sufficient inroads with the CD100 range. Soon, companies like Bajaj, TVS, and Escorts followed suit. Gradually the size of the market expanded and so did the players. Today the motorbike market has a large array of players including Japanese heavyweights like Honda and Suzuki.

Exhibit 1.1
BAJAJ THROUGH THE DECADES
Through the 60's, 70's and the 80's Bajaj scooters was almost a generic brand to the scooter category. It dominated the Indian market and had a near monopoly situation.

However, a traditional scooter making company with such deep-rooted legacy and experience in the said industry has been able to shrug off the image of a family driven vehicle into a more yuppie, younger and definitely more dynamic segment with a range of bikes to suit the taste and lifestyle of the age group.

The company carried out a large number of internal and external changes to realign with the changing nature of the market. Especially, the efforts to reach out to the new segments were more pronounced. In the late 80's the classic "Hamara Bajaj" advertising campaign from the erstwhile HTA now JWT, created very strong visual imagery of a home grown scooter brand. The visual alongside shows one of the old advertisements of the company's scooter, which catered to a more Pan-India profile. However, a few critical factors, pertinent to the macro environmental factors; i. shifting demographic trends: a very young population in India, with rising disposable income, that can own a vehicle at a far more younger age as compared to, say, 10 years back. ii. Rapid urbanization of smaller towns and with it the problems of traffic and distances to travel, together with lack of intra-city public transportation iii. The third aspect is more of a global concern of rising oil prices and its cost benefit analysis by Indian consumers with scooter versus motorbikes. iv. High growth passenger car segment and easy finance options made car buying easier further helped by falling prices and families opting for the comfort and safer climes of a car as against the scooters.

Taking advantage of the environment and the growth opportunities realized in the motorbike segment, Bajaj quickly consolidated its core business and moved more aggressively in this segment. The motorbike models launched prominently featured the brand names unlike in the past where the name Bajaj was more prominent. This was more for the reason that the company still carried the scooter image in its core and that could have diluted the imagery in the new segment. Today brand names like Pulsar, Calibre, Avenger, DTSI feature more prominently as against in the past when most scooter brands were referred as Bajaj Chetak or Bajaj Super or Bajaj 150... The company also changed the corporate logo and a new Tag Line was incorporated in the logo; "Inspiring Confidence", perhaps making an effort to get closer to the younger audience.

Today, Bajaj may not be the No.1 brand in the category, but it firmly stands as number 2 after Hero Honda, giving it a run for its money. Hero Honda, started off as a motorbike company, (therefore it is traditionally known as a motorbike company). hence the challenges to them were altogether different. But, Bajaj remains a classic example of how a company adjusts to the shifting trend in the consumer and his buying preferences and makes itself relevant across segments.

Defining Consumer Behavior

If you were asked to define ***consumer behavior,*** you might say it refers to the study of how a person buys products. However, this is only part of the definition. Consumer behavior really involves quite a bit more, as this more complete definition indicates:

> *Consumer behavior reflects the totality of consumers' decisions with respect to the acquisition, consumption, and disposition of goods, services, activities, and ideas by (human) decision-making units [over time].*[2]

This definition has some very important elements, summarized in Exhibit 1.2. Here is a closer look at each element.

Consumer Behavior Involves Products, Services, Activities, and Ideas

Consumer behavior means more than just how a person buys tangible products such as bath soap, digital music players, and automobiles. It also includes consumer's use of services, activities, and ideas, such as going to the doctor, visiting a theme park, signing up for Salsa classes, taking a trip, donating for a cause or even remembering to vaccinate a child on a specific date or week (the now imminently unputdownable "Pulse Polio" campaign, epitomized by Mr. Bachchan with his proverbial line "Do boond jindagi ke". Another example of consumer behavior involves choices about the consumption of time, such as whether to watch a certain television program (and for how long) and the use of time in ways that show who we are and how we are different from others.[4] Because consumer behavior includes the

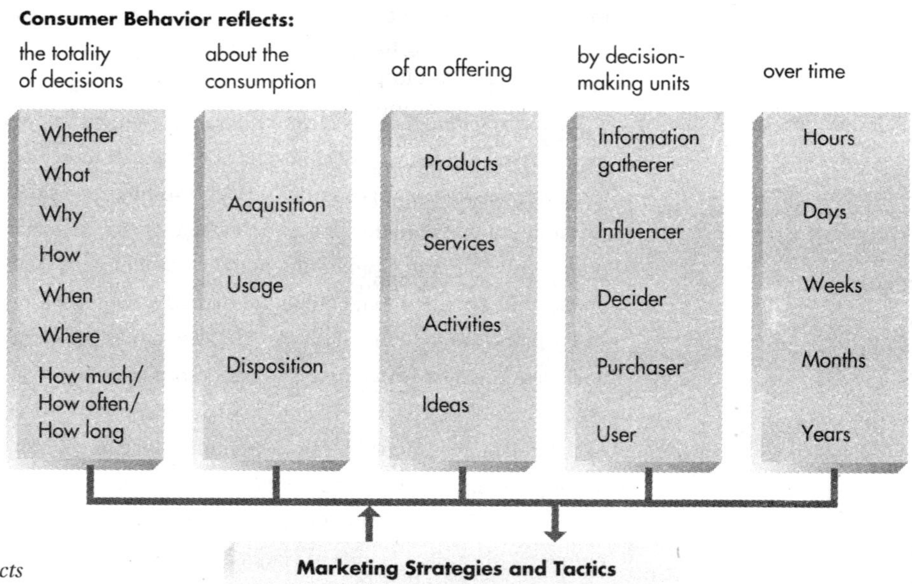

Exhibit 1.2
WHAT IS CONSUMER BEHAVIOR?
Consumer behavior reflects more than how a product is acquired by a single person at any one point in time. Think of some marketing strategies and tactics that try to influence one or more of the dimensions of consumer behavior shown in this exhibit.

consumption of many things—products, services, activities, ideas—we use the simple term ***offering*** to encompass these entities and make reading easier.

Consumer Behavior Involves More Than Buying

The manner in which consumers buy is extremely important to marketers. However, marketers are also intensely interested in consumer behavior related to using and disposing of an offering:

- *Acquiring.* Buying represents one type of ***acquisition*** behavior. As shown later in this chapter, acquisition includes other ways of obtaining products and services, such as leasing, trading, or borrowing. Exhibit 1.3 shows when U.S. consumers are most likely to be out shopping, a highly visible form of acquisition behavior.
- *Using.* After consumers acquire an offering, they typically use it. Although researchers have studied acquisition in great depth, ***usage*** is at the very core of consumer behavior.[5] Usage has symbolic implications for the consumer and therefore is important for marketing strategy and tactics. The products we use during a typical festival, say Diwali, (Diyas, Sweets, Gifts, new clothes, confetti's) may symbolize the event's significance, our efforts to clean the house, prepare for the Pooja in the evening and after exchanging pleasantries and sweets with neighbors and relatives, then by night settle for a round of gambling (officially allowed only on this day, as it is considered auspicious). The music we enjoy (Shakira or Andrea Bocelli) and the jewelry we wear (Swatch watches or belly button rings) can also symbolize who we are and how we feel. Moreover, usage influences other behaviors important to marketers. For instance, dissatisfied or angry consumers may communicate negative experiences to others, sometimes with devastating results.[6] Think of how negative word-of-mouth can hurt ticket sales for a Hollywood film, as one example.
- *Disposing.* Finally, consumer behavior examines ***disposition:*** how consumers get rid of an offering they previously acquired. Disposition behavior can have extremely important implications for marketers.[7] Consumers who are concerned about how disposition affects the environment will seek out products that are biodegradable, are made from recycled materials, or do not pollute when disposed of—creating profitable opportunities for marketers who can address these concerns. For instance, when ecologically minded consumers renovate their kitchens, they can install new counters made from recycled materials, such as

Exhibit 1.3

illustrates the typical buying occasions and products sought by an average Indian homemaker.

The Different Shopping Trips

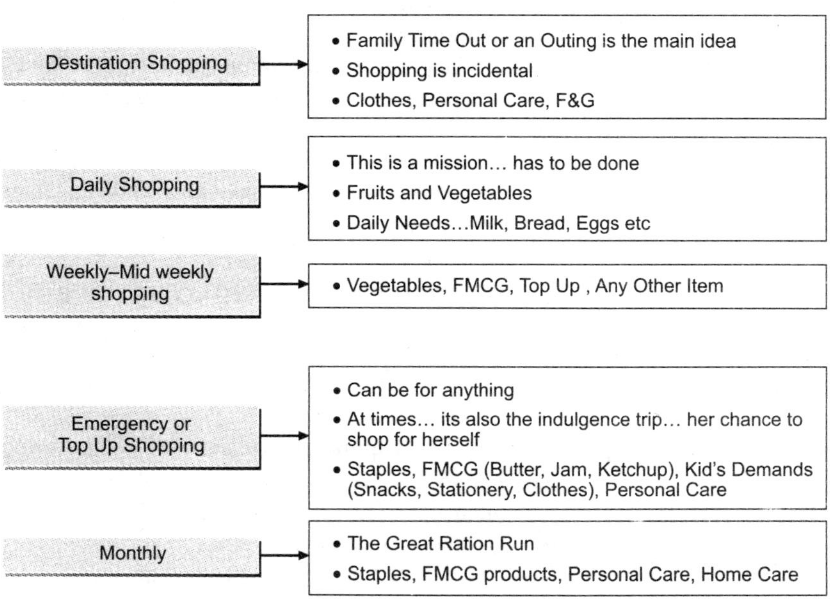

ShetkaStone (made from recycled paper) or Vitracrete (made from recycled traffic lights).[8]

Consumer Behavior Is a Dynamic Process

Consumer behavior suggests that the sequence of acquisition, consumption, and disposition can occur over time in a dynamic sequence. As shown in Exhibit 1.2, this sequence can occur over a matter of hours, days, weeks, months, or even years. To illustrate, assume that a family has acquired and is using a new car. Usage provides the family with information—whether the car drives well, is reliable, is impressive, and does little harm to the environment—that affects when, whether, how, and why the family will dispose of the car by selling, trading, or junking it. Because the family always needs transportation, disposition of the car is likely to affect when, whether, how, and why its members acquire another car in the future.

Entire markets are designed around linking one consumer's disposition decision to other consumers' acquisition decisions. For example, when consumers buy used cars, they are buying cars that others have disposed of. From eBay's online auctions to Goodwill Industries' secondhand clothing stores, from consignment stores to used book stores, many businesses exist to link one consumer's disposition behavior with another's acquisition behavior. Markets have also developed in response to decisions about time consumption. At the Hong Kong International Airport, as at many major airports, travelers who want to make productive use of layovers between flights can shop in airport stores, freshen up with a shower, and recharge cell phone or laptop batteries while checking e-mail.[9]

Consumer Behavior Can Involve Many People

Consumer behavior does not necessarily reflect the action of a single individual. A group of friends, a few coworkers, or an entire family may plan a birthday party, decide where to have lunch, or visit a golf course. Moreover, the individuals engaging in consumer behavior can take on one or more consumer roles. In the case of an automobile purchase, for example, one or more family members might take on the role of information gatherer by collecting information about different models. Others might assume the role of influencer and try to affect the outcome of a decision. One or more members may take on the role of purchaser by actually paying for the car, and some or all may be users. Finally, several family members may be involved in the disposal of the car.

Consumer Behavior Involves Many Decisions

Consumer behavior involves understanding whether, why, when, where, how, how much, how often, and for how long consumers will buy, use, or dispose of an offering (look back at Exhibit 1.2).

Whether to Acquire/Use/Dispose of an Offering Consumers must decide whether to acquire, use, or dispose of an offering. They may need to decide whether to spend or save their money when they earn extra cash.[10] How much they decide to spend may be influenced by perceptions of how much they recall spending in the past.[11] They may need to decide whether to order a pizza, clean out their bulging closets, or go to a movie. Some decisions about whether to acquire, use, or

Exhibit 1.4

maps the expenditure basket of a typical household. It is no longer the fight for 'roti kapda and makaan'. It is about other important things in life as depicted by the grid below. Groceries, utilities and investments account for 55% of an average monthly household expenditure

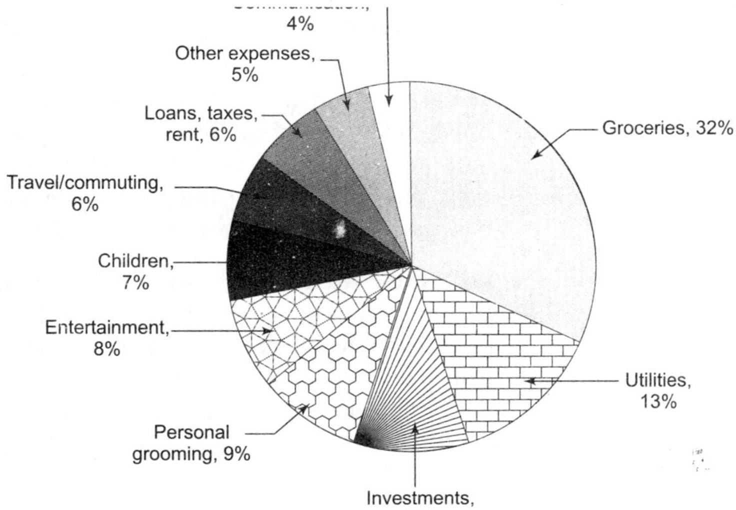

dispose of an offering are related to safety concerns or are motivated by a desire to reduce economic risk, social risk, or psychological risk.

What Offering to Acquire/Use/Dispose of Consumers make decisions everyday about what to buy; in fact, average monthly household expenditure is Rs.7612/- for an average Indian household across SEC A,B,C, D & E.. In some cases we make choices among product or service *categories,* such as buying food versus downloading new music or signing up for health insurance. In other cases we choose between *brands,* such as the decision between acquiring a Nokia cell phone or a Motorola cell phone. Our choices multiply daily, as marketers introduce new products, new sizes, and new packages. Exhibit 1.4 shows the expenditure basket of a typical household.

Why Acquire/Use/Dispose of an Offering Consumption can occur for a number of reasons. Among the most important, as you will see later, are the ways in which an offering meets someone's needs, values, or goals. For example, some consumers have body parts pierced as a form of self-expression. Others do it to fit into a group. Still others believe body piercing is a form of beauty or that it enhances sexual pleasure.[13] The now legendary "Coffee House" in Kolkata located in College Street is a melting pot of art, culture, music and politics, that has bred a warehouse of talent in related fields. The strategic location of the Coffee House which was close to the Calcutta University was an added advantage for the target audience to throng the place.The store's conscious efforts to keep the ambience laidback, with minimal frills and focus on the food with coffee at rock bottom prices made the greatest impact on the possible target audience it wanted.

Sometimes our reasons for using a product or service are filled with conflict, which leads to some difficult consumption decisions. Teenagers may smoke, even though they know it is harmful, because they think smoking will help them gain acceptance. Low-fat margarine is probably healthier than regular margarine, but many consumers avoid it because its taste has been described as similar to "melted plastic."[15] Some consumers may be unable to stop acquiring, using, or disposing of products. They may be physically addicted to products such as cigarettes, drugs, or alcoholic beverages, or they may have a compulsion to eat, purge, gamble, or buy. At times, consumers who want to acquire or consume an offering may not be able to do so because what they want is unavailable. A common sight at most PDS outlets in India or a particular prescription drug going out of stock briefly. Infact, the recent Dengue alert in the city of Delhi led frantic families and individuals looking for mosquito repellants which had a portability factor, like lotions, gels or even crème. Unsought brands like Odomos from Balasara did brisk business, even leading to a brief scarcity of the brand too.

Why Not to Acquire/Use/Dispose of an Offering Marketers also want to know why consumers do *not* acquire, use, or dispose of an offering. For example, consumers may put off buying a personal video recorder because they doubt they can handle the technology or they doubt it offers anything special. They may believe that technology is changing so fast that their purchase will soon be outdated. They may even believe that some manufacturers will go out of business, leaving them without after-sale support or service.

How to Acquire/Use/Dispose of an Offering Marketers gain a lot of insight by understanding the ways in which consumers acquire, consume, and dispose of an offering.

Ways of Acquiring an Offering How do consumers decide whether to pay for an item with cash, a check, a debit card, a credit card, or an electronic payment system? In China, where bank notes are in short supply and the use of counterfeit money is widespread, the government is encouraging consumers to use debit cards.[17] On the Internet, more than 56 million consumers use the PayPal service to pay for their purchases rather than typing in credit card numbers or mailing checks.[18] The following are some of the ways consumers acquire an offering:

- *Buying.* Although we typically recognize buying as a common form of acquisition behavior, consumers can acquire products and services in other ways.
- *Trading.* Consumers could receive a product or service as part of a trade. For example, some stores allow consumers to trade in old CDs or DVDs as partial payment toward new ones.
- *Renting or Leasing.* Goods like automobiles, tuxedos, carpet cleaners, furniture, vacation homes, and computers can be rented or leased through stores and dealers or online.[19]
- *Bartering.* Thousands of businesses and consumers worldwide engage in the practice of bartering; businesses alone exchange more than $8 billion yearly in goods and services. As an example, the Malaysian government recently bartered palm oil for high-tech systems made by a Chinese firm.[20]
- *Gift Giving.* Consumers can also acquire products as gifts. Gift giving is common throughout the world, and most societies have many gift-giving occasions. Each society also has formal and informal rules that dictate how gifts should be given, what is appropriate as a gift, and what is an appropriate response to gift giving. Marketing efforts sometimes aim to induce gift giving on occasions ranging from Mother's Day to Boss's Day, as shown in Exhibit 1.5.
- *Finding.* In some instances consumers simply find goods that someone else has lost (hats left on the bus, books left at the gym, umbrellas left in class) or thrown away.

Exhibit 1.5

Indian Florist Association helps online buyers shop and send flowers to anywhere in India and for any occasion

- *Theft.* Goods can also be acquired through theft. Some marketers have developed products to deter this mode of acquisition. For example, antitheft devices like The Club, LoJack, and car alarms attempt to reduce the likelihood of car theft. Theft is also hurting publishing companies, movie studios, and musical artists who produce copyrighted materials in digital form. Consumers download and swap an estimated 2 billion songs and movies each month without authorization.[21]
- *Borrowing.* Another method of acquisition is by borrowing. Although we typically think of borrowing as a willing and conscious exchange between two people, some types of "borrowing" are illegal and border on theft. It is not uncommon for some consumers to pay for new clothes, wear them, and then return them for a full refund.

Ways of Using an Offering In addition to understanding how consumers acquire products and services, marketers want to know how consumers use an offering.[22] For example, marketers have found that consumers are using their cars and vans as minihomes, complete with phones, faxes, radios, stereos, TVs, DVD players, and refrigerators, and that this usage is reducing demand for traditional features such as stick shifts.[23] For obvious reasons, marketers want to ensure that their offering is used correctly. As an example, makers of camera phones face the challenge of educating consumers about how to print images, not just e-mail them.[24] Improper usage of some offerings, such as cough medicine, can create health and safety problems for some consumers.[25] Because of these hazards, potentially dangerous products must have warning labels; unfortunately, many consumers ignore label warnings and directions. Therefore, to make these warnings more effective, marketers must understand how consumers process label information.

Ways of Disposing of an Offering Finally, consumers deciding how to dispose of products have several disposal options:[26]

- *Finding a New Use for It.* Using an old toothbrush to clean rust from tools or making shorts out of an old pair of jeans are some of the ways consumers continue to use an item instead of disposing of it.
- *Getting Rid of It Temporarily.* Renting or lending an item is one way of getting rid of it temporarily.
- *Getting Rid of It Permanently.* Throwing away an item represents the most common option for getting rid of it permanently, although consumers may choose to

trade it, give it away, or sell it. Some consumers refuse to throw away things they regard as special, even if the items no longer serve a functional purpose. Other consumers are interested in collecting items.[27] Consumers collect many things, from teddy bears and toy trains to DVDs and dolls, creating a $30 billion market for buying, selling, transporting, storing, and insuring collectible items.[28]

Exhibit 1.6

Transitions: Marriages in India are like festivals and the preparations that go behind it extend over months and at times years too.

When to Acquire/Use/Dispose of an offering The product seasonality may be an important rationale to acquire a product, but environment is equally significant when the product is being acquired. It is an age-old practice in most families to purchase bullion reserve as a means of security and eventually use it up for daughter's or son's marriage. However, the recent real estate boom means availability of alternate investment options and more and more households considering it which till now was a bastion of corporate entities. Similarly, for more daily use products, "Ready to Eats" is increasingly gaining acceptance, replacing the fixated Indian mindset of "making and consuming fresh". With more and more women of the house stepping out to work, "Ready to Eats" are considered a nice relaxation option on weekends, when cooking can be given a holiday. Companies even pitch their products according to the requirement of the customer or try creating one. Increased passenger car advertisements during year-end induces customers to avail benefits on lowered prices of the models to be phased-off in that year.

Moreover, when we consume can be affected by traditions imposed by our families, our culture, and the area in which we live. South Indians' natural affinity towards his idlis and dosas even while traveling up-North, is more out of a cultural attachment. His clothes, attitudes and approach to life will be very different from anybody in North India. All this will play a critical role in his buying behaviour pattern. In New Delhi, most Tamilians will prefer to buy their grocery from the famed "Rama Stores" at downtown Munirka, which is virtually a warehouse of specialized South Indian grocery items. Our decisions about when to acquire or use an offering are also affected by knowing when others might or might not be buying or using it. Thus we might be motivated to travel by air, eat dinner, work out, or get a haircut when we know that others will *not* be doing so. In addition, we may wait to purchase an offering until we know it will be on sale—and even if we have to line up to buy something popular, we are likely to continue waiting if we see many people joining the line behind us.[33] In many cases, we acquire a product for later consumption. Research shows that waiting to consume a pleasurable product such as candy increases our enjoyment, although it decreases our enjoyment of the anticipated usage.[34]

Another decision we commonly face is when to acquire a new, improved version of a product we already own. This can be a difficult decision when the current model still works well or has sentimental value. However, marketers may be able to affect whether and when consumers buy upgrades by providing economic incentives for trading up from older products.[35]

Where to Acquire/Use/Dispose of an Offering Consumers have more choices of where to acquire, use, and dispose of an offering than ever before. Infact, shopping habits are changing as more consumers buy groceries, clothing, and a wide variety of other products at large format retail outlets like Big Bazaar or Westside or Pantaloons. Beyond traditional stores and outlets, technology now allows us to buy by mail, over the telephone, from TV, over the Internet, and using wireless handheld devices.

The Internet has dramatically changed where we acquire, use, and dispose of goods. The biggest success story of online shopping is that of the railway ticketing through the IRCTC portal, now tipped as the largest e-commerce site in Asia (outside Japan). With over one million registered customers and an average of over 3,200 bookings per day, the IRCTC site is the largest B2C site in the country. Of IRCTC's turnover of around Rs.4 billion through services like catering and bottled drinking water supply at the stations and on board trains, the online ticketing service during 2002-03 fiscal contributed about Rs.500 million. The average turnover of the railways through internet booking is about Rs.80 million every month.

In addition to acquisition decisions, consumers also make decisions about where to consume various products. For example, the need for privacy motivates consumers to stay home when using products that determine whether they are ovulating, pregnant, or diabetic. On the other hand, wider availability of wireless communication connections allows consumers in public places to make phone calls, check e-mail, read news headlines, play computer games, and download photos or music from anywhere in the world. Consumers can even make charitable donations via cell phone.[41]

Finally, consumers make decisions regarding where to dispose of goods. Should they toss an old magazine in the trash or the recycling bin? Should they store an old photo album in the attic or give it to a family member? Older consumers, in particular, may worry about what will happen to their special possessions after their death and about how to divide heirlooms without creating family conflict. These consumers hope that as a result of their decisions, heirs will have mementos that serve as a legacy.[42]

Clearly, marketers and retailers try to influence consumers' decisions about where to acquire, consume, and dispose of products. As an example, many restaurants give consumers the option of buying meals to eat on-site or to take out for consumption elsewhere. Dell's PC recycling program is a good example of influencing disposal decisions. For a low shipping fee, consumers can send their old PCs to Dell, which then reclaims some components and discards hazardous parts without harming the environment.

How Much, How Often, and How Long to Acquire/Use/Dispose of an Offering
Consumers must make decisions about how much of a good or service they need; how often they need it; and how long they will spend in acquisition, usage, and disposition.[43] Usage decisions can vary widely from person to person and from culture to culture. For example, consumers in India drink an average of only 5 nine-ounce bottles of soft drinks per year, whereas consumers in China drink 17, and consumers in America drink 280.[44]

Sales of a product can be increased when the consumer (1) uses larger amounts of the product, (2) uses the product more frequently, or (3) uses it for longer periods of time. Bonus packs such as the one shown in Exhibit 1.7 help motivate consumers to buy more of a product, but does stockpiling lead to higher consumption? In the

Exhibit 1.7
BONUS PACKS
Consumer promotions like bonus packs prompt consumers to buy and perhaps use more of an offering than they would have bought or used without the promotion.

case of food products, consumers are more likely to increase consumption when the stockpiled item requires no preparation.[45] Usage may also increase when consumers sign up for flat-fee pricing covering unlimited consumption of telephone services or other offerings. However, because many consumers who choose flat-fee programs overestimate their likely consumption, they often pay more than they would with per-usage pricing.[46]

Some consumers experience problems due to excessive consumption or a compulsion to engage in more acquisition, usage, or disposition than they need. Such compulsions can occur in spending, gambling, smoking, exercising, drug abuse (including legal drugs), and eating. With obesity come related problems, from diabetes to heart failure. An estimated 25 million Indians have diabetes, and this is forecasted to grow to 57 million by 2025. Doctors say the government has failed to register the scale of the impending crisis. Excessive consumption can cause many kinds of problems. As an example, doctors are blaming a rise in drug-resistant strains of bacteria on consumers' excessive use of antibiotics.[48]

As you can see, consumer behavior reflects the multitude of factors revealed in Exhibit 1.2, which is why marketers must go beyond simply understanding which products a consumer buys.

What Affects Consumer Behavior?

What affects consumers as they make their acquisition, usage, and disposition decisions? The many factors are organized into four broad domains, as shown in the model in Exhibit 1.8, which also serves as an organizing framework for this book.

The four domains of consumer behavior are (1) the psychological core, (2) the process of making decisions, (3) the consumer's culture, and (4) consumer behavior outcomes. Although the four domains are presented in separate sections of this book, each domain is related to all the others. For example, to make decisions that affect outcomes like buying new products or using products for symbolic reasons, consumers must first engage in processes described in the psychological core. They need to be motivated, able, and have the opportunity to be exposed to, perceive, and attend to information. They need to think about this information, develop attitudes about it, and form memories.

The cultural environment also affects what motivates consumers, how they process information, and the kinds of decisions they make. Age, gender, social class, ethnicity, families, friends, and other factors affect consumer values and lifestyles and, in turn, influence the decisions that consumers make and how and why they make them. Let us consider each domain separately and illustrate the interrelationships among the domains with an example of a vacation decision.

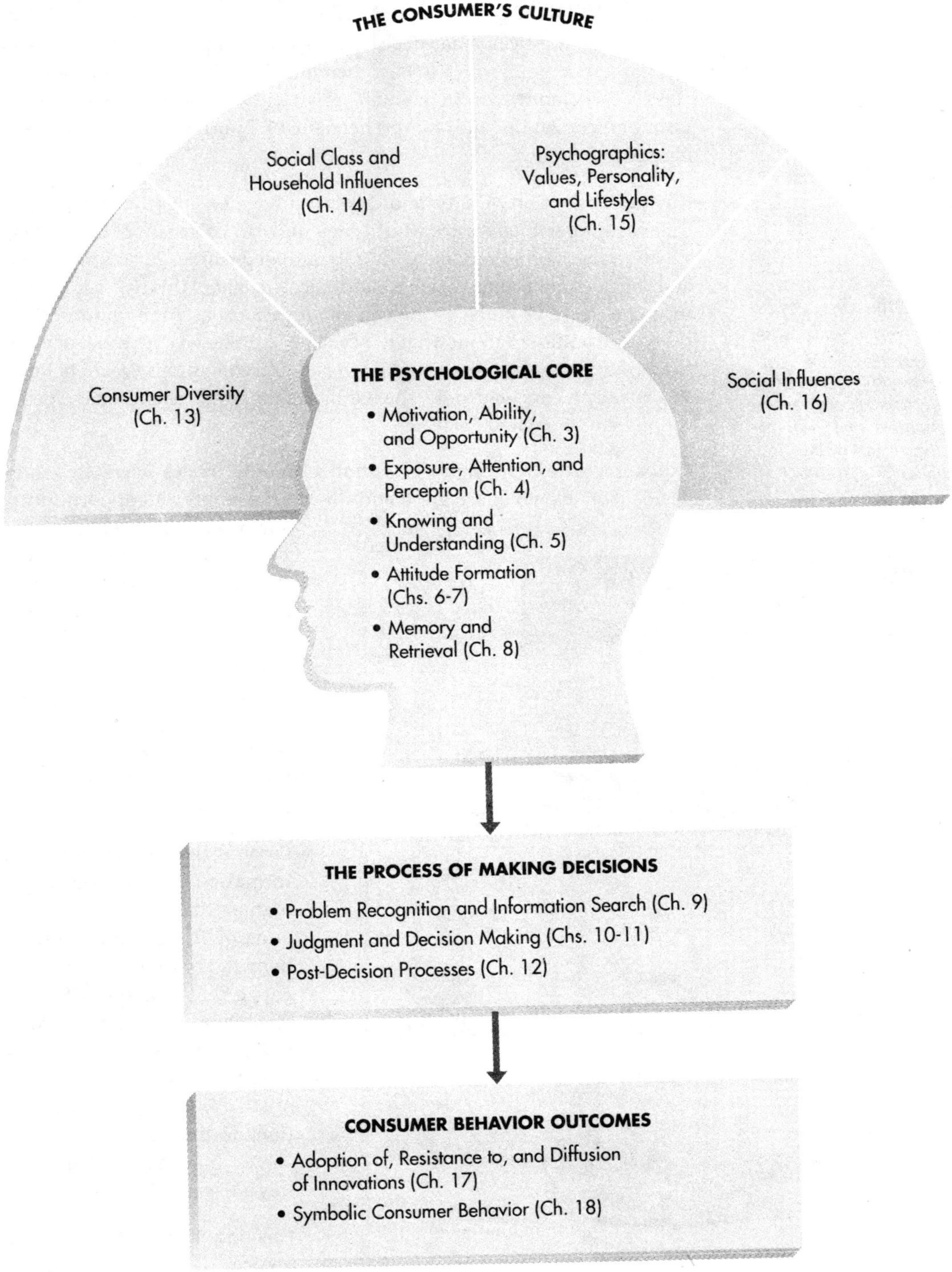

Exhibit 1.8

A MODEL OF CONSUMER BEHAVIOR *Consumer behavior encompasses four domains: (1) the consumer's culture, (2) the psychological core, (3) the process of making decisions, and (4) consumer behavior outcomes. As the exhibit shows, Chapters 3–18 of this book relate to the four parts of this overall model.*

The Psychological Core: Internal Consumer Processes

Before consumers can make decisions, they must have some source of knowledge or information upon which to base their decisions. This source—the psychological core—covers motivation, ability, and opportunity; exposure, attention, and perception; categorization and comprehension of information; and formation and change in attitude.

Having Motivation, Ability, and Opportunity Consider the case of a hypothetical consumer named Jessica who is deciding on a ski vacation. In Jessica's mind, a vacation decision is very risky—her vacation consumes lots of money and time, and she does not want to make a bad choice. In light of this risk, Jessica is very motivated to learn as much as she can about various vacation options, think about them, and fantasize about what they will be like. She has put other activities aside to give herself the opportunity to learn and think about this vacation. Because Jessica already knows how to ski, she has the ability to determine what types of ski vacations she would find enjoyable.

Exhibit 1.9

Categorizing a vacation Vacation can be a weekend vacation or a quick getaway or a planned long vacation-the consumers decide what kind of option to choose from.

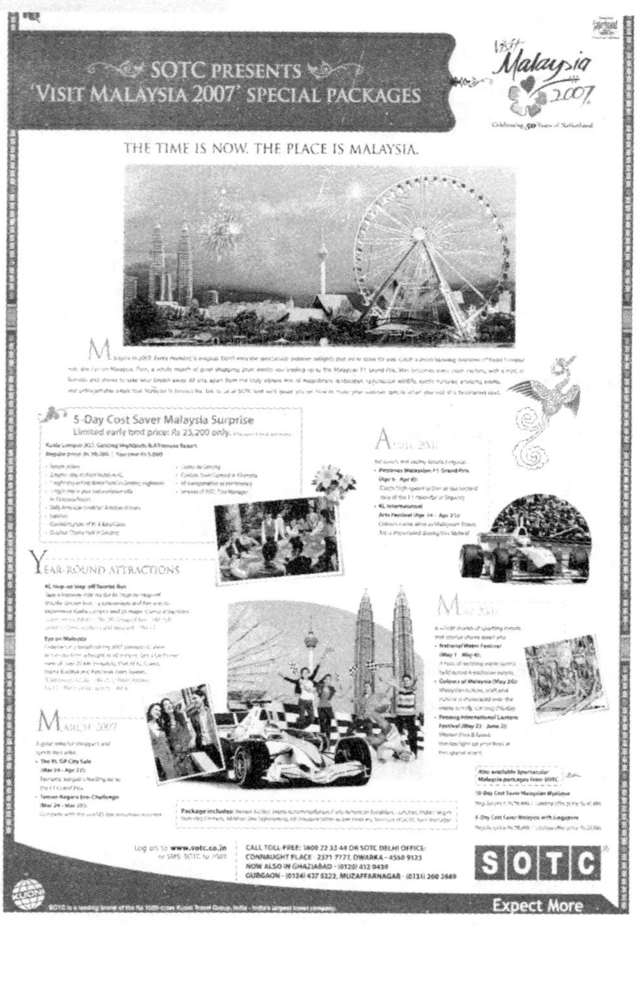

Exposure, Attention, and Perception Because Jessica is greatly motivated to decide where to go on vacation and she has the ability and opportunity to do so, she will make sure she is exposed to, perceives, and attends to any information she thinks is relevant to her decision. She might look at travel ads and websites, read travel-related articles, and talk with friends and travel agents. Note, though, that Jessica will probably not attend to *all* vacation information; she is likely to be exposed to information she will never perceive or pay attention to.

Categorizing and Comprehending Information Jessica will use the information that she does perceive and attempt to categorize and comprehend it. For example, she might categorize the vacation in Exhibit 1.9 as something other than a ski vacation and therefore will not consider it further. She might infer that Kitzbühel, Austria, is a reasonably priced vacation destination because a website shows information consistent with this interpretation.

Forming and Changing Attitudes Jessica is likely to form attitudes toward the vacations she has categorized and comprehended. She may have a favorable attitude toward Kitzbühel because a website describes it as affordable, educational, and fun. However, her attitudes might undergo considerable change as she encounters new information. Attitudes do not always predict our behavior. For example, many of us probably have a positive attitude toward working out. Nevertheless, our positive attitude and our good intentions do not always culminate in a trip to the gym. For this reason, attitudes and choices are considered as separate topics.

Forming and Retrieving Memories One reason that our attitudes may not predict our behavior is that we may or may not remember the information we used to form our attitudes when we later make a decision. Thus Jessica may have *formed* memories based on certain information, but her choices will be based only on the information she *retrieves* from memory.

The Process of Making Decisions

The processes that are part of the psychological core are intimately tied to the process of making decisions. The process of making consumer decisions involves four stages: problem recognition, information search, decision making, and post-purchase evaluation.

Problem Recognition and the Search for Information Problem recognition occurs when we realize we have an unfulfilled need. Jessica realized she needed a vacation, for example. Her subsequent search for information gave her insight into where she might go, how much it might cost, and when she might travel. She also examined her financial situation. Elements of the psychological core are invoked in problem recognition and search because once Jessica realizes that she needs a vacation and begins her information search, she is exposed to information, attends to and perceives it, categorizes and comprehends it, and forms attitudes and memories.

Making Judgments and Decisions Jessica's decision is characterized as a *high-effort decision,* meaning that she is willing to invest a lot of time and exert mental and emotional energy in making it. She identifies several decision criteria that she thinks will be important in making her choices: the trip should be fun and exciting, safe, educational, and affordable. Not all decisions involve a lot of effort. Jessica also faces low-effort decisions such as deciding what brand of toothpaste to take on the trip. Again, the psychological core is invoked in making decisions. With a high-effort decision, Jessica will be motivated to expose herself to lots of information; she will think about it deeply, analyze it critically, and form attitudes about it. She may have lasting memories about the information she sees because she has thought about it so much. With a low-effort decision, such as what brand of toothpaste to buy, she would probably conduct a less extensive information search, do less information processing, and form less enduring attitudes and memories.

Making Post-Decision Evaluations Evaluating the decision is the final step of the decision-making process. This step allows the consumer to judge whether the decision was the correct one and whether to purchase the product or service again. When she returns from her vacation, Jessica will probably evaluate the outcome of her decisions. If her expectations were met and the vacation is everything she thought it would be, she will feel satisfied. If the vacation exceeds her expectations, she will be delighted. If it falls short, she is will be dissatisfied. Once again, aspects of the psychological core are invoked in making post-decision evaluations. Jessica may expose herself to information that validates her experiences, she may update her attitudes, and she may selectively remember aspects of her trip that were extremely positive or negative.

The Consumer's Culture: External Processes

Why did Jessica decide to go on a skiing trip in the first place? In large part, our consumption decisions and how we process information are affected by our culture. ***Culture*** refers to the typical or expected behaviors, norms, and ideas that characterize a group of people. It can be a powerful influence on all aspects of human behavior. Jessica had certain feelings, perceptions, and attitudes because of the unique combination of groups to which she belongs and the influence on her values, personality, and lifestyle.

Diversity Influences Jessica is a member of many regional, ethnic, and religious groups that directly or indirectly affect the decisions she makes. For example, her decision to ski at a place far from home is fairly typical for a working woman from North America. It is doubtful that a consumer from the Third World or a single woman from a Hindu culture would have made the same vacation choice. Also, her age, gender, and educational background may all affect her impressions of what constitutes a good vacation, accounting for her interest in a sophisticated European ski trip.

Social Class and Household Influences Because Jessica is a member of the upper middle class and has moved in with her parents, these social and household influences may have had an effect on her decision to go to a luxurious European ski resort with friends rather than skiing with her family in a rustic ski area near home.

Values, Personality, and Lifestyles The choices Jessica makes are based, in part, on her beliefs, her personality, and her activities, interests, and opinions. Thus, she may be attracted to a European ski trip because she wants a vacation that she thinks will be exciting and out of the ordinary. She also anticipates that this vacation will test her skills and give her a sense of accomplishment.

Reference Groups and Other Social Influences When Jessica sees groups of others she perceives as similar to herself, she regards them as ***reference groups,*** people whose values she shares and whose opinion she values. She might also want to emulate the behavior of people whom she admires, even if she does not know them personally. Thus well-known athletes, musicians, politicians, or movie stars sometimes serve as reference groups, influencing the psychological core and the decision-making process by affecting how we evaluate marketplace information and the choices we make. Reference groups can also make us feel as if we should behave in a certain way. Jessica may feel some pressure to go to Kitzbühel because her friends think that doing so is cool. In addition, Jessica's personality may affect her decisions. Because she is an extrovert and a moderate risk taker, she wants a vacation that is exciting and allows her to meet new people.

Consumer Behavior Outcomes

As the conceptual model in Exhibit 1.8 indicates, the psychological core, decision-making processes, and the consumer's culture affect consumer behavior outcomes such as the symbolic use of products and the diffusion of ideas, products, or services through a market.

Consumer Behaviors Can Symbolize Who We Are The groups we belong to and our own sense of self can affect the ***symbols*** or external signs we use, consciously or unconsciously, to express our identity. For example, while skiing on vacation, Jessica may wear a North Face ski parka and Bollé goggles to communicate her status as an experienced skier. She might also take home objects that symbolize her vacation, such as postcards and T-shirts.

Consumer Behaviors Can Diffuse Through a Market After she makes her vacation decision, Jessica may tell others about her prospective trip. Her choice of vacation destination therefore becomes known to other consumers and may influence their vacation decisions as well. In this way, the idea of going to Kitzbühel on vacation may diffuse, or spread, to others. Had Jessica resisted going to Kitzbühel (perhaps because she thought it was too expensive or too far), she might have communicated information that made others less likely to vacation there. Thus the diffusion of information can have both negative and positive effects for marketers.

In the following chapters we expand on the concepts outlined in Exhibit 1.8. We first consider the psychological core (Part One) and then delve into decision-making processes (Part Two). We next consider how the consumer's culture affects consumer behavior (Part Three) and how individual and cultural factors affect consumer behavior outcomes (Part Four). We conclude by examining consumer welfare issues (Part Five).

Clearly, every consumer is unique and is affected by a unique set of background factors. Consider the vacation choices shown in Exhibit 1.10, and try to imagine the background factors that predispose consumers to choose these as vacation options.

Exhibit 1.10

VACATION

The Indian consumer is on the go, and the urge for travel is fuelled by low-cost airlines, the mushrooming of the on-line travel industry, and the availability of a wide range of destinations and accommodations. Indians are spending 30 percent more on vacations than in 2002. Given that, and the surge of tourist traffic into India, it is hardly surprising that the World Travel and Tourism Council (WTTC) has estimated that by 2020, tourism in India could contribute US$ 189.3 billion to India's GDP. The new Indian is more than willing to share his newfound wealth and prosperity on all the good things in life, vacationing definitely being one of them. Some common forms of vacationing prevalent in Indian settings are:

1. The Weekend getaway: Hectic corporate lifestyles urge most people today to take these quick 2-3 days weekend trips to a destination closer to the city. The focus remains on relaxation and simply chilling out. Destinations and hotels marketing such concepts focus on the ambience, the location, facilities provided and of course the cost of the package. Often companies sponsor such trips and even training programmes or internal board meetings are held on such off-site locations, hence mixing work and play.

2. The Annual Vacation: The Annual holidays which most families take are usually clubbed with vacations at school in and around summer. These are long holidays planned over months and the visits involve planning for both the location and also for the travel. Focus remains on the location(s) to visit and the sharing experience within the peer group is an important ritual

3. The Festival Fervor: A something in between the getaway and the annual vacation, where one plans for a break between or after festivals. Not popular amongst corporates but definitely a regular amongst families in the 9 to 5 job; government servants.

4. The compulsive vacationer: Basically, the variant of a compulsive shopper who makes vacation a routine with time periods fixed along with impromptu trips. Destinations could be exotic to the un-chartered areas. The focus is on absorbing and soaking in the changed setting.

Who Benefits from the Study of Consumer Behavior?

The final question we address in this chapter is *why* people study consumer behavior. The reasons are as varied as the four different groups who use consumer research: marketing managers, ethicists and advocates, public policy makers and regulators, and consumers.

Marketing Managers

The study of consumer behavior provides critical information to marketing managers for developing marketing strategies and tactics. We can emphasize this point by examining the American Marketing Association's definition of ***marketing.***

> *Marketing is an organizational function and a set of processes for creating, communicating, and delivering value to customers and for managing customer relationships in ways that benefit the organization and its stakeholders.*

According to this definition, marketing managers must clearly understand what consumers value in order to effectively market a product or service. Marketers also must look beyond single transactions to determine how they can connect with consumers on an ongoing basis. The study of consumer behavior provides insights that help marketers design, deliver, and communicate appropriate offerings and strengthen relationships with consumers. In Chapter 2 we expand on the role of marketing research and the strategic and tactical decisions it supports.

Ethicists and Advocacy Groups

Marketers' actions sometimes raise important ethical questions. Consumers who are particularly concerned about ethical marketing sometimes form advocacy groups to create public awareness of inappropriate practices. They also influence other consumers as well as the targeted companies through strategies such as media statements and boycotts. For example, the Department of Consumer Affairs being a nodal Department in the field of consumer protection has initiated a number of steps to promote a responsible and responsive consumer movement in the country. Such measures include use of mass media for promoting consumer awareness and encouraging consumers involvement through Governmental and non-governmental organizations etc. In pursuance of the same "Jago Grahak Jago" advertising campaign was developed urging consumers to check all facets of an item that they purchase thoroughly, including weight, date of manufacture/expiry, labeling requirements etc. We explore various ethical issues throughout this book and go into more detail in Chapter 20, "The Dark Side of Consumer Behavior and Marketing."

Consumers sometimes band together to form cooperatives—institutions in which consumers minimize costs and control marketing practices by acting as both owners and consumers. In many segments of Indian economy, cooperatives are playing a predominant role in the credit sector despite of the keen competition from nationalised and private sector banks. Cooperatives are disbursing nearly 46% of the total agricultural credit. They are distributing 36% of the total fertilisers in the country. The share of cooperatives in sugar production is nearly 55%, in spindlege 10%, in yarn production 22.1% and in coverage of handlooms 55%. The cooperatives are playing a very important role in the public distribution system to serve the weaker sections of the community. Nearly 28% of the rural fair price shops are within the cooperative fold. Cooperatives have also played an effective role in exports.

Public Policy Makers and Regulators

Lawmakers and public policy groups strive to protect consumers from unfair, unsafe, or inappropriate marketing practices. In the 1960s, President Kennedy declared that consumers have the right to safety, to information, to choice, and to be heard. The right to a clean environment and protection for minorities and the poor were added later. Many governmental groups develop detailed regulations and enforce laws related to these basic rights. Consider the regulatory limits on tobacco marketing, designed to discourage underage consumers from starting to smoke and to inform consumers of smoking's health hazards. The United States, European Union, and other areas ban cigarette advertising on television, radio, and in certain other media; they also require warning labels on each pack. The United Kingdom goes even further, forbidding tobacco marketers from using Internet promotions and sponsoring major events such as Formula One racing.[52] In India also cigarette and liquor advertising is banned and only surrogate advertising is allowed. Any form of sponsorship and endorsements directly by the tobacco and the liquor company is also not allowed.

In protecting the right to be informed, consumer researchers have investigated deceptive and misleading advertising. Therefore, understanding how consumers comprehend and categorize information is important to recognizing and guarding against misleading advertising. Researchers want to know what impressions an ad creates and whether these impressions are true. Not long ago, the FDA expressed concern about ads for anti-AIDS drugs that show people with AIDS and those who are HIV-positive engaging in vigorous activities. Through research, the San Francisco health department had discovered that gay men exposed to such ads were more willing to participate in unsafe sex. After the FDA asked the drug manufacturers to more clearly explain the limitations of their products, Pfizer added a notice stating that its Viracept drug does not cure AIDS or prevent HIV.[53] The advertising regulatory body in India, ASCI, lays down some guidelines and norms for effective management of the advertising practices within the country. ASCI believes that more and more consumers are questioning the claims made by organizations through their advertisements. Therefore, it becomes the moral responsibility of ASCI to ensure that agencies follow clearly laid down guidelines and norms. ASCI encourages the public to complain against advertisements which they consider to be false, misleading, offensive or unfair. All complaints are evaluated by an independent Consumer Complaints Council (CCC) which has 21 members - 12 from civil society and 9 from advertising practitioners.

Consumer researchers also investigate advertising to children. Research has shown that children under the age of 6 lack the cognitive abilities to understand that advertisements are trying to persuade them. Consequently, many people believe that young consumers need to be protected against messages that may depict products in overly glamorous or attractive ways. In another protective measure,

U.S. policy makers passed the Children's Online Privacy Act to prevent online marketers from collecting personal data from children under 13 without parental notification and consent.[54] You will learn more about this and related issues in Chapter 19, "Consumerism and Public Policy Issues." For now, the important point is that consumer behavior can be quite useful to regulators and government agencies in developing laws and policies to protect consumers—and that marketers' decisions are affected by public policy actions.

Academics

Consumer behavior is important in the academic world for two reasons. First, academics disseminate knowledge about consumer behavior when they teach courses on the subject. Second, academics generate knowledge about consumer behavior when they conduct research focusing on how consumers act, think, and feel when acquiring, using, and disposing of offerings. In turn, such academic research is useful to marketing managers, advocacy groups, regulators, and others who need to understand consumer behavior.

Exhibit 1.11
ADVERTISEMENT FOR RECYCLING
Understanding consumer behavior can help make a better environment for us all, as the trend toward recyling shows.

Consumers

An understanding of consumer behavior can help make a better environment for consumers. For example, research indicates that we better understand the differences between brands when we can view a chart, matrix, or grid comparing brands and their attributes.[55] Thus, matrices such as those presented in *Consumer Reports* are likely to help many consumers make more effective decisions.

Product and service developments designed to protect certain consumer segments have also grown out of understanding how consumers behave. As discussed in other parts of this chapter, many people want to protect children against violent video games, invasion of privacy online, inducements to start smoking, and other stimuli they consider inappropriate. Some companies have changed their marketing voluntarily, whereas others have waited until legislators and regulators forced changes in their marketing.

Finally, consumer research on disposition behavior has the potential to affect programs that conserve natural resources. Exhibit 1.11 shows an ad that aims to educate consumers about the benefits of recycling. You can learn more about consumer behavior and websites that relate to consumer behavior issues by visiting the website for the Association for Consumer Research at www.acrwebsite.org.

Summary

The term *consumer behavior* actually goes beyond the subject of consumer purchasing. It involves understanding the set of decisions (what, whether, why, when, how, where, how much, how often) that an individual or group of consumers makes over time about the acquisition, use, or disposition of products, services, ideas, or activities.

The psychological core exerts considerable influence on consumer behavior. A consumer's motivation, ability, and opportunity affects his or her decisions and influences what a consumer is exposed to, what he or she pays attention to, and what he or she perceives. These factors also affect how a consumer categorizes or interprets information, how he or she forms and changes attitudes, and how he or she forms and retrieves memories. Each of these aspects of the psychological core has a bearing on the consumer decision-making process, which involves (1) problem recognition, (2) information search, (3) judgment and decision making, and (4) evaluation of satisfaction with the decision.

Consumer behavior is also affected by the consumer's culture, and the typical or expected behaviors, norms, and ideas of a particular group. Consumers belong to a number of groups, share their cultural values and beliefs, and use their symbols to communicate group membership. Consumer behavior can be symbolic and express an individual's identity. In addition, consumer behavior is indicative of how forcefully or quickly an offering can spread throughout a market.

Marketers study consumer behavior to gain insights that will lead to more effective marketing strategies and tactics and help build relationships with consumers. Ethicists and advocacy groups are also keenly interested in consumer behavior. Public policy makers and regulators consider consumer behavior when designing protective laws and regulations. Finally, the study of consumer behavior can improve consumers' own lives as marketers learn to make products more user-friendly and to show concern for the environment.

Questions for Review and Discussion

1. How is consumer behavior defined?
2. What three broad categories of consumer activity do marketers and researchers study in consumer behavior?
3. What are some of the factors in the psychological core that affect consumer decisions and behavior?
4. What are some of the external processes that influence consumer decisions and behavior?
5. How is marketing defined?
6. How do public policy decision makers and marketers use consumer research?

Exercises

1. Answer the following questions about a product or service category in which you are interested:
   a. How can this product or service be acquired? (Try to think of more than one way.) What are the implications for marketing strategy?
   b. How is the product or service consumed? How can marketers use this information when developing marketing strategy?
   c. How can the product or service be disposed of? How might this factor influence the next acquisition?
2. Based on the definition of consumer behavior presented in the first part of the chapter, identify the consumer behavior activities you have engaged in today.
3. How might a study of the way children process advertisements be useful to public policy makers? What kinds of industries might be affected by findings from such research? Explain your answer.
4. Consider the time period in which acquisition, consumption, and disposition take place when answering these questions:

a. What products, services, or categories are typically acquired over the course of days? Over the course of weeks or months? How does the timing affect marketing decisions about these offerings?

b. What products, services, or categories are typically used over the course of months? Over the course of years? How does the timing affect marketing decisions about these offerings?

c. What products or categories are typically disposed of over the course of days or weeks? How does the timing affect marketing decisions about these offerings?

5. Locate an ad that aims to influence the disposition of an offering, and answer the following questions about it:

a. Referring to Exhibit 1.2, identify the specific consumer decisions and the decision-making units that might be affected by this ad.

b. Which aspects of the consumer's culture are mentioned or implied in this ad? How do you think these aspects are likely to affect the consumer's response to the ad?

More Exercises from the Adaptor

1. In the context of the case at the start of the Chapter on Bajaj, evaluate the advertising done by Bajaj for scooters in the past and for the motorbike today identifying the following factors:
   a. The difference in the target audience which the two advertisements from different generations are trying to address
   b. The segment of customers that they address and the product proposition
   c. Finally, give your viewpoints on how a company like Bajaj has integrated the changing lifestyle of the Indian consumers in their company vision
2. Evaluate how the advent of large retail stores are putting a pressure on the traditional Kirana or grocery outlets and how a discerning metro consumer will evaluate the existence of the two formats particularly in the context of his buying approach.
3. The effects of the rising economic prosperity in India are felt across markets and product categories, besides buying behaviour. In the context of the following products, discuss how buying approaches have changed
   a. Watches
   b. House
   c. Consumer Loans

Chapter 2 Developing and Using Information About Consumer Behavior

LEARNING OBJECTIVES

After studying this chapter, you will be able to:

- Outline some of the research methods used to understand consumer behavior.
- Identify the different types of people and organizations that conduct consumer research.
- Explain how companies use consumer research to make marketing decisions.
- Discuss some of the ethical issues in consumer research.

INTRODUCTION

Exploring the Indian Affluent: A Study on the Indian Affluent by Technopak India

Consumer Research study across India has picked up particularly in the last two-three years. The unprecedented economic boom and its fallouts have meant serious implications for consumers and therefore an impact on their buying behavior. Housewives traditionally relied on a grocery list to make their purchases, but new researches and observations indicate that with the advent of the modern retail formats, housewives are wary of carrying a grocery list in such locations. Infact, lists that are carried now remain more of a mental checklist of items that need to be bought; the rest is dependant on store and situational influences, which impact a lot of purchase.

Segments which were pre-dominant earlier have broken up into niches or sub-segments and marketers have to make adequate efforts through research, qualitative or quantitative to identify emerging segments. Chapter 1 illustrates the case of Bajaj and its transformation from a traditional scooter manufacturing company to establishing its presence in the growing motorcycle market. Today's marketers are employing research agencies or have their own in-house departments which are continuously involved in data warehousing and mining to explore such emerging markets.

A similar study conducted by Technopak India about the Luxury Trends in India in 2006, across 4000 consumers in 12 cities, covering 17 products and services, throws some interesting insights into a segment which was never really explored in-depth and whatever opinion was formed of it, largely remained restricted to a very superficial level. The Indian Luxury Trends 2006 study attempts to demystify the Indian Affluent, in terms of his segment classification, his aspirations, taste, lifestyle and broad indicators to his shopping trends.

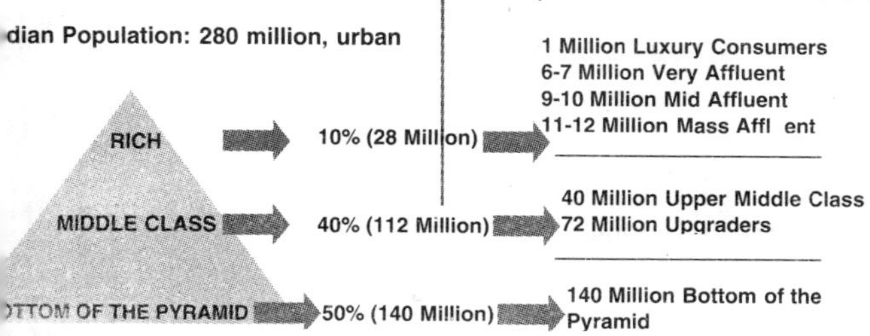

Exhibit 2.1
THE POPULATION DIVIDE ON SOCIAL CLASS HIERARCHY

Indian Population : 280 million, urban

An assessment of the Indian population as depicted in Exhibit 2.1 illustrates the affluent class as just 10% of the 280 million urban population. But the potential within the segment is fast emerging as a trend. In the latter Exhibit 2.2 the further dissection of the 10% has been classified into four key segments and each segment in itself has some key differentiators. The study has been able to classify the affluent class and each sub set has been examined individually on the aspects of Emotions, Aspirations and Lifestyle. Infact, with the rising economic prosperity, particularly noteworthy in the urban sectors, there are new entrants in the segments.

Exhibit 2.2
A CLASSIFICATION OF THE INDIAN AFFLUENT SHOWS THE PATTERNS OF THE AFFLUENT:

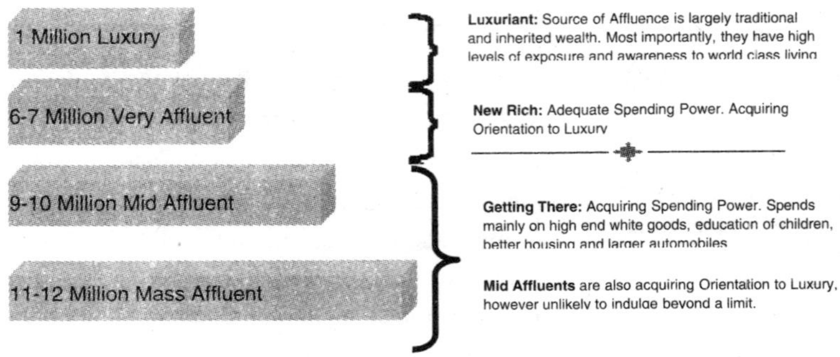

Exhibit 2.3
MARKET SPEND ALLOCATION

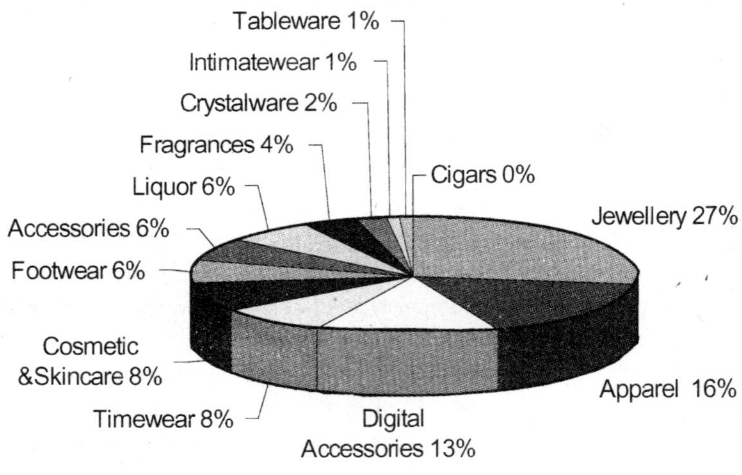

The trends that seem to be noteworthy today are the rise of the new generation affluent who are beyond the traditionally rich. These new generation affluent are an off-spring of the economic boom. The Luxury Trend study broadly outlines five key segments from where this segment has risen:

- CEO's and other senior professionals in their thirties
- Entrepreneurs in myriad new businesses e.g. Technology, Manufacturing, Services
- Returning "Prodigal children"
- Franchisees, Small and Medium Retailers
- Others

As we go back to Exhibit 2.2 we find that the Mid Affluent and the Mass Affluent are the critical segments which have the potential in the future to grow. Their current focus is on Housing, Travel, Education, High end vehicles and Electronic gadgets, lifestyle products. But in the future the categories expected to see further growth after this segment has settled down. The key categories of growth will be men's clothing, women's jewellery, women's accessories including handbags and Footwear, watches and Gourmet Food and Wines. The final picture as exhibited in 2.3 represents how the affluent class decides on the spend across different product categories. The India Luxury Trends 2006, from the Technopak study classifies the Luxury households into the following attitudinal segments:

1. **The Arrived:** The most affluent group. Within the group there is the first generation affluent- the celebrity, the New Rich and the Used to Luxury- Addict. They are the largest segment comprising 49% of the target group.
2. **The Actualized Ascetic:** This group largely comprises of self made men, whether professionals or business people, who are in their late 40's and early 50's. Though they have the purchasing power, they shun all kinds of ostentation. They are the smallest group comprising just 15%.
3. **The Climbers:** These are really the learners. They comprise of climbers- who want to project a lifestyle which will give them admission into the "inner circle", yet lack the discernment that comes from grooming and exposure. They comprise 19% of the universe.
4. **The Laggards:** They are most non chalant to luxury consumption. This group would typically have the highest proportion of college drop outs and plain graduates who are in business and a very few who have done well as office executives. 17% of the total consuming base.

Consumer Behavior Research Methods

Researchers collect and analyze two types of data for marketing purposes: primary and secondary. Data collected for its own purpose is called primary data. When marketers gather data using surveys, focus groups, experiments, and the like to support their own marketing decisions, they are collecting primary data. Data collected by an entity for one pur pose and subsequently used by another entity for a different purpose is called secondary data. For example, after the government collects census data for tax purposes, marketers can use the results as secondary data to estimate the size of markets in their own industry.

A number of tools are available in the consumer researcher's "tool kit" for gathering primary data, some based on what consumers say and some on what they do. Researchers may collect data from relatively few people or compile data from huge samples of consumers. These tools are valuable precisely because they are so different. Each can provide unique insights that, when combined, reveal very different perspectives on the complex world of consumer behavior. This is research with a purpose: to guide companies in making more informed decisions and achieving marketing results.[2]

Surveys

One research tool with which we are all familiar is the ***survey,*** a written instrument that asks consumers to respond to a predetermined set of research questions. Some responses may be open-ended, with the consumer filling in the blanks; others may ask consumers to use a rating scale or check marks. Surveys can be conducted in person, through the mail, over the phone, or using the Web. Procter & Gamble, for example, conducts about 1,500 online consumer surveys every year and obtains results 75 percent faster than with traditional survey methods—at half the cost.[3]

Although companies often undertake specialized surveys to better understand a specific customer segment, some research organizations carry out broad-based surveys that are made available to marketers. The Indian Census study undertaken once in 10 years is a nation wide study attempting to understand the population demographics and the various aspects in the context of age, language, marital status, gender, educational qualification, and a range of other important parameters affecting the demographic factors, while evaluating the population profile. The Pulse Polio campaign of the government is a successful attempt to use the census study and carry forward the immunization campaign.

Survey data can also tell marketers something about media usage and product purchase. The data exhibited as 2.4 is an illustration of how consumers respond to the changing trends in the Indian retail scenario. Research houses like IMRB or ORG-MARG in India have been consistently trying to unearth facts and trends about how Indian consumers are responding to or are most likely to respond to changing trends. In a study by Images-KSA Technopak the India Retail Report 2005, highlights that between 1999-2006 the share of organized retail has gone up by 3.5% which in rupee terms works to some Rs.280 billion. Moving forward, organized retailing is projected to grow at the rate of 25%-30% p.a. and is estimated to reach an astounding INR 1000 billion by 2010. Further, its contribution to total retailing sales is likely to rise to 9% by the end of the decade.

Exhibit 2.4
IMRB'S RETAIL STUDY SHOWS THE BUYING POINTS OF THE HOUSEWIVES HAVE NOT ALTERED ACROSS SEC. THE TRADITIONAL FORMAT HAS LARGELY REMAINED THE PREFERRED DESTINATION, AS COMPARED TO THE MODERN FORMATS.

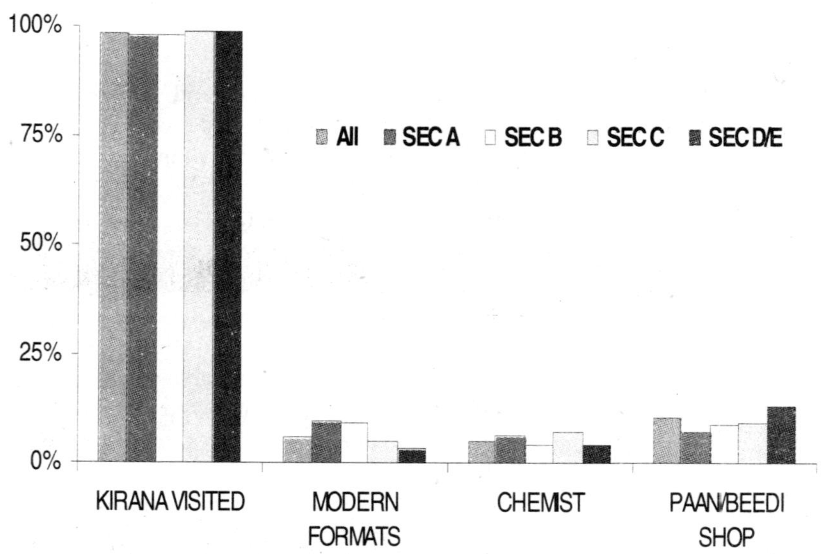

	1999	2002	2005
Total Retail (in billion INR)	7000	8250	10000
Organized Retail (in billion INR)	50	150	350
% Share of Organized Retail	0.70%	1.80%	3.5%

Infact, this whole retail revolution is not restricted to the metros and the tier-II cities, prominently, Surat, Lucknow, DehraDun, Vijaywada, Bhopal, Indore, Vadodara, Coimbatore, Nasik, Bhubaneswar, Varanasi and Ludhiana also seem to be witnessing the winds of change. With consumption in metros already being exploited, manufacturers and retailers of products such as personal computers, mobile phones, automobiles, consumer durables, financial services etc are increasingly targeting consumers in tier II cities and towns. In addition, petro-retailing efforts of petroleum giants scattered through out the country's landscape have also ensured that smaller towns are also exposed to modern retailing formats. Favorable demographic and psychographic changes relating to India's consumer class, international exposure, availability of increasing quality retail space, wider availability of products and brand communication are some of the factors that are driving the retail in India. Over the last few years, many international retailers have entered the Indian market on the strength of rising affluence levels of the young Indian population along with the heightened awareness of global brands and international shopping experiences and the increased availability of retail real estate pace.

Focus Groups

Unlike a survey, which may collect input from hundreds of people responding individually to the same questionnaire, a ***focus group*** brings together groups of 6 to 12 consumers to discuss an issue or an offering. Led by a trained moderator, the people in the focus group express their opinions about a given product or topic, particularly useful in identifying and testing new product ideas. Often the researcher does not have prior insights into how the group might feel. Instead, a group's views become known only as the discussion unfolds. Focus groups provide qualitative insights into consumer attitudes, as opposed to the quantitative (numerical) data resulting from surveys.

Not all focus groups are conducted in a formal research room. In an in-house focus group conducted amongst housewives and working women in the age-group of 28-35 years for cooking oil, most participants where encouraged to mingle within themselves and the moderator moved around trying to initiate discussions on the key points pertaining to: (i) The brands purchased and consumption pattern (usage quantity and frequency); (ii) The reasons for purchasing the current brand; (iii) Knowledge about types of cooking oil; (iv) Influence of communication and promotion; (v) Effects of sales promotion schemes in deciding. The participants in such an uncontrolled or informal setting are able to respond better and also the responses are more realistic.

A related technique is the computer-based focus group, in which consumers go to a computer lab where their individual comments are displayed anonymously on a large screen for viewing by the group. This method can help researchers gather information on sensitive topics, as can focus groups conducted by telephone or online rather than in person. However, the anonymity prevents researchers from collecting other relevant data, such as nonverbal reactions conveyed by facial expressions and body language that would be available in a traditional focus group.

Some companies convene customer advisory boards, small groups of customers that meet with marketing and service executives once or twice a year (face-to-face, online, or by phone). As a representative sample of customers, the board can knowledgeably discuss the company's offerings, competitive products, future needs, acquisition and usage problems, and related issues. Board meetings serve not just as research, but also as a tool for strengthening customer relations.[6]

Interviews

Like focus groups, interviews involve direct contact with consumers. Interviews are often more appropriate than focus groups when the topic is sensitive, embarrassing, confidential, or emotionally charged. They provide more in-depth data than surveys when the researcher wants to "pick consumers' brains." A researcher who wants to really understand the symbolic significance of a brand to consumers, for example, may ask respondents open-ended questions about what the brand means to them; how and when they purchase and use it; and the people, activities, and events they associate with it. When Marico planked brand Saffola as a way to the healthy heart platform, the communication was targeted towards the housewives and particularly the middle-aged for whom the risk of heart related disorders was more common. In order to make the proposition more effective and to drive home the message more effectively to the desired target audience, the brand tied up with the Mumbai Dabbawalas, who carry home cooked food from home to offices. The brand tied for a merchandise promotion with the dabbawalas and the effectiveness of the message was further reinforced. The promotional campaign was cost effective, yet the reach and impact of the event was efficient.

In some interviews, researchers ask customers about the process they use to make a purchase decision. One marketing research company assigns professional interviewers to tape-record consumers' thoughts while they shop for groceries. This research helps marketers understand how factors in the shopping environment affect purchasing. For example, a company might learn that a consumer didn't buy a certain cereal because it was placed too close to the laundry detergent.[8]

Exhibit 2.5

Exhibit 2.5

SAFFOLA HEALTH PLATFORM

Through planking Saffola cooking oil as a way to the healthy heart platform, the company targeted housewives and the middle-aged audience

Traditional interviews require a trained interviewer who attempts to establish rapport with consumers. Interviewers also note nonverbal behaviors like twitches, fidgeting, eye shifting, voice pitch changes, and folded arms and legs as clues to whether the respondent is open to the discussion or whether certain questions are particularly sensitive. Researchers often record interviews for later transcription so they can examine the results using qualitative or quantitative analysis. Sometimes researchers videotape nonverbal responses that cannot be captured in the transcription process and analyze the interviews later to identify patterns or themes. As a result, interviews can be an expensive data collection method.

Storytelling

Another tool for conducting consumer research is ***storytelling,*** in which consumers tell researchers stories about their experiences with a product. Maruti, for its Wagon-R brand introduced an advertising campaign in 2005-06 weaving interesting stories around its brand with the help of people who have interesting stories to share, and how the brand becomes an integral part of the story. The campaign was effectively able to resonate with the changing psychographic profile of the Indian metro population, who are not necessarily chasing a 9-5 dream, but a dream of their own. In one such advertisement, the hero, Ramesh Rao, who worked for a blue chip multinational, definitely a very cushy job, quits to follow his dream of being an adventure sports guide. He also owns a Wagon R.

Although storytelling involves the real stories of real consumers, sometimes marketers ask consumers to tell or write stories about hypothetical situations that the marketer has depicted in a picture or scenario.[10] The idea is that a consumer's needs, feelings, and perceptions are revealed by the way he or she interprets what is depicted in the picture or scenario. For example, researchers may show a picture of a woman at the entrance to a Hot Topic store with a thought bubble above her head and ask consumers to write what they imagine the woman is thinking. Such stories can provide valuable information about what consumers think of a particular store, purchase situation, and so on.

Use of Photography and Pictures

Some researchers use a technique in which they show pictures of experiences that consumers have had. This helps consumers remember their experiences and report them more completely.[11] Researchers may also ask consumers to draw or collect pictures, either their own photographs or clippings from magazines, to represent their thoughts and feelings about the topic at hand (e.g., What does Ivory soap mean to me?). Still another practice is to ask consumers to assemble a collage of pictures that reflects their lifestyles. Researchers then ask questions about the pictures and the meaning behind them. Having the consumer write an essay can help integrate the images and thoughts suggested by the pictures.[12]

For example, Wrigley's marketers asked teenagers to select pictures and write a story about Juicy Fruit Gum. The company learned that teens chewed the gum when they craved sweets. With this insight, Wrigley's ad agency launched the "Gotta Have Sweet" campaign—and Juicy Fruit sales climbed.[13]

In addition, some researchers use pictures to learn how consumers perceive other consumers and the products they use. A car company might ask consumers to sort pictures into categories that reflect different types of product users, such as a Ford truck user, a Toyota SUV user, and so on. One stocking manufacturer used picture research to better understand women's experiences with nylon stockings. Results from traditional research methods indicated that women hated wearing stockings. However, consumers' pictures, coupled with interview results, revealed that stockings made them feel sexy, sensual, and attractive. With this knowledge, the company developed new ads depicting a less "executive" and a more "sexy" view of women in stockings.[14]

Diaries

Asking consumers to keep diaries can provide important insights into their behavior, including product purchasing and media usage. Marketers have, for example, asked preteens and teenagers to keep diaries of their everyday lives. These documents often reveal how friends and family affect decisions about clothes, music, fast foods, videos, concerts, and so on.[15] When Unilever was planning a new deodorant, it asked a group of women to keep an "armpit diary" noting how often they shaved, what their underarms looked like, and how frequently they used deodorant. Finding that the women were concerned about the condition of their underarm skin, Unilever created a moisturizing deodorant product and promoted its skin-care benefits.[16]

In the Indian context the concept of keeping a diary is not prevalent and most research agencies actually have a continuous tracking system, which helps in assessing the consumer trends over a period of time. The IMRB "Wallet Monitor" is an exercise by IMRB that helps in assessing the consumer and his wallet, especially his spending patterns and the implications for evaluating the changing expeniture levels. The enclosed exhibit 2.6 is a data from the IMRB "Wallet Monitor" representing how products are classified on the basis of need sets and the average number of trips which consumers are willing to take for buying the categorized products.

Exhibit 2.6
FROM THE IMRB "WALLET MONITOR"

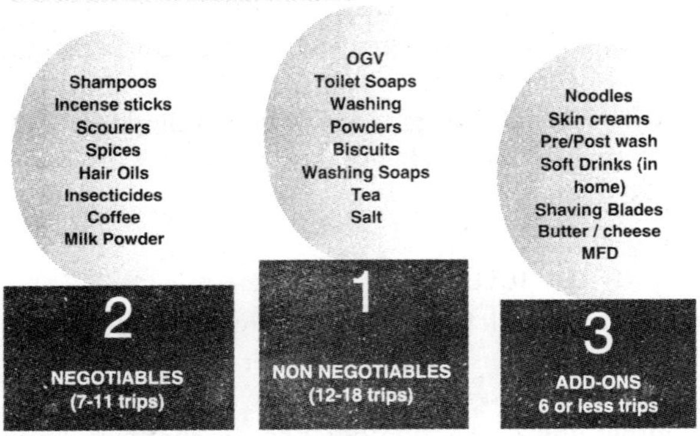

Experiments

Consumer researchers can conduct experiments to determine whether certain marketing phenomena affect consumer behavior. For example, they might design an experiment to learn whether consumers' attitudes toward a brand are affected by the brand name, as opposed to factors such as product features, package, color, logo, room temperature, or the consumer's mood. By measuring emotional arousal, salivation levels, and eye movements of participants, marketers may determine which ads are most arousing and attention getting or which products are preferred. Ford is testing brain scanning technology as a way to gauge European consumers' reactions to a new vehicle in development.[18]

During experiments, researchers randomly assign consumers to receive different "treatments" and then observe the effect of these treatments. For example, consumers might be assigned to groups that are shown different brand names. The researchers collect data about participants' attitudes toward the name and compare attitudes across groups. In a taste-test experiment, they might randomly assign consumers to groups and then ask each group to taste a different product.

An important aspect of such experiments is that the groups are designed to be identical in all respects except the treatment, called the ***independent variable.*** Thus, in a taste-test experiment, only the taste of the food or beverage is varied. Everything else is the same across groups—consumers eat or drink the same amount of the product, at the same temperature, from the same kind of container, in the same room, in the presence of the same experimenter, and so on. After consumers taste and rate the product, researchers can compare the groups' responses to see which taste is preferred.

Researchers also use experiments to determine what attracts consumers' attention and affects their purchase decisions. One researcher has designed a virtual shopping environment in which consumers use a computer to "walk down" store aisles, "pick up" products, and "put" them in their shopping baskets (or not). By varying package colors, space arrangements, layouts, and product features, and then comparing how consumers' attention and behavior differ across different store situations, researchers can determine what makes a retail environment most effective.[19] Nike has put certain high-end athletic shoes into a virtual environment called "There" to test consumer reaction. Consumers who download "There" software can see the Nike shoes from different angles, try pairs on (in the virtual sense), "buy" a pair, and move more quickly through the virtual world.[20]

Field Experiments

Although experiments are often conducted in controlled laboratory situations, sometimes marketers conduct experiments in the real world, known as "field experiments." One type of field experiment, a ***market test,*** reveals whether an offering is likely to sell in a given market and which marketing-mix elements most effectively enhance sales. Suppose marketers want to determine how much advertising support to give to a new product. First they would select two test markets with similar size and demographic composition. They would then spend a different amount of money on advertising in each market. By observing product sales in the two markets over a set period, the marketers would be able to tell which level of advertising expenditure resulted in higher sales.

With the "eating out" culture on the rise in urban India, most restaurants offer consumers a mix of local flavours. However, concept restaurants like Thai, Continental, Italian, Lebanese etc. are gradually making inroads into the Indian palette. Also with more and more Indians now making overseas tours, the acculturation process is faster. More and more restaurants which are opening today offer the consumers the unusual and in most cases they are after a introduction to a select audience, as a part of a field experiment process.

Conjoint Analysis

Many marketers use the sophisticated research technique of ***conjoint analysis*** to determine the relative importance and appeal of different levels of an offering's attributes. To start, researchers identify the attributes of the offering, such as package size, specific product features, and price points. Next, they determine the levels to be tested for each attribute (such as large or small size). Then they ask consumers to react to a series of product concepts that combine these attributes in different ways. For example, researchers might ask how likely consumers are to buy a large package of Tide laundry detergent that has added stain removal power and costs $4.75; they might also ask how likely consumers are to buy a small package of Tide that does not have added stain removal power and costs $2.50. By analyzing the responses to different combinations, the researchers can see how important each attribute (e.g., size, price) and each level of that attribute (e.g., $2.50 versus $4.75) is to consumers' purchase decisions. Fuji Film has used conjoint analysis to learn how brand, price, and packaging influence film buyers.[22] Academic researchers have also used this methodology to understand how much weight consumers give to environmental factors versus price and other attributes when they buy wooden furniture.[23]

Observations

At times, researchers observe consumers to gain insight into potentially effective product, promotion, price, and distribution decisions (see Exhibit 2.4) . Not long ago, American Express hired a research firm to videotape 2,000 consumers checking out at two California supermarkets. The goal was to see whether American Express should display its gift cards near the checkout—along with competing gift cards—or in a separate display elsewhere. Using computers to categorize 2,000 customers' facial expressions and actions on the tape, the researchers were able to tell American Express which location attracted the most attention and yielded the highest sales.[24]

Some companies conduct ***ethnographic research,*** in which researchers observe (and perhaps videotape) how consumers behave in real-world surroundings. In contrast to interviews and focus groups, ethnographic research does not involve interaction between researchers and consumers, only observation (as shown in Exhibit 2.7). This method allows marketers to see what consumers actually *do,* not what they *say* they do. In an in-house observation study conducted at the New Delhi railway station book counter of A.H. Wheeler, on platform no. 1, field observers found that between 1:00-3:00pm slot the book seller had SKU's in the form of books, newspapers and magazines displayed which completely contrasted with the SKU's kept between the 3:30-5:30pm slot. Further probe revealed that the difference in SKU was due to the pattern of trains that arrived and departed in those time slots and therefore the profile of customers who flocked the platform during those time periods. In the 1:00-3:00pm the trains were usually running across smaller cities and as passenger trains or EMU's. However, in the 3:30-5:30pm time slot the Rajdhani Express departs and the Shatabdi arrives, which connect the metros and profile on these trains or attending to these trains are upscale.

In another twist on observational research, some marketers use Web tracking software to observe where consumers go and what they do on the Internet. This technology shows researchers which websites consumers visit, which pages they look at, how long they visit each site, and related data. By analyzing consumer browsing patterns, marketers can determine how to make websites more user friendly and better target online advertising, as well as make other decisions about Web-based marketing activities.[26] However, privacy advocates are concerned that Web tracking—especially when conducted without the consumer's knowledge or consent—is intrusive.

Exhibit 2.7
OBSERVATIONAL RESEARCH
At the Fisher-Price Playlab, researchers observe children's reactions to determine whether they like Fisher-Price toys.

Purchase Panels

Although the research described so far studies individual consumers, sometimes marketers electronically research the behaviors of large numbers of respondents. This kind of research, conducted by IRI and other firms, simply records whether a behavior occurred; for instance, Campbell Soup uses IRI to track soup purchases in U.S. stores.[28] Such behavioral data may be collected from special panel members, from consumers chosen to be representative of the general population, or from the marketer's target market. Every time panel members go shopping, the cash register records their purchases. By merging purchase data with demographic data about panel members, marketers can tell who is purchasing a product, whether those consumers are also buying competitors' products, and whether the purchase was motivated by a coupon or other sales promotion tactic. Marketers can also use this data to determine whether, for example, the shelf space allocated to a product, or added advertising in the test area, affected panel members' purchases.

Database Marketing

Marketers can dig deeper into consumer behavior if they combine different forms of consumer research into a common database. This database might contain information about targeted consumers' demographics and lifestyles combined with data about their purchases in various product categories over time, their media habits, and their usage of coupons and other promotional devices. Using ***data mining,*** the company then searches for patterns in the database that offer clues to customer needs, preferences, and behaviors.[29]

Wal-Mart is at the cutting edge of the data-mining movement. It follows every piece of merchandise from warehouse to store shelf by using radio frequency identification tags. Every item sold at the checkout is tracked, along with the price, the time of sale, and the store location, and then reported hourly and daily by product, by category, by store, by supplier, and so on. Wal-Mart also analyzes what else goes into the shopping cart, store by store and region by region, for clues to pricing products in different categories. Finally, data mining helps the company identify promising new store locations and profile each store's shoppers so it can stock the right assortment of goods in appropriate quantities.[30]

However, some question whether such techniques invade consumer privacy (see Chapter 20, "The Dark Side of Consumer Behavior and Marketing," for more detail). More marketers are collecting consumer data online and analyzing the information for promotional purposes, such as to plan e-mail communications or build website traffic. Although companies view e-mail as fast and cheap compared with other communication methods, consumers are inundated with electronic messages. Therefore, to trigger a response, an e-mail campaign must be based on consumer needs—for instance, provide information the consumer requested—and should tailor the content and timing to each individual.[32] Often when consumers use free services like emails, online greeting cards services, free music downloads or even when making an e-commerce transaction, they agree to abide by all the rules and regulations that govern the use of the site.

It is even possible to use clickstream data from websites to analyze consumer behavior. One study looked at consumers' use of websites to buy automobiles and found that the best predictor of purchase was not the use of sophisticated decision-making aids or the number of repeat visits consumers made to the site but rather how long they browse and navigate through the site.[34]

Types of Consumer Researchers

Many types of entities use market research to study consumer behavior for different reasons, as shown in Exhibit 2.8. On the one hand, organizations such as consumer goods and service companies, ad agencies, and marketing research firms conduct research to make decisions about marketing a specific product or service. On the other hand, government organizations and academics conduct research to protect consumers or simply to understand why and how consumers behave as they do.

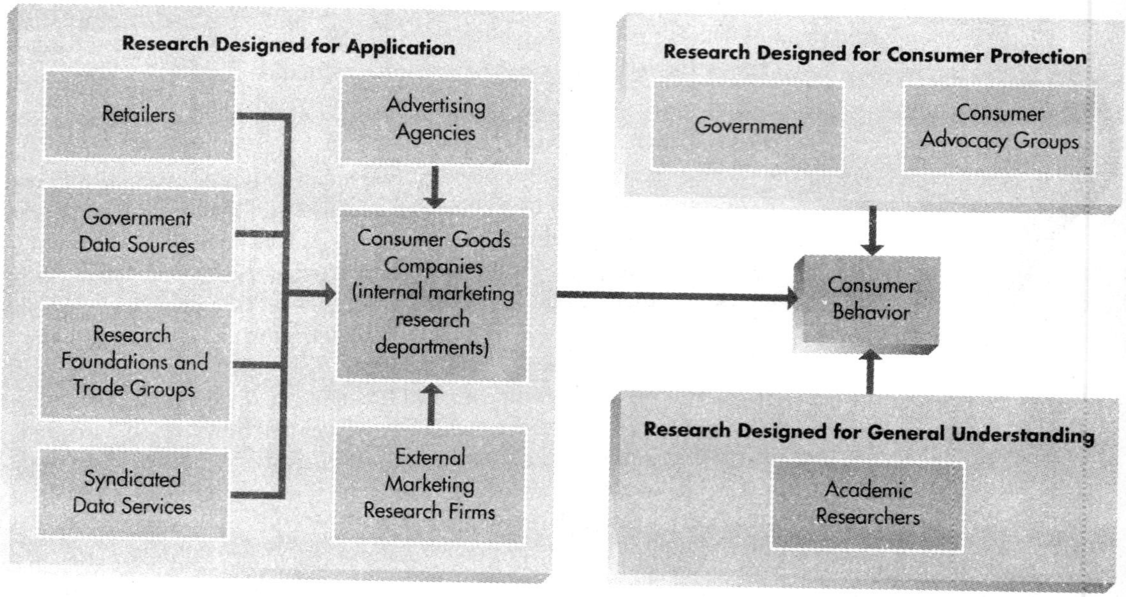

Exhibit 2.8

WHO CONDUCTS CONSUMER RESEARCH? *A number of different organizations conduct research on consumers, although they differ in their objectives. Some do research for application, some for consumer protection, and others to obtain general knowledge about consumers.*

In-house Marketing Research Departments

The benefits of conducting "in-house" research are that the information collected can be kept within the company and that opportunities for information to leak to competitors are minimized. However, internal departments are sometimes viewed as less objective than outside research firms, since they may have a vested interest in the research results. For example, employees may be motivated to show that the company is making good decisions, which may unwittingly bias the nature of their research or the outcomes they report. Consequently, some companies use outside research companies to gather their consumer research.

External Marketing Research Firms

External research firms often help design a specific research project before it begins. They develop measuring instruments to measure consumer responses, collect data from consumers, analyze the data, and develop reports for their clients.

Some marketing research firms are "full service" organizations that perform a variety of marketing research services; others specialize in a particular type of research. NOP World, for instance, conducts media research, ethnographic research, and other consumer behavior research. In its Starch Ad Readership studies, panels of approximately 200 readers of a specific magazine go through a recent issue with a trained interviewer. The interviewer asks whether consumers have seen each ad in the issue and, digging deeper, whether they saw the picture in the ad, read the headline, read the body copy, and saw the ad slogan. The company compiles reports about the percentage of respondents who saw each part of each ad and sells the results to advertisers who want to determine whether their ads are seen and read more than other

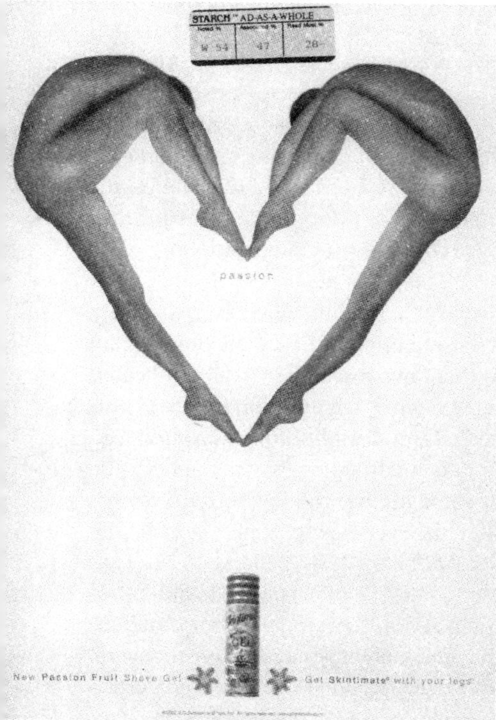

Exhibit 2.9
A "STARCHED" AD
Companies like Starch collect data on what, if anything, consumers remembered from an ad. The numbers noted on the stickers placed at the top of the ad indicate the percentage of respondents sampled who remembered having seen or read various parts of the ad.

ads in the issue or in the product category. Exhibit 2.9 shows an ad for which STARCH scores have been tabulated.

Research in India has been always been present in various forms either through a process of formal or informal research. There has been commissioned research as well as policy research. However, in the last three-four years particularly, research has undergone a transformation. Most companies are now beginning to realize the importance of a qualified research and they are, therefore, not hesitating to hire external agencies to support the activities of their organization. Companies today are even hiring resource persons with research background. Advertising agencies are beginning to realize the increased accountability factor as the key to the client's investments and hence every rupee spent is being questioned. The research agencies have evolved over time. Collaborations with multinational research agencies, mergers and global agencies too who have been in India for a long time are re-aligning themselves and gearing up for a larger frame of operation. There has also been advent of specialized agencies, like Technopak who focus on single sectors. Agencies like IMRB, ORG-MARG, Indica Research, AC Nielsen to name a few, have already re-aligned themselves and are ready to face the challenges of the new India. Development of in-house econometric tools, increased use of technology, data warehousing & mining are being increasingly considered as essential means to envisage new areas of research, as opposed to being considered as merely ornamental.

Advertising Agencies

Some advertising agencies have their own in-house research departments to test advertising concepts as part of the service they provide to clients. Coke's Indian foray has received mixed results not without some success. However, noticeable in the cola war between Pepsi and Coke was the advertising agency's attempt to explore the dominant sub-cultural traits and how it has a Pan-India Appeal. The successful advertising campaign focused on the product's universal appeal and how the regional traits were showcased, be it the rustic from Punjab or the Mumbai Tapori or the Nepali tourist guide, all dominant traits, all of which have a universal appeal too.

Agencies may also conduct advertising pretesting, using drawings of ads or finished ads, to make sure that an ad is fulfilling its objectives *before* it is placed in the media. In addition, agencies often conduct tracking studies to monitor the effectiveness of advertising over time. For example, tracking studies can determine whether the percentage of target market consumers who are aware of a brand has changed as a function of the amount, duration, and timing of its advertising.

Exhibit 2.12

Syndicated Data Services

Syndicated data services are companies that collect and then sell the information they collect, usually to firms that market products and services to consumers. For example, the research firm Yankelovich Partners collects data on consumer lifestyles and social trends in 90-minute interviews at the homes of approximately 2,500 adults. Its annual reports describing current and projected lifestyle trends help advertising agencies and company marketers develop content for promotional messages, choose media, identify new product ideas, plan positioning strategy, and make other marketing decisions.

Syndicated research in India has been there for a long time, however, the rapid churn in the market conditions and the increasing uncertainty of the markets are compelling corporates to either commission their own research or avail syndicated research from the market. Though Custom research is big in India, of-late syndicated research is seeping into gradually. The ORG retail audit (now AC Nielsen Retail Audit) has been there for a long time and most agencies, particularly the advertising agencies have been availing the retail audits which is by far the most comprehensive research Pan-India on the SKU turnover, region, zone, state, district and even city. Another research house IMRB's offshoot TGI INDIA is an international product from Kantar Media Research (KMR) - WPP's specialist global research agency offering media research services. TGI offers single source database combining products, brands, media, demographics and lifestyles. There are several large international houses like the Interpublic Group's NFO WorldGroup already operating successfully in India.

Nielsen is a syndicated data service that tracks the TV viewing habits of 375,000 U.S. consumers using diary reports or, in 10,000 households, an electronic device called a people meter. When family members turn on a TV equipped with a set-top people meter, they use a special remote control to record their presence rather than noting the information in a viewing diary. The people meter records who watches which shows and for how long.[36] Based on this data, Nielsen assigns a rating that indicates the number and percentage of all households watching a particular TV program, and a specific commercial, along with demographic analyses of the audience.

By combining demographic and TV viewing behavior, Nielsen can also examine who is watching which shows. Networks, cable stations, and independent channels use this information to determine whether TV shows should be renewed and how much they can charge for advertising time on a particular show. In general, advertisers will pay more to advertise on very popular shows (those with higher Nielsen ratings). Advertisers who buy Nielsen data can assess which TV shows they should advertise in, based on the match between the demographic characteristics of the viewers and of the sponsor's target market.

Retailers

Large retail chains often conduct consumer research. By using electronic scanners to track sales of a brand or product category, they can determine which are their best- and worst-selling items. They also use scanner data to examine the relationship between sales of an item and the item's location in the store and to see how consumers respond to coupons, discounts, and other promotions.

Because salespeople often interact directly with customers, retailers sometimes use research to measure customer satisfaction and determine how they can improve service quality.

Research Foundations/Trade Groups

Many research foundations and trade groups collect consumer research. A ***research foundation*** is a nonprofit organization that sponsors research on topics relevant to the foundation's goals. The Market Research Society of India is a non-profit autonomous market research body formed by a large fraternity of research suppliers and users spread across India. Established in January 1988, the MRSI is involved in maintaining standards of excellence in the market research industry. MRSI was also responsible for carrying out the path-breaking Socio Economic Classification (SEC) Study, which provided the fundamental basis for classifying urban Indian consumers. Today most organizations use the SEC indicator for market classification and estimation. Another body ESOMAR is also actively involved in the research environment of India. With 4,400 members in 100 countries, ESOMAR, founded in 1948, aims to promote the value of market and opinion research in illuminating real issues and bringing about effective decision-making.

Specialized trade groups may also collect consumer research to better understand the needs of consumers in their own industries. A ***trade group*** is an organization formed by people who work in the same industry, such as the Recording Industry Association of America, a group whose members are involved in the recorded music industry through recording, distribution, or retailing activities. This organization has sponsored a host of research projects, including studies to understand how American music tastes have changed over the years.

Government

Unlike the organizations just mentioned, government agencies do not use research to help market an offering. However, marketers frequently use government research for marketing purposes; for instance, they can examine census data to estimate the size of various demographic markets (see Exhibit 2.10). Many government studies are designed for consumer protection. Agencies such as the Consumer Products Safety Commission, the Department of Transportation, and the Food and Drug Administration research product features and set safety standards or recall unsafe products.

As per the code of conduct laid down by the MRSI (Market Research Society of India) all research agencies have to adhere to the condition that the research is conducted honestly, objectively, without unwelcome intrusion and without disadvantage to informants, and that it is based upon the willing co-operation of the public. Members of the general public must be assured absolutely that personal and/or confidential information supplied during the course of a marketing research study will not be made available without their agreement to any individual or organisation, whether private or official, outside the researcher's own organization. Research should also be conducted according to the accepted principles of fair competition, as generally understood and accepted, and to high technical standards. Marketing and social researchers should always be prepared to make available the necessary information whereby the quality of their work and the validity of their findings can be adequately assessed.

	Total population	Total	White	Black or African American	American Indian and Alaska Native	Asian	Native Hawaiian and other Pacific Islander	Some other race
Median age (years)	35.3%	35.6%	37.7%	30.2%	28.0%	32.7%	27.5%	24.6%
% DISTRIBUTION								
Total population	100.0	100.0	100.0	100.0	100.0	100.0	100.0	100.0
Under 18 years	25.7	25.3	23.5	31.4	33.9	24.1	31.9	35.9
Under 1 year	1.4	1.3	1.2	1.6	1.7	1.3	1.6	2.2
1 to 4 years	5.5	5.3	4.9	6.5	6.9	5.3	6.8	8.5
5 to 13 years	13.2	13.0	12.0	16.5	17.6	12.0	16.3	17.9
14 to 17 years	5.7	5.7	5.4	6.8	7.7	5.5	7.2	7.3
18 to 64 years	61.9	62.1	62.2	60.4	60.5	68.1	62.9	61.1
18 to 24 years	9.6	9.6	8.9	11.0	11.6	11.1	13.7	15.0
25 to 44 years	30.2	30.3	29.6	30.9	30.9	36.0	32.6	34.2
45 to 64 years	22.0	22.2	23.7	18.6	18.0	21.0	16.6	11.9
64 years and over	12.4	12.6	14.4	8.1	5.6	7.8	5.2	3.0

Exhibit 2.10
U.S. CENSUS DATA *The U.S. government collects primary data on the size and composition of the population every 10 years. Many marketers analyze this data to learn more about the demographics of certain target markets.*

Source: U.S. Censes Data from the U.S. Censes Bureau, Census, 2000.

Consumer Organizations

Independent consumer organizations also conduct research, generally for the purpose of protecting or informing consumers. Consumers Union is an independent, nonprofit testing and information organization designed to serve consumers. The organization publishes the well-known *Consumer Reports* magazine. Many of the products described in *Consumer Reports* are tested in Consumers Union's independent product-testing lab, and the results are posted on the organization's website (*www.consumersunion.org*).

Academics and Academic Research Centers

Although academic research involving consumers can be used for marketing and may have implications for public policy, studies often are designed simply to enhance our general understanding of why consumers behave as they do. Indeed, much of the research reported in this book describes state-of-the-art consumer behavior studies conducted by academics. Academics sometimes develop research centers focusing on a specific aspect of consumer behavior. For example, to gain a better understanding of media consumption, researchers from the Ball State University's Center for Media Design spent a full day with 101 consumers. By observing these consumers from the time they woke up to the time they went to sleep, researchers learned that consumers actually spend more time with TV, radio, newspapers, and online media than is reflected in conventional media research. Ball State Professor Bob Papper concludes, "Multitasking poses a huge challenge for the advertising world—not just how to measure it, but how to interpret and evaluate it."[39]

Marketing Implications of Consumer Behavior

As you learn about consumer behavior in this course, you may wonder how and why marketers use different concepts and techniques. This section is the first of many highlighting the marketing implications of consumer behavior. Starting with Chapter 3, you will find numerous sections titled "Marketing Implications" that illustrate how marketers apply consumer behavior concepts in the real world. In general, consumer research helps marketers develop product-specific plans as well as broader strategies for market segmentation, targeting, and positioning. Research also supports more informed decisions about product, promotion (marketing communications), price, and place (distribution).

Developing a Customer-Oriented Strategy

One hundred years ago, companies held a production-oriented view of marketing, focusing their activities on efficiently producing products. Later they shifted to a sales emphasis, developing tactics designed to move the most units of the product. The prevailing view today is that marketing activities are designed *to fulfill customers' needs.* This customer-oriented, market-driven approach automatically makes consumer research pivotal within the company. In other words, marketers must conduct considerable research to understand and describe the various segments or groups of targeted consumers—all of whom may have different needs—as part of the process of developing offerings that actually meet customers' needs. This consumer orientation guides research practices in each of the strategic and tactical marketing decisions described below.

How Is the Market Segmented? All consumers in a market are unlikely to have the same needs and wants. Consider car and SUV buyers. When Ford was planning a gas-electric hybrid version of its Escape SUV, it identified market segments by gender, environmental consciousness, technology orientation, and rough-road driving. More women than men were buying the regular gas Escape SUV—and many were first-time SUV buyers—yet there was also a sizable segment of men, both "greenies and geeks," who were interested in powerful, spacious, all-wheel-drive hybrid vehicles. Digging deeper, the company learned that consumers in this segment were more affluent, better educated, older, and watched less TV than the segment of non-hybrid Escape owners. Segmenting the market and understanding consumer needs helped Ford design the new hybrid SUV and create communications to reach the specific segment for that vehicle.[40]

How Profitable Is Each Segment? Knowing the size of a market segment can be important, because marketers can profit by concentrating on large segments that competitors are not targeting. Consumer research can also help marketers identify underserved segments—consumers who have clearly identifiable needs that are not being met. On the other hand, research can also reveal which segments are less profitable. In a study by Lowe research titled as "Study of Lowe Faces" studied over 10,000 married women who responded to Pathfinders' P:SNAP (Study of Nation's Attitudes and Psychographics): 2005, the study was able to classify the Indian women into five distinct classification as shown in exhibit 2.11. The segments, broadly an outcome of qualitative research, illustrate how each profile can be a basis for psychographic segmentation and helps in understanding the target audience a little more closely.

What Are the Characteristics of Consumers in Each Segment? After determining how the market is segmented and whether it is potentially profitable, marketers need to learn about the characteristics of consumers in each segment. This helps marketers project whether the segment is likely to grow or to shrink over time, which affects future marketing decisions. For example, condominium marketers project sales increases as baby boomers enter retirement in the coming years.

Are Customers Satisfied with Existing Offerings? Marketers often do considerable research to learn whether consumers are currently satisfied with the company's offerings. To illustrate, Harley-Davidson executives regularly ride with members of the Harley Owners Group to find out firsthand what satisfies motorcycle buyers and what else they're looking for. Combining this information with data from other satisfaction research helps the company come up with new product ideas and determine how to promote new bikes to current and potential customers.[42]

Selecting the Target Market

Understanding consumer behavior helps marketers determine which consumer groups might represent the best targets for marketing tactics.The "Incredible India" campaign from the Ministry of Tourism, Govt. of India is an attempt to showcase the country in a new light. The average tourist perception and knowledge about India does not go beyond a "Varanasi" or "Jaipur" or "Taj Mahal". The effort aims to break the exiting myths and showcase the other varied destinations that India has to offer. Another adage about the country was in the context of the tourist's complaints of misbehavior, cheating and at times even criminal assault by the locals. The campaign is also an attempt to also cleanse the internal systems and the local campaign launched as "Atithi Devo Bhava" is a part of the same, where the general public is educated about the status of the guest being equivalent to God and to be treated likewise.

Marketers also use their knowledge of consumer behavior to identify who is likely to be involved in acquisition, usage, and disposition decisions. Although Virgin Mobile mainly targets teenage and young adults who use cell phones, its research shows that parents are the primary decision makers in this market and often consult with other parents prior to a purchase. Virgin Mobile's research also indicates that family subscriber plans can be more costly than parents realize. "The message we're trying to get out is: With family plans, you're handing [teens] a

Exhibit 2.11

MRS. URBAN INDIA: ALONGSIDE EACH PROFILE ARE ALSO INDICATOR BRANDS WHICH HAVE BEEN PROFILING SUCH HOUSEWIVES IN THEIR ADVERTISEMENTS

- **Mrs 'Hasmukh' Popular: 27%** :popular, role model , Independent-minded , not self-sacrificing , perfect all
  - Tata Tea Gold, Lifebuoy, Saffola, Whirlpool
- **Mrs 'Pataka' Cool: 12%:** cool metro woman, still young, goes out the most, consulted by her husband, optimistic
  - Femina, Livon, Moods
- **Mrs 'Gharelu' Homepride:** 18%:sacrificing maa, would save rather than splurge, husband relies heavily on her wisdom
  - Cadbury's Bournvita, Catch Masala, Clinic Plus
- **Mrs 'Hey Bhagwan!' Moaner:** 12%: cooks, cleans, saves, hoards and dresses plainly, husband takes major decisions, having gold jewellery, belongs to the lower middle class
  - Moov, Mortein Coils
- **Mrs 'Meri Awaaz Suno' Attention Seeker:** 31%: family is not modern , doesn't like the idea of staying in a joint family , dresses up even when she goes to the market
  - Everest Pav Bhaji Masala, Active Wheel, Nilkamal Furniture

credit card with an antenna on it," says the company's vice president-brand and communications.[44]

Positioning

Another strategic choice is how an offering should be positioned in consumers' minds. The desired image should reflect what the product is and how it is different from the competition. The American Express Platinum Card launch in India uses the tag line, "Membership Changes Everything", showcasing Abhishek Bachahan, who is making an effort to fit into the shoes of his illustrious father, Amitabh Bachchan.

How Are Competitive Offerings Positioned? Consumer research can show how consumers perceive and categorize different brands in the marketplace, providing interesting perspectives on how a marketer's offering should be positioned. Marketers sometimes conduct research to see how consumers view other brands in comparison with their own and plot the results on a graph called a "perceptual map." Brands in the same quadrant of the map are perceived to offer similar benefits to consumers. The closer various companies are to one another, the more likely they are to be competitors.

How Should Our Offerings Be Positioned? Companies use consumer research to understand what image a new offering should have in the eyes of consumers. Nokia's launch of 1100 series of handsets in India focused on the theme of "Made for India", highlighting the durability, robustness and toughness of the handsets. The earthly setting of the communication and highlighting the features through the medium was effective for target audience to understand. The handset also integrated an in-built torch, considered a necessary item particularly for the suburban and rural areas. As an entry level handset and priced at an affordable range, Nokia attempted to target the lower end of the market, essentially the SEC C,D & E. This was also the time when the incoming call charges were made free and a substantial chunk of fence sitters were waiting to consider and buy the product. The Nokia 1100 series offered the consumer a lower hardware cost to consider the category.

Should Our Offerings Be Repositioned? Yet another use of consumer research is to help marketers reposition existing products (i.e., change their image). Consider how the World Gold Council, a trade group, decided to reposition gold jewelry. Through focus group research, the council determined that women enjoy wearing fine gold jewelry, but they didn't perceive available products as either exciting or stylish. It also learned that gold jewelry's competition was not silver and platinum jewelry but a broad array of luxury goods that women might buy for themselves. The research findings prompted recommendations that jewelers create pieces with updated, edgier styling. It also helped the council reposition gold jewelry through ads tapping into the positive feelings women have toward wearing gold.[47]

Developing Products or Services

Developing products and services that satisfy consumers' wants and needs is a critical marketing activity. Marketers apply consumer research when making a number of decisions about products.

What Ideas Do Consumers Have for New Products? First, marketers need to design an offering that has the benefits desired by target consumers. For example, focus groups helped one company uncover a new product idea. Mothers participating in the groups complained that their children didn't want to use soap. In response, the firm created a bar of soap with a plastic toy inside. The more children wash, the more they can see the toy.[48]

What Attributes Can Be Added to or Changed in an Existing Offering? Marketers often use research to determine when and how to modify or tailor a product to meet the needs of new or existing groups of consumers. To illustrate, Virgin Mobile asked 2,000 of its teenage customers about their color preferences for cell phones. Originally, the company was planning to make an all-white cell phone—building on the popularity of the white Apple iPod digital music player—but the teens rejected the idea as "a knockoff" and asked for blue with a silver interior, which Virgin Mobile put into production (see Exhibit 2.12).[49]

What Should Our Offering Be Called? Consumer research plays a vital role in decisions about product and brand names. Goodyear conducted considerable consumer research when naming its tires. It chose the name Eagle Aquatech EMT (for extended mobility technology) for a tire that, when flat, can go for 50 miles at 55 miles per hour on wet surfaces.[50] Other companies create brand names like Obsession (for perfume) and Country Hearth (for bread), because consumer research suggested that these names would be understood, easy to remember, and suggestive of the brand's benefits.

What Should Our Package and Logo Look Like? Many marketers use consumer research to test alternative packaging and logos. Research shows, for instance, that consumers are likely to think that food (including cookies) is good for them if it comes in green packaging.[51] This information is valuable in the design of packages for products with a "healthy" positioning. Consumer research is also a valuable resource for companies revising logos. When Citizens Bank, a division of Royal Bank of Scotland, acquired Charter One bank, the company wanted to update its logo without losing the images and color that consumers knew and recognized from the various divisions. The new logo retains the "C" formerly used by Citizens Bank and adds four arrows pointing inward, echoing the Royal Bank of Scotland's logo. It also includes the Charter One brand and the distinctive green color that Citizens Bank has used for many years in its branches in New England and the mid-Atlantic states.[52]

Exhibit 2.12
VIRGIN MOBILE AD
Virgin's research on teens helped them determine the popularity of activities such as text-messaging.

Making Promotion (Marketing Communications) Decisions

Consumer research can help companies make decisions about a wide range of promotional/marketing communications tools. These include advertising, sales promotions (premiums, contests, sweepstakes, free samples, coupons, and rebates), personal selling, and public relations.

What Are Our Advertising Objectives? Consumer research can be very useful in determining what objectives should guide the development of advertising. It may reveal, for example, that very few people have heard of a new brand, suggesting that the primary advertising objective should be to enhance brand-name awareness. Other research may suggest that consumers have heard of the brand but don't know anything about it. In this case the advertising objective should be to enhance brand knowledge. If consumers know the brand name but don't know the characteristics of the brand that make it desirable, the advertising should aim to enhance brand knowledge and brand attitudes. And if consumers know neither the brand name nor the product's benefits, the advertising should educate the target market about both.

After consistent research Faber found that Indian cooking requires a lot of oil and spices, thereby releasing a lot of oily smoke into the kitchen. This oily smoke clogs the traditional mesh filter of kitchen chimney very frequently and cleaning the mesh filter is a big hassle as it takes hours to clean. Faber's Baffle Chimneys were convenient to clean and use. Faber's baffle filter structural design of curves and cups-like strips ensure that all the oil and heavy grease particles get trapped at the bottom without it getting choked. Being hollow, the baffle filter can be washed easily using detergent in lukewarm water. Hence, it's easy to maintain. It needs to be washed once in two or three months, while the traditional filters have to be washed once every 10 days. While launching their new range of Baffle Chimneys Faber found that the existing customers were already using the net chimneys that came with the old model of Faber chimneys. They offered an easy up gradation scheme and also highlighted the benefits of the baffle chimneys so that the existing customers realized the differences and were willing to upgrade at a marginal cost. The innovation was also supported through the trade and channel support with the help of company engineers, who made door to door campaign to effectively promote the scheme.

What Should Our Advertising Look Like? If a marketer wants to establish brand-name awareness, research about making ads more memorable might prove relevant and useful. For example, a brand name is better remembered when the ad in which it is placed contains interesting and unusual visuals that relate to it. If the visuals are interesting but unrelated, consumers may remember the visuals but forget the name.

Consumer research can also help marketers understand which visuals should accompany ad copy. Recent research indicates not only that a car with "power" is desirable to both men and women but also that the word *power* means different things to different people. Men associate power with excitement, whereas women associate it with being able to maneuver quickly and safely out of tight or dangerous situations.[54] This information suggests the use of clearly distinct visuals and associated copy depending on whether the ad is designed to appeal to men or women. Marketers can also learn, through research, how different groups respond to different wording. For example, saying a product is a good "value for the money" does not work in Spain. Instead, marketers use the phrase "price for product."[55] Research also shows that it is beneficial for firms using e-mail to increase website traffic to customize their e-mail messages based on their knowledge of different consumers in the target market.[56]

Exhibit 2.13
BP BEYOND PETROLEUM AD
To help make consumers aware of its products, British Petroleum advertised on billboards and bus shelters in many major U.S. cities.

Where Should Advertising Be Placed? When marketers start to select specific media vehicles in which to advertise, they find demographic and lifestyle data and data from companies like Nielsen and Mediamark very useful. As noted earlier, research shows that more people split their time among many different media; moreover, many use recording technology to avoid television commercials. With this knowledge, marketers are choosing media with better targeting or more consumer exposure in mind. Not long ago, the oil and gas company BP decided to polish its image with a campaign called "Beyond Petroleum" (see Exhibit 2.13). The goal was to show that BP is involved in a wide range of energy products, including environmentally friendly ones, using messages such as "Solar, natural, gas, wind, hydrogen. And, oh yes, oil." To reach opinion leaders and build awareness, BP advertised on billboards and bus shelters in New York City, Chicago, and Washington, D.C. Research showed that awareness was up and the company was viewed more favorably after the campaign started.[57]

When Should We Advertise? Researchers may reveal seasonal variation in purchase due to weather related needs; variations in the amount of discretionary money consumers have (dependence of which may be related to a special occasion or a festival) holiday buying patterns, and the like. Companies like Archie's Gallery in India are now aggressively trying to promote events which were unheard of some 10 years back. Valentine's Day or Father's Day or Mother's Day were occasions or rituals of the West and particularly markets like India never espoused on such themes. However, the new generation and particularly the teenage markets have begun to relate and reciprocate to such rituals through materialistic and non-materialistic forms. Research on such variations can help marketers decide on the most effective timing of advertising. The Indian Television prime time slot is fixed at 8.00-11.00pm. The advertisers profile during this slot varies drastically with the afternoon slot of 12.00-3pm reserved for the housewives. The prime time slot of family has a gamut of products ranging from FMCG, durables, processed foods to readymade garments, OTC drugs, on line matrimonial sites and even baby products, social messages on AIDS, primary health and education and Pulse Polio too. The afternoon slots have advertisers targeting the housewives and their range of requirements and relevance.

Has Our Advertising Been Effective? Finally, advertisers can undertake studies to determine whether advertising has been effective. This research can be gathered at various points in the advertising development process. Some times marketers or ad agencies conduct research called advertising *copy testing* or *pretesting*, which tests ads for their effectiveness before they are placed in the media. If the advertising objective is brand-name awareness and the tested ad does not enhance awareness, the company may replace it with a new ad.

Effectiveness research can also take place after the ads have been placed in the media. The STARCH scores described earlier in the chapter are one way of assessing how effective ads are in building brand-name awareness. In addition, advertisers sometimes conduct tracking studies to see how effective their advertising is in achieving particular objectives over time, as BP did in assessing the outcome of its "Beyond Petroleum" campaign.

What About Sales Promotion Objectives and Tactics? When developing sales promotions, marketers can use research to suggest sales promotion objectives and identify appropriate tactics. Pepsi, for instance, targets young African American consumers in marketing its soft drinks. Through research, Pepsi discovered that this segment lags the general U.S. population in owning computers with Internet access. One year, the company developed a sales promotion offering scholarships, computers, software, and 12-packs of Pepsi as prizes for students who submitted the best "Write your own history" essay during Black History Month. Pepsi changed its Black History Month promotion the following year, mounting a sweepstakes with Apple computers as prizes.[59]

Sometimes the tactics are so effective that a promotion exceeds its objectives, as S.C. Johnson & Son's experience shows. To promote its Raid bug killer in Thailand, Johnson offered to pay one baht (about 2 cents) for every dead bug and allow participants to bid for prizes using the bounty they earned. The promotion captured the public's imagination as people turned in thousands of bugs.[60]

When Should Sales Promotions Take Place? Companies can also use consumer research to time their sales promotions. Consider Del Monte Beverages, maker of World Fruits juices, which conducted research to uncover the characteristics and behavior patterns of its target market in Great Britain. The company discovered that the segment of frequent purchasers, men and women ages 25 to 44, usually take two vacations per year, preferably to foreign destinations. To boost brand awareness and sales, World Fruits launched a "Win an Exotic Adventure with a Twist" promotion during the winter months, when this segment is thinking about vacations. Top prizes were vacations in New Zealand, Brazil, India, Italy, and Ecuador—all countries that supply World Fruits ingredients.[61]

Have Our Sales Promotions Been Effective? Consumer research can answer this question. Del Monte can examine brand awareness after the World Fruits promotion with pre-promotion levels, for instance. It can also research market share statistics and other measures of high sales. Pepsi can count the number of entries in its "Write your own history" campaign and use research to find out whether the African American target market is buying more Pepsi soft drinks.

How Many Salespeople Are Needed to Serve Customers? By tracking store patronage at different times of the day or on different days of the week, retailers can determine the appropriate number of store personnel needed to best serve customers.

How Can Salespeople Best Serve Customers? Finally, research can be helpful when managers are selecting salespeople and evaluating how well they serve customers. For example, although there is some debate about it, one general finding suggests that the more similar the salesperson is to the customer, the more effective he or she will be.[62] Research has shown that salespeople can better serve customers when the salespeople are in a good mood.[63] This information implies that managers should devise tactics to enhance the moods of their sales personnel.

Making Pricing Decisions

The price of a product or service can have a critical influence on consumers' acquisition decisions. It is therefore very important for marketers to understand how consumers react to price and to use this information in their pricing decisions.

What Price Should Be Charged? Why do prices often end in 99? Consumer research has shown that people perceive \$.99, \$9.99, or \$99.99 to be cheaper than \$1.00, \$10.00, or \$100.00. Perhaps this is one reason that so many prices end in the number 9.[64]

Although economic theory suggests that a decrease in price will increase the likelihood of purchase, consumer research shows this isn't always so. A low price may make consumers suspect the product's quality, since higher price generally means higher quality.[65] Research shows that consumers have complicated reactions to price. For example, if catalog customers can save \$8 on shipping charges, they will spend an average of \$15 more on catalog purchases—a finding that has caused some catalog marketers to absorb shipping fees.[66]

Also, when making a purchase, consumers consider how much they must pay in relation to the price of other relevant brands or the price previously paid for that product, so marketers must be aware of these reference prices.[67] When buying multiple units of a service for one bundled price (such as a multiday ski pass), consumers may not feel a great loss if they use only some of the units, because they have difficulty assigning value to each unit. In contrast, when consumers buy multiple products for one bundled price (such as a case of wine), they are likely to increase their consumption because unit costs seem low.[68] Recent research indicates that the price consumers are willing to pay for a given item can be affected by the price of unrelated products they happen to see first. To illustrate, the price you would be willing to pay for a T-shirt may vary depending on whether the prices you noticed on shoes in the store next door were high or low.[69]

How Sensitive Are Consumers to Price and Price Changes? Research also suggests that consumers have varying views of the importance of price. Some consumers are very price sensitive, meaning that a small change in price will have a large effect on consumers' willingness to purchase the product. Cruise lines, for example, have found that lower prices help fill their ships.[70] Other consumers are price insensitive, meaning they are likely to buy and use the offering regardless of price. Demand for brewed coffee generally remains steady despite price increases, which means Starbucks is unlikely to lose many customers when it hikes the prices of its lattes and espressos.[71] Marketers can use research to determine which consumers are likely to be price sensitive and when. For fashion or prestige goods in particular, a high price symbolizes status. Thus some consumers, particularly those seeking status, may be less sensitive to the price of a product and pay more than \$50 for a simple T-shirt with a prestigious label.

When Should Certain Price Tactics Be Used? Research on consumer behavior also helps us understand when consumers are likely to be most responsive to various pricing tactics. Historical data, for example, shows that consumers are very responsive to price cuts on linens and sheets during January. These "white sales" are effective because consumers have come to anticipate them and are unlikely to buy these products after Christmas without a financial incentive to do so.

Exhibit 2.14
APPLE COMPUTER STORE
Apple designed its stores to make the environment warm and inviting to customers.

Making Distribution Decisions

Another important marketing decision involves the manner in which products or services are distributed. Here, too, marketers use consumer research when considering how to get their products to customers.

Where Are Target Consumers Likely to Shop? Marketers who understand the value consumers place on time and convenience have developed distribution channels that allow consumers to acquire or use goods and services whenever and wherever it is most convenient for them. For example, 24-hour grocery stores, health clubs, and catalog ordering and online ordering systems give consumers flexibility in the timing of their acquisition, usage, and disposition decisions. As another example, consumers can now shop for cars through the Internet, auto brokers, warehouse clubs, giant auto malls, and used-car superstores, as well as traditional auto dealers.

How Should Stores Be Designed? Supermarkets are generally designed with similar or complementary items stocked near one another because consumer research shows that customers think about items in terms of categories based on similar characteristics or use. Thus stores stock countertop cleaners near bathtub cleaners because both have similar uses, and they stock peanut butter near jelly because those are often used together. Consumer research can also help marketers develop other aspects of their retail environments. Research has shown that bright colors and loud, up-tempo music make consumers move quickly through a store. Softer, subdued colors and gentler music have the opposite effect.[72] According to research, consumers feel less satisfied shopping in stores with narrow aisles and closely spaced fixtures and merchandise.[73]

Stores and websites can also be designed to exactly convey the image marketers wish them to have. Apple's computer stores are open and modern, with plenty of computers for shoppers to test. Each has a section where shoppers can check e-mail or browse the Web for free, which builds store traffic. The "genius bar," staffed by tech experts, is in the back, drawing customers through the store (and past attractive displays) when they need advice (see Exhibit 2.14). "We wanted an atmosphere that was inviting—not intimidating—forward-looking, warm, interactive," explains the head of Apple retail operations. "And it makes you feel intelligent just by being there."[74]

Ethical Issues in Consumer Research

Although marketers rely heavily on consumer research in the development of successful goods and services, the conduct of this research raises important ethical issues. As the following sections show, consumer research has both positive and negative aspects.

The Positive Aspects of Consumer Research

Both consumers and marketers can benefit from consumer research. Consumers generally have better consumption experiences, and marketers can learn to build stronger customer relationships by paying attention to consumer research.

Better Consumption Experiences Because consumer research helps marketers become more customer focused, consumers can get better designed products, better customer service, clearer usage instructions, more information that helps them make good decisions, and more satisfying postpurchase experiences. Consumer research (by government and consumer organizations) also plays a role in protecting consumers from unscrupulous marketers.

Potential for Building Customer Relationships From the marketer's perspective, consumer research is helpful for identifying ways of establishing and enhancing relationships with customers. Consumers will be motivated to develop and continue a relationship with companies that seem to understand them and want to serve their needs. Consumer research can also show marketers how to build and retain a loyal customer base.

The Negative Aspects of Consumer Research

Consumer research is a very complex process, with a number of potentially negative aspects. These include the difficulty of conducting research in foreign countries, the high costs of conducting research, concerns about invasion of privacy, and the use of deceptive practices.

Tracking Consumer Behavior in Different Countries Marketers who want to research consumer behavior in other countries face special challenges. For instance, focus groups are not appropriate in all countries or situations. U.S. marketers often put husbands and wives together in a focus group to explore attitudes toward products like furniture. However, this approach won't work in countries like Saudi Arabia where women are unlikely to speak freely and are highly unlikely to disagree with their husbands. Focus groups must also be conducted differently in Japan, where cultural pressures dictate against disagreeing with the views of a group.

In India the focus group discussions have now been explored more by research agencies. These are custom focus groups or syndicated, like the IMRB car clinic. The annual IMRB car clinic is a wonderful experience on how respondents across age groups, genders and diversified social class profile respond on passenger car vehicles. The scope of coverage ranges from (i) Current car ownership; (ii) Brand owned and why; (iii) Process of owning; (iv) Key influences in buying; (v) Role of dealer and dealer points; (vi) Pre-purchase and while purchase steps followed; (vii) Post purchase behavior.

Telephonic Interview are not popular forms of interviews conducted locally, unless the respondents are known and on the panel of the research agencies for some time. Lack of skilled manpower and training also deters most agencies to adopt telephonic route for interviews. At a minimum, researchers should word questions carefully and check that the meaning is being accurately conveyed by first translating questions into the other language and then back into English.

Secondary data across markets may not be comparable owing to the heterogeneity in the background of each nation. Also the timing and procedure of data collection may also alter from country to country, which is why it is best to evaluate country data individually rather than comprehensively trying to evaluate them. Countries may also use different categorization schemes for describing demographics like social class and education level. Moreover, different or fewer syndicated data sources may be available in other countries, which limits the research available to marketers.

Potentially Higher Marketing Costs Some consumers worry that the process of researching behavior leads to higher marketing costs, which in turn translates into higher product prices. Some marketers, however, argue that they can market to their customers more efficiently if they know more about them. For example, product development, advertising, sales promotion costs, and distribution costs will be lower if marketers know exactly what consumers want and how to reach them.

Invasion of Consumer Privacy A potentially more serious and widespread concern is that marketers' conduct and use of research—especially database marketing—may invade consumers' privacy. Consumers worry that marketers know too much about them and that personal data, financial data, and behavioral data may be sold to other companies or used inappropriately without their knowledge or consent. This issue is discussed in more detail later in the text, in the context of public policy decisions (see Chapter 19) and the dark side of marketing (Chapter 20).

Deceptive Research Practices Finally, unscrupulous researchers may engage in deceptive practices. One such practice is lying about the sponsor of the research (e.g., saying it is being conducted by a nonprofit organization when it is really being conducted by a for-profit company). Another deceptive practice is promising that respondents' answers will remain anonymous, when in fact the company is adding identifying information to individual answers so the company can use the data to market to these consumers later on. Unscrupulous researchers may also promise to compensate respondents but fail to deliver on this promise.[75]

Summary

Consumer research is a valuable tool that helps marketers design better marketing programs, aids in the development of laws and public policy decisions regarding product safety, and promotes our general understanding of how consumers behave and why. Researchers for-profit and nonprofit organizations utilize a variety of research tools, including techniques that collect data on what consumers say (surveys, focus groups, interviews, storytelling, use of photography, diaries, conjoint analysis) and techniques that collect data on what consumers do (observations, purchase panels, experiments, database marketing). These tools may involve data collection from relatively few individuals or from many individuals and may study consumers at a single point in time or track their behavior across time.

Many types of organizations collect consumer research. Some firms have internal marketing research departments; others use external research firms to conduct studies. Advertising agencies and syndicated data services are two types of outside agencies that collect consumer research information. Large retail chains often use electronic scanners to track sales of a brand or product category. Research foundations and trade groups, as well as the government and consumer organizations, also collect consumer information. Many academics and academic research centers conduct consumer research to enhance our general understanding of consumer behavior, although this research may have application purposes as well.

Marketers utilize consumer research information to understand how markets are segmented and to determine the characteristics of consumers in each segment. Consumer research information is also helpful in selecting a target market and deciding how an offering should be positioned. Research is essential to marketing-mix decisions, although it raises some ethical issues. The positive aspect is that consumer research supports a consumer-oriented view of marketing and can help companies improve consumption experiences and strengthen customer relationships. However, some critics point out that research may invade consumers' privacy and lead to higher marketing costs. In addition, unscrupulous marketers can misuse consumer information.

Questions for Review and Discussion

1. How do researchers use surveys, focus groups, interviews, and storytelling to learn about consumer behavior?
2. How do experiments differ from field experiments?
3. Why do researchers use observation and purchase panels to study consumer behavior?
4. How is primary data different from secondary data?
5. What is a perceptual map and why do researchers use it?
6. What are some of the positive and negative aspects of consumer research?

Exercises

1. Look up any three of the following sites on the Web and determine in (a) whether they provide primary or secondary data, (b) which research tools they use, and (c) whether they design research for a specific industry or for many industries.

   www.claritas.com
   www.currentanalysis.com
   www.secondarydata.com
   www2.acnielsen.com
   www.npd.com
   www.qualtalk.com
   www.maritzresearch.com

2. Ask a friend to identify a favorite possession. Interview your friend to find out as much as you can about it. Ask your friend to find photographs from

magazines that best symbolize why that item is meaningful. Then ask him or her to keep a diary for a few days that indicates whether and how he or she used the possession. Finally, conduct a focus group with a few of your friends about their special possessions. What do these combined tools reveal to you about these possessions?

3. Imagine you're a marketing manager for Burger King. You need consumer research to support future decisions about menu items and promotions. Which research tool(s) would you use to uncover the answers to the following questions—and why?
   a. Do Burger King customers prefer the chain's french fries over those of McDonald's?
   b. Which Burger King sandwich is the most popular in California, in Texas, and in Florida?
   c. Do coupons increase sales of the discounted menu items?
   d. Would Burger King sell more burger sandwiches if it added bacon and cheese without raising the price?
   e. Which media vehicles do Burger King customers prefer?
   f. What condiments, if any, do take-out customers add to Burger King burgers eaten at home?
   g. What new side dishes should Burger King introduce?
4. Choose two of the following websites and follow the indicated links to the page where each company invites consumer comment about products, problems, and ideas. What type of consumer data are these two companies collecting along with comments? How can the companies use the information gathered from these consumer comments in their marketing activities? What other data would you recommend that the companies request from consumers who initiate contact with them—and why?

   www.gatorade.com (feedback link)
   www.ford.com (contact link)
   www.apple.com (contact link)
   www.tylenol.com (customer service link)

More Exercises from the Adaptor

1. The exercise is to be done in groups of four. The project is based on observational method of data collection. The group will have to identify a retail outlet of any kind selling any kind of product/services. The group will have to spend a substantial number of days in the outlet to ascertain the following:
   a. The consumer preferences while buying the product (brand)
   b. The decision making process (either for high or low involvement product)
   c. Retailer response in easing or helping purchase decisions
   d. Time spent in buying the product (brand)
   e. The relationship of buying and the buyer behavior model
   f. Accompanies while buying; family, friends, relatives...
   g. Individual or group decisions
   h. Store choice
   i. Effect of window display

   The groups are not required to speak to the consumers but gather as much as data as they can through observational form. However, at any time if any specific aspect needs to be clarified or probed, the group can establish communication with the store-owner.

PART

2

The Psychological Core

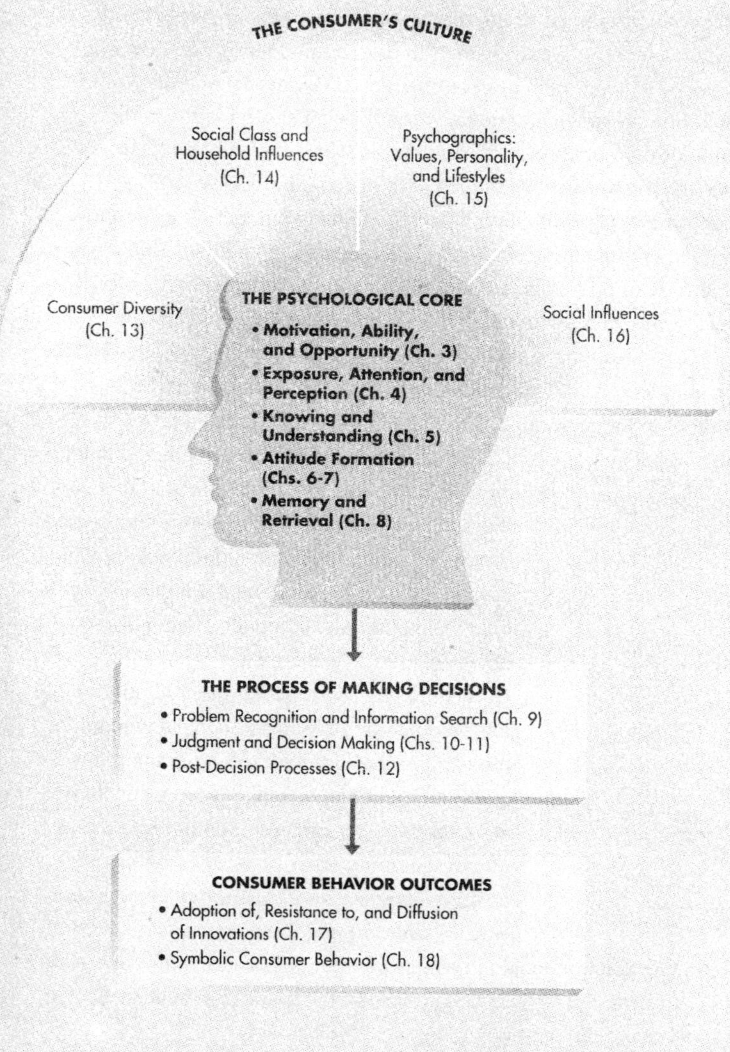

Consumer behavior is greatly affected by the amount of effort that consumers put into their consumption behaviors and decisions. Chapter 3 describes three critical factors that affect effort: the (1) motivation, (2) ability, and (3) opportunity consumers have to engage in behaviors and make decisions.

Chapter 4 discusses how consumers come into contact with marketing stimuli (exposure), notice them (attention), and perceive them. Chapter 5 continues the topic by discussing how consumers compare new stimuli with their existing knowledge (a process called categorization) as well as attempt to understand or comprehend the data on a deeper level.

Chapter 6 describes what happens when consumers exert a great deal of effort forming and changing attitudes. Chapter 7 discusses how attitudes can be influenced when consumer effort is low.

Finally, because consumers are not always exposed to marketing information when they actually need it, Chapter 8 focuses on the important topics of consumer memory and retrieval.

Chapter 3

Motivation, Ability, and Opportunity

INTRODUCTION

LEARNING OBJECTIVES

After studying this chapter, you will be able to:

- Explain why consumers' motivation, ability, and opportunity to process information, make decisions, or engage in behaviors is important to marketers.
- Identify the influences and outcomes of consumer motivation, ability, and opportunity to process information, make decisions and engage in behaviors.

Hyundai Santro: The Sun(rise)shine car

Santro's launch in India in 1998 was a well-timed launch for the company and also for the automobile industry per se. The Maruti bandwagon was there between 1982 and 1998, dominating most of the market and segments. The proverbial Maruti 800, Zen, Esteem and Gypsy seemed to be dragging for far too long and the market looked for innovation in any form, either a new model or a new segment or a car that offered space and power yet not being slotted in the large sedan segment. Santro's launch from Korean stable was a mixed bag of apprehension and skepticism. The Korean experience with India so far was with LG and Samsung. The common perception about Korean brands was that they were low-cost, high technology product and backed with consistent innovation. The similarity ends at the country of origin since the durables and the automotives are two very different categories to have anything in common. At an average price of Rs.350,000 ($8000) ex-showroom and with an on-road price of Rs.400,000 ($8500) the car was noticeable for its tall boy shape, a pioneering effort from Hyundai, something not seen on Indian roads.

The car in itself may not have been a unique product but it was able to fill the void that was there for sometime offering a range and choice to the customer, who seemed to have grown tired of the Maruti platter and the range they offered. Santro was compact, spacious and powerful in its segment, offering enough legroom space and a power of 1100 cc. The typical diffusion of innovation cycle worked for the car and the brand picked up in the metros and mini-metros. It also packed in a successful advertising campaign with Shahrukh Khan (another pioneering attempt, as before that celebrity endorsement in automotive segment was unheard of) and the brand was quick to get noticed. There has been no looking back since then, for Brand Santro and a series of innovative features like e-rlx, zing, etc. helped the brand create an impact in the A3 segment, till than dominated by Maruti.

However, Santro has now targeted a completely new segment in the passenger car market; the entry level car buyers who invariably upgrade from a scooter or are first time car buyers. Through a series of external and internal realignment process it has been able to target this segment that is steadily growing. External, which was its quickness to grasp the opportunity in the emerging markets where Maruti 800 was no more being considered an entry level car. Internal, which was a pricing strategy that was penetrative in nature pricing the car at Rs.275,000 ($6200) ex-showroom that suited the up-grader or the first time buyer, in terms of affordability. NCAER data on demand of consumer durables in Exhibit 3.1 is an illustration of how the lower end of the market is growing.

Exhibit 3.1
NCAER DATA ON DEMAND OF CONSUMER DURABLES

	1995-96	2001-02	2005-06	2009-10
CARS	276	788	1560	3466
MOTORCYCLES	760	2599	4663	8369
CTV REGULAR	1785	4580	6295	9957
REFRIGERATORS	1850	3006	4335	6774
WHITE GOODS	3437	6024	8727	13,149

Source: NCAER, Figures in '000

The data above represents the potential in the market and how the lower end of the market particularly the motorcycles segment had enough opportunity to be tapped currently and in the near future. The motives in this segment to upgrade are quite different while evaluating an existing car owner.

Consumer Motivation and Its Effects

Motivation is defined as "an inner state of arousal," with aroused energy directed to achieving a goal.[2] The motivated consumer is energized, ready, and willing to engage in a goal-relevant activity. For example, if you learn that a much-anticipated cinema will be aired across cinema halls, you may be motivated to be at the cinema hall early next day. Consumers can be motivated to engage in behaviors, make decisions, or process information, and this motivation can be seen in the context of acquiring, using, or disposing of an offering. Let's look first at the effects of motivation, as shown in the middle of Exhibit 3.2.

Goal-Relevant Behavior

One outcome of motivation is goal-relevant behavior. When motivation is high, people are willing to do things that make it more likely they will achieve their goals. For example, if you are motivated to buy a good car, you will research vehicles online, visit dealerships, take test drives, and so on. Likewise, if you are motivated to lose weight, you will buy low-fat foods, eat smaller portions, and exercise. Motivation not only drives behaviors consistent with a goal but also creates a willingness to expend time and energy engaging in these behaviors. Thus someone motivated to see a movie may spend extra money and drive through a massive traffic snarl to reach the hall and also wait for tickets by standing in the queue for an hour.

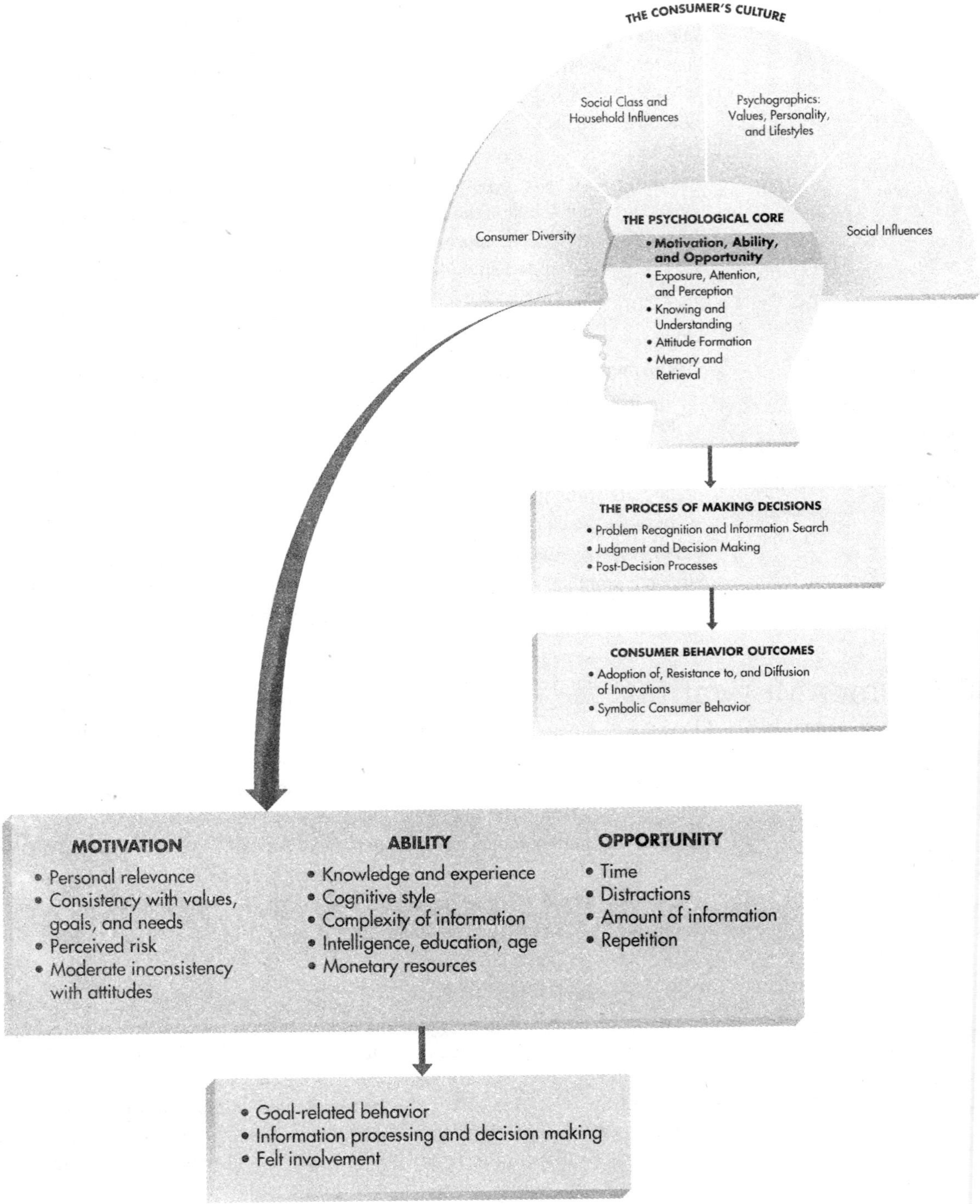

Exhibit 3.2

CHAPTER OVERVIEW: MOTIVATION, ABILITY, AND OPPORTUNITY *Motivation, ability, and opportunity (MAO) to engage in various consumer behaviors is affected by many factors. Outcomes of high MAO include (1) goal-relevant behavior, (2) high-effort information processing and decision making, and (3) felt involvement.*

High-Effort Information Processing and Decision Making

Motivation also affects how we process information and make decisions.[3] When consumers are highly motivated to achieve a goal, they are more likely to pay careful attention to it, think about it, attempt to understand or comprehend information presented about it, evaluate that information critically, and try to remember it for later use. Doing all this takes a lot of effort. For example, if you are motivated to watch the new cinema at the multiplex, you may scour newspaper looking for the show timings and the location of the multiplexes. One may also try and call up the place for free home delivery of tickets or online ticket bookings.

When consumers have low motivation, however, they devote little effort to processing information and making decisions. For example, your motivation to purchase the best pad of paper on the market is likely to be low. You wouldn't devote much attention to learning about the characteristics of paper pads or examining paper pads. Nor would you think about what it would be like to own and use various types of pads. Once in the store, you are unlikely to spend much time comparing brands. You may use decision-making shortcuts, such as deciding to buy the cheapest brand or the same brand you bought the last time.[4] The purchase of most common grocery products falls into the same category.

Most research on consumer behavior has focused on consumers' motivation to process information *accurately*, as just described. However, recent research is aimed at understanding a different type of motivation in information processing, called ***motivated reasoning.*** When consumers engage in motivated reasoning they process information in a way that allows them to reach a particular conclusion they want to reach.[5] For example, if you have a goal of losing weight and you see an ad for a diet product, you might process the ad deeply, trying to use your good judgment and accurately determine how good the product is. Alternatively, you might process the ad in a biased way so as to convince yourself that the product will indeed work for you. We may be particularly prone to motivated reasoning when our egos are at stake or when we desperately hope we can achieve a particular goal (like weight loss).[6] The concept of motivated reasoning is rather new—so most of the discussion that follows focuses on motivation to process information accurately.

Felt Involvement

A final outcome of motivation is that it evokes a psychological state in consumers called *involvement*. Researchers use the term ***felt involvement*** to refer to the psychological experience of the motivated consumer.[7] Felt involvement can be (1) enduring, (2) situational, (3) cognitive, or (4) affective.[8]

Enduring Involvement ***Enduring involvement*** exists when we show interest in an offering or activity over a long period of time.[9] Car enthusiasts are intrinsically interested in cars and exhibit enduring involvement in them. Enthusiasts engage in activities that reveal this interest (e.g., going to car shows, reading car magazines, visiting dealerships). A consumer might express enduring involvement in any object or activity—downloading the latest software or working out, for instance. However, most consumers exhibit enduring involvement for relatively few offerings or activities.

Situational Involvement In most instances, consumers experience ***situational (temporary) involvement*** with an offering or activity. For example, consumers who exhibit no enduring involvement with cars may be involved in the car-buying process when they are in the market for a new car. After they buy the car, their involvement with new cars declines dramatically. Involvement with gift giving is often situational. Involvement is usually high only when the consumer is trying to achieve the goal of deciding on a gift.

Cognitive Involvement Researchers distinguish between cognitive and affective involvement.[10] ***Cognitive involvement*** means that the consumer is interested in thinking about and processing information related to his or her goal. The goal therefore includes learning about the offering. An avid traveler, planning for Machu Pichu in Peru, is likely to scour through all possible literature on the destination planned including working out all logistical details too.

Affective Involvement ***Affective involvement*** means that the consumer is willing to expend emotional energy in or has heightened feelings about an offering or activity. The consumer who listens to music to experience intense emotions is exhibiting affective involvement. The problem of female foeticide especially in urban India is a growing menace. Early sex determination, now considered a crime in India, leads to termination of pregnancy and the process goes on till the woman conceives with a male child, risking herself and the child in the womb to undue health concerns often leading to deaths or permanent physical disorders. The male-female sex ratio also gets altered in the process and some regions of Punjab, Haryana and parts of Delhi are the worst hit. The Ministry of Health and Urban Welfare has been strongly campaigning against such practices and now it has become mandatory to put messages across hospitals, nursing homes and other medical centres, that pre-birth sex determination is completely illegal and banned in such locations. The government also comes out with several promotional messages and advertisements that highlight the "Girl Child" aspect and there are several schemes of the government that encourage people to have girl child.

Objects of Involvement

In analyzing consumer involvement and its influence on behavior, we can also identify the various objects with which consumers may be involved. These include involvement with product categories, brands, ads, media, and decisions.

Involvement with Product Categories As many of this chapter's examples indicate, consumers may exhibit cognitive and/or affective involvement in a certain product category, such as cars, computers, or clothes.[12] On the other hand, research suggests that even when consumers have minimal interest in a product category or branded products, they may exhibit involvement with specific brands.[13]

Involvement with Brands Consumers can also exhibit cognitive and/or affective involvement with a brand, a phenomenon called *brand loyalty*. As you will see in later chapters, brand-loyal consumers consistently purchase the brand, hold strong beliefs about its quality, are devoted to it, and often resist competitors' efforts to attract them. Yet, whether consumers remain involved with a brand that has violated their expectations or trust depends, in part, on the brand's personality and the extent to which they are emotionally attached to the brand.[14]

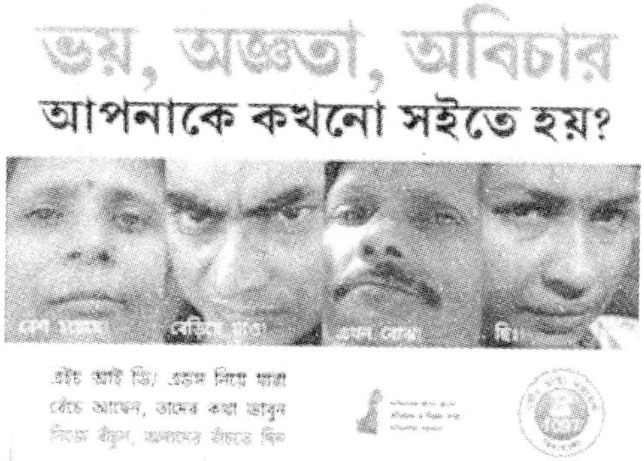

Exhibit 3.3
CREATING INVOLVEMENT IN THE AD
Consumers become involved in ads like this because the ad is relevant to problems consumers might have themselves

Involvement with Ads Involvement with ads may be revealed by consumers' motivation to attend to and process information contained in the ad (see Exhibit 3.3). Typically, involvement in an ad is high if consumers view the advertised message as relevant to them.[15] Consumers can also become involved in an ad simply because they find it interesting. Ads for shaving cream that present sports questions and ask readers to "make the call" usually elicit involvement among sports fans. In Japan, ads that emphasize interpersonal relationships, social circumstances, and nonverbal expressions generate more involvement than ads with clearly articulated and spoken messages.[16] Other methods for stimulating involvement in ads and motivation to process ads are discussed later in the chapter.

Involvement with a Medium Consumers may get involved with the medium in which an ad is placed. Television, for example, is a fairly low-involvement medium because viewers are typically passive and do not have to think much to process what they see. An exception to the rule is the rise of the reality television formats where the viewers are also given discretionary powers to control the future of the programmes. Indian Idol, Sa Re Ga Ma Pa or Fame Gurukul are some of the reality TV shows that have gained acceptance and also popularity. Print media such as magazines and newspapers usually generate higher levels of involvement because readers must interact with these media. Consumers can also be involved in a specific TV or radio program or a particular magazine or newspaper.[18] When companies advertise during TV shows in which consumers become involved, the ads tend to be more effective.[19] However, research suggests that higher levels of involvement with a TV show can sometimes reduce involvement in ads because an interesting show can be distracting and suspend processing of an ad. Finally, when a computer is present, consumers associate it with the Internet as an information-gathering medium and are likely to think more about a product and search for additional details about it.[20]

Involvement with Decisions and Behaviors Consumers involved in certain decisions and behaviors are experiencing ***response involvement***.[21] For example, consumers may be highly involved in the process of deciding between brands. Someone who loves shopping may browse a lot and not buy anything. Consumers can also find the act of using certain products or services involving. Many people enjoy playing video games or attending sporting events because these activities are highly involving.

Specifying the Object of Involvement Consumers can be involved with many different entities, so it is important to specify the *object of involvement* when using the term *involvement*. For instance, brand-loyal consumers are highly involved in the brand, but because they believe their brand is the best, they are unlikely to be involved in making a decision about which brand to buy. Likewise, consumers can be very involved in an ad because it is funny, interesting, or novel—yet, they may show little involvement in the advertised brand because they are loyal to other brands.

What Affects Motivation?

Motivation is influenced by the extent to which the ad, brand, product category, or other characteristic is personally relevant to consumers. Consumers see something as personally relevant and important when it is (1) consistent with their values, goals, and needs; (2) risky; and/or (3) moderately inconsistent with their prior attitudes.

Personal Relevance

A key factor affecting motivation is the extent to which something is ***personally relevant***—that is, the extent to which it has a direct bearing on and significant consequences or implications for your life.[22] For example, if you learn that your laptop computer's battery is being recalled because it can overheat and cause a fire, you will probably find this issue to be personally relevant. Careers, college activities, romantic relationships, a car, apartment or house, clothes, and hobbies are likely to be personally relevant because their consequences are significant for you. Research indicates that the prospect of receiving a customized (and therefore more personally relevant) product will motivate consumers to disclose private information, although they are less likely to reveal details that could be embarrassing.[23]

In addition, something may be personally relevant to the extent that it bears on your ***self-concept,*** or your view of yourself, and the way you think others view you. Self-concept helps us define who we are, and it frequently guides our behavior. When we buy clothing, we are often making a statement about who we are—a professional, a student, or a sports fan. Some consumers find brands like Harley-Davidson to be relevant to their self-concept; owning this brand is important to their self-definition and is personally relevant. *Red,* a U.K. women's magazine, positions itself as being for the reader's "me time," making itself relevant by appealing to the woman's self-concept as a busy, productive woman entitled to a small indulgence.[24]

We will be motivated to behave, process information, or engage in effortful *decision making* about things that we feel are personally relevant. And we will experience considerable involvement when buying, using, or disposing of them. Think about all the behaviors you engaged in when deciding where to go to college—obtaining applications and information packets, searching the Web, visiting campuses, and so on. You probably devoted considerable time and effort to processing the information about each school and deciding where to go. Chances are, you found the task of making this decision personally involving and felt interest, enthusiasm, and perhaps anxiety during the process.

marketing IMPLICATIONS

Marketers can enhance consumers' motivation to process promotional materials by trying to make the information as personally relevant as possible. Salespeople can explore consumers' underlying reasons for a purchase and tailor sales pitches to those reasons. Similarly, ads can be geared toward consumers' special concerns. Consumers seeking positive outcomes such as advancement or achievement will find an ad more personally relevant if it appeals to those outcomes. In contrast, consumers seeking to avoid negative outcomes such as developing cavities or getting AIDS will find an ad more personally relevant when it tells them how to avoid those outcomes (see Exhibit 3.4).[25] The Skin Cancer Foundation recently ran TV and Internet ads aimed at convincing parents to put sunscreen on their children and avoid skin damage that may lead to skin cancer later in life. Because parents want to keep their children from harm, this campaign was personally relevant.[26]

Exhibit 3.4
PUBLIC SERVICE AD
This public service ad is personally relevant to parents since it warns them of the dangers of leaving children unattended when they are near water.

Values, Goals, and Needs

People perceive something as personally relevant when it is consistent with their values, goals, and needs. In turn, this relevance fuels their motivation to process information, make decisions, and take actions.

Values Consumers are more motivated to attend to and process information when they find it relevant to their ***values***—beliefs that guide what people regard as important or good. Thus, if you see education as extremely important, you are likely to be motivated to engage in behaviors that are consistent with this value, such as pursuing a degree. (You'll read more about values in Chapter 15.)

Goals A second factor affecting personal relevance and motivation is goals.[27] A ***goal*** is a particular end state or outcome that a person would like to achieve. You might have goals for saving money, getting a good job after graduation, or meeting an attractive member of the opposite sex at Friday's party. Some goals are specific to a given behavior or action and determined by the situation at hand. If you are tired, one of your goals for the evening might be to go to bed early. If you are often late for class, one of your goals might be to arrive on time. Other goals may be much more abstract and endure over a long period, such as being a good student, being cool, or looking beautiful.[28] Note that if you perceive you have failed in achieving a behavioral goal (such as saving a certain amount of money), you will have less motivation and, subsequently, perform even more poorly in relation to that goal.[29]

Whether the goals are situational and concrete or enduring and abstract, consumers are likely to be very motivated to engage in behaviors that are relevant to achieving their personal goals. Goals help consumers organize product knowledge and assist in the transfer of effort and behavioral intention from one product to another, depending on the degree to which the products fulfill a common goal.[30] Further, a marketer's strong persuasive appeal will stimulate more information processing and more favorable attitudes when consistent with a consumer's self-regulation goal of promotion (such as advancement) or prevention (such as security).[31] Finally, consumers often have a goal of seeing themselves in a positive light. As a result, they may overestimate the positive outcome of actions such as buying a lottery ticket or underestimate the likelihood of such problems as becoming ill—and fail to take preventive steps.[32]

As shown in Exhibit 3.5, goal-attainment activities follow a certain pattern. After we set a goal (such as to lose four pounds this month), we are motivated to form a goal intention, plan to take action (identify low-fat foods and join a gym), implement and control the action (through diet and exercise), and evaluate success or failure in

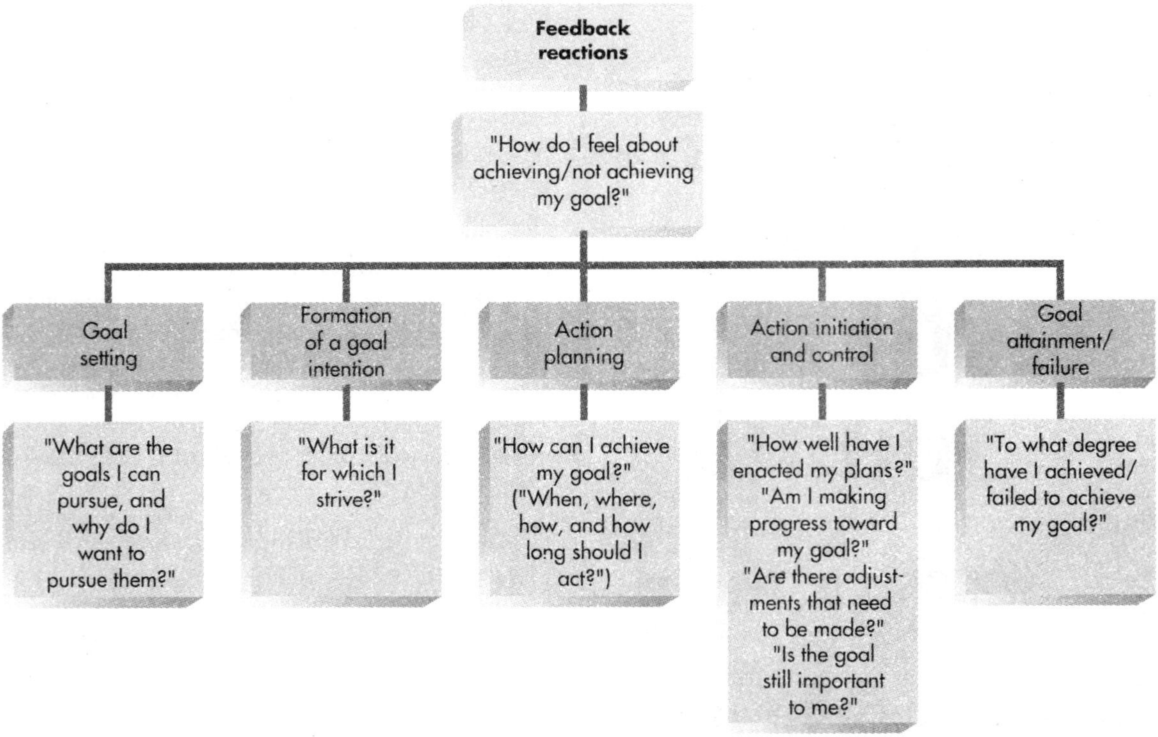

Exhibit 3.5

GOAL SETTING AND PURSUIT IN CONSUMER BEHAVIOR *The process of setting and pursuing goals is circular: how a person feels about achieving or not achieving a goal affects what new goals that person sets and why. This process affects the individual's motivation to initiate or continue behaviors relevant to the goal that has been set.*

attaining the goal (by weighing ourselves at the end of the month). Finally, we use what we learned by achieving or not achieving the goal as feedback for future goal setting.[33] Thus, setting and pursuing goals is a highly motivating, relevant factor driving behavior.

Needs A third and very powerful factor affecting personal relevance and motivation is needs. A ***need*** is an internal state of tension caused by disequilibrium from an ideal or desired state. As this definition indicates, each need has an equilibrium level at which it is in a state of satisfaction. The consumer feels tension when there is any departure from this equilibrium and is motivated to find some way of fulfilling the need. For example, at certain times of the day, your stomach begins to feel uncomfortable. You realize it is time to get something to eat, and you are motivated to direct your behavior toward certain outcomes (e.g., going to the refrigerator or ordering take-out food). Eating satisfies your need and removes the tension—in this case, hunger. Once you are motivated to satisfy a particular need, objects unrelated to that need seem less attractive. Thus if you are motivated to find food when you feel hungry, products such as shampoo will not seem as attractive as popcorn or other snacks.[34]

Just as needs can lead us toward a product or service, they can also keep us away. For example, have you ever put off going to the dentist? If so, you were probably motivated by a need to avoid pain. Consumer researchers call behavior motivated by a desire to approach something good *promotion-focused* and behavior motivated by a desire to stay away from something bad *prevention-focused*.[35]

A variety of needs can operate in a given situation. But what needs do consumers experience? One well-known theory of needs is based on the research of psychologist Abraham Maslow.[36] Maslow grouped needs into the five categories shown in Exhibit 3.6: (1) physiological (the need for food, water, and sleep); (2) safety (the need for shelter, protection, and security); (3) social (the need for affection, friendship, and acceptance); (4) egoistic (the need for prestige, success, accomplishment, and self-esteem); and (5) self-actualization (the need for self-fulfillment and enriching experiences). Within this hierarchy, lower-level needs generally must be satisfied before higher-level needs become activated. Thus before we can worry about prestige, we must meet lower-level needs for food, water, and so on.

Although Maslow's hierarchy brings useful organization to the complex issue of needs, some critics suggest it is too simplistic. First, needs are not always ordered exactly as in this hierarchy. For example, some consumers place a higher priority on buying lottery tickets than on acquiring necessities such as food and clothing. Second, the hierarchy ignores the intensity of needs and the resulting effect on motivation. Finally, the ordering of needs may not be consistent across cultures. In some societies, for example, social needs and belonging may be higher in the hierarchy than egoistic needs.

Exhibit 3.6
MASLOW'S HIERARCHY OF NEEDS

Maslow suggested that needs can be categorized into a basic hierarchy. People fulfill lower-order needs (e.g., physiological needs for food, water, sleep) before they fulfill higher-order needs.

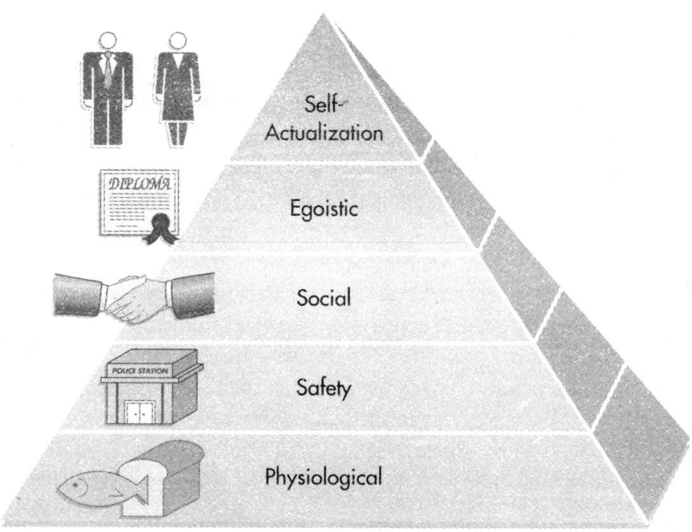

Types of Needs Another way to categorize needs is as (1) social and nonsocial needs or (2) functional, symbolic, and hedonic needs[37] (see Exhibit 3.7).

- *Social needs* are externally directed and relate to other individuals. Fulfilling these needs thus requires the presence or actions of other people. For example, the need for status drives our desire to have others hold us in high regard; the need for support drives us to have others relieve us of our burdens; the need for modeling reflects a wish to have others show us how to behave. We may be motivated to buy products like Hallmark cards or use services such as Friendster.com because they help us achieve a need for affiliation.[38] Other products may be valued because they are consistent with our need for status or our need to be unique.[39] We also have antisocial needs—needs for space and psychological distance from other people. Plane seats that are too close together violate our need for space and motivate us to escape the confining environment.

- *Nonsocial needs* are those for which achievement is not based on other people. Our needs for sleep, novelty, control, uniqueness, and understanding, which involve only ourselves, can affect the usage of certain products and services. We might purchase the same brand repeatedly to maintain consistency in our world—or we might buy something totally different to fulfill a need for variety.

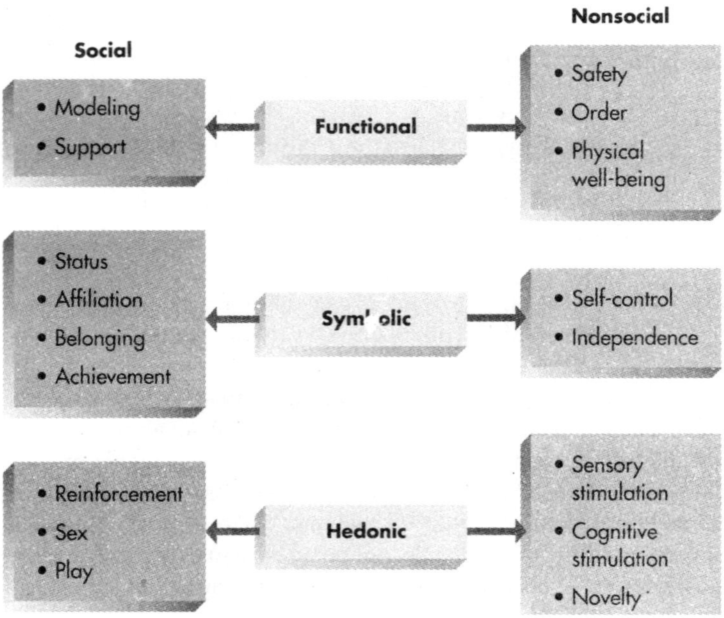

Exhibit 3.7
CATEGORIZING NEEDS

Needs can be categorized according to whether they are (1) social or nonsocial and (2) functional, symbolic, or hedonic in nature. This categorization method helps marketers think about consumers' needs.

- *Functional needs* may be social or nonsocial. Functional needs motivate the search for products that solve consumption-related problems. For example contemplating between a car with safety features (ABS Airbag) at an additional cost or a car without safety features at a lower cost is linked to the functional benefits of the car. Alternatively for working women, putting the child in a day care centre or hiring a full time nanny at home is a contemplation based on cost, convenience and safety aspects for the child.
- *Symbolic needs* affect how we perceive ourselves and how we are perceived by others. Achievement, independence, and self-control are symbolic needs because they are connected with our sense of self. Similarly, our need for uniqueness is symbolic because it drives consumption decisions about how we express our identity.[40] The need to avoid rejection and the need for achievement, status, affiliation, and belonging are symbolic because they reflect our social position or role. For example, some consumers might wear Jimmy Choo shoes to express their social standing.
- *Hedonic needs* include needs for sensory stimulation, cognitive stimulation, and novelty (nonsocial hedonic needs) and needs for reinforcement, sex, and play (social hedonic needs). These ***hedonic needs*** reflect our inherent desires for sensory pleasure. If the desire is intense enough, it can inspire fantasizing about specific goods, simultaneously pleasurable and discomforting.[41] Consumers may buy CDs and perfume for the sensory pleasure they bring or go to luxury shopping centres such as the Santushti complex in Delhi. For the same reason, some products with fake fat or no sugar have failed because they have not met hedonic needs.
- *Needs for cognition and stimulation* also affect motivation and behavior. Consumers with a high need for cognition[43] (a need for mental stimulation) tend to be highly involved in mentally taxing activities like reading and are more likely to actively process information during decision making. People with a low need for cognition may be more involved in activities that require less thought, such as watching TV, and less likely to actively process information during decision making. Consumers also need other kinds of stimulation. Those with a high optimum stimulation level enjoy high levels of sensory stimulation and tend to be involved in shopping and seeking brand information.[44] They also show heightened involvement in ads. Consumers with thrill-seeking tendencies enjoy activities like skydiving and whitewater rafting. In contrast, consumers who feel overstimulated want to get away from people, noise, and demands—a desire revealed in the popularity of vacations at monasteries and other sanctuaries.

Characteristics of Needs Each of the preceding needs has several characteristics:

- *Needs are dynamic.* Needs are never fully satisfied; satisfaction is only temporary. Clearly, eating once will not satisfy our hunger forever. Also, as soon as one need is satisfied, new needs emerge. After we have eaten a meal, we might next have the need to be with others (the need for affiliation). Thus needs are dynamic because daily life is a constant process of need fulfillment.
- *Needs exist in a hierarchy.* Although several needs may be activated at any one time, some assume more importance. You may experience a need to eat during an exam, but your need for achievement may assume a higher priority—so you stay to finish the test. Despite this hierarchy, many needs may be activated simultaneously and influence your acquisition, usage, and disposition behaviors. Thus your decision to go out for dinner with friends may be driven by a combination of needs for stimulation, food, and companionship.
- *Needs can be internally or externally aroused.* Although many needs are internally activated, some needs can be externally cued. Smelling pizza cooking in the apartment next door may, for example, affect your perceived need for food.
- *Needs can conflict.* A given behavior or outcome can be seen as both desirable and undesirable if it satisfies some needs but fails to satisfy others. The result is called an ***approach-avoidance conflict*** because you both want to engage in the behavior and want to avoid it. Teenagers may experience an approach-avoidance conflict in deciding whether to smoke cigarettes. Although they may believe that others will think they are cool for smoking (consistent with need for belonging), they also know that smoking is bad for them (incompatible with need for safety).
- An ***approach-approach conflict*** occurs when someone must choose between two or more equally desirable options that fulfill different needs. A consumer who is invited to a career-night function (consistent with achievement needs) might experience an approach-approach conflict if he is also invited to attend a basketball game with friends (consistent with affiliation needs) on the same evening. This consumer will experience conflict if he views both options as equally desirable.
- An ***avoidance-avoidance conflict*** occurs when the consumer must choose between two equally undesirable options, such as going home alone right after a late meeting (not satisfying a need for safety) or waiting another hour until a friend can drive her home (not satisfying a need for convenience). Conflict arises because neither option is desirable.

Identifying Needs Because needs influence motivation and its effects, marketers are keenly interested in identifying and measuring them. Yet, consumers are often unaware of their needs and have trouble explaining them to researchers. Inferring consumers' needs based only on behaviors is also difficult because a given need might not be linked to a specific behavior. In other words, the same need (affiliation) can be exhibited in various and diverse behaviors (visiting friends, going to the gym), and the same behavior (going to the gym) can reflect various needs (affiliation, achievement). Consider the activity of shopping. One study found that when women shop in drugstores, they are seeking information about items that provide peace of mind (satisfying needs for safety and well-being). When they shop in club stores, they are seeking adventure and entertainment (satisfying the need for stimulation).[45]

Inferring needs in a cross-cultural context is particularly difficult. For example, some research indicates that U.S. consumers use toothpaste primarily for its cavity-reducing capabilities (a functional need). In contrast, consumers in England and some French-speaking areas of Canada use toothpaste primarily to freshen breath (a hedonic need). French women drink mineral water so they will look better (a symbolic need), whereas German consumers drink it for its health powers (a functional need).[46]

Given these difficulties, marketers sometimes use indirect techniques to uncover consumers' needs.[47] Essentially, these techniques ask consumers to interpret a set of relatively ambiguous stimuli such as cartoons, word associations, incomplete sentences, and incomplete stories. For example, using Exhibit 3.8, one consumer might reveal needs for esteem by interpreting the man in the cartoon as thinking, "My friends will think I'm really cool for riding in this car!" Another might reveal needs for affiliation by filling in the cartoon with "I could take all my friends for rides with me."

When one study asked cigarette smokers why they smoked, most said they enjoyed it and believed that smoking in moderation was fine. However, when they were given incomplete sentences like "People who never smoke are _______," respondents filled in the blanks with words like *happier* and *wiser.* And when given sentences like "Teenagers who smoke are _______," respondents answered with words like *crazy* and *foolish.* These smokers were clearly more concerned about smoking than their explicit answers indicated.[48]

Survey

A. Cartoon drawing:
What do you think the people in this cartoon are thinking?

B. Sentence completion:
Fill in the blanks with the first word that comes to your mind:

1. The perfect gift ______________________________.
2. The gifts I still treasure ______________________________.
3. If I give a gift to myself ______________________________.

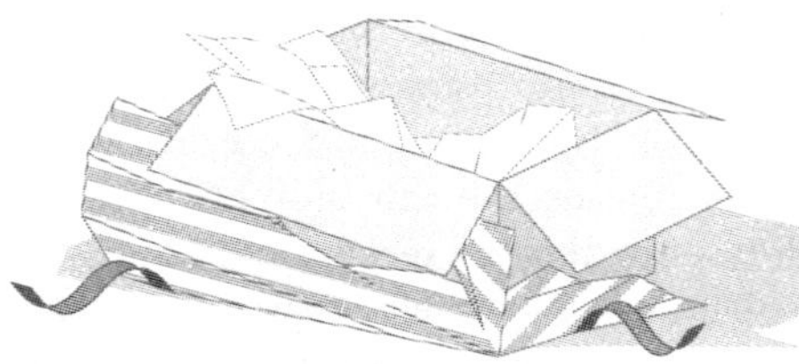

C. Tell a story:
Tell a story about the gift being unwrapped in this picture.

Exhibit 3.8
UNCOVERING CONSUMERS' NEEDS

Marketers sometimes uncover consumers' needs using ambiguous stimuli like cartoon drawings, sentence completion tasks, and tell-a-story tasks. The idea is that consumers will project their needs, wishes, and fantasies onto these ambiguous stimuli.

marketing IMPLICATIONS Consumers' needs, values, and goals have some important implications for marketers.

Segmenting markets based on needs

First, marketers can use needs to segment markets. Dabur, a trusted name in most Indian households made a foray into the processed food market pushing a host of brands in various product categories. They entered the sweetened fruit juice segment, with a brand titled, "Dabur Real" fruit juices. However, the same company when targeting the more health conscious and serious profile, introduced a zero-sweetener low-cal drink titled, "Dabur Real Activ". Similarly, advent of brown breads and other forms of high-fiber breads from both local and national brands signals that more and more consumers are switching to health based options, opening up a new segment of consumers.

Creating new needs

Sometimes marketers attempt to create new needs. For instance, the Italian automaker Ferrari launched its F-1 Clienti program to create a need for a new car-racing experience. Customers willing to pay $1 million (or more) to buy a retired Ferrari race car can drive it on Grand Prix courses, tutored by a racing champion and supported by a professional pit crew. According to Ferrari, the F-1 Clienti program allows customers to have "an experience they can't get elsewhere."[50]

Developing need-satisfying offerings

Marketers can also identify currently unfulfilled needs or develop better need-satisfying alternatives. W, a prominent chain of stores spread across India focused on the women's readymade garment segment by introducing branded apparels. Branded readymade apparels in the women's segment are not very popular and most women prefer to scour for clothes where comfort, design, fit and price are critical. W introduced a range of clothing for women, where the focus was on design, fit, comfort and a wide range. Priced at a premium, discerning shoppers could find a wide range under one roof and the ambience and store layout augmented the shopping experience. W's success is based on the research about women psychology while shopping and evaluating need sets as a build-up to the items purchased. Chapter 17 explains more about research and the development of new products.

The importance of developing need-satisfying offerings operates cross-culturally as well. McDonald's has successfully satisfied international consumer's desire for fast food by altering menus according to cultural differences. In India, the strictly vegetarian leaning of the average diner has meant that McDonald's offers a separate strictly vegetarian platter and a large number of its menu are altered and suited to the local taste. Products like beef are a complete no no and non-vegetarian items are showcased as separate offerings and not mixed with the vegetarian items.

Managing conflicting needs

Companies can develop new products or use communications to resolve need conflicts. For instance, the marketers of Propecia, a prescription tablet for treating male baldness, must promote the drug's benefits while countering the perception that it will reduce sexual desire (which it can).[53]

Appealing to multiple goals and needs

Marketers may want to create bundled offerings that allow consumers to achieve more than one goal or satisfy more than one need during a single consumption episode.[54] For instance, a pizza restaurant might offer healthy fruit juices or smoothies (so consumers can achieve their goals of losing weight or eating better) as well as a wide variety of specialty pizzas (so consumers can satisfy hedonic needs or cravings for variety).

Enhancing communication effectiveness

By suggesting that the offering fulfills a need, value, or goal, marketers can increase the likelihood that consumers will process the message (ad, sales message, etc.) and engage in desired behaviors. The makers of Head and Shoulders shampoo, for example, recognize that consumers have a strong need to be accepted by others. The manufacturer effectively appeals to this need by suggesting that having dandruff will lead to social rejection. Thus needs are an effective way of positioning a product or service.[55] Companies should also develop marketing communications that portray the offerings as relevant to consumers' needs, values, and goals. The ad in Exhibit 3.9 is designed to appeal to both functional and hedonic needs.

Perceived Risk

Another factor affecting personal relevance and motivation is ***perceived risk,*** the extent to which the consumer is uncertain about the personal consequences of buying, using, or disposing of an offering.[56] If negative outcomes are likely or positive outcomes are unlikely, perceived risk is high. Consumers are more likely to pay attention to and carefully process marketing communications when perceived risk is high. As perceived risk increases, consumers tend to collect more information and evaluate it carefully.

Perceived risk can be associated with any product or service, but it tends to be higher in the following circumstances:

- Little information is available about the offering.
- The offering is new.
- The offering has a high price.
- The offering is technologically complex.
- Brands differ fairly substantially in quality, so the consumer might make an inferior choice.
- The consumer has little confidence or experience in evaluating the offering.
- The opinions of others are important, and the consumer is likely to be judged on the basis of the acquisition, usage, or disposition decision.[57]

Exhibit 3.9

APPEALING TO FUNCTIONAL AND HEDONIC NEEDS

Maggi's line extension in the last one year is an attempt to offer the goodness of traditional Indian cereals with Maggi's core product appeal remaining intact

Perceptions of risk vary across cultural groups. In particular, high levels of risk tend to be associated with many more products in less-developed countries, perhaps because the products in these countries are generally of poorer quality.[58] Also, perceived risk is typically higher when travelers purchase goods in a foreign country.[59] In addition, risk perceptions vary within a culture.[60] For example, Western men take more risks in stock market investments than women take, and younger consumers take more risks than older ones take. Clearly the women and older consumers in these examples perceive greater risks with various decisions.

Types of Perceived Risk Researchers have identified six types of risk:[61]

- ***Performance risk*** reflects uncertainty about whether the product or service will perform as expected. If a car buyer is uncertain whether a new or used vehicle will be reliable, perceived performance risk is high. The Maruti Service Master's

"True Value" program is a novel exercise by the company to bring in credibility and trust in the selling and purchasing of the second hand cars directly with Maruti.

- ***Financial risk*** is higher if an offering is expensive. For instance, a home is an expensive purchase, and the level of risk associated with this kind of monetary investment is high. When consumers perceive high product-category risk due to high price levels, research suggests that buying decisions can be improved by researching specific offerings using recommendation agent websites such as MySimon and Epinions.com.[63]
- ***Physical (or safety) risk*** refers to the potential harm a product or service might pose to one's safety. Many consumer decisions are driven by a motivation to avoid physical risk. For example, some U.S. and Canadian consumers concerned about crime or terrorism are hiring private security guards to patrol their neighborhoods.[64]
- ***Social risk*** is the potential harm to one's social standing that may arise from buying, using, or disposing of an offering. According to research, antismoking ad messages that conveyed the severe social disapproval risk of smoking cigarettes were more effective in influencing teens' intensions not to smoke than ad messages stressing health consequences such as disease.[65]
- ***Psychological risk*** reflects consumers' concern about the extent to which a product or service fits with the way they perceive themselves. For example, if you see yourself as an environmentalist, buying disposable diapers may be psychologically risky.
- ***Time risk*** reflects uncertainties over the length of time that must be invested in buying, using, or disposing of the product or service. Time risk may be high if the offering involves considerable time commitment, if learning to use it is a lengthy process, or if it entails a long commitment period (such as a health club that requires a three-year contract).

Risk and Involvement As noted earlier, products can be described as either high- or low-involvement products. Some researchers have classified high- versus low-involvement products in terms of the amount of risk they pose to consumers. Consumers are likely to be more involved in purchasing products such as homes and computers than in purchasing picture frames or coffee because the former generate higher levels of performance, financial, safety, social, psychological, or time risk and can therefore have more extreme personal consequences.

High risk is generally uncomfortable for consumers. As a result, they are usually motivated to engage in any number of behaviors and information-processing activities to reduce or resolve risk. To reduce the uncertainty component of risk, consumers can collect additional information by conducting online research, reading news articles, engaging in comparative shopping, talking to friends or sales specialists, or consulting an expert. Consumers also reduce uncertainty by being brand loyal (buying the same brand as last time), ensuring that the product should be at least as satisfactory as the last purchase.

In addition, consumers attempt to reduce the consequence component of perceived risk through various strategies. Some consumers may employ a simple decision rule that results in a safer choice. For example, someone might buy the most expensive offering or choose a heavily advertised brand in the belief that this brand is of higher quality than other brands.

marketing IMPLICATIONS Perceived risk has a number of marketing implications (see Exhibit 3.10).

Reducing risk perceptions
When perceived risk is high, marketers can either reduce uncertainty or reduce the perceived consequences of failure. MailFrontier, an antivirus, antifraud software company, uses the slogans "Ask me about nothing" and "E-mail is good again" to convey that its product reduces the uncertainty that consumers feel when opening e-mail messages they fear might contain a virus or be fraudulent.[66]

Enhancing risk perceptions
When risk is low, consumers are less motivated to think about the brand and its potential consequences. Marketers sometimes need to enhance risk perceptions to make their messages more compelling. For example, Merck advertises its Varivax chicken pox vaccine by warning that children could require hospitalization or even die due to complications from the disease.[67] Interestingly, consumers do not always see a particular action as risky, even when it is. As one example, many consumers doubt they will have negative outcomes from unprotected sex, which explains why condom sales are not higher. Marketers can also enhance consumers' understanding of how personal behavior can create risky negative outcomes. Research shows that when consumers think about the role their own behavior plays in acquiring AIDS, they are more likely to follow the advice in ads designed to reduce that risk.[68]

Exhibit 3.10
MARKETING AND PERCEIVED RISK
This ad tries to enhance the perceived risk consumers feel about losing their money to pickpockets when they travel.

Inconsistency with Attitudes

A final factor affecting motivation is the extent to which new information is consistent with previously acquired knowledge or attitudes. We tend to be motivated to process messages that are moderately inconsistent with our existing knowledge or attitudes because they are perceived as moderately threatening or uncomfortable. Therefore, we try to eliminate or at least understand this inconsistency.[69] For example, if a consumer sees a car ad that mentions slightly negative information about the brand she currently owns—such as the brand getting lower gas mileage than a competitor—she will want to process the information so she can understand and perhaps resolve the uncomfortable feeling.

On the other hand, consumers are less motivated to process information that is highly inconsistent with their prior attitudes. Thus someone who is loyal to the Heinz brand would not be motivated to process information from a comparative ad suggesting that Heinz is bad or that other brands are better. The consumer would simply reject the other brands as unviable options.

Consumer Ability: Resources to Act

Motivation may not result in action unless a consumer has the ability to process information, make decisions, or engage in behaviors. ***Ability*** is defined as the extent to which consumers have the necessary resources to make the outcome happen.[70] If our ability to process information is high, we may engage in active decision making. As shown in Exhibit 3.2, knowledge, experience, cognitive style, complexity of information, intelligence, education, age, and money are factors that affect consumers' abilities to process information about brands and make decisions about, and engage in, buying, usage, and disposition.

Product Knowledge and Experience

Consumers vary greatly in their knowledge about an offering.[71] They can gain knowledge from product or service experiences such as ad exposures, interactions with salespeople, information from friends or the media, previous decision making or product usage, or memory. A number of studies have compared the information-processing activities of consumers who have a lot of product knowledge or expertise with consumers who do not.[72] One key finding is that knowledgeable consumers, or "experts," are better able to think deeply about information than equally motivated but less knowledgeable consumers, or "novices." These differences in prior knowledge clearly affect how consumers make decisions. For example, consumers trying to lease a car rarely understand the concept of capitalized costs (the figure used to determine lease payments), how these costs are determined, or the need to negotiate lower costs to lower their payments. The inability to understand these costs may result in a less than optimal decision.[73]

Consider also cases in which less knowledgeable consumers try to process the government-mandated information in a prescription drug ad. Although these ads used to contain highly technical information that was difficult for consumers to understand, many companies are trying to make this information "user friendly" so that the ad content is consistent with consumers' abilities to process it.

One study found that novices and experts process similar amounts of information but in different ways.[74] Experts were able to process information stated in terms of attributes (what the product has—such as a Pentium chip), whereas novices could do so only when the information was stated in terms of benefits (what the product can do for the consumer—such as enhance efficiency). Still, novices may be able to process information when marketers provide a helpful analogy.[75] In particular, an analogy will be persuasive when consumers have the ability to transfer their knowledge of one product's attributes to an unfamiliar product and can allocate the resources needed to process this mapping.[76]

Cognitive Style

Consumers can differ in ***cognitive style,*** or their preferences for ways information should be presented. Some consumers are adept at processing information visually, whereas others prefer to process information verbally. For example, some consumers prefer to check a map, and others prefer to read directions when planning to reach a destination. One important aspect of cognitive style is ***cognitive complexity.***[77] A cognitively complex individual is more likely to engage in complicated processing of information from marketing communications, accepting new and/or contradictory

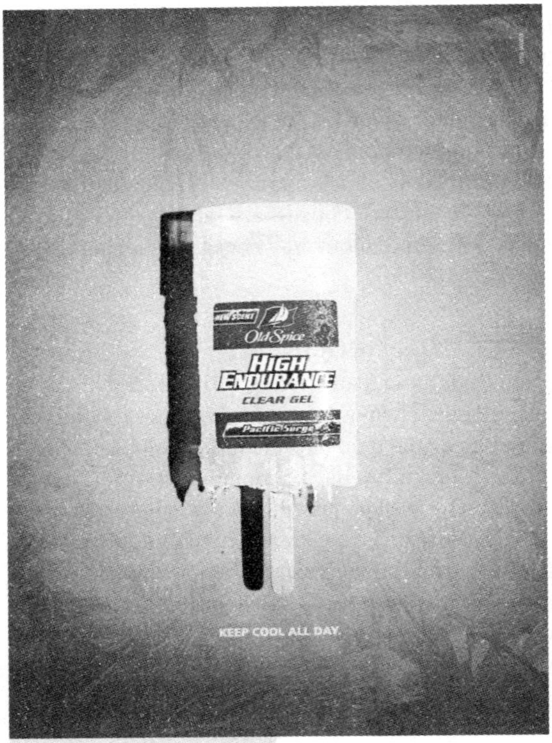

Exhibit 3.11
LEARNING BY ANALOGY
Old Spice creates the impression that the product is cool to the touch by drawing an analogy between the product and a popsicle.

information, making finer distinctions when processing information, and considering a greater diversity of information when making a decision.

Complexity of Information

The complexity of the information to which consumers are exposed can also affect their ability to process it. Even individuals who prefer cognitive complexity may be stymied when information gets too technical or complicated; as information becomes more complex, our ability to process it decreases. What makes information complex? Studies indicate that consumers find technical or quantitative information more difficult to handle than nontechnical and qualitative data,[78] which inhibits processing. Many technological and pharmaceutical products entail complex information. In addition, research shows that messages containing pictures without words tend to be ambiguous and therefore hard to process.[79] Information may also be complex if the individual must sift through a huge volume of it. More consumers look online for complex information about health or medicines because Web search functions help them search efficiently. Knowing this, the patient advocacy group Citizens for the Right to Know maintains an English-language site (*rtk.org*) and a Spanish-language site (*espanol.rkt.org*) to help consumers search through complex information about health-plan coverage.[80] Exhibit 3.11 shows one way of making a message simple.

Intelligence, Education, and Age

Intelligence, education, and age have also been related to the ability to process information. Specifically, consumers who are more intelligent and more educated can better process more complex information and make decisions. Age also accounts for differences in processing ability. Older children seem to be more sensitive to the fact that the benefits of searching for information sometimes outweigh the costs, whereas younger children don't seem to have this same ability.[81] Old age has been associated with a decline in certain cognitive skills and thus reduced ability to process information. In one study, older consumers took more time to process nutrition information and made decisions that were less accurate compared with younger consumers.[82]

Money

Obviously, the lack of money also constrains consumers who might otherwise have the motivation to engage in a behavior that involves acquisition. Although motivated consumers who lack money can still process information and make buying decisions, they are definitely constrained in their immediate ability to buy from marketers.

marketing IMPLICATIONS Factors affecting ability suggest several implications for marketers.

Understand consumers' knowledge and processing styles
First, marketers should be sure that target consumers have sufficient prior knowledge to process marketing communications. If not, the company may need to develop educational messages as a first step.

Match communications with knowledge and processing styles
Marketers also need to be sensitive to the potentially different processing styles, education levels, and ages of target consumers. For example, highly motivated but visually oriented parents may not be able to assemble toys for their children if the written instructions are too complex and, thus, incompatible with their processing style. Putting instructions in both words and pictures covers both processing styles.

Facilitate ability
Because a lack of money constrains purchase behaviors, marketers can facilitate first-time and repeat buying by providing monetary aid. Car manufacturers have enhanced consumers' purchasing ability—and boosted sales—by offering low- or no-down-payment programs, low financing rates, and rebates. Marketers can also provide education and information (through advertising, websites, point-of-purchase displays, and other communications) that help consumers better process information, make more informed decisions, and engage in consumption behaviors.

Consumer Opportunity

The final factor affecting whether motivation results in action is consumers' opportunity to engage in a behavior. For example, a consumer may be highly motivated to work out and have sufficient money to join a health club (ability); however, he may be so busy that he has little opportunity to actually go. Thus even when motivation and ability are high, someone may not take action because of lack of time, distractions, and other factors that impede the ability to act.

Time

Time can affect the consumer's opportunity to process information, make decisions, and perform certain behaviors. Some studies show that consumers are more likely to buy things for themselves during the festival season, simply because this is one of the few opportunities when time-pressed consumers actually go shopping. Time affects leisure-time consumption behavior, as well. Knowing that would-be gardeners have little time (or patience) to plant, weed, and water, companies are successfully marketing seed-embedded mats, low-maintenance plants, and fast-maturing trees.[84]

Consumers under time pressure to make a decision will engage in limited information processing. For example, a consumer who has to buy 30 items in a 15-minute grocery shopping trip will not have time to process a lot of information about each item. According to research, time-pressured consumers not only process less information but also put more weight on negative information; they are quicker to reject brands because of negative features.[85] When the motivation to process information is low, consumers feeling moderate time pressure will tend to process information systematically. However, if time pressure is quite high or quite low, consumers are unlikely to process details systematically.[86] In an advertising context, consumers have limited opportunity to process information when a message is presented in a short period; when they cannot control the pace of message presentation, as is the case with TV and radio ads; or when they fast-forward through commercials.[87]

Distraction

Distraction refers to any aspect of a situation that diverts consumers' attention. For example, an important exam can divert a consumer's attention from a yoga class she really wants to take. If someone talks while a consumer is viewing an ad or making a decision, that distraction can inhibit the consumer's ability to process the information. Certain background factors in an ad, such as music or attractive models, can also distract consumers from an advertised message.[88] Consumers may be distracted from TV commercials if the program during which the commercials appear is very involving.[89] Interestingly, one study suggests that consumers who are distracted when sampling a good-tasting food product are more likely to actually choose that item.[90]

Amount of Information

The amount of information present can also affect consumers' opportunity to process a message. PepsiCo learned the hard way that its targeted consumers for PepsiOne, a low-calorie soft drink, needed real information from the introductory advertising messages—not just edgy imagery—to make a purchase decision. Facing lower-than-expected sales, the company revamped its ads to provide details about PepsiOne's taste and diet benefits.[91]

Repetition of Information

Whereas consumers' ability to process information is limited by time, distraction, and the quality and complexity of the information, one factor—repetition—actually enhances it.[92] If consumers are repeatedly exposed to information, they can more easily process it because they have more chances to think about, scrutinize, and remember the information. Advertisers who use television and radio in particular, must therefore plan to get their messages to the target audience more than once, to enhance the opportunity for processing. However, research suggests that when a brand is unfamiliar, consumers may react negatively to repeated advertising, thereby reducing communication effectiveness. In contrast, consumers show more patience for repetition of ads attributed to known, familiar brands.[93]

Control of Information

Consumers remember and learn more when they can control the flow of information by determining what information is presented, for how long, and in what order. With print ads, for example, consumers have a lot of control over which messages they pay attention to, how long they spend processing each message, and the order in which they process the messages (see Exhibit 3.12). They therefore have more opportunity to select what is appropriate for their own needs and goals, process the information, and apply it to consumption decisions. In contrast, consumers who hear radio commercials or watch television commercials have no such control, so they have less opportunity to process and apply the information.[94] As consumers

Exhibit 3.12
CONSUMERS ARE IN CONTROL WITH PRINT ADS
Print ads have the advantage of letting consumers process information at their own pace. This is important when the information is complex and lengthy

become proficient in controlling the information flow, they have the opportunity to put more effort toward processing the information content rather than focusing on the control task.[95]

marketing IMPLICATIONS Often marketers can do little to enhance consumers' opportunities to process information, make careful decisions, or engage in purchase, usage, or disposition behaviors. For example, advertisers cannot make living rooms less distracting during TV commercials or give consumers more time for shopping. However, companies can play some role in enhancing opportunity.

Repeat marketing communications and make them easy to process
Repeating marketing communications (up to a point) increases the likelihood that consumers will notice and eventually process them. Marketers can also increase the likelihood of processing by presenting messages at a time of day when consumers are least likely to be distracted and pressed for time. Communications should be stated slowly and in simple terms so consumers can understand them. One caution: Although repetition increases the opportunity to process information, it can also reduce consumers' motivation to process it!

Reduce distraction and time-pressured decision making
Marketers can make decisions less time pressured. For example, retailers may extend their hours so consumers can take advantage of the store, product, or service at times that are least distracting and least time pressured. Many catalog companies and all online shopping sites allow consumers to place orders 24 hours a day. Marketers can also offer ancillary services, such as extended shopping or service hours that remove time constraints.

Reduce purchasing/using/learning time
In addition, marketers can reduce the amount of time needed to buy or use an offering and the time needed to learn how to access information about it. Charles Schwab, for example, reduces learning time on its website by allowing consumers to enter questions in plain English.[96] The result: Consumers spend less time figuring out how to search and more time analyzing information for investment decisions.

In stores, clear signs and directories can help consumers locate goods more quickly and increase the likelihood that they will actually buy the goods.

Provide information

Sometimes the simple availability of information enhances consumers' abilities to process it, make decisions, and engage in consumer behaviors. In Zimbabwe, consumers are increasingly becoming overweight, given the influx of fast food and processed food. Some of these consumers are joining Weight Watchers and benefiting from the availability of information about the fat and calorie content of different foods, which gives them the opportunity to make healthier choices.[97]

Summary

Motivation reflects an inner state of arousal that directs the consumer to engage in goal-relevant behaviors, effortful information processing, and detailed decision making. We are motivated to notice, approach, and think about things that are important and personally relevant. Motivated consumers often experience affective or cognitive involvement. In some cases, this involvement may be enduring; in other cases, it may be situational, lasting only until the goal has been achieved. Consumers can also be involved with product categories, brands, ads, the media, and consumption behaviors. Consumers experience greater motivation when they see a goal or object as personally relevant—meaning that it relates to their needs, values, and goals; when it entails considerable risk; or when it is moderately inconsistent with their prior attitude.

Even when motivation is high, consumers may not achieve their goals if their ability or opportunity to do so is low. If consumers lack the knowledge or experience, intelligence, education, or money to engage in a behavior, process information—especially complex information—or make a decision, they cannot achieve a goal. In addition, they may not achieve the goal if they are attending to information that is incompatible with their processing styles. Highly motivated consumers may also fail to achieve goals if lack of time, distractions, insufficient information, or lack of control over information flow limit the opportunity to do so.

Questions for Review and Discussion

1. How is motivation defined, and how does it affect felt involvement?
2. What are some objects of involvement for consumers?
3. What determines the ranking of needs in Maslow's hierarchy?
4. How does perceived risk affect personal relevance, and what are six types of perceived risk?
5. In what ways can ability affect consumer behavior?
6. Identify some of the elements that contribute to consumer opportunity for processing information and making decisions.

Exercises

1. Randomly select ten advertisements from a magazine. Develop questions designed to assess a consumer's involvement in an ad (both cognitive and affective) and motivation to process information from the ad. Select a sample of 20 to 30 consumers to look at the ads and answer the questions. Which types of ads tend to evoke higher involvement? Which types of ads tend to evoke lower involvement? How do these ads tend to differ in terms of (a) recognition of consumers' needs, (b) structure and content, and (c) assumption of consumer knowledge or expertise?
2. Develop your own projective test, depicting some purchase or usage situation for a product or service of your choice. What kinds of needs are revealed by your test? What are the implications for the marketer of that product or service?
3. Watch TV and the associated ads for half an hour.

At the end of your viewing, write down the ads you remember. Use the concepts of motivation, ability, and opportunity to describe why you processed and remembered these commercials. What was it about the ad, your prior knowledge or use of these products, or the environment in which you viewed the ads that made them memorable?

4. Visit a Web retail site (such as *staples.com, hot-topic.com,* or *barnesandnoble.com*) and carefully examine the description and information provided about one of the featured products. Also read the site's descriptions of shipping and payment options. What perceived risks are being addressed by the information on this site? How does the retailer either reduce risk perceptions or enhance risk perceptions with respect to the featured product or the shipping and payment options?

5. Select a high-involvement product you are interested in buying, such as a new car or a new computer system. Identify the factors that make this product personally relevant to you, such as how it relates to specific goals or needs. Next, consider how product knowledge/experience, age, and money affect your ability to process marketing information about this product and make a purchase. Finally, analyze how the opportunity factors related to time, distraction, and information affect your behavior toward making this purchase. What can marketers of this type of product do to enhance your motivation, ability, and opportunity to buy from them?

More Exercises from the Adaptor

1. Differentiate the approach taken while purchasing a laptop and a desktop. Critically evaluate the factors accounted for while buying either of those product categories.

chapter **4**

Exposure, Attention, and Perception

LEARNING OBJECTIVES

After studying this chapter, you will be able to:

- Discuss why marketers are concerned about consumers' exposure to marketing stimuli and what traditional and nontraditional tactics they use to enhance exposure.
- Explain the characteristics of attention and how marketers can try to attract and sustain consumers' attention to products and marketing messages.
- Describe the major senses that are part of perception and outline why marketers are concerned about consumers' sensory perception.

INTRODUCTION

Product Placement Grows More Prominent

With celebrity endorsement and testimonials now becoming stale and suffering from lack of effectiveness, marketers have been making numerous attempts to showcase their brands. Product placement in movies has been there for sometime now, however, the process of formal and serious approach towards the same is in ferment. It all started with Maine Pyaar Kiya in the early 90's and then with movies like Yadeein, Baaghban and now the latest Dhoom series, where the marketers have been trying to place their products strategically. The attempt here is visibility and should not seem as the characters being captive prisoners of the brand. When Amitabh Bachchan was showcased as the bank employee working for ICICI bank in Baaghban, he was merely extending his endorsements onto cinema as a medium. In most cases, wherever product placements are showcased, character is an endorser of the brand in a real time situation. Unlike the West, marketers have still not made attempts to place brands irrespective of the character who will be using it.

The concept has still not caught on in television as a medium though. Kaun Banega Crorepati (KBC) has made some initial foray however, the fine line of separation between endorsement and product placement is quite diffused. Compaq is a brand endorsed by the anchor, and thus product placement in the programme is an extension to his endorsement deal. Airtel's or Santro's sponsorship are more of a programme sponsorship.

By some estimates, the value of product placements and associative marketing around Bollywood films will go up to Rs 200 crore this year from Rs 80 crore last year. "That's almost a 150% rise," says Navin Shah, chief executive officer, P9 Integrated, the movie marketing arm of the Percept Group.

Exhibit 4.1

A key driver of product placements has been the star or stars in a movie, though, the situation in a film could also be the cause of involvement. For instance, in the just-released Namaste London, the heroine, who is an Indian living in Britain, attempts to flee her country of origin, India. In that scene, she lands at a Western Union Money Transfer office to pick up cash deposited by her friend in London. The episode brings out the aspect of speed with which money can be transferred at Western Union. In another scene from the same movie, the father of the heroine, in search of a suitable husband for her, is seen uploading the resume of his daughter on bharatmatrimony.com. He also makes a list of prospective suitors for her from the website. In Honeymoon Travels, for instance, Tata Starbus (from Tata Motors), has bought into the concept of the film by offering the means of travel for the six couples who take a bus ride as part of their tour package. This is not the first time that Tata Motors has adopted such a strategy. In 2002, the company's sports utility vehicle Tata Safari was an integral part of Ram Gopal Varma's Road.

Bollywood films, of course, are replete with subtle and blatant examples of product placements. But the question is: can marketers make that crucial shift from making their choice based on the star or situation to buying into the concept of a film?

In consumer behavior terms, product placement is all about exposure, attention, and perception. If consumers are to register any message about a product after exposure in some medium, they must pay attention to the product. Whether they do so depends on a host of factors, such as whether the product is relevant to them, prominent, or surprising in its context. Whether consumers are affected by exposure to product placement also depends on whether they can actually perceive the product (if the package is not obscured or the product appears long enough to be noticed). This chapter examines exposure, attention, and perception in detail, along with the resulting marketing implications. As Exhibit 4.2 indicates, what consumers comprehend, the attitudes they have, and what they remember from exposure, attention, and perception all affect the decisions they make and the actions they take.

Exposure

Before any type of marketing stimulus can affect consumers, they must be exposed to it. ***Exposure*** reflects the process by which the consumer comes into physical contact with a stimulus. ***Marketing stimuli*** are messages and information about products or brands communicated by either the marketer (via ads, salespeople, brand symbols, packages, signs, prices, and so on) or by nonmarketing sources (e.g., the media, word of mouth). Consumers can be exposed to marketing stimuli at the buying, using, or disposing stages of consumption. Because exposure is critical to consumers' subsequent processing of any stimulus, marketers must ensure that consumers are exposed to stimuli that portray their offering in a favorable light.

marketing IMPLICATIONS

Marketers start the process of gaining exposure by selecting media, such as radio, product placements, and the Internet, and by developing promotions for the targeted consumers. The battle of Pepsi and Coke in India has forced both the cola majors now to look at regional markets with a regional approach. The national heroes in Sharukh or Aamir may not have regional fan following, especially in the conservative markets of East and South India. Both brands look for local heroes, for endorsements and in the currently running Coke advertisement of Aamir Khan in a train, where everybody steals a sip from the Coke bottle; he is replaced by southern star Vikram in the local version of the advertisement. Similarly, Pepsi has also been using local celebrities and stars with a local fan following that helps create a relationship and identification with the brand. Tapping regional markets in India has always been a challenge for multinational brands and heterogeneity of the markets creates an even bigger challenge for the companies. After having developed insights on the relatedness

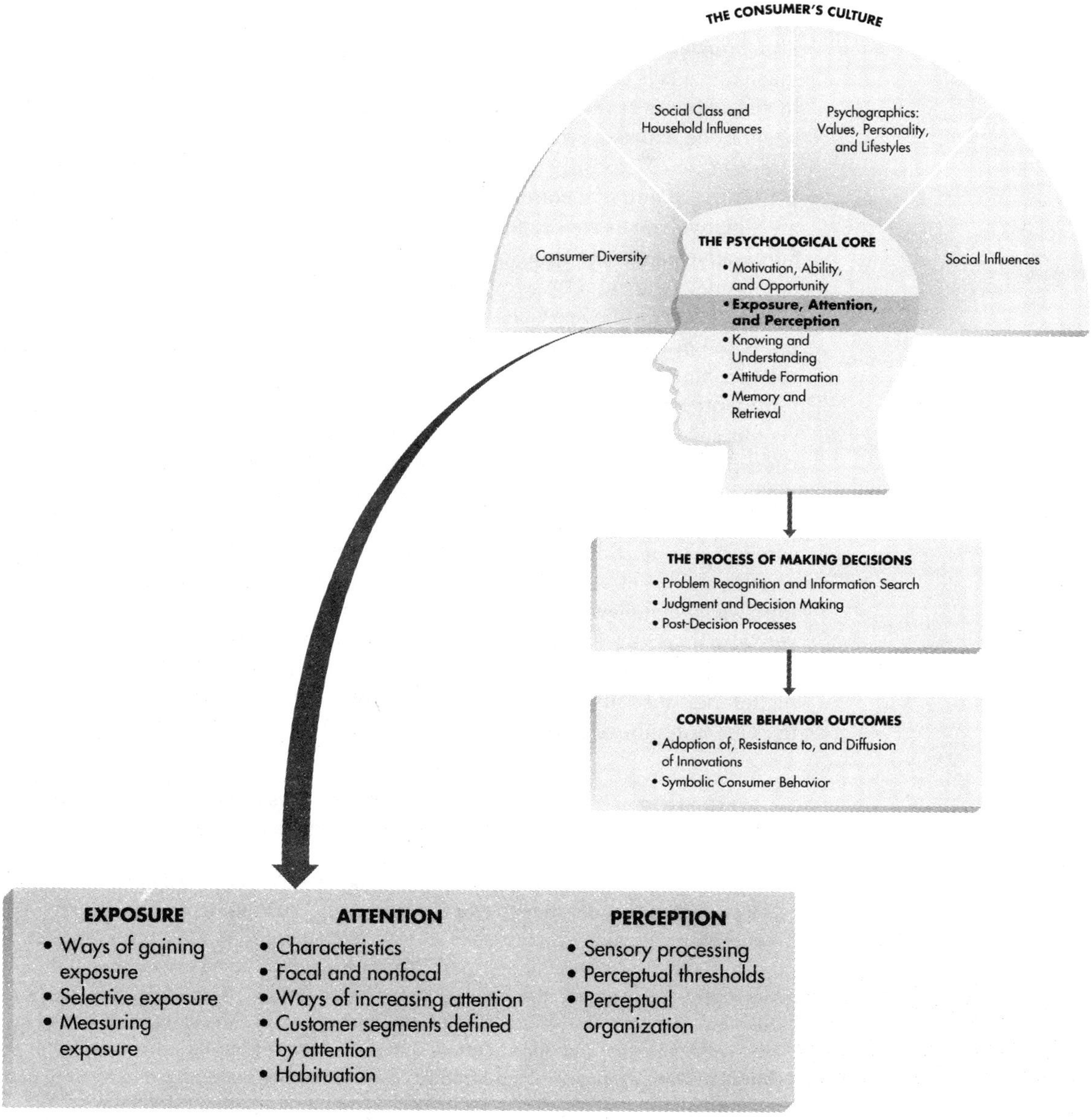

Exhibit 4.2

CHAPTER OVERVIEW: EXPOSURE, ATTENTION, AND PERCEPTION *Consumers do some processing of a stimulus (e.g., an ad, brand) once they have been exposed to it, pay attention to it, and perceive its characteristics. Once it is perceived, consumers may examine it more closely.*

aspect of the brand, companies try and also explore various media vehicles and types to reach target markets. Project Shakti from Unilever India is a novel attempt to reach the vast rural markets of India without the use of any formal media vehicle or type. It uses people from the villages as spokesperson and salesperson for the brand. It works, since word of mouth and trust on fellow villagers is an effective form of communication and promotion in rural belts of India.

Factors Influencing Exposure

The *position of an ad within a medium* can affect exposure. Exposure to magazine ads is greatest when they appear on the back cover because the ad is in view whenever the magazine is placed facedown. Also, consumers are most likely to be exposed to ads placed next to articles or within TV programs that interest them.[3] Exposure to commercials is greatest when they are placed at the beginning or end of a commercial break within a program because consumers are still involved in the program or are waiting for the program to come back on. Some advertisers are sponsoring commercial-free TV programs in which the company gets product placement or airs a single ad before or after the show. Movie Channels like Zee Cinema and Star Gold showcase special films at special times without any commercial break or with just one break. The attempt, being to rope in audience at the start of the programme, and create environment for him/her to sit right through the end of the cinema.

Moreover, *product distribution* and *shelf placement* affect exposure. The more widespread the brand's distribution (the more stores in which it is available), the greater the likelihood that consumers will encounter it. Likewise, the location or the amount of shelf space allocated to the product can increase consumers' exposure to a product. Consumers are most likely to be exposed to products that are featured in an end-of-aisle display or that take up a lot of shelf space. Products placed from waist to eye level get more exposure than those placed higher or lower. Exposure also increases for products placed at points in the store where all consumers must go and spend time. For example, sales of some products increase because of higher exposure in point-of-purchase displays at checkout counters in supermarkets, automotive stores, and restaurants.[5]

marketing IMPLICATIONS

In addition to the traditional ways of reaching consumers, such as strategic placement of television commercials or effective product displays and shelf placement, marketers are testing other ways of gaining exposure for marketing stimuli. Cadbury's India tied up with Reliance Mobile (RIM) to highlight their message "Kuch Meetha Ho Jaye" after RIM subscriber's obtained their results of High School through SMS based format. As soon as the candidate punched in his roll no. his results came on the screen through SMS and followed by the sponsor's message "Pappu Pass Ho Gaya" or "Kuch Meetha Ho Jaye". The entire exercise was cost-effective and established instant connectivity with the audience. Saffola's popular cooking oil brand's tie-up with the Mumbai Dabbawalas, was an attempt to reinforce the goodness of a healthy heart platform.

Cash-strapped governments in some cities are allowing companies to place ads on public buses, garbage trucks, police cars, even subway tunnels. In China, Beijing bus shelters and subway stations are plastered with ads for Internet sites and other offerings.[7] In Egypt, some advertisers use feluccas (boats that sail along the Nile River) to advertise brands.[8] In England, Panasonic helps defray its transportation costs by selling advertising space on the backs and sides of its delivery trucks.[9] Using "human directionals"—people in crazy outfits who stand on street corners waving their hands and shouting information—is one way that retailers and home developers affect consumers' exposure to the store or development. And although Internet users resent uninvited messages from companies, many will agree to receive e-mail or instant messages if they can control their timing.[10]

Exhibit 4.3

A look at how viewership falls in a mid-programme commercial break performance

TG: 4+ years, Men/W'men, SEC ABC, C&S Homes.
Market: Hindi Speaking Markets

Commercial Break Performance: TVRs

Programme	12/3/2007	14/03/2007	15/03/2007	13/03/2007	Grand Total
KAHAANI GHAR GHAR KI	6.88	6.185	6.125	5.225	6.10375
KYUNKI SAAS BHI KABHI BAHU THI	6.725	6.77	6.77	5.115	6.345

Programme Performance: TVRs

Programme	12/3/2007	14/03/2007	15/03/2007	13/03/2007	Grand Total
KAHAANI GHAR GHAR KI	8.43	7.91	7.77	6.55	7.665
KYUNKI SAAS BHI KABHI BAHU THI	8.3	8.79	8.74	7.24	8.2675

(***Source:*** *TAM*)

Selective Exposure

While marketers can work very hard to affect consumers' exposure to certain products and brands, ultimately consumers control whether exposure occurs or not. In other words, consumers can actively seek certain stimuli and avoid others. Readers of *Vogue* magazine selectively expose themselves to its fashion-oriented ads, whereas readers of *Car and Driver* choose to look at different kinds of ads. Some readers may ignore the ads altogether. The same holds true online; in fact, a growing number of consumers are using software to block "pop-up" ads that would otherwise open while a Web page is loading.[11]

Consumers' avoidance of marketing stimuli is a big problem for marketers.[12] One survey reveals that 54 percent of U.S. consumers and 68 percent of German consumers avoid ads.[13] Consumers can simply leave the room during a TV ad, do something else during the ad, or avoid it entirely by zipping and zapping. With ***zipping,*** consumers record television shows and fast-forward through the commercials when viewing the shows. Consumers zip through up to 75 percent of the ads in recorded shows—yet, they can still identify the brand or product category of many ads they zip through.[14] Although digital video recorders like Tivo allow consumers to skip ads easily, users choose to watch specific ads that seem relevant and interesting.[15] Exhibit 4.3 illustrates how possible viewership falls in a popular programme during commercial break.

With ***zapping,*** consumers avoid ads by switching to other channels during commercial breaks. Approximately 20 percent of consumers zap at any one time; more than two-thirds of households with cable TV zap regularly. Men zap significantly more than women do. People are more likely to zap commercials at the half-hour or hour mark than during the program itself.[16] Knowing this, television networks are trying to hold viewers through such techniques as airing 30-second or 60-second minimovies in the middle of a commercial block.[17]

One reason consumers want to avoid ads is because they are exposed to so many that no one can possibly process them all. One issue of the fashion magazine Vogue, for instance, typically contains more than 500 pages of ads, and other magazines—such as those targeting brides—may contain up to 1,000 advertising pages per issue.[18] Consumers avoid ads for product categories that they don't use, which means the ads are irrelevant to them; they also tend to avoid ads they have seen before because they know what these ads will say.

Many adult consumers want to limit their children's exposure to ads because youngsters have difficulty distinguishing between ad messages and other types of media content. Marketers who advertise sugary or fatty foods have come under fire by parents and regulators in the United States, Great Britain, and elsewhere as concerns mount over childhood obesity, for example. One marketer taking steps to respond is Kraft Foods, which has stopped advertising Oreos and similar snacks during TV shows targeted to children under 12 years old.[19] Yet, limiting children's exposure to ads for inappropriate products—such as R-rated movies—is not easy because of massive multimedia campaigns that combine TV, billboards, and other media. Recognizing this, Warner Brothers attempts to shield children by not advertising its R-rated films on TV shows where 35 percent or more of the audience is younger than 17.[20]

Unsolicited messages from telemarketers, through email or SMS has become a menace today and most consumers are now up in arms against such attempts to intrusion in privacy. Particularly, the telemarketing attempts of credit card companies, cellular service providers and banking services companies are under scanner, wherein the Supreme Court of India has come out with a directive against such activities and companies can be severely penalized. Considering the growing dissatisfaction among consumers over unsolicited telemarketing calls, the Telecom Regulatory Authority of India (TRAI) has initiated a consultation process with the aim of reducing the bulk of unsolicited commercial communications (UCC). TRAI (Telecom Regulatory Act of India) has set up a central 'do not call' (DNC) registration service, allowing consumers to register their mobile numbers with the service providers (spammers) to keep those calls at bay.

Measuring Exposure

Why would advertisers pay over Rs.2.5 lakhs for a single 10-second spot during the popular game show, Kaun Banega Crorepati? In part, because of projections of exposure rates indicating that hundreds of millions of consumers around the world watched the preceding year's game. Marketers are very interested in determining which media will generate exposure to their marketing stimuli and whether the desired exposure rates have actually been reached.

As discussed in Chapter 2, many marketers use data from specialized research firms to track consumer exposure to TV, radio, billboards, websites, and other media. Still, measuring exposure is not easy, and marketers are clamoring for more complete and accurate measures. For example, traffic counters are sometimes used to track the number of cars that drive by billboards every day. Unfortunately, the counters cannot track pedestrians, nor can they distinguish how many consumers are in each car or whether anyone actually looked at a particular billboard. Better measures are on the way as researchers test consumer-carried devices for counting the number of people who actually pass billboards or transit ads and learning about their characteristics and behaviors.[22]

In addition, advertisers are concerned about measuring exposure to websites and online advertising. At present, advertisers have no way of knowing exactly how many consumers see an Internet ad, although they can track the number who click through to an ad. Also, different methods of counting Web traffic and ad exposures often yield very different numbers. During one recent month, the NetRatings research firm calculated 94.4 million visitors for Yahoo!, whereas comScore

Networks put the number of visitors at 116.3 million. Marketers are therefore pushing for standardization in the way Internet exposure levels are measured.[23]

Attention

Attention is the process by which we devote mental activity to a stimulus. A certain amount of attention is necessary for information to be perceived—for it to activate our senses. Furthermore, after consumers perceive information, they may pay more attention to it and continue with the higher-order processing activities discussed in the next few chapters. This relationship between attention and perception explains why marketers need to understand the characteristics of attention and find ways of enhancing attention to marketing stimuli.

Characteristics of Attention

Attention has three key characteristics: (1) it is selective, (2) it is capable of being divided, and (3) it is limited.

Attention Is Selective *Selectivity* means that we decide which items we want to focus on at any one time. The number of stimuli to which we are exposed at any given time is potentially overwhelming. As you pay attention to this book, you may simultaneously hear noise from an open window and smell popcorn popping in a microwave oven. You are also exposed to hundreds of marketing stimuli every day. When you go to a store, you are exposed to numerous products, brands, ads, displays, signs, and prices all at the same time. Consumers are generally unable to examine all these marketing stimuli simultaneously, so they must somehow determine which are worthy of processing. For instance, research shows that people pay less attention to things they have seen many times before.[24] Because attention is selective, consumers can control what they focus on. When they use a search engine to look for information online, they are selective about what they focus on—which is why Office Depot and other marketers buy sponsored links alongside product-related search results.[25]

Attention Can Be Divided A second important aspect of attention is that it is capable of being divided. Thus we can parcel our attentional resources into units and allocate some to one task and some to another. For example, we can drive a car and talk at the same time. We can allocate attention flexibly to meet the demands of things in our environment, but we also have the potential to become distracted when one stimulus pulls our attention from another. If we are distracted from a product or ad, the amount of attention we devote to it will be greatly reduced.[26] Knowing that viewers can divide their attention, TV networks reinforce their brands and flash reminders of upcoming shows at the bottom of the screen during programs. "Viewers are more confused than ever about what is on TV and when it is on," says a CBS executive. "It is incumbent on us to help them navigate our programming."[27]

Attention Is Limited A third, and critical, aspect of attention is that it is limited. Although we may be able to divide our attention, we can attend to multiple things only if processing them is relatively automatic, well practiced, and effortless.[28] Imagine that you are watching TV and, at the same time, listening to your friends talk. If the conversation turns serious, you will need to turn down the TV so you can devote your attention to your friends. The fact that attention is limited explains why consumers browsing in an unfamiliar store are less likely to notice new products than when those same consumers browse in a familiar store. Consumers will inevitably miss some products when they try to pay attention to many unfamiliar products.

Focal and Nonfocal Attention

These three characteristics of attention raise questions about whether we give our attention to something in our peripheral vision even if we are already focusing on something else. For example, when we read a magazine article, can we process the information in an adjacent ad—even if our eyes are concentrating on the article and we are not aware of the ad? When we drive down the highway, can we process any information from a roadside billboard even if we are focusing only on the road?

Exhibit 4.4
HEMISPHERIC LATERALIZATION

The two hemispheres of our brain specialize in processing different types of information. When a stimulus is in focal *vision, it is processed by* both *hemispheres. When it is in* peripheral *vision (i.e., it is not being focused on), it is processed by the* opposite *hemisphere. Information presented in the left visual field is therefore processed by the right hemisphere.*

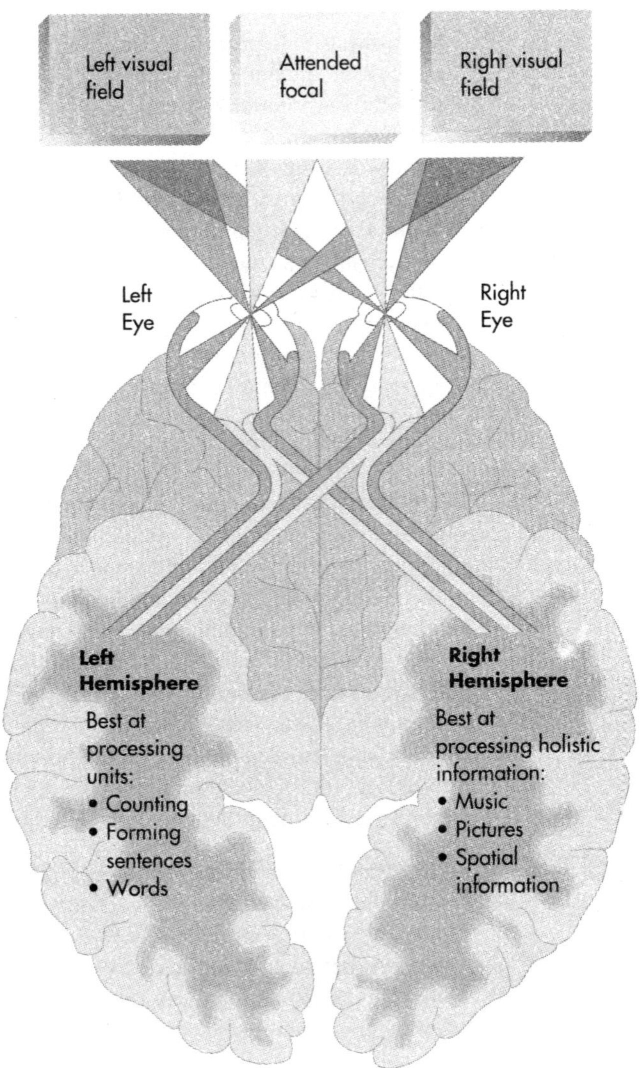

Preattentive Processing To the extent that we can process information from our peripheral vision even if we are not aware that we are doing so, we are engaged in ***preattentive processing.*** With preattentive processing, most of our attentional resources are devoted to one thing, leaving very limited resources for attending to something else. We devote just enough attention to an object in peripheral vision to process *something* about the object. But because the amount of attention is so limited, we are not aware that we are absorbing and processing information about that object.

Hemispheric Lateralization Our ability to process information preattentively depends on (1) whether the stimulus in peripheral vision is a picture or a word and (2) whether it is placed in the right or left visual field (to the right side or the left side of the object on which we are focused). These factors are influential because of how the two halves of the brain—the two hemispheres—process information (see Exhibit 4.4). The right hemisphere is best at processing music, grasping visual and spatial information, forming inferences, and drawing conclusions. The left hemisphere is best at processing units that can be combined, performing tasks such as counting, processing unfamiliar words, and forming sentences.[29]

Interestingly, stimuli placed in the right visual field (ads on the right side of the focal article or billboards on the right side of the road) tend to be processed by the left hemisphere; those in the left visual field tend to be processed by the right hemisphere. Stimuli on which we focus directly are processed by both hemispheres. These findings suggest that people will most likely preattentively process stimuli such as pictures in ads if the pictures are placed to the left of a magazine article because the processing takes place in the right hemisphere—the hemisphere that is best at processing visual stimuli. Likewise, stimuli such as brand names or ad claims are most likely to be preattentively processed if they are placed in the right visual field because they will be processed by the left hemisphere. Several studies have confirmed that consumers' ability to preattentively process pictures, brand names, or claims in ads depends on whether the ad is placed in the right or left visual field.[30]

Preattentive Processing, Brand Name Liking, and Choice Although we may notice and devote some minimal level of processing to stimuli placed in peripheral vision, an important question is whether such preattentively processed stimuli affect our liking for an ad or brand or our decisions to buy or use a particular brand. In fact, some research suggests that consumers will like the same brand name more if they have processed it preattentively than if they have not been exposed to it all.[31] Preattentive processing makes a brand name familiar, and we tend to like things that are familiar.[32]

Other evidence suggests that stimuli processed preattentively can affect consumer choices. In one study, consumers were more likely to consider choosing a product if they had previously been preattentively exposed to an ad containing that product than if they had not been exposed to the ad. In this case, preattentive processing of the ad affected consumers' consideration of the product, even though they had no memory of having seen the ad.[33]

marketing IMPLICATIONS

Although consumers can process information preattentively, the information will have more impact when consumers devote full attention to it. Unfortunately, a marketing stimulus competes with many other types of stimuli (including other marketing stimuli) for consumers' attention. Moreover, consumers may have limited motivation and opportunity to attend to marketing stimuli in the first place. Consequently, marketers try to attract consumers' attention by making the stimulus (1) personally relevant, (2) pleasant, (3) surprising, and (4) easy to process.

Making stimuli personally relevant

One of the most powerful ways for a stimulus to be perceived as personally relevant is for it to appeal to your needs, values, or goals.[34] If you are hungry, you are more likely to pay attention to food ads and packages. A second way to make stimuli personally relevant is by showing sources similar to the target audience. You are more likely to notice individuals whom you perceive as similar to yourself.[35] Many advertisers use "typical consumers," hoping that consumers will relate to these individuals and thereby attend to the ad.

A third way to make stimuli personally relevant is using dramas—ministories that depict the experiences of actors or relate someone's experiences through a narrative—to enhance consumers' attention. Some dramas unfold through a series of ads, whereas other ads convey an entire story in 30 seconds, drawing the consumer into the action and making the ad more relevant to the consumer. A fourth way to capture attention and draw a consumer into the ad is to ask rhetorical questions—those asked merely for effect.[36] No one really expects an answer to a rhetorical question like "How would you like to win a million dollars?" because the answer is so obvious. These questions appeal to the consumer by implicitly including the word *you* and by asking the consumer (if only for effect) to consider answering the question.

Making stimuli pleasant

People tend to approach things that are inherently pleasant. Marketers can use this principle to increase consumers' attention to marketing stimuli by doing the following:

- Using slice of life: A very popular and universal appeal used singularly by several advertisers, be it for corporate communications or reinforcing brands the ploy has been effective across categories. From the "Hamara Bajaj" and VIP "Kal Bhi Aaj Bhi Kal Bhi" to Cadbury's "Taste of Life" and the most recent advertisements of Maruti Alto through the "Bundon Mein Jane Kya Naya Hain" have all been attempts to capture life's myriad hues and shades. The quintessential Indian flavour may largely remain the same, but capturing the dynamism of the changing Indian lifestyle. Our strong cultural rootings and lineage helps advertisers establish instant connectivity with such a platform. However, on the flip side, there is always the danger of sounding almost similar and brand differentiators may be difficult to identify. But it definitely makes the stimuli pleasant thus also increasing the possibility of the stimuli being noticed.
- Using music: Our inclination to films and particularly its music has always been visible in our lives. Be it the truck driver on the highway or the city cab driver or the early morning office traffic or the public transport buses, Listening to music is common to all, either through radio or a player. The Indian music industry has seen a drop in turnover in recent years but is has stabilized a little during the last year and is worth Rs 463 crore at present with a growth of about 3 per cent. In India, while the content has increased the same has not reflected on the amount of revenues for the music companies. In fact, it has been estimated that the total loss of the music industry is largely on account of piracy. The impact of the music through use in communication in the form of jingles or even a parody has always been well received. The sound and the pattern of music may have changed, with

Exhibit 4.5
ATTRACTING ATTENTION THROUGH THE UNEXPECTED
We tend to pay attention to things that are unexpected, as this ad illustrates.

a lot of western influence, but music is integral to our lives and best resonated in the classic song, "Mera Joota Hai Japani, Patloon Englishtani, Sar Pe Lal Topi, Phir Bhi Dil Hai Hindustani"

- Using Humour: Fevicol and M-Seal have started a generation of new generation slap-stick humour which has caught on with the masses very well. The problem with humour remains that, do consumers recall the message? Yet, more and more advertisers today have felt that if consumers smile, then luck would smile on their brands too. Automobiles, telecom, banking, FMCG and numerous other categories have been using humour as a popular means of creating noticeability. However, the Fevicol and M-Seal advertisements will remain pioneers in introducing humour in a more organized form in Indian advertising.

Making stimuli surprising

Consumers are also likely to process a stimulus when it is surprising due to novelty, unexpectedness, or a puzzle.

- *Using novelty.* We are more likely to notice any marketing stimulus (a product, package, or brand name) that is new or unique—because it stands out relative to other stimuli around us. Direct mail and e-mail advertising are relatively new to Chinese consumers, for example, so they not only pay attention, they open such messages far more often than U.S. and European consumers do.[44] Companies can attract attention using novel advertising formats such as magazine ads with graphics that appear to move or digital messages that freeze when surrounding messages continue to move.[45] Although novel stimuli attract attention, we do not always like them better. For example, we may dislike food that tastes different from what we usually eat. Thus the factors that make a stimulus novel may not be the same factors that make it likable.

- *Using unexpectedness.* Unexpected stimuli are not necessarily new, but their placement or content differs from what we are used to, arousing curiosity and causing us to analyze them further to make sense of them (see Exhibit 4.5).[46] Athletic shoe marketer Adidas aroused considerable curiosity when it hired athletes to play soccer matches while dangling from a giant brand-adorned billboard high above a busy Tokyo shopping street. The tactic attracted so much attention that city authorities, concerned about crowd control, would not allow match times be publicized.[47] Also, unexpectedness can affect the extent to which consumers perceive an ad as humorous.[48]
- *Using a puzzle.* Visual rhymes, antitheses, metaphors, and puns are puzzles that attract attention because they require resolution. Consumers tend to think more about ads that contain these elements. However, consumers from other cultural backgrounds may have difficulty understanding some puns and metaphors in U.S. ads that American consumers can easily comprehend.[49] Although ads that use a puzzle may capture attention, they are not necessarily effective in achieving other objectives (like persuasion) if consumers cannot solve the puzzle.

Making stimuli easy to process

Although personal relevance, pleasantness, and surprise attract consumers' attention by enhancing their motivation to attend to stimuli, marketers can also enhance attention by boosting consumers' *ability* to process stimuli. Four characteristics make a stimulus easy to process: (1) its prominence, (2) its concreteness, (3) the extent to which it contrasts with the things that surround it, and (4) the extent to which it competes with other information.

- *Prominent stimuli.* Prominent stimuli stand out relative to the environment because of their intensity. The size or length of the stimulus can affect its ***prominence.*** For example, consumers are more likely to notice larger or longer ads than to notice smaller or shorter ones.[50] This is why larger ads in yellow pages directories generate more phone calls than smaller ads.[51] Pictures in an ad capture attention regardless of size; increasing the amount of the ad devoted to text increases attention to the entire message.[52] Making words prominent by the use of boldfaced text also enhances consumers' attention. In addition, loud sounds can enhance prominence. Television and radio stations sometimes turn up the volume for commercials so they will stand out relative to the program. Loud rock or dramatic classical music can serve the same purpose.

  Prominence explains marketers' use of large or multiple in-store displays. After Dole installed additional coolers to display its fruits in supermarkets, its sales results in those stores improved by more than 25 percent. And the California Tree Fruit Commission has found that expanding display size by just 1 percent can boost sales of the featured foods by about 19 percent.[53] Also, movement makes an ad more prominent, which is why attention to commercials tends to be enhanced when the ad uses dynamic, fast-paced action.[54] Moving billboards and moving store displays are other examples. The state of New Mexico recently used back-lit billboard displays mounted on trucks to promote its Trek for Trash campaign.[55]

Concrete words	Abstract words
Apple	Aptitude
Bowl	Betrayal
Cat	Chance
Cottage	Criterion
Diamond	Democracy
Engine	Essence
Flower	Fantasy
Garden	Glory
Hammer	Hatred
Infant	Ignorance
Lemon	Loyalty
Meadow	Mercy
Mountain	Necessity
Ocean	Obedience

Exhibit 4.6
CONCRETENESS AND ABSTRACTNESS

We may pay more attention to things that are concrete and capable of generating images than to things that are abstract and difficult to represent visually.

- *Concrete stimuli.* Stimuli are easier to process if they are concrete rather than abstract.[56] ***Concreteness*** is defined as the extent to which we can imagine a stimulus. Notice how easily you can develop images of the concrete words in Exhibit 4.6 compared with the abstract words. Concreteness applies to brand names, as well. Consider the brands of well-known dishwashing liquids. The name Sunlight is much more concrete than the names Dawn, Joy, or-

Palmolive and may therefore have an advantage over the others in attention-getting ability.

- *Contrasting stimuli.* A third factor that makes stimuli easier to process is contrast. Notice in Exhibit 4.7 that the Palmolive bottle stands out much better than two bottles on the left and other two on the right, thanks to color contrast. Similarly, color newspaper ads are more likely to capture attention because they are surrounded by black and white, just as a black-and-white TV ad is likely to stand out when aired during shows or ads in color. Wine makers have found that packaging their wine in blue bottles instead of the traditional green or amber profoundly affects sales because the blue bottles stand out on the shelf.[57] Although research indicates that consumers are more likely to consider yellow pages ads in which color is used only for the sake of attracting attention, they are more likely to actually call the companies when the color enhances the product's appeal in an appropriate manner.[58]
- *The amount of competing information.* Finally, stimuli are easier to process when few things surround them to compete for your attention.[59] You are more likely to notice a billboard when driving down a deserted rural highway than in the middle of a congested, sign-filled city. You are also more likely to notice a brand name in a visually simple ad than in one that is visually cluttered.

Customer Segments Defined by Attention

One set of researchers asked the following question: If we do pay attention to things that are relevant, pleasant, surprising, and easy to process, can we identify groups or segments of consumers who are more affected by relevance, pleasantness, surprise, and ease of processing? To answer this question, the researchers hooked up consumers to eye-tracking devices that monitored the focus of their visual attention on a print ad. The ad was divided into basic parts like picture, package shot, and headline, and was categorized as big or small, in color or black and white. The researchers identified three groups of consumers by what specifically captured their attention in the ad.

One group paid minimal attention to the ad because the elements in the ad were not relevant to them. A second group spent a longer time looking at the ad and seemed to focus on things that were visually pleasant, such as the picture. The last group spent the longest time looking at the ad. These consumers were affected by the size of the ad, but they devoted equal amounts of time to the picture, package, headline, and body text. The researchers concluded that this group may have attended to each element because the product was personally relevant and its purchase potentially risky. Hence consumers needed a period of sustained attention to properly evaluate the ad's information.[60]

Exhibit 4.7
CONTRAST AND ATTENTION
The Palmolive bottle stands out and attracts attention only when its color contrasts with (is different from) the bottles that surround it. What implications does contrast have for merchandising products?

Habituation

When a stimulus becomes familiar, it can lose its attention-getting ability, a result called ***habituation.*** Think about the last time you purchased something new for your apartment or room (such as a plant or picture). For the first few days, you probably noticed the object every time you entered the room. As time passed, however, you probably noticed the item less and less to the point where you probably do not notice it at all now. You have become habituated to it.

marketing IMPLICATIONS

Habituation poses a problem for marketers because consumers readily become habituated to ads, packages, and other marketing stimuli. The most straightforward solution is to alter the stimulus every so often. Advertisers sometimes develop multiple ads that all communicate the same basic message but in different ways. Habituation is also the reason that marketers sometimes change product packaging to attract consumers' attention anew.

Perception

After we have been exposed to a stimulus and have devoted at least some attention to it, we are in a position to perceive it. ***Perception*** occurs when stimuli are registered by one of our five senses: vision, hearing, taste, smell, and touch.

Perceiving Through Vision

What arouses our visual perception?

- *Size and shape.* Size attracts attention. When choosing among competing products, consumers tend to buy products in packages that appear taller.[61] Moreover, consumers perceive that packages in eye-catching shapes contain more of a product.[62]
- *Color.* Color is an extremely important factor in visual perception. Research suggests, in fact, that color determines whether we see stimuli.[63]
- *Color dimensions.* A given color can be described according to three dimensions: hue, saturation, and lightness. *Hue* refers to the pigment contained in the color. Researchers have classified colors into two broad categories or color hues: warm colors such as red, orange, and yellow, and cool colors such as green, blue, and violet. *Saturation* (also called "chroma") refers to the richness of the color, leading to distinctions such as pale pink or deep, rich pink. *Lightness* refers to the depth of tone in the color. A saturated pink could have a lot of lightness (a fluorescent pink) or a lot of darkness (a mauve).
- *Effects of color on physiological responses and moods.* Color can also influence our physiological responses and moods. Color psychologists have discovered that warm colors generally encourage activity and excitement, whereas cool colors are more soothing and relaxing. Thus cool colors are more appropriate in places such as spas or doctors' offices, where it is desirable for consumers to feel calm or spend time making decisions.[64] In contrast, warm colors are more appropriate in environments such as health clubs and fast-food restaurants, where high levels of activity are desirable.[65] One study found that deeper and richer colors (greater saturation) and darker colors evoked more excitement than did less deep and lighter colors.[66]

- *Color and liking.* Colors can have a great effect on consumers' liking for a product. Pears, the evergreen glycerin soap expanded into the non-glycerin soap market with an array of colourful soaps in Blue, Green and Pink. Each soap variant offered a specialty in terms of bath or hygiene or beauty soap. The colours offered a desirability element to the soap and also helped in differentiating the soaps from one another. Most shampoos and conditioners also offer variants and the classification is based on colour, typically a yellow for egg, green for amla, brown for shikakai, so on and so forth.

marketing IMPLICATIONS Because colors can have a great effect on consumers' liking for a product, marketers often rely on the advice of "color forecasters" when deciding which colors to use in products and on packages. For example, the Color Association of the United States and the Color Marketing Group provide information to manufacturers and designers about the colors consumers are likely to prefer two to three years into the future. These forecasts are very important: the right color can make consumers believe they are buying products that are very current. Researchers have also found differences among social classes in color preferences. Hot, bright colors have historically appealed to lower-end markets, whereas deep, rich colors have historically appealed to higher-end markets.[68] Still, blue continues to be the favorite color of American teens and adults alike.[69]

Perceiving Through Hearing

Sound represents another form of sensory input. A major principle determining whether a sound will be perceived is its auditory intensity.[70] Consumers are more likely to notice loud music or voices and stark noises. When the announcer in a radio or TV ad speaks more quickly, the faster pace disrupts consumer processing of the information, yet a low-pitched voice speaking syllables in a faster-than-normal rate actually induces more positive ad and brand attitudes.[71] When a company uses one person to speak the voice-over lines during many ads or plays the same jingle in many commercials, consumers come to associate those sounds with the product or brand. McDonald's and other firms consciously seek to define a certain *sonic identity*—using sounds such as music or voices to support a brand's image.[72] Further, consumers infer product attributes and form evaluations using information gleaned from hearing a brand's sounds, syllables, and words, known as *sound symbolism.*[73]

marketing IMPLICATIONS Fast music, like that played at aerobics classes, tends to energize; in contrast, slow music can be soothing. The type of music being played in a retail outlet can have an interesting effect on shopping behavior.[74] Specifically, a fast tempo creates a more rapid traffic flow, whereas a slow tempo can increase sales as much as 38 percent because it encourages leisurely shopping (although consumers tend to be completely unaware of this influence on their behavior).[75] However, a fast tempo is more desirable in restaurants because consumers will eat faster, thereby allowing greater turnover and higher sales.[76] Music can also affect moods.[77] Likable and familiar music can induce good moods, whereas discordant sounds and music in a disliked style can induce bad moods. This effect is important because, as you will see in later chapters, bad moods may affect how people feel about products and consumption experiences.[78]

Perceiving Through Taste

Food and beverage marketers must stress taste perceptions in their marketing stimuli. For example, the major challenge for marketers of low-calorie and low-carbohydrate products is to provide healthier foods that still taste good. Yet, what tastes good to one person may not taste good to another, and consumers from different culture backgrounds may have different taste preferences. Interestingly, tasting or sampling a product is the in-store marketing tactic that most influences consumer purchasing, even though standalone in-store displays for particular brands—perceived through vision—are the marketing tactic that shoppers notice the most.[79] Exhibit 4.8 shows the influence of various in-store tactics perceived through vision, hearing, touch, and taste.

marketing IMPLICATIONS Marketers often try to monitor consumers' tastes through taste tests. Many food and beverage products are thoroughly taste tested before they are introduced. Sometimes, however, these taste tests can backfire, as happened when Coca-Cola introduced new Coke. Because Coca-Cola's market share among younger consumers had been shrinking relative to Pepsi's, Coca-Cola created a cola that tasted more like Pepsi. This decision was bolstered by blind taste tests in which consumers preferred the newer formula to the old one. But Coca-Cola failed to realize the power of the brand name. Longtime Coca-Cola drinkers were firm in their preference for the original formula. Thus when

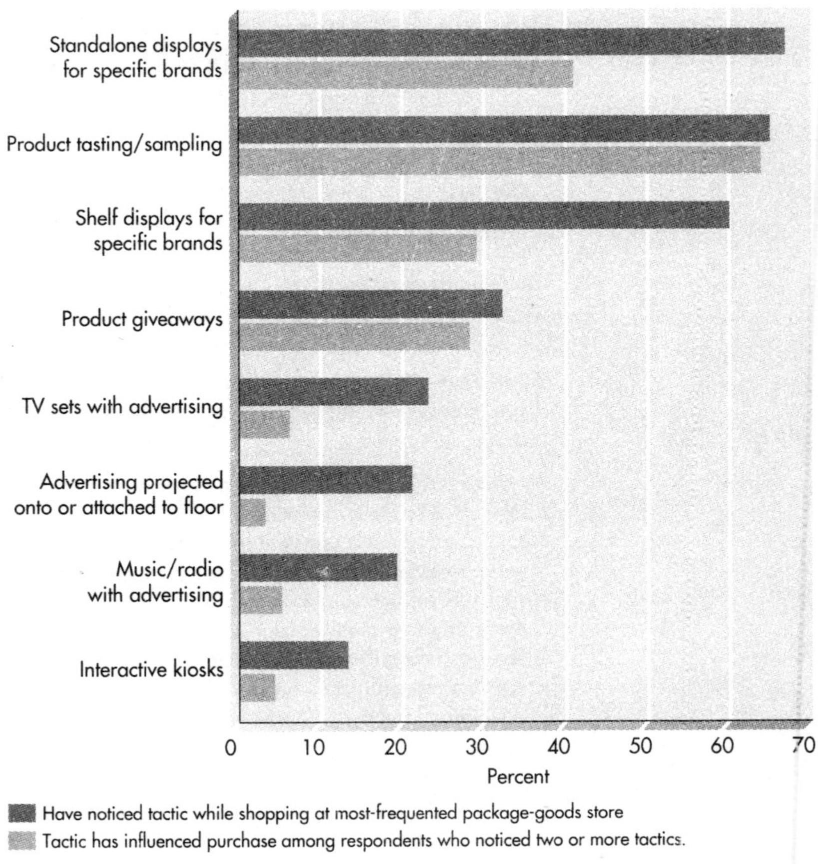

Exhibit 4.8
IN-STORE MARKETING TACTICS
Although standalone displays and product sampling were noted most often by customers, sampling most often influenced purchase.

the old and new formulas were identified by name, consumers strongly preferred the original formula. New Coke provoked such a public outcry that Coca-Cola had to reintroduce the old formula as "Coca-Cola Classic."

Perceiving Through Smell

If you were blindfolded and asked to smell an item, you would probably have a hard time identifying it; most consumers do.[80] However, consumers also differ in their ability to label odors. Compared with younger consumers, the elderly have a harder time identifying smells,[81] and men in general are worse at the task than are women.[82] Marketers are concerned with the effects of smell on consumer responses, product trial, liking, and buying.

Effects of Smells on Physiological Responses and Moods Like the other senses, smell produces physiological and emotional outcomes. For example, the smell of peppermint is arousing, and the smell of lily of the valley is relaxing.[83] In fact, some studies report that people can feel tense or relaxed depending on whether a scent is present and what it is.[84] This theory has been key to the development of aromatherapy. Some of our most basic emotions are also linked to smell. For example, children hate having their security blankets washed, in part because washing removes the smells that comfort the child. In addition, the smell of the ocean or of freshly baked cookies can revive very emotional and basic childhood memories.[85]

Smells and Product Trial Companies can expose consumers to marketing stimuli through their sense of smell. Smell (often in combination with other sensory perceptions) can entice consumers to try and buy a food product. Krispy Kreme designs its outlets so customers can smell—and see—the doughnuts fresh out of the oven.[86] Scratch-and-sniff advertisements expose consumers to fragrances and other types of products that involve the use of smell. Also, some perfume and cologne ads are doused with the product to increase sensory processing. However, this technique can backfire, because some consumers are offended by scented ads, and some even have allergic reactions to the smells.

Smell and Liking Retailers also realize that smells can attract consumers. The concept of smell has been proverbial in India, since the time "Itaar" was sold. Typically, the "Itaar" seller used to apply a drop on the wrist for discerning buyers to experience the smell and also soak into the aroma of the fragrance customers are considering to buy. Today, outlets like Barista or Coffee Café Day rely on the smell that the coffee beans generate to create an in-store ambience which is stirring and invigorating, but most of all brings the customer closer to the core product. Companies like Body Shoppe rely on the store's common smell appeal across all outlets.

Smell and Buying Research has found that providing a pleasant-smelling environment can have a positive effect on shopping behavior by encouraging more attention to relevant stimuli that consumers encounter and encouraging consumers to linger longer.[88] In one study, shoppers in a room smelling of flowers evaluated Nike shoes more positively than did consumers in an odor-free room.[89] Tesco, a U.K. grocery chain, seeks to stimulate coffee purchases by fitting its store-brand coffee packages with special aroma-releasing valves that let the scent waft out.[90]

marketing IMPLICATIONS Obviously, we like some products—for example, perfumes and scented candles—for the smell they produce. However, we may like other products, such as mouthwashes and deodorants, because they mask aromas. One company has introduced a spritzer that hides cigarette smells on hair and clothing.[91] Smell can also work to marketers' disadvantage. For example, many consumers dislike the smell of plastic containers used to pack prepared deli salads.[92] Further, one problem with using scent in the ambient retail environment is that consumers might dislike the scents or find them irritating. In addition consumers value some products because they have no smell, such as unscented deodorants, carpet cleaners, and laundry detergents. Finally, consumers' preferences for smells differ across cultures. Spices that are commonly used in one culture can literally make consumers ill in another. Only one smell (cola) is universally regarded as pleasant, which is good news for companies such as Coke and Pepsi that are expanding globally.[93]

Perceiving Through Touch

Although we know far less about the sense of touch than of smell, we do know that touch (both what we touch with our fingers and how things feel as they come in contact with our skin) is a very important element for many products and services, although individual preferences for touch vary.[94]

Effects of Touch on Physiological Responses and Moods Like the other senses, touch has important physiological and emotional effects. Depending on how we are touched, we can feel stimulated or relaxed. And research has shown that consumers who are touched by a salesperson are more likely to have positive feelings and are more likely to evaluate both the store and salesperson positively. In addition, customers who are touched by the salesperson are more likely to comply with the salesperson's requests.[95] Yet, the effectiveness of being touched in sales situations differs from culture to culture. Compared with U.S. consumers, those in Latin America are more comfortable with touching and embracing. In Asia, however, touching between relative strangers is seen as inappropriate.[96]

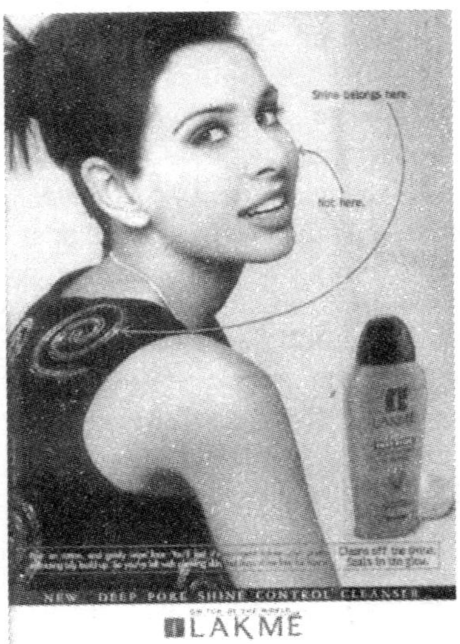

Exhibit 4.9
EMPHASIZING TOUCH
Brands like Lakme focus on the product and its goodness by illustrating it through physical appeals

Touch and Liking Consumers like some products because of their feel (see Exhibit 4.9). Some buy skin creams and baby products for their soothing effect on the skin, or they go to massage therapists to experience tactile sensations and feel relaxed. When considering products with material properties, such as clothing or carpeting, consumers prefer goods they can touch and examine in stores, compared with products they can see and read about online or in catalogs.[97] Clearly, the way clothing feels when worn is a critical factor in purchasing decisions for those products. Knowing that consumers prefer to try products before they buy, the REI chain of sporting goods stores invites shoppers to test any product on display, from boots to bicycles. REI stores also have climbing walls and other simulated outdoor areas so shoppers can gauge how products feel in use before they make a purchase decision.[98]

When Do We Perceive Stimuli?

Our senses are exposed to numerous inputs at any given time. To perceive each one would be overwhelming and extremely difficult. Fortunately, our sensory processing is simplified by the fact that many stimuli do not enter conscious awareness. For us to perceive something, it must be sufficiently intense. Stimulus intensity is measured in units. The intensity of a smell can be measured by the concentration of the stimulus in a substance or in the air. Stimulus intensity of sounds can be measured in decibels and frequencies, and stimulus intensity of colors can be measured by properties like lightness, saturation, and hue. In the area of touch, stimulus intensity can be measured in terms of pounds or ounces of pressure.

Absolute Thresholds The ***absolute threshold*** is the minimum level of stimulus intensity needed for a stimulus to be perceived. In other words, the absolute threshold is the amount of intensity needed to detect a difference between something and nothing. Suppose you are driving on the highway and a billboard is in the distance. The absolute threshold is that point at which you can first see the billboard. Before that point, the billboard is below the absolute threshold and not sufficiently intense to be seen.

marketing IMPLICATIONS

The obvious implication is that consumers will only consciously perceive a marketing stimulus when it is sufficiently high in intensity to be above the absolute threshold. Thus if images or words in a commercial are too small or the sound level is too low, consumers' sensory receptors will not be activated and the stimulus will not be consciously perceived.

Differential Thresholds Whereas the absolute threshold deals with whether a stimulus can be perceived, the ***differential threshold*** refers to the intensity difference needed between two stimuli before people can perceive that the stimuli are different. Thus the differential threshold is a relative concept; it is often called the ***just noticeable difference (j.n.d.).*** For example, when you get your eyes checked, the eye doctor often shows you a row of letters through different sets of lenses. If you can detect a difference between the two lenses, the new lens is sufficiently different to have crossed the differential threshold.

The psychophysiologist Ernst Weber first outlined the basic properties of the differential threshold in the 19th century. ***Weber's Law*** states that the stronger the initial stimulus, the greater the additional intensity needed for the second stimulus to be perceived as different. This relationship is outlined in the following formula: where S is the initial stimulus value, Δs is the smallest change (Δ) in a stimulus capable of being detected, and K is a constant of proportionality.

To illustrate, imagine that consumer testing found that 1 ounce would need to be added to a 10-ounce package before consumers could notice that the two packages weighed different amounts. Suppose we now have a 50-ounce box and want to know how much we must add before consumers could detect a difference. According to Weber's Law, $K = 1/10$ or 0.10. To determine how much would need to be added, we would solve for Δs as follows:

marketing IMPLICATIONS

The answer is .10 of the package weight, or 5 ounces.

The differential threshold has several important marketing implications.

When marketers do not want a differential threshold to be crossed

Sometimes marketers *do not* want consumers to notice a difference between two stimuli. During 1997 Maggi changed its formulation. It was during that time that Indo Nissin - a Japanese company launched its Noodles brand "Top Ramen" with lot of promotion and with Sharukh Khan endorsing the brand. TopRamen gave Maggi a run for its money. The change in taste of Maggi was a mistake. The consumers rejected the new taste of Maggi. And in 1999 Maggi was compelled to relaunch Maggi Noodles with the original taste. Similarly, Pepsi during the 1999 cricket world cup launched Pepsi-Blue coinciding with the Blue coloured dress of the Indian Team. The very colour of the drink, blue, irked the consumers, who also perceived it to be detergent concentrate. The product was summarily rejected and ironically it also coincided with the dismal performance of the Indian Cricket team.

When marketers do want a differential threshold to be crossed

In other instances marketers do want consumers to perceive a difference between two stimuli. For example, McDonald's once increased the size of its regular hamburger patty by 25 percent but left the price the same, hoping that consumers would notice the change.[101] Many marketers hope that consumers can tell the difference between an old and an improved product. However, sometimes consumers cannot make the distinction because differential thresholds vary from sense to sense. For example, since our sense of smell is not well developed, we often fail to differentiate the smell of two versions of the same object.

Subliminal Perception The concept of the perceptual threshold is important for another phenomenon—subliminal perception. Suppose you are sitting at a movie and are exposed to messages like "Eat popcorn" and "Drink Coke." However, each message is shown on the screen for only a fraction of a second, so short a time that you are not consciously aware of them. Stimuli like these, presented below the threshold level of awareness, are called subliminal messages, and our perception of them is called ***subliminal perception.***

Subliminal perception is different from preattentive processing. With preattentive processing our attention is directed at something other than the stimulus, for instance, at a magazine article instead of an ad in our peripheral vision. With subliminal perception our attention is directed squarely at the stimulus. Also, with preattentive processing the stimulus is fully present—if you shift your attention and look directly at the ad or billboard, you can easily see it. In contrast, subliminal stimuli are presented so quickly or are so degraded that the very act of perceiving them is difficult.

marketing IMPLICATIONS

The question of whether stimuli presented subliminally affect consumers' responses has generated considerable controversy in the marketing field. A widely known but fraudulent study in the advertising industry claimed that consumers at a movie theater were subliminally exposed to messages on the movie screen that read "Eat popcorn" and "Drink Coke." Reportedly, subliminal exposure to these messages influenced viewers' purchase of Coke and popcorn.[102] Although advertising agencies deny using such stimuli, and the original popcorn-Coke study has been discredited, some people claim that marketers are brainwashing consumers and attempting to manipulate them. These people also believe that ads containing these stimuli are effective.[103] This perception is perhaps fostered by the availability of self-help tapes with subliminal messages that claim to help consumers stop smoking, lose weight, and feel more relaxed.

Does Subliminal Perception Affect Consumer Behavior? Despite public concern, research suggests that subliminal perception has limited effects on consumers.[104] Such stimuli have not been found to arouse motives like hunger. Nor do subliminally presented sexual stimuli affect consumers' attitudes or preferences. Research has also failed to show that subliminal stimuli affect consumers' explicit memory for ads or brands. As a result, the advertising community tends to dismiss subliminal perception research.

Interestingly, however, there is some evidence that stimuli presented below the threshold of conscious perception can reach our sensory registers. Researchers have found that if consumers are subliminally exposed to a word (e.g., *razor*), that word is recognized faster than words to which they have not been exposed subliminally.[105] Moreover, some preliminary evidence suggests that stimuli perceived subliminally can affect consumers' feelings. Consumers in one study were found to have stronger responses to ads with sexual subliminal implants than to those without.[106] Thus stimuli perceived subliminally are somehow analyzed for their meaning, and they can elicit primitive feeling responses. However, these effects do not appear to be sufficiently strong to alter consumers' preferences or to make an ad or brand more memorable. Exposing consumers to the message at or above the threshold level of awareness should have just as much or more impact, making the use of subliminal stimuli unnecessary.[107]

How Do Consumers Perceive a Stimulus?

Some research has focused on how individuals organize or combine the visual information they perceive. Consumers tend not to perceive a single stimulus in isolation; rather, they organize and integrate it in the context of the other things around it. Also, many stimuli are really a complex combination of numerous simple stimuli that consumers must organize into a unified whole using ***perceptual organization.*** This process represents a somewhat higher, more meaningful level of processing than simply having stimuli register on our sensory receptors. Marketers have borrowed some basic principles from Gestalt psychology to understand this phenomenon. These include the principles of figure and ground, closure, and grouping.

Figure and Ground The principle of ***figure and ground*** suggests that people interpret incoming stimuli in contrast to a background. The figure is well defined and in the forefront, whereas the ground is indefinite, hazy, and in the background. In other words, the figure is the focal point of attention and perception, and the ground is everything else around it. The key point is that individuals tend to organize their perceptions into figure-and-ground relationships, and the manner in which this process occurs will determine how the stimulus is interpreted. Advertisers should therefore plan for important brand information to be the figure, not the background, and avoid letting the background detract from the figure. Advertisers often violate this principle when using sexy or attractive models in ad messages, with the result that the model becomes the figure and focal point, leaving the product or brand unnoticed.

Closure ***Closure*** refers to the fact that individuals have a need to organize perceptions so that they form a meaningful whole. Even if a stimulus is incomplete, our need for closure will lead us to see it as complete. We therefore try to complete the stimulus. The key to using the need for closure, then, is to provide consumers with an incomplete stimulus. For example, putting a well-known television ad on the radio is effective in getting consumers to think about a message. The radio version of the ad is an incomplete stimulus, and our need for closure leads us to picture the visual parts of the ad. Likewise, severely cropping objects in ads so that they appear ambiguous may be one way of getting consumers to think about what the object is and to gain closure.[108]

Grouping ***Grouping*** refers to the fact that we often group stimuli to form a unified picture or impression, making it easier to process them. We view similar or nearby objects as belonging together. Marketers can often influence the image or perception of a product or service by grouping it with other stimuli. For example, in Exhibit 4.7, the green bottles are grouped together, and they are seen as different from the bluish green bottle.

In advertising, companies sometimes include more than one brand or product in an ad message to generate exposure through grouping. In merchandising, marketers often create a unified impression by displaying related items as a group. Consumers may perceive a table setting as elegant when the napkins, napkin holders, wine goblets, silverware, dishes, and serving bowls are cleverly grouped.

Summary

For a marketing stimulus to have an impact, consumers must be exposed to it, allocate some attention to it, and perceive it. Consumers need a basic level of attention to perceive a stimulus before they can use additional mental resources to process the stimulus at higher levels. Exposure occurs when the consumer is presented with a marketing stimulus. Knowing that consumers' exposure to marketing stimuli is selective, marketers use a variety of tactics to increase stimulus exposure.

Attention occurs when the consumer allocates processing capacity to the stimulus. Attention is selective, divided, and limited. Even tactics such as product placement do not guarantee that consumers will directly attend to marketing stimuli, although consumers may attend to them preattentively. Making a marketing stimulus personally relevant, pleasant, surprising, or easy to process enhances its attention-getting properties. Consumers perceive a stimulus using one of their five senses: vision (through size and color stimuli), hearing (through sound intensity, pitch, pace, and other characteristics), taste (especially for food and beverages), smell (affecting responses, moods, trial, liking, and buying) and touch (affecting responses, moods, and liking).

Perceptual thresholds determine the point at which stimuli are perceived. The absolute threshold is the lowest point at which an individual can experience a sensation. The differential threshold is the minimal difference in stimulus intensity needed to detect that two stimuli are different. The differential threshold is important both when marketers do not want consumers to notice a difference between two stimuli (as in a size decrease) and when they do (as in the case of product improvements). Consumers can sometimes perceive things outside their conscious level of awareness, a phenomenon called subliminal perception, but this seems to have a limited impact on consumers' motives or behaviors. Finally, perceptual organization occurs when consumers organize a set of stimuli into a coherent whole, affected by the Gestalt principles of figure and ground, closure, and grouping.

Questions for Review and Discussion

1. How do zipping and zapping affect consumers' exposure to stimuli such as products and ads?
2. What is attention, and what are three key characteristics?
3. In what ways do prominence and habituation affect consumer attention?
4. What is perception, and what methods do we use to perceive stimuli?
5. Differentiate between the absolute threshold and the differential threshold, and explain how these concepts relate to Weber's Law.
6. Name three Gestalt principles of perceptual organization.

Exercises

1. Select a good or service that would typically be considered high in involvement and one that would be considered low in involvement. Design an advertisement to encourage attention to and perception of each chosen good or service. How are these two situations similar? How are they different? Exchange your work with a classmate, and explain your rationale for each advertisement. Critique your classmate's work as he or she critiques yours on the basis of how effectively each ad attracts attention and perception.
2. Browse through a copy of one of your favorite magazines and find three ads you think are most effective for generating exposure, attention, and perception. Also find three ads that are ineffective for each process. What makes the good ones effective? What do you think is wrong with the others, and how could they be improved?
3. Watch TV for one hour (and record it if possible). During this period, describe the ads that got your attention. Why were they successful in attracting you? For which ads did you want to engage in zipping or zapping, and why?
4. Identify as many examples as you can in which marketers want consumers to perceive a just noticeable difference between their product and a competitor's, or between an old product and a new one. Also find examples in which marketers do not want consumers to perceive such a difference. Consider not only visual aspects of the product or service, such as how big or small it is, but other perceptual differences as well (how it tastes, feels, smells, sounds).
5. Visit a local shopping mall and examine the interiors of three or four stores. Describe the physiological and psychological responses that different stores try to create. How do they do so through the use of color, brightness, and contrast? What other sensory stimuli do these stores use to encourage consumer response?
6. Read about color trends and future color predictions in the press releases and reports of the Color Marketing Group (*www.colormarketing.org*). What colors are expected to be popular in the next few years, and why? Choose a particular product, such as a specific car model, and explain how the color forecasts you reviewed might affect the marketing of that product.
7. Examine the homepages of two competing online retailers, such as *Amazon.com* and *Barnesandnoble.com*. How does each site use the principles of perceptual organization to focus consumer attention on specific offerings? How does each make its stimuli pleasant, surprising, or easy to process? Which home page appears to be most effective in attracting your attention and perception—and why?

More Exercises from the Adaptor

Visit any organised retail format and identify how consumers approach buying for high and low involvement goods and focus on the following aspects critically:

1. The deliberations in the product category and the time taken to assess the products
2. The number of brands evaluated in both the cases
3. Differences in spend levels in both the cases.

chapter **5**

Knowledge and Understanding

LEARNING OBJECTIVES

After studying this chapter, you will be able to:

- Describe the connection between consumer knowledge and consumer understanding, be able to explain what affects these processes, and show why marketers must take both into account.
- Discuss how and why concepts like schemas, associations, images, categories, and prototypes are relevant to marketers.
- Distinguish between categorization and comprehension and describe how product features, price, and other marketing elements can induce consumers to make correct or incorrect inferences about products.

INTRODUCTION

Making the Apple iPod Iconic

Just as Sony once dominated the market for portable CD music players, Apple Computer's iPod is the undisputed star among portable digital music players (see Exhibit 5.1). Launched in 2001, the iPod became so wildly popular that within three years, reports that some stores were running out before Christmas made business headlines. The iPod became a huge hit not because of low price—many iPod models are priced significantly higher than competing products—but because of two benefits for which Apple is well known: user-friendly operation and style.

Before the iPod, Apple's signature product was the Macintosh personal computer, known for its ease of operation and forward-looking design. Likewise, iPods are sleek and slender and have clever features for selecting or shuffling songs. Yet, Apple's early ads provided no details about the product's technology, price, or features, focusing instead on the fun and feeling of owning an iPod. The brand's cachet was enhanced as celebrities were spotted wearing iPods, and sales soared. Despite increased competition, the iPod captured more market share over time, due in part to a steady stream of new models. Other firms have jumped on the bandwagon, offering iPod add-ons or forging a marketing connection to the iPod, as BMW did with the "iPod your BMW" campaign. "The iPod is not just a consumer-electronics device; it's a cultural icon, and Apple understands that," says an industry analyst. "By making strong associations with other very strong brands, it establishes the iPod as a platform, ultimately using that as a way to get the iPod experience into consumers' hands."[1]

The tremendous success of the iPod illustrates many of this chapter's concepts. First, some consumers have a number of favorable associations linked with various electronics brands. Moreover, electronics brands have different images and personalities, which means consumers view them as distinct from one another. Consumers have prior knowledge that allows them to categorize brands and products as specific types of electronic entertainment products. In fact, many consider iPod the prototypical brand of digital music players, a product group seen as a subcategory of electronic

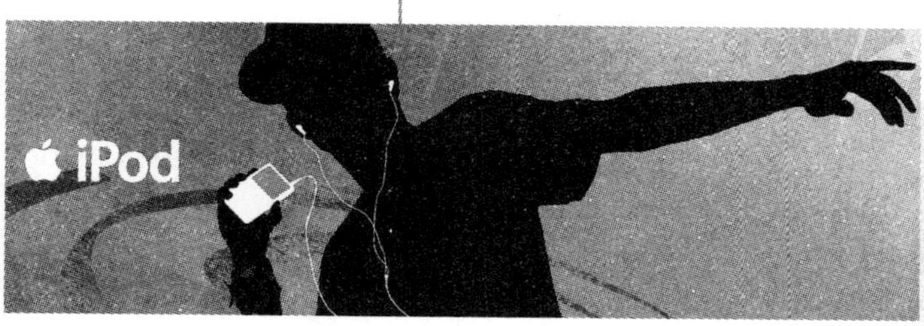

Exhibit 5.1
APPLE IPOD
The iPod's image was driven in part by the image of its maker — Apple.

entertainment products. Finally, consumers' knowledge serves as a basis for interpreting information from iPod ads and its associations with other brands.

In the preceding chapter, you learned how consumers pay attention to and perceive things. This chapter goes a step further, asking how consumers understand the world around them. To answer this question, we need to know how consumers relate what they observe to what they already know—their prior knowledge. As Exhibit 5.2

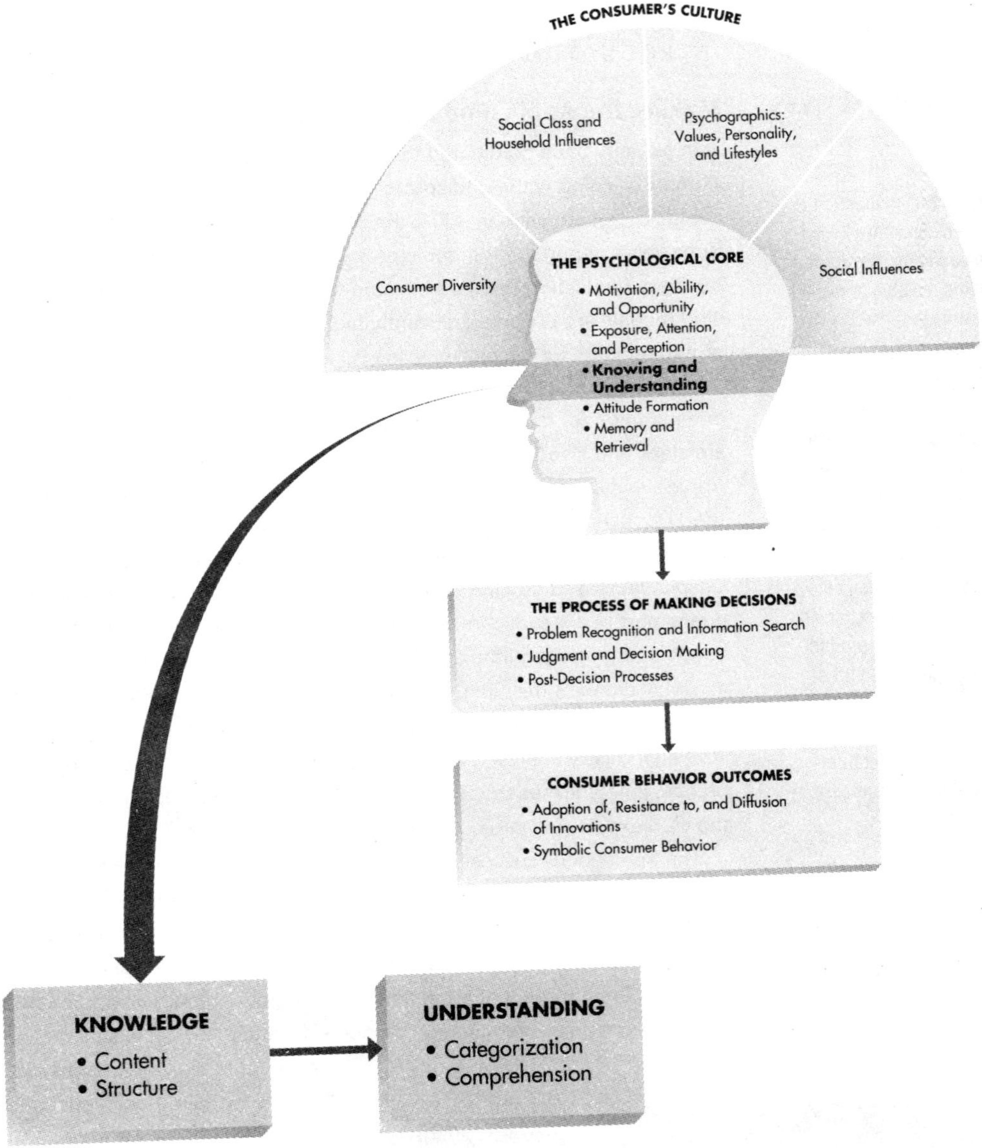

Exhibit 5.2
CHAPTER OVERVIEW: KNOWLEDGE AND UNDERSTANDING *We categorize information that we perceive by comparing it with what we already know. Prior knowledge includes two basic domains: content and structure. Once something is categorized, we use prior knowledge to comprehend more about it.*

shows, this chapter describes two broad domains of knowledge: knowledge content (stored information) and knowledge structure. The chapter also describes how prior knowledge is used for understanding, including categorization and comprehension.

Overview of Knowledge and Understanding

Knowledge content reflects the information consumers have already learned about brands, companies, product categories, stores, ads, people, how to shop, how to use products, and so on. Companies sometimes use marketing to develop, add to, or change consumers' knowledge content; increasingly, they try to link their brands to other knowledge that consumers may have, as in Exhibit 5.3.[2] ***Knowledge structure*** refers to the way consumers organize knowledge. Consumers often organize knowledge into categories, storing similar things in the same category. For example certain brands of toothpastes like Meswak may be stored in a category called Herbal Toothpastes. These brands, alongwith others such as Colgate and Pepsodent may be stored in a more general category called toothpaste. All these brands plus dental floss and other related products may be stored in an even broader category called dental hygiene products.

Prior knowledge is essential for two aspects of consumer understanding: categorization and comprehension. ***Categorization*** is the process of labeling or identifying an object that we perceive in our external environment based on its similarity to what we already know. Thus you might label Trident dental gum as a dental hygiene product as opposed to a candy product and relate it to your knowledge of other dental hygiene products. ***Comprehension*** is the process of using prior knowledge to understand more about what has been categorized. For example you might relate the picture, headline and ad copy in a Colgate ad and understand that "Colgate is good for teeth and can achieve some of the same benefits as brushing."

Exhibit 5.3

MARKETERS USE ADS, PACKAGES, AND PRODUCT ATTRIBUTES TO ENHANCE CONSUMERS' KNOWLEDGE ABOUT AN OFFERING

Marketers often want consumers to know more about their products (for example, that Olay now has a new body wash product). Ads, packages, and product attributes are useful ways of getting this knowledge across.

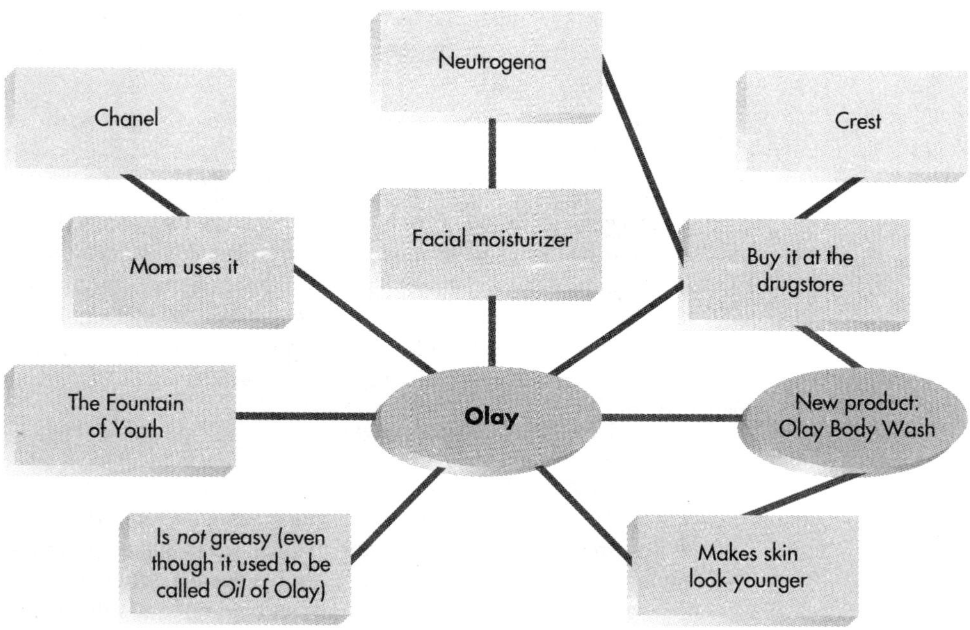

We say that we "know" something when we have encountered it before and have somehow come to understand what it means and what it is like. Knowing therefore has to do with our prior knowledge—both what we have encountered (knowledge content) and how that knowledge is organized (knowledge structure). Further, we tend to direct our consumption and search behaviors in ways that take full advantage of such prior knowledge.[3]

Knowledge Content

The content of our knowledge reflects the set of things we have learned in the past and may consist of many facts. For example, you may know that a banana has about 100 calories, that Nagpur is the Orange (fruits) city of the country, and that you need to change your car's oil every 5,000 miles. These facts are not stored as random facts; rather, they are generally linked to or associated with a concept. The set of associations linked to a concept is called a ***schema.***[4] A schema for the concept "banana" has many associations—for example, it has 100 calories, is yellow, bruises easily, and the peel can be very slippery if stepped on. A schema is elaborated when we have many associations linked to the concept.

Schemas and Associations

The associations in schemas can be described along several dimensions.[5]

- *Types of associations.* Consumers have many *types of associations.* One schema for banana might include associations that reflect (1) the attributes of a banana (yellow, long, soft, has a lot of potassium); (2) its benefits (nutritious, low in fat); (3) people who use it (athletes who lose a lot of potassium through sweating); (4) times when it is used (as a snack, for breakfast); (5) places it is used (at home, at school); (6) ways it is used (peeled, sliced); (7) places it is purchased (at a grocery store); (8) places it is grown (in South America); and so on.
- *Favorability.* Associations can also be described in terms of their *favorability.* The notion that a banana has 100 calories might be evaluated as favorable. The fact that eating too many can make you constipated might not be evaluated as favorable.
- *Uniqueness.* Associations vary in their *uniqueness*—that is, the extent to which they are also related to other concepts. "Greasiness" is not unique to McDonald's, but the Golden Arches and Ronald McDonald are.
- *Salience.* Associations vary in their *salience,* or how easily they come to mind. For example, a consumer might always retrieve the association of Golden Arches upon hearing the McDonald's name. Less salient associations may be retrieved only in certain contexts. Thus the association that McDonald's offers meatless McVeggie Burgers may be less salient, and a consumer may think about it only if someone starts talking about vegetarian meals.[6]

Types of Schemas

We have schemas for many entities. The banana example is an illustration of a *product category* schema; however, we also have schemas for *brands* For example, parents' schema for the Bata shoe brand includes good fit and durability, although the company is using ads to add "fashion" to consumers' schema, as well, in search of sales. Consumers often use associations with brands and other product features to predict what the benefits of the product will be.[8] We also have schemas for people, like our mothers, Amitabh Bachchan, teenagers, working-class people, and so on. We have schemas for services and for stores, although the associations linked to a store such as Big Bazaar may be quite different from the associations linked to Kirana Stores. We have schemas for salespeople (door to door salesperson, salesperson at the retail store), ads (Coke ads, Benetton ads), companies (Dabur, Tata), places (Kerala, Rajasthan), countries (South Africa, Somalia, Switzerland), and animals (tiger, one-horned rhino, cheetah). We even have a schema for ourselves, called a self-schema. We even have a schema for ourselves, called a *self-schema.*

Images

An image is a subset of associations that reflect what something stands for and how favorably it is viewed.[9] For instance, our ***brand image*** of McDonald's may be favorable, and it may include such associations as a family-friendly place and fast food. An image does not represent *all* the associations linked to a schema—only those that are most salient and make the brand different from other brands in the category. Thus although we may know that McDonald's serves some low-fat foods, this knowledge need not be used to form our brand image. We also have images for other marketing entities like stores, companies, places, and countries. We also have images for other marketing entities like stores, companies, places, and countries. Pantaloon group's strong presence in the country through its flagship stores through both food and non-food outlets help it gain favorable associations. Similarly, Wal-Mart the popular US retail chain's imminent entry into India has created enough anticipation with a large section of the audience who have heard of a Wal-Mart or have visited one. Consumer associations can therefore be created either through a direct experience with the brand or through word of mouth. Exhibit 5.4 shows the world's most valuable brands.

In addition, schemas can include associations that reflect the ***brand's personality***—that is, how the consumer would describe the brand if it were a person.[11] Consumers from one study described the Whirlpool brand as gentle, sensitive, quiet, good natured, flexible, modern, cheerful, and creative. Researchers found that these associations suggested a modern and family oriented suburban woman who is neighborly, successful, attractive, and action-oriented. Whirlpool's personality was quite different from Kitchen Aid's, whose name personified a smart, aggressive, glamorous, wealthy, elegant, and fashionable career woman. When Whirlpool began

Exhibit 5.4
THE MOST VALUABLE BRANDS IN THE WORLD

Their global presence and strong sales make Coco-Cola, Disney, and others among the world's most valuable brands.

Rank	Brand (home country)	Known for
1	Coca-Cola (U.S.)	Soft drinks
2	Microsoft (U.S.)	Software
3	IBM (U.S.)	Computer technology
4	General Electric (U.S.)	Lightbulbs, engines, medical technology
5	Intel (U.S.)	Computer chips
6	Disney (U.S.)	Entertainment
7	McDonald's (U.S.)	Fast food
8	Nokia (Finland)	Cell phones
9	Toyota (Japan)	Cars and trucks
10	Marlboro (U.S.)	Tobacco

Source: Diane Brady, Robert D. Hoff, Andy Reinhardt, Moon Ihlwan, Stanley Holmes, and Kerry Campbell, "Cult Brands: The *Business Week*/Interbrand Annual Ranking of the World's Most Valuable Brands Shows the Power of Passionate Consumers," *Business Week*, August 2, 2004, pp. 64ff.

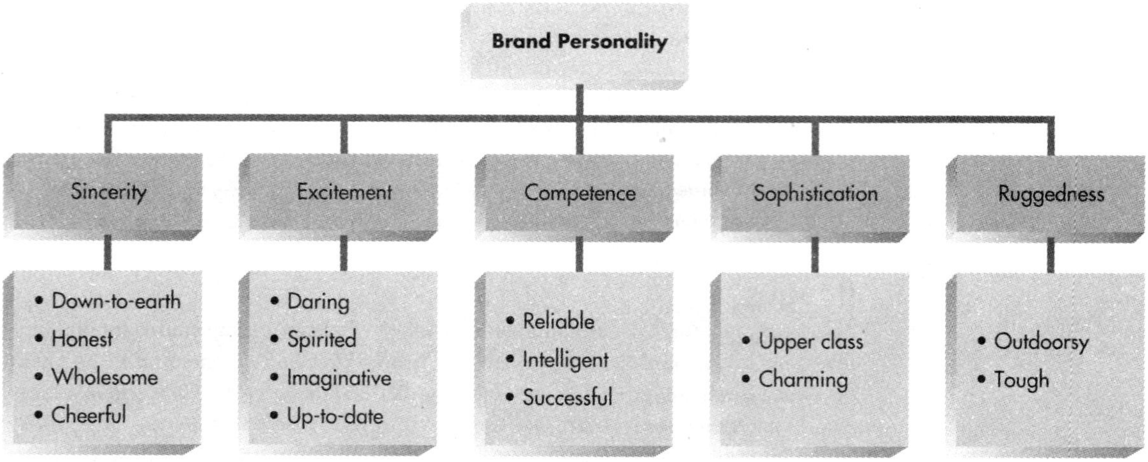

Exhibit 5.5

A BRAND PERSONALITY FRAMEWORK *One researcher found that many brands can be described according to one or more of the five personality types depicted here. Which dimensions best characterize Pepsi's brand personality? Which describe the personalities of Dell? Volkswagen? Google? Smucker's?*

expanding in Europe, it used an advertising campaign to create a brand personality linked to powerful goddesses. The success of this campaign led Whirlpool to adapt the campaign for U.S. markets, where it is targeting working mothers.

Sometimes brand personalities are embodied in brand characters like the Asian Paints- Gattu, Pillsbury Dough Boy and, Dog in the HMV logo. Think about the personality exemplified by each of these characters and how the character's personality says something about the personality of the brand. One study found that many brands could be described according to their position on the five brand personality dimensions shown in Exhibit 5.5.

marketing IMPLICATIONS

Because schemas, images, and personalities are important to consumer knowledge, marketers must work on creating these elements, developing them, changing them, and protecting them.

Creating new schemas, images, and personalities

When an offering is new, the marketer has to create a schema, image, and/or personality to help consumers understand what it is, what it can do for them, and how it differs from competitive offerings. Creating schemas is especially important for new products because consumers may not yet understand what these new products are or what they offer. When Maggi was launched in 1982, the company and the concept were new to the market but the product was already existing. The challenge was to get consumers to try the product and find for themselves the "difference" between Maggi and ordinary noodles. It introduced the now proverbial tag line, "Fast to Cook. Good to eat", something that Maggi has been using. However, over the years, with Doctor's intervention and parents' overall education about the contents of Maggi, a negative perception was created. Fear of Ajinomoto as an ingredient and the flour (maida) base of the product created strong health deterrents, especially in the segment that it targeted, the children. Realizing this Maggi launched a new version of the product as "Maggi Atta Noodles" and "Daal Atta Noodles" showcasing the goodness of wheat as opposed to Flour. It repositioned this new range as "Taste Bhi. Health Bhi."

Creating schemas and images for a company is also important so that consumers understand the general types of products produced by the firm. With the privatization in the Insurance sector, after the IRDA bill was passed, a host of new players entered the market which was dominated till then, by the state sponsored Life Insurance Corporation of India. As per IRDA provisions, MNC's could operate in India through a JV with any Indian company. Indian companies like Bajaj, ICICI, HDFC, Bharti to name a few entered with foreign JV's. However, the noise level created was so high and each player speaking almost the same language it became difficult for prospective customers to discriminate between two offers. Around this time, ICICI Prudential introduced a brand character "Chintamani- No Chinta Only Mani". The character resonated the very middle class sentiment of an Indian, who was trying to make both ends meet and add to that the woes of tax saving. The character helped the brand create a distinct visibility for itself in a high clutter-high noise level market.

- A ***brand extension*** occurs when a firm uses the brand name from a product with a well-developed image, like Tata Salt, on a product in a different category, such as Tata Indica (Cars). Other brand extension examples include Maggi Noodles to Maggi Soups and Amul Butter to Amul Cheese.
- ***Licensing*** occurs when a firm sells the rights of the brand name to another company that will use the name on its product. For example, the popular movie "Krrish" licensed out its name to several companies including names like Pantaloons, Lifebouy and with children's comic books.
- A ***brand alliance*** occurs when two companies' brand names appear together on a single product, as in MTV-Citibank Credit Card. Similarly, Big Bazaar, the retail brand and the ICICI credit card, both appear on the Big Bazaar ICICI Credit Card.

One consequence of brand extensions, license agreements, and alliances is that consumers develop an image for the new brand by transferring to it their associations and favorable feelings from the original brand's schema.[18] If consumers think that Amul Butter has a better taste and has the goodness of butter, necessary associations will get transferred to Amul cheese also. However, firms need to be careful about which associations they want to transfer to the brand extension. Putting promotional emphasis on a brand extension's attributes can focus consumers' attention on the attributes, not the brand, and make the extension seem less attractive.[19]

One concern about brand extensions is that they may make the brand schema less coherent and dilute the brand image.[20] If the Amul name appears on too many different products—processed foods, Ready to Eats, or Jams & Squashes— consumers may be confused about what Amul stands for. On the other hand, consumers may accept a brand extension better when the brand name is already linked to products that are quite different from one another. This is because consumers can find some attributes or benefits of at least one of the product categories that make it seem like the brand extension is a good product.[21]

Although existing brands can affect consumers' perceptions of a brand extension, marketing messages about a brand extension can sometimes influence consumers' perceptions of the existing brand(s) as well.[22] For example, if a consumer has a bad experience with Amul cheese, the negative feelings generated from the cheese may affect the image of Amul Butter. Given these potential problems, marketers need to be concerned about the long-term effects of these strategies.[23]

At a more fundamental level, creating associations linked to an offering helps to position the offering so consumers understand what it is and what it competes against. For example, in the United Kingdom, the Body Shop's association with social responsibility differentiates it from supermarkets offering natural cosmetics products, such as Sainsbury's active:naturals product line.[24]

Developing existing schemas, images, and personalities

Although marketers must sometimes create new schemas, in other cases they must develop or elaborate a schema—that is, add information to an existing schema so that consumers understand more about it.[25] One way to develop schemas is with multiple brand extensions. Although the name Arm & Hammer was once associated only with baking soda, the extension of the name to such categories as kitty litter, carpet deodorizer, and refrigerator deodorizer has reinforced its deodorizing image. Another way is to link the product to sponsorship in an appropriate sporting event, as a way of strengthening and developing the existing schema and personality.[26] A third way is to highlight additional features and benefits, as Avis Rent A Car has done with ads focusing on superior customer service as well as other aspects of its offering.[27]

Changing schemas, images, and personalities

Sometimes consumers' schemas, images, and brand personalities contain associations that require change. When a brand image becomes stale or outdated or when negative associations develop, marketers need to find ways to add new and positive associations. Roohafza, the popular sherbet from Hamdard was going through the classic life cycle decision, where most consumers had gone awry with the brand. Somehow in the Northern part of the country where the brand had some stranglehold was beginning to face heat from competition, especially from the aerated drinks category and consumers also seem to feel stagnated with the brand. At this time, the brand re-launched with the new message; "Pyaar Ka Haath Badaiye. Roohafza Pijiye. Roohafza Pilayea". The sherbet was now positioned as an add-on to Lassi, Milk Shakes, Ice-creams to enhance the taste of the products. The thick syrupy nature of the product helped in making the perfect concoctions.

Protecting brand images

Brand images may be threatened during crises that involve potential harm, such as reports of contaminated products or health problems linked to specific products. The cola majors in India, Pepsi and Coke, both faced a severe problem in the summer of 2006, when certain reports from the NGO, Centre for Science and Environment declared that both the cola brands contained harmful pesticides and the levels were far higher than what the 2003 report of the organization revealed. Faced with such severe allegations, Pepsi and Coke, initially created an uproar about deliberate scandalizing and tried to knee jerk out of it. Eventually, when the news started to trickle pan-India, states started to systemically ban the companies operating regionally. Having realized the uproar, both companies now reworked on a new strategy to reinstill consumer faith and confidence. In the case of Pepsi, Rajeev Bakshi, the company's Managing Director started appearing on infomercials and highlighting the safe conditions in which Pepsi is manufactured and under strict test conditions and standards, finally making the product absolutely safe to drink. Coke followed suit, but used their very popular celebrity, Aamir Khan to talk the same language.

How a company responds to a crisis affects its brand image, but research indicates that consumers' prior expectations also play a critical role. Companies whose customers held a strong positive image of the brand prior to the crisis suffered less image damage than companies whose customers had lower expectations. Thus firms with weaker brand images should be prepared to act aggressively in supporting their brands after a crisis.[30] Interestingly, firms with a "sincere" brand personality may have difficulty reestablishing strong customer relations after a crisis because fundamental perceptions of the brand have deteriorated. In contrast, firms with an "exciting" brand personality may actually have an easier reinvigorating customer relationships after a crisis because consumers are less surprised by nonroutine experiences with such brands.[31]

Scripts

Schemas represent our knowledge about objects or things.[32] A ***script*** is a special type of schema that represents knowledge of a sequence of events. For example, you may have a script for how to arrange roses bought from the store: you open the cellophane wrapping, get scissors, fill a vase with water, run the roses under water, cut them, and then arrange them in the vase. This knowledge helps you accomplish tasks quickly and easily. In contrast, when you do something for the first time, such as assembling a piece of Ikea furniture, having no prior script may prolong the task.

marketing IMPLICATIONS Scripts help marketers understand how consumers buy and use an offering. In turn, marketers use this knowledge to make marketing decisions that improve products or services. Marketers may also perform tasks that are part of consumers' scripts. In other cases, marketers may want consumers to consider using a particular brand or product as part of a scripted activity—incorporating hands-free devices as part of their cell phone usage script, for example. Interactive shopping and advertising are changing the way consumers perform scripted activities such as buying products and processing ads. Amazon.com, for instance, offers wish lists as a way for consumers to quickly identify, buy, and ship gifts they know are wanted by family and friends.

Knowledge Structure

Although schemas and scripts reflect the content of what we know, our lives would be utter chaos if we did not have some way of organizing or structuring our knowledge. Fortunately, as shown in the next sections, we are adept at organizing our knowledge and categorizing information.

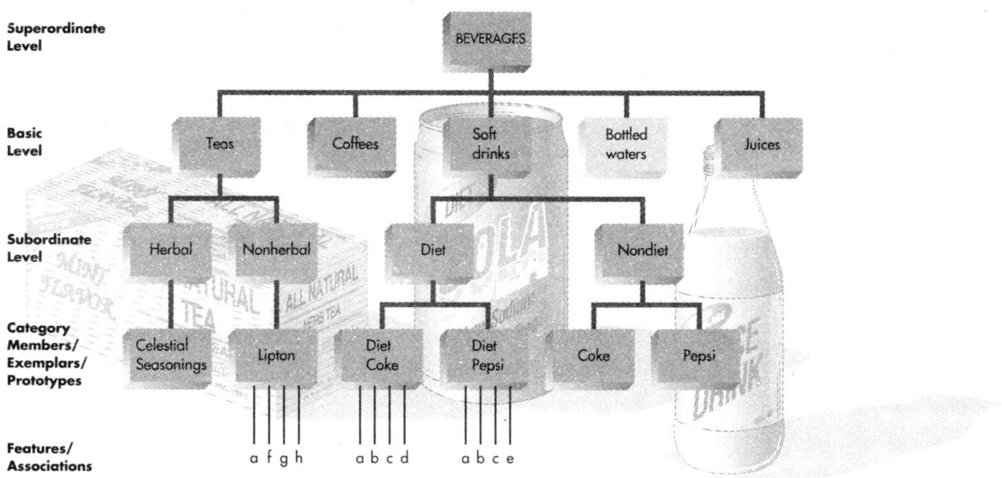

Exhibit 5.6

TAXONOMIC CATEGORY STRUCTURE *Objects can be organized in ordered, hierarchically structured categories, with similar objects in the same category. For example, herbal and nonherbal teas are subordinate to the basic-level category of teas. Teas, coffees, and soft drinks are members of the superordinate category, beverages. The letters under each brand signify attributes linked with each brand. Brands with the same letters have the same attributes. For example, the three brands share a common attribute "a" (e.g., caffeine) while only Diet Coke and Lipton share attribute "b" (e.g., artificial sweetner).*

Categories and Their Structure

Objects can be organized into ***taxonomic categories.***[33] A taxonomic category is a specifically defined division within an orderly classification of objects with similar objects in the same category. For example, although we have schemas for Coke, Pepsi, Diet Coke, and so on, these schemas can be clustered in a category called soft drinks. Moreover, we may use subcategories to cluster specific brands and separate them from others. Thus we might have one subcategory for diet soft drinks and a different subcategory for nondiet soft drinks. In turn, soft drinks may be part of a larger beverage category that also includes coffees, teas, juices, and bottled water, as shown in Exhibit 5.6.

Graded Structure and Prototypicality Things that are in the same taxonomic category share similar features, and the features they share are different from the features of objects in other categories. So a category member such as Diet Coke shares many associations with members of its own category of diet colas but shares few associations with members of other categories. Note that in Exhibit 5.6, Diet Coke has associations a–d, and Diet Pepsi has many but not all of the same associations (a–c and e). Lipton tea has associations a and f–h, which means it has few associations in common with Diet Coke.

Even though category members share similar features, not every member is perceived to be an equally good category member. For example, you might perceive a kingfisher to be a better example of the category "bird" than a robin is. Likewise, you might view Coke as a better example of a soft drink than Crush is. The fact that category members vary in how well they are perceived to represent a category illustrates the principle of ***graded structure.***[34]

Within a category, you as a consumer can rank specific category members according to how well you believe they represent the category. The category ***prototype*** is that category member perceived to be the best example of the category. Thus a robin is a prototypical bird, and iPod is a prototypical digital music player. Exhibit 5.7 identifies brands generally regarded as prototypes in their product categories.

Product category	Prototypical brands
Children's entertainment	Disney
Laundry detergent	Tide
Digital music player	iPod
Cell phone	Nokia
Film	Kodak
Toothpaste	Crest
Electronics	Sony
Peanut butter	Skippy
Tuna fish	Starkist
Soup	Campbell's
Bologna	Oscar Mayer
Ketchup	Heinz
Bleach	Clorox
Greeting cards	Hallmark
Motorcycle	Harley-Davidson
Grape jelly	Welch's
Copiers	Xerox
Gelatin	Jell-O
Hamburgers	McDonald's
Baby lotion	Johnson & Johnson
Tools	Black & Decker
Cold cereal	Kellogg's
Tissue	Kleenex
Acetaminophen	Tylenol

Exhibit 5.7
PROTOTYPICAL BRANDS

Brands viewed as the best examples of a product category are called prototypical brands. Prototypical brands tend to have many features in common with other brands in the category, are encountered frequently, and may have been the first entrant in the product category.

What Affects Prototypicality? Several factors affect whether a consumer regards something as a prototypical category member.[35] The first is shared associations: a prototype shares the most associations with other members of its own category and shares the fewest with members from different categories. Potato chips are a prototypical snack food because they have associations common to many snack foods (taste good, salty, finger food, come in many varieties, are high in carbohydrates and fats) and few associations in common with other categories such as dinner foods. A second feature that affects prototypicality is the frequency with which an object is encountered as a category member. Amazon.com is regarded as a prototypical place to buy books on the Internet because consumers are likely to have frequently encountered its name when online or when searching for online sources of books. The first or "pioneer" brand in a category may also be a prototype because it sets a standard against which brands introduced subsequently are compared. Amazon.com is a prototypical brand in this regard as well.

marketing IMPLICATIONS

Prototypes are the main point of comparison used by consumers to categorize a new brand. Therefore, a brand can develop its identity by being positioned as either close to or different from the prototype.

Positioning close to the prototype

Positioning a brand as close to the category prototype is appropriate when the goal is to appeal to a broad segment of consumers. Because the prototype best defines the category and is well liked, a new brand positioned as similar to it may appeal to a large segment of consumers. Comparative advertising may be a useful tool for making a brand seem similar to a prototype. If a challenger brand such as Barnesandnoble.com comes into the market and directly compares itself to Amazon.com, the challenger may be seen as similar to the prototype.[36]

Positioning away from the prototype

An alternative strategy is to position the new brand away from the prototype. For instance, targeting U.S. consumers in their twenties, Toyota positions its Scion xB as having more distinctive styling than the popular Honda Civic.[37] This is a good strategy when the brand is different from others (particularly from the prototype) and the point of difference represents a credible reason for buying. It is also appropriate when the goal is to appeal to consumers with specific needs. For example, Cranium positions its "Apples to Apples" word game as a catalyst for interaction rather than a win-or-lose situation. The fun is in the heated discussions that accompany the play: "there's no right and wrong, no one ever feels dumb," says Cranium's marketing chief.[38] Positioning away from the prototype can work with pricing as well, because consumers judge whether a product's price is high or low through comparisons with several category members, not just the prototype.[39]

Correlated Associations Although graded structure reflects one way knowledge is structured, another way depends on whether the associations linked to category members are correlated, or go together. For example, in the category of automobiles, car size is positively correlated with safety (larger cars are generally safer), and engine size is negatively correlated with miles per gallon (the bigger the engine, the fewer miles per gallon). If consumers believe that car size, miles per gallon, and safety are correlated, they may infer that a new car with a large engine is safe but not very fuel efficient—inferences that may or may not be true of the brand. Thus ***correlated associations*** can significantly affect the inferences that consumers make about a new brand seen as a member of a particular category and the kinds of communications marketers need to make to overcome potentially false inferences.

Hierarchical Structure A final way in which taxonomic categories are structured is hierarchically. As Exhibit 5.6 indicates, taxonomic categories can be hierarchically organized into basic, subordinate, and superordinate levels. The broadest level of categorization is the ***superordinate level,*** where objects share a few associations but also have many different ones. Diet Coke and Fiji bottled water, both members of the beverages category, have some common associations as well as many that are different.

Finer discriminations among these objects are made at the ***basic level.*** Beverages might be more finely represented by categories such as teas, coffees, and soft drinks. The objects in the teas category have more in common with each other than they do with objects in the coffee category. The finest level of differentiation exists at the ***subordinate level.*** For example, soft drinks might be subdivided into categories of diet and nondiet soft drinks. Here, members of the diet soft drink category have more associations in common with each other than they do with members of the nondiet category. Consumers often have many levels of subcategorization; for beverages, they may consider whether soft drinks are diet or nondiet, colas or not colas, caffeinated or decaffeinated.

Consumers use more associations to describe objects in progression from the superordinate to the basic to the subordinate levels. They may apply associations such as "drinkable" and "used throughout the day" to all members of the beverages category. However, they may add other associations—carbonated, served cold, sold in six-packs—to describe members of the soft drink category, then add the associations of no calories and artificial sweeteners to describe members at the subordinate diet drink level.

marketing IMPLICATIONS

Understanding consumers' hierarchical category structure helps marketers identify their competitors. It also gives marketers a tool for analyzing and influencing consumers' perceptions of category attributes and prototypical products.[40] Although consumers often make choices among brands at the basic or subordinate level, in some cases they choose from brands that belong to a common superordinate category. For example, if you are deciding whether to order a pizza or snack on microwave popcorn, you are making a decision among products that belong to different basic categories within a common superordinate-level category (snack food). The brands in both categories might be compared based on higher-order attributes that link the brands to the same superordinate-level category (convenience, price, taste). And although pizza restaurants might not normally think about competing with popcorn brands, they are rivals in this situation. In line with this thinking, Hormel wants consumers to think about its chili as a side dish for hamburgers and other foods, "as much of a staple as salt, pepper, or mustard," says the senior product manager. Positioning it as more versatile may make consumers think about chili when they are planning all kinds of meal accompaniments.[41]

Establishing a competitive position

By understanding consumers' superordinate-category structure, marketers can glean a broad view of their competition and use this understanding to establish an appropriate competitive position. Understanding subordinate categories also helps marketers determine which attributes to emphasize so consumers will properly categorize their offering. For example, nonalcoholic beer is positioned as a subordinate category of beer, which suggests that its advertising should not only stress features central to beer (great beer taste) but also clarify its subordinate-category membership by promoting associations that put it in this subordinate category (has no alcohol).

Exhibit 5.8
NATURAL THINGS
In this ad, Catch suggests that it's water is part of a derived category of "things made by nature"

Designing retail stores and sites
Basic, subordinate, and superordinate category levels also have implications for consumer search and the design of retail stores and sites. Generally, grocery stores are designed so that objects in taxonomically similar categories are shelved together, as are items in the same basic- and subordinate-level categories. For example, most grocery stores have a dairy (superordinate level) section with shelves for milk, yogurt, cheese, eggs, and so on (basic level). Within each of these sections are subordinate categories of items such as low-fat, nonfat, and whole milk. Retail websites also group products according to category (such as cameras or books). Placing items in ways that are consistent with the structure of consumers' knowledge helps consumers find products efficiently. This is why White Wave markets its soymilk by packaging it in milk cartons and placing it in the refrigerated milk section of the store as a subcategory of milk.[42]

Goal-Derived Categories

In addition to taxonomic categories, we may also organize our prior knowledge according to ***goal-derived categories.*** A goal-derived category contains things that consumers view as relevant to the goal (see Exhibit 5.8). Sometimes we assign things to the same category because they serve the same goals—even though they belong to different taxonomic categories.[43] For example, when traveling on an airplane, you might see in-flight movies and peanuts in the same category because all are part of the goal-derived category "things that make air travel more pleasant." Because we have many goals, we can have many goal-derived categories. For example, if you are on a diet, you might form a category for "foods to eat on a diet."

Consumers frequently encounter certain goals and therefore have firmly established categories of prior knowledge for those goals. For example, if you give a lot of parties, the goal-derived category of "things to buy for a party" probably consists of a fairly stable and constant set of products. In contrast, you may create relevant categories on a situation-by-situation basis for less frequently encountered goals. Yet, category structure is flexible: the same object can be part of a goal-derived and a taxonomic category. Thus Diet Coke might be part of the taxonomic categories diet colas, soft drinks, and beverages. It might also be a member of the following goal-derived categories: things to have for lunch, things to take on a picnic, and things to drink at a ball game.

Like taxonomic categories, goal-derived categories also exhibit graded structure. Consumers regard some members as better examples of a particular category when they best achieve the goals of the category. As an example, lettuce is lower in fat and calories, so it is a better example of foods to eat on a diet than baked crackers. Because goal-derived categories exhibit graded structure, consumers can also identify prototypes of goal-derived categories. As with taxonomic categories, the frequency with which an item is encountered as a category member affects its prototypicality. We tend to classify lettuce as a prototype for things to eat on diet and would probably rate it as more prototypical than a food that is equally appropriate but encountered less frequently, like kohlrabi.

marketing IMPLICATIONS Positioning a product or service as relevant to a goal can be an important marketing objective. To illustrate, Special K is positioned as consistent with the goal-derived category of "things to keep you thin." Wal-Mart discounts all manner of goods and services—including gasoline—to maintain its prototypical position in the goal-derived category of "saving money."[44]

Supermarkets also apply goal-derived category structures when planning store design. Many stores display baby bottles, diapers, baby food, and juice in the same aisle despite their taxonomic differences (diapers are usually seen as similar to tissue, baby juice as similar to juice for older kids, and baby food as similar to other foods). Because these products are part of a goal-derived category—things you need to take care of a baby—they are shelved together so parents can easily find the items and decide which brands to buy. Similarly, websites can be designed with consumers' goal-derived categories in mind. Yatra.com is a new travel related site that offers visitors to the site complete planning from travel, stay, pick up/drop, planning for a holiday of any kind (Weekend getaway versus vacations). A joint venture of Reliance Capital, TV 18 and NVP, it's the first online site that offers the complete travel related support.

Why Consumers Differ in Their Knowledge

Several background factors affect our knowledge structure and content. These include the cultural system in which consumers exist and the consumer's level of expertise based on prior knowledge.

The Cultural System The cultural system in which consumers exist affects their knowledge base in many ways:

- *Different associations linked to a concept.* The associations linked to a concept may vary considerably across cultural systems.[45] For their Platinum Cards, American Express used Abhishek Bachchan as their endorser. Abhishek's stature as the rising star, son to a legendary father and engaged to the most beautiful and successful woman in India, was the right credential required to endorse a product like the Platinum Card. However, such legacy may not be relevant outside of India, where Abhishek is less known and can be a deterrent if used him as a global endorser.
- *Different category members.* Although consumers may have similar goal-derived categories such as "things to have for breakfast," cultural groups vary considerably in what they regard as relevant category members. In India category members may consider including Paratha, Poha, Idli, Uttapam and Upma. In the United States, category members might include cereal, bagels, fruit, and eggs; in Japan, category members include fish, rice, and pickled vegetables.
- *Different category prototypes.* Category prototypes and members may vary across cultures, requiring companies to position brands differently for different cultures. The popular Kingfisher beer in India is a colorful brand and is now extended to a variety of product categories like Airlines, Aerated Water, Pubs etc.

The brand is targeted as a fun beer and positions itself as the "King of Good Times". Today, the beer is exported to several countries around the world but a similar positioning may necessarily not work, owing to strong "country of origin" effect that might affect the brand's entity while going global.

- *Different correlated associations.* Culture may affect whether associations are correlated and the direction of their correlation. For example, in the United States megastores like Costco and Wal - Mart tend to price products lower than small stores because the large stores are often discounters. In India, however, perceptions about such large stores is that they are high priced and do not offer room for bargains, a common habit of most Indian shoppers.
- *Different goal-derived categories.* Consumers in different cultures may not only have different members in goal-derived categories but, in fact, have different goal-derived categories. For example, the goal to have clothing that looks sexy is not likely to apply in cultures with strict religious values.

Level of Expertise Consumers vary in their ability to process information based on how much prior knowledge they have. Experts are people whose prior knowledge is well developed, in part because they have had a lot of experience and familiarity with an object or a task. Experts' knowledge differs from that of novices in several ways.[46] First, experts' overall category structure is more developed than the category structure of nonexperts. They have more categories, more associations with concepts in a category, and a better understanding of whether associations in a category are correlated. Also, they learn brand information appropriate for a variety of usage situations and organize such information by product subcategories; in addition, they tend to learn less about a new product than nonexperts do.[47] Finally, experts have more subordinate-level categories and can therefore make finer distinctions among brands. For example, car experts would have many subordinate categories of cars such as vintage cars and roadsters. Note that consumers are sometimes overconfident in their knowledge and think they know more than they actually do.[48]

Another important point is that when experts are exposed to a marketing message, they form expectations against which they evaluate their actual experiences with that product. If product performance fails to measure up to expectations, experts are more likely to perceive a wider discrepancy between the experience and their message-generated expectations than nonexperts.[49] Still, people who consider themselves experts tend to search for information and make decisions differently from those who do not consider themselves experts, which in turn, affects how companies market to these groups.

Using Knowledge to Understand

Consumers' decisions are not influenced by simply attending to and perceiving stimuli. Individuals must also interpret or give meaning to the objects they perceive in light of their prior knowledge.

Categorization

A first step in this process occurs when consumers categorize an object. Categorization occurs when consumers use their prior knowledge to label, identify, and classify something new. Consumers might categorize iMac as a type of computer, eBay as a site to bid on merchandise, and *Entertainment Tonight* as a place to get the scoop on celebrities. Once we have categorized an object, we know what it is, what it is like, and what it is similar to. How we categorize an offering has many implications for marketers, since categorization affects how favorably we evaluate an offering, the expectations we have for it, whether we will choose it, and how satisfied we may be with it. Research shows, for instance, that consumers who are exposed to brand extensions can more quickly categorize the parent brand correctly. Given the speed at which consumers are exposed to marketing stimuli when shopping, this faster categorization can be an advantage for the parent brand.[50]

Consumers do not always categorize things correctly. During the launch stage of 8-PM, a popular brand of malt whisky from the Radico Khaitan group, the company faced an unusual problem. Through the advertisements that it aired about two warring generals from different countries retiring at the end of the day with a glass of 8-PM whisky, created consumer perception that it was a scotch whisky, which it was not. Similarly, India's new found confidence and economic boom may be a recent phenomenon, still permeating into the western world. For any exports from India, the "Country of Origin" perceptions may be still the dogmatic approaches prevalent in the Western world.

Once consumers have categorized an offering, they may not be able to categorize it differently. The popular health drink from Beecham's (SKB), Horlicks has a larger and stronger market in the eastern parts of the country. Most consumers also had a perception that Horlick's is more an ailing man's energy drink, who is trying to recuperate from the bout of sickness. Horlick's is now making aggressive attempt with a newly developed marketing communication exercise, titled "Aepang Opang Chapang" trying to bring back the fun and excitement in shaking the dregs of the cup and sipping it in one shot. The campaign is targeted towards children and the range of flavours like Chocolate, Vanilla and Strawberry created excitement in the range too. Horlicks has also introduced two new versions, one for infants, Horlicks Junior and the other for adults in the age group of 35-45, Horlicks Lite.

marketing IMPLICATIONS

Categorization is a basic psychological process that has far-reaching implications for marketers, including the following:

Inferences

- If we categorize a product as a member of a category, we may infer that the product has features or attributes typical of that category. For example, we may infer that because a particular brand is a computer, it comes with both a monitor and a hard drive for data storage. These inferences may be correct in many but not all cases. Thus marketers of a novel new product should help consumers categorize the product in a way that positively influences perceptions, such as selling a unique digital camera in the camera department of a store rather than in the computer department.[54]

Elaboration

- Categorization influences how much we think about something. We tend to be more motivated to think about or process information that we have trouble categorizing. We are more motivated to watch ads that are different from the typical ad, and we are more motivated to think about products that look different from others in the category.[55] Seeing a Honda Accord with a spoiler and racing stripes might prompt elaboration because these features suggest a mixture of the sports car and compact car categories.

Evaluation

- Categorization also influences how we feel about an object, also known as our "affect" toward it. Once we categorize something as a member of a category, we may simply retrieve our evaluation of the category and use it to assess the object.[56] For example, if we hate lawyers and see an ad for a lawyer, we may use the category-based affect and decide that we hate this one, too. Likewise, if our category for chocolate bars contains positive affect, we may retrieve and use this affect to evaluate a new brand in the category.

Consideration and choice

- Whether and how we label an offering affects whether we will consider buying it. If a new phone/fax/printer is categorized as a phone, we will consider it if we are in the market for phones. If it is categorized as a printer, we won't consider it if we are in the market for phones.

Satisfaction

- Finally, categorization has important implications for consumer expectations and satisfaction.[57] If we categorize something as a skin moisturizer, we will expect it to meet all the performance characteristics of products in that category; if it does not, we are likely to be dissatisfied.

Comprehension

While categorization reflects the process of identifying an entity, comprehension is the process of extracting higher-order meaning from it. Marketers are concerned with the two aspects of comprehension. The first is ***objective comprehension***—whether the meaning that consumers extract from a message is consistent with what the message actually stated. The second is ***subjective comprehension,*** the different or additional meaning consumers attach to the message, whether or not these meanings were intended.[58]

Objective and Subjective Comprehension ***Objective comprehension*** reflects whether we accurately understand the message a sender intended to communicate. Interestingly, many people miscomprehend marketing messages due to the way the information is presented (its language) or differences between the sender's and the receiver's prior knowledge—or both. ***Subjective comprehension*** reflects what we think we know, whether or not it is accurate. Marketing mix elements such as price and advertising can play a powerful role in influencing what we think we know. To illustrate, you may infer that a specific brand of dental gum is as powerful at whitening teeth as whitening toothpastes because the package uses white sparkles, the model in the ad has very white teeth, and the package uses terms like whitening agent. Yet, the product may not actually be such a powerful whitening agent. The inferences that consumers make and why certain marketing communications prompt these inferences raise some important public policy implications.

Miscomprehension Although marketing communications such as ads and packaging are often fairly simple, consumer research reveals that achieving objective comprehension can sometimes be quite a challenge for marketers. ***Miscomprehension*** occurs when consumers inaccurately receive the meaning contained in a message. Several studies have found a surprisingly high level of miscomprehension of TV and magazine ads, across all demographic segments. The estimated rate of comprehension was only about 70 percent for TV ads and 65 percent for print ads. Moreover, the rates of miscomprehension for directly asserted information and implied information were fairly equal, as were miscomprehension rates for programming, editorial material, and advertising.[59]

Consumers sometimes fail to understand how to use a product. This tendency has led to some rather bizarre warning signs on products, as Exhibit 5.9 illustrates. Like the animation characters, Superman and Spiderman from the west, an indigenously developed local character, Shaktiman created a massive fan following across India. The character had an earthy appeal and it particularly influenced the large rural and suburban population. The stunts performed by Shaktiman on the show were copied by the children and it led to some critical accidents and deaths of teenage kids. A lot of products endorsed by Shaktiman were lapped up by children and a feeling that having these products endorsed by Shaktiman would make them like Shaktiman, permeated their minds. The advertising council, the government and several ministries were involved in creating the now mandatory line, in all advertisements where stunts are being displayed. The line read; "The following stunts have been performed by experts in safety conditions, and may please be not tried at home or elsewhere".

Effect of MAO Miscomprehension is clearly affected by lack of motivation, ability, or opportunity (MAO) to process messages. Consumers seem most likely to miscomprehend something when their motivation to process it is low.[61] Even when consumers have high motivation, however, their comprehension may not be accu-

Exhibit 5.9
COMPREHENSION AND PRODUCT WARNINGS

Consumers do not always understand how to use products, and may use them in inappropriate ways. Unfortunately, sometimes it is difficult for manufacturers' in other countries to convey the exact usage description they mean.

Products	Warnings
On a hair dryer:	Do not use while sleeping
On a bag of corn chips:	You could be a winner! No purchase necessary! Details inside.
On a bar of soap:	Directions: use like regular soap
On frozen dinners:	Serving suggestion: defrost
On a hotel provided shower cap:	Fits one head
Printed on *the bottom* of a Tiramisu dessert:	Do not turn upside down
On bread pudding product:	Product will be hot after heating
On packaging for an iron:	Do not iron clothes on body
On sleep aid:	Warning: may cause drowsiness
On jar of peanuts:	Warning: contains nuts
On packet of nuts:	Instructions: open packet, eat nuts
On a child Superman costume:	Wearing of this garment does not enable you to fly
In some cases, manufacturers' labels for products used in other countries do not always convey the intended meaning.	
On a string of Christmas lights:	For indoor or outdoor use only
On a Korean kitchen knife:	Warning: keep out of children
On a Japanese food processor:	Not to be used for the other use

rate. Regarding ability, one study found that although consumers want to see nutritional information on packaging (implying high motivation to process it), most do not comprehend it once they read it.[62] Still, comprehension may improve with expertise and ability, which is why adults often better comprehend the finer points of a message than young children do.[63] Also, consumers are more likely to miscomprehend messages when they have limited opportunity to process them. Miscomprehension is generally greater when messages are complex, shown for only a few seconds, and viewed only once or twice. Finally, experts are better able to comprehend information about a highly innovative product when prompted by marketing messages that help make the connections and tap existing knowledge in more than one category.[64]

Effect of the Cultural System The cultural system can also affect comprehension and miscomprehension. Low-context cultures such as those in North America and northern Europe generally separate the words and meanings of a communication from the context in which it appears. Consumers in these cultures place greater emphasis on what is said than on the surrounding visuals or the environmental context of the message. But in high-context cultures (such as many in Asia), much of a message's meaning is implied indirectly and communicated visually rather than stated explicitly through words. The message sender's characteristics, such as social class, values, and age, also play an important role in the interpretation of a message.[65]

Because cultures differ in the level of attention they pay to the content and context of the message, we might expect differences in consumers' comprehension of the same message across cultures. For example, when the Michigan-based Big Boy fast-food chain opened its first restaurant on a busy street in Thailand, some local customers mistook its giant Big Boy statue for a religious icon, not a marketing feature.[66] Miscomprehension can also occur because of the way consumers interpret the meaning of a marketing message translated from another language (see the bottom part of Exhibit 5.9 for examples). Language differences further raise the possibility of miscomprehension; in fact, marketers risk miscomprehension if they do not use language as consumers in a culture do. In India, for example, so many people mix Hindi and English that advertisers are doing the same in their messages. Thus Pepsi ads in India say, "Yeh Dil Maange More" (translation: "The heart wants more"), and Coke's slogan there is "Life ho to aisi" (translation: "Life should be like this").[67]

Culture also affects the meaning consumers attach to words.[68] For example, in the United Kingdom, a *billion* is "a million million," whereas in the United States a billion means "a thousand million." Likewise, in the United Kingdom a movie that is a *bomb* is a "success"; in the United States, a *bomb* means a "failure." One U.S. airline promoted its "rendezvous lounges" in Brazil; however, among the Brazilians the phrase implied "a room for lovemaking."

Improving Objective Comprehension Fortunately, consumer researchers have provided some guidelines for improving objective comprehension.[69] One obvious method is to keep the message simple. Another is to repeat the message—stating it multiple times within the same communication and repeating it on multiple occasions. Finally, comprehension can be improved by presenting the message in different forms, such as visually and verbally in a television commercial.

Subjective Comprehension

Subjective comprehension describes the meanings consumers generate from a communication, whether or not these meanings were intended.[70] Public policy makers are often concerned that what consumers take away from an ad may be different from what the ad objectively states. In a complaint filed with the Advertising Standard Council of India (ASCI) for the General Motors Tavera advertisement, featuring a group of Indian cricketers using the Tavera to play cricket. The advertisement developed by Rediffusion DY&R was thought to promote rash and negligent driving and as per ASCI directive, actions portrayed in the visuals depicted in the TVC, show dangerous practices and manifest a disregard for safety without justifiable reason. The advertisement had to be edited and revised to create positive influence in the consumer minds.

Levels of Subjective Comprehension Some researchers consider that subjective comprehension can be described in terms of several comprehension levels. In this scheme each level indicates more thinking or elaboration.[72] For example, suppose a consumer sees an ad for a car CD player that says, "If you have an FM radio in your car, you can play CDs." The ad also states that the advertised CD player comes with a six-disc magazine. The consumer exposed to this ad might think, "I guess if you only have an AM radio, you can't install a CD player in your car." At a higher level of elaboration, the consumer might make logical inferences derived directly from what the ad says. In this example, she might logically infer that CD players and FM radios involve similar electronic interconnections because the radio is necessary for this CD player to work. At even higher levels of elaboration, the consumer might make inferences based on her general knowledge; thus she may infer that because the CD player has a six-disc magazine, it might also have programmable functions. At the highest level, the consumer might think about or imagine future interactions with the stereo. Here, she may think that such a system would be attractive to thieves and therefore might wonder whether getting one also requires getting a car security system.

marketing IMPLICATIONS

Like categorization, subjective comprehension involves some interaction between what is in a message and what consumers know. As a result, a marketer can strongly influence what consumers subjectively perceive from a message by designing or structuring it in a way that is consistent with prior knowledge. Sometimes, when consumers know little about a new product, marketers may be able to convey information effectively by drawing an analogy between the product and something with similar benefits. For example, a marketer may try to communicate the idea that a particular brand of boots is waterproof, soft, and lightweight by using the analogy of a duck.[73]

Marketers are often successful in designing an ad so that consumers form the "correct" inferences about the offering. At times, however, marketers may (knowingly or unknowingly) create inferences that do not accurately characterize a product or service and result in miscomprehension.[74] Situations in which marketers deliberately create false inferences about an offering raise some important ethical and legal implications, as discussed further in Chapter 19.

Consumer Inferences

Specific elements of the marketing mix can work with consumers' prior knowledge to affect the correct or incorrect inferences they make about an offering. The following sections describe how brand names and symbols, product features and packaging, price, distribution, and promotion can affect the inferences consumers make about products.

Brand Names and Brand Symbols Subjective comprehension of a marketing communication can be based on the inferences consumers make from a brand symbol. The Pillsbury Dough Boy has slimmed down over the years because the company's marketers are afraid that consumers will infer that he is fat from eating Pillsbury products.

Brand names can also create subjective comprehension and inferences. For example, alphanumeric brand names like BMW's Z4 roadster 2.5i tend to be associated with technological sophistication and complexity. In addition, consumers tend to make inferences when they evaluate a brand extension by carrying over certain features linked to the parent brand.[75] Moreover, foreign brand names may create inferences based on cultural categories and stereotypes. Thus Häagen-Dazs, a German-sounding name, may evoke favorable associations when applied to ice cream even though it is manufactured in the Bronx. As a result, marketers marketing internationally should not only consider linguistic factors when translating brand names for another culture, but they should also examine how consumers in that culture process different types of brand names.[76]

Descriptive names can also create inferences. Brand names such as Obsession for perfume, Speedo for bathing suits, and Surevue for contact lenses may create inferences about the particular brand's benefits.[77] On the other hand, Procter & Gamble changed the brand name of its Oil of Olay skincare products to simply *Olay* because, says an executive, "Many consumers thought oil meant a greasy product."[78] Finally, companies marketing products whose quality cannot be observed can communicate quality to consumers by offering a warranty, selling through a credible retailer, or forging an alliance with another reputable brand. Under these circumstances, consumers are likely to infer that the allied product would lose its reputation or its future profits if the quality claims were untrue.[79]

Inferences Based on Misleading Names and Labels Although some brand names may accurately characterize a product's attributes and benefits, others have been called misleading because they create false inferences about the product's benefits. For example, consumers may infer that "lite" olive oil has fewer calories when it is really only "lite" in color.[80] This confusion has prompted the development of labeling laws to ensure that product names and ingredients accurately describe the offering. The FPI, a body of the Food Processing Ministry has laid down clear guidelines for labeling instructions on the product packaging, which should discriminate between vegetarian and non-vegetarian ingredients. For a product with all vegetarian ingredients, a bold green dot on the packaging and for all non-vegetarian ingredients a bold brown dot is mandatory, so that consumers know beforehand and are cautioned about the presence of (non)objectionable ingredients in the products.

Inferences Based on Inappropriate or Similar Names Some brand names lead to inappropriate inferences about the product. Fiat, in India had launched a diesel sedan version, titled as Fiat Petra, which was showcased more as a diesel car in the initial launch, inspite of the fact that the name Petra had stronger connotations of being petrol driven car. The car's superior performance and better features get offset, because of inadequate publicity, improper dealer support and a wrong perception of being a diesel car. Other names fail because they do not create unique associations or inferences that differentiate the brands. The challenge for Web-based marketers is to find a name that suggests what they do and helps them stand out the crowd. "A fanciful name that is well branded—and examples of this are plentiful: Intel, Yahoo!—will resonate in the consumer's mind and conjure the supplier of specific products and services," says one Web marketing expert. "A generic domain name lacks that distinctive association."[83]

Sometimes brand or company names are too similar, and consumers may inadvertently infer that the brands are similar or made by the same company. Typically these situations create legal battles, with companies fighting over who can use the original brand name. [1]William Grant & Sons Ltd. filed an action to restrain McDowell & Co. Ltd., from copying the trade dress of Glenfiddich Scotch whisky. Grant had been exporting various whiskies to India since 1946 and Glenfiddich Single Malt Whisky since 1978. The Glenfiddich Single Malt Whisky was sold in a green bottle and black cylindrical cartons bearing a label with a distinctive trade dress and unique features, which included a stag device that Grant contended had become exclusively associated with them and a thistle device which Grant alleged was a Scottish symbol indicating origin of the product. Grant claimed trademark infringement and passing off alleging that McDowell used a label with a similar trade dress as the Glenfiddich label, including also a green bottle, a black cylindrical carton and stag and thistles devices.

Product Features and Packaging Consumers can also subjectively comprehend aspects of an offering based on inferences they make from the product and the way it is packaged.

Inferences Based on Product Attributes Knowledge that two attributes tend to be correlated in a product category may lead consumers to infer that the presence of one attribute in a brand implies the other. Thus consumers may infer that a product with a low repair record also has a long warranty.[85] Consumers may make inferences about products based on package size. A consumer who encounters a large, multipack item may use prior knowledge about the correlation between price and package size to infer that the large-sized brand is also a good buy.[86] Also, when two companies form a brand alliance for marketing purposes, consumers tend to infer that the brand attributes are similar even when one is incompletely described in the ads.[87] Moreover, when consumers search for information about whether a product will deliver a particular benefit, exposure to irrelevant information leads to inferences that the product will not necessarily perform as desired.[88] In highly competitive categories, where differences between products seem minimal, consumers may perceive the dominant brand's advantages in observable attributes yet infer that the brand has disadvantages in some unobservable attributes.[89]

Inferences Based on Country of Origin Knowledge about a product's country of origin can affect how consumers think about it.[90] Just as we stereotype people based on where they were born, we also stereotype products based on where they are made. Research shows that consumers in developing countries infer higher quality from brands that are perceived as foreign.[91] Many Latin American consumers, for instance, infer that foreign telephone companies offer better service and quality than local companies.[92] Consumers are less likely to make inferences about a brand based on its country of origin when they are highly motivated to process information about that brand or when their processing goal guides attention away from origin information.[93]

Furthermore, country of origin inferences can also work to create an advantage for one company and a disadvantage for another. In one study, Japanese consumers inferred that the quality of Japanese-made products was higher than the quality of American-made products—even when the Japanese products were not superior. [2]International retailers need to understand that Indian consumers don't shop and buy the same products as the rest of the world. India is very similar to the EU -the number of states and union territories number 35 and languages, cultures, habits and consumer preferences are different in every one of them. An international retailer looking to enter India needs to be extremely well-versed with local retail culture and know-how. Exhibit 5.10 shows the map of India's Income class where the real driver of the Indian retail sector is the bottom 80 per cent of the first layer and the upper half of the second layer of the income map. This segment of about 40 million households earns USD 4,000-10,000 per household and comprises salaried employees and self-employed professionals.[2]

Inferences Based on Package Design Package characteristics can also create inferences. Although consumers may make inferences about one brand if its packaging looks much like that of the category prototype, they do not necessarily react negatively to the nonprototype brand.[95] At the same time, packaging can suggest a brand's uniqueness. When DS Group launched its range of Catch Spring Mineral Water, to differentiate it from other mineral water and to showcase the premium nature of the product, Catch introduced packaging which was premium in look and appeal. It also helped in highlighting the product differentiator with emphasis on bottling in high quality Pet bottles.

Sometimes packages are designed to look like the packages of well-known brands. [3]A financial company, Quantum Asset Management Co Pvt. Ltd. (Quantum Mutual Fund) in one of their advertisements used the visual in their advertise-

Exhibit 5.10
MAP OF INDIA'S INCOME CLASSES

Map of India's income classes

	1994-95	1999-00	2005-06
• **RICH** (Annual income > US$ 4,700) **Benefit Maximisers:** Own cars, PCs	1 million households	3 million households	6 million households
• **CONSUMING** (US$ 1,000- 4,700) **Cost-benefit optimizers:** Have bulk of branded consumer goods, 70% of two-wheelers, refrigerators, washing machines	29 million households	55 million households	75 million households
• **CLIMBERS** (US$ 500-1,000) **Cash-constrained benefit seekers:** Have at least one major durable (mixer, sewing machine/television)	48 million households	66 million households	78 million households
• **ASPIRANTS** (US$ 350-500) **New entrants into consumption:** Have bicycles, radios, fans	48 million households	32 million households	33 million households
• **DESTITUTES** (Less than US$ 350) **Hand to mouth existence:** Not buying	35 million households	24 million households	17 million households

ments of an earlier run advertisements by Smokin Joe's of "Pizaxx – Har Snack ka Big Baap" that Smokin' Joe's was advertising in mass media (since March 2006), as part of the campaign for their new product – Pizaxx, which is a pizza snack. The agency and the company were charged with plagiarism and the financial company had to withdraw the advertisement.

Inferences Based on Color Finally, consumers can make inferences about an offering based on its color or the color of its package. We have color categories stored in prior knowledge. The category of things that are green includes mint, grass, trees, and leaves as members and has associations like refreshing, new, organic, peaceful, and springlike. Because of this category-based knowledge, consumers can make inferences about a stimulus based on its color. They may infer that a brand of green toothpaste that comes in a green package is refreshing, minty, and healthy.

Knowing that colors can affect consumers' inferences, some companies have taken legal steps to protect the color of their brand. Owens-Corning gained trademark protection for its pink home-insulation products, and Keds gained trademark protection for the blue rectangular label on the heels of Keds shoes. Such protection prohibits other firms from using these colors on their products and reduces the possibility that consumers will categorize the product incorrectly or draw false inferences about a knockoff product.[98]

Because category content varies with culture, the meaning associated with colors and consumers' inferences based on color will also vary.[99] For example, Western consumers usually associate white with purity and cleanliness, whereas in Asian countries white signifies death. Green is a popular color in Muslim countries but is negatively perceived in Southwest Asia. Black has negative overtones in Japan, India, and Europe but is perceived positively in the Middle East. Marketers must therefore consider these cultural differences when marketing in other cultures.

Price At times, consumers make inferences about a product or service based on its price. For example, category-based knowledge suggests that price and quality are correlated, so a consumer may infer that a high-priced product is also high in quality.[100] Consumers often make this inference when they believe brands differ in quality, when they perceive high risk in choosing a low-quality product, and when they have no information—such as a known brand name—to assess quality before buying.[101] In such instances, consumers may simply use price as a shortcut to infer quality. However, consumers' perceptions of quality tend to be less influenced by price, and they are less likely to discount information that is inconsistent with their perceptions when they are unconcerned about coming to a decision quickly and are exposed to only a small amount of information.[102] When consumers receive a product as a free gift with the purchase of another item, they infer that the gift has a lower value and will therefore expect to pay less for the product when offered separately.[103]

Retail Atmospherics and Display Category-based knowledge about aspects of the distribution mix, such as retail design, displays, layout, merchandising, and service, can also affect consumers' inferences. For example, the inferences you make walking into a Kirana Store are likely to be different from the inferences you

Exhibit 5.11

WHICH ATMOSPHERIC ELEMENTS EXERT THE MOST INFLUENCE?

Certain atmospheric elements are perceived by consumers to impact their shopping and buying behavior.

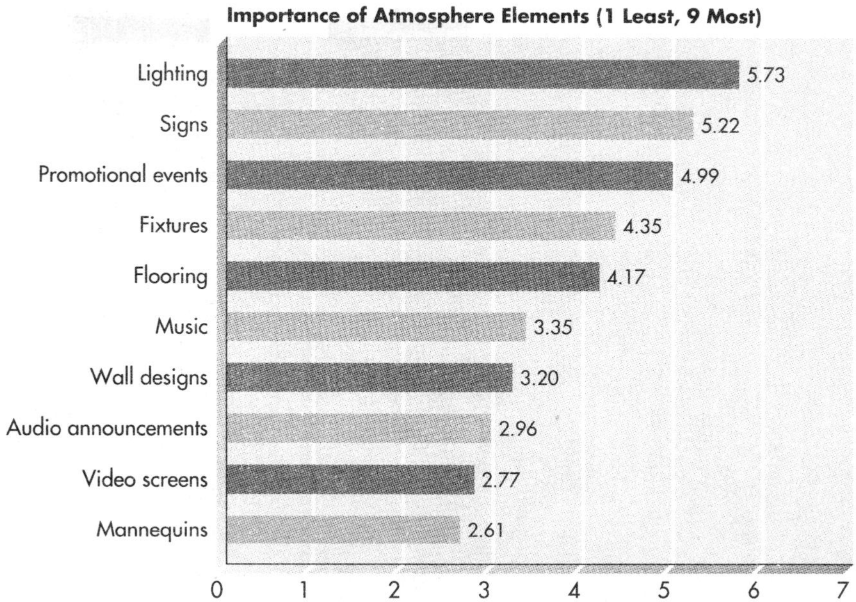

make entering a more upscale, service-oriented store like Foodland or Spencer's. Research indicates that an aesthetically pleasing retail atmosphere causes consumers to infer positive quality perceptions of socially communicative products such as gifts (but not of utilitarian products such as household appliances) and affects consumers' intentions to shop at the store.[104] Consumers also infer differences among brands based on how products are displayed in stores. Further, the display context can lead consumers to rely less on prior knowledge and more on external cues—meaning a brand's positioning could be undermined by inappropriate retail display decisions.[105] Exhibit 5.11 shows that lighting and signs are the two atmospheric elements that consumers say exert the most influence on their in-store behavior.

Atmospherics are a major tool used by retailers to develop, elaborate, and change their store images. When fashion firm Comme des Garcons opened stores in Berlin, Barcelona, and other European cities, it deliberately chose locations outside traditional shopping districts. Untouched by architects, each store's previous use was clearly recognizable from the nearly raw décor, just the kind of edgy urban context the firm wanted for displaying its avant-garde clothing.[106]

Advertising and Selling Advertising and selling efforts clearly affect the inferences consumers make about an offering. In personal selling and advertising, inferences can be based on body language. An advertisement that shows a woman touching a man's hand for longer than a second could lead us to believe that they are romantically involved. Consumers might infer that a salesperson with a weak handshake is not interested in their business. The nonverbal aspects of communication are particularly important in Asian cultures.[107] In Japan, for example, a verbal "yes" often means "no"; the speaker's body language communicates the true intent.[108] In addition, consumers who feel that a salesperson is deliberately trying to persuade, and not just inform, them—especially by the use of hard-sell or pressure-selling tactics—may be less likely to buy the product.[109]

Physical space, or the distance between people, may also be interpreted differently in different cultures. Compared with Westerners, Asians tend to leave more distance between people and prefer limited physical contact. A U.S. salesperson who is accustomed to less space and more contact may give Asian consumers the impression of being pushy and unacceptably physical. However, compared with U.S. consumers, Latin American consumers are comfortable with less distance between people and may infer that a U.S. salesperson who maintains more distance is standoffish.[110]

Exhibit 5.12
STIMULATING INFERENCES WITH PICTURES
An ad for branded petrol from HP depicts the essence of the product and what it can do to you

Pictures Advertisers frequently use pictures to stimulate inferences. In Exhibit 5.12, HP showcases through a strong visual the effect that power can create. The branded petrol segment with the high octane series had all the top 3-4 lube players entering the market, and HP introduced Power as their brand name.

Language Just as specific words like brand names or adjectives can affect inferences, the way in which words are structured into sentences can also affect subjective comprehension.[111] The word structure of the hypothetical ad in Exhibit 5.13 can lead to the following (potentially incorrect) inferences:

- *Juxtaposed imperatives.* The headline contains two sentences placed next to one another (juxtaposed). Consumers might interpret the headline as saying, "The Starfire AD7 gives you luxury and sportiness at its finest," even though the ad does not actually make this statement.
- *Implied superiority.* Another inference commonly made from advertising is implied superiority. The statement "nobody gives you more," as in the exhibit, could be technically true if all brands offered equal performance benefits. Nobody gives you more of what? Because this is an incomplete comparison statement, consumers are likely to fill in a comparison object (right or wrong) and interpret such a statement as implying superiority—that is, "This brand is the best."
- *Incomplete comparisons.* Ads sometimes provide a comparison but leave the object or basis of comparison either incomplete or ambiguous, which can lead to incorrect inferences.[112] The statement "it's less expensive" in Exhibit 5.13, for example, does not indicate what the Starfire AD7 is less expensive than. Is it less expensive than the other brands listed in the ad, last year's model, or the most expensive car on the market?
- *Multiple comparisons.* Some ads make comparisons with multiple brands. For example, the ad in Exhibit 5.13 states that the Starfire AD7 performs better than a Porsche in interior comfort, better than an RX7 in braking ability, and better than a Corvette in smoothness of ride. However, consumers may infer that the AD7 is better than all these brands on all these attributes. Readers may also infer that the Porsche offers the best interior comfort because it is the standard for comparison. Note that the ad could still technically be true if the Porsche were less comfortable than an RX7 and a Corvette but marginally less comfortable than the AD7.

Exhibit 5.13

A HYPOTHETICAL CAR AD

The way a message is worded can affect our inferences. What do you think this ad is saying? Is it really saying what you think? How does the wording affect what you comprehend?

Headline: **Experience luxury and sportiness at its finest. It's the AD7 from Starfire.**

Body copy: Automotive World's toughest tests found that no other brand gives you more than Starfire's AD7. It performs better than the Porsche in interior comfort, has better braking ability than the RX7, has a smoother ride than the Corvette, and it's less expensive.

Tag: **Starfire's AD7. Nobody gives you more.**

Exhibit 5.14

AD STIMULI USED IN ONE STUDY *Consumers may inappropriately conclude that the second version of this ad (the partial comparative ad) says that the brand is superior to the compared brand on all attributes. Actually, the ad says that the brand is superior compared to the first attribute only.*

NC Advertisement

NEW DAZZLE TOOTHPASTE IS
THE BRAND FOR YOU.
HERE ARE 4 REASONS WHY.

REASON #1: EFFECTIVE CLEANING ABILITY
Independent clinical tests conducted at Stanford, Harvard, and Northwestern dental schools have documented Dazzle's cleaning ability — Dazzle removes plaque!

REASON #2: POWERFUL WHITENERS
Other clinical tests have shown that Dazzle is effective in removing stains from your teeth.

REASON #3: A REFRESHING TASTE
Recent tests conducted by Consumer Reports have shown that 9 out of 10 consumers tested liked the refreshing taste of Dazzle.

REASON #4: AN ALL-NATURAL FORMULA
Dazzle is all natural — it contains no artificial colors or preservatives.

NEW ***DAZZLE*** *FLUORIDE TOOTHPASTE*

Try New Dazzle Toothpaste!
A Complete Toothpaste for Today's Consumer!

PC Advertisement

NEW DAZZLE TOOTHPASTE IS
THE BRAND FOR YOU.
HERE ARE 4 REASONS WHY.

REASON #1: MORE EFFECTIVE CLEANING ABILITY
Independent clinical tests conducted at Stanford, Harvard, and Northwestern dental schools have documented Dazzle's cleaning ability — Dazzle removes twice the amount of plaque than Crest!

REASON #2: POWERFUL WHITENERS
Other clinical tests have shown that Dazzle is effective in removing stains from your teeth.

REASON #3: A REFRESHING TASTE
Recent tests conducted by Consumer Reports have shown that 9 out of 10 consumers tested liked the refreshing taste of Dazzle.

REASON #4: AN ALL-NATURAL FORMULA
Dazzle is all natural — it contains no artificial colors or preservatives.

NEW ***DAZZLE*** *FLUORIDE TOOTHPASTE*

Try New Dazzle Toothpaste!
A Complete Toothpaste for Today's Consumer!

CC Advertisement

NEW DAZZLE TOOTHPASTE IS
THE BRAND FOR YOU.
HERE ARE 4 REASONS WHY.

REASON #1: MORE EFFECTIVE CLEANING ABILITY
Independent clinical tests conducted at Stanford, Harvard, and Northwestern dental schools have documented Dazzle's cleaning ability — Dazzle removes twice the amount of plaque than Crest!

REASON #2: MORE POWERFUL WHITENERS
Other clinical tests have shown that Dazzle is effective in removing stains from your teeth. In fact, Dazzle has been proven to get teeth over 60% whiter than Crest.

REASON #3: A MORE REFRESHING TASTE
Recent tests conducted by Consumer Reports have shown that 9 out of 10 consumers tested preferred the refreshing taste of Dazzle over the taste of Crest.

REASON #4: AN ALL-NATURAL FORMULA
Unlike Crest, Dazzle is all natural — it contains no artificial colors or preservatives.

NEW ***DAZZLE*** *FLUORIDE TOOTHPASTE*

Try New Dazzle Toothpaste!
A Complete Toothpaste for Today's Consumer!

In addition, language can lead to misleading inferences drawn from comparative ads, as Exhibit 5.14 shows. This exhibit shows three versions of the same ad for a hypothetical brand of toothpaste called Dazzle. The first ad is a noncomparative ad—it simply describes the brand's benefits, but makes no competitive comparisons. The second is a partial comparative ad. It compares Dazzle to Crest, but only on the benefit of cleaning ability. The third is a direct comparative ad that compares the product to Crest on all benefits. Partial comparative ads can be misleading because consumers are likely to infer that the advertised brand is better than the compared brand on all benefits, not just the stated one.[113]

Ethical Issues

These inferences raise a number of interesting ethical and public policy questions. On the one hand, marketers are apparently able to use marketing mix elements (such as brand name, visuals, price, store atmosphere, and ad copy) to not only make their brand look better but also to mislead consumers. On the other hand, some may argue that consumers allow themselves to be misled by marketers and that marketers cannot be held accountable for inaccurate inferences and miscomprehension of ads. What do you think? See Chapter 20 for further discussion of the potential negative effects of marketing.

Summary

We understand something in the environment by relating it to our prior knowledge. Knowledge content is represented by a set of associations about an object or an activity linked in schemas and scripts. Understanding the content of consumers' knowledge is important because marketers are often in the position of creating new knowledge—that is, developing brand images or personalities, creating brand extensions, or positioning a brand—as well as developing existing knowledge or changing knowledge through repositioning.

Our knowledge is also organized or structured into categories. Objects in one category are similar to objects in the same category and different from objects in other categories. Objects within a category exhibit graded structure, meaning some are better examples of the category than are others. The best example of the category is the prototype. Knowledge may be hierarchically organized, with similar objects organized in basic, subordinate, or superordinate levels of categorization, and objects within a category may have associations that are correlated. Categories may also be organized around things that serve similar goals. How consumers organize knowledge has marketing implications for product positioning, product development, and retail design. Consumers differ in their knowledge in part because of different cultural systems and in part because some consumers are simply more informed than others.

Prior knowledge combined with information from the external environment affects how we categorize something and what we comprehend. Categorization has far-reaching implications for what we think about a product, how we feel about it, what we expect from it, and whether we choose and will be satisfied with it. One way of thinking about comprehension is to ask whether consumers accurately understand what was stated in a message, a concept called objective comprehension. Consumers often fail to accurately acquire the meaning of marketing communications. Limited motivation, ability, and/or opportunity to attend to and process a message often affect comprehension. A second aspect of comprehension is subjective comprehension, or what consumers think they know or have understood from a message, which may not always match what a message states. Consumers may fail to accurately understand what is explicitly stated in a communication because they form inferences based on marketing elements. Unscrupulous marketers can take advantage of consumers' tendencies to make inferences and deliberately mislead consumers, raising ethical and public policy issues.

Questions for Review and Discussion

1. What is a schema, and how can the associations in a schema be described?
2. How do brand extensions, licensing, and brand alliances relate to schemas, brand images, and brand personalities?
3. What is a category prototype, and what affects prototypicality?
4. What does it mean to say that consumers organize knowledge according to goal-derived categories?
5. How do culture and level of expertise affect a consumer's knowledge base?
6. In what way is objective comprehension different from subjective comprehension and miscomprehension?
7. What are some examples of ways in which a company can use the marketing mix, in combination with consumers' prior knowledge, to affect the inferences consumers make about a product?

Exercises

1. Identify five brands from the FMCG sector and list the extensions that they have carried out on either line or brand. Identify the extended brand's current status and its performance aspect in terms of the parent brand.
2. Take a well-known brand and describe its associations. Based on these associations, state what its brand personality might be. Then indicate how this knowledge would facilitate your brand name, packaging, pricing, advertising, and product decisions.
3. Go to the supermarket and to a large department store and find as many examples of brand extensions as you can. For each, indicate the following:
   a. Whether you think they are good brand extensions or not, and why.
   b. Whether any negative effects might be associated with these brand extensions.

   Then take a new product for which no brand extensions exist. Indicate new product categories this brand might successfully extend to.
4. Go to a retail website (such as Amazon.com, eBay.com, or Travelocity.com). Think about how the Web experience alters the basic "shopping-for-products" script that consumers would enact in a typical store. Does this site enable you to perform activities that you would normally perform if you were actually shopping for products in a store? How could the site be improved to enable you to perform scripted activities more easily?
5. Find a brand that is positioned close to the category prototype and another that is positioned away from the category prototype. Why do you think marketers chose to position these brands in this way?
6. Illustrate the principles of basic-, subordinate-, and superordinate-level categories for a product category of your choosing. In one case, assume that consumers' subordinate-category structure is complex; in another case, assume it is simple. Now assume that one of the manufacturers is planning to introduce a new brand. Indicate in which case the new brand will compete with the brands the firm already makes.
7. Find an advertisement that contains juxtaposed imperatives, implied superiority, multiple comparison inferences, or incomplete comparisons.
   a. Let half the class work for the Division of Advertising Practices at the Federal Trade Commission. The commission is charging the company with creating misleading advertising. Argue that the ad is misleading and explain why the advertiser is at fault. Indicate how the ad should be rewritten, or use added or different visuals to create inferences that are more likely to be correct about the product.
   b. The other half of the class works for the legal division of the company. Argue that the ad is not misleading and that advertisers should not be held accountable for the incorrect inferences consumers may make about the brand.

8. Think about a personal goal you want to achieve, such as losing weight or learning to speak Italian. Identify at least 10 goods or services that you would include as members of this goal-derived category, then rank these members from most to least prototypical. Which is the prototypical member of this category, and why? Now consider how the marketing of this prototype might affect your decision to buy or use it in achieving your goal. How is the company using its marketing mix to position its product or service as relevant to your goal? What other steps might this company take to strengthen this position?
9. Visit a local retailer and examine two competing products from a single category, such as two shampoo brands or two cell phone brands. What inferences do you draw from the brand names and symbols? Do the brand names accurately characterize each product's features and benefits? How does the packaging affect the inferences you make about each product? If either product mentions country of origin, how does this influence your thinking about it? What inferences do you make about these products based on color? Contrast and compare your responses for each competing product. Overall, which product carries the most favorable associations and inferences, and why?

More Exercises from the Adaptor

1. Identify five brands from the FMCG sector and list the extensions that they have carried out on either line or brand. Identify the extended brand's current status and its performance aspect in terms of the parent brand.

References

[1] Source: http://www.ladas.com/BULLETINS/1994/1194Bulletin/India_SpeedyCourtDecisions.html

[2] Source: The Great Indian Retail Story: Ernst & Young

[3] Source: Advertising Standard Council of India

chapter **6**

Attitudes Based on High Consumer Effort

LEARNING OBJECTIVES

After studying this chapter, you will be able to:

- Discuss how marketers can apply the cognitive response and theory of reasoned action (TORA) models to understand and influence consumers' attitudes based on high-effort thought reactions.
- Describe some of the methods for using the communication source and the message to favorably influence consumers' attitudes.
- Explain how and why a company might try to change consumers' attitudes by influencing their feelings.

INTRODUCTION

Cadbury's Dairy Milk Pass Ho Gaya

Since its origin in India, Cadbury's Dairy Milk (CDM) as a brand has continuously been working on market penetration strategies, where new segments and sub-segments have continuously been identified by the company.

CDM was considered as a surrogate of parental affection for children. Chocolates were then meant for kids only and were seen as an indulgence product and some of the negative associations with it were–too much of it was bad and bad for health. With communication consciously addressing kids, consumption also got restricted within the same segment resulting in brand stagnation. In 1994, the company made an effort to expand the consumer base by making CDM aspirational and desirable to the adult segment. Extensive brand audits on the consumer pulse revealed that Cadbury Dairy Milk moments were spontaneous, carefree, special, real moments. So, what if these 'moments' were brought back to life even for adults? To increase category relevance, give consumers a taste of life the Cadbury Dairy Milk way - real, fun and free. Integrate the "real" chocolate of Cadbury Dairy Milk to "real" feelings. This gave rise to the famous Cadbury's "Taste of Life" communication, which completely changed the format in which chocolates were sold and CDM was able to break itself free from the clutter.

After a point in time, brands like Kit Kat and Cadbury's own brand Perk introduced a new variant of chocolate in wafer, which was considered younger, trendy, futuristic, exciting, and smart. Added to that was a spurt of imported brands like Lindt, Ritter, & Van Houten, which created their own niche. CDM started to find that the market again was starting to stagnate. Research also revealed that "Real Taste of Life Campaign" cut ice only with the metro audience, the barriers of Middle/Bottom end consumers still remained to be addressed and as a result, brand growth rate was slower than the chocolate market growth.

In the second phase, CDM tried to get across to a larger section of the audience, and it tried to capture the essence of India and tried to introduce CDM as a

Exhibit 6.1

substitute for sweetmeat and positioned itself as a brand, "Kuch Meetha Ho Jaye". Efforts were made for the "Indianisation" of the brand and to increase width of consumption by entering the Indian mind-space - Make CDM part of Indian customs and mores.

This campaign was later supplemented with Amitabh Bachchan being brought in to endorse the brand. The proposition of Kuch Meetha Ho Jaye was not removed and remained the main brand promise. Having tapped into the traditional customs where sweets were an integral part of all activities, CDM moved on to another important plank of integrating with Indian culture, the sharing of all good news with a box of sweets, an idea extended further with the "Pappu Pass Ho Gaya" campaign. Amitabh Bachchan remained an essential part of both the campaigns and the strategy helped increase brand penetration (especially in smaller towns) leading to a brand growth of around 40%.

The success of the CDM strategy was purely based on how a brand initially tries to extend from a segmentation strategy, as a part of a market development strategy to further create new associations and thus work towards market penetration strategy. CDM's efforts to make the brand relevant by developing new associations like festivals, marriages, sharing a good news etc., clicked well with the masses and extended the product's usage platform from a limited usage situation to an extended buying situation.

What Are Attitudes?

An ***attitude*** is an overall evaluation that expresses how much we like or dislike an object, issue, person, or action.[2] Attitudes are learned, and they tend to persist over time. Our attitudes also reflect our overall evaluation of something based on the set of associations linked to it. This is why we have attitudes toward brands, product categories, ads, people, types of stores, activities, and so forth.

The Importance of Attitudes

Attitudes are important because they (1) guide our thoughts (the ***cognitive function***), (2) influence our feelings (the ***affective function***), and (3) affect our behavior (the ***connative function***). We decide which ads to read, whom to talk to, where to shop, and where to eat, based on our attitudes. Likewise, attitudes influence our behavior in acquiring, consuming, and disposing of an offering. Thus, marketers need to change attitudes in order to influence consumer decision making and change consumer behavior.

The Characteristics of Attitudes

Attitudes can be described in terms of five main characteristics: favorability, attitude accessibility, attitude confidence, persistence, and resistance. ***Favorability*** refers to how much we like or dislike an attitude object. ***Attitude accessibility*** refers to how easily and readily an attitude can be retrieved from memory.[3] If you went to a movie last night, you can probably remember with relative ease what your attitude toward it was, just as you can easily remember your attitude toward an important object, event, or activity (such as your attitude toward your first car).

Attitudes can also be described in terms of their strength, or ***attitude confidence.*** In some cases we hold our attitudes very strongly and with a great deal of confidence, whereas in other cases we feel much less certain about them. Attitudes may also vary in their ***persistence,*** or endurance. The attitudes we hold with confidence may last for an extremely long time, whereas others may be very brief. Finally, attitudes can be described in terms of their ***resistance*** to subsequent change.[4] Consumers may change their attitudes easily when they are not loyal to a particular brand or know little about a product. However, attitude change is more difficult when consumers are brand loyal or consider themselves experts in the product category.

Forming and Changing Attitudes

Marketers can better create or influence consumers' attitudes toward new offerings and novel behaviors when they understand how attitudes are formed. This understanding also helps marketers plan strategies for changing consumer attitudes about existing offerings and established behaviors. Exhibit 6.2 summarizes general approaches to attitude formation and change processes, providing a useful overview of the topics discussed in this and the next chapter.

The Foundation of Attitudes

As Exhibit 6.2 shows, one approach to attitude formation suggests that attitudes are based on *cognitions (thoughts)* or beliefs.[5] This means that attitudes can be based on thoughts we have about information received from an external source (such as advertising, salespeople, the Internet, or a trusted friend) or on information we recall from memory. One study shows that ad messages with information about product function—what a product's features can do, for example—can provoke thinking about the product and stimulate positive product attitudes.[6]

A second approach suggests that attitudes are based on *emotions*. Sometimes we have a favorable attitude toward an offering simply because it feels good or seems right. Likewise, we can acquire attitudes by observing and vicariously experiencing the emotions of others who use an offering. For example, if you see that people riding a roller coaster are having fun, you may believe that you will, too. In fact, research suggests that both the hedonic aspect (related to the experience of product use) and the utilitarian aspect (related to the product's function) affect attitudes toward product categories and individual brands.[7]

Exhibit 6.2

GENERAL APPROACHES TO ATTITUDE FORMATION AND CHANGE

As discussed in Chapter 3, consumers' processing differs depending on whether elaboration is high or low. Processing can also be either cognitive or affective. This leads to four basic ways in which consumers can form attitudes. This chapter examines the ways attitudes can be formed and changed when consumer effort is high.

Attitudes are based on:

Consumers' elaboration (consideration) of a message (based on their motivation, ability, and opportunity [MAO])	**Cognitions (thoughts)**	**Affect (feelings/emotions)**
High Effort Central-Route Processing (Chapter 6)	The cognitive response model The expectancy-value model	Emotional processing Affective responses Attitude toward the ad
Low Effort Peripheral-Route Processing (Chapter 7)	Simple beliefs • Simple inferences • Attributions • Heuristics	The mere exposure effect Classical conditioning Attitude toward the ad Mood

The Role of Effort in Attitude Formation and Change

How much extensive thinking or *elaboration* consumers put forth affects their attitude formation and change processes, as well. As discussed in Chapter 3, consumers may sometimes have high motivation, ability, and opportunity (MAO) to process information and make decisions. When MAO is high, consumers are more likely to devote a lot of effort toward and invest considerable personal involvement in forming or changing attitudes and making decisions. Some researchers have used the term ***central-route processing*** to describe the process of attitude formation and change when thinking about a message requires some effort.[8] Processing is central because consumers' attitudes are based on a careful and effortful analysis of the true merits or central issues contained within the message. As a result of this extensive and laborious processing, consumers form strong, accessible, and confidently held attitudes that are persistent and resistant to change.

When MAO is low, however, consumers' attitudes are based on a more tangential or superficial analysis of the message, not on an effortful analysis of its true merits. Because these attitudes tend to be based on peripheral or superficial cues contained within the message, the term ***peripheral-route processing*** has been used to describe attitude formation and change that involves limited effort (or low elaboration) on the part of the consumer.

This chapter focuses on several ways in which consumers form and change attitudes when effort (i.e., MAO) is high. The next chapter focuses on how consumers form and change attitudes when effort is low. Because attitudes tend to be more accessible, persistent, resistant to change, and held with confidence when consumers' MAO to process information is high, much of the chapter focuses on what affects the favorability of consumers' attitudes.

Exhibit 6.3 serves as a framework for the ideas discussed in this chapter. It shows that when consumers are likely to devote a lot of effort to processing information, marketers can influence consumer attitudes either (1) *cognitively*—influencing the thoughts or beliefs they have about the offering, or (2) *affectively*—influencing the emotional experiences consumers associate with the offering. Furthermore, marketers can try to influence consumers' attitudes through characteristics of the source used in a persuasive communication, the type of message used, or some combination of both. After attitudes are formed, they may play a powerful role in influencing consumers' intentions and actual behavior.

The Cognitive Foundations of Attitudes

Researchers have proposed various theories to explain how thoughts are related to attitudes when consumers devote a lot of effort to processing information and making decisions. This chapter focuses on the cognitive response model and expectancy-value models.

The Cognitive Response Model

The basic idea behind the cognitive response model is that consumers' thought reactions to a message affect their attitudes. ***Cognitive responses*** are the thoughts we have when exposed to a communication. These thoughts can take the form of recognitions, evaluations, associations, images, or ideas.[9] Suppose a man sees an

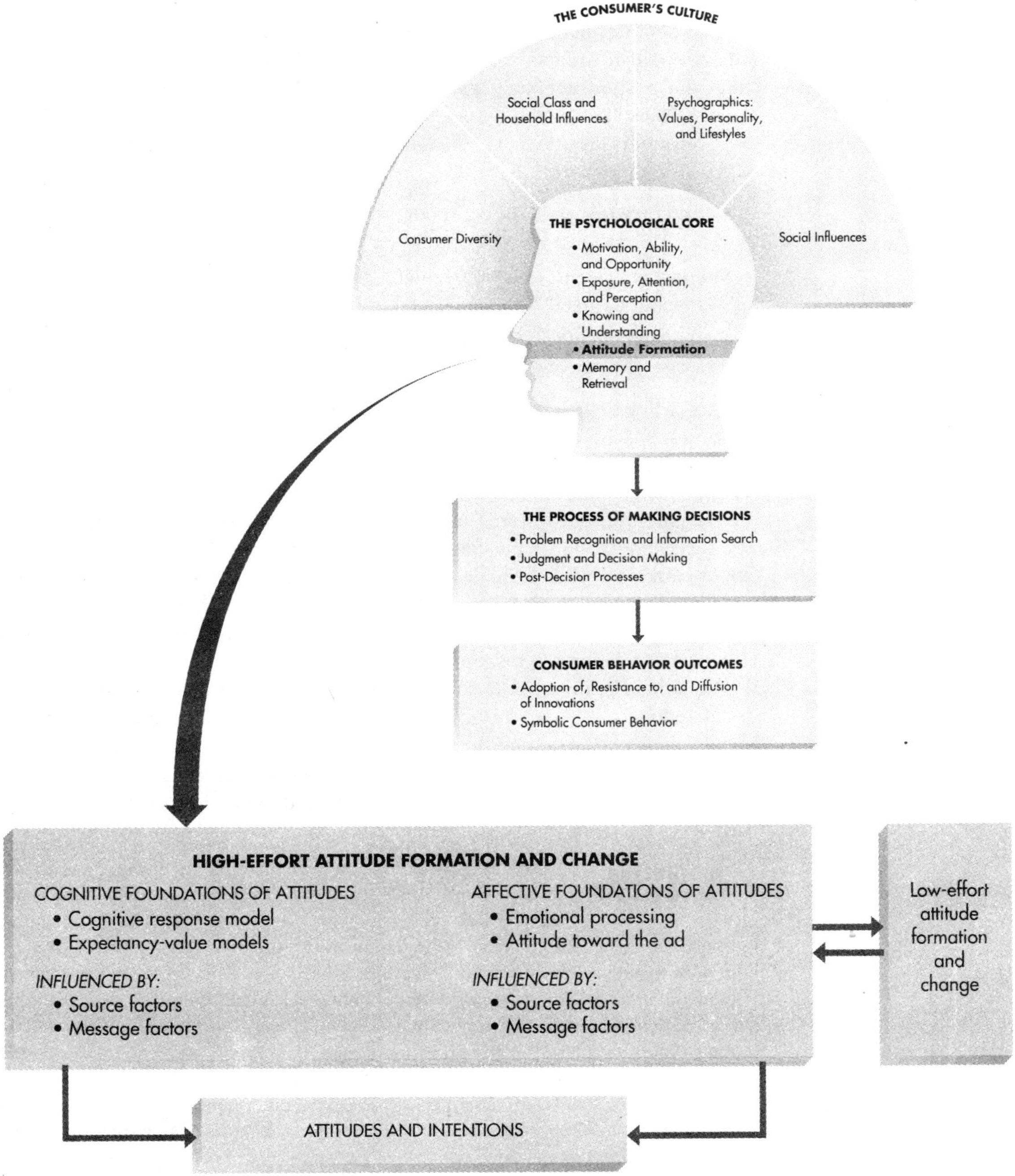

Exhibit 6.3

CHAPTER OVERVIEW: ATTITUDE FORMATION AND CHANGE, HIGH CONSUMER EFFORT *Following the first two stages (exposure, attention, and perception; and knowledge and understanding), consumers can either form or change their attitudes. This chapter explains how consumers form high-effort attitudes based on both cognition and affect. It also shows how marketers can influence attitudes through source factors (credibility, company reputation, and similarity) and message factors (argument quality, emotional appeals, etc.).*

ad for the impotency drug Cialis. In response to this ad, he might think, "I really need a product like this," "This product will never work," or "The guy in the ad was paid to praise this product." The cognitive response model predicts that these spontaneously generated responses will influence his attitude toward Cialis.[10]

Consumers' cognitive responses to communications can be classified in three ways:

- ***Counterarguments (CAs)*** are thoughts that express disagreement with the message ("This product will never work" or "This product will not cure my problem").
- ***Support arguments (SAs)*** are thoughts that express agreement with the message ("This sounds great" or "I really need a product like this").
- ***Source derogations (SDs)*** are thoughts that discount or attack the source of the message ("The guy is lying" or "The guy in the ad was paid to say this").

According to the cognitive response model, these responses affect consumers' attitudes. Specifically, counterarguments and source derogations result in a less favorable initial attitude or resistance to attitude change. In the Cialis example, thoughts like "It will never work" or "The guy was paid to say this" are likely to lead to a negative attitude toward Cialis. Thus consumers do not blindly accept and follow suggestions made in persuasive messages; rather, they can use their knowledge about marketers' goals or tactics to effectively cope with or resist these messages.[11] In fact, consumers do think about how marketers try to influence consumer behavior—and, in turn, these thoughts allow consumers to formulate counterarguments or support arguments in response to marketing activities.[12]

Note that the presence of support arguments results in positive attitudes. As a result, thoughts like "This sounds great" or "I really need something like this" tend to create a more positive attitude toward the offering. According to the cognitive response model, consumers exert a lot of effort in responding to the message—enough effort to generate counterarguments, support arguments, and source derogations.

marketing IMPLICATIONS Although marketers want consumers to be exposed to and comprehend their marketing messages, they also want consumers' responses to be positive instead of negative. Consumers who generate counterarguments and source derogations will have weak or even negative attitudes toward an offering. Marketers can combat this problem by testing marketing communications for cognitive responses before placing ads in the media. By asking consumers to think aloud while they view the ad or to write down their thoughts right after seeing it, marketers can classify the responses, identify problems, and strengthen the message.

Consumers tend to generate more counterarguments and fewer support arguments when message content differs from what they already believe. Thus a message supporting handgun control will generate a lot of counterarguments among National Rifle Association members. This ***belief discrepancy*** creates more counterarguments because consumers want to maintain their existing belief structures and do so by arguing against the message.[13] Consumers also generate more counterarguments and fewer support arguments when the message is weak. For example, saying that Gillette disposable razors come in many colors is not a strong and compelling reason to buy one. In such a situation, consumers may derogate the source (Gillette) or generate counterarguments ("Who cares about color?").[14]

In contrast, consumers come up with more support arguments and fewer counterarguments when they are involved with the TV program in which a commercial appears. In such cases, the program distracts consumers from counterarguing, thereby enhancing the persuasive impact of the message.[15] Finally, consumers react more favorably to communications when they are in a good mood: they often want to preserve this mood, so they resist counterarguing.[16]

Expectancy-Value Models

Expectancy-value models explain how consumers form and change attitudes based on (1) the beliefs or knowledge they have about an object or action and (2) their evaluation of these particular beliefs.[17] According to this model, you might like a Volkswagen because you believe it is reliable, modestly priced, and stylish—and you think it is good for a car to have these traits.

A variety of expectancy-value models have been proposed in psychology and marketing. These models differ in terms of the components of attitude and how these components should be measured. They also differ in whether they examine consumers' evaluation of a product attribute or its importance.

The ***theory of reasoned action (TORA)*** provides an expanded picture of how, when, and why attitudes predict consumer behavior. Exhibit 6.4 and the "Components of the TORA Model" feature explain the basic concepts and show how they are applied. Although research suggests that TORA applies to consumers in different cultures, the power of the model is stronger with U.S. consumers.[18]

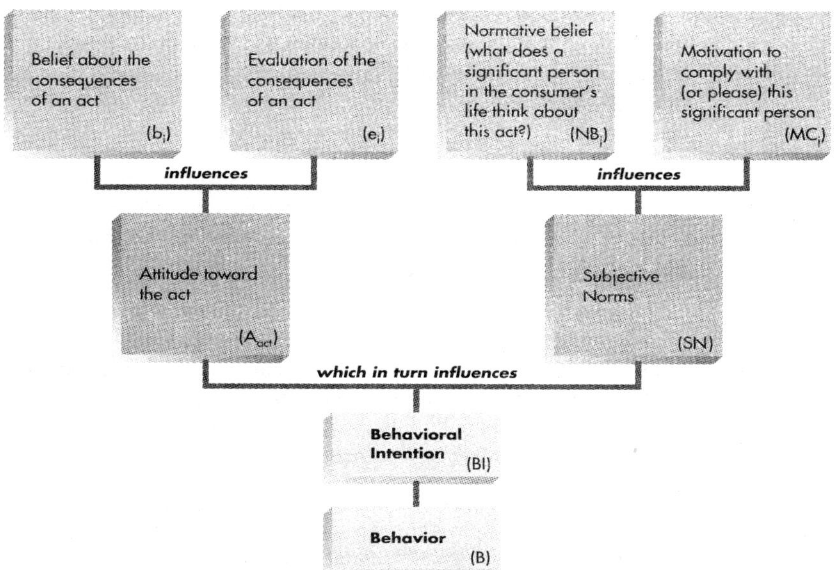

Exhibit 6.4

THE THEORY OF REASONED ACTION *According to TORA, behavior is a function of our intent to behave (BI), which is determined by our attitude toward performing that behavior (A_{act}) as well as the influence of others' opinions (SN). To form A_{act}, the beliefs we have about the consequences of performing the behavior (b_i) are multiplied by an evaluation of the consequences (e_i) and summed. Similarly, SN is a function of beliefs about what important people think (NB_j) and the motivation to comply with these people (MC_j). The Components of the TORA Model exhibit on pages 132–133 shows these concepts in action.*

The TORA model improves on previous models in several important ways. First, it incorporates the principle of ***attitude specificity;*** that is, the more specific the attitude is to the behavior of interest, the more likely the attitude will be related to the behavior. This means that if we are trying to understand consumers' acquisition, usage, and disposition behaviors, we will be more successful if we examine attitudes toward engaging in these behaviors as opposed to attitudes toward offerings in general. Thus knowing a consumer's attitude toward *buying* a Volkswagen should predict car purchase behavior better than the attitude toward the *object itself* (the Volkswagen).

Second, the TORA model looks not only at how consumers' attitudes are formed or changed but also at how other people in the social environment influence consumer behavior. In some situations, ***normative influences*** from others can play a powerful role in how people behave. For example, if you had a positive attitude toward signing an organ donation card, you still might not do so because you thought your parents would be horrified. Normative influences can also make you behave a certain way despite your negative attitude toward doing something. You might have a negative attitude toward eating fast food but do so anyway because of pressure from your friends.

Third, rather than trying to explain behavior per se, the TORA model seeks to predict the intention (tendency) to act. Thus rather than trying to predict whether you will actually buy a Toyota, the TORA model seeks to predict whether you will *intend* to buy one. Trying to predict behavioral intentions from attitudes is much easier than trying to predict actual behaviors because many situational factors could cause a consumer not to engage in an intended behavior.[19] For example, you may *intend* to buy a Volkswagen, but you do not because you are short of money. In addition, an extension of TORA known as the theory of planned behavior seeks to predict behaviors over which consumers have incomplete control by examining perceived behavioral control.[20]

marketing IMPLICATIONS

The TORA model helps marketers understand not only what attitudes consumers have but also why consumers have these attitudes and how attitudes can be changed.

Diagnosing existing attitudes

Marketers can use the TORA model to understand why consumers may like or dislike an offering and whether consumers want to engage in or resist a behavior. In particular, this model can help marketers understand a brand's perceived strengths and weaknesses and identify other influential people who might also be targeted (based on their beliefs and their influence over others). Analyzing these factors is a useful way for marketers to diagnose their products' performance in the marketplace.

Devising strategies for attitude change

This model also provides very useful guidance on how marketers can change attitudes, intentions, and (marketers hope) behavior through four major strategies:

1. *Change beliefs.* One possible strategy would be to change the strength of the beliefs that consumers associate with the consequences of acquiring an offering. Specifically, marketers could try to (1) strengthen beliefs that the offering possesses positive, important consequences or (2) lessen the belief that there are negative consequences. Although marketers commonly use this strategy when consumers are more likely to consider the message, it is difficult to induce such a change when consumers have strong prior beliefs. For instance, Anchor, a popu-

Components of the TORA Model

The most basic proposition of the model is that **behavior (B)** is a function of a person's **behavioral intention (BI)**, which in turn is determined by (1) the person's **attitude toward the act (A_{act})** and (2) the **subjective norms (SN)** that operate in the situation. The model then specifies what affects these two components. Consistent with most expectancy-value models, A_{act} is determined by the consumer's *beliefs* (b_i) about the consequences of engaging in the behavior and the consumer's *evaluation* (e_i) of these consequences. Subjective norms are determined by the consumer's *normative beliefs* (NB_i)—or what the consumer thinks someone else wants him or her to do—and the consumer's *motivation to comply* (MC_j) with this person.

Here is an example to clarify how the model works. First we identify the consumer's most important beliefs about the consequences of engaging in the behavior. Suppose a consumer named David would like to take skydiving lessons and his beliefs about the consequences are that it will be fun, educational, dangerous, and possibly cost a lot of money. Thus we have determined what beliefs (b_i) David has about skydiving lessons, and we have determined that he has four of them ($i = 4$). These beliefs can vary in terms of how strongly they are held, and this can be assessed using a subjective probability scale ranging from –3 (very unlikely) to +3 (very likely) (see the exhibit on the opposite page). We can see that David thinks it is very likely that skydiving lessons will be fun ($b_1 = +3$), somewhat likely they will be educational ($b_2 = +2$) and dangerous ($b_3 = +2$), and slightly likely that they will cost a lot of money ($b_4 = +1$). Each consequence can now be evaluated in terms of how desirable (how bad [–3] to good [+3]) it is. The exhibit on the next page shows that David rates the consequences of potential danger and cost as negative ($e_3 = -3$ and $e_4 = -1$) but rates the fun and educational aspects positively ($e_1 = +3$ and $e_2 = +2$). To determine David's attitude toward taking skydiving lessons (A_{act}), multiply each belief strength rating (b_i) by its associated evaluation rating (e_i) and add these multiplied totals (as specified by the model). From these computations, we can see that David has a positive attitude toward taking skydiving lessons ($A_{act} = +6$).

To predict behavioral intentions, however, we must also examine David's subjective perceptions of the normative influences, also known as subjective norms. There are likely to be people whose opinions and beliefs will affect what David does. We see in the exhibit that there are four people ($j = 4$) whose opinions matter to David. He can estimate whether each person believes he should or should not take the lessons. This is the normative belief (NB_j) component. We see in the exhibit that David's father is somewhat negative about it ($NB_1 = -1$) and his mother is very negative ($NB_2 = -3$), but his two friends think he should take the lessons ($NB_3 = +1$ and $NB_4 = +3$). David can also think about how motivated he is to comply with the beliefs of each person mentioned (the MC_j component). As shown in the exhibit, these components are also measured on a seven-point subjective probability scale. In this case David is motivated to comply with each person, particularly his girlfriend ($MC_3 = +3$). To determine the subjective norm (SN), we multiply each NB by its associated MC and then add these products. Here, the SN is positive but near zero, meaning that David is likely to feel some ambivalence about normative influence because the opinions of these other people are contradictory.

Finally, the model predicts that behavioral intentions (BI) are determined by the combination of a person's attitudes (A_{act}) and the normative influences that operate in the situation (SN). In this case David is likely to take the lessons because his attitudes are positive and, overall, others have slightly positive feelings about him doing so. Note that A_{act} and SN do not always have an equal impact on BI. In some cases, consumers' behavioral intentions are guided more by what they think (A_{act}); in other cases, they are guided more by the opinions of others (SN).

APPLYING THE THEORY OF REASONED ACTION

Here TORA is used to determine David's intention of taking skydiving lessons. His attitude toward the act (A_{act}) is a function of his beliefs about the consequences (e.g., it will be fun, educational, etc.) as well as his evaluation of these consequences. The strengths of his beliefs are rated on a likelihood scale from –3 to +3 (how likely will skydiving be fun, educational, etc.). His evaluations about these beliefs are rated on a scale of very bad (–3) to very good (+3). For example, it is very good that skydiving is fun; it is very bad that skydiving is dangerous. These numbers are multiplied and added to get a +6 (a positive attitude toward the act of taking skydiving lessons). Another aspect of the model (SN) is based on the opinions of important people in David's life as well as how much he values these opinions. These are also multiplied and summed to get a score of +1. Thus, David is likely to feel some ambivalence about taking lessons because the opinions of significant persons in his life are contradictory.

A_{act}

Skydiving lessons will be...	b_i	e_i	$b_i \times e_i$
fun	+3	+3	+9
educational	+2	+2	+4
dangerous	+2	–3	–6
expensive	+1	–1	–1
			A_{act} = +6

b_i The likelihood that skydiving lessons will be... (fun, educational, dangerous, expensive).

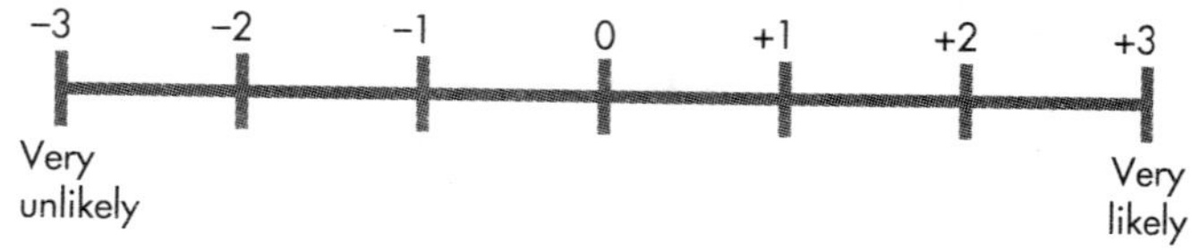

e_i If skydiving is... (fun, educational, dangerous, expensive), this is good.

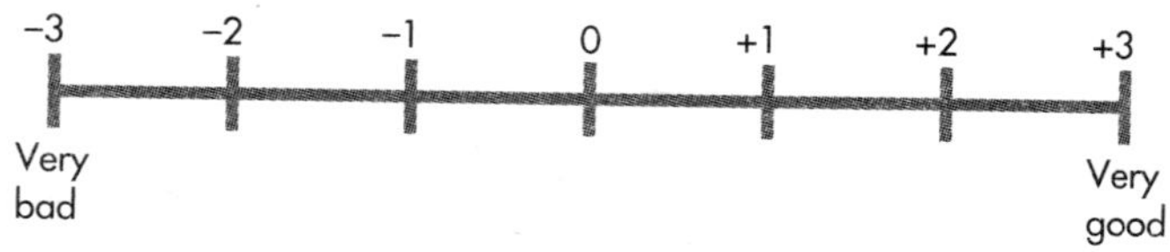

SN (Subjective Norms)

What do significant others think (NB_j) and how much do I care (MC_j)?	NB_j	MC_j	$NB_j \times MC_j$
Mother	–3	+2	–6
Father	–1	+2	–2
Girlfriend	+1	+3	+3
Best friend	+3	+2	+6
			SN = +1

NB_j What significant people think I should do

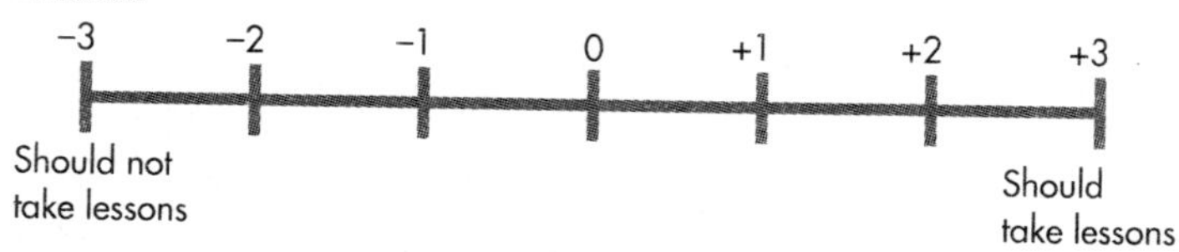

MC_j How much do I care about what these people think?

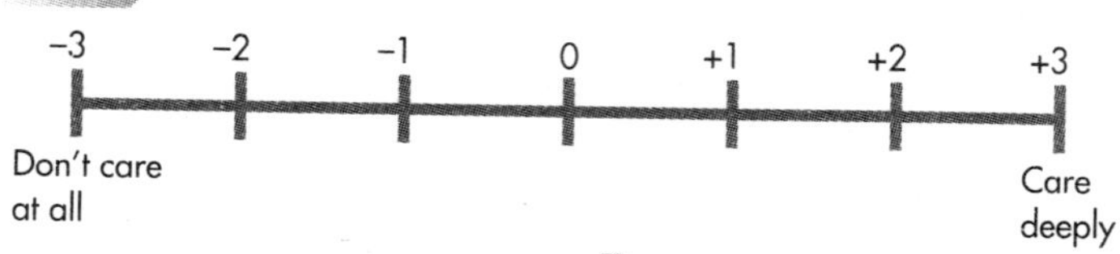

larly known company in electrical equipments related to retail markets had a long standing reputation, at least in the branded segment, where most competitors were local and quality remained a concern. The same company decided to move to the dental care market, initially with toothpastes. This was a major challenge for the company, since consumers knew Anchor more as a company into electrical devices. Brand extension in this case meant removal of consumer mental blocks about Anchor and then establish it as a toothpaste company also. However, the toothpaste market is a high growth high investment market, where brands like Colgate, Pepsodent and Close-Up were the big three, ruling the roost. There were umpteen number of regional and niche brands who operated in the periphery trying to make a mark. Anchor believed that entering into an unrelated market such as toothpaste, with a known name will at least create some associations in the consumer's mind, as alternatively launching a new brand in a such an intensive market would be a task far more time consuming and difficult to establish.

With the growth in the banking sector and the advent of the private players like HDFC, ICICI, ABN Amro etc. to name a few, the pressure to perform on the nationalized banks has also increased. Efficient customer services, banking after banking hours, 24- hours banking, net banking and a host of features offered by these private banks have truly defined the nature and approach of banking in India. The challenge, however is for the nationalized banks who have been trying to cope with such winds of change and realign themselves with the new order.

2. Change evaluations. Another strategy for changing attitudes is to change consumers' evaluations of the consequences. Consumers' attitudes become more positive when their beliefs are more positive or less negative. The NECC (National Egg Coordination Committee) campaign on "Sunday Ho Ya Monday, Roz khao Ande" was a campaign developed in the late 80's as an effort to encourage audiences to eat egg. In an orthodox and religiously inclined society like India, egg is a non-vegetarian platter and our per capita consumption of egg is one of the lowest in the world, at 37 eggs. However, domestic production of eggs at 37 billion eggs makes us the fifth largest producer of eggs in the world. With such surplus, NECC's effort to encourage more and more people to eat eggs was chiefly to offset the rising production and falling prices. The campaign focused with a humor laced appeal to consider the goodness of egg and the endless ways of preparing eggs in different ways. NECC also came out with a recipe book for egg lovers.

3. *Add a new belief.* A third strategy is to add a new belief altogether; adding another set of positive beliefs would make the consumer's attitude more positive. This strategy is particularly effective when a brand has inferior existing features, lower perceived quality, or a higher price compared with its competitors.[25] Note that adding novel attributes to a low-complexity product is likely to encourage positive beliefs and a more positive attitude toward that product.[26] A good example of this strategy is presented in Exhibit 6.5.

4. *Target normative beliefs.* A fourth strategy is to develop communications that specifically target strong normative beliefs as a way of influencing behavior. Seagram's campaign for party revelers during New Year focused on how groups take turns to drink so that drinking and driving is not mixed. Within a group, if some people drink, then at least one in the group drinks responsibly or as per traffic norms, so that everybody can enjoy and party. On the other hand, condom ads have been unsuccessful in increasing sales because they have *not* stressed normative beliefs (what others will think of you if you don't use them).[28] Note that the importance of normative beliefs varies across cultures. In countries that stress group values over the individual (such as Japan, among other Asian nations), appeals to normative beliefs take on greater significance.[29]

How Cognitively Based Attitudes Are Influenced

In the previous sections, you saw how cognitive responses and beliefs can affect consumers' attitudes. In this section, you will see how marketing communications can affect consumers' cognitively based attitudes when the processing effort is extensive. As Exhibit 6.2 shows, the communication source and the message influence how favorable an attitude will be.

Communication Source

Among consumers who process information extensively, those with attitudes based on cognitions are likely to be influenced by believable information. This means marketing messages must be credible to generate support arguments, restrict counterarguments and source derogations, and increase belief strength. Several factors, including source credibility and company reputation, enhance the credibility of a message.

Exhibit 6.5
MAHARASHTRA UNLIMITED
Most people's perception about Maharashtra is restricted to Mumbai and images that conjure of a typical city life. The tourism campaign highlighted other places of interest in the state.

Source Credibility In many marketing messages, information is presented by a spokesperson, usually a celebrity, an actor, a company representative, or a real consumer. In a sales situation, the salesperson is a spokesperson for the company and the offering. Both the ***credibility*** of these sources and the credibility of the company influence consumers' attitudes.[30] According to research, consumers tend to evaluate product information more thoughtfully when source credibility is low than when source credibility is high.[31]

In general, sources are credible when they have one or more of three characteristics: trustworthiness, expertise, and status. First, someone who is perceived as trustworthy is more likely to be believed than someone who is not. Because consumers tend to see other consumers' opinions as less biased than persuasive words from official sources, mouthshut.com, pagaalguy.com, and other websites invite consumers to post reviews of offerings and read reviews that others have posted.

Second, we are more likely to accept a message from someone who is perceived as knowledgeable or *an expert* about the topic than from someone who has no experience with it. For this reason, a salesperson who demonstrates extensive product knowledge will be more credible than an uninformed one. Third, someone with a high position or status in society can also be perceived as credible, which is why many firms feature their CEOs or founders in ads. As a part of their global initiative and to showcase energy independence, Ford is planning to launch a series of advertisements showcasing their Chairman and CEO Bill Ford. Bill Ford talks about how Ford has been trying to reduce the trips to the petrol pumps and help gain better mileage on the cars. The advertisement also features the Ford Escape Hybrid and Bill Ford's pledge to make 250,000 ethanol-capable vehicles. The series is to start from North America and extend globally into countries where Ford has its operations. In Latin America, having products endorsed by famous and respected people is an effective technique, particularly in Venezuela and Mexico. Pepsi, for example, features the Latin pop star Shakira in some Spanish-language ads.[34]

Research has shown that credible sources have considerable impact on consumers' acceptance of the message when consumers' prior attitudes are negative, when the message deviates greatly from their prior beliefs, when the message is complex or difficult to understand, and when there is a good "match" between the product and endorser, as between soccer star David Beckham and the Adidas shoes he promotes.[35] Moreover, source credibility can influence consumer attitudes by influencing consumers' confidence in their thoughts about the ad message.[36] On the other hand, credible sources have less impact when consumers hold their existing attitude with confidence (so even a credible source will not convince them otherwise) and when they have a high degree of ability to generate their own conclusions from the message (they have a lot of product-relevant knowledge, particularly if based on direct experience).[37] Also, consumers are less likely to believe that a source is credible when the source (e.g., a celebrity) endorses multiple products.[38]

marketing IMPLICATIONS Amitabh Bachchan and Sachin Tendulkar have been successful endorsers because consumers perceive these celebrities as honest and successful in their respective fields. Likewise, consumers might perceive a salesperson who has an "honest face" as a credible source of information. Interestingly, a simple two-word ad in the *Wall Street Journal* that stated "Honest Stockbroker" attracted a number of clients.[40] Ordinary people can also be perceived as credible endorsers. Companies such as Tata Steel, Fortis Hospitals and India Post have featured employees in their advertising campaigns because the employees add realism and, in many cases, are similar to the target market. In addition, Latin American consumers tend to give positive evaluations to ads featuring real people.[42]

Because of their skill, sports figures like Sachin Tendulkar and M.S. Dhoni have been successful expert sources for athletic apparel and equipment, as well as other products. Expert sources can also be popular, another factor that can contribute to an effective ad. Interestingly, one survey indicated that women endorsers are often seen as more popular and credible than male endorsers.[44] However, the company or product risks losing some credibility if a celebrity endorser gets into trouble or quits.

A low-credibility source *can* be effective in some circumstances. In particular, if a low-credibility source argues against his or her own self-interest, positive attitude change can result.[45] Political ads, for example, often feature a member of the opposing party who endorses a rival candidate. In addition, the impact of a low-credibility source can actually increase over time (assuming a powerful message). This ***sleeper effect*** occurs because the memory of the source can decay more rapidly than the memory of the message.[46] Thus consumers may remember the message but not the source.

Company Reputation When marketing communications do not feature an actual person, consumers judge credibility by the reputation of the company delivering the message.[47] People are more likely to believe—and change their attitudes based on—messages from companies that have a reputation for producing quality products, for dealing fairly with consumers, or for being trustworthy. On the Internet, a company can enhance its reputation and engender positive reactions by sponsoring content on relevant websites; banner ads that are highly targeted to a site's audience can elicit positive attitudes toward the company, as well.[48] More specifically, a brand's perceived trustworthiness exerts more influence on consumers' consideration and behavior than its expertise.[49]

marketing IMPLICATIONS Knowing that reputation influences consumer perceptions and credibility, many companies devote considerable time and money to developing a positive image through corporate advertising. As Exhibit 6.6 shows, specific aspects of a company's reputation—such as its environmental record and its treatment of employees—can affect buyers' attitudes and behavior. Many companies use advertising and public relations to communicate their involvement in environmental initiatives, thereby polishing their corporate images. For instance, the energy company BP has spent millions of dollars on its image-building "Beyond Petroleum" ad campaign, which focuses on the firm's environmental conservation efforts.

The Message

Just as consumers evaluate whether the source is credible when their processing effort is high, they also evaluate whether the message is credible. Three factors affect the credibility of a message: the quality of its argument, whether it is a one-sided or two-sided message, and whether it is a comparative message.

Argument Quality One of the most critical factors affecting whether a message is credible concerns whether it uses strong arguments.[50] ***Strong arguments*** present the best features or central merits of an offering in a convincing manner. SAIL has been consistently speaking of "There's a little bit of SAIL in everybody's life", a message strongly represented through the visuals showcasing use of steel in our daily lives. Messages can also present supporting endorsements or research such as the *Good Housekeeping* Seal or *Consumer's Digest* Best Buy designation (see Exhibit 6.7). Strong arguments are likely to be more persuasive if consumers are exposed to such messages after thinking about what they could have done differently to avoid a purchasing experience that led to an undesirable outcome.[51] Strong arguments also have a greater effect on behavioral intentions when consumers focus on the process of using the product rather than on the outcome of using it, especially for low- to moderate-involvement products.[52] In particular, the combination of a strong argument plus implicit conclusion in an ad message engenders more favorable brand attitudes and buying intensions among consumers with a high need for cognition.[53]

GOOD COMPANY

Whereas Westerners have a reputation for being earthy, Northeasterners are actually more impressed by companies known for being eco-friendly.

Percentage of Americans who say that the following factors influence their decision to buy a given product:

	GENDER		REGION			
	Men	**Women**	**Northeast**	**Midwest**	**South**	**West**
Safe for the environment	76%	84%	83%	81%	78%	80%
Company is known for using environmentally friendly practices	65%	75%	78%	71%	68%	67%
Company is known for treating workers well	62%	69%	67%	63%	69%	60%
Portion of sale goes to charity	46%	62%	53%	58%	56%	50%

Source: Reprinted with permission from the October 2003 issue of *American Demographics*. Copyright Crain Communications, Inc. 2003.

Exhibit 6.6
IS THE COMPANY ECO-FRIENDLY?

Consumers vary in terms of the importance of eco-friendliness in their decisions depending on gender and region of the country.

Infomercials—commercial messages that can last 30 to 60 minutes—allow companies enough time to fully explain complicated, technologically advanced, or innovative goods and services. Pidilite Industries recently launched a series of infomercials showcasing the product's unique attributes and demonstrating the product application. Celebrities are also showcased as a part of the infomercials to bring the image factor. 'Cadbury's has a complete webisodes featuring the meetha moments' episodes that look like a possible extension of the advertisements that they showcase. Sunsilk, a popular brand of shampoo has launched its own blog site, sunsilkgangofgirls.com which features a complete list of things which girls can do while on the site, including chats, starting online forums and even watch interactive gog tv.

marketing IMPLICATIONS

If messages are weak and not very compelling, consumers are unlikely to think they offer credible reasons for buying. Saying that you should buy a particular brand of mattress because it comes in decorator fabrics is not very convincing. Nevertheless, messages do not always have to focus on substantive features of the product or service. Less important features can actually play a key role in influencing attitudes when brands are similar and many competitors emphasize the same important attributes.[57] Also, a message should match the amount of effort consumers want to use to process it. A message that is either too simple or too complicated is unlikely to be persuasive.[58]

Exhibit 6.7
ARGUMENT QUALITY
When a company announces that its products or services have won awards or endorsements, the company's advertising can become more credible and convincing to consumers.

One- Versus Two-Sided Messages Most marketing messages present only positive information. These are called ***one-sided messages.*** In some instances, however, a ***two-sided message,*** containing both positive and negative information about an offering, can be effective. For example, Buckley's Mixture has captured 12 percent of the Canadian cough syrup market using blunt two-sided ad messages such as "It tastes awful. And it works" and "Relief is just a yuck away."[59] Like strong message arguments, two-sided messages may affect attitudes by making the message more credible (that is, they increase belief strength) and reducing counterarguments. When consumers see negative information in an ad, they are likely to infer that the company must be honest, which adds to source credibility.[60] By providing reasons for consumers to be interested in the offering despite these problems, the ad encourages consumers to add a new belief.

marketing IMPLICATIONS

Two-sided messages seem to be particularly effective when (1) consumers are initially opposed to the offering (they already have negative beliefs) or (2) they will be exposed to strong countermessages from competitors.[61] Two-sided messages are also well received by more intelligent consumers who prefer messages that are neutral and unbiased. Not long ago, the Hardee's restaurant chain aired a campaign that both acknowledged consumers' complaints and trumpeted the introduction of Thickburgers. The campaign's slogan, "It's how the last place you'd go for a burger will become the first," was a direct appeal to transform negative attitudes into positive attitudes.[62] However, the use of two-sided advertising is not always in the marketer's best interest. In general, the positive effects of two-sided messages on brand attitudes occur only if the negative message is about an attribute that is not extremely important.

Comparative Messages ***Comparative messages*** show how much better the offering is than a competitor's. Two types of comparative messages have been identified.[63] The most common type is the *indirect comparative message,* in which the offering is compared with unnamed competitors (such as "other leading brands" or "Brand X"). For example, Suzuki introduced its midsize XL-7 sport-utility vehicle using ads that poked fun at the impracticalities of larger, competing sport-utility vehicles. The headline "We're big (for a Suzuki), but not too big" reinforced the comparison.[64] This strategy can improve consumers' perceptions of a moderate-share brand relative to other moderate-share brands (but not the market leader).[65]

With *direct comparative advertising,* advertisers explicitly name and attack a competitor or set of competitors on the basis of an attribute or benefit. This approach is usually used when the offering has a feature that is purportedly better than that of a competitor's. Not long ago, Cingular Wireless aired an ad comparing the size of its high-speed data network and five other service features to those of rival Verizon and inviting consumers to "just look at the facts."[66] Salespeople in a personal-selling situation frequently use this technique to convince consumers of the advantages of their brand over the competition. Comparative advertising is also used in political advertising, where it generates more counterarguments and fewer source derogations than negative political advertising. This may be due to the different styles of information processing that the two types of messages encourage.[67] However, in the case of political advertising, consumers exposed to negative messages find them less useful for decision making and have more negative attitudes toward political campaigns than consumers exposed to positive political advertising.[68]

In general, research shows that direct comparative messages are effective in generating attention and brand awareness and positively increasing message processing, attitudes, intentions, and behavior (see Exhibit 6.8).[69] They do not, however, have high credibility, as noted earlier. These messages are particularly effective for new brands or for those with a low market share that are attempting to take sales away from more popular brands.[70] Essentially, the new or low-share brand can enhance attitudes by highlighting how it is different from or better than other brands—which gives consumers a credible reason for purchasing the brand. In fact, comparative advertising that stresses differentiation can spur consumers to note the dissimilarities with competing brands.[71] Messages in which the two brands being compared are perceived as dissimilar will elicit more elaboration, especially among consumers with a low need for cognition, precisely because the brands are different.[72] Comparative messages are especially effective when they contain other elements that make them believable—such as a credible source or objective and verifiable claims (a strong argument)[73]—and when the featured attribute or benefit is important within the product category.[74]

Research shows that consumers who originally receive information in a noncomparative message and are then exposed to a comparative message will revise their evaluations more than when subsequently exposed to another noncomparative message. The reverse is also true: consumers who originally receive information in a comparative message and are then exposed to a noncomparative message will revise their evaluative judgments to a greater degree than when subsequently exposed to another comparative message.[75]

Exhibit 6.8
COMPARATIVE ADVERTISING
Subhiksha has been trying to showcase the lowest prices by doing a comparison with other supermarkets and kirana stores and thereby bringing out the price differentials for discerning consumers to judge on their own.

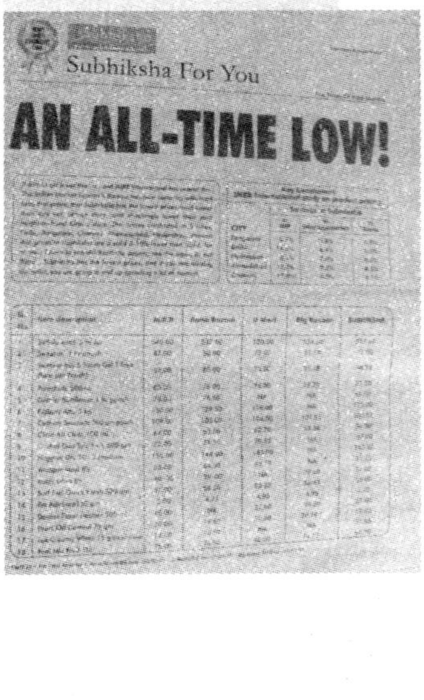

marketing IMPLICATIONS

Direct comparative messages are best used when consumers' MAO to process the message is high. When MAO is high, consumers exert more effort in processing the message and are less likely to confuse the advertised brand with its competition.[76] Marketers must also be careful that all information contained in the message is factual and verifiable; otherwise, competitors may consider taking legal action. In addition, although it is widely used in the United States and Latin America, comparative advertising is illegal in some countries and closely regulated in the European Union.[77] And some consumers do not like comparative advertising. Japanese consumers, for example, respond better to a softer sell than they do to comparative ads.[78] Finally, advertising that compares a company's new, improved product to the same company's original product will be effective only when the improved functions are seen as atypical for that product. Otherwise, consumers are likely to discount the novelty of the new functionality.[79]

The Affective (Emotional) Foundations of Attitudes

Most of the consumer research on attitudes when MAO and processing effort are high has focused on the cognitive models of attitude formation. Now, however, researchers are recognizing that consumers might exert a lot of mental energy in processing a message on an emotional basis. Emotional reactions, independent of cognitive structure, may serve as a powerful way of creating attitudes that are favorable, enduring, and resistant to change.[80] This section examines when and how attitudes can be changed through consumers' feelings when MAO and processing effort are high.

When ***affective involvement*** with an object or decision is high, consumers can experience fairly strong emotional reactions to a stimulus. These feelings can, in turn, influence attitudes. In this case the consumer's *feelings* act as a source of information, and consumers will rely on these feelings to evaluate the stimulus.[81] Feelings are more likely to play a key role in attitude change when they fit with or are viewed as relevant to the product or service being offered.[82] For example, someone who is in love might have a *more positive attitude* toward an expensive perfume or a nice restaurant than someone who is not experiencing this emotion. Feelings can also be a factor when consumers see others experiencing strong emotion while using an offering or when situational factors hamper the consumer's effort to develop a cognitive attitude.[83] Thus consumers under severe time pressure could simply recall a previous emotional experience rather than develop a cognitive attitude.

In marketing situations, certain factors can activate experiences or episodes from memory that may be associated with strong emotions.[84] For example, you might experience positive emotions such as joy and excitement if you suddenly see an ad for the car you have just bought. If you are a dog lover, you might experience affective involvement toward a message featuring a cute dog. Several book shops try and provide personalized services to the customers, by making personal recommendations to them. Usually such book shops are set up by entrepreneurs more for the love of books, than for commercial purposes. Book lovers and buyers prefer visiting such outlets as purchase process is more fulfilling and satisfying. Book shops in Delhi like Fact & Fiction are case in point of such types of outlet.

Exhibit 6.9
AN EMOTIONAL APPEAL
This ad used feelings and emotions to sell a high-technology product. Rather than stressing technical aspects (the cognitive approach), this ad is emphasizing emotions such as happiness, excitement, and "being spirited." Can you think of other products or services that could be sold in a simular manner?

When consumers are emotionally involved in a message, they tend to process it on a general level rather than analytically.[86] This process involves the generation of images or feelings, called ***affective responses*** (or ARs),[87] rather than cognitive responses. Affective responses are particularly important when the ad builds toward a "peak emotional experience."[88] Consumers can either recall an emotional experience from memory or vicariously place themselves in the situation and experience the emotions associated with it.[89] These feelings will then influence attitudes. For example, Kodak's "Share Moments, Share Life" ad campaign reminds consumers of the positive feelings generated by pictures of family and friends.[90] In addition, consumers focused on goals such as their hopes and aspirations tend to rely on their affective responses to an ad, whereas consumers focused on their responsibilities and obligations tend to rely more on message content.[91]

Cross-cultural differences can also influence the effectiveness of ***emotional appeals.*** One study found that messages evoking ego-focused responses (such as pride or happiness) led to more favorable attitudes in group-oriented cultures, whereas empathetic messages led to more positive attitudes in individualist cultures.[92] The reason for this apparent reversal is that the novelty or uniqueness of these appeals increases the motivation to process and consider the message.

Negative emotions can sometimes have a positive effect on attitude change. In one study the exposure to a public service announcement about child abuse initially created negative emotions (sadness, anger, fear) but then led to a feeling of empathy, and this response led to a decision to help.[93] In addition, consumers can actively try to avoid decisions associated with strong negative emotions by making choices to minimize these emotions.[94]

Note that cognition can still influence whether experienced feelings will affect consumer attitudes. For feelings to have a direct impact on attitudes, consumers must cognitively link them to the offering.[95] To illustrate, if you saw a bank ad showing a tender scene of a father holding his baby, you might experience an immediate emotional response (warmth and joy). However, this feeling will affect your attitude toward the bank only if you consciously make a connection between the feeling and the bank ("This bank makes me feel good" or "I like this bank because it cares about people"). Also, an advertising message that relies on emotional appeal will be more effective in helping heavy users of the product access the brand name than in helping light users access the brand name.[96]

marketing IMPLICATIONS

Marketers can try to influence emotions as a way of affecting consumer attitudes. In particular, marketers can try to ensure that the emotions experienced in a particular situation will be positive. Car salespeople, for example, often try to do everything possible to make customers happy so that they will develop positive attitudes toward the dealer and the car. The importance of creating positive emotions also explains why airlines, financial institutions, and other service providers place a high value on being friendly. In the recent spate of private airlines entering into fray through the Open Sky policy of the Civil Aviation Ministry, Kingfisher Airlines introduced itself in the full service airlines category. It has been continually featuring on product augmentation through in-flight experience, focusing on the food, in-flight entertainment and also the seating facilities, all in the economy class. The focus is to provide business class facilities to the customers at economy class rates, thereby putting pressure on other full service airlines to realign accordingly.

Marketing communications can potentially trigger strong emotions in consumers, although the ability to trigger these emotions is typically quite limited—ads are better at creating low-level moods than they are at creating intense emotions. Nevertheless, in situations where affective involvement in the product or service is often high, marketers may be able to generate the images and feelings necessary to change attitudes. This outcome most often occurs in product and service categories in which a strong pleasure-seeking or symbolic motivation is present—when feelings or symbolic meanings are critical. Mercedes has traded its informational advertising approach for a more emotional appeal. One ad depicts an intimate scene between a father and a son standing in a showroom, communicating that the car is durable enough to hand down from father to son.

How Affectively Based Attitudes Are Influenced

When MAO and effort are high and attitudes are affectively (emotionally) based, several strategies shown in Exhibit 6.2 can be employed to change attitudes. As with cognitively based attitudes, marketers can use characteristics of the source and the message to change consumers' attitudes by affecting their emotions.

The Source

Perceived ***attractiveness*** is an important source characteristic affecting high-effort emotionally based attitudes. Research on source attractiveness suggests that when consumers' MAO and effort are high, attractive sources tend to evoke favorable attitudes if the sources are appropriate for the offering category (e.g., a luxury automobile, fashion, cosmetics, and beauty treatments).[98] This effect has been called the ***match-up hypothesis*** (the source should match the offering). The relevant attractive source probably enhances attitudes, either by making the ad informative and likable or by affecting consumers' beliefs that the product must be good. A source that is attractive but not relevant can distract the consumer from the message's ideas.[99]

When golfer Tiger Woods agreed to endorse American Express, some observers wondered whether he could sell financial services; other believed that his image of success and hard work fit well with the company.[100] Still, research suggests that the match-up hypothesis may be even more powerful for expert sources than for attractive sources, which is why Tiger Woods's endorsement may be particularly effective for golf-related products.[101] When Woods unexpectedly switched from Nike clubs, which he promotes, to a competing brand, Nike responded by testing driver designs to address Woods's needs. In this case, publicity about Woods returning to Nike gear could give the brand a big boost.[102]

The relationship between attractiveness and attitude change applies to selling encounters as well. Consumers perceive physically attractive salespeople as having more favorable selling skills and are more likely to yield to their requests.[103] Customers also tend to be attracted to and buy from salespeople who are perceived as similar to themselves.[104]

marketing IMPLICATIONS Marketers need to remember that although attractiveness is most often thought of in terms of physical features, sources can also be attractive if they are perceived as similar, likable, or familiar (in terms of physical appearance or opinions).[105] Cricket is more of a religion in India and cricket stars enjoy god-like status in the country. Marketers have never missed out on opportunity to showcase successful and upcoming cricketers as endorsers, endorsing anything from cars to cola. The effect of the sports has even meant that several marketers have even gone ahead to use successful cricketers from other cricketing nations too, particularly, Australia. Brett Lee, Ricky Ponting to Wasim Akram, Shoaib Akhtar, Brian Lara, Stephen Fleming to name a few have all been featured selling some home grown brand. The status of such cricketers usually, are not restricted to a local sports hero, but goes beyond the national boundaries. A name like Shane Warne draws enough respect in India as much as it does in Australia. Given the popularity of the sports regionally, Sachin and Warne are considered in the same league.

The Message

Just as marketers can use characteristics of the source to understand and influence affective processing, they can also use characteristics of the message to influence consumers. In particular, emotional appeals and fear appeals are two important message characteristics.

Emotional Appeals Marketers sometimes attempt to influence consumers' attitudes by using appeals that elicit emotions such as love, desire, joy, hope, excitement, daring, fear, anger, shame, or rejection. Disgust can be a powerful emotion that, even when stimulated unintentionally through humor or another aspect of an ad message, can engender negative attitudes and purchase intensions toward a brand or company.[107] The positive emotions are intended to attract consumers to the offering, whereas the negatives are intended to create anxiety about what might happen if consumers do not use the offering.

Messages can also present situations that express positive emotions with the hope that consumers will vicariously experience these emotions. In these situations marketers can induce consumers to imagine how good the product will make them feel or look. As an example, one ad for the impotency drug Viagra shows a happy, dancing couple.[108] Similarly, McDonald's Happy Meals ads concentrate on the emotions surrounding this offering. "For parents, Happy Meal means happy memories; for kids, it means fun, favorite toys, and [entertainment] properties, and favorite food," explains a McDonald's executive. "The area between those is 'special moments,' which gave us the line 'Happy Meals for happy times.'"[109] Note that emotional appeals based on conflicting emotions (such as both happiness and sadness) can result in less favorable attitudes among consumers who are not as accepting of such contradictions.[110]

Yet, emotional appeals may limit the amount of product-related information consumers can process.[111] This is because consumers may be thinking more about feeling good than about the product's features, which inhibits cognition about the product and its benefits. Thus emotional appeals are more likely to be effective when the arousal of emotions relates to product consumption or usage, which is common when hedonic or symbolic motivations are important. [2]Maruti's traditional image of tried, tested and trusted was for long an adage that came with all the makes and models that it has launched. From Wagon-R to Alto, all Maruti models, are known for economy, wide service network and experience in small car efficiencies. However, the Swift launch was a radically different launch both for the company and also for the consumers who were used to a very different Maruti till then. One, the shape of the car in itself was quite unique. "It is a melting pot of Italian flair and French quirkiness," enthuses an auto analyst. Perhaps the Swift's biggest plus is its price. Introduced at Rs.387,000 for the base model, it was close to about Rs.50,000 less than its competitors. Even the top-end version was Rs.70,000 cheaper than the Hyundai Getz GLS. Another novel aspect about the car was the colours in which it was available. The conventional white colour was missing and instead, the car was available in two kinds of colours. Elegance colours -- gold, silver, black and azure grey; and energy colours orange, red, blue and green. The Suzuki name was put upfront and instead of calling it as Maruti Suzuki Swift, it was named as Suzuki Swift or simply Swift. The car received a very positive response and there was even a waiting time on the car. For a company that has been known more for its value-for-money proposition -- from the 800 to the Esteem -- that's important. "It's not as if our cars weren't style statements. It's just that with Swift, we have made a break from the past," reveals a company official. Research suggests that emotional appeals more effectively influence consumer behavior when the type of product being advertised has been on the market for some time (an old market). In contrast, ads featuring expert sources and strong arguments are more effective for younger markets.[113]

marketing IMPLICATIONS

Typically, marketers attempt to arouse emotions using techniques such as music, emotional scenes, visuals, sex, and attractive sources. Chevrolet Optra highlighted on the feature of sliding roof by using Karva Chauth, a popular North India festival, as the theme and the husband taking his wife on a drive and helping her see the moon through the sliding roof. A gesture on the husband's part as extremely touching and emotional and where the car feature elicits more spontaneity in the act. Note, however, that arousing emotions is a challenge unless the message has personal relevance.[115]

Fear Appeals ***Fear appeals*** attempt to elicit fear or anxiety by stressing the negative consequences of either engaging or not engaging in a particular behavior (see Exhibit 6.10). By arousing this fear, marketers hope consumers will be motivated to think about the message and behave in the desired manner.[116] Itchguard a popular skin cream from Paras Pharmaceuticals targets the fear factor of having an urge to itch in public or running for privacy to satisfy the urge and then being caught to face a bigger embarrassment. But is fear an effective appeal? Early studies found that fear appeals were ineffective because consumers' perceptual defense helped them block out and ignore the message (due to its threatening nature).[118] This research provides one explanation for why the surgeon general's warning on cigarette packages and ads has been largely ineffective. However, more recent research indicates that fear appeals can work under certain conditions.[119]

marketing IMPLICATIONS

When can fear appeals be effective? First, the appeal must suggest an immediate action that will reduce the fear. Second, the level of fear must be generally moderate.[120] If the fear induced is too intense (as it was in early studies), the consumers' perceptual defense will take over and the message will not have an impact. Third, at higher levels of involvement, lower levels of fear can be generated because the consumer has a higher motivation to process the information.[121] Factors such as personality, product usage, and socioeconomic status also have an impact on the effectiveness of fear appeals.[122] Finally, the source providing the information must be credible; otherwise, the consumer can easily discount the message by generating counterarguments and source derogations.

Attitude Toward the Ad

Although most attitude research has focused on consumers' attitude toward the brand, some evidence suggests that the overall ***attitude toward the ad*** ***(A_{ad})*** in which the brand is advertised will influence brand attitudes and behavior.[123] In other words, if we see an advertisement and like it, our liking for the ad may rub off on the brand and thereby make our brand attitude more positive. Most A_{ad} research has been done in the context of low effort processing. However, researchers are finding that A_{ad} can also have an impact when consumers devote considerable effort to processing the message. Three major factors have been found to lead to a positive A_{ad} in this context.[124]

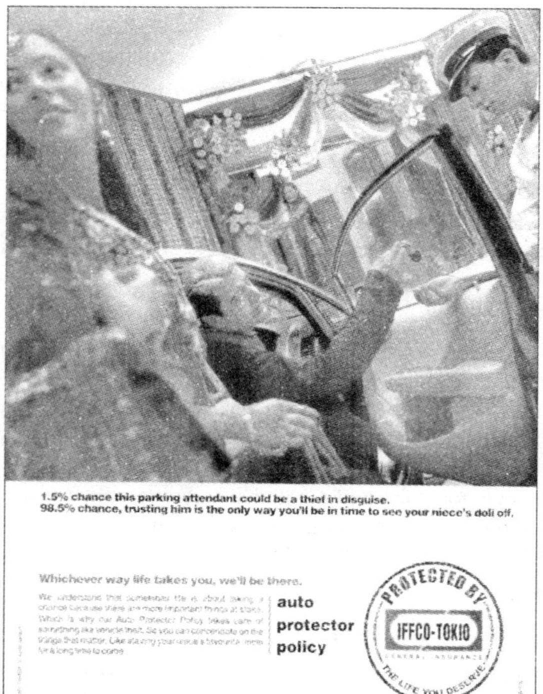

Exhibit 6.10
FEAR APPEAL
This ad uses fear of having your car stolen to get consumers to think about the quality of their insurance company.

First, more *informative* ads tend to be better liked and generate positive responses.[125] These reactions to the ad will, in turn, have a positive influence on brand attitudes, a factor called the ***utilitarian*** (or ***functional) dimension.*** For example, consumers often like promotions on the Internet because these are seen as more informative than promotions in other media. On the other hand, consumers may have negative attitudes toward ads that are not informative. A good example is the rising negativity toward political ads that are viewed as "mudslinging" and that provide little useful information about the candidates.[126]

Second, consumers can like an ad if it creates positive feelings or emotions (the ***hedonic dimension***).[127] We tend to like ads that either make us feel good or elicit positive experiences from memory. This positive attitude can transfer to the brand and make beliefs about the brand (b_i) more positive as well.[128] Marketers are also using a variety of techniques to make online advertising seem hip and fun. Cadbury's Dairy Milk (CDM) features on its website a link to meethamoments.com, where there are three webisodes, featuring three different stories, where the brand CDM, is the hero and the stories revolve around it. Besides webisodes there are numerous activities like Downloads, the commercials streaming videos and even contests for children to bring in the interactivity aspect with their target audience.

Third, consumers can like an ad because it is interesting—that is, it arouses curiosity and attracts attention. When consumers exert a lot of effort and thoughtfully elaborate on a message, it can be viewed as interesting and generate a positive A_{ad}. Amul's popular outdoor messages are a rage and the topicality of the message brings in even more consumer involvement and curiosity for the next message. The locations of the outdoor signages have not changed over the years and consumers make special trip to those locations to view the topical message posted currently.

When Do Attitudes Predict Behavior?

Marketers are interested not only in how attitudes are formed and can be changed but also in knowing whether, when, and why attitudes will predict behavior. The TORA model comes closest to providing this information by predicting which factors affect consumers' behavioral intentions. However, as previously noted, what we intend to do does not always predict what we actually will do. Therefore, marketers also need to consider which factors affect the attitude-behavior relationship. These are some of the factors that affect whether a consumer's attitudes will influence his or her behavior:

- *Level of involvement/elaboration.* Attitudes are more likely to predict behavior when cognitive involvement is high and consumers elaborate or think extensively about the information that gives rise to their attitudes.[131] Attitudes also tend to be strong and enduring and therefore more predictive of a consumer's behavior when affective involvement is high. Thus attitudes toward emotionally charged issues such as owning a handgun or getting an abortion tend to be strongly held and related to behavior. What if consumers are faced with inconsistencies about a brand and learn, for example, that it rates higher against competitors on one attribute but lower on another attribute? Here, the attitude-behavior relationship is weakened if consumers do not to resolve the inconsistency through elaboration.[132]
- *Knowledge and experience.* Attitudes are more likely to be strongly held and predictive of behavior when the consumer is knowledgeable about or experienced with the object of the attitude.[133] When making a computer decision, for example, an expert is more likely to form an attitude that is based on more detailed and integrated information than is a novice. This attitude would then be more strongly held and more strongly related to behavior.
- *Analysis of reasons.* Research shows that asking consumers to analyze their reasons for brand preference increases the link between attitude and behavior in situations where behavior is measured soon after attitudes are measured. Marketers should take this finding into account when planning consumer research to support a new product introduction.[134]
- *Accessibility of attitudes.* Attitudes are more strongly related to behavior when they are accessible or "top of mind."[135] Conversely, if an attitude cannot be easily remembered, it will have little effect on behavior. Direct experience (product usage) generally increases attitude accessibility for attributes that must be experienced (e.g., tasted, touched), whereas advertising can produce accessible attitudes for search attributes (e.g., price, ingredients), especially when the level of repetition is high.[136] Also, consumers asked about their purchase intentions toward a product in a particular category are more likely to choose brands toward which they have positive and accessible attitudes; research itself can make attitudes more accessible for brands in that category, thereby changing behavior.[137]

- *Attitude confidence.* As noted earlier, sometimes we are more certain about our evaluations than at other times. Thus another factor affecting the attitude-behavior relationship is attitude confidence. Confidence tends to be stronger when the attitude is based on either a greater amount of information or more trustworthy information. And when we are confident, our attitudes are more likely to predict our behaviors.[138] Not surprisingly, strongly held attitudes have more influence on consumers' consideration and choice of brand alternatives than weakly held attitudes.[139]
- *Specificity of attitudes.* Attitudes tend to be good predictors of behavior when we are very specific about the behavior that they are trying to predict.[140] Thus if we wanted to predict whether people will take skydiving lessons, measuring their attitudes toward skydiving in general would be less likely to predict behavior than measuring their attitudes specifically toward skydiving lessons.
- *Attitude-behavior relationship over time.* When consumers are exposed to an advertising message but do not try the product, their attitude confidence declines over time. Marketers should therefore plan their advertising schedules to reactivate consumer attitudes and attitude confidence through message repetition. On the other hand, trial-based brand attitudes are likely to decline over time even though advertising-based attitudes do not. As a result, marketers should use communications to reinforce the effects of the trial experience and thereby reactivate the attitude.[141]
- *Situational factors.* Intervening situational factors can prevent a behavior from being performed and can thus weaken the attitude-behavior relationship.[142] You might have a very positive attitude toward a Porsche, but you might not buy one because you can't afford it. If you had gone to buy the car, your attitude might not have resulted in a purchase if the dealer was out of stock. In other circumstances, the usage situation may alter the attitude. For example, your attitudes toward different wines might depend on whether you are buying wine for yourself or for a friend.
- *Normative factors.* According to the TORA model, normative factors are likely to affect the attitude-behavior relationship. As one example, you may like going to the ballet, but you do not do so because you think your friends will make fun of you. Although your attitude is positive and should lead to the behavior of attending the ballet, you are more motivated to comply with normative beliefs.
- *Personality variables.* Finally, certain personality types are more likely to exhibit stronger attitude-behavior relationships than are others. Individuals who like to devote a lot of thought to actions will evidence stronger attitude-behavior relationships because their attitudes will be based on high elaboration thinking.[143] Also, people who are guided more by their own internal dispositions (called low self-monitors) are more likely to exhibit similar behavior patterns across situations and therefore more consistent attitude-behavior relationships.[144] People who are guided by the views and behaviors of others (called high self-monitors), on the other hand, try to change their behavior to adapt to every unique situation. Thus a high self-monitor's choice of beer might depend on the situation; a low self-monitor would choose the same beer regardless of the circumstances.

Summary

When consumers' MAO to engage in a behavior or process a message is high, consumers tend to expend a lot of effort in forming their attitudes and devote considerable effort to message processing. An attitude is a relatively global and enduring evaluation about an offering, issue, activity, person, or event. Attitudes can be described in terms of their favorability, accessibility, confidence, persistence, and resistance. Consumers' thoughts and feelings in response to this situation can affect their attitudes, either through a cognitive or an affective route to persuasion.

The cognitive response model holds that attitudes can be based on cognitive responses, the thoughts that consumers have in response to a stimulus. Three categories of cognitive responses are counter-arguments, support arguments, and source derogations. Expectancy-value models also explain how attitudes form and change. The theory of reasoned action (TORA), one such model, predicts that intentions are affected by consumers' attitudes toward the act and normative factors. The TORA model also suggests that marketers can influence consumers' attitudes and intentions by (1) changing beliefs, (2) changing evaluations, (3) adding a new belief, and (4) targeting normative beliefs.

Under elaborative processing, messages can be effective if they (1) have a credible source, (2) have a strong argument, (3) present positive and negative information (under certain circumstances), or (4) involve direct comparisons (if not the market leader). Attitudes are also formed from feelings or emotions such as joy and fear.

Consumers can experience emotions by being affectively involved with a communication or when the message involves an emotional appeal. In either case the consumer processes the communication, and the positive or negative feelings that result can determine attitudes. When attitudes are affectively based, sources that are likable or attractive can have a positive impact on affective attitude change. Emotional appeals can affect communication processing if they are relevant to the offering (the match-up hypothesis). Fear appeals are a specific type of emotion-eliciting message. A consumer's attitude toward the ad (A_{ad}) can play a role in the attitude change process if the ad is informative or associated with positive feelings. The A_{ad} can then rub off on brand beliefs and attitudes.

Finally, attitudes will better predict a consumer's behavior when (1) involvement is high, (2) knowledge is high, (3) reasons are analyzed, (4) attitudes are accessible, (5) attitudes are held with confidence, (6) attitudes are specific, (7) the attitude-behavior relationship does not decline over time, (8) no situational factors are present, (9) normative factors are not in operation, and (10) we are dealing with certain personality types.

Questions for Review and Discussion

1. What are attitudes, and what three functions do they serve?
2. How does the cognitive response model differ from expectancy-value models of attitude formation?
3. What role does credibility play in affecting consumer attitudes based on cognitions?
4. What are the advantages and disadvantages of offering a two-sided message about a product?
5. Contrast emotional and fear appeals. Why is each effective? Which do you consider most compelling for products in which you are interested?
6. What three factors may lead to a positive attitude toward the ad (A_{ad}) when consumers devote a lot of effort to processing a message? How can marketers apply these factors when designing advertising messages?

Exercises

1. Collect three advertisements (from either magazines or TV) that you think would generate elaborative processing. Perform a detailed analysis of these ads in terms of the following:
   a. What type of cognitive responses might consumers have when seeing/reading these ads? (Be sure to identify counterarguments, support arguments, and source derogations.) Based on these responses, how effective do you think each ad will be in changing attitudes?
   b. Applying the TORA model, what types of attitude-change strategies are these ads using?
   c. What kinds of affective responses (feelings or emotions) might occur? How would these responses affect the attitude change process?
2. Find three ads that you think will generate a fair number of cognitive or affective responses from consumers. Show these ads to a sample of 15 consumers and ask them to think out loud about their reactions while reading the ads. Record these responses either on tape or by hand. Then classify the responses into the categories of counterarguments, source derogations, support arguments, and affective responses. Use this information to answer the following questions:
   a. What are the major strengths of each ad?
   b. What are the major weaknesses of each ad?
   c. How could each ad be improved?
3. Find ten magazine ads that you think will elicit elaborative processing. Analyze these ads for the types of source and message factors discussed in the chapter. Based on this analysis, answer the following questions:
   a. Which types of source and message factors are most frequently used?
   b. Which ads do you think are most effective and why?
   c. Which ads do you think are least effective and why?
4. Interview three people who engage in personal selling for a business. Develop a short questionnaire that will identify the types of strategies they use to persuade consumers to buy particular products. First, ask some open-ended questions about how the salespeople try to influence consumers. Then ask some specific questions regarding the source and message factors discussed in the chapter. Be sure to ask how often the salespeople use each technique and how effective they think the techniques are. Summarize this information and answer the following questions:
   a. Which types of persuasion techniques are most likely to be used in a personal selling situation?
   b. Which message factors are most effective and why?
   c. Which message factors are least effective and why?

More Exercises from the Adaptor

1. Collect information on the following brands, in the context of the following parameters:
   a. Mysore Sandal Soap
   b. Burnol
   c. Iodex
2. The information may be collected from two different age groups, one in the age group of 18-25 years and the other in the age group of 35-50 years.

References

[1] Source: http://www.meethamoments.com/

[2] Source: http://www.rediff.com/money/2005/jul/

chapter **7**

Attitudes Based on Low Consumer Effort

LEARNING OBJECTIVES

After studying this chapter, you will be able to:

- Outline some of the challenges and opportunities faced by marketers trying to change consumers' attitudes when processing effort is low.
- Discuss how consumers form beliefs based on low processing effort and explain how marketers can influence those beliefs.
- Describe the ways consumers form attitudes through affective reactions when cognitive effort is low.
- Highlight how marketers can use the communication source, the message, and the context to influence consumers' feelings and attitudes when processing effort is low.

INTRODUCTION

[1]The Indian Whisky Market: Make it Large

The Indian spirits and liquor market is currently tipped to be one of the largest markets in the world, along with markets like the US and Thailand. The range of options available from premium whisky (not scotch) to scotch has all shown promising growth. Brown spirits account for nearly 96 per cent of the Indian liquor market, pegged at around 88 million cases annually. It must be mentioned that whisky dominates the consumption pattern and India is one of the few growing regions for the flavour globally. However, the sales volume of premium whiskies is only around 1.5 million cases, as the bulk of IMFL consumption comes from segments priced below Rs.250 per quart. Premium Indian whiskies have seen sedate growth in recent years when they remained largely ineffective in attracting consumer upgradation and watched some of their core consumers dabble in white spirits occasionally. Indian "molasses" whisky has about 90% of the Indian market and the domestic industry is fighting a fierce rearguard to ensure that it does not lose its dominant position. It is also much cheaper at 200 rupees for a bottle of entry-level Indian whisky compared to some 3,000 rupees for a bottle of single malt Scotch whisky such as Glenfiddich. The Indians are prodigious whisky drinkers, downing 570-million litres in 2004, 40% more than the second largest consumers The United States, and the total is set to grow. Major drinks companies including the Edrington Group, Moet Hennessy and Diageo are jockeying for position.

In this milieu, the problem of government ban on spirit and cigarette advertising and promotion has created pressure on the companies. Subliminal and surrogate advertising seems to be the norm of the day, with most brands focusing on selling their packaged drinking water or musical cassettes and CD's or even playing cards and snacks items. The primary attempt being to keep the brand top of mind in terms of recall and this is further reinforced through direct promotions at Pubs and bars. Another attempt that brands have been trying to create

Exhibit 7.1
ASSOCIATING FASHION WITH SPIRITS

One of the ways in which brands have been attempting to showcase their appeal by associating themselves with certain themes or events or causes or even music

is a distinct image and appeal about themselves by associating themselves with events, causes, themes or even creating conscious attempts to relate themselves to certain brands of music.

Within this domain, some of the premium brands of whisky like Royal Stag, Royal Challenge, Signature, and Blender's Pride have been trying to create imagery based differentiation. The Royal Stag "Make it Large" appeal or Blender's Pride's association with the fashion industry are all attempts to create a distinct appeal for itself. The market is fiercely competitive with price points that do not separate the brands much from each other. Besides, with product differentiators being minimal, it creates all the more reasons for marketers to focus on appeals based on consumer's self expression.

The rising incomes, economic prosperity and the boom in the BPO/ITES sector, has given rise to a profile of audience, which is younger (18+, the legal age for drinking), high on disposable resource, and who does not hesitate to experiment with the finer things of life. Unfortunately, with such high duties of around 525%, imported scotch is still out of bound for this segment, which makes the Indian made premium whisky market the next obvious choice. Out of the total sales of 88 million cases, this segment contributes to around 1.5 million cases and is growing at a fast pace.

The different approaches used by McDowell's and Seagram's illustrates how marketers can influence our attitudes even when we make effort to process a message or when mainline advertising for such products are banned. Because consumers tend not to actively process message arguments or become emotionally involved in such kind of messages, marketers must employ other techniques to create positive evaluations of their brands, raise awareness of need situations, and stimulate purchasing and consumption (see Exhibit 7.1). This chapter discusses how marketers use techniques such as sex, humor, attractive sources, and emotion to influence attitudes when consumers make little effort to process the message.

High-Effort Versus Low-Effort Routes to Persuasion

When consumers are either unwilling or unable to exert a lot of effort or devote a lot of emotional resources to processing the central idea behind a marketing communication, we characterize it as a low-effort situation. Here, consumers are unlikely to think about what the product means to them, relate empathetically to the characters in the ad, or generate arguments against or in support of the brand message. As a result, when processing effort is low, consumers usually do not form strong beliefs or accessible, persistent, resistant, or confident attitudes.

You saw in Chapter 3 that low-effort situations are those in which consumers do not have the motivation, ability, or opportunity (MAO) to process the information provided. In these situations, consumers tend to be passive recipients of the message. Marketers addressing such situations must therefore use a strategy that takes into account this lower level of processing.

One way to do this is to create communications that use a different route. Instead of focusing on the key message arguments, the message will be more

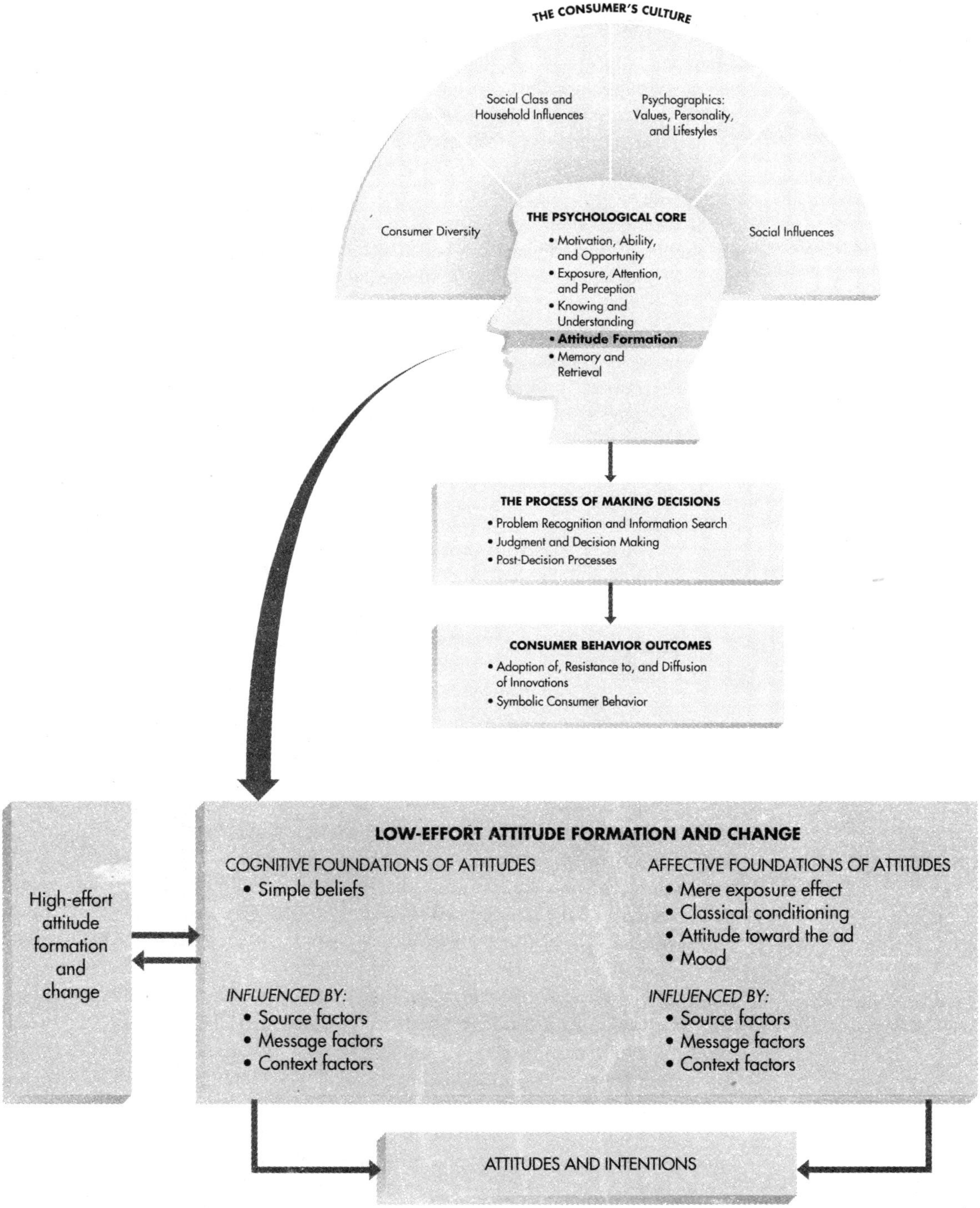

Exhibit 7.2

CHAPTER OVERVIEW: ATTITUDE FORMATION AND CHANGE: LOW CONSUMER EFFORT *Just as in high-effort cases, attitudes can be formed cognitively and affectively in low-effort situations; however, the specific processes are different. Low-effort cognition involves simple beliefs, and affect involves mere exposure, classical conditioning, attitude toward the ad, and mood. Marketers can also influence consumer attitudes cognitively and affectively using source, message, and context factors.*

effective if it takes the ***peripheral route to persuasion.***[2] Processing is called *peripheral* when consumers' attitudes are based not on a detailed consideration of the message or their ability to relate to the brand empathetically but on other easily processed aspects of the message, such as the source or visuals, called ***peripheral cues.*** In particular, consumer attitudes can persist over time if peripheral cues such as visuals are related to the offering.[3]

Just as there are both cognitive and affective routes to persuasion when processing effort is high, so too can consumers form low-effort attitudes in both a cognitive and an affective manner. Marketers can try to design their ads to enhance the likelihood that consumers' thoughts (the cognitive base), feelings (the affective base), or both will be favorable. Exhibit 7.2 provides a framework for thinking about the peripheral bases of consumer behavior.

Marketers need to understand how consumers form attitudes with low effort because, in most cases, consumers will have limited MAO to process marketing communications. Think about the countless marketing messages you receive every day. How many actually attract your attention and stimulate you to think about the ad and how you feel about the offering? Consider how you normally watch TV. Chances are you have limited exposure to ads because you are channel surfing. You may comprehend very little about the messages because you are watching them in a distracting environment, or you may even tune them out because they feature products you do not care about. These behaviors pose challenges for marketers.

Cognitive Bases of Attitudes When Consumer Effort Is Low

Chapter 6 explained how consumers' beliefs form an important cognitive basis for their attitudes. When processing effort is low, attitudes may be based on a few simple and not very strong beliefs, because consumers have not processed the message deeply. Interestingly, because these beliefs are not very strong, marketers may actually be *more* successful in changing them than when processing effort is high. The attitudes of low-effort consumers may be less resistant to attack than those of high-effort consumers because the low-effort people may "let their guard down" and not resist the message or develop counterarguments.

When processing effort is low, consumers may acquire simple beliefs by forming ***simple inferences*** based on simple associations. For example, consumers may infer that a brand of champagne is elegant because it is shown with other elegant things, such as a richly decorated room or a woman in an evening dress. Likewise, if an ad is perceived to be similar to the prototypical ad for a product or service category, consumers may believe that the offering is just like the prototypical brand and develop similar attitudes toward both.[4] As noted in Chapter 5, inferred beliefs about the brand may also come from consumers' superficial analysis of the brand name, country of origin, price, or color.

In addition, consumers can form simple beliefs based on attributions or explanations for an endorsement.[5] If consumers attribute an endorsement to the endorser's desire to earn a lot of money, they will not find the message believable. On the other hand, if they perceive that the endorser truly cares about the offering, the ad may be more credible. For example, when Accu-check from Roche was looking for a celebrity to endorse its line of Home Monitoring Blood Glucose Meter, it found an able support in the form of Wasim Akram, the Pakistani all rounder, who himself suffered from Diabetes and thus could endorse the product based more on his personal experience and not as a celebrity alone.

Finally, consumers can aid judgments by forming ***heuristics,*** or simple rules of thumb, that are easy to invoke and require little thought.[7] For example, consumers could use the heuristic "If it is a well-known brand, it must be good" to infer that brands with more frequent ads are also higher in quality.[8] A special type of heuristic is the ***frequency heuristic,*** with which consumers form a belief based on the number of supporting arguments.[9] They may think, "It must be good because there are ten reasons why I should like it." Research also indicates that consumers are actually likely to have stronger beliefs when they hear the same message repeatedly, this is known as the ***truth effect.***[10] Rather than having to think about and evaluate the information, consumers find it easier to use their familiarity with the message as a way of judging its accuracy ("This 'rings a bell' so it must be true").

How Cognitive Attitudes Are Influenced

Marketers need to consider multiple factors when trying to influence cognitive attitudes. One is the strength and importance of consumers' beliefs. Another is the likelihood that consumers will form favorable beliefs based on the inferences, attributions, and heuristics they use in processing the message. In designing communications that overcome these hurdles, marketers must consider three major characteristics of a communication: (1) the source, (2) the message, and (3) the context in which the message is delivered.

Communication Source

Characteristics of the source play an important role in influencing consumers' beliefs when processing effort is low. Credible sources can serve as peripheral cues for making a simplified judgment, such as "Statements from experts can be trusted" or "Products endorsed by an expert must be good."[11] Note that source expertise is used here as a simple cue in judging the credibility of the message, and unlike the case in high-effort situations, little cognitive effort is required. Marketers may also increase the chances that consumers will believe the endorsement by ensuring that the endorser does not advertise many other products.

The Message

The message itself can influence attitudes in a number of ways when consumers' processing effort is low.

Category- and Schema-Consistent Information Many elements of a communication affect the inferences that consumers make from a message. For example, consumers may infer that a brand has certain characteristics based on its name ("Healthy Choice soups must be good for me"). We may make inferences about quality based on price, as discussed earlier, or about attributes based on color, such as when blue suggests coolness. Thus in designing ads for low-effort consumers, marketers pay close attention to the immediate associations consumers have about easily processed visual and verbal information. These associations are likely to be consistent with category and schema information stored in the consumer's memory.

Many Message Arguments The frequency heuristic can also affect consumers' beliefs about the message. As a simplifying rule, consumers do not actually process all the information but simply form a belief based on the number of supporting arguments. The Blind School at Lodhi Road, New Delhi has the city's crème-de-la-crème coming for buying candles and diyas. The place not only sells the best confetti for Diwali but the gesture of buying from blind children is also a reason for the city's hobnobbers to congregate at such a venue.

Exhibit 7.3
SIMPLE MESSAGE
When effort is low, consumers will not process a lot of information. In these cases, advertisers need to provide simple and unusual messages such as this one for Amar Ujala

Simple Messages In low-processing situations, a simple message is more likely to be effective because consumers will not process a lot of information. Marketers often want to convey basic information about why a particular brand is superior, especially when it has a point of differentiation that distinguishes it from the competition. However, rather than overloading low-processing consumers with detailcd information about the brand, marketers should use a simple message that focuses on one or two key points . The "Trusted Everywhere" Duracell ad campaign, for example, focused on how the battery's long life helps people at critical moments. One of the ads shows a rescue team searching for lost hikers by the light of battery-operated headlamps. "Unless we are continually educating consumers about the difference, they tend to forget over time," says Duracell's president.[13] Another good example is the ad in Exhibit 7.3. For food products being marketed on the basis of convenience, marketers should focus attention on one important functional benefit through a literal, direct assertion, such as "Maggi- 2 Minute Noodles. Fast to Cook. Good to Eat"

Involving Messages Marketers will sometimes want to *increase* consumers' involvement with the message to ensure that the information is received. One common strategy is to increase the extent to which consumers engage in ***self-referencing,*** or relating the message to their own experience or self-image. Studies show that a self-referencing strategy can be effective in developing positive attitudes and intentions, especially if it's used at moderate levels and involvement isn't too low.[15] Similarly, remembering and using the consumer's name in a personal selling context will increase purchase behavior.[16] Also, consumers will have more favorable attitudes toward a brand that is highly descriptive on a personality dimension that they consider important or self-descriptive.[17] Finally, a mainstream ad with dominant culture cues may stimulate self-referencing among members of a subculture and lead to favorable ad attitudes. If the ad has subcultural cues rather than dominant culture cues, however, it will induce self-referencing and positive ad attitudes only among members of that subculture.[18]

marketing
IMPLICATIONS

Marketers can increase self-referencing by (1) directly instructing consumers to use self-reference ("Think of the last time you had a good meal . . ."), (2) using the word *you* in the ad, (3) asking rhetorical questions ("Wouldn't you like your clothes to look this clean?"),[19] or (4) showing visuals of situations to which consumers can easily relate. When a rhetorical question within an ad attracts special attention, however, it stimulates consumers to wonder why the question is there, shifting processing effort to message style instead of keep consumers focused on message content.[20]

The ***mystery ad*** (also called the "wait and bait" ad), which doesn't identify the brand until the end, if at all, is another way to arouse consumer curiosity and involvement. Some movies have used a version of such ads to build audience interest in advance of their release dates. For instance, the opening moments of a preview for *Eternal Sunshine of the Spotless Mind* informed audiences that "the following is a paid advertisement from Lacuna Inc." A "doctor" then touted the benefits of his method for erasing troubling memories but was interrupted by star Jim Carrey, who asked, "This is a hoax, right?" The idea, said the studio's head of marketing, "was to wake people up in the theater" and have them react as Jim Carrey did, prompting more involvement in the preview and in the movie.[21] According to research, the mystery ad is particularly effective in generating category-based processing and storing brand associations in memory.[22]

Marketers can employ other techniques to increase situational involvement and processing effort, as well. Scratch-and-sniff ads often increase processing effort simply because many consumers cannot resist the excitement of trying something new. Also, inviting consumers to experience simulated product usage online increases consumer involvement and advertising effectiveness more than an online ad message alone.[23] This is why the Lego site features interactive games that invite players to create virtual cities, animals, and vehicles using virtual Lego blocks as a demonstration of the product's functionality and the fun.[24] In Exhibit 7.4, Ernst & Young draws consumers into the message by challenging them to look at the illustration in different ways.

Exhibit 7.4
INCREASING ACTIVE PROCESSING
This ad tries to draw consumers into the message by challenging them to look at the image in different ways.

Message Context and Repetition

Although source and message factors can influence consumers' attitudes, the context in which the message is delivered can affect the strength of consumers' beliefs and the prominence (or salience) of those beliefs to the consumers. In particular, a company can use message *repetition* to help consumers acquire basic knowledge of important product features or benefits, enhancing the strength and salience of their beliefs. Consumers do not try to process this information actively; rather, the constant repetition increases recall through effortless or ***incidental learning.*** For example, you may have a prominent belief about milk's health benefits because you've been exposed repeatedly to the decade-long "Got Milk?" milk mustache campaign, which has helped boost sales of milk products over the years.[25]

Second, repetition may enhance brand awareness, make a brand name more familiar,[26] make it easier to recognize in the store, increase the likelihood that consumers will remember it and be better able to process it when making a decision,[27] and increase confidence in the brand.[28] A large number of companies involved in retail sales have started using alternate medium like Internet to explore the possibility to publicize their brands. FMCG companies like HLL, P&G and even Dabur have been trying to exploit the web and its endless possibilities. Separate budgets have now been earmarked by companies to explore the possibility of the internet as a medium. Third, as you have seen, repetition can make claims more believable (the truth effect)—an effect that gets even stronger when ads are spaced out over time.[30] And fourth, TV commercials that air within the context of similar programming (i.e., humorous ads aired during comedy shows) are more likable and better understood by consumers expending low processing effort.[31] Similarly, ads that fit in the context of the magazines where they appear elicit more positive feelings and are better remembered than ads not in tune with magazine context.[32]

Affective Bases of Attitudes When Consumer Effort Is Low

The establishment of low-level beliefs based on peripheral cues is not the only way that consumers can form attitudes about brands with little effort. Attitudes can also be based on consumers' affective or emotional reactions to these easily processed peripheral cues. These low-effort affective processes may be due to (1) the mere exposure effect, (2) classical conditioning, (3) attitude toward the ad, and (4) consumer mood.

The Mere Exposure Effect

According to the ***mere exposure effect,*** we tend to prefer familiar objects to unfamiliar ones. Thus our attitudes toward an offering such as a new style of clothing should change as we become more and more familiar with it, regardless of whether we perform any deep cognitive analysis of it. The mere exposure effect may explain why many of the top 30 brands in the 1930s are still in the top 30 today. It also explains why the music industry likes to have recordings featured on the radio or on TV music videos. Through repeated exposure, consumers become familiar with the music and come to like it.

Because most demonstrations of the mere exposure effect have occurred in tightly controlled laboratory studies, some experts question whether it generalizes to the real world.[33] It is also possible that repeated exposure reduces uncertainty about the stimulus or increases consumers' opportunity to process it[34] and that these factors (rather than mere familiarity) are what affect consumers' attitudes. Yet, research shows that mere exposure can help an unknown brand compete against other unknown brands if product performance characteristics are equivalent and consumers invest little processing effort at the time of brand choice.[35] Research also indicates that when consumers can easily process the information from a stimulus to which they have been exposed in the past, they mistakenly believe that the ease in processing is due to liking, truth, or acceptability.[36]

marketing IMPLICATIONS

If the mere exposure effect is valid, marketers may be able to enhance consumers' liking for a new product or service by repeatedly exposing consumers to the offering or messages about it. Research suggests that when consumers' MAO is low, marketers need to devise creative tactics for increasing exposure to products and messages, perhaps by using the right medium, the right placement within the medium, optimal shelf placement, and sampling.

Consistent with the mere exposure effect, the advertising industry certainly recognizes the importance of developing and maintaining brand-name familiarity. According to advertising authority Leo Bogart, repetition is used to impress "the advertised name upon the consumers' consciousness and make them feel comfortable with the brand."[37] Building brand familiarity is important in many categories; for example, Burger King faced a tough battle when it entered the Japanese market because McDonald's is so well known and strongly preferred there.[38]

However, repeated exposures build familiarity and liking only up to a point.[39] After this, consumers typically experience ***wearout,*** which means they become bored with the stimulus, and brand attitudes can actually become negative.[40] In fact, research shows that once a persuasive ad has effectively reached the targeted consumer segment, wearout causes a loss of persuasiveness.[41] When consumers are familiar with a brand, however, wearout may occur later.[42] Also, the use of rational arguments to promote a well-known brand in a mature product category tends to be less effective than the use of affectively based tactics because consumers have been exposed to the product information many times before.[43] Still, in low-effort processing situations, brand evaluations do not suffer when consumers are repeatedly exposed to messages about product features.[44]

Marketers can overcome the problem of wearout by creating different executions for the same message or variants on the same offering—which is why many advertisers develop a series of ads rather than a single execution.[45] The goal is to get the same message across in many different ways, the way the "Incredible India" campaign showcases different destinations across India, from beaches, mountains, historical destinations, religious circuits to obscure locations. The core theme of "Incredible India" remains common with stunning visuals of the locations highlighted being displayed.

Classical Conditioning

One way of influencing consumers' attitudes without invoking much processing effort is ***classical conditioning.*** Classical conditioning became well known from a study in the 1900s by the Russian scientist Ivan Pavlov. Normally, hungry dogs will salivate automatically just at the sight of food. Pavlov discovered that he could condition hungry dogs to salivate at the sound of a bell. How did he do that?

Exhibit 7.5
CLASSICAL CONDITIONING
These diagrams illustrate the basic process of classical conditioning. An unconditioned stimulus, or UCS (e.g., food or pleasant scenes), will automatically produce an unconditioned response, or UCR (e.g., salivation or positive affect). By repeatedly pairing the UCS with a conditioned stimulus, or CS (e.g., a bell or soft drink), the CS can be conditioned to produce the same response, a conditioned response, or CR (e.g., salivation or positive affect). Can you think of any other situations in which this process occurs?

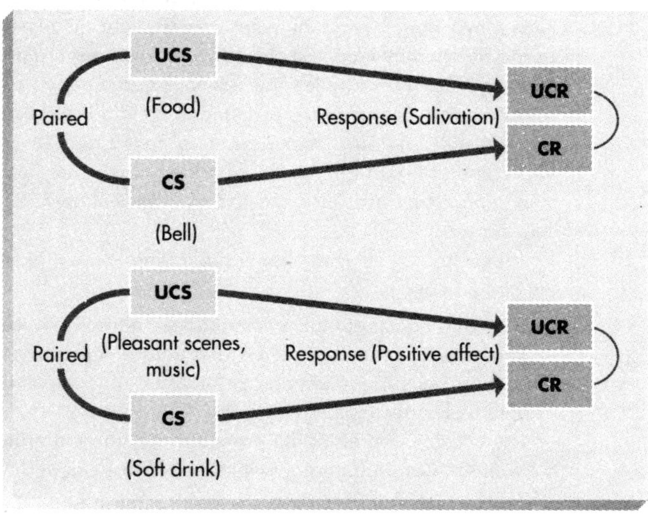

According to Pavlov, the food was an *unconditioned stimulus (UCS)*, and the salivation response to the food was an *unconditioned response (UCR)* (see Exhibit 7.5). A stimulus is unconditioned when it automatically elicits an involuntary response. In this situation, the dogs automatically salivated when they saw meat powder. In contrast, a *conditioned stimulus (CS)* is something that does not automatically elicit an involuntary response by itself. Until Pavlov rang the bell at the same time the food was presented, the bell alone was not capable of making the dogs salivate. By repeatedly pairing the conditioned stimulus (the bell) with the unconditioned stimulus (the meat powder), the involuntary unconditioned response (salivation) was created. The dogs associated the food and the bell so closely that eventually just the ringing bell made them salivate. Because the response could now be evoked in the presence of the conditioned stimulus, the response was said to be a conditioned response (CR). (This is the same phenomenon that makes cats come running when they hear the can opener.)

marketing IMPLICATIONS

What possible significance can salivating dogs have for consumer behavior? In fact, classical conditioning theory is sometimes used to explain the effectiveness of marketing communications. Here, however, the unconditioned response is not a physiological one like salivating but rather a psychological one like an emotion. As Exhibit 7.5 shows, certain unconditioned stimuli (such as a happy scene or a catchy jingle) automatically elicit an unconditioned emotional response such as joy or warmth. By repeatedly pairing one of these unconditioned stimuli with a conditioned stimulus such as the brand name, marketers may be able to evoke the same emotional response (now the conditioned response) to the conditioned stimulus, the brand name itself. Similarly, consumers might be conditioned to have a negative emotional response to an offering such as cigarettes if ads by health advocacy groups repeatedly show the product with stimuli that automatically elicit a negative emotional response (such as pictures of stained teeth).

In one of the first consumer studies to demonstrate classical conditioning, subjects viewed a slide of a blue or beige pen that was matched with a one-minute segment of either pleasant or unpleasant music. Subjects who heard pleasant music selected the pen they viewed with that music 79 percent of the time, whereas only 30 percent of those who heard the unpleasant music selected the pen they had viewed.[46] Although these findings were subject to alternative interpretations (subjects may simply have done what they thought the experimenter wanted them to do, or the music may have put the consumers in a more positive mood),[47] more recent and more tightly controlled studies have found support for the classical conditioning phenomenon. For example, by using unconditioned stimuli such as *Star Wars* music and pleasing pictures, experimenters have affected consumers' attitudes toward such conditioned stimuli as geometric figures, colas, and toothpaste.[48] Research has also shown that attitudes created by classical conditioning can be fairly enduring over time.[49]

These studies suggest that conditioning is most likely to occur under the following circumstances:

- The conditioned stimuli–unconditioned stimuli link is relatively novel or unknown. This is why marketers often use unique visuals, such as pictures of beautiful scenery, exciting situations, or pleasing objects, as unconditioned stimuli to create positive feelings.
- The conditioned stimulus precedes the unconditioned stimulus *(forward conditioning)*. Conditioning is weaker when the unconditioned stimulus is presented

Exhibit 7.6
THE DUAL-MEDIATION HYPOTHESIS

This hypothesis explains how attitudes toward the ad (A_{ad}) can influence attitudes toward the brand (A_b) and intentions (I_b). When you read an ad, you can have responses (C_{ad}) that are both cognitive (this ad has information about a brand) and affective (positive feelings from finding the ad). These responses may cause you to like the ad (A_{ad}), which can then either (1) make you more accepting of brand beliefs (C_b), leading to a more positive brand attitude (A_b), or (2) give you positive feelings that simply transfer over to the brand (I like the ad, so I like the brand). Both processes lead to an increase in intention to purchase.

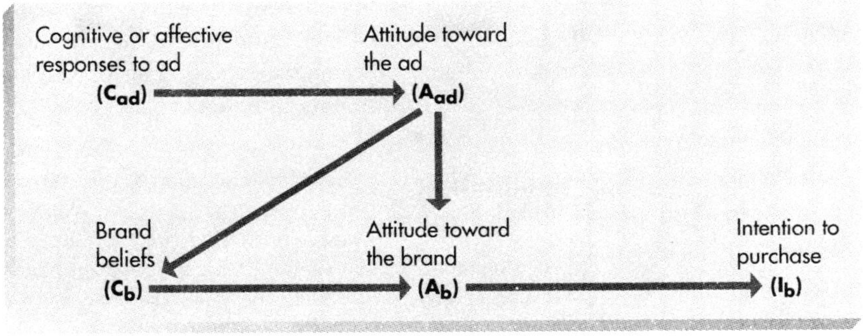

first *(backward conditioning)* or at the same time as the conditioned stimulus *(concurrent conditioning)*.

- The conditioned stimulus is paired consistently with the unconditioned stimulus.
- The consumer is aware of the link between the conditioned and unconditioned stimuli.
- A logical fit exists between the conditioned and unconditioned stimuli, such as between tennis star Andre Agassi and Head, the racket brand he has endorsed for many years.[50]

Interestingly, the first condition can cause problems for marketers because unconditioned stimuli are often well-known celebrities, music, or visuals for which consumers possess many associations. This situation might suggest that highly visible celebrities are not as effective in creating a classical conditioning effect. Other research suggests that this problem can be overcome by using highly familiar stimuli such as popular songs and personalities because they elicit very strong feelings in many situations. Not all marketers avoid endorsers who are associated with multiple brands. Upcoming cricket stars like Dhoni feature in numerous products, through brands like Videocon, Brylcreem, Pepsi, Sonata to name a few and it also adds on to the appeal of Dhoni.

Attitude Toward the Ad

Another concept that has been useful in understanding the affective bases of attitudes in low-effort situations is the consumer's attitude toward the ad (A_{ad}). Sometimes consumers like an ad so much that they transfer their positive feelings from the ad to the brand.[52] Thus you may decide that you really like Sprint/Nextel because you find its wireless phone ads interesting, or Pepsi because its soft-drink ads are quite humorous.

One study found that beliefs or knowledge about the brand did not fully account for brand attitudes and that A_{ad} provided a significant additional explanation—brands with liked ads were evaluated more favorably.[53] Furthermore, research in India, Greece, Denmark, New Zealand, and the United States revealed that the A_{ad} principle was globally applicable.[54] In fact, an Advertising Research Foundation project suggests that attitudes toward ads may be the best indicator of advertising effectiveness.[55]

The ***dual-mediation hypothesis*** is a somewhat more complex explanation of the relationship between consumers' liking for an ad and brand attitude (see Exhibit 7.6).[56] According to this hypothesis, consumers can have a favorable attitude toward an ad either because they find it believable or because they feel good about it. Thus the dual-mediation hypothesis proposes that A_{ad} can affect brand attitudes (A_b) either through believability or liking. These responses, in turn, may positively affect consumers' intentions to purchase (I_b).

marketing IMPLICATIONS

The clear implication of the attitude-toward-the-ad theory is that by providing ads that are pleasing, marketers may be able to make consumers' brand attitudes more positive as well. Thus by using techniques such as humor, music, pleasant pictures, and sex (all of which will be discussed in more detail shortly), marketers can develop positive attitudes toward the ad. Kamasutra condoms were pioneers in introducing condom advertising, which was bold and explicit. It was a concept which was taboo, brought forth by the brand, through a series of highly provocative advertisements, featuring Pooja Bedi. The campaign was sufficiently effective and created the right noise level. Over the years, Kamasutra has been regularly advertising, with several new themes and appeals being showcased. After the launch campaign, they followed it up with another very provocative and bold campaign focusing on the origins of Kamasutra and some featuring lessons from it. The bolder, provocative and overt advertisements have been replaced with more subtle and added finesse to its communications, representing the changing dynamism of the society. Exhibit 7.7 showcases one of the new advertisements from the new series.

In addition, the effect of ad attitudes on brand attitudes may depend on whether consumers already have a strong attitude toward the brand. When brands are well known and attitudes about them have been formed, consumers may not like the brand more just because they like the ad. However, when brands are new or not well-known, consumers' liking for the ad can play a more significant role in their liking for the brand.[58] Studies also suggest that the effect of attitude toward the ad on attitude toward the brand dissipates over time.[59] In other words, as memory of the ad fades, liking for the ad and the brand also becomes weaker.

Exhibit 7.7
AFFECTIVELY PLEASING AD

The new series of Kamasutra condom ads showcases the product in a more subtle and passive overtones as against the earlier aggressive and overtly sexual ads.

Mood

Affective attitudes can also be influenced by the consumer's mood. Here, a stimulus creates a positive or a negative mood; in turn, this mood can affect consumers' reactions to any other stimulus they happen to evaluate. Thus we are more likely to say that we like something if we are in a good mood or say that we dislike something when we are in a bad mood. Mood can therefore bias attitudes in a *mood-congruent direction.* Note that mood is different from classical conditioning because mood (1) does not require a repeated association between two stimuli and (2) can affect consumers' evaluations of any object, not just the stimulus.

According to one study, consumers in a good mood who have a tentative preference for a particular brand tend to ignore negative information about that brand as well as information about a competitor.[60] Still another study found that although consumers tend to like a brand extension less when the product is not very similar to the parent product, consumers in a good mood are more likely to like a brand extension that is moderately similar to the parent product than consumers who are not in a good mood.[61] Moreover, research shows that consumers in a good mood tend to give more weight to positive information when evaluating a product, whereas consumers in a bad mood tend to give more weight to the negative information.[62]

Researchers have examined how lighting influences mood. They found that brighter in-store lighting tends to increase the extent to which shoppers examine and handle merchandise.[63] Brighter lighting does not, however, increase the amount of time consumers spend shopping or the number of purchases they make. Color is also a factor. Warm colors such as red, orange, and yellow tend to be more stimulating and exciting, whereas cool colors such as blue, green, and violet tend to be more soothing.[64]

Consumers may like a brand better when they are put in a good mood by its ads or the programs in which the ads appear. Research has focused on the kinds of emotions or moods that ads invoke and the variety of ways these factors might affect consumers' ad and brand attitudes.[65] One study identified three major categories of affective responses: (1) *SEVA* (surgency, elation, vigor, and activation), which is present when the communication puts the consumer in an upbeat or happy mood; (2) *deactivation feelings*, which include soothing, relaxing, quiet, or pleasant responses; and (3) *social affection*, which are feelings of warmth, tenderness, and caring.[66] Another study found that ad-induced feelings of warmth and humor could have a direct and positive impact on brand attitudes.[67] Thus when ads for Huggies disposable diapers picture tender moments between babies and parents, they may also generate positive feelings for the Huggies brand.

marketing IMPLICATIONS

On the assumption that mood affects consumer behavior, retailers can use physical surroundings and the behavior of store employees to put consumers in a good mood. Warm colors are more likely to draw customers to an outlet but can also create tension, whereas cool colors are more relaxing but do not attract customers.[68] Thus when the goal is to stimulate quick purchases or activity, warm colors are more appropriate, which is why discount stores such as Target often use a red-based color scheme. Warm colors are also appropriate for health clubs, sports stadiums, and fast-food restaurants, where a high level of activity and energy is desirable.

On the other hand, cool colors are more appropriate when the goal is to have consumers feel calm or spend time deliberating. Stores that sell expensive consumer goods are a good example. Apple Computer's stores have white floors, white ceilings, and polished stainless steel walls to bring consumers in, encourage them to linger, and provide a clean, uncluttered environment for showcasing high-tech products.[69] Other businesses that should incorporate cool colors are doctors' offices, hotel rooms, spas, banks, resorts, and upscale restaurants.

How Affective Attitudes Are Influenced

When consumers apply little processing effort and form attitudes based on feelings, the same three factors that influence cognitive reasoning also influence affective attitudes: the communication source, the message, and the context. Again, these factors are based on low-effort processes such as mere exposure, classical conditioning, attitude toward the ad, and mood.

Communication Source

Under conditions of low effort, two factors play a major role in determining whether or not the communication source evokes favorable affective reactions: its physical attractiveness and its likability. These two factors help to explain why marketers like to feature celebrities in ads.

Attractive Sources Many ads feature attractive models, spokespersons, or celebrities, reflecting the long-held belief that beauty sells—especially in the beauty business. Kolkata based Emami signed on Madhuri Dixit in 2002 for a range of products from talc, hair oil, skin cream and three shampoos under the "Beauty Secrets by Madhuri" brand. The attempt here was to have Madhuri share her knowledge of her beauty tips and secrets, which she had collected on her global trips across the world. Alternatively, Bangalore based Jewels De Paragon, used Maharani Gayatri Devi, who is well over 80 years as their endorser for the brand Arisia Diamonds. When consumers' motivation to process an advertised message is low, attractive sources will enhance the favorability of consumers' brand attitudes regardless of whether the message arguments are strong or weak.[71] Consumers also rate ads with physically attractive models as more appealing, attractive, eye-catching, impressive, and interesting than ads with unattractive models. These ratings may affect consumers' attitudes toward the products these models sponsor.[72]

Moreover, attractiveness can have beneficial effects on advertiser believability and actual purchase.[73] These effects can occur for both male and female models (consumers are most strongly attracted to models of the opposite sex) and have been found to operate for direct-mail responses, point-of-purchase displays, and personal-selling interactions as well.[74] Race may be an important factor,[75] as well. The Parsi community in India is a closely knit one and prefers to socialize within itself. The key influences on the community are mainly from their religious leaders and the wise men in the community, who keep the community integrated.

Note that we also discussed attractive sources in the context of high affective involvement (Chapter 6). In the former case, attractive sources directly influence brand-based attitudes because these sources are directly relevant to the product considered (perfume, fashion, lingerie, etc.) and are thus a central part of the message. In the present context of low-effort processing, attractive sources serve as a peripheral cue used to increase situational involvement and generate a positive attitude toward the ad.

Likable Sources The likability of the source can influence affective attitudes.[76] For example, Amitabh Bachchan's likability and credibility has made him an effective spokesperson for the Pulse Polio Campaign. Likable sources may serve as unconditioned stimuli, create a positive mood that affects consumers' evaluations of the ad or brand, and make consumers feel more positive about the endorsed products. Although physically attractive sources can also be likable, sometimes the source can be physically unattractive but have features or a personality that consumers like.

We also tend to like people of average looks because they are more similar to ourselves and we can better relate to them. The Red and White Bravery Award is a classic example of how a brand can differentiate itself with a platform, built purely on the common man appeal and how their efforts to reward gallantry make heroes out of ordinary men. Red and White as a cigarette brand has been able to draw sufficient mileage out of associating itself with such an event, chiefly because the platform creates a strong brand differentiator and second a distinct brand image.

Celebrity Sources Physical attractiveness and likability explain why celebrities and well-known cartoon characters are among the most widely used sources. In this case, celebrities essentially increase the likelihood that consumers will like the ad (A_{ad}). In particular, celebrity sources can be effective when they are related to the offering (the match-up hypothesis).[81] [2]Preity Zinta's famous testimonials in the Bharat Shah case created her image as the bold and brave new face of the Indian women. Her resplendent beauty and talent was already evident through the many films and endorsements she did. This piece of bravery, where most witnesses in the case were turning hostile, projected her as a woman not just with beauty, but with a mind of her own. She went on to even receive the Red & White Bravery Awards for this year. The Brawny man, who appears on Georgia-Pacific's paper towels, recently got a complete makeover, with new hair color, new hair style, and new clothing.[83] Interestingly, spokescharacters may engender trust even if they are not directly relevant to the advertised product—and trust, in turn, influences brand attitude.[84] According to research, spokescharacters may be most effective in ads for hedonic services such as restaurants.[85]

Companies sometimes pay huge sums to get a celebrity to endorse their products: Basketball star LeBron James, for instance, has a $90 million contract to endorse Nike shoes.[86] Teenage consumers find athletes to be especially influential endorsers: the sports stars stimulate discussion about the brand and encourage brand loyalty.[87] Nonprofit organizations also use celebrities to attract attention and influence attitudes. Nicole Kidman and other celebrity endorsers for UNICEF "are of huge value," says the nonprofit's head of celebrity relations. "When a celebrity talks, people listen; there is no better messenger."[88] Using a celebrity endorser entails some risk because the spokesperson might become ill, break the law, or have another problem that could put the brand in a negative light. However, research shows that a company can actually enhance its reputation by associating with an endorser who is perceived by consumers as having little blame for a problem (such as falling ill).[89]

The Message

Just as the source can influence consumers' feelings and moods, so too can characteristics associated with the message. These message characteristics include pleasant pictures, music, humor, sex, emotional content, and context.

Pleasant Pictures Marketers frequently use pleasant pictures to influence consumers' message processing. Visual stimuli can serve as a conditioned stimulus, affect consumers' mood, or make an ad likable by making it interesting. Research has generally supported the view that pleasant pictures can affect ad and brand attitudes when they are processed peripherally, beyond the effect they have on beliefs about the product.[90] A picture of a sunset, for instance, can influence the choice of a soft drink.[91]

Numerous advertisers employ high-powered special effects rivaling those used in the movies. In one ad a Budweiser truck turns into a racing car; in another a speeding car turns into the Exxon tiger (through a process called *morphing*). Internet advertising often uses eye-catching visuals to catch consumers' attention and generate positive attitudes as well. A key goal of these ads is to look cool, thereby creating positive feelings about the ad.[92]

Music Music has been an integral part of most successful commercials produced locally. The Hamara "Bajaj" to "VIP" Kal Bhi Aaj Bhi Aaj Bhi have developed their own jingles, which have been etched in consumer's mind. Alternatively, some marketers have even used liberal doses of Bollywood music to create the impact. Either in the form of parody or original, all of them have been used in liberal doses. The recent Raymond's ad using the classic, "Aaj Kal Tere Mere Pyaar Ke Charche Har Jaban Paar" to the Radio Mirchi Advertisements where the bollywood songs are interestingly juxtaposed with everyday situations is an example of the trend of playing a popular film scene, now with songs turning an integral part of advertisements.

The popularity of music as a marketing device should not be surprising, given that music has been shown to stimulate a variety of positive effects.[95] First, music can be an effective conditioned stimulus for a classical conditioning strategy. Second, music can put the consumer in a positive mood and lead to the development of positive attitudes. Third, music can be effective in generating positive feelings such as happiness, serenity, excitement, and sentimentality. Finally, music can stimulate emotional memories. If a song in an ad reminds you of your high school days or of an old boyfriend or girlfriend, the emotions associated with these memories may transfer to an ad, brand, store, or other attitude object. Several studies have found that music can have a positive effect on purchase intentions.[96]

Whether music evokes a positive affective response depends on the music's structure. Exhibit 7.8 shows several musical characteristics and the emotional responses they may elicit. The style of music used and the product meanings it conveys can vary considerably across different cultures.[97] Marketers must therefore be careful to match their music to the desired affective responses.

Humor An ad can use humor in many different ways, including puns, understatements, jokes, ludicrous situations, satire, and irony. Humor is common in TV advertising: 24 to 42 percent of all commercials contain some form of humor.[98] Although not as widespread in other media as in television, use of humor is nevertheless extensive, particularly in radio.[99] The popularity of humor as a message device is not surprising because it increases liking of both the ad and the brand.[100]

Consumers often rate humorous ad campaigns very positively. Consumers often rate humorous ad campaigns very positively. Many advertisers of low- involvement products have used humor, including Fevicol, M-Seal and Chiclets. Humor helped Joy dish detergent capture 20 percent of the market in Japan largely

Exhibit 7.8

MUSICAL CHARACTERISTICS FOR PRODUCING VARIOUS EMOTIONAL EXPRESSIONS

Research has pinpointed the specific effect that various aspects of music can have on feelings. As shown here, the mode, tempo, pitch, rhythm, harmony, and volume of music can influence whether individuals feel serious, sad, sentimental, serene, humorous, happy, excited, majestic, or frightened.

	Emotional expression								
Musical element	**Serious**	**Sad**	**Sentimental**	**Serene**	**Humorous**	**Happy**	**Exciting**	**Majestic**	**Frightening**
MODE	Major	Minor	Minor	Major	Major	Major	Major	Major	Minor
TEMPO	Slow	Slow	Slow	Slow	Fast	Fast	Fast	Medium	Slow
PITCH	Low	Low	Medium	Medium	High	High	Medium	Medium	Low
RHYTHM	Firm	Firm	Flowing	Flowing	Flowing	Flowing	Uneven	Firm	Uneven
HARMONY	Consonant	Dissonant	Consonant	Consonant	Consonant	Consonant	Dissonant	Dissonant	Dissonant
VOLUME	Medium	Soft	Soft	Soft	Medium	Medium	Loud	Loud	Varied

Source: Gordon C. Bruner, "Music, Mood, and Marketing," *Journal of Marketing*, October 1990, p. 100. Reprinted by permission.

Exhibit 7.9
THE USE OF HUMOR
This ad uses humor to get across the point about how a cricket crazy nation responds to the World Cup.

by featuring comedian Junji Takada in a series of offbeat ads. Another good example is the ad in Exhibit 7.9.

Humor appears to be more appropriate for low-involvement offerings in which generating positive feelings about the ad is critical.[102] Humor is also most effective when it is tied or related to the offering. Otherwise, consumers will only pay attention to the humor and ignore the brand.[103] One study suggests that consumers who feel the need to seek out amusement and wittiness develop more favorable attitudes toward humorous ads. Moreover, these consumers may have less favorable attitudes toward ads with lower levels of humorous content.[104] How consumers react during a TV ad affects their evaluations of the message, as well. In one study, consumers rated TV ads as more humorous when a peak of humor occurred after a peak of surprise. In fact, the late peak of surprise was a key element in stimulating the humorous reaction.[105]

marketing IMPLICATIONS

Humor tends to work best on TV and radio because these media allow for greater expressiveness than other media.[106] Marketers also use humor even in company annual meetings or conferences or corporate night-outs, through stand-up comedians or through use of stage actors. Mahabano Kotwal, Veer Das and Ash Chandler are common names in the corporate sector who are regularly involved in entertaining audience through their variety of stand-up comedy. Humor is more effective with certain audiences than with others. In particular, younger, more educated males tend to respond most positively—apparently because aggressive and sexual types of humor appear more frequently than other types of humor, and men enjoy this more than women do.[108] Also, humor appears to be more effective for consumers who have either a lower need for cognition or a positive attitude toward the advertised brand.[109]

Finally, humor can be used effectively for consumers throughout the world. One study examined humorous ads from Germany, Thailand, South Korea, and the United States and found that most humorous ads in all four countries contained the same basic structure—contrasts between expected/possible and unexpected/impossible events.[110] However, ads in Korea and Thailand tended to emphasize humor related to group behavior and unequal status relationships, whereas the other two countries focused the humor on individuals with equal status. In all four countries, humor was more likely to be used for pleasure-oriented products. Not all countries appear to employ humor more for low-involvement products than high-involvement ones. German and Thai ads, for example, used humor equally for both types of products. Finally, U.K. marketers tend to use humorous ads more than U.S. marketers.[111]

Sex Sex as a communication technique appears in two major forms: sexual suggestiveness and nudity. Sex as a communication technique appears in two major forms: sexual suggestiveness and nudity. Sexual suggestiveness involves situations that either portray or imply sexual themes or romance. In India, sex and nudity is taboo and barring the odd condom advertisements, most advertisers refrain from getting into any controversy. The moral guardians of the society work overtime, especially in Indian context, where the controversy surrounding such advertisements may even have a negative impact on the brand too. Exhibit 7.10 showcases an advertisement of an Indian condom company. As another example, Godiva Chocolatier has used romantic images of a naked beauty on horseback, long hair covering her torso, to evoke the Lady Godiva legend on ads in international airports. The point is to position the brand "as a rich, decadent, sensuous indulgence for women," says Godiva's European marketing director.[114] Interestingly, research shows that consumers prefer mildly provocative ads and that such ads can even be effective in promoting social causes that have some connection to sex (match-up hypothesis).[115]

Although the percentage of ads with sexual overtones has not changed over the years, the type of sex appeal has. From 1964 to 1984, the use of sex in the United States became more overt and blatant.[116] As the country became more conservative in the late 1980s, ads became lighter, more playful, and more subtle—suggestive rather than blunt.[117] Ads became more blatant again until 2004, when controversy over Janet Jackson's "wardrobe malfunction" caused both public and regulatory backlash, prompting many advertisers to tone down the use of sexual references and imagery.[118]

Exhibit 7.10
EXPLICIT ADVERTISING
Sometimes ads contain explicit features to generate attention or elicit emotions toward a product or service. Here we see an ad from India of a condom company, relying on bold visuals to draw attention to the product and the brand.

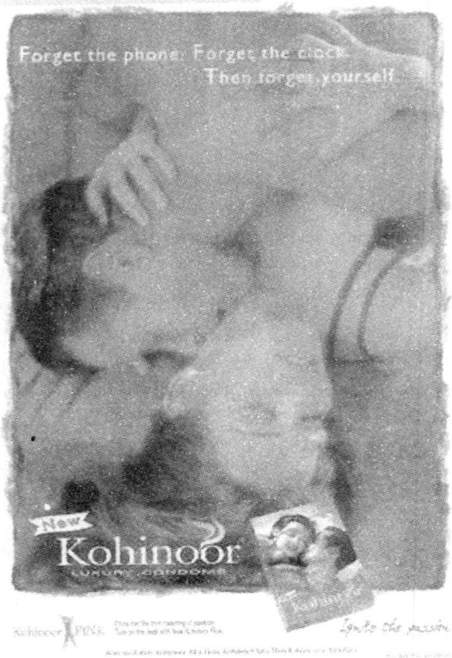

marketing IMPLICATIONS

Research on sexual themes in messages suggests that they can be effective in several ways. Sexual messages attract the consumer's attention,[119] and they also have the ability to evoke emotional responses, such as arousal, excitement, or even lust, which can affect consumers' moods and their attitudes toward the ad and the brand.[120] However, this effect is not guaranteed. For some consumers, sexual messages can create negative feelings such as embarrassment, disgust, or uneasiness, any of which would have a negative effect. In particular, research has found that women are more likely to react negatively to ads with sexy female models.[121] Women also react more negatively to nudity in general, but more positively to suggestiveness.[122] Men are much more likely than women to buy a product featured in an ad with sexual content. Yet 61 percent of the consumers surveyed in a recent study said they would be less likely to buy products advertised with sexual imagery. In this research, 53 percent of the respondents preferred love imagery over sex imagery in advertising.[123]

One survey indicated that 84 percent of females and 72 percent of males believe that TV ads place too much emphasis on sex.[124] In another survey, 49 percent said they have been embarrassed in front of friends or family by sexy TV ads, and 47 percent indicated they would not buy a product if they found an ad offensive.[125] The lesson for marketers is that sexual themes should be used very carefully and should not be demeaning, sexist, or offensive.

Whether consumers will have a positive or negative reaction to a sexual ad often depends on whether the sexual content is appropriate for the product/service. One study found that using a seductive model to sell body oil was very appealing, but having a nude model endorse a ratchet set was not.[126] Thus sexual themes would be relevant for products such as perfume, cologne, suntan lotion, and lingerie but inappropriate for tools, computers, and household cleaners.

Finally, consumer reaction to sexual messages varies from culture to culture. In some societies, such as in Europe, sexual attitudes are fairly open, and the use of sex in advertising is more widespread than in other countries. In other areas (such as Muslim and Asian countries), attitudes are more conservative, and the use of sex is much more restricted. Showing intimacy and kissing, as is done in many ads in the United States, would be totally inappropriate and even offensive in many Asian countries.[127] Consumers in different countries reacted differently to a public-service ad for breast cancer awareness in which men admired an attractive woman wearing a sundress while an announcer states, "If only women paid as much attention to their breasts as men do." Japanese consumers appreciated the humor, but French consumers disliked the sexual overtones and light treatment of a serious problem.[128]

Emotional Content Marketers can plan communications to accommodate or enhance consumers' existing MAO and processing effort in the presence of cognitive attitudes. The same holds true for affective attitudes, which is where emotionally involving messages come into play.

One special type of emotional message is called ***transformational advertising.***[129] The goal of a transformational ad is to associate the experience of using the product with a unique set of psychological characteristics. These ads try to increase emotional involvement by making the use of the product or service a warmer, more exciting, more pleasing, and richer experience, as opposed to informational ads, which seek only to present factual information. Coca-Cola, for example, uses transformational advertising to convey that "Coke is a part of the pleasure of everyday life, the pleasure of aliveness, relaxation, and being connected," says the company's chief marketing officer. Its "Make It Real" campaign focuses on memorable experiences such as driving cross-country and learning basketball tips from a sports star.[130]

Dramas can also increase emotional involvement in a message. A drama message has characters, a plot, and a story about the use of the product or service.[131] This type of message aims to involve consumers emotionally and influence positive attitudes through both sympathy and empathy.[132] Web retailer Amazon.com recently hosted Amazon Theater, a series of five- to ten-minute mini-movies about characters facing poignant or comic challenges. Each movie featured a number of products sold on the Amazon site. For example, one movie told the story of two strangers—wearing clothing and accessories that can be purchased on Amazon—who meet during a subway ride. Credits at the end of each movie listed all products, along with a link to learn more and buy. An Amazon official observed that consumers were "watching and shopping in great droves during lunchtime," with as many as half a million consumers visiting the site in a one-hour period.[133]

Message Context The program or editorial context in which an ad appears can affect consumers' evaluation of the message. First, ads embedded in a happy TV program may be evaluated more positively than those in sad programs, especially if the ads are emotional.[134] Similarly, how well we like the program can affect our feelings about the ad and the brand.[135] One explanation is that the programs influence us to process information in a manner consistent with our mood. Or, according to the excitation transfer hypothesis, we may mistakenly attribute to the ad our feelings about the TV program.[136]

One note of caution: A TV program can become too arousing and distract viewers from the ads. In an interesting study that compared consumers' reactions to ads during the Super Bowl, ad responses in the winning city were inhibited in contrast to those in the losing and neutral cities.[137] Another study shows that placing ads in violent programs can inhibit processing and ad recall.[138]

Summary

Marketers can use a variety of techniques to change consumers' attitudes when motivation, ability, and opportunity (MAO) are low and the effort consumers use to process information, make decisions, or engage in behavior is also low. When attitudes of low MAO consumers are based on cognitive processing, the message should affect their beliefs, which may be formed by simple inferences, attributions, or heuristics. Marketers can also affect the salience, strength, or favorability of consumers' beliefs on which attitudes are based. Credibility of the source, information consistent with the offering category, a large number of message arguments, simple arguments, and the extent of repetition can influence one or more dimensions of beliefs.

According to the mere exposure effect, when effort (MAO) is low, consumers' attitudes toward an offering become more favorable as they become more familiar with it. Classical conditioning predicts that consumers' attitudes toward an offering (the conditioned stimulus) are enhanced when it is repeatedly paired with a stimulus (the unconditioned stimulus) that evokes a positive emotional response (the unconditioned response). This effect is most likely to occur when the unconditioned stimulus is novel, when the consumer is aware of the link, when the conditioned and unconditioned stimuli fit together, and when the conditioned stimulus precedes the unconditioned one. Furthermore, if consumers like a particular ad (attitudes about the ad are called A_{ad}), these feelings may be transferred to the brand (attitudes about the brand are called A_b). Consumers' moods and their tendency to evaluate an offering in accordance with their moods can also affect attitudes toward an offering.

Finally, marketers can use marketing communications to induce favorable attitudes based on affective processes when consumers' motivation, ability, opportunity, and effort are low. Characteristics of the source (attractiveness, likability); the message (attractive pictures, pleasant music, humor, sex, emotionally involving messages); and the context (repetition, program or editorial context) can influence affective attitudes.

Questions for Review and Discussion

1. What role do source, message, context, and repetition play in influencing consumers' cognitive attitudes?
2. What is the mere exposure effect, and why is it important to consumers' affective reactions?
3. How does classical conditioning apply to consumers' attitudes when processing effort is low?
4. Explain the dual-mediation hypothesis. What are the implications for affecting consumers' brand attitudes?
5. In low-effort situations, what characteristics of the message influence consumers' affective response?
6. What are the advantages and disadvantages of featuring celebrities in advertising messages?
7. Why must marketers consider local attitudes when planning to use sex in ad messages for different countries?

Exercises

1. Watch at least four hours of commercial television. Prepare a chart that lists all the techniques discussed in this chapter across the top as columns (attractive source, likable source, visuals, music, humor, sex, emotion, simple message, repetition, and so on). For each ad, tally which techniques are used. Also, briefly assess the effectiveness of each ad in terms of creating positive A_{ad} and A_b, attitudes about the ad and the brand. After collecting this information for all ads viewed during the four hours, answer the following questions:
   a. Which techniques are used most frequently?
   b. In your judgment, which ads tend to be the most effective in influencing attitudes toward the ad and the brand? Why?
   c. In your judgment, which ads tend to be the least effective? Why?
2. Collect five magazines that are directed at different target audiences. Prepare a chart that lists all the techniques discussed in this chapter across the top as columns (attractive source, likable source, visuals, humor, sex, emotion, simple message, repetition, and so on). Down the side of this chart, generate a running list of the different product and service categories that appear in the ads. For each ad in each magazine, make a tally of the type of product advertised and the type(s) of techniques used. Then answer the following questions:
   a. Which techniques are used most frequently?
   b. Do certain techniques tend to be used more often for certain product or service categories?
   c. Do the magazines in general use certain techniques more often for certain target audiences?

More Exercises from the Adaptor

1. Pick up any product category and evaluate its advertising in the last 4 decades between 1970-2007 and critically observe how the format of advertising has changed. The visual appeals, the language of the advertisements and the kind of target audience they are targeting. The changes may be evaluated keeping the time period into account and how the changing dynamism of the society is captured through these advertisements.

References

[1] Source: http://www.The Hindu Business Line High in spirits.mht

http://www.The Hindu Business Line Rising up to the challenge.mht

http://www.The Hindu Business Line Seagram garners 25 pc share of premium Indian whisky market.mht

[2] Source: http://www.indiafm.com/stills/partiesn-events/Preity_Zinta_receives_Red_and_White_bravery_award/index.html

chapter 8 Memory and Retrieval

LEARNING OBJECTIVES

After studying this chapter, you will be able to:

- Distinguish between sensory memory, short-term memory, and long-term memory, and discuss why marketers must be aware of these types of memory.
- Understand how the processes that enhance memory can help marketers plan more effective strategies.
- Explain what retrieval is, how it works, and how marketers try to affect it.

INTRODUCTION

McDonald's pricing reminisces memory

Marketers sometimes use nostalgia to drive a point. In a price sensitive market like India, McDonald's has been focusing on the price point very aggressively. One of the platform through which it emphasizes the price point is the throwback days of reduced prices. The range of products it offers like, Burgers, Ice Creams, Drinks, McPuff etc. all at the Rs.20/- price point. This is reinforced through the series of advertisements, commercials and in-store publicity that the company deploys to highlight the price platform.

Exhibit 8.1 is a popular television commercial of a retired army officer who visits a McDonald's store and after listening to the prices of the burger; he is quickly transformed to his active days and starts giving orders as if on a battle field. He also takes out a photograph of his heydays when in the service and the caption, "Ho gayi Purani Yaadein Taaza" typifies the days of lower prices. Infact, what is even more synchronic about the series, are the link they finally establish to the global positioning of the brand, "I'm lovin' it."

The McDonald's Happy Price Menu is also a part of their global plank, with an adaptation in the communication. The series also has other such related situations where yesteryears film stars are also showcased in their popular characters (like a Dilip Kumar look-alike in the garb of Salim) to highlight the platform of "Ho gayi Purani Yaadein Taaza".

A retired army officer goes to McDonald's and orders for one Chicken McGrill.

Hearing the price as low as Rs 20 from the manager, he goes back to his old days...

...of serving in the army and orders an attack. As the others around him witness the...

...abrupt change in him, the VO plays, "Ho gayi purani yaadein taaza? McDonald's...

Exhibit 8.1

McDonald's uses price points to push their products. The low pricing is a metaphor to the golden days, when prices of all products were very low and a discerning customer is forced to take a walk back on memory lane.

...ka happy prize menu. Aaj bhi only...

...twenty rupees." Super: "I'm lovin' it."

The campaign has been successful in creating appeal in the urban youth in the age group of 18-25 years. For the kids it has a separate set of communication promoting merchandise & toys, which is run separately. In essence therefore, the plank works successfully with a bisection of consumers, who perceive McDonald's to be expensive and on the other hand the youth in schools and colleges, eating out, can explore McDonald's as an option.

What's driving the popularity of nostalgia marketing? Consumers in today's fast-paced, information-intensive age are feeling overwhelmed by the new and unfamiliar, which leaves them more receptive to familiar products, songs, and images. Reminders of familiar offerings can also enhance brand awareness and brand knowledge because consumers already have a rich storehouse of personal experiences associated with these offerings in memory. Many of these memories reflect a quieter, more peaceful time. Hearing the name of an old product, seeing an old ad, or hearing an old jingle reminds consumers of their positive feelings about this earlier time and generates positive attitudes toward both the ad and the advertised brand. All these concepts are covered in this chapter.

What Is Memory?

Consumer memory is a vast personal storehouse of knowledge about products, services, shopping excursions, and consumption experiences. In essence, memory reflects our prior knowledge. ***Retrieval*** is the process of remembering, or accessing, what we have stored in memory.

We can store and remember information such as what brands or services we have used in the past; features of these products or services; how, where, when, and why we bought them; their price; how, where, when, and why we used them; and whether or not we liked them. We can store and remember information about old products we have disposed of, such as a favorite car we sold. We also have memories of special experiences—for example, a concert we attended with friends. The information we store and can retrieve is learned from many sources—marketing communications, the media, word of mouth, and personal experience.

Our memory and ability to retrieve information depend at least in part on our motivation, ability, and opportunity (MAO) to process the information to which we have been exposed. Our ability to carry out day-to-day activities clearly depends on our being able to put new information into our memory and retrieve old information when we need it.

Knowledge, Attitudes, and Memory

We began to discuss certain aspects of memory and retrieval in the preceding three chapters. Chapter 5 noted that information stored in memory affects whether and how we interpret and categorize objects. Chapters 6 and 7 indicated that attitudes are part of our memory—they represent stored summary evaluations of objects. Moreover, we can and often do recall attitudes when we make decisions. Thus memory and retrieval are affected by how we know and understand information through attention, categorization, and comprehension—and by attitude formation processes.

Memory, Retrieval, and Decision Making

How do memory and retrieval influence the way we act and the decisions we make? If you need soap, you might simply remember the brand you bought the last time and buy it again the next time you go shopping. You may decide to buy season tickets to a sporting event because you can vividly remember what a good time you had when you went with your friends. You may decide not to go to a certain restaurant because you remember the bad service from your last visit. We often receive information about an offering at one time and use that information to make purchase, usage, or disposition decisions at another time. Memory and retrieval make this two-stage process possible.

What Are the Types of Memory?

Memory represents more than the prior knowledge we discussed in Chapter 5. Exhibit 8.2 indicates three types of memory: sensory memory (echoic and iconic memory), short-term memory (imagery and discursive processing), and long-term memory (autobiographical and semantic memory). Let us look at what type of memory means.

Sensory Memory

Assume for a minute that as you are talking to the person seated next to you at a dinner party, you happen to overhear other guests talking about a new movie you want to see. You do not want to appear rude, so you try to pay full attention to your dinner partner, but you really want to hear what the others are saying about the movie. Even though you cannot listen to both conversations simultaneously, you can store, for a relatively short period, bits and pieces of the other conversation. So you might be listening to your dinner partner but switch your attention to the other conversation once you hear the word *amazing*. As another example, assume that you are doing your homework in front of the TV. Your roommate comes in and says, "That's a great commercial!" Although you have not been listening, right after your roommate makes this statement, you realize that you heard the words *Mountain Dew*. You realize it is a Mountain Dew commercial, and you say, "Yeah, I really like that one, too."

The ability to store sensory experiences temporarily as they are produced is called ***sensory memory.*** Sensory memory uses a short-term storage area called the sensory store. Sensory memory operates automatically, and if we quickly switch our attention to our sensory store, we may be able to interpret what is in it. If we do not analyze this information right away, however, it disappears from the sensory store, and we cannot determine its meaning.

Echoic and Iconic Memory Our sensory store can house information from any of the senses, but ***echoic memory***—memory of things we hear—and ***iconic memory***—sensory memory of things we see—are the most commonly studied.[3] The Mountain Dew example illustrates echoic memory. Here is another example: You may have found that when someone asks you a question and you are not really listening, you can say, "What did you say?" and actually "play back" what the person said. Iconic memory is at work when you drive by a sign and see it quickly, only to realize after you pass that it was a sign for Applebee's.

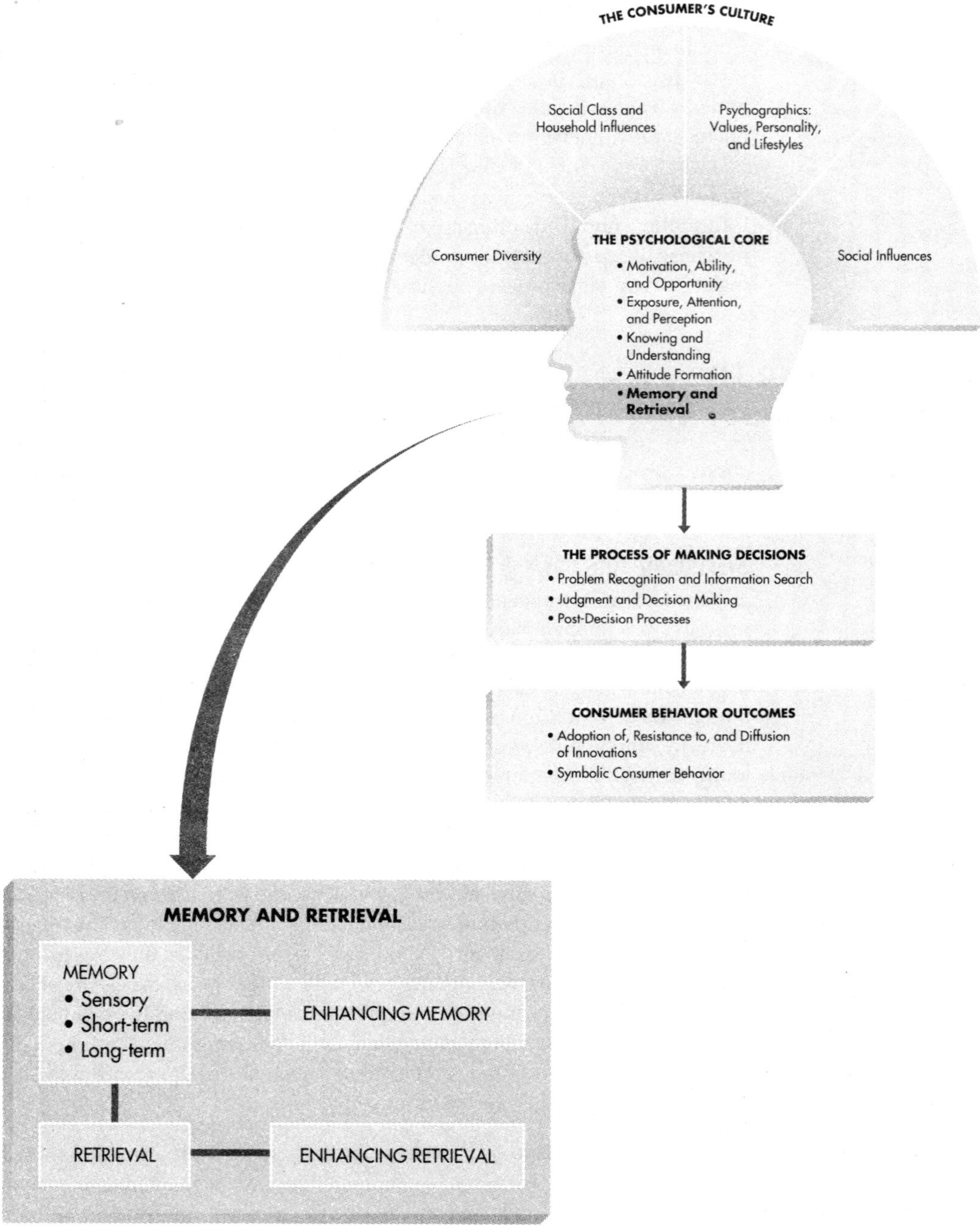

Exhibit 8.2

CHAPTER OVERVIEW: MEMORY AND RETRIEVAL *We can identify three types of memory: sensory memory, short-term memory (STM), and long-term memory (LTM). Once information is in memory, it can then be retrieved (recognized or recalled). This chapter shows (1) what influences the transfer of information from STM to LTM and (2) what affects the likelihood that information will be retrieved from memory.*

Characteristics of Sensory Memory Information in sensory memory is stored in its actual sensory form. In other words, we store *amazing* as it sounds, and we store it exactly, not as a synonym. Information in sensory memory is also short-lived, generally lasting from a quarter of a second to several seconds.[4] If the information is relevant, we will be motivated to process it further, and it may enter what is called short-term memory. However, if we do not analyze that information, it is lost.

Short-Term Memory

Short-term memory (STM) is the portion of memory where we encode or interpret incoming information in light of existing knowledge.[5] The processes of knowing and understanding discussed in Chapter 5 occur in short-term memory. As you read this book, you are using your short-term memory to comprehend what you read. You also use short-term memory when you watch a TV commercial or make a decision in a store. Short-term memory is very important because it is where most of our information processing takes place. Marketers should minimize auditory distractions during ads that convey information using text, because the sounds compete for attention that consumers need to encode and then interpret the words.[6]

Exhibit 8.3
STIMULATING IMAGERY
By using a visual illustration of a straight old man and a bent old man the brand showcases the effect Ranipal starch might drive in.

Imagery and Discursive Processing The information in short-term memory can take one of several forms. When we think about an object—say, an apple—we might use ***discursive processing*** and represent it by the word *apple*. Alternatively, we could represent it visually as a picture of an apple or in terms of its smell, its feel, what it sounds like when we bite into it, or what it tastes like. Representing the visual, auditory, tactile, gustatory, and/or olfactory properties of an apple uses ***imagery processing.***[7] Unlike the case of discursive processing, an object in imagery processing bears a close resemblance to the thing being represented.[8] Thus if you were asked to describe an apple and a car, imagery processing would ensure that you preserve their relative sizes. Exhibit 8.3 is an ad that stimulates imagery processing.

For both imagery and discursive processing, information in short-term memory varies in how much we elaborate on it.[9] When MAO is low, short-term memory might consist of a simple reproduction of a stimulus—for example, the word *skier* or a picture of a skier. When MAO is high, however, consumers can use elaborated imagery processing to engage in daydreams, fantasies, and visual problem solving, or elaborated discursive processing to think about upcoming events or work out solutions to current problems. For example, if you are thinking about a skiing vacation, you may develop an elaborate fantasy about lounging around the fireplace at a resort hotel, drinking hot cider, and feeling the ache of your tired muscles and the company of your friends. You might also use discursive processing to compare the prices and attributes of various resorts. All this information, whether represented as images or words, can serve as important input for decisions.

Characteristics of Short-Term Memory Short-term memory has two interesting characteristics:

- Short-term memory is limited. We can hold only a certain number of things in short-term memory at any one time. For example, if you have to go to the store right now and buy two items, chips and hot dogs, you will have little trouble remembering what to buy. But suppose you have to buy nine items: chips, hot dogs, coffee, cookies, baking soda, plastic wrap, toothpaste, spaghetti sauce, and dog food. Chances are high that you will forget one or more of these items unless you make a shopping list.
- *Short-term memory is short-lived.* The information held in short-term memory is very short-lived unless that information is transferred to long-term memory. Unless we actively try to remember information, it will be lost. This explains why we sometimes learn someone's name only to forget it two minutes later.

marketing IMPLICATIONS

Short-term memory, particularly imagery processing, has many interesting implications for marketers.

Imagery can create liking for the product

First, imagery processing is used often and can affect how we behave. The vacation we choose, for example, may be greatly influenced by our imagery of what it will be like. We value some of the products we buy (for example, novels or music) because of the imagery they provide.[10] Thus a product's ability to stimulate multisensory imagery might affect how much we like that product. You may, for example, like novels that are so descriptive that you can actually imagine the sights, sounds, smells, and tastes experienced by the characters in the book.

Imagery can stimulate memories of past experiences

Second, we value some products or promotional tools because they promote imagery that allows us to vicariously experience a past consumption experience. Thus you might keep a sports program or ticket stub because it evokes imagery that allows you to relive the event. As another example, VIP the popular suitcase company in the 80's had introduced this campaign of "Kal Bhi Aaj Bhi Kal Bhi", which harped on the nostalgia element of the brand and its existence of over 4 decades in the market. It showcased the girl's marriage and a flashback of how VIP the brand was always there since the girl was growing up and as she leaves today for her new abode, VIP will be there with her.

Imagery affects evaluation

Third, the use of imagery can affect the way we evaluate products. Using imagery processing, we may be able to process a lot of information about something simply because more information helps to flesh out the image. Nordstrom.com and Bluefly.com, for example, encourage imagery by allowing consumers to zoom in on the product to get a closer look at it. This closer look may help consumers better imagine what it might be like to own these products, which can in turn help them better evaluate it. However, adding more information when using discursive processing, like providing lists of attributes, may lead to information overload.

Imagery affects satisfaction

Finally, imagery may affect how satisfied we are with a product or consumption experience. We may create an elaborate image or fantasy of just what the product or consumption experience will be like (how great we will look in a new car or how relaxing a vacation might be) only to find that it does not materialize as we had imagined. If reality disconfirms our imagery, we may feel dissatisfied. Some marketers use pictures to help consumers establish realistic imagery. Lands' End, for example, helps online shoppers envision clothing in use by clicking to see how a certain item looks on a virtual model set to each consumer's measurements.

Long-Term Memory

Long-term memory (LTM) is that part of memory where information is permanently stored for later use. Research in cognitive psychology has identified two major types of long-term memory: autobiographical and semantic memory.[12]

Autobiographical Memory ***Autobiographical,*** *or* ***episodic, memory*** represents knowledge we have about ourselves and our past.[13] It includes past experiences as well as emotions and sensations tied to these experiences. These memories tend to be primarily sensory, mainly involving visual images, although they may also include sounds, smells, tastes, and tactile sensations. In a consumer context, we may have autobiographical memories that relate to acquisition, such as buying a specific product or making a specific shopping trip. And we may have autobiographical memories regarding consumption or disposition, such as attending a particular concert or throwing away a well-worn but loved product. The ad in Exhibit 8.4 shows how autobiographical memory can be used in advertising.

Exhibit 8.4
AUTOBIOGRAPHICAL MEMORY
This ad stimulates autobiographical memories of growing up and how age starts catching up more than one can realize it.

Because each individual has a unique set of experiences, autobiographical memory tends to be very personal and idiosyncratic. If you were asked to remember the road test you took when you got your driver's license, you might have stored in long-term memory the sequence of events that occurred on that day: what car you drove, what your route was, how nervous you were, what your instructor told you to do, and what happened after you passed (or failed!).

Semantic Memory A lot of what we have stored in memory is not related to specific experiences. For example, we have memory for the concept called "dog." We know that dogs have four legs, are furry, wag their tails, and so on. This knowledge is true of all dogs and is not tied to any dog in particular. Knowledge about the world that is detached from specific episodes is called ***semantic memory.***

marketing IMPLICATIONS Much of the knowledge we have stored in cognitive categories reflects semantic memory. Thus many of the marketing implications previously presented about knowledge stored in categories also relate to semantic memory. Autobiographical memory, however, is also important to marketers.

Affecting decision making

Each consumer has a large storehouse of consumer-related experiences whose affective associations can influence the way products and services are evaluated. For example, if you ate at a particular restaurant and found a hair in your food, the memory of this experience might prevent you from eating there again. Positive experiences would have the opposite effect. When selecting a restaurant, you might recall a previous episode in which the food was fabulous or the service incredible—memories that would clearly influence your decision about eating there again.

Promoting empathy and identification

Autobiographical memories can play a role in creating identification with characters or situations in ads. For example, arranged marriages in India being an event in itself, where invariably the would be bride's father has to go through a process, which is fairly long, cumbersome, at times embarrassing and even to the extent of showcasing the bride more than once to the prospect. Exhibit 8.5 will instantly help audiences relate to the drudgery and the pain of selection, rejection and selection.

Exhibit 8.5
PROMOTING IDENTIFICTION
Any consumer who has had the unfortunate experience of going through the drudgery of looking for a prospective suitor can reminisce with the advertisement

Cueing and preserving autobiographical memories

As the introduction to this chapter suggested, consumers value some products because they promote autobiographical memories by creating feelings of nostalgia—a fondness for the past.[14] Consumers often find it important to preserve memories of graduations, weddings, the birth of a child, and so on. Entire industries for products such as digital cameras and photo printers, video cameras, and diaries focus on consumers' desires to document these autobiographical memories. The scrapbook industry has become a $1.2 billion business.[15] Consumers in many cultures want to preserve autobiographical memories.[16] Consumers who have moved from one country to another sometimes build shrines in their houses to remind them of the culture they left behind. In the Niger Republic, consumers highly value possessions that remind them of their friends, family, and important events in their lives.

Reinterpreting memories

Research shows that advertising can even affect consumers' autobiographical memories. One study had consumers sample various good- and bad-tasting orange juices and then watch ads that described the products' good taste. Those exposed to the ads remembered the bad-tasting juice as being better tasting than it actually was.[17]

How Memory Is Enhanced

Because we must attend to something before we can remember it, many of the factors that affect attention (described in Chapter 4) also affect memory. Several additional processes, however, including *chunking, rehearsal, recirculation,* and *elaboration,* also affect memory.[18] These processes are useful for influencing short-term memory or for increasing the likelihood that information will be transferred to long-term memory—with important implications for marketers.

Chunking

Traditionally, researchers have believed that the most individuals can process in short-term memory at any one time is three to seven "chunks" of information. Later studies suggest that the number may be closer to three or four.[19] A ***chunk*** is a group of items that is processed as a unit. For example, phone numbers are typically grouped into three chunks: the area code, the exchange, and four numbers.

Exhibit 8.6
RECIRCULATION
IThe "Intel Inside" campaign featured in various computer advertisements and this is another instance of reinforcing Intel's stand on computers

Rehearsal

Whereas chunking increases the likelihood that information will not be lost from short-term memory, rehearsal affects the transfer of information to long-term memory. ***Rehearsal*** means that we actively and consciously interact with the material we are trying to remember. We can either silently repeat the material or actively think about the information and its meaning, as we would when studying for an exam. In marketing contexts, rehearsal is likely to occur only when consumers are motivated to process and remember information. If you are motivated to find the best car on the market, you might study the characteristics of various models so you do not forget them.

Recirculation

Information can also be transferred to long-term memory through the process of ***recirculation.*** Water is recirculated when it goes through the same pipe again and again. In the same way, information is recirculated through your short-term memory when you encounter it repeatedly. Unlike rehearsal, with recirculation we make no active attempt to remember the information. Rather, if we do remember, it is because the information has passed through our brain so many times. For example, you can probably recall the names of the streets adjacent to yours or the name of a store near your home—even if you have never gone down these streets, been to the store, or tried to memorize them. Why? Simply because you see them almost every day. Recirculation may be at work in Exhibit 8.6.

Elaboration

Finally, information can be transferred into long-term memory if it is processed at deeper levels, or ***elaborated.***[20] We can try to remember information through rote memorization or rehearsal; however, this type of processing is not always effective. If you have ever memorized material for an exam, you probably noticed that you forgot most of what you learned within two or three days. More enduring memory is established when we try to relate information to prior knowledge and past experiences. If you see an ad for a new product, for instance, you might elaborate on the ad information by thinking about how you would use the product in your day-to-day life. As a result, you may have a better memory for the brand and what the ad said about it.

marketing IMPLICATIONS Marketers can apply the concepts of chunking, rehearsal, recirculation, and elaboration when trying to help consumers remember their brands, communications, or offerings.

Chunking

Because we can more easily process smaller as opposed to larger pieces of information at any one time, marketers can increase the likelihood that consumers will hold information in short-term memory and transfer it to long-term memory by providing larger bits of information that chunk together smaller bits. For example, acronyms reduce several pieces of information to one chunk. Brand names like IBM and KFC are examples of chunking in a marketing context. Similarly, marketers can facilitate consumers' memory for telephone numbers by providing words rather than individual numbers or digits (800-GO-U-HAUL). Advertisements might draw conclusions that summarize or chunk disparate pieces of information into a single attribute or benefit. For example, an ad that discusses a food product's calorie, fat, sodium, and sugar content might chunk this information into a conclusion about the product's healthfulness.

Rehearsal

When motivation is low, marketers may use tactics to enhance motivation and perpetuate rehearsal. In the early 80's, Taj Mahal Tea, had introduced Taj Mahal Tea Bags and the jingle for the ad went, "Dip Dip Dip, add sugar and add milk and it's ready to drink". The phrase Dip Dip Dip became so popular that even today substantial segments of population who use tea bags refer it as "Dip Dip". Engaging jingles and slogans may be a useful means of inducing rehearsal. Sometimes they work too well, as you may know from going through the day singing a commercial's jingle. Rehearsal isn't always good for marketers. One study found that consumers who rehearsed the price paid for a product on the last occasion by physically writing it down (when paying by check or entering the amount into financial management software, for example) had lower repurchase intentions for that product.[21] The memory of the price presumably made more obvious what consumers had to give up to obtain the product.

Recirculation

Recirculation is an important principle for marketing because it explains why repetition of marketing communications affects memory, particularly in low-involvement situations.[22] Marketers can strengthen the effect of recirculation by creating different ads that repeat the same basic message. The slogan line which Maruti today uses, "Count on us" is used across all advertisements of Maruti and the caption also has a toll free number for viewers to make calls. Today the slogan is also put across in Maruti showrooms, car windowpanes and even as bumper stickers. This is also the thinking behind palmOne's recent airport campaign for the Treo smart phone. The company put up as many as 30 posters at departure and arrival gates, baggage claim areas, and other high-traffic airport areas, repeating the same basic message using a variety of executions, so consumers see the Treo name four, five, or even six times as they walk to or from the plane.[23]

Recirculation may also explain why communications that repeat the brand name frequently, either within an ad or across communications, tend to produce better memory for the brand name. With the telecom boom, particularly in the mobile telephony business, marketers are making aggressive attempts to garner maximum subscriber base on to their kitty. The increased mobility of the consumers also help telecom operators to target roaming customers, by placing strategic hoardings and signage on airport or railway station stretches and even inside the airports and railway stations. According to research, planning spaced exposures by alternating messages in involving media such as TV commercials and less involving media such as billboards can be a highly effective repetition strategy for marketers.[25] However, when one brand repeatedly advertises product claims that are similar to claims promoted repeatedly by a close competitor, the repetition may actually confuse consumers rather than enhance memory.[26]

Elaboration

Several strategies familiar from previous chapters enhance the likelihood that consumers will elaborate on information. For example, unexpected or novel stimuli can attract attention and induce elaboration.[27] [1]The 'Digen Verma' promotion campaign was one of the most interesting and innovative teaser campaigns ever made in India. Designed and executed by Everest Integrated Communications Designed and executed by Everest Integrated Communications (Everest), it was a series of teaser campaigns launched by Parle Agrochemicals for its mango drink Frooti, which aroused the curiosity of the public, especially teenagers. The enigma called 'Digen Verma' was everywhere, in buses, film halls, colleges, cyber cafes and shopping malls. 'Just who is Digen Verma?' That's what the nation seemed to be have been wanting to know. In the 15 days that the campaign lasted in (February 2001), Digen Verma seemed to have become the most talked about faceless name in the country. Also, an advertising agency study indicates that consumers who pay attention to a particular TV program and think about it are more likely to remember the commercials.[28] Elaboration may explain why children and seniors tend to remember less from marketing communications than do other age groups. The elderly may have less ability to elaborate on information, perhaps because their short-term memory is more limited. Children may elaborate less because they have less knowledge, which makes it more difficult for them to think extensively about a message.[29] Elaboration may also explain why moderate levels of humor in an ad enhance both encoding and retrieval of the product's claims, whereas strong humor inhibits elaboration of the claims.[30]

What Is Retrieval?

In Chapter 5, you learned that knowledge is organized into categories and linked to associations. These categories and associations also relate to the concepts of memory and retrieval.

Organization of Long-Term Memory

Memory researchers have attempted to represent the organization of long-term memory, or prior knowledge, as a series of ***semantic (or associative) networks.*** Exhibit 8.7 represents one consumer's memory or prior knowledge about the category called "vacations," specifically the associations the consumer has to a St. Moritz ski vacation, a member of the "ski vacation" category. That category, in turn, is part of the higher-order "luxury vacation" category. The St. Moritz ski vacation concept is connected to a set of links (called associations and beliefs in previous chapters). How did these links get there? They were learned and remembered based on personal experiences or information the consumer heard or read. Some links represent autobiographic memories, whereas others represent semantic

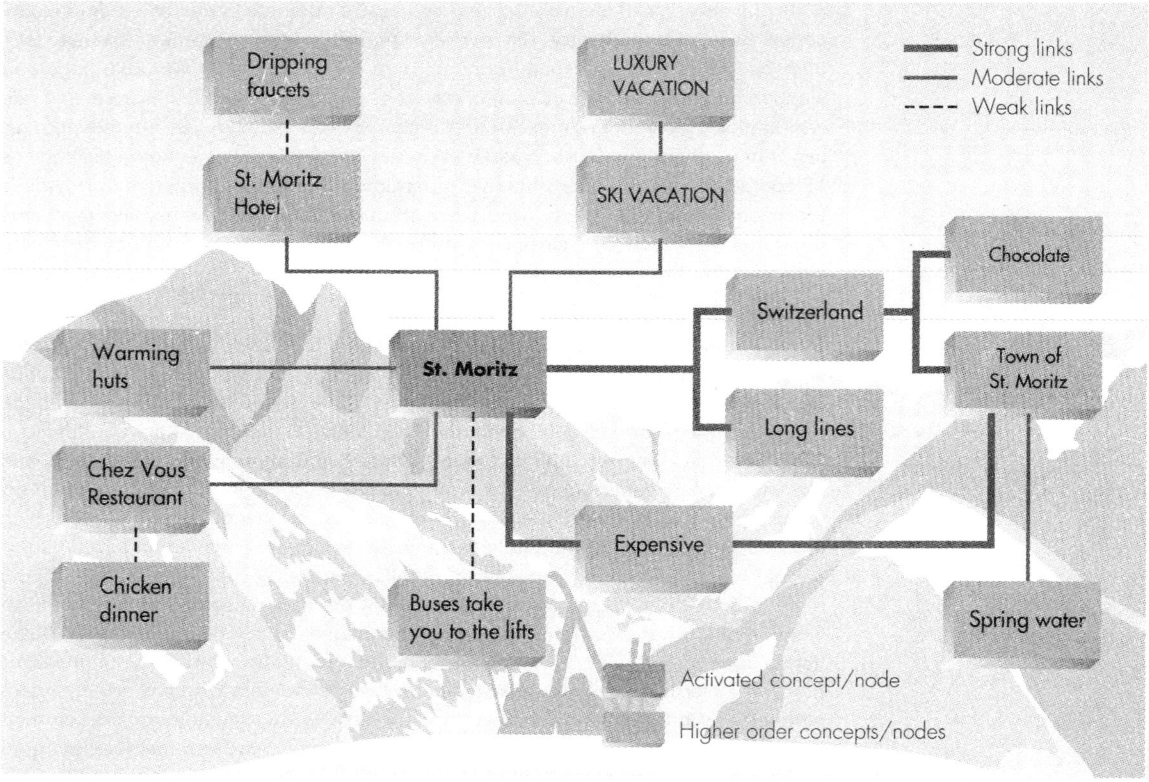

Exhibit 8.7
A SEMANTIC (OR ASSOCIATIVE) NETWORK

A semantic network is a set of concepts connected by links. When one concept is activated, others may become activated via the links. Concepts connected by strong links are more likely to activate each other than those connected by weak links.

memory. The group of associations or links connected to the "St. Moritz ski vacation" concept is called a semantic (or associative) network.

Notice that the links in the semantic network shown in Exhibit 8.7 vary in strength. Strong links, depicted by the thick lines, are firmly established in memory. Others, depicted by the dashed lines, are weakly established in memory. Some links are strong because they have been rehearsed, recirculated, chunked, and elaborated extensively. Others are weak because they have been encountered infrequently, have not been accessed in a long time, or have been processed on a very limited basis. The entire semantic network represents what is available in this consumer's memory about the concept called "St. Moritz ski vacation."

The Semantic Network

We have a considerable amount of information available in our memory but are able to retrieve or access only some of it at any given time.[31] We have all been in situations in which we try to remember something but cannot. Two factors about the semantic network affect what we remember: trace strength and spreading of activation.[32]

Trace Strength The first factor affecting the semantic network is the strength of the links or associations, known as ***trace strength.*** The stronger the link that connects information to the category, the more ***accessible*** the information is and the easier it is to retrieve from memory. You are more likely to remember that BMW is "the ultimate driving machine" if you have a strong association connecting the car with its slogan. Marketers often try to strengthen our memory links. Lifebuoy's relaunch in the urban markets in the 90's saw a plethora of brands like Lifebuoy Plus, Gold, Liquid Soap to name a few all targeted the health and hygiene platform and today the brand is synonymous to health and hygiene. [2]The Unilever website proclaims about Lifebuoy as, "Lifebuoy's goal is to provide affordable and accessible hygiene and health solutions that enable people to lead a life without fear of hygiene anxieties and health consequences". [3]The Lifebuoy 'Swasthya Chetna' ('Health Awakening') campaign – the single largest rural health and hygiene education programme ever undertaken in India – adopts a multi-stage approach over two or three years to ensure handwashing becomes part of everyday life. The more marketers can engage in recirculation, or encourage consumers to rehearse or elaborate on information, the greater the likelihood that the link will be strengthened and consumers will be better able to retrieve that information.

Spreading of Activation A second factor explaining what gets retrieved from memory is called ***spreading of activation.*** Think of a semantic network as a kind of electric network. Strong links have the potential for generating high-voltage current, and weak links have the potential for generating low-voltage current. Using the example in Exhibit 8.7, if a concept like St. Moritz is activated in the consumer's semantic network, the strong link between "St. Moritz" and "expensive" will activate or make the consumer think about "expensive." Because the current connecting St. Moritz and expensive is very strong, the electrical potential from this current will spread to adjacent items in the semantic network, particularly along strong links. This spreading of activation will likely lead the consumer to remember the town of St. Moritz. The activation of the concept "St. Moritz" may also activate "Switzerland" and "long lines." Activation from "Switzerland" may, in turn, spread to the concept "chocolate."

Of course, concepts like Switzerland, chocolate, and expensive are linked to many semantic networks, not just to one. Our consumer may think about chocolate when prompted to think about St. Moritz, but chocolate may be strongly linked to other semantic networks that can be cued through spreading of activation. This consumer may start thinking that she recently bought chocolate at a Godiva store, which may lead her to remember a friend she saw there. Spreading of activation explains why we sometimes have seemingly random thoughts as the activation spreads from one semantic network to another.

MAO can influence spreading of activation. If motivation and opportunity to process information are high, the number of activated links can also be quite high. On the other hand, when motivation or opportunity are low, only the closest and strongest links might be activated. Individuals with more knowledge about a concept will have a greater ability to process a more detailed semantic network, bringing forth any number of associations.[34]

Because strong links enhance an item's accessibility from memory, they are very important to marketers. The weak links are not unimportant, however. Activation spreads to every link in the semantic network, although the activation may not be sufficient to cause consumers to remember an item. A concept that has been activated but not sufficiently to make it retrievable from memory is said to have been ***primed.*** It has been given a jump start. Suppose our consumer is trying to remember how she got to the lifts at St. Moritz. The "buses" link is not strongly established in her memory. Activating St. Moritz might prime the bus concept, but the activation is too weak for the consumer to remember the bus. If she later drives by a school, the activation of school might cue buses, and this activation might be sufficient for her to remember that she got to the ski lift in St. Moritz by taking a bus.

Retrieval Failures

Trace strength and spreading of activation help to explain forgetting—the failure to retrieve information from memory. Forgetting is a fact of life. You might forget to get your car serviced or forget that you are cooking hard-boiled eggs (until they explode). Retrieval failures clearly affect consumers' purchase, consumption, and disposition behaviors.

Decay In some cases, we forget things because trace strength fades; that is, memory links ***decay*** over time, often because they are not used. Thus we tend to forget events from childhood because they happened so long ago. The likelihood of decay is reduced when we are repeatedly exposed to information through recirculation or when we retrieve it often from memory. Sometimes the details or attributes of the information we have learned decay.[35] For example, we might have heard a lot of detailed information about a new movie, such as what the plot was about and who starred in it. Yet, later we may remember only something general about it ("I've heard it was good").

That consumers can forget attributes explains some interesting marketing phenomena. For example, consumers may have equally strong memories for brands about which they have heard either very bad or very good things. They forget the information stated about the brands; all they remember is that the brands were in the news. Forgetting also explains the sleeper effect, discussed in Chapter 6, in which consumers show more positive attitudes toward a bad ad as time passes. Researchers believe that over time, consumers forget that an ad lacked credibility and simply remember what the source said about the brand. In essence, memory for the source decays more rapidly than memory for the message.[36]

Interference Spreading of activation and trace strength explain a second cause of forgetting: interference.[37] ***Interference*** occurs when semantic networks are so closely aligned that we cannot remember which features go with which brand or concept. Suppose you are watching a car ad that focuses on the car's safety. If you have a lot of information about similar cars stored in memory, you might confuse which attribute is associated with which car. In addition, when consumers are exposed to two or more ads with similar contextual elements, the similarity interferes with brand recall.[38] Competitive advertising also affects interference. When an established brand is promoting a new attribute, consumers' knowledge of the brand's old attributes interferes with retrieval of the new one. Yet, when competitive advertising is present, consumers are able to suppress older attribute information and effectively retrieve the new attribute information, which works to the brand's advantage.[39]

Interference also affects marketing across cultures. For instance, a study of how interference affects bilingual consumers concluded that second-language messages are not retrieved as well as first-language messages. To reduce interference, marketers should therefore use visual and textual cues that reinforce each other, facilitating the processing of second-language messages and thereby improving retrieval.[40]

Moreover, interference can result when one concept is activated so frequently that we cannot activate a different one. Suppose you are trying to recall all 50 states or the items that you have on your grocery list. Chances are you can recall several items very easily and a few more with some difficulty, but the last ones are impossible to remember. The reason is that in trying to remember the missing items, you keep remembering the items you have already recalled, and this interferes with your ability to activate the missing ones.[41] Repeatedly activating the memory trace for the items you have remembered inhibits activation of the other items.

Primacy and Recency Effects Decay and interference can be used to explain ***primacy*** and ***recency*** effects—that is, the fact that the things we encountered first or last in a sequence are often most easily remembered. As an example of primacy effects, you are likely to remember the first ad you saw during a commercial break because there was no other advertising information to interfere with it. That information may also be less likely to decay if you rehearse it. The primacy effect explains why, when you study for an exam, you tend to remember best the material you studied first.

As an example of recency effects, you are more likely to remember what you ate for breakfast this morning than what you ate a week ago because (1) this morning's information has not yet decayed, and (2) there is much less information interfering with the retrieval of this information. Based on primacy and recency effects, many advertisers believe that the best placement for an ad is either first or last in a commercial sequence or in a magazine. Some research supports the importance of being first; evidence in support of being last is not as strong.[42]

Retrieval Errors

What we do remember is not always accurate or complete; our memory may be subject to distortion or confusion. You might remember that your friend told you about a great new movie, but it was really your neighbor who told you about it. In addition, memory may be selective, meaning that we retrieve only some information, often the information that is either very positive or very negative. In anticipating a vacation, you may remember the good things that happened on your last vacation but not the bad things. Finally, memory may be distorted. If you had a bad experience with a product, you may later remember experiences that were bad but that did not actually happen. Perhaps you remember that a waitress who treated you badly at a restaurant clunked your coffee down loudly on the table. While this "memory" is consistent with the "bad waitress" experience, it might not have actually happened.[43]

What Are the Types of Retrieval?

Consumers can retrieve information through two retrieval systems: explicit and implicit memory.

Explicit Memory

Explicit memory is memory of some prior episode achieved by active attempts to remember it. In this situation, you are consciously trying to remember something that happened in the past. For example, you would use explicit memory to remember what you ordered during a recent trip to In-N-Out. Consumers try to retrieve information from explicit memory by either recognizing it or recalling it.

- ***Recognition*** occurs when we can identify something we have seen before, such as brand recognition (we remember having seen the brand before) and ad recognition (we remember having seen the ad before). Brand recognition is particularly critical for in-store decisions because it helps us identify or locate the brands we want to buy. Logos on brands or packages may be particularly effective at enhancing brand recognition.
- ***Recall*** involves a more extensive activation of the links in memory, as when we see a Snapple display and use recall to retrieve knowledge about Snapple as input for decision making. *Free recall* exists when we can retrieve something from memory without any help, such as what we had for dinner last night. *Cued recall* exists if we are asked the same question (What did we have for dinner last night?) but need a cue (Was it a vegetarian dish?).

Implicit Memory

Sometimes we remember things without conscious awareness, a phenomenon called ***implicit memory.*** Suppose as you drive down the highway at high speed, you pass a billboard bearing the word *Caterpillar* (tractors). Later you are asked whether you remember seeing a billboard and, if so, what was on it. You do not remember seeing a billboard, let alone what it was for; you have no explicit memory of it. But if you are asked to say the first word you can think of that begins with *cat-*, you might answer "caterpillar." You might have encoded something about the billboard without being aware of having even seen it, and hence you might have some information about Caterpillar stored in memory.

How can you have implicit memory of something you cannot explicitly remember? In part, the answer relates to priming. Your brief exposure to the Caterpillar name activated or primed it in your memory. The activation level was not sufficient for the name to be consciously retrieved; however, when you are asked for a word that begins with *cat-*, this activation brings "caterpillar" to mind.

marketing IMPLICATIONS

Retrieval is clearly an important concept for marketers.

Retrieval as a communication objective

The objective of marketing communications is often to increase retrieval of the brand name, product attribute, or brand benefit.[44] In other cases, the objective of a communication might be to increase consumers' recognition of the brand name, logo or brand symbol, package, advertisement, ad character, brand benefit, and so on. Newer competitors in an established industry work particularly hard to increase consumers' awareness of their brand names. [4]Oh! Calcutta a popular restaurant in Kolkata started with authentic bengali cuisines, cuisines which are off beat and which most begali houses today may avoid or refrain from cooking owing to the drudgery of cooking. Oh! Calcutta is the destination for such clinetele and today as the chain expands across cities, the distinct food and the ambience of the restaurant has become a hallmark of the place. The first retrieval of communication is through the distinct name that it bears and followed by the physical evidences that it provides for.

Retrieval affects consumer choices

One study found that Japanese consumers' use of a bank declined as their recognition of the name of the bank declined.[46] Getting consumers to recognize or recall specific claims or slogans is also critical. Furthermore, knowing and remembering this information may serve as useful input to consumers' attitudes, and consumers may invoke this information when making choices among brands. However, the most memorable ads are not necessarily the most effective in generating the desired effect—inducing purchase behavior, for example. Nor are they necessarily effective in achieving objectives such as linking information to the specific brand. In one study, consumers who watched the Super Bowl and its commercials incorrectly attributed the advertising slogan of one telecommunications firm to as many as 13 other companies.[47] Further, although consumers are not always able to retrieve the actual price information for a product when they are in the store, they are proficient at recognizing when a price is a good deal.[48]

Recall relates to advertising effectiveness

Research shows that it is important for marketers to develop appropriate measures of recognition, recall, and implicit memory when pretesting advertisements.[49] Exhibit 8.8 shows a report from a company that assesses consumers' recall of commercials. Researchers showed consumers a TV commercial and, after 24 hours, asked the consumers what they remembered. This particular page covers cued recall. The percentages indicate how many people remembered the tested ad.

Exhibit 8.8

RECALL RESULTS FOR A 30-SECOND COMMERCIAL

Some marketing research companies measure the effectiveness of TV commercials by whether consumers can recall them 24 hours after they have aired. This company measures the percentage of program viewers who can recall the commercial if they are given the name of the product or brand. Recall by various demographic groups is provided.

COMMERCIAL	IN-VIEW 30" GTE CORPORATION, "DESERT CC" BASE	PROVED COMMERCIAL REGISTRATION* PCR%
Total Sample, Men	(142)	46
By income (excl. DK/NA/Ref)		
Under $30,000	(71)	44
Over $30,000	(52)	46
By age (excl. DK/NA/Ref)		
18–34	(98)	46
35–49	(44)	46
Total Sample, Women	(165)	50
By income (excl. DK/NA/Ref)		
Under $30,000	(87)	46
Over $30,000	(57)	56
By age (excl. DK/NA/Ref)		
18–34	(84)	50
35–49	(79)	51
30" PCR NORMS	**MEN**	**WOMEN**
All commercials	29	33
All corporate	27	32
18–34	28	33
35–49	26	31

* Proved Commercial Registration (PCR) is defined as the percent of qualified viewers of the program who, given the brand name/product, can recall and accurately describe the commercial on the day following the telecast.

	PITTSBURGH	MINNEAPOLIS	SAN DIEGO
Date	6/18	6/19	6/18
Program	Barnaby Jones	S.W.A.T.	Quincy
Time	8:18 p.m.	7:14 p.m.	8:15 p.m.

How valuable recognition or recall is to marketers depends, in part, on how consumers typically buy the product. If they typically go through a store aisle and look for the brand they habitually buy, purchase is based on recognition—meaning recognition of the brand name, package, and logo is important. In other cases, product purchase is based on recall. For example, if you are thinking about where you might go for lunch today, the list of restaurants you will consider will probably depend on those you can recall from memory. In such cases, marketers should use message strategies that encourage consumers to think about the brand and product, which enhances recall at the moment when choices are actually being made.[50]

Implicit memory is also important to marketers. Although ad agencies typically measure consumers' explicit memory by what they recall and recognize from an ad, the concept of implicit memory suggests that consumers may have some memory of information in an advertising message even if they do not recognize or recall it. Thus advertisers may try to use measures of implicit memory to gauge whether their ads have affected consumers' memory.

Consumer segments and memory

Unfortunately, although retrieval is an important objective for marketers, not all consumers can remember things equally well. In particular, elderly consumers have difficulty recognizing and remembering brand names and ad claims.

How Retrieval Is Enhanced

Given the importance of retrieval, marketers need to understand how they can enhance the likelihood that consumers will remember something about specific brands. Consumers cannot recognize or recall something unless it is first stored in memory; chunking, rehearsal, and similar factors increase the likelihood that an item will be stored and available for retrieval. Four additional factors—some related to trace strength and spreading of activation—also affect retrieval: (1) the stimulus itself, (2) what it is linked to, (3) the way it is processed, and (4) the characteristics of consumers.

Characteristics of the Stimulus

Retrieval is affected by the salience (prominence) of the stimulus (the message or message medium). It is also affected by the extent to which the item is a prototypical member of a category, whether it uses redundant cues, and the medium that is used to convey information.

Salience Something is salient if it stands out from the larger context in which it is placed because it is bright, big, complex, moving, or prominent in its environment.[51] If you saw a really long commercial or a multipage ad, it might be salient relative to the short commercials or single-page ads that surround it. A visually complex figure in an ad will be salient relative to a simple background, and an animated Internet ad will be salient relative to motionless ones. Also, ads and demonstrations that offer consumers specific criteria to evaluate the promoted product compared with competing products enhance the salience of those attributes. As a result, consumers can more easily encode and retrieve information based on those salient attributes.[52]

The salience of a stimulus affects retrieval in several ways (see Exhibit 8.9). For one thing, salient objects tend to attract attention to themselves, drawing attention

Exhibit 8.9
SALIENCE
The visuals in the advertisement are distinct and create noticeability factor for the brand Fevicol.

away from things that are not salient. Because they are prominent, salient stimuli also induce greater elaboration, thereby creating stronger memory traces.[53] This might explain why some research has shown that consumers tend to remember longer commercials better than shorter ones and bigger print ads better than smaller ones. Their length or size makes them salient.[54]

Prototypicality We are better able to recognize and recall prototypical or pioneer brands in a product category (see Chapter 5 for a discussion of prototypicality). Because they have been frequently rehearsed and recirculated, the memory trace for prototypical brands is strong. These brands are also likely to be linked to many other concepts in memory, making their activation highly likely. The fact that we tend to remember these brands may explain why they have been so successful over time and why so many companies fight to establish themselves as category leaders.[55] Coca-Cola, for example, is engaged in intense marketing efforts to establish itself as the market leader in Brazil, Spain, and other countries. Thanks to in-store promotions and other techniques, its Femsa subsidiary has dramatically increased sales in Mexico, where consumers now drink more Coca-Cola per capita than consumers in any other nation—3,200 ounces per year—making the brand the prototypical soft drink.[56]

Redundant Cues Memory is enhanced when the information items to be learned seem to go together naturally. Thus our memory of brand names, advertising claims, and pictures presented in ads is better when these elements convey the same information (see Exhibit 8.10). Marketers can also enhance consumers' memory for brands by advertising two complementary products together (such as Special K with Tropicana orange juice) and explaining why they naturally go together.[57] Research indicates that event sponsorship enhances memory when the brand is prototypical—due to prominence in the marketplace—and when the event relates to the brand's core meaning.[58]

The Medium in Which the Stimulus Is Processed Advertisers often wonder whether certain media are more effective than others at enhancing consumer memory, an area that researchers are still exploring. Currently, advertisers are trying to determine whether spending money on Internet ads is a good use of advertising rupees. Some research suggests that consumers tend not to look at or remember Internet ads, whereas other studies suggest that these ads can be as or even more effective in generating brand memory than ads shown in traditional media.[59]

Exhibit 8.10
REDUNDANT CUES
The Amul advertisements and hoardings are not anymore about butter, which is redundant but the topicality of the message that is more relevant.

What the Stimulus Is Linked To

Retrieval can also be facilitated by what the stimulus is linked to in memory. The associative network concept explains a related way of facilitating retrieval—providing retrieval cues. A ***retrieval cue*** is a stimulus that facilitates the activation of memory.[60] For example, if you want to remember to go to a sale at Big Bazaar, you might leave a note on your refrigerator that says, "Big Bazaar." When you see the note later, you remember the sale. The note serves as a retrieval cue.

Retrieval cues can be generated internally or externally. Internally, a thought can also cue another thought, as in "Today is December 8. Oh, my gosh, it's Mom's birthday!" An external stimulus such as a vending machine, a Web banner, or an in-store display could also serve as a retrieval cue—"Oh, there's the new candy bar I've been hearing about." These same retrieval cues can be used to activate images stored in autobiographical memory. If you see an advertisement for your favorite brand of ice cream, this cue might activate both your positive feelings about ice cream and your memory of past experiences with ice cream. Pictures or videos of ourselves engaging in an activity can serve as powerful retrieval cues to stimulate memories.[61] What constitutes an effective retrieval cue may differ from culture to culture. One study found that sounds serve as effective retrieval cues for English-language ads, whereas visuals serve as effective retrieval cues for Chinese-language ads.[62]

Brand Name as a Retrieval Cue One of the most important types of retrieval cues is the brand name. If we see brand names such as Panasonic, Kellogg, and Reebok, we can retrieve information about these and related brands from memory. Research has found, however, that the impact of brand name as a retrieval cue is not the same for recognition as it is for recall.[63] Unfamiliar brands have a particular retrieval advantage when the name of the brand fits well with the product function, whereas familiar brands have a retrieval advantage when the name features unusual spelling.[64] Images that are closely related to the brand name serve as retrieval cues, as well. In fact, ads that omitted a key element (such as an image) related to the brand name can generate more effective retrieval than ads containing that key element.[65]

If marketers want consumers to recognize the brand on the store shelf, it is important to have high-frequency words or names to which consumers have been heavily exposed—for example, Colgate or Surf. On the other hand, if the goal is to have consumers recall the brand and its associations, it is more important to have

Exhibit 8.11
THE PACKAGE AS RETRIEVAL CUE
The Air India Maharaja is the distinct face of the brand and the visible presence of the Maharaja across airlines offices and travel agent offices is a strong retrieval cue for the consumers

brand names that (1) evoke rich imagery (Pure Magic or Temptations), (2) are novel or unexpected (Hookah Bar or Orient Express), or (3) suggest the offering and its benefits (Maggi 2 Minute Noodles or Kitchen King).

Other Retrieval Cues In addition to brand names, logos and packages can also act as retrieval cues. The Air India Maharaja is the distinct character helps in recalling the brand more easily and distinctly as depicted in Exhibit 8.11. Category names are another type of retrieval cue. Thus encountering the product categories "cars," "cookies," or "computers" might cue the names of specific brands from these categories from memories. Moreover, the visual properties of typefaces can serve as retrieval cues to the advertised product's benefits. This is why fast-food companies like Wendy's use distinctive and instantly recognizable lettering for their brand names.[66]

marketing IMPLICATIONS Retrieval cues have implications for consumers' purchasing decisions. Consumers often remember very little advertising content when they are actually making a decision in the store.[67] The reason is that advertising is typically seen or heard in a context completely different from the purchase environment. One way to handle this problem is to place a cue from the ad on the brand's package or on an in-store display, to activate advertising-related links in memory.[68] Thus, packages are sometimes labeled "as seen on TV." Another strategy is to place well-known cues from ads on the package, such as the Pillsbury Doughboy from the product advertisements in all their products featured at the shelf, including atta, cake mixes, maida or other related products.

Retrieval cues also have important implications for marketers. First, these cues can affect what consumers remember from ads.[69] Some research has shown that the most effective retrieval cues match the cues actually used in an ad. Therefore, if an ad uses a picture of an apple, then a picture of an apple and not the word *apple* is the most effective retrieval cue. If the ad uses a particular word, then the actual word and not a picture of what it represents is the most effective retrieval cue. Other research has shown that music can serve as an effective retrieval cue for ad content, affecting consumers' memories of pictures in an ad.

Interestingly, some marketers have developed features to help consumers generate their own retrieval cues. For example, Hallmark.com offers a free reminder service to consumers who register and then list the people and special occasions they want to remember (by sending greeting cards or in other ways). The site will send an e-mail reminder of each birthday, anniversary, or other noteworthy occasion well in advance. This service not only acts as a retrieval cue, but also facilitates searching and decision making—issues discussed in the next set of chapters.

How a Stimulus Is Processed in Short-Term Memory

Another factor affecting retrieval is the way information is processed in short-term memory. One consistent finding is that messages processed through imagery tend to be better remembered than those processed discursively. For instance, research shows that elderly consumers' memory for information from advertising can be improved if they form a mental image of things in the ad, like the claims it makes. Imagery apparently creates a greater number of associations in memory, which, in turn, enhances retrieval.[70] The reason may be that things processed in imagery form are processed as pictures *and* as words. This ***dual coding*** provides extra associative links in memory, thereby enhancing the likelihood that the item will be retrieved. Information encoded verbally, however, is processed just one way—discursively—so it has only one retrieval path.

Nevertheless, imagery processing is not necessarily induced by pictures alone. When you read a novel, you can often generate very vivid images about the story and its characters. In this way, verbal information can also possess imagery-generating properties. Inducing imagery via pictures, high-imagery words, or imagery instructions may result in dual coding.[71] Dual coding is one reason that marketers often use the audio portion of well-known TV ads as radio commercials. When consumers hear the familiar verbal message, they may provide their own imagery of the visual part. The fact that they have engaged in coding of both the verbal message and its associated visuals facilitates retrieval of one if the other is present.

Consumer Characteristics Affecting Retrieval

Finally, both consumers' mood and expertise can affect retrieval.

Mood Mood has some very interesting effects on retrieval.[72] First, being in a positive mood can enhance our recall of stimuli in general. Second, we are more likely to recall information that is consistent with our mood. In other words, if we are in a positive mood, we are more likely to recall positive information. Likewise, if we are in a negative mood, we will recall more negative information. From a marketing perspective, if an advertisement can influence a consumer's mood in a positive direction, the recall of relevant information may be enhanced when the consumer is feeling good.

Several explanations account for these mood effects. One is that feelings consumers associate with a concept are linked to the concept in memory. Thus your memory of DisneyWorld may be associated with the feeling of fun. If you are in a fun mood, the fun concept may be activated, and this activation may spread to DisneyWorld.[73] Researchers have also suggested that people process information in more detail when mood is intense than when it is weak. More detailed processing, in turn, leads to greater elaboration and higher levels of recall.[74] Another study found that mood influences both elaboration and rehearsal, two processes that enhance memory. In this research, consumers in a positive mood were more likely to readily learn brand names and engage in brand rehearsal.[75]

Expertise Chapter 5 mentioned that compared with novices, experts have more complex category structures in memory with a greater number of higher- and lower-level categories and more detail within each category. Therefore, experts' associative networks are more interconnected than the networks of novices. The complex linkages and the spreading of the activation concept explain why experts can recall more brands, brand attributes, and benefits than novices.[76]

Summary

Memory consists of three memory stores, each with different types of memory. Sensory memory (iconic and echoic) involves a very brief analysis of incoming information. Short-term memory represents active working memory and involves imagery and discursive processing. Long-term memory represents the permanent memory store, covering both autobiographical and semantic memory. Consumers will lose information from the sensory store and from short-term memory if they do not further process the information.

Long-term memory can be represented as a set of semantic networks with concepts connected by associations or links. Although long-term memory reflects what we have stored, not everything is equally accessible, indicating that memory and retrieval are different phenomena. To enhance the likelihood that information in long-term memory is stored and to reduce the likelihood that stored information will be lost, marketers can enhance memory using chunking, recirculation, rehearsal, and elaboration.

Retrieval is the process of remembering information that is stored in memory. Consumers can retrieve information when concepts are activated in memory, making the information accessible. Concepts may also be activated by the spreading of activation. Even if the activation potential is not sufficient to retrieve an item, the activation may be sufficient to prime the concept in memory, making that concept more easily retrievable when other cues are present. If a concept or a link to it is not activated often, that concept will "decay" in memory. We may fail to retrieve information, or we may retrieve information that is not accurate.

There are two types of retrieval tasks: those that ask whether we can remember things we have previously encountered—an explicit memory task—and those that *reveal* memory of things for which we have no conscious memory—an implicit memory task. Marketers often use recall and recognition as measures of explicit memory. Because of their importance to retrieval, both recall and recognition serve as objectives for marketing communications, influence consumer choice, and have important strategic implications. Factors that facilitate recognition and recall include characteristics of the information (its salience, prototypicality, and redundancy), what it is linked to (retrieval cues), the way it is processed (particularly in imagery mode), and characteristics of consumers (mood and expertise).

Questions for Review and Discussion

1. How are sensory, short-term, and long-term memory linked?
2. What four techniques can enhance consumers' memory?
3. Why are some links in a semantic or associative network weak, whereas others are strong?
4. How can retrieval failures and errors affect consumer memory?
5. How does recognition differ from recall?
6. What is implicit memory, and how can it affect a consumer's ability to retrieve a brand name?
7. How do mood and expertise affect retrieval of memories?

Exercises

1. Recall a train journey that you have taken while in school and a train journey that you have off late taken up in the last six months. Compare between the two journeys and evaluate the following aspects closely:

a. The time taken for both the journeys & the destinations covered

b. The activities undertaken in the journey

c. The accompaniment in both the journeys

d. The process of food procurement and consumption

e. Any other differences observed while making the two journeys

At the end of the exercise the student must be able to evaluate how the format of journeys have changed and how it also the role of memory and message retrieval.

2. Given the results of question 1, suggest how each marketer could make the information in its ad more memorable for consumers.
3. Collect a set of autobiographical memories from members of your class about a common consumer behavior experience (what they did on their last vacation, how they spent a holiday). Compile this information, and analyze it to determine what implications it might have for marketers (vacation marketers, retailers selling holiday items, and so forth).
4. At one time, Cadillac created a TV commercial using actor Dennis Franz, who plays Detective Andy Sipowicz on ABC's *NYPD Blue*. The commercial showed the actor pulling out a notepad and warning a Mercedes driver that he would write him up for driving a luxury car without enough horsepower. The Mercedes driver asked whether Franz was some kind of cop. The actor winked at the camera and said, "Something like that." NBC and CBS refused to run the ad.[77] Using the concepts of spreading of activation, priming, and interference, explain why the networks acted as they did.
5. Collect a set of ads from a magazine. Analyze each ad and determine whether the marketer was trying to establish recall or recognition of information in the ad. Why is recall or recognition an important objective for this marketer? Do you think the marketer was successful in achieving the objective for this ad? Why or why not?
6. Visit a popular website such as CNN.com, MSNBC.com, or Travelocity.com. Browse several of the main pages, noting the advertised brands and products. Do any of these ads use trace strength to make the information more accessible to consumers? Do any use chunking or rehearsal? How does salience operate in this situation? Based on your analysis, is the Internet a particularly good or poor medium for advertising these brands? Explain your answer.
7. After you have completed exercise 1, select one product category that was represented in the advertising you were exposed to. Go to the supermarket, and walk through the aisle where those products are stocked and find the advertised brand. How do the brand and packaging act as retrieval cues? What redundant cues, if any, are present on the package or at the point of purchase to enhance your memory of this brand? How does the appearance of the supermarket aisle interfere with your memory of this brand or its attributes and benefits? What suggestions can you offer to this marketer for improving its advertising, packaging, or shelf display to enhance memory and retrieval?Exercise:

More Exercises from the Adaptor

1. Recall a train journey that you have taken while in school and a train journey that you have of late taken up in the last six months. Compare between the two journeys and evaluate the following aspects closely:
   a. The time taken for both the journeys and the destinations covered
   b. The activities undertaken in the journey
   c. The accompaniment in both the journeys
   d. The process of food procurement and consumption
   e. Any other differences observed while making the two journeys

   At the end of the exercise the student must be able to evaluate how the formats of journey have changed and how it also changes the role of memory and message retrieval.

References

1 Source: http://www.icmr.icfai.org/casestudies/catalogue/Marketing/MKTG005.htm

2 Source: http://www.unilever.com/ourbrands/personalcare/lifebuoy.asp

3 Source: http://www.unilever.com/ourvalues/environmentandsociety/casestudies/health/indiallifebuoy.asp

4 Source: http://www.thisismyindia.com/entertainment/eating-out.html

PART

3

The Process of Making Decisions

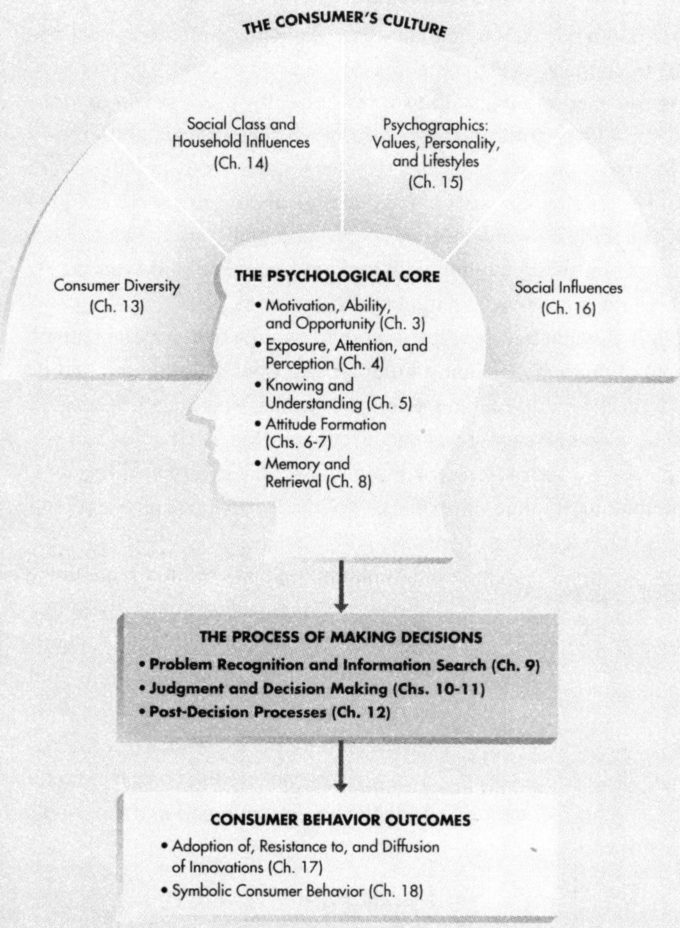

Part Three examines the sequential steps in the consumer decision-making process. Chapter 9 explores the initial steps of this process—problem recognition and information search. Consumers must first realize they have a problem to solve before they can begin the process of making a decision about it. They must then collect information to help make this decision.

As with attitude change, decision making is affected by the amount of effort consumers expend. Chapter 10 examines the decision-making process when consumer effort is high and explores how marketers can influence this extensive decision process. Chapter 11 focuses on decision making when consumer effort is low and discusses how marketers can influence this kind of decision process. Chapter 12 looks at how consumers determine whether they are satisfied or dissatisfied with their decisions and how they learn from choosing and consuming products and services.

chapter **9**

Problem Recognition and Information Search

LEARNING OBJECTIVES

After studying this chapter, you will be able to:

- Describe how consumers recognize a consumption problem and show why marketers must understand this part of the decision-making process.
- Discuss what happens when consumers conduct an internal search to solve a consumption problem and identify some of the ways in which marketers can affect internal searches.
- Explain why and how consumers conduct an external search to solve a consumption problem identify opportunities and the challenges that marketers face in trying to influence such searches.

INTRODUCTION

Mouthshut.com: Compare and contrast

Consumers in today's era have a tough choice to make with so many product options to choose from. In the past consumers relied on word of mouth or on advertising and other forms of communication to know about the product and to make its critical evaluation. A lot of trust and responsibility was also placed on the retailer and his sales persons to take decisions. However, technology and its advent seems to be gradually helping consumers to take more and more judicious and effective decisions. The traditional channels of information gathering have not withered away, but have been supplemented with technology and related avenues through which consumers are now making holistic decisions.

mouthshut.com is a website that helps visitors to the site gather complete information on a host of products including Automobiles, Books, Computers, Education, Electronics, Entertainment, Fashion, Food and Drinks, Health and Beauty, Household, Internet, Media, Personal Finance, Sports and Travel. The site has a veritable list of options to choose from and gives consumers a complete review of existing users and their experiences with the brand. Some treat this as a blog site, however, mouthshut.com cannot be confused with a blog.

A discerning visitor to the site can log and view the various postings made by the users of the brands on any product item selected. On the site, you can write reviews, read reviews, rate reviews and even compare the products. The site can also give the visitors the complete feature specification of the brand and the model

Exhibit 9.1
GETTING INFORMATION ON THE INTERNET
mouthshut.com provides useful information to the consumers before the final selection of the brand is made.

decided and sometimes helps the consumers even find out from where the best deal can be obtained.

[1]The site also has had its fair share of criticism through other websites like petitiononline.com, which has serious allegations against the site and believes that the website only aims to promote a few popular brands who pay heavily to get their products showcased. They also feel that the owners of the site gang up and post heavily to create biasness for a certain range of products, which misleads the consumer. However, such allegations do come by in business and mouthshut.com believes in moving on and creating a more aware and knowledgeable customer.

As shown in Exhibit 9.2, problem recognition, internal search, and external search represent the early stages of the consumer decision-making process. Although these processes often proceed sequentially, they can also occur simultaneously or in a different order. For example, consumers may be searching for information and suddenly realize that they have another problem to be solved. Also, consumers will not necessarily go through every stage in the exact order every time. However they occur, these three stages are useful in explaining the basic processes that characterize consumer decision making.

Problem Recognition

The consumer decision process generally begins when the consumer identifies a consumption problem that needs to be solved ("I need a new camera" or "I'd like some new clothes"). ***Problem recognition*** is the perceived difference between an ideal and an actual state. This is a critical stage in the decision process because it motivates the consumer to action.

The ***ideal state*** is the way consumers would like a situation to be (having an excellent camera or wearing attractive clothing). The ***actual state*** is the real situation as consumers perceive it now. Problem recognition occurs if consumers become aware of a discrepancy between the actual state and the ideal state ("My camera is too old" or "My clothing is out of date"). Exhibit 9.3 shows how a marketer contrasts the ideal and the actual states. The greater the discrepancy between the actual and the ideal states and the higher the level of motivation, ability, and opportunity (MAO), the more likely the consumer is to act. If consumers do not perceive a problem, their motivation to act will be low.

Problem recognition relates not only to acquisition, but also to consumption and disposition. Consumers can recognize problems such as needing to decide what to make for dinner, which item of clothing to wear, or whether to replace an old appliance. Hindustan Unilever Ltd.'s Sunlight brand focuses on the "colour-stay" feature of the detergent and with a strong regional presence in the Eastern part of India, the brand has been focusing on a detergent feature, which most brands have not looked at. The regional appeal of the brand comes from the detergent's product attributes that make it ideally conditioned for the climate and weather of the region, followed by the positioning of "colour-stay" that acts as a strong proposition. Because problem recognition stimulates many types of consumer decision making, it is important to understand what contributes to differences between the ideal and the actual states.

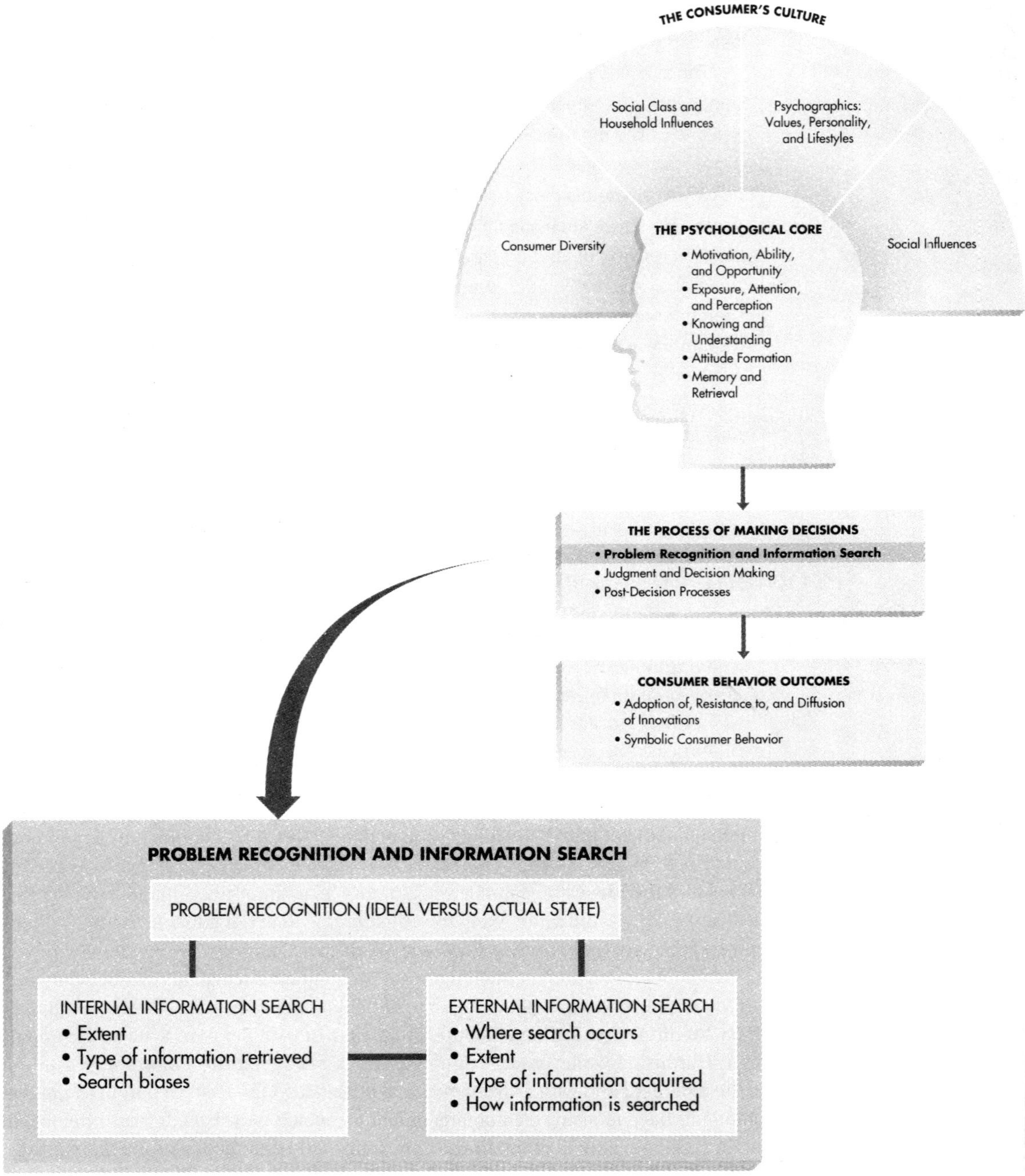

Exhibit 9.2

CHAPTER OVERVIEW: PROBLEM RECOGNITION AND INFORMATION SEARCH *The first step in the consumer decision-making process involves problem recognition (the consumer recognizes a problem that needs to be solved). Next, the consumer searches for information to solve the problem either internally from memory or externally from outside sources (such as experts, magazines, ads). How much consumers search, what they search for, and the process they go through are all discussed in this chapter.*

Exhibit 9.3
IDEAL VS . ACTUAL STATE
This ad is a good illustration of problem recognition and the difference between the actual and ideal state.
The actual state is a Sunday night party with a stinking mess and the ideal state is a clean set of utensils.

The Ideal State: Where We Want to Be

Where do we get our notion of the ideal state? Sometimes we rely on simple expectation, usually based on past experience, about everyday consumption and disposition situations and how products or services fulfill our needs. For example, we consider how we might look in certain clothes, how clean our house should be, how much fun it would be to vacation in a particular location, which old products we should keep, and so on. The ideal state also can be a function of our future goals or aspirations. For example, many consumers might want to drive a car that will provide them with social status (a Lexus, Mercedes, or Porsche) or to join a club that will bring them the admiration or acceptance of others (see Exhibit 9.4).

Both expectations and aspirations are often stimulated by our own personal motivations—what we want to be based on our self-image—and by aspects of our own culture. Some societies are more materialistic than others, and therefore the desire for many goods and services may be higher in those cultures. Likewise, social class can exert an influence: many consumers want to be accepted by members of their class or to raise their social standing, leading them to aspire to a higher ideal state. Reference groups also play a critical role, because we strive to be accepted by others and because reference groups serve as a guide to our behavior.

Finally, major changes in personal circumstances, such as getting a promotion or becoming a parent, can instigate new ideal states. When you graduate and start a new job, you are likely to develop new ideal states related to where you live, what you wear, what you drive, and so forth. Since China has opened its markets to international products, many local consumers have become interested in Western goods that were formerly unavailable, thereby creating a new ideal state. Noting this demand, Procter & Gamble has used brand-oriented advertising and extensive distribution to help its Rejoice brand capture nearly 30 percent of the shampoo market in China. [2]Alternatively in India Rejoice has been launched by P&G to specifically meet the unique needs of Indian consumers. First, P&G in association with the market research firm ACNielson, spoke to a cross-section of 1500 consumers across the length and breadth of India and found that 'smooth, detangled hair' is one of the top unmet needs by ordinary shampoos. Hair tangles are a problem more acute in India because majority of Indian women keep their hair long, and the longer the hair the more it tangles. Rejoice's patented 'Micro- Silicone' conditioning technology gives twice as smooth, detangled and easy to comb hair than ordinary shampoos or the combination of home remedies such as henna, amala ,reetha and shikakai. Second, given the diversity of Indian consumers and their varied hair needs, P&G has launched Rejoice in three unique variants: Rich, Complete, and Silky Clean. For example, Rejoice shampoo's low conditioning Silky Clean variant is specially suited for the heavy-oiling consumers in South and East India; while

Exhibit 9.4
AN IDEAL STATE
Many people desire to live a life of luxury. The Jaguar XJ Super V8 can help consumers achieve this ideal state.

the rich variant is more suited for dry climate condition of North India. Thirdly, quality products at the right price are of special concern to the discerning majority of Indian masses. Keeping this in mind, Rejoice shampoo was made available at an affordable Rs.2 for 7.5ml sachets, Rs.39 for a 100ml bottle and Rs.75 for a 200ml bottle.

The Actual State: Where We Are Now

Like your perception of the ideal state, your perception of the actual state can be influenced by a variety of factors. Often these are simple physical factors, such as running out of a product, having a product malfunction (your camera breaks down) or grow obsolete (the computer has insufficient memory), or unexpectedly needing a service (a cavity requires dental work). Needs also play a critical role. If you are hungry or thirsty or if friends make fun of your clothes, your actual state would not be acceptable. Finally, external stimuli can suddenly change your perceptions of the actual state. If someone tells you that Mother's Day is next Sunday, for example, you might suddenly realize you have not bought a card or present yet. Or opening your closet door may make you realize it is too full.

marketing
IMPLICATIONS

Putting consumers in a state of problem recognition may stimulate the decision process and lead to acquisition, consumption, or disposition of a product or service. Marketing efforts can influence this process. Without problem recognition, marketing efforts are likely to be less effective because the consumer may not be motivated to process information.

In general, marketers use two major techniques to try to stimulate problem recognition. First, they can attempt to create a new ideal state. For example, consumers did not think much about the performance of their athletic shoes in the 1970s. However, today we are continually bombarded with newer and better products that will make us run faster and jump higher—a new ideal state. Some consumers are even willing to pay more than $150 for new higher-tech shoes.

Second, marketers can try to create dissatisfaction with the actual state. The itasveer.com site provides visitors the option to upload their pictures and send orders for online prints. With the advent of digital cameras, most users upload the pictures and leave it at that. In the days of camera, consumers religiously carried the film rolls to the shop and ordered for prints and of course there was the uncertainty of some pictures not developing or some having problems in pictorial representation. But digital camera has replaced all that, however with a spanner that necessarily the consumers do not go for picture developing etc, resulting the pictures taken idle away in the hard disk of the computers. istasveer.com provides a unique opportunity for consumers to upload their pictures online and order prints through the site itself and further pay online too. Another good example is the ad in Exhibit 9.5. Also, major tobacco companies are touting the lower toxins or carcinogens in some new cigarette brands.[5] (See Chapter 20 for an in-depth look at the dark side of marketing.)

Whether they create a new ideal state or stimulate dissatisfaction with the actual state, marketers are more likely to have their product or service chosen if they position it as the solution to the consumer's problem. In the highly competitive cooking oil segment, marketers have used various propositions to sell their brands. Saffola's stand of healthy heart and its focus on the "touching 40 segment" focuses on the problems associated with the age and how Saffola provides an alternative.

Internal Search: Searching for Information from Memory

After problem recognition has been stimulated, the consumer will usually begin the decision process to solve the problem. Typically, the next step is ***internal search.*** As you saw in Chapter 8, almost all decision making involves some form of memory processing. Each consumer has stored in memory a variety of information, feelings, and past experiences that can be recalled when making a decision. For example, at the beginning of the chapter, you saw that consumers who are thinking about buying a car will retrieve their memories of experiences with different car brands.

Because consumers have limited capacity or ability to process information—and because memory traces can decay over time—consumers are likely to recall only a small subset of stored information when they engage in internal search. As a result, researchers are very interested in determining (1) the extent of the search; (2) the nature of the search; and (3) the process by which consumers recall information, feelings, and experiences and enter them into the decision process.

How Much Do We Engage in Internal Search?

The degree of internal search can vary widely from the simple recall of only a brand name to more extensive searches through memory for relevant information, feelings, and experiences. On a general level, researchers know that the effort consumers devote to internal search depends on their MAO to process information.

Exhibit 9.5
CREATING DISSATISFACTION WITH THE ACTUAL STATE
This ad tries to create dissatisfaction with the actual state by showing a typical consumer who has had a problem with hackers breaking into her computer. If consumers can relate to this situation, they will be dissatisfied that they do not have protection from hackers and be motivated to purchase the Symantec system.

Thus consumers will attempt to recall more information when felt involvement, perceived risk, or the need for cognition is high. In addition, consumers can engage in active internal search only if information is stored in memory. Consumers with a greater degree of knowledge and experience therefore have a greater ability to search internally. Finally, consumers can recall information from memory only if they have the opportunity to do so. Time pressure or distractions will limit internal search.

What Kind of Information Is Retrieved from Internal Search?

Much of the research on the role of internal search in consumer judgment and decision making has focused on what is recalled. Specifically, researchers have examined the recall of four major types of information: (1) brands, (2) attributes, (3) evaluations, and (4) experiences.[7]

Recall of Brands The set of brands that consumers recall from memory whenever problem recognition has been stimulated is an important aspect of internal search that greatly affects decision making. Rather than remembering all available brands in any given situation, consumers tend to recall a subset of two to eight brands known as a ***consideration*** or ***evoked set.***[8] For example, someone buying bottled water might ordinarily consider Evian and Perrier rather than all possible brands. With product proliferation, however, the number of offerings has increased dramatically. Nestlé alone offers more than 68 water brands (including Perrier), which means more brand competition for inclusion in the consideration set.[9]

In general, the consideration set consists of brands that are "top of mind," or easy to remember, when making a decision. Some U.S. consumers fly rather than take the train — even when the train is faster and cheaper—simply because they do not consider the possibility of train travels. Conversely, in China, airlines are using marketing to encourage consumers to consider flying rather than taking the train or bus when they travel long distances. In India, trains are the preferred mode of transport for majority of Indian population, but now with the advent of the low cost airlines, consumers, especially in the urban areas, are now even considering air travel as opposed to train. Average distance traveled in India being so large, journeys are usually overnight, which if replaced by air travel can be squeezed to a few hours. Unfortunately, the problem in most cases is of connectivity, as most of the flight coverage is within the metros, mini-metros and a few tourist destinations. A small consideration set is usually necessary because our ability to recall brand information decreases as the size of the set increases. However, even if we do not recall the entire set from memory, stored information aids the recognition process. For example, stored information can help consumers recognize services in the yellow pages or identify brands on the shelf. The Korean brands' foray in India was distinct as it embarked on an aggressive advertising campaign backed by low-cost and high technology products. Before the entry of LG's and Samsung's of the world the market in India either had a Japanese V or an Indian player. The Indian was cost-effective and the Japanese was high on cost and technology both. The Korean brands redefined the market with low cost and high technology products. However, such a platform had to be adequately showcased, which was adequately covered through aggressive and high visibility advertising.

Studies indicate that consideration sets vary in terms of their size, stability, variety, and *preference dispersion* (the equality of preferences toward brands or products in the set). On more familiar occasions and in more familiar locations, such as the occasion of buying snacks at the neighborhood movie theater, consumers have consideration sets that are less stable, are larger in size, and have slightly more variety. In such situations, consumers tend to have stronger preferences for one or two items in the consideration set. This research suggests that a company should enhance its product's linkage with an occasion familiar to consumers—such as movie-going—to increase the chance that the product will be retrieved from memory as part of the consideration set.[12]

According to research, brands that are recalled are more likely to be chosen.[13] However, simply being recalled does not guarantee that a brand will be in the consideration set, because consumers can recall and then reject undesirable alternatives. Also, consumers' choices can be altered by simple manipulation of which brands they recall, even though this may not change their product preferences. Thus if consumers cannot recall brands from memory to form a consideration set, the set will tend to be determined by external factors such as availability on the shelf or suggestions of salespeople.[14]

Researchers have looked at the following factors that increase the possibility of consumers recalling a particular brand during internal search and including that brand in the consideration set:

- *Prototypicality.* When consumers engage in internal search, they more easily recall brands that are closest to the prototype or that most resemble other category members, making these more likely to be included in the consideration set than brands that are not typical of the category.[15] For example brands like Burnol, Dettol, Iodex or Moov come as immediate response brands when evaluating the necessary product category for consideration. This brand is more likely than other brands to be in the consideration set when problem recognition for the product exists.

- *Brand familiarity.* Well-known brands are more easily recalled during internal search than unfamiliar brands because the memory links associated with these brands tend to be stronger. As a result, companies need to repeat marketing communications continually to keep brand awareness high and associations strong. In Asian cultures, ads with high-meaning pictures and words (e.g., Superman fences with a picture of Superman) are very effective in increasing brand-name recall.[17] Even in low-MAO situations where little processing occurs, incidental ad exposure can increase the likelihood of inclusion in the consideration set.[18] This explains why global brands such as Sony, IBM, McDonald's, Mercedes, and Coca-Cola have high familiarity worldwide and are likely to be in many consumers' consideration sets. Brand familiarity helps consumers recognize which of the many available brands in the store should be attended to and reduces misidentification of brands.[19]

- *Goals and usage situations.* As discussed in Chapter 5, consumers have goal-derived and usage-specific categories in memory, such as drinks to bring to the beach, and the activation of these categories will determine which brands they recall during internal search.[20] Thus marketers can attempt to associate products with certain goals and usage situations. Air Deccan's launch in India through the civil aviation's open-sky policy marked a complete departure from how Indians rated air travel as. Air travel was expensive and was restricted to

Exhibit 9.6
RETRIEVAL CUES IN ADVERTISING
The Michelin Man is a well-known icon which helps consumers to remember to place this brand of tires in the consideration set.

the corporates and to the affluent class, when flying at individual cost. Air Deccan's low cost option and with tickets even available at 99 paise, the concept was a runaway success and today several airlines who run on the low cost format have a revenue model similar to what Air Deccan introduced with. Armed the low cost tag, Air Deccan today is making attempts to provide connectivity to the interiors of India.

- *Brand preference.* Brands for which the consumer has positive attitudes tend to be recalled more easily and be included in the consideration set more often than brands that evoke negative attitudes.[22] This principle highlights the importance of developing positive brand attitudes. Unilever's Dove brand, for instance, has been associated with moisturizing since the soap debuted in 1955. Unilever has built on positive attitudes toward Dove by extending the brand to body washes, deodorants, and cleansing cloths.[23]
- *Retrieval cues.* By strongly associating the brand with a retrieval cue, marketers can increase the chance that the brand will be included in the consideration set (see Exhibit 9.6). Think of the Mc Donald's Golden Arches or the Subhiskha outlets, with the distinct Green and Red colour. Packaging can be an important retrieval cue for food products. Gatorade, for instance, uses a curvy, easy-grip bottle with a green pop-up top as a retrieval cue, much as an hourglass bottle has long served as a retrieval cue for Coca-Cola.[24]

Recall of Attributes For a variety of reasons, we access only a small portion of the information stored in memory during internal search. Often we cannot remember specific facts about a product or service because our memory of details decreases over time. Thus the attribute information we recall tends to be in summary or simplified form rather than in its original detail. We would be more likely to remember that a car gets good gas mileage or that it is not expensive than to remember the actual miles per gallon or the exact price.

Nevertheless, consumers can often recall *some* details when they engage in internal search, and the recalled attribute information can strongly influence their brand choices.[25] As a result, researchers have been very interested in determining which factors influence the recall of attribute information in the information search and decision-making processes. These are some of the major variables they have identified:

- *Accessibility or availability.* Information that is more accessible or available—having the strongest associative links—is the most likely to be recalled and entered into the decision process.[26] Information that is perceived as being easy to recall is also more likely to be accessible.[27] Marketers can make information more accessible by repeatedly drawing attention to it in marketing communications or by making the information more relevant.[28] Wal-Mart ads repeatedly stress low prices, hoping that consumers will remember this attribute when they decide where to shop.

- *Diagnosticity.* ***Diagnostic information*** helps us distinguish objects from one another. If all brands of computers are the same price, then price is not diagnostic, or useful, in making a decision. On the other hand, if prices vary, consumers can distinguish between them, so the information is diagnostic.[29] If information is both accessible and diagnostic, it has a very strong influence in the decision-making process.[30] If accessible information is not diagnostic, it is less likely to be recalled.

  Research shows that negative information tends to be more diagnostic than positive or neutral information because the former is more distinctive.[31] In other words, because most brands are associated with positive attributes, negative information makes it easier to categorize the brand as different from other brands. Unfortunately, consumers tend to give negative information greater weight in the decision-making process, increasing the chances that the alternative with the negative qualities will be rejected. Thus some marketers must avoid associating their products and services with negative information, plan a two-sided message campaign, or divert attention away from the negative feature. In addition, marketers can identify which attributes tend to be most diagnostic for a particular product or service category and seek a competitive advantage on one or more of these attributes. In Japan, many consumers like strong drinks, so Budweiser actively markets Buddy beer, which has 6 percent alcohol (versus 5 percent for other brands).[32]

- *Salience.* Research has clearly shown that consumers can recall very ***salient*** (prominent) ***attributes*** even when their opportunity to process is low.[33] The Apple iPod's distinctive white ear buds serve as a salient attribute for consumers interested in digital music players, for example. In addition, price is a highly salient attribute for many consumers. Note that consumers do not always have a strong belief about the salience of an attribute.[34] Thus, a marketer of stereo systems can improve consumers' recall of its products' sound quality by providing information which makes this attribute more salient, which in turn facilitates brand choice.[35] Moreover, by repeatedly calling attention to an attribute in marketing communications, marketers can increase its salience and its impact on the decision.[36] For example, in light of recent research, wine makers are now promoting the positive health benefits of drinking red wine, such as a lower incidence of heart disease.[37]

  Note, however, that an attribute can be highly salient but not necessarily diagnostic. If you are buying a watch, for example, the attribute "tells time" would be highly salient but not very diagnostic. For information to be recalled and entered into the decision, it must have ***attribute determinance,*** which means being both salient and diagnostic.[38] SBI's (State Bank of India) campaign focused on the theme, "Simply Banking" establishes the connectivity with the customers on the basic function that the bank provides, which is banking related services. Within the said industry, it provides, ATM connectivity, after banking hour facilities, credit facilities and several other features related to banking, hence reinforce the salience and diagnosticity of the strength attribute.

- *Vividness.* Vivid information is presented as concrete words, pictures, or instructions to imagine (e.g., imagine yourself on a tropical beach) or through word-of-mouth communication. For example, a picture of a hand holding the Canon Elph digital camera, which is the size of a credit card, is vivid information.[40] Vivid information is easier to recall than less dramatic information but tends to influence judgment and decision making only when consumers have not formed a strong prior evaluation, especially one that is negative.[41] In addition, vividness affects attitudes only when the effort required to process the information matches the amount of effort the consumer is willing to put forth.[42] Otherwise, vivid and nonvivid information affect consumer attitudes in about the same way.

- *Goals.* The consumer's goals will determine which attribute is recalled from memory. For example, if one of your goals in taking a vacation is to economize, you are likely to recall price. Marketers can identify important goals that guide the choice process for consumers and then position their offerings in the context of these goals, such as offering economy vacation packages.

Recall of Evaluations Because our memory for specific details decays rapidly over time, we find overall evaluations or attitudes (that is, our likes and dislikes) easier to remember than specific attribute information. In addition, our evaluations tend to form strong associative links with the brand. This is why it is important for a company to encourage positive consumer attitudes toward its brands. To illustrate, the Dutch company Philips Electronics recently launched a new ad campaign to change the way consumers size up its brand. With competitors such as Samsung and Sony positioning their brands as not just technically advanced but cool as well, Philips wants consumers to have a stronger overall evaluation of its brand. Today, says the chief marketing officer, the Philips brand is "seen as a dull, solid, reliable brand but nothing really special, nothing sparkling."[43]

Evaluations are also more likely to be recalled by consumers who are actively evaluating the brand when they are exposed to relevant information. For example, if you are ready to buy a new computer and suddenly see an ad for a particular brand, you will probably determine whether you like the brand when you see the ad. This activity is called ***online processing.***[44] Afterward, you will more likely recall this evaluation rather than the specific information that led to it. Many times, however, consumers do not have a brand-processing goal when they see or hear an ad. In such cases they do not form an evaluation and are therefore better able to recall specific attribute information, assuming that involvement was high and the information was processed.[45] Marketers should also be aware that consumers are more likely to use online processing in evaluating family brands when the brands within that family have low variability and share many attributes.[46]

Recall of Experiences Internal search can involve the recall of experiences from autobiographical memory, in the form of specific images and the effect associated with them.[47] Like information in semantic memory, experiences that are more vivid, salient, or frequent are the most likely to be recalled. For example, if you have an experience with a product or service that is either unusually positive or unusually negative, you are likely to recall these vivid experiences later. Furthermore, if you repeatedly have a positive experience with a product or service, it will be easier to recall these experiences. For example, some bowling alleys now offer loud music and flashing lights to appeal to younger bowlers and make the experience more fun and exciting.[48] Research suggests that although advertising may affect how accurately consumers can recall their product experiences, their recall of the product's evaluations is not necessarily affected.[49]

marketing IMPLICATIONS Obviously, marketers want consumers to recall positive experiences related to certain products or services. To illustrate, many Japanese consumers have developed a desire for new products that look old, such as motorcycles, cars, kimonos, and cameras, because these products are reminders of simple, happy times.[50] Marketers often deliberately associate their products or services with common positive experiences or images to increase their recall from memory. Prudential and Sony are just two of many firms that film ads at the Grand Canyon because it is the "quintessential breathtaking experience," and they hope that consumers will tie this positive memory to their brands.[51]

Is Internal Search Always Accurate?

In addition to being influenced by factors that affect what we recall, we all have processing biases that alter the nature of internal search. These search biases can sometimes lead to the recall of information that results in a less-than-optimal judgment or decision. Three biases have important implications for marketing: confirmation bias, inhibition, and mood.

Confirmation Bias ***Confirmation bias*** refers to our tendency to recall information that reinforces or confirms our overall beliefs rather than contradicting them, thereby making our judgment or decision more positive than it should be. This phenomenon is related to the concept of selective perception—we see what we want to see—and occurs because we strive to maintain consistency in our views. Thus when we engage in internal search, we are more likely to recall information about brands we like or have previously chosen than about brands we dislike or have rejected. Furthermore, when the confirmation bias is operating, we are more likely to recall positive rather than negative information about favored brands. This response can be a problem because, as mentioned earlier, negative information tends to be more diagnostic.

Nevertheless, we sometimes recall contradictory evidence. In fact, we may recall moderately contradictory information because we had consciously thought about it when we first tried to understand it.[52] In most instances, however, consumers tend to recall information that reinforces their overall beliefs.

Inhibition Another internal search bias is associated with limitations in consumers' processing capacity.[53] In this case, all the variables that influence the recall of certain attributes—such as accessibility, vividness, and salience—can actually lead to the ***inhibition*** of recall for other diagnostic attributes.[54] In buying a house, for example, a consumer might recall information such as the selling price, number of bathrooms, and square footage, but not recall other important attributes such as the size of kitchen and the name of the school district. Inhibition can also lead to a biased judgment or decision because consumers may remember but ignore important and useful information.

Mood You saw in Chapter 8 that consumers engaged in internal search are most likely to recall information, feelings, and experiences that match their mood.[55] With this in mind, marketing communications that put consumers in a good mood through the use of humor or attractive visuals can enhance the recall of positive attribute information.

marketing IMPLICATIONS

From a marketing perspective, confirmation bias presents a real problem when consumers search internally for only positive information about the competition. One way marketers attack this problem is to draw attention to negative aspects of competitive brands in comparative advertising. Microsoft, for example, recently ran a magazine ad in Europe comparing the cost of running its Windows computer operating system to the cost of running Linux, a competing operating system. The ad said that Linux was more expensive than Windows on a megabit-per-second basis, information that a Microsoft spokesperson observed was valuable for "comparing the various technology offerings."[56] By presenting comparative information in a convincing and credible way, marketers may be able to overcome confirmation bias.

Inhibition is an important aspect of internal search for two reasons. First, consumers may not always consider key aspects of a brand when making a decision because they recall other, more accessible attributes instead. In particular, if these nonrecalled attributes reflect features that differentiate the brand from others (i.e., if the attributes are diagnostic), the company may want to highlight them in marketing communications. For example, although price advertising is pervasive in the PC market, Dell Computer does not want consumers to forget one of its key differentiating features—service—so it features this attribute (in addition to price) in its advertisements. Marketers can sometimes offset the effect of their brand's disadvantages and/or their competitors' advantages by drawing attention to more vivid or accessible attributes. Dove premium pricing according to Indian standards could have been a deterrent to its purchases. However, with the company deciding to focus on the 1/4th moisturising cream platform in the soap deflected attention from the belief that it is priced high.

External Search: Searching for Information from the Environment

Sometimes a consumer's decision can be based entirely on information recalled from memory. At other times, information is missing or some uncertainty surrounds the recalled information. Then consumers engage in an ***external search*** of outside sources, such as dealers, trusted friends or relatives, published sources (magazines, pamphlets, or books), advertisements, the Internet, or the product package. Consumers use external search to collect additional information about which brands are available, as well as the attributes and benefits associated with brands in the consideration set.

Two types of external search are prepurchase search and ongoing search. ***Prepurchase search*** occurs in response to the activation of problem recognition. As an example, consumers seeking to buy a new car can get information by visiting dealers, searching mouthshut.com and other websites, checking quality rankings, talking to friends, and reading Consumer Reports. ***Ongoing search*** occurs on a regular and continual basis, even when problem recognition is not activated.[59] A consumer might consistently read automotive magazines, visit automotive websites, and go to car shows because of a high degree of enduring involvement in cars. Exhibit 9.7 contrasts these two types of searches.

Exhibit 9.7
TYPES OF INFORMATION SEARCHES

Consumers can engage in two major types of external search. Prepurchase search occurs in response to problem recognition; the goal is to make better purchase decisions. Ongoing search results from enduring involvement and occurs on a continual basis (independent of problem recognition). Here consumers search for information because they find searching enjoyable (they like to browse).

	Prepurchase Search	Ongoing Search
Determinants	• Involvement in the purchase • Market environment • Situational factors	• Involvement with the product • Market environment • Situational factors
Motives	To make better purchase decisions	• Build a bank of information for future use • Experience fun and pleasure
Outcomes	• Increased product and market knowledge • Better purchase decisions • Increased satisfaction with the purchase outcome	• Increased product and market knowledge leading to – future buying efficiences – personal influence • Increased impulse buying • Increased satisfaction from search, and other outcomes

Researchers have examined five key aspects of the external search process: (1) the source of information, (2) the extent of external search, (3) the content of the external search, (4) search typologies, and (5) the process or order of the search.

Where Can We Search for Information?

For either prepurchase or ongoing search, consumers can acquire information from five major categories of external sources:[60]

- *Retailer search.* Visits or calls to stores or dealers, including the examination of package information or pamphlets about brands
- *Media search.* Information from advertising, online ads, manufacturer-sponsored websites, and other types of marketer-produced communications
- *Interpersonal search.* Advice from friends, relatives, neighbors, coworkers, and/or other consumers, whether sought in person, by phone, online, or in another way
- *Independent search.* Contact with independent sources of information, such as books, non-brand-sponsored websites like Shopping.com, government pamphlets, or magazines
- *Experiential search.* The use of product samples, product/service trials (such as a test-drive), or experiencing the product online

Traditionally, retailer and media search, followed by experiential search, have been the most frequently used forms of search. These increase when involvement is higher and knowledge is lower.[61] This finding is significant for marketers because such sources are under their most direct control. Other research indicates that consumers browse two or more sources of information (such as the Internet and catalogs) before making a buying decision. Therefore, marketers and retailers should ensure that brand information is consistent across the various sources.[62]

Consumers increase their use of interpersonal sources as their brand knowledge decreases. Apparently, when consumers' knowledge is limited, they are motivated to seek out the opinions of others. Furthermore, when consumers believe that their purchase and consumption of certain items (usually hedonic or symbolic products and services such as fashion, music, and furniture) will be judged by others, they tend to seek out interpersonal sources.[63]

Experiential search is also critical for hedonic products and services. Given the importance of sensory stimulation, consumers want to get a "feel" for the offering, so they often try on clothing or listen to a stereo before they buy. The launch of Dabur Real Activ was followed by the launch of Dabur Real, which was a sweetened juice as compared to Real Activ, which was a zero-sweetener, focused on the health conscious segment. The product's taste was very different from a sweetened juice, which most consumers had not tasted before. By offering free samples at stores and busy traffic intersections the brand tried to create a pre-purchase notion about the taste of the brand.

Cultural characteristics play a role in external search as well. According to research, consumers who are members of subcultural groups and not culturally assimilated—fully integrated into the surrounding culture—tend to conduct a wider search of external sources. And members of subcultural groups who identify with the surrounding culture are more likely to search for information among media advertisements. Thus marketers should create informative advertising messages when targeting these consumer segments.[65] Finally, independent search tends to increase as available time increases, but time spent on this type of search is still generally quite low.

Internet Sources The Internet has dramatically altered the way consumers shop and search for information. Without leaving their keyboards, consumers can rapidly search through mounds of data online, locate any specific details needed to make purchase decisions, and buy. In fact, consumers can use the Internet to get information from all five of the sources just mentioned. Sometimes consumers search for specific information; at other times they simply browse.[66] Speed, user control, and two-way communication capability are key elements of website interactivity for consumers conducting online searches.[67] Consumers without broadband connections dislike waiting for websites and ads to load; in such situations, the effectiveness of elaborate display graphics in providing information and encouraging purchases is limited.[68] In general, consumers who have a pleasant online experience with a company's website will have more positive attitudes toward the site and its brands.[69]

In addition to conducting keyword searches on sites such as Yahoo! and Google, consumers can use shopping agents such as Shopping.com to organize search results according to price, retail source, and other attributes. Yet, one study shows that consumers do not always assess accurately whether a shopping agent's recommendations are appropriate and effective in a particular buying situation. As a result, consumers may make poor buying decisions by using an inferior shopping agent and choosing offers that should have been avoided.[70] According to another study, when consumers using a shopping agent receive recommendations of unfamiliar products, they check additional recommendations of familiar products as a context in which to evaluate the unfamiliar products.[71]

Information Overload Consumers today have access to so much information that they can actually become overloaded; depending on how the information is structured, an overload can lead to a decline in decision quality.[72] For example, entering a common keyword on an Internet search site can sometimes return more than 100,000 references. In response, some search sites now apply more efficient search techniques that prioritize results by identifying the most popular or frequently accessed sites.[73] Search sites such as About.com have subject-matter experts selecting the most important information and narrowing the choice set according to specific criteria. Shopping agents bring order to results by presenting items according to price or another attribute selected by the user. Although some retailers try to thwart shopping agents, believing the price comparisons are too easy, a growing number are paying for links or ads on popular shopping sites so they can make it into the consumer's choice set.[74]

Simulations Advances in technology and graphics have dramatically improved the online experience. Website developers can now simulate the retail experience as well as product trials by creating sites that incorporate special and interactive effects including audio, video, zoom, panoramic views, streaming media, and three-dimensional product representations that can be manipulated.[75] Creating a virtual product experience has a positive effect on consumer product knowledge and brand attitude, thereby reducing perceived risk and increasing purchase intention.[76] Barbie.everythinggirl.com site provides a complete range of activities for the visitor to the site, starting from collector's items, shopping items, tips for parents, chats, online quizzes etc., which involves the visitors completely. Magicbricks.com is an online property information site providing complete details on properties, real estate agents, property developers and the best deals available across various Indian cities.

The Online Community The Internet makes it easy for consumers to share information in an online community. People with a common interest or condition related to a product or service can communicate with each other via messages on Web pages, text chat, electronic bulletin boards, and other places.[78] Research indicates that the most common interactions focus on product recommendations and how-to-use-it advice.[79] Often this information is very influential in the decision process because it is not controlled by marketers and is therefore seen as more credible. Knowing this, Jeff Bezos, founder and CEO of Amazon.com, does not try to prevent consumers from posting negative reviews of products. Even though the company may lose a few sales, Bezos believes that his site serves as an online community of "neighbors helping neighbors make purchase decisions."[80]

An increasing number of retailers and manufacturers are tracking consumers' online information search and purchase patterns to provide additional assistance and recommendations. For example, consumers who rent DVD movies online from Netflix are encouraged to rate each, using a system of one to five stars, so the site can recommend other movies based on what each consumer liked and didn't like. In addition, each movie is accompanied by the combined star rating of all Netflix customers. In this way, Netflix brings additional movies into the consideration set and gives consumers more information on which to make a decision.

marketing IMPLICATIONS As consumers become more accustomed to using the Internet for search and shopping, they are buying online more frequently, making bigger purchases, and choosing a wider variety of products than in the early days of the Internet. Hometrade.com launched the first online share trading portal with a lot of fanfare, using Shahrukh Khan, Hrithik Roshan and Sachin Tendulkar, three of the hottest celebrities. The product flopped miserably, in contrast to today's situation, where there are numerous online companies starting ICICI Direct.com onwards who are doing successfully. Hometrade.com as a product was never understood in the early days of the internet and high profile advertising campaign only misled prospective consumers. Facilitating extended searches for even inexpensive items like books can boost sales significantly, as Amazon.com learned with its "Search Inside the Book" feature, which lets consumers read pages from individual books.[82] When shopping for homes and other major purchases, many consumers use the Internet to search for information and then complete the purchase in person, although a small number will buy with a click or call without any personal experience of the offering.[83]

Many consumers see product choice as riskier when they lack access to experiential information until after they have completed an online purchase.[84] This accounts, in part, for the high percentage of online shoppers—as many as 53 percent—who choose to click away before finalizing a purchase.[85] Sometimes consumers search but abandon their online shopping carts because of frustration over the time and effort needed to check out; some do not buy because they get no information about shipping fees and taxes until they reach the final screen.[86] PC Connection, a retailer selling computers online and through catalogs, found that 46 percent of its shoppers were abandoning their carts before making the purchase. As a result, it has adopted technology that recalculates the total order cost, including shipping and any taxes, as consumers add items to their carts. Just as important, consumers can examine their carts and make changes without leaving the merchandise page they are viewing.[87]

To learn which online tactics are most effective for their site and products, marketers need to track consumers' search and purchase behaviors using appropriate measurements. As one example, an Internet retailer would track how many of its shoppers abandon their carts before the checkout process is complete, whereas an online advertiser would track the percentage of consumers exposed to each ad who actually click to read more.[88] Exhibit 9.8 shows some common measures of con-

Exhibit 9.8
SELECTED MEASURES OF ONLINE CONSUMER ACTIVITY

Marketers are very interested in how consumers search online. Here are some common measures used to measure and evaluate this activity.

Measurement	Purpose
Ad impressions	To determine the opportunity for communication by tracking how many consumers are exposed to a particular Web ad.
Unique visitors	To determine the extent of message exposure by measuring how many different consumers visit the site during a given period.
Click-through rate	To determine ad effectiveness by tracking how many consumers who are exposed to a message actually click on it for additional ad information.
Percentage of repeat visits	To determine consumer loyalty by tracking how many visitors in a given period have visited the site previously.
Frequency of visits	To determine consumer loyalty by tracking how often each visitor visits the site in a given period.
Top entry page	To determine message and offer effectiveness by tracking the first page on which most visitors enter the site.
Top exit page	To determine message and offer effectiveness plus interactivity response by tracking the page from which most visitors leave the site.
Visitor path	To determine message and offer effectiveness plus interactivity response by tracking, in page order, how consumers navigate the site.
Conversion rate	To determine offer effectiveness by tracking the percentage of visitors who actually buy.
Cart abandonment rate	To determine offer and interactivity effectiveness by tracking the percentage of visitors who put items in their shopping carts but fail to complete the checkout process.

Sources: Michael Totty, "So Much Information . . ." *Wall Street Journal,* December 9, 2002, p. R4; Subodh Bhat, Michael Bevans, and Sanjit Sengupta, "Measuring Users' Web Activity to Evaluate and Enhance Advertising Effectiveness," *Journal of Advertising,* Fall 2002, pp. 97–106.

sumer activity online. Note that with Internet usage expanding worldwide, marketers need to develop strategies for regional and local markets because marketing activities that are effective within a given market will not be effective everywhere.

How Much Do We Engage in External Search?

Much of the research on external search has concentrated on examining how much information consumers acquire prior to making a judgment or decision. One of the key findings is that the degree of search activity is usually quite limited, even for purchases that are typically considered important.[90] Researchers have found that more than one-third of Australian car buyers made two or fewer trips to the dealer before buying.[91] Note that as more consumers shop on the Internet, search activity will increase because online sources are very convenient. Nevertheless, information search can vary widely from a simple hunt for one or two pieces of information to a very extensive search relying on many sources. In an attempt to explain this variance, researchers have identified a number of causal factors that relate to our motivation, ability, and opportunity to process information.

Motivation to Process Information In general, as the motivation to process information increases, external search will be more extensive. Six factors increase our motivation to conduct an external search: (1) involvement and perceived risk, (2) the perceived costs and benefits of search, (3) the nature of the consideration set, (4) relative brand uncertainty, (5) attitudes toward the search, and (6) the level of discrepancy of new information.

- *Involvement and perceived risk.* To understand how involvement relates to external search, recall the distinction from Chapter 3 between situational involvement—a response to a particular situation—and enduring involvement—an ongoing response. Higher situational involvement will generally lead to a greater prepurchase search,[92] whereas enduring involvement relates to an ongoing search regardless of whether problem recognition exists.[93] Thus consumers with high enduring involvement with cars or trucks are more likely to read automotive magazines, visit car shows and car-related websites, and engage in other efforts to gain knowledge about cars or trucks on a regular basis.

  Because perceived risk is a major determinant of involvement, it should not be surprising that when consumers face riskier decisions, they engage in more external search activity. One of the key components of perceived risk is uncertainty regarding the consequences of behavior, and consumers use external search as a way to reduce this uncertainty.[94] Consumers are more likely to search when they are uncertain about which brand to choose than when they are uncertain about a specific attribute. Consumers also search more when they are evaluating services rather than products because services are intangible and hence perceived as more uncertain.[95] Finally, consumers will have higher motivation to search if the consequences are more serious, such as those entailing high financial or social risk. This is why consumers often search more extensively for information about higher-priced products or services.

- *Perceived costs and benefits.* External search activity is also greater when its perceived benefits are high relative to its costs.[96] In these situations, consumers who search will benefit by reducing uncertainty, increasing the likelihood of making a better decision, obtaining a better value, and enjoying the shopping process. The costs associated with external search are time, effort, inconvenience, and money (including traveling to stores and dealers). All these factors place psychological or physical strain on the consumer (especially if the distance between stores is great). In general, consumers tend to continue searching until they perceive that the costs outweigh the benefits. The desire to reduce searching costs explains why many supermarkets now offer a variety of nontraditional items like jewelry, electronics, and furniture, becoming places "where people do all their gift shopping."[97] Note that shopping on the Internet greatly reduces the costs of searching. Even so, consumers tend to minimize their initial search investment, delay further searches after making a choice, and underestimate the future costs (both search and usage) of switching to another offering.[98]

- *Consideration set.* If the consideration set contains a number of attractive alternatives, consumers will be motivated to engage in external search to decide which alternative to select. On the other hand, a consideration set that contains only one or two brands reduces the need to search for information.
- *Relative brand uncertainty.* When consumers are uncertain as to which brand is the best, they are more motivated to engage in external search.[99]
- *Attitudes toward search.* Some consumers like to search for information and do so extensively.[100] These consumers generally have positive beliefs about the value and benefits of their search. In particular, extensive search activity appears to be strongly related to the belief that "when important purchases are made quickly, they are regretted."[101] Other consumers simply hate to search and do little.

  Researchers have identified two groups of Internet searchers.[102] Experienced searchers are the most enthusiastic and heaviest users of the Internet, whereas moderate and light users see it as a source of information only, not a source of entertainment or fun. To appeal to the latter group, some companies have created interesting and engaging games to stimulate consumers to search.[103]
- *Discrepancy of information.* Whenever consumers encounter something new in their environment, they will try to categorize it by using their stored knowledge. If a stimulus does not fit into an existing category, consumers will try to resolve this incongruity by engaging in information search, especially when incongruity is at a moderate level and the consumer has limited knowledge about the product category.[104] Consumers are likely to reject highly incongruous information.[105] Marketers can capitalize on this tendency by introducing moderate discrepancies between their brand and other brands. For example an advertisement for Airtel Broadband services focuses on how it sets young minds on fire. The communication talks about how young minds have endless questions and queries, which may necessarily not be answered impromptu. The Airtel broadband connection and the connectivity help in answering all such questions. Typically with most broadband advertisements speaking of better connectivity and reduced costs of connection, this breaks through the clutter.

The same general process applies to the search for information about new products. If a new product is moderately discrepant or incongruent with existing categories of products, the consumer will be motivated to resolve this discrepancy.[107] In particular, consumers explore the most salient attributes in greater depth, rather than search for a lot of additional attributes. From a marketing perspective, this behavior suggests that positioning new products as moderately different from existing brands may induce consumers to search for more information that might, in turn, affect their decision process. A good example is a computer drive that can record DVDs, as compared with traditional drives that play prerecorded DVDs. This moderate discrepancy might stimulate consumers to search for additional product information that could ultimately affect their decision to buy.

Ability to Process Information External search is also strongly influenced by the consumer's ability to process information. Researchers have studied how three variables affect the extent of external information search: (1) consumer knowledge, (2) cognitive abilities, and (3) demographic factors.

- *Consumer knowledge.* Common sense suggests that expert consumers search less because they already have more complex knowledge stored in memory. However, research results on this subject have been mixed.[108] Part of the problem stems from the way in which knowledge is defined. Some studies have measured *subjective knowledge,* the consumer's perception about what he or she knows relative to others. *Objective knowledge* refers to the actual information stored in memory that can be measured with a formal knowledge test. Researchers have linked objective knowledge to information search, although both types of knowledge are somewhat related. One study found that subjective knowledge influences where consumers search for information as well as the quality of their choices.[109]

  Specifically, several studies have found an inverted-U relationship between knowledge and search.[110] Consumers with moderate levels of knowledge search the most. They tend to have a higher level of motivation and at least some basic knowledge, which helps them to interpret new information. Experts, on the other hand, search less because they have more knowledge stored in memory, and they also know how to target their search to the most relevant or diagnostic information, ignoring that which is irrelevant—except when the search involves new products. Because experts have more developed memory structures, they have an advantage in learning novel information and can acquire more information about new products.

- *Cognitive abilities.* Consumers with higher basic cognitive abilities, such as IQ and the ability to integrate complex information, are not only more likely to acquire more information than consumers with little or no knowledge, but are also able to process this information in more complex ways.[111]

- *Demographics.* As researchers continue to investigate whether certain types of consumers search more than others, they have discovered a few consistent patterns. For instance, consumers with higher educations tend to search more than less educated consumers. This is because more educated consumers have at least moderate levels of knowledge and better access to information sources.[112]

Opportunity to Process Information Consumers who have the motivation and ability to search for information must still have the opportunity to process that information before an extensive search can take place. Situational factors that might affect the search process include (1) the amount of information, (2) the information format, (3) the time available, and (4) the number of items being chosen.

- *Amount of information available.* In any decision situation, the amount of information available to consumers can vary greatly, depending on the number of brands on the market, the attribute information available about each brand, the number of retail outlets or dealers, and the number of other sources of information, such as magazines or knowledgeable friends. In general, consumers do more searching as the amount of available information increases, suggesting that the Internet can generate greater external search. If information is restricted or not available, however, consumers have a hard time engaging in extensive external search.
- *Information format.* The format in which information is presented can also strongly influence the search process. Sometimes information is available from diverse sources or locations, but consumers must expend considerable effort to collect it. In buying insurance, for example, consumers may have to contact different agents or companies to collect information about individual policies. In contrast, presenting information in a manner that reduces consumer effort can enhance information search and usage, particularly when the consumer is in the decision mode.[113] For example, in an effort to increase the use of nutritional information, researchers provided a matrix that makes this information easier for consumers to search, thereby improving opportunity.[114] A related study found that consumers increase their use of nutritional information when the rewards of good nutrition are made more explicit.[115] In addition, consumers will engage in more leisurely exploratory searches if information surrounding an object is visually simpler and less cluttered.[116]
- *Time availability.* Consumers who face no time restrictions have more opportunity to search. If consumers are under time pressure, however, they will severely restrict their search activity.[117] Further, consumers will spend less time getting information from different sources as time pressure increases.[118] Note that time pressure is one of the main reasons that consumers search and shop on the Internet. One study found that when consumers revisit a website for search reasons, they spend less total time on the site because they look at fewer pages, not because they spend less time looking at each page.[119]
- *Number of items being chosen.* When consumers are making a decision about multiple items, research suggests that they will conduct a more extensive search with less variability in search patterns than if the decision involves the purchase or use of only one item.[120]

marketing IMPLICATIONS

The extent to which consumers search for external information has important implications for marketing strategy. If many consumers tend to search extensively for a particular product or service, marketers can facilitate the decision process by making information readily available and easily accessible at the lowest cost and with the least consumer effort. To do this, marketers should look at the design of their product packaging, websites, ads, and other promotional materials with an eye toward providing information that will alter consumers' attitudes and change their buying behavior. As an example, Eastwood, which makes car refurbishing tools, saw sales soar after making changes that caused search engines to list its website near the top of results on searches for "auto tools" and related phrases.[121] Exhibit 9.9 shows how a company uses a kiosk to make brand-related information easily available.

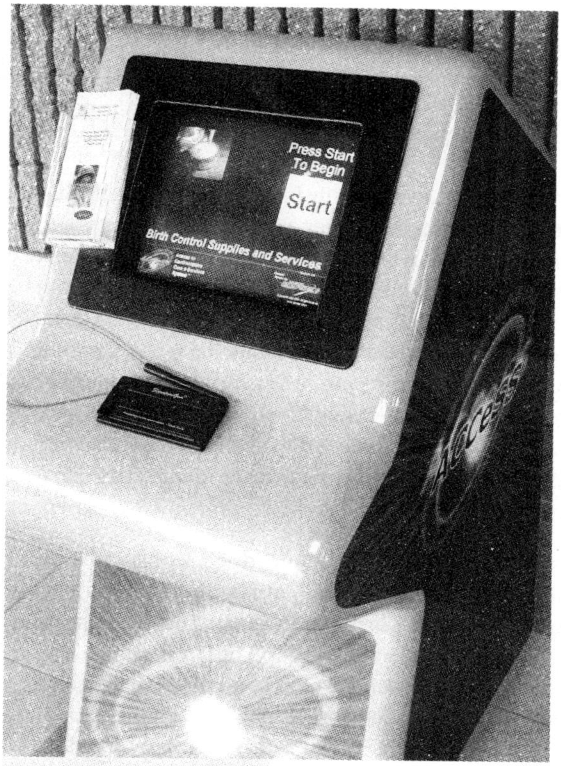

Exhibit 9.9
MAKING INFORMATION READILY AVAILABLE
This kiosk makes it easy for women to acquire birth control information.

Companies should also provide information about salient and diagnostic attributes, particularly if the brand has a differential advantage. Otherwise, if consumers cannot get the information they need, they may eliminate the brand from their consideration set. Novices, in particular, tend to be influenced by visual cues such as pictures and colors that focus their attention on selected attributes, which affects their external search and, ultimately, their brand choices.[122]

Moreover, marketers can segment the market for a product or service according to search activity. For example, one study identified six clusters of searchers in the purchase of a car.[123] Another found that consumers who search online for cars are younger, better educated, and conduct more searches than those who do not use the Internet—and they would have searched more extensively if they could not use the Internet.[124] A study of high-tech markets revealed that older consumers tend to search information channels that provide fairly non-complex information, whereas better-educated consumers tend to search all information channels.[125] Once marketers determine which types of search activities are most likely to occur for their product or service, they can plan to meet the information needs of the consumers in targeted segments. Low-search consumers, for example, will focus on getting a good deal, whereas high searchers will need a lot of attention and information to offset their low levels of confidence and prior satisfaction. Marketers can be very selective in providing low searchers with information, emphasizing only those attributes that are most salient and diagnostic.

Marketers can attempt to stimulate external search by providing information in a highly accessible manner. For example, most automobile companies provide the complete details on the models, price, finance options, dealer locations and even the exchange options on the existing cars that customer have. Through this process the consumer is able to carry with him a sizeable amount of information even before he checks out the first car dealer for all the possible information he wants. Such opportunities for additional search may lead low searchers to information that will change their attitudes and affect their buying decisions. Marketers can provide consumers with incentives to search, as well. For example, after Gap.com posted an online coupon good only in Gap stores, the chain was flooded with consumers clutching coupons as they examined merchandise.[127]

What Kind of Information Is Acquired in External Search?

Researchers are interested in the types of information that consumers acquire during an external search because this information can potentially play a crucial role in influencing the consumers' judgments and decision making. When searching external sources, consumers usually acquire information about brand name, price, and other attributes.

Brand Name Brand name is the most frequently accessed type of information because it is a central node around which other information can be organized in memory.[128] Thus when we know the brand name, we can immediately activate other relevant nodes. For example, if we know the brand name is LIC, Indian Airlines, or NIIT, we can draw on a wealth of prior knowledge and associations.

Price Consumers search for price information not only because it tends to be diagnostic but also because it can be used to make inferences about other attributes such as quality and value.[129] One study found that when price and quality are not directly correlated for a product category, consumers who use quality-screening smart agents to search for purchase options online are actually more sensitive to price differences.[130] Still, the search for price is less important than we might expect (due to the low overall extent of search), and it does not become more important when price variations increase and costs are higher.[131] Furthermore, the importance of price can depend on the culture. As an example, although consumers in Japan have not traditionally been fond of discounters, many now flock to discount stores such as Uniqlo and Jusco in search of bargains.[132]

Other Attributes After searching for brand name and price, consumers will search for additional, information depending on which attributes are salient and diagnostic in the product or service category. Most Indian consumers look for best deals on prices, easy finance options and fuel efficiency and better coverage of aftersales service stations. Consumers are more likely to access information that is relevant to their goals. For example, if a major goal in choosing a vacation is to maximize excitement, a consumer would probably collect information about a location's available activities, nightlife, and visitors. When consumers switch goals from one purchase occasion to the next, as when looking for an economy car versus one that is fast, the search they perform for the second task is more efficient because they can transfer the knowledge from the first task.[134]

Is External Search Always Accurate?

Consumers can be just as biased in their search for external information as they are during internal search. In particular, consumers tend to search for external information that confirms rather than disconfirms their overall beliefs. In one study, consumers with a strong price-quality belief tended to search more for higher-priced brands.[135] Unfortunately, confirmation bias can lead consumers to avoid important information, resulting in a less-than-optimal decision outcome. Thus if a lower-priced, high-quality brand were available, consumers might never acquire information about it and therefore never select it for purchase.

marketing IMPLICATIONS Marketers have to make the specific information that consumers seek easily and readily available by emphasizing it in advertising, on a package, in pamphlets, on websites, or through the sales force. In addition, companies must remember that consumers are less likely to choose a brand that performs poorly on attributes that are accessed frequently. Therefore, marketers should be sure that their offerings perform well on attributes that are heavily accessed, including price. When marketers promise to match the lowest price that consumers can find, such policies spark more extensive searching when search costs are low (as consumers look for the lowest price) but less extensive searching when search costs are high (and consumers perceive that the policy signals low prices).[136] Finally, some companies pay search engines such as Yahoo! to make brand information available in a prominently positioned sponsored link when consumers perform certain key word searches. Brands like LG, Hero Honda, Hutch, Samsung, Airtel are big spenders on the Indian Cricket circuit but they also believe that sponsored links are important for reaching consumers who conduct external searches online.

How Do We Engage in External Search?

External search follows a series of sequential steps that can provide further insight into the consumer's decision. These steps include orientation, or getting an overview of the product display; evaluation, or comparing options on key attributes; and verification, or confirming the choice.[138] Researchers have examined the order of information acquisition during evaluation, in particular, because they assume that information acquired earlier in the decision process plays a more significant role than information acquired later.[139] For example, once a brand emerges as the leader early in the search process, subsequent information acquisition and evaluation is distorted in favor of that brand.[140]

Search Stages Consumers tend to access different sources at different stages of the search process. In the early stages, mass media and marketer-related sources tend to be more influential, whereas interpersonal sources are more critical when the actual decision is made.[141] Consumers are more likely to access information that is especially salient, diagnostic, and goal-related earlier in the search process. However, if they can recall salient, diagnostic information from memory, they will have little need to search for it externally. Thus consumers will search first for information on attributes that provoke greater uncertainty or are less favorable.[142] Consumers also tend to search first for brands that have a higher perceived attractiveness, again pointing to the importance of developing positive attitudes. Finally, research indicates that consumers who are new to a product or service category will start by searching for information about low-risk, well-known brands, progress to a search of lesser-known brands, and then consolidate the information leading to a preference for brands that provide the greatest utility.[143]

Searching by Brand or Attribute Two major types of processes are (1) ***searching by brand,*** in which consumers acquire all the needed information on one brand before moving on to the next, and (2) ***searching by attribute,*** in which consumers compare brands one attribute at a time.[144] A good example of the latter strategy is price-comparison shopping. Consumers generally prefer to process by attribute because it is easier.

Also, consumers are very sensitive to the manner in which information is stored in memory and the format in which it is presented in the store.[145] If information is organized by brand, as is the case in most stores where all the information is on packages, consumers will process information by brand. Experts, in particular, tend to process by brand because they have more brand-based knowledge. The fact that consumers are accustomed to processing by brand may bias processing, however, even when information is organized by attribute.[146] In addition, different search strategies affect our decision process differently.[147] Consumers who process by brand remain high in uncertainty until the very end of the search process, whereas those who search by attribute gradually reduce their uncertainty.

Nevertheless, consumers with less knowledge will take advantage of opportunities to process by attribute, such as by viewing information in a matrix in *Consumer Reports* or in another format that simplifies searching. One study found that presenting lists of nutritional information in the grocery store is popular with consumers. The *Consumer Reports'* Rating Charts, which provide information about the top brands and best buys in various product categories in a simple format, are popular sources of information. As noted earlier, search engines and shopping agents also make it easier for consumers to process by attribute, especially price.

Summary

This chapter examined the three initial stages of the consumer judgment and decision-making process. Problem recognition, the first stage, is the perceived difference between an ideal state and the actual state. When a discrepancy exists between these two states, the consumer may be motivated to resolve it by engaging in decision making.

Internal search is the recall of information, experiences, and feelings from memory. The extent of internal search generally increases as motivation (involvement and perceived risk), ability (knowledge and experience), and opportunity (lack of time pressure and distractions) increase. In general, aspects of an offer that are more salient, diagnostic, vivid, and related to goals are the most likely to be recalled. Several biases exist in internal search: confirmation bias, in which information that reinforces our overall beliefs is remembered; inhibition, in which the recall of some information can inhibit the recall of other attributes; and mood, our tendency to recall mood-congruent information.

When consumers need more information or are uncertain about recalled information, they engage in external search, acquiring information from outside sources through prepurchase search (in response to problem recognition) or ongoing search (which continues regardless of problem recognition). During external search, consumers can acquire information from retailers, the media, other people and independent sources, and by experiencing the product. Retailer and media search account for the highest level of search activity, but interpersonal sources increase in importance as consumer knowledge decreases and normative factors increase. Consumers find the Internet a fast and convenient way to search for information.

The extent of external search can vary widely, depending on motivation, ability, and opportunity to search, but it is usually rather limited. Consumers will conduct a more extensive search when they have a higher motivation and opportunity to process information. Situational factors affect the consumer's opportunity to process the information. Brand name and price are the most accessed attributes in an external search. Consumers also tend to exhibit a confirmation bias in their external search. More salient and diagnostic information tends to be accessed earlier. Finally, consumers tend to process either by brand or by attribute. Attribute search is easier and preferred, but often the information is not organized to facilitate such processing.

Questions for Review and Discussion

1. How does a discrepancy between the ideal state and the actual state affect consumer behavior?
2. What factors affect the inclusion of brands in the consideration set, and why would a company want its brand in the consideration set?
3. How does confirmation bias operate in internal and external searches for information?
4. What six broad groups of sources can consumers consult during external search? Where does the Internet fit in these groups?
5. How do involvement, perceived risk, perceived costs and benefits, and the consideration set affect a consumer's motivation to conduct an external search?
6. When would a consumer be more likely to conduct an external search by brand rather than by attribute? Which search process would a marketer prefer consumers to use—and why?

Exercises

1. Find 20 magazine, television, or radio advertisements that you think are trying to instigate problem recognition in consumers. Then group these ads into those you think are (a) trying to influence the ideal state and (b) trying to create dissatisfaction with the actual state. Relate each group of ads to the factors discussed in the chapter on influencing the ideal state and the actual state. Which types of ads do you think are effective and why?
2. Interview five consumers to determine their knowledge about a product or service category for which you think motivation, ability, and opportunity to process are high. Ask consumers to discuss the following:
   a. All the brands they would consider
   b. What they know about each brand
   c. Their evaluations of each brand
   d. Any prior experiences they have relative to these brands

   After obtaining this information, ask consumers which brand they would choose if they had to pick one right now and whether they would want any additional information before deciding. Finally, analyze this information in terms of the principles discussed in this chapter: recall of brands, attributes, evaluations, and experiences. Do your findings support or contradict these concepts? If so, why? How does internal search relate to the desire for external search?
3. Interview five consumers about their external search activity regarding a product or service category for which you think motivation, ability, and opportunity to search are high. Be sure to ask them questions about the following:
   a. Which brands they would search for information on
   b. Which types of information they would look for
   c. Which sources of information they would use
   d. How much time they would take

   Analyze the answers in terms of the external search principles discussed in this chapter: the extent, content, and sources of search. Do your findings support or contradict these concepts?

More Exercises from the Adaptor

1. You have decided to buy a car after having spent six months in your first job. What would be various steps taken by you to buy the car. Imagine that after having spent 7 years you plan to buy a second car, what would be differences in approach to buy the second car. Illustrate the differences clearly between the first and second situation.

References

1 Source:http://www.petitiononline.com/banms201/petition.html

2 Source: http://www.pg-india.com/hp/rejoice.pdf

chapter **10**

Judgment and Decision Making Based on High Consumer Effort

LEARNING OBJECTIVES

After studying this chapter, you will be able to:

- Distinguish between judgment and decision making, and indicate why both processes are important to marketers.
- Identify the major types of cognitive models for high-effort decision making and discuss some ways marketers can try to influence decisions made with these models.
- Explain how consumers make affective decisions in high-effort situations.
- Understand what consumers do when facing noncomparable decisions.
- Outline the four contextual factors that can influence high-effort consumer decisions, and outline how marketers try to affect consumer behavior within such contexts.

INTRODUCTION

Housing boom in India

The housing boom in India, which started about four years ago is still moving at a scorching pace. The boom is unprecedented. It is not just visible in the metros and the mini-metros but it is also spreading its wings in the hinterlands. Smaller cities like Vizag, Bhopal, Gorakhpur, Nagpur, to name a few are also witnessing the housing boom. A few questions that crop up are the reasons for the boom, how long it will last and the sustainability factor. The economic prosperity and one of the felt effect or the outcome is investments in real estate. Today the credit industry has also flourished with falling interest rates and the banks are also willing to increase credits to the customer. Also, more and more realtors are offering housing at affordable costs and with multiple options to choose from. Therefore, as earlier buying a property was more like buying a dwelling place on which prospects spent savings of their lifetime, today it is also an investment and consumers are willing to explore.

[1]The multiplier effect of investment in housing has grown over the past years as the proportion of outstanding housing loans as percentage of GDP increase from 3.4 per cent in 2001 to 7.25 per cent by 2005. This is quite indicative of the potential that exists in the proportion of investment in housing in other developed and emerging economies. The proportion of investment in housing to the Gross Domestic Product (GDP) is 54 per cent in USA, 57 per cent in UK, 40 per cent in the European Union, 17 per cent in Thailand, 34 per cent in Malaysia and 7 per cent in China. The emergence of housing on the national map as a critical sector continues to engage policy makers, regulators and the players on the ground. While the Government has continued its commitment towards housing by way of supportive fiscal measures, the Reserve Bank of India (RBI) has cautioned the industry about the potential problems arising out of the

Exhibit 10.1
THE HOUSING BOOM IN INDIA
The sudden spurt in the housing, particularly in the retail market is backed by falling interest rates and housing being considered as an investment option.

overheating of the sector and the need to maintain a watchful surveillance on the developments.

Some key aspects which have come up for review are the approaches to buying houses. One is that it has now come out more as an investment option and secondly no more are the consumers restricting themselves on the location of the houses. As these houses become investment option, the focus is more on getting the cheapest option, irrespective of the conventional factors on which houses were bought. Location, distance from nearest amenities, access to schools, hospitals and other public facilities are not a concern till the house is considered for the purpose of staying. Backed by easy credit and flexible payment options, the consumer is willing to consider the house as an option to invest.

How consumers buy houses points out the importance of knowing the types of judgments that consumers make (such as for staying versus investment) and the criteria that influences consumers' decisions most (location, propensity to invest the seed money, return on investment and even resale value). In addition, marketers must understand the emotions and feelings that influence consumer decisions (for example buying a house as one's first house and buying it as one of the multiple investments are buying decisions with different objectives.). This chapter examines consumer judgment and decision making when motivation, ability, and opportunity to process are high, the next stages in the overall model of consumer behavior (see Exhibit 10.2). By carefully analyzing the factors that enter into judgment and decision making, marketers can acquire valuable insights that help them develop market offerings to consumers.

High-Effort Judgment Processes

Think about the last time you went to a restaurant. While reviewing the menu, you probably considered some items and thought about how good they would be before making your final choice. You were making ***judgments,*** evaluations or estimates regarding the likelihood of events. Judgment is a critical input into the decision process, but it is not the same as ***decision making,*** which involves making a selection between options or activities.

In a consumer context, *judgments* are evaluations or estimates regarding the likelihood that products and services possess certain features or will perform in a certain manner.[2] Judgments do not require the consumer to make a decision. Thus if you see an ad for a new Italian restaurant, you can form a judgment as to whether you will like it, how different it will be from other Italian restaurants, or how expensive it will be. These judgments can serve as input into your decision about whether to eat at the restaurant, but they do not require an actual choice.

In addition, judgment and decision making can involve us in different processes. One study found that consumers searched attributes in a different order during a judgment task as opposed to a decision task.[3] In another study, higher levels of brand familiarity made it easier for consumers to remember information for a judgment but lowered memory in a decision task.[4] Consumers can also act on different preferences depending on whether the task involves choice or a judgment (especially when the product category is unfamiliar).[5] Given the importance of judgment in consumers' information processing, marketers need to understand judgment processes, particularly estimations of likelihood, judgments of goodness or badness, and predictions of the likelihood that the two events will occur together.

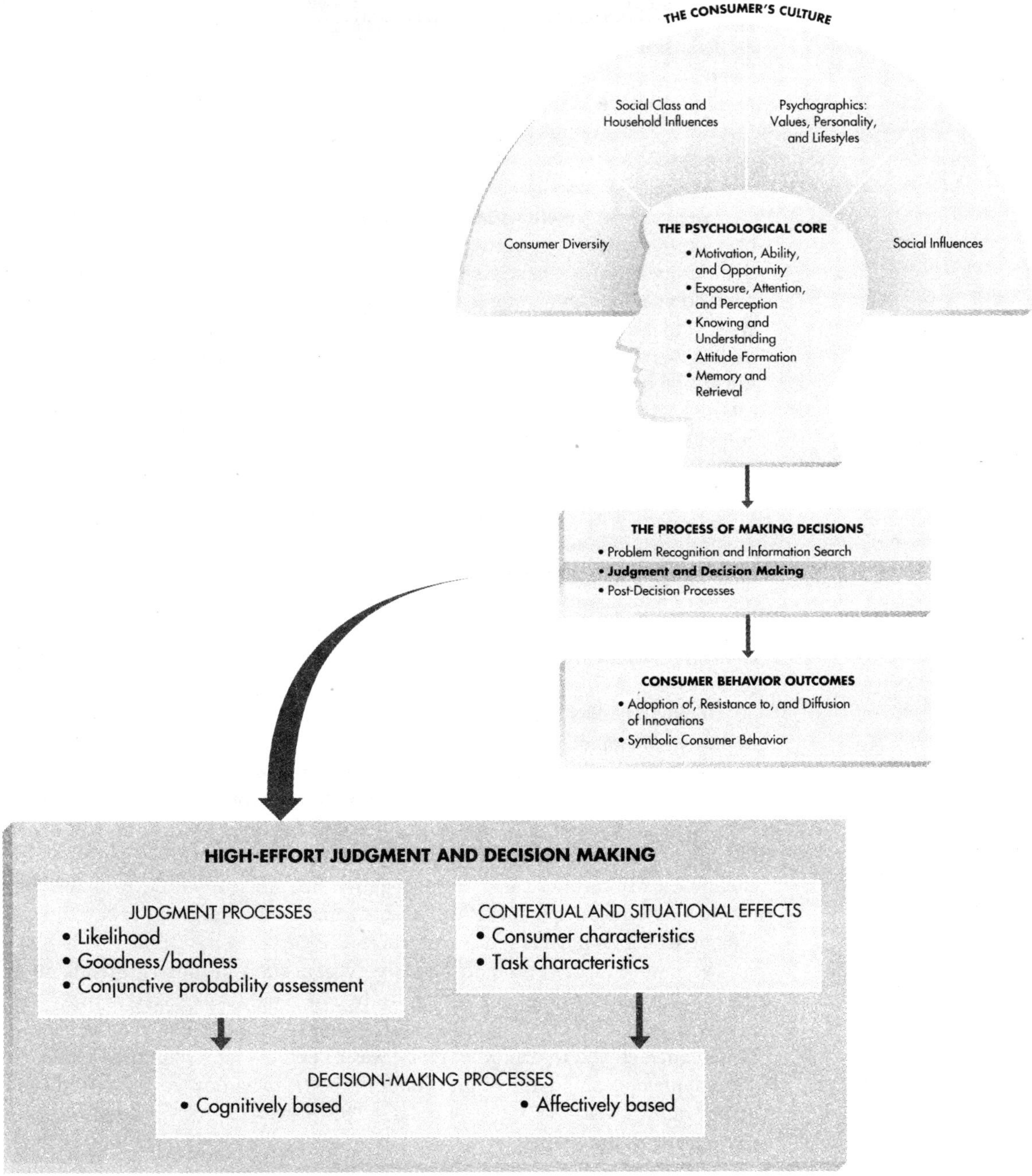

Exhibit 10.2

CHAPTER OVERVIEW: JUDGMENT AND DECISION MAKING BASED ON HIGH CONSUMER EFFORT *After problem recognition and search, consumers can engage in some form of judgment or decision making, which can vary in terms of processing effort (from high to low). This chapter looks at high-effort judgment and decision processes. Judgments are estimates of how likely something is to occur or how good or bad something is. These serve as inputs into decision making, which can be cognitively or affectively based. The decision-making process can also be influenced by contextual factors such as consumer characteristics, task characteristics, decision framing, and group presence.*

Judgments of Likelihood and Goodness/Badness

An ***estimation of likelihood,*** our determination of the probability that something will occur, is at the very core of consumer information processing. Estimations of likelihood appear in many consumer contexts. For example, when we buy a good or service, we can attempt to estimate its quality and the likelihood that it will satisfy our needs. When we buy clothing, we can estimate the likelihood that others will approve of it. When we view an ad, we can assess the likelihood that it is truthful.

Judgments of goodness/badness are our evaluation of the desirability of the offering's features. If you were planning a trip, you might judge how good or bad it is that Europe is fun and expensive. Most of the research on this kind of judgment has been done in the context of the attitude models covered in Chapter 6. These models suggest that a consumer combines individual judgments into an overall evaluation of goodness or badness in order to form an attitude about the product or service. Affect is important, as well: when consumers monitor their feelings toward an offering, they may form judgments of goodness or badness more quickly and consistently based, in part, on the intensity and direction of their affective response.[6]

Anchoring and Adjustment In making estimations of likelihood and goodness/badness, consumers employ an ***anchoring and adjustment process.***[7] They will first anchor the judgment based on some initial value and then adjust or "update" the evaluation as they consider additional information. The initial value can be information or an affective response readily available from memory; or it can be attribute information from the external environment that is encountered first.[8] Consumer values and normative influences can also be strong determinants of the initial value.

To illustrate, Starbucks Coffee has a very positive image in Japan—one survey ranks it at the top of all Japanese restaurant brands.[9] This factor led a local chain to change its name to Seattle Coffee, hoping to form a positive initial anchor and encourage consumers to see the shops as similar to Starbucks. Additional information from ads or experience may adjust this initial value upward or downward, but the judgment is more likely to be positive, based on Starbucks's image. If the prior evaluation of Starbucks had been negative, the anchor would probably have resulted in a negative judgment. Thus the same anchor can lead to two different judgments depending on how it is perceived.

The nature of the initial anchor is very important because it greatly affects the outcome of the judgment. In one study, consumers were asked to make judgments about ground beef samples. Researchers told one group that the beef was 75 percent lean and told another that it was 25 percent fat. Even though these two statements contain identical information, the "lean" group gave the beef much higher ratings than the "fat" group did.[10] This process, known as *framing,* is discussed later in the chapter.

Anchoring and adjustment can occur in two other ways. First, when one or more products are *bundled* into a single offer, the most important item serves as the anchor, and consumers make adjustments based on evaluations of the remaining items.[11] Second, when low-ability or low-knowledge consumers are evaluating *new* products, they give greater weight to information acquired later in the process, an example of the recency effect.[12]

Imagery, or visualization, also plays a major role in judgment. Consumers can try to construct an image of an event, such as how they will look and feel behind the wheel of a new car, to estimate its likelihood or judge its goodness or badness. Visualizing an event can actually make it seem more likely, because consumers may form a positive bias when they imagine themselves using the product.[13] Imagery may also lead consumers to overestimate how satisfied they will be with a product or service.[14] Moreover, when consumers who anticipate satisfaction engage in imagery, they allocate more mental resources to vivid attributes and weigh those attributes more heavily in forming preferences.[15]

Biases in Judgment Processes It is important to note that judgments are not always objective. Bias may affect consumer judgment in a variety of ways:

- *Confirmation bias.* If consumers are susceptible to a confirmation bias (see Chapter 9) and they acquire and process only confirming evidence, they will be more confident in their judgment than if they acquired negative information. This bias can lead to less-than-optimal choices for future purchases. When consumers are overconfident, they are unlikely to engage in an external information search, because they believe they know almost everything.[16]
- *Self-positivity bias.* When consumers believe they are less vulnerable to a risk than others are, they have a self-positivity bias. A study on AIDS found that consumers' self-positivity bias ("I am less likely to get AIDS than others") can be reduced if important information is made more accessible.[17] In another study of health messages, self-positivity bias was found to hinder message processing, although risk-behavior message cues reduced this bias and encouraged more precautionary thoughts and actions.[18]
- *Negativity bias.* With a negativity bias, consumers weight negative information more heavily than positive information when forming judgments. Studies have found this bias when the consumer is highly motivated to form as accurate a judgment as possible about a brand. Under marketplace conditions, however, the negativity bias tends to be lessened when consumers are familiar with a brand—and may even be reversed when consumers are committed to the brand.[19] Brand commitment also minimizes the negativity bias that may result from spillover, which occurs when consumers exposed to a marketing message change their evaluations of brand attributes that are not mentioned in the message.[20]
- *Mood and bias.* Mood can bias consumer judgment.[21] Essentially, your mood serves as the initial anchor for your judgment. If you are in a good mood when shopping for a CD, you will probably respond positively to new music you hear. In part, this is because consumers want to preserve a good mood, so they avoid negative information.
- *Prior brand evaluations.* When consumers judge a brand to be good based on past exposure, they may subsequently fail to learn (and view as important) information about the brand's attributes that are diagnostic of its actual quality.[22] In effect, the favorable brand name "blocks" learning about quality-revealing product attributes.

marketing IMPLICATIONS Marketers can increase the probability that judgments of their products and services will be anchored by a positive initial value if they focus consumers' attention on certain attributes. For example, by focusing attention on sleek styling, Apple has made its iPod the anchor for digital music players. Judgment of a product can also be affected by exposure to other products.[23] Thus to affluent consumers concerned about personal safety, the spacious $350,000 Mercedes Maybach may seem overly showy compared with the more discreet Bentley GT luxury coupe. As a result, Bentley has a long waiting list for coupes, whereas Mercedes sold only 600 Maybachs in the model's first year.[24]

When consumers are exposed to a brand extension, the existing brand name and its positive associations serve as a positive anchor for judgments of the new product. For example, Amul is the market leader in the pasteurized butter segment and commands a distinct leadership status in the market. Based on positive consumer reaction to the original products, the company has successfully introduced numerous brand extensions, including cheese, shakes, cold coffee, Ghee, Milk and Lassi to name a few.

A product's country of origin can serve as an anchor and influence subsequent judgments.[26] For example, domestic brands in China have had to mount vigorous marketing campaigns because many consumers prefer Western versions of the same product. In line with this trend, younger consumers in China are choosing Coca-Cola over local soft-drink brand Jianlibao.[27]

Priming consumers with positive feelings before giving them information will lead them to evaluate the offering more positively.[28] For instance, Nike has built considerable positive feelings and goodwill by raising $20 million for champion biker Lance Armstrong's cancer research foundation through the sale of yellow "Live Strong" bracelets.[29] The humorous ad in Exhibit 10.3 is another example of priming good feelings. Ads suggesting that consumers engage in imagery, like imagining a delicious pizza, can also produce positive judgments. Finally, priming consumers to think about their family ties may help in marketing some offerings. Research shows that consumers primed to consider their ties are more likely to take a financial risk because their family can help cushion a monetary loss. However, consumers are less likely to take a social risk when thinking about family ties because of how a negative outcome might effect their family.[30]

Exhibit 10.3
ANCHORING A JUDGMENT

The light humor created by NECC showcases the variety of cuisines that can be made from a good healthy chicken. The campaign was particularly effective post the fear of bird flu virus attack in the country when most consumers were wary of eating chicken

Conjunctive Probability Assessment

When consumers estimate the likelihood that two events will occur simultaneously or that two attributes are related, they are using ***conjunctive probability assessment.*** According to research, prior expectations influence its accuracy.[31] Thus consumers might expect that a rich flavor means high calories or that nationally advertised brands are of higher quality than local ones. When consumers use diagnostic attributes, their judgment improves because they can detect actual relationships between variables. For instance, experts are less guided by country-of-origin stereotypes and more by actual attributes when information is unambiguous.[32]

Sometimes, however, consumers are not adept at making conjunctive probability judgments, and they think a relationship exists when in fact it does not.[33] Such ***illusory correlation*** is apt to occur when information is ambiguous. To illustrate, just as smokers mistakenly thought "clean," smokeless cigarettes were safer, they may also mistakenly believe that low-toxin and natural cigarettes are safer.[34] This raises ethical issues, as Chapter 20 discusses. On the other hand, companies need to address inaccuracies that affect their marketing of goods and services. To illustrate, Hyundai was originally introduced to Western nations as a budget automotive brand. Now the company is targeting more upscale markets and must overcome perceptions of low quality. This is why Hyundai is spending millions to advertise quality indicators such as advanced features and five-year warranty coverage.[35]

High-Effort Decision-Making Processes

In any consumer choice situation, consumers face many available options, often choosing from a set of products, services, brands, or courses of action. They first evaluate the options in the consideration set (see Chapter 9), find those in the ***inept set*** unacceptable, and treat those in the ***inert set*** with indifference.[36] When faced with novel product categories, buying situations, or consumption contexts, consumers try to create a consideration set with easy-to-compare options.[37] Remember that consumers must decide how and when to dispose of an offering, not just how to acquire it. Thus to engage in most forms of consumer behavior, consumers must make some type of decision—even if they decide not to select any of the alternatives, which may happen when a great deal of uncertainty exists.[38]

Researchers studying how consumers combine information acquired from internal and external search to make a decision have proposed various models of the decision-making process. A basic assumption underlying many of these models is that consumers behave in a cognitive and rational manner, choosing the offering with the best combination of features to satisfy their needs. Thus when buying a new car, consumers might investigate a set of brands in terms of styling, reliability, fuel efficiency, and other salient attributes before selecting the one that maximizes their utility. Consumers do not always operate in such a rational manner, however. In high-elaboration situations, strong feelings might cause a consumer to buy a new PC even when the old PC is still functional. Therefore, researchers want to know how consumers make choices when the decision is more hedonic or emotional in nature.

Another important finding is that the decision process can vary according to the situation because consumers are highly adaptive to the task.[39] Each choice situation can vary greatly, not only in terms of the types of brands and information evaluated but also in the consumers' motivation, ability, and opportunity (MAO) to process information. As a result, the process consumers use to select a car is likely to be very different from the process they use to choose a house, a computer, or any other type of offering. Moreover, the decision context can change over time as new brands are introduced and information becomes outdated.

Decision-making styles can vary across cultures.[40] Some North Americans, for example, tend to be analytical, rely on factual information, and search for solutions to problems. In contrast, in Asian cultures, and particularly in Japan, logic is sometimes less important than the *kimochi*—the feeling. Similarly, many Saudi Arabians are more intuitive in their decision making and avoid persuasion based on empirical reasoning. Russians may place more emphasis on values than on facts, and Germans tend to be theoretical and deductive. In North American and European cultures, decisions are usually made by individuals who control their own fate. In Asian cultures the group is of primary importance, and actions arise at random or from other events, rather than being controlled by individuals.

It is important to recognize that consumers do not follow a uniform process every time they make a decision.[41] Instead, they construct a strategy depending on the nature of the task, and they may employ a number of decision rules, either alone or in combination, that can vary, sometimes just because the consumer wants a change.[42] So even though a number of decision-making models have been proposed—including the cognitive and affective models described in the following sections—each may accurately describe decision making under certain circumstances.

High-Effort Thought-Based Decisions

Cognitive models describe the processes by which consumers combine information about attributes to reach a decision in a rational, systematic manner. The various models discussed here are not intended to describe the same process. Rather, they identify *different* processes that may occur when consumers make a decision. Which model a consumer follows depends on both the consumer and the nature of the situation. Furthermore, the situations that different models fit may lead to entirely different selections by the consumer. Finally, consumers may employ a combination of models rather than just one and may not necessarily be aware of the exact process they are following.

Types of Decision Processes

Cognitive models can be classified along two major dimensions: compensatory versus noncompensatory nature, and brand versus attribute processing (see Exhibit 10.4).

Compensatory Versus Noncompensatory Models With ***compensatory models,*** consumers choose the brand that has the greatest number of positive features relative to negative. These models are a type of mental cost-benefit analysis in which a negative evaluation on one attribute can be compensated for (hence the name *compensatory*) by positive features on others. To illustrate, the "Made in China" tag and the "Made in Japan" tag have different connotations for the Indian consumer. The Japanese products have a better implied value as compared to a Chinese make. However, this evaluation can be overcome if the products rate highly on other aspects, such as reliability and price.

With a ***noncompensatory model,*** negative information leads the consumer to immediately reject the brand or service from the consideration set. In the preceding example, knowing that a product is foreign-made might prevent some Indian consumers from considering it further. Noncompensatory models are easier to implement and require less cognitive effort than compensatory models.

Exhibit 10.4
TYPES OF COGNITIVE CHOICE MODELS

Cognitive decision-making models can be classified along two major dimensions: (a) whether processing occurs one brand at a time or one attribute at a time, and (b) whether they are compensatory (bad attributes can be compensated for by good ones) or noncompensatory (a bad attribute eliminates the brand).

	Compensatory	**Noncompensatory**
Processing by Brand	Multiattribute models	Conjunctive model Disjunctive model
Processing by Attribute	Additive difference model	Lexicographic model Elimination-by-aspects model

Brand Versus Attribute Models In making a decision, consumers may evaluate *one brand at a time.* Thus a consumer making a PC purchase might collect information about a Dell model and make a judgment about it before moving on to the next brand. This type of ***brand processing*** occurs frequently because the environment—advertising, dealerships, and so on—is often organized by brands.

Attribute processing occurs when consumers compare across brands, *one attribute at a time.* A good example is price-comparison shopping in which consumers compare each brand on price and select the one with the desired price. Although most consumers prefer attribute processing because it is easier than brand processing, they cannot always find information available in a manner that facilitates it. This accounts for the increasing popularity of shopping agents. Interestingly, one study found that the inclusion of an attribute in a shopping agent's recommendations list gives that attribute more prominence.[43] Also note that consumers tend to value tangible attributes more heavily than intangible attributes.[44]

Compensatory Brand-Processing Models

Much research has focused on brand-based compensatory models, also called ***multiattribute models.*** One multiattribute model, the theory of reasoned action (TORA), was discussed in Chapter 6. Under TORA, consumers' attitudes toward an intended act, coupled with their belief about what significant people in their lives think is appropriate behavior, predict their intentions of buying, using, or disposing of an offering. Note that when considering multiple attributes, consumers tend to give more weight to those that are compatible with their goal orientation, whether related to promotion needs (seeking advancement and achievement) or prevention needs (seeking security and safety).[45]

Various other multiattribute models have been proposed.[46] These models differ in the components they include, usually one or more of these three: (1) belief strength, (2) evaluation, and (3) the importance consumers attach to the attribute or outcome. The boxed insert on page 228 discusses a multiattribute model based mainly on belief strength and importance.

marketing IMPLICATIONS

Brand-based compensatory models are very useful in identifying which alternatives consumers may choose or reject. This is because they identify the beliefs consumers have about the outcomes or attributes associated with buying, using, or disposing of a product or about the attributes that characterize the product. These models also help marketers understand which outcomes or attributes associated with the product need to be reinforced or changed.

If consumers do not strongly believe that positive outcomes or attributes are associated with a decision, marketers should stress these outcomes or attributes through marketing so as to strengthen consumers' beliefs. For example, DaimlerChrysler markets its ultracompact Smart car by stressing fuel efficiency and ease of parking and maneuvering. This helps consumers recognize the positive benefits that compensate for the car's small size.[47] The ad in Exhibit 10.5 helps consumers compare air-conditioners on a feature to feature basis.

If marketers analyzing consumer decisions find product weaknesses, they should address these shortcomings by altering the product and communicating the improvements to consumers. Thus after Volkswagen recalled thousands of cars in Europe because of leaky fuel pumps, the company not only fixed the problem, but it began to offer a better warranty to reassure consumers and protect its market share.[48] However,

Illustration of Two Compensatory Models

Here's an example of one multiattribute model that uses belief strength and importance weights as its two components. Belief strength represents how strongly consumers hold each belief (some beliefs are held more strongly than others); importance weights represent how important each belief is to a decision (some beliefs are more important than others). The model can be outlined as follows:

$$A_b = \sum(b_i \times I_i)$$

where A_b represents an attitude toward the brand; b_i is the belief strength associated with attribute i, a judgment of likelihood; and Ii is the importance of the attribute. The model can easily be applied to a decision context if we assess A_b for each option in the consideration set. The consumer would choose the option for which he or she has the strongest attitude.

Consider the following example. Suppose Elena wants to go to graduate school at school A, school B, or school C and that the most salient attributes of each school she is considering are qualifications of the faculty, prestige, cost, and distance from home. As shown in the following exhibit, Elena rates b_i and I_i for each option, one at a time. The model then predicts that Elena will select school A because it is rated the most prestigious with the best faculty.

Using the *additive difference model,* Elena first compares school A and school B on the attribute of superior faculty. Using the b_i rating, for example, she finds a difference of +1. She moves on to the prestige attribute, where the difference is +2. Elena continues this process for the other attributes to get a total additive difference of +3, establishing a preference for school A. She repeats the process by comparing school A and school C, again finding that school A is seen as a better choice. (Note that because school A is seen as better than the other two choices, there is no need to compare school B and school C).

Remember that consumers do not formally make these ratings when they make a decision. The numbers are a way of quantifying the mental cost-benefit analysis that consumers might engage in. Nevertheless, compensatory models are useful in helping us identify which factors are most influential in making a decision.

	Description	Outcome or Consequences of the Decision	How Important is Each Outcome (*1 = not at all; 7 = very important*)	How Strong is Elena's Belief that the Outcome Characterizes the Alternative (*−3 = very weak; +3 = very strong*) School A	School B	School c	Alternative Chosen and Why
The Multi-Attribute Model	Decisions are made by brand-based processing. Each alternative's outcome importance weight is multiplied by its belief strength. These totals are then summed across outcomes. The brand with the highest weighted score is chosen.	Has superior faculty	6	+3	+2	+3	School A is chosen because the sum of its importance weights times their outcome ratings [6x(+3)]+[4x(+3)]+[3x(−1)]+[2x(+1)]=29. This value is higher than the summed products of the other alternatives (School B=[6x(+2)]+[4x(+1)]+[3x(+1)]+[2x(−1)]=17, and School C=[6x(+3)]+[4x(−2)]+[3x(+2)]+[2x(0)]=16).
		Is a more prestigious institution	4	+3	+1	−2	
		Has more expensive tuition	3	−1	+1	+2	
		Is far from home	2	+1	−1	0	
		Weighted Total (sum of each belief strength 3 its importance)		**29**	**17**	**16**	

How do the belief strength ratings compare across alternatives?

	Description	Outcome	*School A vs. School B*	*School A vs. School c*	*School B vs. School c*	
The Additive Difference Model	Belief strengths about attributes are compared across brands. The brand with the highest total additive difference across the outcomes is chosen.	Has superior faculty	(+3)–(+2)=+1	(+3)–(+3)=0	(+2)–(+3)=–1	School A is chosen because the additive difference of its belief strength ratings compares more favorably with both School B (+3) and School C (+3). School B isn't seen as any better than School C (additive difference = 0).
		Is a more prestigious institution	(+3)–(+1)=+2	(+3)–(–2)=5	(+1)–(–2)=+3	
		Has more expensive tuition	(–1)–(+1)=–2	(–1)–(+2)=–3	(+1)–(+2)=–1	
		Is far from home	(+1)–(–1)=+2	(+1)–(0)=+1	(–1)–(0)=–1	
		Additive Difference	**+3**	**+3**	**0**	

Exhibit

HOW ELENA MIGHT CHOOSE A GRADUATE SCHOOL: COMPENSATORY MODELS*

**Models are compensatory because, for any given alternative, a high rating on one outcome can compensate for a low rating on another outcome.*

Exhibit 10.5
COMPARING ATTRIBUTES TO HELP CONSUMERS DECIDE
This ad helps consumers decide which air conditioners to buy by comparing Voltas with all the brands on a feature to feature basis.

when companies make changes to remove competitive disadvantages, although they are often able to draw consumers from competitive offerings, they are also reducing differentiation. Therefore, marketers should consider the long-term effects of improvements.[49]

Decision models can help marketers identify weaknesses of competitors and plan for targeting these in marketing communications, especially comparative ads. This is important: Research shows that consumers with little commitment to a brand will put more weight on negative information because they perceive it as more diagnostic.[50] Most retailers in India do not deal with stockists, dealers or distributors during the peak business hours which are usually in the morning, between 8-10am and in the evening between 5-9pm. The reason being, that the salespeople at the counter can concentrate better on the customers, rather than having to deal with the stockists, dealers or distributors.

Compensatory Attribute-Processing Models

According to the ***additive difference model,*** brands are compared by attribute, *two brands at a time.*[52] Consumers evaluate differences between brands on each attribute and then combine them into an overall preference. This process allows tradeoffs between attributes—that is, a positive difference on one attribute can offset a negative difference on another.

marketing IMPLICATIONS

The additive difference model helps marketers determine which attributes or outcomes exhibit the greatest differences among brands and use this knowledge to improve and properly position their brand. If a brand performs below a major competitor on a certain attribute, the company needs to enhance consumers' beliefs about that product's superiority. On the other hand, if a brand performs significantly better than competitors on a key attribute, marketers should enhance consumer beliefs by positioning the offering around this advantage. Mahesh Lunch Home, set up in 1971, a Manglorean food joint located at Juhu in Mumbai is a popular sea food joint which started off by catering largely to the office crowd, but gradually became a favorite of the crème-de-la-crème of the city. Over the years it has added several menus on the platter but its core strength still lies in the authentic Manglorean style sea food that it makes, the unique selling proposition of the outlet.

Noncompensatory Brand-Processing Models

The compensatory models we have discussed require consumers to exert a significant amount of effort in evaluating each brand on many attributes. Often consumers are not willing to put forth this much effort and instead opt for a simpler noncompensatory process. With noncompensatory brand-processing models, consumers use key attributes to evaluate brands and then eliminate those that are not adequate on any one attribute.[54] These models are called noncompensatory because a negative rating on a key attribute eliminates the brand.

A common feature of noncompensatory models is that the decision process proceeds in a simple, sequential manner. Consumers set up ***cutoff levels*** for each attribute and reject any brand below the cutoff. For example, some consumers use fuel efficiency as a key attribute and first reject gas-guzzling cars, then use environmental friendliness as an attribute to eliminate others. This has worked to the advantage of the Toyota Prius, which gets 50 miles to the gallon due to its hybrid engine and has lower smog-forming emissions than conventional cars.[55] Consumers tend to choose cutoffs that set up the largest difference between accepted and rejected alternatives. Noncompensatory models can be differentiated in terms of cutoff levels and whether the comparison proceeds by brand or by attribute.

Conjunctive Model Using a ***conjunctive model,*** consumers set up *minimum* cutoffs for *each* attribute that represent the absolute lowest value they are willing to accept.[56] For example, a consumer might want to pay less than $20 per month to charge a brief vacation and therefore reject an alternative with a higher monthly cost. Thus the Carnival cruise line has arranged financing to allow consumers to charge a $299 three-day cruise and pay $14 per month for two years. "Some people still perceive cruising as too expensive," says a Carnival executive. "This just helps us get over that hurdle."[57] Because the cutoffs represent the bare minimum belief strength levels, the psychology of a conjunctive model is to rule out unsuitable alternatives (i.e., get rid of the 'bad ones') as soon as possible, which consumers do by weighing negative information.

Disjunctive Model The ***disjunctive model*** is similar to the conjunctive model, with two important exceptions. First, the consumer sets up *acceptable* levels for the cutoffs—levels that are more desirable (i.e., find the "good ones"). So even though $20 per month may be the highest monthly payment a consumer will accept for a vacation, $14 per month may be more acceptable. Second, the consumer bases evaluations on several of the *most important* attributes, rather than on all, putting the weight on positive information.

marketing IMPLICATIONS

Identifying consumers' cutoff levels can be very useful for marketers. If an offering is beyond any of the cutoffs that many consumers set, it will be rejected frequently. This means marketers must change consumers' beliefs about these attributes. For example, more consumers in China are considering SUVs because of the cargo capacity and the safety of a larger vehicle, but they are very price-conscious as well. So Great Wall and other local manufacturers make SUVs similar to Japanese or American models but priced below 84,000 yuan (about $10,000). Meanwhile, Japanese and Western automakers want to change Chinese consumers' beliefs by emphasizing the sophistication, styling, and quality of their SUVs, which are often priced above the equivalent of $14,000.[58]

In addition, research suggests that marketers can hurt themselves by adding unwanted or unneeded features to a product or service, because these give the consumer a reason for rejecting the brand.[59] One study found that when two brands offered collector's plate and golf umbrella premiums, the brands were less desirable than when the offer was not made.[60]

Noncompensatory Attribute-Processing Models

Two noncompensatory models in which consumers process by attribute are the lexicographic and elimination-by-aspects models.

Lexicographic Model With the ***lexicographic model,*** consumers order attributes in terms of importance and compare the options one attribute at a time, starting with the most important. If one option dominates, the consumer selects it. In case of a tie, the consumer proceeds to the second most important attribute and continues in this way until only one option remains. A tie can occur if the difference between two options on any attribute is below the just noticeable difference: one brand priced at $2.77 and one priced at $2.79 would likely be seen as tied on price. Another common example of a lexicographic strategy is price-comparison shopping, where the most important attribute is, of course, price.

Elimination-by-Aspects Model The ***elimination-by-aspects model*** is similar to the lexicographic model but incorporates the notion of an *acceptable cutoff.*[61] This model is not as strict as the lexicographic model, and more attributes are likely to be considered. Consumers first order attributes in terms of importance and then compare options on the most important attribute. Those options below the cutoff are eliminated, and the consumer continues the process until one option remains.

marketing IMPLICATIONS

Knowing how consumers use attribute-processing models helps marketers identify determinant attributes and understand the order in which consumers evaluate attributes. Thus if many consumers are employing a lexicographic model and a brand is weak on the most important attribute, the company needs to improve on this feature in order to be selected. Also, marketers can try to change the order of importance so that a major brand advantage is the most critical attribute. Dell has done this with its high-definition widescreen plasma TVs, making price the most critical attribute, whereas Pioneer, Panasonic, and other global competitors emphasize screen size, new technology, or another attributes.[62] In Exhibit 10.6, Color Plus is trying to make the attribute of fabric design the most important.

Exhibit 10.6
STRESSING ONE ATTRIBUTE THROUGH MARKETING

Color Plus has always stressed on the fabric design and quality, two key ingredients in the brand's success. They were pioneers in introducing advertising that concentrated on the product rather than models wearing the product, as they took away the attention from the product.

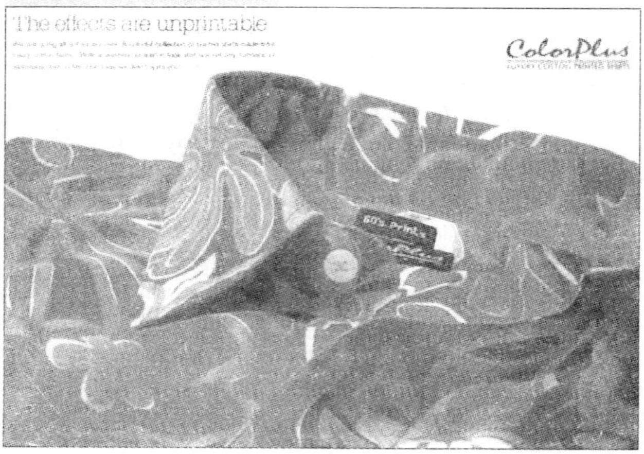

Multiple Models That Characterize Decision Making

Consumers often use a combination of decision-making strategies.[63] When many options are available, they can use a noncompensatory strategy (conjunctive model) to reduce the size of the consideration set and eliminate poor options and then use a more thorough model (a compensatory strategy) to evaluate the remaining ones. Or they might use bits and pieces of various strategies in constructing a decision process.[64] Often, making one decision leads to yet another decision. In such cases, consumers can either directly evaluate each alternative based on its specific

Exhibit 10.7
SWITCHING TO A COMPENSATORY MODEL
Oil companies have been criticized for their impact on the environment. However, this ad stresses some positive things that they do (hoping to compensate for any negative impressions).

characteristics or evaluate each based on the characteristics of the options they make available in later decisions.[65]

Consumers also tend to consolidate or stabilize their brand preferences as they make initial tradeoffs in the decision process—preferences that remain stable as consumers continue using attributes to make subsequent choices among available options.[66] Moreover, as consumers learn more about the alternatives or about the decision task, they may change their strategy to adjust to their new knowledge by reordering the importance of attributes or employing a different strategy.[67] And, as noted earlier, consumers may change decision rules just for the sake of change. Thus consumers tend to be opportunistic and adaptive processors.

marketing IMPLICATIONS Given that different models can lead to different choices, marketers may sometimes want to change the process by which consumers make a decision. For example, if most consumers are using a compensatory strategy, switching them to a noncompensatory strategy may be advantageous, particularly if competitors have a major weakness. By convincing consumers not to accept a lower level on an important attribute—that is, not to compensate for the attribute—marketers might prompt some consumers to reject competitors from consideration. [2]Maruti had re-introduced their popular model as Zen-Classic, complete with all the features of the retro look. It had all the contemporary features of the Zen, with a change in design. The Classic had the retro look with round headlights and a vertical chrome grill. The bumpers too got the retro treatment and were replaced with slim chrome bumpers. It featured revised interiors with classic wood finish louvers on the dashboard and an all new speedometer make.

When consumers are rejecting a brand with a noncompensatory strategy, marketers can try to switch them to a compensatory strategy by arguing that other attributes compensate for a negative. A good example is the ad in Exhibit 10.7. For instance, Precept MC Lady brand golf balls attracted considerable attention after a man used them to win a statewide tournament. Initially, men were put off by the feminine name. However, those who tried the balls liked their performance, and stores began referring to this brand as the "Laddie." The performance and the informal name change helped make the brand America's top-selling golf ball.[69]

High-Effort Feeling-Based Decisions

The common feature of cognitive models is that decision making proceeds in a sequential and rational manner. Researchers now realize, however, that consumers also may make decisions in a more holistic manner on the basis of feelings or emotions—***affective decision making.***[70] Thus consumers sometimes make a decision simply because it feels right, rather than as the result of a detailed and systematic evaluation. Or they may decide that the chosen option feels like a perfect fit, regardless of prior cognitive processing.[71] Emotional processing can sometimes overwhelm rational thought, leading consumers to select an option that is inconsistent with their rational preferences—a decision they may regret later.[72]

As you saw in Chapter 6, brands can be associated with positive emotions such as love, joy, pride, and elation, as well as with negative emotions such as guilt, hate, fear, anxiety, anger, sadness, shame, and greed. These emotions can be recalled to play a central role in the decision process, particularly when consumers perceive them as relevant to the product or service.[73] This affective processing is frequently experience based.[74] In other words, consumers select an option based on their recall of past experiences and the feelings associated with them.

Consumer feelings are particularly critical for offerings with hedonic, symbolic, or aesthetic aspects.[75] One study found that when the decision outcome will be realized far in the future, some consumers commit themselves in advance to choosing a highly hedonic experience (such as taking a cruise), even if it means avoiding more necessary choices (such as saving money for college).[76] Further, consumers who are especially concerned with aesthetic elements will give criteria of visual appearance more importance when formulating buying intentions for a wide range of products.[77]

In choosing a restaurant, clothing, music, entertainment, or art, for example, consumers will often base their choice on positive associated feelings. A study of rock music found that emotional, sensory, and imagery responses were the most critical in determining liking and intent to purchase recorded music.[78] American outlets in India like Ruby's Tuesday, TGI Friday, Taco Maker offer an all American experience not just in the cuisines offered, but also in terms of the restaurant ambience too. The ambience and the décor add to the physical evidence and for most diners the experience of the ambience along with the food is equally important.

Emotions also play a key role in deciding what we consume and for how long.[80] We consume products and services that make us feel good more often and for longer periods than offerings that do not. Moreover, we expect more enjoyment from a consumption experience when it will follow a less pleasing consumption experience—and the expectation of this contrast can affect our decisions even when we do not have this exact experience.[81] Note that offerings can serve as a means of removing or reducing negative emotions. Sometimes consumers buy a product, such as jewelry, simply to make themselves feel better. In other situations, they may make a choice because of a negative feeling, buying a product out of guilt or shame.

Negative emotions can also be associated with difficult choices that involve conflict, such as trading off greater safety versus lower price in a car, and consumers will often choose the option that avoids the negative emotion.[82] Consumers who are facing emotionally difficult tradeoffs between price and quality cope with potentially negative emotions related to quality by choosing the offering with the best quality.[83] Some consumers may simply avoid making trade-offs between conflicting attributes.[84] Further, brands that require a lot of effort to evaluate may create negative emotions and be selected less frequently than those requiring less effort.[85] When consumers evaluate the outcome of a purchase, they compare what they actually received with what they would have received if they had chosen differently. If a different option would have led to a better outcome, they will regret their actual choice and may switch to the brand they didn't buy on the next purchase occasion.[86]

Exhibit 10.8
STIMULATING IMAGERY THROUGH ADVERTISING
Advertisement for the Incredible India campaign creates strong visual imagery to attract prospective audience.

Imagery plays a key role in emotional decision making.[87] Consumers can attempt to imagine themselves actually consuming the product or service and use any emotions they experience as input for the decision. In choosing a vacation, for example, you can imagine the excitement you might experience from each destination. If these images are pleasant (or negative), they will exert a positive (or negative) influence on your decision process. Imagery can also ignite consumer desire for and fantasizing about certain products.[88] Inviting consumers to interact with a product through an online demonstration can evoke vivid mental images of product use and increase purchase intentions.[89] As shown in Exhibit 10.8, ads can encourage consumers to imagine themselves in a certain situation.

Adding information actually makes imagery processing easier, because more information makes it easier to form an accurate image (whereas it may lead to ***information overload*** under cognitive processing). Moreover, imagery encourages brand-based processing because images are organized by brand rather than by attribute. Also, companies that design new products by including customers in imagining visual imagery—creating a new image rather than recalling one from memory—can produce more original product designs.[90]

Consumers can use *both* cognitive and affective processing in making a decision. Or they can use yet another combined strategy, starting with a compensatory or noncompensatory cognitive model to narrow down the choice set and then using imagery and emotions to make the final decision.[91] In buying a house, for example, consumers often use price, square footage, and number of rooms to narrow the choices, then select the home that "feels right."

marketing IMPLICATIONS

Marketers can employ a variety of advertising, sales, and promotion techniques to add to the emotional experience surrounding an offering. Good service or pleasant ambiance in a restaurant or store, for example, can produce positive feelings and experiences that may influence future choices. To differentiate itself by providing a pleasant ambiance, the South African retailer Shoprite opens spacious stores with colorful décor, bright lighting, and well-organized shelves plus low prices. Building on its success in Africa, the chain is expanding into India as well.[92]

Decision Making When Alternatives Cannot Be Compared

In the decision-making models discussed thus far, consumers compare alternatives from the same product or service category on the basis of similar attributes or emotions. However, consumers often need to choose from a set of options that may not be directly comparable on the same attributes. For instance, you might be trying to select entertainment for next weekend and have a choice of going to the movies, eating at a nice restaurant, renting a video, or attending a party. Each alternative has different attributes, making comparisons more difficult.

In making these ***noncomparable decisions,*** consumers adopt either an alternative-based strategy or an attribute-based strategy.[93] Using the ***alternative-based strategy*** (also called top-down processing), they develop an overall evaluation of each option—perhaps using a compensatory or affective strategy—and base their decision on it. If you were deciding on weekend entertainment, you could evaluate each option's pros and cons independently and then choose the one you like the best.

Using the ***attribute-based strategy,*** consumers make comparisons easier for themselves by forming abstract representations of comparable attributes. In this type of bottom-up processing, the choice is constructed or built up. To make a more direct comparison for an entertainment decision, for example, you could construct abstract attributes such as fun or likelihood of impressing a date. Because abstractions simplify the decision process, consumers tend to make them even when the options are easy to compare.[94]

Note that both strategies can be employed in different circumstances. When the alternatives are less comparable, consumers tend to use an alternative-based strategy because it is harder to make attribute abstractions.[95] Alternative-based strategies also suit consumers who have well-defined goals, because they can easily recall the various options and their results. If your goal is to find fun things to do with a date, you could immediately recall a set of options like going to a movie or eating out, along with your overall evaluation of each option. You would then pick the option with the strongest evaluation. On the other hand, when consumers lack well-defined goals, they tend to use attribute-based processing.

One final point about noncomparable choice is that price is often the one attribute on which alternatives can be compared directly. Consumers typically use price to screen alternatives for the consideration set rather than as the main basis of comparison among noncomparable alternatives. Thus in your decision among entertainment alternatives, you might use cost to generate a set of options that are reasonably affordable, then use an alternative- or attribute-based strategy to make the final decision.

Does Context Affect How Decisions Are Made?

Consumers use different strategies in different decision contexts or even for the same decision in different time periods. The best strategy for a specific decision depends both on the consumer and on the nature of the decision.[96] This final section looks at four ***contextual effects*** on decision making: consumer characteristics, task characteristics, task definition or framing, and the presence of a group.

How Consumer Characteristics Can Affect Decision Making

A variety of factors related to consumers affect the nature of the decision process. Consistent with the overall processing model, these factors can be grouped according to consumers' motivation, ability, and opportunity to elaborate on information when making a decision.

Motivation to Process Although we are more likely to use any of the decision processes described in this chapter when motivation to process is high, the models still differ in the amount of effort they require. As our incentive to make a correct decision increases, we consider the alternatives more carefully,[97] and the likelihood that we will use a more active compensatory (versus noncompensatory) model increases. We also use a greater number of attributes to make a decision as our involvement increases.[98] On the other hand, if we perceive the decision to be too risky or if it entails an unpleasant task, we may delay making a decision.[99]

Consumers who are in a good mood are more willing to process information and take more time in making a decision than those who are not in a good mood.[100] When in a good mood, consumers pay closer attention to the associative network of brands being considered and elaborate a higher number of attributes connected with each brand, which can result in more extreme (positive or negative) evaluations.[101] Another study showed that consumers in a high-arousal mood—feeling very happy or very sad, for instance—tend to process information less thoroughly. Recall is affected, as well: consumers in a bad mood are more likely to accurately recall what a marketing message said.[102]

Mood can also influence the nature of the evaluation. One study found that consumers in a good mood rated a set of audio speakers more positively than did consumers in a bad mood when their mood was subconsciously influenced by music (awareness caused the consumers to adjust for mood).[103] Moreover, when consumers receive information about a product's attributes before evaluating it, their mood will influence their judgment in situations where they would ordinarily judge the category using hedonic, not utilitarian, criteria.[104] Interestingly, consumers may deliberately manipulate their mood when intuition suggests that a mood change could improve decision performance.[105]

Ability to Process Consumers are more likely to understand their preferences and decisions when they can relate the evaluation of a product to its features.[106] When consumers have this "consumption vocabulary," they can use more attributes and information in making a decision. Expert consumers have more brand-based prior experience and knowledge and, as a result, tend to use brand-based decision strategies.[107] These consumers know how to identify diagnostic information and ignore irrelevant attributes in their decision making. When consumers consider complex information, they may simplify the processing task by focusing more on brand effects and less on attributes, especially if they face more than one complex choice task.[108] Finally, consumers in different cultures tend to use different decision strategies when confronted with information incongruity. North American consumers form evaluations based on attribute information, whereas East Asian consumers form evaluations based on both source and attribute information.[109]

Opportunity to Process As time pressure increases, consumers initially try to process faster.[110] If this does not work, they base their decision on fewer attributes and place heavier weight on negative information, eliminating bad alternatives with a noncompensatory strategy such as a conjunctive model. Time pressure, one of the major reasons that consumers fail to make intended purchases, can reduce the number of impulsive purchases and shopping time.[111] Consumers may also delay making a decision if they feel uncertain about how to get product information.[112] However, consumers feeling time pressure will defer decisions less when the choice entails high conflict and when the offerings under consideration display common bad features but unique good features.[113] Moreover, whether a consumer is present- or future-oriented can lead to different motivations and choices for different products.[114] *Present-oriented consumers* want to improve their current well-being and prefer products that help them do so, such as relaxing vacations and entertaining books. *Future-oriented consumers* want to develop themselves and select life-enriching vacations and books.

How Task Characteristics Can Affect Decision Making

In addition to consumer characteristics, task characteristics can influence decision making. Researchers have studied two task characteristics: the consideration set and information availability.

The Consideration Set The number and types of alternatives in the consumer's consideration set are key determinants of the decision-making process. [3]Evolving markets such as India face marketing challenges which are quite different from the ones found in developed markets in terms of managing brand association, pricing and levels of consumers' aspirations. For instance, the price war initiated by the well-known brands in the detergent category has literally eliminated the premium segment in terms of price. There are too many price points and stock-keeping units (SKUs) across brands in the soaps and confectionery categories. Even in the case of durables, the introduction of product line variants in general is much more than what it was in the past. Larger consideration sets require additional cognitive effort to make a decision. As consumers, we typically handle this increased load by adopting a combined strategy—narrowing down the set with a noncompensatory model, followed by a compensatory or affectively based strategy.[117] The influence of the consideration set depends on its composition, on the consumer's goal, and on the consumer's aversion to extreme options.

Composition Merely changing the alternatives in the consideration set can have a major impact on the consumer's decision, even without a change in preferences.[118] Adding inferior brands to the set increases decision accuracy and decreases effort. This ***attraction effect*** occurs because the inferior brands increase the attractiveness of the dominant brand, making the decision easier.[119] Interestingly, when product information is presented numerically, as in graphs or charts, the attraction effect is weakened—whereas when information is in words, our greater knowledge increases the attraction effect.[120] The attraction effect may not occur at all if we are more conscious of price and less conscious of quality.[121] Note that not all brands in a consideration set are equally considered.[122] If consumers focus on one specific alternative, they are more likely to select it and be willing to pay more for it than for the other alternatives.[123] If they focus on one brand at a time, they tend to judge that brand more positively than the average of the best brands within that category.[124]

The composition of the consideration set is also extremely important because our evaluation of a brand depends on the other brands to which it is compared. In particular, if one brand is clearly more attractive or dominant than others, making a choice does not require much effort.[125] We are more selective in our use of information and process by brand under these conditions. Yet if the brands are similar in attractiveness, we must put more effort into making a decision—perhaps using a compensatory or detailed noncompensatory process.[126] If the consideration set excludes a neutral or midpoint option (one that is neither extremely positive nor extremely negative), we are likely to be more risk averse and prefer the option that is most positive on a key attribute.[127] If the consideration set is large, having an option with the ideal combination of attributes simplifies our choice and strengthens our preference for the chosen alternative.[128]

Consumer's Goal When the consumer's primary objective is to make a decision, he or she may use trivial attributes to help finalize the decision. For example, if three brands in the consideration set are perceived as equivalent with the exception that one contains a trivial attribute, the consumer is likely to choose the brand with the trivial attribute (arguing that its presence may be useful). If, however, two of the three brands in the consideration set have a particular trivial attribute, the consumer is likely to choose the one without that attribute (arguing that the attribute is unnecessary). In both cases, the consumer used the trivial attribute to complete and justify the final decision.[129] Another study found that when the goal is to make a decision, consumers may judge products with unique, positive attributes and shared negative attributes as more favorable than products with unique, negative attributes that share positive attributes.[130] Finally, consumers whose goal is to influence others will use this context to construct a consideration set with different alternatives than a consideration set constructed in the absence of an influence goal.[131]

Extremeness Aversion Consumers tend to have an ***extremeness aversion,*** meaning that options perceived as extreme on a particular attribute will seem less attractive than those perceived as intermediate. This is why people often find moderately priced options more attractive than options that are *either* very expensive or very inexpensive. For example, Nestle had introduced its range of mineral water at Rs.12/- price point, whereas competitor brands offered theirs at Rs.10/- price point. Unable to differentiate between what Nestle offered on a Rs.2/- price premium, consumers refrained from Nestle. When consumers see the attributes of one alternative as being equally dispersed (rather than very close together or very far apart), they will view this as the compromise option even when it is not at the overall midpoint among options.[133] In situations where options lack correlated benefits and costs, expanding the consideration set to include a wider range of options increases the contrast with the extremes. Thus adding lower-priced options makes the intermediate options seem more costly, whereas adding higher-priced alternatives makes the intermediate options seem less costly.[134] When one option is perceived to be moderately (but not extremely) inconsistent with the consideration set's product category, it will be preferred only if consumers perceive no real risk in the decision.[135]

marketing IMPLICATIONS

By examining the nature of consumers' consideration sets, marketers can develop some interesting strategies. One way to try to gain an advantage is by promoting comparisons with inferior rather than with equal or superior competitors. This maximizes the attraction effect and results in a more positive evaluation of the brand. Also, marketers can increase sales of a high-margin item simply by offering a higher-priced option.[136] Thus Panasonic could increase the sales of a $179 microwave oven by offering a slightly larger model at $199. The higher-priced model might not sell well, but it would make the lower-priced model look like a good deal. Another technique is to sell a new, improved model alongside the old model at the same price, which makes the new one look better.

Availability of Information The amount, quality, and format of the information also affect the decision strategy employed. When a consumer has more information, the decision becomes more complex, and the consumer must use a more detailed decision strategy. Having more information will lead to a better choice only up to a point; after that, the consumer experiences information overload.[137] As an example, pharmaceuticals firms are legally required to provide detailed prescription information and disclose side effects in their ads, yet the sheer amount of information probably overwhelms many consumers. As another example, one study found that consumers in Romania and Turkey have experienced great confusion in judging quality and making choices because "there are so many alternatives now."[138] Marketers should therefore present a few key points rather than a flood of information. Too little information can hamper decision making, however, resulting in poorer-quality decisions and a lower level of satisfaction. A lack of both products and information has been a major problem in some former communist countries.[139]

If the quality of information we acquire from either internal or external search is useful or diagnostic, our processing effort is reduced and we make better decisions.[140] Essentially, we can narrow the consideration set relatively quickly because we need fewer attributes. One study shows that when consumers lack information about a certain feature, they will use their interpretation of this missing information to support their choice of the option that is superior on the common feature.[141] A focus on quality information further suggests that marketers can benefit from being selective about the information they provide rather than by always focusing on quantity.

However, if the available information is ambiguous, consumers are more likely to stay with their current brand than to risk a new competitive brand—even a superior one.[142] Consumers also can compare numerical attribute information faster and more easily than they can compare verbal information.[143] For example, to help parents select video games, a group of video game manufacturers developed a numerical rating system to indicate the amount of sex and violence in their games.

The format of the information—the way it is organized in memory or in the external environment—greatly influences the type of decision strategy employed. In one study, consumers were less likely to choose the cheapest brand of consumer electronics product when the offerings were organized by model (similar offerings by different companies grouped together) rather than by brand.[144] Thus companies with high-priced brands would want the display to be organized by model, and

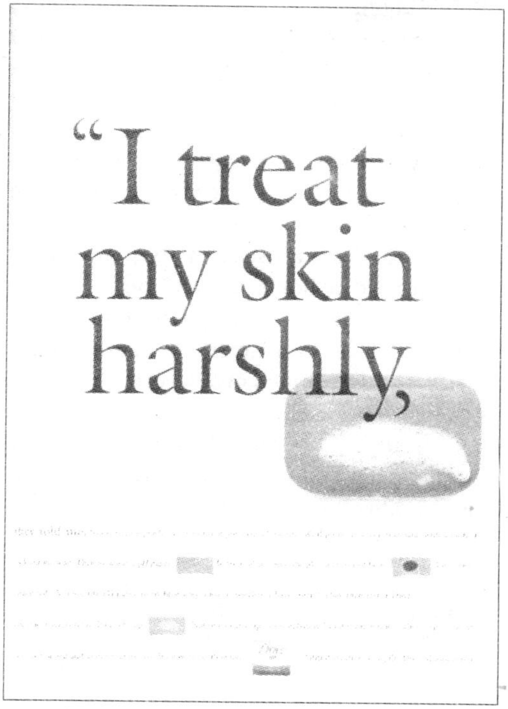

Exhibit 10.9
ORGANIZING INFORMATION
The advertisement for Dove compares the soap to any ordinary soap and illustrates the softness element of the brand as compared to any other ordinary brand. It also further reinforces Dove's stand of 1/4th moisturising lotion.

companies offering low-priced brands would prefer a brand-based display.

If information is organized by brand, consumers will likely employ a brand-based strategy such as a compensatory, conjunctive, or disjunctive model. If information is organized by attribute or in a matrix, consumers can use an attribute-processing strategy. Providing information to consumers in a format that requires less effort increases decision effectiveness and accuracy.[145] When researchers presented consumers with a narrative message about vacations, the consumers used holistic processing to sequence and evaluate the information. The narrative structure is similar to the way consumers acquire information in daily life, so processing was easier. In processing the narrative, consumers did not consider individual features, which meant negatives had less impact.[146] Another study found that organizing yogurt by flavor, not brand, encouraged more comparison shopping on the basis of attribute processing.[147] Sometimes consumers will even restructure information into a more useful format, especially a matrix.[148]

How Decision Framing Can Affect Decision Making

A third contextual influence on the decision process is the way in which the task is defined or represented, called ***decision framing.*** This is an important influence because the frame serves as the initial reference point or anchor in the decision process. All subsequent information is processed in light of it. For example, a frame for a car purchase might be (1) buy an economical car I can afford or (2) buy a car that will impress my friends. Clearly, consumers will use different models and process information differently under these two frames.

Early research on framing studied people's willingness to take risks in a gamble. Results showed that people are more willing to take risks when a choice is framed as a loss rather than as a gain.[149] One study examined consumer preferences for two different coupons.[150] Consumers were asked to choose between two coupons they could use when buying a jar of spaghetti sauce. With one they would get a free can of soup (a 49-cent value), and with another they would buy a can of soup and get 49 cents off the total. The first condition was framed as a gain (get something free), and the second was a reduced loss (49 cents off). Even though the coupons had the same value, more consumers opted for the free can of soup. Other research has found that messages framed in terms of loss are more persuasive when consumers are in a good mood, whereas messages framed in terms of gain are more persuasive when consumers are in a bad mood.[151] As the next sections show, either consumers can frame their decisions or their decisions can be framed by exposure to external stimuli.

Framing by the Consumer The decision-framing process begins with the consumer's knowledge of the purchase situation.[152] Consumers then activate that portion of memory related to their goals and the situation. For example, the goals to "get food that is on my diet" and "get food that makes me feel good" would probably activate different brands and information from memory and result in different decision processes. Also, the context in which the product will be used can influence the decision process. Thus you are likely to use different consideration sets, decision criteria, and levels of decision effort when buying beer for yourself and when buying beer for a party. You might buy lower-priced beer for a party because you need a large quantity, but you might be more concerned about image as well.

Research involving mouth-related products (mouthwash, mints, gums, and so on) found that where the product would be used (at home or away from home) and who would use the product (the purchaser or someone else) determined which products were purchased.[153] Another study asked consumers to rate the importance of different attributes for four situations: (1) lunch on a weekday, (2) snack during a shopping trip, (3) evening meal when rushed for time, and (4) evening meal with the family when not rushed for time.[154] Results indicated that attribute importance depended on the situation. Speed and convenience were the most important attributes for situations 1 and 3, whereas variety of menu and popularity with children were most critical for situation 4.

Exhibit 10.10
FRAMING BY THE CONSUMER'S GOAL
Marketers can sometimes position the product in terms of the consumers' goal categories. In this ad, Microsoft is creating a different positioning for Windows XP as software for downloading educational material.

marketing IMPLICATIONS

The decision-framing process has important implications for both positioning and market segmentation. First, marketers can position the product or service in consumers' goal-related or usage categories. That way, when consumers frame the decision, they will be more likely to consider the brand and important related information. Exhibit 10.10 is a good example of this strategy. Second, marketers can identify and market to large segments of consumers who have similar goal-related or usage-context categories. Thus Procter & Gamble markets its $200 SK-II Air Touch electric makeup applicator to women who want their faces to look flawless.[155]

External Framing Decisions can also be framed by how the problem is structured in the external environment, such as vanaspati ghee in its purest form is even safer than the various kind of white oil like Corn, Groundnut, Coconut and Kardi oil. [156] Framing the time period can affect decisions as well. Consumers perceive health hazards as being more immediate and concrete if framed as occurring every day, but less immediate and more abstract if framed as occurring every year.[157] In another study, industrial buyers who used low price as an initial reference point were less willing to take risks than those with a medium- or high-price point.[158] Likewise, consumers react more positively when marketers frame the cost of a product as a series of small payments (pennies a day or a few dollars a month) instead of as a large one-time expense.[159] Moreover, because of framing, a product presented in the context of higher-priced options will be judged as less expensive than one evaluated in the context of lower-priced options.[160]

Whether a decision is framed positively (How good is this product?) or negatively (How bad is this product?) influences the evaluation differently.[161] Consumers are more likely to choose a brand with negatively framed claims about a competitor when elaboration is low, but higher elaboration may lead them to conclude that the tactics are unfair.[162] In general, under low motivation and low processing opportunity, a negatively framed message is more effective than a positively framed one.[163] Research also shows that consumers with a low need for cognition are more susceptible to the influence of a negatively framed marketing message.[164] When a decision is framed in terms of subtracting unwanted options from a fully loaded product, consumers will choose more options with a higher total option price than if the decision is framed in terms of adding wanted items to a base model.[165]

Priming certain attributes, such as reliability and creativity, can significantly alter judgments of both comparable alternatives like brands of cameras and noncomparable alternatives like computers or cameras.[166] This priming causes consumers to focus their processing on specific attributes rather than on abstract criteria. Research on charitable contributions found that providing consumers with a high anchor point by asking for $20 increased contributions relative to a low anchor point like a penny.[167] Priming hedonic or symbolic attributes—such as associations—with political concerns (e.g., reduce toxic waste) rather than with functional ones (e.g., no more hassles) can produce a higher willingness to pay for items or social programs.[168] Finally, one study found that consumers primed to respond to a question about liking a product answered more quickly than when primed to respond to a question about disliking a product.[169]

How Group Context Can Affect Decision Making

A fourth contextual influence on the decision-making process occurs when a consumer makes a decision in the presence of a group, such as deciding what to order when dining out with other people. As each member of the group makes a decision in turn, he or she attempts to balance two sets of goals: (1) goals that are attained by the individual's action alone *(individual-alone)* and (2) goals that are achieved

Exhibit 10.11
GOAL CLASSES THAT AFFECT CONSUMER DECISION MAKING

Consumers are not always able to achieve both individual-alone and individual-group goals when making decisions in the context of a group. Trying to achieve individual-group goals can result in either group-variety or group-uniformity, while trying to achieve individual-alone goals allows the consumer to satisfy his or her own taste through the decision.

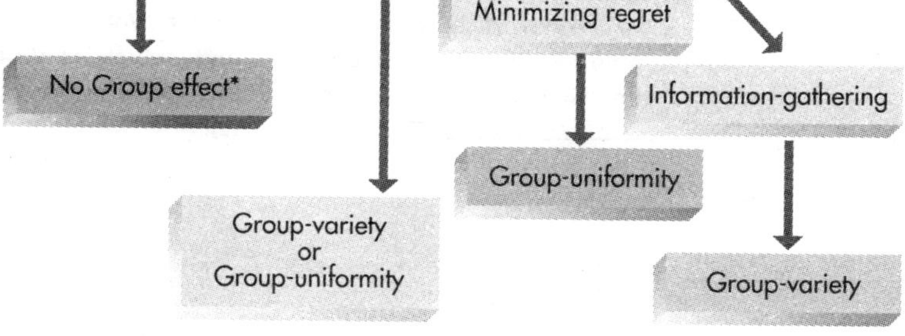

Note. — In cases where informational social influence is present during the decision process, an outcome of group uniformity or variety seeking can result.

depending on both the individual and the group *(individual-group)*.[170] Because consumers may have to choose a different alternative to achieve each set of goals, they cannot always achieve both sets of goals simultaneously in group settings.

In a group, consumers face three types of individual-group goals, as shown in Exhibit 10.11:

- *Self-presentation.* Consumers seek to convey a certain image by the decisions they make in a group context. When consumers want to use unique choices as positive self-presentation cues or to express their individuality, the result will be variety seeking at the group level. Yet, consumers are often more concerned about social norms and therefore make similar choices to blend in, resulting in uniformity at the group level.
- *Minimizing regret.* Consumers who are risk averse and want to minimize regret will tend to make choices that are similar to those made by the rest of the group, leading to uniformity at the group level. This allows group members to avoid any disappointment they might feel if someone else's choice seemed better than their own.
- *Information gathering.* Consumers can learn more about the different choices each has made through interaction with other group members. Whether members actually share choices or simply share their reactions, the result is variety in the totality of choices within the group when consumers see information-gathering as a priority. However, when group members are more concerned with self-presentation or loss aversion than with information gathering, they will make similar choices, resulting in group uniformity.

When making a decision in a group context, we try to balance these three individual-group goals with our individual-alone goals. In most group situations, the result is group-uniformity, even though individual members may ultimately feel less satisfied by the outcome.

marketing IMPLICATIONS

The findings about contextual influences on decision making have important implications because marketers can use communications to influence reference points and the way decisions are framed. For example, targeting recent immigrants, Western Union reframed the use of its money-transfer services to emphasize the emotional aspect of sending money to family members still at home, rather than the speed or cost.[171] Sales promotions generally are more successful when framed as gains rather than as a reduced loss—consumers prefer to get something for free rather than getting a discount. Consumer decisions can be framed by the location of products in the store, which influences comparisons. Finally, marketers can use communications to make individual-group goals a higher priority in group situations, leading to more uniformity of choice in favor of the advertised brand. Beer marketers, for instance, often show group members enjoying only the advertised brand, which reinforces strong social norms and encourages consumers to order that brand when they drink in a social setting.

Summary

Judgments involve forming evaluations or estimates regarding the likelihood of events, whereas decisions entail a choice between options or courses of action. Two major types of judgments are estimations of likelihood and judgments of goodness or badness, both of which can be made by recalling past judgments from memory, using either imagery or an anchoring and adjustment process. Consumers may have difficulty making conjunctive probability assessments, which involves determining how two attributes vary together.

Among the decision-making models that consumers may use alone or in combination are (1) compensatory brand-processing models, including the multiattribute (expectancy-value) model; (2) compensatory attribute-processing models, including the additive difference model; (3) noncompensatory brand-processing models, including the conjunctive and disjunctive models; and (4) noncompensatory attribute-processing models, including the lexicographic and elimination-by-aspects models. Decisions can also be based on emotions or feelings, using a type of holistic processing in which emotions or images play a key role. Often consumers cannot directly compare alternatives but must make a decision, so they use an alternative-based strategy to make overall evaluations for each option or an attribute-based strategy to make comparisons using abstract representations of attributes.

Finally, contextual or situational factors can exert a strong influence on the decision process. These contextual factors can be grouped according to (1) consumer characteristics, such as their motivation, ability, and opportunity to process; (2) task characteristics, such as the nature of the consideration set and the information available; (3) decision framing, either by the environment or by the consumer; and (4) the presence of a group, which causes consumers to try to balance individual-alone goals with individual-group goals.

Questions for Review and Discussion

1. How does consumer judgment differ from consumer decision making?
2. What is the anchoring and adjustment process, and how does it affect consumer judgment?
3. How do consumers use compensatory and noncompensatory decision-making models?
4. Why do marketers need to know that attribute processing is easier for consumers than brand processing?
5. In what ways do emotions and feelings influence consumer decision making?
6. What four contextual elements affect consumer decision making?

Exercises

1. On the basis of the mini case discussion on the housing boom in India, collect information on the following:
   a. How have approaches in buying car and houses have changed in the last 25 years
   b. What are the parameters for judgments for both product categories?
   c. What are the sources of finance options (personal) for finance in both cases?
   d. What are the attributes evaluated for purchase in both the cases?
2. Select a product or service category for which you expect the consumers' motivation, ability, and opportunity to process information to be high. Ask five consumers to describe in detail how they would go about making a decision for this product or service category. First ask them which brands they would consider (the consider-

ation set), and then ask them to describe the specific steps they would go through in making a decision. Which brand would they choose? After collecting this information, answer the following questions:

a. How do the descriptions provided by the consumers compare with the decision models discussed in this chapter?

b. How do these processes vary for different consumers?

c. Why did one brand tend to be chosen over another?

d. If these processes were representative of many consumers, how might this information be used to develop a marketing strategy?

3. Pick a product or service category that is likely to generate high-elaboration decision making. Identify the most salient attributes for the decision, and collect information about these attributes. Ask ten consumers to rate each attribute in terms of the b_i and I_i ratings from the compensatory model (see the box on page 228) for three major brands in this category. Based on this information, answer the following:

a. What are the strengths and weaknesses of each brand?

b. How would each model described in this chapter provide insights into consumers' decision processes in this situation?

c. How would the information you have collected aid in designing marketing strategy?

More Exercises from the Adaptor

1. On the basis of the mini case discussion on the housing boom in India, collect information on the following:

a. How have approaches in buying cars and houses changed in the last 25 years?

b. What are the parameters of judgments for buying these product categories?

c. What are the sources of finance options (personal) for finance in both cases?

d. What attributes are evaluated for purchase in both the cases?

References

1 Source: Report on Trend and Progress of Housing in India 2005, National Housing Bank

2 Source: http://auto.indiamart.com/cars/maruti-zen-classic/

3 Source: http://www.blonnet.com/catalyst/2005/05/26/stories/2005052600170200.htm

chapter **11**

Judgment and Decision Making Based on Low Consumer Effort

LEARNING OBJECTIVES

After studying this chapter, you will be able to:

- Identify the types of heuristics that consumers can use to make simple judgments under low effort, and why marketers need to understand these heuristics.
- Show how the hierarchy of effects, decision heuristics, and operant conditioning explain consumers' low-effort decision making.
- Discuss the thought-based strategies of performance tactics, habit, brand loyalty, price-related tactics, and normative influences that consumers use to simplify low-effort decision making.
- Describe the feeling-based strategies of affective tactics, variety seeking, and impulse purchasing that consumers use to simplify low-effort decision making.

INTRODUCTION

Food retail in India gets organized

With a population of billion plus the majority of which lives in the rural heartlands of the country, there are more mouths to feed than there are hands to deliver. The markets are highly skewed with disparity across regions. Add to that the geographical and climatic uncertainties affecting the agricultural business. However, a quiet revolution which is affecting the retail business of food and agriculture will have a key role to play. The corporate sector is now increasingly realizing the importance of India's vast agricultural dominance and seeking every possible option. Contract farming is one of the most successful forays from the corporate sector, where the farmers have a dedicated customer base, without the middleman affecting the business. The farm fresh products are processed at the farm level and through the cold chain, forwarded to open markets or retailed through exclusive retail outlets.

[1]Reliance Fresh's foray into the food retail market is a pioneering attempt. Beginning with vegetables and fruits, these `Fresh' outlets, are starters, in the Rs 25,000-crore agri and retail business venture of the company, which will have its presence across 784 cities and 6,000 towns in the country. Bharti has already been in strategic tie-up with the UK based Rothschild group initially targeting the export markets. [2]The company recently announced that it was investing with Rothschild Group, a European private equity group, in a venture called Field Fresh, which will export onions, chilies, okra and other vegetables to Western retailers, including Tesco of Britain.

Exhibit 11.1
FOOD RETAIL IN INDIA
The farm fresh products are processed at the farm level and then forwarded to open markets or retailed through exclusive retail outlets

From the consumer perspective,the market is growing too and there is an increasing acceptance of the organized retail formats in the food category. Earlier, our perception of modern retail formats as restricted to only clothes, fashion accessories, music, movies and durable products. Food retail was perceived as expensive and the apprehension of the food being not "Fresh" was the key deterrent for most consumers. However, changing lifestyles, increasing percentage of working women, lack of disposable time and inversely proportional disposable income has meant that more and more consumers are willing to explore the option of food retail also. These on-stop shops offer range and quality on the same platter and as far as freshness is concerned, stores ensure that the supply chain ensures fresh supplies at all peak time of purchases.

Outlets like Reliance Fresh, Subhiksha and even Mother Dairy's Safal (an old hat in the industry) have been making continual efforts to smoothen and make the supply chain more efficient, benefits of which can be passed on to the consumers, the prime among them being low price and freshness. Alternatively, the farmers in the supply chain also gain out of it, with assured customers and better prices. The "food chain" benefits both ends of the continuum.

When consumers have low motivation, ability, and opportunity (MAO) to process information (as when purchasing everyday products), their judgment and decision processes are different and involve less effort than when they have high MAO (as when buying luxury goods). This chapter examines the nature of low-effort judgment and decision making—the next stage in the overall model, as shown in Exhibit 11.2. The focus here is on the cognitive and affective shortcuts or heuristics that consumers use to make judgments and decisions and the marketing implications of this behavior.

Low-Effort Judgment Processes

Chapter 10 showed that when effort is high, consumers' judgments—such as estimations of likelihood and goodness/badness—can be cognitively complex. In contrast, when MAO is low, individuals are motivated to simplify the cognitive process by using heuristics to reduce the effort involved in making judgments.[3] Two major types of heuristics are representativeness and availability.

Shortcuts in Making Judgments: The Representativeness Heuristic

One way that consumers can make simple estimations or judgments is to make comparisons to the category prototype or exemplar. This categorization process is called the ***representativeness heuristic.***[4] For example, if you want to estimate the likelihood that a new toothpaste is of high quality, you might compare it with your prototype for toothpaste, such as Colgate. If you see the new brand as similar to the prototype, you will assume that it is also of high quality. This is why many store brands have packaging that is similar to that of the leading brands in various product categories, hoping that outward similarity will suggest to the consumer that the products possess the same good qualities.

Like any shortcut, the representativeness heuristic can also lead to biased judgments. In the opening example, some consumers automatically assumed that McDonald's offered no healthy foods; others assumed that McDonald's could not

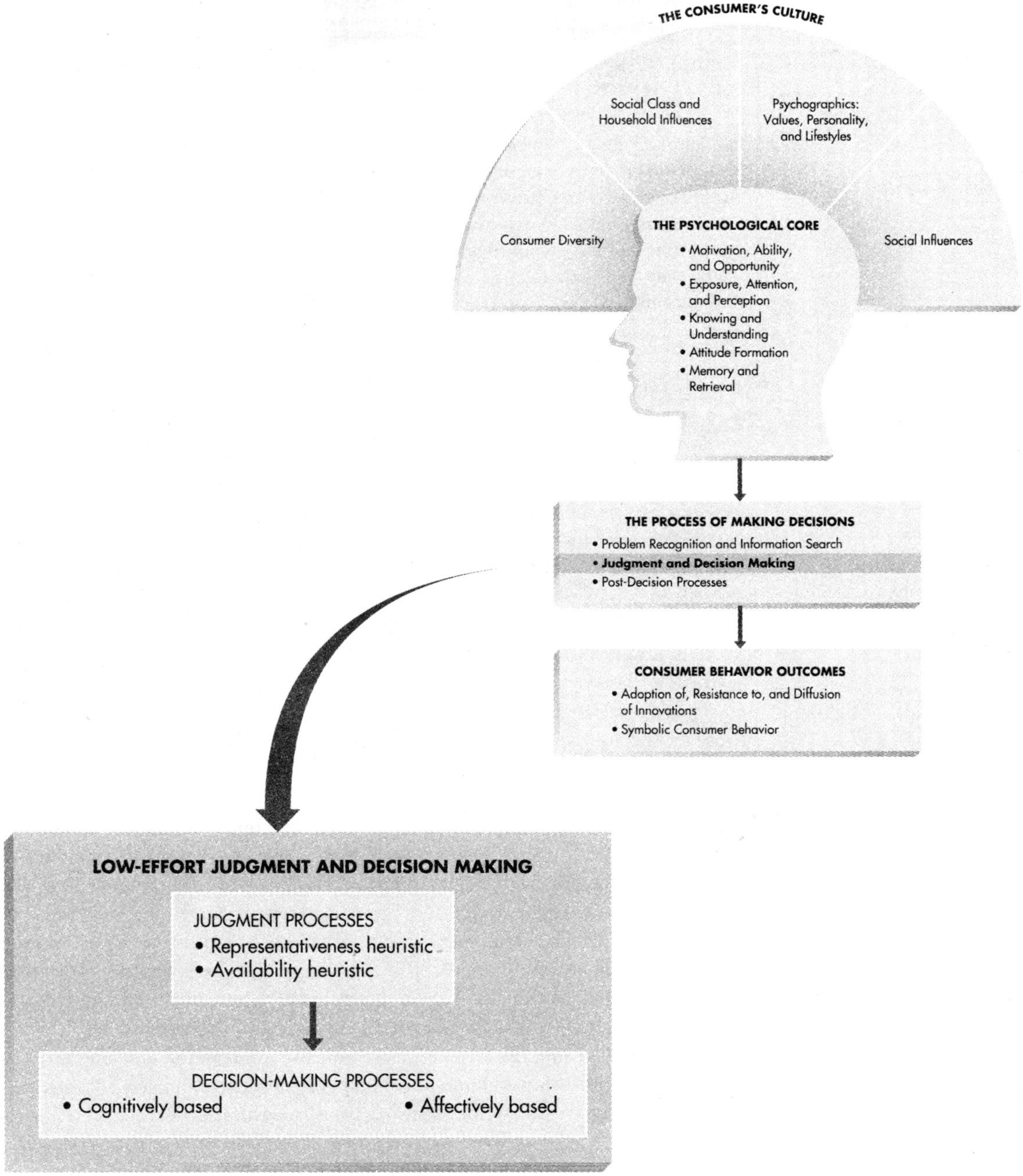

Exhibit 11.2

CHAPTER OVERVIEW: JUDGMENT AND DECISION MAKING: LOW CONSUMER EFFORT

In low-effort processing situations, consumers tend to use heuristics or ways of simplifying the judgment or decision. Both cognitively based heuristics (performance-based tactics, habit, price-related tactics, brand loyalty, and normative influences) and affectively based heuristics (affect-related tactics, variety seeking, and impulse) are used to make decisions.

make a good salad. To overcome these biased judgments, McDonald's added menu items made from high-quality fruit and vegetable ingredients.

marketing IMPLICATIONS The representativeness heuristic is an important marketing factor because it suggests that companies position products or services close to a prototype that has positive associations in consumers' minds. However, when the shortcut leads to biased judgment, marketers must take steps to overcome it. In the 1960s, radios and electronics made in Japan were considered the prototype for poor-quality merchandise. Japanese firms spent many years producing and heavily marketing high-quality products to overcome this bias. Now Korean electronics firms and car makers are working to overcome the same bias.[6] For example, Samsung Electronics is using marketing to showcase its brand as high quality, high-tech, and high style.[7]

Shortcuts in Making Judgments: The Availability Heuristic

Judgments can also be influenced by the ease with which instances of an event can be brought to mind, a shortcut called the ***availability heuristic.***[8] Consumers are more likely to recall more accessible or more vivid events, which influences their judgments—even though they may be unaware of this effect.[9] To illustrate, suppose that years ago you purchased a CD player that needed constant repair. Today you may still recall your anger and disappointment when you see this brand. Your experiences greatly color your estimations of quality for this brand, even though the brand might actually have few breakdowns today.

Word-of-mouth communication is another example of accessible information that leads to use of the availability heuristic. If a friend tells you about all the problems she had with her CD player, this information is likely to affect your estimates of quality, even though her experience might have been an isolated event.

These judgments are biased because we tend to ignore ***base-rate information***—how often the event really occurs—in favor of information that is more vivid or accessible. One study demonstrated this effect in the context of estimating the probability of refrigerators breaking down.[10] One group was given a set of case histories told by consumers, and another was given actual statistics about the incidence of breakdown. People who read the case histories provided breakdown estimates that were 30 percent higher than those of the statistics group. Another study found that consumers can use both base-rate and case information, but their judgment depends on how the information is structured.[11] As case history information becomes more specific, consumers rely less on base rates. Another reason we do not use more base-rate information is that it is often not available.

A related bias is the ***law of small numbers,*** whereby people expect information obtained from a small sample to be typical of the larger population.[12] If friends say that a new CD by a particular group is really good or that the food at a particular restaurant is terrible, we believe that information, even if most people do not feel that way. In fact, reliance on small numbers is another reason that word-of-mouth communication can be so powerful. We tend to have confidence that the opinions of friends or relatives are more reflective of the majority than they may actually be.

marketing IMPLICATIONS

Marketers can attempt to either capitalize on the availability bias or overcome it. To capitalize, they can provide consumers with positive and vivid product-related experiences through the use of marketing communications, or they can ask consumers to imagine such situations. Both strategies will increase consumers' estimates that these events will occur. Or marketers can attempt to stimulate positive word-of-mouth communication. For example, Kwality Wall's brand Cornetto has been trying to extend the 2006 summer campaign of "pleasure up" to the young teenager, through the launch of its webisode, spillurdil.com. The site features a complete guide to all things that fascinate the teen population of 10-18 years, starting with the cursor arrow, which immediately changes into a cupid's arrow to the various sub-links on romantic sms'es, confessions, and crushes. The format tries to establish a one to one relationship with the logger and thus reinforce the essence of the brand, Cornetto.

Marketers can attempt to overcome the availability bias by providing consumers with base-rate information about the general population. If this information is vivid and specific, it can help consumers make a less biased judgment. The classic Lalitaji communication for Surf (a Unilever brand) showed a discerning housewife in the form of Lalitaji, who exemplified the typical no-nonsense Indian housewife and her further claim that, $^{1}/_{2}$ kg Surf is equivalent to 1 kg ordinary washing powder and therefore she goes on to say, "Surf ke Khariddari mein hi samajdari hai". The Internet is an excellent vehicle for providing base-rate information. To illustrate, consumers interested in buying books or music at Amazon.com can see a summary rating and read reviews submitted by other consumers. The availability bias is also a common problem in the context of sweepstakes and lotteries. Consumers often overestimate the likelihood of winning, even though their chances are exceedingly small, because they are exposed to highly vivid and available images of winners in the media. Regulators have attempted to overcome this bias by requiring marketers to clearly post the odds of winning.

The availability bias is quite common in marketing research that uses focus groups to evaluate marketing programs. As discussed in Chapter 2, focus groups consist of as many as 12 consumers who give their opinions on topics ranging from product design to advertising messages. Even though these groups contain a very small number of consumers, marketing managers sometimes mistakenly view the group's responses as mirroring those of the general consumer population.[15] Companies can overcome this problem by checking the findings with a quantitative study using a larger, more representative consumer sample.

Low-Effort Decision-Making Processes

Most low-effort judgment and decision situations are not very important in consumers' lives. Clearly, career and family decisions are far more important than deciding which toothpaste or peanut butter to buy. Thus the consumer usually does not want to devote a lot of time and effort to these mundane decisions.[16] In a typical shopping trip, a consumer might purchase 30 to 40 items. Spending even five minutes on each decision would stretch the shopping trip to several hours. Researchers are therefore interested in examining just how consumers make decisions in these low-elaboration situations.

How Does Low-Effort Decision Making Differ from High-Effort Decision Making?

In the discussion of high-effort decision making in Chapter 10, you saw that consumers have certain beliefs about each alternative that are combined to form an attitude that leads to a behavior or a choice. In other words, the consumer engages in *thinking*, which leads to *feelings*, which results in *behaving*. This progression, known as the ***hierarchy of effects***, is outlined in Exhibit 11.3.

Herbert Krugman was among the first researchers to recognize that this traditional hierarchy of effects might not describe all consumer decision-making situations.[17] In studying how television advertising affects consumers, Krugman noticed that even though viewers could recall ads, the ads appeared to have little impact on viewers' attitudes toward the brand—a finding that is inconsistent with the belief-attitude link. Krugman hypothesized that advertising influences consumers through a process called ***passive*** (or ***incidental***) ***learning***. He saw television as a primarily low-involvement medium to which viewers do not pay close attention. Viewers also do not link the advertised product or ad to their previous experiences or beliefs. However, through the constant repetition of ad messages, viewers can pick up and retain messages passively. They can therefore possess low-level beliefs about the product, a kind of basic familiarity, but not form a strong attitude. As a result, consumers can make purchase decisions without a strong attitude. If a consumer does develop a strong attitude, this tends to occur *after* purchase when the product is being used.

Thus if a consumer sees an ad for Crocin, he would probably not pay very close attention to it. Yet, if he sees the ad repeatedly, he would acquire a basic awareness of the brand and the key claims that it is stronger than aspirin and relieves headache pain faster. If he goes to the store to purchase Crocin, this low level knowledge may be enough to influence is choice. But only after trying the product will he decide whether he likes or dislikes this brand.

Consistent with Krugman's theory, researchers have proposed an alternative hierarchy of effects for low-effort situations that follows a *thinking-behaving-feeling* sequence.[18] The consumer enters the decision process with a set of low-level beliefs based on brand familiarity and knowledge obtained from repeated exposures to advertising, in-store exposure, or prior usage. These beliefs serve as the foundation for the decision or behavior, in the absence of any attitude. After making the decision and while using the product, the consumer evaluates the brand and may or may not form an attitude, depending on how strongly the brand is liked or satisfies needs. Exhibit 11.3 compares this model with the traditional hierarchy of effects.

Exhibit 11.3
HIERARCHY OF EFFECTS
When effort is high, consumers actively evaluate brands before making a decision and purchasing. In low-effort situations, consumers think very little before deciding, and beliefs (often based on basic familiarity) lead directly to choice. Consumers make evaluations after the choice, once they have used the product.

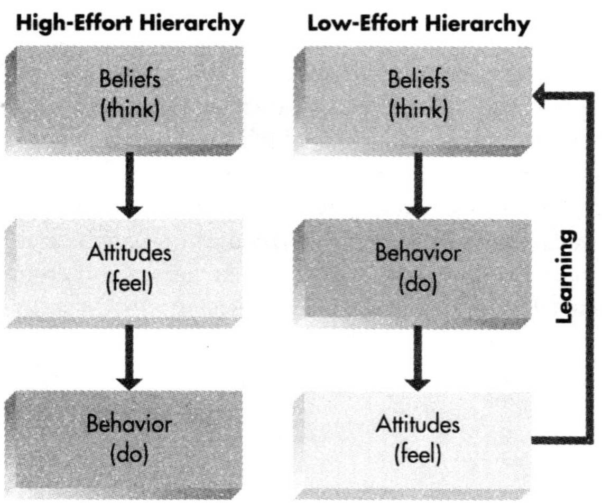

Some researchers have challenged the belief-behavior link in the low-involvement hierarchy, saying that consumers sometimes engage in "pure affective choice," making a decision based solely on how they feel rather than on what they think.[19] For example, you might select a flavor of gum or a new DVD based on positive feelings rather than on any beliefs or knowledge. Here, the sequence would be feeling, behaving, and then thinking. This type of decision making, which clearly does occur, suggests that consumers can process in both a cognitive and affective manner—a factor in many low-elaboration situations.

Using Simplifying Strategies When Consumer Effort Is Low

Low-effort purchases represent the most frequent type of decisions that consumers make in everyday life. One study of in-store examination of laundry detergent purchases found that the median amount of time taken to make a choice was only 8.5 seconds.[20] Another study of coffee and tissues found very low levels of decision activity, particularly among consumers who purchased the product frequently and possessed a strong brand preference.[21] Findings were similar for analgesics.[22] Some research has examined consumer decision processes across a number of product categories and has even questioned whether there is any decision process at all.[23]

A decision process probably does occur in low-effort situations, but it is simpler, involves less effort, and is qualitatively different from the processes that occur when MAO is high. Two other factors influence the low-MAO decision process. First, the goal is not necessarily to find the best possible brand, called *optimizing*, as is the case with high-elaboration decisions. To optimize here would require more effort than consumers are typically willing to expend. Instead, consumers are more willing to ***satisfice***—that is, to find a brand that simply satisfies their needs. It may not be the best, but it is "good enough." The effort required to find the best may simply not be worth it.[24]

Second, most low-elaboration decisions are made frequently and repeatedly. In these decisions, consumers may rely on previous information and judgments of satisfaction or dissatisfaction from past consumption. Think of all the times you have purchased toothpaste, breakfast cereal, and shampoo. You have acquired information by using these products and from seeing ads, talking to friends, and so forth. Thus you do not need to search for information every time you are in the store. You can simply remember previous decisions and use that information to make your next choice.

In these common, repeat-purchase situations, consumers can develop decision heuristics called ***choice tactics*** for quick, effortless decision making.[25] Rather than comparing various brands in detail, consumers apply these rules to simplify the decision process. The study of laundry detergents mentioned earlier supports this view.[26] When consumers were asked how they made their choice, several major categories of tactics emerged, including *price tactics* (it's the cheapest or it's on sale), *affect tactics* (I like it), *performance tactics* (it cleans clothes better), and *normative tactics* (my mother bought it). Other studies have identified *habit tactics* (I buy the same brand I bought last time), *brand-loyalty tactics* (I buy the same brand for which I have a strong preference), and *variety seeking tactics* (I need to try something different). Similar results were produced in a study of shampoo and laundry detergent in Singapore.[27] Related patterns of choice-tactic usage were found in a comparison of consumers in Germany, Thailand, and the United States.[28]

Consumers can develop a choice tactic for each repeat-purchase, low-elaboration decision in the product or service category. If the consumer's decision is observed only once, it will appear very limited. Because all prior purchases serve as input to the current decision, it is important to look at a whole series of choices and consumption situations to fully understand consumer decision making. Thus low-effort decision making is very dynamic in nature.

Learning Choice Tactics

The key to understanding low-elaboration decision making is knowing the manner in which consumers learn to use their choice tactics. Certain concepts from the behaviorist tradition in psychology are relevant to understanding the way consumers learn. ***Operant conditioning*** views behavior as a function of previous actions and of the reinforcements or punishments obtained from these actions.[29] For example, while you were growing up, your parents may have given you a reward for making good grades or an allowance for mowing the lawn. You learned that these are good behaviors, and you were more likely to do these things again in the future because you were compensated for them.

Reinforcement

Reinforcement usually comes from a feeling of satisfaction that occurs when we as consumers perceive that our needs have been adequately met. This reinforcement increases the probability that we will purchase the same brand again. For example, if you buy Liquid Tide and are impressed by its ability to clean clothes, your purchase will be reinforced and you will be more likely to buy this brand again. One study found that past experience with a brand was by far the most critical factor in brand choice—over quality, price, and familiarity.[30] Other research has shown that information consumers receive from product trials tends to be more powerful and influential than that received from advertising.[31] The thoughts and emotions experienced during a trial can have a particularly powerful influence on evaluations.[32]

Note that consumers often perceive few differences among brands of many products and services.[33] They are unlikely to develop a positive brand attitude when no brand is seen as clearly better than another. However, as long as the consumer is not dissatisfied, the choice tactic he or she used will be reinforced. Suppose you buy the cheapest brand of paper towels. If this brand at least minimally satisfies your needs, you are likely to buy the cheapest brand again—and it may be a different brand next time. Thus reinforcement can occur for either the brand or the choice tactic.

Punishment

Alternatively, consumers can have a bad experience with a product or service, form a negative evaluation of it, and never purchase it again. In operant conditioning terms, this experience is called *punishment*. If you did something bad when you were growing up, your parents may have punished you to make sure you would not behave that way again. In a consumer context, punishment occurs when a brand does not meet our needs and we are dissatisfied, so we learn not to buy that brand again. Punishment may also lead consumers to reevaluate the choice tactic and use a different tactic for the next purchase. If you buy the cheapest brand of trash bags and the bags burst when you take out the trash, you could either employ a new tactic (buying the most expensive or the most familiar brand) or upgrade your tactic (buying the cheapest *national* brand).

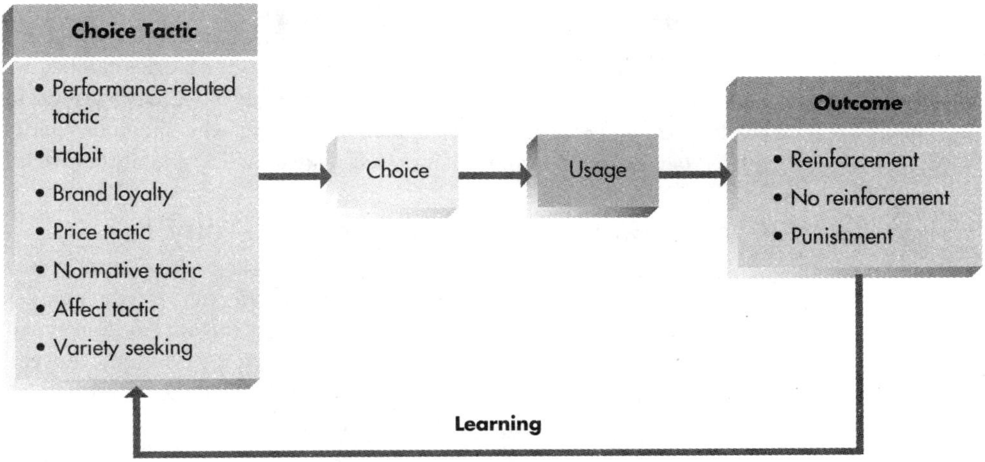

Exhibit 11.4

THE LEARNING PROCESS *This diagram shows how the outcome of a decision can help consumers learn which choice tactic to apply in a given situation. After consumers apply one of the seven basic types of tactics to make a choice, they take the brand home and use it. During consumption, they can evaluate the brand, which results in one of three basic outcomes: reinforcement (satisfaction leading to positive attitude and repurchase), no reinforcement (leading to tactic reinforcement, but no attitude toward the brand), or punishment (leading to a negative attitude, no repurchase, and tactic reevaluation).*

Repeat Purchase

Consumers learn when the same act is repeatedly reinforced or punished over time, as summarized in Exhibit 11.4. This process occurs whenever we buy a common, repeat-purchase product. Thus we learn and gradually acquire a set of choice tactics that will result in a satisfactory choice in each decision situation. Decision-making models have traditionally ignored the key role of consumption in the decision process, focusing more attention on the processing that occurs immediately prior to the decision. But clearly what takes place while the product is being consumed has important implications for future acquisition, usage, and disposition decisions. In other words, whether the consumer forms a positive or negative evaluation of the brand or tactic can be an important input into future decisions.

Choice Tactics Depend on the Product

The choice tactics we use often depend on the product category we are considering.[34] For example, we might be brand loyal to Heinz ketchup but always buy the cheapest trash bags. The tactic we learn for a product category depends on which brands are available and our experiences with them. The amount of advertising, price variations, and the number and similarity of brands also influence the type of tactic we employ.[35] Interestingly, the study from Singapore mentioned earlier found a greater similarity in the tactics consumers use for the same product in different cultures (the United States and Singapore) than for products in the same culture.[36] In general, our experiences help us learn what works for each product, and we use these tactics to minimize our decision-making effort for future purchases.

Low-Effort Thought-Based Decision Making

Each tactic consumers learn for making low-elaboration decisions can have important implications for marketers. As in high-elaboration decisions, these strategies can be divided into two broad categories: thought-based and feeling-based decision making. This section examines cognitive-based decision making, which includes performance-related tactics, habit, brand loyalty, price-related tactics, and normative influences.

Performance as a Simplifying Strategy

When the outcome of the consumption process is positive reinforcement, consumers are likely to use ***performance-related tactics*** to make their choices. These tactics can represent an overall evaluation (works the best) or focus on a specific attribute or benefit (gets clothes cleaner, tastes better, or has quicker service). Satisfaction is the key: satisfied consumers are likely to develop a positive evaluation of the brand or service and repurchase it based on its features.

Exhibit 11.5
EMPHASIZING PRODUCT QUALITY

Sometimes ads make a simple statement about product quality like this one for New Balance which makes the claim: "N is for mileage, not image."

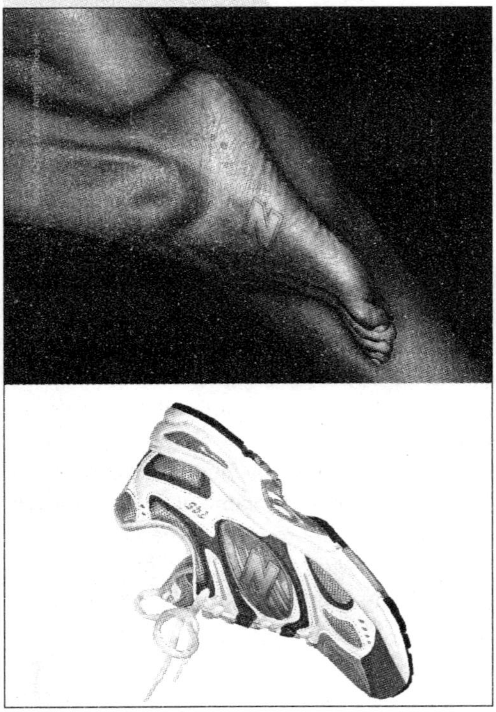

marketing IMPLICATIONS

A principal objective of marketing strategy should be to increase the likelihood of satisfaction through product or service quality. Only then can a brand consistently achieve repeat purchases and loyal users. Campbell's soup, for example, has provided quality products for years, as evidenced by its 75 percent market share.[37] Holiday Inn operators must comply with a variety of standards for hotel room furnishings, amenities, even breakfast offerings so customers will have a consistent, high-quality experience whether they stay in a Holiday Inn in Paris, Rotterdam, or Boston.[38] Another example is the ad in Exhibit 11.5.

Advertising can play a central role in influencing performance evaluations by increasing the consumer's expectation of positive reinforcement and satisfaction and lessening the negative effects of an unfavorable consumption experience.[39] Because we see what we want to see and form our expectations accordingly, marketers should select product features or benefits that are important to consumers, help to differentiate the brand from competitors, and convince consumers they will be satisfied if they buy the product. To illustrate, to compete with Gillette's three-blade Mach3 razor, Schick emphasizes the four blades in its Quattro razor as a point of differentiation, saying the result is "the closest shave ever."[40]

Sales promotions such as free samples, price deals, coupons, or premiums (gifts or free merchandise) are often used as an incentive to get the consumer to try the product or service. Marketers hope that if consumers find the product satisfactory, they will continue to buy it when the incentives are withdrawn. These strategies work only if product performance satisfies and reinforces the consumer. They will not overcome dissatisfaction resulting from poor quality or other factors. Snapple failed in Japan, despite heavy promotion, because its beverages had features that Japanese consumers loathe: a cloudy appearance and stuff floating in the bottle.[41] Another caution is that consumers may perceive a price promotion as a signal of lower quality when they are not category experts, when the promotion is not typical of the industry, and when the brand's past behavior is inconsistent.[42]

Habit as a Simplifying Strategy

Humans are creatures of ***habit.*** Once we find a convenient way of doing things, we tend to repeat it without really thinking: following the same routine every morning, driving the same route to work or school, shopping at the same stores. We do these things because they make life simpler and more manageable.

Sometimes consumers' acquisition, usage, and disposition decisions are based on habit too. Habit is one of the simplest, most effortless types of consumer decision making, characterized by: (1) little or no information seeking and (2) little or no evaluation of alternatives. However, habit does not require a strong preference for an offering; rather, it simply involves repetitive behavior and regular purchase.[43] Decision making based on habit also reduces risk.[44] Consumers know the brand will satisfy their needs because they have bought it a number of times in the past. Research supports the effect of habit on low-priced, frequently purchased products. Yet, the longer consumers wait to make their next purchase in a product category, the less likely they are to buy the brand they habitually purchase.[45]

marketing
IMPLICATIONS

Habit-based decision making has several important implications for marketers who want to develop repeat-purchase behavior and to sell their offerings to habitual purchasers of both that brand and competing products.

Developing repeat-purchase behavior

Getting consumers to acquire or use an offering repeatedly is an important marketing objective because repeat purchases lead to profitability. Marketers can use an operant conditioning technique called ***shaping*** that leads consumers through a series of steps to a desired response: purchase.[46] Companies often use sales promotion to shape repeat purchasing. First, they might offer a free sample to generate brand trial, along with a high-value coupon to induce trial (see Exhibit 11.6 for product samples from Thailand). To illustrate, Procter & Gamble offers new parents free samples of Pampers disposable diapers, along with coupons to encourage trial purchase. The next step for marketers might be to provide a series of lower-value coupons to promote subsequent repurchase. Companies hope that when they end the incentives, consumers will continue to buy by habit. Procter and Gamble's Pampers in the Indian market has been there for over a decade now, with focus largely on the product benefi ts.[3] In Rs.70 crore diaper market, most players have focused on the product and its absorption

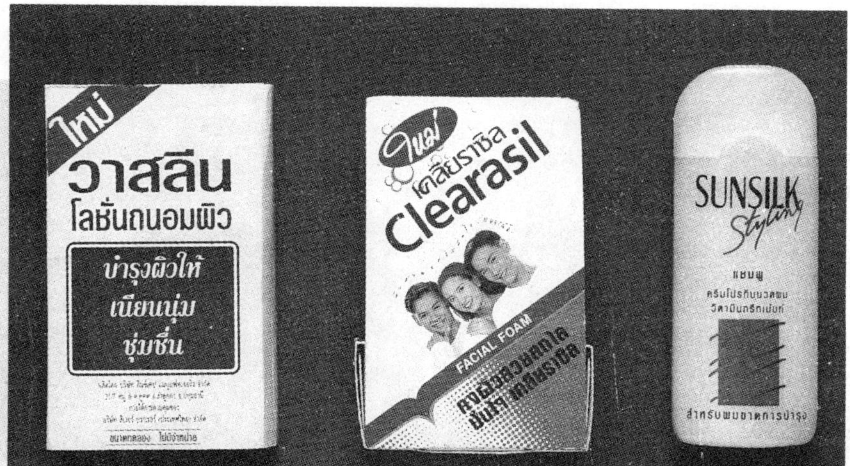

Exhibit 11.6
FREE SAMPLES
Here are three samples of skin products from Thailand, where sampling is a frequently used marketing tool. Many samples are given out in shopping centers. What types of product samples do you receive?

issue. However, Pampers is now addressing the issue of a sound sleep and how important it is for babies. It tries to educate parents about a cranky and irritant baby. The reason why the baby behaves that way could be absence of a sound sleep, due to frequent bed-wetting.

Marketing to habitual purchasers of other brands

A variety of marketing opportunities are available for marketers targeting habitual purchasers of a competing brand. The major goal is to break consumers' habits and induce them to switch to another brand. Because the habitual consumer does not have a strong brand preference, this goal is easier to achieve than it is for brand-loyal consumers. For example, the Kurkure launch from Pepsi foods was targeted to the snacking segment, which wanted a low-oil and low-fat option. The snack is baked unlike namkeen or potato chips, which is fried, thus making it safer for even kids and adults alike. The product was typically positioned as a family snack also, unlike branded potato chips, which targets the youth or children.

Sales promotion techniques to induce brand switching include pricing deals, coupons, free samples, and premiums intended to capture consumers' attention and get them to try the new brand. Procter & Gamble has used coupons generated at the supermarket checkout to target users of a competing dishwashing product. Several booksellers and publishers try and sell their publication by hard selling them, at strategic locations like, outside an examination centre or in front of an educational institution. The idea being to closely target the actual user of the product. Competing with Coca-Cola, PepsiCo has used free music downloads during Super Bowl season and sweepstakes promotions during the summer to attract consumers and encourage repeat purchasing. "It's about growing our business and grabbing our share of summer," says its chief marketing officer.[50]

Marketers can also break habits by introducing *a new and unique benefit* that satisfies consumers' needs better than existing brands. This differential advantage then needs to be heavily advertised to get the word out to consumers. [4]Tata Gold from Tata Tea was a unique product which combined the flavor of leaf tea and the colour of the CTC tea. The brand's novel initiative came from the learning that tea connoisseurs preferred to blend their tea at home, to get the benefit of both color and flavor in their tea, which Tata Gold was able to encash on. Priced at a premium in the branded tea market, the brand's unique product mix was able to create a niche for itself in the highly competitive packaged tea market. Another example of offering unique product benefits is, the launch of Scotch Brite sponge and particularly the scouring pads in India. Most Indian households have oil based cuisines which invariably make the cooking utensils stained with obstinate oil marks. Cleaning them through home grown tools like coconut scrubs, pumice stones or at times the metallic medicine stubs. Scotch Brite scouring pads offered the twin benefit of removing

Exhibit 11.7
STORE AND WINDOW DISPLAY

With organized retailing permeating the food and non-food outlets, the focus is now on the display of products so that consumers have an ease of search and attention.

obstinate oil stains from the utensils and also keeping them scratch proof, which was not possible before with the harsh scrubbing tools.

Finally, *distribution policies* are very important for habitual purchasing. In general, the greater the amount of shelf space a brand has in the store, the more likely the brand is to get consumers' attention. A product's location may be enough to capture the habitual consumer's attention and plant the idea to buy something else. An end-of-aisle display may increase a brand's sales by 100 to 400 percent.[53] In one study, eye-catching displays increased sales of frozen dinners by 245 percent, laundry detergent by 207 percent, and salty snacks by 172 percent.[54] In another study, sales of cough and cold syrups rose by 35 percent with in-store promotions linked to a point-of-purchase brand display.[55] Thus marketers often try to develop interesting displays, such as the award-winning units shown in Exhibit 11.7.

Marketing to habitual purchasers of one's own brand

Marketers do not want their brand's repeat-purchase customers to break the buying habit. Because habitual consumers are susceptible to competitors' deals, marketers need to offer *comparable deals* to build resistance to switching. This is why a fare cut by any one airline is usually matched immediately by all major competitors.

Distribution and proper inventory control are also important to prevent habitual consumers from switching to another brand. Without a strong preference, consumers are more likely to break the habit and buy another brand if their usual brand is out of stock, rather than to go to another store. In one study, 63 percent of consumers said they would be willing to buy another brand of groceries and canned foods if their preferred brand were not available.[56] Widespread distribution can ensure that the consumer is not forced to buy something else. For Coke, other soft drinks, and teas to be successful in Japan, they must be widely available in that country's vast network of vending machines.[57] Finally, *advertising* can induce resistance to switching. By occasionally reminding the consumer of a reason for buying the brand and keeping the brand name "top of mind," marketers may be able to keep consumers from switching.

Brand Loyalty as a Simplifying Strategy

Brand loyalty occurs when consumers make a conscious evaluation that a brand or service satisfies their needs to a greater extent than others do and decide to buy the same brand repeatedly for that reason.[58] Essentially, brand loyalty results from *very* positive reinforcement of a performance-related choice tactic. Note that the level of commitment to the brand distinguishes brand loyalty from habit. The stronger this evaluation becomes over time, the higher the degree of brand loyalty. If you buy Heinz ketchup and decide that it is thicker and tastes better than other brands, you will purchase it again. If this evaluation is reinforced repeatedly, you will develop strong brand loyalty. Consumers can also be ***multibrand loyal,***[59] or committed to two or more brands they purchase repeatedly. For example, if you prefer and purchase only Coke and Sprite, you exhibit multibrand loyalty for soft drinks.

Brand loyalty results in low-effort decision making because the consumer does not need to process information when making a decision and simply buys the same brand each time. However, because of their strong commitment to the brand or service, brand-loyal consumers have a relatively high level of involvement with the *brand* whether their involvement with the product or service category is high or low. Thus even though ketchup might typically be thought of as a low-involvement product, the brand-loyal consumer can exhibit a high level of involvement toward the brand Heinz.

marketing IMPLICATIONS

Brand-loyal consumers form a solid base on which companies can build brand profitability. By identifying the characteristics of these consumers, marketers might discover ways to strengthen brand loyalty. Unfortunately, this task is difficult because marketers cannot obtain a general profile of the brand-loyal consumer that applies to all product categories.[60] In fact, the extent to which a consumer is brand loyal depends on the product category; the consumer who is loyal for ketchup may not be loyal for peanut butter. This means marketers must assess brand loyalty for each specific category.

Identifying brand-loyal customers

One way marketers can identify brand-loyal consumers is to focus on consumer purchase patterns. Consumers who exhibit a particular sequence of purchases (three to four consecutive purchases of the same brand) or proportion of purchases (seven or eight out of ten purchases for the same brand) are considered brand loyal.[61] The problem is that because brand loyalty involves both repeat purchases *and* a commitment to the brand, purchase-only measures do not accurately distinguish between habitual and brand-loyal consumers. To truly identify the brand-loyal consumer, marketers must assess both repeat-purchase behavior and brand preference. In one study a measure that looked only at repeat-purchase behavior identified more than 70 percent of the consumer sample as brand loyal. Adding brand preference as a qualifier reduced the percentage to less than 50 percent.[62]

Despite these problems, purchase-only measures of brand loyalty are still widely used in marketing. With the availability of scanner data and online buying information, marketers now have a wealth of information about consumer purchase patterns they can analyze to understand how coupons or pricing changes affect buying. Nevertheless, if the goal is to study brand loyalty, an approach that measures both purchase patterns and preference is preferable.

Developing brand loyalty

Because brand-loyal consumers have a strong brand commitment, they are more resistant to competitive efforts and switching than other consumers. Thus a major goal of marketing is to develop brand loyalty. Hindustan Lever has done this in India by creating products that deliver unique and valued benefits: a cleaning power that works with two buckets of water rather than four and products packaged in tiny quantities with small prices to fit local incomes.[63] However, the widespread use of pricing deals in the United States has gradually eroded consumer loyalty toward many brands, leading more consumers to buy on the basis of price. Therefore, marketers are now striving to develop consumer loyalty through nonprice promotions. (Note that in Europe, firms use fewer price promotions, and brand loyalty has remained relatively stable.[64])

Exhibit 11.8
USING QUALITY TO ENCOURAGE BRAND LOYALTY

Eastern India based Arambagh Hatcheries focuses on hygiene, cleanliness as well as technology to sell quality products both in the domestic and export markets.

Developing brand loyalty through product quality

One obvious and critical way to develop brand loyalty is to provide the consumer with a high-quality product that leads to satisfaction. With a nation boasting of more vegetarian population and religion based orthodox society it is the meat eating fraternity, under pressure. Most poultry, meat and fish markets are located at the secluded corners of the market and owing to the nature of the product and with improper hygienic conditions maintained, the place invariably dirty and reeking. Even the meat eating population sometimes abstains from such zones, marked at the market place. Of late a large number of regional and national players, noticing the potential in the market for frozen meat and poultry products are offering the consumers clean and hygienic place for buying meat. Godrej and Arambag Hatcheries, to name a few, have introduced their own retail stores and also using the services of other channels to stock and sell their products. Consumers develop a strong and positive association with the brand, owing to the environment in which they sell and also the company's credibility in the case of national brands. Recent evidence suggests that consumers will become brand loyal to high-quality brands if products are perceived to be priced fairly, which is why some companies have lowered prices on major brands.[66]

Developing brand loyalty through sales promotions

Many companies cultivate brand loyalty through sales promotions. One approach is to use a coupon premium, whereby the consumer saves special coupons, proof-of-purchase seals, or UPC codes to acquire gifts or prizes free or for a small cost. Domino's Pizza's continuous effort to push their brand works at the locality level, where the stores do house to house promotion. The effectiveness of the promotion is best measured through the coupons attached to the leaflets and the flyer given out. The customers are required to redeem such coupons by announcing their unique coupon code before they place their orders. Domino's keeps track of the coupon convertibility and discovers its effectiveness too.

Frequent-flyer programs build loyalty by encouraging consumers to fly repeatedly on a particular airline so they can earn points to exchange for free trips or other offerings. Similar programs are used by hotels, credit card companies, and other marketers. The frequent flier programmes from Indian Airlines or Jet Airways have been immensely successful with passengers availing free tickets not just for themselves, but for their families as well. They ensure to register for the mileage points while traveling and even prefer to book with a single airline for most of their journeys, ensuring that the loyalties remain with the brand, which is rewarded too. Marketers must take care in planning loyalty rewards and program requirements. The reward should have some connection with the brand if it is to increase accessibility of favorable brand associations. Yet, if the reward is too valuable, it will draw more attention than the brand itself.[68] Also, research shows that consumers perceive more value in a loyalty program when they think they have an advantage in earning points.[69] Moreover, consumers who must do more to earn loyalty points will tend to choose luxury rewards (especially when they feel guilty about luxury consumption).[70]

Marketing to brand-loyal consumers of other brands

Marketers want to induce brand-loyal users of competitive brands to switch to their brands. However, because these consumers are strongly committed to other brands, getting them to switch is extremely difficult. As a result, it is usually better to avoid these consumers and try to market toward nonloyal or habitual consumers, except when a brand has a strong point of superiority or differentiation compared with the competition. In this case the superior attribute might be enough to persuade brand-loyal consumers to switch. For example, Flickr's online photo-sharing service attracted 200,000 users in a year by offering something that Web-based competitors lacked: the ability to link comments to images so friends or family can have a running dialogue with the photographer.[71]

Exhibit 11.9
MONEY-SAVING STRATEGIES

Consumers can use different types of money-saving strategies in their shopping. Which type of shopper are you?

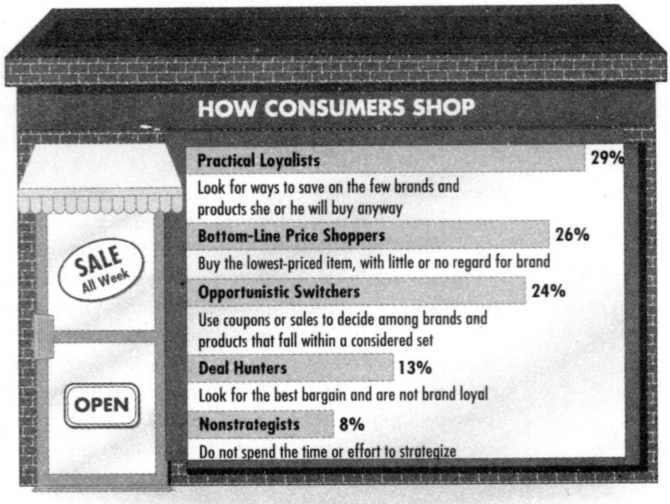

Price as a Simplifying Strategy

Consumers are most likely to use ***price-related tactics*** such as buying the cheapest, buying the brand on sale, or using a coupon when they perceive few differences among brands and when they have low involvement with the brands in the consideration set. One study found that nine out of ten shoppers entered the store with some strategy for saving money (see Exhibit 11.9).[72] Although price is a critical factor in many decisions, consumers generally do not remember price information, even for a brand they have just selected.[73] This is because price information is always available in the store, so consumers have little motivation to remember it. Note that consumers who worry about losing money are more concerned about price, whereas those who are sensitive to gains look at brand features as well as price.[74]

marketing
IMPLICATIONS

Sometimes marketers mistakenly assume that consumers always look for the lowest possible price. Although this assumption is certainly true in some instances, a more accurate statement is that consumers have a ***zone of acceptance*** regarding what constitutes an appropriate range of prices for a particular product or service category.[75] As long as the brand falls within this price range, consumers will consider it but reject brands falling either above or below the range. For instance, consumers initially shunned wipe products because they cost more than paper towels and cleaning fluids. After marketers revamped their wipes to promote the germ-killing benefits, consumers began to buy—although some still use price as a primary criterion for choice.[76]

Consumers may also reject products that are priced too low because they infer that something is wrong with the product. Buyers would be suspicious if a pair of expensive designer jeans were on sale for $9.99. And, as noted earlier, consumers sometimes use price as a heuristic to judge product or service quality (higher price means higher quality). This is one reason why Japan's Aeon stores have had less success marketing discounted clothing than marketing discounted processed foods and bottled water.[77] Also, framing can be a factor: Under low motivation and low processing opportunity, consumers will respond more to a negatively framed message than a positively framed one.[78] Finally, retailers should be aware that consumers view store design (layout and ambiance) as a pricing cue and will expect higher prices at stores that look upscale.[79]

Price Perceptions Consumer perceptions play an important role in the use of price-related tactics. Remember that for consumers to perceive two prices as different, the variation must be at or above the just noticeable difference. Thus consumers might not care if one brand of toothpaste is priced at Rs.23.50 and another at Rs.24.75. Consumers also compare a product's price with an internal reference price for such products, based on past prices paid, competing product prices, and other factors.[80] Moreover, they pay attention to the individual prices of products when considering the value of an offer bundling two or more products at a special price. Consumers perceive more value when the discount applies to the product that they weight most heavily in evaluating the overall bundle.[81]

In addition, perceptual processes figure in the consumer's reaction to different price points. Researches have consistently indicated that consumers perceive odd prices (those ending with an odd number) as significantly lower than even prices (those ending with an even number); a DVD priced at Rs.3999/- will be perceived as less expensive than one priced at Rs.4000/-. Consumers tend to be more responsive to price decreases than they are to price increases.[83] Lowering the price of an offering will therefore increase sales to a greater degree than increasing price by the same amount will decrease sales. Moreover, when a company heavily discounts a product on an infrequent basis, consumers will perceive the average price as lower than if the product goes on sale often but with less of a price reduction.[84]

An interesting study found that when companies put restrictions on the deal, such as a purchase or time limit, consumers perceive the deal as more valuable—but only when motivation to process is low.[85] How companies describe the deal can make a difference. One study found that comparing the sale price to the "regular price" worked better in the store, whereas comparison to competitors' prices was more effective at home.[86] Also, paying for products in a foreign currency (as when traveling) affects price perceptions and spending behavior: when the foreign currency is valued as a multiple of the home-country currency (such as 4 Malaysian ringgits = $1), consumers tend to spend more than when the foreign currency is valued as a fraction (such as .4 Bahraini dinar = $1).[87]

The Deal-Prone Consumer Marketers are interested in identifying ***deal-prone consumers*** because this segment is suitable for more directly targeted price-related strategies, but research findings on this issue have been mixed. One study found that deal-prone consumers are more likely to be lower-income, older, and less educated than non-deal-prone consumers; other studies have found that higher-income consumers have better access to price information and are therefore more able to act on it.[88] Part of the problem is that consumers react differently to different types of deals: some will be more responsive to coupons, whereas some will be more responsive to price cuts and to rebates.[89]

marketing IMPLICATIONS

Pricing strategy is clearly important to marketers, and they can use a variety of pricing techniques, including coupons, price-offs, rebates, and two-for-ones as long as the savings are at or above the just noticeable difference and within the zone of acceptance. The shampoo market in India is valued at Rs 4.5 bn with the penetration level at 13% only, but with unique innovations in packaging, like the sachets, it caters to the urban and the rural population in the same spirit. For the rural market, consumption being low, a sachet serves as an ideal SKU and for the urban markets, for lower per unit consumption household it serves as an ideal SKU.

The importance of deals is evidenced by the deep price cuts supermarkets have made, spurred by stiff competition from Wal-Mart, Costco, and other discounters. A number of U.S. and European brands have lowered their prices in response to competition from store brands, which are promoted as equal in quality to national brands but priced lower. Large households are big buyers of store brands, although affluent households are buying more store brands than ever before.[90] In the United Kingdom private-label brands are very profitable and have the choicest spots on supermarket shelves.[91] The ability to search for lower prices is the reason that many consumers shop on the Internet. However, some companies prefer not to attract consumers who use price-comparison sites. The head of marketing for John Lewis Direct, a U.K. catalog company, says, "Customers recruited from these sites have generally been the least profitable, as they don't come back. They are often seeking the cheapest deals . . . and show little loyalty."[92]

The importance of value

Consumers are looking for good value—that is, a high-quality brand at a good price. Fast-food chains such as Burger King, McDonald's, and Taco Bell therefore seek to satisfy consumers by offering special "value meals." But *value* does not always mean lower price. Consumers will pay more if they believe the offering provides an important benefit.[93] European consumers, for instance, will pay more for the convenience of premeasured laundry detergent tablets marketed under such well-known brands as Wisk and Tide.[94] One way for marketers to deliver value without lowering prices is to provide a differential benefit and convince consumers that the brand is worth the extra cost. For example, Colgate bet—correctly—that consumers would pay more for Total toothpaste, which has a special germ-fighting ingredient.[95] In Mexico, cosmetics are extremely important to a woman's appearance, and many Mexican women will spare no expense in purchasing these products.[96]

Special pricing

If marketers use pricing deals too often, consumers will perceive the special price as the regular price and will not buy unless the brand is on sale—resulting in lost profits. This has happened in the past to food chains such as Arby's and Domino's. Too many deals can also damage brand loyalty as consumers become too deal oriented and switch brands more often. Thus deals tend to work best when they are used intermittently and selectively. Lower brand loyalty has become a major concern in numerous product categories in the United States and is the reason many firms want to move toward brand-building strategies such as advertising and sampling.[97]

The use of pricing deals also varies with the country. Coupons are common in the United States: nearly 50 percent of all retailers use them, and consumers save $3 billion annually by redeeming coupons.[98] Many Web-based sellers use online coupons to attract and retain customers; however, excessive discounts can hurt profitability, as the now closed Vitamins.com site learned after offering $25 off a purchase of $25.01 or more.[99] The trend in the United Kingdom and Italy has been toward fewer coupons of higher value.[100] Coupons are not used in every country; retailers will not accept them in Holland and Switzerland, and the retail infrastructure in Russia and Greece cannot accommodate them.

Price consciousness is not static

As might be expected, consumers tend to be more price conscious in difficult economic times than in times of prosperity. For more than a decade, the sluggish Japanese economy has contributed to the growing popularity of discount stores in a country that once scorned them, and coupon use also increased there.[101] In China, consumers have become even more price conscious now that Carrefour, Wal-Mart, and other discount retailers are expanding in the big cities.[102]

Normative Influences as a Simplifying Strategy

Sometimes other individuals can influence consumers' low-elaboration decision making. A college freshman may buy the brand of laundry detergent his mother uses at home; a sophomore might buy clothing that her friends like. Our use of such ***normative choice tactics*** can result from (1) *direct influence,* in which others try to manipulate us; (2) *vicarious observation,* in which we observe others to guide our behavior; and (3) *indirect influence,* in which we are concerned about the opinions of others. Normative tactics are particularly common among inexperienced consumers who have little knowledge. Note that chat groups on the Internet can increase the importance of normative influence in decision making because consumers can talk to each other so easily.

marketing
IMPLICATIONS

If normative tactics are particularly evident in a product or service category, companies can emphasize these motivations in advertising. A good example of this strategy is an ad for Ritz crackers that shows how pleased party guests will be when you "serve it on a Ritz." Consumers often buy expensive imported products to impress others. Marketers can also attempt to stimulate word-of-mouth communication, as described in Chapter 16.

Low-Effort Feeling-Based Decision Making

The final category of low-effort strategies covers decisions based more on feelings than on cognitive processing. These types of strategies include affective tactics, variety seeking, and impulse purchasing.

Feelings as a Simplifying Strategy

At times, consumers will select a brand or service because they like it, even though they may not know why. This behavior relies on very basic, low-level feelings, or ***affect.*** Affect differs from cognitive strategies such as performance-related attitudes in that it does not necessarily result from a conscious recognition of need satisfaction and is usually weaker than an attitude. Simply being in the presence of someone you like who is smiling happily can make you smile and feel happy—and, in turn, have a positive influence on your evaluation of a product.[103]

Affect is most likely to be part of the decision process when the offering is hedonic (rather than functional) and when other factors, such as performance evaluations, price, habit, and normative influences, are not in operation. If you buy Heinz ketchup because it best satisfies your needs or if you usually buy only the cheapest brand of paper towels, affect is less likely to influence your decision. However, when these factors do not operate in low-effort situations, affect can play a central role.

Affect Referral ***Affect-related tactics*** use a form of category-based processing.[104] In other words, we associate brands with global affective evaluations we recall from memory when making a choice, a process called ***affect referral*** or the "How do I feel about it?" heuristic.[105] For example the name Archie's Gallery conjures favorable images in our minds and our thoughts get across to positive feelings like gifting, love, festivals (see Exhibit 11.10 for another example). In one study, consumers choosing between a healthy dessert and a less healthy chocolate cake chose the dessert associated with the most positive affect (the cake) when they had little opportunity to think about the choice. When they had more time to think, however, they chose the healthier dessert, suggesting that affect referral is more of a factor when processing effort is low.[106]

Whenever a consumer encounters a new brand, he or she can also compare it to other brands in the same category. To the extent that the new brand is similar to previously encountered brands, the affect associated with that category can be transferred to the new instance and influence choice.[107] On the other hand, if the new brand is perceived as dissimilar, the consumer is more likely to switch to piecemeal processing, evaluating attributes in the manner described in Chapter 10.[108] For example, teens may perceive the original Jell-O product as old-fashioned and therefore dislike it. However, they may have a very different reaction to X-treme Gel Sticks, a version of Jell-O that comes in unusual flavors like cotton candy and is eaten from push-up packaging. Because the product name, the flavors, and the packaging are all dissimilar to traditional Jell-O attributes, teens may be able to evaluate the attributes of the newer product on their own terms rather than in light of their affect for Jell-O.[109]

Exhibit 11.10
ADVERTISING BASED ON AFFECT
Sometimes marketers try to generate positive feelings and associate them with the product. This ad for HelpAge India tries to promote their range of new year cards and how the sale benefits the old people directly.

Brand Familiarity

Affect can also be generated from ***brand familiarity*** (through the mere exposure effect). In one study, beer drinkers with well-established brand preferences could not distinguish their preferred brand from others in a blind taste test.[110] However, when the beers were identified, consumers rated the taste of their preferred brand significantly higher than the others. Another study found that "buying the most familiar brand" was a dominant choice tactic for inexperienced purchasers of peanut butter. Even when the quality of the most familiar brand was manipulated to be lower than unfamiliar brands, consumers still greatly preferred the familiar brand.[111]

These findings were replicated in a study in Singapore, suggesting that the impact of brand familiarity may be a cross-cultural phenomenon.[112] Another study found that brand name was a more important heuristic cue in a low-elaboration situation than in a high-elaboration one.[113] Coca-Cola, the world's most valuable brand, is a household name due, in part, to its consistent, highly visible marketing.[114] Yet, aggressively promoted local brands such as Crazy Cola that work hard to gain brand familiarity are outselling Coke and other global brands in Siberia and other areas. Very young children can be influenced by brand names accompanied with visual cues like the Froot Loops toucan.[115]

Visual Attributes Affect plays a key role in determining aesthetic responses to marketing stimuli, especially when visual properties are the only basis for judgment. In yellow pages advertising, for example, consumers are more likely to consider firms with color ads and more likely to call those with product-enhancing color.[116] One study showed that two key aspects of a product's design generate more positive affective responses to the product.[117] These are *unity*, which means that the visual parts of the design connect in a meaningful way, and *prototypicality*, which means that the object is representative of its category.

marketing IMPLICATIONS

Given that feelings can play an important role in the decision process, marketers can attempt to create and maintain brand familiarity, build category-based associations, and generate affect through advertising that creates positive attitudes toward the ad. By creating positive affect toward their brand, marketers can increase the probability that it will be selected (all other things being equal).

The power of brand name familiarity was demonstrated years ago when Coca-Cola changed its formula. Even though most consumers preferred the taste of New Coke in blind taste tests, a strong preference for the old formula resurfaced when brand names were identified. In fact, the demand for the old brand was so strong that the company reintroduced Coca-Cola Classic under public pressure. As shown in Exhibit 11.11, Colgate is a highly familiar and positively evaluated brand of toothpaste. In Romania and Turkey, buying well-known brand names is very important because it increases a consumer's prestige.[118] Most of the status brands, however, are foreign.

Many companies now engage in ***co-branding***, an arrangement by which two brands form a partnership to benefit from the power of two.[119] Examples include co-branding exercises in the airlines, credit card, publications and the oil companies. Companies like ICICI, Indian Airlines, HPCL, Bharat Petroleum, Bennett and Coleman all have strategic tie-ups within themselves. Off-late the large retail outlets like Big Bazaar, Planet M, Westside and Shopper's Stop have also entered into strategic co-branding exercise with various credit card companies. Food chains like McDonald's global alliances are also extended into India, particularly, the tie-up with Disney, through the sale of Disney merchandise.

Brands that have positive cross-cultural affect can be marketed internationally. The country of origin plays different roles for different product categories, in a heterogeneous market like India. For electronic items and for the automotive segment the Japanese influence has been the strongest, whereas for fashion and lifestyle related aspects the American and European influence has been predominant. Our food habits being conservative, the influences upon it have been more regional. Our experimentation has not gone beyond Chinese cuisines, and that too an adapted version of it. In particular, hedonic offerings—those that involve style or taste—rely heavily on affective associations. The marketing philosophy at Frito-Lay is "If you can make people feel better about what they are eating, the propensity to consume more is there."[125] Finally, familiar packaging can play an important role in influencing brand choice, which is why Coca-Cola introduced plastic versions of its familiar glass bottle.

Exhibit 11.11
BRAND NAME FAMILIARITY AND POSITIVE AFFECT

Consumers tend to have more positive feelings towards, brands that are more familiar relative to brands that are unfamiliar. The Colgate brand is a well-known toothpaste that has been around since 1937.

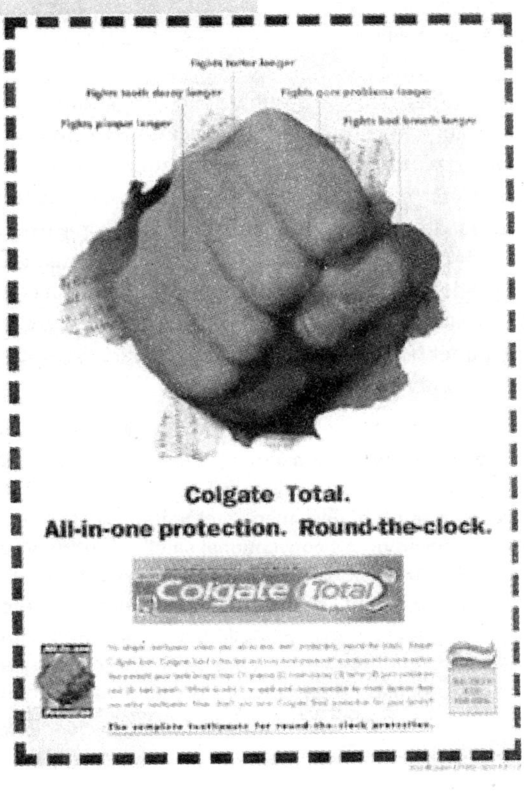

Decision Making Based on Variety-Seeking Needs

Another common consumer-choice tactic in low-effort situations is to try something different, a phenomenon called ***variety seeking.*** A consumer might regularly buy Johnson's baby shampoo but one day have an urge to try Pantene shampoo—then return to the baby shampoo for later purchases. Consumers engage in variety seeking for two major reasons: *satiation* and *boredom.*[126] If you had the same food for dinner every night or listened to only

Exhibit 11.12
COURTING VARIETY SEEKERS

Bingo a recently launched snacking item from ITC caters to the variety seeking behavior of the customer by offering a range of snacking items.

one CD over and over, satiation would occur and you would be driven to do something different. Consumer decisions that occur repeatedly can become monotonous; this is why some consumers switch for the sake of change, even though they would have derived more immediate enjoyment from repeating their usualchoice.[127] Another reason consumers seek variety in public situations is because they expect others will evaluate their decision more positively.[128]

Note that variety seeking is not expressed in every product category. It is most likely to occur when involvement is low, there are few differences among brands, and the product is more hedonic than functional.[129] It also tends to occur when consumers become satiated with a particular sensory attribute of a product, such as smell, taste, touch, and visual appearance.[130] Marketers can therefore reduce boredom simply by providing more variety in a product category.[131]

Consumers are motivated to relieve boredom because their level of arousal falls below the ***optimal stimulation level (OSL)***—an internal ideal level of stimulation.[132] Repetitive purchasing causes the internal level of stimulation to fall below the OSL, and buying something different is a way of restoring it. In addition, certain consumers need more stimulation and are less tolerant of boredom than others. These ***sensation seekers*** are more likely to engage in variety seeking and are often the first to try new and trendy products, making them a good market for new offerings.[133]

Note that purchasing something different is only one way to seek stimulation. Consumers can also express their variety drive by engaging in vicarious exploration and use innovativeness.[134] ***Vicarious exploration*** occurs when consumers collect information about a product, either from reading or talking with others, or putting themselves in stimulating shopping environments. For example, many people like to go to stores simply to look around or browse—not to buy, just to increase stimulation. ***Use innovativeness*** means using products in a new or different way, the way a consumer might use an aluminum can that held soup to organize nails in a workshop or use baking soda to deodorize a kitty litter box. Consumer use innovativeness actually led Arm & Hammer to introduce a new kitty litter deodorizer product.

marketing IMPLICATIONS Marketers should recognize consumers' need for variety and accommodate these needs when appropriate. For example, Tide in India launched a series of perfumed detergents, namely Mogra and Jasmine to create a difference in the product's conventional smell and offer product related differentiation to the market. The company hopes consumers will express their need for variety by buying Tide in a different scent than choosing another brand. In the soft-drink category, Coca-Cola's Sprite Remix is targeted toward teens who crave new flavors and want to be able to add fruit juice or other ingredients to change the taste entirely.[136] Interestingly, the largest increase in flavored soft drinks occurred in single-serve sizes, which involves less risk than buying a 6- or 12-pack (lending support to the variety-seeking theory).

Marketers can attempt to induce brand switching among variety seekers by encouraging consumers to "put a little spice into life" and try something different. The newly launched Bingo offers competition to its rival Kurkure by launching a range in the similar product category. Not only the shapes are different, but the tastes are different too in the variants offered. In the potato chip segment also Bingo offers a wider range from the conventional flavors to the off beat ones like, Masala Chanch or Paneer Tikka Masala. However, consumers may not like *too* much variety. For example, KFC consumers began to cry "No more" in response to the chain's many menu additions.[138] Note that simply altering the way the product assortment is presented (how items are arranged on the store shelves, for example) can increase consumers' perceptions of variety and trigger higher consumption, a finding that is particularly relevant for food retailers.[139]

Buying on Impulse

Another common type of decision process that has a strong affective component is the ***impulse purchase,*** which occurs when consumers suddenly decide to purchase something they had not planned on buying. Impulse purchases are characterized by (1) an intense or overwhelming feeling of having to buy the product immediately, (2) a disregard for potentially negative purchase consequences, (3) feelings of euphoria and excitement, and (4) a conflict between control and indulgence.[140] Consumers in Asian countries, where interdependence and emotional control are emphasized, tend to engage in less impulse purchasing than consumers in Western countries, where personal independence and hedonistic pleasures are emphasized.[141] Some research suggests that impulse purchases are prompted by consumers' self-control failure.[142] Such purchases are often triggered by the consumer's exposure to an external stimulus, such as an in-store display, catalog, Web ad, or TV ad with a phone number.

Researchers estimate that anywhere from 27 to 62 percent of consumer purchases can be considered impulse buys.[143] However, it is important to distinguish between impulse buying and partially planned purchases, or those for which the consumer has an intention to buy the product category but uses the store display to decide which brand to select. When this distinction is made, the proportion of impulse purchases is usually lower.[144] The tendency to engage in impulse purchasing varies; some consumers can be considered highly impulsive buyers, whereas others are not.[145] The tendency to buy on impulse is probably related to other traits such as general acquisitiveness and materialism, sensation seeking, and a liking for recreational shopping.[146] If the costs of impulsiveness are made salient or if normative pressure such as the presence of others with a negative opinion is high, consumers will engage in less impulse purchasing.[147]

marketing
IMPLICATIONS

Many stores organize their merchandise to maximize impulse purchases. Card shops position commonly sought items such as greeting cards near the back so consumers will have to pass a number of displays containing higher-margin, impulse items. As discussed earlier, eye-level and eye-catching displays, including end-of-aisle displays and blinking lights, can increase sales dramatically—mostly from impulse purchases.[148] This is why suppliers pay high prices for the best display space in a store.[149] In addition, package design can increase impulse purchases. For instance, L'Oreal put new iridescent-colored sleeves on its Fructis hair-care products to attract shopper attention at the point of purchase.[150]

Impulse purchasing tends to decline in difficult economic times. In Japan, for example, the lengthy economic recession has led many consumers to buy only what they need, such as clothes and items for children. As a result, marketers have had to reposition many products as necessities rather than as impulse items.[151] On the other hand, consumers still splurge on selected luxuries when money is tight, such as fine dining or even exclusive watches.

Summary

This chapter examined the nature of consumer judgment and decision making when motivation, ability, and opportunity—and consequently elaboration—are low. In these situations, consumers often make judgments using simplified heuristics or decision rules. When using the representativeness heuristic, consumers base their judgments on comparisons to a category prototype. When using the availability heuristic, they base their judgments on accessibility of information. Consumers can use choice tactics that are either cognitively based (performance, habit, brand loyalty, price, normative) or based on feelings (affect, variety seeking, impulse). They learn these tactics over repeat purchase occasions through a process similar to operant conditioning.

Performance-related tactics are more likely to be employed when the consumer's needs have been satisfied and the consumer has formed positive attitudes based on consumption, which is why product or service quality is so important. Some consumers purchase by habit or simple repetitive behavior. Marketers want to encourage consumers to continue buying certain brands while inducing users of competing brands to switch. Brand loyalty represents the most desirable situation for marketers because the consumer is strongly committed to the brand and buys it repeatedly. Marketers can build brand loyalty by offering high-quality products and by providing incentives for repeat purchasing. Price-related tactics can be effective when consumers perceive few differences among brands or when economic motives are extremely important. As long as the price of the brand or service falls within the zone of acceptance, the consumer will consider buying it. When the consumer is inexperienced, has little knowledge, or considers the opinion of others very important, the decision may be guided by normative tactics. In this case, marketers can emphasize normative motivations in their ad messages.

Consumers' use of affect-related tactics implies that marketers should attempt to build and maintain brand familiarity and positive attitudes toward their ads. In addition, marketers need to be aware that some consumers will switch brands because of a need for variety. Finally, many purchases are made on impulse, and marketers can organize the purchase environment to induce such activity.

Questions for Review and Discussion

1. How do base-rate information and the law of small numbers bias judgments made on the basis of the availability heuristic?
2. How is the high-effort hierarchy of effects similar to and different from the low-effort hierarchy?
3. What operant conditioning concepts apply to consumer learning?
4. Why is quality an important ingredient in cognitive-based decision making?
5. What is brand loyalty, and what role does it play in low-effort decision making?
6. How do price and value perceptions affect low-effort decision making?
7. When is affect likely to be more of a factor in low-effort decision making?
8. If habit is a simplifying strategy, why do consumers sometimes seek variety?

Exercises

1. Interview ten consumers about their decision-making behavior for the following product categories: peanut butter, laundry detergent, canned vegetables, coffee, and ice cream. Ask the consumers to indicate (a) how much time and effort they take in making a decision and (b) how they select the brand they purchase (which choice tactics do they use?). Summarize the responses for each consumer individually and for all consumers; also, answer the following questions:
   a. On average, how much time and effort do consumers spend on these decisions?
   b. What are the major types of tactics employed for each category?
   c. How do the tactics differ for the product categories?
   d. Do consumers use the same or different tactics across product categories?
   e. What are the marketing implications of your findings?
2. Pick two common product categories where low-elaboration decision making is likely to occur. Go to your local store and observe 20 consumers making a choice for these two products. Record the amount of time taken and the number of brands examined. If possible, ask consumers why they chose the brand they did immediately after the choice. (Be sure to get the store's permission first.) Summarize this information, and answer the following questions:
   a. How much time and effort did consumers typically devote to these decisions? Are your findings consistent with those reported in the chapter?
   b. What were the most common types of choice tactics employed?
   c. Did the types of choice tactics differ between product categories? If so, why do you think this occurred?
3. Pick ten product or service categories in which low-elaboration decision making is likely to occur. For each category, try to identify the type of choice tactic you would typically use.
   a. Does this tactic differ across categories?
   b. If so, why?
   c. How do you think you learned to use these tactics?

More Exercises from the Adaptor

1. In certain product categories like shampoos, writing pens, watches, tourism destinations, to name a few where the options to choose form increased many times in the last three – four years. Classify products on low and high involvement (preferably five each) and identify the complete range available and further how have marketers defined segment markets to classify the same.d. What attributes are evaluated for purchase in both the cases?

References

1 Source: http://www.blonnet.com/2006/11/04/stories/2006110405820100.htm

2 Source: http://www.iht.com/articles/2006/05/26/business/wbfood.php

3 Source: http://www.blonnet.com/catalyst/2003/12/11/stories/2003121100020300.htm

4 Source: http://indica.co.za/tata_tea/articles/20051011_highs.htm

chapter 12 Post-Decision Processes

LEARNING OBJECTIVES

After studying this chapter, you will be able to:

- Distinguish between the post-decision dissonance and post-decision regret that consumers may experience after acquisition, consumption, or disposition.
- Explain how consumers can learn from experience and why marketers need to understand this post-decision process.
- Discuss the ways in which consumers judge their satisfaction or dissatisfaction with a decision and show how marketers can influence such judgments.
- Describe how consumers may dispose of something, why this process is more complex for meaningful objects, and what influences consumer recycling behavior.

INTRODUCTION

ICICI Bank: Hum Hai Naa

Banking in India post nationalization in 1969 projected a picture of a laid back approach, where the basic focus was driven towards savings and deposits. Most retail customers with banks operated within the dictate laid down by banking regulations. Aspects like, banking between 10-2pm, Saturday half day, Sunday off day, lag time to get drafts made and numerous other facets (bottlenecks) with which the retail customer at the bank was conditioned too. After liberalization in 1991 and with banking sector also opening, the industrial credit arm of the government expanded into retail banking in 1994 with ICICI bank.

[1]After Shri K.V. Kamath took over as MD and CEO of the bank in 1996, ICICI went through a series of takeovers and new product launches between 1996 and 1999. [2]With 364 branches, 46 extension counters, a network of 1,050 ATMs, multiple call centers and well-developed Internet banking, the Mumbai-headquartered ICICI bank can provide financial services all over India. Its customers often use multiple channels, and they are increasingly turning to electronic banking options. Business from the Internet, ATMs and other electronic channels now comprises 50% of all transactions, up from 5% just two years ago.

In the process of growing its business to this level, ICICI Bank has distinguished itself from other banks through its customer relationships. ICICI Bank Executive Director Chanda Kochhar says, "In an increasingly competitive environment where customers are becoming more demanding and financial services are getting commoditized, ICICI realized the key differentiator would be customer focus."

ICICI today has not just expanded into numerous divisions like Insurance, Mutual Funds, Securities, and Commodity trading, but even their core banking business has extended into a multitude of activities, providing benefits to the customers. [3] The ICICI ATM today is not just a point for cash withdrawal, but it can also be used for Mobile prepaid card recharge, buying Internet Packs (ATN - Any Time Net), payment of Donations (Anytime Blessing), Mutual Funds Transactions, Bill

Exhibit 12.1
MAKING CUSTOMER SATISFACTION A PRIORITY

ICICI bank's foray into internet banking, 8-8pm extended banking hours, well connected ATM's offer customer not just extended banking services, but also an efficient and well established customer services also.

Payments, Flexi Top Ups and Calling Cards.
ICICI's aggressive and customer driven approach on the filp side has also been able to open the market. Nationalized banks like SBI, Corporation Bank etc. have had to realign themselves and a host of other private banks have followed suit. HDFC Bank, UTI Bank, IDBI Bank to name a few have always been known as the follower in the segment after ICICI's aggressive opening in the Indian Banking sector which redefined how customer driven banking is done.

The ICICI Bank example illustrates several key topics in this chapter. First, it highlights the importance of customer satisfaction as the foundation of a successful business. Second, it shows how customer satisfaction depends on good performance creating positive feelings and perceptions of equity (a fair exchange). Third, it illustrates how consumers learn about offerings by experiencing them directly, as customers do when they use the various services of ICICI, or vicariously by viewing the bank's advertisements. Finally, it shows how a company can encourage customers to stay loyal by offering innovative and new range of services to them. All these phenomena occur after the consumer has made a decision. This chapter examines the four post-decision processes shown in Exhibit 12.2: dissonance and regret, consumer learning, satisfaction/dissatisfaction, and disposition— all of which have important implications for marketers.

Post-Decision Dissonance and Regret

Consumers are not always confident in their acquisition, consumption, or disposition decisions. They may feel uncertain as to whether they made the correct choice or even regret the decision they made, as the following sections show.

Dissonance

After you make an acquisition, consumption, or disposition decision, you may sometimes feel uncertain about whether you made the correct choice. You might wonder whether you should have bought a shirt or dress other than the one you did, or whether you should have worn something else to a party, or whether you should have kept an old teddy bear instead of throwing it away. ***Post-decision dissonance*** is most likely to occur when more than one alternative is attractive and the decision is important.[2]

Post-decision dissonance can influence consumer behavior because it creates anxiety that the consumer would like to reduce, especially when motivation, ability, and opportunity (MAO) are high. One way of reducing dissonance is to search for additional information from sources such as experts and magazines. This search is very selective and is designed to make the chosen alternative more attractive and the rejected ones less attractive, thereby reducing dissonance.

Regret

Post-decision regret occurs when consumers perceive an unfavorable comparison between the performance of the chosen option and the performance of the unchosen options. If you consider three cars before making your purchase decision and then find out that the resale value of the car you bought is much lower than either of the two options, you may regret your purchase and wish you had chosen one of the other cars. In fact, research indicates you may feel regret even if you have

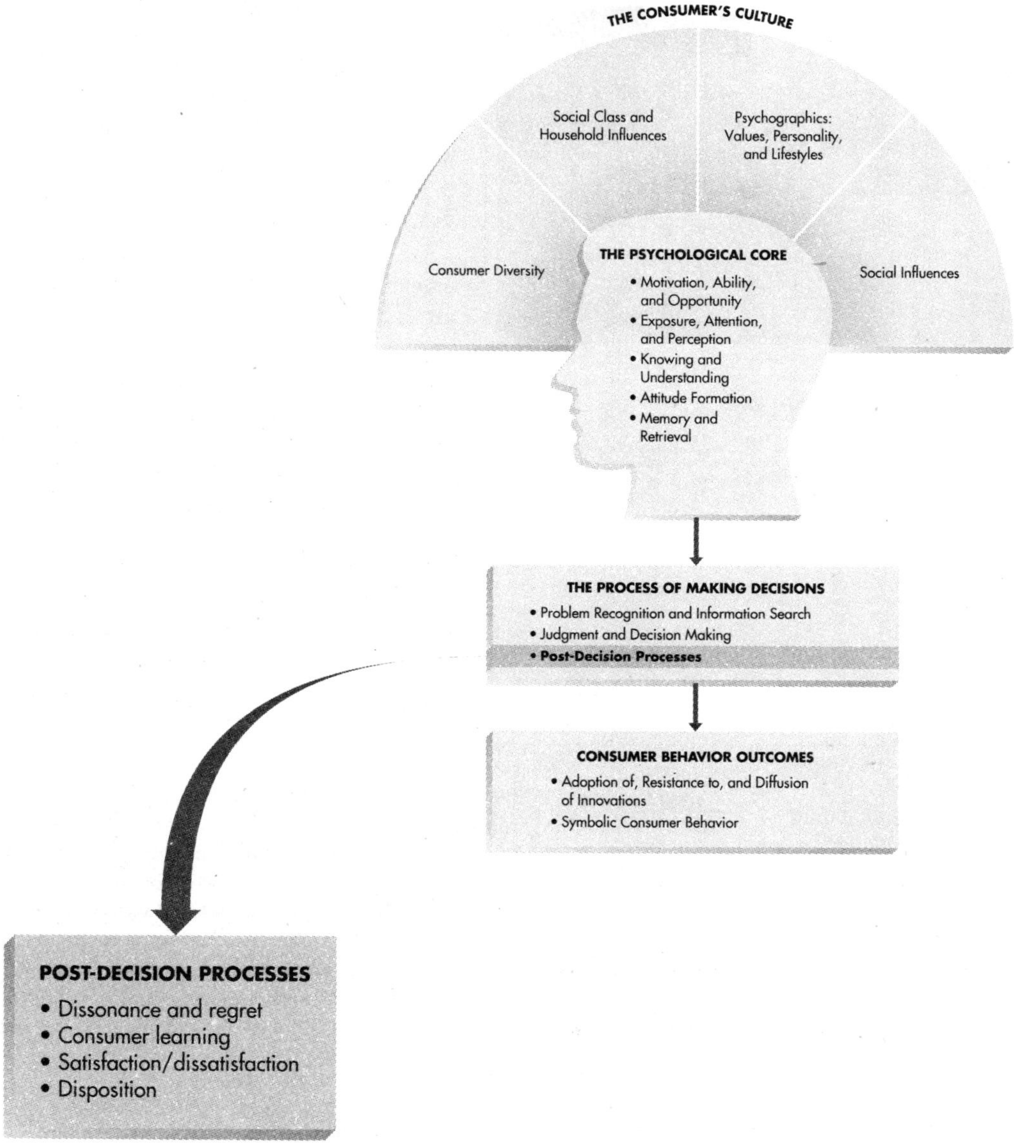

Exhibit 12.2

CHAPTER OVERVIEW: POST-DECISION PROCESSES *The decision does not end after consumers make a choice or a purchase. Consumers can experience dissonance (anxiety over whether the correct decision was made) or regret after a purchase, learn about the offering by using it, experience satisfaction or dissatisfaction with it, and eventually dispose of it. This chapter examines the theories and implications underlying each of these important processes.*

Exhibit 12.3
ADVERTISING BASED ON FEELINGS OF REGRET

In this ad, Porsche uses the theme "buyer's remorse" to encourage consumers to think about how good they will feel after buying the Carrera 4S model.

no information about the unchosen alternatives—especially if you cannot reverse your decision, have a negative outcome from your chosen alternative, or have made a change from the status quo. Your feelings of regret can also directly influence your intention to buy the same kind of car again.[3] Porsche has used regret in an ad promoting its Carrera 4S model (see Exhibit 12.3).

Researchers are also investigating how the consumer's anticipation of post-decision regret can affect a decision about making a purchase, how pre- and postpurchase price comparisons of alternatives affect regret, and how the outcome of a purchase decision affects future purchase decisions. One study suggests that if consumers who receive postpurchase information want to avoid feeling regret after a decision, they should postpone their purchases for a longer period.[4] Suppose consumers are dissatisfied with the outcome of a purchase and decide to switch to a different alternative. Will they regret switching? Even if this new alternative turns out to have a negative outcome, research shows that consumers will feel less regret because they believe their decision to switch was justified.[5]

marketing IMPLICATIONS

By helping consumers reduce post-decision dissonance and regret, marketers can diminish any negative feelings related to the product or service. They accomplish this by helping consumers obtain supporting information. For example, consumers who purchase a BMW receive a copy of *BMW Magazine,* which is filled with interesting facts and "feel good" information about the car. This supporting information reduces dissonance and helps consumers develop a positive attitude toward the vehicle. Consumers may also reduce dissonance and regret by reading supporting information in advertisements after a purchase. A good example is the ad in Exhibit 12.3.

Learning from Consumer Experience*

Earlier chapters explained how consumers acquire knowledge through processes such as information search, exposure to marketing communications, and observation of others. From a practical perspective, we most often think about this type of consumer learning because much of it is under the direct control of the company, which provides information through marketing communications. However, these efforts are often limited because of their low credibility.[6] Consumers assume that these messages are intended to persuade them to buy the offering and are therefore generally skeptical about the marketing claims.

* This section draws heavily from an article by Stephen J. Hoch and John Deighton, "Managing What Consumers Learn from Experience," *Journal of Marketing,* April 1989, pp. 1–20.

Experiences that occur during acquisition, consumption, or disposition, however, can be equally—if not more—important sources of consumer knowledge for several reasons. First, the consumer tends to be more motivated to learn under these circumstances. Actually experiencing an event is more involving and interesting than being told about it, and the consumer has more control over what happens. Simply investigating the various buying alternatives is a learning experience. However, if consumers become too attached to the alternatives during the decision process, they may feel uneasy after making a choice because they had to forgo the other alternatives.[7]

Second, information acquired from experience is more vivid and therefore easier to remember than other types of information.[8] Finally, information about attributes that must be experienced through taste, touch, or smell exerts a stronger influence on consumers' future behavior when it comes from experience or product trial than when it is acquired from advertising or word of mouth.[9] For example, an ad can state that a product will taste good, but actually eating it is more likely to result in a strong attitude. On the other hand, repeated exposure to ads can approximate the effect of direct experience when it comes to search or informational attributes such as price or ingredients.[10] If an ad is repeated often enough, it can result in strong beliefs about these characteristics.

A Model of Learning from Consumer Experience

Consumers can learn from experience by engaging in a process of ***hypothesis testing.*** On the basis of past experience or another source such as word of mouth or advertising, consumers can form a hypothesis or expectation about a product or service, a consumption experience, or a disposition option and then set out to test it. Such hypotheses are important because without them consumers are less likely to gather the evidence they need to learn. Researchers have proposed that consumers go through four basic stages in testing hypotheses for learning: (1) ***hypothesis generation***, (2) exposure to evidence, (3) encoding of evidence, and (4) integration of evidence and prior beliefs (see Exhibit 12.4). The following example illustrates these four stages.

Suppose a consumer is watching TV and sees an exciting ad for a new Jim Carrey movie. She also remembers some of his previous movies, such as *Lemony Snicket's A Series of Unfortunate Events* or *Fun with Dick and Jane.* Based on all this information, she generates a hypothesis about the quality of the new movie ("It must be great"). Next, she seeks out ***exposure to evidence*** to either confirm or disprove this hypothesis by going to see the new movie. While watching it, she can assess whether or not it is in fact great, a step called ***encoding the evidence.*** After watching the movie, the consumer can ***integrate the evidence*** with her existing knowledge or beliefs. If she really likes it, confirming her hypothesis, she may have learned that "you can always count on a Jim Carrey movie to be great." However, if she does not like it, as was the case for some consumers who saw *The Majestic,* she may form the new belief that "not all Carrey films are great, and I must be careful in the future."

Consumers can form hypotheses in relation to any aspect of consumer behavior: acquisition (this offering will fulfill my needs, buying from eBay will be fun), consumption (sitting in a hot tub will be soothing, listening to the concert will be fun), or disposition (getting rid of my old PC will be easy). Learning from experience is also important when consumers use a shopping agent or react to recommendations from sites such as Netflix, a DVD rental service. Using feedback from

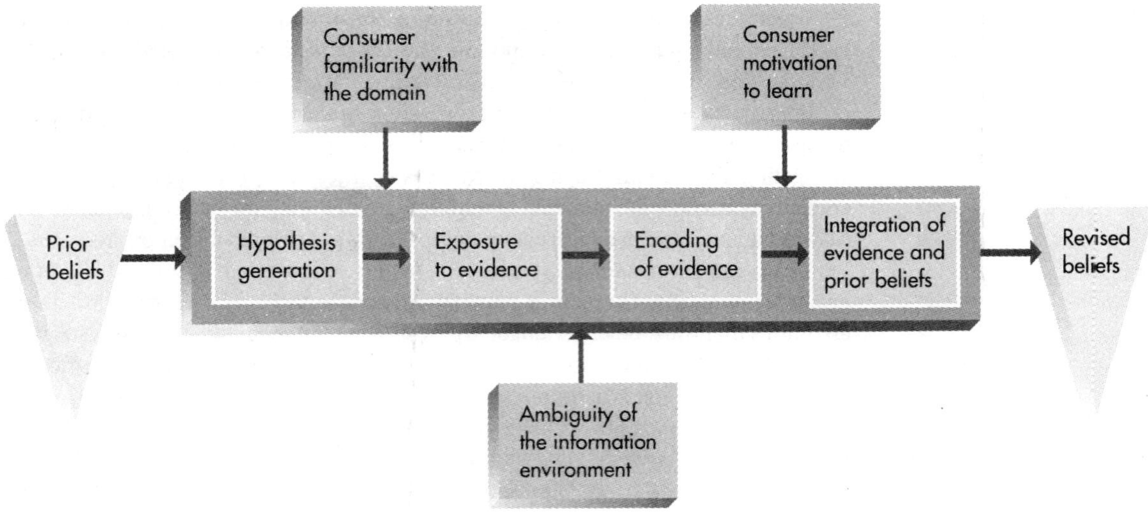

Exhibit 12.4

A MODEL OF LEARNING FROM EXPERIENCE *Consumers can acquire a lot of information about products and services by actually experiencing them. This learning process starts with prior beliefs (such as "Jim Carrey movies are great"). Upon seeing an ad for a new Jim Carrey movie, the consumer can generate hypotheses ("I'll bet this new movie is really good"), get exposure to the evidence (see the movie), encode the evidence (evaluate whether or not it is good), and integrate the evidence with prior beliefs (relate current evaluation with past perceptions). If the movie is not good, the consumer will revise beliefs (not all Jim Carrey movies are good). This entire process is influenced by consumer familiarity, motivation to process, and the ambiguity of the information.*

repeated hypothesis tests, the agent or site learns what the consumer likes and can present more appropriate options.[11]

The consumer's hypothesis and experience of brand personality also influence learning. If a firm with a "sincere" brand personality suffers a crisis, it may have difficulty reestablishing strong customer relations because fundamental perceptions of the brand have deteriorated. However, firms with an "exciting" brand personality may reinvigorate customer relationships more easily after a crisis because consumers are less surprised by nonroutine experiences with such brands.[12]

What Affects Learning from Experience?

Four factors affect learning from experience: (1) motivation, (2) prior familiarity or ability, (3) ambiguity of the information environment or lack of opportunity, and (4) processing biases.

Motivation When consumers are motivated to process information, they will generate a number of hypotheses and seek out information to confirm or disprove them, actively engaging in the process of learning from experience. But when motivation is low, consumers will generate few or no hypotheses and will be less likely to learn unless the learning process involves the simpler processes of classical or operant conditioning (see Chapters 7 and 11). Nevertheless, marketers can still facilitate the learning process when motivation is low, as you will see later in this chapter.

Prior Knowledge or Ability Consumers' prior knowledge or ability affects the extent to which they learn from experience. When knowledge is high, consumers are likely to have well-defined beliefs and expectations and are therefore unlikely to generate new hypotheses. Also, experts are less likely than those with moderate knowledge to search for information.[13] Both of these factors inhibit learning. In contrast, low-knowledge consumers lack skills to develop hypotheses to guide the learning process.[14] Without guiding hypotheses, consumers have difficulty collecting evidence and learning. Thus moderately knowledgeable consumers are the most likely to generate hypotheses and learn from experience. Interestingly, experts do have an advantage in learning information about new products and services, thanks to their more extensive knowledge base.[15]

Ambiguity of the Information Environment or Lack of Opportunity Some situations do not provide the opportunity for consumers to learn from experience, which means consumers may lack sufficient information to confirm or disprove hypotheses.[16] Such ***ambiguity of information*** occurs because many offerings are similar in quality and consumers can glean little information from the experience. Moreover, making the initial choice in a context of ambiguity affects consumers' certainty about the decision and, if the actual experience is uninformative, can lead to persistent preferences for the chosen option's attributes.[17]

Ambiguous information can strongly affect consumers' ability to learn from experience. When consumers have difficulty determining product quality (for such products as beer and motor oil), they tend to support their hypotheses with information from advertising or word of mouth. The main reason is that consumers cannot disprove the information by experiencing the product, so they see the product as consistent with their prior expectations.[18] Thus for many years consumers believed that Listerine prevented colds because the claim could not be disproved by usage. Obviously, the marketer in such a situation has an unfair advantage, which is why deception in advertising is an important topic (see Chapters 4 and 19).

On the other hand, when evidence is unambiguous and the product is clearly good or bad, consumers base their perceptions on actual experience and are able to learn a great deal. Unambiguous information tends to be better remembered and to have a greater impact on future decisions.[19] When evidence is ambiguous, evaluations by both experts and novices are strongly influenced by country-of-origin expectations (e.g., the knowledge that a product was made in Japan), but when evidence is unambiguous, experts ignore this information and make evaluations based on actual quality.[20]

Processing Biases Two biases in information processing—the confirmation bias (Chapter 9) and overconfidence (Chapter 10)—can pose major hurdles to the learning process, particularly when evidence is ambiguous.[21] Specifically, these biases inhibit learning by making consumers avoid both negative and highly diagnostic information. For example, a consumer who believes that all Japanese products are of high quality may ignore contrary evidence and learn nothing new about these products.

Negative information is important to the learning process because it provides a more balanced picture of the situation and allows us to more accurately test hypotheses. Research has also shown that the acquisition of disproving evidence has a strong and rapid impact on consumer learning.[22]

marketing IMPLICATIONS

Ambiguous information and processing biases often inhibit consumer learning about products and services. From a marketing perspective, these learning principles can have important strategic implications, depending on the market position of the product or service.[23]

Top-dog strategies. A product or service that is the market leader or has a large market share is called a *top dog*. Limitations on learning are advantageous to top dogs because consumers will simply confirm existing beliefs and expectations and display overconfidence, particularly when the motivation to learn is low. Thus consumers are less likely to learn new information that might lead to brand switching.

When motivation to learn is high, however, the consumer will try to acquire information that could be disproving and lead to a switch. Marketers can employ three strategies in this kind of situation. First, the top dog can reinforce the agenda by stating specific claims that justify consumers' evaluation of the brand. For example, in its global advertising, Heinz ketchup tries to give consumers a reason why "Mine's Gotta Have Heinz."[24] Second, marketers can encourage consumers not to acquire new information, which is called *blocking exposure to evidence*. Here, marketers are trying to convey the idea "Why change if it works?" Finally, if evidence about the top dog is unambiguous, the consumer simply needs reinforcement of why the brand is satisfying—called *explaining the experience*—and encouragement to try it. For example, KFC, the market leader in Shanghai, touts its quality and value compared to that of small local food vendors. In the United States, the company uses the phrase "Chicken Capital USA" to emphasize its major point of differentiation.[25]

Underdog strategies. Unlike top dogs, *underdogs* (lower-share brands) have everything to gain by encouraging consumer learning because new information may lead to switching. Thus the underdog gains an advantage by motivating the consumer to learn (see Exhibit 12.5). When the consumer is not motivated, underdogs face a more difficult task; they must instigate learning by reducing either the product's costs or its perceived risk.

First, the underdog needs to do everything possible to facilitate comparisons with the market leader, such as using comparative ads, setting up side-by-side displays, or providing information online. India's first quartz television, Binatone introduced the concept of comparative advertising in the country, wherein through a tabular format, Binatone tried to showcase their product's superiority as against other brands, essentially, non-quartz televisions.[26] Nevertheless, overconfidence and confirmation biases may stack the odds against these efforts, and the underdog is unlikely to succeed unless it has a strong and distinct advantage.

Second, marketers can disrupt the agenda by employing advertising to create expectations as well as promotions such as sampling to provide the actual experience. If the evidence is ambiguous, expectations are unlikely to be disconfirmed. Restaurants introducing new cuisines, generally, invite food critics to come and savour the new platter on the menu. Their experience and critical review in the press attracts the customers to the store. Food critics like Vir Sanghvi, Sabina Sehgal Saikia et al. are well-known.

Finally, facilitating product trial is critical when the motivation to learn is low but evidence is unambiguous, because evidence will lead to a positive learning experience. Two common means of encouraging product trial are sampling and coupons. Although chicken dishes make up one-third of McDonald's menu, consumers may think of KFC or other

Exhibit 12.5
ENCOURAGING LEARNING TO FACILITATE SWITCHING

In a market dominated by LIC, new entities like AIG focus on the heritage of the company to help customers learn about the organization and help in switching.

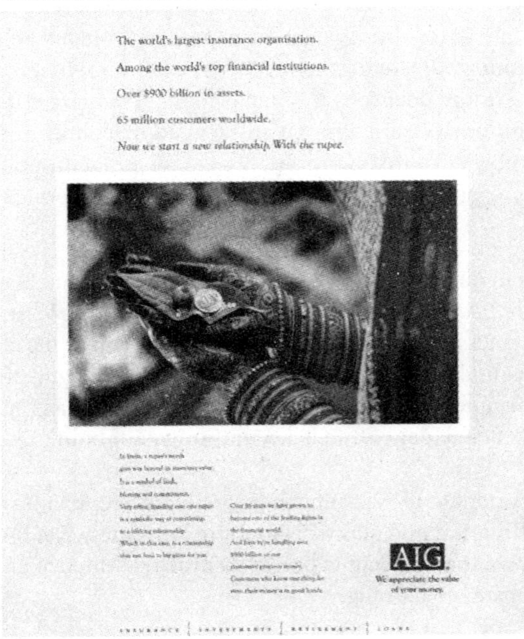

Exhibit 12.6
FACILITATING TRIAL
This ad facilitates trial by encouraging consumers to "Buy in the festival period and get a chance to be a millionaire. Through the 21 Day 21 millionaire scheme

chains rather than McDonald's when they want fast-food chicken. Sampling can be an effective means to get consumers to check out new range of Chicken menus at McDonalds and thus help consumers overcome perceptions that KFC is the only major outlet for chicken.

How Do Consumers Make Satisfaction or Dissatisfaction Judgments?

After consumers have made acquisition, consumption, or disposition decisions, they can evaluate the outcomes of their decisions. If their evaluations are positive—if they believe their needs or goals have been met—they feel ***satisfaction.*** Thus you could feel satisfied with the purchase of a new DVD player, the choice of a red wine, or the way you cleaned a cluttered closet. You might also be pleased with a buying experience, a salesperson, or a retail outlet.[29] Satisfaction can be associated with feelings of acceptance, happiness, relief, excitement, and delight.

When consumers have a negative evaluation of an outcome, they feel ***dissatisfaction.*** Dissatisfaction occurs if you did not enjoy a movie, did not like the taste of a breakfast cereal, were unhappy with a salesperson, or wished you had not thrown something away. Dissatisfaction can be related to feelings of tolerance, distress, sadness, regret, agitation, and outrage.[30]

Most of the research on satisfaction and dissatisfaction has focused on products and services for which the consumer can make an evaluation of both *utilitarian dimensions,* or how well the product or service functions (good or bad), and *hedonic dimensions,* or how it makes someone feel (happy, excited, delighted or sad, regretful, angry).[31] Consumers make a conscious comparison between what they think will happen and actual performance.[32]

Consumers' evaluations and feelings are generally temporary and can change over time. The fact that we are satisfied now does not necessarily mean we will be satisfied the next time. Consumers' satisfaction evaluations also tend to be tied to specific consumption situations—we are satisfied (or not) with the offering as we are using it at the current time. In these ways, satisfaction differs from an attitude, which is relatively enduring and less dependent on the specific situation (see Chapter 5).[33] Note also that a post-decision evaluation can differ from a pre-decision evaluation in that after using the product, a consumer may judge different attributes and cutoff levels than before.[34] For example, after trying frozen microwave pizza, you might like the taste less than you thought you would.

Levels of satisfaction vary with consumer involvement, consumer characteristics, and time.[35] Specifically, high-involvement consumers tend to express a higher level of satisfaction immediately after purchase, probably due to their more extensive evaluation. However, their satisfaction declines over time. On the other hand, lower-involvement consumers exhibit a lower level of satisfaction initially, but their level of satisfaction tends to increase with greater usage over time.

marketing IMPLICATIONS

Satisfied customers form the foundation of any successful business. Customer satisfaction leads to repeat purchase, brand loyalty, and positive word of mouth.[36] One study of 100,000 automotive customers found that consumers with different characteristics have different satisfaction thresholds and therefore different repurchase tendencies, even at the same reported satisfaction level.[37] Still, a study of Swedish consumers suggests that satisfaction is especially important for companies that rely on repeat business.[38] Online retailer Amazon.com attributes 63 percent of its sales to repeat customers.[39] Marketers should also aim for satisfaction when responding to customers who communicate a question or concern, for two reasons: (1) these tend to be highly loyal customers and (2) these consumers will influence others through word of mouth after the contact.[40]

It is important to consider how much satisfied customers will spend with a company over the long run, not just in a single transaction. For Toyota's Lexus vehicles, the lifetime value of a satisfied, loyal customer is $600,000 in repeat business.[41] For Disney theme parks, the value of a loyal customer can be $50,000.[42] Even a 5 percent increase in customer retention can raise profits by 25 to 85 percent.[43] Research by J.D. Powers & Associates shows that consumers who are satisfied with the maintenance and repairs provided by a car dealership are more likely to return there for service (giving the dealership more business) and more likely to buy the same brand of car again (giving the car manufacturer more business).[44]

Monitoring customer satisfaction. Not surprisingly, many companies now actively monitor customer satisfaction through the use of market surveys. For example, the JD power Survey for Tire as shown in Exhibit 12.7, illustrates the tire companies' customer satisfaction by showing a comparison between the tire companies' and the industry average of customer satisfaction. The JD power annual survey in India is an indicator which most automotive companies sufficiently illustrate to consumers as a parameter to evaluate the brand. In conducting such research, marketers need to measure not only satisfaction but also customer wants and expectations.[47] However, marketers should be aware that when consumers expect to evaluate a product or service, they tend to pay closer attention to negative aspects during consumption and therefore provide less favorable quality and satisfaction evaluations—unless they have low expectations at the outset.[48]

Interestingly, most consumers find enjoyment and satisfaction in their buying experiences. One study found that more than 90 percent of durable-goods purchases

Exhibit 12.7

THE JD POWER CONSUMER SATISFACTION INDEX FOR TIRES

The JD Power survey for tires in India showcases the industry versus company average for consumer satisfaction

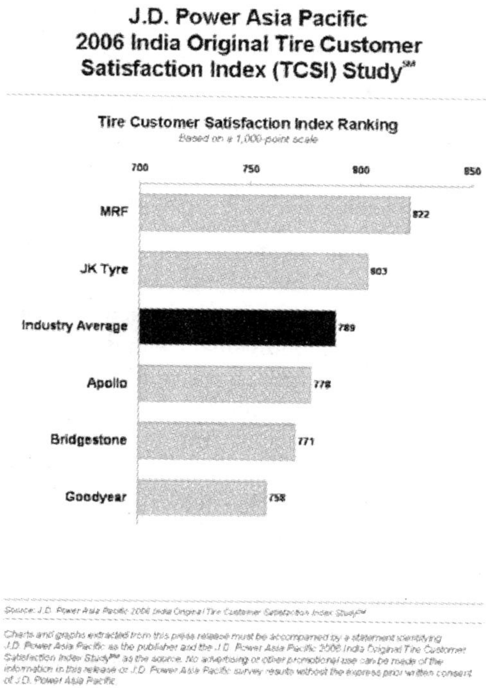

were associated with positive feelings.[49] Satisfaction levels also tend to be similar in most European countries.[50] In fact, consumers worldwide are generally satisfied. As a result, some companies are going a step further to focus on building customer loyalty as an indicator of success in the form of willingness to repurchase and to recommend the product or service to others.[51]

The costs of dissatisfaction. Dissatisfaction can lead to a variety of negative outcomes, including negative word-of-mouth communication, complaints, and reduced purchases with resulting lower profits. If a department store lost 167 customers a month, it would lose $2.4 million in sales (and $280,000 in profit) over the course of just one year.[52] A study of European consumers found that it takes 12 positive experiences to overcome one negative one and that the cost of attracting a new customer is five times the cost of keeping an existing one.[53] Addressing dissatisfaction issues can improve customer satisfaction and company performance.

Today, even though consumers in formerly communist countries like Romania have more product choices than ever before, they experienced significant levels of dissatisfaction after the fall of communism.[54] One reason is that these consumers have had difficulty judging quality, and as a result products do not always live up to expectations. Another is that the consumers tend to buy cheaper products in open-air markets where there is no guarantee of quality.

The Disconfirmation Paradigm

The most central concept in the study of satisfaction/dissatisfaction is disconfirmation, diagrammed in Exhibit 12.8. ***Disconfirmation*** occurs when there is a discrepancy, positive or negative, between our prior expectations and the product's actual performance (see the red arrows in the exhibit).[55] In this case, ***expectations*** are desired product/service outcomes and include "pre-consumption beliefs about overall performance, or . . . the levels or attributes possessed by a product (service)."[56] For example, you might expect a Japanese car to be reliable and fuel efficient, expectations based on advertising, inspection of the product, prior experience with similar offerings, and the experiences of other referent consumers.[57]

Satisfaction Based on Expectations ***Performance*** measures whether these expected outcomes have been achieved. Performance can either be *objective*—based on the actual performance, which is fairly constant across consumers—or *subjective*—based on individual feelings, which can vary across consumers. The objective performance of a car describes how well it runs, how economical its gas mileage is, or how often it needs repair, whereas subjective performance might include an assessment of how stylish it is or "how good it makes me feel." Research suggests that disconfirmation is based more often on subjective than objective performance.[58] Better-than-expected performance leads to a *positive disconfirmation* and to satisfaction. If performance is as good as expected, a *simple confirmation* has occurred, and this condition will also lead to satisfaction. In contrast, if performance is lower than expected, the result is *negative disconfirmation* and dissatisfaction.

Customers' evaluation of services is also susceptible to disconfirmation.[59] Here, customers have expectations related to price and service performance and to intangible characteristics of the facilities and personnel (including characteristics such as reliability, responsiveness, assurance, and empathy).[60] When *Consumer Reports* surveyed users of wireless telephone services, it found that no wireless

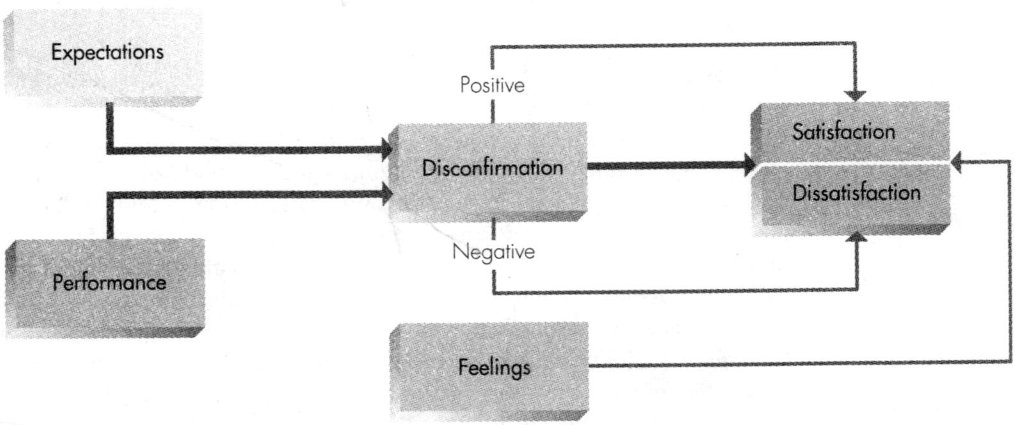

Exhibit 12.8

THE DISCONFIRMATION PARADIGM *Here the disconfirmation paradigm shows how satisfaction or dissatisfaction can occur. Using an example of a new Jim Carrey movie, the consumer enters the situation with expectations ("Jim Carrey movies are funny"). She can then go see the movie and evaluate it (performance). If she evaluates it as funnier than she expected, positive disconfirmation has occurred and she will be satisfied. If the movie is not funny, a negative disconfirmation and dissatisfaction result. Note that expectations (the likelihood of seeing the movie as funny), performance (whether the movie actually is good), and feelings (positive or negative emotions during viewing) will also affect satisfaction/dissatisfaction (independent of disconfirmation).*

carrier met consumers' expectations of static-free calls, signal availability, calls being completed, and calls not dropped. Noting that 35 percent of the customers surveyed were thinking about switching, the magazine concluded that "overall levels of satisfaction are lower than for most other services we measure."[61]

One study of Swedish consumers found that average levels of performance and expectations can predict overall levels of service satisfaction.[62] To set high expectations of its services, Ukrops' Super Markets stresses "perfectly packed groceries" (even outlining the packing process on the bag) to avoid customer discontent over broken eggs, crushed bread, and soggy ice cream.[63] One way online retailers such as Lands' End avoid dissatisfaction is by providing plenty of information, such as clearly indicating the cutoff date for ordering merchandise to be delivered by Christmas.[64] Research also finds that if consumers participate in a service expecting to achieve a goal such as weight loss, they are more satisfied when they successfully follow the service instructions and achieve the goal.[65]

Other Influences on Satisfaction Exhibit 12.8 shows that performance, expectations, and feelings can affect satisfaction, *independent* of disconfirmation (as reflected by the blue arrows).[66] To fully understand why satisfaction or dissatisfaction occurs, we must account for all these dimensions together and separately. The simple fact that a product performs well will have a positive influence on satisfaction, independent of expectations.[67] This is particularly true in the case of consumer durables, where risk and involvement are higher. Thus a consumer might not have any expectations about how a new computer may perform and be pleasantly surprised when she sees what it can do. Likewise, the poor performance of a product or service alone can lead to dissatisfaction.[68] If you buy a new DVD player and it does not work well, you could be dissatisfied—even without any prior expectations.

Positive expectations about product or service performance can actually increase the likelihood of satisfaction thanks to the process of *selective perception* by which consumers tend to see what they want to see.[69] In a now classic case, seven of ten consumers participating in a blind taste test preferred the taste of New Coke (which was similar to Pepsi) over the original Coke formula. However, expectations led many consumers to believe that they liked the old Coke better, and they refused to accept the new product.

In addition, positive and negative ***post-decision feelings*** can help to explain satisfaction or dissatisfaction judgments independent of disconfirmation.[70] If consumers feel good (or bad) while using the product or service, they are more likely to be satisfied (or dissatisfied), independent of their expectations and evaluations of performance. Consumers who are happy or content are most likely to be satisfied, followed by those who experience pleasant surprise. Dissatisfaction is most likely to strike consumers who feel angry or upset, followed by those who experience unpleasant surprise.[71] One study found that consumers' post-decision feelings were a positive function of the expectations of the consumption experience and a major influence on satisfaction.[72] Your mood also can color post-decision evaluations, particularly when the consumption experience itself is not strongly emotional.[73] For example, you might tend to like a new CD if you are in a good mood when you hear it.

Note that the disconfirmation paradigm is similar to the learning process described earlier. The difference is that satisfaction and dissatisfaction are based on a formal evaluation and feelings, whereas the learning process may not be. For example, you can test the hypothesis that rock music is loud or that Mexican food is spicy without making an assessment of like or dislike. Nevertheless, satisfaction or dissatisfaction can still be an important element of the learning process because it provides us with information. Finally, research suggests that consumer satisfaction with products need not be transaction-specific and is subject to change. Satisfaction can also be affected by social influences such as family members and may be closely related to consumers' satisfaction with their own lives.[74]

marketing IMPLICATIONS Based on the disconfirmation paradigm, marketers need to be very demanding about product or service quality and performance. Better performance leads to fulfilled expectations and satisfaction. Employees who work for Ritz-Carlton hotels confirm customers' expectations of exceptional service in a variety of ways. As one example, an employee of the Ritz-Carlton in Osaka, Japan, once plunged into the hotel swimming pool to find a contact lens lost by a hotel guest.[75] A second important implication is that the expectations created by marketers about product performance can influence the level of consumer satisfaction or dissatisfaction. Raising consumers' expectations of how well the product or service will perform can increase ratings of product performance.[76] When Pizza Hut first opened in China, it knew that pizza was unfamiliar to most Chinese consumers. The firm therefore developed tabletop cards to inform diners that pizza is a healthy food with natural ingredients, creating positive expectations.[77] Another example is the ad in Exhibit 12.9.

Exhibit 12.9
SETTING PERFORMANCE EXPECTATIONS
Ads sometimes create expectations for product performance. Babco creates strong expectations by claiming that their vises will last a lifetime, and "you'll retire before we do."

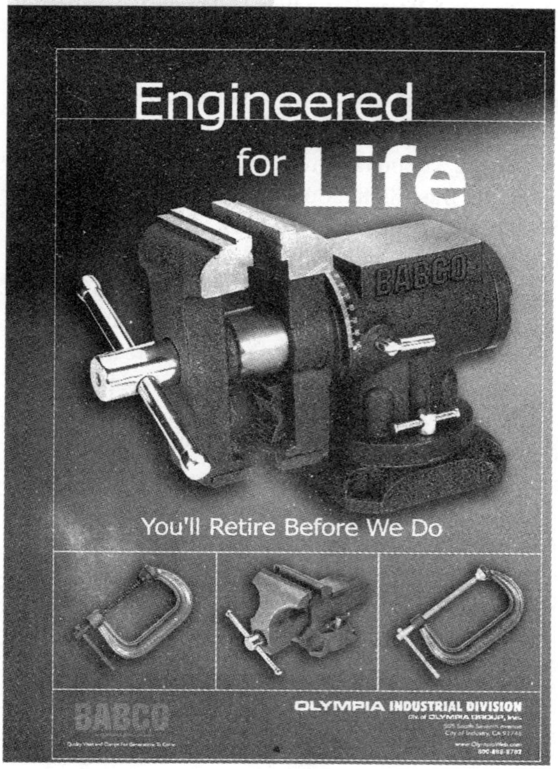

Providing consumers with a good warranty or guarantee can create positive expectations that will lead to satisfaction.[78] [4] Bharti's telecom foray especially in the process of making itself telecom major meant that a significant role was played by a successful Customer Relationship Management programme. [5] With over 38 million as a subscriber base, Bharti's biggest challenge is to keep those customers and keep them satisfied. This is ensured through a highly efficient and well established IT support that Bharti has developed over the years. According to Amrita Gangotra, vice president of Information Technology at Bharti; "For telecom, IT is like bread and butter. We believe it plays two significant roles-it works as a support system, and it can also be a business driver. Thus IT is very important to us". A complex web of WAN in place with a mix of leased lines and E1 and E3 lines, an extranet in place through which it extends different applications to its dealers and partners, a range of high-end servers from Sun and HP, millions of records being processed everyday, with storage in terabytes, and a storage area network (SAN). As far as software is concerned, some of the applications that are running on its network are billing, fraud management, revenue assurance and data warehousing. They also have some internal-facing applications like Oracle Financial and Oracle HRMS. However, in developing countries such as Turkey and Romania, many products are of poor quality and lack warranties. Moreover, consumers often do not understand how to use the products (there are few instructions), which leads to further dissatisfaction.[80]

Marketers are setting themselves up for a potential negative disconfirmation and dissatisfaction if customer expectations are too high and companies make promises they cannot keep. To illustrate, many hotels and resorts have met higher customer expectations by improving quality through renovated guest rooms and upgraded facilities. However, the noise and confusion of construction sometimes resulted in guest dissatisfaction—even prompting angry confrontations between annoyed guests and hotel staff.[81]

Marketers should make sure that customers' feelings about buying and using their offerings are as positive as possible. Helping consumers bond with the brand or organization and develop loyalty over the long term is a form of *relationship marketing*. Cheerful, accommodating employees are more likely to generate consumer satisfaction with the purchase and the experience, as shown in the Southwest Airlines example. In addition, marketers can use various promotions to increase positive feelings during consumption. The St. Paul Saints, a Minnesota minor league baseball team, gives fans a good feeling about the team by using fun promotions such as a Jerry Garcia lookalike contest and having players read to young fans in center field.[82] In Hong Kong, a very popular promotion involved trading in old Marlboro boxes for gifts such as lighters, knapsacks, and lanterns.[83] Finally, corporations and nonprofits can build relationships with consumers and contributors by encouraging active involvement and identification with the organization through communication and other marketing activities.[84]

Attribution Theory

Another theory that is useful in determining how and when dissatisfaction occurs is ***attribution theory.*** This theory was developed by social psychologists to explain how individuals find explanations or causes for effects or behavior.[85] In other words, if someone you do not know suddenly kisses you on the cheek, you would be motivated to attribute or find an explanation for this event—but how would you do this? In a marketing context, when a product or service does not fulfill needs, the consumer will attempt to find an explanation. According to attribution theory, three key factors influence the nature of this explanation:

- *Stability.* Is the cause of the event temporary or permanent?
- *Focus.* Is the problem consumer or marketer related?
- *Controllability.* Is the event under the customer's or marketer's control?

Customers are more likely to be dissatisfied if the cause is perceived to be permanent, marketer related, and not under the customer's control. Suppose you find a crack in the windshield of your new car. If you perceive that this is only a chance or temporary occurrence, beyond the control of the marketer (maybe a rock hit the window while you were driving), or your own fault, you will probably not be dissatisfied. On the other hand, if you discover that many other consumers have a similar problem—that is, the cause is more permanent, company related, and under the company's control—you will probably be dissatisfied.

Attribution theory has also found support in research on services, such as a study in which consumers were dissatisfied with a travel agent if a problem was permanent and under the firm's control.[86] Further, in a study of passengers delayed at an airport, attributions were found to explain the desire either to complain or to fly the same airline again. If consumers saw the delay as permanent and under the airline's control, they were more likely to complain and less likely to fly the airline again.[87]

Another study showed that attribution can affect satisfaction when consumers participate in producing a good or service (such as self-check-in at a hotel). Specifically, consumers who can choose whether to participate are likely to attribute at least part of any negative outcome to their own involvement, whereas they will attribute a good part of any positive outcome to their own participation.[88] Satisfaction with services also depends on whether the consumer holds the company responsible for the outcome and believes the outcome stems from a stable or unstable cause.[89]

marketing IMPLICATIONS Attribution theory can provide marketers with guidance in how to deal with potential or existing perceptions of consumer dissatisfaction. If the cause of the dissatisfaction actually is permanent, marketer related, and under the marketer's control, something must be done to correct the problem or provide the consumer with restitution. In the banking industry, which counts almost two dissatisfied consumers for every satisfied one, many banks are marketing value-added services such as financial advice, stock quotes, and bill payment in an attempt to satisfy customers.[90]

When a service failure occurs, research indicates that consumers prefer recovery efforts that correspond to the type of failure experienced.[91] In the case of a process failure such as inattentive service, restoring good service and quickly apologizing can reduce dissatisfaction and help restore satisfaction. Restitution is often provided, as well. Maruti's biggest call back of cars happened in 1995 when the pinion had a defective steel casing and resulting that most axles used to break down. The company realizing the problem quickly ordered back all the cars manufactured in the same lot number and replaced the defective pinion. Such instances illustrate companies'concerns and care for their customers.

Alternatively, when consumers perceive that the cause of the dissatisfaction is permanent, marketer related, and under the firm's control when in fact it is not, marketers need to correct these misperceptions. Providing consumers with logical explanations for failure, especially if it was not the company's fault, or providing some form of compensation such as a gift or refund can often reduce feelings of dissatisfaction.[92] For example, Pepsi once faced a serious potential consumer dissatisfaction problem when a syringe was reportedly found in a can of Diet Pepsi. Once the company learned that the problem was temporary and not under its control (a consumer had tampered with the can), management quickly launched a media campaign to correct any consumer misperceptions by explaining that the company and its employees had nothing to do with the incident.

Equity Theory

Equity theory is another approach developed by psychologists that is useful in understanding consumer satisfaction and dissatisfaction. This theory focuses on the nature of exchanges between individuals and their perceptions of these exchanges. In marketing, it has been applied to examining the exchange between a buyer and a seller or a more general institution.[93]

According to equity theory, consumers form perceptions of their own inputs and outputs into a particular exchange. They then compare these perceptions with their perceptions of the salesperson, dealer, or company. For example, when buying a stereo, a consumer's inputs might include information search, decision-making effort, psychological anxiety, and money. The output would be a satisfactory sound system. Seller inputs might include a quality product, selling effort, and a financing plan; a fair profit might constitute the output.

For equity to occur, the buyer must perceive ***fairness in the exchange.*** Thus the stereo buyer might perceive a fair exchange if he or she purchased a desirable system at a fair price. Satisfaction is even higher if consumers perceive that they have gotten a bargain.[94] If the consumer perceives inequity in the exchange—for example, the salesperson did not pay enough attention to the consumer or the deal was not fair—he or she will be dissatisfied. For equity to occur, a perception of fairness must exist on both sides of the exchange, with the consumer perceiving that the seller is also being dealt with fairly. Nevertheless, fairness perceptions tend to be self-centered—that is, biased more toward buyer outcomes and seller inputs than to buyer inputs and seller outcomes.[95]

Moreover, research shows that consumers judge the equity of the payment exchanged for service usage by asking themselves, "Am I using this service enough, given what I pay for it?" They will perceive the exchange as more equitable when they have high expectations of service usage levels at first or when the service performance exceeds their normative expectations. And when they perceive the price/usage exchange to be more equitable, they will be more satisfied.[96]

The principles of equity theory complement the disconfirmation paradigm in that equity theory specifies another way dissatisfaction can occur. In other words, both types of processes can be in operation at the same time. However, whereas the disconfirmation paradigm focuses on expectations and performance, equity theory is concerned with more general interpersonal norms governing what is wrong or right and with a consideration of the outcomes for both the seller and buyer, not just the buyer.

marketing IMPLICATIONS

Equity theory highlights the importance of fairness in marketing exchanges. As long as consumers perceive that their inputs and outputs are equitable in relation to those of the seller, they will be satisfied. This is true in terms of the offering itself as well as interactions with the seller's employees when resolving a complaint. In other words, consumers who perceive that they have been treated fairly in the complaint process will be more satisfied, more likely to buy again, and more likely to make positive word-of-mouth comments.[97] However, if an inequity exists, consumers will be dissatisfied. In fact, the Internet is among the top 10 categories of businesses about which consumers complain—especially registering complaints about products ordered online.[98] In Turkey, retail service is generally very poor, leading to dissatisfaction. Consumers often have to wait a long time for service, and after-sale service is frequently bad.[99]

The clear implication is that marketers must work toward providing fair exchanges. This is not always easy because consumers' perceptions of fairness tend to be biased toward themselves. One area in which marketers can most directly affect equity perceptions is the salesperson-customer interaction. In these exchanges, salespeople must make every effort to ensure that their inputs match customer inputs by listening to consumer needs, answering questions, and trying to provide a good deal. The same principles also apply to Internet transactions, where sites like Amazon.com emphasize customer service for a fair exchange. Fairness can also be stressed in advertising messages (see Exhibit 12.10).

Promotions can also increase perceptions of fairness in an exchange. Providing consumers with a lower price or with a free item of merchandise can make con-

Exhibit 12.10
INCREASING PERCEPTIONS OF FAIRNESS
Companies like Hindustan Unilever Ltd.'s foray in the rural heartlands of India with Project Shakti reinforces the companies' perception of fairness, making consumers feel the honest and integrative approach in business operations

sumers feel that they are getting more out of the exchange. This is why many cosmetics companies give consumers free products such as tote bags with a purchase. In addition, companies must ensure that outputs are satisfactory by providing a quality product at a fair price. Subhiksha and Big Bazaar's foray in offering low cost grocery in smaller and bulk purchase respectively have meant that consumers come flocking because of such advantages.

Responses to Dissatisfaction

Marketers must understand the nature of consumers' responses to dissatisfaction because a variety of mostly negative consequences can result. Specifically, dissatisfied consumers can decide to (1) take no action, (2) discontinue purchasing the product or service, (3) complain to the company or to a third party and perhaps return the item, or (4) engage in negative word-of-mouth communication.[100] The last two behaviors in particular have been of great interest to consumer researchers.

Complaints

Surprisingly, the majority of dissatisfied consumers do not complain.[101] Nevertheless, even a few consumer complaints can indicate marketing-related problems that need attention. When consumers complain, they can voice their dissatisfaction to a manufacturer, the retail outlet, regulatory agencies, or the media. Sometimes consumers can take even more drastic action by seeking formal redress through legal means or from governmental regulatory bodies. Complaints can be related to a variety of matters, such as the offering, the store, salespeople, or related services. Many consumers have been complaining about problems with cellular phone service, including confusing and misleading ads, complicated fees, and poor service.[102] Thus marketers need to focus on when complaints are likely to occur and what types of people tend to complain.

When Complaints Are Likely to Occur Complaining is more likely to occur when motivation, ability, and opportunity are high. Complaining is also more likely as the level of dissatisfaction or the severity of the problem becomes greater.[103] In equity theory terms, the unfairness of the exchange is higher and the consumer is more motivated to act.[104] Yet, the severity of the dissatisfaction alone does not explain complaining behavior. In particular, consumers are less likely to act if they perceive that complaining will take a lot of time and effort, their chances of benefiting from it are low, and the product or service is insignificant.[105]

The more the blame or attribution for dissatisfaction is placed on someone else, particularly on the company or society in general, the greater the motivation and likelihood of complaining.[106] Thus consumers are more likely to complain when they feel removed from the problem—that is, when the perceived cause is permanent, marketer related, and volitional.[107] If dissatisfaction is so strong that complainers want "revenge" against the company, they will even resort to a suboptimal alternative, such as switching to a more costly competing product. In part, this desire for revenge depends on how fairly or how rudely complainers believe they have been treated by the company.[108]

You might expect that consumers who are aggressive and self-confident would be more likely to complain than those who are not[109] or that consumers with more experience or knowledge ability about how to complain might be more likely to do so than their less savvy counterparts. Neither idea has been strongly supported by evidence, although findings suggest experience may influence the likelihood of complaints. Interestingly, consumers are more likely to complain when they have the time and formal channels of communication. Lack of opportunity, methods, and knowledge about how to complain has been a major problem in many developing countries.[110] However, the opportunity to complain is now influencing the way businesses operate.

Other studies have examined whether demographic and socioeconomic factors are related to complaining behavior. Although the findings have been somewhat mixed, there are several slight tendencies. Complainers tend to be younger, have higher income levels, and be less brand loyal than noncomplainers.[111] Researchers have also found that complaining behavior may vary by ethnic group. For example, Mexican American consumers are more likely to complain about certain aspects of goods and services such as delay or nondelivery than are other consumers.[112] Puerto Rican consumers are less likely to complain than mainland U.S. consumers because of cultural norms and values.[113]

Complainer Types Finally, research has suggested that there are different types of complainers.[114] *Passives* are the least likely to complain. *Voicers* are likely to complain directly to the retailer or service provider. *Irates* are angry consumers who are most likely to engage in negative word of mouth, stop patronage, and complain to the provider but not to a third party such as the media or government. *Activists* engage heavily in all types of complaining, including to a third party. Interestingly, some companies feel that listening to the "customer from hell" actually improves their business because these critics often provide good suggestions.[115] For instance, Holiday Inn learned from surveys that customers were unhappy with the design of the shower, which was too small and tended to collect dirt. In redesigning its hotel bathrooms, the company paid very close attention to everything from the angle of the shower head to elbow room to grout (which captures dirt).[116]

marketing IMPLICATIONS

Although a large percentage of consumers do not complain, it is still in the marketer's best interests to be responsive when they do. In one study, 90 percent of managers said satisfying the customer was the primary reason for responding to complaints.[117] Responding in writing, especially with a coupon or gift, can have a noticeable impact on consumer evaluations.[118] Speedy response is important: 57 percent of the consumers in one survey said that how quickly a website responds to e-mail influences their decision to buy from that site in the future.[119] Yet, 45 percent of the big companies included in a recent study did not tell consumers how quickly they could expect a response to an e-mailed complaint or inquiry.[120] Clearly, consumers will be more satisfied and more likely to buy again if they get a speedy response, especially if it involves money reimbursement or a fair exchange/refund policy. Speedy response is valued in many cultures: Research confirms that it leads to higher customer satisfaction in Singapore, for instance.[121]

Note that dissatisfied consumers who have been treated fairly can become even more loyal in the future. For example, a consumer who set up a complaint website to publicize his problems with a Sony electronics product converted the site to an enthusiastic fan site after the company contacted him to resolve the problem.[122] However, if consumers experience more than one problem with a company, their satisfaction and repurchase intent will drop, even if the problems are quickly resolved. In fact, they will rate the second problem as even more severe than the first and are more likely to see a pattern in which the company is to blame.[123] Thus companies not only need an efficient and responsive mechanism for handling problems, but they must make changes to avoid similar lapses in the future.

Positive disconfirmation of warranty and service expectations—a response that is better than expected—can result in satisfaction with complaint resolution.[124] [6] Monsoon in India reiterates images of faulty and broken down roads, water clogging, open sewers and overall a "go-away soon" psyche haunts most of us. Goa, a state thriving on tourism, witnesses a surge, particularly in winters. But of late the state has been promoting the concept of "Goa in the rains". Depending mainly on tourism, the state has tapped the monsoon advantage. Almost all hotels and the state-run Tourism Development Corporation have been offering the `monsoon package' at almost half the seasonal price. As a result, most of the popular beaches here were packed with tourists despite heavy rains, though the Mumbai deluge had an impact on the inflow this year. Note that marketers and customers still experience some problems in developing countries, where service is generally poor and warranties are nonexistent.[126]

Sometimes it is in the company's best interest to encourage complaining because dissatisfied consumers who do not complain are more likely to stop buying.[127] But when companies are too responsive to complaints—that is, too eager to please—customers may actually be more likely to complain, even when a complaint is not justified, because they perceive a greater likelihood of compensation.[128] In particular, consumers are more likely to complain when the cause is ambiguous and the party responsible for the problem is not obvious. Still, by encouraging complaints when justified and actively managing customer problems, the company can retain valued consumers.

Responding by Negative Word of Mouth

When consumers are unhappy with a product or service, they are often motivated to tell others in order to relieve their frustration and to convince others not to purchase the product or do business with the company. ***Negative word-of-mouth communication*** is more likely to occur when the problem is severe, consumers are not happy with the company's responsiveness, and consumers perceive that the company is at fault.[129]

Negative word of mouth can be particularly troublesome because it tends to be highly persuasive and very vivid (and therefore easily remembered), and consumers place great emphasis on it when making decisions.[130] Furthermore, it is more damaging than complaints because consumers are communicating with other people who might stop (or never begin) doing business with the company. [7] The Pesticide problem in Pepsi and Coke during 2006 and its impact on the Asia Pacific region was quite talked about, especially with Sunita Narain's claim through her NGO, CSE after the results of the study, which sampled 57 finished drink products from 25 different Indian Coca-Cola and PepsiCo plants."Clearly unacceptable as we know that pesticides are tiny toxins and impact our bodies over time," CSE Director Sunita Narain said when the group's findings were released. The impact of the campaign in the Asia Pacific region had a far reaching impact and it took some time for the beverage giants to restore normalcy.

marketing IMPLICATIONS Marketers need to be responsive to negative word of mouth. Most important, they should make an effort to identify the reason for or source of the difficulty so they can take steps to rectify or eliminate the particular problem with restitution or marketing communications. In the above mentioned pesticide issue affecting Pepsi and Coke, a slew of Public Relations exercises by the companies through editorials, advertorials and advertisements. [8] They also tried to attack the CSE's findings in advertorials published in Indian newspapers. And Coca-Cola had posted background information on its testing and quality procedures done at labs in Hyderabad, California, and London for its Indian drink lineup on the Web site of its Indian subsidiary. It had even offered to take Indian customers on guided tours of its processing plants as a goodwill measure.

Is Customer Satisfaction Enough?

Although customer satisfaction should be an extremely important goal for any firm, some companies have questioned whether satisfaction alone is enough to keep customers loyal. As evidence they point out that 65 to 85 percent of customers who defect to competitors' brands say they were either satisfied or very satisfied with the product or service they left.[133] Other studies have found a low correlation between satisfaction and repurchase.[134] Thus customers may need to be "extremely satisfied" or need a stronger reason to stay with a brand or company.[135] Moreover, loyalty depends on whether the product is competitively superior, consumers find its superiority desirable and subject to adoration, the product can be embedded in a social network, and the company works to maintain the network.[136]

A key goal for any marketer should therefore be ***customer retention,*** the practice of working to satisfy customers with the intention of developing long-term relationships with them. A customer-retention strategy attempts to build customer commitment and loyalty by continually paying close attention to all aspects of customer interaction, especially after-sales service. A good example of this strategy is seen in Exhibit 12.11. This approach not only strengthens relationships with customers, but also increases profits. Specifically, profits can be increased through repeat sales, reduced costs, and referrals.[137]

Exhibit 12.11

ENCOURAGING SATISFACTION AND LOYALTY

Providing strong guarantees is one way to increase customer satisfaction and loyalty. A good example is this guarantee from L.L.Bean.

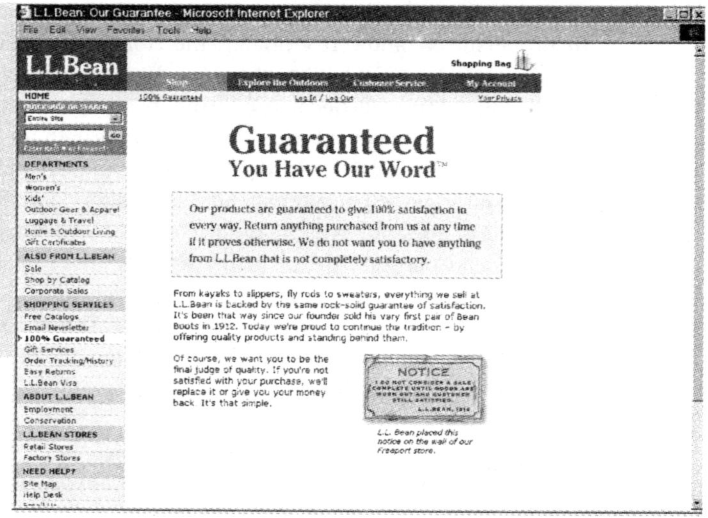

marketing IMPLICATIONS

Given the cost of acquiring new customers and the potential profit in repeat purchasing, companies should take steps such as the following to retain their customers:[138]

- *Care about customers.* Two-thirds of consumers defect because they believe that the company doesn't care about them. Thus, a little caring can go a long way. The local grocery shop or the chemist shop or even the cigarette and Pan shop establishes connection with their customers, by either remembering their product (brand) preferences, or through their names and at times even their cryptic codes like "Mataji ka Paan" or "Sharmaji ka brand" et al. Such connectivity helps establish a relationship with the customer, because he or she feels the retailer is making a genuine effort to understand and relate to him or her.
- *Remember customers between sales.* Companies can contact consumers to make sure they are not having any problems with the offering or to acknowledge special occasions such as birthdays and anniversaries. Most restaurants like the House of Ming in Taj Mahal Hotel, Delhi maintain their database of customers. For any new product or event launch at the restaurant, the regular customers are sent mailers or invites. Chef Lo Ka Yan's return to the House of Ming in 1998 was a "back to home" theme showcased by the restaurant, because he set up the restaurant when it had started and then had gone off to Europe. So the Chef's return was targeted to all the patrons who longed for the Chef and his cuisines. The gesture went well with the customers, who received the mailers and established the standing of the restaurant.
- *Build trusting relationships.* Provide consumers with expertise and high-quality products and services. Maruti Service Masters (MSM) keeps a track of its customers who come to their service stations located in Delhi and Chennai. After the service is over, MSM regularly updates the customers on the mileage covered and sends reminders on when the next service will fall due on the basis of approximation done for the total distance the vehicle would have covered. Such tracking helps the customers to get their vehicles serviced on time and also makes them feel special, that someone is concerned about their vehicle.
- *Monitor the service-delivery process.* Consumers need the company most when an offering requires service or repairs. Companies should make every effort to respond and show concern in these situations. Being a busy sector, the Delhi-Mum-

bai air sector has a number of flights operating in a given day. Low cost and full service aircrafts operate on the sector, invariably creating air traffic congestion. The civil aviation department has now introduced a differential airport charges for peak and off-peak hours dissuading the low cost airlines from operating during peak hours, catering to the business.

- *Provide extra effort.* Companies that go above and beyond the call of duty are more likely to build lasting customer relationships than companies that take the minimalist approach. Dell, for instance, set up a dedicated service center in China, one of its fastest-growing markets, to identify potential problems and offer technical support so local customers have their systems "back up and running as quickly as possible," says a Dell vice president.[143]

Disposition

Another important process at the postacquisition stage is disposition.

The Many Ways We Can Dispose of Something

At the most basic level, *disposition* is the throwing away of meaningless or used-up items without any thought. This process occurs on a regular basis for most consumers. Recent studies, however, suggest that disposition is a much richer and more detailed process than researchers once thought.[144]

Disposition is an action we take toward possessions. Although we tend to think of possessions as physical things, they can be defined much more broadly as anything that reflects an extension of the self, including one's body and body parts, other persons, pets, places, services, time periods, and events. For example, you could end a relationship, give a friend an idea, donate an organ, abandon an unhealthy lifestyle, use up all your leisure time, or discontinue a health club membership. Thus the study of disposition relates to all these types of possessions.

Many options are available when a consumer decides that a possession is no longer of immediate use. As outlined in Exhibit 12.12, the item can be (1) given away, which can include passing it along or donating it with or without a tax deduction; (2) traded to someone else or traded in as part of the purchase of a new item; (3) recycled; (4) sold; (5) used up; (6) thrown away; (7) abandoned, which means discarding it in a socially unacceptable way; or (8) destroyed.[145] Note that disposition can be *temporary* (loaning or renting the item) or *involuntary* (losing or destroying the item).[146] Here we will focus on permanent, voluntary disposition.

Consumers often have logical and reasonable motives behind their disposition actions.[147] For example, people sell things to earn an economic return and come out ahead. In contrast, they donate something without a tax deduction and pass an item along out of desire to help someone, as well as not wanting the product to go to waste. Situational and product-related factors can also affect disposition options.[148] For example, when consumers have limited time or storage space, they may be more likely to dispose of a possession by throwing it away, giving it away, or abandoning it. Consumers disposing of a possession of high value are likely to sell it or give it to someone special rather than throw it away. In general, the frequency of different disposition behaviors varies by product category.

Research has examined how consumers dispose of unwanted gifts.[149] They can be laterally recycled (swapped, sold, or passed on to someone else), destroyed, or returned. Destruction is a way of getting revenge against the giver but is usually more of a fantasy than a real action. Retailers need to be aware that returning a gift to a

Exhibit 12.12
DISPOSITION OPTIONS

Disposition often means throwing things away; however, there are many additional ways of disposing of an offering (e.g., give away, trade, recycle). In addition, disposition can involve one person (personal focus), two or more people (interpersonal focus), or society in general (societal focus).

A TAXONOMY OF VOLUNTARY DISPOSITION

Methods	Personal Focus	Interpersonal Focus	Societal Focus
Give away: usually to someone who can use it.	Necessarily requires another person as receiver.	Donate body organs; give clothes to the needy; give a baby up for adoption; give an idea to a friend.	Give land to new settlers; give surplus food to the poor; give military advice to an ally.
Trade or exchange it for something else.	Skin grafts; trade sleep time for work time; trade work time for shopping for bargains.	Trade a car; trade stock; barter; exchange ideas with a colleague; switch boyfriends. Swap meets.	Trade tanks for oil; exchange effluent water for a golf course.
Recycle: convert it to something else.	Convert barn beams to paneling; make a quilt of scraps; turkey sandwiches after Thanksgiving.	Recycle newspapers; recycle aluminum cans; manufacturers' recycling of defective parts.	Recycle waste water; convert a slum to a model neighborhood; recycle war ruins as national monuments.
Sell: convert it to money.	Necessarily requires another person as buyer; prostitution; sell one's artwork; sell ideas.	Businesses; sell blood; sell ideals to attain political goals.	Sell wheat; sell weapons; sell land.
Use up: consumption is equivalent to disposal.	Eat food; drive car using up the fuel; shoot ammo; spend one's time; burn wood.	Use employee's time and energy; use someone else's money; use the neighbor's gas.	Use natural fuels or electricity; use a nation's productive capacity; use people as soldiers in wars.
Throw away: discard in a socially acceptable manner.	Put things in the trash; flush the toilet; use a garbage disposal; discard an idea.	Neighborhood cleanup; divorce; end a relationship; resign or retire from a job.	Dump garbage in the oceans; bury nuclear waste.
Abandon: discard in a socially unacceptable manner.	Abandon car on the roadside; abandon morals; abandon an unhealthy, unhappy lifestyle.	Abandon one's child or family; abandon a pet on someone's doorstep; abandon another's trust.	Abandon Vietnam; abandon the Shah of Iran; abandon old satellites in space; abandon the poor.
Destroy: physically damage with intent.	Tear up personal mail; commit suicide; burn house down; shred old pictures.	Raze a building; murder; euthanasia; cremation; abort a child; commit arson.	Conduct war; genocide; execute prisoner; carry out a revolution; burn a flag.

Source: Melissa Martin Young and Melanie Wallendorf, "Ashes to Ashes, Dust to Dust: Conceptualizing Consumer Disposition of Possessions," in Proceedings, Marketing Educators' Conference, (Chicago, American Marketing Association, 1989), pp. 33–39. Reprinted by permission.

store can be a negative emotional experience for consumers. Disposition can involve more than one individual, as when consumers give old clothes to someone, sell a car, or participate in a neighborhood cleanup, or it can consist of activities of a collective or societal nature, such as dumping garbage in the ocean or recycling waste water.[150]

By combining the personal, interpersonal, and societal arenas with the eight types of disposition identified in Exhibit 12.12, we can see that disposition encompasses a wide variety of behaviors. Consumer researchers have only begun to explore these options, focusing mostly on personal disposition. Much work is needed to achieve a more thorough understanding of disposition.

Disposing of Meaningful Objects

Although disposition often means simply getting rid of unwanted, meaningless, or used-up possessions, the process is more involved for certain significant items. Possessions can sometimes be important reflections of the self that are infused with significant symbolic meaning.[151] They define who we are, and they catalog our personal history.[152] In these situations, disposition involves two processes: physical detachment and emotional detachment.

We most often think of disposition in terms of ***physical detachment,*** the process by which the item is physically transferred to another person or location. However, ***emotional detachment*** is a more detailed, lengthy, and sometimes painful process. Often, consumers remain emotionally attached to possessions long after they have become physically detached. For example, it may take a person years to come to grips with selling a valued house or car. Selling of jewellery or sending the child to a hostel are similar examples that sometimes result in grief and mourning. In fact, some have a difficult time disposing of even not-so-valued possessions—as evidenced by overstuffed basements, closets, and garages. Even when an item can be traded in for a discount on a new replacement, emotional attachment enhances the value consumers perceive in the old item, complicating the disposition and purchase decision.

The disposition process can be particularly important during periods of role transition, such as puberty, graduation, and marriage.[154] In these instances consumers dispose of possessions that are symbols of old roles. Upon getting married, for example, many people dispose of items that signify old relationships, such as pictures, jewelry, and gifts. The disposition of shared possessions is a critical process during divorce. Two types of such disposition have been identified: *disposition to break free,* in which the goal is to free oneself from the former relationship, and *disposition to hold on,* in which the intent is to cling to possessions with the hope that the relationship can be repaired.[155]

The more common pattern is breaking free. Sometimes the partners attempt to be fair and distribute possessions evenly. One of the partners—usually the initiator of the divorce—will give most of the possessions to the other partner just to relieve guilty feelings. In still other situations, the division of assets can involve a lot of conflict and bitter disagreements as the former partners are motivated by rivalry, punishment, and a desire to cling to power in the relationship.[156]

Consumers also specify how their possessions will be distributed upon death. This process can include giving away valued items to important family members, other individuals, and organizations such as charities and schools, as well as distributing monetary wealth through a will. The subject of intergenerational transfers and inheritance has been of great interest to social scientists.[157]

marketing IMPLICATIONS Marketers need to understand disposition for several reasons. First, disposition decisions often influence later acquisition decisions because a consumer who decides to dispose of a particular item often acquires another. Someone who must buy a new refrigerator because the old one stopped working may decide that the old one did not last long enough and eliminate this brand from future consideration. By understanding why consumers dispose of older brands, particularly when a problem has occurred, marketers may be able to improve their offerings for the future.

Second, marketers have become interested in the way that consumers trade, sell, or give away items for secondhand purchases. Used-merchandise retail outlets and websites, flea markets, garage sales, and classified ads in newspapers and online are becoming more widespread as consumers increasingly choose to sell or trade old items rather than throw them away. The number of used-merchandise retailers has grown at a rate ten times that of conventional retailers.[158] Flea markets are quite popular, not only because they are a different way of disposing of and acquiring products but also because of the hedonistic experience they provide.[159] Consumers enjoy the process of searching and bargaining for items, the festive atmosphere—almost like a medieval fair—and the social opportunities. This is also true of consumers who use sites such as eBay and Craigslist to search for and buy goods.

Third, product disposition behaviors can sometimes have a major impact on society in general. For example, if product life can be extended by getting consumers to trade or resell items, waste and resource depletion could be reduced. As another example, the state of Texas was having a tremendous problem with litter on its highways and streets. The increasing number of private vehicles on the roads of Delhi also means pressure on the infrastructure and the traffic. Congestions, violated traffic rules and road rage are the order of the day. Delhi Traffic Police's attempt to penalize the violators seems to be of no avail as penalty amount is abysmally low. However, the recent drive as per the dictate of the Delhi High Court for Traffic violators to fall in line, and a higher penalty amount along with the Delhi Traffic Police discipline vigil helped get the notorious Delhi traffic in place. [9]According to the traffic police's official announcement, the special traffic police teams deployed across the Capital have prosecuted 4,571 violators, collected Rs.17,64,100 in fines, punched 1,333 driving licenses, and impounded 220 vehicles.

Fourth, by examining broad disposition patterns, we can gain insights that might not otherwise have been possible. To illustrate, one study examined household garbage to identify group differences in food consumption.[160] Researchers found that region of the country accounted most strongly for differences in consumption patterns, followed by cultural status. For instance, people from the southern India consume more coffee than people in up north, especially filter coffee. The key point is that trace analysis may yield more accurate information than self-report questionnaires.

Finally, disposition patterns can sometimes serve as economic indicators.[161] The earlier culture and norm of the society about product disposition has drastically changed, especially in the urban metropolis. With rising economic prosperity and favorable GDP indicators, disposals have got affected. The practice of stocking old clothes and exchanging it for utensils have been done away with. Now old clothes are given away to the menial staff employed at home.

Recycling

We live in an age in which natural resources are rapidly being depleted. Because we can no longer squander resources, the study of disposition behaviors can provide valuable insights for the development of recycling programs. In light of this fact, a

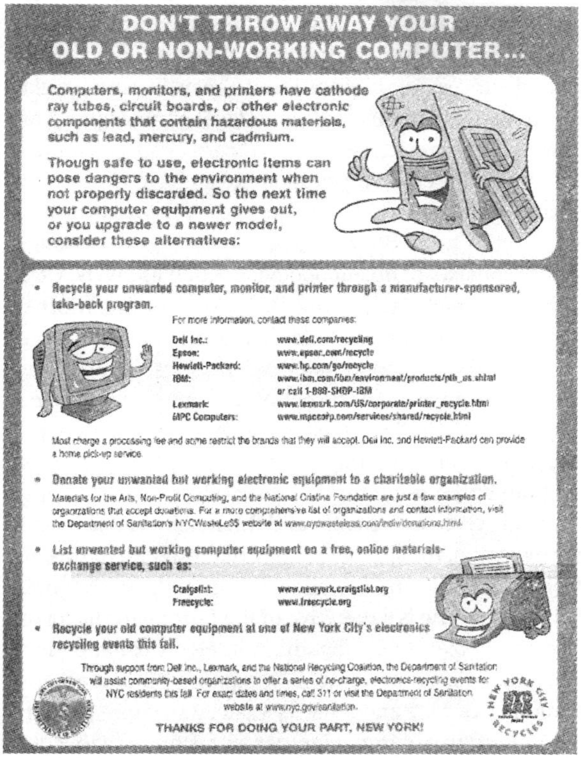

Exhibit 12.13
ENCOURAGING RECYCLING
Here is an ad that encourages consumers to think about recycling more.

number of researchers have been interested in examining factors that relate to recycling.[162] Attitudes toward specific actions such as saving bottles and separating papers have shown promise as predictors of recycling behavior.[163] In addition, research suggests that attitudes toward recycling influence waste recycling and recycling shopping behaviors.[164] Unfortunately, variables such as demographics and psychographics are not strong predictors. What appears to be most useful in understanding consumer recycling is the motivation, ability, and opportunity to recycle.

Motivation to Recycle Consumers are more likely to recycle when they perceive that the benefits outweigh the costs, including money, time, and effort.[165] Immediate benefits or goals include avoiding filling up landfills, reducing waste, reusing materials, and saving the environment. Higher-order goals are to promote health and avoid sickness, achieve life-sustaining ends, and provide for future generations.[166] Note that these benefits are likely to vary across segments. For example, focusing on environmental effects may have little meaning in low-income neighborhoods where family members are being killed in the streets.[167] Also, consumers who perceive that their efforts will have an impact are more motivated to recycle than consumers who do not.[168] Having a clean, convenient place to bring recyclable materials improves consumer motivation, as well. [10] Delhi is a particularly interesting case in point, because it has one of the biggest and most vibrant recycling bases in the country. The wastepickers, of whom there are 100,000 in Delhi, are therefore, the base of a large recycling pyramid, handling between 9 to 15 percent of the solid waste generated in the city. In Delhi, which generates over 7000 MT waste daily, this comes to a substantial amount. There is a range of materials which are picked up and recycled by this sector. These include plastics, paper, glass, and metals. Studies estimate that the amounts this informal labour forces saves the three Municipalities is a minimum of Rs. 6 lakhs (approx.. 12,000 USD) daily. It is also seen that a piece of plastic, for example, increases 700% in value along the recycling chain, before it is even reprocessed. Chintan, an NGO, is trying to organize waste pickers, enabling them to access information, knowledge, assistance from them and each other in times of need and above all, to see themselves as they are : people who are amongst the most important pulses of the city.

Ability to Recycle Consumers who know how to recycle are more likely to do so than those who do not.[170] One study of German consumers found that a lack of knowledge led to incorrect disposal and therefore less recycling.[171] Consumers must also possess general knowledge about the positive environmental effects of recycling and must remember to recycle as part of their daily routine.

Opportunity to Recycle If separating, storing, and removing recyclable materials is difficult or inconvenient, consumers will usually avoid doing so. A program in Germany that offered color-coded, large plastic containers on wheels for recyclable materials was quite popular and successful. In addition, to recycle on a regular basis, consumers must break old waste disposal habits and develop new ones. Providing easy-to-use containers also helps consumers in this regard. Also, consumers who buy products such as soft drinks for consumption on the go have less opportunity to recycle the empty bottles and cans.[172] But even one-time-use products can be conveniently recycled. [11] With the IT Boom in India, recycling e-waste is a huge concern. E-waste generally consists of obsolete devices such as DVDs, CDs, floppies, tapes and electronic components including chips, processors, mother boards, printed circuit boards and industrial electronics. Experts say e-waste contains many hazardous substances like heavy metals, PVC plastics, brominated flame retardants. While the density of e-waste in the country is on the rise, at present there is no e-waste recycling plant in India. Recently the representatives of the National Association of Software and Service Companies and the Manufacturers' Association of Information Technology have committed themselves to establishing a nodal agency that will develop a socially acceptable and financially viable model for electronic waste (e-waste) recycling. An agreement has been signed to this effect to promote the "Waste from Electronic and Electrical Equipment (WEEE) programme" in the city. The WEEE programme is a directive of the European Union on the restriction of the use of certain hazardous substances in electrical and electronic equipment and ensures their proper recycling. [12] By signing the agreement, both associations declared to reduce, recycle and reuse e-waste. Bangalore, with its 1,322 software companies and 36 hardware companies, generates more than 8,000 tonnes of e-waste each year.

marketing IMPLICATIONS Clearly, marketers can facilitate recycling by increasing consumers' MAO to recycle (see Exhibit 12.13). Special incentives such as lotteries and contests can increase motivation. Messages that focus on the negative consequences of not recycling and that are conveyed by personal acquaintances appear to be most effective in increasing motivation.[174] [13] For example the recent efforts of the The Delhi Metro Rail Corporation and the National Cadet Corps to launch a joint campaign involving NCC cadets guiding commuters at busy Metro stations, has been quite effective. These cadets encourage commuters to stand in queue and help women, disabled and elderly passengers and also distribute handouts on Metro etiquette. Neighborhood block leaders can also be effective. The only drawback is that all these techniques must be reintroduced periodically because their effects are usually temporary.

Marketers can increase consumers' ability to recycle by teaching them how to recycle through personal communications from community or block leaders, flyers, or public service announcements. These messages must be personally relevant and easy to remember. Also, offering tags to place on the refrigerator door can remind consumers to recycle.[176] By providing separate containers so recyclable items can be easily put out and collected along with the trash, recycling programs can increase the opportunity to recycle. [14] One such instance of the Delhi government's recent drive to separate the garbage into different disposal bins is a novel approach. The blue and the green bin represent the dry and wet garbage disposal boxes respectively.

Finally, making products and packaging as environmentally friendly as possible—and promoting the benefits—can help marketers attract consumers who like the convenience of *not* having to recycle. As the Indian industry of food packaging board grows, a substantial part of this growth can be attributed to increasing sales of elemental chlorine free (ECF) paper. ECF uses a pulping process that eliminates chlorine and hypochemicals in the manufacturing system, producing healthier food grade, non-contaminating and odour-free packaging material. Companies were using ECF material for pharma exports of domestic products as well. [15] One of the challenges for companies like ITC was to get the sweets, or 'mishti' industry in the country to switch to ECF board from the recycled packaging boards being used at present. With almost 50 per cent of India's 'mishti' industry being based in eastern India, ITC has launched a campaign in Kolkata. Last year, 1500 shops were tapped in Kolkata and 100 of these agreed to use ECF as packaging material for their products.

Summary

Consumers sometimes develop post-decision dissonance—a feeling of anxiety or uncertainty regarding a purchasing decision after it has been made. They are motivated to reduce this dissonance by collecting additional information that is used to upgrade the chosen alternative and downgrade the rejected ones. On occasion, they may feel regret when they perceive an unfavorable comparison between the performance of the chosen option and the performance of the unchosen options. In turn, feelings of regret can directly influence the consumer's intention to buy the same product in the future.

Consumers can learn from experience through a process of hypothesis testing in which they try to confirm or disprove expectations by actually engaging in acquisition, consumption, or disposition. This process is influenced by motivation, prior knowledge (familiarity), ambiguity of information, and two types of biases: the confirmation bias and overconfidence. Marketers can use several strategies to influence the learning process, depending on whether the offering is a top dog or an underdog.

Satisfaction is both a subjective feeling and an objective evaluation that a decision has fulfilled a need or goal. Dissatisfaction occurs when consumers have negative feelings and believe that their goals or needs have not been fulfilled. Marketers need to keep consumers satisfied because losing customers can be very costly in the long run. Three major theories of satisfaction/dissatisfaction are (1) the disconfirmation paradigm (that satisfaction occurs when performance disconfirms expectations in a positive way and that dissatisfaction results from negative disconfirmations); (2) attribution theory (that dissatisfaction results when the cause of a problem is determined to be permanent, marketer related, and under marketer control); and (3) equity theory (that satisfaction results when the buyer perceives fairness in the exchange). Two major ways that consumers can respond to dissatisfaction are by complaining and by engaging in negative word of mouth.

Finally, consumers can dispose of products in a variety of ways. This process has important implications for marketing strategy and an understanding of consumer behavior. Recycling, which is one form of disposition, depends on consumers' motivation, ability, and opportunity to act.

Questions for Review and Discussion

1. How does post-decision dissonance differ from post-decision regret, and what effect do these have on consumers?
2. Describe how consumers acquire information about goods and services by learning from experience with them.
3. Describe the strategies for dealing with consumer learning that can be used by companies with high market share, and contrast these with strategies used by companies with low market share.
4. How do expectations and performance contribute to disconfirmation?
5. Define attribution theory and equity theory, and explain how they relate to dissatisfaction.

6. Why is complaining important to marketers and how should complaints be handled?
7. In what eight ways can consumers dispose of something?
8. Why is it important for marketers to consider both physical and emotional detachment aspects of consumer disposition?

Exercises

1. Pick five durable or nondurable product or service categories. Develop a set of questions to ask consumers to tell (1) how satisfied they are with the offerings in each category, (2) recall any instances when they have been dissatisfied in the past, (3) indicate how they dealt with the situation when they were dissatisfied, and (4) identify how they felt about the company or retailer response (if any). Administer this questionnaire to at least 15 consumers. Based on the data, try to answer the following questions:
   a. With what types of products or services are consumers most satisfied? Why do you think this is the case?
   b. For what products or services are consumers most dissatisfied? Why do you think this is the case?
   c. What are the most common responses to dissatisfaction?
   d. How well have the companies handled dissatisfaction?
2. Interview two marketing professionals (from different companies), either by phone or in person. Ask them to describe in detail (1) how important satisfaction/dissatisfaction is to their business, (2) how they try to generate satisfaction, and (3) what kinds of experiences they have had with dissatisfied consumers and how they handled these problems. Summarize your findings for each topic.
3. Pick five durable and five nondurable products. Develop a set of questions to determine how consumers disposed of each product the last time they needed to do so. Administer the questionnaire to at least ten consumers. Summarize the responses, and answer the following questions:
   a. For each product category, which are the most frequently used methods of disposition?
   b. Which product categories are most alike in terms of disposition patterns? Why?
   c. Which product categories are most dissimilar in terms of disposition patterns? Why?
4. Make an inventory of at least 30 of your possessions. For each, indicate when and how you plan to dispose of it. Also provide detailed reasons for this behavior. Then summarize this information, and answer the following:
   a. Which possessions will be the easiest to dispose of and why?
   b. Which possessions will be the hardest to dispose of and why?
   c. What are your most frequent disposition options and why?

More Exercises from the Adaptor

1. Illustrate from your personal experience how has been your relationship with:
   a. your neighboring kirana shop and how has it culminated over the years. Explain specifically the reasons for how has it flourished over the years.
   b. the dealer/retailer from where you/your family bought the last customer durable.
   c. Explain in detail the differences in the relationship established between the two and the reasons for such differences
2. How have automobile companies changed their approach towards marketing of their products? Also bring our the differences seen in the last ten years. How has the approach changed? Why have the approaches differed over the years?

References

[1] Source: http://www.icicibank.com/Pfsuser/aboutus/newsroom/history/history.htm

[2] Source: http://www.teradata.com/t/page/114733/index.html

[3] Source: http://www.icicibank.com/pfsuser/channels/atm/services_at_atm.htm

[4] Source: http://www.expresscomputeronline.com/20041011/casestudies14.shtml

[5] Source: http://www.cellular-news.com/story/23093.php

[6] Source: http://www.businessweek.com/globalbiz/content/aug2006/gb20060810_826414.htm?chan=globalbiz_asia_today%5C's%20top%20story

[7] Source: http://www.hindu.com/2007/04/10/stories/2007041014130100.htm

[8] Source: http://www.ecologycenter.org/iptf/Ragpickers/indexragpicker.html

[9] Source: http://www.expressindia.com/fullstory.php?newsid=55274#compstory

[10] Source: http://www.hindu.com/2005/05/13/stories/2005051307760500.htm

[11] Source: http://www.hindustantimes.com/StoryPage/StoryPage.aspx?id=b203d9f8-453b-4d90-88a9-2552d1f317e0&&Headline=NCC+does+its+bit+for+Metro

[12] Source: http://www.thehindubusinessline.com/2007/02/26/stories/2007022603691500.htm

[13] Source: http://www.hindustantimes.com/StoryPage/StoryPage.aspx?id=b203d9f8-453b-4d90-88a9-2552d1f317e0&&Headline=NCC+does+its+bit+for+Metro

[14] Source: http://www.thehindubusinessline.com/2007/02/26/stories/2007022603691500.htm

[15] Source: http://www.itcportal.com/newsroom/press_31jan06b.htm

PART

4 The Consumer's Culture

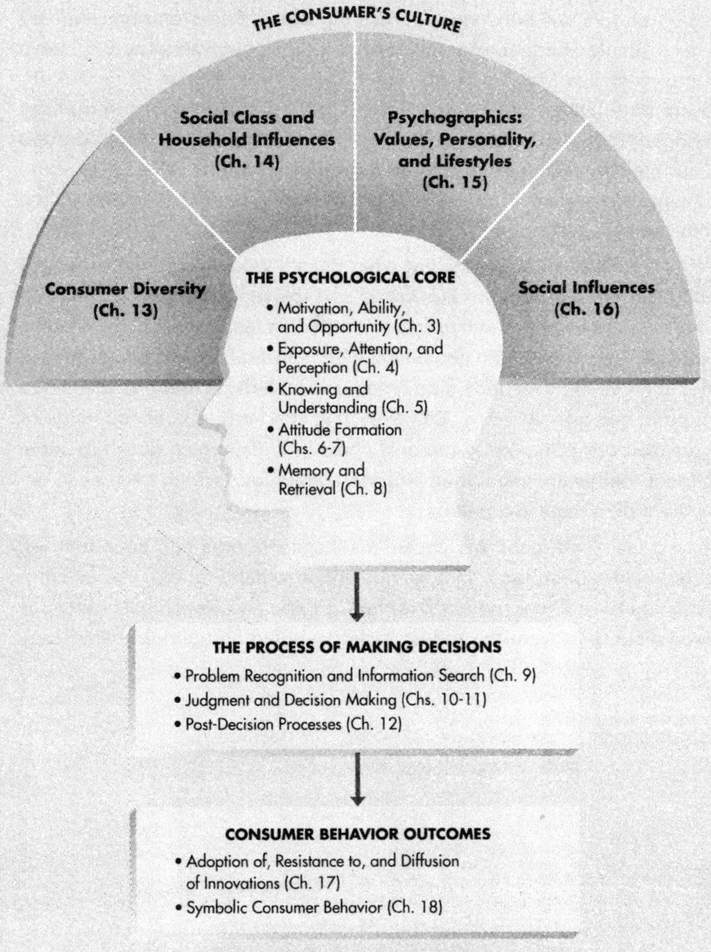

Part Four reflects a "macro" view of consumer behavior, examining how various aspects of the consumer's culture affect behavior. Chapter 13 focuses on diversity, specifically on the roles that age, gender, sexual orientation, and regional, ethnic, and religious influences play in consumer behavior. Chapter 14 explores how social class is determined in various cultures and how, in turn, it affects consumer decisions and behaviors. The chapter also looks at various types of households and families and discusses the effect of household members on acquisition and consumption decisions.

The combination of diversity, social class, and household influences can affect our values, personality, and lifestyle, the topics covered in Chapter 15. Moreover, as Chapter 16 explains, our behavior and decisions can be influenced by certain individuals, specific groups (such as friends, coworkers, club members) and various media.

Because all of these factors influence consumer behavior, they have many implications for marketers.

chapter 13 Consumer Diversity

LEARNING OBJECTIVES

After studying this chapter you will be able to:

- Explain how the consumer's age affects acquisition, consumption, and disposition behavior, and why marketers need to consider age influences when planning marketing activities.
- Describe how gender and sexual orientation each affect consumer behavior and how marketers can create more effective marketing by understanding these two influences.
- Discuss how regional, ethnic, and religious influences can affect consumer behavior and why marketers must consider such influences when targeting specific groups.

INTRODUCTION

McDonald's India: I am loving it

[1] On McDonald's launch in India during 1996 its North Zone Managing Director, Vikram Bakshi quoted on being asked whether the menu will be altered to suit the Indian palette,: "We will surely take into consideration the Indian requirements and a variety of vegetarian dishes will be part of our regular course". [2] Circa 2006 and according to Vikram Bakshi, it was necessary to adapt the company's offerings while keeping the core brand values consistent across cultures. "The menu has evolved over the years as a result of constant innovation and our customers' needs," says Bakshi. "Local creations like McAloo Tikki Burger, Curry Pans, Wraps Pizza McPuff, and McVeggie are established departures from what we had in our introductory restaurant offerings." Today 70 percent of our menu is 'Indianized', and the McAloo Tikki burger is our highest selling product. While the menu may be different in some ways, the McDonald's experience around the world is consistent, offering quality, great service, cleanliness, and value.

The complete reversal of statement is not what Bakshi would have really thought when McDonalds launched in India. [3] The brand and the products were familiar to most Indian's but the platter it offered had to suit the Indian taste. India is the world's vegetarian's paradise. Nearly all of the one billion people living here eat meat only occasionally, or not at all. Beef never shows up on the menu. India is home to the Hindu religion, which preaches non-violence. Believers fear the karmic consequences of harming other creatures. McDonalds is the only chain in India, which does not serve beef and pork. Most menus are vegetarian and there are a few, which have been developed suiting the Indian taste and palette.

The [4] US-based fast food giant, McDonald's success in India had been built on four pillars: limited menu, fresh food, fast service and affordable price. Intense competition and demands for a wider menu drive-through and sit-down meals - encouraged the fast food giant to customize product variety without hampering the efficacy

Exhibit 13.1
FOCUSING ON THE INDIAN PALETTE

McDonald's local creations like McAloo Tikki Burger, Curry Pans, Wraps Pizza McPuff, and McVeggie are a favorite with the consumers

of its supply chain. The restaurant started operations in 1996, after getting a FIPB clearance in 1991-92, but the company was busy establishing the perfect cold chain. Between 1992 and 1996, when McDonald's opened its first outlet in India, it worked frenetically to put the perfect supply chain in place. It trained the local farmers to produce lettuces or potatoes to specifications and worked with a vendor to get the perfect cold chain1 in place. It explained to the suppliers precisely why only one particular size of peas was acceptable (if they were too large, they would pop out of the patty and get burnt).

This example illustrates several diversity influences that affect consumer behavior, all of which are discussed in this chapter (see Exhibit 13.2). In a culturally heterogeneous market like India, McDonald's attempt to offer a unique platter that caters to a Pan India taste is pioneering and focuses on how global companies can adapt themselves to local needs and tastes. In the McDonald's example the attempt was not just to offer a localized menu, but issues like fresh food, fast service and affordable price were well addressed too. Finally, consumer behavior can vary among subgroups of individuals with unique patterns of ethnicity and religion, due to different traditions, customs, and preferences. Clearly, to develop and implement effective marketing strategies and tactics, companies must understand how these diversity influences affect consumers.

How Age Affects Consumer Behavior

Marketers often segment consumers by age. The basic logic is that people of the same age are going through similar life experiences and therefore share many common needs, symbols, and memories, which, in turn, may lead to similar consumption patterns.[2] Regardless of country, age groups are constantly shifting as babies are born, children grow up, adults mature, and people die. This section opens with an overview of U.S. age trends and continues with an examination of four major age groups being targeted by marketers: (1) teens and Generation Y, also called the "millenniums," (2) Generation X, (3) boomers, and (4) seniors.

Age Trends in the United States

The median age of U.S. consumers, which was 32.9 years in 1990, is currently 36 years, reflecting a huge bulge in the 40- to 60-year-old population. Adults aged 18 and over now make up more than 74 percent of the overall U.S. population (see Exhibit 13.3). Thanks in part to better medical care and healthier lifestyles, people are living longer, making the senior market an attractive target for marketers with offerings geared to this age group. The number of adults aged 20 to 34 (spanning Generations X and Y) had been declining, but that trend is turning around, opening new opportunities for marketers to build and sustain brand loyalty during these critical household formation years.[3]

Teens and Generation Y

Your own experience may confirm that teenagers have more influence in household purchases and more financial independence than ever before. Given the high number of two-career families and single parents, teens often shop for themselves and are responsible for more decisions than previous generations.[4] They tend to do more shopping on weekends, and females shop more than males do.[5] Friends are also a major source of information about products, and socializing is one of the

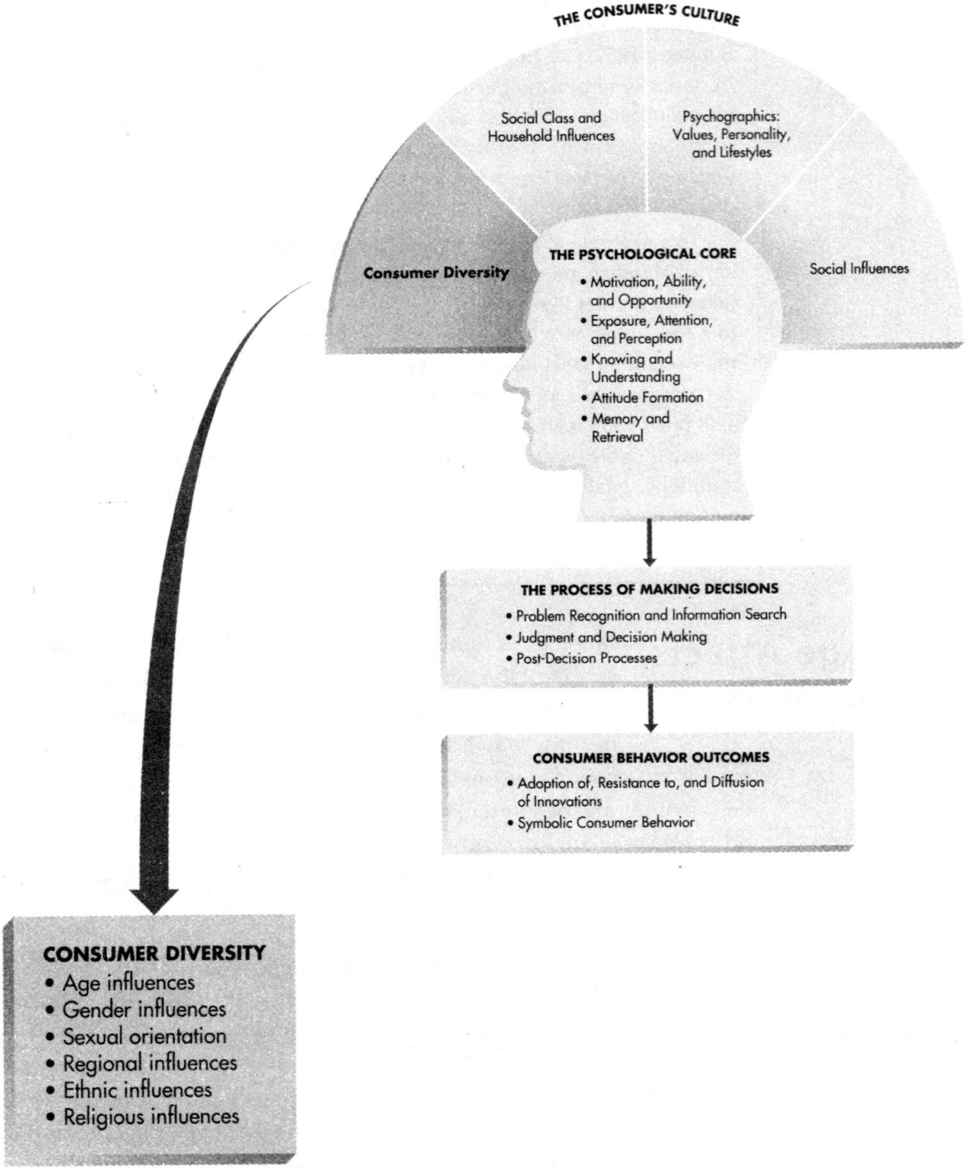

Exhibit 13.2

CHAPTER OVERVIEW: CONSUMER DIVERSITY *This chapter examines how diversity influences such as age, gender, sexual orientation, the region in which one lives, ethnic groups, and religion can affect consumer behavior.*

Exhibit 13.3

THE U.S. POPULATION BY AGE *Consumers up to the age of 18 comprise 26 percent of the U.S. population; by comparison, consumers aged 65 and older comprise just 12 percent of the population.*

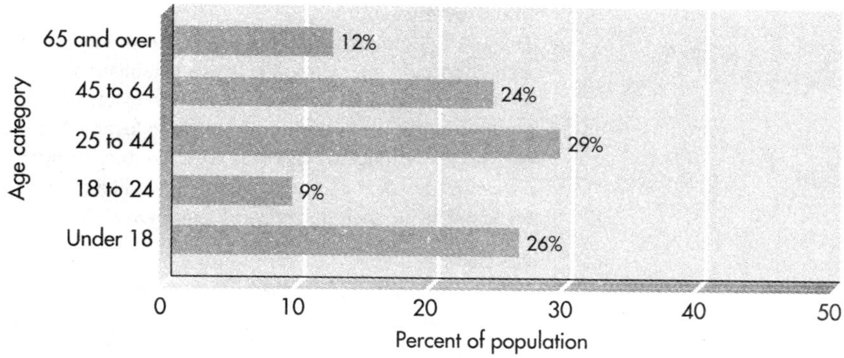

major reasons teens like to shop. Having grown up with recycling, many teens will weigh a product's environmental impact before buying.

A study of 27,000 teens in 44 countries reveals common characteristics and attitudes that cross national boundaries in six distinct segments.[6] The "Thrills and Chills" segment, including teens in the United States, Germany, England, and other European countries, consists of fun-seeking, free-spending consumers from mainly middle-class or upper-class backgrounds. Teens in the "Resigned" segment, covering Denmark, Sweden, Korea, and other countries, have low expectations of the future and of material success, and they are alienated from society. Teen "World Savers" in Hungary, the Philippines, Venezuela, and several other countries are characterized by altruism, good grades, and high career aspirations. Teen "Quiet Achievers" in Thailand, China, Hong Kong, and other nations conform to societal norms and are ambitious for success. "Bootstrappers" in Nigeria, Mexico, the United States, India, and other countries are family-oriented achievement seekers with hopes and dreams for the future. Finally, "Upholders" in Vietnam, Indonesia, Taiwan, and other nations are dutiful and conforming, seeking a rewarding family life and upholding traditional values.

Both teens and 20-something consumers, being born in the years 1979 through 1994, are part of ***Generation Y.*** Generation Y is media and tech savvy, using PCs, the Internet, cell phones, DVD players, and many other high-tech products to communicate, play games, do homework, and shop.[7] Among consumers under 24 years old, for example, the market for cell phones tops $16 billion annually; many in their twenties have no other phone than a cell phone.[8] Approximately 4 million U.S. consumers reach the age of 21 every year, making them eligible for adult offerings such as liquor that are off-limits to younger consumers—which is why Courvoisier is targeting urban men in their twenties.[9]

marketing IMPLICATIONS The number of U.S. teens is expected to reach 35 million by 2010.[10] Their personal purchasing power is a substantial $108 billion, not counting $47 billion more in family purchases.[11] Around the world, teens' similarity of tastes, attitudes, and preferences for music, movies, athletic shoes, clothing, and video games is partly due to popular entertainment, such as MTV, and partly due to the Internet. Nonetheless, teens in different regions exhibit some differences, which is why MTV and other marketers are careful to research and address local tastes and behaviors.[12]

Brand loyalty

The fact that initial purchases of many offerings are made during the teenage years is also important, since brand loyalties established at this time may carry into adulthood. As an example, 50 percent of female teens have developed cosmetic brand loyalties by the age of 15.[13] To encourage early brand loyalty, Macy's recently created a special website just for teenagers because "we'd like the younger customers to think of Macy's as a destination. And as they grow up, we'd like them to continue to think about Macy's for themselves, their homes, and their own children," says a Macy's executive.[14]

Positioning

Some marketers position their products as helpful for dealing with the adolescent pressures of establishing an identity, rebelling, and being accepted by peers. For instance, Clairol created XtremeFX hair color for male teens.[15] In the United Kingdom and in Asia, credit and debit card companies are targeting teens under age 16 because they are more likely than their parents to embrace the credit culture and use their cards to buy online.[16] As you know, teens can also be trendsetters, particularly in areas such as fashion and music, which is why companies such as MTV, Coca-Cola, and Pepsi are constantly researching what teens want (see Exhibit 13.4).[17] Companies in Japan have found that the nation's high school girls have an uncanny ability to predict which products will be hits because a fad that catches on with teens usually becomes a big trend among consumers in general.[18] However, teen tastes can change very quickly, and popular products or stores may become overexposed and quickly lose their cachet.[19]

Exhibit 13.4
TARGETING TEENS
Sometimes marketers try to target teens specifically. This ad for Winterfresh is a good example, as it depicts a popular activity among teens.

Advertising messages

Effective advertising often incorporates symbols, issues, and language to which teens can relate. Because music and sports tend to be the universal languages of teenagers, popular music and sports figures are frequently featured in ads. However, teens are often wary of blatant attempts to influence them.[20] Thus messages need to talk *to* teens, not at them. Furthermore, because they have grown up with videos and computers, today's teens seem to process information faster.[21] As a result, they prefer short, snappy phrases to long-winded explanations. For example, an antismoking ad campaign used the tagline "Tobacco: tumor-causing, teeth-staining, smelly puking habit."[22] Note, however, that using slang can sometimes be dangerous because a phrase may already be out-of-date by the time the ad appears, which can make the product or service look "uncool." Finally, marketers should note that many teenagers are less concerned about advertising messages and more concerned with price.

Media

Marketers can target Generation Y through certain TV networks (especially MTV), TV programs (such as *The O.C.*), magazines (such as *Teen People*), popular-music radio stations, and the Internet (see Exhibit 13.5).[23] Target also publishes a magalog—magazine-catalog combination—featuring lifestyle articles interspersed with product information, a technique used by American Eagle Outfitters and others targeting teens.[24] Marketers of sports-related products can reach teens through special-interest magazines, TV shows, and websites

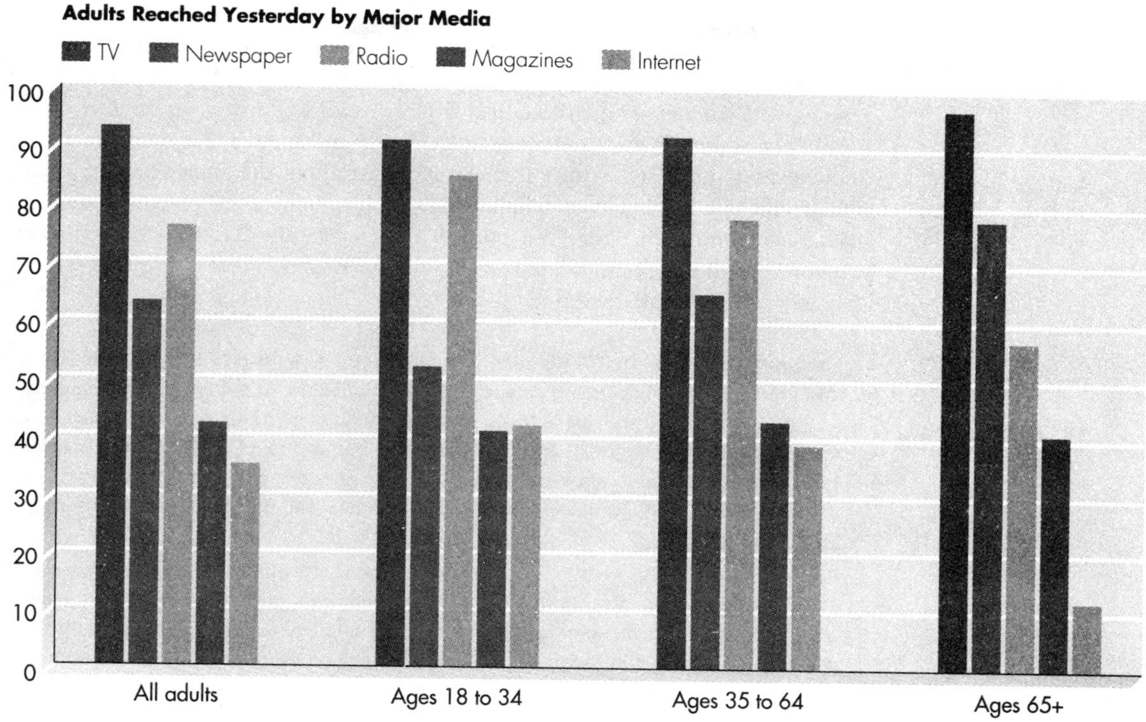

Exhibit 13.5
WHO'S TUNING IN?
As you can see, usage of the different types of media varies by age.

devoted to snowboarding and other sports.[25] However, teens tend not to be loyal to individual sites unless there is a specific appeal. This is why Nike and Alloy post new videos and interactive features to draw teens back again and again.[26]

Other marketing activities

Some marketers reach teens through recreation or special events. Heeling Sports, which makes specialized sneakers, sends teen product ambassadors to perform at amusement parks, malls, skate parks, and college campuses.[27] In addition, marketers are rethinking their distribution strategies to get their products into stores where teens and Generation Y consumers shop. Thus Viacom's Simon Spotlight Entertainment division decided to sell books such as *He's Just Not That Into You* through the clothing chain Urban Outfitters.[28]

Generation X

Individuals born from 1965 to 1976 are often called ***Generation X.*** Within this diverse group of 49 million, some underachievers at 30 or beyond still hang on to their Generation X "angst," while older members of this group are building careers, having families, and buying homes.[29] Nonetheless, Xers who believe that they may not be able to match or surpass their parents' level of success may feel a bit disillusioned and less materialistic than other age groups. In fact, compared with consumers who were 30 to 40 years old a decade ago, fewer Xers own their own homes today.[30] Nevertheless, they tend to find success and achievement in being at the cutting edge of technology and try to balance their work and personal lives.

Some Xers are boomerang kids, returning home to live after college or, to save money, not moving out until well into their thirties.[31] Because parents pay for many essentials, boomerang kids have more discretionary income to spend on entertainment and pleasure and are more likely to buy items like a new car or electronics than Xers who must pay utility bills and other housing costs. Boomerangers also feel less pressure to settle down than earlier generations and often delay marriage. This trend has led to closer relationships with parents, who are often seen as friends or roommates. Boomerangers also influence family decisions to remodel or expand the house, creating opportunities for construction firms, furniture manufacturers, and other marketers.[32]

marketing IMPLICATIONS

The Generation X market represents more than $120 billion in spending power. This group takes the time to research a purchase and likes to customize offerings to their personal needs and tastes.[33] It is a key segment for music, movies, budget travel, beer and alcohol, fast food, clothing, athletic shoes, and cosmetics.[34] Xers are also important targets for marketers of PCs, DVDs, online services, video games, and other tech-related offerings.

Advertising messages

Born and bred on TV, Xers tend to be cynical about obvious marketing techniques.[35] They sometimes find objectionable ads that contain exaggerated claims, stereotypes, unpopular products like cigarettes and alcohol, sexually explicit content, and political, religious, or social messages. However, Xers do react positively to messages they see as clever or in tune with their values, attitudes, and interests (see Exhibit 13.6). For example, Heineken and Mountain Dew have used alternative music and fast-paced videos in ads to attract Xers.[36] As another example, Toyota stopped using 1960s music and started using hip-hop and heavy metal songs in car commercials targeting this segment.[37]

Exhibit 13.6
TARGETING GENERATION X

Nabisco is targeting Generation X with this trendy appeal.

Media

Marketers can reach Xers through media vehicles such as popular or alternative music radio stations and network or cable TV, although this group watches less TV than other groups do.[38] Magazines such as *Spin* and music-related publications and messages displayed at concerts, sporting events, and popular vacation spots can also be effective. Thus, Mountain Dew, among other companies, sponsors extreme sporting events such as the X Games to reach Xers through special interests.[39] Increasingly, marketers are using the Internet to reach these Web-savvy consumers.[40] For instance, to get Xers to donate to charity, ReliefRock offered an online benefit rock music concert rather than send direct-mail letters.[41] To promote its car insurance, State Farm Insurance has run fast-paced online ads that pop up when Xers visit Rollingstone.com and other sites that target this segment.[42]

Boomers

The 78 million ***baby boomers*** born between 1946 and 1964 make up the largest demographic group in the United States. Because of their numbers and the fact that many are in their peak earning years, boomers have considerable buying power and are an influential consumer segment. Although boomers are a diverse group, they share many common experiences of the dynamic world of the 1960s and 1970s in which they grew up. Boomers strongly value individualism and want the freedom to do what they want, when and where they want.[43] Most boomers grew up with TV and, as they get older, tend to watch more—and they spend more time browsing the Internet than other groups.[44]

Some researchers have identified five subgroups of boomers, based on five-year divisions (1946–1951, 1951–1956, and so on). Others suggest three subsegments: leading boomers (born 1946–1950), core boomers (1951–1959), and trailing boomers (1960–1964). Consumers in these subgroups have life experiences in common and may share more attributes with each other than with other segments.[45] If this is true, the oldest and youngest groups would tend to be the most different. Some experts have even suggested the name Gappers for the youngest group (born between 1963 and 1969) because its members fall between boomers and Xers in terms of interests and behavior patterns.[46] Moreover, research suggests that boomers around the world, like teens around the world, share certain attitudes and values. For example, a majority of U.K. boomers believe that life today is more stressful than it was 50 years ago—a view echoed by most boomers in Mexico, France, and Hong Kong.[47]

Exhibit 13.7
TARGETING BOOMERS
Concern for the future and famiiy protection is a high priority for many baby boomers who now have children.

Seniors

In the ***gray market*** of consumers over 65, women outnumber men because women tend to live longer.[48] Because information-processing skills tend to deteriorate with age, seniors are less likely to search for information and more likely to have difficulty remembering information and making more complex decisions.[49] Thus they tend to engage in simpler, more schematic processing.[50] Further, poor recognition memory makes them susceptible to the "truth effect" (believing that often-repeated statements are true—see Chapter 8).[51] As a result, they sometimes need help or education when making decisions, as discussed in Chapter 19.[52]

marketing IMPLICATIONS Because baby boomers have so much buying power, they are the target for many products and services, including cars, housing, travel, entertainment, recreational equipment, and motor homes.[53] Real estate developers are adding whirlpools, bedroom fireplaces, upscale kitchens, and other amenities for baby-boom house buyers.[54] Harley-Davidson has profited by producing heavyweight motorcycles—priced at $17,000 or more—for this segment.[55] Boomers are also heavy consumers of financial services as they look toward retirement and simultaneously pay for their children's college educations.[56] The life insurance ad in Exhibit 13.7 is directed at baby boomers concerned about providing for their children. Time-pressured boomers still like fast food, but many are buying gourmet sandwiches from Cosi, Panera, and other restaurant chains as a healthier and more varied alternative to burgers and fries.[57]

An aging population

Because boomers are getting older, marketers who fail to modify their offerings for this large segment will suffer from a shrinking market share. Some firms are developing offerings specifically for the needs of baby boomers. For example, apparel marketers have created jeans in larger sizes and different styles to accommodate the middle-aged physique.[58] The Chico's chain has grown to more than 450 stores by specializing in loose-fitting casual clothing for baby-boom women.[59] DesignerShoes.com, which sells shoes online and in a Boston store, stocks high-fashion shoes (instead of "sensible" shoes) in larger, wider sizes needed by boomers.[60] Offerings that help boomers look and feel young, such as personal care products, fitness goods and services, and cosmetic surgery, are especially attractive to boomers who are sensitive to the idea of aging.[61] Thus, Procter & Gamble has been successful with "Rejuvenating Effects" toothpaste and anti-aging Olay cream for boomer women.[62]

Seniors represent a critical and growing market for health-related and medical products and services and retirement communities (particularly in Florida and the South).[63] Mature consumers already spend more than twice the national average on prescription drugs, accounting for more than 40 percent of all U.S. pharmaceutical sales.[64] In Japan, where consumers 65 and older will soon account for 20 percent of the population, companies are marketing such age-specific offerings as a health-monitoring talking robot cat and home nursing services.[65]

Marketing communications

Marketers can target boomers through the use of media geared to this group's interests, including oldies rock 'n' roll radio and TV programs, activity-specific publications and TV shows, and lifestyle-related events such as home shows and sporting events.[66] Seniors prefer public television, CNN, and premium pay cable, but they may have more difficulty processing TV messages because of deteriorating processing skills.[67] Marketers should recognize that seniors perceive advertisements with positive older role models as more credible than those with younger models.[68] However, because of America's youth culture, seniors are less likely to appear in ads—or to be depicted positively—a situation that is changing over time.[69] Thus models in ads for seniors should represent active, contributing members of society, and messages should focus on only a few key attributes.

Specialized sales techniques and promotions

Retailers can design their outlets to provide a more age-friendly shopping environment for boomers and seniors, with features such as wider aisles and well-lit aisles and parking lots.[70] Gap is already testing clothing stores geared specifically to boomers' preferences. Boomers and seniors value sales service, as well, which is why Chico's also differentiates itself on the basis of personalized assistance.[71] Many marketers use special promotions such as senior citizen discounts to attract and retain boomer and senior consumers. Some seniors are heavy users of these discounts and take advantage of them in many product and service categories.[72] However, because older consumers who seek social interaction from telemarketing calls may not recognize fraudulent offers, consumer education can help this segment avoid being victimized by scams (see Chapter 19).[73]

Age Trends in India

Unlike in the US, age profiling in India is more skewed and does not have homogeneity and clear classification as like the US markets. The regions in India have a strong rural and urban divide where the demographic and psychographic profiles are very different. With a total population of 1,028,610,28 (Source: Census 2001), only 28% of it lives in the urban areas, which only makes a quarter of the population living in the urban heartlands. However, in terms of age the population is fairly young, of which 55% are below 24 yrs of age and 109 million people will enter the "employable age" in the next 5 years. As much as 54 percent of India's population is below 25 and 80 percent are below the age of 45. Dependant population, which is below 15 and above 64, is an all time low of .81 percent.

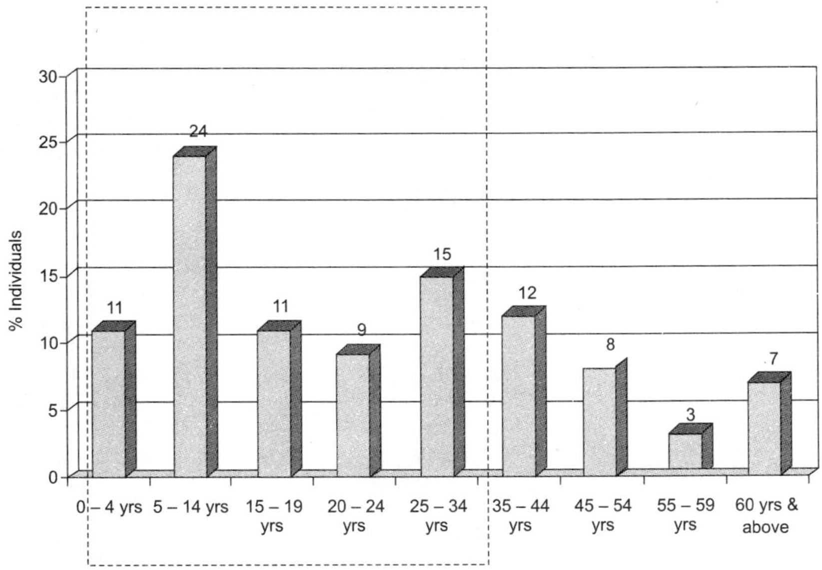

Source: Census of India, 2001

Exhibit 13.8
AGE TRENDS IN INDIA
A young population of which 55% is below 24 yrs of age and 109 million people will enter the "employable age" in the next 5 years A young population of which 55% is below 24 yrs of age and 109 million people will enter the "employable age" in the next 5 years

The population is however, male skewed as illustrated in Exhibit 13.19 and the male to female ratio is 54:46, and the percentage keeps on changing every year with increasing problems of female foeticide being reported from even urban areas .

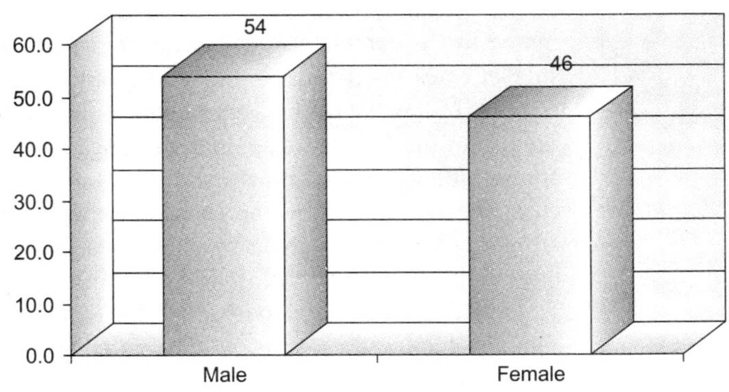

Source: Census of India, 2001

Exhibit 13.19
SEX RATIO
The skewed sex ratio in India is a representation of the traditional thought process of perceiving the girl child of still being a liability.

Unlike the US markets where the population is segregated as; Seniors, Boomers, Generation X and Teens & Generation Y, the Indian population segregation would be more feasible on the parameters of dwelling in geographic region, sex, and age.

The Rural and Urban divide

The rural and urban population divide in India has long been been a matter of debate, given that over 70% of the Indian population living in the rural heartlands. In a agrarian economy, where the majority of rural population depends on agriculture, the statistics of expenditure, consumption and even lifestyles pattern have even dichotomy within the rural population (See exhibit 13.20). However, the rural India has reduced its dependence on agriculture and a little less than half of the rural GDP is from non-agricultural activities. This is creating a different kind of rural market. NCAER occupation data shows a decline in cultivators, and there is enough evidence of dual sector households.

Exhibit 13.20
TALE OF TWO RURALS
The differences in the inter- rural population are more visible

Category	Developed Rural (% of households in each group owing the product)	Developing Rural
Size (million hh)	43	90
Per cent of rural population	32	68
Two Wheeler	10	5
Cars/Jeep	0.8	0.3
Refrigerator	8	2
Colour TV	12	3
Telephone	9	3
Toothpaste	45	27
Toothpowder	36	36
Branded Tea/Coffee	11	1
Packaged atta	8	4
Toilet/Floor cleaner	7	3
Oil 13	7	
Press reach	34	19
TV reach	57	34

*Punjab, Haryana, Gujarat, Maharashtra, Karnataka, Kerala
Source: IRS 2002/HIG Analysis

The aspect of population migration from rural to suburban and to urban locations also affects households both in the origin location and also in the migrated households. Alternatively, the urban population is also undergoing a radical change. The metros and the mini metros (usually the state capitals) have long dominated most markets and consumption trends, however it's the newer and the smaller cities where the new India is unfolding. A look at the population indexes in terms of India's top urban agglomerations in Exhibit 13.21 is an illustration of how the urban markets are also changing. Agglomerations are a "continuous urban spread which includes a town and its urban outgrowths, or two or more physical contiguous towns together and any adjoining urban outgrowths of such towns". Examples of outgrowths are railway colonies, university campuses, port areas, military camps, satellite towns.

For long, companies have been trying to model the rural market as a dearer version of urban markets and was considered aspirational in nature. However, companies are beginning to realize that the rural and urban divide is specific to both markets and individual needs are required to be addressed.

Urban Agglomeration	State/Union Territory*	District	Population (%)			Literates (%)		
			Total	Male	Female	Total	Male	Female
Greater Mumbai	Maharashtra	Thane, Mumbai (Suburban) and Mumbai	16,368,084	54	46	12,66,186	58	42
Kolkata	West Bengal	Nadia, North 24 Parganas, Hugli, Haora, Kolkata and South 24 Parganas	13,216,546	55	45	10,009,727	56	44
Delhi	Delhi	All 9 districts of Delhi	12,791,458	51	49	9,053,324	59	41
Chennai	Tamil Nadu	Thiruvallur, Chennai and Kancheepuram	6,424,624	52	48	4,769,591	54	46
Bangalore	Karnataka	Bangalore	5,686,844	52	48	4,340,36	55	45
Hyderabad	Andhra Pradesh	Medak, Hyderabad and Rangareddi	5,533,640	53	47	3,363792	56	44
Ahmedabad	Gujarat	Gandhinagar and Ahmedabad	4,519,278	53	47	3,363,792	56	44
Pune	Maharashtra	Pune	3,755,525	57	43	2,867,828	56	44
Surat	Gujarat	Surat	2,811,466	54	46	2,025,489	61	39
Kanpur	Uttar Pradesh	Kanpur Nagar	2,690,486	53	47	1,960,125	54	46
Lucknow	Uttar Pradesh	Lucknow	2,266,933	52	48	1,559,335	56	44
Nagpur	Maharashtra	Nagpur	2,122,965	54	46	1,672,611	54	46
Patna	Bihar	Patna	1,707,429	53	47	1,193,736	59	41
Indore	Madhya Pradesh	Indore	1.639,044	52	48	1,167,209	57	43
Vadodara	Gujarat	Vadodara	1,492,398	53	47	1,157,035	55	45
Bhopal	Madhya Pradesh	Bhopal	1,454,830	51	49	1,000,580	57	43
Coimbatore	Tamil Nadu	Coimbatore	1,446,034	49	51	1,112,744	54	46

Source: Census of India 2001

Exhibit 13.21

Exhibit 13.22 is an illustration of the divide that exists in the markets, which may not be in terms of population index, however it illustrates that the dichotomy must be examined. Another critical aspect on population is the states, where each state differs from one another. The most heavily populated state is Uttar Pradesh and some of the North-East states are the lowest in population. Exhibit 3.23 is an illustration of the statewise population and each state has its unique sub-cultural traits, which are very different from the other, creating a melting pot of culture. There are 18 official languages and 1652 distinct dialects spoken across various states.

Total/ Rural/ Urban	Total number of households	Total number of households availing banking services	Availability of assets						
			Radio, Transistor	Television	Telephone	Bicycle	Scooter, Motor Cycle, Moped	Car, Jeep, Van	None of the specified assets
1	2	3	4	5	6	7	8	9	10
Total	191,963,935	68,230,642	67,415,133	60,649,623	17,549,991	83,838,450	22,484,686	4,801,899	66,198,648
Rural	138,271,559	41,639,949	43,539,732	26,149,263	5,218,884	59,150,303	9,222,638	1,780,493	55,988,658
Urban	53,692,376	26,590,693	23,875,401	34,500,360	12,331,107	24,688,147	13,262,048	3,021,406	10,209,990

Source: Census 2001

Exhibit 13.22

Number of Households Availing Banking Services and Number of Households Having Each of the Specified Asset

Exhibit 13.23

**

**

Units in million

States	Individuals	Households
Uttar Pradesh	122.3	28.1
Maharashtra	79.2	21.7
West Bengal	63.5	17.5
Andhra Pradesh	60.3	18.5
Bihar	60.3	15.6
Tamil Nadu	53.3	16.2
Madhya Pradesh	45.6	12.3
Karnataka	42.6	11.5
Rajasthan	42.4	10.3
Gujarat	40.9	10.8
Orissa	28.9	8.6
Kerala	26.5	7.3
Assam	20.1	5.5
Jharkhand	20.0	5.4
Punjab	19.9	4.8
Haryana	16.9	4.3
Chhattisgarh	15.8	4.5
Delhi	12.1	13.2
Uttaranchal	6.6	1.7
Himachal Pradesh	4.9	1.3
Goa	1.2	0.3
Chandigarh	0.7	0.2
Jammu & Kashmir	0.7	0.2
All India	784.6	210.1

The Segregation on Sex Ratio

Though the sex ration in India is skewed but the women population is undergoing both demographic and psychographic profile changes. The population of working women has increased and this has led to more out of home mothers, creating new opportunities in day care and changing consumption basket. Exhibit 13.24 illustrates statewise male-female sex ratio and for states the ratio is quite alarming. However, the female population of working versus non-working also has heterogeneity and marketers reflect the same in their communication, as shown in Exhibit 13.25.

Age trends in India

As discussed earlier the relative population in India is fairly young and nearly 55% (see Exhibit 13.26) of it is within the working workforce. However, half of it is not within the working population. There is another large base of population which is waiting to enter the workforce, hence making the dependency ratio very low. With such low dependency ratios and high working population base, the household income base is bound to rise.

With the economic reforms in India in an accelerated pace now, it is significant to assess the population dynamics over the years and how have they settled down. The population profile is listed as: (i) The pre-independence workforce, which settled down in the post independence era (much like the US war time and depression era population) born in the later part of 19th century and early 21st century and superannuated between 1940's – 1950's.; (ii) The off springs of the pre-independence workforce forms the second set of population, reaching superannuation between

Exhibit 13.24

Population Break up

S. No.	State	Persons	Males	Females	Sex ratio
1	Jammu & Kashmir	10,143,700	5,360,926	4,782,774	892
2	Himachal Pradesh	6,077,900	3,087,940	2,989,960	968
3	Punjab	24,358,999	12,985,045	11,373,954	876
4	Chandigarh	900,635	506,938	393,697	777
5	Uttaranchal	8,489,349	4,325,924	4,163,425	962
6	Haryana	21,144,564	11,363,953	9,780,611	861
7	Delhi	13,850,507	7,607,234	6,243,273	821
8	Rajasthan	56,507,188	29,420,011	27,087,177	921
9	Uttar Pradesh	166,197,921	87,565,369	78,632,552	898
10	Bihar	82,998,509	43,243,795	39,754,714	919
11	Sikkim	540,851	288,484	252,367	875
12	Arunachal Pradesh	1,097,968	579,941	518,027	893
13	Nagaland	1,990,036	1,047,141	942,895	900
14	Manipur**	2,166,788	1,095,634	1,071,154	978
15	Mizoram	888,573	459,109	429,464	935
16	Tripura	3,199,203	1,642,225	1,556,978	948
17	Meghalaya	2,318,822	1,176,087	1,142,735	972
18	Assam	26,655,528	13,777,037	12,878,491	935
19	West Bengal	80,176,197	41,465,985	38,710,212	934
20	Jharkhand	26,945,829	13,885,037	13,060,792	941
21	Orissa	36,804,660	18,660,570	18,144,090	972
22	Chhattisgarh	20,833,803	10,474,218	10,359,585	989
23	Madhya Pradesh	60,348,023	31,443,652	28,904,371	919
24	Gujarat	50,671,017	26,385,577	24,285,440	920
25	Daman & Diu	158,204	92,512	65,692	710
26	Dadra & Nagar Haveli	220,490	121,666	98,824	812
27	Maharashtra	96,878,627	50,400,596	46,478,031	922
28	Andhra Pradesh	76,210,007	38,527,413	37,682,594	978
29	Karnataka	52,850,562	26,898,918	25,951,644	965
30	Goa	1,347,668	687,248	660,420	961
31	Lakshadweep	60,650	31,131	29,519	948
32	Kerala	31,841,374	15,468,614	16,372,760	1058
33	Tamil Nadu	62,405,679	31,400,909	31,004,770	987
34	Pondicherry	974,345	486,961	487,384	1001
35	Andaman & Nicobar Islands	356,152	192,972	163,180	846

Source: Census 2001

Exhibit 13.25

WORKING WOMAN AND THE HOUSEWIFE

Psychographic profiles of the differences between the career women and the traditional housewife is gradually shrinking.

1990's-till date. They were the first generation of achievers who came from small towns and large families. Taking advantage of the newly created job opportunities- especially in the government sector- the strivers laid the foundation of the "great Indian Middle class". A respectable and secure life; (iii) [5] Their offsprings were the first generation of achievers, a population that today forms a sizeable working population and an equally large number is waiting to enter the workforce segment. These children were brought up to see higher education as their only means of economic salvation. These people are born during 1960-1980 and are today bearing the fruits of the economic boom.

Exhibit 13.26

Population Mix in urban and rural India

Rural	Urban			
Age Group	**No.**	**%**	**No.**	**%**
Age Group : 12-14 years	58763	10.5	21516	8.6
Age Group : 15-19 years	75725	13.5	34466	13.6
Age Group : 20-29 years	125381	22.3	61224	24.2
Age Group : 30-39 years	111756	19.9	51399	20.3
Age Group : 40-49 years	78145	13.9	38371	15.2
Age Group : 50 years+	112511	20	45663	18.1
Source: IRS 2006				

On the other side of this population divide is India's economic history, which is segregated into; (i) the Post Independence era to 1980's; (ii) the decade of 1980-1991; (iii) the economic reform of 1991 and thereafter. [6] Today, the post liberalization generation is coming of age. In 2006 there were 100 million 17-21 year olds in India. Six out of the 10 households today have a liberalization childhood.

How Gender and Sexual Orientation Affect Consumer Behavior

Clearly males and females can differ in traits, attitudes, and activities that can affect consumer behavior. The following sections discuss a few key issues that have been the focus of consumer research, because complete coverage of the contrasts between men and women is beyond the scope of this text. Remember that these sections describe only general tendencies, subject to considerable individual variation.

Sex Roles

In most cultures, men and women are expected to behave according to sex-role norms learned very early in childhood. Until recently, males in Western society were expected to be strong, assertive, the primary breadwinner, and emotionless and were guided by ***agentic goals*** that stress mastery, self-assertiveness, and self-efficacy.[74] Women, on the other hand, have been guided more by ***communal goals*** of forming affiliations and fostering harmonious relations with others and have been expected to be relatively submissive, emotional, and home oriented.

On a very general level, men tend to be more competitive, independent, externally motivated, and willing to take risks.[75] Expressing "man-of-action" masculinity may take the form of hypercompetitive breadwinner behavior or a rebel approach (including entrepreneurial breadwinner behavior).[76] In contrast, women tend to be cooperative, interdependent, intrinsically motivated, and risk averse. Over time, however, female and male roles have been evolving. [7] Today as more and more urban Indian middle class women are joining the workforce; it puts a pressure on the family. Traditional careers as teachers, secretaries to high profile careers in the corporate sector are all being juggled across by women. Delayed marriages leading to late-born children and sometimes not having children at all are the new norms of the society. [8] Today 23% of the Indian households have working wives and this number has jumped up from [9]1% to 15% in a decade's time.

Traditional sex roles are changing in many countries, even those that are very conservative and male dominated. For example, in India, where arranged marriages are still the norm, women's attitudes toward careers, marriage, and the family are undergoing radical changes as more women build careers—especially in high-tech firms—and seek independence.[78] Note, however, that sex roles and appropriate behavior are dictated by society and may vary from one culture to another. In the United States, for example, some men feel uncomfortable hugging each other, whereas this behavior is widely accepted in European and Latin societies, often as a greeting. In certain Muslim countries, the very strict sex roles allow women few rights and require that they be completely covered and kept out of view.

Gender and Sexual Orientation

Gender refers to a biological state (male or female), whereas ***sexual orientation*** reflects a person's preference toward certain behaviors. *Masculine* individuals (whether male or female) tend to display male-oriented traits, and *feminine* individuals tend toward female characteristics. In addition, some individuals can be *androgynous,* having both male and female traits. Sexual orientations are important because they can influence consumer preferences and behavior. For example, women who are more masculine tend to prefer ads that depict nontraditional women.[79]

In India the subject of gays, lesbians, homosexuals is considered taboo and such people are socially ostracized. [10]According to a United States government fact book, India has a population of more than 1.65 billion people, making it the largest democracy of the world. While no statistics exist for the number of Indians who are gay, according to 2001 figures, the country had roughly four million people living with HIV. Homosexual sex is outlawed in India and many provinces and localities strictly enforce sodomy laws. [11] Section 377 of the Indian Penal Code states 'Whoever has carnal intercourse against the code of nature with any man, woman or animal, shall be punished with imprisonment for life'. In India's large urban centres such as Delhi and Bombay, while homosexuality is slowly becoming a topic of conversation, the general reaction is still one of hostility and ridicule. The threat of legal action - combined with social ostracism - is enough to deter all but the least vulnerable from coming out. The threat is real for gay men who, like their counterparts around the world, for want of better places are forced to meet in public parks, public toilets and similar places. Here they are open to persecution by the police who are primarily interested in extorting whatever they can from their victims.

Differences in Acquisition and Consumption Behaviors

Despite sex-role changes, men and women still exhibit a number of differences in their consumption behaviors. Females are more likely to engage in a detailed, thorough examination of an ad message and then make extended decisions based on product attributes (similar to high MAO decision making), whereas males are selective information processors, driven more by overall themes and simplifying heuristics (similar to low MAO decision making).[84] Males tend to be more sensitive to personally relevant information (consistent with agentic goals), and women pay attention to both personally relevant information and information relevant to others (consistent with communal goals).[85]

Whereas men are more likely to use specific hemispheres of their brain for certain tasks (the right side of the brain for visual and the left side for verbal), women use both hemispheres of their brain for most tasks. Men also appear to be more sensitive to trends in positive emotions experienced during consumption, such as feeling enthusiastic and strong, whereas women display a tendency for negative emotions, such as feeling scared and nervous.[86] In addition, men and women differ in the symbolic meaning they attach to products and services.[87] Women are more likely to have shared brand stereotypes for fashion goods, whereas men are more consistent in their images of automobiles.

In general, females see shopping as a pleasurable, stimulating activity and a way of obtaining social interaction. Men, on the other hand, view shopping merely as a way of acquiring goods and regard it as a chore, especially if they hold traditional sex-role stereotypes. These patterns also hold true in other countries such as Turkey and the Netherlands. Finally, men and women tend to exhibit different eating patterns. In particular, women are more likely to engage in compensatory eating— making up for deficiencies such as lack of social contact or depression that they overcome by eating.

As gender roles are changing their impact on marketing of products as also in their promotion is also undergoing radical changes. Vicks Vaporub's new advertisement showcases the father taking care of the child, since the mother is out of town (assumption that she is out on business tour) is a stark contrast to the advertisements aired from the last three decades, wherein the mother looks after the child at home. The joint family system in India is crumbling and being replaced with nuclear families thus changing the role and status of the individuals in the family. Case in point is the Vicks Vaporub advertisement. [12] Unlike the West, we are a society of consensus seekers. We rely a great deal on our family. Even our purchase decisions are made jointly.

Now the father of the family is taking more and more responsibility within the house and is forced to integrate more feminine traits as the women in the house steps out to work. Similarly, the woman too is undergoing a reflective change in her approach towards the family and also to her self. She is more indulgent, willing to experiment and appreciates her own leg space (Exhibit 13.27 illustrates an advertisement targeting the working women).

The media and communication industry are gradually adapting themselves to such changes. The media and media vehicles are making constant efforts to identify the relevant target audience and target them. Earlier, women's magazine only meant Femina in English and Grihshobha or Meri Saheli in the vernacular medium. Today there are numerous options to choose from, both in the mainstream and vernacular languages. Similarly, television has also adapted itself to the changing needs of the society. Soaps and news channels rule the roost, but cricket and films (especially blockbuster premieres) are also quite popular now. Reality shows are also finding a slot for themselves, in a family where wholesome entertainment definition is changing. Exhibit 13.28 gives an indication of the programme mix which households are watching.

Exhibit 13.27
TARGETING THE WORKING WOMEN
Increasingly automobile companies are realizing the potential of the working women as the target audience in the family for the second car

Exhibit 13.28
Most Viewed One Hour Slot in 2005 (All India)

Rank	Channel	Programme	Date	Day	Start Time	End Time	TVR
1	Star Plus	Kaun Banega Crorepati	05/08/2005	Fri	21:00	21:59	13.8
2	Sony	Indian Idol-Grand Finale	05/03/2005	Sat	21:00	21:59	11.5
3	Star Plus	Kahani+Kyunki*	08/02/2005	Tue	22:00	22:59	11.3
4	Star Plus	Kahani+Kyunki*	04/01/2005	Tue	22:00	22:59	11.3
5	Star Plus	Kahani+Kyunki*	03/01/2005	Mon	22:00	22:59	11.3

* Kahaani Ghar Ghar Ki+; Kyunki Saas Bhi Kabhi Bahu Thi   Source: TAM
Source: The Marketing Whitebook, Businessworld 2006

How Regional Influences Affect Consumer Behavior

Because people tend to work and live in the same area, residents in one part of the country can develop patterns of behavior that differ from those in another area. For example, a consumer from New England might enjoy lobster and appreciate colonial architecture, whereas someone from Texas may prefer barbecues and rodeos. This section explores how the region in which people live can affect their consumer behavior, both within the United States and in various regions across the world.

Regions With in the United States

Although we can speak of an overall U.S. culture, the United States is a vast country in which various regions have developed distinctive identities based on differing ethnic and cultural histories. For example, California and the Southwest were originally part of Mexico and therefore reflect a Mexican character; the Southwest also has Native American and frontier roots. The eastern seaboard from New England to Georgia reflects the region's roots as the original 13 British colonies. The great expanses of the West and Northwest are reflected in the free-spirited personalities of these regions, and the Deep South from Louisiana to Florida owes some of its character to agriculture, especially the cotton-growing industry, as well as the rebellion of the Confederacy during the Civil War. Finally, the Midwest is noted for its farms and agriculture.

These statements represent very broad generalizations. Although each region also has many unique influences and variations that are too numerous to mention, regional differences can affect consumption patterns. Immigration patterns, such as a large number of Mexican-born consumers moving into California and Texas, can add ethnic influences to certain regions as well.[105] For instance, due to strong Mexican influence, consumers in the Southwest prefer spicy food and dishes such as tortillas and salsa. Interestingly, some Tex-Mex foods, including nachos and chili dogs, were actually developed in the United States and are only now becoming popular in Mexico.[106] Because considerable variation exists in values and lifestyles among consumers within a region, researchers have looked for ways to describe consumers on the basis of more specific characteristics, a technique called *clustering*.

Clustering is based on the principle that "birds of a feather flock together."[107] This suggests that consumers in the same neighborhood tend to buy the same types of cars, homes, appliances, and other products/services.[108] Systems such as Mosaic (from Experian) and PRIZM NE (from Claritas) group areas and neighborhoods into more precise clusters based on consumers' similarities on demographic and consumption characteristics. These systems can define a cluster according to similarity of income, education, age, household type, degree of urbanity, attitudes, and product/service preferences, including the type of car owned and preferred radio format. The systems summarize and group all this information using sophisticated statistical techniques such as multivariate regression.

To illustrate, Exhibit 13.29 presents the 66 major types of neighborhoods derived from PRIZM NE.[109] This system uses data from the U.S. Census, automobile registrations, consumer surveys, magazine subscription lists, and other sources to identify clusters or groups of consumers. The 66 clusters can be grouped into the 14 larger clusters in Exhibit 13.30, based on degree of urbanization and socioeconomic status. Note that because clusters are based on common characteristics, not on geography, consumers from different areas of the country may be grouped in the same cluster. These more precise clusters help marketers segment and target consumers more effectively than using broad regional classifications.

marketing IMPLICATIONS

Marketers can develop a product, service, or communication to appeal to different regions of the United States. McDonald's sells bratwurst in Minnesota, burritos in California, and lobster sandwiches in Maine.[110] Many marketers in Texas infuse their ads with a distinct western flavor, whereas ads directed toward the East Coast may take on a more urban theme. Also, some products are identified with certain regions: Florida orange juice, Hawaiian macadamia nuts, Maine lobsters, and Texas beef are a few examples. Smaller firms catering to local tastes can develop a loyal following in certain regions. Even though Frito-Lay sells more potato chips across America than all its smaller competitors combined, Utz potato chips are popular in Pennsylvania and Jays potato chips are popular in Chicago.[111]

Marketers can use clustering systems to help find new customers, learn what their customers like, develop new products, buy advertising, locate store sites, and target through media.[112] Hyundai uses PRIZM to target consumers in Bohemian Mix

PRIZM$_{NE}$ TARGET FINDER REPORT RANKED BY SEGMENT

PRIZM$_{NE}$ Clusters			Demographic Descriptors				
Social Group	**#**	**Nickname**	**Income Level**	**Cluster Type**	**HH Composition**	**Adult Age**	**Education**
S1	01	Upper Crust	Wealthy	Suburban	Couples	Age 45+	College Grad+
S1	02	Blue Blood Estates	Wealthy	Suburban	Families	Age 35–64	College Grad+
S1	03	Movers & Shakers	Wealthy	Suburban	Couples	Age 35–64	College Grad+
U1	04	Young Digerali	Upscale	Urban	Mix	Age 25–44	College Grad+
T1	05	Country Squires	Wealthy	Town	Families	Age 35–64	College Grad+
S1	06	Winner's Circle	Wealthy	Suburban	Families	Age 25–54	College Grad+
U1	07	Money & Brains	Upscale	Urban	Mix	Age 45+	College Grad+
S2	08	Executive Suites	UpperMid	Suburban	Sngl/Cpls	Age 25–44	College Grad+
T1	09	Big Fish, Small Pond	Upscale	Town	Couples	Age 45+	College Grad+
C1	10	Second City Elite	Upscale	2nd City	Couples	Age 45+	College Grad+
T1	11	God's Country	Upscale	Town	Couples	Age 35–64	College Grad+
C1	12	Brite Lites, Li'l City	UpperMid	2nd City	Sngl/Cpls	Age 25–54	College Grad+
C1	13	Upward Bound	Upscale	2nd City	Families	Age 25–54	H.S./College
S2	14	New Empty Nests	UpperMid	Suburban	Couples	Age 65+	College Grad+
S2	15	Pools & Patios	UpperMid	Suburban	Couples	Age 45+	College Grad+
U1	16	Bohemian Mix	Midscale	Urban	Singles	Age <35	College Grad+
S2	17	Beltway Boomers	UpperMid	Suburban	Families	Age 35–64	H.S./College
S2	18	Kids & Cul-de-Sacs	UpperMid	Suburban	Families	Age 25–54	H.S./College
S2	19	Home Sweet Home	UpperMid	Suburban	Mix	Age 25–44	H.S./College
T1	20	Fast-Track Families	UpperMid	Town	Families	Age 25–54	H.S./College
S3	21	Gray Power	Midscale	Suburban	Sngl/Cpls	Age 65+	H.S./College
S3	22	Young Influentials	Midscale	Suburban	Singles	Age <35	H.S./College
T2	23	Greenbelt Sports	Midscale	Town/Rural	Mix	Age 25–54	H.S./College
C2	24	Up-and-Comers	Midscale	2nd City	Mix	Age <35	H.S./College
T1	25	Country Casuals	UpperMid	Town/Rural	Couples	Age 35–64	H.S./College
U1	26	The Cosmopolitans	Midscale	Urban	Sngl/Cpls	Age 55+	H.S./College
C2	27	Middleburg Managers	Midscale	2nd City	Sngl/Cpls	Age 55+	H.S./College
T2	28	Traditional Times	Midscale	Town/Rural	Sngl/Cpls	Age 55+	H.S./College
U1	29	American Dreams	Midscale	Urban	Mix	Age 25–44	H.S./College
S3	30	Suburban Sprawl	Midscale	Suburban	Sngl/Cpls	Age 25–44	H.S./College
U2	31	Urban Achievers	LowerMid	Urban	Singles	Age <35	H.S./College
T2	32	New Homesteaders	Midscale	Town	Families	Age 25–44	High School
T2	33	Big Sky Families	Midscale	Rural	Families	Age 25–54	High School
C2	34	White Picket Fences	Midscale	2nd City	Families	Age 25–44	High School
C2	35	Boomtown Singles	LowerMid	2nd City	Singles	Age <35	H.S./College
S3	36	Blue-Chip Blues	Midscale	Suburban	Families	Age <45	High School
T2	37	Mayberry-ville	Midscale	Rural	Mix	Age 35–64	High School
T3	38	Simple Pleasures	LowerMid	Town/Rural	Sngl/Cpls	Age 65+	High School
S3	39	Domestic Duos	Midscale	Suburban	Sngl/Cpls	Age 55+	High School
U2	40	Close-In Couples	LowerMid	Urban	Sngl/Cpls	Age 55+	High School
C2	41	Sunset City Blues	LowerMid	2nd City	Sngl/Cpls	Age 65+	High School
T3	42	Red, White & Blues	LowerMid	Town	Mix	Age 25–44	High School
T3	43	Heartlanders	LowerMid	Rura	Sngl/Cpls	Age 45+	High School
S4	44	New Beginnings	LowerMid	Suburban	Mix	Age <35	High School

Continued

Exhibit 13.29

SIXTY-SIX CUSTOMER SEGMENTS DERIVED FROM PRIZM, NEW EVOLUTION *Marketers can classify consumers according to household- and geographic-level data. The logic is that consumers are more likely to share similar characteristics and behaviors with others who have similar demographic traits. PRIZM divides U.S. consumers into 14 different groups and 66 different segments. Which segment do you belong to?*

PRIZM$_{NE}$ TARGET FINDER REPORT RANKED BY SEGMENT *(Continued)*

PRIZM$_{NE}$ Clusters			Demographic Descriptors				
Social Group	#	Nickname	Income Level	Cluster Type	HH Composition	Adult Age	Education
T3	45	Blue Highways	LowerMid	Rural	Mix	Age 25–44	High School
S4	46	Old Glories	Downscale	Suburban	Singles	Age 65+	High School
C3	47	City Startups	Poor	2nd City	Singles	Age <35	H.S./College
T4	48	Young & Rustic	Downscale	Town	Mix	Age <35	High School
S4	49	American Classics	LowerMid	Suburban	Sngl/Cpls	Age 65+	High School
T3	50	Kid Country, USA	LowerMid	Town	Families	Age <45	High School
T3	51	Shotguns & Pickups	LowerMid	Rural	Families	Age 25–44	High School
S4	52	Suburban Pioneers	LowerMid	Suburban	Mix	Age <45	High School
C3	53	Mobility Blues	Downscale	2nd City	Mix	Age <35	High School
U2	54	Multi-Culti Mosaic	LowerMid	Urban	Mix	Age 25–44	High School
T4	55	Golden Ponds	Downscale	Town/Rural	Sngl/Cpls	Age 65+	Some H.S.
T4	56	Crossroads Villagers	Downscale	Rural	Sngl/Cpls	Age <45	High School
T4	57	Old Milltowns	Downscale	Town	Sngl/Cpls	Age 65+	Some H.S.
T4	58	Back Country Folks	Downscale	Rural	Sngl/Cpls	Age 55+	Some H.S.
U3	59	Urban Elders	Poor	Urban	Singles	Age 55+	Some H.S.
C3	60	Park Bench Seniors	Poor	2nd City	Singles	Age 55+	Some H.S.
U3	61	City Roots	Downscale	Urban	Sngl/Cpls	Age 65+	Some H.S.
C3	62	Hometown Retired	Downscale	2nd City	Sngl/Cpls	Age 65+	Some H.S.
C3	63	Family Thrifts	Downscale	2nd City	Families	Age <45	Some H.S.
T4	64	Bedrock America	Downscale	Town/Rural	Families	Age <35	Some H.S.
U3	65	Big City Blues	Downscale	Urban	Mix	Age <45	Some H.S.
U3	66	Low-Rise Living	Poor	Urban	Mix	Age <35	Some H.S.

Source: Copyright © Claritas, Inc. Reprinted with permission.

and other clusters. Within weeks of mailing test-drive offers to consumers in these and other targeted clusters, Hyundai was seeing more test drives and making more sales at a lower cost per vehicle sold.[113] Retailers can use clustering to identify neighborhoods of consumers most likely to purchase certain merchandise. Petco, which sells pet products, uses clustering to pinpoint neighborhoods where home ownership is high, because "usually renters don't own animals," says a company manager.[114] Clustering systems are also available for Germany, Australia, South Africa, and other countries. Experian's Global Mosaic system clusters consumers in other countries into 14 common lifestyle categories so global marketers can target consumers with similar characteristics in different parts of the world.[115]

Regions Across the World

Clearly, the area of the world in which a consumer resides can influence consumption patterns; as you've learned, cross-cultural variations exist in just about every aspect of consumer behavior. Here are just a few examples of how regions across the world differ in their consumer behavior.

Consumers in different countries vary dramatically in the way they spend their income. Six times as many cars pack the roads in Western Europe as in Eastern Europe. The most Coca-Cola is consumed in North America, followed by Latin America and the European community. The lowest consumption occurs in Asia, the Middle East, and Africa. The top chocolate markets are Switzerland, Britain, and Germany. The need for doctors is highest in Asia, including Indonesia, Thailand,

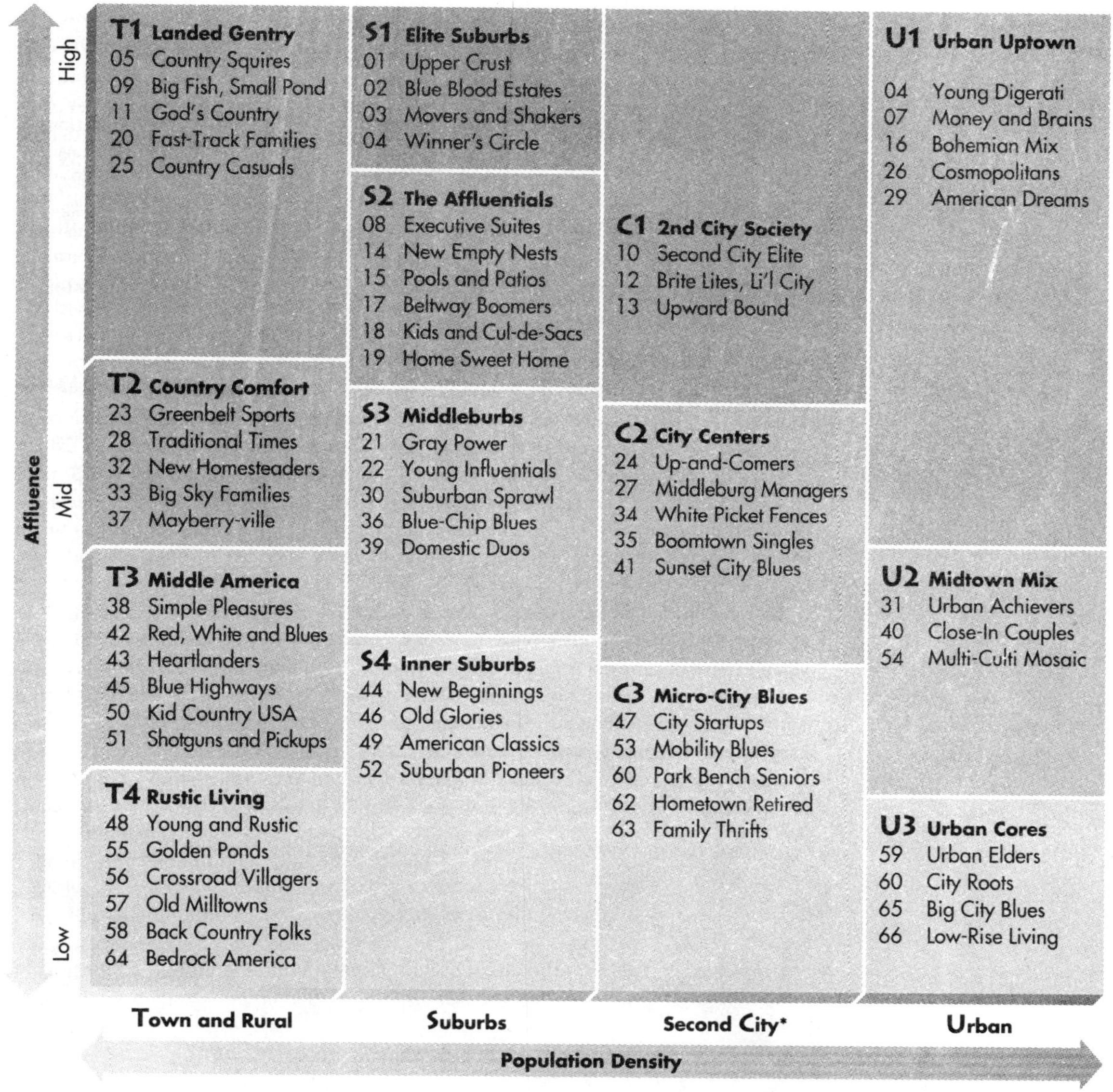

Exhibit 13.30
PRIZM CLUSTERS
PRIZM NE's social groups are based on population density ("urbanicity") and affluence.

Malaysia, India, and Pakistan. Finally, the fastest-growing restaurant cuisines in the United States are Thai, Indian, Vietnamese, and Cajun.[116]

Although some nations are strongly associated with certain products (such as beer in Germany and sushi in Japan), the consumption of specific types of products is forbidden in certain regions. For example, drinking alcohol and smoking are not allowed in Muslim countries, and religious restrictions forbid the consumption of pork in Israel and beef in India. Food preferences in one part of the world can sometimes appear exotic to people in other areas. The Chinese eat fish stomachs and soup made from bird saliva, natives of Thailand like deep fried chicken heads and claws, and the Iraqis snack on dried, salted locusts.[117]

* Smaller cities outside of the nation's metropolitan core.

Just as in the United States, regional differences in consumer behavior can occur within a specific region of the world. To illustrate, consumers in western India are generally more affluent and more favorably disposed toward premium products, whereas consumers in the north and east are more price conscious. Those in the south tend to be more conservative and utilitarian consumers. Also, in northern India the staple food and drink are wheat and tea; in the south, rice and coffee. Southern Indians tend to be more health conscious and to buy more health and beauty aids and cosmetics because of a desire for fair skin. Finally, southern Indians tend to go to the movies more often and to watch more regional TV due to local language differences, which is why advertising tends to be concentrated in the cinema and on regional TV broadcasts.

marketing IMPLICATIONS

Marketers need to understand global differences in consumer behavior so they can alter marketing strategy, where necessary, to appeal to specific regions and countries, as is the case in Exhibit 13.31. As an example, money-back guarantees give U.S. consumers confidence, but Latin Americans do not believe them because they never expect to get their money back. Also, the strategies of using famous endorsers or being the official product of a sporting event are much more effective in Venezuela and Mexico than in the United States.

Many companies adjust their brand positioning and marketing activities to accommodate global consumer differences.[118] McDonald's, for instance, created the spicy Prosperity Burger as a special menu item for Lunar New Year celebrations in Indonesia, South Korea, and other Asian nations.[119] In Brazil, the chain has offered northeastern specialties such as *acaraje, bobo de camarao,* and *vatapa.*[120] To draw consumers in Japan, where stores are generally small, Office Depot had to downsize its cavernous warehouse stores and reduce the number of office-supply products on the shelves.[121] And Procter & Gamble developed different versions of a TV ad for

Exhibit 13.31
REGIONAL MARKETING
McDonald's adapts its promotions to different regions of the world. This Hello Kitty plush doll giveaway was popular in Asian regions such as Hong Kong.

Pampers disposable diapers to account for variations in slang and accent in different regions of the German-speaking world.

Not heeding important cross-cultural differences can embarrass a company and cause products to fail. In Germany, Vicks had to change its brand name to Wicks, because the former term is slang for sexual intercourse. Adapting strategies to local differences does not ensure success, however. Despite educational programs mounted by Western pharmaceuticals firms, sales of antidepressants remain low in east Asia because mental illness still carries a stigma there, and many consumers are treated by alternative healers rather than psychiatrists.[122] Finally, marketers should remember that, as in the United States, consumers in different parts of one country may exhibit different consumer behavior. Consumers in Beijing and Shanghai prefer different foods, for instance—differences that are common in many of China's 2,000 cities.[123] This again shows why marketers must take regional differences into account.

States of India

Regional influences in India have been referred to as more of a state influence and Indians differ from each other on various levels (culture, languages, religion) and that impacts media consumption behavior. So there is so much to explore on an All India / State wise prospective to reach ones prospective consumer. There are 28 states and 7 union territories, 18 official languages and 1652 distinct dialects. In terms of religion also there are four predominant sects of Hindus, Muslims, Sikhs and Christians, in addition to which it is the homeland to the Buddhists and the Jains too.

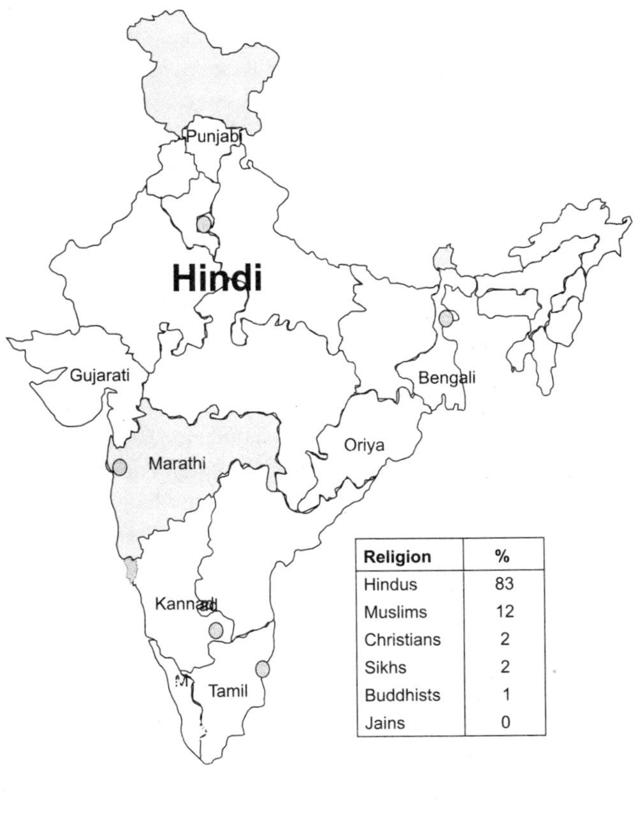

Religion	%
Hindus	83
Muslims	12
Christians	2
Sikhs	2
Buddhists	1
Jains	0

Exhibit 13.32
STATES AND LANGUAGES OF INDIA
India speaks approximately 18 different languages not counting the local dialects which add to 1652 types of them spoken in the various regions of the country.

In an indepth study in Census 2001 data on state exhibited as 13.33 illustrates the details of an earlier data presented as Exhibit 13.23. The statewise data gives in-depth details on the states of India and how they stand up on the asset ownership. States like Uttar Pradesh have the highest popualtion but are not the most affluent states. Assets and amenities penetration never rises above 50% in any category. Alternatively, Maharastra with the second highest population fares better than Bihar and West Bengal. In terms of household ownership of cars, Delhi ranks number one, followed by Goa

How Ethnic Influences Affect Consumer Behavior

Ethnic influences are another major factor that affects consumer behavior. It is important to emphasize that the generalizations about ethnic groups discussed in this chapter are only broad group tendencies and may or may not apply to individual consumers. Marketing to any consumer group requires careful research to get beyond stereotypes and identify specific characteristics and behavioral patterns that can be addressed using appropriate strategies and tactics.

Throughout the history of the United States, individuals from many different cultures have come to America, creating not only a unique national culture but also a number of subcultures or ***ethnic groups*** within the larger society. Members of these ethnic groups share a common heritage, set of beliefs, religion, and experiences that set them apart from others in society. Larger groups include the Hispanic, African American, Asian, Italian, Irish, Jewish, Scandinavian, and Polish subcultures.

These groups are bound together by cultural ties that can, in turn, strongly influence consumer behavior. Moreover, through the process of ***acculturation,*** members of a subculture must learn to adapt to the host culture. During acculturation, consumers acquire knowledge, skills, and behavior through social interaction, modeling the behavior of others, and reinforcement or receiving rewards for certain behaviors.[124] Acculturation is strongly influenced by family, friends, and institutions such as the media, place of worship, and school and combines with traditional customs to form a unique consumer culture.

Ethnic Groups Within the United States

The majority of U.S. consumers (commonly referred to as *Anglos*) can trace their ancestry back to one or more European nations. However, immigration and population trends are greatly changing the demographic profile of the United States. According to the U.S. census, the three largest ethnic groups within the U.S. population are African Americans (12.9 percent of the population), Hispanic Americans (12.5 percent), and Asian Americans (4.2 percent).[125] By 2030, nearly half the youth population of the United States will be non-Anglo—primarily Hispanic (see Exhibit 13.34).[126] As a result, the U.S. population is increasingly diverse.

Clearly, U.S. population trends have huge implications for marketers. Collectively, the three main U.S. subcultures control $1.5 trillion in buying power. Their buying power could surpass $4 trillion by the end of the decade as these groups continue to grow much faster than the general U.S. population.[127] Small wonder that many firms are targeting certain ethnic groups with appropriate marketing approaches. However, marketers need not focus on only one group. ***Multicultural***

State wise details	Total/ Rural/ Urban	Total number of households	Total number of households availing banking services	Availability of assets: Radio, Transistor	Television	Telephone	Bicycle	Scooter, Motor Cycle, Moped	Car, Jeep, Van	None of the specified assets
	1	2	3	4	5	6	7	8	9	10
INDIA	Total	191,963,935	68,230,642	67,415,133	60,649,623	17,549,991	83,838,450	22,484,686	4,801,899	66,198,648
INDIA	Rural	138,271,559	41,639,949	43,539,732	26,149,263	5,218,884	59,150,303	9,222,638	1,780,493	55,988,658
INDIA	Urban	53,692,376	26,590,693	23,875,401	34,500,360	12,331,107	24,688,147	13,262,048	3,021,406	10,209,990
JAMMU & KASHMI	Total	1,551,768	566,133	1,010,563	631,256	105,234	198,324	121,188	48,444	399,767
JAMMU & KASHMIR	Rural	1,161,357	344,778	716,578	334,834	26,380	106,850	44,724	17,014	362,009
JAMMU & KASHMIR	Urban	390,411	221,355	293,985	296,422	78,854	91,474	76,464	31,430	37,758
HIMACHAL PRADESH	Total	1,240,633	738,589	595,414	661,782	204,684	112,931	92,149	32,282	354,966
HIMACHAL PRADESH	Rural	1,097,520	631,029	513,296	552,905	152,552	99,328	67,587	19,812	334,849
HIMACHAL PRADESH	Urban	143,113	107,560	82,118	108,877	52,132	13,603	24,562	12,470	20,117
PUNJAB	Total	4,265,156	2,068,489	1,680,595	2,887,050	807,629	3,060,716	1,348,872	246,132	488,253
PUNJAB	Rural	2,775,462	1,269,055	1,067,450	1,700,192	329,247	2,057,300	749,719	102,020	368,824
PUNJAB	Urban	1,489,694	799,434	613,145	1,186,858	478,382	1,003,416	599,153	144,112	119,429
UTTARANCHAL	Total	1,586,321	948,975	788,182	680,881	157,180	489,837	189,366	42,329	407,213
UTTARANCHAL	Rural	1,196,157	671,508	614,430	385,975	53,012	309,688	73,636	15,026	360,211
UTTARANCHAL	Urban	390,164	277,467	173,752	294,906	104,168	180,149	115,730	27,303	47,002
HARYANA	Total	3,529,642	1,596,593	1,390,731	1,869,903	448,796	1,766,624	669,664	150,460	849,104
HARYANA	Rural	2,454,463	1,041,557	962,736	1,078,836	151,428	1,134,333	324,711	60,069	714,016
HARYANA	Urban	1,075,179	555,036	427,995	791,067	297,368	632,291	344,953	90,391	135,088
DELHI	Total	2,554,149	1,302,645	1,277,675	1,903,744	886,608	959,875	714,671	332,201	359,844
DELHI	Rural	169,528	78,892	79,001	117,334	33,475	82,567	35,129	12,322	23,877
DELHI	Urban	2,384,621	1,223,753	1,198,674	1,786,410	853,133	877,308	679,542	319,879	335,967
RAJASTHAN	Total	9,342,294	2,699,220	3,206,757	2,625,016	749,364	3,384,319	1,226,395	233,148	3,762,760
RAJASTHAN	Rural	7,156,703	1,716,486	2,266,596	1,186,690	247,961	2,266,268	521,775	118,181	3,369,415
RAJASTHAN	Urban	2,185,591	982,734	940,161	1,438,326	501,403	1,118,051	704,620	114,967	393,345
UTTAR PRADESH	Total	25,760,601	11,365,316	10,202,702	6,439,629	1,444,166	17,899,061	2,671,188	578,993	5,218,143
UTTAR PRADESH	Rural	20,590,074	8,627,075	7,849,601	3,296,351	496,161	14,649,539	1,378,316	304,014	4,407,805
UTTAR PRADESH	Urban	5,170,527	2,738,241	2,353,101	3,143,278	948,005	3,249,522	1,292,872	274,979	810,338
BIHAR	Total	13,982,590	2,984,496	3,882,745	1,267,766	312,350	5,682,084	509,177	127,159	6,925,037
BIHAR	Rural	12,660,007	2,360,437	3,353,519	700,149	131,073	5,078,742	310,071	82,578	6,499,484
BIHAR	Urban	1,322,583	624,059	529,226	567,617	181,277	603,342	199,106	44,581	425,553
SIKKIM	Total	104,738	31,106	38,002	32,392	13,792	448	1,820	2,367	51,511
SIKKIM	Rural	91,723	22,571	32,320	23,079	8,420	323	1,260	1,415	48,904
SIKKIM	Urban	13,015	8,535	5,682	9,313	5,372	125	560	952	2,607

Continued

Exhibit 13.33

Number of Households Availing Banking Services and Number of Households Having Each of the Specified Assets

Exhibit 13.33 *Continued*

State wise details	Total/ Rural/ Urban	Total number of households	Total number of households availing banking services	Availability of assets						
				Radio, Transistor	Television	Telephone	Bicycle	Scooter, Motor Cycle, Moped	Car, Jeep, Van	None of the specified assets
	1	2	3	4	5	6	7	8	9	10
ARUNACHAL PRADESH	Total	212,615	79,292	82,841	54,640	19,539	37,030	14,387	5,051	98,111
ARUNACHAL PRADESH	Rural	164,501	47,059	59,588	25,896	6,772	27,035	7,308	2,328	86,762
ARUNACHAL PRADESH	Urban	48,114	32,233	23,253	28,744	12,767	9,995	7,079	2,723	11,349
NAGALAND	Total	332,050	52,789	107,995	60,194	17,402	27,034	9,222	11,713	189,054
NAGALAND	Rural	265,334	30,574	79,787	30,118	6,409	20,296	5,294	6,379	165,554
NAGALAND	Urban	66,716	22,215	28,208	30,076	10,993	6,738	3,928	5,334	23,500
MANIPUR	Total	397,656	34,745	170,869	96,107	21,128	151,020	44,162	12,167	157,829
MANIPUR	Rural	296,354	18,804	113,086	49,112	8,447	94,110	20,610	5,799	137,186
MANIPUR	Urban	101,302	15,941	57,783	46,995	12,681	56,910	23,552	6,368	20,643
MIZORAM	Total	160,966	51,121	67,554	32,904	22,745	4,985	9,915	5,452	81,935
MIZORAM	Rural	79,362	12,692	25,542	5,085	2,797	1,830	1,968	865	51,340
MIZORAM	Urban	81,604	38,429	42,012	27,819	19,948	3,155	7,947	4,587	30,595
TRIPURA	Total	662,023	175,198	188,744	156,935	34,693	202,398	25,988	7,196	330,331
TRIPURA	Rural	539,680	111,389	138,229	83,573	11,140	149,134	10,631	4,169	301,518
TRIPURA	Urban	122,343	63,809	50,515	73,362	23,553	53,264	15,357	3,027	28,813
MEGHALAYA	Total	420,246	87,497	134,323	87,785	25,100	46,060	12,150	11,308	231,746
MEGHALAYA	Rural	329,678	41,882	95,421	34,760	5,176	39,009	5,024	4,250	205,362
MEGHALAYA	Urban	90,568	45,615	38,902	53,025	19,924	7,051	7,126	7,058	26,384
ASSAM	Total	4,935,358	1,013,252	1,489,742	903,126	214,203	2,289,426	257,023	101,167	2,006,045
ASSAM	Rural	4,220,173	632,093	1,207,270	508,212	79,364	1,985,318	139,978	48,737	1,826,013
ASSAM	Urban	715,185	381,159	282,472	394,914	134,839	304,108	117,045	52,430	180,032
WEST BENGAL	Total	15,715,915	5,781,591	6,073,279	4,173,596	1,052,629	8,264,357	790,322	297,634	4,727,771
WEST BENGAL	Rural	11,161,870	3,076,221	4,093,465	1,494,335	200,230	6,059,054	341,227	135,005	3,799,330
WEST BENGAL	Urban	4,554,045	2,705,370	1,979,814	2,679,261	852,399	2,205,303	449,095	162,629	928,441
JHARKHAND	Total	4,862,590	1,465,831	1,282,074	838,732	162,815	2,446,821	454,436	74,617	1,923,641
JHARKHAND	Rural	3,802,412	806,537	895,245	253,814	32,341	1,873,209	151,114	22,012	1,684,316
JHARKHAND	Urban	1,060,178	659,294	386,829	584,918	130,474	573,612	303,322	52,605	239,325
ORISSA	Total	7,870,127	1,905,716	1,862,036	1,218,877	310,846	4,089,049	618,753	84,875	3,226,907
ORISSA	Rural	6,782,879	1,339,221	1,440,408	625,940	111,644	3,351,768	306,651	42,126	3,009,290
ORISSA	Urban	1,087,248	566,495	421,628	592,937	199,202	737,281	312,102	42,749	217,617
CHHATTISGARH	Total	4,148,518	1,000,575	969,027	892,003	157,330	2,482,261	448,689	56,011	1,337,139
CHHATTISGARH	Rural	3,359,078	634,858	725,013	421,264	34,960	1,954,310	196,610	19,699	1,199,048
CHHATTISGARH	Urban	789,440	365,717	244,014	470,739	122,370	527,951	252,079	36,312	138,091
MADHYA PRADESH	Total	10,919,653	3,048,800	2,281,329	3,236,446	674,855	4,673,887	1,318,355	195,047	4,602,640
MADHYA PRADESH	Rural	8,124,795	1,714,498	1,411,799	1,369,062	158,343	3,107,981	486,940	72,623	4,099,959

Continued

Exhibit 13.33 *Continued*

State wise details	Total/ Rural/ Urban	Total number of households	Total number of households availing banking services	Availability of assets						
				Radio, Transistor	Television	Telephone	Bicycle	Scooter, Motor Cycle, Moped	Car, Jeep, Van	None of the specified assets
	1	2	3	4	5	6	7	8	9	10
MADHYA PRADESH	Urban	2,794,858	1,334,302	869,530	1,867,384	516,512	1,565,906	831,415	122,424	502,681
GUJARAT	Total	9,643,989	3,648,745	2,910,568	3,731,727	1,202,761	3,598,297	2,035,331	330,803	3,596,904
GUJARAT	Rural	5,885,961	1,757,732	1,445,190	1,271,481	325,697	1,726,407	696,613	107,314	2,916,421
GUJARAT	Urban	3,758,028	1,891,013	1,465,378	2,460,246	877,064	1,871,890	1,338,718	223,489	680,483
MAHARASHTRA	Total	19,063,149	9,175,825	6,843,363	8,410,197	2,686,081	5,731,801	2,513,953	642,064	7,016,634
MAHARASHTRA	Rural	10,993,623	4,333,606	2,946,401	2,717,806	481,112	3,112,816	878,525	177,497	5,518,912
MAHARASHTRA	Urban	8,069,526	4,842,219	3,896,962	5,692,391	2,204,969	2,618,985	1,635,428	464,567	1,497,722
ANDHRA PRADESH	Total	16,849,857	5,229,627	3,644,190	5,302,519	1,445,424	5,531,090	1,687,507	215,878	7,739,831
ANDHRA PRADESH	Rural	12,676,218	3,850,064	2,336,629	2,702,661	498,673	3,797,888	652,057	65,952	6,738,636
ANDHRA PRADESH	Urban	4,173,639	1,379,563	1,307,561	2,599,858	946,751	1,733,202	1,035,450	149,926	1,001,195
KARNATAKA	Total	10,232,133	4,092,035	4,728,781	3,783,346	1,307,008	3,084,050	1,478,026	313,654	3,569,912
KARNATAKA	Rural	6,675,173	2,350,550	2,813,899	1,416,971	379,957	1,858,848	486,479	90,708	2,865,088
KARNATAKA	Urban	3,556,960	1,741,485	1,914,882	2,366,375	927,051	1,225,202	991,547	222,946	704,824
GOA	Total	279,216	203,214	161,432	177,330	81,372	87,925	108,179	29,563	54,745
GOA	Rural	140,755	97,079	76,650	78,221	30,544	43,108	46,737	9,613	33,802
GOA	Urban	138,461	106,135	84,782	99,109	50,828	44,817	61,442	19,950	20,943
KERALA	Total	6,595,206	3,370,034	3,903,341	2,560,680	1,257,615	1,216,832	659,520	262,507	1,795,041
KERALA	Rural	4,942,550	2,479,299	2,908,735	1,594,344	774,009	776,684	365,363	141,113	1,481,290
KERALA	Urban	1,652,656	890,735	994,606	966,336	483,606	440,148	294,157	121,394	313,751
TAMIL NADU	Total	14,173,626	3,234,770	6,172,203	5,595,386	1,592,540	6,014,940	2,280,742	309,595	4,589,040
TAMIL NADU	Rural	8,274,790	1,465,062	3,193,451	2,013,409	420,853	3,299,103	888,461	88,481	3,314,616
TAMIL NADU	Urban	5,898,836	1,769,708	2,978,752	3,581,977	1,171,687	2,715,837	1,392,281	221,114	1,274,424

Source: Census 2001

Exhibit 13.34

ETHNIC COMPOSITION OF UNDER-18 U.S. CONSUMERS

In the coming years, the Hispanic American, African American, Asian American, and other non-Anglo youth population will continue to grow much faster than the Anglo youth population in the United States. By 2030, projections indicate that non-Anglo youngsters under 18 will comprise nearly half of the total U.S. youth population.

We are the World

Ethnic kids and teens are fueling growth in the youth market.

(UNDER AGE 18)	2001	2010	2020	2030	% CHANGE (2001–2030)
Total Youth	71.0 mil	72.5 mil	77.6 mil	83.4 mil	+18%
Hispanic	11.3 (16%)	13.7 (16%)	17.2 (22%)	21.0 (25%)	+85%
Non-Hispanic White	45.2 (64%)	42.7 (59%)	42.4 (55%)	42.3 (51%)	–6%
Non-Hispanic Black	10.7 (15%)	11.3 (16%)	12.2 (16%)	13.2 (16%)	+24%
Asian/ Pacific Islander	3.2 (5%)	4.0 (6%)	5.0 (7%)	6.1 (7%)	+94%
Other Non-Hispanic	0.7 (1%)	0.7 (1%)	0.8 (1%)	0.9 (1%)	+27%

(in millions, % of total youth) *Percentages may not equal 100 due to rounding*

marketing, the use of strategies that appeal to a variety of cultures at the same time, is quite popular. Soft Sheen-Carson, which originally specialized in hair-care products for African American consumers, has broadened its focus through multicultural marketing. "Because we are a culture that comes in many hues," says the company president, "the advertising should be reflective of the multihues that we come in."[128] To be effective, this approach requires both a long-term commitment and consideration of ethnic groups from the outset, rather than as an afterthought.[129]

Hispanic American Consumers Hispanic Americans represent one of the largest, most diverse, and fastest-growing ethnic groups in the United States today, more than 42 million strong. This subculture can be divided into four major groups: Mexican Americans (58.5 percent), living primarily in the Southwest and California; Puerto Ricans (9.6 percent), centered in New York; Central and Southern Americans (8.6 percent); and Cuban Americans (3.5 percent), located primarily in southern Florida.[130]

Hispanics can also be divided into several groups based on their level of acculturation to the host culture: (1) the *acculturated,* who speak mostly English and have a high level of assimilation; (2) the *bicultural,* who can function in either English or Spanish; and (3) the *traditional,* who speak mostly Spanish.[131] The rate of acculturation tends to be slow, usually taking four generations, because 80 percent of all Hispanics marry other Hispanics. However, some Hispanic Americans resist assimilation and desire to maintain their ethnic identity.[132] And although more than 75 percent of Hispanic youth are bilingual, the proportion of consumers speaking Spanish at home, more than 70 percent, is increasing.[133]

The median age of the Hispanic American population is 26—well below the overall U.S. median age of 36—although the median age of Cuban Americans is 41 and the median age of Mexican Americans is 24.[134] Other important demographics include a lower divorce rate than the general population, reflecting strong family and religious values; larger families, with an average of 2.2 children versus fewer than 2 for the general U.S. population; a higher proportion of blue-collar occupations; a median income lower than the general population; and a lower level of education.[135] Note, however, that both education and occupational levels are now rising dramatically.[136]

The consumer's level of acculturation affects consumption patterns, as does the ***intensity of ethnic identification.***[137] Consumers who strongly identify with their ethnic group and are less acculturated into the mainstream culture are more likely to exhibit the consumption patterns of the ethnic group. Strong Hispanic identification leads to a higher level of husband-dominant decisions (discussed in greater detail in Chapter 14).[138] Furthermore, strong identifiers are more likely to be influenced by radio ads, billboards, family members, and coworkers and are less likely than weak identifiers to use coupons.[139]

marketing IMPLICATIONS

Marketers are using a variety of marketing activities to reach Hispanic Americans. Here are a few examples showing how marketers apply their knowledge of consumer behavior to successfully target consumers in this subculture.

Product development

Marketers are building customer loyalty by developing offerings specifically for Hispanic Americans. Cosmetics firms such as Revlon, Maybelline, Cover Girl, Estée Lauder, and L'Oréal have developed cosmetics designed for consumers with darker skin.[140] Frito-Lay created a line of zestier Doritos snacks for the Hispanic American segment; within a year, the products were ringing up more than $100 million in annual sales.[141] And McDonald's has been successful with a Mexican-style Fiesta Menu in southern California.[142]

Media targeting

Because Hispanic Americans tend to be concentrated in certain areas and share a common language, many can be targeted with Spanish-language media, including TV, radio, print, billboards, and websites. Not surprisingly, Hispanic American consumers are heavy users of these media, leading to unprecedented growth in advertising sales.[143] Thus, when Miller Brewing wanted to boost sales of its beer to Hispanic Americans, it arranged with the Spanish-language TV network Univision to sponsor World Cup soccer matches and boxing programs.[144]

Advertising messages

More marketers are developing ads targeting Hispanic Americans, including Procter & Gamble, AT&T, and Toyota.[145] Advertising is particularly important in this segment because many Hispanics prefer prestigious or nationally advertised brands. When Hanes started an advertising campaign targeting Hispanic consumers in Chicago and San Antonio, its pantyhose sales increased by 8 percent.[146] Corona Beer, Mexico's best-selling brand, has boosted U.S. sales by advertising to blue-collar Hispanic workers and linking some promotions to Cinco de Mayo celebrations.[147] Messages stressing family themes repeatedly win the praise of Hispanic American consumers during ad tests.[148] Advertising can address different Hispanic segments. In an ad based on the theme, "Coke and your favorite meal," the soft drink was shown with a taco for Mexican Americans, pork loin for Cubans, and chicken and rice for Puerto Ricans.

Exhibit 13.12
MULTICULTURAL MARKETING

This ad is a good example of multicultural advertising. Several ethnic groups are represented in it.

Hispanic Americans tend to react positively to ads using ethnic spokespeople, who are perceived as more trustworthy, leading to more positive attitudes toward the brand being advertised.[149] This approach is most effective in environments where ethnicity is more salient (the group is in the minority).[150] Ads with verbal or visual cues that draw attention to ethnicity can trigger "ethnic self-awareness" and generate more favorable responses from the targeted group.[151] Marketers who develop ads specifically for Hispanic Americans or other groups should remember that although members of the overall culture may be exposed to the messages, they are unlikely to react in the same way as the targeted group, because they are less familiar with the cues in the ads.[152] Also, some advertisers try to make ethnic representation in ads proportional to the group's size relative to the general population.[153]

Simply translating an advertising message into Spanish for the Hispanic community can lead to inadvertent blunders.[154] For instance, a Coors Light campaign, "Turn It Loose Tonight," was translated literally into Spanish but was interpreted as meaning "Have the Runs Tonight" by Hispanics in the Southwest.

Accommodation theory can also apply when marketers develop advertising for Hispanics. This theory predicts that the more effort a source puts into communicating with a group by, for example, using role models and the native language, the greater the response by this group and the more positive their feelings. As predicted by accommodation theory, advertising in Spanish increases perceptions of the company's sensitivity toward and solidarity with the Hispanic community, creating positive feelings toward the brand and the company.[155] However, using Spanish messages exclusively can lead to negative ad perceptions. Many ads directed toward Hispanic Americans are delivered in English because viewers are often bilingual or highly acculturated. Thus effective strategy may involve both English and Spanish, which is how Anheuser-Busch plans its TV commercials for Hispanic Americans.[156]

Distribution

More marketers are tailoring the distribution of products and services for Hispanic American consumers. El Guero and Delray Farms in Chicago, Fiesta Market in Texas, Vallarta Foods in Los Angeles, and Varadero supermarkets in southern Florida are full-scale Hispanic markets with a broad selection of Hispanic foods and other products.[157] Building on this subculture's focus on the family, the discount store Target positions children's clothing and baby products near the front of stores located in areas with a high Hispanic American population.[158]

African American Consumers

More than 35 million African Americans live in the United States, and this population is expected to exceed 45 million by 2020.[159] African Americans represent a large and diverse group consisting of many subsegments across different levels of income and education, occupations, and regions. Among African American households, nearly 30 percent have an income of $50,000 or higher; 46 percent are homeowners; and more are single-parent families headed by women than in the general population. The South is home to more than half of all African American consumers, with a high proportion living in major urban areas. Nearly 15 percent of African Americans have college degrees, compared with 24 percent of the overall U.S. population.[160]

As with any subculture, African American consumers have some similarities to the general population and also differ in certain ways. For example, African Americans are more likely to believe that people should feel free to live, dress, and look the way they want to.[161] They also do not necessarily aspire to desert their heritage and assimilate with the majority culture.[162] Yet, as incomes rise, a strong desire to preserve a cultural identity develops.

A defining element in the consumption patterns of African Americans is the importance of style, self-image, and elegance. Consumption patterns are also related to a strong desire to be recognized and show status. According to research, African Americans often buy premium brands of boys' clothing to make a statement about themselves.[163] African Americans have preferences for distinctive fashion and music—touching off trends that often are emulated by members of the general population, particularly teenagers.[164]

marketing IMPLICATIONS

African American consumers have a total buying power exceeding $500 billion, and their buying power is multiplying every year.[165] Furthermore, they respond positively to offerings and communications targeted toward them and are less likely to trust or buy brands that are not advertised.[166]

Product development

Many marketers focus primarily on products for the unique needs of the African American market, the way Soft Sheen-Carson and African Pride have created hair care brands for this market.[167] In addition, marketers that make products for the broader U.S. population are now branching out to design products specifically for black consumers; L'eggs, for instance, sells panty hose shades for darker skin.[168] Clothing manufacturers are designing styles more flattering for the physique of African American women. They are also featuring colorful styles based on African kente cloth.

Media targeting

African Americans watch more TV and have more positive attitudes toward ads than do Anglo consumers.[169] According to research, strong ethnic identifiers among African American consumers act more positively than weak identifiers to ads placed in racially targeted media.[170] In fact, 82.3 percent of African American consumers seek out information from magazines specifically aimed at them.[171] Thus marketers such as Colgate-Palmolive reach African Americans through targeted magazines such as *Ebony* and *Essence*.[172] African American TV networks (such as Black Entertainment Television) and targeted websites such as BET.com also are good media vehicles. African American radio stations have long been a cultural lifeline and represent an efficient advertising vehicle.[173] Mercedes, for example, relied primarily on radio in a campaign targeting affluent African American car buyers in Baltimore, Philadelphia, and Washington, D.C.[174] And direct marketing works well: Kraft sends a free recipe magazine, *Food and Family*, to households in areas with large African American populations.[175]

Advertising messages

Some of the largest U.S. advertisers, including General Motors, Procter & Gamble, and Johnson & Johnson, are investing in ad campaigns specifically for this segment.[176] As noted earlier, subcultures such as African Americans will identify more strongly and have more positive evaluations when the advertising source is of the same ethnic group as the target.[177] Thus advertising for this segment should take the unique values and expectations of African Americans into account rather than simply using an Anglo strategy (see Exhibit 13.35).[178] The director of ethnic marketing for Coors Brewing says that thanks to targeted ads, "the attitude of African American young males toward our company and toward the Coors Light brand has increased significantly."[179] As another example, when Maybelline was planning ads targeting African American women, it learned that they want to be treated like all

Exhibit 13.35
TARGETING BY ETHNIC INFLUENCE
Ads directed at African Americans need to express the strong values of this group. This ad for Wal-Mart stresses the value of education and heritage.

other women and to be depicted as strong, contemporary, and self-confident—information the company used to create appropriate messages.[180]

Marketers must also be aware of the effect that African American models and actors in ads may have on consumers outside the targeted segment. According to Coors's director of ethnic marketing, the targeted advertising has boosted the beer's overall sales, not just sales to African American consumers, "because African American consumers in urban markets have a lot of influence on what's cool with the general market."[181] On the other hand, one study found that some Anglo consumers had less favorable attitudes and were less likely to purchase the product when ads featured African American rather than Anglo actors.[182] This problem is more pronounced when Anglo consumers are prejudiced toward non-Anglos. Yet, research suggests that younger Anglo consumers are more accepting of non-Anglo actors, which may reduce the problem over time.[183]

Distribution

Marketers can also adjust distribution strategies to appeal to African American consumers. KFC outlets in largely African American neighborhoods have played upbeat music and dressed employees in traditional African garb with kente ties, vests, and kufu hats.[184] In areas where African Americans represent more than 20 percent of the population, J.C. Penney has developed "Authentic African Boutiques" that offer clothing, handbags, hats, and other accessories imported from Africa.

Asian American Consumers

Asian Americans are the third-largest and fastest-growing major subculture in the United States. The number of Asian Americans doubled in the last decade to more than 10 million and is expected to increase even more rapidly in the coming years.[185] The largest concentrations are in California cities, New York City and its suburbs, and Hawaii, where more than 65 percent of the population is of Asian descent. Growth has also been high in other urban areas, including Chicago and Washington, D.C.[186]

The Asian American community is even more diverse than the Hispanic American and African American groups because it consists of people from more than 29 countries, from the Indian subcontinent to the Pacific Ocean, each with its own values and customs. The six largest groups include immigrants from China, the Philippines, India, Korea, Vietnam, and Japan.[187] In light of this tremendous diversity, marketers should research the specific subsegment to be targeted and not rely on broad statements about Asian Americans as a group.

Despite this diversity, Asian Americans tend to exhibit several similar consumption patterns. One common denominator of most Asian cultures is the strong emphasis on the family, tradition, and cooperation.[188] These consumers shop frequently and enjoy shopping with friends. They want brand names and are willing to pay for top quality, even though they react positively to bargains. Also, Asian Americans frequently recommend offerings to friends and relatives.[189] Thus Consolidated Restaurants in Seattle ran a two-week campaign in Japanese promoting its eateries on mainstream radio stations. "We know there is a significant Japanese population that's bilingual and they're going to talk to each other," says the marketer who created the campaign.[190] Asian Americans are more than twice as likely as the average consumer to check prices and products on the Internet before they buy.[191] Consumers in this group also tend to save money, be highly educated, have higher computer literacy, and hold a higher percentage of professional and managerial jobs than the general population.[192] More than half live in integrated suburbs as opposed to ethnic areas such as a Chinatown, and most tend to be highly assimilated by the second and third generations.

marketing
IMPLICATIONS

Because Asian Americans are a rapidly growing group with buying power approaching $450 billion in annual purchases, this subculture is attractive to many marketers.[193] Another reason is that the median income for Asian Americans is nearly $55,000, well above the overall U.S. median income of $43,000. Moreover, 22 percent of Asian American households have an annual income of $100,000 or more, compared with 14 percent of overall U.S. households earning at this income level.[194]

Product development

Marketers are increasingly offering products designed with Asian Americans in mind.[195] More companies now offer cosmetic shades that blend better with Asian skin colors and teach consumers appropriate skin care techniques. The Pleasant Company has also developed dolls for the Asian American market. One company mistakenly offered golf balls in a four-pack instead of the usual three-pack, not knowing that the word *four* sounds similar to the word for death in both Japanese and Chinese and is therefore considered unlucky.

Media targeting

To reach this very diverse group, marketers often use native-language newspapers, magazines, TV, and radio. Ford has done this, placing newspaper ads in Mandarin, Korean, and Cantonese and running TV commercials in Cantonese, Mandarin, and Vietnamese.[196] Citibank has used direct mail to attract Chinese American depositors with an offer of a gold medallion in exchange for a minimum deposit of $30,000.[197] The Internet is an excellent way to reach Asian Americans: Charles Schwab, for instance, has a Chinese language version of its brokerage website, and HSBC, a global bank, has sponsored the Chinese language World Cup soccer site.[198] Also, satellite TV allows Asian American immigrants to see shows produced in their homelands, interspersed with culturally appropriate programs produced in the United States and accompanied by ads for U.S. products.[199]

Advertising messages

Messages delivered in the native language are often more effective. Despite the diversity of languages within this subculture, marketers may find the effort worthwhile when many consumers from a single subgroup are concentrated in an area. For instance, Toyota dealers in Seattle air commercials on the International Channel in Mandarin, Cantonese, Tagalog, Vietnamese, and Korean.[200] Taking advantage of the popularity of Yao Ming and other basketball stars recruited from China, the National Basketball Association has promoted the sport with ads in Chinese-language newspapers in six U.S. cities.[201] Asian Americans tend to respond to subtle messages that focus on tradition, the family, and cooperation.[202] Interestingly, one study found that Asian models tend to be overrepresented in business settings and underrepresented in home and family settings.[203]

Promotions and distribution

Linking promotions to the language, interests, or lifestyles of a particular Asian American group can be quite successful. To illustrate, Pacific Place shopping center in Seattle draws Japanese American shoppers by printing coupons and special offers in English on one side and Japanese on the other. Moreover, marketers can design or modify distribution channels for Asian American consumers. The United Savings Bank in San Francisco decorates its branches in popular colors of red and gold.[204]

[13] In India, ethnic groups usually cover the Parsis and the North Eastern population of India. However, unlike the USA, UK, and Australian Censuses, the national Census of India does not recognize racial or ethnic groups within India but recognizes many of the tribal groups as Scheduled Castes and Tribes Organizations and individuals not affiliated with India's national census have classified India into racial/ethnic groups. These racial and ethnic groups are debated. According to the Joshua Project, there are 2,334 ethnic groups in India. The Indian people are descended from more or less all of the peoples that historically settled in the subcontinent including the Caucasoid groups of Dravidians, Indo-Aryans, Iranians, Bactrians, Europeans, Greeks, Hepthalites, Arabs, the Australoid Austro-Asiatics, the Mongoloid Tibeto-Burmans, Kushans, Turks, Mughals, and a few African Siddis exist as well.

It should be noted that Dravidian, Indo-Aryan, Austro-Asiatic and Tibeto-Burman are linguistic terms and cannot be directly taken as ethnic terms. It simply means a speaker of a language belonging to a particular linguistic family. The speakers of these languages descend from a plethora of different ethnic groups that eventually adopted one or more set of languages. The traits of each of these groups can be found in at least some small segments of the population, but over a period of time these superficial differences in appearances have blurred to a great extent. The framework of the culture of the Indian people comes from these various ethnic groups who contributed to Indian civilization as it is today.

Ethnic Groups Around the World

Ethnic subcultures exist in many nations. It is beyond the scope of this book to discuss each of the numerous ethnic groups around the world, but a few examples should illustrate their importance and the challenges and opportunities of reaching specific groups within a particular country.

In Canada, the French-speaking subculture has unique motivations and buying habits.[205] Compared with the rest of the Canadian population, French Canadians use more staples for original or "scratch" cooking; drink more soft drinks, beer, wine, and instant beverages; and consume fewer frozen vegetables, diet drinks, and hard liquor. Patriotism and ethnic pride are extremely strong, and this theme has been successfully incorporated into marketing by Kodak, McDonald's, KFC, and others.[206]

The former Soviet Union was a diverse country, with more than 100 different ethnic groups speaking more than 50 different languages. The breakup of this large nation yielded a number of countries with strong ethnic cores, including Russia, the Baltic countries (Lithuania, Estonia, and Latvia), Belorussia, and Ukraine.

In Thailand more than 80 percent of the population is of Thai origin, but several sizable ethnic subcultures still flourish. The largest, 10 percent of the population, has Chinese roots, and this segment has influenced the Thai culture to a significant degree.[207] Chinese consumers in Thailand exert a powerful economic force because they own many businesses; their influence is also felt in art, religion, and food. This ethnic group has assimilated very well into the main Thai society. Other smaller ethnic groups in Thailand include people of Laotian, Indian, and Burmese origin.

India has a diverse ethnic population, with more than 80 languages and 120 dialects spoken in the country. Some villagers need travel only 30 miles from home to reach a destination where they are not able to speak the language. KFC and Pizza Hut, both owned by Yum Brands, have done well in India by customizing their American-style menus to the tastes of consumers in specific cities, with local ingredients and flavors that appeal to each subsegment.[208]

The Influence of Religion

A final type of subculture is based on religious beliefs. Religion provides people with a structured set of beliefs and values that serve as a code of conduct or guide to behavior. It also provides ties that bind people together and make one group different from another. According to a recent survey, the majority of Americans are either Protestant or Catholic. By comparison, only a small fraction of Americans identify themselves as being Jewish, Mormon, Muslim, or a follower of another religion.[209]

Although individual differences certainly come into play, some religious influences or traditions can affect consumer behavior. One study found that Jewish consumers were more likely than non-Jews to be exposed in childhood to information from print media, group memberships, and special training; to seek information from TV, magazines, and other media; to adopt new products; to provide information to others; and to remember more information.[210] A study of weekend leisure activities found that the price of the activity was the most important factor for Protestants, whereas companionship was more critical for Jews, and Catholics were more likely to prefer dancing.[211] Born-again Christians, on the other hand, were less likely to buy on credit, purchase national brands, or attend rock concerts and movies.[212]

Religion can also prevent consumption of certain products or services. Mormons are prohibited from using liquor, tobacco, and caffeine, including cola. Orthodox Jews do not eat pork or shellfish, and all meat and poultry must be certified as kosher. Muslims cannot eat pork or drink liquor. Catholic consumers may choose to abstain from eating meat on Fridays during the season of Lent.

Religious subcultures are clearly present in many parts of the world. In India, for example, most of the population is Hindu, but large groups of Muslims, Christians, and Sikhs exhibit different patterns of consumption. Because Hindus are predominantly vegetarian, Indian manufacturers of food and cosmetics must use vegetable-based rather than animal-based oils and shortening in their products. The Sikh religion forbids the consumption of beef and tobacco, and the sale of such products is low in areas where many Sikhs live. Finally, the color green has significance for Muslims, which has led to its frequent use on product packages for this group.

marketing IMPLICATIONS

Marketers can segment the market by focusing on religious affiliation, delivering targeted messages and promotions, or using certain media. They can target Christian consumers through religious radio stations, cable TV networks, and TV programs, which reach millions of U.S. consumers. A number of marketers reach Christian consumers through commercials on Salem Communications' Christian music radio stations in Dallas, Atlanta, Los Angeles, and Chicago.[213] In addition, marketers can advertise in one of the many publications geared to specific religious affiliations.

Marketing tactics should demonstrate understanding and respect for the beliefs and customs of the targeted group—and in close-knit groups, word of mouth is a powerful communicator. Thus Denali Flavors, an ice cream company in Michigan, has gained a loyal following among born-again Christians who like the company's strong support of Christian causes. As another example, Target sponsored part of a national concert tour of the Newsboys, a Christian music group, and promoted this sponsorship through local media in each concert city as well as in-store materials playing up the connection.[214]

In planning distribution, marketers can consider stores such as King's House in Scottsdale, Arizona, which specializes in religious products. And more religious institutions are opening gift shops, snack bars, even fitness centers, providing distribution opportunities for suitable goods and services.[215] Finally, marketers sometimes use religious themes to sell products. A common example is special products or packages produced during times of religious holidays. However, for broad appeal and to avoid alienating certain groups, some marketers avoid products or messages with overt religious meaning. To illustrate, the teen retail chain Hot Topic will not sell products emblazoned with religious symbols. "If someone who isn't familiar with our store walks by our window display and is offended by what they see, we won't carry it," explains the general merchandise manager.[216]

In a large secular nation like India, religion has always been a debatable issue, especially with a large base of Hindu population, exceeding over 80 per cent (as shown in Exhibit 13.37). There is a large base of muslim population that exists in India and forms the largest religious group after Hindus (see Exhibit 13.36 for mus-

Exhibit 13.36
MUSLIM POPULATION BREAKUP

Half of the Muslim population in India is based in UP and West Bengal

		Muslim Population, 2001 (in Millions)			
		Approximation I	Approximation II	Approximation III	Average
	India	132.79	138.57	128.67	133.54
1.	UP	30.26	32.99	30.25	31.17
2.	W. Bengal	18.96	22.02	30.25	19.98
3.	Bihar	16.26	16.56	16.26	16.36
4.	Maharashtra	9.55	10.63	9.35	9.84
5.	Kerala	6.77	8.52	7.42	7.57
6.	Assam	6.27	9.02	7.55	7.61
7.	AP	6.76	7.76	6.75	7.09
8.	Karnataka	6.16	6.55	6.15	6.29
9.	J&K	6.46	5.16	5.17	5.59
10.	Gujarat	4.47	4.48	4.42	4.46
11.	Rajasthan	4.52	4.96	4.55	4.68
12.	MP	4.03	4.36	4.02	4.14
13.	Tamil Nadu	3.36	3.66	3.35	3.45
14.	Delhi	1.36	1.65	1.36	1.46

lim population break up). However, from the marketers perspective, religion has never been the basis of segmenting markets. They have been used to profile target audience in communication and promotion. The little sardar kid playing around with a toy Maruti car — Petrol Khatam Hi Nahin Honda (The petrol never finishes) in the Maruti 800 advertisement, showcases a Sikh family. Films have also used religious settings to showcase characters.

Exhibit 13.37

The religion mix of the Indian population

Religions of India

Religion	Persons	Percent
All Religions	1,028,610,328	100.00%
Hindus	827,578,868	80.456%
Muslims	138,188,240	13.434%
Christians	24,080,016	2.341%
Sikhs	19,215,730	1.868%
Buddhists	7,955,207	0.773%
Jains	4,225,053	0.41%
Others	6,639,626	0.645%
Religion not stated	727,588	0.07%

Source: Census of India, 2001

The other exhibit 13.38 illustrates how the growth patterns have happened for the religious sub groups. The most notable is the growth in the muslim population at 36 percent, contrasted with very low literacy rates. [14] Contacts between India and other cultures have led to the spread of Indian religions throughout the world, resulting in extensive influence of Indian thought and practice on Southeast and East Asia in ancient times and, more recently, in the diffusion of Indian religions to Europe and North America. Within India, a vast majority of people engage in rituals that are motivated by religious systems originated in the past but are continuously evolving. Religion, then, is one of the most important facets of Indian history and contemporary life. A number of world religions originated in India, and others that started elsewhere found fertile ground for growth there.

Census information for 2001

Composition	Hindus	Muslims	Christians	Sikhs	Buddhist	Jains	Others
% total of population 2001	80.46	13.43	2.34	1.87	0.77	0.41	0.65
10-Yr Growth % (est '91–'01)[13][b]	20.3	36.0	22.6	18.2	24.5	26	103.1
Sex ratio* (avg. 933)	931	936	1009	893	953	940	992
Literacy rate (avg. 64.8)	65.1	59.1	80.3	69.4	72.7	94.1	47.0
Work Participation Rate	40.4	31.3	39.7	37.7	40.6	32.9	48.4
Rural sex ratio[13]	944	953	1001	895	958	937	995
Urban sex ratio[13]	894	907	1026	886	944	941	966
Child sex ratio (0–6 yrs)	925	950	964	786	942	870	976

Source: The First Report on Religion: Census of India 2001

Exhibit 13.38

Growth index for the different religions in India

Summary

Six major aspects of consumer diversity have important effects on consumer behavior: age; gender; sexual orientation; and regional, ethnic, and religious differences. Age is a key factor because people of the same age have similar life experiences, needs, symbols, and memories that may lead to similar consumption patterns. Teens have significant spending power and influence family purchasing, as well. Generation Y consists of consumers in their twenties. Consumers who make up Generation X were born between 1965 and 1976. Baby boomers, born 1946 to 1964, are the largest age category in the United States. Seniors in the 50 and older segment can be divided into two groups: the ***young again*** and the gray market, neither of which wants to be thought of as old.

Gender differences also affect consumer behavior. Sex roles are changing as more women delay marriage, become financially independent, and build careers; men are learning to become more sensitive and caring. Men and women also differ in terms of consumer traits, information-processing styles, decision-making styles, and consumption patterns. In addition, more marketers are using sexual orientation to target gay and lesbian consumers for various goods and services.

Consumption patterns may differ in various regions of the United States and the world, leading some marketers to tailor strategies specifically to these regions. Clustering helps marketers describe consumers in different regions based on similar demographic and consumption characteristics rather than by geographic location only. The three largest U.S. ethnic groups are African Americans, Hispanic Americans, and Asian Americans. Changing population trends require marketers to target carefully and understand the consumer behavior of each group. Many marketers are taking a multicultural approach, trying to appeal to several subcultures instead of just one. Marketers who want to sell in other countries must also be familiar with important ethnic groups in other areas. Finally, religious values and customs can influence consumer behavior and form the basis of marketing strategies.

Questions for Review and Discussion

1. What type of U.S. consumers are in the Generation X, Generation Y, and baby boomer segments?
2. What is the difference between gender and sexual orientation, and why is this distinction important for marketers?
3. What is clustering, and why do marketers use it?
4. What are the three main subcultures within the U.S. population?
5. How do acculturation and intensity of ethnic identification affect consumer behavior?
6. Define the accommodation theory, and explain its importance for marketers who target Hispanic Americans.
7. Why would a company adopt multicultural marketing rather than targeting a single subculture?
8. Why do marketers have to consider regional influences when targeting consumers within the United States or in another country?
9. Identify some of the ways in which religion can influence consumer behavior.

Exercises

1. Pick a product or service category that individuals of all age groups consume. Conduct a detailed research analysis of the marketing techniques used to attract the four demographic segments discussed in this chapter in the following areas: (a) brands or services offered, (b) package design, (c) advertising content, (d) media selection, (e) sales promotion, and (f) distribution strategy. Collect this information via a library search, a content analysis of advertising messages and media used, in-store visits, and interviews with marketers. Then answer the following questions:
   a. Which techniques are used to market to multiple age groups?
   b. Which techniques are used to appeal to specific age groups? How do these techniques differ from age group to age group?

2. Conduct a detailed research analysis of the marketing techniques used to appeal to males and females in the following areas: (a) brands or services offered, (b) package design, (c) advertising content, (d) media selection, (e) sales promotion, and (f) distribution strategy. Collect this information in the same manner as described in exercise 1, and then answer the following questions:
   a. Which techniques are used to market to both males and females?
   b. Which specific techniques are used to appeal to males? To females?
3. You have been assigned to develop a marketing strategy for a new fruit drink that provides high energy and is high in nutrients. It is also light and very refreshing, especially on a hot day. How would you market this product in different regions of the world? Develop a detailed marketing plan for two regions that addresses the advertising message, media selection, distribution, and sales promotion.
4. You are developing a marketing strategy for a fashion clothing store chain that wants to specialize in providing products for one of the three main subcultures in your area. The stores plan to sell medium- to high-priced clothing for either Hispanic, African American, or Asian American women. Develop a questionnaire to collect information about acquisition and consumption patterns among the group you will target (of which you are not a member). Be sure to ask questions that will provide insight into your decisions about (a) store design, (b) products offered, (3) pricing, and (4) advertising. Administer this questionnaire to at least ten members of the chosen groups. Summarize the key findings of your research and make a recommendation in each of the areas mentioned.
5. Pick three product/service categories that you think will show consumption differences across different religious subcultures. Design a questionnaire to assess major consumption patterns for each of these products/services and administer it to at least five consumers in each of the major subcultures. Summarize the responses, and answer the following questions:
   a. How do these cultures vary in terms of consumption?
   b. How would marketing efforts differ for the groups?

More Exercises from the Adaptor

1. Identify advertisments, films, documentaries accessible on public domain and illustrate how various ethnic groups have been showcased in the them and how have they evolved over the years. Also illustrate the changing role of genders in India in the marketing and promotion of products.

References

[1] Source: http://www.mcspotlight.org/media/press/indiaxprs_9oct96.html

[2] Source: http://www.businessweek.com/innovate/content/may2006/id20060508_952455.htm

[3] Source: http://www.cbsnews.com/stories/2007/04/02/asia_letter/main2640540.shtml

[4] Source: http://www.icmr.icfai.org/casestudies/catalogue/Operations/McDonald%20Food%20Chain-Operations%20Case%20Study.htm

[5] Source: India's Youth and their career opportunities, Marketing Whitebook, Businessworld, 2006

[6] Source: The New Improved Consumer, Marketing Whitebook, Businessworld, 2006

[7] Source: Sunday Supplement, The Times of India, 6th May 2007

[8] Source: Marketing Whitebook 2006, Businessworld

[9] Source: Sunday Supplement, The Times of India, 6th May 2007

[10] Source: http://www.sodomylaws.org/world/india/innews065.htm

[11] Source: http://www.achillesheel.freeuk.com/article08_13.html

[12] Source: The Marketing Whitebook 2006, Businessworld

[13] Source: http://en.wikipedia.org/wiki/acial_groups_in_India_%28historical_definitions%29

[14] Source: http://www.photius.com/religion/india_religious_life.html

chapter **14**

Social Class and Household Influences

LEARNING OBJECTIVES

After studying this chapter, you will be able to:

- Define the social class hierarchy and identify the major determinants of social class standing.
- Explain how social class influences consumer behavior, particularly consumption, and why marketers must consider these influences when planning strategy and tactics.
- Discuss three key forces that are, over time, changing social class structure in many countries.
- Describe the various types of households and families, and explain how the family life cycle and other forces affect household structure.
- Understand the roles that household members play in acquisition and consumption decisions, and show how companies can use their knowledge of these roles to market more effectively.

INTRODUCTION

The Rising Indian Middle Class

The story of the Indian Middle Class has been much written about especially its two important facets, the growth within the segment and population moving out of the segment. [1]In Chapter 13 we discussed how the Indian population has evolved over the years and how the classification is done in a pre and post independence era, followed by the era of permits, rationing and scarcity, which gave rise to a new generation of strivers, who laid the foundation of the great Indian middle class, taking the advantage of the newly created job opportunities in the government sector.

The middle class, as defined in the NCAER data, is a segment of population that falls in the income segment as defined in Exhibit 14.2. [2]The average middle class consumption per capita per year works out to Rs.12,546. A little more than 40 per cent of the total consumption of this class is accounted for by the top one third; the 'upper middle class', which enjoys an average consumption of Rs.20,196 per capita per year, more than twice as much as the Rs.9,896 average for the 'lower middle class'.

[3]McKinsey defines the middle class as households with annual disposable income of $4,380-21,890, which totaled 13 million households or 50 million people

Exhibit 14.1

THE GREAT INDIAN MIDDLE CLASS

The 241 million people belonging to the middle class as a whole (23 per cent of total population) accounted for Rs.3,02,534 crore of total consumption (42 per cent).

in 2005. Overall average real household disposable income would reach Rs 318,896 by 2025 from 113,744 in 2005, a compound annual growth rate of 5.3 per cent. India has seen high growth in sales of cars and mobile phones in the past couple of years, with the total number of wireless subscribers up 68 per cent to 166 million in March from the same month in 2006. Domestic car sales topped 1 million units in 2006/07. Shopping malls are springing up in major cities like New Delhi and Mumbai, and signs of increasing prosperity are visible in the rising number of luxury foreign cars on the roads.

Exhibit 14.2

The segment of Lower Middle, Middle and Upper Middle forms a large base

Income Class	Number of Households (AAGR in %) 1995-96 to 1998-99		
	Urban	Rural	Total
Lower	-10.8	-4.5	-5.5
Lower-Middle	0.9	7.7	5.6
Middle	5.3	7.8	6.6
Upper Middle	9.9	8.6	9.3
High	21.5	14.3	18.6

*Inflation adjusted, comparable over time

Source: NCAER

Initially, the rise of the middle class was attributed more towards an income growth, but what has significantly affected the changes are: [4]The Striving class which is now wanting to seize every possible opportunity. The "I can" attitude in the self-employed class, the rise of the women not just as a working class but ones managing their home, Education and health driven society, pragmatism in consumption and preference for "real value" products and services, the format of entertaining ourselves, comfort to borrow to fund for future consumption and comfort with consumption.

[5]McKinsey's report divides the population into five groups: globals, strivers, seekers, aspirers and deprived. The globals are India's urban elite, with their new cars and frequent trips abroad. Strivers and seekers are the middle class, with rising incomes and robust consuming habits. Aspirers are those who seek to break into the middle class, but haven't made it yet. The deprived are those who earn less than $5.40 (U.S.) a day.

Exhibit 14.3

Classification from the "The Bird of Gold" The Rise of the Indian Consumer Market

	Deprived	Aspirers	Seekers	Strivers	Globals
1985 - (755)	93%	6%	1%		
1995 - (928)	80%	18%	2%		
2005 estimate - (1,107)	54%	41%	4%	1%	
2015 forecast - (1,278)	35%	43%	19%	1%	1%
2025 forecast - 1,429)	22%	36%	32%	9%	2%

Figures may not add up to 100%, due to rounding

Source: McKinsey Global Institute

The accompanying chart shows how Indian society is being transformed. Just 20 years ago India was an impoverished, mostly agrarian country; 93 per cent of its people were deprived and only a tiny sliver at the top was middle or upper class. Today, the number of deprived is way down, though they still make up the majority. By 2025, if all goes well, the great majority of India's people will be well-off, middle class or on their way to a better life.

This example about the rise of the middles class in India illustrates how social class and household influences affect consumer behavior (see Exhibit 14.4). The concept of social class implies that some people have more power, wealth, and opportunity than others do, which makes a difference in what and how consumers buy. The opening example also illustrates how some consumers can raise their social standing—a process called upward mobility—whereas others may fall to lower levels through downward mobility—changes that clearly affects consumer decisions and behavior. In addition, the structure and size of a household can influence acquisition and consumption decisions. It is important to remember that the generalizations about social class and household in this chapter are broad group tendencies and may or may not apply to individual consumers..

Social Class

Most societies have a ***social class hierarchy*** that confers higher status to some classes of people than to others. These social classes consist of identifiable groups of individuals whose behaviors and lifestyles differ from those of members of the other classes. Members of a particular social class tend to share similar values and behavior patterns. Note that social classes are not formal groups with a strong identity, but rather loose collections of individuals with similar life experiences.[2]

Many societies view these distinctions as important because they recognize that everyone has a necessary role to play for society to function smoothly. However, some roles, such as medical doctor or executive, are more prestigious and more valued than others, such as toll taker or janitor. Nevertheless, the concept of social class is not inherently negative. Even with the inequalities, social class distinctions can help individuals determine what their role in society is or what they would like it to be (their aspirations). Furthermore, all levels of the social class hierarchy make an important contribution to society.

Types of Social Class Systems

Most societies have three major classes: high, middle, and lower. Often, however, finer distinctions are made. For example the Socio Economic Classification (SEC) study in India takes into account the occupation and education of the Chief Wage Earner (CWE) of a household. The grid as shown in Exhibit 14.5 divides the society in five segments; viz.; SEC A, B, C, D, E. On one side of the grid lies the educational qualification and on the other the chief wage earner's profession/occupation, covering service class to the business community

Although most societies have some kind of hierarchical structure, the size and composition of the classes depend on the relative prosperity of a particular country.[4] For example, compared with the United States, Japan and Scandinavia have an even larger and more predominant middle class with much smaller groups above and below. This means there is greater equality among people in those two countries than in other societies. The Japanese structure represents a concerted government effort to abolish the social class system and mix together people from all levels of society.[5] Despite this effort, the highly competitive and

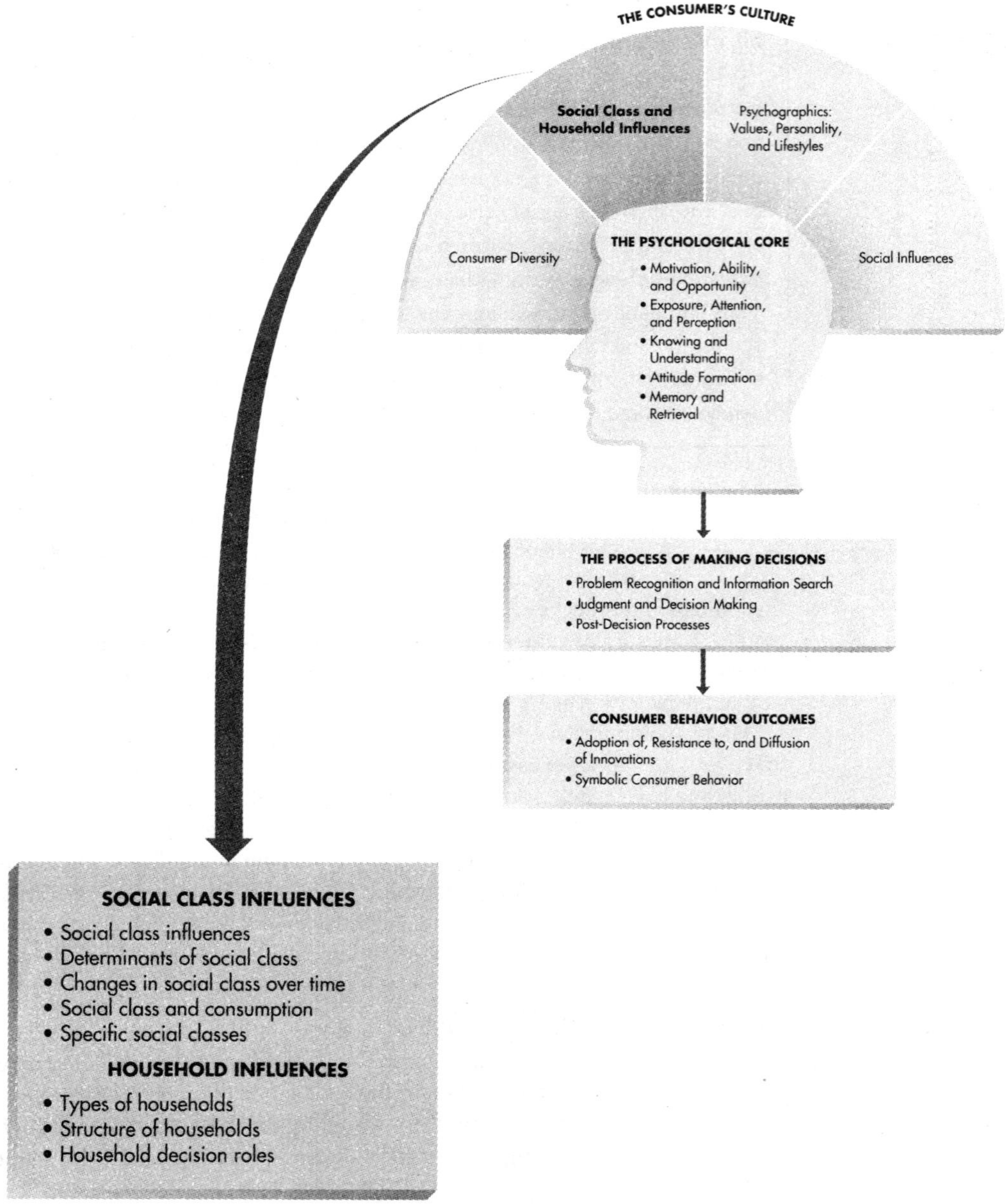

Exhibit 14.2

CHAPTER OVERVIEW: SOCIAL CLASS AND HOUSEHOLD INFLUENCES

This chapter examines social class and household influences on consumer behavior. The first section discusses the determinants of social class (e.g., occupation, education, income), changes in social class over time, and how social class affects consumption. Next is a discussion about household influences on consumer behavior, including the various types of households, trends in household structure, and the decision roles that household members play in acquiring and using an offering.

selective Japanese educational system still restricts entry to higher status positions in the executive and prestigious government ranks. In developing areas such as Latin America and India, on the other hand, the largest concentrations are in the lower classes. Most Latin households are truly poor, whereas India displays a more varied middle class of 241 million people, which is 23 percent of the population (see Exhibit 14.4). In China, the middle class accounts for about 16 percent of the population, including managers, entrepreneurs, professionals, and governmental officials.[6]

In formerly communist countries that stressed equality and sameness, the status hierarchy has changed rapidly. Many citizens now have the opportunity to increase their status, which serves as a strong motivation to "get ahead."[7] At the same time, this sudden social climbing can be frightening because it entails a feeling of venturing into the unknown.

	CWE Education						
CWE Occupation	Illiterate	Literate no school/ school upto 4 years	School 5-9 years	SSC/ HSC	Some college but not grad	Gard/ post grad general	Gard/ Post grad prof.
Unskilled worker	E2	E2	E1	D	D	D	D
Skilled worker	E2	E1	D	C	C	B2	B2
Petty trader	E2	D	D	C	C	B2	B2
Shop owner	D	D	C	B2	B1	A2	A2
Business sman/Industrialist							
-no employees	D	C	B2	B1	A2	A2	A1
-1-9	C	B2	B2	B1	A2	A1	A1
-10+	B1	B1	A2	A2	A1	A1	A1
Self employed professional	D	D	D	B2	B1	A2	A1
Clerical/salesman	D	D	D	C	B2	B1	B1
Supervisory level	D	D	C	C	B2	B1	A2
Officers/executive-jr.	C	C	C	B2	B1	A2	A2
Offier/executive-middle/sr.	B1	B1	B1	B1	A2	A1	A1

Exhibit 14.5
THE SEC GRID
The SEC grid is a useful tool for market estimation

Interestingly, the upper classes in most societies are more similar to each other than they are to other classes within their own countries because the upper classes tend to be more cosmopolitan and international in orientation.[8] The lower classes, on the other hand, are the most likely to be culture bound and tend to be the most different from other classes in terms of lifestyles, dress, and eating behaviors. The middle classes are most likely to borrow from other cultures because this practice may represent a means of achieving upward social mobility.

For example, the Indian Middle Class as also illustrated in the opening piece is a segment which is divided into Lower Middle, Middle Class and Upper Middle Class. Each of these three segments has unique traits. The large segment of the urban middle class today is a picture of confidence and "willing to experiment" kind of phenomenon. The strivers of the 70's and the 80's are now the achievers and

Exhibit 14.4
CLASS STRUCTURE BY CULTURE

The relative sizes and structures of social classes vary by culture. Japan and Scandinavia, for example, are characterized by a large middle class with few people above or below. India and Latin America, on the other hand, have a greater proportion of individuals in the lower classes. The United States has a large middle class but also has significant proportions in the upper and lower classes.

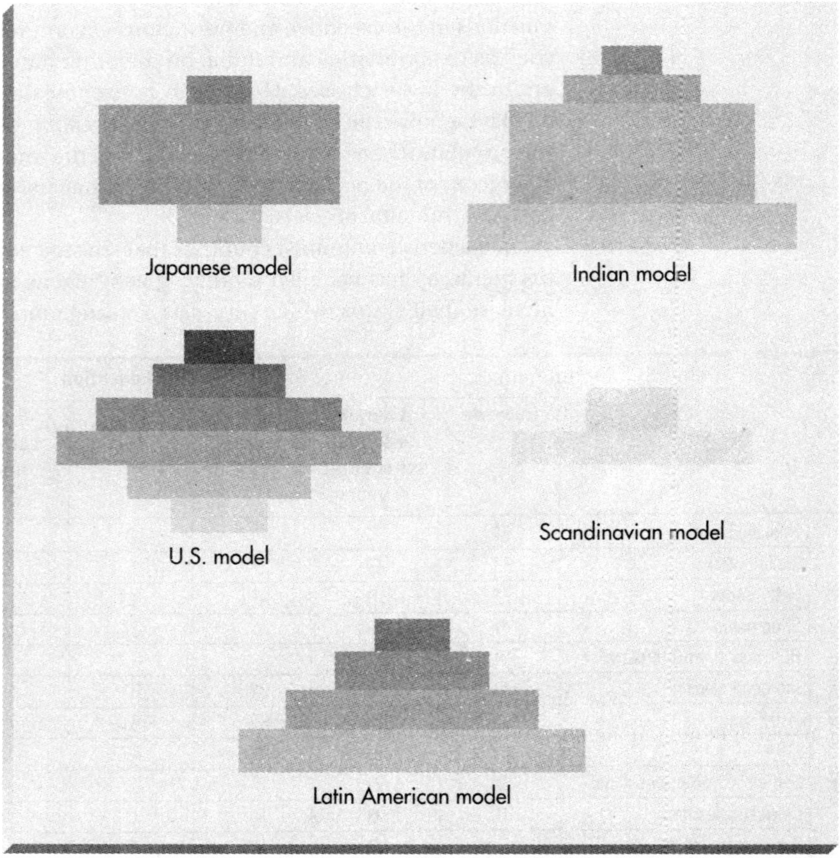

there are more first generation entrepreneurs coming out from this segment. Infosys, Subhiksha, or for that matter some of the start up IT companies like bazee.com are some of the cases in point, where these entrepreneurs came from humble backgrounds. The McKinsey Bird of Gold report on the Indian consumers classifies the Indian consumers into five distinct segments of Deprived, Aspirers, Seekers, Strivers and Globals, illustrating the mindset of the segment and how each one of them have evolved over time.

Finally, a particular social class may contain different economic substrata. Specifically, families whose income level is 20 to 30 percent over the median of their class are considered ***overprivileged*** because they have funds to buy items beyond the basic necessities.[9] ***Class average*** families are those whose income level is average for their social class. They can therefore afford the type of symbols expected for their status, such as a house, a car, and appropriate clothing. The ***underprivileged,*** who have incomes below the median, have trouble meeting class expectations.

Social Class Influences

Social class structures are important because they strongly affect norms and values and, therefore, behavior. Given that members of a social class interact regularly with each other (both formally and informally), people are more likely to be influenced by individuals in their own social class than by those in other classes. Note that social class influence is not a cultural straitjacket; it merely reflects the fact that people with similar life experiences are likely to exhibit similar lifestyles and behaviors.[10]

The norms and behaviors of consumers in one class can also influence consumers in other social classes. A traditional and commonly cited theory of class influence is the ***trickle-down effect***, whereby lower classes copy trends that begin in the upper classes. As one example, clothing styles that are introduced in the upper class often become popular with other groups. The trickle-down effect occurs because those in lower classes may aspire to raise their social standing by emulating the higher classes. They also accept upper-class influence if they lack the cultural knowledge to make their own judgments of what is and is not acceptable.[11] For example, the middle class often looks to the upper class for guidance on what is "cultural" in music, art, and literature.

More recently, however, the universal validity of the trickle-down theory has been questioned. In some instances, a ***status float*** can occur, whereby trends start in the lower and middle classes and then spread upward. This has occurred with tattoos, which began in the lower classes and moved into the upper classes. It also happened with blue jeans, which first gained popularity in the 1950s and 1960s among lower- and middle-class U.S. youths because it symbolized rebellion against the establishment.[12] Eventually this message gained popularity among upper-class youths who wanted to revolt against their parents, and jeans ultimately evolved into a global fashion item, complete with designer labels.

How Social Class Is Determined

Examining how social class affects consumer behavior requires a way of classifying consumers into different social classes. Unfortunately, this is a complex task, and the exact determinants of social class have been the subject of considerable debate over the years.

Income Versus Social Class Many people believe more money means higher social standing. You may be surprised to learn, however, that income is not strongly related to social class for several reasons.[13] First, income levels often overlap social classes, particularly at the middle and lower levels. For example, in India there are the trading communities whose income might be far higher than the white collar workers, yet do not have higher social standing. For instance in Exhibit 14.5, the petty trader with educational qualification not beyond SSC/HSC may have higher income than an officer/executive with SSC/HSC qualification, but his social standing may not be the same. Second, income increases greatly with age, but older workers do not automatically achieve higher social status. Finally, in many countries an increasing number of dual-career families generate a higher than average income but not necessarily higher status. Thus, although income is one factor related to social class, other factors play key roles as well. Finally, in many countries an increasing number of dual-career families generate a higher than average income but not necessarily higher status. Thus, although income is one factor related to social class, other factors play key roles as well.

Occupation	Score	Occupation	Score
Physician	88	Mechanic	31
Lawyer	88	Photographer	30
Marketing professor	83	Bank teller	29
Psychologist	82	Hotel receptionist	29
Architect	80	Mail carrier	27
Civil engineer	77	Plumber	27
High school teacher	75	Shoe salesperson	25
Computer scientist	73	Bartender	24
Airplane pilot	68	Farmer	24
Accountant	65	Carpenter	22
Marketing manager	58	Truck driver	21
Actor	52	Hairdresser	19
Athlete	49	Waiter/waitress	19
Sales representative	48	Machine operator	19
Musician	46	Baker	19
Office supervisor	37	Janitor	18
Police detective	38	Crossing guard	17
Secretary	35	Farmworker	17
Firefighter	33	Maid	16

Source: Reprinted from Gillian Stevens and Joo Hyun Cho, "Socioeconomic Indexes and the New 1980 Census Occupational Classification Scheme," *Social Science Research*, vol. 14, pp. 142–168. Copyright © 1985 by Academic Press with permission from Elsevier.

Exhibit 14.5
STATUS LEVELS OF VARIOUS OCCUPATIONS
A variety of indexes have been developed to classify different occupations in terms of their status level. This exhibit presents the status scores of a sample of occupations, using one of these indexes. What major factors do you think cause some occupations to be high in status and others to be low?

Some researchers have argued that income can be a better predictor of consumer behavior than social class. However, a more common view is that both factors are important in explaining behavior in different situations.[14] Social class tends to be a better predictor of consumption when it reflects lifestyles and values and does not involve high monetary expenditures, such as for clothes or furniture. For example, middle-class and lower-class consumers favor different styles of furniture, and middle-class consumers tend to spend more money on home furnishings even when income levels are roughly similar. Income, on the other hand, is more useful in explaining the consumption of offerings unrelated to class symbols—such as boats—but that do involve substantial expenditures. Both social class and income are needed to explain behaviors that involve status symbols and significant expenditures such as buying a house or car.

Although income cannot explain social class, social class can often explain how income is used. As one illustration, upper-class consumers are more likely to invest money, whereas the lower classes are more likely to rely on savings accounts in banks. The key point is that social class aids in the understanding of consumer behavior and that social standing is determined by a variety of factors in addition to income.

Occupation and Education The greatest determinant of class standing is occupation, particularly in Western cultures. Specifically, some occupations, especially those that require higher levels of education, skill, or training, are viewed as higher in status than others. Moreover, individuals with the same occupation tend to share similar income, lifestyles, knowledge, and values.

Researchers can easily measure occupation by asking consumers what they do for a living. They can then code the responses and compare them with published scales of occupational prestige, such as the widely used socioeconomic index (SEI) or the Nam and Powers scale.[15] Exhibit 14.5 shows rankings for a sample of occupations.

Note that the perceived status of an occupation may vary from culture to culture. Compared with the United States, for example, professors have higher status in Germany, Japan, China, Thailand, and Nigeria because those countries place more emphasis on education. Engineers typically have higher status in developing countries than they do in developed countries because of the important role engineering plays in integrating industry and technology into society.

Education also plays a critical role because it is one of the key determinants of occupation and therefore social class. In fact, educational attainment is considered the most reliable determinant of consumers' income potential and spending patterns.[16] In India, education has always been given priority, particularly in the working class segment. [6]Infact, it is considered to provide the skills that will provide the escape velocity to move to a higher station in life. Though literacy rates in a country like India is low (see Exhibit 14.8) yet education has been an integral part of the grooming for the large middle class population. 7The India Science Report, for instance, shows that India had a total of 48.7 million graduates in 2004, sharply up from 20.5 million in 1991. And while just around 29 per cent of those enrolled for graduate courses went in for science in 1995-96, now there are only 35 per cent.

Exhibit 14.8

Literacy rates in India

Year	Literacy Rate (%)			Number of Schools	
	Persons	Males	Females	Primary	Upper Primary
1951	18.33	27.16	8.86	215036	14576
1961	28.31	40.40	15.34	351530	55915
1971	34.45	45.95	21.97	417473	93665
1981	43.56	56.37	29.75	503763	122377
1991	52.21	64.13	39.29	566744	155926

Note: Literacy rates of 1951, 1961 and 1971 relate to population aged five years and above. The rates for the years 1981 and 1991 relate to the population aged seven years and above.
Source: EFA India: Year 2000 Assessment

Other Indicators of Social Class Factors such as area of residence, possessions, family background, and social interactions can also indicate class level. The neighborhood in which we live and the amount and types of possessions we have are visible signs that often communicate class standing. In terms of family background, researchers distinguish between ***inherited status,*** which is adopted from parents at birth, and ***earned status,*** which is acquired later in life from personal achievements.[18] Inherited status is the initial anchor point from which values are learned and from which upward or downward mobility can occur. As mentioned previously, members of a social class often interact with each other, so the company we keep also helps us to identify our social standing.

The relative importance of these determinants of social class varies from country to country. In formerly communist countries such as Romania, for example, money and possessions are now the strongest determinants of social standing, as opposed to the former criterion of position in the Communist party.[19] In the Arab world, status is determined primarily by social contacts and family position, both of which are considered far more important than money.[20]

Social Class Indexes All of the preceding factors must be taken into account to determine social class standing, and sociologists have developed a number of indexes to accomplish this task. In recent years, tools such as the *Index of Status Characteristics* and the *Index of Social Position* have been criticized as out-of-date and inappropriate for gauging the status of dual-career households.[21] Therefore, researchers now use more current indexes such as the ***Computerized Status Index (CSI)*** (see Exhibit 14.6). This index assesses consumers' education, occupation, area of residence, and income. In contrast to the use of informants for the reputational method, the CSI is easy for interviewers to administer and for consumers to answer.

When consumers are consistent across the various dimensions, social class is easy to determine and ***status crystallization*** occurs. Sometimes, however, individuals are low on some factors but high on others. Thus a new doctor from an inner-city neighborhood might be inconsistent on factors such as occupation, income, neighborhood, and family background. In such situations, consumers can experi-

Interviewer circles code numbers (for the computer) which in his/her judgment best fit the respondent and family. Interviewer asks for detail on occupation, then makes rating. Interviewer often asks the respondent to describe neighborhood in own words. Interviewer asks respondent to specify income—a card is presented to the respondent showing the eight brackets—and records R's response. If interviewer feels this is overstatement or under, a "better-judgment" estimate should be given, along with explanation.

EDUCATION:	Respondent	Respondent's spouse
Grammar school (8 yrs or less)	–1	–1
Some high school (9–11 yrs)	–2	–2
Graduated high school (12 yrs)	–3	–3
Some post high school (business, nursing, technical, 1 yr college)	–4	–4
Two, three years of college—possibly Associate of Arts degree	–5	–5
Graduated four-year college (B.A./B.S.)	–7	–7
Master's or five-year professional degree	–8	–8
Ph.D. or six/seven-year professional degree	–9	–9

R's age: ___

Spouse's age: ___

OCCUPATION PRESTIGE LEVEL OF HOUSEHOLD HEAD:
Interviewer's judgment of how head-of-household rates in occupational status.

(Respondent's description—ask for previous occupation if retired, or if R is widow, ask husband's: ________________________________)

Chronically unemployed—"day" laborers, unskilled; on welfare	–0
Steadily employed but in marginal semi-skilled jobs; custodians, minimum-pay factory help, service workers (gas attendants, etc.)	–1
Average-skill assembly-line workers, bus and truck drivers, police and firefighters, route deliverymen, carpenters, brick masons	–2
Skilled craftsmen (electricians), small contractors, factory foremen, low-pay salesclerks, office workers, postal employees	–3
Owners of very small firms (2–4 employees), technicians, salespeople, office workers, civil servants with average-level salaries	–4
Middle management, teachers, social workers, lesser professionals	–5
Lesser corporate officials, owners of middle-sized businesses (10–20 employees), moderate-success professionals (dentists, engineers, etc.)	–7
Top corporate executives, "big business" in the professional world (leading doctors and lawyers), "rich" business owners	–9

AREA OF RESIDENCE:
Interviewer's impressions of the immediate neighborhood in terms of its reputation in the eyes of the community.

Slum area: people on relief, common laborers	–1
Strictly working class: not slummy but some very poor housing	–2
Predominantly blue-collar with some office workers	–3
Predominantly white-collar with some well-paid blue-collar	–4
Better white-collar area: not many executives, but hardly any blue-collar either	–5
Excellent area: professionals and well-paid managers	–7
"Wealthy" or "society" type neighborhood	–9

TOTAL FAMILY INCOME PER YEAR:

TOTAL SCORE ______

Under $5,000	–1	$15,000 to $19,999	–4	$35,000 to $49,999	–7
$5,000 to $9,999	–2	$20,000 to $24,999	–5	$50,000 and over	–8
$10,000 to $14,999	–3	$25,000 to $34,999	–6		

Estimated Status ______

(Interviewer's estimate:__________ and explanation:________________________________)

R's MARITAL STATUS: Married ______ Divorced/Separated ______ Widowed ______ Single ______ (CODE ______)

Exhibit 14.6

THE COMPUTERIZED STATUS INDEX

The CSI attempts to assess consumers' social class by measuring the various key determinants—education, occupation, area of residence, and income—and combining them to form an overall index. The higher the score, the higher the social standing.

ence stress and anxiety because they do not know exactly where they stand.[22] It is also difficult for marketers to neatly categorize such consumers into one social class or another.

How Social Class Changes over Time

Social class structures are not necessarily static, unchanging systems. Three of the key forces producing an evolution in social class structures in many countries are: (1) upward mobility, (2) downward mobility, and (3) social class fragmentation.

Upward Mobility

In many cultures, consumers can raise their status level through ***upward mobility,*** usually by educational or occupational achievement. In other words, lower- or middle-class individuals can take advantage of educational opportunities, particularly a college education, to gain entry into higher-status occupations. "Education is the biggest ticket to the middle class," says one economist about upward mobility opportunities for lower-class consumers.[23] Though the number of graduates and post graduates is high in a country like India, however, they do not have as many job opportunities. Disguised unemployment is the norm in most cases and with a high agrarian base there is a sizeable volume of population which wants to settle down even after higher studies into their domestic business or agricultural farmlands.

[8]As discussed earlier, unlike most advanced nations education in India is not a ticket to a job, but a security blanket. India's education system turns out millions of graduates each year, many skilled in IT and engineering. This manpower advantage underpins India's recent economic advances, but masks deepseated problems within India's education system. While India's demographics are generally perceived to give it an edge over other countries' economies (India will have a youthful population when other countries have ageing populations), if this advantage is restricted to a small, highly educated elite, the domestic political ramifications could be severe. The thrust on elementary education over the last two decades and the growing aspirations of poor communities resulting from their participation in a political democracy have already led to a situation where most children at age six are enrolling in schools/learning centres and residential bridge courses. However, the poor quality of these schools and their rudimentary physical and human infrastructure often lead to children dropping out of the school system without learning or continuing in it with limited learning.

Clearly, upward mobility is not guaranteed. The lower classes, particularly minorities, still face restricted economic and cultural resources as well as educational opportunities. They are therefore statistically less likely than the upper classes to have access to higher-status occupations.[26] Individuals from higher-status families are twice as likely to maintain their status as members of lower classes are to achieve a higher status. Even after achieving upward mobility, an individual's behavior can still be heavily influenced by his or her former class level because the behaviors associated with the social class in which we grew up were strongly learned.[27]

Note that the degree of upward mobility may vary across cultures. Typically, Western nations offer the greatest number of opportunities for upward advancement, although opportunities for upward mobility have actually decreased in Canada and the United States during some periods. Even in traditionally rigid class societies such as Great Britain, upward mobility has increased recently. In formerly communist countries, old party and state bureaucrats have formed the new upper classes because they have the skills and economic knowledge to thrive in the modern environment. In Arab countries, the upper and middle class are growing rapidly as a result of oil money and an increase in Western college education. The size of the middle class has been exploding in many developing countries because international trade is making affordable goods more available, dual-career families are earning greater income, and more professionals like managers and accountants are needed to support growing economies. As discussed initially, the rise of the middle class in India is particularly spawning a new generation of achievers.

Downward Mobility

Downward mobility, or moving to a lower class, is an increasing trend in some industrialized societies. In the past 15 years, millions of U.S. families have slid downward as jobs were sent overseas or eliminated by technology and companies lowered wages or laid off workers.[32] Although many parents dreamed of providing their children with a better life and higher status, some children may have difficulty reaching their parents' status level, a phenomenon labeled ***status panic.***[33] Meanwhile, because of increasing material desires, more upper-middle- and middle-class families are having difficulty maintaining a lifestyle characteristic of their status level. Even households with sizable retirement portfolios can feel the pinch when stock market gyrations erode the value of their holdings, which in turn can affect current consumption behavior and consumption patterns after retirement.[34]

The problem of downward mobility is particularly an issue in formerly communist countries such as the Czech Republic, Hungary, and Poland, where the elimination of government-subsidized jobs led to very high unemployment. With skyrocketing prices and sluggish economic conditions, many people feel worse off than before, leaving many to face a loss of class status.

Regardless of the causes, downward mobility creates disappointment and disillusionment. People in this situation face a constant struggle to provide for the family, fight off depression, and maintain a sense of honor. Sometimes acquisition and consumption can help protect personal self-worth. For example, a consumer might buy a new truck or other item to feel good about himself or herself.[35] Because middle-class consumers in Japan are accustomed to conveying status through the purchase of luxury goods, many have continued to spend lavishly despite the country's prolonged economic problems.[36] Alternatively, downward mobility can lead to a loss of possessions, such as a prized car or home, or to a decrease in consumption if people choose to spend less on items that are less important.

Social Class Fragmentation

Interestingly, the old social class distinctions are beginning to disintegrate—a phenomenon called ***social class fragmentation***—due to several factors.[37] First, both upward and downward mobility have blurred class divisions. Second, the increased availability of mass media, especially TV and the Internet, is exposing consumers worldwide to the values and norms of diverse classes and cultures, leading some to incorporate the idiosyncrasies of these groups into their own behavior. A third reason for social class fragmentation is that advances in communication technology

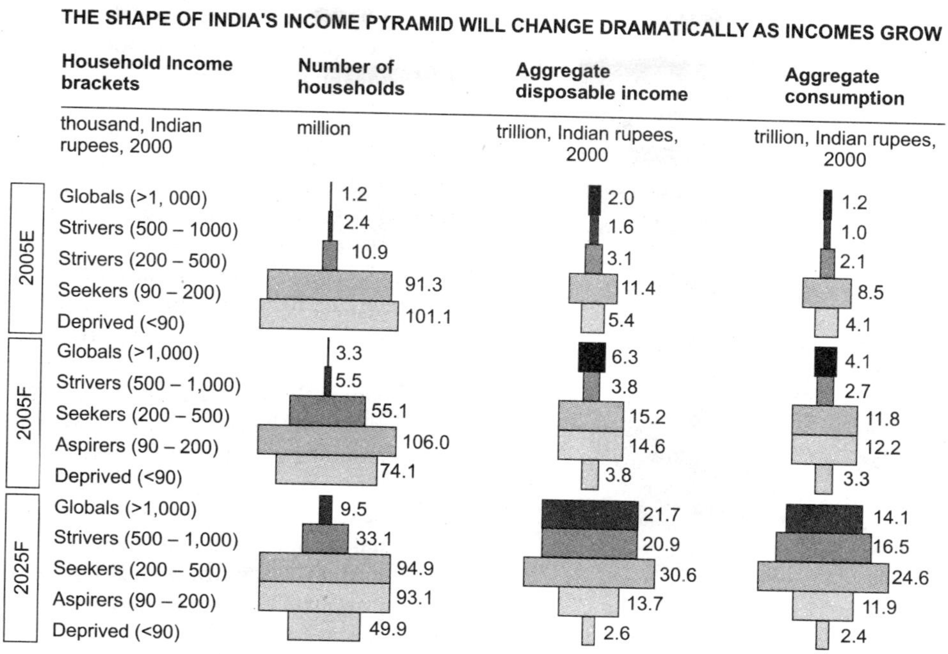

Exhibit 14.10

G10 THE MCKINSEY STUDY OF THE INDIAN CONSUMER

The McKinsey Study classifies the Indian population into five different social classes of Deprived, Aspirers, Seekers, Strivers and Globals.

have increased interaction across social class lines, as when Internet users chat online without regard to social class. These factors have led to the emergence of many social class subsegments with distinct patterns of values and behavior. The United States now has dozens of classes ranging from the suburban elite (super rich families) to the hardscrabble (poor, single-parent families). Similar trends are occurring in other countries as well. Exhibit 14.10 illustrates the McKinsey Global Institute's classification of the Indian market into five distinct categories of Deprived, Aspirers, Seekers, Strivers and Globals.

Taking an expensive cruise indicates status in Thailand, and the same is true of having a rock garden or a golf club membership in Japan. In Brazil, eating in fast-food restaurants such as McDonald's and Burger King is a status symbol for lower-middle-class consumers. In India, the new found status symbol of the corporates is exclusive membership of clubs. The corporate culture of the '90s has brought a considerable change in the definition of a club. Today, signature golf courses rate high on the preferred membership list. And at a Rs 9-lakh refundable deposit for a 10-year individual membership, the DLF Golf and Country Club, designed by Arnold Palmer, is one of the most expensive clubs in the country.

How Does Social Class Affect Consumption?

Social class is often viewed as a cause of or motivation for consumer acquisition, consumption, and disposition behaviors. This section examines three major topics: (1) conspicu-

Exhibit 14.8
CONSPICUOUS CONSUMPTION
Consumers may judge each other based on the type of watch they wear. This ad implies that wearing a Roger Dubuis watch is a mark of status and prestige.

ous consumption and status symbols, (2) compensatory consumption, and (3) the meaning of money.

Conspicuous Consumption and Status Symbols

Conspicuous consumption, also related to social class, is an attempt to offset deficiencies or a lack of esteem by devoting attention to consumption.[39] Conspicuously consumed items are important to their owner because of what they tell others. The visibility of these goods and services is critical because their message can be communicated only if others can see them. Conspicuous consumption can be observed in most social classes.[40] Individuals at all levels can "keep up with the Joneses"—acquiring and displaying the trappings that are characteristic of a respected member of their class. In the Arab world the newly rich upper classes engage in the conspicuous consumption of items such as airplanes. Conspicuous consumption competition also occurs in formerly communist countries, where someone who cannot keep up with others might be "the shame of the village."[41]

In addition, consumers can engage in ***conspicuous waste.*** For example, wealthy individuals may buy houses they never use, pianos that no one plays, and cars that no one drives.[42] Yet, some consumers are moving away from conspicuous consumption toward "experience facilitators" or items and pastimes that set them apart from the crowd.[43] For example, many consumers who have satisfied their desire for material possessions are paying for out-of-the-ordinary experiences, such as adventure travel tours.[44]

Status Symbols and Judging Others

Highly related to conspicuous consumption is the notion that people often judge others on the basis of what they own. In other words, goods or services become ***status symbols*** to indicate their owners' place in the social hierarchy.[45] Someone who owns an expensive watch or car will likely be viewed as upper class (see Exhibit 14.8). Taking an expensive cruise indicates status in Thailand, and the same is true of having a rock garden or a golf club membership in Japan. In Brazil, eating in fast-food restaurants such as McDonald's and Burger King is a status symbol for lower-middle-class consumers.[46]

[9]In India, the new found status symbol of the corporates is exclusive membership of clubs. The corporate culture of the 90's has brought a considerable change in the definition of a club. Today, signature golf courses rate high on the preferred membership list. And at a Rs 9 lakh refundable deposit for a 10 year individual membership, the DLF Golf and Country Club, designed by Arnold Palmer, is one of

the most expensive clubs in the country.

Consumers' quest to acquire items that reflect not only their current social class but also their class aspirations can explain some acquisitions and consumption behavior. Middle-class consumers, for example, characteristically display a strong desire to own a nice house in a respectable neighborhood so that others will judge them in a positive manner. By acquiring items that members of their own social class cannot typically afford, consumers can increase their perception of self-worth. Even relatively affordable luxuries—like a $6 Panera sandwich or the lowest-priced Mercedes car—"enable less affluent consumers to trade up to higher levels of quality, taste, and aspiration," says a Boston Consulting Group expert. "These are the luxuries that continue to sell even when the economy is shaky, because they often meet very powerful emotional needs."[47]

Interestingly, status symbols can sometimes move in a reverse direction, which is called a ***parody display.***[48] For example, middle- and upper-class Brazilians now feel hip if they sip caipirinhas (a specialty drink once identified with the lower class) and practice capoeira, a blend of dance and martial arts that was traditionally popular among the lower class.[49] In addition, if certain status symbols become widely possessed, they can lose their status connotations and become ***fraudulent symbols.*** To illustrate, recognizing that luxury brands are often copied by low-price knockoffs for the mass market, Coach and others have redesigned their products with more subtle logos. The new products are unmistakably upscale but don't "scream 'Coach, Coach, Coach,'" observes a Coach designer.[50]

Compensatory Consumption

Compensatory consumption behavior, also related to social class, is an attempt to offset deficiencies or a lack of esteem by devoting attention to consumption.[51] A consumer who is experiencing frustration or difficulties, particularly in terms of career advancement or status level, may compensate for this lack of success by purchasing desired status symbols, such as a car, house, or nice clothes. These acquisitions help restore lost self-esteem.

Traditionally, compensatory consumption typified the acquisition patterns of the working classes, who would mortgage their future to buy a house, car, and other status symbols. More recently, however, many middle- and upper-middle-class U.S. consumers have exhibited compensatory consumption behavior. Some of these consumers have not enjoyed the level of career advancement and prosperity that their parents did, due in part to increased job competition, corporate downsizing, and economic uncertainty. To offset their disappointment, a number of consumers will seek gratification through compensatory consumption.[52] Knowing this, some marketers have created new luxury brands that are somewhat more affordable than their existing luxury brands. The Great Kabab Factory, a fine dining restaurant at the Radisson Hotel, has now introduced a stand alone restaurant for customers, who might get intimidated with a five star hotel's appearance, look and price perceptions and in its place would prefer in its place a more toned down version of the restaurant in the hotel to a concept of stand alone restaurant at the Sector 18 Market NOIDA, UP.

The Meaning of Money

An important concept related to social class is money. At the most basic level, economists define *money* as a medium of exchange or standard of payment. Under this view, money fulfills a very functional or utilitarian purpose, enabling people to acquire items needed for everyday living. Often, however, money comes to symbolize security, power, love, and freedom.

Consumers learn the meaning of money early in childhood. Parents easily discover that they can control their children through rewards and punishments based on money and buying or not buying things.[54] Children learn that if they behave, get good grades, or do their chores, their parents will buy things for them. This early learning later translates into adult life when money is viewed as a means of acquiring things that will not only bring happiness and fulfillment but also a sense of status and prestige. In some societies this can lead to an almost insatiable desire and quest for making money, which is enhanced by media coverage of those who have "made it" and the belief that "it could happen to anyone, including me" (see Exhibit 14.9). This belief is one reason that state lotteries are popular among certain classes.

Exhibit 14.12
MARKETING A STATE LOTTERY
State lotteries are popular among certain classes because of the belief that "it could happen to anyone, including me." This illustrates the importance of money.

Marketers must understand money and what it stands for in order to understand consumption patterns. Money allows consumers to acquire status objects as indicators of social class standing. It is also viewed as a way to rise to a higher level by acquiring more. Yet, the ongoing growth in credit and debit card usage shows that money need not involve physical cash. Even in nations like Kenya, where cash has long been the accepted payment method, more consumers are qualifying for credit cards so they can acquire goods and services now but pay the bill at a later date.[55] Shoppers in a growing number of nations can set up electronic wallets that enable them to easily make purchases online. Consumers in the Netherlands can sign up for the MiniTix electronic wallet and then just click to have the amount of any purchase electronically transferred to an online retailer.[56]

Of course, different consumers treat money in different ways. Some will spend money to acquire what they want now, whereas others will engage in self-denial to save. One study found that spenders tend to be healthier and happier than self-deniers, who tend to have more psychosomatic illnesses and are more unhappy about finances, personal growth, friends, and jobs.[57] Over time, consumers who consistently spend more than they have will be deeply in debt and may even have to declare bankruptcy.

Money as Both Good and Evil Money can be perceived as the just reward for hard work and can lead to the acquisition of needed items, a higher quality of life, and the ability to help others and society in general. On the downside, the quest for money can lead to obsession, greed, dishonesty, and potentially harmful practices such as gambling, prostitution, and drug dealing (see Chapter 20). The quest for money can also lead to negative emotions such as anxiety, depression, anger, and helplessness.[58] Although people generally respect wealthy individuals, they often disdain the obsessive desire for money, which means wealthy people may feel alienated from others.[59] Moreover, individuals who do not share their wealth with others may be seen as selfish and greedy. Interestingly, consumers with yearly household incomes under $25,000 donate about 4 percent of their income to charities, whereas consumers with household incomes of $100,000 or more actually contribute a smaller percentage (less than 3 percent) to charities.[60]

Money and Happiness The popular belief (especially in Western countries) that money can buy happiness is rarely true. Examples of very wealthy individuals whose lives were generally unhappy include Howard Hughes (the subject of the movie *Aviator*) and J. Paul Getty. After some people acquire tremendous wealth, money can become meaningless and no longer highly desired. Furthermore, wealthy people can often afford to hire others to handle many of activities that they formerly enjoyed, such as gardening and do-it-yourself projects. And, of course, money simply cannot buy love, health, true friendship, and children, among other things. Thus the relentless pursuit of money may not end in the fulfilled dreams that many think it will.

The Consumption Patterns of Specific Social Classes

Earlier sections examined how social class influences acquisition and consumption in general. This section extends the discussion by examining, in broad generalities, the consumption patterns of specific social classes. Although class distinctions are becoming increasingly blurred, for the sake of simplicity, this discussion will focus on (1) the upper class, (2) the middle class, (3) the working class, and (4) the homeless. Remember that these are broad tendencies; marketers must delve deeper to identify subsegments of consumers with specific and unique consumption patterns.

The Upper Class

The ***upper class*** of most societies is a varied group of individuals who include the aristocracy, the new social elite (or nouveaux riches), and the upper middle class (professionals). In the United States, the upper class usually means "old money" consumers—the 1 percent of U.S. society whose ancestors acquired great wealth and power a century ago and who now live on inherited money. These consumers tend to save and invest money more than members of other classes.[61] Still, many are price-conscious.[62] When shopping for holiday gifts, only 49 percent visit upscale stores; the remainder shop at midrange stores such as Macy's and at discount and outlet stores.[63] Upper-class consumers are also more likely than other classes to carefully research their purchases and to use product characteristics, not price, as an indicator of quality.

Although small, the upper class is diverse, and its members share a number of common values and lifestyles that relate to consumption behavior. These consumers tend to view themselves as intellectual, political, and socially conscious, leading to an increase in behaviors such as attending the theater, investing in art and antiques, traveling, giving time and money to charities and civic issues, and belonging to private clubs.[64] Self-expression is also important, resulting in the purchase of high-quality, prestige brands in good taste. Small wonder that this group is an attractive market for luxury offerings. Rolls-Royce, which markets high-end cars like the $320,000 Phantom, says that its average customer has a net worth of more than $30 million.[65]

The nouveaux riches are upper-class consumers who have acquired a great deal of status and wealth in their own lifetimes. A characteristic tendency of this group is to collect items that are symbols of acquired wealth and power, such as furniture, art objects, cars, fine jewelry, or airplanes (see Exhibit 14.10). In London, for example, wealthy consumers are paying $5 million or more for luxury penthouses to be designed and placed on the roof of historic apartment buildings.[66]

These days, most millionaires do not fit the traditional image of tycoons with stately mansions. In fact, one-third of all U.S. households with assets topping $1 million are headed by consumers aged 39 and younger.[67] The average U.S. millionaire is 54 years old, is married with three children, and has an average household net worth of $9.2 million.[68] More than 72 percent of U.S. millionaires hold college or graduate degrees, and 67.5 percent have annual household incomes of $100,000-plus.[69] At the top end of the spectrum, more than 265,000 U.S. households have a net worth exceeding $10 million.[70]

[10]The Indian upper class is also growing and there are an estimated 7,11,000 individuals with liquid cash of over $1,00,000, and the number is expected to increase to 1.1 million, growing annually at 11.6 per cent by 2009. These individuals have cumulative liquid wealth of $203 billion which is expected to rise by 12.2 per cent per year to $322 billion by 2009. The India Luxury Trends 2006 divides consumers for luxury goods into 4 categories: (i) Luxuriented: Source of affluence is largely traditional and inherited wealth. Most importantly, they have high levels of exposure and awareness to world class living; (ii) New Rich: Adequate spending power and acquiring orientation to luxury. (iii) Getting there: Acquiring spending power and spends mainly on high end white goods, education of children, better housing and larger automobiles. (iv) Mid Affluents: Also acquiring orientation to luxury, however unlikely to indulge beyond a limit. What is also noteworthy is the rise of the new generation entrepreneurs who have originated from the middle class background. The earlier trend of upper class identified through inherited wealth or the family run business are now being replaced with more strivers making into the achiever segment.

Exhibit 14.13
TARGETING UPPERCLASS CONSUMERS
Some products and services are marketed for certain classes like this watch fair, showcasing exclusive and premium watches

The Middle Class

The U.S. ***middle class*** consists of primarily white-collar workers, many of whom have attended college (although some have not earned a degree). Although the values and consumption patterns of middle-class consumers vary, many look to the upper class for guidance on certain behaviors such as proper dining etiquette, clothing (especially important for those with aspirations of upward mobility), and popular leisure activities such as golf and tennis. This tendency extends to theater attendance, vacations, and adult education classes for self-improvement. Middle-class values can also determine the types of products and brands that middle-class consumers acquire and consume. As just one example, compared with lower-class consumers, a higher percentage of middle-class consumers subscribe to premium cable channels and satellite dish TV.[71]

Similar middle-class behavior patterns have been found in other countries. For example, the middle class in Mexico has many similarities to the U.S. middle class, spending much of its disposable income on cars, clothing, vacations, and household goods. Yet, lower-middle-class households in Mexico have a lower average income (around $14,400) compared with their American counterparts.[72] In Russia, 5 million consumers make up the middle class, with an average monthly income of $500. Roughly 85 percent of this group own cars, and many prefer fast-food restaurants from the West.[73] In fact, the middle class is growing in many developing countries, with the greatest change occurring in parts of East Asia (China, India, Indonesia, and South Korea).[74]

The Working Class

The ***working class*** is mainly represented by blue-collar workers. The traditional stereotype is of a hard-hatted, middle-aged man, but this image is changing as the working class becomes younger, more ethnically diverse, more female, somewhat more educated, and more alienated from employers.[75] Working-class consumers heavily depend on family members for economic and social support in many areas, including job opportunities and advice—particularly for key purchases and help during difficult times.[76] As a result, they tend to have more of a local orientation socially, psychologically, and geographically than other classes. For example, working-class men exhibit strong preferences for local athletic teams, news segments, and vacations (typically taken less than two hours from home). The working class has also demonstrated the strongest resistance to the foreign car invasion in the United States and to abandoning the macho symbol of a large and powerful car or truck.

Consumers in the working class are more likely to spend than to save; however, when they do save, many choose savings accounts over investments. In addition, working-class consumers are more likely to judge product quality on the basis of price (higher price means higher quality), to shop in mass merchandise or discount stores, and to have less product information when purchasing.[77] And they may exhibit distinctly different product preferences, compared with consumers in other social classes. For instance, only 15 percent of U.S. adults with an income below $25,000 say they drink wine, compared with 52 percent of adults in the top income bracket and 28 percent in middle-income brackets.[78] Finally, working class consumers have remained relatively resistant to change over the years, tending to continue behavior patterns that reflect traditional sex roles.

The working population in India is a large population with a sizeable proportion of it engaged in the primary sector - agriculture. Statistics from the Census study, conducted in 2001, represents the population profile of male and female in the working community. A large base of population, 72%, lives in the rural heartlands and a sizeable proportion of it is currently engaged in agriculture. Though disguised employment, landless labors, bonded labors exist, yet the people employed in this area all add up to the working class population involved in the primary sector. The population involved in the secondary sector or the industrial sector has reduced over the years, yet the core sector growth has been visible, particularly in the last three to four years. Notable is the fact that the pattern of manufacturing is now moving towards high end and high technology products, which require more skilled and semi-skilled workers. With growth in the services sector and particularly the IT and ITES sectors more and more employment opportunities are creating a larger workforce.

Exhibit 14.14
THE WORKING CLASS IN INDIA
Work Participation Rates : (Excluding J & K)

Total Workers		Number	Rate
Persons		314,131,370	37.46%
Males		224,363,807	51.55%
Females		89,767,563	22.25%
Main Workers (Working for at least 183 days a year)			
Persons		285,932,493	34.10%
Males		221,658,584	50.93%
Females		64,273,909	15.93%
Marginal Workers (Working less than 183 days a year)			
Persons		28,198,877	3.36%
Male		2,705,223	0.62%
Females		25,493,654	6.32%
Percentage of Main Worker Engaged In:			
	Persons	Males	Females
Primary Sector	67.5%	63.6%	81.2%
Secondary Sector	12.0%	13.1%	8.0%
Tertiary Sector	20.5%	23.3%	10.8%

Data Source: 1991 Census of India

The Homeless

At the low end of the status hierarchy are ***homeless*** consumers who lack shelter and live on the streets or in makeshift structures, cars, or vacant houses.[79] The homeless represent a very sizable segment of society in some countries. In the United States, the homeless population is estimated to be as high as 7 million.[80] This group, which is growing in size, is made up primarily of drug and alcohol abusers, former mental patients, members of female-headed households, and those who have experienced financial setbacks. Homeless consumers are not necessary unemployed: according to a survey in Austin, Texas, where an estimated 6,000 homeless people live, 51 percent of the respondents were employed but not earning enough to afford a permanent residence.[81]

An overriding characteristic of the homeless is the struggle for survival. With little or no income, homeless consumers have difficulty acquiring daily necessities such as food and medical care.[82] They are not helpless but rather are a "resourceful, determined, and capable group that proactively deals with its lack of resources in the consumer environment."[83] They tend to maintain their self-esteem by distancing themselves from more dependent individuals on welfare or in shelters and from institutions like the Salvation Army, accepting their street role identity, or telling fictitious stories about past or future accomplishments.[84]

A particularly important survival activity for homeless consumers is *scavenging*, finding used or partially used goods that others have discarded. Thus homeless consumers are often secondhand consumers, scavenging for what they need in garbage cans or dumpsters and going to restaurants or stores that are known to discard edible food. Many vary their scavenging patterns to avoid detection as they move between areas to find the needed items, making this therefore a mobile or nomadic society. Despite their poverty, most homeless consumers have some valued possessions, and they get the maximum use out of items, discarding something only if they have absolutely no further use for it.

Homelessness is a matter of concern for a country like India where every winter nearly 2,000 homeless people die in India. According to the latest census report, there are 13 million homeless households in India and each of these households has 5-6 members. This issue is of greater concern in the urban areas and with population migration quite rampant between the rural to the urban heartlands, the issue has become graver. The aspect of homelessness also means resettlement in most cases, for which there are no adequate back up plans by the government. In Chennai City 40 per cent of the population lives in slums - there are 69,000 families who have been identified to be living on government land and are to be relocated to areas far removed from the city. Delhi, where sub-standard settlements house as much as 70 per cent of the city's population, leads the way in environmental activism. In 1997, Hyderabad was distributing land titles and housing loans to the urban poor, but during the TDP tenure the state leased large areas of land at heavily subsidized rate to business groups, international airports, cinemas, shopping complexes, hotels, corporate hospitals, and railway tracks. Over 10,000 houses of the 'weaker members of society' have been demolished to make way for the new face of 'Cyber bad'.

marketing IMPLICATIONS

Social class can serve as an effective way of segmenting the market, thereby influencing product or service development, messages, media selection, and channel member selection.

Product or service development

Social class motives and values can determine which offerings consumers desire. For example, to satisfy their need for prestige and luxury, many upper-class consumers prefer high-end automobiles, imported wines, fancy restaurants, exotic or deluxe vacations, and couture clothing. The working class, on the other hand, wants good quality at a fair price, and many offerings are designed to fulfill this desire. Examples include family-rate motels, buffet restaurants, and economy or used cars. In Mexico, the Elektra retail chain caters to working-class customers by making credit available for purchases of televisions and other appliances.[85]

Sometimes marketers develop different product lines for different classes. Anheuser-Busch, for example, offers Michelob for the upper middle class (with a super-premium price), Budweiser for the middle class (premium price), and Busch for the working class (low price). Furthermore, Heineken is perceived as an upper-class beer, Coors and Miller as middle class, and Old Style as lower middle.[86] Procter & Gamble has even developed a premium line of Pampers disposable diapers called Baby Stages of Development. Designed for middle- and upper-class consumers, the line is marketed on the basis of innovative features rather than price.[87] Also, marketers can create products that appeal to consumers' aspirations for upward mobility. Thus the designer Michael Kors now offers moderately priced clothing based on his high-end apparel line, fashions he calls "carpool couture" that "look aspirational."[88]

Messages

Advertisers targeting a particular social class within the larger population can be effective by tapping into the group's distinctiveness; when targeting the upper classes, for instance, the advertiser might suggest the group's status as a small, elite group.[89] Other messages for the upper classes might focus on themes of "just reward for hard work," "you've made it," or "pamper yourself because you deserve it." Certain offerings can be advertised as coveted status symbols; thus, Jaguar advertises its XJ8 as a car that wealthy consumers lust after because of the unique combination of "beauty and brains" (see Exhibit 14.11). Messages for the working class might take on a more localized orientation, focusing on home and friends as well as favored activities such as hunting, watching sports events, and getting together at the local bar. In addition, messages can use typical members of a social class as role models. The ad in Exhibit 14.12, for example, represents an appeal to the working class.

Media exposure

The classes also differ in their exposure to certain media. Advertisers try to reach the upper classes, especially the nouveaux riches, through targeted magazines and newspapers such as the *Robb Report* (whose readers' average income is $755,000 a year), *Town and Country,* and the *New York Times.*[90] Many upper-class consumers watch public TV stations and cultural shows and are also more likely to fit the profile of the Internet shopper, with higher income and education.[91] Lower-class consumers tend to be heavy watchers of TV and less likely to read magazines and newspapers, compared with other classes. Middle-class consumers, particularly those with only some college, are unique because they tend to be heavy TV watchers and magazine readers.

Exhibit 14.11
ADVERTISING A STATUS SYMBOL
The Rolex watch is a strong status symbol for upper-class consumers.

Channel member selection

Marketers targeting upper-class consumers can make goods available through channel members that sell exclusive merchandise with personalized service.[92] For example, the high-fashion Bijan boutique on Rodeo Drive in Los Angeles sells by appointment only. With an average of only five customers a day, Bijan sells bulletproof, chinchilla-lined jackets for $27,000 and perfume in Baccarat crystal bottles for $1,500. Specialty stores such as Prada and Hermes appeal to the upper class by showcasing status products in luxurious settings.[93] Conspicuous consumption can play a role when consumers want to acquire items in the "correct" store, especially if they can be seen doing so.[94] Even mass merchandisers are selling products with a bit more snob appeal. Target sells "cheap chic" apparel and housewares very similar to those offered by pricier retailers.[95] Discount stores such as Wal-Mart and dollar stores such as Dollar Tree attract working-class consumers with value pricing of quality goods.

Note of caution

Marketers have had difficulty in using social class as a segmentation variable for several reasons. As noted earlier, a variety of factors such as occupation and income can have opposite effects on social class, which makes social class difficult to measure. Also, variations within a class make social class a better predictor of broad behavior patterns, such as conspicuous product-level choice, than of specific behaviors such as brand choice. Finally, because of social class fragmentation, traditional social class distinctions may be becoming too broad to be truly useful. Therefore, marketers are using technology to segment markets more effectively and target more precisely. "Marketers can now pinpoint the class status and buying patterns of just about everyone in the U.S. on a neighborhood-by-neighborhood basis,"[96] thanks in part to database marketing, the Internet, direct mail, and other tools.

How the Household Influences Consumer Behavior

As discussed earlier, social class is an important influence on the behavior of consumers within a household. However, some researchers argue that the household itself is the most important unit of analysis for consumer behavior because households make many more acquisition, consumption, and disposition decisions than individuals do. This section defines families and households, examines the different types of households, and describes the family life cycle. After exploring some major trends that affect household structure and consumer behavior, the chapter closes with a look at how families influence decision making and consumption.

Types of Households

A *family* is usually defined as a group of individuals living together who are related by marriage, blood, or adoption. The most typical unit is the ***nuclear family,*** consisting of a father, mother, and children. The ***extended family*** consists of the nuclear family plus relatives such as grandparents, aunts, uncles, and cousins. Nearly 4 million U.S. families have three or more generations of parents living with children and grandchildren.[97] In the United States we often think of *family* in terms of the nuclear family, whereas in many countries the extended family is the defining unit. Although the family is important almost everywhere in the world, some countries and cultures exhibit a stronger family orientation than others. In Japan and China, for example, the family is a focal point, and most people feel a very strong sense of obligation to it.[98]

Family in India is considered a social security blanket and the traditional mindset still follows the age old adage, 'the family which lives together, eats together'. Though conventional family structures are breaking down and joint families are few in the urban towns, yet values, traditions and norms laid down by the family are inherently visible in the family members, even while staying in nuclear households. The rural heartlands, however, present a contrasting picture of the family, where the cohesiveness and the intention to stay together is more visible. Contrastingly, in the urban households the family is increasingly under pressure to disintegrate. Increasing opportunities in urban metropolis and the lure of the amenities in the bigger towns are irrepressible for most households. [11]A study conducted in 2003, by JWT shortlisted 24 families from all over India- DINKs(Double Income No Kids) in Bangalore, affluent Punjabis in Lajpat Nagar, New Delhi, a middle class family from small town India (Bareilly), middle class family in Mumbai, an MNC executive family, an extended family in Warangal, and so on. The JWT focused on anthropology issues and spent seven-days with the family to watch their interplay. The key issues that cam out of the surveyed families were; (i) The World in your home: The effects of consumerism and western lifestyle is beginning to take its toll on households; (ii) The Head of the family: Earlier the father was the unquestioned head of the family, a role which is now diluting and today the authoritarian approach is being replaced

Exhibit 14.12

WORKING-CLASS APPEAL *This ad appeals to working-class values and product preferences (i.e., having a large vehicle to tow things such as a trailer as well as having a "big fat juicy" cheeseburger.*

with managing of inter-personal relationships; (iii) The importance of self: The aspect of "We" to "Me" is gradually becoming the norm today in most households; (iv) Uncertainty: Retrenchment, lay-offs or a passing boom can affect confidence of consumers. [12]However, joint families are still prevalent and well-suited to modern Indian life, especially for the 67 percent of Indians who are farmers or agricultural workers or work in related activities. As in most primarily agricultural societies, few individuals can hope to achieve economic security without being a part of a cooperating group of kinsmen. The joint family is also common in cities, where kinship ties can be crucial to obtaining scarce jobs or financial assistance. Numerous prominent Indian families, such as the Tatas, Birlas, and Sarabhais, retain joint family arrangements even as they work together to control some of the country's largest financial empires. However, the joint family structures in the urban and the rural areas are very different. Most urban metropolis may have joint families, under a single roof, but they stay as separate households, contrast to rural and suburban joint families, where the cohesiveness and a concept of single household still exists.

Household is a broader term that includes a single person living alone or a group of individuals who live together in a common dwelling, regardless of whether they are related. This term includes cohabiting couples (an unmarried male and female living together), gay couples, and singles who are roommates. Because the number of households is on the rise—increasing by 1.35 million each year—marketers and researchers are increasingly thinking in terms of households rather than families.[99]

The traditional stereotype of the American family consisted of a husband as the primary wage earner, a wife who was a nonwage earner at home, and two children under the age of 18. Yet, only 6 percent of families fit this profile. Trends such as later marriages, cohabitation, divorce, dual careers, boomerang children, longer life, and a lower birth rate have greatly increased the proportion of nontraditional families.[100] However, the number of single-parent households headed by women has increased three times faster than the number of two-parent households.[101] Note that 29 percent of all U.S. households consist of married couples without children (because of a conscious choice to have none or because the children have left home).[102] Exhibit 14.13 shows how U.S households are expected to change by the end of this decade

	2000		2010		2000-2010
	number	percent	number	percent	percent change
All households	**110,140**	**100.0 %**	**117,696**	**100.0 %**	**6.9 %**
Families	**77,705**	**70.6**	**80,193**	**68.1**	**3.2**
Married couples	60,969	55.4	61,266	52.1	0.5
with children younger than 18*	24,286	22.1	23,433	19.9	–3.5
with children 18+ only	5,318	4.8	6,884	5.8	29.4
with no children	31,365	28.5	30,950	26.3	–1.3
Single fathers	1,523	1.4	1,660	1.4	9.0
Single mothers	7,473	6.8	7,779	6.6	4.1
Other families	7,741	7.0	9,488	8.1	22.6
Nonfamilies	**32,434**	**29.4**	**37,503**	**31.9**	**18.0**
Men living alone	10,898	9.9	12,577	10.7	15.4
Women living alone	16,278	14.8	18,578	15.8	14.1
Other nonfamilies	5,258	4.8	6,347	5.4	20.7

* Includes those with children both younger than age 18 and 18 and older.
Note: Numbers in thousands and percent of all households by type, 2000-2010; and percent change 2000-2010.
Numbers may not add to total due to rounding.

Exhibit 14.13
CHANGES IN HOUSEHOLD TYPES *By the end of this decade, the profile of the U.S. family will change dramatically. In particular, the segment of nontraditional families (singles living alone, couples without children, divorced families) is on the rise. Here are some specific projections for each type of household.*

In India, contrastingly, the concept of households is on the rise as joint families are crumbling and more so in bigger cities, where a large population migrates for job opportunities, higher studies, specialized coaching or for preparation of competitive examinations. Today, there are localities earmarked as a hub where such kind of households exists. For instance, Ber Sarai or Katwaria Sarai in South Delhi are small localities nestled behind India's finest engineering college, Indian Institute of Technology- Delhi, and young boys from the remotest areas of India prepare for their Civil Services exams. Today as more and more girls are pursuing careers, they need to step out of their homes and at times even move to different cities. Paying Guest accommodations, especially, suited to the requirements of the working girls or women are being created.

Households and Family Life Cycle

Households can further differ in terms of the ***family life cycle.*** As shown in Exhibit 14.14, families can be characterized in terms of the age of the parents and how many children are living at home.[103] Thus families progress from the bachelor stage (young and single) through marriage and having children to being an older couple without children at home. Households may also consist of unmarried singles, couples without children (younger and older), and older couples who delay having children. Various changes such as death or divorce can alter household structure by, for instance, creating single-parent households. The many arrows in Exhibit 14.14 illustrate how households can change over time.

Marketers must consider the great variation in needs over the family life cycle and the effect on consumer behavior within households. In general, spending increases as households shift from young singles to young married and then remains high until falling sharply at the older married or older single stages.[104] However, this pattern depends on what is purchased. New parents tend to spend more on health care, clothing, housing, and food (and less on alcohol, transportation, and education). The U.S. market for baby products alone is worth nearly $9 billion.[105] As their families grow, parents spend more on housing and furnishings, child care, and related household services. Young empty nesters spend more on vehicles and clothing; older single households and couples spend more on home-based products, health care, and travel. Finally, households in the midst of a life cycle change are more likely to switch brand preferences and be more receptive to marketing efforts.[106]

These stages do not capture all types of households. Notably missing are same-sex couples and never-married single mothers, two important market segments. Gays and lesbians, for example, represent anywhere from 11 to 23 million consumers in the United States and are relatively affluent and highly educated (see Chapter 13).[107] In addition, more than 4 million women are never-married mothers between 15 and 44 years old.[108] The largest proportion are teenagers at lower income levels.

Also, many households consider pets (cats, dogs, birds, fish, or other animals) to be important family members. More than 60 percent of U.S. families (mostly married couples with no children under 18 years old) own pets; in all, these households spend more than $23 billion yearly on pet-related goods and services.[109] Some consumers buy pet mansions, give their pets greeting cards, and dress their pets for holidays.[110] Also, many consumers view pets as surrogate siblings or children (owners can experience, in a limited way, what it is like to have children), an important influence on household spending.

Exhibit 14.14
CHANGES IN ROLES AND STATUS IN FAMILY LIFE CYCLE *The new generation of retired individuals is high on resources and also willing to enjoy life*

Family Life Cycle trends are significantly changing in the Indian context. Chapter 13 illustrates how the population is classified into different stages of evolution from the pre-independence to a post-independence era. This population classification when mapped on the family life cycle graph shows some interesting trends. The bachelorhood stage of the workforce born and brought up between the 1940's to the 1960's was about scarcity and more of resettlement in a post independence era. Contrast that to the bachelorhood of population born between 1960's to the 1980's which was a period of economic transition and surplus. This dichotomy helped in creating a new generation of achievers from the strivers of the earlier generation. The upbringing and parenting patterns in both these population segments also was different and created diverse backgrounds of thought processes, which affected the way parenting to them was defined. Today, family life cycle roles and status are prominently segmented on psychographic profile. Exhibit 14.14 illustrates the profile of the population who grew up between 1940 and 1960, now superannuating, a stark contrast in psychographic profiling as compared to their parents, who lived through scarcity and dependency.

Changing Trends in Household Structure

Five main factors are altering the basic structure and characteristics of households. These include (1) delayed marriage, (2) cohabitation, (3) dual careers, (4) divorce, and (5) smaller families.

Delayed Marriage In many Western societies, an increasing number of individuals are either delaying or avoiding getting married. Today the median age at which U.S. men first marry is 27; for U.S. women, the median age is 25.[111] As a result, 27 percent of all U.S. households (27 million people, more women than men) consist of one person living alone.[112] Delayed marriage may occur because career is seen as a higher priority, because it is more acceptable for a man and a woman to live together before marriage, or because consumers with college loans want to reduce their debt first.

The trend toward delayed marriage is important for marketers because single-person households exhibit unique consumption patterns. For example, single men spend more on alcohol, new cars, clothes, and education than married men do. Compared with married women, single women tend to spend more on new cars, shoes, entertainment, candy, and housing (to live in a safe area).[113] Single men are more likely than married men to give gifts of jewelry, watches, and clothes, whereas single women are more likely than married women to give housewares and small appliances. In general, singles tend to have more discretionary income and therefore can spend more than couples of the same social class and income level.[114] Not only do singles spend more on restaurant meals, they eat out more often.[115]

By delaying marriage, couples typically find themselves in a better financial position and can pay more for a home and furnishings, baby clothes, and housekeeping services. Parents over 35 with children under 6 spend more than younger parents do on housing, home maintenance, furnishings, child care, transportation, and food. Also, when couples delay marriage, they also delay having children, which has led to an increase in the use of fertility drugs and the incidence of twins and triplets.[116]

Cohabitation As a result of changing social norms, more consumers are deciding to live with members of the opposite sex outside marriage. Among the 5 million opposite-sex U.S. households, more than half have never been married. Most of the cohabitors (38 percent) are aged 25 to 34, and 20 percent are aged 35 to 44.[117] The highest percentage of unmarried couples living together is in Sweden.

Compared with married couples, cohabitating individuals tend to be more self-oriented. Many view possessions as personal rather than joint items in case the relationship does not endure.[118] Nevertheless, many unmarried partners share expenses, and because both individuals are likely to work, they often have higher discretionary income than married couples of a similar age (with a nonworking spouse). Thus unmarried couples are more frequent consumers of entertainment, transportation, and vacations than are married couples.

Dual-Career Families The increasing number of dual-career families has had a dramatic impact on household behavior. In general, the two major types of dual-career families are (1) those in which the woman is concerned about career advancement and personal fulfillment and (2) those in which the woman works out of financial necessity and considers her employment "just a job."[119] The latter group tends to be more like the traditional housewife in terms of outlook and behavior, whereas the former group is more contemporary and progressive.

Dual-career families have several important implications for consumer behavior. First, having two incomes increases discretionary spending.[120] One study found that dual-career families spend more than other families do on child care, eating out, and services in general. Likewise, dual careers mean that the wife is bringing more financial resources to the family, giving her more influence over family decisions for expensive or important purchases such as vacations, cars, and housing.

Second, the increased burden of having both career and family, or role overload, leaves less time for cooking, housekeeping, shopping, and other activities.[121] This is why dual-career families particularly value offerings that save time, such as microwaveable meals, prepared foods, housekeeping, child care, fast food, and food delivery services. Because women in such households have limited shopping time, they are more likely to be brand loyal, buy impulsively, and buy from catalogs or online.

Third, more husbands are taking on household responsibilities, including shopping, cooking, and—for a small but growing percentage of families—staying home to care for children.[122] As a result, more ads are geared toward men who are, for example, sharing some responsibility for household cooking. In Asia, however, such ads received a negative response from both men and women because sex roles are viewed more traditionally, even though more men are handling more housework.

Divorce More than four of every ten U.S. marriages is likely to end in divorce.[123] Although the trend has recently leveled off, many divorces still occur each year, and these separations have important implications for consumer behavior.[124] Going through a divorce represents a major transition in which consumers perform a number of critical tasks, such as disposing of old possessions, forming a new household, and creating new patterns of consumption.[125] Divorce can lead to a major change in lifestyle, and acquiring goods and services can be an integral part of forming a new identity and relieving stress during this transition. For example, a recently divorced consumer might buy a new house, car, furniture, or clothing; get a new hairstyle; or go to singles clubs to assume a new image or to feel better.

Divorce also influences household structure. First, if the couple was childless, the newly divorced often adopt many of the singles' acquisition and consumption patterns discussed earlier. However, these new singles are typically older and have greater discretionary income for housing, transportation, and clothing if they are working. Second, divorce creates single-parent families when children are involved. Estimates are that one in three families in the United States now has only one parent, and most of these families have a female head-of-household, although the proportion of single fathers is growing.[126] Because the single parent must earn an income and raise children, products or services that offer convenience—such as packaged or fast foods—are a necessity.[127] Compared with their married counterparts, single parents are likely to have lower than average incomes, spend relatively less on most things, and be renters rather than homeowners.

Finally, divorced individuals with children are remarrying with greater frequency, creating more stepfamilies.[128] Demographers estimate that more than one-third of U.S. families are of this type. In nearly two-thirds of stepfamilies, children live with their biological mother; many such families are lower in income and education and are more youthful than intact families. Due to potential stress and conflicting emotions, about half these families will also end up in divorce. Like other households, stepfamilies can have unique consumption needs. For example, children who travel between families require duplicate supplies of clothes, toothbrushes, and toys.[129]

Smaller Families In many countries, the average household size is getting smaller. In particular, boomer and Xer couples are having fewer children because of dual careers, financial burdens, and concern for overpopulation—some couples believe that having more than two children is socially irresponsible. The average family size in the United States is now 3.14 people.[130] Smaller family size means more discretionary income to spend on recreational items, vacations, education, toys, and entertainment. Smaller families also can spend more on each child. The trend toward smaller families has been key in Japan, where parents with fewer children are spending more on education, cultural activities, and clothing.[131] Childless married couples are one of the fastest-growing types of households. Clearly, these households have more discretionary income than other households. Compared with couples who have children, childless couples spend more on food, restaurant meals, entertainment, liquor, clothing, and pets.[132]

The Indian family and household structures are also going through a phase of evolution where the traditional thought process and the conventional wisdom is making way for new influences and value systems. Issues like delayed marriages and therefore late children or deciding not to have children, failed marriages, dual careers, nuclear families and cohabitation have become the norm of the society. [13]Take for instance, divorce rates in India which are amongst the lowest in the world. 11 marriages out of 1,000 marriages (around 1 marriage out of 100 marriages) ends up in divorce in India. This figure was even low in 1990. In 1990, 7.40 marriages out of 1,000 marriages ended up in divorce in India. The divorce rate is even lower in the villages. However, these days divorce rates in India's urban sphere are shooting up as a result of increasing pressure on individuals to perform many roles together with lack of compromise.

The working women population is increasing and today conventional careers like teachers, secretarial positions or even NGO attachments are being sidelined for more demanding career choices. Extended working hours, travel programmes and demanding working patterns put pressure on women in the family. Earlier the women were safely cocooned in the protection of the family, today the environment is equally challenging for her as it is for men. Today, as India has more working women than any other country in the world, at all levels of skill – from a surgeon to an airline pilot to a bus conductor or a menial labourer, her role and status in the family too are increasingly challenging.

Today, women are even delaying marriages and even children or deciding to have no children at all to consolidate their careers. Ironically, the concept of child marriage is still prevalent in the same country. The median age is still very low for marriage in India, this trend of delayed marriages is prevalent in the bigger cities and metros. [14]National Family Health Survey, conducted in 1998-99, reports that 50% percent of women who were in ages 20-24, were married before the age of 18 years, indicating a decline of 4% points during the period between the data collection for the two surveys of 1992-93 and 1998-99. Reported percentages of girls in ages 20-24, marrying before age 18 were 58.6% for rural and 27.9% for urban areas. The survey also reported that in Bihar almost 3 out of 4 girls (71%) in ages 20-24 were married before age 18 years and in Rajasthan more than 2 out of 3 (68.3%) of the girls in ages 20-24 were married before they reached 18 years. In Madhya Pradesh this percentage was 64.7, in Andhra Pradesh it was 64.3% and in Uttar Pradesh it was 62.47%. Other States reporting high percentages were Maharashtra (47.7%), Karnataka (46.3%), West Bengal (45.9%), Haryana (41.5%), and Gujarat and Assam (40.7%). The States reporting lower percentages were Manipur (9.9%), Goa (10.1%) Himachal Pradesh (10.7%), Punjab and Mizoram (11.6%), and Kerala (17.0%).

As influences of the West seep steadily, aspects like cohabitation is now being considered an acceptable norm, however, limited. [15]With domestic violence on the rise, the govt. of India has now integrated a new law for the protection of women; it will extend equal benefit to women in live-in relationships as it will to married women. In other words, this means an official recognition to live-in relationships. Under the new proposal, the Government has defined violence against women in such a way that it makes no distinction between a woman who is married and one who is in a live-in relationship. [16]The boom in the BPOscape of the Indian IT milieu has brought winds of change now been blowing across the country for the last few years. Economic independence, coupled with self-assurance and liberated spending power has brought about a change in the social structure as traditional units dissolve and new ones come into shape. Recent years have witnessed a rise in live-in relationships, especially among urban couples working in BPO units across the country. A concoction of love and convenience gives birth to a live-in relationship as young BPO professionals shed inhibition and traditional notions. The entry of MNCs and the setting up of BPOs in the country have helped redefine the way young minds think and function as social mores are transformed.

marketing IMPLICATIONS

Marketers are recognizing the importance of nontraditional households and developing offerings that cater to their unique needs. Products and services that offer convenience can be marketed specifically to dual-career and divorced households. Because more husbands from dual-career families and single or divorced men shop for groceries and other items, retailers are increasingly targeting men.[133] Wives in dual-career households have more clout in expensive decisions, so marketers of costly products and services must appeal to both husband and wife. Nontraditional families are also being targeted: Hallmark has developed greeting cards that deal with stepfamily and cohabitation relationships.[134]

Single men and women, in particular, are an attractive target for many marketers. In Germany, Wal-Mart has had great success with "Singles Shopping" nights. Unmarried men and women wheel their shopping carts down the aisles (alone or with their children) to meet other singles while passing displays of convenience products such as frozen dinners and displays of items that foster romance, such as wine and candles. Wal-Mart reports that sales are up by 25 percent on singles nights.[135]

Roles That Household Members Play

A key aspect of households is that more than one individual can become involved in acquisition and consumption. This section discusses various elements of household consumer behavior, with particular emphasis on ***household decision roles*** and how household members influence decision processes.

In a multiperson household, members may perform a variety of tasks or roles in acquiring and consuming a product or service:

- *Gatekeeper* Household members who collect and control information important to the decision.
- *Influencer* Household members who try to express their opinions and influence the decision.
- *Decider* The person or persons who actually determine which product or service will be chosen.
- *Buyer* The household member who physically acquires the product or service.
- *User* The household members who consume the product

Each role can be performed by different household members and by a single individual, subset of individuals, or the entire household. For example, in deciding which movie to rent or download, parents might make the final decision, but the children may play a role, either directly (by stating their preferences) or indirectly (when parents keep their children's preferences in mind). One parent may actually obtain the movie, but the entire family may watch (or consume) it. Parents are often the deciders and purchasers of items consumed by their children such as clothing, toys, food, and movies (see Exhibit 14.15). Similarly, more than 70 percent of men's underwear and fragrance is purchased by wives and girlfriends. Exhibit 14.16 divides household purchases into nine categories, depending on the decision maker and the user.

Household decision roles can be ***instrumental,*** meaning that they relate to tasks affecting the buying decision, such as when and how much to purchase. Roles can also be ***expressive,*** which means they indicate family norms such as choice of color or style.[136] Traditionally, the husband fulfilled the instrumental role and the wife the expressive role, but sex-role changes are altering this pattern. Women, for example, are now involved in 65 percent of decisions about buying the household's first computer.[137]

Conflict can often occur in fulfilling different household roles based on (1) the reasons for buying, (2) who should make the decision, (3) which option to choose, and (4) who gets to use the product or service.[138] For example, because all family members have increased their computer usage, conflict often arises over who gets to use the computer and for how long.[139] In general, households resolve conflicts through problem solving, persuasion, bargaining, and politics, with persuasion

Exhibit 14.15

MARKETING TO PARENTS AND CHILDREN

Although young children are the users or consumers of many products and services, parents usually decide what to purchase.

This ad seeks to convince parents about the goodness of Fisher Price toys and how they help the child learn and grow with them

EXHIBIT 14.16

BUYERS AND USERS

Household purchase decisions can be made by one, some, or all members of the family. Acquired products and services may be consumed by one, some, or all members. Here is an example of three cells that result from crossing these two factors. Can you think of examples that would fit into the other six cells?

A Purchase Decision Maker

Consumer	One member	Some members	All members
One member	1	2 Tennis racket	3
Some members	4 Sugar Pops	5	6
All members	7	8	9 Refrigerator

For Example:

1. Mom and Dad go to buy a new tennis racket for Mom. Dad advises Mom on her purchase. Some members are decision makers and one member is a consumer: cell 2.
2. Mom goes to the grocery store to buy Sugar Pops cereal for her children. She'll never eat the stuff. One member is a decision maker and some members are consumers: cell 4.
3. Mom, Dad, and the kids go to the department store to buy a refrigerator. All members are decision makers and all are consumers: cell 9.

and problem solving the most frequently used.[140] Note, however, that resolution is often not systematic and rational, but rather a "muddling-through" process in which the household makes a series of small decisions to arrive at a solution.[141] Moreover, many households avoid rather than confront conflict.

Marketers should recognize that household decisions are more frequent in some circumstances than in others. Specifically, joint decisions are more likely when the perceived risk associated with the decision is high, the decision is very important, there is ample time to make a decision, and the household is young. In addition, household members can influence each other in terms of brand preferences and loyalties, information search patterns, media reliance, and price sensitivities.[142]

The Roles of Spouses

Husbands and wives play different roles in making decisions, and the nature of their influence depends on the offering and the couple's relationship. In examining husband-wife influence, a landmark study conducted in Belgium (and replicated in the United States) identified four major decision categories:[143]

- A ***husband-dominant decision*** is made primarily by the male head-of-household (e.g., the purchase of lawn mowers and hardware).
- A ***wife-dominant decision*** is made primarily by the female head-of-household (e.g., children's clothing, women's clothing, groceries, and toiletries).
- An ***autonomic decision*** is equally likely to be made by the husband or the wife but not by both (e.g., men's clothing, luggage, toys and games, sporting equipment, and cameras).
- A ***syncratic decision*** is made jointly by the husband and wife (e.g., vacations, refrigerators, TVs, living room furniture, financial planning services, and the family car).

As spouses come closer to a final decision, the process tends to move toward syncratic decision making and away from the other three types, particularly for more important decisions. These role structures are only generalities, however; the actual influence exerted depends on many factors. First, a spouse will have greater influence when he or she brings higher financial resources to the family and he or she has a high level of involvement in the decision.[144] Second, demographic factors, such as total family income, occupation, and education, are also related to the degree of husband-wife influence.[145] Combined, these factors provide a spouse with a perception of power in the decision-making situation. The higher the degree of perceived power, the more likely the spouse will exert influence.

When the family has a strong traditional sex-role orientation, certain tasks are stereotypically considered either masculine or feminine, and more decisions tend to be husband dominated than in less traditional families.[146] For example, Mexican American families tend to have a strong traditional orientation and are characterized by more husband-dominant decisions. Yet, sex-role changes, as noted earlier, are influencing husband-wife decisions. In Thailand, for instance, nearly half of the husbands surveyed said they decided what foods their households would eat and that they did the family food shopping, traditionally considered the wife's role.[147] In the United States, joint decision making is most common among Anglo families; husband dominance is more likely in Japanese American families; and wife dominance is more prevalent in African American families.

Researchers have found support for the four major patterns of spousal decision roles in a number of countries, although the United States, France, and the Netherlands exhibited a higher level of joint decision making than Venezuela and Gabon, where autonomous decisions were more prevalent.[148] Other aspects of spousal decision making have also been studied. For example, through the processes of ***bargaining*** (which involves a fair exchange) or ***concession*** (in which a spouse gives in on some points to get what he or she wants in other areas), couples tend to make equitable decisions that result from compromises.[149] Couples do not typically follow a formal, systematic process for making decisions; instead, they use an informal process in which they have limited awareness of each other's knowledge and decision strategy.[150] Husbands and wives are generally not good at estimating their spouse's influence and preferences, although each learns from the outcome of previous decisions over time and tends to adjust decision behaviors accordingly.[151]

Alternatively, the man's role of being a patriarch in the family who was considered the supreme guardian is now increasingly under pressure. As the woman of the house steps out to work, he is stepping in to help in household chores. Looking after the children, cooking, household shopping are some of the chores that the man in the house is sharing today. According to tradition and deeply embedded culture formats, the man's status was god like and he was therefore, referred to as "Pati Parmeshwar". Today, his role is more defined as a pati and not parmeshwar, which means he is a more humane character that the family can relate to.

The Roles of Children

Children play an important role in household decisions by attempting to influence their parents' acquisition, usage, and disposition behavior. The most common stereotype is that children nag until their parents finally give in. Research finds that the success of such attempts depends on the type of offering, characteristics of the parents, age of the child, and stage of the decision process.[152] Children are more likely to use influence for child-related products such as cereals, cookies, snacks, cars, vacations, and new computer technologies. For clothing and toys, children often use the argument that "everyone else has one," and because parents want to avoid being identified as "scrimpers," they will often give in.[153]

Interestingly, children consistently overestimate how much influence they have in most decisions.[154] Children tend to have less influence when parents are more involved in the decision process or are more traditional and conservative. Working and single parents, on the other hand, are more likely to give in because they face more time pressures.[155] When parents place more restrictions on TV watching, they tend to yield less, but children's attempts to influence parents increase as parents watch more TV with them.

Another important finding is that the older the child, the more influence he or she will exert.[156] One reason is that younger children tend to have lower involvement in the decision process, and parents are more likely to refuse younger children's requests. As evidence, teens believe they have greater influence when the decision is important to them and the family. Older children also generate their own income, giving them more power.[157] Even when the family includes two or more children, parents exert the most influence over decisions about buying and consuming new offerings.[158]

One study examined the strategies adolescents use in trying to influence parental and family decision making, which include bargaining (making deals), persuasion (trying to influence the decision in their favor), emotional appeals (using emotion to get what they want), and requests (directly asking).[159] Parents, in turn, can use not only the same strategies on their children but also expert (knowledge), legitimate (power), and directive (parental authority) strategies.

The type of household determines the nature of children's influence:

- Authoritarian households stress obedience.
- Neglectful households exert little control.
- Democratic households encourage self-expression.
- Permissive households remove constraints.

Children are more likely to have direct decision control in permissive and neglectful families and to influence decisions in democratic and permissive ones.[160] Also, children's influence varies at different stages of the decision process. It is greatest at the earliest stages of decision making (problem recognition and information search), and declines significantly in the evaluation and choice phases.[161] However, because three out of five parents take their children along when grocery shopping, children may have more influence over grocery purchases than over other purchases.

marketing IMPLICATIONS Marketers need to recognize that household decision roles exist and may be performed by different household members. Thus appealing only to deciders or purchasers may be a narrow and relatively ineffective strategy. Marketers who exclusively target children for toys or breakfast cereals, for example, ignore the fact that parents are usually influencers, deciders, and purchasers of these products. Similarly, marketers of men's underwear must take into account that women make the majority of decisions and purchases of these items. Therefore, marketers should determine which family members are involved in each acquisition decision and appeal to all important parties.

For example, Mattel designed the colorful My Scene cell phone specifically for preteens. Knowing that parents will be buying the phone and paying for its usage, Mattel's marketing "needs to resonate with the mom or dad," says one of the phone's marketers.[162] Online marketers know that children use the Internet to send e-mail, play games, visit websites of popular TV shows, and do homework.[163] Older children are heavier Internet users in the United States and United Kingdom, whereas younger children are a significant part of the online population in Spain and Italy.[164] Some websites that target kids allow them to shop without credit cards by, with parental permission, setting up special accounts.[165] Websites for children under 13 must comply with the Children's Online Privacy Protection Act and obtain parental permission before collecting information from children (see Chapters 19 and 20 for more on regulation and ethical issues).[166]

Marketers sometimes direct their efforts toward the entire family. For instance, the Nickelodeon Family Suites Holiday Inn in Orlando, Florida, is designed to appeal to both children and their parents. Children like sleeping in rooms decorated with SpongeBob SquarePants and other Nickelodeon characters. Meanwhile, parents like the hotel's family-friendly touches, including wake-up calls featuring the voices of Nickelodeon characters and refrigerators that are not prestocked with expensive snacks and beverages. "Every parent I've ever talked to hates the fact that those items are in the refrigerator already," says Nickelodeon executive.[167]

It is important to recognize that most of the research mentioned in this chapter focused rather narrowly on decision making. More study is needed to better understand the variety of events, interactions, and processes that can occur when households consume products and services.[168]

Summary

Individuals in a society can be grouped into status levels (upper, middle, and lower), making up a social class hierarchy. Class distinctions are significant because members of a particular class share common life experiences and therefore values and consumer behavior patterns, although many variations occur within groups. Individuals are most likely to be influenced by members of their own class because they regularly interact with them. Still, influence can cross class lines through the trickle-down effect (when lower classes copy upper-class values and behavior) or the status float effect (when trends start in the lower classes and spread upward).

A variety of factors determine social class, the most critical of which are occupation and education. Researchers use a battery of items, such as the Computerized Status Index, to measure social class. Three major trends producing an evolution in social class structure are upward mobility, downward mobility, and social class fragmentation. Social class influences consumer behavior in three major ways: (1) through conspicuous consumption, the acquisition and display of status symbol offerings to demonstrate social standing; (2) through compensatory consumption, trying to offset some deficiency by engaging in greater than usual consumption; and (3) through the meaning of money.

Households include both families and unrelated people living together, as well as singles. The proportion of nontraditional households has increased because of factors such as (1) later marriages, (2) cohabitation, (3) dual-career families, (4) divorce, and (5) smaller families. Households exert considerable influence on acquisition and consumption patterns. Members can play different roles in the decision process (gatekeeper, influencer, decider, buyer, and user). Also, husbands and wives vary in their influence in the decision process, depending on whether the situation is husband dominant, wife dominant, autonomic, or syncratic. Children can influence the decision process by making requests of parents. The nature of this influence partly depends on whether the household is authoritarian, neglectful, democratic, or permissive. In general, the older the child, the greater the influence.

Questions for Review and Discussion

1. What is the social class hierarchy?
2. What are the determinants of social class?
3. Why is social class fragmentation taking place?
4. Why would a consumer engage in conspicuous consumption and conspicuous waste?
5. How does parody display differ from status symbols?
6. Under what circumstances does compensatory consumption occur?
7. Why might a company develop different offerings for consumers in different social classes?
8. Define the nuclear family, extended family, and household.
9. What five key factors have altered the basic structure and characteristics of households?
10. What are the five roles that a household member may perform in acquiring and consuming something?

Exercises

1. Design a battery of questions to measure social class standing. (The CSI in Exhibit 14.6 can be used as a starting point.) Make sure to include all the determinants of social class. In addition, pick one product and one service that you think will vary across social class in terms of consumer behavior and develop a series of questions to measure the acquisition and consumption of this product and service (i.e., how much time is spent, what information is collected, where it is purchased, what brands are considered and selected, and so on). Administer this questionnaire to at least 15 consumers who represent the range of social classes, and divide the respondents into three major groups (upper,

middle, and lower class). Summarize how the three groups vary in terms of consumption behavior for both the product and service.

2. A travel service has hired you to develop a marketing strategy for a vacation package. The company wants to offer different packages to different social classes. Develop a complete package and marketing strategy for each of the following: the upper class, the middle class, and the working class. Be sure to discuss (1) services offered (including destination, accommodations, and so on), (2) pricing, (3) the advertising message, and (4) media targeting. Summarize the key differences among the three marketing strategies.
3. Pick three products and services that households consume. Conduct an interview of individuals from five families, and ask them to provide a thorough description of the processes used to acquire, consume, and dispose of these products or services. Summarize this information by answering the following questions:
   a. Which specific roles do household members play in the decision process?
   b. What is the nature of husband-wife interaction in the decision?
   c. Which role do children play in the process?
   d. How do household consumption patterns for these products and services differ from individual consumption patterns?
   e. Who disposes of the products and services and why?

More Exercises from the Adaptor

1. Changing family and social structures are best reflected through films, music and music lyrics or even advertisements and communication fraternity. From your understanding of the chapter and particularly the perspectives presented on India, how do you reflect on the statement and illustrate with answers?

References

1 Source: The Marketing Whitebook, Businessworld, 2006- India's youth and their career opportunities

2 Source: http://www.blonnet.com/2005/01/22/stories/2005012201860700.htm

3 Source: http://www.expressindia.com/fullstory.php?newsid=85926#compstory

4 Source: The New Improved Indian Consumer, Rama Bijapurkar, Businessworld, 28th December 2003

5 Source: http://www.theglobeandmail.com/servlet/story/RTGAM.20070509.wibasia09/BNStory/Business/columnists

6 Source: The New Improved Indian Consumer, Rama Bijapurkar, The Marketing Whitebook, Businessworld, 2006

7 Source: http://www.rediff.com/money/2005/dec/19guest1.htm

8 Source: http://www.chathamhouse.org.uk/pdf/research/asia/BPindiaeducation.pdf

9 Source: http://www.india-today.com/iplus/2000_1/status.html

10 India Luxury Trends Study by Technopak India, 2006

11 Source: The Marketing Whitebook, Businessworld, 2006

12 Source: http://countrystudies.us/india/83.htm

13 Source: http://www.divorcerate.org/divorce-rate-in-india.html

14 Source: http://www.indianngos.com/issue/population/resources/articles3.htm

15 Source: http://www.ibnlive.com/news/livein-relationship-now-a-serious-affair-for-govt/24727-3.html

16. Source: http://timesofindia.indiatimes.com/articleshow/msid-780296,curpg-1.cms

chapter **15**

Psychographics: Values, Personality, and Lifestyles

LEARNING OBJECTIVES

After studying this chapter, you will be able to:

- Define values and the value system, and show how they can be described.
- Identify some values that characterize Western cultures, outline the main factors that influence values, and describe how values can be measured.
- Discuss the personality characteristics most closely related to consumer behavior patterns and show why these are important from a marketing perspective.
- Explain how lifestyles are represented by activities, interests, and opinions, and describe how psychographic applications in marketing combine values, personality, and lifestyle variables.

INTRODUCTION

Surf Excel: Never have stains been so welcome

The story of Surf is 44-year old in India, which had a humble beginning from the Hindustan Lever (now Hindustan Unilever) stable. The brand lived through the 60's, 70's and 80's on the platform of 'washes whitest' and the classic Lalitaji icon that the brand created is still etched in the consumers' minds. Lalitaji symbolized the no-nonsense housewife, who always looked for the best bargain. She was the icon which first represented the empowerment of the Indian housewife in Indian ads. She was the traditional, middle class housewife who was educated and smart — someone nobody could take for a ride. The Indian housewife could identify completely with Lalitaji and she became a runaway success. The brand at that point tried to reposition itself as a superior product as compared to any other ordinary detergent powder. [1]The differentiator was showcased through a tough non-compromising person like Lalitaji, who said, "Adha Kilo Surf Ek Kilo Saste Powder Ke Barabar Hota Hai." Surf at that point in time worked on this positioning for two reasons. First, it was already an established brand with over two decades of market presence behind it and second, Nirma, an economy brand was eating into its market share, with a low price plank.

The Lalitaji campaign worked for some time, after which, the changing nature of the market and new consumer trends forced Surf to focus on a different platform to retain its market and get across to new consumer segments. The brand for some time made efforts to sustain its market presence and market share by introducing perceptible changes in the brand through features like Power Boosters, cues like 'new improved Surf', to name a few. [2]However, around 1990's the brand was again under pressure with the imminent launch of Ariel from P&G, Surf had to rethink on its franchise and looked at line extension through Surf Excel. The brand was successful in the premium end of the market and created sufficient inroads for itself. [3]However, in the process the parent brand Surf remained under pressure and therefore in 2004 had to be withdrawn. Around this time Surf Excel also consolidated itself by launching newer variants through Surf Excel.

[4]One of the key value drivers for Surf Excel was stain removal which was a paradigm shift from the earlier platform of more lather and therefore cleaner clothes. Most housewives had the perception that more lather gives better cleaning. One of the challenges for brand Surf Excel was to remove this notion and hence the

platform of stain removal was used and it worked. [5]Later the brand went on to develop a new formulation of Surf Excel detergent that produced less lather, helping to conserve water.This made a big difference in the dry Southern states of India where many people spend more money on the water needed for washing than they do on detergents. Washing clothes accounts for almost a quarter of all the water used in the states of Tamil Nadu and Andhra Pradesh. In May 2004, Surf Excel was relaunched in these two states, promising to save people two buckets of water a day without compromising on stain removal. Independent research by the C.P. Ramaswami Trust, an NGO that works on water conservation, has verified this claim. Advertisements endorsed by the Indian film celebrity, Revathi, promoted the message of cleaner clothes without more lather. Sales of Surf Excel have increased by over 50% in Tamil Nadu and Andhra Pradesh since its relaunch.

The campaign was extended pan India later and Shabana Azmi, who had a more national presence, was showcased to focus on the water conservation aspect. The brand later took the platform of stain removal to a higher value driver and used the proposition of stains are welcome, as it said, "Surf Excel Hain Na". Today the brand proclaims, "Daag Achhe Hai". Continual shifting and moving on process has helped the brand value to reach deep in the consumer minds and today the brand is synoynomous with stain removal.

Exhibit 15.1
STAINS ARE WELCOME FOR SURF EXCEL
A brand like Surf Excel has evolved over the last forty four years of its existence from brand Surf to Surf Excel, it has been continually offering a common value proposition as a stain remover with different executions

Surf Excel has been continuously innovating and offering new value drivers to the consumers in an attempt to keep the brand fresh and alive in their minds. As a part of brand reinforcement strategy it helps, since the core value driver has remained unchanged and most propositions only consolidate the stand.

Together values, personality, and lifestyles constitute the basic components of psychographics, the description of consumers based on their psychological and behavioral characteristics (see Exhibit 15.2). Traditionally, psychographics measured consumer lifestyles, but more modern applications have broadened its approach to include concepts such as the consumers' psychological makeup, their values and personality, and their behavior with respect to specific products (usage patterns, attitudes, and emotions). Marketers use psychographics to gain a more detailed understanding of consumer behavior than they can get from demographic variables like ethnicity, social class, age, gender, and religion. The following sections examine the major components of psychographic research in greater detail, beginning with values.

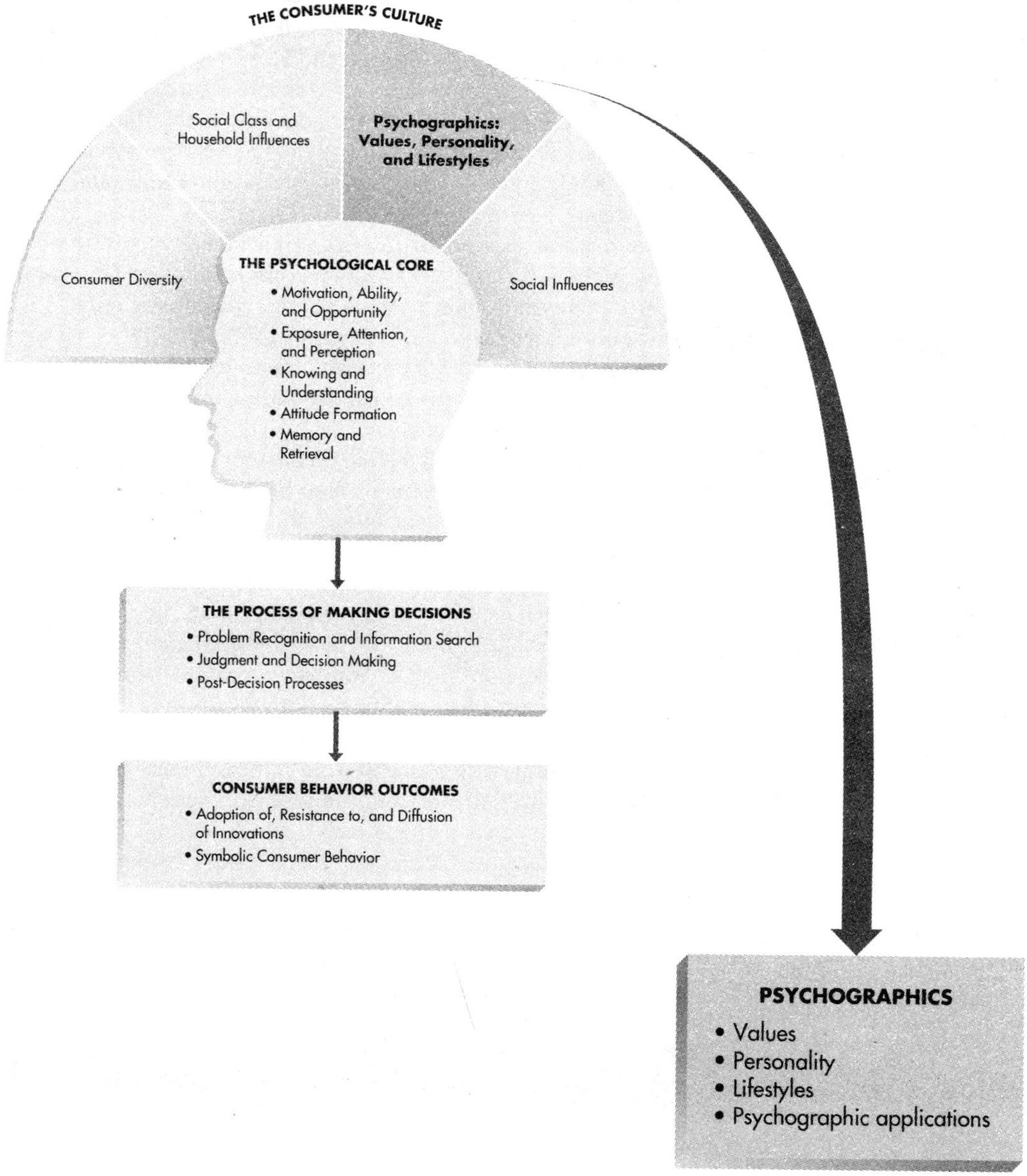

Exhibit 15.2

CHAPTER OVERVIEW: PSYCHOGRAPHICS: VALUES, PERSONALITY, AND LIFESTYLES *Previous chapters demonstrated how membership in certain cultural groups (regional, ethnic, social class, etc.) can affect group behaviors. This chapter examines the effect of these cultural influences on an individual level—namely, on values (deeply held beliefs), personality (consumer traits), and lifestyles (behavioral patterns that are manifestations of values and personality). Each of these factors is useful in understanding consumer behavior; in addition, marketers often combine them to obtain an overall psychographic profile of consumers.*

Values

Values are enduring beliefs that a given behavior or outcome is desirable or good.[2] For example, you may believe that it is good to be healthy, keep your family safe, have self-respect, and be free. As enduring beliefs, your values serve as standards that guide your behavior across situations and over time. Thus how much you value the environment generally determines the extent to which you litter, recycle, or buy products made from recycled materials. Values are so ingrained that most people are not consciously aware of them and have difficulty describing them.

Our total set of values and their relative importance constitute our ***value system.*** The way we behave in a given situation is often influenced by how important one value is relative to others.[3] For instance, deciding whether to spend Saturday afternoon relaxing with your family or exercising will be determined by the relative importance you place on family versus health. You feel value conflict when you do something that is consistent with one value but inconsistent with another equally important value. This is why parents who place equal value on convenience and concern for the environment may experience value conflict if they buy disposable diapers for their babies. Similarly, smoking cigarettes may cause conflict for teenagers if they value health and social acceptance equally.

Because values are among the first things children learn, value systems are often in place by age 10. As you will see in Chapter 16, people learn values through the process of socialization, which results from exposure to reference groups and other sources of influence.[4] You may therefore value education because your parents went to college and because they and your teachers encouraged this value. Likewise, the value you place on money, high-tech products, or the environment may come from your exposure to the opinions of family, friends, or the media. The Cartoon Network, for example, airs anger management spots during children's shows such as *Dragon Ball Z,* which features violent conflicts between characters.[5] Because individuals learn values through exposure to others in institutions and cultures, people within the same group often hold similar values.

Acculturation is the process by which individuals learn the values and behaviors of a new culture (see Chapter 13). For example, immigrants arriving in the United States must learn new values to acculturate to American life. Consumers are more likely to adopt the values of a new culture if they view that culture as attractive and having values similar to their own. Acculturation is also faster when people in the new culture are cohesive, give a lot of verbal and nonverbal signals about what their values are, and express pride in the values they hold.[6]

How Values Can Be Described

Values can vary in terms of their specificity. At the broadest level are ***global values,*** which represent the core of an individual's value system. These values, which are highly enduring, strongly held, and abstract, apply in many situations. To illustrate, because much of U.S. political philosophy is based on the idea of freedom, that value permeates many domains of our lives. We believe that we should have the freedom to speak, go where we want, dress as we please, and live where we want.

One of the many ways of characterizing global values is depicted in Exhibit 15.3. This scheme divides global values into seven categories: maturity, security, pro-

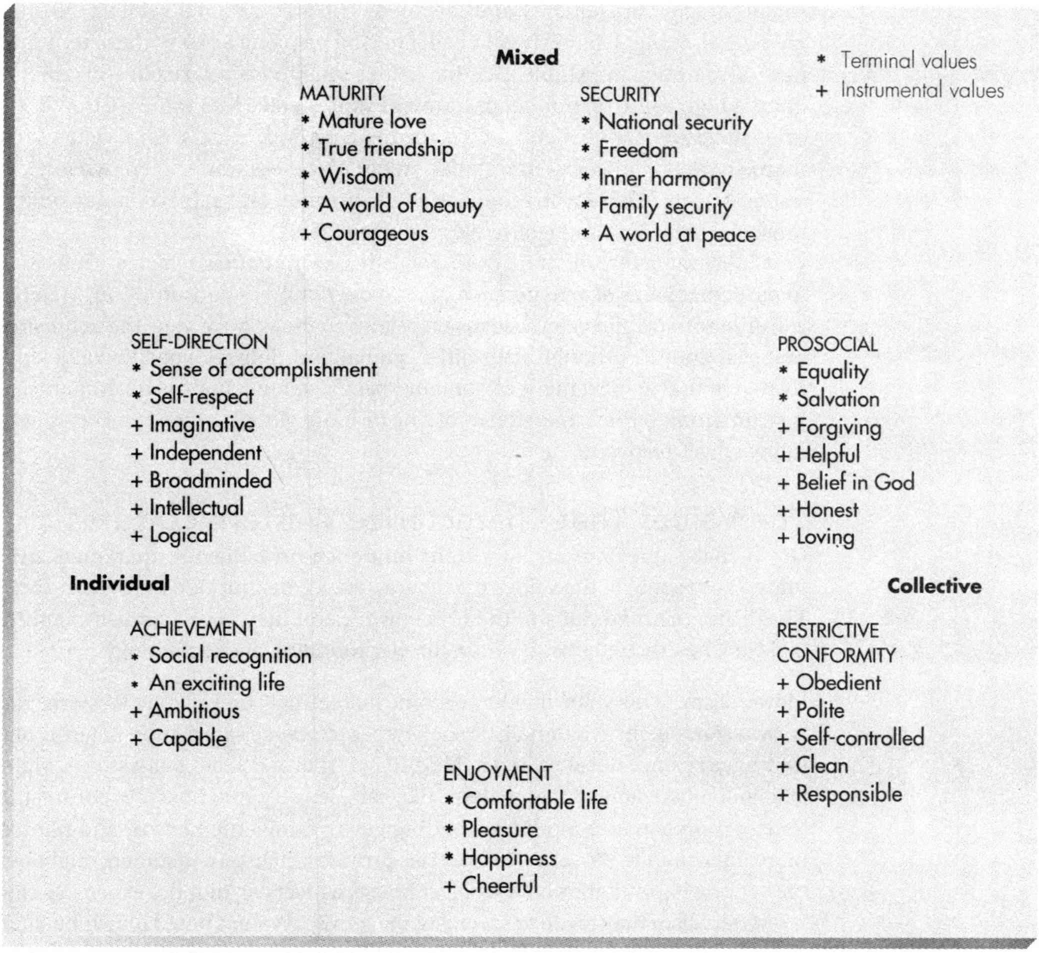

Exhibit 15.3

GLOBAL VALUES AND VALUE CATEGORIES

One scheme for classifying global values identifies seven major categories. Some values are individual oriented (e.g., self-direction, achievement); others are more collective or group oriented (e.g., prosocial, restrictive conformity). Note that categories close to each other are similar; those farther apart are less so. Terminal values (or highly desired end states) are marked with an asterisk (*); instrumental values have a plus sign (+).

social behavior (doing nice things for others), restrictive conformity, enjoyment, achievement, and self-direction. Note that similar categories are placed close together. Thus achievement and self-direction reflect a similar orientation toward the individual as a person, whereas prosocial behavior and restrictive conformity reflect values that relate to how an individual should deal with others.

Within the seven domains there are two types of global values: terminal and instrumental. ***Terminal values*** (shown with an asterisk) are highly desired end states, and ***instrumental values*** (shown with a plus sign) are those needed to achieve these desired end states. For example, the two terminal values in the prosocial category are equality and salvation. The instrumental values of loving, forgiving, helpfulness, honesty, and belief in God help one achieve these terminal values.[7] Also notice in Exhibit 15.3 that values tend to be polarized: consumers who place a high value on one set of terminal values place less value on the set on the opposite side of the figure. This means that individuals who value security, maturity, and a prosocial orientation might place less value on enjoyment (on the opposite side). Those who emphasize self-direction and achievement would value prosocial behaviors and restrictive conformity less.

Global values are different from ***domain-specific values,*** which are relevant only to particular areas of activity, such as religion, family, or consumption. Materialism is a domain-specific value because it relates to the way we view the acquisition of material goods. Although they differ, global and domain-specific values can be related in that achievement of domain-specific values (such as health) and can be instrumental to the achievement of one or more global values (such as inner harmony or self-respect).

The Values That Characterize Western Cultures

Given that values are an important influence on behavior, marketers need to understand some of the values that characterize consumption in Western societies. These include materialism, the home, work and play, individualism, family and children, health, hedonism, youth, the environment, and technology.

Materialism One value that has become increasingly prevalent in Western cultures is ***materialism.***[8] In a materialistic society, people gauge satisfaction in terms of what they have or have not acquired in life and in terms of desired possessions. Materialistic individuals tend to value items like cars, jewelry, and boats. In contrast, symbolic items such as a mother's wedding gown, family mementos, and photos are more important to those low in materialism.[9] Materialistic consumers might believe they will be happy if they have a bigger house, a nicer car, or more expensive clothes.

Materialism may relate to several of the terminal values noted in Exhibit 15.3. For example, possessions may be instrumental in achieving the higher-order value of social recognition. Or materialism may reflect a high value on accomplishment, if people judge self-worth by what they have acquired or their achievement of a comfortable life. Some people value materialism more highly than others. Not everyone is unhappy with a low-paying job or little discretionary income. Members of communes and certain religious orders have chosen a lifestyle that rejects material possessions.[10] Also, growing numbers of people have changed their priorities, rejected materialism, and decided to simplify their lives by making and spending less. One study noted that the value conflict between the individual orientation of materialism and the group orientation of family-oriented values is associated with a reduced sense of well-being, which may help to explain the movement away from materialism.[11]

Nevertheless, U.S. consumers generally have a materialistic bent, and studies of Japanese and Chinese consumers also reveal an increasing emphasis on a materialistic lifestyle.[12] The desire for material goods is particularly acute in formerly communist countries such as the Czech Republic and Romania, where consumers strive to acquire as many Western goods as possible, including a car and fashionable clothing.[13] In a developing economy like India too, the spurt of economic boom and prosperity in a given segment of the society, encourages compulsive consumption and makes the consumer materialistic in approach. Product disposability, dual ownership, impulse buying or even travelling distances to buy a brand are its characteristics. In a materialistic society, consumers will be receptive to marketing tactics that facilitate the acquisition of goods, such as phone-in or on-line orders and credit card payments, and to messages that associate acquisition with achievement and status, like ads for a Rolex watch. Special sales, two-for-one deals, bonus packs, and warehouse clubs have done exceptionally well in the United States and Japan, perhaps in part because of consumers' materialistic tendencies. These marketing tactics allow consumers to buy some products cheaply, thus saving money to buy other things.[14] Consumers also want to protect their possessions, creating opportunities for services such as insurance and security companies that protect consumers against loss, theft, or damage.

Home Many consumers place a high value on the home and believe in making it as attractive and as comfortable as possible. According to a CRIS Infac report, new housing CAGR has been 3.4% over a time period of 1998-99 to 2003-04 from 26.04% to 30.85% respectively. Particularly, in the metros the boom has been more visible, where there has been a surge in purchasing a house. Because the outside world is becoming more complex, exhausting, and dangerous, consumers often consider their home their haven, but they still look for opportunities to connect with others rather than focusing exclusively on their homes.[15] The home is "command central"—a place to coordinate activities and pool resources before family members enter the outside world. More than 53 million Americans use online banking to control family finances from their home computers.[16] Take-out and delivery services, DVD rentals or downloads, pay-per-view television, computer or Web-based games, and shopping from home are increasingly popular. Home-improvement retailers such as Lowe's and crafts chains such as Michael's are experiencing growth as consumers lavish attention on their homes.

Work and Play Consumers in the United States appear to have a rather schizophrenic approach toward work and play. We're working harder and longer than ever before, partly due to corporate downsizing and an emphasis on productivity. In fact, when career-minded consumers go on vacation, nearly half choose to stay in touch by checking in regularly (through phone calls, e-mails, or faxes).[17] Yet, we increasingly value work for its instrumental function in achieving other values such as a comfortable lifestyle, family security, and accomplishing our life goals. Thus the idea of valuing work itself and delaying gratification to the exclusion of leisure and pleasure is less characteristic of U.S. consumers than it was a century ago. Alternatively, in Indian markets the concept of work hard and party harder is permeating rapidly. Work cultures demand extended working hours, extending beyond the 8-hour schedule. It becomes imperative for the employees to look at vacations, getaways, weekend breaks more proactively—a culture which was not pronounced before. Today a large chunk of corporate India is exploring new destinations, new ideas of relaxation and even innovative ways to train manpower by mixing work and pleasure. White water rafting at Rishikesh or remote destinations like Shoghi in Himachal Pradesh are being picked up by corporate India for training, skill building, annual reviews mixing with pleasure and relaxation in the evening. These are some of the new ways corporate India relaxes and unwinds.

Perhaps because people are working more, many value leisure time as much as they value money and will pay for services so they can spend more nonwork time on leisure activities. The culture of eating out in India is usually a family affair, with a sit-down meal and soaking in the ambience of the restaurant, which is why McDonald's in India focuses more on family restaurants. However, the culture of home delivery in meals is also coming in, particularly in the metros, where changing lifestyles of households often leaves little time for cooking. Hence, ordering food at home is more out of a convenience than a luxury. Moreover, the distinction between work and home life is blurring because technological advances such as e-mail and electronic conferencing allow many people to work at home. A study of working mothers found that a strong concern was "juggling, balancing, and fitting it all in" with the "endless array of competing demands" of work and home.[19] However, not everyone in every culture shares the same values of work and play. In the Netherlands, research identified two main groups among young people: those who value work as a means to achieve something and those who say, "You can work your whole life, so let's have fun now."[20]

Individualism U.S. culture, in particular, has long placed a high value on individualism. The traditional "rugged individualist" consumer values independence and self-reliance, tending to see the individual's needs and rights as a higher priority than the group's needs and rights.[21] Marketers who target men for products such as hunting gear often use advertising imagery and words to make explicit the connection between owning and using these products and expressing rugged individualism. Despite the frontier roots of individualism in America, a backlash is developing among some consumers who worry about violence and other possible negative consequences of unbridled individualism.

Even in a generally individualistic society, there are *allocentric* consumers who prefer interdependence and social relationships. In contrast, *idiocentric* consumers tend to put more emphasis on individual freedom and assertiveness. The behavior of these consumers reflects such differences: Idiocentric consumers in the United States exhibit more interest in sports and adventure, financial satisfaction, gambling, and brand consciousness. Allocentric consumers, on the other hand, exhibit more interest in health consciousness, group socializing, reading, and food preparation.[22]

Strikingly similar, in India today, delayed marriages or even the decision to have no kids is a mindset change implying gradual change in our cultural traits and attitude. Individualism, a common trait in the Western culture, is now seeping in and with the break-up of the traditional joint family structure, such trends are even more visible.

Family and Children Cultures also differ in the values they place on their families and children. Parents in Europe and Asia, for example, tend to value education more than U.S. parents. Among Asian hggggmiddle-class families, educating children is second in priority only to providing food. This is why children's books have been the largest sellers among Time Life's offerings in the Asian market, representing 55 percent of sales.[23]

Children in India as discussed in Chapter 13 particularly, hold a special place in the social setting. They are perceived as the flag bearer of the generation, at times social security and in some cases there is even a peer pressure to have children. However, across generations Indians have always tried to give their best to their children. Education, career, financial security or social security, parents have always been there to ensure the best for their child. The generations of strivers and achievers have been oriented with the paraphernalia of education being the platform and the stepping stone to success. This thought process created a fear and insecurity, even leading to emphasis on career and stability. The psychology runs through generations.

Exhibit 15.4
VALUING CHILDREN
The advertisement appeals to parents who are concerned and involved in the process of parenting

Health Many U.S. consumers place a high value on health for reasons of self-esteem (the way the body looks) and due to concerns about longevity and survival. The value of health is reflected in the popularity of foods low in fat, calories, carbohydrates, salt, sugar, or cholesterol—as well as foods with special nutritional benefits. Unilever offers a line of functional foods, called nutraceuticals, such as its Take Control spread, which helps lower cholesterol levels and reduce the risk of heart disease.[27] Gatorade drinks are marketed to consumers who work out or play sports, with the benefit of replacing fluids and electrolytes.[28] Growing concern over pesticides, additives, food-related illnesses, and contaminants has enhanced demand for organic and vegetarian foods. Heinz is only one of many companies launching organic versions of foods such as ketchup (see Exhibit 15.5).[29] Sales at specialized chains like Whole Foods and Trader Joe's are rising year after year.[30] In Europe, health concerns have led to a deep-seated resistance to genetically modified foods.[31]

The emphasis on health has also paved the way for dieting services like Weight Watchers, health clubs, and diet aids. Hospitals now offer aerobics, kick-boxing, and aquatics classes to promote wellness. Magazines like *Health* and *Runners' World* also exemplify health values. In addition, more consumers are turning to health food stores and alternative medicine for treating and preventing illnesses.[32] Antismoking campaigns, bans on smoking in public places, and tobacco and alcohol warning labels in many Western nations are consistent with health values.[33]

Values and behavior can differ, however. Although many consumers talk about a healthy diet. The problem of obesity is now beginning to creep into India and it is expected that [6]India's 300 million-strong middle-class is prone to developing obesity much earlier in life. Chairperson of the Delhi Diabetes Research Centre, Ashok Jhingan said, "It's a very serious condition as obesity can lead to diabetes, heart disease and early heart attacks. Many teenage girls are already suffering from diseases like polycystic ovarian syndrome, which is a condition that occurs in overweight females and disrupts menstruation, and other children have hypertension." Director of the Diabetes and Metabolic Diseases at Fortis hospital, New Delhi; Anoop Misra said, "India's economic liberalization in the early 1990's has brought in a lot of western ways of living which we did not have before. This includes the mushrooming of fast food restaurants and increased availability of snacks like crisps and chocolates which have increased the carbohydrate and fat intake of children." (See Chapters 19 and 20 for more on this issue.) Still, healthier foods don't always sell well: Neither Coca-Cola's nor Pepsi's low-calorie, low-carbohydrate colas have been big hits.[36] On the other hand, offerings such as plus-size clothing outlets and dating services for overweight people have flourished.[37]

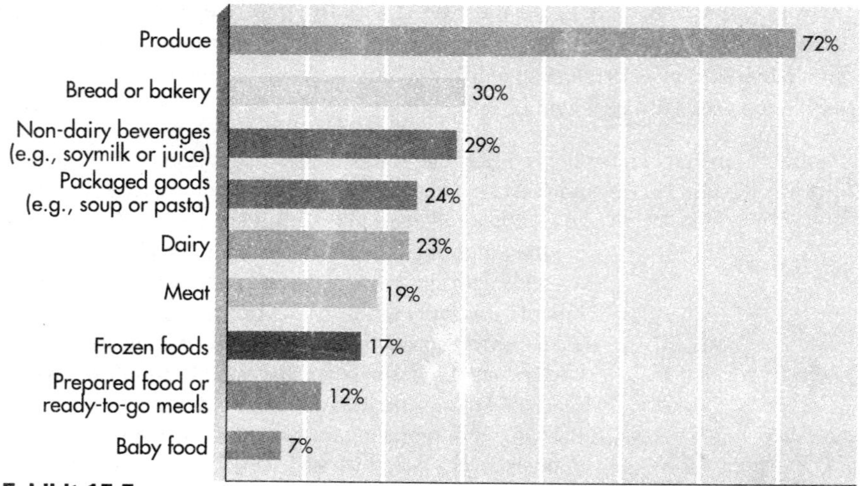

Exhibit 15.5
MOST POPULAR CATEGORIES OF ORGANIC FOODS

Consumers are increasingly buying organic foods. These are the most popular items.

Hedonism Consumers are increasingly operating on the principle of ***hedonism,*** or pleasure seeking, and they desire products and services that simply make them feel good, such as luxury cars, home entertainment centers, and exciting vacations. [7]In India a new found concept of babymooning is finding its place in the upscale metro households. The appeal of this brief but indulgent experience — known as a babymoon in the travel industry parlance — is pure escape, for pregnant women, working or non-working, who go through the pang. The travel agents are carving out increasingly customised packages to target different life stages. Some of the favourite spots for babymooners are London, a castle outside Salzburg, Austria, which offers lymph drainage for the legs and a lovely lakeside, the valleys of Switzerland and Italy. According to gynecologists, the second trimester is the safest time for pregnant women to travel in. A babymoon is not only about pampering, but about slowing down enough to savour the pregnancy. It helps a mother keep in touch with her sensuality, with her body, and to embrace the change that is happening in her life.

Hedonism has led to some interesting eating patterns that contradict health values, witnessed by the success of the Chicago Steakhouse chain and Häagen-Dazs ice cream on the one hand, and Healthy Choice fat-free chocolate chip cookies and fat-free frozen yogurt on the other.[40] Furthermore, despite concerns over health, consumers will not switch to low-fat, low-calorie varieties unless they taste good. Sweets occupy a special position in Indian culture and households. However, with rising diabetes problems in the country, sweets have now become a symbol of antithesis of a diabetes patient. [8]But in recent years the use of Sugar Free has become commonplace. Now it is not only on airlines and in restaurants that one is offered sugar-free sachets and powders to sweeten your beverages, the average household stocks them too. Apart from Sugarfree, which seems to be the most popular (it has got 80 per cent of the market by virtue of being the first mover), there is the relatively recent entrant – Equal, as well as latest arrival, a 'natural' sweetener, Steviocal.

Youth Youth in India, are one of the largest segments in the consuming class. [9]The median age of India in 2000 was 24 and by 2025 will be 31, projecting a still very young population, significantly being accounted for as a consuming class. The age structure of India's population is also favourable. 44 per cent of the population is in the under-19 age bracket, with their literacy rate pegged at over 75 per cent. Going forward, the working population (19-60 year olds) is expected to increase from 485 million to 615 million by 2010 with an educational base of 21 million professionals and 90 million graduates/post graduates. The household mix is also changing fast. By 2006-07, the consuming class will form around 46 per cent of the total households as compared to around 17 per cent during 1995-96, according to an NCAER report. The combination of these fundamental factors, age and household mix, has led to the emergence of a huge consumer base for various products and services. Marketers are making attempts to target this segment more aggressively. Advertising messages also indicate the value we place on youth, as illustrated by Pepsi's "Be Young. Have Fun. Drink Pepsi" campaign theme. As another example, when Honda targeted Generation Y for its Element vehicle, the ads featuring images of college kids frolicking on the beach actually attracted boomers as buyers. As a result, the average age of an Element owner is just over 40, not 20-something as Honda had expected.[43]

The Environment Environmental protection has assumed important value across most developed and developing nations who are interested in conserving natural resources, preventing pollution, and supporting environmentally friendly goods, services, and activities. [10]In the early 90's Delhi was one of the world's 10 most polluted cities with vehicles accounting for 70 per cent of polluting emissions. Pollution levels exceeded World Health Organization standards by nearly five times. Then, the Supreme Court stepped in through public interest litigation by the Centre of Science and Environment in 1996 that resulted in a series of Supreme Court orders, the major step being introduction of CNG for public transport in 1998. Today, in Delhi compared to 1997, carbon monoxide levels are down 32 per cent, sulphur dioxide levels, 39 per cent. Delhi is a showpiece example of making air quality safe with its entire public transport fleet converted to Compressed Natural Gas (CNG) on a massive scale —80,000 CNG vehicles including 9,000 buses and 110 CNG stations. Delhi has banned taxis, buses and auto rickshaws older than 15 years. Though, the great vehicle explosion continues in Delhi. Yet, this rush of clean vehicles keeps the air relatively sparkling. The initiative was entirely driven by the judiciary's pushing and prodding and with the support of the State Government the initiative today is a showcase for other metros of the country. The Honda Insight and Toyota Prius are just two of a growing number of cars that run more cleanly and deliver more fuel efficiency—as much as 71 miles per gallon for an Insight on the highway. Among environmentally conscious consumers, 90 percent buy products with recycled parts or packaged in re cycled materials. Many also buy from firms that offer earth- friendly products or contribute some profits to environmental causes. Businesses can profit from many aspects of environmental values. Re Cellular, for instance, recycles 10 tons of cell phones every day for use in other areas, thus keeping them out of local landfills.

Technology Consumers in many cultures are fascinated by technological advances. More than ever before, consumers in the United States, Japan, and other nations believe that computers, cell phones, digital cameras, and the Internet improve the quality of their lives. On the horizon are nanotech-enhanced products such as paint that doesn't peel and light yet powerful tennis rackets.[49] Nevertheless, technological changes can be so rapid that we have trouble keeping up, resulting in a renewed emphasis on simplicity or at least on managing complexity. This trend is reflected in the rise of magazines like *Real Simple* and *Organic Style*, which show readers how to incorporate basic or all-natural products into their daily lives. Still, products with features that work automatically are popular because they make it easier for consumers to use the products properly.[50] For example, many cell phones are programmed for voice activation so consumers can make calls without pushing any buttons. Thus consumers appear to value technology more for what it can do to make life easier than for the technological advance per se—making technology an instrumental rather than a terminal value.

Why Values Change

Because societies and their institutions are constantly evolving, value systems are also changing. In addition to the key trends already discussed, U.S. values are moving toward casualness in living, more liberal sexual attitudes, greater sophistication in behavior, a change in sex roles, and the wish to be modern.[51] Furthermore, although the United States was different from Western Europe 100 years ago, both cultures, and to a certain extent Japan as well, are becoming more similar in values, even though differences still exist. This increase in value consistency is driven in part by the increase in global communication. For example, Western Europeans regard some U.S. consumption patterns as attractive. Affluent Japanese consumers are starting to place greater value on personal preferences, a balanced life, and experiences and less value on traditional expectations, work, and possessions.[52]
[11]The Western influence has gradually begun to permeate the Indian subcontinent also, evidences of which are found aplenty in what we eat, what we see and even at time our thought process. Three key issues that bother us are the first one - Pursuit of Wealth, the second one - Power of Western Media and the third and final one - Western Complex, which may be the most damaging of them.

Exhibit 15.6
UNDERSTANDING CULTURE AND VALUES
The sense of collectivism is high in a country like India where family is high on the priority and even households also present a picture of cohesiveness.

Influences on Values

How do values differ across groups of consumers? This section explores the ways that culture, ethnicity, social class, and age can influence our values.

Culture and Values People in different countries are exposed to different cultural experiences, which leads to cross-cultural differences in values. One study found that the three most important values among Brazilians are true friendship, mature love, and happiness, whereas U.S. consumers named family security, world peace, and freedom.[53] Inner harmony ranked 4th in importance among Brazilians but 13th in the United States. These values all differ from the beliefs of consumers in China, where the most important values are preserving the best that one has attained, being sympathetic to others, having self-control, and integrating enjoyment, action, and contemplation. A study of women in Germany, France, and the United Kingdom found that the value of "having a familiar routine" is most important for German women, but only 10th in importance for the British and 23rd for the French.[54]

In a classic study, Geert Hofstede found that cultures can vary along four main value dimensions:[55]

- *Individualism versus collectivism.* The degree to which a culture focuses on the individuals rather than the group
- *Uncertainty avoidance.* The extent to which a culture prefers structured to unstructured situations (see Exhinit 15.6)
- *Masculinity versus femininity.* The extent to which a culture stresses masculine values (as defined by Hofstede) such as assertiveness, success, and competition over feminine values such as quality of life, warm personal relationships, and caring
- *Power distance.* The degree to which a society's members are equal in terms of status

All cultures can be classified according to these four dimensions. Understanding where a given culture falls may provide insight into cross-cultural differences. For example, research showed that tipping in restaurants is less likely to occur in countries where power distance and uncertainty avoidance are low, feminine values are strong, and individualism is high.[56] Another study found that humorous ad themes are more likely to focus on groups in collectivist societies like Thailand and South Korea and on unequal status relationships in countries with high power distance like the United States and Germany.[57]

Ethnic Identification and Values Ethnic groups within a larger culture can have some values that are different from those of other ethnic subcultures. As noted in Chapter 13, Hispanic Americans strongly value the family and home; similarly, African American and Asian American consumers place a high value on the extended family.[58] Consumers in different countries may have different ethnic values. For example, consumers in China tend to hold the traditional Confucian value of respect for older family members. Knowing this, Nestlé advertises milk-based meal supplements to adults by appealing to their respect and responsibility for aging parents.[59]

Family values are deeply embedded in the Indian psyche. A child imbibes most of them by the time he reaches his 10th year. A large part of this value system is carried forward by the child, for the rest of his life. Generally, Indians have tremendous loyalty to the family. For instance, parents make enormous sacrifices for their children. They support them until they can stand on their own feet. On the other side, children consider it their duty to take care of their aged parents. [12]In India, the family is a dominant institution in the life of an individual and in the life of the community. For the Hindu family, extended family and kinship ties are of utmost importance. In India, families adhere to a patriarchal ideology, follow the patrilineal rule of descent, are patrilocal, have familialistic value orientations, and endorse traditional gender role preferences. The Indian family is considered strong, stable, close, resilient, and enduring. Historically, the traditional, ideal and desired family in India is the joint family. A joint family includes kinsmen, and generally includes three to four living generations, including uncles, aunts, nieces, nephews, and grandparents living together in the same household. It is a group composed of a number of family units living in separate rooms of the same house. These members eat the food cooked at one hearth, share a common income, common property, are related to one another through kinship ties, and worship the same idols. The family supports the old; takes care of widows, unmarried adults, and the invalids; supports members going through periods of unemployment; and provides security and a sense of support and togetherness. The joint family has always been the preferred family type in the Indian culture, and most Indians at some point in their lives have participated in joint family living.

Social Class and Values Different social classes hold specific values, as discussed in Chapter 14, which in turn affects their acquisition and consumption patterns. As countries in Eastern Europe and other nations embrace market economies, the size of the global middle class is increasing dramatically, along with middle-class values of materialism and a desire for less government control over their lives and greater access to information. Upper-upper-class consumers value giving back to society, which spurs them to become active in social, cultural, and civic causes. These consumers also prize self-expression as reflected in their homes, clothing, cars, and other forms of consumption.[60]

Age and Values Members of a generation often share similar values that differ from those of other generations. For example, your grandparents may value security over hedonism, not because they are older but because they grew up during the Great Depression and suffered economic hardship as children. They therefore view hedonic activities as frivolous and unacceptable. Likewise, baby boomers who grew up in the 1960s—a time of political upheaval, self-indulgence, and rebellion—value hedonism, morality, self-direction, and achievement.[61] Note that it is sometimes very difficult to distinguish values we acquire with age from those we learn from our era. Nevertheless, differences by virtue of age or cohort do exist, and they influence the way we behave as consumers.

marketing IMPLICATIONS Marketers need to understand how consumer values affect consumption patterns, market segmentation, new product development, ad development strategy, and ethics.

Consumption patterns

Consumers usually buy, use, and dispose of products in a manner consistent with their values.[62] Thus marketers can know more about what consumers like if they understand their values. For example, those who value warm relationships with others are more likely to buy gifts and send cards than those who place less value on relationships.[63] Consumers buy personal care products at The Body Shop because of the value the company places on naturalness and health as well as its emphasis on societal values, such as buying ingredients from poor Brazilian tribes.[64] Interestingly, most international marketing blunders occur because companies do not understand the values of a particular culture.[65] Marketers sometimes adopt an ethnocentric perspective, assuming that consumers in other cultures hold values similar to their own. Campbell's soup failed in South America because in that region, a mother's behavior is judged by the amount of time and dedication she devotes to domestic duties. Serving canned soup is like saying you do not care enough about your family.

[13]The ready-to-eat (RTE) industry, still nascent in India, is estimated to be around Rs 50 crore and growing at 30 per cent a year. [14]In India, the launch of "Ready to Eat" (RTE) was considered to be favourably accepted in the target market. But it has been tougher to cook up a storm in the Indian market than anyone expected. Indians proved remarkably attached to freshly cooked meals. [15]The growing number of nuclear families, an increase in household incomes and a significant rise in the number of single working men and women professionals in the past decade, have opened the opportunity for the RTE segment. However, the real challenge for the promotion of ready meals lies in category creation – of establishing relevance in the lives of con-

sumers by highlighting the convenience of the offer and making it a part of regular household purchase market.

Market segmentation

Marketers can identify groups of consumers who have a common set of values different from those of other groups, a process called ***value segmentation.*** For example, Honda segmented the car market based on the value consumers place on environmental issues and then identified some specific demographic variables that described a particular group: primarily married men in their thirties with high incomes and a technical job or an interest in technology or the environment.[66] Then Honda designed the Insight, powered by both gasoline and electricity, to appeal to this group. Like other car manufacturers, Honda offers brands and models for different value segments, such as the Acura brand for materialistic, achievement-oriented consumers.

Marketers also can use values to understand the attributes that consumers in a particular segment are likely to find important in a product and that may therefore motivate them to choose one brand over another. When buying clothes, individuals who value status might look for attributes like price and luxury, whereas those who value fitting in with the crowd might look for clothing that is trendy.[67] One study found that women's perfume preferences can be grouped according to value segments such as the Fledgling Career Woman, Working-Class Woman, Frustrated Professional, Traditional Housewife, Successful Professional, and Senior Set Woman. In this research, women with higher levels of self-confidence were found to prefer more subtle fragrances.[68]

New product ideas

Values can influence consumers' reactions to new and different products. For example, consumers who value change highly are likely to react very differently to innovations like e-mail compared with those who value change less.[69] The more a new product is consistent with important consumer values, the greater the likelihood of its success. For example, good-tasting, microwavable, low-fat, and low-calorie frozen entrees succeeded in part because these items are consistent with multiple values like hedonism, time, convenience, health, and technology. ITC's Ready to Eat brand, Aashirwad, has been showcased as a product, which gives the woman of the house, holiday on Sunday, even from cooking. It says, "Aaj Sunday hai. Aaj Chutthi Hai."

Ad development strategy

Examining the target segment's value profile can help marketers design more appealing ads.[71] The more compatible the ad copy is with consumers' values, the more likely consumers are to become involved in the message and find it relevant. [16]The Bajaj rejuvenation strategy in the mid 80's is a classic case of how brand's can revive themselves from nowhere. The company desperately needed a selling factor and its machines could not achieve one on their own. Newer and technically more savvy brands like Kinetic and Vespa had inundated the market and Bajaj was becoming redundant and one of their flagship brand Chetak had a seven month stock pile-up. The automotive company couldn't boast of any technical superiority as there was none. They said they would take at least 18 months to revamp the product, but till then they couldn't afford losses. So the ball was in the advertising agency's court. After much brainstorming, the advertising agency decided to add an emotional punch to an otherwise normal piece of machinery. The communication targeted the middle class and presented Chetak as a friend of the family they could depend on. For the makers of both the ad and the two-wheelers it was an effort to get the brand back into the groove. An emotional pull was necessary. The ad brought out the dependability of the product. It hit an emotional nerve with its reliance value. Whether to carry luggage, to celebrate youth or just for family outings, Bajaj was there for you.[72] Clearly, marketers must connect product attributes and benefits to consumer values

Exhibit 15.7
VALUE BASED TO MATERIAL BASED
A Brand like Bajaj today targets compulsive consumers from the traditional value based advertising it did earlier, representating a gradual shift in the societal norms.

because these represent the end state consumers desire to achieve—the driving force behind their consumption of the product. A good example of this strategy is the ad in Exhibit 15.7.

Marketers must also avoid communications that conflict with cultural values. As one example, the clothing retailer Benetton created a stir with several ads, including one showing a nun kissing a priest, which was particularly offensive in predominantly Catholic countries like Italy and France.[73] Consumer groups in Thailand protested an ad that showed Hitler eating an inferior brand of potato chips and being transformed into a good guy by eating the advertised brand.[74]

Ethical considerations

Consumers use values to gauge the appropriateness of others' behaviors—including the behavior of marketers. For example, those who value morality might disapprove of products such as X-rated videos and cigarettes, consumption practices like prostitution and gambling, and sexually explicit ads. Consumers also evaluate marketers' behavior for fairness, ethics, and appropriateness.[75] As Chapter 20 explains, marketers should be aware that consumers may boycott, protest, or complain about practices that seem inconsistent with their values of fairness. Knowing that consumers are increasingly concerned about the risks and cost of prescription drugs—a product category that accounts for $4.4 billion in annual direct-to-consumer advertising—Johnson & Johnson now makes safety the main focus of its TV commercials.[76]

How Values Can Be Measured

To segment the market by values, marketers need some means of identifying consumers' values, gauging their importance, and analyzing changes or trends in values. Unfortunately, values are often hard to measure. One reason is that people do not often think about their values and may therefore have a hard time articulating what is really important to them. Another reason is that people may sometimes feel social pressure to respond to a values questionnaire in a certain way to make themselves look better in the eyes of the researcher. Therefore, marketers usually use less obtrusive or more indirect ways of assessing values.

Inferring Values from the Cultural Milieu The least obtrusive way to measure values is to make inferences based on a culture's milieu. For example, advertising has often been used as an indicator of values.[77] Advertising in India has also evolved from being value based to more hedonistic appealing. Increasingly as society becomes more materialistic and consumers compulsive, marketers make attempts to illustrate the feelings and the process of acquiring the product through their own communication as illustrated in Exhibit 15.7.Researchers can also use ads to uncover cross-cultural differences in values and to track trends in values. One study found that because the People's Republic of China, Taiwan, and Hong Kong are at different levels of economic development and have different political ideologies, different values were reflected in each country's ads.[78] At the time, ads from China focused on utilitarian themes and promised a better life; Hong Kong ads stressed hedonism and an easier life; and Taiwan ads fell between the other two. Given the economic changes occurring in China, it is not surprising that the trend in local advertising is already moving away from more utilitarian themes to focus on variety in products and product assurances.[79] Marketers can infer values just by looking at product names. Product names reflecting values of materialism (MGM Grand Hotel), hedonism (Obsession perfume), time (Minute Rice), technology (Microsoft), and convenience (Reddi-wip topping) are common in the United States.

Marketers can also identify values reflected in magazine titles (such as *Money*), book titles, TV programs, and the types of people regarded as heroes or heroines. Even comic books have been used to indicate consumer values. According to research, materialism is portrayed as a valued trait in comic books like *Archie, Uncle Scrooge,* and *Richie Rich.*[80] This study also found that materialism was sometimes viewed as good (bringing happiness and goodwill) and sometimes viewed as bad, abusive, and hurtful. Popular songs are also indicators of values. Many people are concerned that violent song lyrics are an indication of a decline in values, for instance.

One criticism of cultural milieu as an indicator of values is that researchers never know whether culture reflects values or creates them. For example, was Madonna's "Material Girl" successful because consumers value materialism, or did the song promote an attitude that other consumers emulate? In light of this problem, researchers have introduced other methods to measure values.

Means-End Chain Analysis Marketers can use the ***means-end chain analysis*** to gain insight into consumers' values by better understanding which attributes they find important in products. Armed with this information, researchers can work backward to uncover the values that drive consumer decisions.[81] Suppose a consumer likes light beer because it has fewer calories than regular beer. If a researcher asks why it is important to have a beer with fewer calories, the respondent might say, "Because I don't want to gain weight." If the researcher asks why not, the consumer might respond by saying, "I want to be healthy." If asked why again, the consumer might say, "Because I want to feel good about myself." This example is illustrated in the top line of Exhibit 15.8.

Note that this means-end chain has several potential levels. First, the consumer mentioned an important attribute followed by a concrete benefit that the attribute provides. Then the consumer indicated that this benefit was important because it served some instrumental value. This entire process is called a *means-end chain,* because the attribute provides the means to a desired end state or terminal value (in this case, self-esteem). Looking at Exhibit 15.8, you can also see that a particular attribute can be associated with very different values. For example, rather than valuing light beer for its health benefits, some consumers may like light beer because they drink it in a social context that leads to a greater sense of belonging. Second, the same value may be associated with very different products and attributes. Thus attributes associated with both light beer and rice may appeal equally to the value of belonging. Third, a given attribute may be linked with multiple benefits and/or values, meaning that a consumer might like light beer because it makes her feel healthier and it facilitates belonging.

Marketers can use means-end chain analysis to identify product attributes that will be consistent with certain values.[82] Not long ago, consumers generally considered sports cars to be expensive and uncomfortable, and ownership took on an aspect of "arrogance and irresponsibility." As a result, manufacturers began offering comfortable cars positioned for "people who have friends" in order to be more in line with current values.[83] The means-end chain model is also useful for developing advertising strategy. By knowing which attributes consumers find important and which values they associate with those attributes, advertisers can better design ads that appeal to these values and emphasize related attributes. Note that the ad need not explicitly link a given attribute with a motive but allows consumers to implicitly make the linkage.

Finally, marketers can use the means-end chain to segment global markets, cutting across national boundaries to appeal to consumers on the basis of specific benefits and related values.[84] To market yogurt, for instance, a company could identify one segment that values health and reach this segment by focusing on product attributes such as low fat, and identify a second segment that values enjoyment and reach this segment through attributes such as fruit ingredients.

Value Questionnaires Marketers can directly assess values by using questionnaires. Some types of questionnaires, such as the material values scale, focus only on specific aspects of consumer behavior.[85] Others cover a range of values. One of the best known of these is the ***Rokeach Value Survey (RVS).*** This questionnaire asks consumers about the importance they attach to the 19 instrumental values and 18 terminal values identified in Exhibit 15.3. This questionnaire is standardized, and everyone responds to the same set of items, which helps researchers identify the specific values that are most important to a given group of con-

Exhibit 15.8
AN EXAMPLE OF MEANS-END CHAINS

According to the means-end chain analysis, product and service attributes *(e.g., fewer calories) lead to* benefits *(e.g., I won't gain weight) that reflect* instrumental values *(e.g., helps make me healthy) and* terminal values *(e.g., I feel good about myself). This analysis helps marketers identify important values and the attributes associated with them. Can you develop a means-end chain for toothpaste or deodorant?*

Product	Attribute	Benefit	Instrumental Value (driving force)	Terminal Value
Light beer (I)	Fewer calories	I won't gain weight.	Helps make me healthy	I feel good about myse f (self-esteem).
Light beer (II)	Fewer calories Great taste Light taste	Less filling Enjoyable/relaxing Refreshing	Good times/fun Friendship Sharing	Belonging
Rice	Comes in boiling bag	Convenient No messy pan to clean up	Saves time	I can enjoy more time with my family (belonging).

Source: Adapted from Jonathan Gutman, "A Means-End Chain Model Based on Consumer Categorization Processes," *Journal of Marketing*, Spring 1982, pp. 60–72 Thomas J. Reynolds and John P. Rochan, "Means-End Based Advertising Reasearch: Copy Testing Is Not Strategy Assessment," *Journal of Busines Research*, March 1991, pp. 131–142.

Exhibit 15.9
VALUE SEGMENTS

Marketers try to segment consumers in terms of the patterns of values they hold and their relative importance. Here, for example, are four major value segments. Segment A places very high importance on security, and segment D tends to stress warm relationships with others. By identifying value segments, marketers can develop messages that appeal to the specific values of these segments.

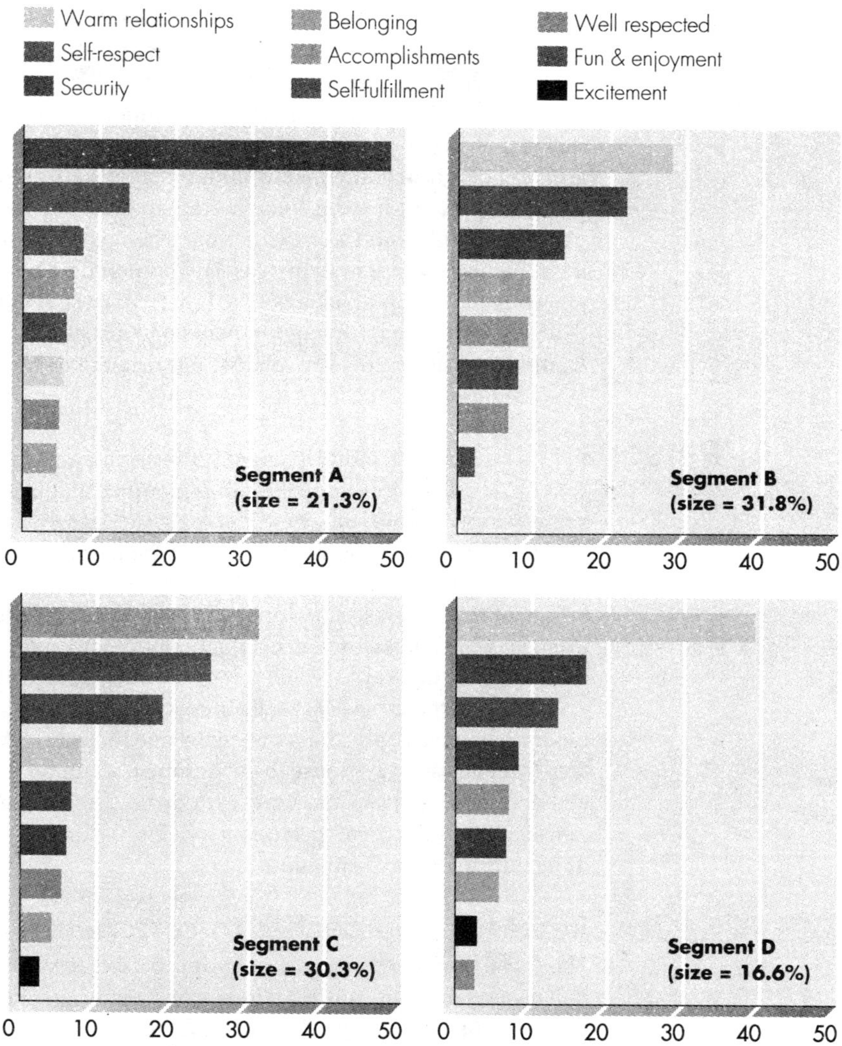

sumers, determine whether values are changing over time, and learn whether values differ for various groups of consumers. One drawback is that some values measured by the RVS are less relevant to consumer behavior (such as salvation, forgiving, and being obedient). Some researchers have therefore recommended using a shortened form of the RVS containing only the values most relevant to a consumer context.[86]

Others have advocated the use of the ***List of Values (LOV).*** Consumers are presented with nine primary values and asked either to identify the two most important or to rank all nine values by importance. The nine values are (1) self-respect, (2) warm relationships with others, (3) sense of accomplishment, (4) self-fulfillment, (5) fun and enjoyment in life, (6) excitement, (7) sense of belonging, (8) being well respected, and (9) security.[87] The first six are internal values because they derive from the individual; the others are external values. The values can also be described in terms of whether they are fulfilled through interpersonal relationships (warm relationships with others, sense of belonging), personal factors (self-respect, being well respected, self-fulfillment), or nonpersonal things (sense of accomplishment, fun, security, and excitement).

In one study, the LOV predicted consumers' responses to statements that describe their self-reported consumption characteristics (e.g., "I am a spender, not a saver"), their actual consumption behaviors (the frequency with which they watch movies or the news, read certain magazines, and engage in activities like playing tennis), and their marketplace beliefs ("I believe the consumer movement has caused prices to increase"). Compared with the RVS, the LOV is a better predictor of consumer behavior, is shorter, and is easier to administer. Finally, the LOV is useful for identifying segments of consumers with similar value systems. Exhibit 15.9 illustrates the relative importance of the nine LOV values in four U.S. segments.[88]

Personality

Although individuals with comparable backgrounds tend to hold similar values, it is important to remember that people do not always act the same way even when they hold the same values. In listening to a sales pitch, one consumer may state demurely that she finds the product interesting but is not ready to make up her mind right now. Another might act more assertively, interrupting the salesperson midway through his pitch to indicate that she has no interest whatsoever in the product. Thus consumers vary in terms of their personality or the way in which they respond to a particular situation.

Personality consists of the distinctive patterns of behaviors, tendencies, qualities, or personal dispositions that make one individual different from another and lead to a consistent response to environmental stimuli. These patterns are internal characteristics that we are born with or that result from the way we have been raised. The concept of personality helps us understand why people behave differently in different situations.

Research Approaches to Personality

The social sciences provide various approaches to studying personality. This section reviews five that consumer researchers apply: psychoanalytic approaches, trait theories, phenomenological approaches, social-psychological theories, and behavioral approaches.

Psychoanalytic Approaches According to psychoanalytic theories, personality arises from a set of dynamic, unconscious internal struggles within the mind.[89] The famous psychoanalyst Sigmund Freud proposed that we pass through several developmental stages in forming our personalities. In the first stage, the oral stage, the infant is entirely dependent on others for need satisfaction and receives oral gratification from sucking, eating, and biting. At the anal stage, the child is confronted with the problem of toilet training. Then in the phallic stage, the youth becomes aware of his or her genitals and must deal with desires for the opposite-sex parent.

Freud believed that the failure to resolve the conflicts from each stage could influence one's personality. For example, the individual who received insufficient oral stimulation as an infant may reveal this crisis in adulthood through oral-stimulation activities like gum chewing, smoking, and overeating or by distrusting others' motives (including those of marketers). At the anal stage an individual whose toilet training is too restrictive may become obsessed with control and be overly orderly, stubborn, or stingy, resulting in neatly organized closets and records, list making, and excessive saving or collecting. These individuals may also engage in extensive information search and deliberation when making decisions. On the other hand, those whose training was overly lenient may become messy, disorganized adults.

Although some of Freud's theories were later questioned by many researchers, the key point is that the subconscious can influence behavior. Consequently, some advertising agencies conduct research to delve deep into consumers' psyches and uncover subconscious reasons why they buy a particular product.[90] This type of research led to the discovery of a deep-seated desire for milk that the dairy industry used in its "Got Milk?" campaign.

Trait Theories Trait theorists propose that personality is composed of characteristics that describe and differentiate individuals.[91] For example, people might be described as aggressive, easygoing, quiet, moody, shy, or rigid. Psychologist Carl Jung developed one of the most basic trait theory schemes, suggesting that individuals could be categorized according to their levels of introversion and extroversion.[92] Introverts are shy, prefer to be alone, and are anxious in the presence of others. They tend to avoid social channels and therefore may not find out about new products from others. They are also less motivated by social pressure and more likely to do things that please themselves. In contrast, extroverts are outgoing, sociable, and typically conventional.

More recent work has found that the trait of stability, or consistency in behavior, when combined with the introversion/extroversion dimension, can be used as a basis to represent various personality types (see Exhibit 15.10). For example, a person who is reliable tends to be high on both introversion and stability. In contrast, a passive person is introverted but neither highly stable nor highly unstable. One interesting feature about this scheme is that the personality types identified by these two dimensions match the four temperaments identified by the Greek physician Hippocrates centuries ago—for example, a phlegmatic person is introverted and stable; a melancholic person is introverted and unstable.

Phenomenological Approaches Phenomenological approaches propose that personality is largely shaped by an individual's interpretations of life events.[93] For example, according to this approach, depression is caused by the way someone interprets key events and the nature of that interpretation, rather than by internal conflicts or traits.

A key concept of the phenomenological approaches is ***locus of control,*** or people's interpretations of why specific things happen.[94] Individuals with an internal locus of control attribute more responsibility to themselves for good or bad outcomes, so they might blame themselves or see themselves as careless when a product fails. Externally controlled individuals, on the other hand, place responsibility on other people, events, or places, rather than on themselves. Thus they might attribute product failure to faulty manufacturing, poor packaging, or the clumsy delivery person.

Locus of control can heavily influence consumers' perceptions of satisfaction in a consumption experience and determine how the consumer feels. To illustrate, consumers who blame themselves for product failure might feel shame, whereas

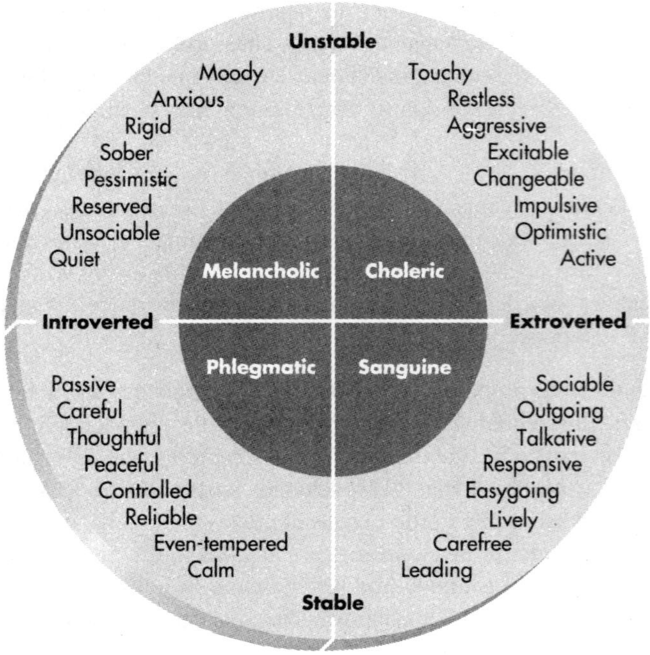

Exhibit 15.10
A TRAIT CONCEPTION OF PERSONALITY TYPES
Consumers can be classified according to whether they have introverted or extroverted personality traits. These traits can lead to the identification of various personality types (e.g., moody, peaceful, lively, and aggressive). Interestingly, these traits can be collected into four major groups that correspond to the basic temperaments identified by the ancient Greek physician Hippocrates many centuries ago. How would you classify your personality according to this scheme?

those who blame product failure on an external source might feel anger and irritation. In addition, someone's life theme or goals (concerns that we address in our everyday lives) can greatly influence the meanings he or she derives from ads.[95] As a result, a person who is more concerned with family might interpret an ad differently than someone who is more concerned with his or her private self.

Social-Psychological Theories Another group of theories focuses on social rather than biological explanations of personality, proposing that individuals act in social situations to meet their needs. The researcher Karen Horney, for instance, believed that behavior can be characterized by three major orientations.[96] *Compliant* individuals are dependent on others and are humble, trusting, and tied to a group. *Aggressive* individuals need power, move away from others, and are outgoing, assertive, self-confident, and tough-minded. *Detached* individuals are independent and self-sufficient but suspicious and introverted. These three orientations are measured by the CAD scale.[97] One study found that assertiveness and aggressiveness were significantly related to styles of interaction with marketing institutions.[98] In particular, highly assertive and aggressive people were likely to perceive complaining as acceptable and to enjoy doing it.

In social-psychological theory, researchers distinguish between state-oriented consumers, who are more likely to rely on subjective norms to guide their behavior, and action-oriented consumers, whose behavior is based more on their own attitudes.[99] Consumers also vary in terms of their attention to information that helps them compare themselves to others (social comparison information). Individuals high on this factor are more sensitive to normative pressure than are those low on this factor.

Behavioral Approaches In contrast to other explanations of personality, behavioral approaches propose that differences in personality are a function of how individuals have been rewarded or punished in the past. According to behavioral approaches, individuals are more likely to have traits or engage in behaviors for which they have received positive reinforcement. They are less likely to maintain characteristics and behaviors for which they have been punished.[100] Thus an individual might be extroverted because parents, caretakers, and other individuals rewarded outgoing behaviors and punished introverted behaviors. Likewise, a consumer might prefer colorful clothing if he or she previously received positive reinforcement for wearing it. Note that these behavioral approaches to personality involve the principles of operant conditioning discussed in Chapter 11.

Courtesy of
Bound USA.

Determining Whether Personality Characteristics Affect Consumer Behavior

Much of the consumer-related personality research has followed the trait approach and focused on identifying specific personality traits that explain differences in consumers' purchase, use, and disposition behavior. A number of studies have attempted to find a relationship between personality and consumer behavior, but reviews of this research generally conclude that personality is not a good predictor of consumer behavior.[101] One major problem is that researchers developed many of the trait measurement instruments for identifying personality disorders in clinical settings, so these instruments may not be applicable for identifying traits related to consumption behaviors.

In addition, consumer researchers have often attempted to use personality traits inappropriately to explain phenomena. One classic study, which employed a detailed instrument to compare Ford and Chevy owners by measuring personality traits, yielded disappointing results.[102] The only significant difference was that Ford owners were more dominant-aggressive (not a very meaningful or useful finding). Thus personality did not appear to be a good predictor of brand choice.

Exhibit 15.11
PERSONALITY AND AD APPEAL
Ad messages are often designed to appeal to certain personalities. This ad is directed towards achievers

Although personality has not been shown to be strongly related to consumer behavior, some researchers believe that more reliable measures of traits, developed in a consumer context, would reveal a relationship.[103] For instance, researchers created a consumer self-confidence scale to examine how this trait affects the choice of higher-price alternatives.[104] The association between personality and consumer behavior may be stronger for some types of consumer behavior than for others. For example, although personality may not be very useful in understanding brand choice, it may help marketers understand why some people are more susceptible to persuasion, particularly like a certain ad, or engage in more information processing. The ad in Exhibit 15.11 shows an ad with personality appeal.

Marketers may also find personality more useful for targeting some product and service categories than others. In particular, our choice of offerings that involve subjective or hedonic features such as looks, style, and aesthetics may be somewhat related to personality. A good example is the selection of a greeting card, which represents a personal message and therefore is an extension of the sender's personality. Finally, certain types of personality traits may be more related to consumer behavior than others. As described below, these include optimal stimulation level, dogmatism, need for uniqueness, need for cognition, susceptibility to influence, frugality, self-monitoring behavior, and national character.

Optimal Stimulation Level Some activities have the potential to provide some sort of physiological arousal. For example, you might feel more aroused when you drive extremely fast on the highway, ride a roller coaster, see a scary movie, or go to new and unfamiliar surroundings. Things that are physically stimulating, emotionally energizing, or novel have arousal-inducing potential. However, highly stimulating activities are not always desirable. According to the theory of ***optimal stimulation level (OSL),*** people prefer things that are moderately arousing to things that are either too arousing or not arousing at all.[105] For example, you might prefer eating at a restaurant that offers moderately imaginative food to eating at one that offers boring food or one that offers very exotic and unusual food.

Even though people generally prefer moderate levels of stimulation, individuals differ in the level of arousal they regard as moderate and optimal. Individuals with a low optimal stimulation level tend to prefer less arousing activities because they want to avoid going over the edge. In contrast, individuals with a high optimal stimulation level are more likely to seek activities that are very exciting, novel, complex, and different. Consumers with a high need for stimulation might enjoy activities like skydiving, gambling, and river rafting.[106] They are also more likely to be innovative and creative.

Individuals with high and low needs for stimulation also differ in the way they approach the marketplace. Those with high stimulation needs tend to be the first to buy new products, to seek information about them, and to engage in variety seeking (buying something different).[107] They are more curious about the ads they see but may be easily bored by them. These consumers are more likely to buy products associated with greater risk, enjoy shopping in malls with many stores and products, and prefer products and services that deviate from established consumption practices.

Dogmatism Consumers can vary in terms of being open- or closed-minded. ***Dogmatism*** refers to an individual's tendency to be resistant to change and new ideas. Dogmatic, or closed-minded, consumers are likely to be relatively resistant to new products, new promotions, and new ads. In support, one study found that Nigerian consumers' acceptance of new products depended on how dogmatic the consumers were. The study also found that Muslims were more dogmatic than Christians.[108]

Need for Uniqueness Consumers who pursue novelty through the purchase, use, and disposition of goods and services are displaying a ***need for uniqueness (NFU).***[109] A need for uniqueness covers three behavioral dimensions: creative choice counterconformity (the consumer's choice reflects social distinctiveness yet is one that others will approve), unpopular choice counterconformity (choosing products and brands that do not conform to establish distinctiveness despite possible social disapproval), and avoidance of similarity (losing interest in possessions that become commonplace to avoid the norm and hence reestablish distinctiveness). In one study, consumers with a high need for uniqueness who were asked to explain their decisions made unconventional choices, showing that they were aware that their choices and reasoning were outside the norm.[110] Thus consumers with a high need for uniqueness may consciously resist conformity by disposing of clothing that has become too popular in favor of emerging fashion trends. They may also express this need by buying handcrafted or personalized items and by customizing products to their own specifications.

Creativity In terms of consumer behavior, creativity means "a departure from conventional consumption practice in a novel and functional way."[111] For instance, if confronted with an everyday problem such as lacking the right ingredients to bake a cake, a consumer high in creativity would locate substitutes for the missing ingredients. This solution would enable the consumer to complete the activity in a novel yet practical way. Moreover, such creativity enhances the consumer's mood, as well.[112] Today a lot of companies are encouraging consumers to also hit their websites. The websites are accordingly being made interactive and encouraging consumers to sign up with their free newsletters or their free updates. [17]Pepsizone.yahoo.co.in, is one such interactive site, where it encourages surfers to create their brand of music, movies, download clippings and even play their popular advertisements.

Need for Cognition Consumers who enjoy thinking extensively about things like products, attributes, and benefits are high in the ***need for cognition (NFC).***[113] Those with a low need for cognition do not like to think and prefer to take shortcuts or rely on their feelings. Consumers with different needs for cognition differ in terms of their product interests, information search, and reaction to different ad campaigns. Specifically, those with a high need for cognition enjoy products and experiences that carry a serious learning and mastery component such as chess, educational games, and TV shows like Nat Geo.They derive satisfaction from searching for and discovering new product features and react positively to long, technically sophisticated ads with details about products or services. They might also scrutinize messages more carefully than other consumers do, considering the credibility or merits of the message.[114] Consumers with a low need for cognition, on the other hand, react more positively to short messages using attractive models, humor, or other cues. These individuals tend to make decisions that involve little thinking.

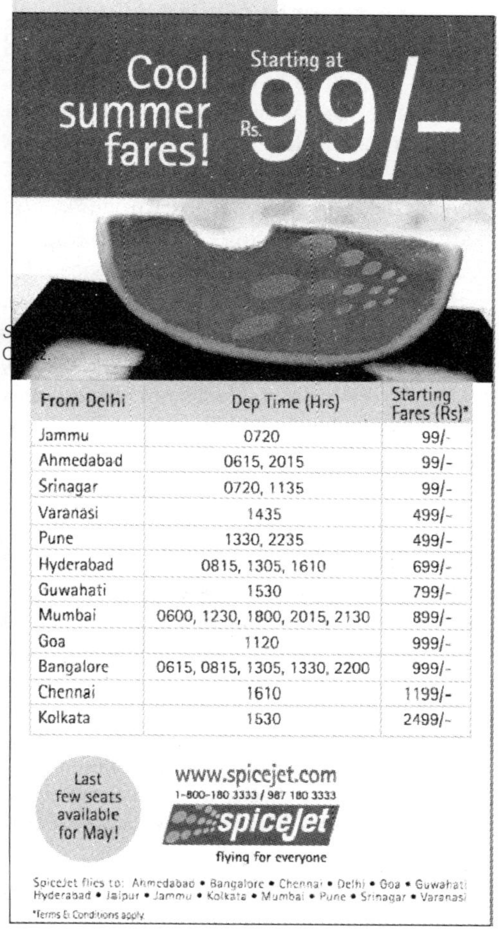

Exhibit 15.12
AD APPEALING TO FRUGALITY
This ad would appeal to consumers who are frugal and value saving money.

Susceptibility to Influence Consumers also vary in their susceptibility to persuasion attempts, especially those that are interpersonal or face-to-face. Some consumers have a greater desire to enhance their image as observed by others and are therefore willing to be influenced or guided by them.[115] Consumers with lower social and information processing confidence tend to be more influenced by ads than are those with higher self-confidence.

Frugality Frugality is the degree to which consumers take a disciplined approach to short-term acquisitions and are resourceful in using products and services to achieve longer-term goals. Consumers who are high on frugality will, for example, pack leftovers for lunch at work (rather than buy take-out food or eat in a restaurant). Research shows that such consumers are less materialistic, less susceptible to the influence of others, and more conscious of price and value than those low in frugality (see Exhibit 15.12).[116] Sometimes governments or companies will actively encourage frugality to conserve scarce resources such as electric power.[117]

Japanese magazines such as *Hot Pepper* appeal to frugality with discount coupons and articles about money-saving restaurants. "Four years ago when the magazine was first published, there were people who said, 'What are coupons?' or 'Discounts are petty,'" says a *Hot Pepper* executive. Now, he says, the featured stores and restaurants are seeing more traffic—and *Hot Pepper* has lots of competition for the attention of frugal-minded consumers.[118]

Self-Monitoring Behavior Individuals differ in the degree to which they look to others for cues on how to behave. High self-monitors are typically sensitive to the desires and influences of others as guides to behavior, and low self-monitors are guided more by their own preferences and desires and are less influenced by normative expectations.[119] High and low self-monitors also differ in their responsiveness to advertising appeals. High self-monitors are more responsive to image-oriented ads and more willing to try and pay more for products advertised with an image consistent with high self-monitoring. In contrast, low self-monitors are generally more responsive to ads that make a quality claim and are more willing to try these products and pay extra for them.

National Character Personality traits can sometimes be used to stereotype people of a particular country as having a ***national character.*** These characterizations represent only very broad generalizations about a particular country; obviously individuals vary a great deal. To illustrate, French people and Italian people are often characterized as emotional and romantic, the British as more reserved; German, French, and U.S. citizens have been characterized as more assertive than their British, Russian, or Italian counterparts. German, British, and Russian consumers can be viewed as "tighter" compared with the "looser" French, Italian, and U.S. consumers.[120] U.S. consumers are also considered more impulsive, risk oriented, and self-confident than Canadians, who are stereotyped as more cautious, restrained, and reserved. Researchers have characterized how countries differ in their needs for achievement, levels of introversion and extroversion, perceptions of human nature, and flexibility.[121] Marketers must consider how differences in national character may influence reactions to advertising and other communications. Not long ago, Nike had to pull a TV commercial in China featuring basketball star LeBron James fighting cartoon characters in martial arts attire after the Chinese government said the ad was insulting to national dignity.[122]

marketing IMPLICATIONS Because some personality traits may be related to consumption behavior, marketers can develop products, services, and communications that appeal to various personality types. For example, ads targeting compliant or extremely self-monitoring consumers should focus on the approval of others, whereas ads and promotions appealing to high optimal stimulation-level consumers or those with a strong need for uniqueness might focus on trying something new and different. Coca-Cola, for instance, used word of mouth to attract consumers to its Burn energy drink as a pub drink distinctly different from Red Bull and other established competitors.[123] The magazine *Sole Collector* and the website niketalk.com (sponsored not by Nike but by sneaker enthusiasts) often feature hand-decorated athletic shoes and other one-of-a-kind sneakers, targeting consumers with a high need for uniqueness.[124]

Lifestyles

Lifestyles relate closely to consumers' values and personality. Whereas values and personality represent internal states or characteristics, ***lifestyles*** are manifestations or actual patterns of behavior. In particular, they are represented by a consumer's ***activities, interests, and opinions (AIOs),*** as in Exhibit 15.13. What people do in their spare time is often a good indicator of their lifestyle. One consumer might like outdoor activities such as skiing or diving, whereas another might prefer to surf the Web or make a scrapbook. Consumers who engage in different activities and have differing opinions and interests may in fact represent distinct lifestyle segments for marketers.

For example, one study identified two lifestyle segments that were most likely to drink and drive: Good Timers, frequent partygoers who are macho and high on sensation seeking, and Problem Kids, youths who frequently display troublesome behaviors.[125] Another lifestyle segment consists of people with an affinity for nostalgia, or the desire for old things.[126] This segment clearly represents a key market for old movies, books, and antiques. Also, consumers are participating in more extreme sports such as snowmobiling—opening opportunities for marketers of related equipment—whereas group sports are losing popularity.[127]

Lifestyle research can help marketers better understand how a product fits into consumers' general behavior patterns. To illustrate, lifestyles related to cooking include Speed Scratch Cooking (using time-saving techniques and equipment to prepare meals) and Investment Cooking (cooking many dishes or a large quantity of food at once but storing some for later consumption).[128]

Finally, consumers in different countries may have characteristic lifestyles. One study found considerable lifestyle differences between Japanese and U.S. women. Japanese women were more home focused, less likely to visit restaurants, less price sensitive, and less likely to drive. Given these preferences, Japanese women would probably spend more time than U.S. women preparing meals at home and would therefore pay more for products that enhance meal quality. Alternatively, an Indian woman, be she a career woman or at home, family is supreme and so she is likely to invest equal amount of time both for her home and work. Popular lifestyle activities among Russian consumers include going to the movies and theater and participating in sports like soccer, ice hockey, and figure skating.[130]

Activities	Interests	Opinions	Demographics
Work	Family	Themselves	Age
Hobbies	Home	Social issues	Education
Social events	Job	Politics	Income
Vacations	Community	Business	Occupation
Entertainment	Recreation	Education	Family size
Club membership	Fashion	Economics	Dwelling
Community	Food	Products	Geography
Shopping	Media	Culture	City size
Sports	Achievements	Future	Life cycle stage

Source: Joseph T. Plumer, "The Concept and Application of Life Style Segmentation," *Journal of Marketing*, January 1974, pp. 33–37. Reprinted with permission.

Exhibit 15.13
ACTIVITIES, INTERESTS, AND OPINIONS

Lifestyles are represented by consumers' activities, interests, *and* opinions. *Here are some major examples of each category. Note that these lifestyles provide a more detailed profile of consumers than their demographics do (the last column).*

marketing IMPLICATIONS

Consumer lifestyles can have important implications for market segmentation, communication, and new product ideas.

Market segmentation

Marketers can use lifestyles to identify consumer segments for specific offerings. [18]For example, eyeing the trend towards busier lifestyles, the concept of Ready To Eat in India is now catching up. Brands like MTR, Kohinoor, and Kitchens of India to name a few, are already there in the market, offering a range. For cooking as well, condiment pastes, purees, or specialized condiments required for a recipe, are all available for the woman of the house to choose from. Take for example, Bengali cuisine which requires specialized condiments, that needs to be mixed and ground in right proportions to get the right taste. To do away with the drudgery or to save time, several companies today offer a range of such condiments.

Lifestyle segmentation also has important cross-cultural implications. For example, one study of 12 European countries used demographics, activities, media behavior, political inclinations, and mood to identify six Eurotype lifestyle segments: Traditionalists (18 percent of the population), Homebodies (14 percent), Rationalists (23 percent), Pleasurists (17 percent), Strivers (15 percent), and Trendsetters (13 percent).[135] Travelers visiting Moscow used to have to settle for a narrow bed in a dingy hotel with little service.[136] Now, Western hotel chains offer services better geared to the typical traveler's lifestyle, such as dry cleaning, room service, and bistros. In Japan, outdoor-oriented consumers are snapping up recreational vehicles—even though many never leave the city.[137] Although alcohol is forbidden in Saudi Arabia, nonalcoholic beers have become popular among young consumers with an active, hip lifestyle.[138] Finally, marketers often monitor lifestyle changes to identify new opportunities. In Florida, Regions Financial bank is opening 20 percent more new accounts after extending banking hours at branches in residential areas so time-stressed customers can handle transactions in person.[139]

Communications

Marketers can design ad messages and promotions to appeal to certain lifestyles, featuring products in the context of desired lifestyles.[140] [19]As Golfing in India becomes popular, more and more developers, sports companies and resorts are trying to develop golf resorts, getting the big names in golfing and golfing equipments and accessories. [20]Reebok's, golfing arm, Greg Norman Collection targets golf courses through a series of promotional activities at some of the most premium golf courses in India. Direct interaction with the golfers and the organizers at the ground helps Reebok understand the user profile, requirements and even create a distinct imagery.

Lifestyles also influence media plans. For example, because many fathers have changed their lifestyle to become more involved in child rearing, parenting magazines are adding a focus on male readers and attracting male-oriented advertising.[143] Now that consumers on the go are increasingly using technology such as digital music players to take entertainment along The surge in private vehicles in India generates a large base of mobile vehicular traffic.. FM Radio, particularly, in the bigger cities like Delhi, Mumbai, Kolkata or Bangalore has been targeting the mobile traffic and has custom made programmes like [21]Radio Mirchi's Bumper to Bumper, a generic name in itself to identify with such traffic. The programming content, focuses on traffic updates, warning about traffic bottlenecks, weather updates and even live coverage of special events. In fact, the Internet can be a very targeted way to communicate with a variety of lifestyle segments, particularly those who surf very often. Teenagers are especially fickle surfers, so a site must generate considerable interest to attract and hold these visitors for any length of time. Sites like pespiszone.com, spillurdil.com, desimartini.com focus on such young crowd and marketers get a dedicated audience on their website.

Finally, media usage patterns may be related to lifestyles.[147] For example, consumers who read magazines and newspapers tend to be educated and hold prestige jobs as well as being involved in community and politics. Interestingly, consumers who love to surf the Internet also tend to be heavy TV watchers.[148] One national survey found connections between seemingly unrelated lifestyles and media usage, such as fishing enthusiasts tending to enjoy listening to Christian rock music and reading *Southern Living* (see Exhibit 15.14).[149]

New product ideas

Often marketers can develop new product and service ideas by uncovering unfulfilled needs of certain lifestyle segments. For example, marketers discovered that many workers who bring their lunch to work were tired of sandwiches. In response, companies such as Oscar Mayer, StarKist, and Libby's developed different varieties of easy-to-pack "lunch kits." After learning that consumers prefer baby food in easy-to-carry plastic packages, Gerber switched from its traditional single-serving glass jars.[150] And Nike is marketing a wristwatch heart monitor to help athletes monitor their health and performance.[151]

Psychographics: Combining Values, Personality, and Lifestyles

This chapter opened by observing that psychographic research today combines values, personality, and lifestyle variables. To illustrate this key point, this last section provides a brief description of several psychographic applications in marketing.

VALS

One of the most widely known psychographic tools is ***VALS,*** formerly known as Values and Lifestyle Survey, conducted by SRI Consulting Business Intelligence. VALS

Exhibit 15.14

LIFESTYLE AND MEDIA CONNECTIONS

This graph illustrates the connection between lifestyles and different types of media such as TV stations and shows, magazines, and radio shows.

analyzes the behavior of U.S. consumers to create segments based on two factors. The first is resources, including income, education, self-confidence, health, eagerness to buy, intelligence, and energy level. The second is primary motivation. Consumers motivated by ideals are guided by intellectual aspects rather than by feelings or other people's opinions. Those who are motivated by achievement base their views on the actions and opinions of others and strive to win their approval. And those who are motivated by self-expression desire social or physical action, variety, activity, and personal challenge.[152]

Combining the resource and motivation variables, VALS has identified eight consumer segments (see Exhibit 15.15). At the low end of the resource hierarchy are Survivors, who have the lowest incomes. Their focus is on survival, so they are not described by a primary motivation. Believers are conservative and motivated by ideals; they have somewhat modest resources and, because they do not change easily, tend to prefer familiar, established products and brands. The other group motivated by ideals is the Thinkers, who are mature, well educated, and actively conduct information searches when planning purchases. Thinkers have more resources and are value oriented in their consumption practices.

The two achievement-oriented segments are Strivers (who have limited discretionary income yet strive to emulate more successful people) and Achievers (who have higher resources, are focused on their work and families, and prefer status-symbol products). In the self-expression segment, Makers value self-sufficiency, buy basic products, and are focused on family, work, and constructive activities. Experiencers have more resources than Makers, stay active, seek stimulation and novelty, and spend money on socializing and entertainment. Innovators have the greatest resource base, with lots of self-confidence, high incomes, and education, so they can indulge in all three primary motivations to some extent. These consumers will accept new products and technologies, and they choose upscale offerings reflective of their personal style.

Other Applied Psychographic Research

Although VALS is probably the best known and most widely used psychographic tool, there are a variety of other ongoing surveys. One of the newer tools is NOP World's LifeMatrix, which examines personal values, lifestyles, and lifestages to segment consumer markets into ten basic categories (see Exhibit 15.16). For instance, "Dynamic Duos" (11 percent of the U.S. population) are married, have successful careers, and are optimistic about what the future may bring. These consumers are heavy Internet users and avid newspaper readers, although they listen to radio only occasionally, and they have the time and money to travel and pursue hobbies.[153] Thinking globally, some of the elements used to develop LifeMatrix are also being included in the company's 30-country studies to better understand what drives consumer behavior in other nations.[154]

Another tool, the Yankelovich MindBase, is a psychographic segmentation system with eight broad segments and 24 subsegments for more precise targeting.[155] Based on attitudes, lifestage data, gender, age, and other inputs, MindBase determines how consumers in each segment behave and why, and then interprets

Exhibit 15.15
VALS AMERICAN SEGMENTS
VALS classifies consumers into eight major segments based on two dimensions: resources (education, income, intelligence, etc.) and primary motivation (ideals, achievement, self-expression), as described in this exhibit. Into which group would you fall?

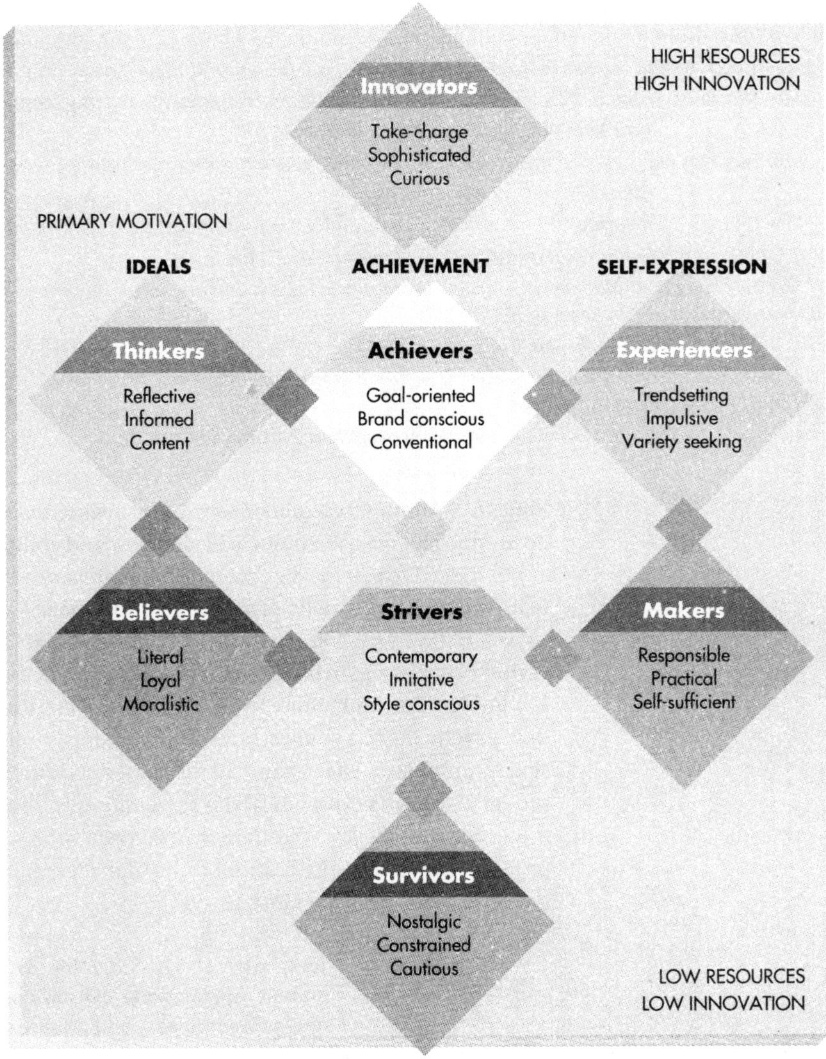

this information for marketing purposes. Consumers in MindBase's "I am at capacity" segment, for instance, have as their motto "Time is of the essence," because they are extremely busy; therefore, this segment values convenience, control, and simplification.

Some researchers question whether psychographic techniques fully capture all the variation in consumers' lifestyles. Rather than relying on the traits measured in the preceding research, one researcher identifies some consumption patterns that do not fit into the VALS framework. These include canonical aesthetics (which relates to traditional Western thought and tastes for art and culture), nurturing mother (in which consumption centers on the home and caring for children), and Jeffersonian America (related to the styles and traditions of a pastoral United

Exhibit 15.16

MRS. URBAN INDIA

Alongside each profile are also indicator brands which have been profiling such housewives in their advertisements

- *Mrs 'Hasmukh' Popular: 27% :popular, role model , Independent-minded , not self-sacrificing , all perfect*
  - *Tata Tea Gold, Lifebuoy, Saffola, Whirlpool*
- *Mrs 'Pataka' Cool: 12%:cool metro woman, still young, goes out the most, consulted by her husband, optimistic*
  - *Femina, Livon, Moods*
- *Mrs 'Gharelu' Homepride: 18%:sacrificing maa, would rather save than splurge, husband relies heavily on her wisdom*
  - *Cadbury's Bournvita, Catch Masala, Clinic Plus*
- *Mrs 'Hey Bhagwan!' Moaner: 12%: cooks, cleans, saves, hoards and dresses plainly, husband takes major decisions, having gold jewellery, belongs to the lower middle class*
  - *Moov, Mortein Coils*
- *Mrs 'Meri Awaaz Suno' Attention Seeker: 31%: family is not modern , doesn't like the idea of staying in a joint family , dresses up even when she goes to the market*
  - *Everest Pav Bhaji Masala, Active Wheel, Nilkamal Furniture*

States).[156] Another researcher warns that segments can shift with societal changes, economic changes, technological changes, and competitive changes.[157]

In India, lifestyle studies are a preliminary stage. The largeness and more significantly the heterogeneity of the population makes it difficult to conduct any kind of pan-India study. A study by P-SNAP Lowe, tracked 10,000 housewives across the country trying to gain meaningful insights into their thought process. The outcome is showcased as in Exhibit 15.17. Though advertising and research agencies conduct psychographic studies, however the scope is limited and does not cover extensive sample sizes. The urban and the rural divide are quite expansive and the same model of analysis does not fit the segment. Even the metros, mini-metros and the A,B,C class towns are so different from each other that it requires individual approach. Add to this, the cultural traits of each region being different that implies strong differentiators in lifestyle too.

marketing IMPLICATIONS

Tools such as VALS, LifeMatrix, MindBase, and other psychographic applications can be useful for market segmentation, new product ideas, and ad development. Pittsburgh's Iron City beer used VALS to improve its image and counteract lagging sales. From research, Iron City discovered that it had two main markets. Makers and Believers were loyal customers for many years. However, the younger market of Strivers and Experiencers was rejecting the brand. To appeal to these important, yet diverse, segments, Iron City developed an ad campaign juxtaposing images of old Pittsburgh with contemporary, vibrant images of the city as the backdrop for Strivers and Experiencers working hard at having fun. By advertising on television programs and radio stations favored by Strivers and Experiencers, Iron City successfully appealed to these segments and increased its sales by 26 percent.[158]

Hyundai has used LifeMatrix data to segment the U.S. market for cars, identify the consumers most likely to buy its brand, choose the most effective media to reach these consumers, and create advertising messages that appeal to these consumers' values and interests.[159] Chris Bole, customer development manager for PowerBar, sees an opportunity to sell to Tribe Wired men by displaying its products in the personal grooming section of drugstores. He comments, "This would be a good example of 'How does this fit into a lifestyle?'"[160]

Summary

Consumers learn values—enduring beliefs about things that are important—through the processes of socialization and acculturation. Our values exist in an organized value system, where some are viewed as more important than others. Terminal values are desired end states that guide behavior in many situations, whereas instrumental values help achieve those desired end states. Domain-specific values are relevant within a given sphere of activity.

Western cultures tend to highly value materialism, the home, work and play, individualism, family and children, health, hedonism, youth, the environment, and technology. Marketers use value-based segmentation to identify groups within the larger market that share a common set of values different from those of other groups. Three methods for identifying value-based segments are inferring values based on the cultural milieu of the group, the means-end chain analysis, and questionnaires like the Rokeach Value Survey and the List of Values.

Personality consists of the patterns of behaviors, tendencies, and personal dispositions that make people different from one another. Approaches to the study of personality include (1) the psychoanalytic approach, which sees personality as the result of unconscious struggles to complete key stages of development; (2) trait theories, which attempt to identify a set of personality characteristics that describe and differentiate individuals; (3) phenomenological approaches, which propose that personality is shaped by an individual's interpretation of life events; (4) social-psychological theories, which focus on the way individuals act in social situations; and (5) behavioral approaches, which view personality in terms of behavioral responses to past rewards and punishments. Marketers are also interested in examining lifestyles, which are patterns of behavior or activities, interests, and opinions, for additional insight into consumers' consumption patterns. Finally, some marketing researchers use psychographic techniques involving values, personality, and lifestyles to predict consumer behavior.

Questions for Review and Discussion

1. Explain the differences between global values, terminal values, instrumental values, and domain-specific values.
2. What are the four main value dimensions along which national cultures can vary?
3. How do marketers use means-end chain analysis, the Rokeach Value Survey, and the List of Values?
4. How does the locus of control affect personality?
5. What are the three components of a consumer's lifestyle?
6. Define psychographics, and discuss its use and potential limitations.

Exercises

1. Conduct a content analysis of the advertisements that appear over four issues of a selected magazine. For each ad, record the type of product or service and whether and how each of the following values is reflected in the message: (a) materialism, (b) youthfulness, (c) the home, (d) work and play, (e) individualism, (f) the family, (g) health, (h) hedonism, and (i) technology. Summarize this information, and answer the following questions:

   a. Which values are most often reflected in the advertisements?

   b. Do certain types of values appear more often for certain types of products?

   c. Which themes appear in relationship to each value?

2. Develop a questionnaire to measure some of the key activities, interests, and opinions of college students. Also develop a series of items to measure the consumption of five product or service categories that may be related to college lifestyles. Administer this questionnaire to 20 fellow students (across different majors if possible). Summarize the results, and answer the following questions:

a. What are the key lifestyle segments of the college students you surveyed?

b. For each segment, are there recognizable consumption patterns in terms of products or services?

c. What general types of marketing strategies would you use to appeal to each group?

3. Visit either the VALS website (www.sric-bi.com) or the Yankelovich website (www.yankelovich.com), and answer one of these online surveys to see how psychographics might describe you as a consumer.

a. How do the questions in this survey compare with the questions you developed for exercise 2?

b. Do you agree that the segment in which the survey placed you, based on your answers, is an accurate description of your lifestyle, personality, and/or values? Explain.

c. In terms of psychographics, what additional details about your values, personality, or lifestyle would help a car manufacturer target you more effectively for a new car purchase? What questions would you add to the survey in order to elicit these details?

More Exercises from the Adaptor

1. Choose any ten categories of products from durables, FMCG, services and telecom and track their advertising in the last 5 years. Elaborate how have they showcased the setting of the product, particularly in the context of the lifestyles and the personality profile of the characters.

References

[1] Source: http://www.rediff.com/money/2004/mar/15spec.htm

[2] Source: http://www.thehindubusinessline.com/catalyst/2004/02/26/stories/2004022600030100.htm http://www.thehindubusinessline.com/catalyst/2005/06/09/stories/2005060900020100.htm

[3] Source: http://www.rediff.com/money/2004/feb/11surf.htm

[4] Source: http://www.chennaionline.com/cityfeature/newlaunches/surf.asp

[5] Source: http://www.unilever.com/ourvalues/environment-society/case-studies/water/india-surf-excel-relaunched-reduce-rinsing-conserve-water.asp

[6] Source: http://www.medindia.net/news/view_news_main.asp?str=1&x=16802

[7] Source: Times of India, Delhi Times, 19th

[8] Source: http://www.blonnet.com/life/2004/12/24/stories/2004122400170400.htm

[9] Source: KSA Technopak Consumer Outlook 2004

[10] Source: http://cities.expressindia.com/fullstory.php?newsid=85665

[11] Source: http://www.freeonlineresearchpapers.com/western-cultures-overbearing-influence

[12] Source: http://family.jrank.org/pages/859/India-Family-Life-Family-Values.html

[13] Source: http://www.thehindubusinessline.com/2004/09/12/stories/2004091201230200.htm

[14] Source: http://www.itcportal.com/newsroom/press_sept20.htm

[15] Source: http://www.thehindubusinessline.com/2004/09/12/stories/2004091201230200.htm

[16] Source: Sunday- Hindustan Times, 13.5.2007

[17] Source: http://pepsizone.yahoo.co.in/home

[18]. Source: http://www.thehindubusinessline.com/2004/09/12/stories/2004091201230200.htm

[19] Source: http://www.tribuneindia.com/2003/20030628/spr-trib.htm#3

[20] Source: http://www.shark.com/gnccorporate/Media/press092705.php

[21] Source: http://us.indiantelevision.com/headlines/y2k7/jan/jan117.htm

chapter 16 Social Influences on Consumer Behavior

LEARNING OBJECTIVES

After studying this chapter, you will be able to:

- Explain how general sources of influence differ in four key ways depending on whether they are delivered via mass media or personally, and whether they are delivered by marketers or others.
- Discuss why marketers must pay particular attention to the influence of opinion leaders.
- Describe the types and characteristics of reference groups and show how each can affect consumer behavior.
- Distinguish between normative and informational influence, and outline how marketers can use their knowledge of these types of influence for more effective marketing.

INTRODUCTION

Hum Tum: Creating Buzz through Hum and Tum

[1]Yash Raj Films (YRF) have been in the film industry for a long time now, particularly Yash Chopra, who is now considered a legendary figure in the industry. YRF started out as a film-making company in 1970. In the last three decades it has grown from strength to strength and today has to its credit India's most enviable film catalogue – of which some films have been the highest grossers in the entertainment business. YRF, over the years, has expanded the distribution of films all over the world – its own as well as films made by other well-known Indian names. YRF has also widened its horizons into Home Entertainment by marketing and distributing DVDs and VCDs of classic Indian films all over the world through its offices in UK, USA, UAE and India.

[2]Yash Chopra's career started around the mid 50's as an Assistant Director to his brother B.R. Chopra when he assisted him in the classic 1957 movie, Naya Daur. In 1959 he independently directed his first film, Dhool Ka Phool, about a very touching story of those times where a girl fearing the social stigma of an unwed mother leaves her child. Though it was a hackneyed plot but the treatment was excellent and quite touching. The film went on to become a hit and since then, there has been no looking back. Yash Chopra directed and produced numerous films and today the mantle has been taken over by his son, Aditya Chopra. Yash Raj Films, the banner under which the company operates has diversified into film production, direction, music, home entertainment. and has set up its own studio (rented and used for home productions).

Exhibit 16.1
HUM TUM

A clever marketing strategy pushing two cartoon characters, Hum and Tum as a part of the film's publicity creating buzz around audiences and inquisitiveness amongst prospects. Add to that, the comic strips that were featured regularly in leading newspapers.

One of their films released in 2004 was Hum Tum, a runaway hit that went on to do well at the box office. [3]The film starring two of the current popular film stars, Saif Khan and Rani Mukherjee explored the much trivialized aspect of love-hate-love relationship between a couple. However, what set the film apart was the setting of the characters, the dialogues, but most of all the cartoon characters created specially as a part of the movie promotion. Taking off from the lead stars, Hum and Tum were showcased as cartoon strips in a major English daily, creating a buzz amongst the target audience about the film. [4]Infact, the film per se was not marketed too aggressively and according to Tarun Tripathi, Marketing Head of Yash Raj Films, just 10-15% of the film budget was used for promotion, unlike the industry norm of 25-30%. Besides, some free-of-cost deals got the movie free publicity worth 30-35 per cent of its budget. The film went on to earn Rs.30 crore from domestic and overseas releases at the end of nine weeks. Hum Tum also emerged as a surprise winner at the box office, particularly in the overseas markets where collections at the end of ninth week stood at Rs.8.16 crore, according to statistics available at the International Business Overview Standard.
The success of the movie was dependent on the curiosity it created through the cartoon characters released much before the film was actually released and second, the connectivity of the character to the film. Infact, lead actor was a creator of the Hum and Tum series in the film. The film and the stars were not marketed so aggressively as in most cases. It was left to the audience to judge for themselves how they found the film, They appreciated the film.

This chapter explores when and why individuals, groups, and various media affect consumer behavior. Sometimes information and pressures, known as social influences, have a strong influence on consumers because the information source is very credible; at other times they have a strong influence simply because the source can communicate information widely. Think about how you would react if your good friend raves about the taste of a new food, for example, or a stranger hands you a new electronic gadget to try. Social influence is also powerful when individuals within groups are in frequent contact and have many opportunities to communicate information and perspectives. Certain people can be quite influential within a group because their power or expertise makes others want to follow what they believe, do, or say.

In addition to communicating information, individuals can influence whether, what, when, where, how, how much, and how often consumers think they should acquire, use, and dispose of an offering. Groups can induce not only socially appropriate consumer behaviors but also socially inappropriate and even personally destructive behaviors, such as the use of illicit drugs. Therefore, marketers need to understand what kinds of social entities create influence, what kinds of influence they create, and what effects their influence attempts can have. Exhibit 16.2 summarizes the social influences that affect consumer behavior.

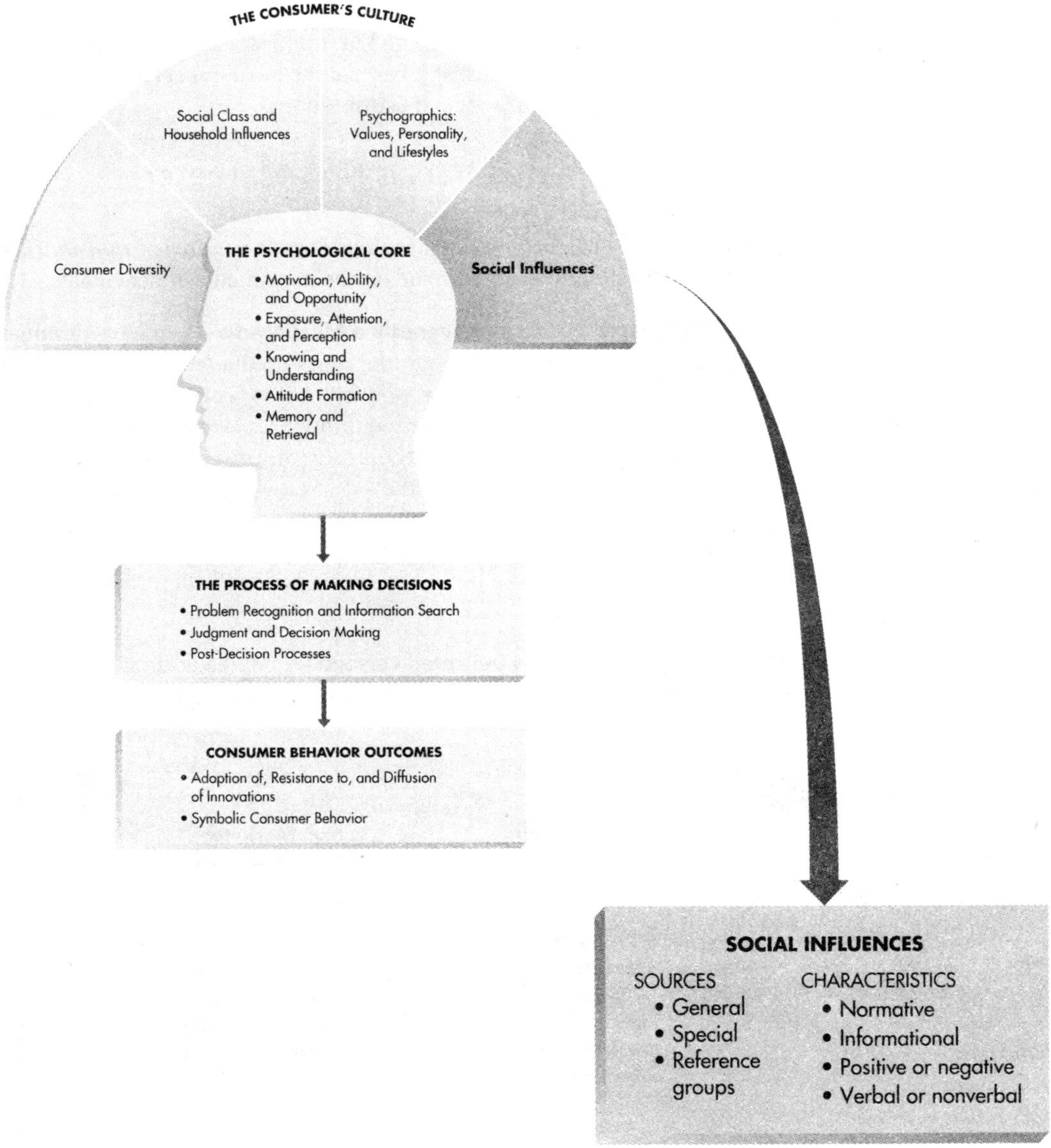

Exhibit 16.2

CHAPTER OVERVIEW: SOCIAL INFLUENCES *This chapter describes various sources of influence (general sources, special sources, and groups) and how they exert influence (by providing normative or informational influence, by providing positive and/or negative information, and by providing information verbally or nonverbally).*

General Sources of Influence

Consumers in the opening example learned about a film through publicity by the cartoon strips created, a unique treatment to the film, and other sources. But which sources had the most impact and why? Exhibit 16.3 offers some answers to these questions.

Marketer-Dominated Versus Non-Marketer-Dominated Influence

Sources of influence can be described as ***marketer-dominated*** or ***non-marketer-dominated*** and be described as delivered via the mass media or personally.

Marketer-Dominated Sources Delivered via Mass Media Marketer-dominated sources that deliver influence through the mass media (cell 1 in Exhibit 16.3) include advertising, sales promotions, publicity, and special events. Big Bazaar's recent sale of 50 per cent off was publicized through local newspapers and it tried to get across to mobile subscribers through SMS, by giving them special offers which they could avail upon showing the SMS to the staff at the outlet. Companies often announce a new offering through special events; the way Maruti launched the Swift, wherein special engineers and sales staff were appointed at the dealer outlets and separate corner was earmarked for Swift to create a distinction.

Marketer-Dominated Sources Delivered Personally Marketer-dominated sources can also deliver information personally (cell 2 in Exhibit 16.3). Salespeople, service

Exhibit 16.3
SOURCES OF INFLUENCE
Social influence can come from marketer- or non-marketer-dominated sources and can be delivered via the mass media or in person. Non-marketer-dominated sources tend to be more credible. Information delivered via the mass media can reach many people but may not allow for a two-way flow of communication.

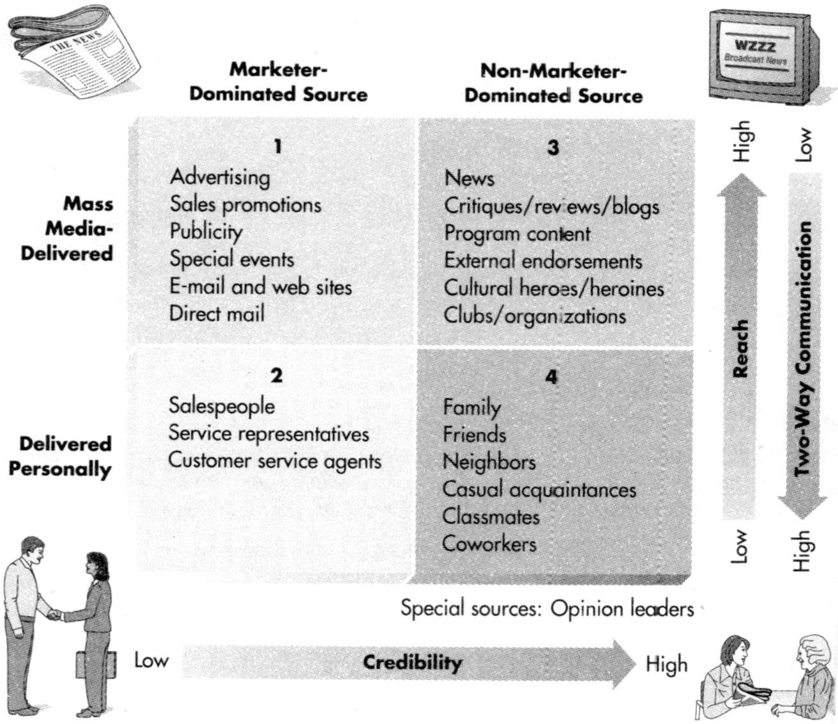

representatives, and customer service agents are marketer-dominated sources of influence who deliver information personally in retail outlets, at consumers' homes or offices, over the phone, via online chat, or at trade shows. In some situations, consumers will respond to a marketing agent, such as a salesperson, by making use of the agent's knowledge and assistance to further their personal goals. Where consumers worry about undue persuasion, however, they will adopt techniques to fend off unwanted attention.[3] Note that buzz-building tactics such as those in the opening example blur the line between marketer-dominated and non-marketer-dominated sources. Sony Ericsson hired actors to get the product into consumers' hands and talk it up, although consumers who came in contact with the actors probably did not know that a company was responsible for the activity. "I have a real issue with stealth," says one promotion expert. "You break the trust if people don't know who you are."[4]

Non-Marketer-Dominated Sources Delivered via Mass Media As cell 3 in Exhibit 16.3 shows, non-marketer-dominated sources delivered via mass media can also wield influence. Consumer behavior may be affected by news items about new products, movies, and restaurants; product contamination; accidents involving products; and incidences of product abuse or misuse. Consumers shopping for a new car may learn about recalls and quality problems from TV coverage, Internet sites, blogs (Weblogs), and other media not controlled by marketers.[5] Certain media sources are particularly influential. Many consumers, for instance, choose movies based on film critics' recommendations; make dining decisions based on restaurant reviews; make buying decisions based on *Consumer Reports* articles; and choose hotels based on the American Automobile Association's ratings. Not long ago, the Czech car manufacturer Skoda wanted to change its low-quality image among U.K. consumers. After Skoda lent test cars to influential journalists from mainstream U.K. publications, the journalists' glowing news reports helped boost the car's sales by 23 percent.[6] Celebrities and other well-known figures may also influence consumers' acquisition, usage, and disposition decisions.

Non-Marketer-Dominated Sources Delivered Personally Finally, consumer behavior is influenced by non-marketer-dominated sources that deliver information personally (cell 4 in Exhibit 16.3). Our consumer behavior can be affected by observing how others behave or by ***word of mouth,*** information about offerings communicated verbally from friends, family, neighbors, casual acquaintances, and even strangers. For instance, according to a Consumer Electronics Association survey, 64 percent of adults find out about new electronics products by talking with friends, family, or work associates; 65 percent of adults ask these people for recommendations when starting to research an electronics purchase.[7] [5]Google, the search engine brand replaced Microsoft as the world's number one ranked brand. The rankings, compiled by market research firm Millward Brown, also put Google ahead of well-established brands like General Electric, No. 2; Coca-Cola, No. 4; Wal-Mart Stores, No. 7; and IBM, No. 9. For Google, which ranked No. 7 a year ago, the jump to the top underscores how quickly the web search leader has become an everyday name. The company uses relatively little advertising, relying instead on word-of-mouth promotion.

How Do These General Sources Differ?

The influence sources shown in Exhibit 16.3 differ in terms of their reach, capacity for two-way communication, and credibility. In turn, these characteristics affect how much influence each source can have with consumers.

Reach Mass-media sources are important to marketers because they reach large consumer audiences. [6]The impact of KBC on Star Plus can be observed by looking at the viewership share of the channel for the 9-10 pm daypart for four weeks prior to the launch of the programme vis-à-vis the launch day for both the years 2000 and 2005 on a 6 metros level. It was observed that while KBC1 in the year 2000 took Star Plus's channel share from 2 to 25 per cent during the 9-10 pm daypart, 2005 saw 10 per cent viewership jump to 38 per cent during the 4 weeks prior to the launch period. This illustrates the popularity of the programme and the kind of viewership it generated. Now satellite TV, the Internet, and other technologies are spreading marketing messages, product news, information about the behavior of public figures, and television programs to an increasingly large audience, expanding marketers' reach to other regions and around the world.

Capacity for Two-Way Communication Personally delivered sources of influence are valuable because they allow for a two-way flow of information. For example, a car salesperson may have more influence than a car ad because the salesperson can tailor sales information to fit the buyer's information needs, rebut counterarguments, reiterate important and/or complex information, ask questions, and answer the buyer's questions. Personal conversations are often more casual and less purposeful than mass-media-delivered information. During a conversation, people are less likely to anticipate what will be said and hence less likely to take steps to avoid information inconsistent with their own frames of reference. Information from a personal source may also seem more vivid than information from the mass media because the person speaking somehow makes it more real, which may make it more persuasive.[10]

Credibility Whereas personal and mass media sources differ in their reach and capacity for two-way communication, marketer- and non-marketer-dominated sources differ in their credibility (see Exhibit 16.3). Consumers tend to perceive information delivered through marketer-dominated sources as less credible, more biased, and manipulative. In contrast, non-marketer-dominated sources appear more credible because we do not believe they have a personal stake in our purchase, consumption, or disposition decisions. [7]We are more likely to believe an indiacar.com article on cars than information from a car salesperson. Because non-marketer-dominated sources are credible, they tend to have more influence on consumer decisions than marketer-dominated sources.[11] [8]Murad Ali Baig's major claim to fame is that he is a renowned automobile journalist. He has been around the world driving cars which also makes him an avid traveler. His favorite occupation is tracking down little known offbeat destinations that he can motor to. [9]His regular columns in cybersteering.com helps consumers gain valuable information about the car they want to buy.

Specific personal and mass-media sources vary in their credibility. We tend to believe information we hear from people with whom we have close relationships, in part because we are more likely to find them credible.[13] Certain celebrities are also regarded as more credible than others. Tiger Woods is a credible source for golf - related equipment; Amitabh Bachchan is credible as a spokesperson for the Pulse Polio Campaign. Similarly, certain media have higher credibility: consumers are more likely to believe articles in the Time magazine than articles in any non-reputed magazine.

marketing IMPLICATIONS

Marketers can build on these differences in credibility, reach, and two-way communication capability to influence consumer behavior in various ways.

Use non-marketer-dominated sources to enhance credibility

When possible, marketers should try to have non-marketer-dominated sources promote their offerings (see Exhibit 16.4). Testimonials and word-of-mouth referrals may have considerable impact, particularly if they are delivered through personal communication.[14] Likewise, the media have tremendous power to influence consumption trends and behavior, making or breaking new styles and altering perceptions of what is cool. [10]The Sonagachi (a red light area in Kolkata, West Bengal) Project - with sex workers in India, illustrates the importance of women initiating a change themselves rather than waiting for 'outsiders' to bring change or act as

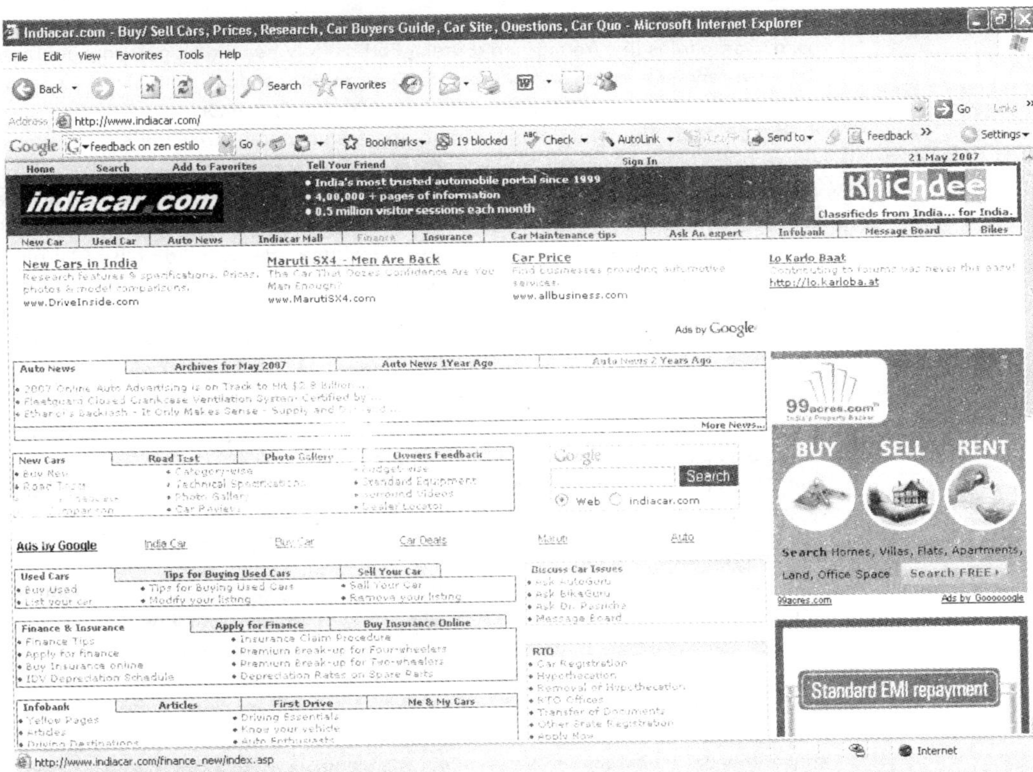

Exhibit 16.4

NNON - MARKETER -DOMINATED SOURCES ENHANCE CREDIBILITY

Non-marketer-dominated sources of influence like Indiacar can have a powerful impact on consumers' purchase decisions because they are regarded as highly credible.

catalysts for change. Sex workers in Sonagachi are successfully negotiating safer sex relationships with clients as well as better treatment from society including from the police. In 1992 the STD/HIV Intervention Project (SHIP) set-up a Sexually Transmitted Diseases (STD) clinic for sex workers to promote disease control and condom distribution. The sex workers themselves decide the programme's strategies. 25 per cent of managerial positions are reserved for sex workers and they hold many key positions. The sex workers are peer educators, clinic assistants and clinic attendants in the project STD clinics. SHIP aims to build sex workers' capacity to question the cultural stereotypes of their society and build in them an awareness about power.

Sometimes consumers have difficulty determining whether information in the media is from a marketer- or non-marketer-dominated source. Some magazine ads are disguised to look like editorial content, and some magazines feature articles that mention the names of their advertisers. [11]ICICI Bank periodically carries a special feature of one page in the Economic Times under the caption: ICICI BANK PRESENTS SME DIALOGUE giving success stories and tips and guidance to SMEs and it becomes difficult to distinguish between an actual news feature and an advertorial, owing to the format in which it is presented. Connecting with a virtual community that is structured around consumers' common interests (such as cooking) can be a credible, effective way for marketers to reach a targeted group.[18]

Use personal sources to enhance two-way communication

Marketing efforts may be more effective when personal information sources are used. Companies like Aquaguard (Eureka Forbes) rely heavily on personal contacts between representatives and customers. Door to door selling, annual maintenance contracts, regular service checks and friendly staff help customers gain confidence on the product. A growing number of companies encourage managers and employees to write blogs, informal online journals with personal opinions and ideas about various topics. The blog by Microsoft's Robert Scoble is widely read because Scoble talks candidly about the industry and even his employer, and he invites readers to respond—which they do. "I get comments on my blog saying, 'I didn't like Microsoft before, but at least they're listening to us,'" Scoble says. "The blog is the best relationship generator you've ever seen. A growing number of companies encourage managers and employees to write blogs, informal online journals with personal opinions and ideas about various topics. Vir Sanghvi's articles and features on food are considered very reliable, as his vast repertoire of knowledge and experience on cuisines has established him as a credible food critic. From Wines, Cheese, upscale vegetables (artichokes, asparagus, broccoli), poultry products and reviewing restaurants, food of the world and the even at times other related issues like hotels to stay et al, make Vir stand out as an authority on the subject.

Use a mix of sources to enhance impact

Because marketer- and non-marketer-dominated sources differ in their impact, the effect on consumers may be greatest when marketers use complementary sources of influence. A vitamin marketer, for example, found that although word of mouth had historically sustained the company, competition forced it to achieve greater reach through advertising. Similarly, given competition from nonbank service providers, word-of-mouth referrals are less effective at enticing consumers to try or stay with a particular bank.[21] Mass-media ads using superstars seem to make less of an impression than in the past, whereas ads combined with favorable word of mouth may have more impact.[22]

Opinion Leaders

A special source of social influence is the ***opinion leader,*** someone who acts as an information broker between the mass media and the opinions and behaviors of an individual or group. Opinion leaders have some position, expertise, or firsthand knowledge that makes them particularly important sources of relevant and credible information, usually in a specific domain. Thus Serena Williams is an opinion leader for sports apparel, not for computers. In rural India, the village headman serves as an opinion leader for TVs, cell phones, and many things. "If I tell [the villagers] I like a particular brand, they'll go out and get it," says the headman of Kaler, a tiny town in Punjab.[23]

Opinion leaders are regarded as non-marketer-dominated sources of influence, which adds to their credibility. Sometimes they are friends or acquaintances; in other cases, they are professionals like doctors, dentists, or lawyers who advise patients and clients. Film critics, restaurant reviewers, and *Consumer Reports* may also be opinion leaders. For instance, Hollywood insider Harry Knowles is seen as an opinion leader because he critiques new movies on his website (*www.aintitcoolnews.com*). Celebrities, models, and leaders of various social groups may also serve as opinion leaders for various offerings. Because they are so credible, opinion leaders can play an important role in consumers' acceptance of new products and services. Exhibit 16.5 identifies several well-known opinion leaders and the categories they influence.

Opinion leaders are part of a general category of ***gatekeepers,*** people who have special influence or power in deciding whether a product or information will be disseminated to a market. For example, the Beijing Telegraph Administration serves as a gatekeeper because it limits the type of information entering China from the Internet. The Chinese government is also a gatekeeper, prohibiting sexually explicit TV shows and music videos from other countries.[24] Even within the

Exhibit 16.5
OPINION LEADERS

Some—but not all—opinion leaders are well-known people. These well-known opinion leaders have the capacity to influence many people.

Who are they?	What are they known for?	Who listens to them?
Anna Wintour, editor of *Vogue*	Approving new designers, designs	- Fashion forward consumers
John Doerr, venture capitalist	Funding Silicon Valley start-ups	- Wall Street
Csoba Csere, editor of *Car and Driver* magazine	Providing information to car buffs	- Car dealers - Car manufacturers - Car buffs
Oprah Winfrey, personality, show host, movie star, book club magnate	Popularizing books, people, and ways of dealing with problems	- Book publishers, book buyers - Women
Matt Drudge, Web reporter	Providing news and gossip on the goings on of Washington	- Everyone in Washington
Walter Mossberg, *Wall Street Journal* columnist	Providing straight facts, in easy to digest language, about which software and hardware is worth buying	- Silicon Valley product managers - Consumers contemplating computer hardware of software purchase

Source: Adapted from Rick Martin and Sarah Van Brown, "The Buzz Machine," *Newsweek,* July 27, 1998, pp. 22–26.

United States, certain people play gatekeeping roles. For example, the search site Yahoo! hires people to keep websites that might compromise the integrity of the Yahoo! directory from being included.[25]

Because their influence can be profound even though opinion leaders are not always well-known people, researchers have studied who opinion leaders are and how to target them. They have observed several characteristics.[26] Opinion leaders tend to learn a lot about products, are heavy users of mass media, and tend to buy new products when they are first introduced. Opinion leaders are also self-confident, gregarious, and willing to share product information. Interestingly, compared with other consumers, opinion leaders may actually use different criteria to evaluate offerings. One study found that movie critics focus on factors like cinematic excellence, whereas the public focuses on whether the film is American made, features popular stars, and offers nonobjectionable content.[27]

People may become opinion leaders because they have an intrinsic interest in and enjoyment of certain products. In other words, they have enduring involvement in a product category.[28] Opinion leaders might also like the power of having information and sharing it with others. Finally, opinion leaders may communicate information simply because they believe their actions will help others.[29]

Opinion leaders have influence because they generally have no personal stake in whether their opinions are heeded, which is why their opinions are perceived as unbiased and credible. In addition, because they have information about and experiences with the product, opinion leaders are often regarded as knowledgeable about acquisition, usage, and disposition options. This is why PC buyers value the comments of opinion leaders such as Walter Mossberg, who writes a technology column for the *Wall Street Journal*—and why PC marketers want Mossberg to review their products. However, simply because they serve as information brokers does not mean that information always flows from opinion leaders to consumers. Indeed, opinion leaders often get information by seeking it from others; they are just as likely to be information seekers as providers.[30]

Whereas opinion leaders are important sources of influence about a particular product or service category, researchers have also identified another special source of influencer—a ***market maven,*** known as someone who seems to have a lot of information about the marketplace in general.[31] A market maven is someone who seems to know everything about what are the best products, where are the good sales, and what are the best stores.

marketing IMPLICATIONS

Marketers use several tactics to influence opinion leaders.

Target opinion leaders

Given their potential impact and the fact that they serve as both seekers and providers of marketplace information, an obvious strategy for reaching opinion leaders is to target them directly.[32] For example, doctors may be targeted to help consumers learn about health-related products and services. The Ghana government had more success with its inoculation programs when health workers contacted and gained the approval of an opinion leader—in this case, the local healer—before approaching the public.[33] Marketers must be able to identify opinion leaders if they are to target them. Exhibit 16.6 shows one scale that researchers use to identify opinion leaders.

Exhibit 16.6

A SCALE MEASURING OPINION LEADERSHIP

Marketers sometimes try to identify opinion leaders because these consumers can be so important to marketing efforts. These scales identify which consumers are opinion leaders and opinion seekers in several product categories.

INITIAL ITEM POOL FOR THE OPINION LEADERSHIP AND OPINION SEEKING SCALES

The questionnaires below ask consumers questions about rock music. A similar version of the questionnaire asks consumers about fashion and environmentally friendly products. Consumers respond to each question using a scale, where 1 means strongly disagree and 7 means strongly agree. People who have a high score on the first scale are classified as opinion leaders in the area of music. Those who score high on the second are opinion seekers in the area of music.

Opinion Leadership

1. Other people rarely ask me about rock CD's before they choose one for themselves. (RS)
2. My opinion on rock [fashion; environmentally friendly products] seems not to count with other people.* (RS)
3. My opinions influence what types of recordings other people buy.
4. Other people think that I am a poor source of information on rock music. (RS)
5. When they choose a rock music recording [fashionable clothing; "green" products], other people do not turn to me for advice.* (RS)
6. Other people rarely come to me for advice about choosing CD's and tapes [fashionable clothing; products that are good for the environment].*
7. People that I know pick rock music [clothing; "green" products] based on what I have told them.*
8. People rarely repeat things I have told them about popular rock music to other people. (RS)
9. What I say about rock music rarely changes other people's minds. (RS)
10. I often persuade other people to buy the rock music [fashions; "green" products] that I like.*
11. I often influence people's opinions about popular rock music [clothing; environmentally correct products.]*

Opinion Seeking

1. When I consider buying a CD or tape [clothes; "green" products], I ask other people for advice.*
2. I don't need to talk to others before I buy CD's or tapes [fashionable clothing; products that are good for the environment].* (RS)
3. Other people influence my choice of rock music.
4. I would not choose a recording without consulting someone else.
5. I rarely ask other people what music [fashions; environmentally friendly products] to buy.* (RS)
6. I like to get others' opinions before I buy a CD or tape [new clothes; "green" products].
7. I feel more comfortable buying a recording [fashion item; product that is good for the environment] when I have gotten other people's opinions on it.*
8. When choosing rock music [fashionable clothing; a "green" product], other people's opinions are not important to me.* (RS)

*Items in the final scales.
(RS): Items reverse scored.

Use opinion leaders in marketing communications

Although opinion leaders' influence may be less effective when delivered through a marketer-dominated source, their expertise and association can still support an offering (see Exhibit 16.7). As an alternative, marketers may use a simulated opinion leader. For example, the major television networks forbid the use of medical professionals or actors playing them to endorse a product. Instead, Mentadent toothpaste has used the wives, husbands, and children of actual dentists. Although these individuals are not experts on toothpaste, their affiliation with real experts presumably gives them some credibility.[34]

Refer consumers to opinion leaders

Finally, marketers can target consumers and ask them to refer to a knowledgeable opinion leader, the way many prescription drug ads suggest that consumers consult their doctors (opinion leaders) about how the product can help. A recent U.K. ad campaign for NiQuitin CQ Lozenges, a nicotine replacement therapy product, focused on the role that pharmacists play in suggesting products for consumers who want to quit smoking. The campaign worked: after a month, recommendations by pharmacy personnel were 5 to 20 percent higher than before the campaign—and consumer sales increased by as much as 34 percent in some areas.[35]

Exhibit 16.7
USING OPINION LEADERS IN ADVERTISING

TSachin Tendulkar in the Adidas advertisements is an example of opinion leader endorsing the product and validating use.

Reference Groups as Sources of Influence

Social influence is exerted by individuals such as opinion leaders as well as by specific groups of people. A reference group is a set of people with whom individuals compare themselves as a guide to developing their own attitudes, knowledge, and/or behaviors.

Types of Reference Groups

Consumers may relate to three types of reference groups: aspirational, associative, and dissociative.

Aspirational reference groups are groups we admire and wish to be like but are not currently a member of. For example, a younger brother may want to be like his older brother and other older children. Some Eastern European youths aspire to be like their U.S. counterparts.[36] According to one U.S. study, consumers aged 18 to 34 most often admire celebrities for their possessions, traits, or lifestyles.[37] Given the high respect accorded to education in Korea, teachers often serve as an aspirational reference group for students in that country.

Associative reference groups are groups to which we actually belong, such as a clique of friends, an extended family, a particular work group, a club, or a school group. The gender, ethnic, geographic, and age groups to which you belong are also associative reference groups with whom you may identify. Exhibit 16.8 shows a case of associative reference group formed around a brand, as is the case with fan clubs and clubs like the HOG group of Harley Davidson (HOG stands for Harley Owners Group). As Exhibit 16.9 shows, each member may think about the brand community in terms of the brand, the marketer, the product, and other customers. Members of a brand community not only buy the product repeatedly, but they are extremely committed to it, share information about it with other consumers, and influence other community members to remain loyal to the group and the brand.

Dissociative reference groups are groups whose attitudes, values, and behaviors we disapprove of and do not wish to emulate. "Gangsta rap" groups promoting violence are dissociative reference groups for some people. U.S. citizens serve as dissociative reference groups to consumers in some Arab countries, and neo-Nazis serve as dissociative reference groups for many people in Germany and in the United States. Research shows that country music fans are a dissociative reference group for many in the United States—even though these consumers may secretly

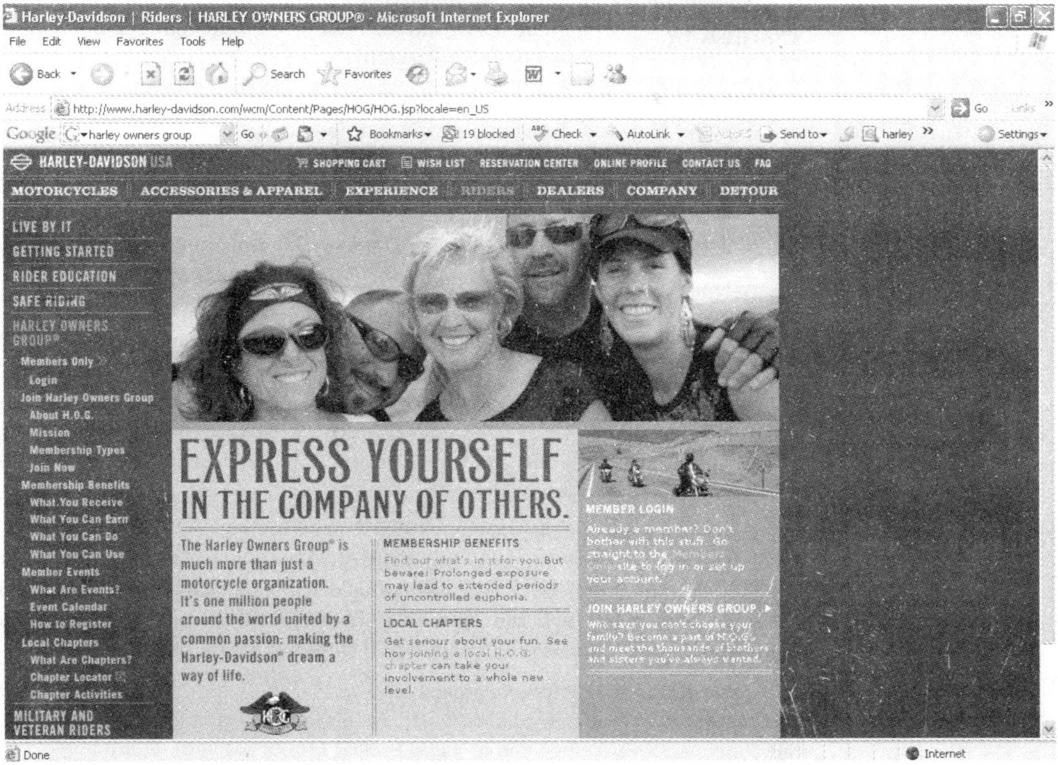

Exhibit 16.8

ASSOCIATIVE REFERENCE GROUPS *TThe Harley Owner's Group is an associative reference group formed around a brand where consumers of the brand come together.*

Exhibit 16.9

CUSTOMER-CENTRIC MODEL OF BRAND COMMUNITY

A consumer who is a member of a brand community thinks about brand names (e.g., Harley Davidson), the product category (e.g., motorcycles), customers who use the brand (e.g., HOG members), and the marketer who makes and promotes the brand.

Customer-Centric Model of Brand Community

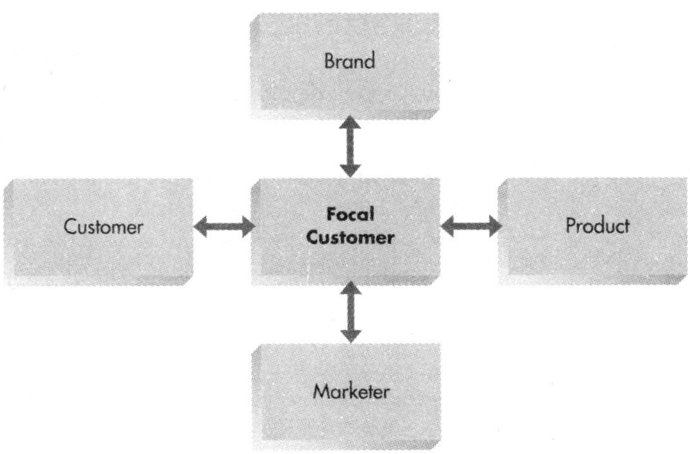

like the music itself.[38] Materialistic consumers and, in some instances, marketers are a dissociative group for participants in Nevada's annual Burning Man event, where self-expression and noncommercial social exchange are the main focus.[39]

marketing IMPLICATIONS The influence of various reference groups has some important implications for marketers.

Associate products with aspirational reference groups

Knowing their target consumers' aspirational reference groups enables marketers to associate their product with that group and use spokespeople who represent it. Because celebrities are an aspirational reference group for some, many companies use celebrities to endorse their products, the way Nokia has hired rappers Jay-Z and Missy Elliott to promote its cell phones to people who admire these rappers.[40]

Accurately represent associative reference groups

It is important to identify and appropriately represent target consumers in ads by accurately reflecting the clothing, hairstyles, accessories, and general demeanor of their associative reference groups.[41] To sell products like skateboards and mountain-climbing equipment, for example, many sports marketers develop promotions featuring actual skateboarders and mountain climbers.[42] New Balance features amateur athletes in ads for its sports shoes, which appear in *Outside, Prevention,* and other publications.[43]

Help to develop brand communities

Marketers can help to create a ***brand community,*** a specialized group of consumers with a structured set of relationships involving a particular brand, fellow customers of that brand, and the product in use.[44] Harley-Davidson does this by organizing events for the 640,000 members of its Harley Owners Group.[45]

Avoid using dissociative reference groups

When appropriate, companies should not use dissociative reference groups in their marketing. McDonald's decided to avoid Ronald McDonald in its promotions in the Middle East because it knew that religious Muslims would not consider a zany, brightly colored clown to be an idol.[46] Similarly, some marketers drop celebrity spokespeople who commit crimes or exhibit other behavior that is offensive to the target market.

Characteristics of Reference Groups

Reference groups can be described according to degree of contact, formality, similarity among members, group attractiveness, density, degree of identification, and the strength of the ties connecting members.

Degree of Contact Reference groups vary in their degree of contact. We may have direct and extensive contact with some reference groups like our immediate circle of friends or family but less contact with our former high school classmates. Reference groups with which we have considerable contact tend to exert the greatest influence.[47] A group with which we have face-to-face interaction, such as family, peers, and professors, is a ***primary reference group.*** In contrast, a ***secondary reference group*** is one that may influence us even though we have no direct contact with its members. We may be members of groups like an Internet chat group or a musical fan club. Although we interact with the group only through such impersonal communication channels as newsletters, its behavior and values can still influence our behavior.

Formality Reference groups also vary in formality. Groups like fraternities, athletic teams, clubs, and classes are formally structured, with rules outlining the criteria for group membership and the expected behavior of members. For example, you must satisfy certain requirements—gaining admission, fulfilling class prerequisites—before you can enroll in particular college courses. Once enrolled, you follow specified rules for conduct by coming to class on time and taking notes. Other groups are more ad hoc, less organized, and less structured. For example, your immediate group of friends is not formally structured and likely has no strict set of rules. Likewise, an informal group of local residents may form a neighborhood watch group. People who attend the same party or vacation on the same cruise also may constitute an informal group.

Homophily: The Similarity Among Group Members Groups vary in their ***homophily,*** the similarity among the members. When groups are homophilous, reference-group influence is likely to be strong because similar people tend to see things in the same way, interact frequently, and develop strong social ties.[48] Group members may have more opportunity to exchange information and are more likely to accept information from one another. Because the sender and receiver are similar, the information they share is also likely to be perceived as credible.

Group Attractiveness Research shows that the attractiveness of a particular peer group can affect how members conform through illicit consumption of drugs and other substances.[49] When members perceive a group as very attractive, they have stronger intentions to conform through illicit consumption behavior. Group attractiveness is much less important, however, when a group can socially punish a member for not conforming to activities the group disapproves of, such as participating in illicit consumption. From a public policy perspective, this implies that making substance abusers seem less attractive may help children and teens resist illicit activities (see Chapters 19 and 20 for more on this issue).

Density Dense groups are those in which group members all know one another. For example, an extended family that gets together every Sunday operates as a dense social network. In contrast, the network of faculty at a large university is less dense because its members have fewer opportunities to interact, share information, or influence one another. In Korea, network density varies by geographic area. A rural village in Korea may have high density because its families have known each other for generations. By contrast, even though Seoul has a high population density (more than 10 million people), many city dwellers may not know one another, making network density low.

Degree of Identification Some characteristics of the individual within a group contribute to the way groups vary. One is the degree of identification a consumer has with a group. Just because people are members of a group does not mean they use it as a reference group. Even though you may be Hispanic or a senior citizen, you need not necessarily regard similar individuals as part of your reference group.[50] The influence that a group has on our behavior is affected by the extent to which we identify with it. One study found that consumers who attend sporting events were more likely to buy a sponsor's products when they strongly identified with the team and they viewed such purchases as a group norm.[51] Moreover, a marketing stimulus that focuses attention on consumers' identification with a certain group (such as ethnic or religious identity) and is relevant to that identification will more likely elicit a positive response.[52]

Exhibit 16.10
TIE-STRENGTH AND SOCIAL INFLUENCE

Strong ties (denoted by the thick red line) are people with whom we have a close, intimate relationship. As relationships become less close and intimate, tie-strength weakens. If you were a marketer, whom would you target in this network? Why?

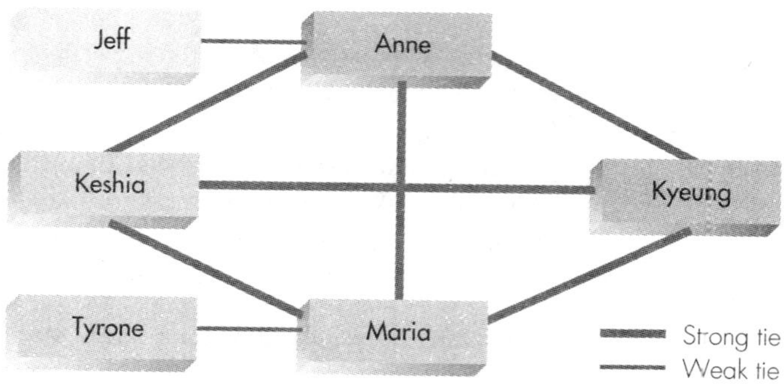

Tie-Strength Another characteristic describing individuals within a group is ***tie-strength.***[53] A strong tie means that two people are connected by a close, intimate relationship, often characterized by frequent interpersonal contact. A weak tie means that the people have a more distant, nonintimate relationship, with limited interpersonal contact. Exhibit 16.10 illustrates these concepts. Here, Anne has three very close friends from school: Maria, Kyeung, and Keshia. She also knows Jeff from her health club; Tyrone is Maria's distant cousin. The solid red lines connect individuals who know one another, with the width of the line indicating how strong the tie is. Thus Anne, Maria, Kyeung, and Keshia are strongly tied to one another. Maria has a weak tie with Tyrone, and Anne has a weak tie with Jeff.

marketing IMPLICATIONS The characteristics that describe reference groups have some important marketing implications.

Understanding information transmission
Homophily, degree of contact, tie-strength, and network density can significantly influence whether, how much, and how quickly information is transmitted between and among consumers within a group. Within dense networks, where consumers are in frequent contact and are connected by strong ties, information about acquiring, using, and disposing of an offering—or related offerings—is likely to be transmitted quickly. The best way for marketers to disseminate information rapidly within a market is to target individuals in dense networks characterized by strong ties and frequent contact.

Formal reference groups as potential targets
Formal reference groups can provide marketers with clear targets for marketing efforts. The Jessica Lal murder case that shook Delhi more for the acquittal of the accused was again put up for fresh investigations, trials and judicial hearing. All this happened because of immense pressure from public, media and pressure from the apex court of the country, the Supreme Court of India. Some of these representations came through formal sources, where citizens came together and in some, the mass and media were mobilized to gain an opinion, which worked in favour of reopening the trial again.

Homophilous consumers as targets
Marketers may use the concept of homophily to market their products. If you log on to Amazon.com and find a book you like, the recommendation system points you to more books you might like based on the purchases of consumers who bought the first book. The principle is that you might share the reading tastes of people that the site considers to be similar to you.

Targeting the network

Sometimes it makes sense for marketers to target the network itself. Verizon, for example, targets families with offers of one large pool of monthly cell phone minutes to be shared among all family members.[55] Health clubs target networks when they offer consumers a discount if a friend joins. Marketers may also encourage referrals by asking consumers to "tell a friend about us."

Understanding the strength of weak ties

Although weak ties may seem to have little potential for marketers, the opposite is true. Because weak ties often serve as "bridges" connecting groups, they can play a powerful role in propagating information *across* networks. In Exhibit 16.10, for instance, Maria serves as a bridge between her four friends and her extended family. Once she gives information to Tyrone, he can communicate it to others with whom he has ties. Weak ties therefore serve a gatekeeping function by transporting information from one group to another.[56] Restaurants and even small shanties selling food sometimes sell more through word of mouth, than through formal publicity. Most cities have such outlets, where the consumers are purely driven through word of mouth promotion. Mahesh Lunch Home in Mumbai, Karims in Delhi, or Nizams in Kolkata are a few examples of food outlets which rely on word of mouth selling.

Marketers can also use weak ties to identify new networks for marketing efforts. For example, direct selling organizations like Tupperware and charitable organizations like the American Cancer Society target individual consumers as selling (or fundraising) agents and rely on their interpersonal networks to reach others.[58] Individuals can tap not only consumers with whom they have strong ties, but also those with whom ties are weak. Girl Scouts sell cookies to friends and relatives plus neighbors, parents' coworkers, and people shopping at grocery stores. Recognizing the value of this technique, marketers try to sell all kinds of products through home parties, from Bible videos and raspberry salsa to personal computers and educational toys.[59]

These types of markets are called ***embedded markets*** because the social relationships among buyers and sellers change the way the market operates.[60] In other words, the social relationship you have with a seller may influence the way you react to his or her selling efforts. You are more likely to buy Girl Scout cookies from your neighbor's daughter than from a girl you have never met because you want to remain on good terms with your neighbor. Your future interactions with her may depend on whether you buy cookies from her daughter.

Reference Groups Affect Consumer Socialization

One way reference groups influence consumer behavior is through socialization, the process by which individuals acquire the skills, knowledge, values, and attitudes that are relevant for functioning in a given domain. ***Consumer socialization*** is the process by which we learn to become consumers and come to know the value of money; the appropriateness of saving versus spending; and how, when, and where products should be bought and used.[61] Through socialization, consumers learn motives and values as well as the knowledge and skills for consumption, although some observers worry that consumer socialization encourages children to see material goods as a path to happiness, success, and achievement.[62] Consumer socialization can occur in many ways, as the following sections show.[63]

People as Socializing Agents Reference groups like family and friends play an important role as socializing agents. Parents may, for example, instill values of thriftiness by directly teaching their children the importance of saving money, letting the children observe them being thrifty, or rewarding children for being thrifty. One study found that direct teaching was most effective for instilling consumer skills in younger children and observational learning was most effective for older children.

Intergenerational influence—information, beliefs, and resources being transmitted from one generation (parents) to the next (children)—affects consumers' acquisition and use of certain product categories and preferred brands.[64] Research shows that children are using brand names as cues for consumer decisions by the time they are 12 years old.[65] Note that parenting styles and socialization patterns vary from culture to culture.[66] In individualistic cultures like Australia and the United States (see Chapter 15), where many parents are relatively permissive, children develop consumer skills at an earlier age. In contrast, children in a collectivist culture such as India, where parents tend to be stricter, understand advertising practices at a later age.

Moreover, parents affect socialization by influencing what types of products, TV programs, and ads their children are exposed to. Some parents are very concerned about children's exposure to violent and sexually explicit programming and products and actively regulate what their children watch and what games they play.[67] Even grandparents can play a powerful socializing role. [12]Besides the influence grandparents have on their grandchildren while they are raising them – such as in academic success and psychological well-being – grandparents also affect grandchildren even when they do not live under the same roof with them. When children face high risk situations such as poverty and parental mental illness, grandparents can make a difference by positively affecting a child's development. Notably, recent findings have supported how grandparents buffer the negative effects of high risk on children. High risk settings that include poverty, parental mental illness, and stressful family events are found to be causes of maternal depression. Maternal depression has notable negative effects on parenting and children's functioning, effects which have been found to be lessened by children's sense of emotional closeness to their grandparents.

The effect of reference groups as socializing agents can change over time. Parents have substantial influence on young children, but their influence wanes as children grow older and interact more with their peers.[69] Similarly, your high school friends probably had a powerful effect on your values, attitudes, and behaviors as a teen, but they likely have much less impact now. Because we associate with many groups throughout our lives, socialization is a lifelong process.

The Media and the Marketplace as Socializing Agents TV programs, movies, music, video games, the Internet, and ads can also serve as socializing agents. Consider the fact that boys are depicted in ads as more knowledgeable, aggressive, active, and instrumental to actions than girls are. These sex role stereotypes can affect children's conceptions of what it is like to be a boy versus a girl.[70] In addition, consumer products may be used as socializing agents, which means our childhood toys might have influenced who we are and what was expected of us.[71] One study found that parents were likely to give their boys sporting equipment, military toys, and vehicles. In contrast, girls were more likely to receive dolls, dollhouses, and domestic toys.[72] Not surprisingly, studies have shown that children of 20 months can already distinguish "boy" toys from "girl" toys. These effects seem to occur at least in part because parents encourage the use of what they consider sex-appropriate toys and discourage cross-sex interests, especially for boys.[73] As children mature, they can become more suspicious of media and marketplace socializing agents; teens are particularly skeptical of advertising claims, some studies show.[74]

Normative Influence

Thus far you have learned about various sources of influence—general, special, and groups. These sources can exert two types of influence, normative and informational (see Exhibit 16.11). Assume that you are at a dinner interview with a prospective employer who tells you she is a vegetarian. Although you love beef, you may be reluctant to order it because you want to make a good impression, so you order a vegetarian dish. Your host has just communicated information about your expected behavior.

Normative influence, which is what you felt in this example, is social pressure designed to encourage conformity to the expectations of others.[75] Chapter 6 discussed normative influences in the context of how they affect our intentions and consumption decisions. The term *normative influence* derives from ***norms,*** society's collective decisions about what behavior should be. For example, we have norms for which brands and stores are "in" as well as norms that discourage stealing and impulse buying.[76] Morals also exert normative influence about what is right and wrong, and they can strongly influence attitudes toward cigarette smoking, for example.[77]

Normative influence implies consumers will be sanctioned or punished if they do not follow the norms, just as they will be rewarded for performing the expected behaviors. To illustrate, a prospective boss may reward you with a job offer or deny you a job, depending on your behavior in the interview. Middle school girls impose sanctions by treating classmates differently when they do not conform to the dress norm.[78] The London department store Harrods bounces consumers who violate its dress code by wearing flip-flop shoes, dirty clothing, or clothing that is too revealing.[79]

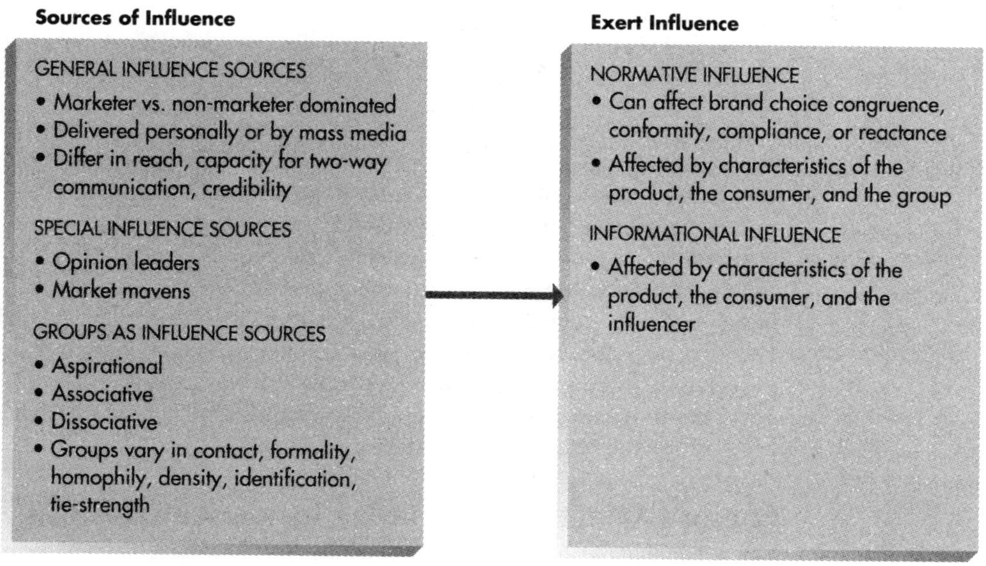

Exhibit 16.11

SOURCES OF INFLUENCE AND TYPES OF INFLUENCE *General influence sources, special influence sources, and specific groups can affect consumer behavior by exerting normative and/or informational influence.*

How Normative Influence Can Affect Consumer Behavior

Normative influence can have several important effects on consumption behaviors.

Brand-Choice Congruence and Conformity Normative influence affects ***brand-choice congruence***—the likelihood that consumers will buy what others in their group buy. If you compare the types of foods, clothes, music, hairstyles, and cars that you buy with the selections of your friends, you will probably find that you and your friends have made similar choices.[80] Friends, family members, and others in your social network may also influence the types of goods and services you buy as gifts.[81] Simply rehearsing what to say in anticipation of discussing a particular brand purchase with others can change the way consumers think and feel about the product and its features.[82]

Normative influence can also affect ***conformity,*** the tendency for an individual to behave as the group behaves. Conformity and brand-choice congruence may be related. To illustrate, you might conform by buying the same brands as others in your group,[83] although brand-choice congruence is not the only way for you to conform. You may also conform by performing activities that the group wants you to perform, such as initiation rites, or by acting the way the group acts. For example, your actions at a party might depend on whether your companions are your parents or your college friends. In each case, you are conforming to a certain set of expectations regarding appropriate behavior. One study found that the norms established by social and brand relationships can influence consumer behavior, as well.[84]

Pressures to conform can be substantial.[85] Research examining group pressure toward underage drinking and drug consumption found that students worried about how others would perceive them if they refused to conform to the expected behavior of the group. Other studies have shown that conformity increases as more people in the group conform. Note that conformity varies by culture. Compared with consumers in the United States, for example, the Japanese tend to be more group oriented and more likely to conform to what group desires.

Compliance Versus Reactance ***Compliance,*** a somewhat different effect of normative influence, means doing what someone asks us to do. You are complying if, when asked, you fill out a marketing research questionnaire or purchase the products sold at a home party. Parents comply with children by purchasing foods or toys or allowing activities (such as parties) that kids request. However, when we believe our freedom is being threatened, a boomerang effect occurs and we engage in ***reactance***—doing the opposite of what the individual or group wants us to do. For example, if a salesperson pressures you too much, you may engage in reactance by refusing to buy whatever he or she is trying to sell.[86]

Factors Affecting Normative Influence Strength

The strength of normative influence depends on the characteristics of the product, the consumer, and the group to which the consumer belongs.

Product Characteristics Researchers have hypothesized that reference groups can influence two types of decisions: (1) whether we buy a product within a given category and (2) what brand we buy. However, whether reference groups affect product and brand decisions also depends on whether the product is typically consumed in private or public and whether it is a necessity or luxury. As shown in Exhibit 16.12, mattresses and hot-water heaters are considered privately consumed necessities, whereas digital cameras and DVD players are considered publicly consumed luxuries. This exhibit reflects predictions, validated in the United States and Thailand, about when reference groups will affect these decisions.

One prediction is that because we must buy necessity items, reference groups are likely to have little influence on whether we buy such products. However, reference groups might exert some influence on whether we buy a luxury item. For example, your friends will probably not influence whether you buy a hot-water heater or whether you buy shoes; because they are necessities, you are going to buy them regardless. But they might influence whether you get an iPod or a DVD player. In part, this is because luxury products communicate status—something that may be valued by group members. Also, luxury items may communicate your special interests and values and thus who you are and with whom you associate.

A second prediction is that products consumed in public give others the opportunity to observe which brand we have purchased. For example, cars are publicly consumed items, which means that other people know whether we drive a Wagon R or a Santro. In contrast, few people see which brand of mattress we buy because we use this product in private. Different brand images communicate different things to people, so reference groups are likely to have considerable influence on the brand we buy when the product is publicly consumed but not when it is privately consumed. Moreover, a publicly consumed product provides opportunities for sanctions, whereas it would be difficult for groups to develop norms and sanctions for

Exhibit 16.12
REFERENCE GROUP INFLUENCES ON PUBLICLY AND PRIVATELY CONSUMED PRODUCTS

Reference groups tend to influence consumption of a product category only when the product is a luxury (not a necessity). Reference groups tend to influence brand only when the product is consumed in public (not when it is consumed in private). Give some examples of your own to illustrate the matrix.

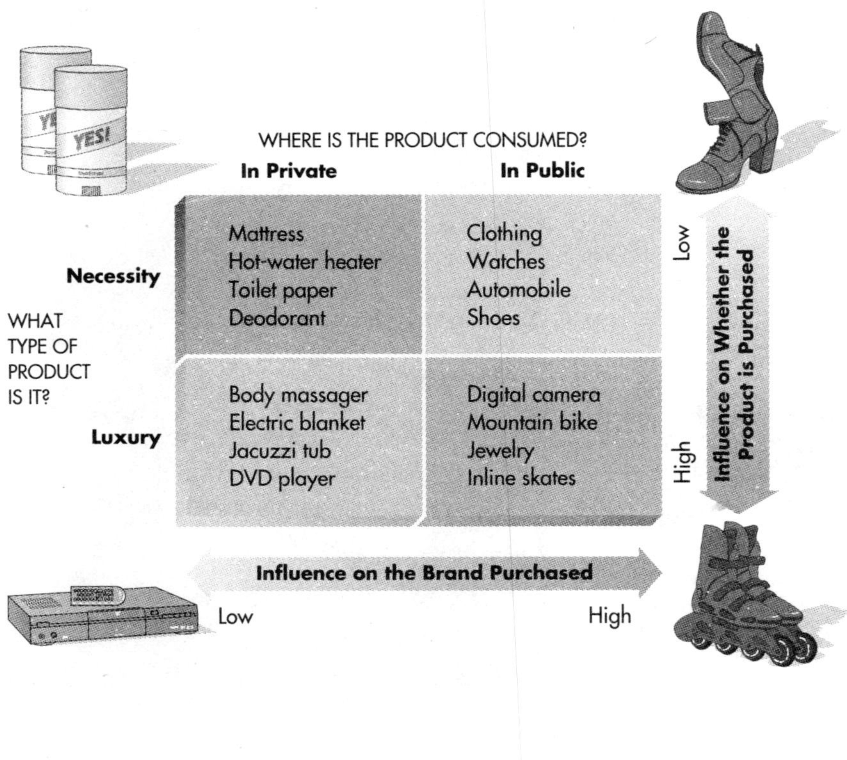

violations when the product is consumed privately. Therefore, reference groups influence product category choice for luxuries but not necessities and influence brand choice for products consumed in public but not those consumed in private.[87]

The significance of the product to the group is yet another characteristic that affects normative influence.[88] Some products, for instance, designate membership in a certain group. A varsity sports jacket may signify membership on a sports team and play a significant role in designating in-group and out-group status. The more central a product is to the group, the greater the normative influence the group exerts over its purchase. Finally, whether a product is perceived as embarrassing may influence acquisition and consumption behavior that occurs in a more public setting.[89]

Consumer Characteristics The personalities of some consumers make them readily susceptible to influence by others.[90] The trait of competitiveness, for instance, can influence conspicuous consumption behavior.[91] Mahindra's Scorpio is positioned towards a target audience who is an achiever and flaunts its wealth. In one of the advertisement it says, "Now other cars will suffer from low self esteem." Exhibit 16.13 illustrates another advertisement from Scorpio focusing on susceptibility to personal influence. Consumers who are susceptible to interpersonal influence try to enhance their self-image by acquiring products that they think others will approve of. These consumers are also willing to conform to others' expectations about which products and brands to buy.

In addition, a personality characteristic called "attention to social comparison information" (ATSCI) is related to normative influence. Exhibit 16.13 shows several items from an ATSCI scale. People who are high on this personality trait pay close attention to what others do and use this information to guide their own behavior. For example, research shows that people feel lower self-esteem when they are exposed to idealized ad images of financial success or physical attractiveness.[93] Not surprisingly, when consumers are susceptible to normative influence, they tend to react more positively to communications highlighting product benefits that help them avoid social disapproval.[94]

Tie-strength also affects the degree of normative influence. When ties are strong, individuals presumably want to maintain their relationships with others, and are therefore motivated to conform to the group's norms and wishes.[95] Normative influence is affected by a consumer's identi-

Exhibit 16.13
SUSCEPTIBILITY TO INTERPERSONAL INFLUENCE AND ATTENTION TO SOCIAL COMPARISON INFORMATION *The Scorpio advertisements target the consumers who flaunt and try to create an impact through influence it makes.*

fication with the group, as well.[96] When a member of a group such as a family or subculture does not identify with that group's attitudes, behaviors, and values, normative reference-group influence will be weak.

Group Characteristics The characteristics of the group can influence the degree of normative influence. One characteristic is the extent to which the group can deliver rewards and sanctions, known as the degree of reward power or ***coercive power.***[97] To illustrate, your friends probably have more influence over your clothing choices than your neighbors do, because friends have greater opportunity and more motivation—greater coercive power—to deliver sanctions if they consider your clothing inappropriate or out of style.

Group cohesiveness and group similarity also affect the degree of normative influence.[98] Cohesive groups and groups with similar members may communicate and interact on a regular basis. Thus they have greater opportunity to convey normative influences and deliver rewards and sanctions. Also, research shows that if a company calls consumers' attention to their cultural identity, increased awareness of membership in a particular group can influence their decisions based on group norms.[99] In addition, normative influence tends to be greater when groups are large and when group members are experts.[100] As an example, you might be more inclined to buy a bottle of wine recommended by a group of wine experts than one recommended by a casual acquaintance.

marketing IMPLICATIONS

Marketers can take a variety of actions based on normative influences and the factors that affect their strength. Exhibit 16.14 shows one example.

Demonstrate rewards and sanctions for product use/nonuse

Marketers may be able to create normative influence by using advertising to demonstrate rewards or sanctions that can follow from product use or nonuse. For example, beer or liquor ads sometimes show friends approving of the purchase or consumption of the advertised brand.

Exhibit 16.14
USING NORMATIVE INFLUENCE

This ad provides normative influence by identifying ways in which the homemaker or the woman of the family takes care of the house and the family members.

Create norms for group behavior

Marketing organizations may create groups with norms to guide consumers' behavior. Members of Weight Watchers, for example, who adhere to the norms (by losing weight) are rewarded by group praise. Because influence is greater when consumption is public rather than private, another marketing strategy is to make a private behavior public. Group discussions about eating behaviors is one way that Weight Watchers makes private information public.

Create conformity pressures

Marketers may also attempt to create conformity. For example, they may actively associate a product with a certain group so that their product becomes a badge of group membership. They may simulate conformity by showing actors in an ad behaving similarly with respect to a product, the way some antismoking campaigns portray teens who do not smoke.[101] Conformity may also be enhanced by publicizing others' conformity, which is what happens at Tupperware parties and at charity fundraisers like telethons.

Use compliance techniques

The ***foot-in-the-door technique*** suggests that marketers can enhance compliance by getting a consumer to agree first to a small favor, then to a larger one, and then to an even larger one. For example, a salesperson may first ask a consumer his or her name and then ask what the person thinks of a given product. After complying with these requests, the consumer may be more inclined to comply with the salesperson's ultimate request to purchase the product.[102] Consumers may comply with large marketing research requests such as filling out a long survey if they have first agreed to a smaller request such as answering a few research questions over the phone.[103]

With the ***door-in-the-face technique,*** the marketer first asks the consumer to comply with a very large and possibly outrageous request, then presents a smaller and more reasonable request. For example, a salesperson might ask a consumer whether she wants to buy a $500 piece of jewelry. When the consumer says no, the salesperson might then ask if she wants to buy a set of earrings on sale for only $25.[104] Because the consumer perceives that the requestor has given something up by moving from a large to a small request, he or she feels obligated to reciprocate by responding to the smaller request.

A third approach is the ***even-a-penny-will-help technique.***[105] With this technique, marketers ask the consumer for a very small favor—so small it almost does not qualify as a favor. For example, marketers collecting money for a charity may indicate that even a penny will help those in need. Salespeople making cold calls may tell prospective clients that even one minute of their time will be valuable. Because people would look foolish denying these tiny requests, they usually comply and, in fact, often give an amount appropriate for the situation.

Ask consumers to predict their behavior

Simply asking consumers to predict their own behavior in taking a certain action often increases the likelihood that they will actually behave in that way.[106] For example, a marketer of products containing recycled parts might ask consumers to predict their behavior in supporting the environment by buying or using products made with reclaimed materials.[107] This may remind consumers that they have not been doing enough to live up to their own standards in supporting the environment—in turn, leading to purchases that will fulfill the consumers' self-prophecy.

Provide freedom of choice

Because reactance usually occurs when people feel their freedom is being threatened, marketers need to ensure that consumers believe they have freedom of choice. For example, a salesperson might show a variety of DVD players, discussing the advantages of each. The consumer will feel a greater sense of control over whether to buy at all, and if so, which item to buy.

Informational Influence

In addition to normative influence, reference groups and other influence sources can exert ***informational influence*** by offering information to help make decisions.[108] For example, chat groups on Internet travel sites exert informational influence by providing travel tips to prospective travelers. Friends exert informational influence by telling you which movie is playing at the local theater, and the media exert informational influence by reporting that certain foods may be health hazards.

How Informational Influence Can Affect Consumer Behavior

Informational influence is important because it can affect how much time and effort consumers devote to information search and decision making. If you can get information easily from a friend, you may be reluctant to conduct an extensive, time-consuming information search when making a decision. Thus if you want a new DVD player and a trusted friend says the brand he just bought is the best he has ever had, you might simply buy the same one.

Although informational influence can reduce information search, it is sometimes important for marketers to increase the likelihood that consumers will engage in information search. For example, few consumers are likely to know about the benefits of a new, superior offering. The company must therefore launch a campaign to build product awareness and encourage consumers to compare products.

Factors Affecting Informational Influence Strength

The extent to which informational influence is strong or weak depends on the characteristics of the product, of the consumer and the influencer, and of the group.

Product Characteristics Consumers tend to be susceptible to informational influence when considering complex products such as electronic appliances that consumers cannot easily understand how to use.[109] Consumers are also more susceptible to informational influence when they perceive product purchase or usage to be risky.[110] Thus consumers may be affected by information they receive about cosmetic surgery, given its formidable financial and safety risks. Consumers may also be more open to informational influence when brands are very different from one another. Because consumers have difficulty determining which brand is best for them when the brands are quite distinct, they attach significance to information learned from others.[111]

Consumer and Influencer Characteristics Characteristics of both the consumer and the influencer affect the extent of informational influence. Such influence is likely to be greater when the source or group communicating the information is an expert,[112] especially if the consumer either lacks expertise or has had ambiguous experiences with the product. For example, given their lack of knowledge and confidence about the home-buying process, first-time home buyers may consider carefully the information conveyed by experts such as real estate agents. Personality traits, such as consumers' susceptibility to reference group influence and attention to social comparison information, should also influence the extent to which consumers look to others for cues on product characteristics.[113]

Like normative influence, informational influence is affected by tie-strength. Individuals with strong ties tend to interact frequently, which provides greater opportunities for consumers to learn about products and others' reactions to them. Note that informational influence may actually affect the ties between individuals. When people establish social relationships that involve sharing information, for example, they may become friends in the process.[114]

Finally, culture may influence the impact of informational influence. One study found that U.S. consumers were more likely than Korean consumers to be persuaded by information-packed ads. Because the Korean culture often focuses on the group and group compliance, Korean consumers may be more susceptible to normative influence than U.S. consumers are.[115]

Group Characteristics Group cohesiveness also affects informational influence. Specifically, members of cohesive groups have both greater opportunity and perhaps greater motivation to share information.

marketing IMPLICATIONS Marketers can incorporate informational influence into their marketing activities in several ways.

Create informational influence by using experts
Because source expertise and credibility affect informational influence, marketers can use sources regarded as expert or credible for a given product category, the way athletic footwear manufacturers use sports stars as spokespeople.

Create a context for informational influence
The likelihood that informational influence will occur depends on the situation. For this reason, marketers should try to create a context for informational influence to occur. One way of creating a context for informational influence is to host or sponsor special events related to the product. Another way is to allow online chats or blogs in a special area of a product's or company's website.[116]

Create informational and normative influence
Marketing efforts may be most successful when *both* normative and informational influence attempts are involved. One study found that only 2 percent of consumers donated blood in the absence of any type of influence, but between 4 and 8 percent did so when either informational or normative influence was present. However, when both forms of influence were used, 22 percent of the consumers donated blood.[117] Also, because source similarity enhances both normative and informational influence, advertisers might enhance influence by using sources that are similar to their target audience. For example, lottery commercials often show sources similar to the target audience winning the lottery. Web-based recommendation systems are another approach to using both normative and informational influence.[118]

Descriptive Dimensions of Information

In the context of consumer behavior, information can be described by the dimensions of valence and modality.

Valence: Is Information Positive or Negative?

Valence describes whether the information is positive or negative. This is very important because researchers have found that negative and positive information affect consumer behavior in different ways.[119] Negative information is more likely than positive information to be communicated. As discussed in Chapter 12, more than half of dissatisfied consumers engage in negative word of mouth. Moreover, dissatisfied consumers talk to three times more people about their bad experiences than satisfied consumers do about their good experiences.[120] In one study, consumers who were dissatisfied with their home rental situation said they told up to ten people about their negative experiences.[121]

Researchers also hypothesize that people pay more attention to and give more weight to negative information than they do to positive information. This means negative information is more influential than positive information is.[122] Most of the information we hear about offerings is positive, so negative information may receive more attention because it is surprising, unusual, and different. Interestingly, one study found that negative movie reviews hurt a movie's box-office performance more than positive reviews enhanced performance—but only during the first week of release.[123]

Negative information may also prompt consumers to attribute problems to the offering itself, not to the consumer who uses it. Thus if you learn that a friend got sick after eating at a new restaurant, you may attribute the outcome to the food (it must be bad) rather than to your friend (he ate too much). Finally, negative information may be diagnostic—that is, we may attach more significance to it because it seems to tell us how offerings differ from one another.

Modality:Does Information Come from Verbal or Nonverbal Channels?

Another dimension describing influence is the modality in which it is delivered—is it communicated verbally or nonverbally? Although norms about group behavior might be explicitly communicated by verbal description, consumers can also infer norms through observation. For instance, a consumer may learn that a can opener is bad by observing someone struggling with it or hearing people discuss their experiences with the product.

The Pervasive and Persuasive Influence of Word of Mouth

Marketers are especially interested in word of mouth, which can affect many consumer behaviors. For example, you may go to see a new movie because your friend said it was great. You may ask a coworker where she gets her hair cut and then go to the same salon. Your neighbor may recommend an electrician, or you may overhear a stranger say that Nordstrom's semiannual sale is next week.[124] More than 40 percent of U.S. consumers ask family and friends for advice when selecting a doctor, a lawyer, or an auto mechanic, although men and women differ in how often they seek advice and from whom (see Exhibit 16.15).[125]

Not only is word of mouth pervasive, it is also more persuasive than written information.[126] One study found that word of mouth was the top source affecting food and household product purchases. It was seven times more effective than print media, twice as effective as broadcast media, and four times more effective than salespeople in affecting brand switching.[127] Online forums and chats, blogs, websites, and e-mail can potentially magnify the effect of word of mouth, because consumers can tell others about good or bad experiences with the click of a mouse.

PERCENT OF MEN AND WOMEN WHO CHOOSE SELECTED PEOPLE AS SINGLE MOST-TRUSTED SOURCE FOR SELECTED PRODUCTS AND SERVICES, FOR THREE MOST-TRUSTED SOURCES, 1995

	First-Ranked	Percent Choosing	Second-Ranked	Percent Choosing	Third-Ranked	Percent Choosing
NEW DOCTOR:						
Men	female relative	26	no one	18	male friend	17
Women	female relative	29	female friend	20	no one	14
WHERE TO GET HAIR CUT:						
Men	no one	38	male friend	25	female relative/friend	12
Women	female friend	45	no one	26	female relative	22
WHAT CAR TO BUY:						
Men	no one	31	male friend	26	male relative	22
Women	male relative	46	male friend	20	no one	19
CAR MECHANIC:						
Men	male friend	40	no one	26	male relative	21
Women	male relative	50	male friend	30	no one	10
WHERE TO GET LEGAL ADVICE:						
Men	male relative	26	male friend	23	no one	17
Women	male relative	31	male friend	16	female relative	14
WHERE TO GET PERSONAL LOAN:						
Men	no one	29	male friend	20	male relative	18
Women	male relative	33	no one	21	professional advisor	12
WHAT MOVIES TO SEE:						
Men	male friend	27	no one	22	female friend	18
Women	female friend	40	no one	19	female relative	15
WHERE TO EAT OUT:						
Men	female friend	26	female relative	21	male friend	21
Women	female friend	42	female relative	18	no one/male relative	11

Source: From Chip Walker, "Word of Mouth," *American Demographics*, July 1995, p.34–35. Reprinted with permission from the July 1995 issue of *American Demographics*. Copyright Crain Communications, Inc., 1995.

Exhibit 16.15

GENDER DIFFERENCES *Men and women differ in how often they ask for advice and from whom they seek the advice. Women are more likely than men to seek word of mouth from others and to use a broader array of sources.*

Knowing this, some companies monitor the Internet to see whether and how their products are being mentioned.[128] Ford, for example, uses special software to find out what consumers are saying online about its vehicles.[129]

Viral marketing, online consumer-to-consumer communication in support of a particular offering, is powerful and credible because the source is non-marketer dominated and the message is delivered personally. To illustrate, Buena Vista Home Entertainment uses viral marketing to promote its DVD movie releases. Recently, it designed instant message backgrounds featuring Lizzie Maguire and other characters for youngsters to download and use in communicating with their friends.[130]

marketing IMPLICATIONS Word of mouth can have a dramatic effect on consumers' product perceptions and an offering's marketplace performance. Many small businesses such as hairstylists, piano instructors, and preschools cannot afford to advertise and rely almost exclusively on word-of-mouth referrals. Doctors, dentists, and lawyers often rely heavily on word of mouth because they fear that extensive advertising will cheapen their professional image. Moreover, product success in some industries (such as entertainment) is ultimately tied to favorable word of mouth.

Preventing and responding to negative word of mouth

Marketers must act to prevent negative word of mouth and to rectify it once it occurs.[131] Rather than ignoring complaints, service providers who empathize with consumers' complaints and respond with free goods or in another meaningful way will be more successful in reducing negative word of mouth. Recently, Wal-Mart decided to respond to criticisms of its employment practices by launching a "Wal-Mart is working for everyone" campaign with positive information about its advancement opportunities, wages, and benefits.[132] In the event of a major crisis, companies must take definite steps to restore consumer confidence (see Exhibit 16.16).[133]

Engineering favorable word of mouth

In addition to creating quality offerings,[134] marketers may try to engineer favorable word of mouth by targeting opinion leaders and using networking opportunities at trade shows, conferences, and public events. Word of mouth or buzz works more positively for films, music and related products where advertising is not pronounced. Infact, the opening example, Hum Tum's promotion was more through word of mouth. Similarly, pharmaceutical companies today are giving away free samples and other gifts in kind, to help the brand stay on top of a doctor's mind while prescribing any kind of related drugs.

Dealing with rumors

Rumors are a special case of negative word of mouth.[136] Companies may use several strategies to deal with false rumors.[137]

- *Do nothing.* Often companies prefer to do nothing because more consumers may actually learn about a rumor from marketers' attempts to correct it. However, this

Exhibit 16.16
RESTORING PUBLIC TRUST

Professional crisis managers recommend these steps when a company is under siege.

DO:	DON'T:
• *Recognize that speed is crucial.* "If you don't have an answer or a solution to the problem, you better be able to tell your audiences that you're working on one," says Rich Blewitt, president of Rowan & Blewitt.	• *Hide what you know.* Being one step behind when evidence of wrongdoing surfaces not only damages your credibility, but also hinders your ability to control the spin, says Victor Kamber, CEO of The Kamber Group.
• *Place customers' interests above your own.* A company must "seem to want to come to the aid of the people in the crisis first, and [put] their own corporate interests last," says Larry Kramer, managing director at GCI Group.	• *Get tied down in the day-to-day details of running the company.* Make this crisis the No. 1 priority. "You've got to have a bunch of people who drop everything and just deal with this," says Mark Braverman, principal, CMG Associates Inc.
• *Take a long-term view.* As the massive Tylenol recall showed, sacrificing a product's image in the short-term can demonstrate responsibility over the long haul.	• *Forget that public perception is more important than reality.* Even if you've done nothing wrong but consumers think you have, their view is what matters, says Steven Fink, president of Lexicon Communications Corp.

strategy can also backfire. When Nike was accused of condoning low wages and abusive conditions in its Asian factories, its image suffered when it did not respond vigorously to the attacks. The company has since responded in various ways, including putting links to labor practices and a virtual factory tour on its website.[138]

- *Do something locally.* Some companies react locally, putting the rumor to rest on a case-by-case basis. Procter & Gamble sent a packet of information about its man-in-the-moon symbol, long rumored to connote devil worship, only to those consumers who called its hotline. In such cases, companies should brief staff members about the rumor and how they should respond to consumers.
- *Do something discreetly.* Companies may want to respond discreetly to a rumor. For example, when rumors circulated that oil companies were contriving oil shortages out of greed, the firms ran a public relations campaign highlighting their socially desirable activities. They did not mention the rumor, but the gist of the campaign clearly ran contrary to the rumor's content.
- *Do something big.* At times, companies may respond with all the media resources at their disposal. They may use advertising to directly confront and refute the rumor, create news refuting the rumor, conduct media interviews to communicate the truth, and hire credible outside opinion leaders to help dispel the rumor.

Tracking word of mouth

Whether word of mouth is positive (like referrals) or negative (like product dissatisfaction or rumors), companies may want to try to identify the source. Through *network analysis,* companies cam try to identify critical information sources by asking where consumers heard the information and then asking all of those sources where, in turn, they heard the story.[139] Marketers can also query consumers about specific details they heard from the source to track the distortion of information and find the key sources responsible for perpetuating it. Then the company can follow up by, for example, thanking or rewarding individuals who communicate positive word of mouth and provide referrals. The company can also design referral-incentive programs that reward both the referrer and referee.[140] Finally, companies should be aware that some institutions can serve as sources of word-of-mouth information. For example, although U.S. consumers may not find the church to be an important clearinghouse for word of mouth, Koreans do.

Summary

Consumers are influenced by many sources—marketer-dominated and non-marketer-dominated, and those that are delivered through the mass media and those that are delivered personally. Consumers regard non-marketer-dominated sources as more credible than marketer-dominated sources. Information delivered personally generally has less reach but more capacity for two-way communication than information from mass-media sources. Opinion leaders (experts in a product category) are special sources of influence that marketers may target through marketing communications.

Reference groups are people with whom individuals compare themselves to guide their values, attitudes, and behaviors. Reference groups are associative, aspirational, and dissociative; they can be described according to their degree of contact, formality, homophily, group attractiveness, density, identification, and tie-strength. Reference groups may play a powerful socializing role, influencing consumers' key actions, values, and behaviors.

These influence sources exert normative and informational influence. Normative influence tends to be greater for products that are publicly consumed, considered luxuries, or regarded as a significant aspect of group membership. Normative influence is also strong for individuals who tend to pay attention to social information. Strong ties and identification with the group increase the likelihood that consumers will succumb to normative influences. Finally, normative influence is greater when groups are cohesive, members are similar, and the group has the power to deliver rewards and sanctions.

Informational influence operates when individuals affect others by providing information. Consumers are most likely to seek and follow informational influence when products are complex, purchase or use is risky, and brands are distinctive. The more expert the influencer and the more consumers are predisposed to listen to others, the greater the informational influence. Informational influence is also greater when groups are more rather than less cohesive.

Social influence varies in valence and modality. Negative information is communicated to more people and given greater weight in decision making than positive information. Marketers are particularly interested in word of mouth, both positive and negative. They may seek out and reward sources of positive information and, when necessary, identify and target sources of negative information, such as rumors. Companies faced with false rumors can do nothing, do something locally, do something discreetly, or do something big.

Questions for Review and Discussion

1. How do sources of influence differ in terms of marketer domination and delivery?
2. Why do companies sometimes target opinion leaders for marketing attention?
3. What are the three types of reference groups, and how can these groups be described?
4. How might consumers respond to normative influence?
5. What three techniques can marketers use to encourage consumer compliance?
6. Differentiate between information valence and modality.
7. Why is word of mouth so important for marketers?

Exercises

1. Keep a word-of-mouth log for 24 hours. Document (a) what information you hear, (b) whether it is positive or negative, (c) what effect you think it will have on your behavior, and (d) why. Think about what implications the entries in your log have for marketers.
2. Take an entry in your word-of-mouth log (from exercise 1) and try to track down the source of the information. Did the information flow within a relatively dense social network, or did it flow across social networks via weak ties? Try to diagram the nature of the information flow within and across various groups.
3. Observe a salesperson trying to make a sale. Try to understand which aspects of his or her selling attempts represent informational influence and which represent normative influence. Was the salesperson successful at inducing a sale? Which concepts from this chapter may explain why or why not?
4. As a marketing manager for a new brand of diet hot chocolate, you want to use an opinion leader to stimulate sales of the brand. How might you identify an opinion leader, and what strategies do you have for using an opinion leader in your marketing communications program?
5. You have recently learned that a lot of positive and negative information is being communicated about the new brand of diet hot chocolate. Should your strategy be to try to bolster the positive information or to stop the negative information? Why?

More Exercises from the Adaptor

1. There have been a spate of sequels launched in the last two years, both in Hollywood and in the Hindi film Industry. Krrish (Koi Mil Gaya), Dhoom 1 and 2, Shrek 1, 2 and now 3. Identify the differences in marketing of the prequel and the sequel and how do you think consumers react to such kind of serialized version of cinema.

References

[1] Source: http://www.yashrajfilms.com/AboutUs/CompanyInfo.aspx?SectionCode=PRO001

[2] Source: http://www.imdb.com/name/nm0007181/

[3] Source: http://www.yashrajfilms.com/Movies/MovieIndividual.aspx?MovieID=66453de4-5f37-4639-8008-ee448ea0e815

[4] Source: http://www.thehindubusinessline.com/2004/08/28/stories/2004082800990500.htm

[5] Source: http://www.smh.com.au/news/biztech/google-brand-tops-the-charts/2007/04/24/1177180618078.html

[6] Source : http://www.indiantelevision.com/special/y2k5/kbc_dviteeya.htm

[7] Source: http://www.indiacar.com/

[8] Source: http://www.chowk.com/show_writer_page.cgi?pen_name=Murad%20Ali%20Baig

[9] Source: http://www.cybersteering.com/pulmain/motoring/motoring.html

[10] Source: http://www.eldis.org/gender/dossiers/Indiasexworkers.htm

[11] Source: http://www.medcindia.org/cgi-bin/Dec05/Banking%20&%20Finance.HTM

[12] Source: http://fycs.ifas.ufl.edu/newsletters/rnycu06/2007/01/protective-role-of-grandparents.html

PART

5 Consumer Behavior Outcomes

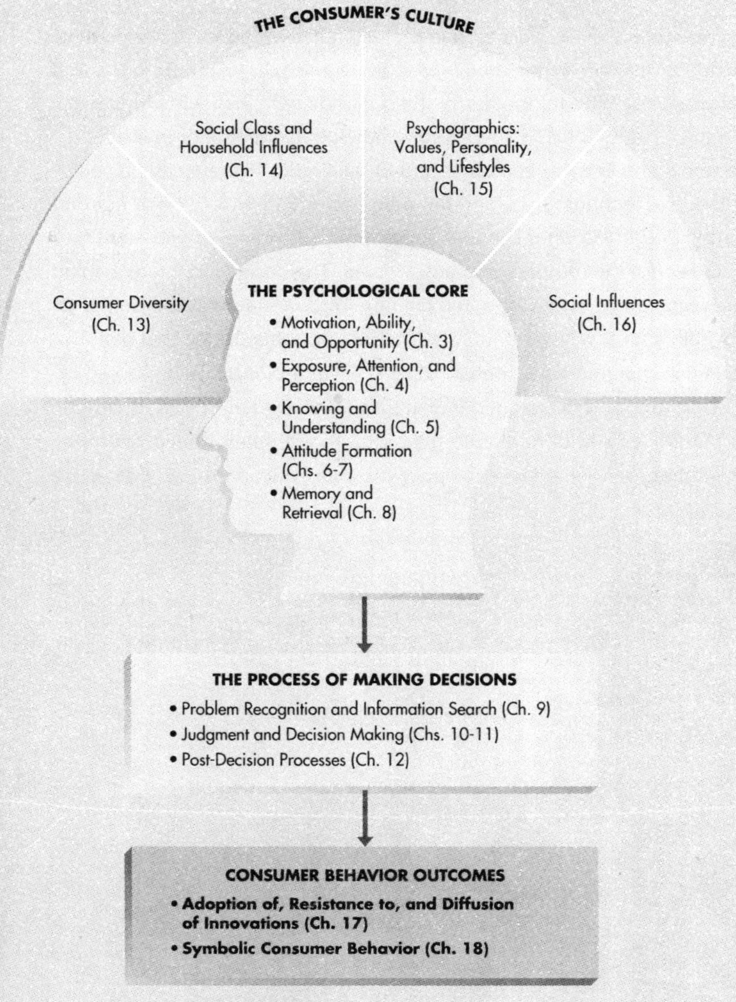

Part Five examines the outcomes of the numerous influences and decision processes discussed in Parts Two, Three, and Four. Chapter 17 builds on the topics of internal decision making and group processes by exploring how consumers adopt innovative offerings and how their adoption decisions affect the spread (diffusion) of a new offering through a market. This chapter also looks at the various factors that make a difference in resistance to an innovation, adoption of an innovation, and diffusion of an offering.

Chapter 18 discusses the fascinating topic of symbolic consumer behavior. Both goods and services can have deep-felt and significant meanings for consumers. These symbolic meanings are affected by rituals related to acquisition, consumption, and disposal. Moreover, the meaning of an offering can be transferred through gift-giving.

chapter **17**

Adoption of, Resistance to, and Diffusion of Innovations

LEARNING OBJECTIVES

After studying this chapter, you will be able to:

- Describe how innovations can be classified in terms of the type of innovation, the type of benefits offered, and the breadth of the innovation.
- Explain how consumers adopt an innovation, why they might resist adoption, and why marketers must understand the timing of innovation adoption decisions.
- Define diffusion and discuss how diffusion curves relate to the product life cycle.
- Outline the main factors that affect adoption, resistance, and diffusion, and show how marketers can use their knowledge of these factors to market more effectively.

INTRODUCTION

The Telecom Boom Takes Over India

[1]The landmark year of India, 1991 ushered in the new telecom policy and with that a complete change of the face of the Indian telecom landscape. Infact, from the mid 80's the market was beginning to transform, Sam Pitroda with his technology working closely with the Govt. of India helped connect the people of India—in far-flung regions and remotest corners, to each other and to the world. His tenacity helped create the concept and technology behind the network of 'STD/PCO' phone booths across the country, in every village. The 600,000 booths, providing employment for a million people, today dot the remotest regions of India. The basic technology behind this network was simple and cheap. Created by Sam Pitroda's team at the Center for Development of Telematics, which he founded in 1984, it was a device that displayed the phone call cost and generated an instant bill at the user's end, instead of at the telephone exchange. This changed Indian telephony. Under Pitroda, C-DoT's key contribution was the RAX, or rural automatic exchange—small, cheap and robust phone switches that helped take telephony to rural India, forming its telecom

Exhibit 17.1
THE MOBILE MANIA

Falling airtime charges, aggressive marketing by telecom operators, cheap and technologically robust hardware makes the mobile market a highly attractive destination in India. It has come a long way, from the time when waiting time to get a phone installed would run into years to now when it is just a phone call away.

backbone. Sam Pitroda then moved on to helping shape telecom policy. In 1987, he was appointed advisor to the Prime Minister of India. In 1989, he became the first chairman of India's Telecom Commission, responsible for all aspects of telecom legislation and development for the country.

[2]Today, the telecom industry has seen a transformation, take for instance the mobile subscriber base touching 100 million by 2006 and 200 million by 2008. The country's mobile services market is forecast to grow by a compound annual rate of 28.3 percent during the next five years, to reach revenues of about $15.6 billion in 2008, according to research firm Gartner Inc. in Stamford, Connecticut. [3]The Telecom Regulatory Authority of India has announced that 41.26 million Indians have subscribed to phone service since the beginning of 2005. Of the 5.33 million phone people who subscribed to phone service in March 2006, 94 percent were solely for mobile phones, bringing the number of Indians with phone service to 140 million. Of those phones, 36 percent are land lines and 64 percent are cell phones. The Telecom Regulatory Authority of India also announced today that 1.3 million Indians have broadband connections.

When mobile telephony came in 1994, the acquisition cost, handset cost as well as the recurring expenditure was too high. At Rs.16.40/- per minute airtime charges, the cost was steep. Add to that handset prices and incoming call charges (incoming calls then were not free). In 1995, bookings opened at Rs.10,000/- and the final entry cost with a basic handset worked close to Rs.25,000/-, a price steep by 1995 standards. The product, considered a luxury product for the crème de la crème had a penetration only at the upper end of the market,. As the product and the services diffused over time, the airtime charges dipped and so did the handset costs. Most operators had by then realised that volumes would be the basis to drive the market and value. Significantly, the market was also moving away from duopoly to accommodate more players, chiefly state run BSNL and MTNL. In 2002, the launch of CDMA changed the market dynamics. As the product had diffused over time into the segment of customers in the initial phase, the next level of customers were seeking lower rates for both services and handset, which the operators were gradually doing.

The Indian cellular market therefore became a classic case of cost based economics. The lower cost of entry brought in more consumers, with high airtime usage. [4]Incidentally the airtime usage cost in India remains the lowest in Asia Pacific. Today operators target SEC C, D and even E segments of the market. The two key drivers to the category, which defined the diffusion process, are the introduction of the prepaid services and the waiver of incoming call charges. The handset companies also manufacture specially designed cellular phones for the Indian consumer and Nokia 1110 is a case in point. Today, the market is flooded with handsets of all price ranges.Add to that the flexibility of choosing any tariff option from the operator. All this makes cellular phone acquisition easier.

The telecom boom in India, particularly in the cellular market, reflects some of the factors that influence consumers' decisions about innovative offerings, the subject of this chapter (see Exhibit 17.2). The first part of the chapter describes the types of innovations, which can vary in both novelty and benefits. Next is a discussion of the factors that affect an individual consumer's resistance to or adoption of a new product. Different groups of consumers adopt products at different rates; those who tend to buy new products first are known as innovators, as this section indicates. Innovators in India were the first to convert to mobile services, the majority of the population then quickly followed. The final section examines the factors that determine how quickly a new product spreads, or diffuses, through a market like India.

Why are South Korean consumers so willing to switch to broadband? First, competition between service providers keeps the price relatively low (lower than in the United States) and results in a wide variety of offerings. Second, the government actively encourages parents to get broadband for the sake of their children's education—a benefit that fits with the high cultural value placed on education. Third, multinationals such as Samsung and LG make it easy by marketing all sorts of related products, from enhanced handsets to Web-controlled smart appliances. And fourth, half of the population lives in the big cities, so word of new innovations (such as higher download speeds) spreads rapidly.[1]

The rapid rise of broadband in South Korea reflects some of the factors that influence consumers' decisions about innovative offerings, the subject of this chapter (see Exhibit 17.2). The first part of the chapter describes the types of innovations, which can vary in both novelty and benefits. South Koreans recognize that broadband is different from dial-up Internet access, but not so different that they are confused about how it works or what its benefits are. Next is a discussion of the factors that affect an individual consumer's resistance to or adoption of a new product. Different groups of consumers adopt products at different rates; those who tend to buy new products first are known as innovators, as this section indicates. Innovators in South Korea were at the forefront in the rush toward broadband, but the majority of the population has quickly followed. The final section examines the factors affecting how quickly a new product spreads, or diffuses, through a market like South Korea.

Innovations

The ability to develop successful new products is critical to a company's sales and future growth. Kraft Foods, for example, regularly rings up $800 million in annual sales just from the new products it launches in a single year.[2] Given the role that new products play in a company's sales and profitability, it is very important for marketers to understand new products and what drives their success.

Defining an Innovation

A new product, or an ***innovation,*** is an offering that is new to the marketplace. More formally, an innovation is a product, service, attribute, or idea that consumers within a market segment perceive as new and that has an effect on existing consumption patterns (see Exhibit 17.3).[3] Services as well as goods can be innovations, as in the introductory example of broadband Internet access and broadband-enabled cell phones. Ideas can also be described as innovations. For example, social marketers have been active in persuading consumers to adopt such ideas as safe sex, smoke-free workplaces, and abstinence from drugs. In Third World countries, social

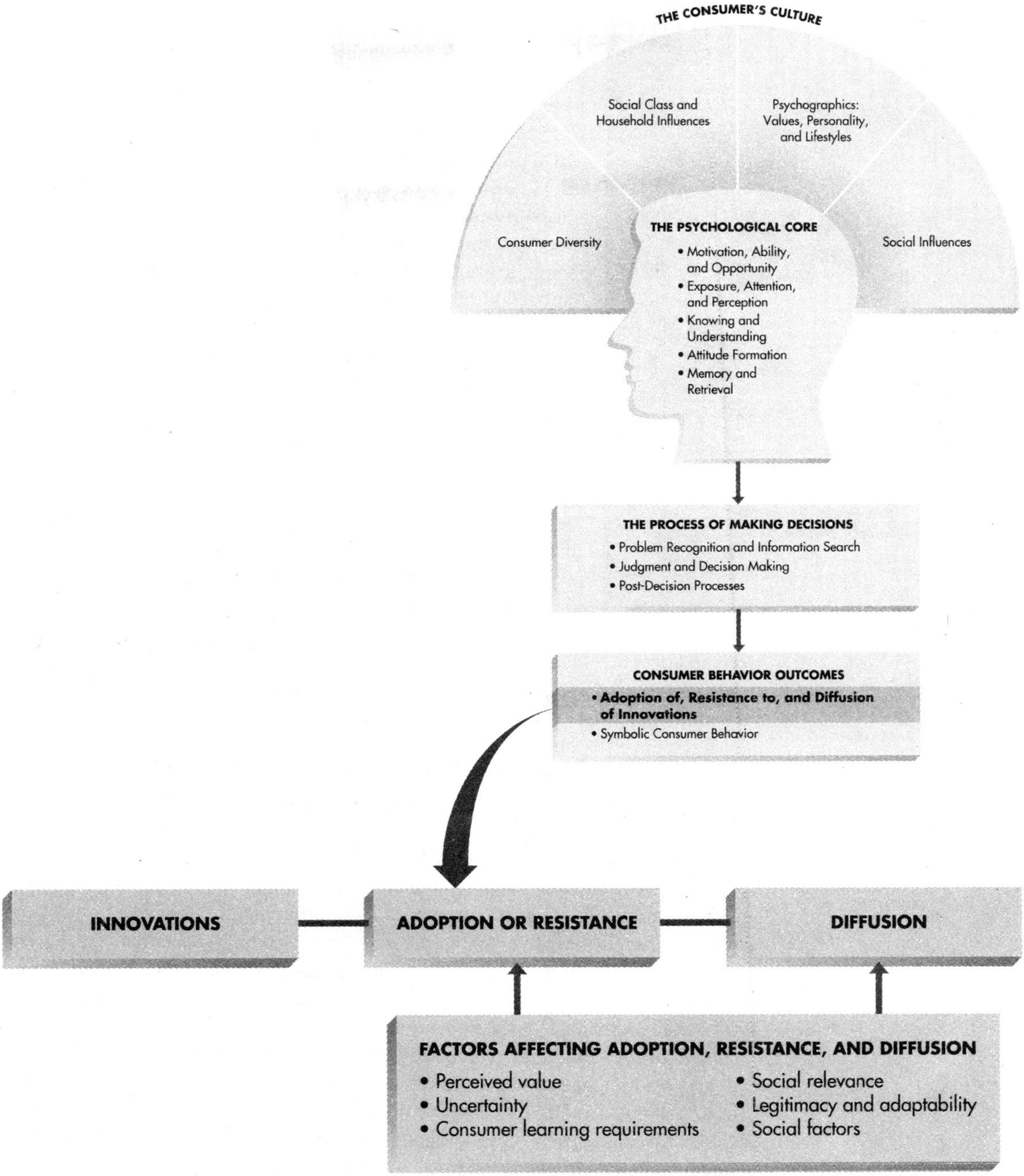

Exhibit 17.2

CHAPTER OVERVIEW: ADOPTION OF, RESISTANCE TO, AND DIFFUSION OF INNOVATIONS *Consumers may decide to adopt (e.g., purchase) or resist a new offering (an innovation). Diffusion reflects how fast an innovation spreads through a market. Adoption, resistance, and diffusion can be influenced by the type of innovation, its breadth, its characteristics, and the social system into which it is introduced.*

Exhibit 17.3
IINNOVATIVE ATTRIBUTES ZIPOUCH'
Launch in India attempts to showcase how food is preserved fresh and odor free in refrigerators and even when the child takes the Tiffin to school

marketers have promoted ideas such as family planning, childhood immunization, and safer and more nutritious food-preparation practices. Often these ideas are supported by related products, such as contraceptives for family planning.[4]

Today, condoms are being marketed more as a measure of AIDS prevention than as a contraceptive. Health centres and AIDS control association like NACO are making attempts to target brothels, slums and places to educate them about safe sex. Also, the shame and hesitation in buying condoms is also being targeted with a new campaign. To help buyers overcome embarrassment associated with buying, using and selling condoms, the United States Agency For International Development (USAID), with support from the Ministry of Health and Family Welfare, has launched a new campaign, Condom Bindas Bol! The aim of the campaign is to increase the use of condoms for avoiding unwanted pregnancies and for preventing sexually transmitted infections including HIV/AIDS.

A second aspect of the definition of innovation is that products, services, attributes, packages, and ideas are innovations if they are perceived as new by consumers, whether or not they actually are new. Propecia, a drug introduced to reduce male baldness, is really the same drug that is sold as Proscar and used to treat prostate problems, although consumers are not likely to know this.[7] On the other hand, research shows that the failure of products that are marketed as new is primarily due to the fact that they don't really provide any unique benefits.[8]

Marketers also define *innovation* with respect to a market segment. Because of small home kitchens and ingrained traditions, the automatic dishwasher is seen as an innovation in Japan, where only seven percent of households own one.[9] Consumers in Third World countries may regard certain appliances and electronic gadgets as entirely new, even though Americans and consumers in other Western countries regard these items as near necessities.

Innovations bring about changes in consumption patterns, altering how, where, when, whether, or why we acquire products. For example, South Korean consumers now do 20 percent of their shopping online, thanks to broadband access.[10] In the Netherlands, consumers can use a handheld scanning device to scan their own groceries while they shop.[11] Both innovations have changed the acquisition process.

Other innovations may change the way we use goods or services. Microwave ovens have changed the way we cook, e-mail has changed the way we communicate, and digital cameras and camera phones have changed the way we take photographs and share them with others. Some innovations influence disposition behavior as well. Increased attention to recycling has brought about innovations such as recyclable and reusable packaging, can crushers, and composters. Finally, online auction sites such as eBay represent an innovation in the way consumers can dispose of unwanted items.

Marketers classify innovations in three main ways: in terms of (1) the type of innovation, (2) the type of benefits offered, and (3) the breadth of innovation.

Innovations Characterized by Degree of Novelty

One way to characterize innovations is to describe the degree of change they create in our consumption patterns.[12]

- A ***continuous innovation*** has a limited effect on existing consumption patterns; it is used in much the same way as the products that came before it. Hybrid gas-electric vehicles such as the Ford Escape hybrid SUV are continuous innovations because drivers must make only minor changes to the way they use and maintain their vehicles. Not surprisingly, most new products are continuous innovations.
- A ***dynamically continuous innovation*** has a pronounced effect on consumption practices. Often these innovations incorporate a new technology. Digital music players equipped with hard-drive storage were originally a dynamically continuous innovation. The product category was pioneered by a Singapore company, Creative Technology, nearly two years before Apple Computer's iPod popularized the innovation.[13] Other examples of dynamically continuous innovations include digital cameras and satellite radio services (that require special receivers).
- A ***discontinuous innovation*** is a product so new that we have never known anything like it before:[14] Airplanes and Internet service providers were once discontinuous innovations that radically changed consumer behavior. Like dynamically continuous innovations, discontinuous innovations often spawn a host of peripheral products and associated innovations. For example, after microwave ovens were introduced, marketers began offering new pans, temperature probes, food products, and cookbooks tailored specifically for microwave cooking.

Based on these three broad innovation types—continuous, dynamically continuous, and discontinuous—innovations can be characterized more specifically according to their degree of novelty on a continuum of newness (see Exhibit 17.4). Discontinuous innovations are the most novel and require the most behavioral change, whereas continuous innovations are the least novel and require the least behavioral change.

Innovations Characterized by Benefits Offered

In addition to their degree of novelty, innovations can be characterized by the benefits they offer. Some new products, services, attributes, or ideas are ***functional innovations*** because they offer functional performance benefits over existing alternatives. For example, hybrid vehicles are more fuel-efficient than traditional gasoline-powered vehicles, a functional performance benefit that helps consumers save money on fuel costs and reduce pollution at the same time. Many functional innovations rely on new technology that allows better performance than existing alternatives. Exhibit 17.5 promotes a functional innovation called InDuo, which tests blood glucose levels in five seconds. The brand also comes with an insulin delivery system that tracks when and how much insulin was last taken.

Aesthetic or ***hedonic innovations*** are new products, services, or ideas that appeal to our aesthetic, pleasure-seeking, and/or sensory needs.[15] New forms of dance or

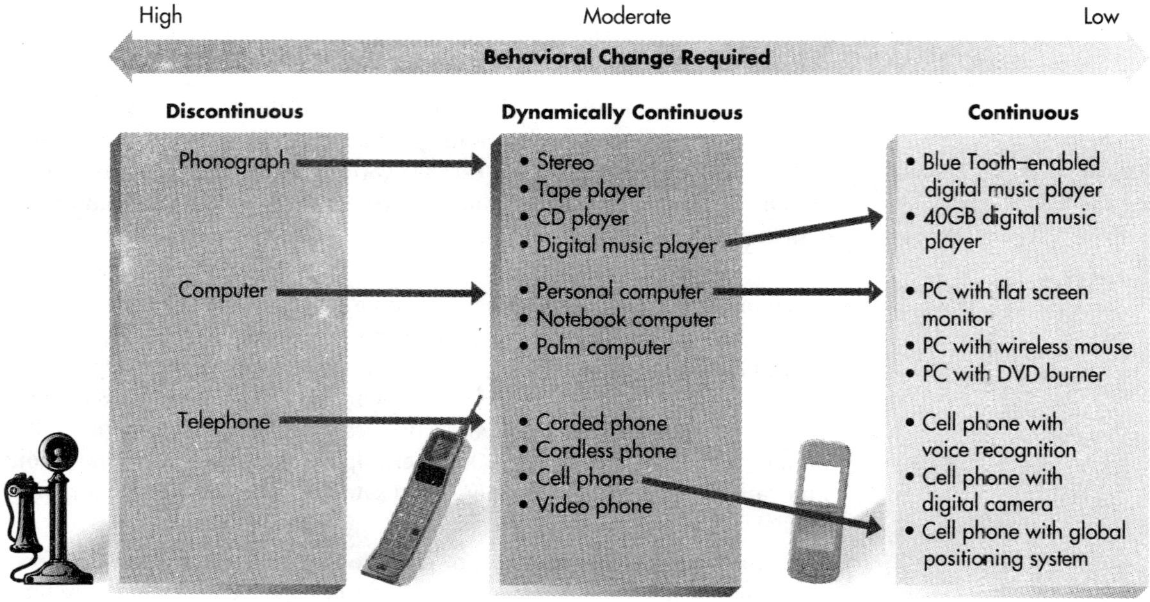

Exhibit 17.4

THE INNOVATION CONTINUUM *Innovations vary in how much behavioral change they require on the part of consumers. Discontinuous innovations (products that are radically new when they are first introduced) require considerable change in consumption patterns, whereas continuous innovations (often extensions of existing products) require very little change.*

exercise, new types of music, new clothing styles, and new types of food all qualify as aesthetic or hedonic innovations. [5]The size of the cooking paste market in India, tipped at Rs.20 crores, might be miniscule but more and more households today are adopting the convenience of the cooking pastes. The drudgery of grounding paste at home, though quality and freshness is unquestioned, is now replaced with the convenience of packaged paste of all possible combinations.

Symbolic innovations are products, services, attributes, or ideas that have new social meaning. In some cases a symbolic innovation is a new offering used exclusively by a particular group of consumers. Using the innovation, therefore, conveys meaning about group membership. New styles of clothing that convey membership in a particular ethnic, age, or gender group may be regarded as symbolic innovations. Movies like Maine Pyaar Kiya, Dil Hain Ke Manta Nahin and yesteryear films of actresses like Sadhna triggered a trend of clothes, hairstyles and even caps suggesting the influence that the films and their stars had on the audience.

In some cases the meaning of the product, not the product itself, is new. For example, although condoms have been around for a long time, their meaning is now couched in terms of preventing the spread of AIDS as opposed to controlling conception. Earrings, once worn by women, are fashionable with men as well. Finally, tattoos, once a symbol of machismo, have gained wide appeal and have different meaning among various consumer groups. Many new products represent blends of innovation types. Thus nutrition bars are designed to offer the functional benefits of protein and vitamins with the hedonic benefit of good taste.

Innovations Characterized by Breadth

Breadth of innovation refers to the range of new and different uses for a particular product. Baking soda, for example, has enjoyed a long life in part because it has been used as a baking ingredient, a tooth polisher, a carpet deodorizer, and a refrigerator deodorizer (see Exhibit 17.6). Teflon, originally developed to keep food from sticking to cookware, is now being used as an ingredient in men's suits. It helps to resist spills, and it retains its resistance through repeated washing and dry cleaning.[18]

Adoption of Innovations and Resistance to Adoption

Because the success of their new offerings is so important to companies, marketers need to understand how a consumer or household makes an ***adoption*** decision for an innovation. Adoption decisions represent a continuation of the choice decisions examined in Chapters 10 and 11. Initially, marketers are interested in whether consumers would even consider adopting an innovation, because consumers sometimes resist adoption. Marketers also want to know how consumers adopt products and how they decide whether to buy an innovation. Finally, marketers are interested in when a consumer buys an innovation, in relation to other consumers.

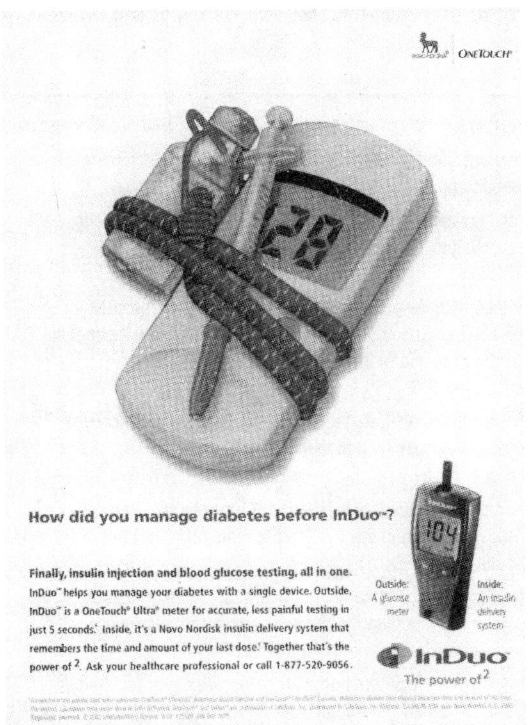

Exhibit 17.5
FUNCTIONAL INNOVATION
Drug companies often introduce functional innovations like the one shown here.

Exhibit 17.6
CHANGING ROLE OF CONDOMS
Increasingly, condoms are now being marketed as an AIDS prevention measure and for safe sex, shifting from the traditional role of a contraceptive. Bold messages such as these are flashed across AIDS prone belts of India.

Resistance to Adoption

Adoption will take place only if consumers do not resist the innovation. ***Resistance*** is consumers' desire not to buy the innovation, even in the face of pressure to do so.[19] Consumers sometimes resist adopting innovations because it is simpler or seems preferable to continue using a more familiar product or service. For example, many consumers resist switching to a new software program or upgrading to a new PC because they fear the new products will be too complicated or will offer few new features that they can actually use.[20]

Resistance may also be high if consumers think that using the product involves some risk. Exhibit 17.7 shows that consumers often resist new technologies because they perceive that the negative effects are likely to outweigh the positive effects.[21] In addition, research shows that consumers with a low need for change and a low need for cognition are the most likely to resist innovations; those with a high need for change and a high need for cognition are the least likely to resist.[22]

Note that resistance and adoption are separate concepts. An individual can resist purchasing an innovation without ever progressing to the point of adoption. If an individual does adopt a product, he or she has presumably overcome any resistance that might have existed initially. Marketers have to understand whether, why, and when consumers resist innovations—because the product will fail if resistance is too high. Marketers typically use a number of tactics to reduce consumers' resistance to an innovation. As discussed later in this chapter, characteristics of the innovation,

Exhibit 17.7
EIGHT CENTRAL PARADOXES OF TECHNOLOGICAL PRODUCTS

Consumers sometimes have mixed reactions to technologies because they create some of the paradoxes noted here. When the negative sides of these paradoxes are salient, consumers will likely resist an innovation.

Paradox	Description
Control/chaos	Technology can facilitate regulation or order, and technology can lead to upheaval or disorder.
Freedom/enslavement	Technology can facilitate independence or fewer restrictions, and technology can lead to dependence or more restrictions.
New/obsolete	New technologies provide the user with the most recently developed benefits of scientific knowledge, and new technologies are already or soon to be outmoded as they reach the marketplace.
Competence/incompetence	Technology can facilitate feelings of intelligence or efficacy, and technology can lead to feelings of ignorance or ineptitude.
Efficiency/inefficiency	Technology can facilitate less effort or time spent in certain activities, and technology can lead to more effort or time in certain activities.
Fulfills/creates needs	Technology can facilitate the fulfillment of needs or desires, and technology can lead to the development or awareness of needs or desires previously unrealized.
Assimilation/isolation	Technology can facilitate human togetherness, and technology can lead to human separation.
Engaging/disengaging	Technology can facilitate involvement, flow, or activity, and technology can lead to disconnection, disruption, or passivity.

Source: From David Glen Mick and Susan Fornier, "Paradoxes of Technology: Consumer Cognizance, Emotions, and Coping Strategies," *Journal of Consumer Research*, vol. 25, September 1998, p. 126. Reprinted with permission of The University of Chicago Press.

the social system in which consumers operate, and marketing tactics all influence consumers' resistance to innovations.

How Consumers Adopt Innovations

In studying consumers' adoption decisions, marketers find it useful to distinguish between high-effort and low-effort decisions. Adoption follows the high-effort hierarchy of effects in a high-effort situation and the low-effort hierarchy of effects in a low-effort situation.

High-Effort Hierarchy of Effects In some cases, the consumer becomes aware of an innovation, thinks carefully about it, gathers as much information as possible about it, and forms an attitude based on this information. If his or her attitude is favorable, the consumer may try the product. If the trial experience is favorable, the consumer may decide to adopt the new product. This ***high-effort hierarchy of effects*** is illustrated in the top half of Exhibit 17.8 and corresponds to the high-effort attitude formation, search, judgment, and choice processes described in earlier chapters.

Consumers' motivation, ability, and opportunity (MAO) determine whether a high-effort adoption process occurs. A high-effort adoption process often takes place when consumers think the innovation incurs psychological, social, economic, financial, or safety risk. For example, the consumer may think that wearing a new style of clothing is socially risky and will wait for others to make the first move. Or the consumer may carefully consider the benefits of buying a DVD player because of the high cost of replacing an entire collection of videotapes with DVDs.

Often a high-effort decision-making process is related to the type of innovation. In particular, consumers are more likely to follow a high-effort decision-making process when the innovation is discontinuous (as opposed to continuous) because they know less about the innovation and must learn about it. Compared with novices, experts with considerable knowledge of the product category need more information before they can understand and appreciate the benefits of a discontinuous innovation.[23] Also, a high-effort adoption process may be used when many people are involved in the decision, as in a family or an organization.[24]

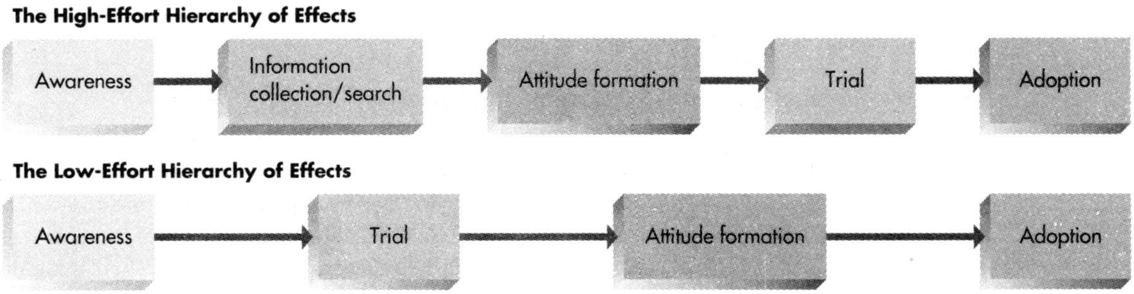

Exhibit 17.8

ADOPTION DECISION PROCESS *The amount of effort we engage in before we decide to adopt an innovation varies. In some cases we engage in considerable effort (e.g., extensive information search and evaluation of an offering). In other cases the adoption process involves limited effort. In such cases we first adopt the innovation and then decide whether we like it.*

Low-Effort Hierarchy of Effects When the new product involves less risk (as might be the case with a continuous innovation) and when fewer people are involved in the buying process, decision making may follow the ***low-effort hierarchy of effects*** illustrated in the bottom half of Exhibit 17.8. Here consumers engage in a trial after they become aware of the innovation. They devote less decision-making effort to considering and researching the product before they try it, and then they form attitudes based on the trial. If their attitudes are positive, they may adopt the innovation. With a low-effort hierarchy of effects, the time between awareness of the innovation and its trial or adoption may be brief.

marketing IMPLICATIONS

Understanding whether consumers' adoption decisions are based on a high- or low-effort adoption process has important implications for marketers. For example, if the adoption involves low effort, marketers need to do all they can to encourage trial because trial affects brand attitudes. Pepsi and Hindustan lever's launch of Lipton Ice tea was a phased launch owing to the newness of the product category. [6]The launch was in phases, "We will launch Lipton iced tea in three cities to begin with, from where we would gradually expand," Pepsi India chief, Rajiv Bakshi said. The brand was not just introduced in phases but relied heavily on sampling also that is, by giving out free samples to familiarize the customers with the product.

If the adoption process is a high-effort one, marketers need to do all they can to reduce the perceived risk associated with adopting the innovation. [7]In the Bhopal Gas Tragedy in 1984, a poisonous vapor burst from the tall stacks of the Union Carbide pesticide plant killing 2,000, and injuring as many as 300,000 lives. A series of studies made five years later showed that many of the survivors were still suffering from one or several of the following ailments: partial or complete blindness, gastrointestinal disorders, impaired immune systems, post traumatic stress disorders, and menstrual problems in women. A rise in spontaneous abortions, stillbirths, and genetic defects in offsprings was also noted. In addition to the human toll, the incident set off a chain reaction at Carbide. [8]By 1985, the company's market value dropped by two-thirds to less than $3 billion, and GAF Corporation's Samuel Heyman accumulated enough stock to mount a hostile takeover bid of $5.3 billion. After working for two decades to expand its consumer products lines, Carbide was forced to sell off its Consumer Products Division, a profitable group that included Glad trash bags, Eveready batteries, Prestone, and STP automotive products. The company took a hit in sales and consumers were wary of buying Union Carbide products, particularly batteries, and their flagship product.

Timing of Innovation Adoption Decisions

Consumers differ in the timing of their adoption decisions. One framework identifies five adopter groups based on the timing of their adoption decisions, as shown in Exhibit 17.9.[27] The first 2.5 percent of the market to adopt the innovation are described as innovators. The next 13.5 percent are called early adopters. The next 34 percent are called the early majority. The late majority represent the next 34 percent of adopters. The last 16 percent of the market to purchase the product are called laggards.

Characteristics of Adopter Groups The adopter groups tend to exhibit different characteristics, as shown in the exhibit. With a new technology product, for instance, research shows that innovators who are enthusiastic about technology

Exhibit 17.9
PROFILE OF ADOPTER GROUPS

Some researchers have identified five groups of consumers that differ in when they adopt an innovation relative to others. Innovators are the first in a market to adopt an innovation, and laggards are the last. Certain characteristics (e.g., venturesomeness) are associated with each adopter group.

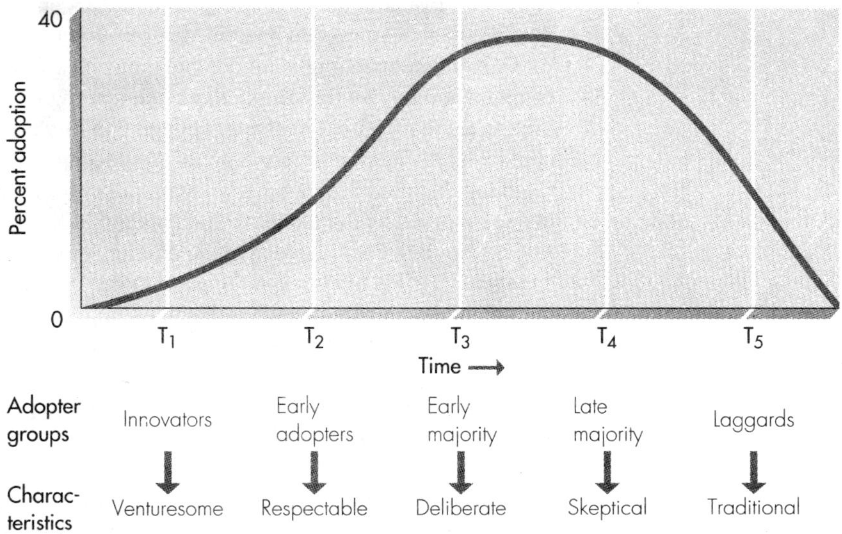

want to be the first to get a new high-tech product, even if there are a few bugs or inefficiencies.[28] As a first step toward gaining entry into the mainstream market, manufacturers of digital media centers—gadgets that connect or incorporate a PC, TV, stereo, and other components of a high-tech home entertainment center—initially targeted innovators.[29] [9]With the current generation set to call the shots, all the cellular operators are targeting for the youth's special attention focusing on their easygoing and freewheeling lifestyle, and their minds all charged up with ideas. Cellular telephony will become a vital connecting link for them. Two of the country's major cellular providers, Idea and Bharti, are both building on targeting the youth brigade. [10]The Nokia N series has been showcasing its brand and its extended range of features, which goes beyond making and receiving calls.

Early adopters are visionaries. They admire a technologically new product not so much for its features as for its abilities to create a revolutionary breakthrough in how things are done. The new generation of parents and children are more technologically drawn than the past. Penetration of durables, technological gadgets and home PC (personal computers) is an evidence of that. [11]Take for instance, the internet market in India, the only country in Asia Pacific with single-digit home access rates, with one in every 14 households with telephones having Internet access via home PC. On the other end of the spectrum, Singapore exhibited a 6% gain over Q3 and is now a country with the highest penetration level among all countries in Asia Pacific. [12]Yet the Indian broadband market is perhaps the only one where presently telecom giants, Internet service providers, cable operators and even the Indian Railways are fighting for a piece of the pie. Proof enough to suggest the huge size of the market and growing receptivity of the product.

The early majority are pragmatists, seeking innovations that offer incremental, predictable improvements on an existing technology. Because they do not like risk, they care deeply about who is making the innovation and the reputation of the company. They are interested in how well the innovation will fit into established technology systems, and they are concerned about the innovation's reliability. They are price sensitive, and they like to see competitors enter the market because they can then compare features and be more assured about the product's ultimate feasibility.

Consumers who represent the late majority are conservatives. They are wary of progress and rely on tradition. They often fear high-tech products, and their goal in buying them is to not get stung. They like to buy preassembled products that include everything in a single, easy-to-use package. Today the mobile operators are targeting the lower end of the market in India, essentially the SEC C, D and E, where the price remains the driver to the category. This segment loosely referred to as ABCD (Aya, Bai, Cook, Driver) of the market, looks for deals and lower tariff rates to convert. [13]This is the famous "Bottom of the Pyramid" segment that C.K. Prahlad defines and according to World Bank estimates will swell to more than 6 billion people over the next 40 years . Such segments use the mobile, more to stay in touch and only receive calls, save for a few emergency calls. Within this segment, for some who reside as migrant population in metros and bigger cities, the mobile also doubles up as an "STD Calling" device since it saves them visits to a PCO for making calls back home. Therefore, the reasons, motives and usage patterns are very different in the latecomers category as compared to the early adopters or early majority.

Laggards are skeptics. Although laggards may resist innovations, marketers can gain insights from understanding why this group is skeptical of an innovation. Why, for example, do some people shun PCs in favor of other methods of storing, analyzing, and communicating information? Do they fear losing or misplacing data not filed in printed form? Do they worry about the security of the information? Or do they believe that PCs are so complex that they will never learn to use one properly?

Application of Adopter Group Categories An important implication of the delineation of adopters into groups is that if an innovation is to spread through the market, it must appeal to every group. Unfortunately, many potentially useful innovations have never gained mass-market appeal because the marketing efforts for them did not acknowledge the characteristics of the adopter groups. For example, Prodigy, a software package for the PC, allowed users to connect to a nationwide computer network via a modem. Users could shop, consult online encyclopedias, check the weather and sports, order airline tickets, and perform other functions.

Although Prodigy featured a relatively new technology at the time (appealing to innovators) and promised an innovative way of getting information and ordering products (appealing to early adopters), it did not appeal to the mass market because it did not fit with the early majority's mindset. Few competitors were producing similar products, so the pragmatic early majority doubted the product would survive and apparently decided that buying it was not a good idea. Moreover, rather than showing how the software was an incremental improvement on existing products, Prodigy's ads tried to create a vision of a new kind of world.[33] Such a strategy may encourage innovators but not early adopters.

Some researchers have criticized the five-category scheme of adopter groups because it assumes these categories exist for all types of innovations. The critics say there may be more or fewer categories, depending on the innovation.[34] Also, the assumption that the number of consumers in the adopter categories forms a bell-shaped curve may not be true. For example, unlike the percentages that form the bell-shaped curve in Exhibit 17.9, certain products may attract the first one percent of adopters as innovators, the next 60 percent as early adopters, the next 30 percent as the early majority, the following five percent as the late majority, and the last four percent as laggards.

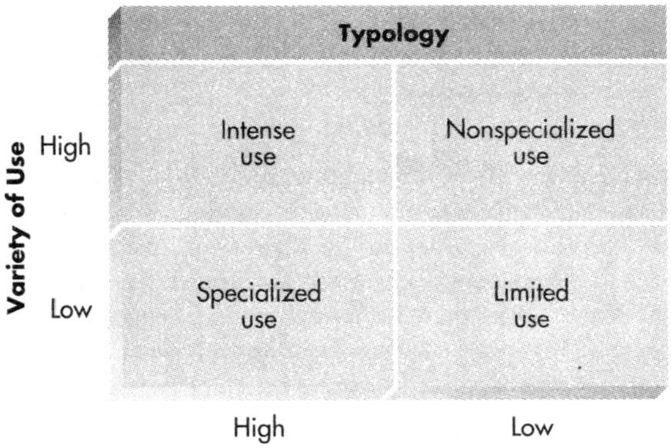

Exhibit 17.10
USE-DIFFUSION PATTERNS FOR HOME TECHNOLOGY INNOVATIONS

In fact, some researchers have rejected the definition of innovators as a certain percentage of people who have adopted a product just after it comes on the market. These researchers believe that innovators are instead those who make a decision to buy a new product despite the fact that they have not heard about it from others.[35] Often such consumers do buy the product soon after it comes to the marketplace, but they do so based on their own feelings, not on the opinions of others.

Other research suggests that examining the rate of use and variety of use can help marketers understand how an innovation diffuses through the market.[36] As an example, the use-diffusion model in Exhibit 17.10 identifies specific types of users of home technology such as PCs: intense users (who have many uses for an innovation and show a high rate of use), specialized users (high rate of use but low variety of use), nonspecialized users (high variety of use but low rate of use), and limited users (low variety of use and low rate of use).

marketing IMPLICATIONS Whether or not marketers accept the five-category adopter scheme, they recognize that consumers who are the first to buy a new product are important for several reasons. First, because innovators adopt new products independently of the opinions of other people, they are more likely to be receptive to information about new products, including information provided by marketers. Second, by virtue of their experience with the innovation, they may also communicate information to others and thus exact informational influence through the adoption decisions of others. Given these issues, many researchers want to better understand who innovators are and how they can be reached through marketing communications and appropriate media.

Demographics

Several of the demographic variables described in Chapters 13 and 14 have been linked with innovators.[37] For example, innovators tend to be younger, more affluent, and better educated than other consumers. In contrast, laggards are older and have less income and education, as well as lower occupational status. Religion is sometimes linked with innovation adoption. Amish consumers, for example, avoid many innovations, including cars, electricity, and telephones.

The link between these demographic variables and innovativeness makes sense. First, highly educated people tend to be heavier users of media and therefore tend to learn about new products earlier than less educated people. Second, high-income consumers can afford to buy innovations, and they may perceive less financial risk in adopting something new. Demographic variables such as culture of origin have also been linked with innovativeness. Consumers in South Korea, Australia, and Japan, for example, are regarded as innovators for new technology, which is why these markets have become launching sites for new high-tech offerings.[38]

Social influence

Innovators have been linked with the social influence factors discussed in Chapter 16.[39] They tend to have a great deal of social influence beyond their immediate groups, and they tend to be opinion leaders. Although this finding has not been observed in all research, it makes sense that innovators have influence because their opinions are shared with and respected by nonadopters.

Personality

Several personality characteristics have also been linked with adoption of innovations.[40] For example, innovators are high in need for stimulation, are inner directed, and are less dogmatic than other consumers. However, the relationships between personality traits and innovativeness are not very strong.[41] Innovators also do less planning and deliberate less than other consumers do when making buying decisions.[42]

Some researchers have proposed that rather than measuring "innate innovativeness" (as a personality trait), a better approach is to examine consumers' willingness to be innovative in a specific consumption domain. For example, an innovator of alternative music might respond positively to statements like "In general, I am among the first in my circle of friends to buy a new alternative-rock CD when it appears" or "I know the names of new alternative-rock acts before other people do." Innovators in the area of fashion, however, might not respond similarly to these statements.[43]

Cultural values

Adoption of innovations has been linked with culture of origin and the values tied to culture. One study of 11 European countries found that innovativeness was associated with cultures that value individualism over collectivism, those that value assertiveness over nurturing, and those that value openness to change over conservatism.[44]

Media involvement

Other research has suggested that innovators are frequent users of the media and rely extensively on external information.[45] They tend to think of themselves as active seekers and disseminators of information.[46] This finding makes sense because to affect others' adoption decisions, innovators must not only get their information somewhere but also be willing to transmit it.

Usage

Finally, innovators may be heavy users within the product category.[47] Consumers who frequently drink soft drinks may be innovators of new beverages because they are in the market often and hence are likely to notice these new products. In addition, innovators are usually experts in the product category, perhaps because of their usage and media involvement.

Diffusion

As increasing numbers of consumers in a market adopt an innovation, the innovation spreads or diffuses through the market. Whereas adoption reflects the behavior of an individual, ***diffusion*** reflects the behavior of the marketplace of consumers as a group. More specifically, diffusion reflects the percentage of the population that has adopted an innovation at a specific point in time. To illustrate, in the United States and Hong Kong, cell phones are already used by more than half of the population. In Africa, however, the diffusion of cell phones is much lower—although adoption is growing faster on this continent than anywhere else in the world, thanks to steady decreases in the price of phones and service (see Exhibit 17.11).[48] As described in the beginning the Indian cellular subscriber base has shown growth trends tipped as one of the fastest in the world. A study released in 2005 by the research firm Gartner stated that the Indian cellular services market had recorded the highest growth across the Asia Pacific and Japan region in 2004 with a CAGR of 67 percent. Revenues from the Indian cellular ser-

Exhibit 17.11
DIFFUSION OF CELL PHONES
India (ex-Japan) is one of the fastest growing cellular phone markets, with the highest airtime usage in the world.

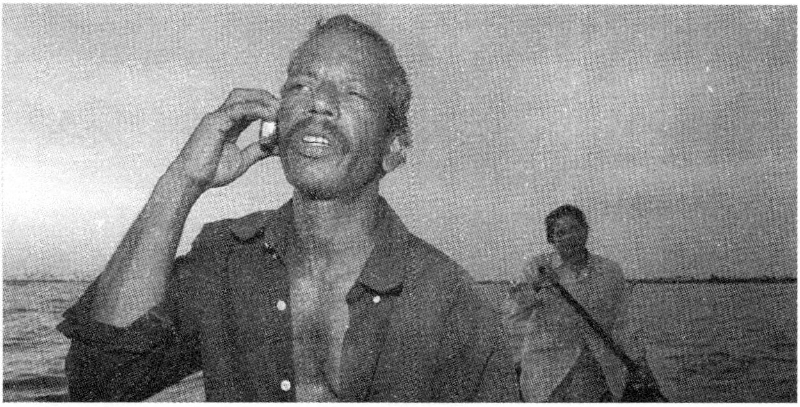

vices market will reach $24 billion by the end of 2009, at a compound annual growth rate (CAGR) of 35.6 percent.

Because marketers are interested in successfully spreading their offering through a market, they want to know how quickly groups of consumers will adopt innovations. This involves two important diffusion issues: how an offering diffuses through the market and how quickly it does so.

How Offerings Diffuse Through a Market

One way to examine how offerings spread through a market is to look at the pattern of adoption over time. From the marketers' perspective, life would be easy if everyone adopted the new offering just as soon as it was introduced into the market. However, this is rarely the case; in fact, several diffusion patterns have been identified.

The S-Shaped Diffusion Curve Some innovations exhibit an ***S-shaped diffusion curve,*** as shown in Exhibit 17.12(a).[49] Following this pattern, adoption of the products begins relatively slowly; as the exhibit shows, a relatively small percentage of the total market has adopted the product between time **1** and time **2** in the Exhibit. After a certain period, however, the rate of adoption increases dramatically, with many consumers adopting the product within a relatively short period of time. Between times **2** and **3,** a dramatic increase occurs in the number of consumers adopting the product. Then adoptions grow at a decreasing rate, and the curve flattens out.

To illustrate, the diffusion of microwave ovens was initially very slow. Then it increased dramatically as consumers became more aware of and knowledgeable about microwave technology and as marketers introduced more products compatible with microwave cooking (snacks, meals, cookware, and so forth). Now there is general acceptance of the microwave, and many consumers have one in their house or workplace, which is why the diffusion rate has again slowed.

The Exponential Diffusion Curve Another type of adoption curve is the ***exponential diffusion curve,*** illustrated in Exhibit 17.12(b).[50] In contrast to the S-shaped curve, the exponential diffusion curve starts out much more quickly, with a large percentage of the market adopting the product as soon as it is available. However, with each additional time period, the adoption rate increases at a slower pace.

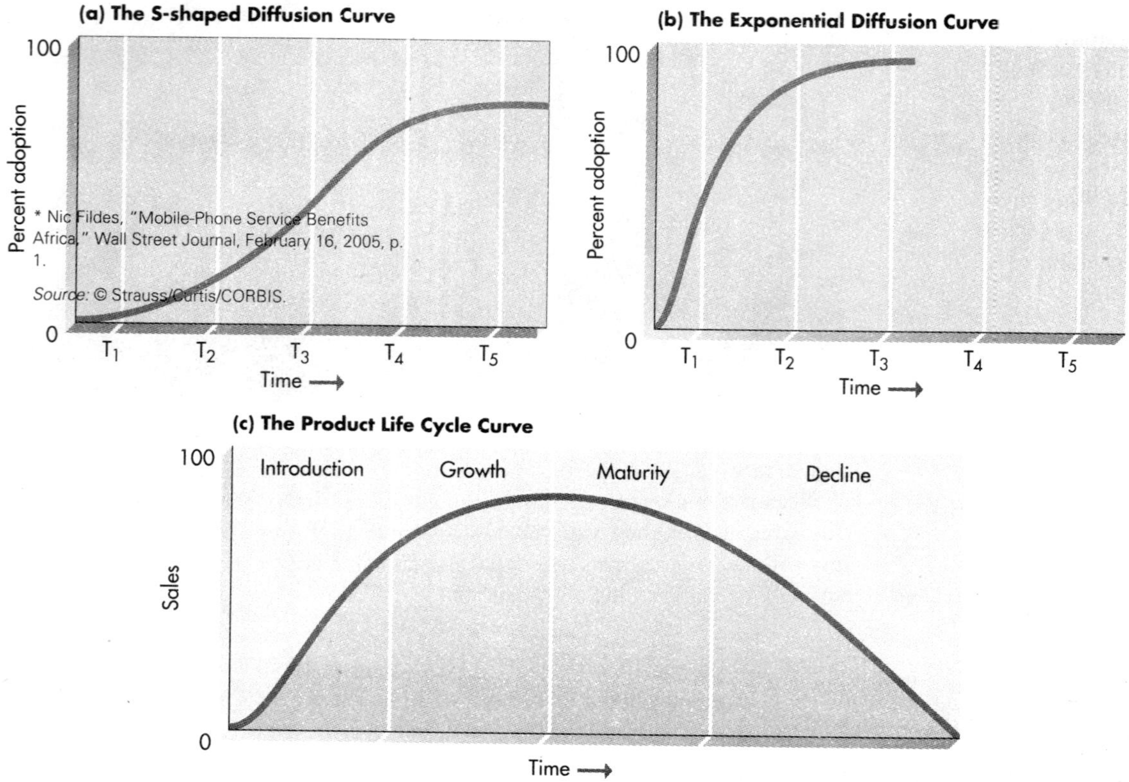

Exhibit 17.12

DIFFUSION AND PRODUCT LIFE CYCLE CURVES *Several diffusion patterns have been identified. (a) With an S-shaped diffusion curve, diffusion starts out slowly, increases rapidly, and then flattens out again. (b) With an exponential diffusion curve, many people adopt the innovation quickly. (c) The product life cycle curve depicts sales (not cumulative diffusion) of an offering over time.*

Factors Affecting the Shape of the Diffusion Curve

Many factors influence the ultimate shape of the diffusion curve. In general, marketers might expect an S-shaped diffusion curve when the innovation is associated with some social, psychological, economic, performance, or physical risk. In such situations, consumers might wait to see how other people use and react to the innovation before adopting it. Diffusion may also be slow initially if consumers are not sure whether the product will be on the market for a long period or whether its use carries high switching costs. The diffusion of computers and CD players followed this S-shaped curve. An S-shaped diffusion pattern might also occur when consumers are physically far apart, do not discuss the innovation with others, or do not share the same beliefs.

In contrast, when the innovation involves little risk, switching costs are low, consumers are similar in their beliefs and values, and/or when people talk often about the product and quickly disseminate knowledge throughout the social system, the product may have a rapid takeoff period that follows the exponential curve for diffusion. Note that these curves reflect only the rate at which consumers in the market adopt, not the time period under analysis. In other words, an S-shaped or an exponential curve could reflect diffusion that has occurred over a 1-year or a

Exhibit 17.13
TREND TOWARD DHABAS
The dhabas of India, located on the highways and patronized by the highway truck drivers have now become a part of urban theme restaurants.

30-year period. Furthermore, the curves could reflect the diffusion of either a functional, symbolic, or hedonic innovation.

How Diffusion Relates to the Product Life Cycle

The ***product life cycle*** concept (illustrated in Exhibit 17.12(c)) proposes that products initially go through a period of introduction, followed by relatively rapid growth as more competitors enter the market and more consumers adopt the product. As competition increases, weaker competitors drop out, and product sales plateau. At some point, however, consumer acceptance wanes, and product sales decline.

Product diffusion and the product life cycle are related but different concepts. Diffusion focuses on the percentage of the market that has adopted the product; diffusion is complete when 100 percent of the market has purchased the product. The product life cycle, on the other hand, deals with sales of the product over time. Moreover, diffusion curves are generally cumulative—that is, they continue to increase or at least level off over time. However, the product life cycle curve may decline as consumers decide not to purchase the product on future occasions. For instance, after an innovation such as the rotary-dial telephone diffused through an entire market, it was replaced by another innovation, the touch-tone phone, and sales of the old product eventually declined as the new innovation took hold.

marketing IMPLICATIONS

Marketers who understand a product's life cycle can try to prevent that product's decline—perhaps by finding new uses for it. For example, nylon has enjoyed a long life cycle given the myriad uses to which it has been put since its introduction in the 1940s—as an ingredient in clothing, rope, fishing lines, and so on. [14]Roohafza, a Hamdard Wakf brand launched in 1904 was initially introduced as a medicinal drink, and was known for its medicinal properties. The distinct red coloured drink contained essential nutrients, electrolytes and was known for its soothing and refreshing properties. However, with the passage of time the brand lost its essence and relevance in the desired target audience. Roohafza has now been repositioned as fun drink and is positioned as a concentrate which can be mixed and had with shakes, lassis, mocktails, without losing its core essence. To the extent that marketers develop new uses for a product or encourage use innovativeness, they can lengthen their product's life cycle.

Marketers can also try to diagnose the likely life cycle pattern of their offering. Just as diffusion curves differ, so too are there different product life cycle curves. A ***fad*** is a successful innovation that has a very short product life cycle. A fad is a successful innovation that has a very short product life cycle. Beyblades, Powerpuff Girls, Pokemon cards, scooters, and certain diets are examples of fads. As energy drinks such as Red Bull became a fad, Pepsi, Cadbury Schweppes, Coca-Cola, and others brought out their own energy drinks to capitalize on consumer interest. Some fads experience a revival years after they first surface. Hula-hoops are back, 40 years or more later. They first became a fad, as a way to stay fit.

A ***fashion*** or trend is a successful innovation with a lengthier and potentially cyclical life. For example, certain aesthetic styles like art deco run in fashion cycles, as do certain styles of clothing like cargo pants and platform shoes. Some types of foods, like Thai or Mexican, run in fashion cycles, as do certain consumption practices (e.g., breast- versus bottle-feeding infants). Dhabas, a popular form of roadside eatery patronized by highway truck drivers conjures images of open fields, charpoys and a tandoor alongside a few glistening Dekchis. Serving hot, fresh food (usually vegetarian) the Dhabas were more like a resting place for the drivers after their long driving through the night. For the city slickers, Dhabas were an occasional indulgence. Today Dhabas are back (see Exhibit 17.13) now more refurbished and as mobility of the urban genre increases and as city limits stretch Dhabas also are integrating into urban console. In contrast, a classic is a successful innovation that has a lengthy product life cycle. Jeans are an American classic, as are rock 'n' roll music, Coca-Cola, and hamburgers.

Although the terms *fad, fashion,* and *classic* have most often been applied to aesthetic or hedonic innovations, they can also describe functional and symbolic innovations because the life cycle of these innovations can be similarly variable.

Influences on Adoption, Resistance, and Diffusion

Knowing that innovations may diffuse quickly or slowly through a market and that the success of a new product depends on how many people within the market adopt it, marketing managers need to understand the factors affecting resistance, adoption, and diffusion. Exhibit 17.2 identifies a number of factors, including characteristics of the innovation and of the social system into which it is introduced.

Characteristics of the Innovation

Characteristics of the innovation that can affect resistance, adoption, and diffusion include perceived value, benefits, and costs.

Perceived Value Consumers perceive that an innovation has value if it offers greater perceived benefits or lower perceived costs than existing alternatives. Products with high perceived value may be more readily adopted than those with low perceived value.

Exhibit 17.14
RELATIVE ADVANTAGE
The advertisement says, 'only Kiwi shoe polish has dysolwax to protect, nourish and shine your shoes. Rich with imported waxes, special dyes and solvents', showcasing the relative advantage of the product

Perceived Benefits An innovation's value to consumers is affected by its perceived ***relative advantage,*** the extent to which it offers benefits superior to those of existing products. As shown in the opening example, South Korean consumers perceive the relative advantage of broadband compared to dial-up Internet access because they appreciate benefits such as being able to download TV programs and control home appliances remotely. Exhibit 17.14 shows another product with a relative advantage.

A product or service offers a relative advantage if it can help consumers avoid risks, fulfill their needs, solve problems, or achieve their goals—criteria that affect consumers' adoption decisions. In fact, research indicates that product advantage is one of the most important predictors of new-product success.[55] Note that a relative advantage is something the product does for the consumer—not something that exists in the product. Thus the relative advantage of hybrid cars such as the Toyota Prius lies not in their features, but in the owners' ability to save money on gasoline and help save the environment.

Marketers must also realize that if consumers do not perceive a new product's advantage over existing alternatives or think the advantage is unimportant, the innovation will face resistance. [15]The launch of Vacummisers by Real Value Appliances in the early 1990's generated enough media attention and used very innovative methods to get the viewers' attention. However, the product failed, owing to the deep rooted cultural traits of Indians in terms of food habits, that of preferring freshly cooked food. The vegetables to be freshly cut and washed and cooked immediately thereafter, unlike what the Vacummiser offered – to cut and store vegetables and use later,. The product was in fact ahead of its times.

Perceived Costs Another aspect of the value of a product is its perceived costs, including the purchase cost and the cost of switching to a new product. The higher the purchase cost, the greater the resistance and hence the slower the diffusion. Consider hybrid gas-electric cars, which incorporate new technology and tend to have a higher initial cost than conventional cars. Although the higher perceived cost slowed adoption at first, consumers saw the relative advantage in a different light after the pump price of gasoline skyrocketed—resulting in higher demand for fuel-efficient cars. In contrast, DVD players have experienced much more rapid diffusion. Thanks to ever-more efficient manufacturing and steadily higher sales volume, players can now be purchased for less than $100, compared with $600 when this innovation was introduced in the late 1990s.[57] The cost of changing from the current product to a new one (called switching costs) can also be an issue. Consumers with extensive collections of videotapes will take the perceived cost of switching into account when they consider whether to buy a DVD player.

marketing IMPLICATIONS

If consumers do not perceive that an innovation has a relative advantage, marketers may need to add one by physically redesigning or reengineering the innovation.

Communicate and demonstrate the relative advantage

The company will need to educate consumers who do not understand what a product is or what its relative advantages are. [16]Proctor and Gamble's Ariel used an innovative way to showcase the difference made by Ariel by sticking two pieces of cloth, one of which was washed with the detergent in leading national dailies. The advertising agency, Leo Burnet, was able to help the housewives touch and feel the difference in the product. In another instance, computer magazines like PC Quest, Data Quest and Computerworld tied up with software developers to attach trial version CD's along with the magazines, thus enabling the readers a chance to access the software.

Use price promotions to reduce perceived costs

If consumers perceive that a product is too costly, the company can use special price-oriented sales promotions such as price-offs, rebates, or refunds to reduce the perceived cost. In price sensitive markets like India, launching premium products are a challenge, since the economy brands are at arm's length to choose from. The plasma television and LCD television market is currently at an introduction stage, where consumers are wary about the price points. However, brands like Samsung and Sony are aggressively trying to push their products. The cricket World Cup, 2007 saw these companies giving promotional offers to encash on the cricket season. Marketers can also provide guarantees or warranties that make the product seem less expensive. Alternatively, the marketer may find a cheaper way to manufacture the product and pass on the savings in the form of lower prices for consumers, which is what marketers of digital watches did.

Provide incentives for switching

If innovations are not adopted because consumers think switching costs are high, marketers might provide incentives for switching. For example, Earthlink eases the transition to its broadband services with an "Easy Switch" tool that moves e-mail address books and other information from the consumer's existing system to the Earthlink system. Companies might also use advertising to inform consumers about the costs associated with not switching.

Finally, marketers might be able to force their innovation to become the industry standard, for instance, by having exceptionally high quality, great ease of use, or low price. MPEG-4, a technology standard for condensing huge video files so they can be easily transferred online, is backed by a large number of companies, including Cisco Systems. Although earlier MPEG technologies became widely accepted standards, Windows Media, RealPlayer, and QuickTime are also trying to win wider acceptance within the industry.[60]

Uncertainty

In addition to characteristics of the innovation, uncertainty surrounding the innovation can affect adoption, resistance, and diffusion. Several aspects of uncertainty are particularly important. One is doubt about what will become the standard product in the industry. Only after Sony modified its digital music players so they would play industry-standard MP3 files did sales jump significantly.[61]

Another aspect is uncertainty about the relative advantage of a product that requires the consumer to make significant behavioral changes.[62] Research shows that

Exhibit 17.15
CONSUMER LEARNING REQUIREMENTS

As the Indian consumer is increasingly getting mobile and looks for newer destinations for holiday, convenience to search for airlines, places to stay and local sightseeing tours are critical decisions which is all made simpler by makemytrip.com

consumers are more uncertain about the usefulness of a discontinuous innovation than about the usefulness of a continuous innovation.[63] Surprisingly, when consumers are confronted by a high-tech product combining a new interface with new functionality, uncertainty actually increases when more information is provided. Researchers suggest this happens because consumers pay more attention to the new interface and, in processing the information, reason through the possible negative outcomes of product adoption.[64]

A third aspect of uncertainty is the length of the product life cycle. If consumers think the product might be a fad, they are likely to be more resistant than if they think it will become a fashion or a classic. For example, you may forgo spending $80 on spike-heeled shoes if you don't believe that they will be in style for very long. Concern over life cycle length is quite legitimate in clothing and high-tech markets, where products are changed or improved at frequent intervals.

marketing IMPLICATIONS

Show product adaptability

When consumers resist innovations because they worry about a short life cycle, marketers might show how adaptable the product is and hence how likely it is to have a long life cycle. For example, marketers of digital video recorders can address consumers' fears of rapid obsolescence by demonstrating how their products may be upgraded, connected to advanced systems, or used in other ways that extend the life cycle by continuing to deliver perceived value.

Consumer Learning Requirements

A third characteristic affecting resistance, adoption, and diffusion is consumer learning requirements—or what consumers need to do to use the innovation effectively.

Compatibility Consumers often resist innovations because they see them as incompatible with their needs, values, norms, or behaviors.[65] The more ***compatible*** the innovation is with consumers' values, norms, and behaviors, the less the resistance and the greater the product diffusion. Leaking taps and pipes are a common problem in India and often even the plumber is wary of coming for miniscule repairs. M-Seal, from Pidilite Industries offers the convenience of hassle free sealing, joining, repairing and insulating ferrous and non-ferrous metals, glass, asbestos, concrete, ceramics, etc. The product available in "Putti" form is less tacky and easy to use. Alternatively, Reckitt Benckiser's brand Robin Blue in powder form was rejected by consumers due to the uneven whiteness it gave and stains it thus created.

Some potentially serious consequences can arise when an innovation is incompatible with consumers' values, goals, and behaviors. One case in particular is marketers' attempts to encourage bottle-feeding by mothers in the developing nations of Latin America, Africa, and Asia. Manufacturers' ads showed pictures of mothers with beautiful, fat, healthy babies. The ad copy read, "Give your baby love and Lactogen." (Lactogen is an infant formula.) The modern look of the ad was attractive to upper-income, well-educated consumers as well as to peasant families who aspired to be like the well educated. Unfortunately, most peasant families could not afford the expensive formula, so they diluted it with water, leaving their babies malnourished. Furthermore, they were unfamiliar with practices like sterilizing nipples and bottles, so the baby bottles became a haven for bacteria, which made the babies sick. The lack of compatibility between the innovation and the consumers' behavior therefore caused unanticipated problems.[68]

Trialability A second aspect of consumer learning requirements is the ***trialability*** of the innovation, or the extent to which the product can be tried on a limited basis before it is adopted. Products like microwaveable meals can easily be tested and tasted in just a few minutes. However, trialability is virtually impossible with some innovations, such as laser eye surgery. Because a trial allows a consumer to see the product's relative advantages and assess the potential risks associated with purchase, products that are easy to try tend to diffuse through the market more quickly than those that do not.

Studies suggest that the degree of importance placed on trialability depends on the type of adopter. Trialability may be very important to innovators and early adopters, because they have little else on which to base the value of the innovation. Trialability may be less important for later adopters, who are likely to know many people who have already adopted the innovation and who can therefore speak to its efficacy.[69]

Complexity Complexity is a final learning requirement related to adoption and diffusion. Diffusion is likely to be slow when consumers perceive they will have difficulty understanding or using a new product. In fact, consumers may form a lower evaluation of a complex product with novel attributes because they worry about the time needed to learn the new features.[70] Digital photography initially diffused at a relatively slow rate because consumers perceived complexity in learning to transfer digital images from the camera to the computer, figuring out the software for enhancing images, and printing high-quality photos.[71] Other products, such as DVD players, have diffused more rapidly, in part because they are easy to use.

marketing IMPLICATIONS Marketers can use several tactics to reduce consumers' resistance to innovations.

Enhance compatibility or reduce complexity
Marketers may be able to reposition an innovation so it appears more consistent with consumers' needs and values. Campbell's soup enjoyed renewed popularity when it was repositioned away from taste and toward nutrition and low calories.[72] Sometimes, however, companies must redesign a product to overcome incompatibility and reduce complexity. For example, because camcorders were initially too complex for the average user, companies like Sharp and Matsushita developed simpler, more user-friendly products.[73]

Educate about compatibility
Companies can use advertising and promotion to show how their innovations actually are compatible with consumers' needs, values, norms, or behaviors. For example, in Third World countries consumers are not used to modern medicine and the techniques used to avoid many dreaded diseases. One way organizations like the World Health Organization have dealt with this situation is to launch educational programs to demonstrate the value of vaccinations and the procedures that can stop disorders like diarrhea.[74] Advertising can also show how a new offering is easier to use or has more benefits than current alternatives, even if it requires new behaviors.

Use change agents
Another way to enhance perceived compatibility is to use change agents such as opinion leaders (see Chapter 16). Marketers in such diverse fields as farming equipment, medicine, and computers have aimed new products at influential and highly respected people who can be convinced of a new product's merits and who will then spread positive word of mouth to others.[75]

Fit with a system of products
Another way to address incompatibility is to design the innovation to fit with a system of existing products. Rin Supreme Bar from Hindustan Lever introduced a Dry-Knit cover to prevent the soap from being wet after use, thereby preventing the soap from melting. The cover also had a facility to be hanged so that the excess water in the soap could be drained out too.

Force the innovation to be the industry standard
Marketers can sometimes work with regulators to require adoption of the innovation. For example, smoke detectors, seat belts, and lead-free gasoline are all innovations that have been forced into usage by government mandate. One reason manufacturers are introducing more hybrid cars is because of state clean-air requirements mandating zero-emission vehicles.[77]

Use promotions to enhance trialability
Companies can stimulate trial through various promotions. Free samples, for example, encourage trial by people who might otherwise resist using the product. [17]Over the past couple of years, freebies and cross-promotions have been rampant in the FMCG business. Companies often tag on a free bar of toilet soap with a tube of toothpaste or offer two toothpaste tubes for the price of one. [18]Colgate has been for quite sometime now offering a family value pack of two toothpastes of 250gms and 100gms along with a free toothbrush.

Demonstrate compatibility and simplicity
Demonstrations, either live or presented in advertising, can show how compatible the product is with existing needs, values, and behaviors and how simple it is to use. The concept of test drive in India has gradually been adopted by several automobile companies. They constantly advertise about the test drives in their product advertisements.

Simulate trial
At times, a company may need to simulate trial rather than having consumers actually try the product. [19]In Auto Expo, 2006 Maruti Suzuki gave unique opportunity to test drive by installing specially designed eight French simulator consoles. Simulators are machines that create (simulate) normal road driving conditions in classrooms, and those installed at the Auto Expo, 2006 international exhibition in the Capital were customised for Indian roads.

Reduce complexity through product redesign
Sometimes companies can change a product to make it less complex, the way Sharp and others simplified their camcorders. As another example, cameras with automatic focusing allow novices to take high-quality pictures without worrying about aperture settings and other complexities.

Social Relevance

A fourth major factor that affects resistance, adoption, and diffusion is the innovation's ***social relevance,*** particularly its observability and social value. Observability is the extent to which consumers can see others using the innovation. In general, the more consumers can observe others using the innovation, the more likely they are to adopt it.[79] In part, consumers learn about new products and their potential benefits when the products are visibly consumed by others. For example, a new shoulder strap designed to distribute the weight of a golf bag gained acceptance among caddies after they saw others using the product.[80] On the other hand, a new scale that announces your body weight is unlikely to be very observable because few people want to weigh themselves in public (or want others to hear their weight!).[81] Thus diffusion is also affected by the public or private nature of the product, as described in Chapter 16.

Social value reflects the extent to which the product has social cachet, which means that it is seen as socially desirable and/or appropriate and therefore generates imitation, speeding diffusion. One study found that farmers adopted certain farming innovations because the innovations were expensive and thus had social prestige value. These studies also found that the earlier someone adopted the innovation, the more prestige was associated with it.[82] Consumers sometimes adopt aesthetic innovations like new fashions, hairstyles, and cars solely on the basis of the social prestige these innovations confer on the user.

Although social value may enhance diffusion, the diffusion of a product based on a prestige image may actually shorten its life cycle because once a product is adopted by the masses, it is no longer prestigious. For example, designer jeans, once associated with prestige and exclusivity, lost prestige when everyone in the market started to wear them.[83]

marketing IMPLICATIONS Marketers can use extensive advertising, promotions, and distribution to overcome problems associated with observability. Observability can also be enhanced by the use of distinctive packaging, styling, and color or unique promotions,[84] using the attention and perception enhancement techniques described in Chapter 4. Associating the product with a well-known person or developing ads to suggest that the consumer will be socially rewarded for using the product may also enhance observability. The social relevance of an innovation can be heightened through advertising—particularly advertising that ties product use with potential social approval. Finally, marketers can enhance social value by associating the product with some social entity, cause, or value. Having a new beverage serve as the official drink of the Olympic team might, for example, enhance its social value.

Legitimacy and Adaptability

Legitimacy and adaptability are two additional factors that influence resistance, adoption, and diffusion, particularly for symbolic and aesthetic innovations.[85] ***Legitimacy*** refers to the extent to which the innovation follows established guidelines for what seems appropriate in the category. An innovation that is too radical or that does not derive from a legitimate precursor lacks legitimacy. For example, rock 'n' roll and later rap music were initially seen as deviant forms of music and thus diffused slowly. In contrast, part of the success of artists like k. d. lang stemmed from their ability to fuse two legitimate music styles (country and rock) into a style that sounded new.

Adaptability, the innovation's potential to fit with existing products or styles, is another factor affecting adoption and diffusion.[86] For example, certain forms of fashion or furniture may be seen as highly adaptable because they can fit with a variety of other fashion or furniture trends. Some functional products, such as PCs, have high adaptability because they can perform a variety of functions.

marketing IMPLICATIONS Marketers may enhance legitimacy by demonstrating how the innovation came into being or marketing in a way that is consistent with consumers' perceptions of what is appropriate for the category. The market for ready-to-eat (RTE) is estimated to be around Rs 50 crore which is growing at 30 per cent a year. The growing number of nuclear families, an increase in household incomes, and a significant rise in the number of single working men and women professionals in the past decade, has opened the opportunity for the RTE segment. The RTE segment now offers options in cuisines of both South and North Indian background. From Punjabi Chole, Mirchi Ka Salan, Lemon Rice, Upma Mix, to a range of options in regional sweets are available under the RTE category.

Conversely, if consumers believe the product lacks adaptability, marketers can show that it has uses beyond its original function. Similarly, Chyawanprash, is an ancient Ayurvedic health tonic, widely used in India, as a rejuvenative energizer and immunity booster. It is often called "the elixir of life" due to its numerous nutritional properties and benefits to the body. However, the association with the product is more during the winters, when consumption goes up, for warding off cough and cold and strengthen immunity. [20]Now, Himani has introduced Sona Chandi Chyawanprash especially for the summer season, which for the first time, mixes the goodness of Amla and other herbs with the super power of precious metals like Gold and silver to ward off the searing summer heat and related problems.

Exhibit 17.16
THE MODERNITY OF THE SOCIAL SYSTEM

The economic boom and the rising prosperity level has led to a new generation of urban affluent customers who look for high value and premium products.

Characteristics of the Social System

Innovations diffuse rapidly or slowly in part because of product characteristics and in part because of the characteristics of the social system into which they are introduced. Both the kinds of people in the target market and the nature of the relationships among the people in the social system will affect the innovation's acceptance.

Modernity Resistance, adoption, and diffusion are affected by the ***modernity*** of the social system, meaning the extent to which consumers in the system have a positive attitude toward change. Consumers in modern systems value science, technology, and education, and are technologically oriented in terms of both the goods produced and the skill of the labor force.[89] The receptivity of consumers toward change, science, and technology is illustrated by the ad in Exhibit 17.16. The more modern the social system, the more receptive its consumers are to new products.

Homophily A second general characteristic of the social system is homophily, or the overall similarity among members of the system. Diffusion is faster when consumers in the market are highly similar in education, values, needs, income, and other dimensions.[90] Why? First, the more similar people's backgrounds are, the more likely they are to have similar needs, values, and preferences. Second, similar people are more likely to interact with one another and transmit information. Third, similar people tend to model each other. Also, normative influence is likely to be higher as homophily grows, increasing the pressure for adopting the innovation and speeding adoption and diffusion.

Physical Distance A third characteristic of the social system is the physical distance between its members. Diffusion tends to be slower when members of the social system are spread apart. Some marketers in Japan have found that high school girls excel at setting trends. No doubt this ability is due to the physical and emotional proximity of girls and their tendency to talk about new products they have seen and used.[91] Likewise, an innovation may experience slower diffusion when consumers are physically separated.[92]

Opinion Leadership A final characteristic of the social system involves the key influencers in the diffusion process. Chapter 16 mentioned that people with credibility, such as experts or opinion leaders, can have considerable influence on adoption and diffusion because they may spread positive or negative product information to others.[93] One study analyzing the diffusion of information about family-planning practices among women in a Korean village found that opinion leaders were very important sources of information. Not only was the information communicated by these women important, but the opinion leaders served as bridges connecting spatially related but separate cliques in the village.[94]

marketing IMPLICATIONS Marketing efforts can influence resistance, adoption, and diffusion by affecting the social system. For example, if members of the target market are very different from one another, companies may need to use targeted communications that show the product's relevance to consumers' unique needs, values, or norms and place the messages in specialized (target-market-specific) media to reach these consumers.

Marketers might also identify consumers who have not adopted the innovation. According to research, nonadopters can be divided into groups with very different characteristics. One group consists of passive consumers who have tried the product but are unlikely to provide much information to others about it. A second is active rejectors who have tried the product but are likely to provide unfavorable word of mouth to others. The third is potential adopters who have not yet tried the product but who may be influenced by active rejectors, active acceptors, or marketers.

Because even a small group can have a big impact on others' adoption decisions, it may be useful to specifically target some of these groups. To illustrate, if potential adopters lack awareness of the innovation, the company can use advertising to build awareness and encourage adoption. Product improvements may, however, be necessary for active rejectors. Thus different marketing strategies may be appropriate for different adopter groups.[95]

Marketing tactics may also affect the nature and extent of word-of-mouth communication. For example, companies can facilitate word of mouth about the new product by targeting opinion leaders. Promotions that target the network, rather than the consumer, can be an effective way of speeding diffusion. Media coverage of an innovation generally has more credibility than communications from the company itself. Special events like trade shows are also ways of showcasing a product, demonstrating its features, and stimulating positive word of mouth. As Chapter 16 indicates, marketers can take a number of steps to track word of mouth, generate positive word of mouth, and counteract negative word of mouth. Because marketing activities can influence diffusion by affecting both the innovation and the social system, it is not surprising that the more intensive the marketing effort, the faster the innovation spreads through a market.[96]

The Consequences of Innovations

Although innovations often offer relative advantages that may not have previously existed, they are not always good for society. Several studies have suggested that negative social and economic consequences may arise from the diffusion of an innovation.

One study examined the diffusion of the steel ax among a tribe of aborigines who lived in the Australian bush.[97] Before the innovation was introduced, the stone ax had served as the tribe's principal tool. It was used only by men and was awarded to them as a gift and as payment for work performed. It was generally regarded as a symbol of masculinity and respect. However, missionaries came into the social system with the steel ax and distributed it to men, women, and children. This distribution scheme disrupted the sex and age roles among tribal members and thus affected the social system.

Innovations may also have negative socioeconomic consequences. For example, a study examining the diffusion of the CAT scanner through the medical community identified two important sociological consequences. First, the innovation tended to diffuse to markets that were generally wealthy, leaving the technology unavailable to families who lived in poorer rural areas. Second, the innovation was expensive and was viewed as driving up health care costs.[98] Given these types of unanticipated social and economic consequences, we as consumers should be careful to avoid adopting a universally pro-innovation bias.

Summary

Innovations are products, services, ideas, or attributes that consumers in a market segment perceive to be new. Innovations can be characterized as functional, symbolic, or hedonic and may vary in the degree of behavioral change their adoption requires. Product innovativeness ranges along a continuum from continuous to discontinuous. Innovations may represent fads, fashions, or classics and hence may exhibit a short, moderate, or long life cycle. Marketers can extend a product's life cycle by enhancing the breadth of the innovation and by encouraging consumers to find innovative uses for familiar products.

Strategies for marketers of innovations include reducing consumers' resistance to innovations, facilitating consumers' adoption of the innovation, and affecting the diffusion of the innovation through the marketplace. A high-effort as opposed to low-effort hierarchy-of-effects adoption process occurs when the innovation is seen as risky. Some individuals, called innovators, are among the first to adopt new products, independently of the decisions of other people. Companies may target innovators because their adoption influences other consumers' adoption decisions through word of mouth or social modeling.

Resistance, adoption, and diffusion are affected by characteristics of the innovation and the social system into which it is introduced. Overcoming resistance is easiest when the innovation is perceived to provide value such as a relative advantage, low price, or low switching costs. Resistance will be lower when the innovation requires minimal learning and when it is highly compatible with existing needs, values, and behaviors; easy to try; easy to use; and low risk. Innovations viewed as high in social relevance, legitimacy, and adaptability encounter less resistance than those regarded as low in such factors. The characteristics of the social system in which the innovation operates also affect resistance, adoption, and diffusion. The more dense the social network and the more homophilous consumers within the social system are, the more likely it is that adopters will transmit information to nonadopters, in turn affecting their likelihood of adoption. However, the diffusion of an innovation may entail some negative social and economic consequences, making a universally pro-innovation bias inappropriate.

Questions for Review and Discussion

1. How can innovations be described in terms of degree of novelty and types of benefits? How does the degree of novelty affect consumers' behavioral change?
2. What is the difference between adoption and diffusion? How does the concept of resistance relate to adoption?
3. Under what circumstances might a consumer follow the high-effort hierarchy of effects in adopting an innovation?
4. How can consumers be categorized in terms of their timing of adoption relative to other consumers?
5. What is the product life cycle, and how does it differ from product diffusion?
6. How do consumer learning requirements and social relevance affect resistance, adoption, and diffusion?
7. What characteristics of the social system affect an innovation's acceptance within a market?

Exercises

1. Read several publications like *BusinessWeek*, *Fortune*, or the *Wall Street Journal* and identify two innovative products and/or services.
   a. Why are these offerings innovations? (Relate your answers to the chapter's definition of an innovation.)
   b. What type of innovations are they—continuous, dynamically continuous, discontinuous? Functional, aesthetic, symbolic?
   c. Describe whether you think adoption and diffusion of these offerings will be fast or slow by using concepts associated with the innovations, such as relative advantage, observability, and legitimacy.
   d. Indicate how marketers might overcome resistance and speed adoption and diffusion for offerings whose diffusion is likely to be slow.
2. Consider a product that you think represents an innovation but that you have not yet purchased. Using the terms discussed in this chapter, indicate why your resistance to this product is high or low.
3. Identify a new product that you consider to be a fad. Why is it likely to be a fad? What can marketers do to enhance the length of this product's life cycle?
4. Think about a new product or service you have recently encountered. How did the social system of which you are a member influence your knowledge about, attitudes toward, and willingness to adopt this innovation?
5. Identify a set of offerings that you consider to be symbolic innovations. How has the meaning of each innovation changed? What cultural forces explain these changes?

More Exercises from the Adaptor

1. The Indian television market has witnessed a distinctive cycle between the periods:
   a. Pre 1982- 1982
   b. 1982-1991
   c. 1991-1995
   d. 1995 onwards

   Analyze specifically how between these time periods the product and the brands have moved with times. Focus specifically on the following issues:
   a. The technology aspect of the product
   b. The environmental factors affecting the category and the players
   c. The pricing aspects of the industry and the changing nature of price tiers and price bands
   d. The country of origin effect
   e. Finally, the changing buyer behavior approaches

References

[1] Source: http://www.dqindia.com/content/top_stories/102122703.asp

[2] Source: http://www.infoworld.com/article/04/09/22/HNmobileindia_1.html

[3] Source: http://www.trai.gov.in/Default.asp#

[4] Source: http://www.apnic.net/mailing-lists/s-asia-it/archive/2002/10/msg00010.html

[5] Source: http://agencyfaqs.com/news/interviews/data/170.html

[6] Source: http://www.fnbnews.com/article/detnews.asp?articleid=15046&sectionid=32

[7] Source: http://www.hu.mtu.edu/hu_dept/tc@mtu/papers/bhopal.htm

[8] Source: http://www.answers.com/topic/union-carbide-corporation

[9] Source: http://www.blonnet.com/catalyst/2002/06/06/stories/2002060600110300.htm

[10] Source: http://wirelessfederation.com/news/category/mtv/

[11] Source: http://www.nielsen-netratings.com/pr/pr_020306_eratings.pdf

[12] Source: http://www.expresscomputeronline.com/20060717/market01.shtml

[13] Source: http://www.changemakers.net/library/temp/fortunepyramid.cfm

[14] Source: http://www.hamdard.com/rooh_afza/roohafza_nutshell.htm

[15] Source: http://economictimes.indiatimes.com/articleshow/1029075.cms

[16] Source: http://economictimes.indiatimes.com/articleshow/1029075.cms

[17] Source: http://www.blonnet.com/iw/2003/04/13/stories/2003041300840700.htm

[18] Source: http://www.colgate.co.in/app/Colgate/IN/OralCare/SpecialOffers.cvsp

[19] Source: http://www.thehindu.com/2006/01/09/stories/2006010910790400.htm

[20] Source: http://www.emamigroup.com/products/your_health/sona_chandi.htm

chapter **18**

Symbolic Consumer Behavior

LEARNING OBJECTIVES

After studying this chapter, you will be able to:

- Discuss how products, special possessions, and consumption activities gain symbolic meaning and how this meaning is conveyed from one consumer to another.
- Highlight how marketers can influence symbolic meaning.
- Distinguish between sacred and profane entities, and show why this distinction is important for marketing strategy.
- Understand the process of gift giving and describe how marketers can use knowledge of this process to market more effectively.

INTRODUCTION

Ka-ching! Consumers Buy (and Sell) Special Somethings on eBay

Auctioning McDonald's Happy Meals toys from 1979, Hawaiian postcards from 1897, pieces of the original Hollywood sign from 1923, and gum chewed by Britney Spears in 2004, eBay is the world's largest marketplace for collectibles. The site facilitates the purchase of $34 billion worth of goods and services every year, from everyday objects to special somethings that draw hundreds of people eager to make the winning bid. Recent prices paid for a Happy Meal toy approximated $200; the 1897 postcard (one of 160,000 postcards listed on any given day) went for $1,085; a section of the 50-foot-high Hollywood sign sold for more than $500; and Britney's gum was purchased for more than $15,000 (see Exhibit 18.1).

What makes these items so special? Often, Happy Meals collectibles tap into adults' nostalgia for childhood visits to McDonald's. Postcards offer an opportunity to own a tiny piece of the past or a memento of a place that has personal meaning, such as the consumer's home town or honeymoon destination. The movie producer who sold the Hollywood sign called it an icon that "epitomizes the entertainment industry," a source of fascination for many consumers. And possessing Britney's gum gives the purchaser a small but direct connection to a well-known celebrity.

According to eBay's research, consumers who unintentionally build a collection do so, in part, because they get pleasure from using these special items in daily life. Consumers who consider themselves collectors tend to buy more frequently and spend more to expand their collections. Some seek out specific items that have meaning because of family traditions, whereas others acquire items that represent their interests or aspirations. Even occasional collectors mob the eBay

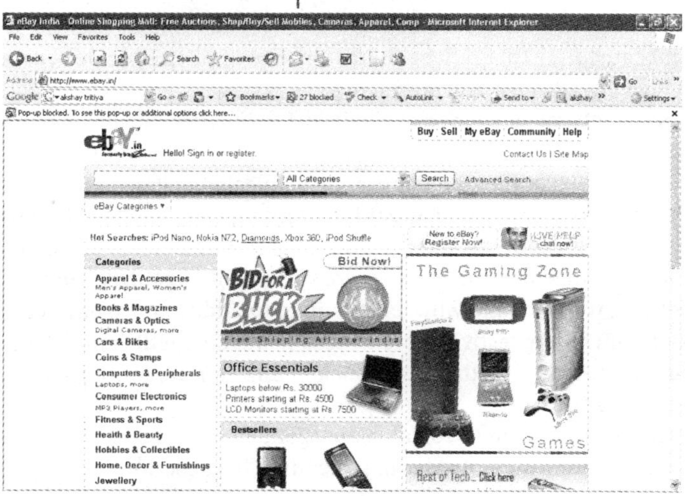

Exhibit 18.1
COLLECTING OBJECTS WITH SYMBOLIC MEANING

The thousands of items sold on eBay provides just one small example of how many consumers collect items and the variety in the types of items they collect.

site when particular items are up for bid, as when 60,000 people visited during a weeklong auction of Walt Disney memorabilia to benefit a children's charity. For $37,500, one consumer won the right to have his name and a funny saying etched on a mock tombstone featured in Disneyland's Haunted Mansion attraction. A Disney spokesperson observed that the company has been part of the childhood experience for many people and "here was a chance to be part of that on a very big scale."[1]

As this opening example shows, some offerings can have symbolic meaning, the focus of this chapter. The first section examines how offerings acquire symbolic meaning, the functions of symbols, and how they affect our self-concept. The next section explains why some offerings are more meaningful than others. Some are special—even sacred—and require consumption practices to keep them so. The final section discusses how meaning is transferred from one individual to another through the process of gift giving (see Exhibit 18.2). Knowing how symbolic meaning affects consumer behavior can help marketers develop suitable strategies for targeting specific markets, creating needs-satisfying offerings, and planning communications that are appropriate for the target market and the offering. In turn, the meaning that marketers or others create in offerings becomes part of consumers' schema or category for the offering—concepts discussed in Chapter 5.

Sources and Functions of Symbolic Meaning

To understand why some consumers would spend thousands of dollars for Britney's gum or their name on a tombstone in the Haunted Mansion, consider where the meaning associated with products and activities like those in the entertainment industry come from and what functions these offerings and practices fulfill. As shown in Exhibit 18.3, this meaning can stem from either our culture or ourselves as individuals.

Meaning Derived from Culture

Part of the meaning associated with products derives from our culture (see Exhibit 18.4).[2] Anthropologists suggest that we have ***cultural categories*** for such things as time (as in work time and leisure time), space (such as home, office, and safe or unsafe places), and occasions (such as festive versus somber events). We also have cultural categories that reflect characteristics of people, such as categories of gender, age, social class, and ethnicity.

Implicit in these cultural categories are ***cultural principles***—ideas or values that specify how aspects of our culture are organized and how they should be perceived or evaluated. For example, the cultural principles associated with "work time" dictate that it is more structured, organized, and precise than leisure time. Cultural principles give meaning to category-related products, which is why the clothing we associate with work time is also more structured, organized, and precise than the clothing we associate with leisure time. In addition, we have categories for occasions, including festive (vibrant, active, and energetic) and somber (dark, quiet, and inactive). The clothing we consider appropriate for those occasions mirrors these qualities.

Cultural categories that relate to social status, gender, age, and ethnicity are particularly relevant to the study of symbolic meaning because we link various

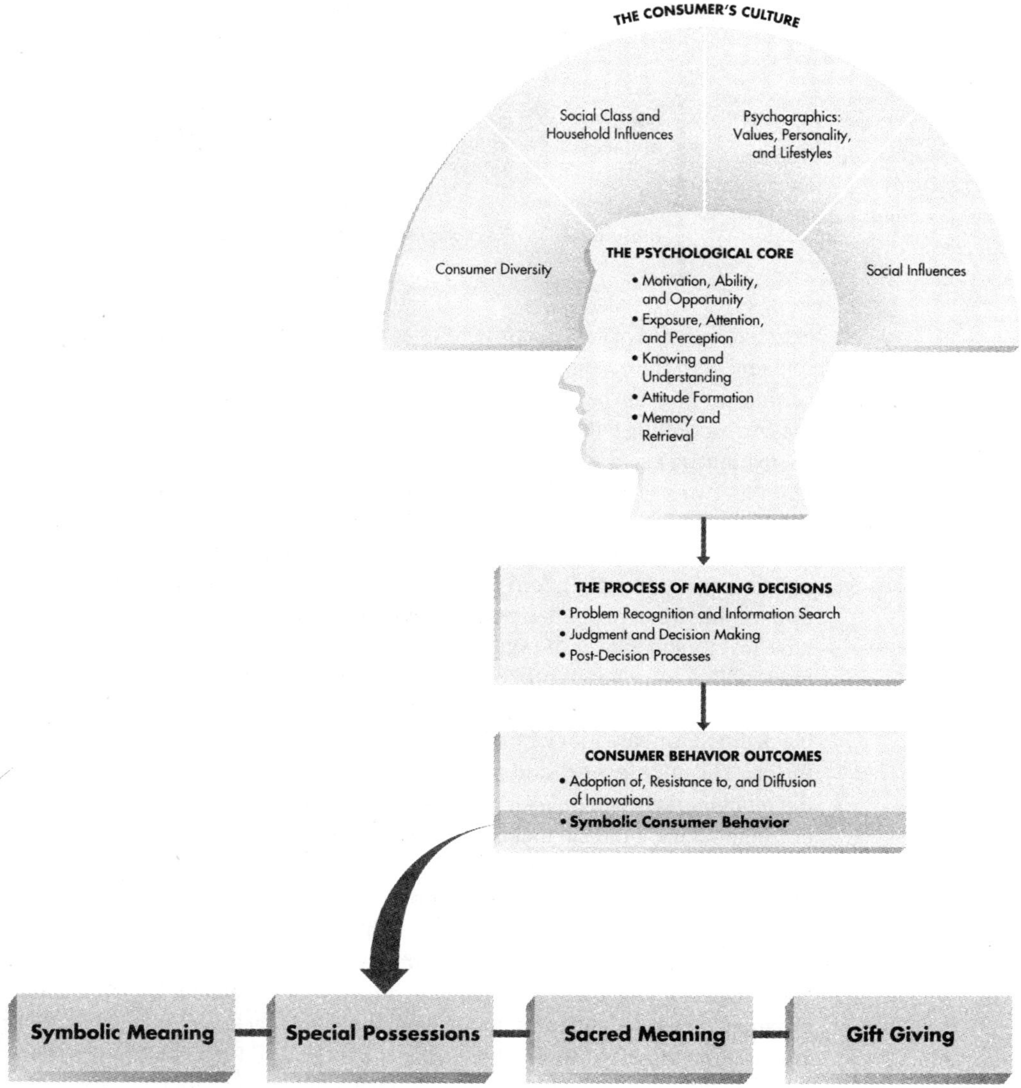

Exhibit 18.2

CHAPTER OVERVIEW: SYMBOLIC CONSUMER BEHAVIOR *Products and consumption activities can symbolize something about ourselves and our relationships with other people. In this chapter, we consider how products and consumption activities take on and communicate meaning. We also discuss that some possessions and consumption activities take on special or even sacred meaning. Finally, we discuss how gift giving can symbolize how we feel toward a gift recipient.*

cultural principles to these categories. For example, the category "women" has historically been associated with concepts like delicate, whimsical, expressive, and changeable. In contrast, the category "men" has historically been associated with concepts like disciplined, stable, and serious. Marketers make products and consumers use them in ways that are consistent with these principles. Thus women's clothing is traditionally more delicate, whimsical, expressive, and changeable than clothing for men. Exhibit 18.4 indicates that by associating and matching product

Exhibit 18.3

THE SOURCES AND FUNCTIONS OF CONSUMPTION SYMBOLS

Consumers use products with various meanings to achieve a set of functions. Combined, these functions help define the consumer's self-concept.

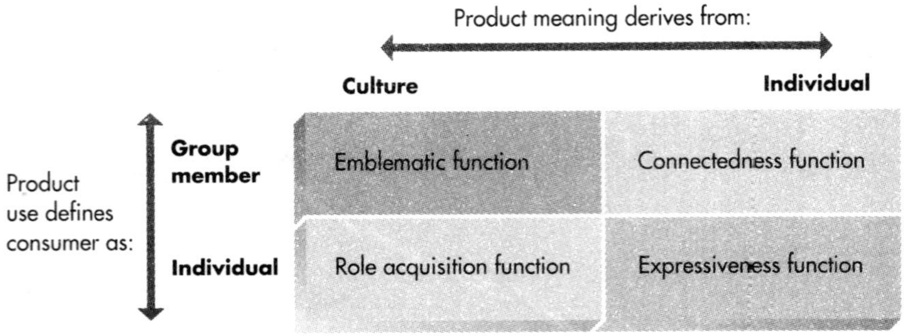

characteristics with cultural principles and categories, we transfer the meaning associated with the cultural principle to the product. For example, we might classify certain clothing as "feminine" or as "suitable for work" because we associate it with the corresponding cultural principles and categories.

Exhibit 18.4 also shows that many agents can play a role in this association and matching process. First, product designers and manufacturers introduce new products whose characteristics reflect cultural principles. [1]The Ambassador car in India has now been running on the Indian roads since its inception in 1948. Originally based on Morris Oxford (United Kingdom, 1948), the Ambassador has been undergoing a series of changes, adapting to customer expectations. The car may have lost its sheen over the years but has "niche" buyers such as government, professionals, luxury hotels and export marketer. The government sector patronizes the brand so completely that today it has become a symbol of bureaucrats and a black tinted Ambassador with a red or a blue light on the top denotes a VIP donning the car. The once favorite and popular car of the Indians has now moved away from the retail markets and focuses completely on institutional markets such as the government sector, a radical makeover of its "Amby" image to a "Power Symbol".

Meaning also comes from nonmarketing sources. Specific people may serve as opinion leaders who shape, refine, or reshape cultural principles and the products and attributes they are linked to (see Chapter 16). [2]Film actresses of the past like Sadhna, Hema Malini and the later years stars like Madhuri Dixit had immense fan following their looks, hairstyles, dresses and at times even mannerisms. Today, the urban women is redefined as smart, sassy, bold and packs a punch in her approach and actresses like Aishwarya Rai, Kareena Kapoor and Priyanka Chopra represent that thought process, not just through the characters they depict but even the numerous endorsements they do. Soaps (Lux), toiletries (Himani) or even Diamonds (Nakshtra)—all represent the feelings and ethos of the new age women, which has evolved over time. They can be agents of change, as when inner-city teens, who are associated with anti-establishment principles, are introduced new styles of clothing that reflected those principles. Hero cycles' attempt to push their upmarket range of teenage bikes was positioned on the anti-establishment image of "Why must...?" trying to break free of rules and creating their own. Such advertisements showcase characters who are on the fringe wondering what to do or not to do and suffer from dilemma.

Journalists also shape cultural principles and the products associated with them. For example, restaurant reviewers may determine whether a restaurant is associated with principles like status, and style editors may determine whether clothes are associated with young and hip categories or with others. Magazines like

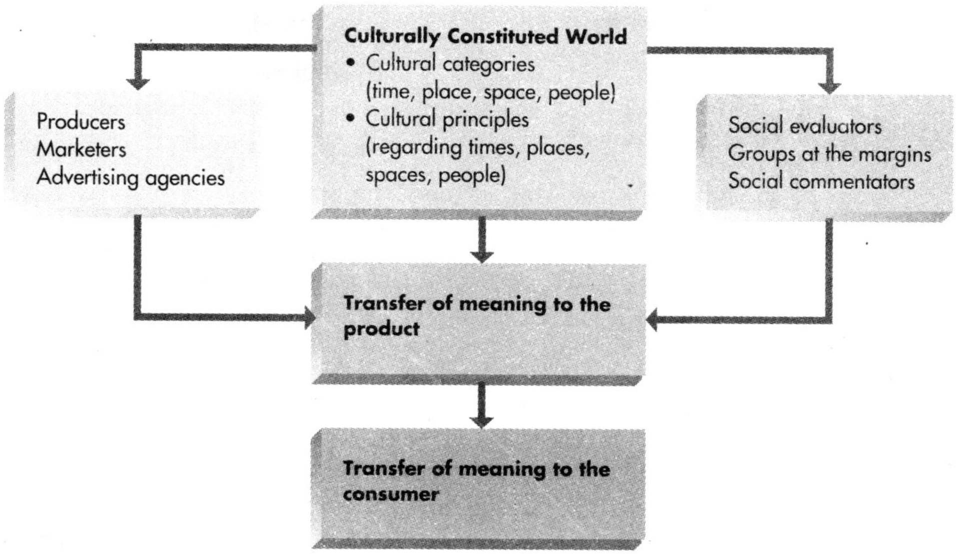

Exhibit 18.4

TRANSFER OF MEANING FROM THE CULTURE TO THE PRODUCT AND TO THE CONSUMER *Meaning that exists at the level of the culture (e.g., youthful) can become associated with a product (e.g., Pepsi). Marketer-dominated groups (e.g., marketers) and non-marketer-dominated groups (e.g., opinion leaders, the media) can play a powerful role in this association process. The meaning associated with the product can in turn be transferred to the consumer who uses it.*

Runner's World communicate meaning associated with the runner category, such as what runner are like, what they wear and eat, and what they like to do. Celebrities like Ricky Martin can also create meaning in products by how they use them. Through all of these sources, the meaning inherent in the product gets transferred to the consumer.

Meaning Derived from the Consumer

In addition to the way products derive symbolic meaning from culture, consumers can develop their own individual meanings associated with products. Whether meaning stems from (1) the culture or the consumer, however, consumption symbols can be used to say something (2) about the consumer as a member of a group or as a unique individual. Combining these two dimensions produces the emblematic, role acquisition, connectedness, and expressiveness functions of symbols described next.

The Emblematic Function

Meaning derived from culture allows us to use products to symbolize our membership in various social groups, what we call an ***emblematic function.*** Dresses are associated with women, and clerical collars are associated with priests. The music we listen to may symbolize our age, and the car we drive may symbolize our social status. Consciously or unconsciously, we use brands and products to symbolize the groups to which we belong (or want to belong[7]). At the same time, people who observe us using these products may consciously or unconsciously categorize and make inferences about us and the groups we belong to (see Chapter 5). Just by looking at someone and his or her possessions, we might be able to tell whether that person is a member of the "surfer," "fraternity type," or "rich kid" social categories.[8] In particular, offerings can serve as geographic, ethnic, or social class emblems.

Geographic Emblems Products can symbolize geographic identification. For example South Indian women traditionally wear the chira (in Telugu, cheela in Tamil) while the men wear a type of sarong, which could be either a white pancha (veshti in Tamil) or a colourful lungi with typical batik patterns. Alternatively, his North Indian counterpart is identified more through Kurta Pyjama or even a Sherwani. The way of wearing Sarees by the north and south Indian women differ too. This besides the fact that in India there are enough regional influences which define their own localised approach to dressing, the essence however remaining the same.

Ethnic Emblems Products and consumption activities can symbolize identification with a specific culture or subculture. African Americans sometimes wear African garb to symbolize identification with that culture. In India, Sikh men wear five Ks as symbols of their ethnic and religious affiliation: *kesh* (hair), *kada* (bangle), *kangha* (comb), *kacha* (underpants), and *kirpan* (dagger). Some consumers use ethnic emblems of other cultures or subcultures to differentiate themselves. To illustrate, clothing and sneakers identified with African American urban culture and music have become popular among Anglo consumers in the United States.[10]

Consumers commonly use food to express ethnic identity. Similarly, food habits differ drastically across India. North, South, East and West have their own local cuisines and today with population migrating across regions, some foods have become national identity. A number of religions, with their own traditions and customs, co-exist in India. [3]The food habits differ across regions and religions. However, the two cultures that have played a pivotal role in the development of the Indian cuisine and food habits are the Hindu and the Muslim traditions. The Portuguese, the Persians and the British have also made important contributions to the Indian cuisine. Foods like Chole Bhature, Puri Sabji or Samosas that originated from North India, are nationally recognised. Ditto for Idli, Dosas or Upmas, south Indian cuisines now have a Pan India presence.

Social Class Emblems Products can also symbolize social class. In China, emblems of status include color TVs, cognac (for older consumers), and fine imported wine (for younger consumers). Among wealthy American consumers, symbols of social class include helicopters, backyard golf courses, private airplanes, and palatial homes. [4]In India, according to a Techopak India Luxury Trends 2006 study, the top five categories of growth in the affluent class are, Jewelry, Clothing, Digital accessories, timewear and cosmetics & skincare. Consider, also, emblems of membership in the upper-upper class (see Exhibit 18.5). The cultural principles of upper- upper-class membership include characteristics of refinement, understated restraint, and discipline. So too do the products and consumption activities of this class. The Techopak study also classifies the affluent Indian women into three different categories, namely "The Butterfly", who is market mover to luxury, well heeled and well educated, is brand conscious, owns the latest gadgets and dines at the most upscale restaurants. Next is "Mrs. Rationality", who is value conscious and

Exhibit 18.5
SOCIAL CLASS EMBLEMS
Louis Vuitton bags are a sign of status and denote upper-class membership in the affluent section.

not ostentatious, she seldom indulges, she has a self made household and is not an impulsive buyer. The last, "Old Luxury", who is grown up with luxury and it is her way of life and is a steady luxury buyer.

The social classes also use different symbols in consumption rituals. In markets like India, where disparity between the social classes is high, it is more distraught and stark. Particularly, in the urban metropolis, the disparities are even more visible. The difference in the neo rich and the traditionally affluent class is also understandable. What creates the bigger challenge for the society is the peer pressure to imitate life styles. Movies like Dhoom and Dhoom 2, glorify living good life even through stealing and conning, which leaves a deep impact on the young minds, particularly at the lower end of the society. Even recent spate of economic offences committed, show a history of average middle class youth committing such crimes, again aspiring for the good life. More and more public schools in bigger cities are discouraging parents to lavish their children with gifts. Some schools even disallow parents from sending sweets and goodies on their birthdays to school, insisting schools privately celebrate that with the class, thereby creating a quasi commonality between diverse social classes.

Gender Emblems Food, clothing, jewelry, and alcoholic beverages are only some of the product categories associated with membership in the male and female gender categories.[18] One study of consumers in France revealed that meat and certain other foods are viewed as "man" foods, whereas celery and other foods are viewed as "woman" foods. In part, associating certain foods with specific gender groups stems from culturally devised notions of fatness and thinness and the appropriateness of these attributes for men and women. The way a food is eaten also reflects its gender appropriateness: steak and meats that may be cut roughly and chewed intensively are viewed in some cultures as more consistent with male characteristics.[19] Other researchers have found gender differences in food preferences, with boys preferring chunky peanut butter, for instance, and girls preferring the smooth variety. These preferences may be related to culturally derived associations with boys (rough) and girls (not rough).[20]

Large, rugged, powerful vehicles are often associated with male characteristics. Consider the boxy, militaristic look of GM's Hummer and the Toyota FJ Cruiser, both marketed primarily to men. Governor Arnold Schwarzenegger added to the Hummer's macho quality when reporters watched him test-drive the SUV during a major auto show.[21] In contrast, the Ford Freestar minivan is so closely associated with women—especially mothers—that the automaker asks its engineers and designers to get a firsthand sense of what pregnant women go through in exiting and entering the car by wearing the weighted Empathy Belly Pregnancy Simulator, which also features a bulging belly sack.[22]

Reference Group Emblems Harley-Davidson is a good example of how products can serve as emblems of membership in a reference group. One reason consumers become outlaw bikers (or adopt outlaw symbols) is that they like being members of a reference group with a counterculture ideology. Consumers may also wear varsity jackets, special hats, particular colors, or gang-designated jewelry to symbolize reference group membership. Conversely, consumers may shun certain products to avoid being seen as members in a reference group—which, in turn, symbolizes membership in another reference group. This is the case in the auto business, where a backlash is forming against gas-guzzling SUVs. "It's a big deal, and it's real," confirms a Chrysler marketing official. Instead of driving SUVs, some consumers look for fuel-efficient hybrid cars (such as the Toyota Prius), joining the movement of consumers who use their buying power to act on their concerns about the environment.[23]

In addition to products, rituals are sometimes important indicators and affirmations of group membership. For example, Annaprashan' is a social ritual among the Hindus, an occasion when the baby breaks its baby food pattern to welcome home-made food. It is as well as a social introduction of the new member of the family in the community. Annaprashan literally means feeding the baby rice for the first time. "Anna" means food, specially rice while "prashan" means to feed. Annaprashan acquires the importance of a religious ceremony. Arranged for the Hindu child generally before teething, this ritual is separate for both boys and girls. In case of the girl child annaprashan is performed on odd months, generally in the 5th or the 7th month, whereas in case of a boy child the ritual is performed in even months either in the 6th or the 8th month. Even rituals like exchanging sweets and pleasantries during festivals like Holi and Diwali reinforce membership within groups.

marketing IMPLICATIONS Marketers can play three roles in establishing the emblematic function of products.

Symbol development

The first role is symbol development, linking a product and its attributes to a specific cultural category and its principles. For example, Patek Philippe watches have characteristics associated with the upper class: timeless style, understated elegance, precision craftsmanship, precious materials, and price tags that range from $4,700 to $600,000.[25] Sometimes marketers need to ensure that product attributes are appropriately linked with cultural principles. Miller, for example, positioned the *lite* in Miller

Lite as meaning "less filling and has fewer carbohydrates"—an appropriate attribute for men—rather than *diet*, which would have made the beer seem more feminine.[26]

Symbol communication

The second role is symbol communication. A company can use advertising to charge a product with meaning through the setting for the ad (whether fantasy or naturalistic, interior or exterior, or rural or urban) and through other details such as the time of day and the types of people in the ad—their gender, age, ethnicity, occupation, clothing, body postures, and so on.[27] Each ad element reinforces the meaning associated with the product.

Symbol reinforcement

The third role is to design other elements of the marketing mix to reinforce the symbolic image.[28] For instance, a company can use various pricing, distribution, and product strategies to maintain a product's status image. It may give the product a premium price, distribute it through outlets with an upscale image, and incorporate certain features that are appropriate only for the targeted segment. However, marketers may hurt a product's symbolic image if the elements of the marketing mix clash with each other.

Symbol removal

Some marketers have made a business of helping consumers erase symbols associated with groups with whom they no longer identify. For example, the tattoo removal market is growing. Consumers often want tattoos removed because they are emblematic of an earlier time of life or an abandoned reference group and therefore impede the development of new personal identities.[29]

The Role Acquisition Function

In addition to serving as emblems of group membership, offerings can help us feel more comfortable in new roles. This function is called the ***role acquisition function*** (look back at Exhibit 18.3).

Role Acquisition Phases Consumers fill many roles in their lives, and these roles constantly change. You may currently occupy the role of student, son or daughter, brother or sister, and worker. At some point in your life (perhaps even now), you may occupy the role of husband or wife, uncle or aunt, parent, divorcee, grandparent, retiree, widow or widower, and so on.

People typically move from one role to another in three phases.[30] The first phase is separation from the old role. This often means disposing of products associated with the role we are leaving, the way children give up security blankets in their transition from baby to child. Consumers who are breaking up a relationship may symbolize the relationship's end by giving away, throwing away, or destroying products that remind them of their former partners.[31] The second phase is the transition from one role to another, which may be accompanied by experimentation with new identities. During this transition, consumers may be willing to accept new possessions or styles they otherwise would have rejected. Consumers may also construct a new identity through plastic surgery, dieting, new hairstyles, branding, body piercing, and tattooing. The final phase is incorporation, in which the consumer takes on the new role and the identity associated with it.

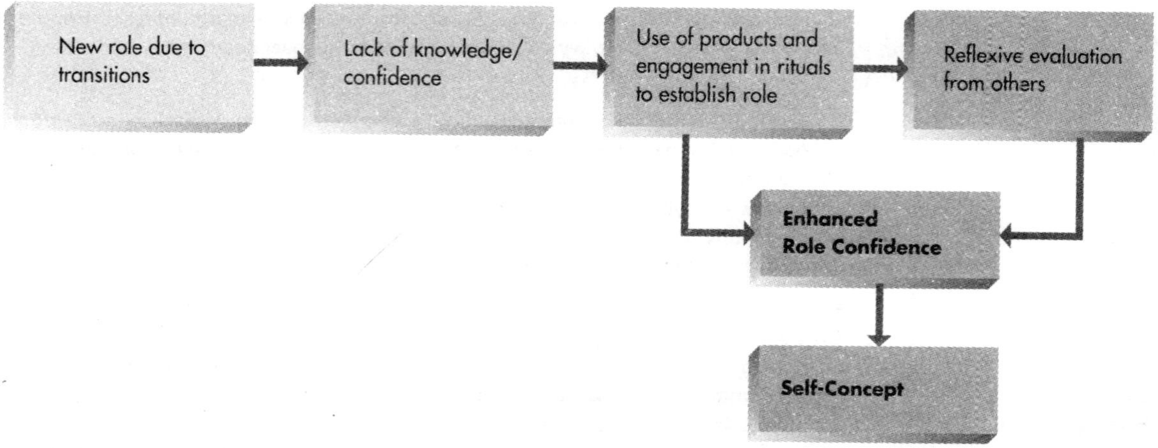

Exhibit 18.6

MODEL OF ROLE ACQUISITION *When we are entering a new role (e.g., parenthood), we may lack some role confidence. As a result, we engage in activities (e.g., have baby showers) and buy groups of products (e.g., strollers) typically associated with that role. These activities and products, along with the way that others react to our behaviors, enhance our role confidence.*

Use of Symbols and Rituals in Role Transitions Exhibit 18.6 illustrates how and why we use symbols and rituals when we acquire a new role. We often feel uncomfortable with a new role because we are inexperienced in occupying it and have little knowledge about how to fulfill it. A common reaction is to use products stereotypically associated with that role. For example, MBAs who are insecure about their job prospects are more likely than other MBAs to use symbols generally associated with the role of businessperson.[32] We often use a group of products to symbolize adoption of a new role. Having the right combination of products is important because without it we may not elicit the appropriate response from others. Imagine the reaction you would get at work if you wore white socks or sneakers with a business suit.

Rituals are also an important part of role transitions. For example, a number of rituals mark the transition from single to married status in the United States—engagement party, wedding shower, bachelor party, rehearsal dinner, wedding, reception, and honeymoon—each with relevant enabling products.[33] The wedding itself includes clothing for the attendants, flowers, wedding gown, musicians, a photographer, and so on. Funeral rituals in different cultures involve symbolic consumption activities, as well, such as presenting or consuming special foods, buying flowers and cards, and displaying pictures or valuables that reflect on both the deceased and the bereaved.[34]

Rituals often involve others whose participation helps validate the role transition. As Exhibit 18.6 shows, we use symbols and engage in rituals to get feedback from participants about whether we are fulfilling the role correctly. This feedback, called ***reflexive evaluation,*** helps us feel more confident in our role and thus validates our new status. Newly minted MBAs, for example, feel more confident in their role when experienced businesspeople acknowledge them as another businessperson. The next section focuses on marital role transitions and products as symbols of this transition process.

Marital Transitions Products are often an important component in the transition from single to married status. As part of separating from the old phase, the couple must decide which of their possessions to dispose of and which to move to their new household. Often presents from old boyfriends or girlfriends are discarded, as are products symbolizing their former single status. As part of the incorporation phase, the couple acquires new products that are culturally appropriate for the married role and that help them create a mutual history. Clearly, different cultures have different marital rituals. For example, in a Hindu household the mother-in-law often gives the keys to the house to the bride following the wedding, symbolically handing over the charge of running the house. The ad in Exhibit 18.7 showcases diamond as a part of the marriage (ring) ceremony.

Exhibit 18.7
MARITAL ROLE TRANSITION SYMBOLS
Jewelery is a precious part of Indian marriages and parents save through ages on the gold jewelery that the daughter will wear for her marriage. Today, diamonds are also showcased as an integral part of such rituals, signifying a more individual appeal to marriage.

A similar process operates in the transition from married to divorced status. Here, each person takes back what was his or hers and they divide their joint possessions. People may deliberately dispose of possessions that remind them of the other person. As one set of researchers notes, "Jettisoning symbols of the ex-spouse . . . may be psychologically necessary in the process of ending the relationship."[35] Some people destroy possessions, which perhaps serves several functions—symbolically representing the destruction of the marriage, punishing the ex-spouse, and eliminating possessions that symbolize the marriage.

People may have difficulty fulfilling other symbolic functions as a result of ending a marriage. For example, one spouse may no longer have the conspicuous consumption items they once used to communicate social status. Thus someone who loses a house and a car (two important symbols of social prestige) may feel a loss of identity. On the other hand, people may acquire products symbolic of their new single status during this role transition, the way some people purchase a sports car.

Cultural Transitions Consumers also may change roles when they move to a new culture, often abandoning or disposing of old customs and symbols and adopting new ones in the process. Research suggests that Mexican immigrants faced different and sometimes difficult experiences in moving to the United States.[36] Among these were living in densely grouped housing, shopping in stores with a sometimes overwhelming number of choices, and dealing with unfamiliar currency. Another study shows that Indians moving to the United States acquired status symbols that they did not need in India, where caste and family designate class membership.[37] Expatriates often face frustrating and formidable barriers to inclusion in a new culture. To reduce these barriers, they may participate in local events and rituals, adapt consumption to local customs, and become brand conscious, even though they may hold on to certain aspects of their home culture, like food, language, videos, photos, and jewelry.[38]

Whether someone abandons or retains possessions that symbolize the old role may depend on how long the role is expected to last. The study of expatriates from India showed that consumers held onto possessions reminiscent of their culture of origin because they still considered the possibility of someday returning to India.

Social Status Transitions Newly wealthy individuals, the "nouveaux riches," use possessions—usually ostentatious ones—to demonstrate their acquired status and validate their role. This is consistent with the model of symbols and role transitions in Exhibit 18.6, which shows the importance of reflexive evaluation from others to indicate successful role performance. As one author notes, "Consumer satisfaction is derived from audience reactions to the wealth displayed by the purchaser in securing the product or service rather than to the positive attributes of the item in question."[39]

marketing IMPLICATIONS Marketers can apply their knowledge of consumers' role transitions in several ways.

Role transitions and target consumers

Consumers in transition represent an important target market for many firms. As Procter & Gamble's global marketing officer says, "Newlyweds are in some ways the ultimate consumer."[40] Many companies target engaged couples who will soon buy offerings related to the wedding, honeymoon, and new housing. Exhibit 18.8 shows one example. De Beers's Diamond Trading Company is targeting women with a campaign that reinforces how wearing jewelry on different hands can symbolize marriage or self-expression. The tag line is "Your left hand says 'we.' Your right hand says 'me.' "[41]

Role transitions as a means for developing inventory

Because product disposition can be an important aspect of role separation, marketers of secondhand products can acquire inventory by marketing to people engaged in role transitions. For example, secondhand stores might target college students before graduation, knowing that in their role transitions many may wish to dispose of student-related paraphernalia such as furniture and clothing. Similarly, online auction sites such as eBay profit when consumers decide to dispose of items made obsolete or irrelevant by role transitions.

Role transitions and product promotions

Marketers may find it useful to promote their products as instrumental in incorporating a new role. Anniversaries, Mother's Day, Father's Day or Valentine's Day, associated more with the western world have seeped into the Indian cultures and norms. Gifting as a part of such rituals has also begun to evolve over time. Valentine's Day today is much awaited time for the teens and youths, when not just greeting cards and flowers but expensive gifts are exchanged like Mobile phones, jewelery and even expensive gadgets like i-pod.

Selling product constellations

Marketers can stress the importance of groups of products to consumers in the process of role acquisition.[44] For example, marketers may appeal to new parents looking for complete layette sets or suites of baby furniture. Businesses featuring product constellations include websites such as TheKnot.com and WeddingChannel.com, which offer access to one-stop shopping for wedding apparel, photographers, florists, limousine companies, catering companies, and related offerings. Company advertising can suggest that consumers will earn positive

Exhibit 18.8
MANAGING RITUALS
The website shaadionline.com positions itself as a complete source for helping consumers manage the wedding ritual.

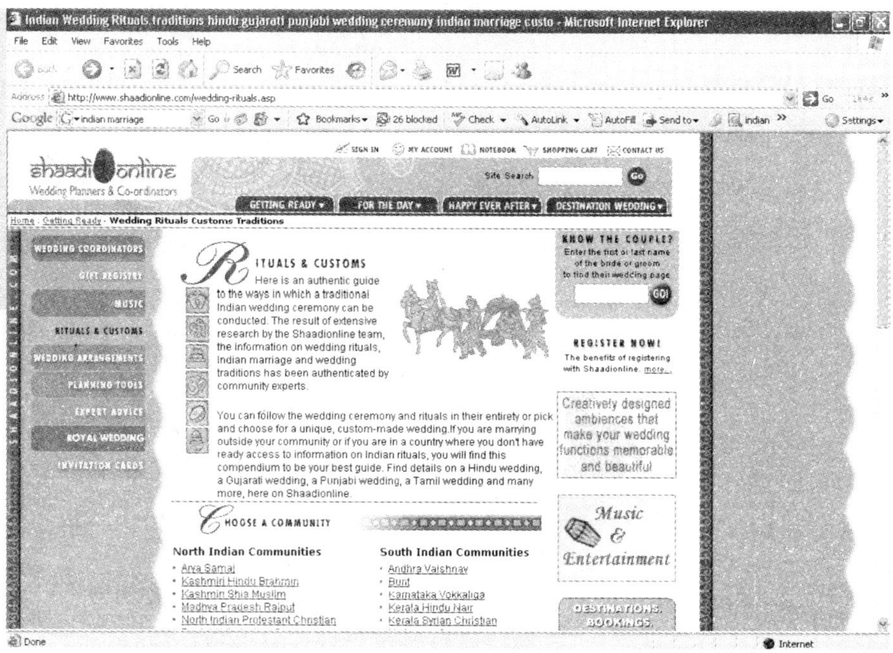

reflexive evaluation from others if they use an appropriate constellation of products associated with a given role.

Managing rituals

Marketers can also be instrumental in developing services that help in planning and implementing rituals surrounding transitions, the way funeral homes perform services in the death ritual. Exhibit 18.8 indicates how a marketer positions itself as a comprehensive source for helping couples manage the wedding ritual.

The Connectedness Function

Although the meaning of offerings that serve emblematic or role acquisition functions comes from the culture, product meaning can also derive from the consumer's role as a member of a group or as an individual (review Exhibit 18.3).[45] Products and consumption activities that serve the ***connectedness function*** express our membership in a group and serve as symbols of personal connections to significant people, events, or experiences in our lives. For example, you may particularly like a painting or a hat because it was a gift from a close friend. Heirlooms and genealogy studies connect people with their ancestors; family photos connect them to their descendants. People may also value ticket stubs, concert programs, and other souvenirs as reminders of special people, events, and places.[46]

Other products and acts can also symbolize connectedness. For instance, Chinese consumers use large round tables in restaurants to symbolize wholeness and the group's connectedness; Chinese New Year celebrations emphasize family ties. During Muslim feasts, everyone shares food from a community plate; those who ask for a separate plate are considered rude. Rituals may also symbolize connectedness. The U.S. ritual of Thanksgiving is marked by numerous symbols of connectedness.[47] Often family members show their commitment by attending the Thanksgiving gathering—even if they have to travel long distances—and significant others also attend the entire meal or come just for dessert, depending on the seriousness of the relationship. Cultures like the United States and England also emphasize family connectedness during the Christmas ritual. In other cultures, such as some Eskimo villages in Alaska, the Christmas ritual has more of a community focus.[48] In India the family holds a significant power over an individual. [5]Although traditional roles are changing, especially in urban areas, there are important values shared by most Indian families. Generally, Indians hold family progress, unity and support in high regard throughout their lives. Many live in an extended family, in which every member has his own role, often determined by age and gender. Elders are supposed to use their experience and wisdom to help guide younger family members. Children are cherished and can look forward to continual family support throughout their lives. In return, children are expected to respect family ties and wishes. Festivals are a common meeting point for families and even migrant populations staying away from families make it a point to be home during festivals. Northern states like Bihar, UP, Rajasthan or Madhya Pradesh have important festivals like Holi, Diwali, Chath, and Teej where families congregate together.

Each family maintains its own traditions that foster connectedness. Members often strongly resist deviating from these traditions (such as trying a new stuffing recipe). Many families foster connectedness by looking at old family photographs or videos and telling family stories. Other families pass certain cherished objects from one generation to the next as symbols of the family's connectedness.[49] This sense of connectedness may not only reaffirm social ties but also make us nostalgic about past times.[50]

The Expressiveness Function

As a symbol, a product has the potential to say something about our uniqueness.[51] This ***expressiveness function*** reflects how unique we are, not how we relate to other people. According to research, Eastern European youths like Western products because these offerings are used to create a distinct appearance that sets them apart.[52] We express our unique personalities through offerings like clothing, home decoration, art, music, leisure activities, and food consumption. Some consumers use body piercing, branding, and tattooing to symbolize their individuality and expressiveness.[53]

marketing IMPLICATIONS The connectedness and expressive functions lead to several marketing implications. [6]Nostalgia Marketing has now become a plank for marketers, especially in the music industry to cash on. Music Company SA RE GA MA launched an album containing twenty one hit tracks handpicked to form an album, which is aptly called 'Flash Back'. These are tunes which are closely tied to the emotions of almost every generation. In fact, the company has turned nostalgia into a money-spinning business. A tune is a trigger which can hurl you back in time instantly. Every generation, as it ages, has a yearning to turn back the clock and return to the simpler times. Marketers have understood this yearning and are using it to their advantage. Of late, Bollywood has been awash with remakes and re-mixes. The global success of Mughal-e-Azam amplifies the point that the faster we hurtle into this millennium, the more desperate is the impulse of a generation to look backwards. McDonald's is marketing its burgers using the look-alikes of Raj Kapoor, Sanjeev Kumar and Rajesh Khanna to seduce the older age group into consuming fast food fare. Indians are quite sensitive to their tradition, and the memories of the past weigh them down. Nostalgia marketing, which is being born, is succeeding because of this vulnerability. While the young India today lives on the dreams of a phosph or escent tomorrow, the old live on the memories of their foggy yesterdays.

Multiple Functions

Because products and rituals can be used symbolically to serve many functions, a given product may serve several functions simultaneously. A set of crystal wine goblets received as a wedding present from the bride's grandparents could serve an emblematic function because their high price tag communicates social status. They may also serve a role acquisition function, helping the newlyweds to internalize their new marital roles. Because they were a present from grandparents, the goblets may also serve a connectedness function—symbolizing the newlyweds' special relationship with their grandparents. Finally, if the goblets are personally appealing to the couple, they may symbolize the newlyweds' individual aesthetic tastes, thus serving an expressiveness function.

We sometimes deliberately use products because they fulfill one or more of the four functions noted in Exhibit 18.3. We may choose to dress in a certain way to communicate the group to which we belong or the unique tastes we have, or we might show off photos or artwork to remind ourselves of certain people or occasions. However, we are not always aware of a product's symbolic function, such as the possibility that an item of clothing symbolizes our gender or our age. We may expect certain types of gifts when we go through role transitions like graduation and marriage, but we are probably not conscious that these products help us adjust to our new role. Finally, we may really like an item we got as a gift without realizing that we react this way because it serves as a reminder of the gift giver.

Symbols and Self-Concept

The symbolic functions of products and consumption rituals are important because together they help to define and maintain our self-concept, our mental conception of who we are.[56] Social identity theory proposes that we evaluate brands in terms of their consistency with our individual identities.[57] According to the theory, our self-concept can be decomposed into many separate identities called ***actual identity schemas,*** including student, worker, daughter, and so on. These identities may be driven, at least in part, by the roles we fulfill. Some identities may be especially salient or central to our self-concept. Our actual identity may be shaped by an ***ideal identity schema***—a set of ideas about how the identity we seek would be realized in its ideal form.

Our actual and ideal identity schemas influence which products we use and which consumption practices we engage in, even among consumers whose self-concept includes objecting to the overcommercialization of contemporary culture[58] (see Chapter 20 for more about the dark side of marketing). The fact that possessions help shape our identity may explain why people who lose their possessions in natural disasters or wars and people who are in institutions like the military, nursing homes, or prisons often feel a loss of identity.[59] In fact, some consumers who lose their possessions experience feelings of grief very similar to the feelings that follow the death of a loved one. Some institutions, such as the military and prisons, deliberately strip individuals of their possessions to erase their old identities.[60] At the other end of the spectrum, a growing number of consumers are posting personal Web pages in which they use words, images, audio, links, and other elements to construct and project identities digitally, shaping and sharing their self-concept within the Internet community.[61]

marketing IMPLICATIONS Marketers need to consider several implications stemming from the preceding concepts.

Marketing and the development of consumer self-concepts

Marketers can play a role in both producing and maintaining an individual's self-concept. Although products may help define who we are, we also maintain our self-concept by selecting products with images that are consistent with it. The profile of the women in India is undergoing a steady change in terms of her outlook and thought process. She might be a career women or a homemaker, yet she has begun to assert herself more positively in households. The traditional role of "Sati Savitri" is now being replaced with an independent and forward thinking outlook.

Marketers are also quick to realize this gradual shift in the roles and status of the women. Even filmmakers are scripting redefined roles. A popular film, Taxi No. 9211, showcased two different kinds of women. One a lower middle class homemaker, wife of a taxi driver, who does not hesitate to leave her errant and ill-tempered husband and the other who leaves her fiancée, when she realizes that he has turned a pauper from a prince. These changing roles are not to be mistaken for negativism but an affirmation for her new role. [7]The new advertisement for Amul Macho underwear is another case in point, generating controversy. The advertisement in question has a newly wed woman entering a 'dhobi ghat' (a place where clothes are washed, generally near the banks of a water body), as other women eye her curiously. Regardless of their stares, the woman opens up her bundle of clothes and pulls out the first garment – Amul Macho underwear belonging to her husband. She then starts brushing it, and through her expressions it is clear that she fancies that the man is still wearing it.

Product fit with self-concepts

Marketers should understand how their product fits with the identities of their target consumers and try to create a fit between the image of the brand and the actual or ideal identity of the consumer. Research has found that the more similar a product's image is to a consumer's self-image, the more the consumer likes the product (see Exhibit 18.9).[64]

Product fit with multiple self-concepts

Because self-images are multifaceted, marketers must also determine whether products consistent with one aspect of the target customers' identity may be inconsistent with another aspect. A new father may react negatively to disposable diapers because even though the product is consistent with his new parent identity, it is inconsistent with his environmentally conscious identity.

Exhibit 18.9

FIT WITH SELF - CONCEPT

This ad suggests that smarter mothers will give Bournvita to their kids but they themselves have to fit into the shoes of a smart mom.

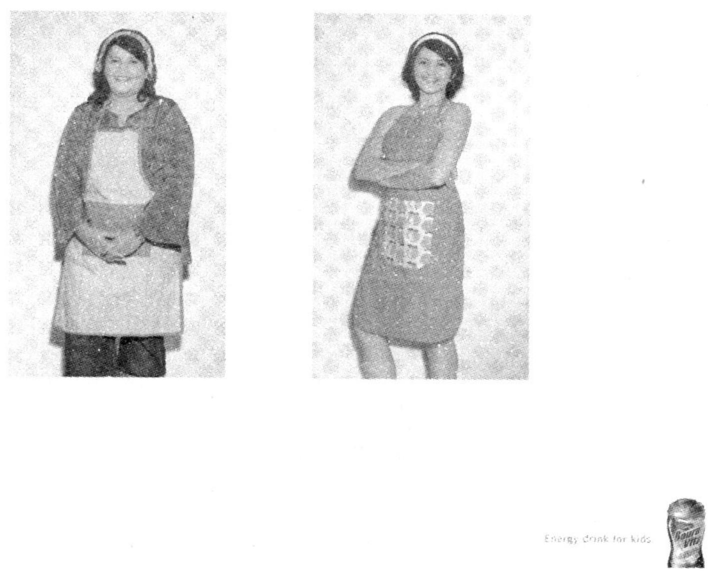

Advertising fit with self-concepts

Finally, advertising should appeal to the identity concept appropriate for the gender and culture of the targeted segment.[65] Thus some ads that target women might emphasize mutual reliance, whereas some ads that target men might emphasize autonomy. Similarly, ads geared toward consumers in China might stress culturally appropriate themes of group goals and achievement, whereas ads for U.S. consumers might stress culturally appropriate themes of personal goals and achievement.

Special Possessions

Some products come to hold a special, valued position in our minds, whether or not they are relevant to our self-concepts.[66] For example, one consumer may regard his lawn mower as a special possession because it is extremely functional, whereas another may view her skis as special because they give such enjoyment. However, neither consumer may view these products as relevant to their self-concept.[67] What products become special and why do they remain so?

Types of Special Possessions

Although almost any possession can be special, researchers have found that special possessions typically fall into one of several categories: pets, memory-laden objects, achievement symbols, and collections.[68]

Pets A $34 billion market for pet-related offerings is partly due to the fact that U.S. consumers tend to regard their pets as very special.[69] Many name their pets, buy them special food and clothes, talk to them, groom them, play with them, photograph them, buy them Christmas presents, take them on vacation, and even buy them health insurance.[70] Often consumers treat pets as family members or as extensions of themselves, and they feel sad or guilty about leaving them alone when they have to go to work or boarding them when the need to travel. These feelings have created profitable opportunities for doggie day car centers, pet sitters, and hotel chains that welcome pets. Now that 64 million U.S. households keep a pet, retailers such as PetsMart and Petco see higher demand for gourmet pet food and other premium products. Petco's CEO states, "People keep projecting onto their animals how they feel about themselves and what they want in their own life. The premium pet-food craze very much reflects human interest in better diets."[71] However, not every culture treats pets as special possessions. For example, cats and dogs are not treasured as pets in the Middle East, and dog owners in Korea typically feed their pets leftovers rather than dog food. Having pets in India is not as common a practice as it is in the west. Save for an occasional dog or a cat, pets have never been well accepted by our society. On the other hand in the western way of living which is individualistic, where children move out early from home, pets become a source of dependence and at times people get emotionally attached to them as if they are family members. Alternatively, in India, family bonding and attachments are more, which may be a reason for pets not being a favored choice. [8]In India, cats for instance are not as popular a pet as dogs, falling prey to deep-rooted superstitions and associations that link them with witchcraft and bad luck. That is the main reason why people in India do not prefer to keep them as pets. Alternate pets like turtles, insects or off-beat ones like python or birds are even rarer pets.

Memory-Laden Objects Some products acquire special meaning because they evoke memories or emotions of special people, places, or experiences.[72] Examples include heirlooms, antiques, souvenirs, and gifts from special people. You may value a ticket stub—otherwise just a piece of paper—because it evokes memories of going to see your favorite band in concert. Similarly, a special song may evoke feelings of sentimentality or nostalgia. Such possessions can be therapeutic for elderly people because they evoke links to other people and happy times. Several researchers report the case of an individual who had to sell a favorite automobile because of a divorce but saved the license plates as a memento of this special possession. Many consumers consider photographs special because they are reminders of special people, and they create "shrines" by displaying photos on bureaus, mantles, and pianos.[73] Possessions that symbolize connectedness clearly have the potential to become special.

Achievement Symbols People also regard possessions that symbolize achievement as special. One researcher who studied the Mormon migration to Utah in the 1800s found that people often moved possessions that demonstrated competence. For example, men brought tools, and women brought sewing machines and other objects that had a practical function but also symbolized domestic achievement.[74] Modern-day symbols of achievement might include college diplomas, sports trophies, recognition plaques, or even conspicuously consumed items like Rolex watches or Porsches.

Collections Collections are special possessions for many. At least one in three U.S. consumers is a collector.[75] Common collectible items include porcelain figurines; model cars; seashells; minerals; CDs; and childhood objects like baseball cards, GI Joe and Barbie dolls, and cookie jars.[76] Uncommon collectibles include spark plugs, junk mail, drain tiles, and airsickness bags. Firms like the Bradford Exchange, the Franklin Mint, and the Danbury Mint produce collectible items for consumers, but rarity makes items particularly special. For example, one collector paid $1.1 million for a 1910 Honus Wagner baseball card—a record price for a single baseball card—because only 50 still exist.[77]

Collectors often view their collections as extensions of themselves—sometimes symbolizing an aspect of their occupation, family heritage, or appearance. Researchers have studied a grocery store owner who collected antique product packages, an engineer who collected pocket watches, a woman named Bunny who collected rabbit replicas, and wealthy women who collected monogrammed silver spoons.[78] For some, collections represent a fantasy image of the self. For example, men who collect baseball cards may be keeping alive the fantasy of themselves as ball players. As is often the case with people who have special possessions, collectors tend to believe that they take better care of their collections than anyone else would.[79] In the past Philately was a popular form of collectible hobby, which has now made way for newer collectible hobbies like, WWF cards, Pokemon cards, Duel Master cards, YU-GI-OH cards. As the culture of writing letters is slowly diminishing, philately as a hobby is fading too. However, there are some new forms of collectible hobbies like, match boxes, erasers or even train tickets to name some. However, the culture of storing, preserving and keeping them as prized possession is not unheard of now, particularly in urban households.

The Characteristics That Describe Special Possessions

Special possessions have several distinct characteristics.[80] First, consumers will not sell them at market value, if at all, and often buy special possessions with little regard for their price. We could never, for example, sell at any price our family pet or a quilt made by our grandmother. Collectors may pay exorbitant prices to acquire particularly sought-after objects like rare coins.

Second, special possessions have few or no substitutes. For example, when our family dog dies, we are unlikely to find or even want to find another dog just like it. Insurance may pay to replace furniture that was damaged in a fire, but new furniture cannot compensate for heirloom pieces that were passed down through generations. In fact, consumers see special possessions as irreplaceable because of the associations with certain events and people in their lives.[81] A third characteristic is that people will not discard special possessions, even when they lose their functional value. Children are often reluctant to part with security blankets and stuffed animals and will keep these favorite objects until they are mere threads of fabric. Do your parents still keep your old report cards, bronzed baby shoes, and cards you or others have given to them?

Special possessions are not always used for their original purpose. Some people who buy Altoids "Curiously Strong" mints retain the tin container for special but unusual purposes, such as to encase a digital music player.[82] Some consumers even believe that a prized possession will lose valued properties if used to fulfill its original function. For example, collectibles such as Barbie dolls and Star Wars toys lose their collectible value if they have been removed from their packaging. One study described a woman who collected nutcrackers but would not consider using them to crack nuts.[83] Special possessions can also evoke powerful emotions like achievement, affection, pride, or passion.[84] If these possessions are lost, destroyed, or otherwise disposed of, we may feel depressed, saddened, or pained.

Finally, consumers frequently personify special possessions. Some people give names to individual items in a collection, name their houses, or use a feminine or masculine pronoun when referring to their cars or boats. Perhaps even more significant, we may treat these possessions as though they were our partners, feeling such commitment and attachment that we are devastated by their loss.[85]

Why Some Products Are Special

Possessions take on special meaning for several reasons, including their symbolic value, mood-altering properties, and instrumental importance. Exhibit 18.10 shows more specific reasons that underlie these three general categories.

- *Symbolic value.* Possessions may be special, in part, because they fulfill the emblematic, role adoption, connectedness, and expressiveness functions noted earlier in the chapter. For example, we may value art, heirlooms, and jewelry because they express our style or because they were gifts and tie us to special people.[86] Thus consumers are very reluctant to part with a possession that has symbolic meaning because it was acquired from a much-loved family member or close friend.[87] Further, cars and houses may be valued for their reflection of social class, whereas a possession like a wedding dress may be valued because it reflects a role transition.

Exhibit 18.10

REASONS WHY POSSESSIONS ARE SPECIAL

Take a possession you regard as special. Most likely it is special to you because it has symbolic value, mood-altering properties, and/or utilitarian value.

Take a possession you regard as special, and answer the following questions using a 7-point scale (1 = not true of me; 7 = very true of me).

This possession is important to me because it . . .

Symbolic Value	Symbolizes personal history	Reminds me of my childhood Reminds me of particular events or places Is a record of my personal history
	Represents achievement	Required a lot of effort to acquire or maintain Reminds me of my skills, achievements, or goals
	Represents interpersonal ties	Reminds me of my relationship with a particular person Reminds me of my family or a group of people I belong to Represents my family heritage or history
	Facilitates interpersonal ties	Allows me to spend time or share activities with other people
	Demonstrates status	Has social prestige value Gives me social status Makes others think well of me
	Is self-expressive	Allows me to express myself Expresses what is unique about me, different from others
Mood-Altering Properties	Provides enjoyment	Provides enjoyment, entertainment, or relaxation Improves my mood Provides comfort or emotional security
	Is spiritual	Provides a spiritual link to divine or higher forces
	Is appearance related	Is beautiful or attractive in appearance Improves my appearance or the way I look
Utilitarian Value	Is utilitarian	Allows me to be efficient in my daily life or work Has a lot of practical usefulness Provides me freedom or independence
	Has financial aspects	Is valuable in terms of money

Source: Adapted from Marsha Richens, "Valuing Things: The Public and Private Meanings of Possessions," *Journal of Consumer Research,* vol. 21, December 1994, pp. 504–521.

- *Mood-altering properties.* Possessions may be special because they have mood-altering properties. For example, trophies, plaques, collections, and diplomas can evoke feelings of pride, happiness, and joy.[88] Pets can evoke feelings of comfort. A consumer in one study described her refrigerator as a special possession because making snacks always cheered her up. Others cited CD players and music as favorite possessions because they put these consumers in a good mood.[89]
- *Instrumental importance.* Possessions may be special because they are extremely useful. A consumer who describes her cell phone or computer as special because she uses it constantly to get things done throughout the day is referring to this possession's instrumental value.

Consumer Characteristics Affect What Is Special

Social class, gender, and age are among the background characteristics that affect the types of things that become special to each of us.

- *Social class.* One study examined the meanings that people of different social classes in England gave to their possessions. People in the business class were concerned about possessions that symbolized their personal history and self-development. Unemployed people were concerned about possessions that had utilitarian value.[90] In addition, consumers who aspire to a higher social class may use particular possessions to associate themselves with that social class, even misrepresenting those products to support the self-image of belonging to the higher class.[91]
- *Gender.* For men, products are special when they symbolize activity and physical achievement and when they have instrumental and functional features. On the other hand, women often value symbols of identity and products that symbolize their attachment to other people.[92] In both Niger and the United States, women identified items that symbolized their children's accomplishments and those that indicated connectedness as special possessions. For U.S. women, these possessions included heirlooms and pictures; for the Nigerian women, they included tapestry, jewelry, and other items passed through generations. Men chose objects that showed material comfort and possessions that indicated mastery over the environment.[93] Men are more likely to collect cars, books, and sports-related objects, and women are more likely to collect jewelry, dishes, and silverware.[94] Exhibit 18.11 identifies special possessions by gender and ages.
- *Age.* Although individuals have special possessions at all ages, what they regard as special changes with age.[95] As Exhibit 18.11 shows, stuffed animals are very important for children, music and motor vehicles are highly prized among adolescents, and photographs take on increasing importance as consumers enter adulthood and old age.

Rituals Used with Special Possessions

We often engage in rituals designed to create, energize, or enhance the meaning of special possessions. These rituals can occur at the acquisition, usage, or disposition stage of consumption.

At the acquisition stage, ***possession rituals*** enable the consumer to claim personal possession of new goods.[96] When you buy new jeans, for example, you may change the length, cut them at the knees, or add embellishments. You may adorn a new car with personal markers like personalized license plates, favorite CDs, a special scent, seat covers, and so on. When you move to a new house or apartment, you hang pictures, buy curtains, and position the furniture.

Possession rituals for previously owned goods include wiping away traces of the former owner.[97] For example, when you buy a new home, you thoroughly clean it, tear down old wallpaper, and take down personal markers like the name on the mailbox. However, it is not always possible to wipe away meaning. In China, for example, consumers often build new houses because of a sense that older structures are "contaminated" by the former occupants.

At the consumption stage, consumers may engage in ***grooming rituals*** to bring out or maintain the best in special products.[98] Some consumers spend hours washing and waxing their cars or cleaning house before visitors arrive. Sometimes the grooming ritual extends to you personally, as when you spend a lot of time making yourself look good for a special event.

Exhibit 18.11
FREQUENTLY NAMED SPECIAL POSSESSIONS BY AGE AND GENDER

The possessions we regard as special may vary by cultural category (e.g., age and gender). Girls differ from boys and older consumers differ from younger ones in the possessions they regard as special. Can you think of other examples using other cultural categories (e.g., social class)?

Age	Males	Females
Middle childhood	Sports equipment* Stuffed animals Childhood toys Small appliances Pillows, blankets	Stuffed animals* Dolls Music Jewelry Books
Adolescence	Music Sports equipment Motor vehicles Small appliances Clothing	Jewelry Stuffed animals Music Clothing Motor vehicles Small appliances
Early adulthood	Motor vehicles Music Photographs Jewelry Memorabilia Artwork	Jewelry Photographs Motor vehicles Pillows, blankets Stuffed animals
Middle adulthood	Photographs Jewelry Books Sports equipment Motor vehicles Small appliances	Dishes, silverware Jewelry Artwork Photographs Memorabilia Furniture
Late adulthood	Small appliances Photographs Motor vehicles Artwork Sports equipment	Jewelry Dishes, silverware Photographs Religious Items Furniture

*Items are listed in order from most to least frequently cited.

Finally, when the offering loses its symbolic meaning, consumers engage in ***divestment rituals***—wiping away all traces of personal meaning. For example, many people remove the address labels before giving away magazines they subscribe to or delete personal files before selling or donating a computer. We might even get rid of a possession in stages, moving it from the living room to the basement before finally selling it or throwing it away. A recent IKEA commercial poked fun at the difficulty some people have in disposing of home furnishings once considered special. In the ad, a woman takes a lamp from her living room out to the curb for garbage pickup. Sad music plays as rain falls and the lamp droops. Then a man jumps out and addresses the audience: "Many of you feel bad for this lamp! That's because you're crazy! It has no feelings! And the new one is much better." As one ad critic noted, the ad "says that a lamp is a lamp is a lamp." So why not buy a new one from IKEA?[99]

Disposing of Special Possessions

People dispose of special possessions for different reasons and in different ways. Studies show that older consumers make disposition decisions during periods of crisis, when they move to an institution, when approaching death, and to mark rites of passage and progression—although some transfer special possessions only after death through a will. Sometimes the consumer hopes that giving the object to a relative will invoke memories, express love, or lead to a symbolic immortality; at other times the consumer is seeking control through disposition decisions and timing. An older consumer generally considers which recipient will best appreciate the special object's meaning, continue to use or care for it, or uphold family traditions, or he or she may simply give it to the person who asks first.[100]

Sacred Meaning

Although many possessions are considered special, some are so special they are viewed as sacred. ***Sacred entities*** are people, things, and places that are set apart, revered, worshiped, and treated with great respect. We may find such entities deeply moving, and we may feel anger and revulsion when they are not respected. In contrast, ***profane things*** are those that are ordinary and hence have no special power. Profane objects are often distinguished from sacred ones by the fact that they are used for more mundane purposes.[101]

Sacred People, Objects, and Places

Movie stars, popular singers, historic figures like John F. Kennedy and Martin Luther King Jr., and religious leaders such as the pope, Buddha, and Gandhi are regarded by many people as sacred. When one of Buddha's fingers was displayed in Hong Kong, 600,000 people waited to view the religious relic.[102] The sacred status of famous people is exemplified by the crowds visiting the graves of celebrities like Princess Diana; driving by or visiting homes of living or dead celebrities, such as Elvis's Graceland; and visiting Mann's Chinese Theater in Los Angeles to touch the famous handprints and footprints in the sidewalk. Japanese and American baseball fans regard Seattle Mariners slugger Ichiro Suzuki as sacred. Suzuki paraphernalia is popular, Japanese reporters cover all his games, and fans travel from afar to watch him play.[103]

One reason why heirlooms and photographs of ancestors take on sacred status is that we may view our ancestors as heroes. A similar phenomenon explains why we treat items associated with famous statesmen such as George Washington and Winston Churchill as sacred. Although not part of our actual past, these heroes were instrumental in formulating national identities. Consumers demonstrate their reverence by visiting the places that mark these historic figures.[104]

Many consumers also regard as sacred such objects as national flags, patriotic songs, art, collections, family recipes, and the Bible and such places as museums, the Vietnam Memorial, the Taj Mahal, and the Great Wall of China (see Exhibit 18.12). These sacred objects and places evoke powerful emotions, sometimes causing people to weep or feel choked up when viewing them. In addition to sacred people, objects, and places, we may identify certain times and events, religious holidays, weddings, births, deaths, and grace before meals as sacred.

The Characteristics That Describe Sacred Entities

Sacred entities involve some mystery or myth that raises them above the ordinary.[105] The pope, for example, is viewed as being almost godlike. And legendary figures such as Jim Morrison, Elvis Presley, Marilyn Monroe, and John F. Kennedy are associated with mystery. Second, sacred entities have qualities that transcend time, place, or

Exhibit 18.12
MARKETING A WONDER
Certain places, like the Taj Mahal are known as one the wonders of the world and they are associated with Indian history.

space. When you enter the Alamo, you may feel as if you were back in the period when the historic fighting took place.

Sacred objects also possess strong approach/avoidance characteristics and create an overwhelming feeling of power and fascination. For example, you may simultaneously desire to be close to but also watch from a distance people you view as heroes and heroines. Encountering sacred entities may evoke certain feelings, such as ecstasy or the sense of being smaller and more humble than the sacred entity. For instance, some people may feel that they have accomplished little in comparison to heroes like Martin Luther King, Jr. Some people feel humbled by the mass of humanity represented by the Vietnam Memorial. Moreover, sacred objects can create strong feelings of attachment, such as the need to take care of and nurture the sacred entity. Often sacred objects involve rituals that dictate how we should behave in the object's presence. To illustrate, many Americans know the right and wrong way to treat the national flag.

Sacredness may be maintained by scarcity and exclusivity.[106] For example, the sacred status of special works of art derives from their uniqueness and the fact that their high price maintains their exclusivity. People like Katharine Hepburn became imbued with sacredness by their desire to be out of the public eye, and limiting their public appearances only made them more interesting to their adoring fans.

How Sacred Objects Are Profaned

Entities that were once sacred can be made profane if they are not treated with due respect or if their sacred status is eliminated through commercialization. In divorce, for example, some people profane things that were sacred or special in the marriage by throwing away, giving away, or selling the wedding ring, wedding dress, family furniture, special automobiles, or family jewelry.[107] We can feel anger and disgust at the profaning of a sacred person or sacred object. In one study, some *Star Trek* fans said they were "barely" able to "stand watching the show" because of the way the series was being commercially exploited.[108]

marketing
IMPLICATIONS

Marketers need to be aware of the sacred meanings of people, objects, places, and events.

Creating and maintaining sacredness

Sometimes marketers create sacredness in objects or people. For example, the promoters of a famous movie star might heighten his sacred status by creating or enhancing his mystery and myth, making him exclusive, and promoting the powerful emotional effect he has on people. Marketers may also help maintain sacredness—for example, by keeping the price of sacred objects like collections, precious works of art, and rare jewelry very high.

Avoiding the profaning of sacred objects
Unsophisticated marketers sometimes profane sacred objects through commercialization. Some consumers believe that Elvis Presley is profaned by commercial Elvis paraphernalia. Selling religious trinkets outside the sacred properties of certain religious sites may profane these places.

Product involvement in sacred activities and rituals
In some cases, marketers sell products regarded as instrumental to the continuation or conduct of sacred occasions and rituals. [9]Sacred rituals in India like the Lakshmi Puja held during Diwali are important to the north Indians as compared to the Durga Puja (Dusshera) for the Bengalis. Pongal, Onam or Ugadi may have different connotations across regions, but signify the heterogeneity in ways rituals are observed in India. Ganesh Chaturthi is a very big festival in Maharashtra, and so is Chath in Bihar or Teej in Rajasthan. Marketers keep track of such rituals and accordingly showcase relevant products which are occasion specific. Akshaya Tritiya is one such momentous occasion, which is considered one of the most auspicious days of the Vedic Calendar. It is believed, any meaningful activity started on this day would be fruitful. Akshaya Tritiya falls on the third day of the bright half of Vaishakh month (April-May), when the Sun and Moon are in exaltation; they are simultaneously at their peak of brightness, which happens only once every year. Buying gold is a popular activity on Akshaya Tritiya, as it is the ultimate symbol of wealth and prosperity. Gold and gold jewelry bought and worn on this day bring never diminishing good fortune. Indians arrange weddings, begin new business ventures, and even plan long journeys on this day.

The Transfer of Symbolic Meaning Through Gift Giving

This chapter has shown how consumers invest products, times, activities, places, and people with symbolic meaning. Some meanings enhance the special and/or sacred status of the product, and some are instrumental in developing or maintaining the consumer's self-concept. However, another important aspect of symbolic consumption involves transferring meaning from one individual to another through gift giving.

The Timing of Gifts

Some gift-giving occasions are culturally determined and timed. In the United States, these include Valentine's Day, Mother's Day, Father's Day, and Secretary's Day.[110] Koreans celebrate the 100th day of a baby's life, and families in China celebrate when a baby is one month old. Koreans also give gifts to elders and family members on New Year's Day. Consumers in cultures around the world also celebrate various gift-giving holidays such as Christmas, Hanukkah, and Kwanzaa.[111] A child's annaprashan is an occasion when the baby breaks its baby food pattern to begin home-made food. The gifts associated with it are utensils. Similarly, the child's Upnayan (thread ceremony) or the mundan (Shaving of the hair) ceremonies are events where gifting is integral and different kinds of products are associated. However, the most common form of gift is money in cash or cheque that has higher utility value and is also considered auspicious.

Some gift-giving occasions are culturally prescribed but occur at a time that is specific to each individual.[112] These are often the transitions discussed earlier: anniversaries, graduations, birthdays, weddings, bridal and baby showers, retirement

Exhibit 18.13

A MODEL OF THE GIFT-GIVING PROCESS

The process of gift giving can be described in terms of three stages: (1) the gestation stage, at which we think about and buy the gift; (2) the presentation stage, at which we actually give the gift; and (3) the reformulation stage, at which we reevaluate our relationship based on the nature of the gift-giving experience. At each stage we can identify several issues that affect the gift-giving process.

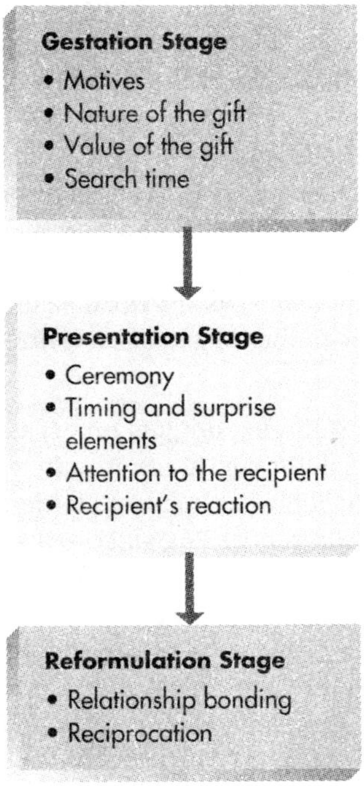

parties, and religious transitions such as baptism, first communion, or bar mitzvah. Still other gift-giving occasions are ad hoc, as when we give gifts as part of a reconciliation attempt, to celebrate the birth of a child, to cheer someone who is ill, or to thank someone for helping us.

Three Stages of Gift Giving

Gift giving consists of three stages, as shown in Exhibit 18.13. In the ***gestation stage,*** we consider what to give the recipient. The ***presentation stage*** occurs with the actual giving of the gift. Finally, in the ***reformulation stage,*** we reevaluate the relationship based on the gift-giving experience.

The Gestation Stage The gestation stage before a gift is given involves the motives for and emotions surrounding giving, the nature and meaning of the gift, the value of the gift, and the amount of time spent searching for the gift.

Motives for and Emotions Surrounding Giving During the gestation stage we develop motives for gift giving.[113] On the one hand, people may give for altruistic reasons—to help the recipient. For example, a relative may give a large cash gift to help a young couple start their married life. We may also give for agnostic reasons because we derive positive emotional pleasure from the act of giving. Or we may give a gift for instrumental reasons, expecting the recipient to give something in return. For example, a student may give a teacher a small gift in hopes of getting a higher grade. Consumers may also give for purely obligatory reasons because they feel the situation or the relationship demands it.

Indeed, sometimes we do not react positively to gifts given by others because we now feel the obligation to reciprocate. Sometimes we give gifts because we want to reduce guilt or alleviate hard feelings. In divorce, for example, the spouse who feels responsible for the breakup tends to give the partner more than a fair share in what is called compensatory giving.[114] Sometimes people have antagonistic motives for gift giving. For example, if you are invited to the wedding of someone you do not like, you might give the couple something you think is not very beautiful. Sometimes givers feel anxiety about giving a gift.[115] They may feel that the gift has to be absolutely perfect or worry if they lack the time or money to find a suitable gift.

The Appropriateness and Meaning of the Gift The appropriateness of the gift depends on the situation and the relationship between the gift giver and recipient. For example, a worker would not give a boss a gift of lingerie because such items are too personal. Likewise, you would not give good friends a token wedding gift because the relationship dictates something more substantial. Although token gifts may not be appropriate on a clearly defined gift-giving occasion, they can be highly significant when no gift is expected. Spontaneously giving a gift, even something small, can signify love and caring.[116] Thus you may feel quite touched when your significant other buys you "a little something." Similarly, token gifts are quite important for recipients with whom we do not have strong ties. It is appropriate and desirable to send holiday and birthday cards to those whom we do not see very often.[117]

The gift may also symbolize a particular meaning to the receiver.[118] For example, gifts can represent values we regard as appropriate for the recipient, such as domesticity for new brides and grooms or a new set of expectations. An engagement ring symbolizes expectations regarding commitment and future fidelity, just as giving golf clubs at retirement symbolizes expectations regarding future leisure. Gifts can also be symbolic of the self, as when giving a piece of art or something that the giver has created.

The Value of the Gift Splurging on gifts on occasions like Bhai Duj or Karva Chauth, both popular north Indian rituals, is quite common and has seen some dramatic changes. Mobile phones, expensive clothes, jewelery and at times even getaways are planned as a part of gifting and celebrations. It replaces the age old norms of gifting sweets and a token money or clothes. The consumer's culture can influence decisions about the value of a gift. In Japan, for example, people lose face if the gift they receive exceeds the value of the gift they have given.[120] Interestingly, consumers perceive that gifts they buy for others are more valuable, in economic terms, than gifts received from others. When giver and receiver had close connections, however, the receiver perceived higher economic value in the gift.[121]

The Amount of Time Spent Searching The amount of time spent searching for a gift symbolizes the nature and intensity of the giver's relationship with the recipient. Men and women differ in how much time and effort they invest in the search for a gift. Women are reportedly more involved in holiday gift shopping than are men.[122] Women also appear to spend more time searching for the perfect gift, whereas men are more likely to settle for something that "will do."[123]

The Presentation Stage The presentation stage describes the actual exchange of the gift. Here, the ritual or ceremonial aspects of the giving process become very important.[124]

Ceremony During the presentation stage, the giver decides whether to wrap the gift and, if so, how. Wrapping the present nicely in appropriate paper helps to de-commodify, or make more personal, a gift that is otherwise mass-produced.[125] Yet, the importance of the gift packaging depends on the formality and spontaneity of the occasion. For example, unanticipated gifts, such as a boss's surprise gift to an assistant or a wife's surprise gift to her husband, may be less formally wrapped and may even be appropriate if left unwrapped.

Timing and Surprise Both the timing and the possibility of surprise may be important in gift giving. For example, although we know that gift giving is part of the Christmas ritual and that the gifts are even prominently displayed under the tree—sometimes for days before the actual exchange—being surprised by what they contain is often a key element. The excitement of unwrapping an item is heightened by having the recipient guess what the package contains. Although surprise is a valued part of the ritual, it is not always achieved. One study found that right before Christmas, some husbands purchase items that have been chosen in advance by their wives. Here, the gift giving is an orchestrated event with the husband playing the role of "purchasing agent."[126]

Attention to the Recipient Paying attention to the recipient can be a critical dimension in the presentation stage. For example, attendees at wedding showers are expected to watch closely as the bride-to-be opens her gifts.

Recipient's Reaction Another aspect is the reaction the giver hopes to elicit from the recipient, the recipient's actual reaction, and the giver's response to the recipient's reaction. If you spent a lot of time and effort looking for the perfect gift and then the recipient opens the package quickly and goes on to the next gift without a word, you will probably feel hurt. As noted earlier, you may also feel anxiety at the presentation stage if you are uncertain about whether the recipient will like your gift.[127]

The Reformulation Stage The reformulation stage marks the third and final stage of the gift-giving process. At this stage, the giver and recipient reevaluate their relationship based on the gift-giving process.

Relationship Bonding A gift may affect the relationship between giver and recipient in different ways, as shown in Exhibit 18.14. A gift can either maintain, strengthen, or weaken the relationship between the giver and receiver. One study found that gifts could strengthen a relationship by communicating feelings of connection, bonding, and commitment. Gifts can also affirm the relationship, validating existing feelings of commitment. Research suggests that a romantic relationship is likely to last longer when one member gives the other a gift to publicly announce their relationship. On the negative side, inappropriate gifts or those showing limited search effort or interest in the recipient's desires can weaken a relationship, creating the perception that the relationship lacks bonding and connection.[128]

Reciprocation The reformulation stage also has implications for how and whether the recipient will reciprocate on the next gift-giving occasion. If you gave someone a nice gift on one occasion, you would generally expect the recipient to reciprocate on the next occasion. If, on the other hand, you gave a gift that weakened the tie between you and the recipient, the latter may not give you a very nice gift or may give no gift at all on the next gift-giving occasion.

Some kinds of gift-giving situations or recipients are exempt from reciprocation.[129] For example, if you give someone a gift because she is ill or has experienced some tragedy (say, her house burned down), you will not expect her to reciprocate. Yet, if someone unexpectedly gives you a Christmas gift, you will usually feel guilty and want to rush out and buy him a gift, too. People of limited financial means (children, students) or of lower status (a secretary as opposed to a boss) may be seen as exempt from giving. Thus it is appropriate for parents to give their children gifts and expect nothing in return. Women have also been reported to feel less obligated to reciprocate in date-related gift giving, perhaps because of culturally prescribed notions regarding men's generally higher economic power.[130] Note that expectations of reciprocation depend on the culture and the relationship between the giver and the recipient. In China and Hong Kong, for instance, where gifts are commonly exchanged during certain festivals and other important occasions, reciprocity is discouraged among family members and close friends because there is no need to build ties through gift giving.[131]

Exhibit 18.14

POSSIBLE EFFECT OF GIFT GIVING ON THE RELATIONSHIP

Gifts can have many different effects on a relationship—effects that range from strengthening to severing the relationship.

Relational Effect	Description	Experiential Themes
Strengthening	Gift receipt improves the quality of the relationship between giver and recipient. Feelings of connection, bonding, commitment, and/or shared meaning are intensified.	Ephiphany
Affirmation	Gift receipt validates the positive quality of the relationship between giver and recipient. Existing feelings of connection and/or shared meaning are validated.	Empathy Adherence Affirming farewell Recognition
Negligible effect	The gift-reciept experience has a minimal effect on perceptions of relationship quality.	Superfluity "Error" Charity Overkill
Negative confirmation	Gift receipt validates an existing negative quality of the relationship between giver and recipient. A lack of feelings of connection, bonding, and/or shared meaning is validated.	Absentee Control
Weakening	Gift receipt harms the quality of the relationship between giver and recipient. There is a newly evident or intensified perception that the relationship lacks connection, bonding, and/or shared meaning, but the relationship remains.	Burden Insult
Severing	Gift receipt so harms the quality of the relationship between giver and recipient that the relationship is dissolved.	Threat Nonaffirming farewell

Source: Julie A. Ruth, Cele C. Otnes, and Frédéric F. Brunel, "Gift Receipt and the Reformulation of Interpersonal Relationships," *Journal of Consumer Research,* vol. 25, March 1999, p. 389. Reprinted by permission of the University of Chicago Press.

marketing IMPLICATIONS

Companies can build on several aspects of gift giving to market more effectively to consumers.

Promoting products and services as gifts

Many marketers promote their products for gift-giving occasions, and often gift-giving occasions are the primary focus of their business. [10]The greeting card market in India is estimated to be around Rs.250 crore in terms of yearly consumer spend. The unorganised sector in the greeting card market will be close to 40 per cent. The organised sector, controlling 60 per cent of the market, is divided between ITC, Archies and Hallmark. These days consumers look for convenience and instant gratification. Communication media like the telephone and e-mail facilitate communication to a great extent. But many greeting card sites are moving from a 'free' to a 'pay' mode. This could be an emerging revenue earning opportunity for content providers. In some cases uncommon gifts are promoted as appropriate for various gift-giving occasions. For example, products from blenders and lingerie to stock certificates and power tools are touted as appropriate Mother's Day gifts. Mortgage companies now offer bridal registries. Rather than buying gifts, gift givers contribute money to the couple's down payment or mortgage. Some retail outlets are known exclusively as gift stores. Here the services the store provides to enhance the presentation of the gift and the salespeople's abilities to point out gifts with special meanings may be important.

Cause-related marketing for frivolous products

Research indicates that consumers who are thinking about buying a product linked with a gift to charity will prefer a higher-priced brand carrying a larger donation when the product is frivolous rather than practical.[133]

Technology and gift shopping

Technology has created major changes in the gift-giving process. Online shopping is faster and more convenient than ever, and many retail sites invite consumers to post "wish lists" showing the gifts they would like for holidays, weddings, and other occasions. Another major change is the growing use of card-sized plastic gift cards. Such gift cards now account for 10 percent of year-end holiday retail sales. The popularity of gift cards is changing the way retailers handle inventory planning. Post Diwali shopping is now a common trend in India, where consumers perceive that with the festival frenzy over, the marketers might be in a haste for stock clearance and give deals and price off on stock. More and more consumers are choosing this option to look for best deals, while the crescendo is reached. It helps the retailer since he clears the stock and the consumer too is benefited, as he gets a good deal.

Ethnicity and holiday shopping

Marketers have also become more sensitive to the ethnic and religious diversity within the United States. For example, because Christmas, Hanukkah, and Kwanzaa are celebrated at about the same time of the year, Archway cookies decided to change its traditional holiday packaging from bells, wreaths, and candles to less culturally specific prints of snowy outdoor scenes.[135]

Alternatives to traditional gifts

Knowing that consumers are tiring of commercialism, hassle, and the materialism surrounding gift-giving occasions like Christmas, some charities are asking consumers to give gifts to people in need. For example, the nonprofit Heifer International's holiday catalog, titled "The Most Important Gift Catalog in the World," invites consumers to purchase "gift" animals such as some geese or a sheep to help families around the world to become self-sufficient. For similar reasons, travel marketers tout travel as a holiday gift. More two-income families have less time, more money, and more distance separating them from loved ones, creating a trend toward travel and family reunions at posh resorts around the world and away from holiday shopping.[136]

Summary

This chapter discussed the symbolic role that products can play. Consumers use some products as conscious or unconscious badges that designate the various social categories to which they belong. Products and rituals hold symbolic significance when people undergo role transitions; serve as symbols of connection to people, places, and times that have meaning; and are symbols of individuality and uniqueness. The combined symbolic uses of products and rituals affect the consumer's self-concept.

Consumers regard some possessions as very special. These objects are nonsubstitutable, irreplaceable, will not be sold at market value if at all, and are purchased with little regard for price. They are rarely discarded, even if their functional value is gone, and they may not even be used for their original purpose. We personify these possessions, may feel powerful emotions in their presence, and feel fear or sadness over their potential or actual loss. In part, possessions are special because they serve as emblems, facilitate role transitions, connect us to others, or express our unique styles. They are special because they indicate personal mastery and achievements or are mood enhancing. Background characteristics such as social class, gender, and age all influence the type of object someone regards as special.

Some entities are so special that they are worshiped, set apart, and treated with inordinate respect—that is, they are sacred. In addition to possessions, people, places, objects, times, and events may take on sacred status. Sacred objects transcend time and space and have strong approach/avoidance powers and great fascination. Consumers care for and nurture these possessions and often devise special rituals to handle them. Sacred objects can be profaned or made ordinary by commercialization, inappropriate usage, or divestment patterns.

Gift giving is a process of transferring meaning in products from one person to another in three phases: gestation, presentation, and reformulation. Such occasions are often culturally prescribed but may vary in the timing. The manner in which the first two phases of gift giving are enacted can affect the long-term viability of the relationship between giver and recipient.

Questions for Review and Discussion

1. Contrast the emblematic function of a product with the role acquisition function; also contrast the connectedness function of a product with the expressive function.
2. What is reflexive evaluation, and how does it affect role acquisition?
3. How does the ideal identity schema relate to a person's actual identity schemas?
4. What are the three main reasons for possessions taking on special meaning?
5. Why do consumers engage in possession, grooming, and divestment rituals?
6. What are sacred entities, and how are they profaned?
7. Identify the three stages of gift giving, and explain how gift giving can affect relations between the giver and the recipient.

Exercises

1. Consider the cultural category of occupational status and the typical clothing of doctors, farmers, waitresses, politicians, businesspeople, truck drivers, and pharmacists. Identify the cultural principles that reflect membership in each of these occupational groups, and explain how the clothing worn by members of each group illustrates these characteristics.
2. Consider two role transitions: graduation and new parenthood. For each, identify the rituals that mark these role transitions and the enabling products that mark their passage. (This task will be easier if you can actually attend a graduation or watch a new parent care for a baby.) Find several advertisements for relevant products or services that may be appropriate as gifts given during the transition rituals. Identify a set of marketing implications regarding marketing to groups undergoing these transitions.
3. Interview someone you know about one or more possessions that they regard as special/sacred. Try to get them to indicate why these possessions are special and compare their answers with the reasons given in the chapter for why possessions are special. What marketing implications can you derive from their responses?

More Exercises from the Adaptor

1. Discuss how gifts and the process of gifting has undergone a change in India and what are the key factors that have influenced such change in approach of Indians.

References

[1] Source: http://www.hmambassador.com/history.asp

[2] Source: http://www.thehindubusinessline.com/life/2006/01/27/stories/2006012700180400.htm

[3] Source: http://www.geocities.com/Tokyo/Shrine/4287/cuisine.htm

[4] Source: India Luxury Trends 2006, Technopak India

[5] Source: http://www.cp-pc.ca/english/india/family.html

[6] Source: http://fecolumnists.expressindia.com/full_column.php?content_id=96374

[7] Source: http://agencyfaqs.com/main1.html

[8] Source: http://pets.indiatimes.com/articleshow/1736285885.cms

[9] Source: http://hinduism.about.com/od/festivalsholidays/a/akshayatritiya.htm

[10] Source: http://www.itcportal.com/newsroom/press_oct21_04.htm

PART

6

Consumer Welfare

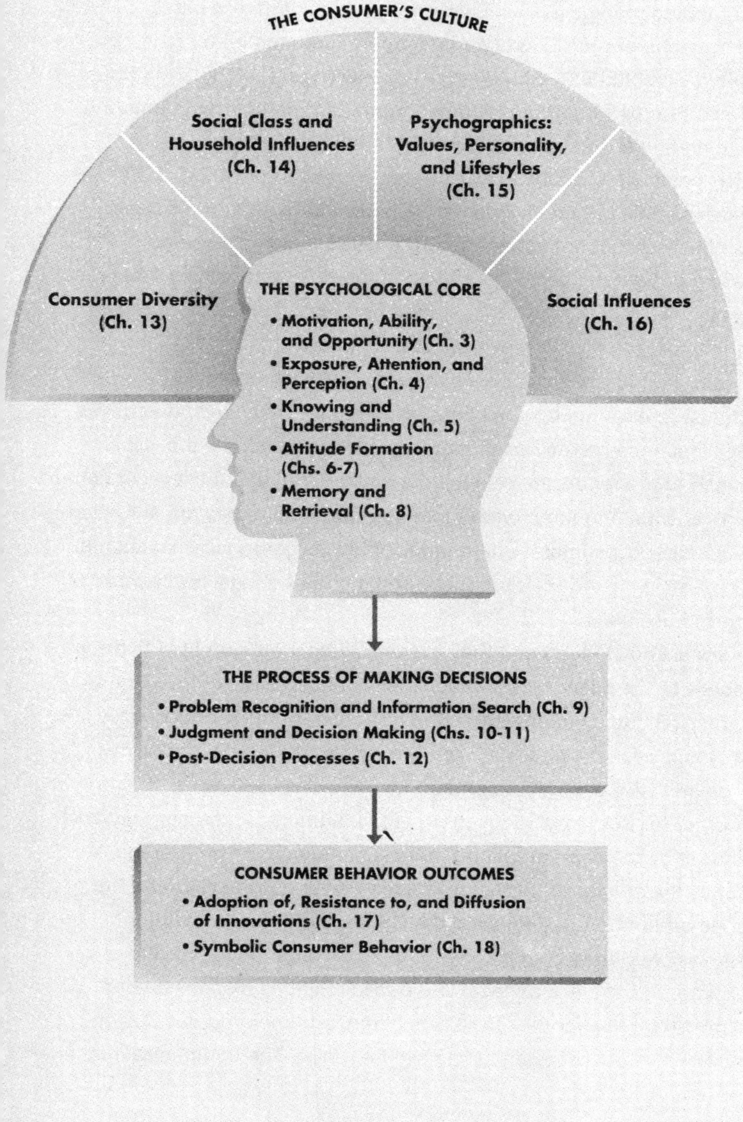

This final section covers two topics related to consumer welfare that researchers have studied with great interest in recent years. Chapter 19 focuses on consumer rights and the groups and trends that are shaping public policy programs to protect consumers and improve our quality of life.

Chapter 20 examines the dark side of consumer behavior and marketing, including the negative outcomes of certain acquisition behaviors (such as compulsive buying) and certain consumption behaviors (such as underage drinking). This final chapter also explores the potential negative effects of marketing and the ways consumers can resist marketing practices, individually and in groups.

chapter **19**

Consumerism and Public Policy Issues

LEARNING OBJECTIVES

After studying this chapter, you will be able to:

- Define consumerism and describe the three types of groups involved with public policy and consumerism.
- Explain how marketing communications can violate consumer rights in four ways.
- Discuss the key product information and safety issues that apply to marketing.
- Show how increased attention to environmental protection is affecting consumer behavior and marketing decisions.
- Summarize some of the consumerism trends that affect marketing in other countries.

INTRODUCTION

There is a pesticide in my Cola

In the summer of August 2006 when the Cola majors had to battle it out amongst themselves for grabbing market share, they were fighting a different battle. Centre for Science and Environment (CSE) in one of its report came out with startling facts. Sunita Narain, Director, CSE quoted in her press release, [1]"The 2006 CSE study tested 57 samples of 11 soft drink brands, from 25 different manufacturing plants of Coca-Cola and PepsiCo, spread over 12 states.

The study finds pesticide residues in all samples; it finds a cocktail of 3-5 different pesticides in all samples — on an average 24 times higher than BIS norms, which have been finalised but not yet notified. The levels in some samples — for instance, Coca-Cola bought in Kolkata — exceeded the BIS standards by 140 times for the deadly pesticide Lindane. Similarly, a Coca-Cola sample manufactured in Thane contained the neurotoxin Chlorpyrifos, 200 times the standard." When the claim was first published on the front pages of Indian newspapers this month that Coca-Cola and PepsiCo beverages were contaminated with pesticides, executives at the two companies were breezily confident that they could handle the issue.

[2]After the launch of the report the cola majors could not gauge the level of controversy it would generate and three weeks into the report later, they are still struggling to win back Indian consumers. One-quarter of India's component states had already imposed partial bans on their products, and a complex legal battle had started to overturn those bans.

Both companies acknowledged that they miscalculated, and stumbled badly, in their initial response to the pesticide allegations. They underestimated how quickly the matter would spiral into a nationwide scandal. They misjudged how quickly local politicians would seize on the issue. And they did not move swiftly themselves to quell the anxieties of their customers.

As soon as Center for Science and Environment, announced its finding that soft drinks manufactured by the two companies in India contained, on an average, more than 24 times the amount of pesticide residue that is considered safe, the companies formed committees in India and the United States to deal with the issue. They commissioned their own laboratory tests to rebut the report and worked in parallel round the clock on legal and public-relations responses. But their decision early on to wait for the lab results before commenting in detail on the accusations, and that decision seems to have backfired. The companies' reti-

Exhibit 19.1
TRUTH IN ADVERTISING
KFC now offers healthier non-fried foods as well as salads.

cence merely fanned consumers' suspicions, and they soon got bogged down in the technicalities of the allegations, instead of focusing on winning back the emotional support of their customers.

Eventually as both the companies had begun to realize the extent of damage, the approach towards damage control was now seen as more of a public relation exercise and win back consumer confidence. Pepsi got its then Managing Director, Rajeev Bakshi, to feature in their advertisements to testify about the safety issue. Alternatively, Coca Cola hired the services of celebrities like Aamir Khan to testify for itself. Free plant visits were organized, should customers want to personally validate for themselves. In all the cola majors approach was more customer driven now.

Today, consumers may have buried the past and moved on and the cola majors may be back aggressively targeting the long-hot Indian summer, but the controversy created sufficient stir in a market and more specifically a country, where public policy issues and interest of consumer welfare were never discussed. Most of the efforts were initiatives of the government, which were not effective to create the noise level and seemed more routine than necessary.

This chapter opens with the definition of consumerism and an overview of the major consumer rights. A brief description of the government agencies, industry regulations, and groups involved in public policy follows. The remainder of the chapter explores specific issues in consumerism, including advertising and selling practices, product safety, and environmental protection. Examining these issues can help marketers better understand the context and processes surrounding how consumers acquire, consume, and dispose of goods and services.

What Is Consumerism?

Consumerism is "the set of activities of government, business, independent organizations, and concerned consumers that are designed to protect the rights of consumers."[2] Note that the key focus is on ***consumer rights.*** In 1962 President John F. Kennedy proposed the Consumer Bill of Rights to guarantee consumers several basic rights fundamental to the effective functioning of our economic system.[3] These are the rights:

- *Right to safety.* Protection from offerings that might be hazardous to health and safety.
- *Right to be informed.* Protection from fraudulent or misleading advertising and other forms of communications and access to the information needed to make an informed decision.

- *Right to choose.* Access to a variety of offerings at competitive prices wherever possible. If choice is restricted, the government will ensure that consumers receive satisfactory quality and fair prices.
- *Right to be heard.* Full and sympathetic consideration of consumer interests in the formation of government policy.

Since 1962, other presidents have added more consumer rights:

- *Right to consumer education.* Access to knowledge about the offerings acquired and consumed.
- *Right to recourse and redress.* Right to a fair settlement of problems encountered.
- *Right to an environment that enhances the quality of life.* Right to live in an environment that is not threatened by pollution and hazardous waste.

[3]In India, the Consumer Protection Act of 1986 covers the issues of consumer welfare and protection. Some of the basic contents of the Act, are stated as:

1. Structure of Consumer Protection Act

The Act envisages a three- tier quasi-judicial machinery at the National, State and District levels.

- *National Consumer Disputes Redressal Commission.* known as "National Commission" deals with complaints involving costs and compensation higher than Rs. One Crore.
- *State Consumer Disputes Redressal Commissions.* known as "State Commission", deals with complaints involving costs and compensation higher than Rs. Twenty Lakhs and less than Rs. One Crore.
- *District Consumer Disputes Redressal Forums.* known as "District Forum, deals with complaints involving costs and compensation less than Rs. Twenty Lakhs.

2. Extent and Coverage of Consumer Protection Act

- The Act applies to all goods and services unless specifically exempted by the Central Government.
- It covers all the sectors whether private, public or cooperative.
- The provisions of the Act are compensatory in nature.
- The provisions of this Act are in addition to and not in derogation of the provisions of any other law for the time being in force.
- The Act envisages establishment of Consumer Protection Councils at the Central and State levels, whose main objects will be to promote and protect the rights of the consumers.

3. Who is a Consumer?

All o]f us are consumers of goods and services. For the purpose of the Consumer Protection Act, the word "Consumer" has been defined separately for "goods" and "services".

(A) For the purpose of "goods", a consumer means a person belonging to the following categories:

- One who buys or agrees to buy any goods for a consideration which has been paid or promised or partly paid and partly promised or under any system of deferred payment;

- It includes any user of such goods other than the person who actualy buys goods and such use is made with the approval of the purchaser.

(B) For the purpose of "services", a "consumer" means a person belonging to the following categories:

- One who hires or avails of any service or services for a consideration which has been paid or promised or partly paid and partly promised or under any system of deferred payment.
- It includes any beneficiary of such service other than the one who actually hires or avails of the service for consideration and such services are availed with the approval of such person.

4. Relife Available to Consumer

Depending on the facts and circumstances, the Redressal Forums may give order for one or more of the following relief.

- Removal of defects from the goods,
- Replacement of the goods;
- Refund of the price paid;
- Award of compensation for the loss or injury suffered;
- Removal of defects or deficiencies in the services;
- Discontinuance of unfair trade practices or restrictive trade practices or direction not
- to repeat them;
- Withdrawal of the hazardous goods from being offered to sale; or
- Award for adequate costs to parties

5. Contents of Consumer Complaint

Procedures for filing complaints and seeking redressal are simple. There is no fee for filing a complaint before the District Forum, the State Commission or the National Commission. (A stamp paper is also not required). Three to five copies of the complaint on plain paper are required to be submitted by the complainant or his authorized agent in person or could be sent by post to the appropriate Forum / Commission.

A complaint should contain the following information:-

(a) The name, description and the address of the complainant.
(b) The name, description and address of the opposite party or parties, as the case may be, as far as they can be ascertained;
(c) The facts relating to complaint and when and where it arose;
(d) Documents, if any, in support of the allegations contained in the complaint.
(e) The relief which the complainant is seeking.

The complaint should be signed by the complainant or his authorized agent. The complaint is to be filed within two years from the date on which cause of action has arisen.

Over the years, these basic consumer rights have formed the foundation for many public policy discussions and decisions as well as much consumer behavior research. Researchers have been especially interested in applying consumer behavior principles, theories, and research methods to better understand consumer issues and offer suggestions to improve consumers' lives. In addition, various government, industry, and advocacy groups and agencies can influence marketing practices and the development of regulations to protect consumer rights.

Groups Involved with Public Policy and Consumerism

Three types of groups play a major role in the formation of public policy decisions to protect the rights and interests of consumers. These include various government agencies, self-regulating industry groups, and consumer groups.

Government Agencies

Many government agencies look after various consumer interests and regulate fair trade. Although the entire list is too lengthy to present here, On the recommendation of the Central Consumer Protection Council following six working groups have been set up in the Ministry to consider ways and means of protecting interests of the consumers in these critical areas. A Standing Committee for Promotion of Consumer Interest has also been constituted with the following terms of reference:

(i) To identify the key concerns of consumers;
(ii) To identify ways and means of giving publicity to educate as well as to address the concerns of consumers;
(iii) To identify ways and means of involving various stakeholders for protecting consumer interest; and
(iv) To identify ways and means of bringing consumer interest to the forefront of all operations, be they in Government, public or private sector.

Whether consumers should protect themselves from products and services or whether the government should intervene on their behalf is the subject of much debate.[4] Some argue that regulation threatens individual freedom of choice and can slow the commercialization of technologies that offer potentially important consumer benefits.[5] On the other hand, government intervention is sometimes necessary because consumers do not or cannot protect themselves adequately. Consumers may not accurately assess the risk inherent in the situation, either because they lack the necessary information or because such hazards occur infrequently.

Consumers exposed to messages about prescription drugs, for instance, would be unlikely to know the details of the clinical evidence (if specifics were mentioned) or be able to knowledgeably compare the scientific evidence with the ad's claims.

Exhibit 19.2

On the recommendation of the Central Consumer Protection Council following six working groups have been set up in the Ministry to consider ways and means of protecting interests of the consumers in these critical areas.

S. No	Name of the Working Group
1.	Food Safety;
2.	Misleading Advertisements;
3.	Drugs, Pharmaceuticals and Medical Devices / Equipments;
4.	Consumer Health & Safety concerning Tobacco Products;
5.	Counterfeit, Fake, Spurious, Contraband products;
6.	To formulate the following New Acts/for including the proposals for amending in the existing Acts relating to Consumer Interest, e.g. a. Product Liability Act; b. Unfair Terms of Contract Act; c. Builders Licensing Boards Act; d. Whistle Blowers Protection Act

This has become a bigger issue since the FDA reinterpreted its guidelines to allow direct-to-consumer advertising of pharmaceutical products, with messages incorporating certain information about risks, limitations, and other vital details.[6] Now that drug companies are spending $4 billion annually on such advertising, concerns have been raised over whether consumers are developing false expectations of drug safety and efficacy, whether doctors are feeling pressure to prescribe drugs that consumers may not need, and whether risk information and clinical evidence are presented in a detailed and balanced way.[7] [4]In India, unlike the OTC (Over the counter) drugs, prescription drugs are not allowed to advertise. There are several governing bodies which look after the regulatory issues like; (i) Central Drugs Standard Control Organization (CDSCO), Ministry of Health & Family Welfare, Government of India provides general information about drug regulatory requirements in India. (ii) Drugs (Price Control) Order 1995 and other orders enforced by National Pharmaceutical Pricing Authority (NPPA), Government of India. (iii) The Drugs & Cosmetics Act, 1940 regulates the import, manufacture, distribution and sale of drugs in India. (iv) Schedule M of the D&C Act specifies the general and specific requirements for factory premises and materials, plant and equipment and minimum recommended areas for basic installation for certain categories of drugs. (v) Schedule T of the D&C Act prescribes GMP specifications for manufacture of Ayurvedic, Siddha and Unani medicines (vi) The clinical trials legislative requirements are guided by specifications of Schedule Y of The D&C Act. (vii) The Narcotic Drugs and Psychotropic Substances Act, 1985 is an act concerned with control and regulation of operations relating to Narcotic Drugs and Psychotropic Substances.

Industry Self-Regulation

Companies are not always “the bad guys” that require constant monitoring to ensure that they deal fairly with consumers. For both ethical and business-related reasons, it is in companies’ best interests to be concerned about consumer welfare because it is so closely tied to consumer satisfaction. As a result, numerous industries have set up mechanisms to self-regulate business activity and correct problems when necessary, generally on a voluntary basis. Industry guidelines help companies determine what is inappropriate—especially critical with newer techniques such as wireless advertising messaging—and show the industry’s responsiveness to consumer concerns, which also improves the industry’s image.[8] Moreover, self-regulation removes the government from an antagonistic role and reduces its caseload.

[5]In an intra-industry complaint filed with Advertising Standard Council of India (ASCI), complaint was lodged against Dabur for Promise Toothpaste, wherein it claimed that after using Promise toothpaste consumers won’t get cavities and won’t even have to visit the dentist”, “New Promise has clove that fights twice as hard and not only removes germs that cause cavities, but also prevents them from coming again”. The nature of complaint was about these claims being grossly misleading.

Even a lifetime use of fluoridated toothpaste cannot guarantee a cavity-free mouth.

The results of various clinical trials show that continuous and sustained use of fluoridated toothpaste with either 1000ppm or 1500ppm fluoride can cause a clinically significant caries reduction of around 25-40%, but never 100% reduction. ASCI recommended that the commercial be suspended from airing and its decision mentioned that, New Promise fights the germs that cause cavities and prevents them from coming back, and therefore prevents cavities", was not substantiated adequately. Claim, "prevents cavities", was an exaggeration which could mislead consumers.

[6]Alternatively in the case of Coca Cola, when a case was filed with the Advertising Standard Council of India, there was an objection raised about an outdoor hoarding displaying the message of a well-known celebrity displaying a Coca-Cola bottle and assuring that it is 100% safe. ASCI reversed the complaint and mentioned in its decision that, "100% safe", "it is according to International standards", and "all the ingredients meet regulations in India", were not substantiated. CCC considered the Advertiser's recent submission that the Hoarding under complaint carries only one claim, "I have 100% confidence that Coca-Cola is absolutely safe", the other claims cited in the complaint being apparently the subjective allegations of the Complainant. Claim of, "Coca Cola is absolutely safe", was substantiated. Earlier CCC decision of upholding the original complaint stands reversed.

The movie industry and the television industry often develop their own standards about airing advertising. Under pressure from the FTC and Congress, the film studios are not airing TV commercials for R-rated movies during programs that attract many viewers below 18 years old.[13] For years, the major television networks have voluntarily refrained from accepting hard liquor ads, although some cable networks and local TV stations allow these ads (often on the condition that they air after 9 P.M. and include a responsible drinking message).[14] As another example, four major TV networks rejected an animal rights campaign promoting vegetarianism because it was considered too controversial.[15] [7]Strict Censor Board regulations and even rigid societal norms acting as moral guardians protect the content of the film and the entertainment industry. Stigmas and taboos associated with discussion on sex and related issues, gross violence and language leads to Censor Board of Film Certification (CBFC) imposing strict guidelines to be adhered to by the people involved. At times sensitive issues pertaining to caste, religion and racial issues have to be also accounted for. CBFC's stated objectives are; (a) the medium of film remains responsible and sensitive to the values and standards of society; (b) artistic expression and creative freedom are not unduly curbed; (c) certification is responsible to social changes; (d) the medium of film provides clean and healthy entertainment; and (e) as far as possible, the film is of aesthetic value and cinematically of a good standard. [8]The classification of films by CBFC is as "U", which is a universal picture and is a Theme and treatment suitable for family viewing including children, followed by UA, where all may not be suitable for children and the theme or dialogues may need explaining by the parents. And the last A, where theme or treatment of the film is adult oriented and it is prohibited for children to watch it.

Finally, companies have the option of taking competitors to court over practices they believe are illegal or unfair. Kimberly-Clark filed suit against Procter & Gamble not long ago, saying that a commercial for Pampers Easy Ups made "false and disparaging claims" about Huggies Pull-Ups training pants. After a judge issued a temporary restraining order preventing P&G from airing the ad, the company changed it and put the modified commercial back on the air. Kimberly-Clark then asked a court to halt the new ad. Although the judge found insufficient grounds for blocking the new ad, Kimberly-Clark planned to continue the legal fight. This type of battle can be extremely costly for both sides, but it also provides a vital venue for companies to fight for changes if they believe they have been harmed by a competitor's practices.[16]

Consumer Groups

In addition to government and industry agencies, more than 100 national organizations and 600 local groups look out for various consumer interests. Among the best-known groups are Ralph Nader's Public Citizen, National Consumer's League, Consumers Union, Consumer Federation of America, Better Business Bureaus, National Wildlife Federation, and Environmental Defense Fund (see Exhibit 19.3). These groups lobby various government agencies to influence the enactment of legislation and assist consumers in dealing with companies.

Groups like Center for Science in the Public Interest monitor companies' marketing activities and publicly comment on objectionable ads or techniques. Concerned about childhood obesity, this group recently asked food companies to stop promoting high-sugar and high-fat foods to young children. In response, Kraft Foods said it would stop advertising cookies and certain snacks to children under 12 and change ingredients to make the foods healthier.[17] Animal rights groups have

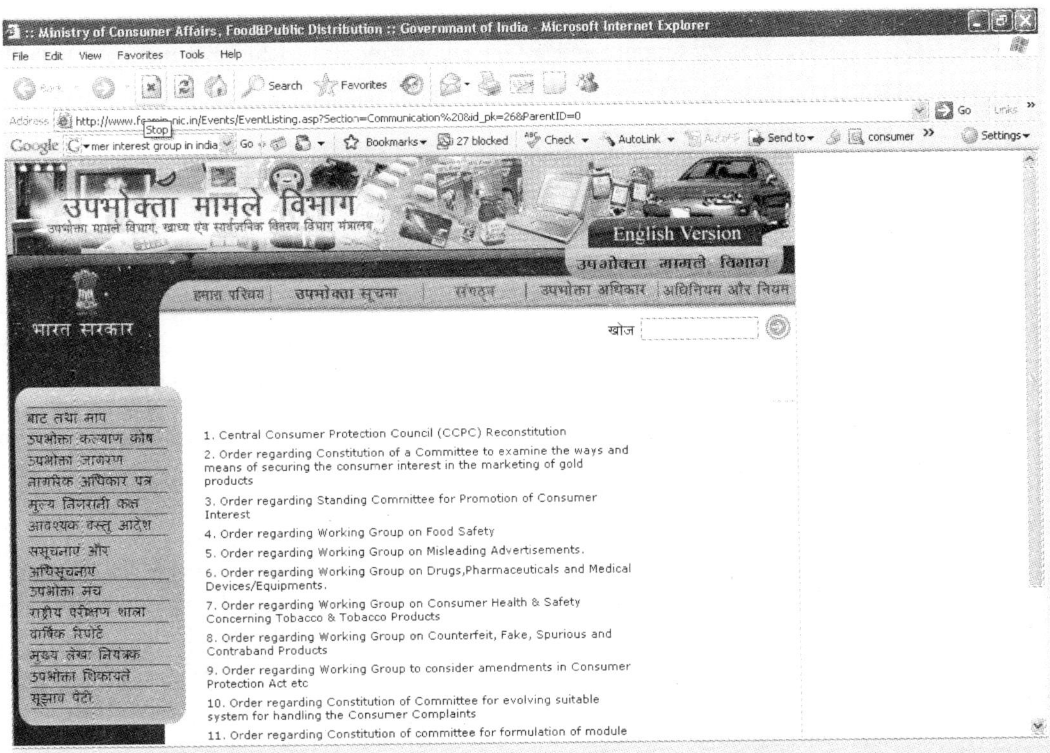

Exhibit 19.3
LOOKING OUT FOR CONSUMERS' INTERESTS
The website of the Ministry of Consumer Affairs gives information on how consumers can gain meaningful information on consumer rights and laws.

put pressure on the National Cattlemen's Beef Association by calling attention to poor treatment of calves and by calling for a veal boycott.[18] EthicAd works with consumer advocates and drug manufacturers to draft voluntary standards for consumer advertising of drugs.[19] Also, various local consumer groups and media organizations help protect consumer rights through hotlines, websites, and investigative reporting. In the Indian context some recent initiatives have been taken both at the Public and Private level in terms of the Consumer Action Groups. [9]The Consumer Online Foundation has complete information on the consumer redressel forum and the various organizations and the consumer courts, listed state wise, which help consumers in voicing their rights and opinions. Consumer Online is an initiative launched by Consumer Online Foundation (COF) to interlink and integrate a comprehensive database of information related to consumers, consumerism and the digital economy. Consumer Online Foundation, is a registered Trust formed with the motive of ensuring that modern technologies and communication medium are used to subserve the greater common good. COF advocates the use of these effective communication tools to ensure improved productivity, enhanced information delivery, reduced transaction costs and efficiency in society. COF manages one of the country's largest resource centres on Consumer law and policy in India and its dedicated band of researchers has been involved in addressing various legal remedies affecting consumers. The COF has adopted a four-pronged strategy of providing (i) Research support; (ii) Information dissemination; (iii) Advocacy support; and (iv) Litigation support to achieve its mandate. In Delhi, for instance the Consumer Rights groups involved are:

- Common Cause
- Consumer Coordination Council
- Consumer Online Foundation(COF)
- Consumers' Forum
- Friedrich-Naumann-Stiftung (FNSt)
- Indian Federation Of Consumer Organizations (Regd.) (IFCO)
- Mahila Dakshita Samiti
- Pragati Sheel Mahila Samiti (PSMS)
- Voluntary Organization In Interest Of Consumer Education (VOICE

Similarly, each state has its own advocacy groups and courts which look after the rights and the rules governing the consumer interests.

How Marketing Practices Violate Consumer Rights

Regulators have long been interested in the types of information provided in marketing communications and the extent to which they violate consumer rights. This section discusses four areas of concern: (1) deceptive advertising and labeling, (2) deceptive selling practices, (3) advertising to children, and (4) privacy on the Internet.

Deceptive Advertising and Labeling

Sometimes marketing communications can leave consumers with information or beliefs that are incorrect or cannot be substantiated, resulting in ***deception.*** For example, Microsoft had to change its ads for handheld computer software because they were found to focus on features available only on higher-priced wireless models.[20] As defined by the FDA, a *deceptive ad* is one that "either through (1) its verbal content, (2) its design, structure, and/or visual artwork, or (3) the context in which it appears causes at least *n* percent of a representative group of consumers to have a common incorrect impression or belief."[21] (The *n* percent—a percentage of affected consumers, as determined by the federal agency—varies and is determined by the nature of the situation and how severe the consequences of the incorrect belief are.) According to the FTC, deception involves (1) a misrepresentation, an omission, or a practice that is likely to mislead the consumer; (2) consumers acting as they normally would in relation to a product or service or in a consumption situation; and (3) a material misrepresentation (one that will affect their choice).[22]

Just because consumers hold an incorrect belief, however, does not necessarily mean that deception is involved. Remember from Chapter 5 that consumers can simply misunderstand the message.[23] This is why advertisers must take care when explaining the facts surrounding their offerings (see Exhibit 19.4). Yet, because mass media is imperfect, every communication is naturally associated with some degree of miscomprehension. However, when a large proportion of consumers hold the same incorrect belief that can be traced to a specific message, then deception is considered to be a problem. According to the FTC, deception occurs when approximately 20 to 25 percent of consumers have an incorrect belief (this percentage may be lower for offerings that affect consumer safety).[24]

The severity of deception is determined by factors such as whether the claim influences behavior, what potentially harmful effects it has on consumers, and the extent to which it creates an unfair advantage in the marketplace.[25] The FTC usually takes action only when the deception causes injury to consumers or unfair losses to competitors. For instance, the agency fined the Home Shopping Network $1.1 million for making deceptive claims in Internet advertising.[26] However, some consumers, such as children or the elderly, may be more susceptible to deception than other groups and may need more protection.[27] One study found that both gender and brand usage can influence whether consumers are susceptible to potential deception in comparative advertising.[28]

Exhibit 19.4
CLARIFYING INFORMATION
This ad clarifies the point that scientific evidence suggests that Dove is less harmful than any other ordinary soap.

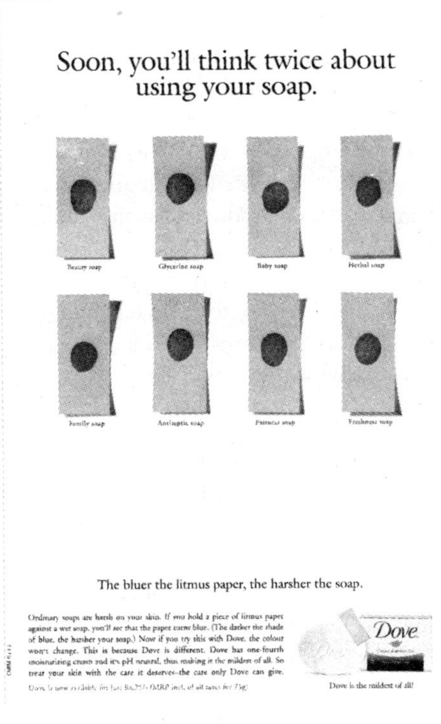

Types of Deception Deception can occur in a variety of ways.[29] The most obvious type is a company's ***false objective claim*** about a product or service. For years Listerine claimed to be the mouthwash that "kills germs that cause colds." After research evidence demonstrated that this claim was not valid, the FTC found Listerine guilty of deceptive advertising. More recently, a judge said that a Listerine ad was misleading when it claimed the mouthwash was as effective as flossing in fighting plaque and gingivitis. Changing the advertising and covering unacceptable wording on product packages cost Listerine an estimated $2 million.[30] Also, some retailers use "exaggerated reference prices" in ads to make consumers believe that a sale price is a really good deal.[31]

As discussed in Chapter 5, the name of the product or service or the label can sometimes be misleading.[32] For example, the winemaker Canandaigua Brands was required to alter the labeling of its white zinfandel and chardonnay wines and to use the phrase *with natural flavors* because these brands add fruit flavors that do not conform to zealously guarded pedigrees.[33] Various regional marketing groups have been actively monitoring produce labels that misrepresent the origin of a fruit or vegetable.[34] In fact, the FTC has established specific guidelines under which companies are allowed to label or promote a product as "Product of U.S.A."

Puffery Certain false or unsubstantiated claims fall outside the realm of regulation, as in the case of puffery. These exaggerated claims, such as a brand being "the world's best," cannot be proven, and most consumers do not believe them.[35] However, if "puff" claims are believed and have a significant effect on behavior, then some type of corrective action may be necessary.[36]

Missing Information Consumers can also be deceived by what is *not* said in an ad. Even when everything stated in the ad is true, consumers can be left with a false impression because *information has been left out,* or qualifications have been presented in an inconspicuous place where consumers may not see them.[37] This type of deception is most likely to occur when a consumer's motivation, ability, or opportunity (MAO) to process are low.[38] For example, regulatory agencies have scrutinized weight-loss ads because some lack information about how many consumers lose weight and fail to mention that weight loss may be temporary.[39]

Allowing Incorrect Inferences to Be Made An ad can be deceptive simply because of the way it *interacts with consumers' beliefs.* Even when everything in the ad is accurate, it may still be deceptive if consumers develop an incorrect inference from it. This situation often occurs when consumers infer unrealistically high levels of attribute performance.[40] In the tobacco industry, advertising for low-tar, low-nicotine, and additive-free cigarettes has been attacked because consumers mistakenly believe these cigarettes are healthier for them. At one point, Philip Morris added a warning to packages of Parliament and other brands telling consumers not to assume that cigarettes labeled as light, ultra light, medium, or mild are "less harmful" or "will help you quit smoking."[41]

In addition, health claims made by a particular food brand can incorrectly cause consumers to believe that all brands in the same category possess the same benefit; however, this can be corrected by printing nutrition information on the package.[42] Research on nutrition information shows that consumers tend to draw misleading generalizations or inferences from one claim about an attribute to other, unmentioned attributes. Shoppers might, for instance, think a product advertised as low fat is also low in cholesterol.[43]

The key point is that what the ad actually says does not determine whether or not it is deceptive. What matters is what the consumer *believes* as a result of the ad. Therefore, consumer research studies that assess customers' reactions to advertising messages play a key role in assessing deceptive advertising.[44]

Regulation of Deceptive Advertising The FTC and FDA are the major agencies that regulate deceptive advertising. When companies, consumers, or other organizations complain about an advertising message and the case is severe enough to warrant attention, these agencies will investigate. If the agencies find evidence of potential deception, they will require the offending company to engage in ***substantiation*** to prove the questionable claims. For instance, the Home Shopping Network was asked to substantiate claims about the effectiveness of three vitamin sprays and an aerosol to help quit smoking.[45] The FDA has become more active in seeking substantiation for nutritional claims made by food products, as well as health claims made by certain dietary supplements (that they prevent cancer, thwart hair loss, and so on).[46] Moreover, the FTC's "Big Fat Lie" initiative has halted numerous misleading promotions of diet aids and helped educate consumers about quick-weight-loss claims.[47]

Although the FDA allows food marketers to advertise certain health claims, the advertising requirements are so stringent that few marketers use them.[48] Yet, health claims can be highly effective in attracting consumer attention and motivating purchases. After Coca-Cola began promoting its Minute Maid Heartwise orange juice on the basis of heart health (the juice contains plant sterols, proven to lower "bad" cholesterol levels), sales jumped significantly.[49] Another good example of this approach is in Exhibit 19.5.

Exhibit 19.5
ADVERTISING A HEALTH CLAIM
Walls made a claim about their new brand of ice cream Moo, that it has calcium equivalent to one glass of milk.

The FTC and FDA have several options if advertising claims cannot be substantiated. The most common one is to issue a ***cease-and-desist order*** forcing the company to immediately discontinue all advertising with the offending claim. At one time, the makers of heartburn medicines Pepsid AC and Tagamet HB were ordered to withdraw advertising that contained unsubstantiated or misleading claims.[50] Depending on the severity of the problem, the FTC can impose fines or punitive damages. In other cases, it may order ***affirmative disclosure,*** altering ad claims to provide correct information. For example, the FTC now wants all weight-loss products to provide information about the chances of weight-loss success and to state that this loss may be only temporary.[51] Unfortunately, affirmative disclosure statements can sometimes contribute to uncertainty, be misunderstood, or be misleading.[52] Research shows that these disclosures are likely to effectively correct invalid inferences only when consumers' MAO to process the information are high.[53]

The agencies may require ***corrective advertising*** when the infraction is considered very severe and merely ceasing the misleading ad will not dissipate consumer beliefs. (This may occur when an ad has been shown so often that the incorrect belief persists long after the advertisement disappears.) In these cases, the company must make a formal statement to correct the false consumer belief. For example, Listerine was required to spend more than $10 million over two years on corrective ads to dispel the belief that Listerine prevents colds.[54] One TV ad stated, "While Listerine will not help prevent colds or sore throats or lessen their severity, breath tests prove Listerine fights onion breath better than Scope." Research has generally supported the effectiveness of corrective ads in eradicating false beliefs.[55] However, one study found that *brand* evaluations were likely to be lower after exposure to corrective ads only when prior brand evaluations were negative.[56] Nevertheless, corrective ads did lead to lower evaluations of the *advertiser* when prior attitudes were positive.

Other agencies and groups also regulate deceptive advertising. As one example, the FCC is quite responsive to consumer complaints about broadcast ads. Various state and local organizations are responsible for monitoring marketing messages that are not national in scope, and the NAD/NARB system provides for industry self-regulation of ad claims. The FTC is also enlisting the help of media outlets in turning away ads for quick-weight-loss products that lack scientifically substantiated claims.[57]

Issues of deceptive advertising and false claims have now become sensitive issues. With the advent of media channels and innovations in the existing options, the consumer's access and reach have increased to issues that concern them. Though, with high illiteracy rate, sellers (at the retail, level) have been taking undue advantage, it becomes important to analyze whether deceptive information and advertising are two separate or single issues. The marketer may make a claim at the company level about a product, on the flip side, the retailer may be misrepresenting to the consumers. Most issues in India are handled, particularly those related to advertising, by the [10]India, ASCI (Advertising Standards Council of India) that govern the advertising norms and practices. The Advertising Standards Council of India is a non- profit self regulatory body set up to deal with complaints pertaining to advertisements and consisting of members from among advertisers, advertising agencies, the media and allied professionals. The Consumer Complaints Council of the ASCI deals with complaints received from Consumers and Industry, against Advertisements which are considered as False, Misleading, Indecent, Illegal, leading to Unsafe practices, or Unfair to competition, and consequently in contravention of the ASCI Code for Self-Regulation in Advertising.

Deceptive Selling Tactics

Deceptive practices can occur in the context of personal selling. Millions of sales transactions are completed every year through personal selling, telemarketing, and similar sales methods. This volume is bound to lead to instances in which consumers are not treated fairly, which is why regulation has been enacted to protect the interests of consumers. Most companies attempt to prevent abuses because it is in their best interest to please consumers. Nevertheless, some problematic practices have required regulatory attention, including (1) the bait-and-switch technique, (2) misrepresentation of the selling intent, and (3) incorrect statements or promises.

The Bait-and-Switch Technique In the ***bait-and-switch*** technique, a retailer draws a customer into the store by advertising a product or service at a very attractive, low price. The retailer then tries to get the consumer to trade up to a higher-priced item by not stocking the advertised item or by making it so unattractive upon closer inspection that the consumer will not want it. Encouraging consumers to trade up to another model is not illegal in itself; it can be an honest attempt to better fulfill the consumer's needs. However, it *is* illegal if the intent is to deceive the consumer.

As an example, the New Jersey Division of Consumer Affairs charged Nationwide Computers and Electronics of engaging in bait-and-switch practices when it failed to stock sufficient quantities of advertised goods, refused to honor rain checks for out-of-stock advertised goods, sold used goods as new, and required consumers to present the actual print advertisement in order to receive the sale price. "When merchants lure customers to a store by advertising a great deal on a specific product and then fail to adequately stock that product, they are engaging in the unlawful practice of baiting and switching," said New Jersey's director of consumer affairs. The electronics retailer settled the charges and promised to change its practices (and ultimately filed for bankruptcy protection).[58]

When the FTC determines that infractions have occurred, it can impose fines and require corrective advertising. Three carpet retailers in the Washington, D.C., area, for example, were ordered to include the following statement in a conspicuous place in their advertisement and to surround the statement with a black border:

> *The Federal Trade Commission has found that we engage in bait-and-switch advertising; that is, the salesman makes it difficult to buy the advertised product, and he attempts to switch you to a higher-priced item.*[59]

Misrepresenting the Selling Intent Consumers are often concerned that if they interact with salespeople, they will feel pressured into buying something they do not want. Salespeople realize this and sometimes devise strategies to "trick" consumers into entering a conversation. For example, salespeople might ask consumers to answer a questionnaire or say that consumers have just won a valuable prize. Using these techniques to get a "foot in the door," the salesperson then attempts to sell a product or service. Poor and elderly consumers are often victims of this type of fraud.

A common example is the ***postcard scheme*** in which consumers receive a postcard promising cash prizes, free vacations, or expensive cars, usually with the announcement "Congratulations! You are a guaranteed winner!"[60] When consumers contact the company, they are subjected to an intense selling effort and pressured to buy worthless or unneeded items. In particular, certain land development projects have engaged in this type of activity. Consumers are encouraged to report misrepresentations through the National Consumer League's toll-free hotline and other avenues. Interestingly, in a study about the ethics of certain sales practices, misrepresentation was one of the most negatively viewed practices.[61]

Incorrect Statements or Promises Another way in which salespeople create legal problems for their company is to make statements, intentionally or not, that cannot be backed up or substantiated. Problem statements can (1) create unintended warranties, (2) dilute the effectiveness of safety warnings, (3) disparage competitive offerings, (4) misrepresent one's own offerings, and (5) interfere with business relationships.[62] Sales managers must therefore carefully educate salespeople about what they can and cannot say and do. In addition, companies that promote apparent "pyramid selling" schemes have been under attack because some salespeople are recruited with promises of big money that is unlikely to materialize.[63] Amway was forbidden to do business in China in 1998 as part of a general crackdown on organizations that use independent representatives for door-to-door sales and allow representatives to make money from the sales made by the people they, in turn, have recruited as reps. Amway adapted and sales of its personal and household products soared after the company opened stores and made other changes required by the Chinese government.[64]

Some selling practices are outright deceptive or fraudulent, and elderly consumers are often victimized by them.[65] For example, unscrupulous telemarketers tell elderly consumers they will win a $1 million if they send a check for a certain amount. In another scheme, salespeople claim to be bank employees and ask for the consumer's account number.[66] One consumer received more than 6,000 calls and pieces of mail for such scams. This situation has led organizations such as the AARP to develop educational programs to help consumers avoid falling victim to fraudulent selling practices.[67]

Despite the potential for abuse and the need for consumer protection, government agencies have often had difficulty regulating personal selling. This is because

(1) many sales interactions are verbal and entail little or no written evidence, (2) the abuses usually occur at a local and individual level, making detection more difficult, and (3) it is hard to monitor compliance with the law. Thus protecting consumers from these selling activities is more difficult than protecting them from deceptive advertising.

Some cases which have generated controversies in Indian advertising are worth mentioning here. [11]1993 saw the first controversy in Indian advertising with the Kamasutra condoms ads which was much talked about because of the nudity and sexual explicitness used in the marketing of the product. [12]Later, in July 23, 1995, a Mumbai tabloid published a photograph of an ad for Tuff shoes that had models Madhu Sapre and Milind Soman posing in the nude with a python wrapped around them, just about covering the vitals. The controversy and protests dragged on for a long time.

Advertising to Children

Advertising to children has been the subject of considerable controversy and debate focusing on the effect these ads may have on young, impressionable consumers. The average child spends more than three hours a day watching television and is exposed to more than 30,000 ads a year.[68] Networks cluster children's programming in certain time periods, making it easy for marketers to target children and spend heavily to promote toys and other products for this segment.[69] However, advertising to children raises a variety of troubling consumer issues.

Issues Related to Children as Consumers One basic problem is that young children, particularly those under seven years old, have not yet developed the cognitive abilities to distinguish between the ad and the program.[70] Even at an age when children can recognize this difference, they still may not understand that the purpose of the ad is to sell them something.[71] Thus young children do not possess the same skepticism as adults and are more likely to believe what they see in ads. Note, however, that children are better at understanding the informational intent ("ads tell you about things") than the persuasive intent.[72]

Another problem is that children can experience difficulties in storing information in long-term memory and retrieving it to use in evaluating ads.[73] Furthermore, ad messages may prey on children's strong needs for sensual satisfaction, play, and affiliation, influencing them to choose material objects over socially oriented options.[74] Critics argue that ads teach children to become materialistic, act impulsively, and expect immediate gratification.

Unfortunately, many parents do not watch television with their children and do not educate or teach them about advertising.[75] As a result, children may be particularly impressionable and subject to having their attitudes and behaviors influenced by ads.[76] For example, some younger children believe that little people inside the television set are speaking directly to them. One study found that children who viewed products advertised in school on Channel One (a daily TV program that reaches 12,000 U.S. schools) liked these products better and had stronger consumption values than those who were not exposed to those ads.[77] Exposure to ads often prompts children to step up requests to parents about buying products, particularly toys, leading to family conflict and disappointed children.[78]

Because they do not understand the costs involved, children have been especially vulnerable to ads encouraging them to call 900 numbers for products or services.[79] In fact, mothers say they have more negative perceptions of this practice than of any other activity directed toward children.[80] Children are also exposed to numerous ads for products that shape, often negatively, their impressions of what it means to be an adult.[81] Over the years, Consumers Union has cited some companies for directing unfair advertising toward children. For example, the consumer group disapproved of Nike and Reebok using emotional appeals and celebrities.[82]

When a character in a TV program is also featured in ad messages—a technique called ***host selling***—children may easily confuse the program with advertising. PBS came under fire for featuring the popular children's character Barney in pledge drives during children's programming. This led many children to ask their parents to "send money to Barney."[83] The NAD has recommended that no program characters appear in ads within the program or even in adjacent programs, and the FCC now prohibits TV stations from using host selling on children's programs.

Another controversy centers on the types of products advertised. Many ads directed at children promote foods that contain a lot of sugar, such as candy and sugar-coated cereals; critics say these ads encourage bad eating habits. For example, children who watch such ads are more likely to ask for these sugar-packed products than to ask for fruit for a snack.[84] Furthermore, children who have been exposed to these ads tend to consume more sugared products and be less educated about nutrition. Companies are responding to such concerns in a variety of ways. For instance, Nickelodeon has SpongeBob Squarepants promoting healthy eating by appearing in special "Nicktritional" labels showing a food's nutritional content.[85] Another example is the vending machine in Exhibit 19.6.

Children's use of the Internet is also a focus for consumer advocates and regulators. Nearly all websites targeting children feature some form of advertising.[86] Although parents can use software to block access to some sites, children may not understand the need to avoid giving out personal data and e-mail addresses on the Internet. Internet access thus raises concerns about family privacy as well as about

Exhibit 19.6
ADVERTISEMENT TARGETED TOWARDS CHILDREN
The NECC Advertisement showcases the goodness of egg and is directed towards both mothers and children

children's ability to differentiate between advertising and nonadvertising material on the Web.

Some Possible Solutions In light of the many issues related to ads targeting children, both the FTC and the FCC have recommended that television stations use a separator between the program and the ad whenever the program is directed toward younger children, particularly on Saturday mornings. They recommend including a message in both the video and audio portion of the broadcast prior to and directly after the ads, such as "We will return after these messages" before the commercial break, followed by "We now return to [name of the program]" at the end of the break.[87] Such separators have successfully helped children to distinguish between ads and programming.[88] The FCC has also ruled that TV stations and cable operators must keep records of their commitment to provide three hours of educational children's programming per week and limit children's advertising to a total of 12 minutes per hour on weekdays and 10.5 minutes per hour on weekends.[89]

In response to the problem of advertising sugary foods to children, the FTC has encouraged the use of public service announcements (PSAs) to teach children proper nutritional habits. Unfortunately, this program has had limited success because the PSAs tend to be shown infrequently and because simply providing children with basic nutritional information is not sufficient to instill good eating habits. In addition, entertaining or emotional appeals tend to be more effective in reaching the stated goals.[90] Other programs have attempted to educate children about nutrition in schools, hoping that the children will influence their parents to be more conscious of nutrition. Companies such as Red Lobster are providing schools with informational packages about nutrition (in this case, the nutrition of seafood).

The advertising industry has developed guidelines for children's advertising that are enforced by the Children's Advertising Review Unit (CARU), a wing of the Council of Better Business Bureaus.[91] These guidelines encourage truthful and accurate advertising that recognizes children's cognitive limitations and does not create unrealistic expectations about what products can do. For example, advertisers are expected to accurately portray a product's size, durability, and benefits, and clearly indicate what comes with the product.[92] A recent study found that most advertisers are following these guidelines. However, violations were more likely to occur on cable TV than on network TV, involve the fast-food industry more than other industries, and relate to the amount of time a prize or premium was highlighted.

Educational initiatives by consumer groups and industry organizations are teaching children about the role of advertising.[93] Overall, however, the issue of advertising to children has not been resolved; some critics even suggest banning *all* advertising directed toward children. This position is obviously very controversial and would be strongly opposed by many companies. Supporters of children's advertising maintain that ads deliver useful information to children; teach positive values such as achievement, success, individualism, and fairness; and provide entertainment.[94] Some supporters also believe that very young children are not old enough to buy or significantly influence buying decisions.

"Children in advertising" have also remained a point of debate in India. The first controversy came up with the "Shaktiman", issue which caused child fatalities. There may be lack of guidelines over acceptable advertising or the use of child models in advertisements; there are however specific laws and a procedure for complaints to the Advertising Standards Council, and control of the Internet is strict, while the Board of Film Certification awards viewing ratings concludes that the laws relating to advertising to children, while better than they were heretofore, are not comprehensive and are often flouted. There is no restriction on advertising to schools, although there are guidelines on the sale of cigarettes and alcohol and the government's emphasis on breastfeeding has led it to prohibit the promotion of commercials on infant milk substitutes.

[14] A survey by AC Nielsen, UTV's research partner, showed that an average child watches TV for about three hours on weekdays and 3.7 hours on weekends The time spent in front of television goes up with age, and the preferred language of viewing is Hindi across all age groups. Apart from the programmes, the children also view a lot of advertisements. A study conducted by Millward Brown and IMRB showed that kids influence decision making on categories beyond those just meant for kids. Data from the study, culled over five years after interviewing 100,000 kids every year across 35 markets in Asia Pacific, including Hong Kong, Manila and Mumbai, showed that recognition of corporate logos happens at the age of six months, brand name requests begin by the age of three years, differentiating between brand values happens by age 10 and brand loyalty begins by the age of 11. By 2030, in the markets studied, there would be 800 million tweens (that's the pre-teen age group between 9-14 years). The research also showed that six out of 10 children pester an average of nine times even after their parents say 'no' to a particular request, and that 80 per cent of all brand purchases by parents with tweens are controlled by their children. In India, the ad spend per year on products meant for kids but purchased by parents, like health drinks, is 12 to 15 per cent of the total Rs.38,000 million. Ad spends per year on products meant for children and also bought by them, like chocolates, is seven to eight per cent.

Privacy on the Internet

Whereas the issues of deceptive advertising and labeling, deceptive selling practices, and advertising to children relate to protecting consumers from incoming information, privacy on the Internet relates to the flow of personal information from the consumer to outside parties. Privacy is not a new consumer issue, but it has received much more attention recently because the Internet offers the opportunity to collect a lot of detailed information about consumers.[95] Key issues of concern are how much and which information marketers should be allowed to collect, how marketers will keep personal information secure, how much information should be made public, how it should be used in marketing, whether consumers consent to the collection and use of information, and how consumers can control the flow and use of information.[96]

One researcher observes that consumers wind up bearing some of the costs for dealing with unwanted marketing communications—both traditional and online messages—and maintaining control of personal information.[97] The extent of consumer concern and willingness to give personal information varies according to the type of information the online marketer wants to collect.[98] Another study suggests that a company can enhance privacy by providing consumers with more control and information about the benefits they may gain (such as customized offers of products or services) when they allow personal information to be collected.[99]

Online companies are involved in a number of self-regulation strategies to protect consumer privacy. Most websites post privacy statements to explain what

Exhibit 19.7
PRIVACY ON THE INTERNET

	Goals	Limitations
TRUSTe	Provides guarantee of privacy protection: • Gives a seal of trust to Web sites that submit to application process • Acts as a clearinghouse for privacy violation reports • Provides a children's privacy seal program	• Limited industry compliance • Critics suggest that guidelines go further in protecting privacy
BBBOnline	Provides seal of approval to Web sites that adequately perform through a self-assessment and pay a fee	• Voluntary nature of member company compliance • Enforcement
Alliance for Privacy	Publishes guidelines for member companies to follow in the collection and dissemination of information	• Voluntary nature of member company compliance • Enforcement

consumer data they gather, what they do with it, how consumers can review it, and how it is protected. Unfortunately, a survey shows that many of these statements do not provide sufficiently complete explanations.[100] Moreover, a study of privacy- and security-related statements indicates that many commercial websites do not post their policies regarding unsolicited consumer contacts, sharing of information with other firms, and allowing consumers to opt out of information sharing.[101] Some organizations grant seals of approval to show consumers that certain websites adhere to specific privacy protection guidelines (see Exhibit 19.7).

Government regulators are monitoring privacy issues and taking action to protect certain consumer groups, such as children and seniors. Both Mrs. Fields Cookies and Hershey have settled FTC charges of collecting personal information online from children under 13 without prior, verifiable consent of the parents.[102] This FTC action was taken under the Children's Online Privacy Protection Act, which addresses privacy issues related to children's use of the Internet, defining what is acceptable and unacceptable behavior for Internet advertisers.[103] Also, knowing that seniors are more vulnerable to being victimized by Internet-based scams, the FBI's Financial Crimes Squad spends a significant amount of time focusing on this group.[104]

Consumers are increasingly worried about "identity theft," or the stealing of personal information over the Internet, especially in the wake of several highly publicized incidents involving theft of thousands of Social Security numbers and credit card numbers.[105] Many consumers—not just in the United States, but around the world—fear their credit card numbers will be intercepted by a third party or misused if submitted through the Internet.[106] Thus manufacturers, technology firms, and online retailers are working hard to increase online security.[107] Congress has passed legislation making Internet identity fraud a crime, and the FBI's Internet Fraud Complaint Center invites consumer complaints about this and other online crimes.[108] The FTC provides assistance when consumers are worried that their identity has been stolen (see Exhibit 19.8). As the Internet evolves, regulators, marketers, and researchers will closely follow consumer attitudes and behavior to uncover important concerns and provide protection against privacy violations and other problems.

Exhibit 19.8
FTC BATTLES IDENTITY FRAUD
When consumers think their identity may have been stolen, they can go this Web page sponsored by the Federal Trade Commission for assistance.

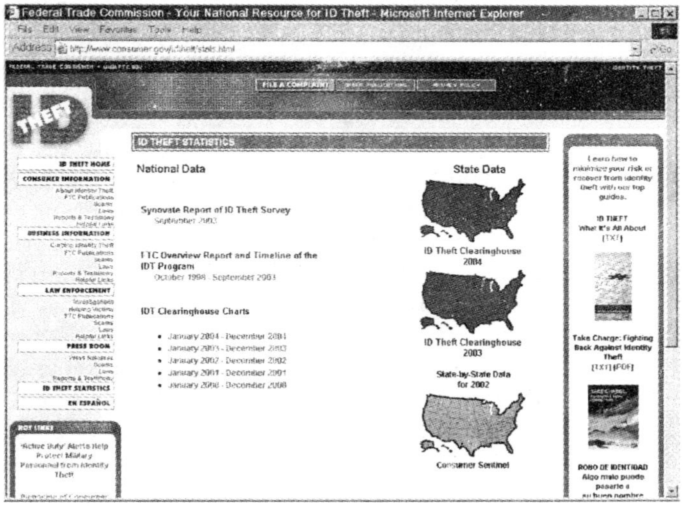

[15]A study was conducted across US and India in the BPO industry to understand the differences and similarities between the privacy perceptions of Indians and Americans. Subjects in both countries spoke of many concepts when asked about what comes to their minds when they hear the word privacy. Overall, subjects in India discussed privacy in terms of personal space and subjects in the US related privac to personal information. While 61% of the subjects in the US related privacy to some form of control of information only 14% of the subjects in India related privacy to these concepts. On the other hand, 48% of the subjects in India related privacy to physical, home and living space, but only 18% of the subjects in the US related privacy to these concepts. In addition, while 50% of the US subjects mentioned either financial information or identity theft or both, these concepts were not discussed by any of the Indian subjects. Typical responses of Indian subjects were: Privacy for me is my personal territory" and "personal privacy". A typical response from a US subject was: Privacy is not allowing other people to have your information. It is protection of your information from outside people.

Product Information and Safety Issues

Government agencies and consumer groups go beyond protecting consumers from unfair practices. They also provide information to help consumers make better decisions and use products and services safely.

Consumer Protection Through Information

The purpose of providing consumers with more and better product information is to help them make more informed decisions. For example, the FDA has paid a great deal of attention to the types of nutrition information provided on food labels, hoping that consumers will purchase and consume these products in a more nutritionally sound manner.[109] As part of this effort, fast-food restaurants are now required to disclose nutrition information about their menu items, with the result that a number of fast-food chains have improved the nutritional content of their offerings. Other types of restaurants may have to provide this type of information in the future, especially to substantiate low-fat or low-salt claims.

Although efforts to inform consumers are instituted with good intentions, a number of problems have arisen, in part because regulators have not based their proposals on a solid understanding of consumer information processing and decision making. Four areas are particularly important for protecting consumers through information: (1) consumer comprehension of information, (2) consumer use of the information, (3) the amount of information provided, and (4) the format of the information.

Can Consumers Comprehend the Information? Unfortunately, the general assumption that consumers can understand and correctly use detailed information when provided is not always valid. For example, a summary of six studies concluded that the vast majority of consumers do not understand basic nutrition information, including common terms such as *calories, fat, carbohydrates,* and *protein.*[110] Also, older consumers (those over 60) are less accurate in their use of nutrition information than younger consumers are.[111] Another study found that a large percentage of consumers do not understand the relationship between the contract interest rate and the annual percentage rate when acquiring a loan.[112]

Thus regulators can expect an information program to help consumers make better decisions only when they are certain that consumers can understand the information they are given. One approach is to use educational pamphlets or informal classes to offer instruction on specific topics. However, these programs have generally been difficult to implement because of a lack of consumer interest, suggesting a low MAO level. Some regulators have developed simpler formats that make it easier for consumers to understand the information, as discussed later in the chapter. And some experts are calling for U.S. marketers to print product warnings and instructions in both English and Spanish so the large segment of Hispanic Americans can read the information.[113]

Will Consumers Use the Information? A second assumption of consumer information programs is that consumers will actually *use* this information. One study found that fewer than 5 percent of consumers examined nutrition information when selecting breakfast cereals.[114] Other research showed that most consumers look at the front of the package only, especially when health claims are made.[115] Also, after an initial flare-up of public interest, fast-food fare is again becoming fattier because some people crave fatty foods and are not motivated to read nutrition information.[116] On the other hand, when the claims made on a food package are inconsistent with the details in the federally required Nutrition Facts panel, consumers are capable of evaluating the panel data and will question the claims rather than the panel data.[117] In fact, nutrition labeling has gotten consumers to pay more attention to certain negative nutrition attributes of foods (such as fats) and benefited highly motivated consumers who are less knowledgeable about nutrition.[118]

Some experts question the validity and usefulness of consumer information programs. Others maintain, however, that even if only 5 percent of consumers use the information, it is still benefiting at least some segment of the population, and one that highly desires it. In support of this view, one study found that consumers who perceive that nutritional information can aid in preventing disease are more likely to read this information on the package.[119] Research also suggests that low-income expectant mothers, in particular, would benefit from nutrition information designed to improve dietary practices.[120] Moreover, some observers argue that even though consumers do not pay attention to this information when making a decision, they still might read it while the product is being consumed, such as at the breakfast table.

Can Consumers Be Given Too Much Information? Another subject of controversy is how much information to provide consumers. Chapter 9 mentioned that providing consumers with too much information can result in information overload, consumer confusion, and poorer decisions.[121] Some argue that consumers seldom acquire enough information to become confused, that they will stop

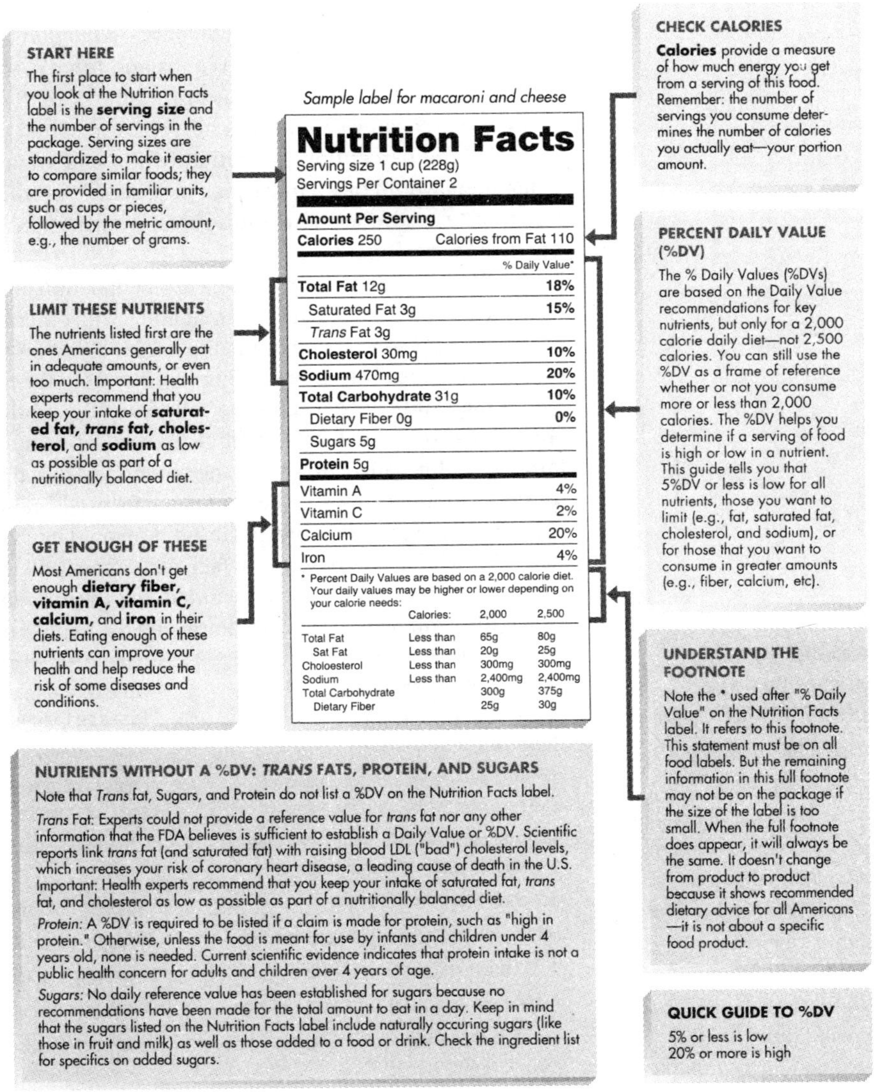

Exhibit 19.9

NUTRITION FACTS LABEL

The Nutrition Labeling and Education Act of 1990 mandated this format for food labeling. Do you think consumers find this format easy to understand?

searching before they reach overload. Regardless, the key point is that more is not always necessarily better. Thus regulators should provide consumers with the most *useful* and *important* information, rather than offering all the details that are available. The value of limited information is a key argument in the fight to shorten the lengthy disclosures required in direct-to-consumer pharmaceutical ads.[122] Such a change may not be successful, however. One study found that consumers who read the entire summary box of risk information in prescription drug ads are less likely to find it useful than consumers who only skim the summary.[123]

Can Information Be Made Easier to Use? In light of these three concerns—comprehension, use, and amount of information—regulators have been vitally interested in developing formats that supply information that is easier both to understand and to use. According to research, formats that make it easier to process information, highlight information so it stands out, or provide a benchmark that allows easy comparisons are more likely to affect consumers' decisions.[124] The Nutrition Facts labeling format was designed to permit easy comparisons of nutritional content for different food items and force manufacturers to follow stricter rules in labeling contents, thereby preventing deceptive claims (see Exhibit 19.9).[125] Some research shows that this label format resulted in somewhat more favorable attitudes and perceptions toward nutrition and an increase in the likelihood that consumers would buy a nutritious product.[126] Another study found that the label improved comprehension of nutrition information but had less impact on the purchase of healthier foods.[127]

Studies indicate that consumers at all education levels can understand nutrition information presented in this format and, as just mentioned, can evaluate the data even in the presence of a conflicting health claim on the package.[128] Further, consumers are more likely to rely on information from the nutrition panel than to rely on claims made on the package, especially when the motivation to process is higher.[129] Some have suggested using verbal (instead of numerical) descriptors to further improve performance. However, when numerical descriptors are used, percentages of nutrient amounts appear to be the most effective.[130] Researchers have suggested that showing "average" values or similar figures would be more effective than using "daily values" as a reference point.[131] In fact, with obesity on the rise, the FDA is shifting its emphasis to calories: "We've concluded that the emphasis on low fat and no fat obscured the central message that calories are the main thing," a top official explains.[132]

Exhibit 19.10
ACCEPTABLE AND UNACCEPTABLE CLAIMS

This table shows wording that the FDA has deemed acceptable and unacceptable for claims about dietary supplements. In general, claims that a product will cure a disease cannot be made without prior FDA approval, whereas claims about supporting or maintaining body functions are acceptable.

Acceptable Wording about Structure or Function	**Unacceptable Wording about Disease Claims**
Maintains healthy lung function	Maintains healthy lungs in smokers
Arouses or increases sexual desire and improves sexual performance	Helps restore sexual vigor, potency, and performance
Helps to maintain cholesterol levels that are already within the normal range	Lowers cholesterol
Supports the immune system	Supports the body's antiviral capabilities
For the relief of occasional sleeplessness	Helps to reduce difficulty falling asleep
'Resolving that irritability that ruins your day'	A reference to helping 'a nervous tension headache'
Helps support cartilage and joint function	A reference to helping 'joint pain'

Source: Chris Adams, "Splitting Hairs on Supplement Claims," *Wall Street Journal,* February 22, 2000, p. B1. Reprinted by permission of *The Wall Street Journal* via The Copyright Clearance Center.

Another example of making information easier for consumers to use is the U.S. government's efforts to standardize the energy-use information provided on various appliances. The goal is to help consumers conserve energy and save money by having the information to compare appliances and choose those that are more energy efficient. The program has had a positive effect on consumer decisions.[133] As another example, to prevent companies from exaggerating claims about a dietary supplement's disease-fighting capabilities, the FDA has established specific guidelines for acceptable wording about a product's claims (see Exhibit 19.10). [16]The Directorate General of Health Services in the Ministry of Health and Family Welfare, is working to integrate Codex standards into national food laws as much as possible. Where specific local needs justify more stringent requirements, specifications are being fixed based on scientific data. India is now reorienting its food laws to emphasize food safety as well as food quality. National standards for both domestic and export trade lay down parameters for pesticide residues, antibiotic residues, heavy metals, aflatoxin, pathogens, and other contaminants. Within India, risk analysis and setting of national standards are supported by new data generated at several research institutes.

Consumer Protection Through Product Safety

Each year consumers suffer a great number of injuries, usually between 15 and 20 million, from product-related accidents. Consumers have the right to be protected from offerings that may be hazardous to their health or safety. A product or service can be potentially harmful to consumers if a problem exists with its quality or features, if it is used by consumers in an unsafe manner, or both.[134]

Product/Service Problems The government, and in particular the CPSC, sets safety standards for each industry. A product or service that fails to meet these standards can be recalled or altered. Procter & Gamble's Adult NyQuil Nighttime, for example, once contained high levels of alcohol (25 percent), and the company was pressured to reduce these levels.[135] The CPSC has also developed child-resistant packaging guidelines for drugs to protect children from accidental poisoning—a real challenge because older adults sometimes have more difficulty opening the packages than children do.[136] Other government agencies actively address consumer problems with products and services. Several years ago, the NHTSA had Firestone recall millions of tires after reports of accidents due to tread separation.[137]

Products for children raise perennial safety issues. Every year World Against Toys Causing Harm releases a list of the ten most unsafe toys.[138] Note, however, that some companies have actively disputed the claims made by activists. Even auto airbags, which can save adult lives, have been seriously questioned for their potential to harm children.[139] The NHTSA also discovered that 50 percent of the time that children are in car seats, they are not buckled in safely. This discovery led to new safety rules for car seats.[140] Some companies are helping educate consumers about safety issues and prevention techniques through public service campaigns (see Exhibit 19.11).

Seat belts are another focus of government regulation and education efforts. U.S. government efforts to regulate this problem began with requiring seat belts to be installed in all vehicles, followed by public service announcements that educated consumers about the importance of usage. Some of the early campaigns utilized fear appeals, depicting the negative and often

Exhibit 19.11
COMPANIES EDUCATE CONSUMERS

Unilever's website gives a complete detail on a World Bank Project, where it has associated itself in India, with one of their flagship brand, Lifebuoy. According to the World Health Organisation, diarrhoea is the largest single cause of preventable death, killing 2.2 million people every year. In 2003, it killed 600 000 children aged under five in India alone. It's been estimated that if everyone washed their hands properly at key times during the day, up to half of all childhood deaths from diarrhoea - one million children - could be avoided.

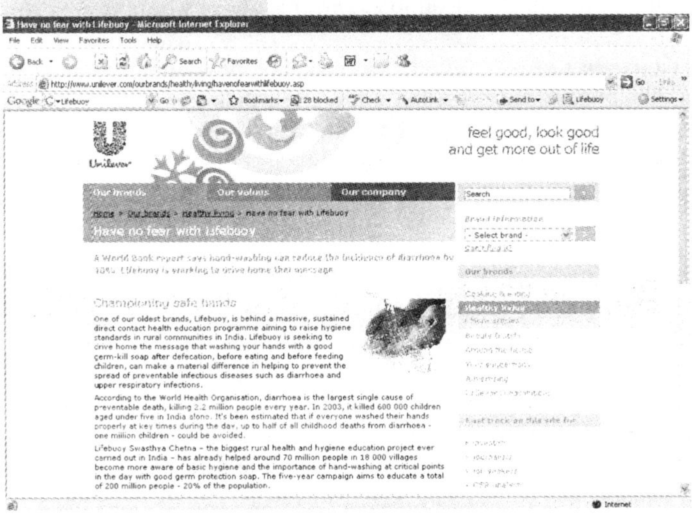

grisly consequences of not wearing seat belts. Even though many states also passed seat belt laws, compliance was much lower than desired, in part because consumers were not accustomed to using seat belts—even though they would agree that buckling up could save their lives.[141] Thus successful driver education programs must not only change consumer attitudes, but should also give drivers experience to instill the habit of using a seat belt.[142]

Voluntary self-regulation can help protect consumers. In recent years, for example, car manufacturers such as Ford, General Motors, and Chrysler have recalled various models to fix safety problems.[143] Nevertheless, when a significant infraction occurs, the CPSC, FTC, FDA, EPA, and NHTSA can intercede and propose an appropriate remedial action.[144] To illustrate, the FDA ordered the diet drug Redux off the market because of concerns that it may cause heart valves to leak and had the antihistamine Seldane taken off the market because of dangerous side effects.[145] On occasion, individual consumers engage in litigation against companies in situations where they believe the company is liable for a specific problem. In a highly publicized case against McDonald's, a woman was awarded $480,000 in damages because she received severe burns from hot coffee that she spilled on her lap.

Incorrect Use of a Product Failure to meet standards accounts for only about 20 percent of product-related injuries.[146] In other cases, injuries occur because consumers use products or services incorrectly. For example, a consumer might combine two combustible chemicals, such as different types of oven cleaners, and cause a fire; spray an insecticide near food preparation areas and poison someone; or use a plunger with a liquid drain opener and accidentally splash the acid on his or her skin.

To reduce these types of dangers, companies are expected to anticipate reasonable risks that may be inherent in the use of a product or service and take steps to avoid them. This expectation is known as the ***doctrine of foreseeability.***[147] Under this doctrine, companies can be held responsible if they do not try to prevent or at least minimize misuses that might occur from normal consumption of a product or service. Research on consumer consumption patterns can be particularly useful in identifying common usage problems. For example, it is reasonable for a company to foresee the potential for a consumer to use a plunger with a liquid drain opener. Sometimes, however, consumer misuses are very hard to anticipate, and the company is not usually held responsible. Using a power mower to cut someone's hair would be unexpected, for example, and this abuse would not be the company's fault.

When potential dangers are identified, the company must attempt either to alter the product or to provide clear instructions on how the consumer can avoid potential problems. One of the key tools for protecting consumers from safety hazards is the warning label. Consumers are clearly warned about the danger of using a plunger with liquid drain opener, for instance. Pesticide labels warn consumers to keep the product away from their hands and face and that the product "should not be taken internally." Unfortunately, these warnings are not always as effective as they should be.[148]

New label formats are being developed that should make it easier for consumers to notice and heed the warning when using the product. The label must be easy to locate, perhaps highlighted by different colors or sizes of type, and simple to understand.[149] Companies can also design packaging and labels for poisonous products to make these items especially unattractive to children.[150] Consumer education programs might also be useful in reducing the number of product-related injuries.[151]

Some products or services are inherently risky. Riding a skateboard, bungee jumping, skydiving, driving a car, riding a bicycle, and using a tanning booth involve serious safety risks to the consumer. In these instances, however, consumers are made aware of these potential dangers and use the product at their own risk. Thus companies are not generally held liable for injuries associated with these products or services unless the injury was due to faulty manufacturing or negligence. The gun industry has been fighting lawsuits brought by municipalities that say guns are an unsafe product. Guns are not currently covered by federal consumer-safety regulations, a situation some antigun groups are trying to change. Meanwhile, the gun industry has mounted a safety campaign showing the proper use of gun locks and is continuing training and education efforts to teach consumers how to use guns safely.[152] [17] The major concern on food safety in India is the physical, chemical and microbial contaminations. The consumer movements, environmental protection agencies and food safety enforcement agencies are increasingly prescribing stricter standards for macro cleanliness, microbial loads, aflatoxins, pesticide residues etc. The Govt. of India has set up a National Codex Committee under the Department of Health, Ministry of Health and Family Welfare which has identified six major areas namely Fish and Marine Products, Cereal, Nuts & Oil Seeds. There exists no comprehensive single standard in India. Standards available are under: (1) Prevention of Food Adulteration (PFA) Act 1954 (2) AGMARK an voluntary grading system operated by Directorate of Marketing Inspection under Ministry of Agriculture (3) Bureau of Indian Standards and (4) Export Inspection & Quality Control act among others. Now Government of India is attempting to develop national standards encompassing all areas of operation. But the pace of its formulation and implementation seems tardy because of the coordination problems between various ministries. In India, for instance, issues concerning use of firecrackers is an issue that the state government's every year warn people about during Diwali. Unlike developed nations where firecrackers are restricted and out of bounds for common public to use, India has a flourishing firecracker market. [18]The firecracker industry, which is worth between Rs 800-1000 crore, comes alive after Ganeshotsav. It gathers momentum after Dassehra when suppliers begin to take stock of firecrackers piled in their godowns from the previous year. This is also the time when prices begin to peak. Most people give in to the spirit of the festive season and do not mind spending a little bit extra. LPG Cylinders are also another concern in terms of how consumers use, store and dispose the product after use. In the 1950's, when LPG came to India, most houses used sagdi or a kerosene stove or chulha. Today, according to the 2001 Census of India, 17.5% of Indian households or 33.6 million Indian households used LPG as cooking fuel in 2001. 76.64% of such households were from urban India making up 48% of urban Indian households as compared to a usage of 5.7% only in rural Indian households. Moving from the conventional systems to the modern and convenient cooking also brought in its share of problems. Prime amongst which was the safety concern. The initiatives from the oil companies, HPCL, IOCL and BPCL tried to introduce safety measures in using the LPG's.

Another important aspect that covers the issue of product information and safety issues is the Infant Milk Substitute (IMS) Act of 1992. The act encourages and makes it compulsory for companies dealing in infant food and milk, follow guidelines as laid down in the act. The Government of India, recognizing the need to protect and promote breastfeeding and to protect expectant and nursing mothers from adverse influences undermining the practice of exclusive breastfeeding; has amended the IMS act 1992 to make it more effective and eliminate all possible loopholes in this act. The new act, 'The Infant Milk Substitutes, Feeding Bottles and Infant Food (Regulation of Production, Supply and Distribution) Amendment Act 2003' was enacted on 2nd June 2003. In addition to the provision of the previous act prohibiting promotion of infant milk substitutes and feeding bottles, the modified act also prohibits promotion of these products on the pretext of distribution of educational or informational material.

Environmental Protection

One final area of consumer rights is the right to an environment that enhances the quality of life—free of hazardous wastes, garbage, and pollutants and with adequate natural resources. Many efforts in this area have focused on developing laws and programs to improve air and water quality and to guard against waste disposal problems, especially hazardous waste.

Environmentally Conscious Behavior

Knowing that motor vehicles are a major cause of air pollution, the U.S. government requires the use of unleaded gasoline and has developed stricter emission control standards to reduce damage to the environment. Authorities in Kathmandu, Nepal, are trying to reduce pollution by replacing diesel-powered vehicles with electric public-transit vehicles.[153] Although many dry cleaning businesses use the chemical perc, a possible human carcinogen, some "green" dry cleaners are responding to public concerns by operating without the use of this chemical.[154]

Another major concern is the increasing amount of trash or garbage in our environment. Projections say that American consumers will generate 40 percent more trash by the year 2010 and that disposed packaging will account for 30 percent of it.[155] In response, many products (such as Lenor fabric softener in Germany; Jergen's lotion; and Lysol, Windex, and Resolve cleaners) are being sold in refillable containers.[156] Consumers in Romania and other countries reduce waste by using refillable bottles for wine, beer, seltzer, oil, and milk. The U.K. supermarket chain Tesco

Exhibit 19.12
HELPING CONSUMERS RECYCLE

This ad focuses on the importance of recycling and how consumers must follow it.

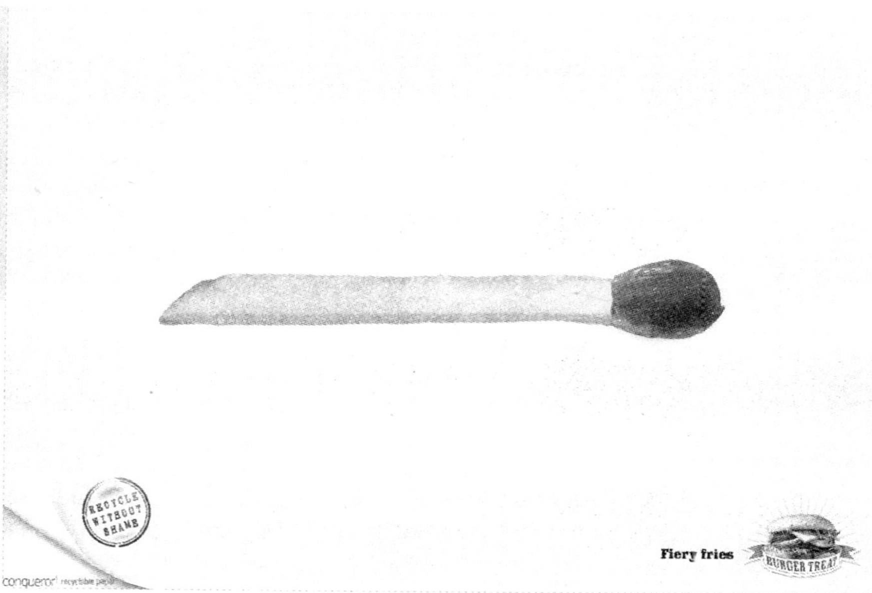

has moved to smaller food packages and replaced cardboard cartons with reusable plastic containers to minimize waste.[157] Companies that use direct-mail advertising have been pressured to give consumers the option of refusing these materials because of the tremendous waste of ink and paper associated with junk mail.[158] One study found that stressing societal benefits, self-efficacy, and behavioral control were the most effective ways to induce consumers to reduce household garbage.[159]

The trend toward the use of environmentally friendly products is growing. Nokia is developing cell phones with recyclable and biodegradable parts so discarded phones will not lie forever in landfills.[160] The ad in Exhibit 19.12 gives consumers information on how they can recycle their old cell phones. The nonprofit Rechargeable Battery Recycling Corporation helps both consumers and businesses protect the environment by recycling batteries and cell phones. More consumers are abandoning caustic cleaning products in favor of those that are milder and less damaging to the environment.[161] Consumers are also returning to natural cleansers such as baking soda, vinegar, and lemon juice, even if these products are sometimes less effective than manufactured cleansers.

One company awards a Green Seal to manufacturers of certain products that meet tough environmental standards. This seal makes it easy for environmentally conscious consumers to identify "green," or environmentally friendly, products. Consumers who have a positive attitude toward ecologically conscious living, a negative attitude toward littering, and a perception that pollution is a problem are more likely to buy ecologically packaged products than products without such attributes.[162] Researchers have also found that a *general environmental concern* has an indirect effect on intentions to purchase environmentally sensitive products.[163] Research about recycling shows that specific beliefs about its importance can directly affect whether consumers engage in recycling behaviors and whether they perceive that recycling is inconvenient.[164] Although many consumers express concern for the environment, studies often show that these feelings still do not play a major role in the purchase of many products.[165] On the other hand, environmentally conscious behaviors are most likely to occur when consumers perceive that their actions will make a difference—called *perceived consumer effectiveness.*[166]

Conservation Behavior

A second important aspect of environmental protection is ***conservation behavior.*** The need to conserve has become increasingly important in light of the rapidly escalating problems of garbage disposal and depletion of natural resources. Companies are now realizing that garbage has been a misused resource and are finding creative ways to make products more durable and to reuse materials. For example, Wellman, Inc., has used old soda bottles to make carpeting, Marcal makes paper towels out of undelivered junk mail, and Prestone recycles old antifreeze rather than making it from scratch.[167] Ecofurniture, made of recycled wood, plastic, or paper, is also growing in popularity.[168]

Government and company programs have been developed to encourage consumers to conserve certain resources, especially energy. In particular, consumer researchers have been interested in three major aspects of conservation behavior: *when* are consumers likely to conserve, *who* is most likely to conserve, and *how* can consumers be motivated to conserve?

When Are Consumers Likely to Conserve? In general, consumers are most likely to conserve when they accept personal responsibility for the pollution problem.[169] For example, consumers who perceive that there is an energy shortage because every consumer (including themselves) is using too much are more likely to accept personal blame for this problem and do something about it. However, one of the major obstacles facing conservation programs is actually *getting* consumers to take personal responsibility. Consumers often do not feel accountable for many environmental problems and are therefore not motivated to act.

Thus for conservation programs to succeed, communications must make the problem personally relevant. For example, in trying to get consumers to conserve energy by turning down the thermostat, communications could focus on how much energy and money the household could save each year and over a long period, such as ten years. Consumers are also most likely to conserve when there are no barriers to doing so, such as the lack of conservation information or salespeople who do not stress conservation.[170]

A study in the Netherlands points out the importance of using social norms to influence consumers' environmental behaviors. This study found that consumers generally perceive that they are more motivated to engage in proenvironmental behavior than other households but are lower in the ability to do so.[171] Further, they believe that ability is the greatest determinant and that their own behavior is influenced by others.

Who Is Most Likely to Conserve? A weak relationship exists between conservation behavior and some demographic characteristics. Younger consumers and individuals with more education are slightly more likely to conserve than other groups.[172] However, researchers have not been able to identify a general profile of "the conserving consumer." Attitudes toward social responsibility and environmental consciousness generally do not relate to conservation behavior.[173] Instead, consumers tend to make environmentally beneficial choices on an activity-by-activity basis.

Physical or structural characteristics of the consumer's residence, such as the type of dwelling and number of appliances, tend to be strongly related to conservation behaviors.[174] Consumers who have fewer appliances and live in apartments and mobile homes are less likely to conserve. A study in the Netherlands found that characteristics of the house, such as the amount of insulation, and behavior of the household members, such as having curtains on the windows and lowering the thermostat when no one is home, were more likely to be related to energy use than factors such as demographics and attitudes.[175]

Researchers have identified three major behaviors of energy conservers: (1) ***efficiency behaviors,*** which include driving fuel-efficient cars and insulating and weatherizing the home; (2) ***curtailment behaviors,*** which include lowering the thermostat setting, turning off unneeded lights, and reducing driving by 10 percent; and (3) ***demand-shift behaviors,*** which include switching to solar heating units and converting from electric appliances to natural gas.[176] Conservation programs are more likely to be effective when they emphasize efficiency behaviors rather than curtailment behaviors.

Can Consumers Be Motivated to Conserve? Many organizations and agencies, both government and private, are trying to motivate consumers to conserve. Ads sometimes encourage consumers to use products or packages that conserve resources or to engage in conservation behaviors. Another approach is to provide consumers with detailed information about conservation through communications, home audits, and appliance labels. Unfortunately, these programs usually have only a limited impact on conservation behavior.[177]

A more promising approach is to provide consumers with incentives to conserve. Providing consumers with a free shower-water flow device, for instance, significantly increased participation in an energy conservation program.[178] Consumers have shown that they prefer incentives such as tax credits to coercive tactics such as higher taxes. In addition, setting goals and providing feedback can be effective in helping consumers curtail energy use.

There is now a growing concern about environmental issues in India. There are some country specific issues, like rising population, increased consumption of energy and rising urbanization leading to issues of carbon emissions to name a few. The population explosion has placed great strain on the country's environment. [19]This rapidly growing population, along with a move toward urbanization and industrialization, has placed significant pressure on India's infrastructure and its natural resources. Deforestation, soil erosion, water pollution and land degradation continue to worsen and hinder economic development in rural India, while the rapid industrialization and urbanization in India's booming metropolises are straining the limits of municipal services and causing serious air pollution problems.

[20]Industrialization and urbanization have resulted in a profound deterioration of India's air quality. India has more than 20 cities with populations of at least 1 million, and some of them--including New Delhi, Mumbai, Chennai, and Kolkata--are among the world's most polluted.

[21]India's energy consumption is increasing rapidly, from 4.16 quadrillion Btu (quads) in 1980 to 12.8 quads in 2001. This 208% increase is largely the result of India's increasing population and the rapid urbanization of the country. Higher energy consumption in the industrial, transportation, and residential sectors continues to drive India's energy usage upwards at a rate faster than even China, which experienced a 130% increase in energy consumption from 1980 to 2001.

[22]Despite of a trend towards urbanization, more than 70% of India's population still lives in rural areas. As the Indian economy develops, one of the greatest challenges that India's local and regional governments face is providing people in rural areas an access to energy. Renewable energy projects - in the form of solar-, wind-, and hydropower-generated electricity - are the key to providing rural areas with energy where power is in short supply. In addition, replacing coal- and other fossil fuel-generated electricity supplied to India's cities with energy from renewable energy sources could aid in reducing air pollution and help to meet the growing energy needs of the country's large metropolises.

[23]India faces significant challenges in balancing its increased demand for energy with the need to protect its environment from further damage. Sheer population growth and urbanization make this task all the more difficult for the Indian government, as increased vehicular ownership contributing to already existing air pollution and urbanization raise the health risks. A rapidly increasing population will also lead to an increase in electricity demand, taxing the already straining power generation, transmission and distribution infrastructure and putting pressure on the power sector to add new capacity to the system.

With depleting resources and the impending issues of environmental damages the culture of recycling is gradually seeping into the country. [24]One of the challenges for a country like India is disposal of Electronic Waste (E-Waste). Waste Electrical & Electronic Equipments (WEEE) consist of computers, monitors, printers, copiers, fax machines, cellular phones, palm tops, lap tops, televisions, music systems, and many other items which are either out of use because of wear and tear or due to change in technology. Since Indian economy is growing very fast the demand of the above items is increasing too; declining prices are further leading to discarding of these machines faster.giving rise to more and more e-waste. As per estimates India generates nearly 500,000 tons of WEEE per annum, of which 60-70% consists of electronic equipments. With the markets growing multi fold, and the rural markets being explored by banking and financial services, retail industry among others, these figures are expected to go up further. Recycling of e-waste therefore, is a major concern today. Organisations like Infotrek Syscom Limited, are working on unique projects of electronic waste recycling processes and procedures.

Consumerism Around the World

Many countries have consumer protection laws, regulatory agencies, and consumer movements, although countries with conservative governments usually impose fewer restrictions on activities.[179] More liberal governments, on the other hand, often seek to protect consumers by creating a more restrictive regulatory environment. In addition, agencies such as the European Food Safety Authority provide information to help national governments protect consumers by regulating products (in this case, foods).[180] Clearly, companies must account for these forces when marketing internationally.

Like the United States, many nations have regulatory agencies to monitor advertising. In France, the Truth in Advertising commission monitors ad messages.[181] In the United Kingdom, advertising is controlled by two organizations: the Advertising Standards Authority (ASA) and the Independent Broadcasting Authority (IBA). The ASA is a self-regulatory agency (including nonindustry members) that monitors nonbroadcast advertising to ensure its honesty and fairness. The IBA is responsible for overseeing radio and television advertising. The British system tends to work more efficiently than similar U.S. organizations because it has better funding and staffing, substantial public participation, stronger remedies for infractions, better organization, and a stronger spirit of cooperation.[182] Limiting children's exposure to advertising is such a high priority in certain countries that Sweden, Norway, and Austria do not allow TV commercials that target children to be aired.[183]

Germany has very strict standards for truth in advertising. Deception occurs when research determines that 10 to 15 percent of reasonable consumers, even gullible ones, perceive a message to be misleading.[184] German deception cases are tried in courts (the same is true in France and Belgium). In one highly publicized German case, Philip Morris was ordered to discontinue an ad campaign claiming that passive exposure to cigarette smoke was no more dangerous than eating cookies.[185]

In the Netherlands, the Commercial Code Commission oversees ads. Not long ago, it ruled that a comical mobile phone ad suggesting that phones drive people insane was distasteful and harmful to mental patients.[136] Industry self-regulation is also common in the United Kingdom, Italy, Belgium, Ireland, Switzerland, and the Netherlands; Germany and Austria permit private litigation against companies as well.

Countries have widely varying laws regarding the legalities of particular marketing practices. In Germany the words *best* or *better* are considered misleading.[187] Finland prohibits newspaper or TV advertising for political groups, religion, alcohol, weight-loss products, or "immoral literature," and the United Kingdom does not allow cigarette or liquor advertising on television. More than 50 European nations have called for bans on tobacco advertising and promotion, even though the European Court of Justice recently overturned a sweeping European Community ban on tobacco ads.[188] After the fall of communism, the Russian government banned cigarette and alcohol ads and then all advertising temporarily until a reasonable set of guidelines could be developed.[189] Regulations regarding advertising to children also vary widely in different countries, which means companies must carefully research local rules when marketing across national boundaries.[190] Other countries often regulate promotion techniques such as premiums, sweepstakes, and free samples more heavily than the United States does.

Advertisers in China have been making wildly exaggerated false claims for years.[191] For example, one ad states that a brand of toothpaste cures cancer, and another claims a soap can wash ten years off a woman's face. Interestingly, local advertisers, and not foreign companies, are the worst offenders. However, the Chinese government is cracking down with comprehensive advertising laws and stiffer enforcement.

Product safety standards are becoming more stringent around the world, particularly in the European Community, which has adopted tougher regulations than the United States.[192] Thus to minimize liability, companies need to maximize product performance and safety. Finally, many consumer activist groups are at work around the world. For example, the environmental movement is strong in many European countries, and the Green Party has been increasing its representation in the German government. International environmental groups such as Greenpeace monitor issues around the globe. Finally, the World Health Organization has been involved in a worldwide effort to control tobacco use and marketing by requiring larger on-pack warnings, restricting certain types of cigarette advertising, and providing more education about the risks of smoking. Tobacco marketers must therefore comply with these rules as well as with local regulations in the 40 nations that have adopted the WHO's program.[193]

Summary

Consumerism is "the set of activities of government, business, independent organizations, and concerned consumers that are designed to protect the rights of consumers" to (1) be safe, (2) be informed, (3) have choices, (4) be heard, (5) receive consumer education, (6) have recourse and redress, and (7) live in an environment that enhances the quality of life. The various influences on consumerism and public policy issues are government agencies, industry self-regulation, and political consumer groups.

A key public policy issue is deceptive advertising and labeling. Ads can be deceptive when they provide false information, leave out relevant information, or interact with consumers' beliefs to mislead. Deceptive selling techniques include the bait-and-switch technique, misrepresentation of the selling intent, and incorrect statements. Several problems are associated with advertising to children. Young consumers do not have the cognitive capabilities to process ads and must sometimes be protected from certain practices. Regulators, advocacy groups, and consumers are also concerned about privacy on the Internet.

The government is working on ways to help consumers become more informed. To be effective, however, information must be easy to understand, be reasonable in amount, be used by consumers, and appear in an easy-to-use format. The consumer's right to safety is ensured by protection from unsafe products and warnings of dangers or risks when present. Environmental protection and conservation behavior are key public policy issues. Around the world, consumerism issues are being addressed by various rules and regulations enforced by governmental agencies and self-regulation groups.

Questions for Review and Discussion

1. What are the main government agencies and industry self-regulation groups that address consumer issues?
2. In the context of regulation, how does affirmative disclosure differ from corrective advertising?
3. How have marketers used deceptive selling tactics on consumers?
4. Why is advertising to children so controversial?
5. What are the main consumer privacy issues related to use of the Internet?
6. How does the doctrine of foreseeability relate to product safety?
7. What influences environmentally conscious consumer behavior?

Exercises

1. Watch or record three hours of Saturday morning children's television. Code or analyze each ad in terms of the following: (a) type of product advertised, (b) message techniques used (fantasy, humor, music, etc.), (c) emotion evoked, (d) key message delivered, and (e) any aspects you think might confuse young children. Summarize this information and answer the following questions:
   a. What are the most frequently advertised types of products or services? Do you see any ethical problems?
   b. What main techniques are used to influence children? Do you believe that these are reasonable marketing practices?
   c. Did you notice any efforts made to educate children and make them more aware of the advertising? Were these efforts effective?
   d. What types of messages are children being exposed to? Do you see any problems with them?
   e. Did any ads or messages seem to be unfair or unethical? If so, why?
2. Acquire and copy three nutrition labels from packages of food products. Ask ten consumers (as different from one another as possible) to describe what this information means. Alternatively, ask the ten consumers a series of multiple-choice questions about the terms contained on the label. Based on your observations, how well do you think the consumers understood the information? What types of consumers were most likely and least likely to understand the material? What could be done to make it more understandable and useful?

3. This chapter briefly discussed several key public policy issues. Select one of the key issues, and conduct a thorough library search for information about it. Use this information to write a more detailed summary report of the key arguments and possible solutions for this issue.
4. This chapter notes that public policy regulation varies throughout the world. Select a particular country and research the nature of regulation for one of the key issues discussed in this chapter. How do the practices in that country differ from those in the United States? How are they similar?
5. On the basis of your understanding of the chapter write about the trends discussed about India and your perspectives on the consumerism in India.

More Exercises from the Adaptor

1. On the basis of your understanding of the chapter write about the trends discussed about India and your perspectives on the consumerism in India.

References

[1] Source: http://www.cseindia.org/misc/cola-in-depth/cola2006/cola_press2006.htm

[2] Source: http://www.indiaresource.org/news/2006/2025.html

[3] Source: http://fcamin.nic.in/Events/EventDetails.asp?EventId=1471&Section=Consumer%20welfare%20Fund&ParentID=0&Parent=1&check=0#

[4] Source: http://www.ipapharma.org/Regulations.asp Source: http://www.thebrandreporter.com/perl/tbr/bwi/tbr_bwi.html?xmlid=183

[5] Source: http://www.ascionline.org/five/cccdecisions.htm

[6] Source: http://www.ascionline.org/five/cccdecisions.htm

[7] Source: http://www.cbfcindia.tn.nic.in/

[8] Source: http://www.cbfcindia.tn.nic.in/planning_movie.htm

[9] Source: http://www.consumeronline.org/guest/aboutco.asp

[10] Source: http://www.thebrandreporter.com/perl/tbr/bwi/tbr_bwi.html?xmlid=183

[11] Source: http://www.cut-up.com/news/detail.php?sid=413

[12] Source: http://www.etstrategicmarketing.com/smNov-Dec2/art7.html

[13] Source: http://www.emeraldinsight.com/Insight/viewContentItem.do;jsessionid=D9C50257B502A37AAAAE1CA67AADB647?contentType=Article&hdAction=lnkpdf&contentId=1576150

[14] Source: http://www.exchange4media.com/kids/KidsFullStory.asp?news_id=11101

[15] Source: http://www.cs.cmu.edu/~ponguru/tprc_2005_pk_lc_en.pdf

[16] Source: http://www.ifpri.org/2020/focus/focus10/focus10_11.pdf

[17] Source: http://www.unctad.org/trade_env/test1/meetings/standards/charles.doc

[18] Source: http://www.kuttyjapan.com/sivakasi-fireworks.asp

[19] Source: http://www.eia.doe.gov/emeu/cabs/indiaenv.html

[20] Source: http://www.eia.doe.gov/emeu/cabs/indiaenv.html

[21] Source: http://www.eia.doe.gov/emeu/cabs/indiaenv.html

[22] Source: http://www.eia.doe.gov/emeu/cabs/indiaenv.html

[23] Source: http://www.eia.doe.gov/emeu/cabs/indiaenv.html

[24] Source: http://www.geepinc.com/RecyclingRevolutionIndia.php

chapter **20**

The Dark Side of Consumer Behavior and Marketing

LEARNING OBJECTIVES

After studying this chapter, you will be able to:

- Describe the behaviors of compulsive buying, consumer theft, and use of black markets, and outline the ethical questions that such behaviors present for marketers.
- Identify the main behaviors that arise from addictive or compulsive consumption and explain the marketing issues that must be considered in relation to these behaviors.
- Discuss the potential negative effects of marketing and what marketers are doing in response.
- Show how consumers resist marketing practices, both individually and in groups.

INTRODUCTION

Is Your Personal Data Private? Is It Safe?

Whenever you use a credit card to buy something—online, in a store, or by mail—your purchase is recorded and stored in the retailer's database (as well as the bank's database). Even when you're just surfing the Web, some sites are collecting personal information about you, and you may not even know it. Many websites place *cookies*—small data files—on your computer's hard drive to track your movement around each site, determine which pages and items you looked at, and note how long you lingered. Some sites require you to provide information such as a phone number or e-mail address before gaining access to coupons, games, or other online features. And your online behavior may be tracked by software that uses that same data to choose which ads you see.

Privacy is a growing concern for consumers who use the Internet (see Exhibit 20.1). For example, after Comcast was criticized by consumer groups and legislators for storing data on its customers' online habits, the company agreed to halt the practice. Many sites post privacy policies to explain their data collection practices. However, consumers may not always understand what the company plans to do with the information. Moreover, companies may change their privacy

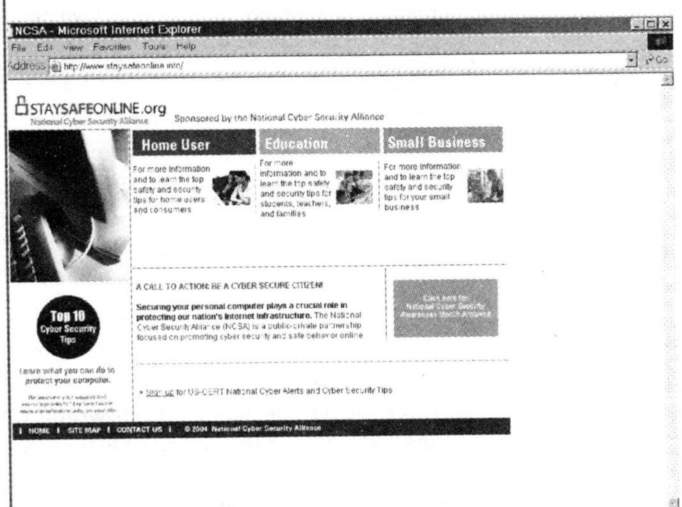

Exhibit 20.1
PRIVACY AND SECURITY
Concerns about privacy and security have prompted parents, teachers, and kids to turn to organizations like StaySafe.org to learn about online safety.

polices or take actions that seem inconsistent with those policies. The pharmaceutical firm Eli Lilly violated its privacy policy by inadvertently revealing the names of people who signed up to receive information from its Prozac.com website. The Federal Trade Commission ordered Eli Lilly to set up a system to protect customer data for the next 20 years and to report every year on its security processes.

In some cases, information sharing benefits consumers because they get merchandise or services in exchange for providing personal information. Although adults can weigh the merits of such tradeoffs, privacy advocates worry that children will not be able to resist divulging family data online in exchange for gifts. And with so much data being gathered and stored by so many organizations, security is an important concern. Not long ago, ChoicePoint, a large information broker, said that personal data about 145,000 consumers had been stolen from its computer system. This is hardly an everyday occurrence, yet several banks and retailers have also reported the loss of consumer data. Sometimes consumers are hoodwinked into revealing information in response to e-mails, letters, or phone calls that appear legitimate but are not.

Each year, more than half a million U.S. consumers fall victim to identity theft, having credit card numbers or other details stolen and used to make fraudulent purchases. The government estimates that $50 billion worth of goods, services, and funds is stolen annually through identity theft. As more questions are raised about the privacy and security of personal data, companies are tightening security, individuals and advocacy groups are pressing for more complete disclosure of how information is gathered and protected, and lawmakers are considering stiffer measures to protect consumers.[1]

The preceding example illustrates several issues discussed in this chapter. Marketers sometimes engage in practices that could seem distasteful or detrimental to consumers, such as invading their privacy. Consumers may look for opportunities to steal personal information and use the data to make purchases or obtain services illegally. In addition, the chapter describes ways that consumers can, individually and in groups, resist marketing efforts seen as inappropriate (such as invasion of privacy) or pressure marketers to take certain steps (such as boosting security or reporting security breaches).

Some of these issues represent part of the "dark side" of *marketing;* others represent the dark side of *consumer behavior.* The latter include deviant consumer behaviors that stem from uncontrollable sources (compulsive buying, compulsive gambling, and smoking and alcohol addictions), as well as consumer behaviors that are deviant because they are illegal (consumer theft, underage drinking and smoking, and black market transactions).

Deviant Consumer Behavior

Much of this book has focused on the behavior of the average consumer in an everyday consumption context. However, sometimes consumer behavior is regarded as deviant if it is either unexpected or not sanctioned by members of the society. Such behavior may be problematic to the consumer and/or to the society in which the consumer operates. As Exhibit 20.2 indicates, some forms of deviant consumer behavior occur during the purchase or acquisition of the

Exhibit 20.2
FRAMEWORK FOR DEVIANT CONSUMER BEHAVIOR

Consumer behavior may be deviant because it involves a physical or psychological abnormality or involves a behavior regarded as illegal. Such deviant behaviors can be associated with the acquisition or usage of offerings.

Stage of the Consumer Behavior Process

Why Deviant?	Deviant acquisition behavior	Deviant usage behavior
Physical/ psychological abnormality	Compulsive buying	Addictive consumption • smoking • drugs • alcohol Compulsive consumption • compulsive gambling • binge eating
Illegal behavior	Consumer theft Black markets	Underage drinking Underage smoking Drug use

product—before consumers even use it. Three types of deviant *acquisition* behaviors are discussed here: compulsive buying, consumer theft, and black markets. The section that follows it focuses on deviant *consumption* behaviors, including addiction, compulsive consumption, and underage smoking and drinking.

Compulsive Buying

Some individuals buy compulsively, purchasing excessive quantities of items they do not need and sometimes cannot afford. Individuals who buy compulsively gain satisfaction from *buying*, not from *owning* (see part a of Exhibit 20.3).[2]

Inside the Compulsive Buying Experience Compulsive buying has a strong emotional component, and the emotions run the gamut from the most negative to the most positive.[3] Compulsive buyers feel anxious on days when they do not buy. In fact, compulsive buying may be a response to tension or anxiety. While in the store, compulsive buyers may feel great emotional arousal at the stimulation evoked by the store's atmosphere. The act of buying, in turn, brings an immediate emotional high and often a feeling of loss of control (see part b of Exhibit 20.3). However, this emotional high is followed by feelings of remorse, guilt, shame, and depression. Compulsive buyers think that others would be horrified by knowing about these spending habits, and some even hide their purchases in a closet or the trunk of a car.

Buying products in excessive amounts seems antithetical to the buying processes described in earlier chapters. Why then do people buy compulsively? The answer to this question is not simple.

Low Self-Esteem First, compulsive buyers tend to have low self-esteem. In fact, the emotional high consumers experience from compulsive buying comes in part from the attention and social approval they get when they buy. The salesperson can bring considerable satisfaction—being a doting helper, telling consumers how attractive they look in a particular outfit, and saying how thoughtful they are to buy such a nice gift. Consumers can also feel that they are pleasing someone: pleasing the salesperson by buying the product and pleasing the company by making purchases. This attention and the feeling that they are pleasing others may temporarily raise

Exhibit 20.3
QUOTES FROM COMPULSIVE BUYERS

Compulsive buying can be an emotionally involving experience. Consumers who engage in compulsive buying often do so for the extra attention or the feeling that they are pleasing someone else. But this emotional high may be followed by serious financial and negative emotional consequences.

Emotional Aspects of Compulsive Buying

a. "I couldn't tell you what I bought or where I bought it. It was like I was an automatic."
"I really think it's the spending. It's not that I want it, because sometimes I'll just buy it and I'll think, Ugh, another sweatshirt."

b. "But it was like, it was almost like my heart was palpitating, I couldn't wait to get in to see what was there. It was such a sensation. In the store, the lights, the people; they were playing Christmas music. I was hyperventilating and my hands were starting to sweat, and all of a sudden I was touching sweaters and the whole feel of it was just beckoning to me. And if they had a SALE sign up, forget it; I was gone. You never know when you're going to need it. I bought ten shirts one time for $10.00 each."
"It's almost like you're drunk. You're so intoxicated;...I got this great high. It was like you couldn't have given me more of a rush."

Factors Influencing Compulsive Buying

c. "The attention I got there was incredible. She waited on me very nicely, making sure it would fit and if it didn't they would do this and that. And I guess I enjoyed being on the other end of that. I had no idea how I was going to pay for it. I never do."
"I never bought one of anything. I always buy at least two. I still do. I can never even go into the Jewel and buy one quart of milk. I've always got to buy two...It's an act of pleasing. I had been brought up to please everybody and everyone around me because that was the way you got anything was to please. So I thought I was pleasing the store."

Financial and Emotional Consequences of Compulsive Buying

d. "I would always have to borrow between paychecks. I could not make it between paychecks. Payday comes and I'd pay all my bills, but then I'd piss the test away, and I'd need to borrow money to eat, and I would cry and cry and cry, and everyone would say, 'Well just make a budget.' Get serious. That's like telling an alcoholic not to go to the liquor store. It's not that simple."

e. "My husband said he couldn't deal with this and he said, 'I'm leaving you. We'll get a divorce. That's it. It's your problem. You did it. You fix it up.'"

"I didn't have one person in the world I could talk to. I don't drink. I don't smoke. I don't do dope. But I can't stop. I can't control it. I said I can't go on like this...My husband hates me. My kids hate me. I've destroyed everything. I was ashamed and just wanted to die."

Source: Thomas O'Guinn and Ronald Faber, "Compulsive Buying: A Phenomenological Perspective," *Journal of Consumer Research,* September 1989, pp. 147–157.

compulsive buyers' self-esteem and act as a reinforcement for buying (see part c of Exhibit 20.3).

Fantasy Orientation A personality trait called fantasy orientation is also linked with compulsive buying. Buying makes compulsive buyers feel more important and more grandiose than they actually are. These fantasy feelings may explain how compulsive buyers temporarily avoid or escape thoughts about the financial consequences of their shopping habits.

Alienation Compulsive buyers tend to be somewhat alienated from society; they have fewer friends and social contacts than most people do. Compulsive buying may therefore provide an opportunity for social gratification. Consumers may feel as if they are friends with a salesperson who has sold them items on repeated occasions. By buying, these consumers may feel more integrated and less alienated than they otherwise would.

Family History Finally, compulsive buyers are more likely to come from families whose members show compulsive or addictive behaviors or emotional disorders, including eating disorders like binge eating. For example, one study of Canadian consumers found that compulsive buyers were more likely to come from families showing problems of alcoholism, bulimia, extreme nervousness, or depression. Some evidence suggests that compulsive buying may be hereditary.

Consequences of Compulsive Buying Compulsive buying is more than an annoying habit. Its financial, emotional, and interpersonal consequences can be devastating. Some compulsive buyers spend roughly 50 percent of their income on purchases. To finance their buying habits, they rely extensively on credit cards. They have significantly more credit cards than the general population and are more likely to carry balances within $100 of their credit limit. Because their credit card debt is so great, they tend to pay the minimum monthly balance. They are also more likely to write checks for purchases, even though they know they cannot afford them. And compulsive buyers are more likely to borrow money from others to make it from paycheck to paycheck (see part d of Exhibit 20.3).[4] A clinical screening test that incorporates many of these elements is shown in Exhibit 20.4. Note that this test is used in the United States but may not be appropriate for consumers in other countries.[5]

1. Please indicate how much you agree or disagree with the statement below. Place an X on the line that best indicates how you feel.

	Strongly agree (1)	Somewhat agree (2)	Neither agree nor disagree (3)	Somewhat disagree (4)	Strongly disagree (5)
a. If I have any money left at the end of the pay period, I just have to spend it.	_____	_____	_____	_____	_____

2. Please indicate how often you have done each of the following things by placing an X on the appropriate line.

	Very often (1)	Often (2)	Sometimes (3)	Rarely (4)	Never (5)
a. Felt like others would be horrified if they knew of my spending habits	_____	_____	_____	_____	_____
b. Bought things even though I couldn't afford them	_____	_____	_____	_____	_____
c. Wrote a check when I knew I didn't have enough money in the bank to cover it	_____	_____	_____	_____	_____
d. Bought myself something in order to make myself feel better	_____	_____	_____	_____	_____
e. Felt anxious or nervous on days I didn't go shopping	_____	_____	_____	_____	_____
f. Made only the minimum payments on my credit cards	_____	_____	_____	_____	_____

Scoring equation = −9.69 + (*Q*1a x .33) + (*Q*2a x .34) + (*Q*2b x .50) + (*Q*2c x .47) + (*Q*2d x .33) + (*Q*2e x .38) + (*Q*2f x .31).
If scoring is ≤ −1.34, subject is classified as a compulsive buyer.

Exhibit 20.4

A CLINICAL SCREENING TEST FOR COMPULSIVE BUYING *Do you have compulsive buying tendencies? Take this screening test to find out.*

Compulsive buying can also wreak devastating emotional and interpersonal consequences. As part e of Exhibit 20.3 indicates, children, spouses, and friends can all be hurt by the spending habits of compulsive buyers. [1]People suffering from Compulsive Shopping Disorder experience a feeling of elation when they shop but feel guilty when they return home and scrutinise their big bags of unwanted/unnecessary items. In India, though CSD is not as widespread, it is clearly on the rise, say psychologists. "CSD could happen to anyone, but is found especially among those suffering from frequent spells of depression," says Dr Aroona Broota, a well-known psychologist in Delhi. [2]On the other hand as the Indian retail sales, now US$200 billion, is about to be transformed with the rapid growth of multiple stores, partial relaxation of controls over foreign companies, and the development of 300 new shopping malls. Organised retailing in India is currently responsible for US$6.4 billion (according to KPMG/ FICCI), but this is expected to grow to US$23 billion by 2010. Such growths bring it's own set of problems. One of the prime amongst them is, compulsive shopping. The lure of the mega malls, organized retail formats and attractive displays create a sense of fondness for the good things in life and continue to remain aspirational in nature.

marketing IMPLICATIONS Compulsive buying raises important ethical questions for marketers; however, research is still needed to clarify these difficult issues.

Do marketing practices foster compulsive buying?
Although research on this issue is scarce, it seems quite likely that enticing sales, attractive displays, doting salespeople, and easily available credit foster compulsive buying.

Are marketers ethically bound to help compulsive buyers?
Marketers might help compulsive buyers through direct actions such as liberal return policies, sales training in compulsive buying, and denials for credit increases or through indirect actions such as contributions to research and treatment organizations.

Consumer Theft

Whereas compulsive buying reflects an uncontrollable desire to *purchase* things, consumer theft reflects a desire to *steal* things.

Prevalence of Consumer Theft When we think of consumer theft, we may think first of shoplifting. For retailers, shoplifting is indeed pervasive and significant, with yearly merchandise losses topping $10 billion. Some types of stores are harder hit by shoplifting than others, as Exhibit 20.5 shows. Yet, consumers also suffer. Because retailers tend to recoup losses by raising prices, a four-person U.S. family winds up spending an estimated $440 more per year.[6] Also, consumers may be inconvenienced by procedures and devices designed to prevent theft, not to mention the possibility of slower service when employees are diverted to antitheft duties.[7]

Consumer theft is a problem for nonretailers as well.[8] For example, automobile insurance fraud has been estimated to exceed $10 billion per year, and hotel theft is also pervasive, with yearly losses exceeding $100 million. Officials at Holiday Inn estimate that a towel is stolen every 11 seconds. Credit card fraud is a problem for Internet businesses in particular. Other common forms of consumer theft include loan fraud; concealing income to avoid taxation; theft of cable TV services; music,

Exhibit 20.5
CONSUMER THEFT

Which types of stores suffer the most losses due to consumer theft?

Type of Retailer	Percentage of Inventory Loss Accounted for by Shoplifters
Apparel specialty stores	46
Family apparel stores	38
Department stores	38
Shoe stores	35
Sporting goods stores	34
Optical stores	32
Drug stores	32
Card, gift, and novelty stores	31
Discount stores	30
Office supply and stationery stores	30
Auto parts, tire, and accessories stores	30
Supermarkets and grocery stores	29
Consumer electronics and appliance stores	29
Jewelry stores	28
Home centers, hardware, and garden stores	23

Source: Created from information in "The WWD List: It Takes a Thief," *WWD,* December 13, 2004, p. 89S, based on the National Retail Security 2003 Survey by the University of Florida's Center for Studies in Criminology and Law.

video, and software piracy; coupon fraud; fraudulent returns; and switching or altering price tags. Financial-aid fraud is on the rise as students and parents falsify their income or submit false tax returns to college aid offices. Although complaints about online auction fraud, in which consumers steal from other consumers, outnumber all other reports of online crimes, consumers are also stealing through stolen or fake credit cards, fake websites, and other methods.[9]

Factors Affecting Consumer Theft Although you may think that consumer theft is driven by economic need, few demographic variables are associated with theft. Some *forms* of consumer theft are associated with certain demographic groups: shoplifting is most common among teens, and credit card fraud is usually associated with better-educated consumers. However, consumers from all walks of life engage in theft. Moreover, many consumers have engaged in some form of theft at one time. For example, roughly two-thirds of the public admit to having shoplifted, and 15 percent admit to concealing income to avoid taxation.[10]

As shown in Exhibit 20.6, two psychological factors seem to explain theft: (1) the temptation to steal and (2) the ability to rationalize theft behavior. As the exhibit indicates, these factors are, in turn, affected by aspects of the product, the purchase environment, and the consumer.

Temptation to Steal The *temptation* to steal arises when consumers want products that they cannot legitimately buy. Some of these desires are driven by real needs, such as the mother who steals baby formula to feed her child. Others reflect greed, as in the case of upper-class consumers who steal money or high-ticket items like jewelry. Some researchers suggest that marketers are involved by perpetuating materialistic tendencies and creating insatiable desires for new goods and services.[11] Consumers may also be tempted to steal items they are too embarrassed to buy through conventional channels (e.g., condoms, pregnancy tests) or that they cannot legally buy (e.g., an underage consumer stealing alcohol).[12]

Exhibit 20.6 shows that environmental factors also affect the temptation to steal. Temptation is greater when consumers think that they can get away with stealing and that it is worth doing. Thus consumers may assess the perceived risks associated with stealing and getting caught and may consider the benefits of having a product or using a service they did not pay for.[13] Of the millions of consumers who have used file-swapping software or websites to share music, few are individually identified, let alone taken to court for copyright violations, which may encourage some consumers to try or continue file-sharing.[14]

Exhibit 20.6
MOTIVATIONS FOR CONSUMER THEFT

Consumers may engage in theft because they (1) feel the temptation to steal and (2) can somehow rationalize their behavior. Various factors associated with the product, the environment, and the consumer can influence temptation and the ability to rationalize.

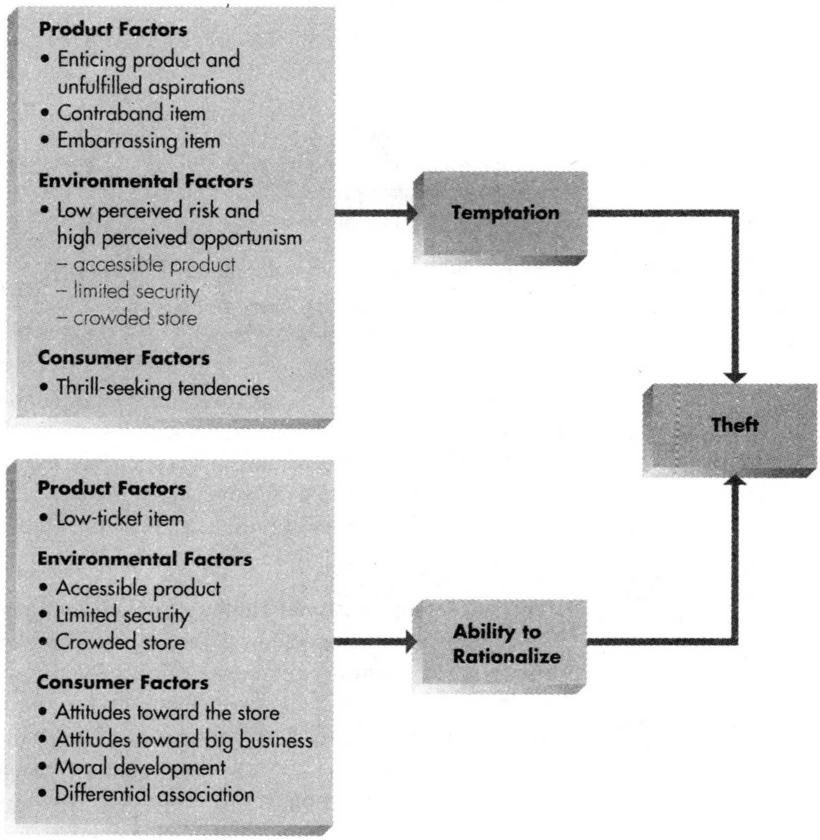

Many factors in the environment affect the perceived risks of shoplifting.[15] Stores may be very noisy or crowded, have little or no security, have lax return policies, have few salespeople, contain nooks and crannies that make it easy to steal without being noticed, or have price tags that are easily switched, making it easier for consumers to steal without being noticed. Sometimes people steal for the thrill of doing something they are not supposed to do. This thrill-seeking tendency has been associated with many forms of consumer theft, including price tag switching and shoplifting.[16]

Rationalizations for Stealing As Exhibit 20.6 shows, consumers also steal because they can somehow *rationalize* their behavior as being either justified or driven by forces outside themselves. For example, consumers may justify stealing a low-ticket item such as grapes from a grocery store or candy from a checkout counter because the item's cost seems so negligible that the word *stealing* hardly seems to apply. Some consumers may believe that stealing is justified because the environment encourages it. Thus the consumer may believe that the marketer "asked for it" by keeping merchandise displays open, having no security guards, or using price tags that can be readily switched. Consumers in crowded stores may become so frustrated by waiting for service that they give up and walk out with their items. They may justify their behavior by deciding that the theft compensates for the inconvenience of the long wait.[17]

In addition, consumers are likely to rationalize when social influences encourage theft, as in the case of someone who shoplifts on a dare.[18] The consumer rationalizes the behavior through thoughts like "my friend made me do it." Interestingly, researchers have little evidence that dares actually play a large role in the shoplifting behavior of teenagers.[19] "Everybody does it" is another rationalization. In one study, 11 percent of the respondents agreed it was wrong to download online music without paying and copy software without paying—but if they believe that "everybody else does it," they may follow suit.[20]

Consumers are also most likely to rationalize theft when stores have a negative public image. If the store is seen as unfriendly, intimidating, or somehow unfair, consumers may see theft as a way of getting revenge against the retailer. Similarly, consumers may steal because they have negative attitudes toward businesses and because they think that large businesses can readily absorb the losses. Some consumers may steal because they feel psychologically distanced from the retailer—they believe that they are dealing with a huge, faceless conglomerate, not a shop owner. In sum, consumers are more likely to rationalize theft behavior when there is less personalization.[21]

Consumers who have weak moral development may not see the act of stealing as wrong. One study found that shoplifters tend to be rule breakers in general. Some speculate that our society's overall level of moral development is changing, so fewer people view theft as wrong. Some evidence suggests that adolescents' moral restraint is weakened simply by observing their peers shoplift. Thus socialization can affect moral development, which in turn can affect consumer theft.[22]

Shoplifting, as compared to the West is low in India, however, this could be so because of absence of organized and large retail formats in India. Isolated incidents continue to trickle, but the trend is yet to catch on. Though, with the retail sector growth showing positive growth signs, the typical problems of the West are bound to permeate into the country. [3]According to RPG Retail CEO Raghu Pillai, "Shoplifting, or shrinkage as we call it, is a global phenomenon. Even the world's largest retailer, Wal Mart, with a turnover of $240 billion, suffers a shrinkage of 0.6 percent, which works out to be more than $1 billion! But that is the way it is. And shrinkage is clearly focused at lifestyle products. We try to prevent it by putting a system and procedures in place. And you do so keeping in mind the environment that we operate in, where everything is kept open and displayed. One can make shrinkage zero by keeping everything locked up, or having security guards all over the place, but the cost of doing that is much higher than the 0.5 to 0.6 percent that one suffers on average. So we budget for that and keep a system in place to ensure that the shrinkage percentage is kept low." [4]As India is one of the world's most dynamic economies, with a majority of its population below 30 years there may be a danger that the dash for growth may generate excessive shrinkage and crime and that management controls could become lax without a tough-minded approach.

marketing IMPLICATIONS

Theft is clearly a pervasive and expensive problem for marketers.

Increased usage of theft-reducing devices

Businesses spend billions of dollars every year trying to prevent or reduce theft through antitheft devices and improved security systems.[23] Some companies combine closed-circuit TVs with sophisticated computer software to track suspicious behavior. The retailer Brookstone, for instance, uses special software to determine the most theft-prone products so it can rearrange displays and checkout procedures to minimize losses.[24] Marketers have also used some unusual tactics to reduce theft, including subliminal audio messages that say things like "Do not steal" and "Stealing is a crime."[25]

Covering the costs of theft

Theft hurts consumers because retailers must raise prices to pay for lost merchandise and equipment, cover theft insurance, and cover the costs of high-priced security systems.[26] Some of the costs are absorbed by consumers through higher prices. In addition, theft adds to research and development costs as firms experiment with newer and better security systems, which also results in higher prices.

Reducing ability to serve customers

Security systems and procedures may interfere with retailers' abilities to service customers. For example, retailers may have to keep merchandise in glass display cases, locked cabinets, and so on.[27] This added security increases consumers' search costs, making it more difficult and more time consuming for consumers to examine products and for salespeople to service customers.

Black Markets

Whereas theft represents situations in which consumers refuse to pay for available items, ***black markets*** represent situations in which consumers *pay* (often exorbitant amounts) for items *not* readily available. The markets are called "black" markets because the sellers are unauthorized, which means the buying-selling process is usually illegal. Some products sold on black markets fulfill basic human needs. Black markets for goods like sugar, salt, blankets, matches, and batteries fulfill functional needs; black markets for drugs, entertainment, and sexual services fulfill experiential needs; and black markets for watches and jewelry may fulfill symbolic needs.

Consumers obtain many types of products through black markets.

- *Legal items in short supply.* Some items sold on the black market are legal but in short supply. For example, some consumers buy blocks of tickets to popular sporting events, plays, and concerts and then sell them later at much higher prices. Black markets for car airbags and Cuban cigars have also been prevalent in the United States in recent years.[28] Some black markets deal with the trade of very basic consumer goods. For example, prisoners will trade money and cigarettes for goods like food, books, and clothing.[29]
- *Brands.* In some cases specific brands are sold on the black market, as mentioned in Chapter 11's opening example. The black market for Levi jeans has been strong in the former Soviet Union. The United States has a black market for frequent-flyer tickets: sellers, who sometimes work through brokers, can get \$12 to \$15 for each 1,000 miles accrued.[30]

- *Illegal items.* Some goods and services that *cannot legally be sold* to consumers are sold through the black market, such as weapons and products used to build bombs.[31] Black markets for drugs are also common. For example, a large global black market exists for the male potency drug Viagra.[32] Counterfeit products such as fake Gucci shoes are also sold through black markets.[33] On the other hand, some New York City consumers who want to avoid the high taxes on cigarette purchases use black-market channels to buy cigarettes smuggled in from low-tax states.[34]

One of the common problems infesting most developing nations today of which India has also been a victim is black market. Starting from movie tickets to essential commodities, there are a plethora of products, which marketers have to sell (much against their wishes) through the black markets. The larger parts of the country, where illiterate and deprived population still reside, the government's of Public Distribution System (PDS) has not been effective. This is owing to the cartelization of the PDS grocer (a government nominated staff) and the private shopkeepers, who hoard and then sell through the black markets. Products like Kerosene, Sugar, Wheat or Rice have to be then bought through the open markets at higher price. [5]At the national level, leakages from the PDS amount to nearly 1.5 times the actual amount of grain needed. A Planning Commission report on the PDS states: "In the year 2003-04, out of 14.07 million tonnes of foodgrain issued to 16 States at BPL (below poverty line) prices from the central pool, only around 5.93 million tonnes were delivered to the poor families." Though the green revolution, the economic reforms of 1991 and the current liberalized policies of the government have been conducive and attempts have been made to provide equal opportunities to people across regions, yet disparities have been predominant. The inherent scarcity of the 50's, 60's and 70's, noticeably in the food grains, LPG and the Kerosene (Kerosene hoarding was rampant through three decades) has now made way for artificial scarcity created by hoarders and black marketers. [6]In 1998, the Bharatiya Janata Party lost power in elections in Delhi and Rajasthan as the cost of vegetables soared by 600 percent. The "onion factor" also contributed to the defeat of the left-leaning, now defunct Janata Party in the 1980 general elections. In both these cases, artificial hoarding and black marketing was the name of the game.

[7]Supplementing this problem has been the problem of counterfeits, clones and duplicates. It is estimated that the size of such market is tantamount to US$ 2.218 billion. It is estimated that out of this market, the entertainment industry is the worst hit. [8]The entertainment industry in India is estimated to be losing up to 80 percent of its revenue due to counterfeiting and piracy.

Products	**Market Value**
Auto Parts	37 percent sold to public.
Books	40 Million
Cable	685 Million
Movies	80 Million
Music	52.7 Million
Software	1.275 Billion
Video Games	85.6 Million

Addictive and Compulsive Consumption

Compulsive buying, consumer theft, and black markets are all forms of deviant *acquisition* behavior. However, in some cases it is not the acquisition process that is deviant but rather how or whether products are *used*. As shown in Exhibit 20.2, consumer behavior can also be deviant when someone loses control over consumption or when consumption is illegal.

Addiction ***Addiction*** reflects excessive behaviors typically brought on by a chemical dependence. Addicted consumers feel a great attachment to and dependence on a product or activity and believe that they must use it to function.[35] Individuals can become addicted to many consumer products and services, including cigarettes, drugs, alcohol, exercise, Internet use, TV, video games, and so on. In many cases, an addiction involves a product that is used repetitively, even if it is dangerous. Although addicted individuals may want to stop consuming the product, they believe that stopping is beyond their control ("I can't help myself"). Often individuals feel shame and guilt over their addiction and try to hide it. Some addicted consumers find strength in programs like Alcoholics Anonymous and Smoke Enders.

Addictive behaviors can be harmful to addicts and to those around them.[36] For example, cigarette smoking is the number one preventable cause of death in the United States and a leading cause of cancer, cardiovascular disease, and chronic obstructive lung disease. The social costs of cigarette smoking are also high. Smokers use more health benefits, take more sick leave, and have more job-related accidents and injuries than nonsmokers do. Although the number of smokers in the United States is declining, smoking is still prevalent, and those who are most vulnerable have the least knowledge about its ill effects. Furthermore, some consumers seem to be switching from cigarettes to cigars and chewing tobacco, although these products are just as harmful.

Compulsive Consumption ***Compulsive consumption*** is an irresistible urge to perform an irrational consumption act. For example, consumers who bet twice their weekly salary on a race horse are not acting rationally, even though compulsive gamblers might behave this way. Similarly, eating two dozen donuts is not rational, but compulsive (binge) eaters might consume food in such quantities.

Compulsive gambling is a special case of compulsive compulsion. An estimated 6 to 9 million Americans are compulsive gamblers. In one study of consumers aged 18 to 24, 85 percent of the respondents said they had gambled, and 5 percent admitted having gambling problems.[37] Compulsive gamblers suffer from a chronic inability to resist impulses to gamble, and they engage in gambling behavior that is disruptive to both themselves and those around them.[38] These consumers are more likely to come from families in which other members exhibited addictive behavior and are more likely to engage in compulsive buying or exhibit alcoholism, be generally impulsive, and view materialism as a measure of success.[39] In fact, scientists have established a strong link between compulsive gambling and consumption of alcohol, tobacco, and illicit drugs.[40]

Typically, compulsive gambling behavior evolves over a series of stages. Sometimes, but not always, the consumer first experiences the pleasure of a "big win."[41] During the second stage, gambling becomes more reckless, losses pile up, and gambling becomes a central force in the individual's life. Because the consumer cannot obtain a legal loan at this point, he or she turns to loan sharks. The compulsive gambler promises to stop gambling but cannot. Faced with rising debt and compulsive gambling urges, many gamblers engage in crimes like forgery and embezzlement. The final stage occurs when the gambler realizes that he or she has hit rock bottom. The psychological and financial consequences of compulsive gambling can be disastrous. One study of 54 compulsive gamblers found that each had accumulated debts of nearly $28,000. Ninety-eight percent had turned to crime.[42]

Despite the popular stereotype of the compulsive gambler as a lower-income consumer, compulsive gamblers represent every ethnic and socioeconomic group in society. However, certain groups are particularly susceptible to compulsive gambling. Teens, for example, are four times more likely to engage in compulsive gambling than adults are.[43] The typical compulsive gambler is 39 years old and married; nearly one-third have incomes between $25,000 and $50,000.

Causes of Addictive and Compulsive Consumption Why do some people become addicted to drugs or alcohol or eat or bet compulsively, whereas others do not? The answers are neither clear nor simple, and many factors have been implicated in the development of addictive and compulsive tendencies.[44]

Inherited Tendencies Some evidence suggests that addictive tendencies are inherited; for example, genetic markers of alcohol addiction have been the topic of much research. Personality has also been linked to compulsive and addictive behavior. To illustrate, alcohol addiction has been linked with low self-esteem, anxiety, depression, sensation seeking, and antisocial personality disorders. Compared with non-addicts, addicts are also more likely to exhibit an external locus of control, believing that control or responsibility for events lies in factors outside of themselves. This may explain why addicts find it hard to stop their addictive behavior. Some of these factors (e.g., depression and low self-esteem), however, may be outcomes of being an addict, not factors that predispose one to becoming an addict.

Family-Related Factors Addictive behaviors may also have their roots in dysfunctional families. For example, children of alcoholics are more likely to become alcoholics, perhaps because they model the behavior of their parents. They may also have developed fewer coping mechanisms for dealing with their parents' addiction, thus making them more susceptible to using escapist means like drugs and alcohol. Clearly, addictive and compulsive behaviors are complex and multifaceted problems.

marketing IMPLICATIONS

Do marketing activities encourage addictive and compulsive behaviors?

Some might argue that marketing activities encourage addictive and compulsive behaviors. For example, cigarettes are heavily advertised in the United States, and the nicotine in cigarettes is addictive. Public policy makers clearly view marketers as perpetuating this form of addictive consumption. As discussed in this chapter, some countries have banned cigarette advertising and require warning labels on cigarette packages, legislative acts that affect marketing practices.

Industry and marketing practices may also perpetuate behaviors like compulsive gambling.[45] Gambling is a fast-growing $900 billion industry, already legal in more than two dozen states and prevalent on many Indian reservations.[46] Floating riverboat casinos have attracted thousands of midwestern consumers. Moreover, cash-strapped states and governments see casinos and lotteries as important revenue generators. Singapore recently lifted a ban on casinos in a bid to boost tourism and job growth.[47] Video Poker machines are available in some states at restaurants, gas stations, convenience stores, and bars. Some 1,400 Internet gambling sites handle

$3 billion in bets every year, creating opportunities for 24-hour gambling—even though U.S. citizens cannot legally bet in online casinos.[48]

Other practices encourage gambling as well. Advertising for gambling is increasing. For example, California and New York each spend roughly $30 million a year on state lottery advertising (see Exhibit 20.7). Furthermore, some casinos have installed real-time monitoring systems that show how much a given consumer is winning or losing. When customers sign up for Harrah's Total Rewards program, the company can track their betting and spending activities in any Harrah's casino. The goal is to target customers with appropriate marketing communications, but people worry that casinos will target people who have gambling problems.[49] Given these trends, it is not surprising that spending on gambling has increased dramatically over the past 20 years.

Exhibit 20.7
FORMS OF GAMBLING
Casinos and lotteries represent common forms of gambling.

Marketing activities that deal with addictive and compulsive consumption

Some marketing activities aim to reduce addictive and compulsive consumption. For example, some states and casinos have established hotlines to help suicidal and emotionally distraught compulsive gamblers. Hotline calls are especially frequent following the Super Bowl—perhaps because the hype surrounding the game makes betting even more enticing to compulsive gamblers.[50] Many casinos post signs and distribute flyers mentioning sources of help for gambling problems. Still, some people are concerned that gambling industry growth will be followed by increases in the number of consumers who become compulsive gamblers and/or an increase in gambling opportunities for those already hooked.

Marketing and overconsumption

Does marketing contribute to other over-consumption problems? For instance, overeating—especially of unhealthy foods—may not be addictive or compulsive, yet it can lead to real problems (such as heart disease). In fact, scientists are alarmed about what is being called a worldwide obesity epidemic.[51] The World Health Organization believes that evidence connecting junk food advertising and childhood obesity is convincing enough that governments should discourage marketing activities that promote unhealthy eating among youngsters.[52] The Center for Science in the Public Interest, an advocacy group, charges that "parents are fighting a losing battle against food marketers" and wants a ban on junk-food commercials during TV programs that draw 25 percent or more of their audience from under-18 consumers.[53] Meanwhile, more companies and media are using marketing to encourage healthier behaviors. McDonald's, which has faced lawsuits over obesity, has introduced healthier menu items[54] and aired commercials urging consumers to get more exercise. *Sesame Street*'s Cookie Monster now tells kids that cookies are a "sometimes food."[55]

Underage Drinking and Smoking

As mentioned earlier, addictions to alcohol and tobacco represent one form of deviant consumer behavior. Illegal use of these products is another deviant consumer behavior.

Prevalence of Underage Drinking and Smoking The National Minimum Drinking Age Act requires states to raise the legal drinking age to 21 in order to receive federal highway funds. Yet, even when minors cannot legally consume alcohol and tobacco, many do.[56] Half of all junior and senior high school students have consumed alcohol, with the average age of first use below 16.[57] Nearly one-third of high school students and nearly 45 percent of college students have engaged in "binge drinking" (drinking more than five drinks in one sitting). Four million children are alcoholics or problem drinkers, and excessive consumption contributes to the deaths of 4,500 underage drinkers every year, including 1,400 college students.[58] One million young consumers begin smoking every year, and 90 percent of new smokers are teenagers. Nearly 12 percent of middle school students and 28 percent of high school students say they are already smoking.[59] These figures are even more dramatic in Asian countries, where there are few bans on cigarette advertising. In the Philippines, half of the consumers between the ages of 7 and 17 smoke.

Exhibit 20.8
PUBLICIZING THE HEALTH CONSEQUENCES OF SMOKING
Cigarette smoking at an early age can lead to serious health consequences, including impotence, lung cancer, and heart disease. Public interest groups and government organizations sometimes call attention to these negative health consequences. A poster put up at a smoking point here on the ceiling of the room, depicts the cremation ground for the smokers.

Consequences of Underage Drinking and Smoking The problem of drinking and smoking by underage consumers has consequences for the individual consumer and for society as a whole.[60] Overuse of alcohol has been implicated in 70 percent of campus violence cases, 68 percent of campus property damage cases, and 40 percent of academic failures. Overuse of alcohol is regarded as the primary discipline, emotional, and physical problem on college campuses. Alcohol is also involved in roughly half of teen highway fatalities, half of all youth suicides, and 90 percent of campus hazing deaths. Almost half of all schools polled say that alcohol is the most serious problem they face. Now that colleges are liable for campus drinking incidents, alcohol is a factor in rising tuition costs because schools must cover their insurance costs. Accidents due to drinking also contribute to the high cost of automobile insurance for young consumers. Mothers Against Drunk Driving (MADD) is one of many consumer groups seeking stricter laws to punish drinking and driving, using social disapproval to pressure students not to drink and drive, and stressing the importance of having a designated driver.

Cigarette smoking at an early age is also harmful, contributing to serious health problems such as lung cancer and heart disease. Moreover, nonsmokers can be harmed through exposure to secondhand smoke. Use of tobacco products also makes young consumers more vulnerable to the problems of addictive consumption, as previously noted. Furthermore, in any given year 75 percent of adolescent smokers have tried to quit smoking but cannot do so.[61] As with underage drinking, public interest groups and government organizations are actively publicizing the negative health consequences associated with smoking (see Exhibit 20.8).

[9]Most countries in Asia do not have a national policy to reduce alcohol consumption. However, in countries with a predominantly Muslim population such as Bangladesh the production, sale, and consumption of alcoholic beverages is prohibited by law. India's constitution declares, "the State shall endeavour to bring about prohibition of the consumption of intoxicating drinks." Even then, since independence in 1947 successive governments have followed different policies on alcohol and currently the central government is encouraging deregulation of alcohol production and liberal imports of alcoholic beverages. Today, both beer and spirits consumption in India have been rising, possibly due to liberalisation of the Indian market. Several foreign companies have taken notice of India's increasing economic liberalisation and have entered into joint ventures with Indian companies. Anhaeuser-Busch entered the market through a joint venture with Bombay based Shaw Wallace and Co Ltd., India's third largest brewer. Guinness entered through a joint venture with United Breweries India. Parallel with the international and more expensive alcoholic beverages, there exist the local, cheap, potent brews, both legal and illicit, which are not computed into the national statistics. In Indian households expenditure on alcohol varies between 3–45 per cent of their income. Alcohol abuse is one of the main killers of young men in India today. But its real impact is on the social and family dynamics that underlie its communities. Domestic violence and an exacerbation of poverty have made alcohol abuse the single most important problem for women in India. Particularly, in the lower strata of the society alcohol related problems like sexual abuse or wife-beating are quite common. The problem of drinking on the other hand also affects urban metropolis, where the economic liberalization and boom in the BPO market has seen rising income level at a lower median age. Today, graduating students serve the BPO industry, thereby getting an access to money and all the liberties associated with it. Spending on food, drinks, clothes, electronic items and automobiles are now increasingly seen as a trend in the market. Drinking in this age group is now becoming more and more prevalent, thereby putting the prospect into risk at an early age. [10]When drinking begins before age 15, youth are four times more likely to turn alcohol addicts and twice as likely to become alcohol abusers. Underage alcohol use is associated with traffic fatalities, violence, unsafe sex, suicide, educational failure, and countless other problems.

[11]Smoking is another recurrent problem in India, since the Portuguese introduced tobacco in India, 400 years ago. In India there are 18 crore people who use tobacco products. A rough break up among the various products would read, four crores using cigarettes, eight crores beedis and six crores other products like gutkha and Zarda. Other hard facts: 55,000 children start smoking in a year; Indians smoke 90 billion cigarettes a year; At an average of Rs. 2 a cigarette, Rs. 180 billions goes up in smoke. According to the Indian Council for Medical Research (ICMR) the cost of treating tobacco related disorders like COPD, CAD and cancers is Rs. 2,776 crores whereas the value of tobacco products sold nationwide is about Rs. 24,400 crores. If this trend goes unchecked 13 per cent of all deaths in India would be solely due

to tobacco. Eight lakh people die every year, 2,200 deaths per day and 90 per hour. The Government of India has passed an anti-tobacco legislation, "The Cigarettes and Other Tobacco Products Act 2003", which came into force on May 1, 2004. This replaces the Cigarette Act 1975. Films are a big influence on the teens, which drives them to smoking. [12]A study done by World Health Organization and Indian Ministry of Health and Family Welfare in 2003 revealed that 76% of Indian movies had tobacco use shown in them. In 1991, 22% of top box office movie hits had lead characters using tobacco on-screen. In 2002, this escalated to 53%. This study also demonstrated that 52.2% of children in India who had their first smoke were influenced by tobacco use depicted in movies. A repeat follow-up study conducted by WHO and Ministry of Health and Family Welfare in India on top box office movie hits during 2004-2005 demonstrated that tobacco use depiction in movies has become more aggressive as compared to previous years. During 2004-2005, 89% of all movies analyzed showed tobacco use and 75.5% movies depicted leading stars using tobacco on screen. Moreover 41% of movies screened had clear and distinct tobacco brand placement. Not surprising, that 33.7% of youth respondents could recall brand use in films too. [13]This has led to a complete ban on showing of on screen smoking and in a directive, Dr Anbumani Ramadoss, Minister for Health and Family Affairs, says categorically that stopping depiction of tobacco use in films is an evidence based public health measure, and that is what he has been strongly advocating since May 31, 2005. India, says Dr Ramadoss, has the world's largest film industry rolling out over 900 films per year. Through cinema theatres, these movies reach 60 million people and through cable television network, they further reach another 70 million people in India. "Influence of cinema is paramount in India," says Dr Ramadoss.

marketing IMPLICATIONS

A number of marketing issues are related to underage drinking and smoking.

Product availability

First, some argue that it is all too easy for underage consumers to buy alcohol and tobacco.[62] Teens can easily get fake IDs, and store clerks are often lax in checking IDs. Indeed, most underage consumers who smoke buy their own cigarettes, usually at convenience stores and gas stations. In one recent nationwide study, less than one-third of middle school students were asked for proof of age when they bought cigarettes.[63]

Exposure to advertising

A second issue is whether kids are exposed to too much advertising for alcohol and tobacco and whether such exposure increases the tendency to buy these products. Arguments that disprove and support this notion have been advanced. A recent survey also showed that only 8 percent of consumers identify advertising as a cause of adolescent drinking (the major causes named were peer pressure and having parents who drink). Other studies show that peer influence, parental smoking, and self-esteem are the major factors affecting smoking. Some argue that alcohol and cigarette advertising has limited effects on underage consumers.[64] One recent study found that cigarette ads prime positive smoker stereotypes, whereas pairing an antismoking ad with a cigarette ad increased the salience of negative smoker stereotypes and reinforced antismoking beliefs and intentions.[65]

The United States bans cigarette commercials on TV, and Canada bans almost all cigarette advertising. Nevertheless, children are exposed to a lot of alcohol and tobacco advertising.[66] One study found that 15 alcohol commercials are broadcast for every hour of sports programs—and children are heavy viewers of sports. Furthermore, only 3 of 685 alcohol ads televised during 122 sporting events advertised drinking in moderation. Most ads depict alcohol as a positive and appropriate behavior of socially active and beautiful people. Alcohol products are also promoted on the Internet. For example, the Jim Beam site has a "virtual bar." Although the site states that consumers must be of legal age to enter and asks for each consumer's birth date, checking the actual age of visitors can be problematic.

Despite the tobacco industry's agreement to avoid marketing to children, some brands continue to be advertised in popular adult consumer publications—magazines that many teens also read, which means these underage consumers are being exposed to cigarette ads.[67] In fact, R.J. Reynolds Tobacco, which markets Camel, Winston, and other brands, settled a lawsuit by agreeing not to advertise in publications where teens represent 15 percent or more of the readership.[68] Most youthful smokers choose the most heavily advertised brands—further implicating advertising as a cause of smoking behavior. Exposure may be even greater as advertisers look for ways to get around advertising bans.[69] For example, in Canada and some parts of Asia, where tobacco advertising is banned, advertisers use sponsorships and licensed goods to stay in the public eye. And because these items are not required to carry the surgeon general's warning label, consumers may not be reminded of the dangers of smoking.[70]

Traditionally, alcohol marketers have voluntarily refrained from advertising hard liquor (anything except beer and wine) on broadcast TV, although some liquor is now advertised on cable TV.[71] Some companies want hard liquor ads on broadcast TV because beer and other competitive products run commercials there; in addition, increases in advertising expenditures have historically been associated with increased alcohol consumption.[72] Moreover, evidence suggests that the more young consumers view alcohol ads, the more they know about these products, and the more likely they are to use them.[73] One study found that 10-year-olds could easily reel off the names of beers and their slogans. Children who were the most aware of these ads were most likely to say that they intended to drink later in life.

A similar effect has been observed with cigarette advertising. Some research shows that teens who smoke are more likely to be aware of and recognize cigarette ads than teens who do not smoke. Adolescents who have the greatest exposure to cigarette advertising in general tend to be the heaviest smokers, and the brands that do the most advertising tend to attract a significantly greater proportion of teenagers than adults. Thus teens appear to be particularly sensitive to advertising for cigarettes. In particular, tobacco and alcohol ads featuring human actors or models have been found to directly produce more positive attitudes toward the ad, the brand, and the product category.[74]

Targeting youth

Third, and perhaps of even more concern, is the suspicion that the cigarette and alcohol manufacturers explicitly target young consumers by portraying advertising images that youths find relevant.[75] The surgeon general, for example, has criticized the alcohol and tobacco industries for using lifestyle appeals that teens find desirable (associating the products with fun, beauty, social acceptance, sports, and sex). Many cigarette ads evoke images such as freedom from authority and independence—themes that clearly appeal to young consumers. Advertising content that shows individuals engaged in risky behavior while consuming alcohol has also been criticized.

Some regulators and critics charge that tobacco advertisers target young consumers by using fictional and cartoon characters, although companies dispute this.[76] As one advertiser noted, children are not demanding Metropolitan Life insurance policies that are promoted by Snoopy and Woodstock.[77] Others argue that even when children are aware of an advertising character associated with a cigarette brand, they may still have an unfavorable image of cigarettes.[78] The alcohol industry stresses that it does not target young consumers and says it has taken great strides to develop ads promoting responsible drinking. Anheuser-Busch alone has spent more than $100 million over the past decade promoting responsible drinking.[79]

Inappropriate messages in mainstream media and ads

Fourth, there is concern that mainstream advertisers and entertainment offerings may be sending inappropriate messages about cigarettes and alcohol. For example, after Anheuser-Busch arranged placements of Budweiser and Bud Light packaging and brand signs within the PG-13 movie *Dodgeball,* some critics argued that too many teens would be exposed to these placements. The company responded that it is careful to make product placements only in movies that appeal to consumers who are 21 and older.[80] In addition, the liquor industry's self-regulatory council enforces its code of responsible practices by acting on complaints about the content of liquor ads, especially the use of overly explicit sexual themes to sell a brand.[81] Meanwhile, tobacco marketers such as Philip Morris are asking movie studios not to feature cigarette brands or brand imagery. "You do not have permission to mention or depict our brands in your films," R.J. Reynolds warned Sony Pictures after noticing a Camel cigarette ad in *Mona Lisa Smile*.[82]

Exhibit 20.9
HEALTH WARNINGS FOR ALCOHOL PRODUCTS
Becasue they are more attention-grabbing and vivid, ads like this may be more effective than labels warning of the dangers of alcohol consumption.

Warning labels and ads

Cigarette and alcohol marketers must take care to display appropriate warnings on product packaging and in ads.[83] Tobacco packages and ads are required to carry the surgeon general's warning regarding the dangers of smoking. Alcohol marketers must comply with federal and state requirements about warning labels that indicate the dangers of drinking and driving and the risks of alcohol to pregnant women. For instance, Arizona requires businesses that sell alcohol to put up posters warning of the risks of drinking while pregnant. However, these warning labels and posters have not been very effective in changing young consumers' behaviors over long periods.[84] Perhaps one reason is that consumers' perceptual defenses make them tune out these messages.

The surgeon general has called for more explicit health warnings on labels. Manufacturers now list alcohol levels on their products so consumers will clearly understand how strong the beverage is. Some researchers are also experimenting with more attention-getting warning labels and messages (see Exhibit 20.9). One study found that when high school students viewed an antismoking ad before a movie in which teen characters smoked, the ad helped reposition the smoking as a tainted activity.[85] Other researchers have suggested that understanding the rituals involved in underage binge drinking can be the basis of public service announcements to reduce this behavior.[86]

Negative Effects of Marketing

Marketing has been implicated as contributing to other negative social outcomes—outcomes that are not necessarily related to deviant acquisition or consumption. Three negative effects are examined here: whether advertising affects self-image; whether it misrepresents or inappropriately depicts certain consumer segments; and whether marketing practices invade consumers' privacy.

Does Advertising Affect Self-Image?

Advertising has long been accused of depicting idealized images of people and their lives. For example, few people have homes like those depicted in ads for household products, and few enjoy holidays in the idealized manner depicted by Hallmark and Royal Caribbean. Advertising may create an idealized image of what one's life *should* be like. If we do not measure up to this idealized image, we may feel dissatisfied. This section considers two questions about advertising and self-image:

- Does advertising make consumers dissatisfied with their appearance?
- Does advertising make consumers materialistic and hence dissatisfied with what they own?

Idealized Body Images Male models shown in advertisements are often trim with well-developed muscles and handsome features. The female models who appear in advertisements are mostly young, very thin, and exceedingly beautiful. Because these ads represent society's conception of the ideal man or woman, they exemplify traits that many men and women will never actually achieve. A particularly salient issue for both men and women is how their body compares to that of thin models.

Obsessions with Thinness American society places great value on thinness as a characteristic of attractive women. As evidence, 70 percent of normal-weight women want to be thinner, and 23 percent of underweight women want to be even thinner than they are.[87] A New Zealand study found that thinness is popular and dieting is considered normal behavior. The same research found that from the 1950s through the 1980s, women depicted in ads got increasingly thinner.[88] Eating disorders such as anorexia and bulimia affect approximately 10 million U.S. women and 1 million men; such disorders are also increasing dramatically among young women in Japan.[89] In another study, 11 percent of men said they would trade more than five years of their lives to achieve personal weight goals—statistics that closely track women's responses.[90] On the other hand, binge eating—which contributes to obesity—is a problem for an estimated 25 million Americans.[91]

This focus on thinness is a relatively recent phenomenon. During the 15th through 18th centuries, being fat was considered fashionable and erotic.[92] Furthermore, being thin is mainly valued in developed countries. In Third World countries, where food is lacking and disease is rampant, higher weight is associated with health and prosperity.[93]

Thinness, Advertising, and Self-Perceptions Certainly, seeing ads with thin models does not make someone become bulimic or anorexic, but do such ads serve as an impetus to consumers with predispositions to eating disorders? Does identification with superthin models create dissatisfaction with one's own body and appearance?[94] Some evidence suggests the answer to these questions is yes.

General Comparison	"God! I wish I looked like that." (written comment about a cosmetic ad before discussion began) "There's certain [ads] that I look at and say, 'Wow! I'd sure like to look like that.'" "In high school, you want to think that you could look like that if you try. Then in college, you realize, 'Oh, forget it.'"
Ads Generating Specific Body Comparisons	"When I see ads, I always look at the chest. I like it when she has no chest. Because, you know, I don't either." "I have wide hips. I always look at the hips. I guess I'm just jealous." "When I look at a model I look at the arms, because my arms are awful."
Negative Self-Feelings from Viewing Ads	"You look at these ads and you feel inadequate, like you can't measure up." "It's frustrating when you start to realize you should look that way—I mean—I can't." "I used to go through these magazines every day and look at [models in the ads] and wish I looked like them. I used to go running every day, and really thought maybe I could look like them. I remember, I even picked one model in particular and cut out ads with her in them. I was pretty obsessed. And I finally realized this wasn't realistic. But I sometimes still look and think, 'Well, maybe.'" "Sometimes [ads with models] can make you feel a little depressed." "They make me feel self-critical." (participant viewing models in swimsuit ads)

Source: Marsha L. Richins, "Social Comparison and the Idealized Images of Advertising," *Journal of Consumer Research,* June 1991, pp. 71–83.

Exhibit 20.10

WOMEN'S REACTIONS TO IDEALIZED BODY IMAGES IN ADS *One study found that women exposed to ads with beautiful and thin models compared the models with themselves or specific parts of their bodies. In some cases, the ads made consumers feel bad about themselves.*

Social comparison theory proposes that individuals have a drive to compare themselves with other people.[95] Consistent with this theory, some research has found that young women do compare themselves with models in advertisements and that such self-comparisons can affect self-esteem.[96] Another study suggests that high school girls who are predisposed to unhealthy weight-loss behaviors frequently read fitness and health magazines because they want ideas about losing weight.[97] Seniors are also affected: according to AARP research, 25 percent of older women are currently dieting and 23 percent plan to diet soon.[98]

One outcome of this comparison process is that consumers feel inadequate if they do not live up to the comparison person. Exhibit 20.10 illustrates the statements female consumers in one study made when they looked at magazine ads that featured beautiful models. Interestingly, some research has also found that consumers who view ads with beautiful models reduce their attractiveness ratings of average-looking women. A potentially strong conclusion, based on the research, is that advertising can have an unintended but negative impact on whether men and women are satisfied with their appearance.[99]

marketing IMPLICATIONS

Fortunately, some companies are becoming more sensitive to the effects of such messages. In the fashion industry, demand for plus-size models is up—perhaps in response to consumers' demands for different types of women in fashion products and ads.[100] New fashion brands such as Abby Z are emerging specifically for plus-size women who want stylish clothing.[101] In general, although some women may be unhappy about how they compare with models in ads, many seem to be more comfortable with themselves and more hostile toward advertisers that perpetuate unrealistic images of women.[102] However, some women will still be willing to use products that entail some risk to achieve an idealized body image benefit. As a result, marketers must be careful to disclose risks (of a pharmaceutical product, for example, or a cosmetic procedure) so that consumers' hopes of a positive outcome will not blind them to any potential negative outcomes.[103]

Materialism Advertising has long been criticized for perpetuating materialistic values and making consumers less satisfied with their lives.[104] For example, as advertising content has increasingly depicted materialistic themes, Americans have become more materialistic. Consumers in other countries have also become more materialistic, a trend that coincides with the purchase of U.S. products and exposure to U.S. ads. Research shows that consumers who watch a lot of TV and who find commercials realistic tend to be more materialistic than consumers who watch less TV.[105] TV shows may provide a biased or distorted view of reality by showing characters who seem to have everything at their disposal.

Family influences can quite strong: The children of materialistic parents tend to be more materialistic.[106] Materialistic adolescents shop more, save less, and are more responsive to marketing efforts.[107] And with more marketing and media emphasis on brands, it is not surprising that children are aware of more than 200 brand names by the time they reach first grade.[108] Does the marketing of child-size versions of traditionally adult luxuries, such as BabyGund diamond necklaces for tots, contribute to materialism as well?[109]

Social comparison theory would predict that if advertising and the media show individuals with many material possessions, consumers might use advertising as a way of judging their personal accomplishments. Consumers who perceive that they are less well off than the comparison population may be less satisfied with their lives and accomplishments. Some evidence supports this idea. Consumers exposed to a lot of advertising tend to overestimate how well off the average consumer is.[110] This misperception sets up a potentially false frame of reference regarding how much the average consumer owns. Further, materialistic consumers may pay undue attention to the possessions of others and make inferences about them based on the possessions they own.[111]

Because the material "good life" often depicted in advertising is out of reach for many, consumers are set up for potential dissatisfaction. Governments in some countries have been reluctant to show U.S. ads out of fear that the ads will set off a wave of demand for products the country cannot produce and/or the people cannot afford.[112] In Russia, children who were used to playing with stones and chalk are now encountering ads for toys such as Lego blocks and Barbie dolls and for foods such as Coca-Cola and chocolate bars. As one consumer noted, "Parents are now in the position of disappointing their children in ways that were once impossible."[113] Although advertising has not been proven to cause materialism and dissatisfaction, the connection is provocative and deserves more research attention.

Does Advertising Misrepresent Segments of Consumers?

Critics also charge that advertising ignores or inaccurately represents key segments in the marketplace.

Ignoring Key Segments Although women represent 50 percent of the population, they are underrepresented in ads for nondomestic products and large-ticket items like cars.[114] Even when women are depicted, the ads often contain male voice-overs. Advertisers have historically believed that male voices are more convincing, more credible, and better at conveying knowledge and expertise than female voices are. When women's voices are used, they are used primarily to speak to dogs, cats, babies, children, and women dieters rather than to the population at large.[115]

Likewise, although African Americans represent roughly 13 percent of the U.S. population and 11 percent of magazine readers, one study found that they appeared in less than 5 percent of all magazine ads and less than 8 percent of TV ads. Only a fraction of U.S. advertising spending is directed toward African American women, despite their buying power.[116] Hispanics and Asians, who are represented in even fewer TV commercials, are often shown in primarily background roles when they appear in ads.[117] Others charge that although marketers are more cognizant of the important Hispanic and African American markets, consumers from countries such as Israel, Poland, Russia, Korea, and Vietnam are often ignored.[118] Sometimes minorities are deliberately excluded from advertising. In Britain, Ford Motor Company was criticized for substituting white faces for black, Indian, and Pakistani workers who appeared in a company brochure.[119] Mature consumers also tend to be underrepresented or, when represented, tend to have minor roles in ads.[120]

Misrepresenting Key Segments Key consumer segments are sometimes represented in advertising in stereotypical or inappropriate ways.[121] For example, women have been represented in gender stereotyped ways (as the mother, wife, homemaker, and sex object), a pattern that holds true whether the products are for men or for women. Women have historically been shown in ads for household cleaning products even though a relatively large number of households are headed by single or divorced men. Women are also more likely than men to be depicted without a paid occupation or shown in lower-status occupations than men—a portrayal that does not accurately represent the status of women in the workforce. In contrast, men and boys have been portrayed as knowledgeable, achieving, independent, active, dynamic, masterful, and important.

Both in the United States and in other countries, women and girls have often been depicted as secondary, dependent, nurturing, in need of help, and concerned about appearance. Although many U.S. ads now play up the independence of teenage girls, many ads in Japan depict teenage girls in inappropriately young poses and scenes.[122] Brewing company ads, notorious for portraying scantily clad women, have been criticized for being sexist and discriminating against women.

Stereotypical images of minorities can also be identified.[123] For example, consistent with ethnic stereotypes regarding work ethic, Asian consumers in ads are more likely to appear in work situations than in family or social roles. Some ads stereotype mature consumers in ways that are unflattering.[124] Depictions of the mature consumer as blue-haired, weak, passive, unproductive, ailing, doddering, foolish, and sexless are not uncommon, and advertisers sometimes use stereotypical terms such as *senior citizens, retirees,* and *golden years.* Mature consumers tend to react negatively to ads that show older people leading nonproductive lives. Because many mature consumers view themselves as being 10 to 15 years younger than their actual chronological age, they react more positively to ads featuring models who are somewhat younger than the consumers themselves are.

marketing IMPLICATIONS

Alienating consumers by excluding or failing to represent them accurately can negatively affect consumers' images of and attitudes toward brands and companies.[125] Consumers may have more extreme reactions to offensive advertising. Some Canadian women, for example, refuse to buy clothing and cosmetic products that are advertised using inaccurate and unrealistic depictions of women. Given the size of these markets, alienating consumers can be very costly. Therefore, many marketers are taking steps to improve their depiction of key consumer segments.

Represent key segments

Many advertisers have made efforts to represent key segments in their advertising.[126] For example, one study found that 26 percent of all commercials shown by ABC, CBS, and NBC during a week of prime-time programming contained African American consumers. Avon, Cover Girl, and other cosmetics firms are using African American celebrities such as Venus and Serena Williams in their ads.[127] The representation of mature consumers in print ads has also been on the rise. Some companies have dropped logos and images that represent minorities in stereotypical ways or have modified their logos to present more positive portrayals. For example, Quaker Oats changed Aunt Jemima from a black mammy to a black homemaker—someone akin to Betty Crocker.[128]

Exhibit 20.11

CHANGING IMAGES OF MEN IN ADS

Some advertisers are depicting less stereotypical images of men, showing them as prominent figures in sensitive roles.

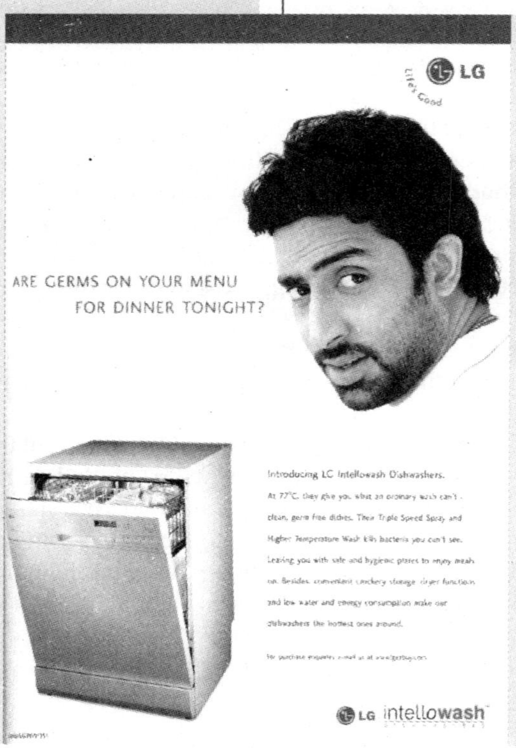

Avoid stereotypes

Advertisers are also representing groups in more positive and less stereotypical ways. Several ads have done well by depicting the mature consumer as wise, spunky, romantic, and individualistic. In general, ads that depict mature consumers as active, take-charge doers are more consistent with mature consumers' views of themselves. Similarly, the portrayal of women in advertising is improving.[129] Car companies have begun to depict women as decision makers, and men are now being shown in activities historically associated with women. Some ads, like the one in Exhibit 20.11, showing dishwasher as product, traditionally a female bastion now shows a male, depicts the rise of the nuclear families and husbands sharing household chores.

Tailor communications to key targets

Companies are also recognizing that they must go beyond simply placing a member of a minority group in an ad. Instead, advertisers need to understand more about these consumers.[130] Many companies, including McDonald's, rely on specialty advertising agencies that have in-depth knowledge of these key target groups.

Do Marketing Practices Invade Consumers' Privacy?

The opening vignette raised concerns about companies invading consumers' privacy by collecting information about them. Many organizations, including retailers, banks, credit reporting agencies, mailing list firms, Internet businesses, telephone companies, and insurance and banking companies, also collect and exchange information about consumers through product registration cards, credit applications, product activity monitoring, sales information, and other techniques.

Sources of Marketing Information Interestingly, much of the information that companies have about consumers is information that consumers themselves provide. For example, marketers can track consumer purchases through scanner data collected at the supermarket checkout. Many catalog companies know a great deal about consumers based on what they buy and which neighborhood they live in. Retailers and banks collect information from the applications that consumers fill out when seeking credit and send many details to credit reporting agencies, which make data available to other credit companies. And companies are always trying to learn more about consumers through marketing research (see Chapter 2).

Considerable consumer information also exists in the public domain in the form of zip codes and census data. The government sells this information to marketers, who use it to update their mailing lists, target people who have moved, determine consumers' likely income based on the type of neighborhood in which they live, and so on.[131]

Consumers' Responses Consumers are clearly uncomfortable with the amount of information marketers have about them.[132] According to research, 78 percent of consumers believe that businesses collect too much personal information, and 88 percent are concerned about threats to their personal privacy. Eighty-two percent perceive a lack of control over how businesses use their personal information, and 41 percent believe that businesses have already invaded their privacy.[133] In a survey about privacy on the Internet, 64 percent of respondents agreed that companies using the Internet should not be allowed to track users for the purposes of sending them marketing messages.[134] In another study, 61 percent of the respondents decided not to use a financial website because of concerns about how their personal data would be handled.[135] Consumers also complain that whereas credit card companies, publishers, and catalog companies (among others) earn money by selling their names to other companies, consumers themselves receive nothing. Furthermore, consumers must spend time sifting through mail and e-mail messages from companies that have bought their names and contact information.[136]

Many consumers do not trust marketers' use of personal information.[137] Consumers worry that companies collect information about them for one purpose but use it for another purpose or sell it to another company without their knowledge. Many also worry about the theft or abuse of personal data. This worry is legitimate—as the opening example showed—and identity theft is a growing international phenomenon. For instance, after the leak of personal information about 121,000 annual admission passholders of the Tokyo Disney resorts, hundreds received phony offers by phone or mail.[138]

Another worry is that personal data such as credit histories may have errors but that protections against such errors may be inadequate. In addition, consumers and marketers disagree on who should control consumer information. For instance, some businesses believe that they own whatever information they legitimately obtain about their customers, and they justify their use of consumer information by saying it helps them to provide better products and services to consumers.[139]

marketing IMPLICATIONS Why are consumers so concerned about marketers' use of personal information?

Horror stories hurt all marketers
A major reason for concern is that a small number of unscrupulous marketers use marketing techniques to defraud consumers, such as companies that use telemarketing to defraud elderly consumers of their life savings.[140] These stories get considerable media attention and tarnish the image of all marketers. Consumers are also wary because information disclosures occurring on other fronts make them worry about the lack of privacy in general. For example, more workers are losing jobs or are being denied jobs because information about their current or past health history has been leaked to current or prospective employers.[141]

Communicating how information helps consumers
Marketers believe that consumers worry about privacy because they really do not understand how the information marketers collect is used and how it might benefit consumers. For example, the information collected by catalog companies on details such as consumers' household characteristics, clothing style preferences, and sizes allows marketers to develop customized catalogs. This practice (1) eliminates waste because marketers can more accurately target consumers, (2) better matches products to consumer needs, and (3) keeps costs down so that savings may be passed on to consumers. Tracking personal information online allows firms to help consumers save time by not reentering that information; in addition, the companies can provide customized messages, products, or services tailored to the needs of specific consumers.

Laws and self-imposed regulation
Consumers are gaining more power against unwanted marketing efforts. In Canada, a privacy code requires direct marketers to give consumers the opportunity to opt out of mailing lists.[142] Although U.S. consumers can write to the Direct Marketing Association or log onto its website (*www.the-dma.org*) and ask that their names not be sold to other companies, many consumers do not know about this option.[143] Millions of U.S. consumers have also added their phone numbers to the FTC's do-not-call list.[144] In Germany, laws prohibit companies from exchanging customer lists. And the European Union (EU) has strict rules governing the transfer of personal information to companies outside the EU.[145]

The U.S. government is giving businesses a last chance to design self-imposed standards for consumer privacy protection. Already, many websites are posting more detailed privacy policies to explain exactly what personal information is being collected online and how that information will be shared, if at all.[146] Online businesses can also reassure consumers by paying for an outside firm to conduct a privacy audit showing how they use personal data.[147] Still, in the aftermath of several highly publicized instances of credit card numbers being stolen, two dozen states are considering laws requiring businesses to notify consumers if their personal information has been stolen or compromised.[148]

How Can Consumers Resist Marketing Practices?

What can consumers do if they are upset about the negative effects of marketing practices? Can consumers change the nature of marketing activities? The answer is yes. Consumers can engage in several forms of consumer resistance.[149]

Individual Resistance Efforts First, consumers who are upset or otherwise dissatisfied with marketing practices can demonstrate dissatisfaction by not patronizing the offending marketer in the future, by complaining and/or by spreading negative word of mouth. These individual consumer resistance strategies can be very effective. For example, Calvin Klein withdrew an ad campaign that showed very young girls in provocatively posed positions in response to public outcry and charges of child pornography.[150]

Advocacy Groups Group strategies are potentially even more powerful than unorganized consumer efforts. Some formally organized advocacy groups engage in resistance by informing the public about business practices they regard as socially inappropriate (see Exhibit 20.12). The Center for the Study of Commercialism, for example, distributes information via videos, pamphlets, books, and conferences and uses lobbying to stop marketing practices such as advertising in schools. *Adbusters,* a magazine published by Canada's Media Foundation, prints articles that make consumers aware of commercial excess.[151] The Center for Food Safety, the Organic Consumers Association, and five other advocacy groups have staged public demonstrations to protest Campbell's Soup's use of ingredients that may be genetically modified, such as soybeans and corn.[152] Teens in Minnesota have formed Target Market, as an advocacy group to discourage underage smoking.[153]

Boycotts A ***boycott*** is an organized activity in which consumers avoid purchasing products or services from a company whose policies or practices are seen as unfair or unjust. Why do consumers join boycotts? At the most basic level, boycotting is a way for consumers to hold companies accountable for perceived actions. Thus many consumers are motivated by the opportunity and likelihood of making a difference. Also, consumers who are particularly susceptible to normative influences of the reference group conducting the boycott will be more likely to participate than those who are less susceptible. Finally, consumers may be seeking to boost or sustain self-esteem by joining the boycott.[154]

Organized boycotts are able to gain publicity and are likely to have more impact than the same number of consumers acting on their own.[155] Consumers have boycotted products made in foreign sweatshops. Nike, for instance, has come under attack for poor working conditions at some overseas factories where its sneakers and clothing are made. In response, Nike has reviewed factory conditions, brought in the nonprofit Fair Labor Association to check some factories, and demanded that many of its factories make major changes if they want to retain the company's manufacturing contracts.[156] People for the Ethical Treatment of Animals recently ended a two-year boycott of Petco after the retailer agreed to stop selling African grey parrots and other large birds.[157] Sometimes boycotts are directed against a company's activities rather than against a product itself.[158]

Exhibit 20.12
ADVOCACY ADVERTISING
Advocacy groups like PETA here raise the issue of caged birds through use of celebrities like John Abraham here, to create a deeper and better impact.

Although only 20 national boycotts were recorded by 1981, the number had risen beyond 250 by the early 1990s.[159] This dramatic increase was partly due to government deregulation of businesses and the underfunding of agencies that monitor business practices.[160] Because of perceptions that the government was not regulating business practices, the public took on the action of doing so. Today, boycotts may be international, national, or local in focus, depending on the issue.

Clearly, boycotts can hurt companies financially. Eight Los Angeles hotels lost a total of $5 million worth of banquet and convention bookings during a four-month union boycott sparked by a labor dispute.[161] However, sales sometimes rise because of boycotts (perhaps because the publicity made the company's name more familiar). For example, StarKist tuna sales rose during a tuna boycott.[162] The primary indicators that a boycott has been successful are not its financial effects, but rather that it (1) changes the offending policies, (2) makes businesses more cautious and responsible in their future activities, and (3) forces changes in the behavior of nontargeted businesses that engage in similarly offensive practices.

Summary

Deviant consumer behavior covers both illegal and psychologically/physically abnormal behavior. Deviant acquisition behaviors include compulsive buying, consumer theft, and black markets; deviant consumption behaviors include addictive and compulsive consumption and underage drinking and smoking. These behaviors are fairly pervasive, and although some (such as black markets) can have certain consumer benefits, most have fairly negative effects on consumers and the social groups in which they operate.

Moreover, critics have questioned whether and/or how much marketing practices influence these behaviors. Advertising has been accused of perpetuating idealized body images, creating materialistic values, failing to represent key consumer segments, misrepresenting key segments, and invading consumer privacy.

In response, many companies are adopting strategies to reduce public criticism and put marketing practices in a more favorable light. At the same time, sophisticated consumers are showing their disapproval of practices regarded as disreputable, objectionable, and/or unethical through individual resistance, support of advocacy groups, and participation in boycotts.

Questions for Review and Discussion

1. What is compulsive buying, and why is it a problem?
2. How do temptation and rationalization affect consumer theft?
3. How does addictive consumption differ from compulsive consumption?
4. What is social comparison theory, and how does it apply to advertising?
5. Why has advertising been criticized for overlooking or misrepresenting certain consumer segments?
6. What can consumers do to resist marketing practices they perceive as unwanted or unethical?

Exercises

1. Using library sources, research retailers' and service companies' yearly losses due to theft, insights about factors affecting theft, whether theft has been increasing or decreasing in recent years, and what marketers are doing to reduce theft. Report your results to the class. Interview consumers about their theft behavior. Ask consumers whether they have ever engaged in theft and why. Discuss your findings with other members of the class. Do the findings support, enhance, or modify the findings shown in Exhibit 20.6?

2. Collect and share magazine advertisements that deal with cigarettes or alcohol. Do these ads suggest that such advertising (a) is excessive, (b) targets youths, or (c) represents images that are attractive to youths?

3. Collect and share magazine advertisements that use models. Use these advertisements and your own personal experience to argue for or against the idea that advertising perpetuates negative body images.

4. Collect and share magazine advertisements that portray women, minorities, and mature consumers. Based on your observations, evaluate whether advertisers misrepresent these key segments or represent them in stereotypical ways.

5. Examine the privacy policies of three Internet retailers. What types of data does each retailer say it collects, and why? Under what circumstances can you review the data each site would be collecting about you? What does each retailer say it plans to do with consumers' personal data? Do you think these sites are addressing consumers' privacy concerns? What can you suggest to improve these privacy policies?\

6. Corporate Social Responsibility is now an established norm for many organizations in India. Identify a few companies and explore what are the advocacy issues which these organizations have adopted. Case in point, as discussed in Chapter 19, Lifebuoy's tie-up with World Health Organisation for the Anti-Diarrhea programme.

More Exercises from the Adaptor

1. Corporate Social Responsibility is now an established norm for many organizations in India. Identify a few companies and explore what are the advocacy issues which these organizations have adopted. Case in point, as discussed in Chapter 19, Lifebuoy's tie-up with World Health Organisation for the Anti-Diarrhea programme.

References

[1] Source: http://in.rediff.com/getahead/2004/sep/08gashop.htm

[2] Source: http://www.retailresearch.org/crime_and_fraud/2007_retail_crime_overseas.php

[3] Source: http://inhome.rediff.com/money/2004/apr/01binter.htm

[4] Source: http://www.retailresearch.org/crime_and_fraud/2007_retail_crime_overseas.php

[5] Source: http://www.centralchronicle.com/20070526/2605301.htm

[6] Source: http://www.iht.com/articles/2007/02/15/news/letter.php

[7] Source: http://www.havocscope.com/Counterfeit/india.htm

[8] Source: United States-India Business Council Newsletter, December 18, 2006, http://www.usibc.com/documents/Dec%2018.06.%20IPR%20News.pdf (accessed: May 8, 2007).

[9] Source: http://www.ias.org.uk/resources/publications/theglobe/globe200103-04/gl200103-04_p4.html

[10] Source: http://www.aa-uk.org.uk/alcoholics-anonymous-reviews/2007/05/underage-drinking-is-big-problem-in.html

[11] Source: http://www.hindu.com/mag/2005/05/29/stories/2005052900130700.htm

[12] Source: http://theseoultimes.com/ST/?url=/ST/db/read.php?idx=4111

[13] Source: http://theseoultimes.com/ST/?url=/ST/db/read.php?idx=4111

Endnotes

(Please note that some of the references in the original edition have been replaced by Indian equivalents for the "glocal" text version. References for added content are given at the end of respective chapters.)

CHAPTER 1

2. Jacob Jacoby, "Consumer Psychology: An Octennium," in ed. Paul Mussen and Mark Rosenzweig, *Annual Review of Psychology* (Palo Alto, Calif.: Annual Reviews, 1976), pp. 331–358. With permission from the *Annual Review of Psychology*, vol. 27, © 1976, by Annual Reviews.
4. See, for example, C.A. Russell, A.T. Norman, and S.E. Heckler, "The Consumption of Television Programming: Development and Validation of the Connectedness Scale," *Journal of Consumer Research*, June 2004, pp. 150–161; S.P. Mantel and J.J. Kellaris, "Cognitive Determinants of Consumers' Time Perceptions: The Impact of Resources Required and Available," *Journal of Consumer Research*, March 2003, pp. 531–538; and J. Cotte, S. Ratneshwar, and D.G. Mick, "The Times of Their Lives: Phenomenological and Metaphorical Characteristics of Consumer Lifestyles," *Journal of Consumer Research*, September 2004, pp. 333–345.
5. Morris B. Holbrook, "What Is Consumer Research?" *Journal of Consumer Research*, June 1987, pp. 128–132; Russell W. Belk, "Manifesto for a Consumer Behavior of Consumer Behavior," *Scientific Method in Marketing*, 1984, AMA Winter Educators' Conference.
6. Jonathan Arndt, "Role of Product-Related Conversations in the Diffusion of a New Product," *Journal of Marketing Research*, August 1967, pp. 291–295; Vijay Mahajan, Eitan Muller, and Frank M. Bass, "New Product Diffusion Models in Marketing: A Review and Directions," *Journal of Marketing*, January 1990, pp. 1–27.
7. Jacob Jacoby, Carol K. Berning, and Thomas F. Dietworst, "What about Disposition?" *Journal of Marketing*, April 1977, pp. 22–28.
8. Nigel F. Maynard, "Waste Not," *Building Products*, July-August 2004, pp. 45+.
10. See Peter Francese, "A New Era of Cold Hard Cash," *American Demographics*, June 2004, pp. 40–41.
11. Joydeep Srivastava and Priya Raghubir, "Debiasing Using Decomposition: The Case of Memory-Based Credit Card Expense Estimates," *Journal of Consumer Psychology*, vol. 12, no. 3 (2002), pp. 253–264.
13. Mathis Chazanov, "Body Language," *Los Angeles Times: Westside News*, April 30, 1995, pp. 10–15.
15. Yumiko Ono, "Buttering Up Customers for Margarine," *Wall Street Journal*, June 7, 1994, pp. B1, B6.
17. Craig S. Smith, "U.S. Bank Cards Fight to Win China's Millions," *Wall Street Journal*, July 17, 1995, pp. B1, B5.
18. "PayPal and Apple iTunes Link Up," *BBC News*, December 10, 2004, *www.bbc.co.uk*.
19. See, for example, Jean Halliday, "Car Renters Flock to the Internet," *Advertising Age*, October 27, 2003, p. 44.
20. "Bartering Makes Comeback Through Evolving Business Networks," *Chicago Tribune*, October 4, 2004, *www.chicagotribune.com;* "High-Tech Exports Bartering for Palm Oil," Asia Africa Intelligence Wire, August 12, 2003, n.p.
21. Tony Mauro, "High Stakes File-Sharing Finds High Court's Ears," *The Recorder*, December 7, 2004, n.p.
22. See, for example, Valerie S. Folkes, Ingrid M. Martin, and Kamal Gupta, "When to Say When: Effects of Supply on Usage," *Journal of Consumer Research*, December 1993, pp. 467–477.
23. Sara Kehaulani Goo, "Americans Shift Down and Out of Manual Transmissions," *Wall Street Journal*, August 19, 1998, pp. B1, B4.
24. Pui-Wing Tam, "Entreaty to Camera-Phone Photographers: Please Print," *Wall Street Journal*, December 28, 2004, pp. B1, B3.
25. Mark A. Le Turck and Gerald M. Goldhaben, "Effectiveness of Product Warning Labels: Effects of Consumer Information Processing Objectives," *Journal of Public Affairs*, Summer 1989, pp. 111–125.
26. Jacoby, Berning, and Dietworst, "What about Disposition?"
27. Russell W. Belk, "Collecting As Luxury Consumption: Effects on Individuals and Households," *Journal of Economic Psychology*, September 1995, pp. 477–490.
28. Laura Bergan, "Collectibles Generate Big Business for Agents," *National Underwriter Property & Casualty-Risk & Benefits Management*, December 26, 2004, p. 46.
33. Rongrong Zhou and Dilip Soman, "Looking Back" Exploring the Psychology of Queueing and the Effect of the Number of People Behind," *Journal of Consumer Research*, March 2003, pp. 517–530.
34. Stephen M. Nowlis, Naomi Mandel, and Deborah Brown McCabe, "The Effect of a Delay Between Choice and Consumption on Consumption Enjoyment," *Journal of Consumer Research*, December 2004, pp. 502–210.
35. Erica Mina Okada, "Trade-ins, Mental Accounting, and Product Replacement Decisions," *Journal of Consumer Research*, vol. 27, March 2001, pp. 433–446.
41. Rebecca Buckman and David Pringle, "Cellphones Help with Disaster Relief," *Wall Street Journal*, January 3, 2005, p. B5; Hassan Fattah, "America Untethered," *American Demographics*, March 2003, pp. 34–41; Hassan Fattah and Pamela Paul, "Gaming Gets Serious," *American Demographics*, May 2002, pp. 39–43.
42. Linda L. Price, Eric J. Arnould, and Carolyn Folkman Curasi, "Older Consumers' Disposition of Special Possessions," *Journal of Consumer Research*, vol. 27, September 2000, pp. 179–201.
43. Morris B. Holbrook and Meryl P. Gardner, "How Motivation Moderates the Effects of Emotion on the Duration of Consumption," *Journal of Business Research*, July 1998, pp. 241–252.

44. Rasul Bailay, "A Hindu Festival Attracts the Faithful and U.S. Marketers," *Wall Street Journal,* February 12, 2001, p. A18.
45. Pierre Chandon and Brian Wansink, "When Are Stockpiled Products Consumed Faster?" *Journal of Marketing Research,* August 2002, pp. 321–335.
46. Joseph C. Nunes, "A Cognitive Model of People's Usage Estimations," *Journal of Marketing Research,* vol. 38, November 2000, pp. 397–409.
48. Elyse Tanouye, "Researchers Report More Patients Ill with Bacterium Resistant to Antibiotics," *Wall Street Journal,* August 24, 1995, p. B9.
52. "News Analysis: Tobacco's Last Stand?" *Marketing,* October 27, 2004, p. 15.
53. Stuart Elliott, "A Campaign for AIDS Drug Adds Warning," *New York Times,* May 10, 2001, p. C1.
54. Robert O'Harrow Jr., "3 Web Firms to Pay Fines for Collecting Data on Children," *Washington Post,* April 20, 2001, p. E03.
55. James R. Bettman, *An Information Processing Theory of Consumer Choice* (Reading, Mass.: Addison-Wesley, 1979).

CHAPTER 2

2. Louise Witt, "Inside Intent," *American Demographics,* March 2004, pp. 35–39.
3. Christopher T. Heun, "Procter & Gamble Readies Market-Research Push," *Information Week,* October 15, 2001, p. 26.
6. "Getting Close to the Customer," *Knowledge@ Wharton,* May 5, 2004, *http://knowledge.wharton.upenn.edu.*
8. Chad Rubel, "Two Research Techniques Probe Shoppers' Minds," *Marketing News,* July 29, 1996, p. 16.
10. Sandra Yin, "Marketing Tools: The Power of Images," *American Demographics,* November 2001, pp. 32–33.
11. Deborah D. Heisley and Sidney J. Levy, "Autodriving: A Photoelicitation Technique," *Journal of Consumer Research,* December 1991, pp. 257–272.
12. Robin A. Coulter, Gerald Zaltman, and Keith S. Coulter, "Interpreting Consumer Perceptions of Advertising: An Application of the Zaltman Metaphor Elicitation Technique," *Journal of Advertising,* vol. 30, Winter 2001, pp. 1–21, January 5, 1999, *www.hbs.edu/units/marketing/zmet;* Morris B. Holbrook, "Collective Stereographic Photo Essays: An Integrated Approach to Probing Consumption Experiences in Depth," *International Journal of Research in Marketing,* July 1998, pp. 201–221.
13. "How Sweet It Is," *American Demographics,* March 2000, p. S18.
14. Lieber and Davis, "Storytelling: A New Way to Get Close to Your Customer."
15. McGee, "Getting inside Kids' Heads."
16. Christine Bittar, "Up in Arms," *Brandweek,* June 18, 2001, pp. 17–18.
18. Julie Schlosser, "Scanning for Dollars," *Fortune,* January 10, 2005, p. 60.
19. Mike Hofman, "Virtual Shopping," *Inc.,* October 1998, p. 88.
20. Tobi Elkin, "Virtual Test Market," *Advertising Age,* October 27, 2003, p. 6.
22. David J. Lipke, "Product by Design," *American Demographics,* February 2001, pp. 38–41.
23. Roy C. Anderson and Eric N. Hansen, "The Impact of Environmental Certification on Preferences for Wood Furniture: A Conjoint Analysis Approach," *Forest Products Journal,* March 2004, pp. 42–50.
24. Joseph Pereira, "Spying the Sales Floor," *Wall Street Journal,* December 21, 2004, pp. B1, B4.
26. Robyn Weisman, "Web Trackers: The Spies in Your Computer," *NewsFactor Network,* November 8, 2001, *www.newsfactor.com/perl/story/14662.html.*
28. Jack Neff, "IRI Snares Campbell Soup Market-Research Account," *Advertising Age,* April 26, 2004, p. 8.
29. Jennifer Lach, "Data Mining Digs In," *American Demographics,* July 1999, pp. 38–45.
30. Constance L. Hays, "What They Know About You," *New York Times,* November 14, 2004, sec. 3, pp. 1, 9.
32. Janet Logan, "Most E-mail Marketing Never Gets Read," *East Bay Business Times,* October 22, 2001, *eastbay.bcentral.com/eastbay/stories/2001/10/22/smallb4.html.*
34. Caterina Sismeiro and Randolph E. Bucklin, "Modeling Purchase Behavior at an E-Commerce Web Site: A Task-Completion Approach," *Journal of Marketing Research,* August 2004, pp. 306–323.
36. Brooks Barnes, "TV Drama: For Nielsen, Fixing Old Ratings System Causes New Static," *Wall Street Journal,* September 16, 2004, p. A1.
39. Joe Mandese, "Observers Rock Research," *Television Week,* March 1, 2004, p. 35.
40. Kathleen Kerwin, "How to Market a Groundbreaker," *Business Week,* October 18, 2004, pp. 104, 106.
42. Dale Buss, "Can Harley Ride the New Wave?" *Brandweek,* October 25, 2004, pp. 20+.
44. Todd Wasserman, "Virgin Mobile's New Call Placed to Teens' Parents," *Brandweek,* December 13, 2004, p. 14
47. Ellen Byron, "Ad Campaign and Sharper Styles Help Gold Shed Its Frumpy Image," *Wall Street Journal,* December 24, 2004, pp. A7, A9.
48. Dale Dauten, "Displaying Failures: A Help to Find Success?" *Chicago Tribune,* August 30, 1998, p. 7.
49. Rob Walker, "Risky Business," *New York Times Magazine,* November 28, 2004, p. 68.
50. Elaine Erickson and Elaine Taylor-Gordon, "Finger on the Pulse," *Brandweek,* December 7, 1998, pp. 30–32.
51. Robert McNatt, "Hey, It's Green—It Must Be Healthy," *BusinessWeek,* July 13, 1998, p. 6.
52. "Citizens, Charter One Take Up RBS Logo in Rebrand," *Europe Intelligence Wire,* December 31, 2004, (n.p.).
54. Judith Langer, "Focus on Women: Three Decades of Qualitative Research," *Marketing News,* September 14, 1998, pp. 21–22.
55. Charlotte Clarke, "Language Classes," *Marketing Week,* July 24, 1997, pp. 35–39.
56. Asim Ansari and Carl Mela , "E-Customization," *Journal of Marketing Research,* May 2003, pp. 131–145.

57. Sandra Yin, "Counting Eyes on Billboards," *American Demographics,* December 2002/January 2003, pp. 24+.

59. "Pepsi Connects with Black History," *American Demographics,* November 2004, p. 33.

60. Wanlapa Rerkkriangkrai, "From Bugs to Bahts: 1.6 Million Mosquitoes Turn into One TV," *Wall Street Journal,* November 6, 2000, p. B1.

61. "Del Monte Squeezes Out More Sales," *Incentive Today,* November–December 2004, p. 8.

62. For example, see Sean Dwyer, Orlando Richard, and C. David Shepherd, "An Exploratory Study of Gender and Age Matching in the Salesperson–Prospective Customer Dyad: Testing Similarity-Performance Predictions," *Journal of Personal Selling and Sales Management,* Fall 1998, pp. 55–69.

63. Jennifer M. George, "Salesperson Mood at Work: Implications for Helping Customers," *Journal of Personal Selling and Sales Management,* Summer 1998, pp. 23–30.

64. Robert M. Schindler and Patrick N. Kirby, "Patterns of Rightmost Digits Used in Advertising Prices: Implications for Nine-Ending Effects," *Journal of Consumer Research,* September 1997, pp. 192–201.

65. Jacob Jacoby, Jerry Olson, and Rafael Haddock, "Price, Brand Name, and Product Composition Characteristics as Determinants of Perceived Quality," *Journal of Applied Psychology,* December 1971, pp. 470–479; Kent B. Monroe, "The Influence of Price Differences and Brand Familiarity on Brand Preferences," *Journal of Consumer Research,* June 1976, pp. 42–49.

66. Laura Bird, "Catalogs Cut Shipping, Handling Fees to Inspire Early Christmas Shopping," *Wall Street Journal,* October 24, 1995, pp. B1, B11.

67. Ziv Carmon and Dan Ariely, "Focusing on the Forgone: How Value Can Appear So Different to Buyers and Sellers," *Journal of Consumer Research,* vol. 27, December 2000, pp. 360–370; Tridib Mazumdar and Purushottam Papatla, "An Investigation of Reference Price Segments," *Journal of Marketing Research,* vol. 37, May 2000, pp. 246–258.

68. Dilip Soman and John T. Gourville, "Transaction Decoupling: How Price Bundling Affects the Decision to Consume," *Journal of Marketing Research,* vol. 38, February 2001, pp. 30–44.

69. Joseph C. Nunes and Peter Boatwright, "Incidental Prices and their Effect on Willingness to Pay," *Journal of Consumer Research,* November 2004, pp. 457–466.

70. Martha Brannigan, "Sailing on Sale: Travelers Ride a Wave of Discounts on Cruise Ships," *Wall Street Journal,* July 17, 2000, pp. B1, B4.

71. Steven Gray and Amy Merrick, "Latte Letdown: Starbucks Set to Raise Prices," *Wall Street Journal,* September 2, 2004, pp. B1, B5.

72. Ronald E. Milliman, "The Influence of Background Music on the Behavior of Restaurant Patrons," *Journal of Consumer Research,* September 1986, pp. 286–289; Richard Yalch and Eric Spannenberg, "Effects of Store Music on Shopping Behavior," *Journal of Services Marketing,* Winter 1990, pp. 31–39; Joseph A. Bellizi, Ayn E. Crowley, and Ronald W. Hasty, "The Effects of Color in Store Design," *Journal of Retailing,* Spring 1983, pp. 21–45.

73. Karen A. Machleit, Sevgin A. Eroglu, and Susan Powell Mantel, "Perceived Retail Crowding and Shopping Satisfaction: What Modifies This Relationship," *Journal of Consumer Psychology,* vol. 9, no. 1, pp. 29–42.

74. Timothy C. Barmann, "Apple Polishes Its Store Layout, Design," *Providence Journal,* April 23, 2004, *www.projo.com.*

75. Kenneth C. Schneider and Cynthia K. Holm, "Deceptive Practices in Marketing Research: The Consumer's Viewpoint," *California Management Review,* Spring 1982, pp. 89–97.

CHAPTER 3

2. C. Whan Park and Banwari Mittal, "A Theory of Involvement in Consumer Behavior: Problems and Issues," in ed. J. N. Sheth, *Research in Consumer Behavior* (Greenwich, Conn.: JAI Press, 1979), pp. 201–231; Deborah J. MacInnis, Christine Moorman, and Bernard J. Jaworski, "Enhancing and Measuring Consumers' Motivation, Opportunity, and Ability to Process Brand Information from Ads," *Journal of Marketing,* October 1991, pp. 32–53.

3. Deborah J. MacInnis and Bernard J. Jaworski, "Information Processing from Advertisements: Toward an Integrative Framework," *Journal of Marketing,* October 1989, pp. 1–23; Scott B. MacKenzie and Richard A. Spreng, "How Does Motivation Moderate the Impact of Central and Peripheral Processing on Brand Attitudes and Intentions?" *Journal of Consumer Research,* March 1992, pp. 519–529; Richard E. Petty and John T. Cacioppo, *Communication and Persuasion* (New York: Springer-Verlag, 1986); Anthony Greenwald and Clark Leavitt, "Audience Involvement in Advertising: Four Levels," *Journal of Consumer Research,* vol. 11, June 1984, pp. 581–592; Ronald C. Goodstein, "Category-Based Applications and Extensions in Advertising: Motivating More Extensive Ad Processing," *Journal of Consumer Research,* June 1993, pp. 87–99; Ellen Garbarino and Julie A. Edell, "Cognitive Effort, Affect, and Choice," *Journal of Consumer Research,* September 1997, pp. 147–158.

4. Wayne D. Hoyer, "An Examination of Consumer Decision Making for a Common Repeat Purchase Product," *Journal of Consumer Research,* December 1984, pp. 822–829.

5. Ziva Kunda, "The Case for Motivated Reasoning," *Psychological Bulletin,* 1990, pp. 480–498; Getta Menon, Lauren G. Block, and Suresh Ramanathan, "We're at As Much Risk as We're Led to Believe: The Effect of Message Cues on Judgments of Health Risk," *Journal of Consumer Research,* March 2002, pp. 533–549; Shailendra Jain and Durairai Maheswaran, "Motivated Reasoning: A Depth-of-Processing Perspective," *Journal of Consumer Research,* 2000, pp. 358–371.

6. Deborah J. MacInnis and Gustavo de Mello, "The Concept of Hope and Its Relevance to Product Evaluation and Choice," *Journal of Marketing,* January 2005, pp. 1+.

7. Richard L. Celsi and Jerry C. Olson, "The Role of Involvement in Attention and Comprehension Processes," *Journal of Consumer Research,* September 1988, pp. 210–224.
8. Marsha L. Richins, Peter H. Bloch, and Edward F. McQuarrie, "How Enduring and Situational Involvement Combine to Create Involvement Responses," *Journal of Consumer Psychology,* September 1992, pp. 143–154; Peter H. Bloch and Marsha L. Richins, "A Theoretical Model for the Study of Product Importance Perceptions," *Journal of Marketing,* Summer 1983, pp. 69–81; Celsi and Olson, "The Role of Involvement in Attention and Comprehension Processes"; Andrew A. Mitchell, "The Dimensions of Advertising Involvement," in ed. Kent Monroe, *Advances in Consumer Research,* vol. 8 (Ann Arbor, Mich.: Association for Consumer Research, 1981), pp. 25–30; Marsha L. Richins and Peter H. Bloch, "After the New Wears Off: The Temporal Context of Product Involvement," *Journal of Consumer Research,* September 1986, pp. 280–285.
9. Michael J. Houston and Michael L. Rothschild, "Conceptual and Methodological Perspectives in Involvement," in ed. S. Jain, *Research Frontiers in Marketing: Dialogues and Directions* (Chicago: American Marketing Association, 1978), pp. 184–187; Richins and Bloch, "After the New Wears Off"; Gilles Laurent and Jean-Noel Kapferer, "Measuring Consumer Involvement Profiles," *Journal of Marketing Research,* February 1985, pp. 41–53.
10. C. Whan Park and S. Mark Young, "Consumer Response to Television Commercials: The Impact of Involvement and Background Music on Brand Attitude Formation," *Journal of Marketing Research,* February 1986, pp. 11–24.
12. Judith Lynne Zaichkowsky, "Measuring the Involvement Construct," *Journal of Consumer Research,* December 1985, pp. 341–352; Laurent and Kapferer, "Measuring Consumer Involvement Profiles."
13. Robin A. Coulter, Linda L. Price, and Lawrence Feick, "Rethinking the Origins of Involvement and Brand Commitment: Insights from Postsocialist Central Europe," *Journal of Consumer Research,* September 2003, pp. 151–169.
14. Jennifer Aaker, Susan Fournier, and S. Adam Brasel, "When Good Brands Do Bad," *Journal of Consumer Research,* June 2004, pp. 1–16; Matt Thomson, Deborah J. MacInnis and C. W. Park, "The Ties that Bind: Measuring the Strength of Consumers' Emotional Attachments to Brands", *Journal of Consumer Psychology,* vol. 15, no. 1, 2005, pp. 77–91.
15. J. Craig Andrews, Syed H. Akhter, Srinivas Durvasula, and Darrel D. Muehling, "The Effect of Advertising Distinctiveness and Message Content Involvement on Cognitive and Affective Responses to Advertising," *Journal of Current Issues and Research in Advertising,* Spring 1992, pp. 45–58; Laura M. Bucholz and Robert E. Smith, "The Role of Consumer Involvement in Determining Cognitive Response to Broadcast Advertising," *Journal of Advertising,* March 1991, pp. 4–17; Darrel D. Muehling, Russell N. Laczniak, and Jeffrey J. Stoltman, "The Moderating Effects of Ad Message Involvement: A Reassessment," *Journal of Advertising,* June 1991, pp. 29–38; Scott B. MacKenzie and Richard J. Lutz, "An Empirical Examination of the Structural Antecedents of Attitude Toward the Ad in an Advertising Pretesting Context," *Journal of Marketing,* April 1989, pp. 48–65.
16. Barbara Mueller, "Standardization vs. Specialization: An Examination of Westernization in Japanese Advertising," *Journal of Advertising Research,* January–February 1992, pp. 15–24.
18. Tammi S. Feltham and Stephen J. Arnold, "Program Involvement and Ad/Program Consistency as Moderators of Program Context Effects," *Journal of Consumer Psychology,* vol. 3, no. 1, 1994, pp. 51–78; Nader Tavassoli, Clifford Schultz, and Gavan Fitzsimons, "Program Involvement: Are Moderate Levels Best for Ad Memory and Attitude toward the Ad?" *Journal of Advertising Research,* vol. 35, no. 5, 1995, pp. 61–72.
19. Kevin J. Clancy and David W. Lloyd, *Uncover the Hidden Power of Television Programming* (Thousand Oaks, Calif.: Sage Publications, 1999), p. 109.
20. Ann E. Schlosser, "Computers as Situational Cues: Implications for Consumers Product Cognitions and Attitudes," *Journal of Consumer Psychology,* 2003, pp. 103–112.
21. Houston and Rothschild, "Conceptual and Methodological Perspectives in Involvement"; Peter H. Bloch, Daniel Sherrell, and Nancy Ridgway, "Consumer Search: An Extended Framework," *Journal of Consumer Research,* June 1986, pp. 119–126; Peter H. Bloch, Nancy M. Ridgway, and Scott A. Dawson, "The Shopping Mall as Consumer Habitat," *Journal of Retailing,* Spring 1994, pp. 23–42; Richard L. Celsi, Randall L. Rose, and Thomas W. Leigh, "An Exploration of High-Risk Leisure Consumption through Skydiving," *Journal of Consumer Research,* June 1993, pp. 1–23; Eric J. Arnould and Linda L. Price, "River Magic: Extraordinary Experience and the Extended Service Encounter," *Journal of Consumer Research,* June 1993, pp. 24–45; Morris B. Holbrook and Elizabeth C. Hirschman, "The Experiential Aspects of Consumption: Consumer Fantasies, Feelings, and Fun," *Journal of Consumer Research,* September 1982, pp. 132–140; Elizabeth C. Hirschman and Morris B. Holbrook, "Experience Seeking: Emerging Concepts, Methods, and Propositions," *Journal of Marketing,* Summer 1982, pp. 92–101; Morris B. Holbrook, Robert W. Chestnut, Terence A. Oliva, and Eric A. Greenleaf, "Play as a Consumption Experience: The Roles of Emotions, Performance, and Personality in the Enjoyment of Games," *Journal of Consumer Research,* September 1984, pp. 728–739.
22. Celsi and Olson, "The Role of Involvement in Attention and Comprehension Processes"; Greenwald and Leavitt, "Audience Involvement in Advertising"; Laurent and Kapferer, "Measuring Consumer Involvement Profiles"; Zaichkowsky, "Measuring the Involvement Construct"; Michael L. Rothschild, "Perspectives on Involvement: Current Problems and Future Directions," in ed. Tom Kinnear, *Advances in Consumer Research,* vol. 11 (Ann Arbor, Mich.: Association for Consumer Research, 1984), pp. 216–217; Andrew A. Mitchell, "Involvement: A Potentially Important Mediator of Consumer Behavior," in ed. William L. Wilkie, *Advances in*

Consumer Research, vol. 6 (Ann Arbor, Mich.: Association for Consumer Research, 1979), pp. 191–196; Petty and Cacioppo, *Communication and Persuasion.*

23. Tiffany Barnett White, "Consumer Disclosure and Disclosure Avoidance: A Motivational Framework," *Journal of Consumer Psychology*, 2004, pp. 41–51.
24. Lorna Stevens, Pauline Maclaran, and Stephen Brown, "Red Time Is Me Time," *Journal of Advertising*, Spring 2003, pp. 35–45.
25. Jennifer L. Aaker and Angela Y. Lee, "'I' Seek Pleasures and 'We' Avoid Pains: The Role of Self-Regulatory Goals in Information Processing and Persuasion," *Journal of Consumer Research*, vol. 28, June 2001, pp. 33–49.
26. "Skin Cancer Prevention," Ad Council website, *www.adcouncil.org.*
27. Sharon Shavitt, Suzanne Swan, Tina M. Lowrey, and Michaela Wanke, "The Interaction of Endorser Attractiveness and Involvement in Persuasion Depends on the Goal That Guides Message Processing," *Journal of Consumer Psychology*, vol. 3, no. 2, 1994, pp. 137–162; Robert Lawson, "Consumer Decision Making within a Goal-Driven Framework," *Psychology and Marketing*, August 1997, pp. 427–449.
28. Richard P. Bagozzi and Utpal Dholakia, "Goal Setting and Goal Striving in Consumer Behavior," *Journal of Marketing*, vol. 63, 1999, pp. 19–32.
29. Dilip Soman and Amar Cheema, "When Goals Are Counterproductive: The Effects of Violation of a Behavioral Goal on Subsequent Performance," *Journal of Consumer Research*, June 2004, pp. 52–62.
30. Ingrid W. Martin and David W. Stewart, "The Differential Impact of Goal Congruency on Attitudes, Intentions, and the Transfer of Brand Equity," *Journal of Marketing Research*, November 2001, pp. 471–484.
31. Aaker and Lee, "'I' Seek Pleasures and 'We' Avoid Pains, pp. 33–49.
32. Ying-Ching Lin, Chien-Huang Lin and Priya Raghubir, "Avoiding Anxiety, Being in Denial, or Simply Stroking Self-Esteem: Why Self-Positivity?" *Journal of Consumer Psychology*, 2003, pp. 464–477.
33. Bagozzi and Dholakia, "Goal Setting and Goal Striving in Consumer Behavior."
34. C. Miguel Brendl, Arthur B. Markman, and Claude Messner, "The Devaluation Effect: Activating a Need Devalues Unrelated Objects," *Journal of Consumer Research*, March 2003, pp. 463–473.
35. Jens Förster, E. Tory Higgins, and Lorraine Chen Idson, "Approach and avoidance strength during goal attainment: Regulatory Focus and the 'Goal Looms Larger' Effect," *Journal of Personality & Social Psychology*, November 1998, pp. 1115–1131.
36. Abraham H. Maslow, *Motivation and Personality*, 2nd ed. (New York: Harper & Row, 1970).
37. C. Whan Park, Bernard J. Jaworski, and Deborah J. MacInnis, "Strategic Brand Concept-Image Management," *Journal of Marketing*, October 1986, pp. 135–145.
38. Martha Visser, "Entrée New," *American Demographics*, December 2003–January 2004, pp. 20–23.
39. Judy Harris and Michael Lynn, "The Manifestations and Measurement of the Desire to Be a Unique Consumer," Proceedings of the 1994 AMA Winter Educators' Conference, Chicago; Kelly Tepper, "Need for Uniqueness: An Individual Difference Factor Affecting Nonconformity in Consumer Responses," Proceedings of the 1994 AMA Winter Educators' Conference, Chicago.
40. Kelly Tepper Tian, William O. Bearden, and Gary L. Hunter, "Consumers' Need For Uniqueness: Scale Development and Validation," *Journal of Consumer Research*, vol. 28, June 2001, pp. 50–66.
41. Russell W. Belk, Güliz Ger, and Soren Askegaard, "The Fire of Desire: A Multisited Inquiry into Consumer Passion," *Journal of Consumer Research*, December 2003, pp. 632+.
43. John T. Cacioppo and Richard E. Petty, "The Need for Cognition," *Journal of Personality and Social Psychology*, February 1982, pp. 116–131; Douglas M. Stayman and Frank R. Kardes, "Spontaneous Inference Processes in Advertising: Effects of Need for Cognition and Self-Monitoring on Inference Generation and Utilization," *Journal of Consumer Psychology*, vol. 1, no. 2, 1992, pp. 125–142; John T. Cacioppo, Richard Petty, and Katherine Morris, "Effects of Need for Cognition on Message Evaluation, Recall, and Persuasion," *Journal of Personality and Social Psychology*, October 1993, pp. 805–818.
44. P. S. Raju, "Optimum Stimulation Level: Its Relationship to Personality, Demographics, and Exploratory Behavior," *Journal of Consumer Research*, December 1980, pp. 272–282; Jan-Benedict E. M. Steenkamp and Hans Baumgartner, "The Role of Optimum Stimulation Level in Exploratory Consumer Behavior," *Journal of Consumer Research*, December 1992, pp. 434–448.
45. Stuart Elliott, "Study Tries To Help Retailers Understand What Drives the Shopping Habits of Women," *New York Times*, January 17, 2001, p. C6.
46. Robert Roth, *International Marketing Communications* (Chicago: Crain Books, 1982), p. 5.
47. H. Murray, *Thematic Apperception Test Manual* (Cambridge, Mass.: Harvard University Press, 1943); Harold Kassarjian, "Projective Methods," in ed. Robert Ferber, *Handbook of Marketing Research* (New York: McGraw-Hill, 1974), pp. 85–100; Ernest Dichter, *Packaging the Sixth Sense: A Guide to Identifying Consumer Motivation* (Boston: Cahners Books, 1975); Dennis Rook, "Researching Consumer Fantasy," in ed. Elizabeth C. Hirschman, *Research in Consumer Behavior*, vol. 3 (Greenwich, Conn.: JAI Press, 1990), pp. 247–270; David Mick, M. De Moss, and Ronald Faber, "A Projective Study of Motivations and Meanings of Self-Gifts: Implications for Retail Management," *Journal of Retailing*, Summer 1992, pp. 122–144; Mary Ann McGrath, John F. Sherry, and Sidney J. Levy, "Giving Voice to the Gift: The Use of Projective Techniques to Recover Lost Meanings," *Journal of Consumer Psychology*, no. 2, 1993, pp. 171–191.
48. Harold H. Kassarjian and Joel B. Cohen, "Cognitive Dissonance and Consumer Behavior: Reaction to the Surgeon General's Report on Smoking and Health,"

California Management Review, Fall 1965, pp. 55–65; see also Kenneth E. Runyon and David W. Stewart, *Consumer Behavior*, 3rd ed. (Columbus, Ohio: Merrill, 1987).

50. Jonathan Welsh, "Checkered-Flag Past Helps Ferrari Unload a Fleet of Used Cars," *Wall Street Journal*, January 11, 2005, p. A1, A10.
53. Robert Langreth, "Bulletins from the Battle of the Baldness Drug," *Wall Street Journal*, December 19, 1997, pp. B1, B12.
54. Ravi Dhar and Itamar Simonson, "Making Complementary Choices in Consumption Episodes: Highlighting versus Balancing," *Journal of Marketing Research*, vol. 36, February 1999, pp. 29–44.
55. Park, Jaworski, and MacInnis, "Strategic Brand Concept-Image Management."
56. Raymond A. Bauer, "Consumer Behavior as Risk Taking," in ed. Robert S. Hancock, *Dynamic Marketing for a Changing World* (Chicago: American Marketing Association, 1960), pp. 389–398; Grahame R. Dowling, "Perceived Risk: The Concept and Its Measurement," *Psychology and Marketing*, Fall 1986, pp. 193–210; Lawrence X. Tarpey and J. Paul Peter, "A Comparative Analysis of Three Consumer Decision Strategies," *Journal of Consumer Research*, June 1975, pp. 29–37.
57. James R. Bettman, "Perceived Risk and Its Components: A Model and Empirical Test," *Journal of Marketing Research*, May 1973, pp. 184–190.
58. Dana L. Alden, Douglas M. Stayman, and Wayne D. Hoyer, "The Evaluation Strategies of American and Thai Consumers: A Cross Cultural Comparison," *Psychology and Marketing*, March–April 1994, pp. 145–161; Ugur Yavas, Bronislaw J. Verhage, and Robert T. Green, "Global Consumer Segmentation versus Local Market Orientation: Empirical Findings," *Management International Review*, July 1992, pp. 265–272.
59. Vincent W. Mitchell and Michael Greatorex, "Consumer Purchasing in Foreign Countries: A Perceived Risk Analysis," *International Journal of Advertising*, vol. 9 no. 4, 1990, pp. 295–307.
60. Anonymous, "Marketing Briefs," *Marketing News*, March 1995, p. 11.
61. Jacob Jacoby and Leon Kaplan, "The Components of Perceived Risk," in ed. M. Venkatesan, *Advances in Consumer Research*, vol. 3 (Chicago: Association for Consumer Research, 1972), pp. 382–383; Tarpey and Peter, "A Comparative Analysis of Three Consumer Decision Strategies."
63. Vanitha Swaminathan, "The Impact of Recommendation Agents on Consumer Evaluation and Choice," *Journal of Consumer Psychology*, 2003, pp. 93–101.
64. "Personal Protection," *The America's Intelligence Wire*, October 23, 2004, n.p.
65. Cornelia Pechmann, Guangzhi Zhao, Marvin E. Goldberg, and Ellen Thomas Reibling, "What to Convey in Antismoking Advertisements for Adolescents," *Journal of Marketing*, April 2003, pp. 1–18.
66. Stuart Elliott, "Antispam Software Company Is Selling 'Nothing,'" *New York Times*, August 1, 2004, *www.nytimes.com*.
67. Abbey Klassen, "Merck Breaks Out Pox Vaccine Spots," *Advertising Age*, June 25, 2001, p. 12.
68. Priya Raghubir and Geeta Menon, "AIDS and Me, Never the Twain Shall Meet: The Effects of Information Accessibility on Judgments of Risk and Advertising Effectiveness," *Journal of Consumer Research*, June 1998, pp. 52–63.
69. Shailendra Pratap Jain and Durairaj Maheswaran, "Motivated Reasoning: A Depth-of-Processing Perspective," *Journal of Consumer Research*, vol. 26, March 2000, pp. 358–371; Joan Meyers-Levy and Alice Tybout, "Schema-Congruity as a Basis for Product Evaluation," *Journal of Consumer Research*, June 1989, pp. 39–54.
70. MacInnis and Jaworski, "Information Processing from Advertisements."
71. Joseph W. Alba and J. Wesley Hutchinson, "Dimensions of Consumer Expertise," *Journal of Consumer Research*, March 1987, pp. 411–454. For an excellent overview of measures of consumer knowledge or expertise, see Andrew A. Mitchell and Peter A. Dacin, "The Assessment of Alternative Measures of Consumer Expertise," *Journal of Consumer Research*, December 1996, pp. 219–239.
72. Eric J. Johnson and J. Edward Russo, "Product Familiarity and Learning New Information," *Journal of Consumer Research*, June 1984, pp. 542–550; Merrie Brucks, "The Effects of Product Class Knowledge on Information Search Behavior," *Journal of Consumer Research*, June 1985, pp. 1–16; Alba and Hutchinson, "Dimensions of Consumer Expertise."
73. Oscar Suris, "New Data Help Car Lessees Shop Smarter," *Wall Street Journal*, July 11, 1995, pp. 1, B12.
74. Durairaj Maheswaran and Brian Sternthal, "The Effects of Knowledge, Motivation, and Type of Message on Ad Processing and Product Judgments," *Journal of Consumer Research*, June 1990, pp. 66–73.
75. Jennifer Gregan-Paxton and Deborah Roedder John, "Consumer Learning by Analogy: A Model of Internal Knowledge Transfer," *Journal of Consumer Research*, December 1997, pp. 266–284.
76. Michelle L. Roehm and Brian Sternthal, "The Moderating Effect of Knowledge and Resources on the Persuasive Impact of Analogies," *Journal of Consumer Research*, September 2001, pp. 257+.
77. Elizabeth C. Hirschman, "Cognitive Complexity, Intelligence, and Creativity: A Conceptual Overview with Implications for Consumer Research," *Research in Marketing*, vol. 3, 1981, pp. 59–99.
78. Richard Yalch and Rebecca Elmore-Yalch, "The Effect of Numbers on the Route to Persuasion," *Journal of Consumer Research*, June 1984, pp. 522–527.
79. Noel Capon and Roger Davis, "Basic Cognitive Ability Measures as Predictors of Consumer Information Processing Strategies, *Journal of Consumer Research*, June 1984, pp. 551–564.
80. Joe Goldeen, "Spanish-Language Web Site Aims to Educate California Latinos on Health Care," *The Record (Stockton, CA)*, April 6, 2004, *www.recordnet.com*.
81. Jennifer Gregan-Paxton and Deborah Roedder John, "Are Young Children Adaptive Decision Makers? A

Study of Age Differences in Information Search Behavior," *Journal of Consumer Research*, March 1995, pp. 567–580.

82. Catherine A. Cole and Gary J. Gaeth, "Cognitive and Age-Related Differences in the Ability to Use Nutrition Information in a Complex Environment," *Journal of Marketing Research*, May 1990, pp. 175–184.
84. June Fletcher and Sarah Collins, "The Lazy Gardener," *Wall Street Journal*, June 6, 2001, pp. W1, W16.
85. Peter Wright, "The Time Harassed Consumer: Time Pressures, Distraction, and the Use of Evidence," *Journal of Applied Psychology*, October 1974, pp. 555–561.
86. Rajneesh Suri and Kent B. Monroe, "The Effects of Time Constraints on Consumers' Judgments of Prices and Products," *Journal of Consumer Research*, June 2003, pp. 92–104.
87. Danny L. Moore, Douglas Hausknecht, and Kanchana Thamodaran, "Time Compression, Response Opportunity, and Persuasion," *Journal of Consumer Research*, June 1986, pp. 85–99; Priscilla LaBarbera and James MacLaughlin, "Time Compressed Speech in Radio Advertising," *Journal of Marketing*, January 1979, pp. 30–36; Shelly Chaiken and Alice Eagly, "Communication Modality as a Determinant of Message Persuasiveness and Message Comprehensibility," *Journal of Personality and Social Psychology*, March 1976, pp. 605–614; Herbert Krugman, "The Impact of Television Advertising: Learning Without Involvement," *Public Opinion Quarterly*, Fall 1965, pp. 349–356; Patricia A. Stout and Benedicta Burda, "Zipped Commercials: Are They Effective?" *Journal of Advertising*, Fall 1989, pp. 23–32.
88. Park and Young, "Consumer Response to Television Commercials"; Deborah J. MacInnis and C. Whan Park, "The Differential Role of Characteristics of Music on High- and Low-Involvement Consumers' Processing of Ads," *Journal of Consumer Research*, September 1991, pp. 161–173; Shelly Chaiken and Alice Eagly, "Communication Modality as a Determinant of Persuasion: The Role of Communicator Salience," *Journal of Personality and Social Psychology*, August 1983, pp. 605–614.
89. Kenneth Lord and Robert Burnkrant, "Attention Versus Distraction: The Interactive Effect of Program Involvement and Attentional Devices on Commercial Processing," *Journal of Advertising*, March 1993, pp. 47–61; Kenneth R. Lord and Robert E. Burnkrant, "Television Program Effects on Commercial Processing," in ed. Michael J. Houston, *Advances in Consumer Research*, vol. 15 (Provo, Utah: Association for Consumer Research, 1988), pp. 213–218; Gary Soldow and Victor Principe, "Response to Commercials as a Function of Program Context," *Journal of Advertising Research*, February–March 1981, pp. 59–65.
90. Baba Shiv and Stephen M. Nowlis, "The Effect of Distractions While Tasting a Food Sample: The Interplay of Informational and Affective Components in Subsequent Choice," *Journal of Consumer Research*, December 2004, pp. 599–608.
91. Betsy McKay, "PepsiCo Tries to Clarify PepsiOne's Image," *Wall Street Journal*, February 25, 2000, p. B4.
92. Rajeev Batra and Michael L. Ray, "Situational Effects of Advertising Repetitions: The Moderating Influence of Motivation, Ability, and Opportunity to Respond," *Journal of Consumer Research*, March 1986, pp. 432–435; Carl Obermiller, "Varieties of Mere Exposure: The Effects of Processing Style and Repetition on Affective Response," *Journal of Consumer Research*, June 1985, pp. 17–30; Arno Rethans, John L. Swazy, and Lawrence J. Marks, "The Effects of Television Commercial Repetition, Receiver Knowledge, and Commercial Length: A Test of the Two-Factor Model," *Journal of Marketing Research*, February 1986, pp. 50–61; Sharmistha Law and Scott A. Hawkins, "Advertising Repetition and Consumer Beliefs: The Role of Source Memory," in ed. William Wells, *Measuring Advertising Effectiveness* (Mahwah, N.J.: Lawrence Erlbaum Associates, 1997), pp. 67–75; Giles D'Sousa and Ram C. Rao, "Can Repeating an Advertisement More Frequently Than the Competition Affect Brand Preference in a Mature Market?" *Journal of Marketing*, 1995, pp. 32–43.
93. Margaret C. Campbell and Kevin Lane Keller, "Brand Familiarity and Advertising Repetition Effects," *Journal of Consumer Research*, September 2003, pp. 292+.
94. Dan Ariely, "Controlling the Information Flow: Effects on Consumers' Decision Making and Preferences," *Journal of Consumer Research*, vol. 27, September 2000, pp. 233–248.
95. Ibid.
96. Fred Vogelstein, "Can Schwab Get Its Mojo Back?" *Fortune*, September 17, 2001, pp. 93–97.
97. Matt Murray, "A Bit of Prosperity and Some Fast Food Fatten Zimbabweans," *Wall Street Journal*, August 8, 1997, pp. A1, A11.

CHAPTER 4

3. Adam Finn, "Print Ad Recognition Readership Scores: An Information Processing Perspective," *Journal of Marketing Research*, May 1988, pp. 168–177.
4. Brian Steinberg, "More Networks Are Pulling the Plugs," *Wall Street Journal*, October 15, 2004, p. B2; Claire Atkinson, "More Marketers Join Ad-Free TV Trend," *Advertising Age*, August 23, 2004, p. 37.
5. John Battle, "Cashing in at the Register," *Aftermarket Business*, September 1, 1994, pp. 12–13.
7. Douglas A. Blackmon, "New Ad Vehicles: Police Cars, School Buses, Garbage Trucks," *Wall Street Journal*, February 20, 1996, pp. B1, B6; Suzanne Vranica, "Think Graffiti Is All That's Hanging in Subway Tunnels? Look Again," *Wall Street Journal*, April 4, 2001, pp. B1, B6; Leslie Chang, "Online Ads in China Go Offline," *Wall Street Journal*, July 30, 2000, pp. B1, B6.
8. Amy Dockser Marcus, "Advertising Breezes Along the Nile River with Signs for Sails," *Wall Street Journal*, July 18, 1997, pp. A1, A11.
9. "Panasonic Signs Deal with RoadAds," *Marketing*, January 8, 2004, p. 6.
10. For more about consumer control of e-mail advertising, see Ray Kent and Hege Brandal, "Improving Email Response in a Permission Marketing Context," *International Journal of Market Research*, Winter 2003, pp. 489+.

11. Steven M. Edwards, Hairong Li, and Joo-Hyun Lee, "Forced Exposure and Psychological Reactance," *Journal of Advertising,* Fall 2002, pp. 83–95.
12. Paul Surgi Speck and Michael T. Elliott, "Predictors of Advertising Avoidance in Print and Broadcast Media," *Journal of Advertising,* Fall 1997, pp. 61–76.
13. Amy L. Webb, "More Consumers Are Ignoring Ads, Survey Shows," *Wall Street Journal Europe,* June 18, 2001, p. 29.
14. Steve McClellan, "It's Inescapable: DVRs Here to Stay," *Television Week,* November 29, 2004, p. 17.
15. Gina Piccalo, "TiVo Will No Longer Skip Past Advertisers," *Los Angeles Times,* November 17, 2004, p. A1; Jeff Howe, "Total Control," *American Demographics,* July 2001, pp. 28–31.
16. Dean M. Krugman, Glen T. Cameron, and Candace McKearney White, "Visual Attention to Programming and Commercials: The Use of In-Home Observations," *Journal of Advertising,* Spring 1995, pp. 1–12; S. Siddarth and Amitava Chattopadhyay, "To Zap or Not to Zap: A Study of the Determinants of Channel Switching during Commercials," *Marketing Science,* vol. 17 no. 2, 1998, pp. 124–138.
17. Bill Carter, "NBC Is Hoping Short Movies Keep Viewers from Zapping," *New York Times,* August 4, 2003, p. C1.
18. Sally Beatty, "Vogue Puts Mortar in E-Commerce," *Wall Street Journal,* January 3, 2005, p. B4.
19. Sarah Ellison, "Kraft Limits on Kids' Ads May Cheese Off Rivals," *Wall Street Journal,* January 13, 2005, p. B3; Todd Wasserman, "Curbing Their Appetite," *Brandweek,* December 6, 2004, pp. 24+; Annie Seeley and Martin Glenn, "Kids and Junk Food: Are Ads to Blame?" *Grocer,* May 15, 2004, p. 30.
20. Bruce Orwall, "Can Hollywood Shelter Kids from Its Ads?" *Wall Street Journal,* September 29, 2000, pp. B1, B4.
22. Cynthia H. Cho, "Outdoor Ads, Here's Looking at You," *Wall Street Journal,* July 12, 2004, p. B3; Bradley Johnson, "Cracks in the Foundation," *Advertising Age,* December 8, 2003, pp. 1, 10.
23. Carl Bialik, "Getting a Grip on Internet Traffic," *Wall Street Journal,* December 30, 2004, pp. B4+.
24. Rik Pieters, Edward Rosbergen, and Michel Wedel, "Visual Attention to Repeated Print Advertising: A Test of Scanpath Theory," *Journal of Marketing Research,* vol. 36, November 1999, pp. 424–438.
25. Mylene Mangalindan, "Web Ads on the Rebound," *Wall Street Journal,* July 25, 2003, p. B1.
26. Scott B. MacKenzie, "The Role of Attention in Mediating the Effect of Advertising on Attribute Importance," *Journal of Consumer Research,* September 1986, pp. 174–195; Richard E. Petty and Timothy C. Brock, "Thought Disruption and Persuasion: Assessing the Validity of Attitude Change Experiments," in eds. Richard E. Petty, Thomas Ostrom, and Timothy C. Brock, *Cognitive Responses in Persuasion* (Hillsdale, N.J.: Lawrence Erlbaum, 1981), pp. 55–79.
27. Joe Flint, "Disappearing Act: The Amount of TV Screen Devoted to Show Shrinks," *Wall Street Journal,* March 29, 2001, pp. B1, B6.
28. L. Hasher and R. T. Zacks, "Automatic and Effortful Processes in Memory," *Journal of Experimental Psychology: General,* September 1979, pp. 356–388; W. Schneider and R. M. Shiffrin, "Controlled and Automatic Human Information Processing: I. Detection, Search, and Attention," *Psychological Review,* January 1977, pp. 1–66; R. M. Shiffrin and W. Schneider, "Controlled and Automatic Human Information Processing: II. Perceptual Learning, Automatic Attending, and a General Theory," *Psychological Review,* March 1977, pp. 127–190.
29. Chris Janiszewski, "Preconscious Processing Effects: The Independence of Attitude Formation and Conscious Thought," *Journal of Consumer Research,* September 1988, pp. 199–209; Joan Meyers-Levy, "Priming Effects on Product Judgments: A Hemispheric Interpretation," *Journal of Consumer Research,* June 1989, pp. 76–87.
30. Janiszewski, "Preconscious Processing Effects"; Chris Janiszewski, "The Influence of Print Advertisement Organization on Affect toward a Brand Name," *Journal of Consumer Research,* June 1990, pp. 53–65.
31. Chris Janiszewski, "Preattentive Mere Exposure Effects," *Journal of Consumer Research,* December 1993, pp. 376–392; Janiszewski, "Preconscious Processing Effects"; Janiszewski, "The Influence of Print Advertisement Organization on Affect toward a Brand Name."
32. Janiszewski, "Preattentive Mere Exposure Effects"; Stewart Shapiro and Deborah J. MacInnis, "Mapping the Relationship between Preattentive Processing and Attitudes," in eds. John Sherry and Brian Sternthal, *Advances in Consumer Research,* vol. 19 (Provo, Utah: Association for Consumer Research, 1992), pp. 505–513.
33. Stewart Shapiro, "When an Ad's Influence Is Beyond Our Conscious Control: Perceptual and Conceptual Fluency Effects Caused by Incidental Ad Exposure," *Journal of Consumer Research,* vol. 26, June 1999, pp. 16–36; Stewart Shapiro, Deborah J. MacInnis, and Susan E. Heckler, "The Effects of Incidental Ad Exposure on the Formation of Consideration Sets," *Journal of Consumer Research,* June 1997, pp. 94–104.
34. Richard L. Celsi and Jerry C. Olson, "The Role of Involvement in Attention and Comprehension Processes," *Journal of Consumer Research,* September 1988, pp. 210–224.
35. Arch Woodside and J. William Davenport Jr., "The Effect of Salesman Similarity and Expertise on Consumer Purchasing Behavior," *Journal of Marketing Research,* May 1974, pp. 198–202.
36. Robert E. Burnkrant and Daniel J. Howard, "Effects of the Use of Introductory Rhetorical Questions versus Statements on Information Processing," *Journal of Personality and Social Psychology,* December 1984, pp. 1218–1230.
44. Sherman So, "Unsolicited Messages Still a Novelty in the Mainland," *Asia Africa Intelligence Wire,* November 9, 2004, n.p.
45. Kate Fitzgerald, "In-Stadium Tech Reinvents Ad Game," *Advertising Age,* October 27, 2003, p. S-6.

46. Staya Menon and Dilip Soman, "Managing the Power of Curiosity for Effective Web Strategies," *Journal of Advertising,* Fall 2002, pp. 1–14; Yih Hwai Lee, "Manipulating Ad Message Involvement through Information Expectancy: Effects on Attitude Evaluation and Confidence," *Journal of Advertising,* vol. 29, no. 2, Summer 2000, pp. 29–42; Joan Meyers-Levy and Alice Tybout, "Schema Congruity as a Basis for Product Evaluation," *Journal of Consumer Research,* June 1989, pp. 39–54. Characteristics of music can also cause surprise; see Kellaris and Kent, "An Exploratory Investigation of Responses Elicited by Music Varying in Tempo, Tonality, and Texture."
47. Geoffrey A. Fowler and Sebastian Moffett, "Adidas's Billboard Ads Give a Kick to Japanese Pedestrians," *Wall Street Journal,* September 29, 2003, pp. B1, B4.
48. Dana L. Alden, Ashesh Mukherjee, and Wayne D. Hoyer, "The Effects of Incongruity, Surprise and Positive Moderators on Perceived Humor in Television Advertising," *Journal of Advertising,* vol. 29, no. 2, Summer 2000, pp. 1–15; Elpers, Mukherjee, and Hoyer, "Humor in Television Advertising: A Moment-to-Moment Analysis."
49. Edward F. McQuarrie and David Glen Mick, "Visual Rhetoric in Advertising: Text-Interpretive, Experimental, and Reader-Response Analyses," *Journal of Consumer Research,* vol. 26, June 1999, pp. 37–54.
50. Finn, "Print Ad Recognition Readership Scores."
51. Avery M. Abernethy and David N. Laband, "The Impact of Trademarks and Advertisement Size on Yellow Page Call Rates," *Journal of Advertising Research,* March 2004, pp. 119–125.
52. Rik Pieters and Michel Wedel, "Attention Capture and Transfer in Advertising: Brand, Pictorial, and Text-size Effects," *Journal of Marketing,* April 2004, pp. 36–50.
53. Roseanne Harper, "Secondary Produce Displays Boost Sales," *Supermarket News,* November 15, 2004, p. 54.
54. S. Shyam Sundar and Sriram Kalyanaraman, "Arousal, Memory, and Impression-Formation Effects of Animation Speed in Web Advertising," *Journal of Advertising,* Spring 2004, pp. 7–17; Werner Krober-Riel, "Activation Research: Psychobiological Approaches in Consumer Research," *Journal of Consumer Research,* March 1979, pp. 240–250; Morris B. Holbrook and Donald R. Lehmann, "Form vs. Content in Predicting Starch Scores," *Journal of Advertising Research,* August 1980, pp. 53–62.
55. Rory McClannahan, "Rio Ranch, N.N., Firm Rolls Out Billboard-Size Advertising Signs for Trucks," *Albuquerque Journal,* January 13, 2004, *www.abqjournal.com.*
56. Mackenzie, "The Role of Attention in Mediating the Effect of Advertising on Attribute Importance."
57. Elizabeth Jensen, "Blue Bottles, Gimmicky Labels Sell Wine," *Wall Street Journal,* July 7, 1997, pp. B1, B6.
58. Karen V. Fernandez and Dennis L. Rosen, "The Effectiveness of Information and Color in Yellow Pages Advertising," *Journal of Advertising,* vol. 29, no. 2, Summer 2000, pp. 61–73.
59. Chris Janiszewski, "The Influence of Display Characteristics on Visual Exploratory Search Behavior," *Journal of Consumer Research,* December 1998, pp. 290–301.
60. Edward Rosbergen, Rik Pieters, and Michel Wedel, "Visual Attention to Advertising: A Segment-Level Analysis," *Journal of Consumer Research,* December 1997, pp. 305–314.
61. Priya Raghubir and Aradhna Krishna, "Vital Dimensions in Volume Perception: Can the Eye Fool the Stomach?" *Journal of Marketing Research,* vol. 36, August 1999, pp. 313–326.
62. Valerie Folkes and Shashi Matta, "The Effect of Package Shape on Consumers' Judgments of Product Volume," *Journal of Consumer Research,* September 2004, pp. 390–401.
63. Peter H. Lindsay and Donald A. Norman, *Human Information Processing: An Introduction to Psychology* (New York: Academic Press, 1973).
64. Ibid.
65. Ibid.
66. Gerald J. Gorn, Amitava Chattopadhyay, and Tracey Yi, "Effects of Color as an Executional Cue: They're in the Shade," *Management Science,* October 1997, pp. 1387–1401.
68. Marnell Jameson, "The Palette Patrol," *Los Angeles Times,* June 13, 1997, pp. E1, E8.
69. Sandra Yin, "Blue Notes," *American Demographics,* December 2003–January 2004, p. 15.
70. Lindsay and Norman, *Human Information Processing.*
71. Amitava Chattopadhyay, Darren W. Dahl, Robin J. B. Ritchie, and Kimary N. Shahin, "Hearing Voices: The Impact of Announcer Speech Characteristics on Consumer Response to Broadcast Advertising," *Journal of Consumer Psychology,* 2003, pp. 198–204.
72. Hannah Booth, "Sound Minds: Brands These Days Need to Sound Good as Well as Look Good," *Design Week,* April 15, 2004, pp. 16+.
73. Eric Yorkston and Geeta Menon, "A Sound Idea: Phonetic Effects of Brand Names on Consumer Judgments," *Journal of Consumer Research,* June 2004, pp. 43–51.
74. Ronald E. Milliman, "Using Background Music to Affect the Behavior of Supermarket Shoppers," *Journal of Marketing,* Summer 1982, pp. 86–91.
75. Colleen Bazdarich, "In a Buying Mood? Maybe It's the Muzak," *Business 2.0,* March 2002, p. 100.
76. Ronald E. Millman, "The Influence of Background Music on the Behavior of Restaurant Patrons," *Journal of Consumer Research,* September 1986, pp. 286–289; Richard Yalch and Eric Spannenberg, "Effects of Store Music on Shopping Behavior," *Journal of Services Marketing,* Winter 1990, pp. 31–39.
77. Mark I. Alpert and Judy Alpert, "The Effects of Music in Advertising on Mood and Purchase Intentions," Working paper No. 85/86-5-4, Department of Marketing Administration, University of Texas, 1986.
78. Gerald J. Gorn, "The Effects of Music in Advertising on Choice Behavior," *Journal of Marketing,* Winter 1982,

pp. 94–101; C. Whan Park and S. Mark Young, "Consumer Response to Television Commercials: The Impact of Involvement and Background Music on Brand Attitude Formation," *Journal of Marketing Research*, February 1986, pp. 11–24; MacInnis and Park, "The Differential Role of Characteristics of Music on High- and Low-Involvement Consumers' Processing of Ads."

79. Kate Fitzgerald, "In-Store Media Ring Cash Register," *Advertising Age*, February 9, 2004, p. 43.
80. Trygg Engen, *The Perception of Odors* (New York: Academic Press, 1982); Trygg Engen, "Remembering Odors and Their Names," *American Scientist*, September–October 1987, pp. 497–503.
81. T. Schemper, S. Voss, and W. S. Cain, "Odor Identification in Young and Elderly Persons," *Journal of Gerontology*, December 1981, pp. 446–452; J. C. Stevens and W. S. Cain, "Smelling via the Mouth: Effect of Aging," *Perception and Psychophysics*, September 1986, pp. 142–146.
82. W. S. Cain, "Odor Identification by Males and Females: Prediction vs. Performance," *Chemical Senses*, February 1982, pp. 129–142.
83. Beryl Leiff Benderly, "Aroma," *Health*, December 1988, pp. 62–77.
84. M. S. Kirk-Smith, C. Van Toller, and G. H. Dodd, "Unconscious Odour Conditioning in Human Subjects," *Biological Psychology*, vol. 17, 1983, pp. 221–231.
85. Pamela Weentraug, "Sentimental Journeys: Smells Have the Power to Arouse Our Deepest Memories, Our Most Primitive Drives," *Omni*, August 1986, p. 815; Howard Erlichman and Jack N. Halpern, "Affect and Memory: Effects of Pleasant and Unpleasant Odors on Retrieval of Happy and Unhappy Memories," *Journal of Personality and Social Psychology*, May 1988, pp. 769–779; Frank R. Schab, "Odors and the Remembrance of Things Past," *Journal of Experimental Psychology: Learning, Memory and Cognition*, July 1990, pp. 648–655.
86. Theresa Howard, "Who Needs Ads When You've Got Hot Doughnuts Now?" *USA Today*, May 31, 2001, p. B3.
88. Maureen Morrin and S. Ratneshwar, "Does It Make Sense to Use Scents to Enhance Brand Memory?" *Journal of Marketing Research*, February 2003, pp. 10–25.
89. Susan Reda, "Dollars and Scents," *Stores*, August 1994, p. 38.

90 Thomas K. Grose, "That Odd Smell May Be Your E-mail," *U.S. News & World Report*, August 6, 2001, p. 33.

91. Tara Parker-Pope, "Body Spritzes Promise to Dispel Smokers' Odors," *Wall Street Journal*, March 31, 1998, pp. B1, B14.
92. Tony Spleen, "Precut Future Debated: Convenience vs. Taste," *Supermarket News*, February 28, 1994, p. 29.
93. Maxine Wilkie, "Scent of a Market," *American Demographics*, August 1995, pp. 40–49.
94. Joann Peck and Terry L. Childers, "Individual Differences in Haptic Information Processing," *Journal of Consumer Research*, December 2003, pp. 430–442.
95. Jacob Hornik, "Tactile Stimulation and Consumer Response," *Journal of Consumer Research*, December 1992, pp. 449–458.
96. Sak Onkvisit and John J. Shaw, *International Marketing: Analysis and Strategy* (Columbus, Ohio: Merrill, 1989).
97. Deborah Brown McCabe and Stephen M. Nowlis, "The Effect of Examining Actual Products or Product Descriptions on Consumer Preference," *Journal of Consumer Psychology*, 2003, pp. 431–439.
98. M. Eastlake Stevens, "REI's X-Treme Sports Retailing," *Colorado Biz*, August 2000, pp. 56–57.
99. Alison Fahey, "Party Hardly," *Brandweek*, October 26, 1992, pp. 24–25.
101. Richard Gibson, "Bigger Burger by McDonald's: A Two Ouncer," *Wall Street Journal*, April 18, 1996, p. B1.
102. Stuart Rogers, "How a Publicity Blitz Created the Myth of Subliminal Advertising," *Public Relations Quarterly*, Winter 1992, pp. 12–18.
103. Martha Rogers and Christine A. Seiler, "The Answer Is No," *Journal of Advertising Research*, March–April 1994, pp. 36–46; W. B. Key, *Subliminal Seduction* (Englewood Cliffs, N.J.: Prentice-Hall, 1973); W. B. Key, *Media Sexploitation* (Englewood Cliffs, N.J.: Prentice-Hall, 1976); W. B. Key, *The Clamplate Orgy* (Englewood Cliffs, N.J.: Prentice-Hall, 1980); Martha Rogers and Kirk H. Smith, "Public Perceptions of Subliminal Advertising: Why Practitioners Shouldn't Ignore This Issue," *Journal of Advertising Research*, March–April 1993, pp. 10–19; Michael Lev, "No Hidden Meaning Here: Survey Sees Subliminal Ads," *New York Times*, June 16, 1991, pp. 22, S12.
104. Sharon Beatty and Del I. Hawkins, "Subliminal Stimulation: Some New Data and Interpretation," *Journal of Advertising*, June 1989, pp. 4–9; Myron Gable, Henry T. Wilkens, Lynn Harris, and Richard Feinberg, "An Evaluation of Subliminally Embedded Sexual Stimuli and Graphics," *Journal of Advertising*, March 1987, pp. 26–32; Dennis L. Rosen and Surendra N. Singh, "An Investigation of Subliminal Embed Effect on Multiple Measures of Advertising Effectiveness," *Psychology and Marketing*, March–April 1992, pp. 157–173; J. Steven Kelly, "Subliminal Embeds in Print Advertising: A Challenge to Advertising Ethics," *Journal of Advertising*, September 1979, pp. 20–24; Anthony R. Pratkanis and Anthony G. Greenwald, "Recent Perspectives on Unconscious Processing: Still No Marketing Applications," *Psychology and Marketing*, Winter 1988, pp. 337–353; Joel Saegert, "Why Marketing Should Quit Giving Subliminal Advertising the Benefit of the Doubt," *Psychology and Marketing*, March–April 1987, pp. 157–173.
105. A. J. Marcel, "Conscious and Unconscious Perception: Experiments on Visual Masking and Word Recognition," *Cognitive Psychology*, June 1983, pp. 197–237; A. J. Marcel, "Conscious and Unconscious Perception: An Approach to the Relations between Phenomenal Experience and Perceptual Processes," *Cognitive Psychology*, September 1983, pp. 238–300.
106. Ronald C. Goodstein and Ajay Kalra, "Incidental Exposure and Affective Reactions to Advertising," Working paper No. 239, School of Management, University of California at Los Angeles, January 1994.
107. Timothy E. Moore, "Subliminal Advertising: What You See Is What You Get," *Journal of Marketing*, Spring 1982, pp. 38–47.

108. Laura A. Peracchio and Joan Meyers-Levy, "How Ambiguous Cropped Objects in Ad Photos Can Affect Product Evaluations," *Journal of Consumer Research*, June 1994, pp. 190–204.

CHAPTER 5

2. Kevin Lane Keller, "Brand Synthesis: The Multidimensionality of Brand Knowledge," *Journal of Consumer Research*, March 2003, pp. 595+.
3. Brian T. Ratchford, "The Economics of Consumer Knowledge," *Journal of Consumer Research*, March 2001, pp. 397–411.
4. Lawrence W. Barsalou, *Cognitive Psychology: An Overview for Cognitive Scientists* (Hillsdale, N.J.: Lawrence Erlbaum, 1992); James R. Bettman, "Memory Factors in Consumer Choice: A Review," *Journal of Marketing*, Spring 1979, pp. 37–53; Merrie Brucks and Andrew A. Mitchell, "Knowledge Structures, Production Systems and Decision Strategies," in ed. Kent B. Monroe, *Advances in Consumer Research*, vol. 8 (Ann Arbor, Mich.: Association for Consumer Research, 1982), pp. 750–757.
5. Kevin L. Keller, "Conceptualizing, Measuring, and Managing Customer-Based Brand Equity," *Journal of Marketing*, January 1993, pp. 1–22; Deborah J. MacInnis, Kent Nakamoto, and Gayathri Mani, "Cognitive Associations and Product Category Comparisons: The Role of Knowledge Structure and Context," in eds. John F. Sherry and Brian Sternthal, *Advances in Consumer Research*, vol. 19 (Provo, Utah: Association for Consumer Research, 1992), pp. 260–267.
6. Stewart Ain, "Hain Celestial Gets a 'Hamburger Helper,'" *New York Times*, January 9, 2005, p. 14.
7. Stuart Elliott, "Can Stride-Rite's Shoes Mean Fun?" *New York Times*, April 6, 2004, *www.nytimes.com.*
8. Stijn M. J. Van Osselaer and Chris Janiszewski, "Two Ways of Learning Brand Associations," *Journal of Consumer Research*, September 2001, pp. 202–223.
9. Burleigh B. Gardner and Sidney Levy, "The Product and the Brand," *Harvard Business Review*, March–April 1955, pp. 33–39; see also David Ogilvy, *Confessions of an Advertising Man* (New York: Atheneum, 1964).
11. Joseph T. Plummer, "How Personality Makes a Difference," *Journal of Advertising Research*, December 1984–January 1985, pp. 27–31; William D. Wells, Frank J. Andriuli, Fedele J. Goi, and Stuart Seader, "An Adjective Check List for the Study of 'Product Personality,'" *Journal of Applied Psychology*, October 1957, pp. 317–319; Jennifer L. Aaker, "Dimensions of Brand Personality," *Journal of Marketing Research*, August 1997, pp. 347–356.
18. Sheri Bridges, Kevin Lane Keller, and Sanjay Sood, "Communication Strategies for Brand Extensions: Enhancing Perceived Fit by Establishing Explanatory Links," *Journal of Advertising*, vol. 29, no. 4, Winter 2000, pp. 1–11; Elyette Roux and Frederic Lorange, "Brand Extension Research: A Review," in eds. Fred von Raiij and Gary Bamoussy, *European Advances in Consumer Research*, vol. 1 (Provo, Utah: Association for Consumer Research, 1993), pp. 492–500; C. Whan Park, Bernard J. Jaworski, and Deborah J. MacInnis, "Strategic Brand Concept-Image Management," *Journal of Marketing*, October 1986, pp. 135–145; David A. Aaker and Kevin L. Keller, "Consumer Evaluations of Brand Extensions," *Journal of Marketing*, January 1990, pp. 27–41; Bernard Simonin and Julie A. Ruth, "Is a Company Known by the Company It Keeps: Assessing the Spillover Effects of Brand Alliances on Consumer Brand Attitudes, *Journal of Marketing Research*, February 1998, pp. 30–42; C. Whan Park, Sung Youl Jun, and Allan D. Shocker, "Composite Branding Alliances: An Investigation of Extension and Feedback Effects, *Journal of Marketing Research*, November 1996, pp. 453–466; MacInnis, Nakamoto, and Mani, "Cognitive Associations and Product Category Comparisons," pp. 260–267; David M. Bousch et al., "Affect Generalization to Similar and Dissimilar Brand Extensions," *Psychology and Marketing*, 1987, pp. 225–237; Susan M. Baroniarczyk and Joseph W. Alba, "The Importance of the Brand in Brand Extension," *Journal of Marketing Research*, May 1994, pp. 214–228.
19. Stijn M. J. Van Osselaer and Joseph W. Alba, "Locus of Equity and Brand Extension," *Journal of Consumer Research*, March 2003, pp. 539–550.
20. Deborah Roedder John, Barbara Loken, and Christopher Joiner, "The Negative Impact of Extensions: Can Flagship Products Be Diluted?" *Journal of Marketing*, vol. 62, January 1998, pp. 19–32.
21. Tom Meyvis and Chris Janiszewski, "When Are Broader Brands Stronger Brands? An Accessibility Perspective on the Success of Brand Extensions," *Journal of Consumer Research*, September 2004, pp. 346–357.
22. Subramanian Balachander and Sanjoy Ghose, "Reciprocal Spillover Effects: A Strategic Benefit of Brand Extensions," *Journal of Marketing*, January 2003, pp. 4–13.
23. Rohini Ahluwalia and Zeynep Gürhan-Canli, "The Effects of Extensions on the Family Brand Name: An Accessibility-Diagnosticity Perspective," *Journal of Consumer Research*, December 2000, pp. 371–381; Zeynep Gürhan-Canli and Durairaj Maheswaran, "The Effects of Extensions on Brand Name Dilution and Enhancement," *Journal of Marketing Research*, November 1998, pp. 464–473; Sandra Milberg, C. Whan Park, and Michael S. McCarthy, "Managing Negative Feedback Effects Associated with Brand Extensions: The Impact of Alternative Branding Strategies," *Journal of Consumer Psychology*, vol. 6, no. 2, 1997, pp. 119–140; Barbara Loken and Deborah Roedder-John, "Diluting Brand Beliefs: When Do Brand Extensions Have a Negative Impact," *Journal of Marketing*, July 1993, pp. 71–84; David A. Aaker, *Managing Brand Equity* (New York: The Free Press, 1991).
24. "Body Shop Leans on Ethical Image," *Marketing*, October 20, 2004, p. 3.
25. C. Whan Park, Bernard J. Jaworski, and Deborah J. MacInnis, "Strategic Brand Concept-Image Management."
26. Kevin P. Gwinner and John Eaton, "Building Brand Image through Event Sponsorship: The Role of Image Transfer," *Journal of Advertising*, vol. 28, no. 4, Winter 1999, pp. 47–57.

27. Kathryn Kranhold, "Avis to Try Even Harder with Ads Touting High Quality of Service," *Wall Street Journal*, February 18, 2000, p. B9.

30. Niraj Dawar and Madan M. Pillutla, "Impact of Product-Harm Crises on Brand Equity: The Moderating Role of Consumer Expectations," *Journal of Marketing Research*, May 2000, pp. 215–226.

31. Jennifer Aaker, Susan Fournier, and S. Adam Brasel, "When Good Brands Do Bad," *Journal of Consumer Research*, June 2004, pp. 1–16.

32. Thomas W. Leigh and Arno J. Rethans, "Experiences in Script Elicitation within Consumer Decision-Making Contexts," in eds. Richard P. Bagozzi and Alice M. Tybout, *Advances in Consumer Research*, vol. 10 (Ann Arbor, Mich.: Association for Consumer Research, 1983), pp. 667–672; Roger C. Shank and Robert P. Abelson, *Scripts, Plans, Goals, and Understanding: An Inquiry into Human Knowledge Structures* (Hillsdale, N.J.: Lawrence Erlbaum, 1977); Ruth Ann Smith and Michael J. Houston, "A Psychometric Assessment of Measures of Scripts in Consumer Memory," *Journal of Consumer Research*, September 1985, pp. 214–224; R. A. Lakshmi-Ratan and Easwar Iyer, "Similarity Analysis of Cognitive Scripts," *Journal of the Academy of Marketing Science*, Summer 1988, pp. 36–43; C. Whan Park, Easwar Iyer, and Daniel C. Smith, "The Effects of Situational Factors on In-Store Grocery Shopping Behavior: The Role of Store Environment and Time Available for Shopping," *Journal of Consumer Research*, March 1989, pp. 422–432.

33. Eleanor Rosch, "Principles of Categorization," in eds. E. Rosch and B. Lloyd, *Cognition and Categorization* (Hillsdale, N.J.: Lawrence Erlbaum, 1978), pp. 119–160; Barsalou, *Cognitive Psychology*.

34. Rosch "Principles of Categorization"; Barsalou *Cognitive Psychology;* Madhubalan Viswanathan and Terry L. Childers, "Understanding How Product Attributes Influence Product Categorization: Development and Validation of Fuzzy Set-Based Measures of Gradedness in Product Categories," *Journal of Marketing Research*, February 1999, pp. 75–94.

35. Lawrence Barsalou, "Ideals, Central Tendency, and Frequency of Instantiation as Determinants of Graded Structure in Categories," *Journal of Experimental Psychology: Learning, Memory and Cognition*, October 1985, pp. 629–649; Barbara Loken and James Ward, "Alternative Approaches to Understanding the Determinants of Typicality," *Journal of Consumer Research*, September 1990, pp. 111–126; James Ward and Barbara Loken, "The Quintessential Snack Food: Measurement of Product Prototypes," in ed. Richard J. Lutz, *Advances in Consumer Research*, vol. 13 (Provo, Utah: Association for Consumer Research, 1986), pp. 126–131; Gregory S. Carpenter and Kent Nakamoto, "Consumer Preference Formation and Pioneering Advantage," *Journal of Marketing Research*, August 1989, pp. 285–298.

36. Gerald J. Gorn and Charles B. Weinberg, "The Impact of Comparative Advertising on Perception and Attitude: Some Positive Findings," *Journal of Consumer Research*, September 1984, pp. 719–727; Cornelia Pechmann and S. Ratneshwar, "The Use of Comparative Advertising for Brand Positioning: Association versus Differentiation," *Journal of Consumer Research*, September 1991, pp. 145–160; Rita Snyder, "Comparative Advertising and Brand Evaluation: Toward Developing a Categorization Approach," *Journal of Consumer Psychology*, vol. 1, no. 1, 1992, pp. 15–30.

37. Sholnn Remand and Norihiko Shirouzu, "Toyota's Gen Y Gamble," *Wall Street Journal*, July 30, 2003, p. B1.

38. Clive Thompson, "The Play's the Thing," *New York Times Magazine*, November 28, 2004, pp. 49+.

39. Ronald W. Niedrich, Subhash Sharma, and Douglas H. Wedell, "Reference Price and Price Perceptions: A Comparison of Alternative Models," *Journal of Consumer Research*, December 2001, pp. 339–.

40. Barbara Loken, Christopher Joiner, and Joann Peck, "Category Attitude Measures: Exemplars as Inputs," *Journal of Consumer Psychology*, 2002, pp. 149–161.

41. Michael D. Johnson, "Consumer Choice Strategies for Comparing Noncomparable Alternatives," *Journal of Consumer Research*, December 1984, pp. 741–753; Michael D. Johnson, "Comparability and Hierarchical Processing in Multialternative Choice," *Journal of Consumer Research*, December 1988, pp. 303–314; James R. Bettman and Mita Sujan, "Effects of Framing of Comparable and Noncomparable Alternatives by Expert and Novice Consumers," *Journal of Consumer Research*, September 1987, pp. 141–154; C. Whan Park and Daniel C. Smith, "Product Level Choice: A Top Down or Bottom Up Process?" *Journal of Consumer Research*, December 1989, pp. 151–162; Stuart Elliott, "Hormel Chili Broadens Its Appeal," *New York Times*, January 18, 2005, *www.nytimes.com*.

42. Lea Goldman, "A Cry in the Wilderness," *Forbes*, May 15, 2000, p. 322.

43. Barsalou, *Cognitive Psychology*.

44. Alexei Barrionuevo and Ann Zimmerman, "Latest Supermarket Special—Gasoline," *Wall Street Journal*, April 30, 2001, pp. B1, B4.

45. Eleanor Rosch, "Human Categorization," in ed. N. Warren, *Studies in Cross-Cultural Psychology* (New York: Academic Press, 1977), pp. 1–49; A. D. Pick, "Cognition: Psychological Perspectives," in eds. H. C. Triandis and W. Lonner, *Handbook of Cross-Cultural Psychology* (Boston: Allyn & Bacon, 1980), pp. 117–153; Bernd Schmitt and Shi Zhang, "Language Structure and Categorization: A Study of Classifiers in Consumer Cognition, Judgment and Choice," *Journal of Consumer Research*, September 1998, pp. 108–122.

46. Joseph W. Alba and J. Wesley Hutchinson, "Dimensions of Consumer Expertise," *Journal of Consumer Research*, March 1987, pp. 411–454; Deborah Roedder John and John Whitney Jr., "The Development of Consumer Knowledge in Children: A Cognitive Structure Approach," *Journal of Consumer Research*, March 1986, pp. 406–417; Merrie Brucks, "The Effects of Product Class Knowledge on Information Search Behavior," *Journal of Consumer Research*, June 1985, pp. 1–16; Deborah Roedder John and Mita Sujan, "Age Differences in Product Categorization," *Journal of Consumer Research*, March 1990, pp. 452–460. See also Andrew A. Mitchell and Peter A. Dacin, "The Assessment of Alter-

native Measures of Consumer Expertise," *Journal of Consumer Research*, December 1996, pp. 219–239; C. Whan Park, David L. Mothersbaugh, and Lawrence Feick, "Consumer Knowledge Assessment," *Journal of Consumer Research*, June 1994, pp. 71–82.

47. Elizabeth Cowley and Andrew A. Mitchell, "The Moderating Effect of Product Knowledge on the Learning and Organization of Product Information," *Journal of Consumer Research*, December 2003, pp. 443–454; Stacy L. Wood and John G. Lynch Jr., "Prior Knowledge and Complacency in New Product Learning," *Journal of Consumer Research*, December 2002, pp. 416–426.
48. Joseph W. Alba and J. Wesley Hutchinson, "Knowledge Calibration: What Consumers Know and What They Think They Know," *Journal of Consumer Research*, September 2000, pp. 123–156.
49. Chingching Chang, "The Interplay of Product Class Knowledge and Trial Experience in Attitude Formation," *Journal of Advertising*, Spring 2004, pp. 83–92.
50. Maureen Morrin, "The Impact of Brand Extensions on Parent Brand Memory Structures and Retrieval Processes," *Journal of Marketing Research*, November 1999, pp. 517–525.
54. C. Page Moreau, Arthur B. Markman, and Donald R. Lehmann, "'What Is It?' Categorization Flexibility and Consumers' Responses to Really New Products," *Journal of Consumer Research*, March 2001, pp. 489–498.
55. Ronald C. Goodstein, "Category-Based Applications and Extensions in Advertising: Motivating More Extensive Ad Processing," *Journal of Consumer Research*, June 1993, pp. 87–99; Mita Sujan, "Consumer Knowledge: Effects on Evaluation Strategies Mediating Consumer Judgments," *Journal of Consumer Research*, June 1985, pp. 31–46.
56. Susan T. Fiske, "Schema Triggered Affect: Applications to Social Perception," in eds. Margaret S. Clark and Susan T Fiske, *Affect and Cognition: The 17th Annual Carnegie Symposium on Cognition* (Hillsdale, N.J.: Lawrence Erlbaum, 1984), pp. 55–78; Susan T. Fiske and Mark A. Pavelchak, "Category-Based vs. Piecemeal-Based Affective Responses: Developments in Schema-Triggered Affect," in eds. Richard M. Sorrentino and E. Tory Higgins, *Handbook of Motivation and Cognition* (New York: Guilford, 1986), pp. 167–203; Joel B. Cohen, "The Role of Affect in Categorization: Toward a Reconsideration of the Concept of Attitude," in ed. Andrew A. Mitchell, *Advances in Consumer Research*, vol. 9 (Ann Arbor, Mich.: Association for Consumer Research, 1982), pp. 94–100.
57. Douglas M. Stayman, Dana L. Alden, and Karen H. Smith, "Some Effects of Schematic Processing on Consumer Expectations and Disconfirmation Judgments," *Journal of Consumer Research*, September 1992, pp. 245–255.
58. David G. Mick, "Levels of Subjective Comprehension in Advertising Processing and Their Relations to Ad Perceptions, Attitudes, and Memory," *Journal of Consumer Research*, March 1992, pp. 411–424.
59. Jacob Jacoby, Wayne D. Hoyer, and David A. Sheluga, *Miscomprehension of Televised Communication* (New York: American Association of Advertising Agencies, 1980); Jacob Jacoby and Wayne D. Hoyer, *The Comprehension and Miscomprehension of Print Communications: An Investigation of Mass Media Magazines* (New York: Advertising Education Foundation, 1987); see also Jacob Jacoby and Wayne D. Hoyer, "The Miscomprehension of Mass-Media Advertising Claims: A Re-Analysis of Benchmark Data," *Journal of Advertising Research*, June–July 1990, pp. 9–17; Jacob Jacoby and Wayne D. Hoyer, "The Comprehension-Miscomprehension of Print Communication: Selected Findings," *Journal of Consumer Research*, March 1989, pp. 434–444; Fliece R. Gates, "Further Comments on the Miscomprehension of Televised Advertisements," *Journal of Advertising*, Winter 1986, pp. 4–10.
61. Richard L. Celsi and Jerry C. Olson, "The Role of Involvement in Attention and Comprehension Processes," *Journal of Consumer Research*, September 1988, pp. 210–224.
62. Jacob Jacoby, Robert W. Chestnut, and William Silberman, "Consumer Use and Comprehension of Nutrition Information," *Journal of Consumer Research*, September 1977, pp. 119–127.
63. Gary J. Gaeth and Timothy B. Heath, "The Cognitive Processing of Misleading Advertising in Young and Old Adults," *Journal of Consumer Research*, June 1987, pp. 43–54; Deborah Roedder and John and Catherine A. Cole, "Age Differences in Information Processing: Understanding Deficits in Young and Elderly Consumers," *Journal of Consumer Research*, December 1986, pp. 297–315; Catherine A. Cole and Michael J. Houston, "Encoding and Media Effects on Consumer Learning Deficiencies in the Elderly," *Journal of Marketing Research*, February 1987, pp. 55–63.
64. C. Page Moreau, Donald R. Lehmann, and Arthur B. Markman, "Entrenched Knowledge Structures and Consumer Response to New Products," *Journal of Marketing Research*, February 2001, pp. 14–29.
65. Edward T. Hall, *Beyond Culture* (Garden City, N.Y.: Anchor Press/Doubleday, 1976); Sak Onkvisit and John J. Shaw, *International Marketing: Analysis and Strategy* (Columbus, Ohio: Merrill, 1989), pp. 223–224.
66. Robert Frank, "Big Boy's Adventures in Thailand," *Wall Street Journal*, April 12, 2000, pp. B1, B4.
67. Scott Baldauf, "A Hindi-English Jumble, Spoken by 350 Million," *Christian Science Monitor*, November 23, 2004, p. 1.
68. Onkvisit and Shaw, *International Marketing*.
69. Wayne D. Hoyer, Rajendra K. Srivastava, and Jacob Jacoby, "Examining Sources of Advertising Miscomprehension," *Journal of Advertising*, June 1984, pp. 17–26; Julie A. Edell and Richard Staelin, "The Information Processing of Pictures in Print Advertisements," *Journal of Consumer Research*, June 1983, pp. 45–61; Ann Beattie and Andrew A. Mitchell, "The Relationship between Advertising Recall and Persuasion: An Experimental Investigation," in eds. Linda F. Alwitt and Andrew A. Mitchell, *Psychological Processes and Advertising Effects* (Hillsdale, N.J.: Lawrence Erlbaum, 1985), pp. 129–156.
70. Mick, "Levels of Subjective Comprehension in Advertising Processing and Their Relations to Perceptions,

Attitudes, and Memory"; Deborah J. MacInnis and Bernard J. Jaworski, "Information Processing from Advertisements: Toward an Integrative Framework," *Journal of Marketing*, October 1989, pp. 1–23.

72. Mick, "Levels of Subjective Comprehension in Advertising Processing and Their Relations to Ad Perceptions, Attitudes, and Memory"; David G. Mick and Claus Buhl, "A Meaning-Based Model of Advertising Experiences," *Journal of Consumer Research*, December 1992, pp. 317–338.
73. Jennifer Gregan-Paxton and Deborah Roedder John, "Consumer Learning by Analogy: A Model of Internal Knowledge Transfer," *Journal of Consumer Research*, December 1997, pp. 266–284.
74. Richard D. Johnson and Irwin P. Levin, "More Than Meets the Eye: The Effect of Missing Information on Purchase Evaluations," *Journal of Consumer Research*, September 1985, pp. 169–177; Frank Kardes, "Spontaneous Inference Processes in Advertising: The Effects of Conclusion Omission and Involvement in Persuasion," *Journal of Consumer Research*, September 1988, pp. 225–233; Alba and Hutchinson, "Dimensions of Consumer Expertise."
75. Michaela Wänke, Herbert Bless, and Norbert Schwarz, "Context Effects in Product Line Extensions: Context Is Not Destiny," *Journal of Consumer Psychology*, vol. 7, no. 4, 1998, pp. 299–322.
76. Shi Zhang and Bernd H. Schmitt, "Creating Local Brands in Multilingual International Markets," *Journal of Marketing Research*, August 2001, pp. 313–325.
77. Teresa Pavia and Janeen Arnold Costa, "The Winning Number: Consumer Perceptions of Alpha-Numeric Brand Names," *Journal of Marketing*, July 1993, pp. 85–99; France Leclerc, Bernd H. Schmitt, and Laurette Dube, "Foreign Branding and Its Effects on Product Perceptions and Attitudes," *Journal of Marketing Research*, May 1994, pp. 263–270; Mary Sullivan, "How Brand Names Affect the Demand for Twin Automobiles," *Journal of Marketing Research*, May 1998, pp. 154–165.
78. Emily Nelson, "P&G Tries to Hide Wrinkles in Aging Beauty Fluid," *Wall Street Journal*, May 16, 2000, pp. B1, B4.
79. Akshay R. Rao, Lu Qu, and Robert W. Ruekert, "Signaling Unobservable Product Quality through a Brand Ally," *Journal of Marketing Research*, May 1999, pp. 258–268.
80. Bonnie B. Reece and Robert H. Ducoffe, "Deception in Brand Names," *Journal of Public Policy and Marketing*, vol. 6, 1987, pp. 93–103.
83. Wendy M. Grossman, "Generic Names Lose Their Luster," *Smart Business*, April 2001, p. 58.
85. Susan M. Broniarczyk and Joseph W. Alba, "The Role of Consumers' Intuitions in Inference Making," *Journal of Consumer Research*, December 1994, pp. 393–407.
86. Gary T. Ford and Ruth Ann Smith, "Inferential Beliefs in Consumer Evaluations: An Assessment of Alternative Processing Strategies," *Journal of Consumer Research*, December 1987, pp. 363–371.
87. Irwin P. Levin and Aron M. Levin, "Modeling the Role of Brand Alliances in the Assimilation of Product Evaluations," *Journal of Consumer Psychology*, vol. 9, no. 1, 2000, pp. 43–52.
88. Tom Meyvis and Chris Janiszewski, "Consumers' Beliefs about Product Benefits: The Effect of Obviously Irrelevant Information," *Journal of Consumer Research*, March 2002, pp. 618+.
89. Alexander Chernev and Gregory S. Carpenter, "The Role of Market Efficiency Intuitions in Consumer Choice: A Case of Compensatory Inferences," *Journal of Marketing Research*, August 2001, pp. 349–361.
90. Sung-Tai Hong and Robert S. Wyer Jr., "Determinants of Product Evaluation: Effects of Time Interval between Knowledge of a Product's Country of Origin and Information about Its Specific Attributes," *Journal of Consumer Research*, December 1990, pp. 277–288; Durairaj Maheswaran, "Country of Origin as a Stereotype: Effects of Consumer Expertise and Attribute Strength on Product Evaluations," *Journal of Consumer Research*, September 1994, pp. 354–365; Sung-Tai Hong and Robert S. Wyer Jr., "Effects of Country of Origin and Product-Attribute Information on Product Evaluation: An Information Processing Perspective," *Journal of Consumer Research*, September 1989, pp. 175–187; Johny K. Johansson, Susan P. Douglas, and Ikujiro Nonaka, "Assessing the Impact of Country of Origin on Product Evaluations," *Journal of Marketing Research*, November 1985, pp. 388–396; Maheswaran, "Country of Origin as a Stereotype"; Wai-Kwan Li and Robert S. Wyer Jr., "The Role of Country of Origin in Product Evaluations: Informational and Standard-of-Comparison Effects," *Journal of Consumer Psychology*, vol. 2, 1994, pp. 187–212.
91. Rajeev Batra, Venkatram Ramaswamy, Dana L. Alden, Jan-Benedict E. M. Steenkamp, and S. Ramachander, "Effects of Brand Local and Non-local Origin on Consumer Attitudes in Developing Countries," *Journal of Consumer Psychology*, vol. 9, no. 2, 2000, pp. 83–95.
92. Stephanie N. Mehta, "BellSouth Pushes Harder in Latin America," *Wall Street Journal*, May 24, 1999, p. B10.
93. Zeynep Gürhan-Canli and Durairaj Maheswaran, "Determinants of Country-of-Origin Evaluations," *Journal of Consumer Research*, June 2000, pp. 96–108.
95. Luk Warlop and Joseph W. Alba, "Sincere Flattery: Trade-Dress Imitation and Consumer Choice," *Journal of Consumer Psychology*, 2004, pp. 21–27.
98. Maxine S. Lans, "Supreme Court to Rule on Colors as Trademarks," *Marketing News*, January 2, 1995, p. 28.
99. Ayn Crowley, "The Two-Dimensional Impact of Color on Shopping," *Marketing Letters*, 1993, pp. 59–69.
100. Donald Lichtenstein and Scott Burton, "The Relationship between Perceived and Objective Price-Quality," *Journal of Marketing Research*, November 1989, pp. 429–443; Etian Gerstner, "Do Higher Prices Signal Higher Quality?" *Journal of Marketing Research*, May 1985, pp. 209–215; Kent Monroe and R. Krishnan, "The Effects of Price on Subjective Product Evaluations," in eds. Jacob Jacoby and Jerry C. Olson, *Perceived Quality: How Consumers View Stores and Merchandise* (Lexing-

ton, Mass.: D. C. Heath, 1985), pp. 209–232; Susan M. Petroshius and Kent B. Monroe, "Effect of Product-Line Pricing Characteristics on Product Evaluations," *Journal of Consumer Research*, March 1987, pp. 511–519; Akshay R. Rao and Kent B. Monroe, "The Moderating Effect of Prior Knowledge on Cue Utilization in Product Evaluations," *Journal of Consumer Research*, September 1988, pp. 253–264; Cornelia Pechmann and S. Ratneshwar, "Consumer Covariation Judgments: Theory or Data Driven?" *Journal of Consumer Research*, December 1992, pp. 373–386.

101. Thomas T. Nagle and Reed K. Holden, *The Strategy and Tactics of Pricing*, 2nd ed. (Englewood Cliffs, N.J.: Prentice Hall, 1995), pp. 84–85.
102. Frank R. Kardes, Maria L. Cronley, James J. Kellaris, and Steven S. Posavac, "The Role of Selective Information Processing in Price-Quality Inference," *Journal of Consumer Research*, September 2004, pp. 368–374.
103. Priya Raghubir, "Free Gift with Purchase: Promoting or Discounting the Brand?" *Journal of Consumer Psychology*, 2004, pp. 181–186.
104. Ann E. Schlosser, "Applying the Functional Theory of Attitudes to Understanding the Influence of Store Atmosphere on Store Inferences," *Journal of Consumer Psychology*, vol. 7, no. 4, 1998, pp. 345–369.
105. Lauranne Buchanan, Carolyn J. Simmons, and Barbara A. Bickart, "Brand Equity Dilution: Retailer Display and Context Brand Effects," *Journal of Marketing Research*, August 1999, pp. 345–355.
106. Amanda Fortini, "Anti-Concept Concept Store," *New York Times Magazine*, December 12, 2004, p. 54.
107. Tsune Shirai, "What Is an 'International' Mind?" *PHP*, June 1980, p. 25.
108. Barbara Mueller, "Standardization vs. Specialization: An Examination of Westernization in Japanese Advertising," *Journal of Advertising Research*, January–February 1992, pp. 15–22.
109. Margaret C. Campbell and Amna Kirmani, "Consumers' Use of Persuasion Knowledge: The Effects of Accessibility and Cognitive Capacity on Perceptions of an Influence Agent," *Journal of Consumer Research*, June 2000, pp. 69–83.
110. Onkvisit and Shaw, *International Marketing*.
111. Richard J. Harris, Julia C. Pounds, Melissa J. Maiorelle, and Maria Mermis, "The Effect of Type of Claim, Gender, and Buying History on the Drawing of Pragmatic Inferences from Advertising Claims," *Journal of Consumer Psychology*, vol. 2, no. 1, 1993, pp. 83–95; Richard J. Harris, R. E. Sturm, M. L. Kalssen, and J. I. Bechtold, "Language in Advertising: A Psycholinguistic Approach," *Current Issues and Research in Advertising*, University of Michigan Press. 1986, pp. 1–26; Raymond R. Burke, Wayne S. DeSarbo, Richard L. Oliver, and Thomas S. Robertson, "Deception by Implication: An Experimental Investigation," *Journal of Consumer Research*, March 1988, pp. 483–494.
112. J. Craig Andrews, Scot Burton, and Richard G. Netemeyer, "Are Some Comparative Nutrition Claims Misleading? The Role of Nutrition Knowledge, Ad Claim Type, and Disclosure Conditions," *Journal of Advertising*, vol. 29, no. 3, Fall 2000, pp. 29–42; Terence Shimp, "Do Incomplete Comparisons Mislead?" *Journal of Advertising Research*, December 1978, pp. 21–27; Harris et al., "The Effect of Type of Claim, Gender, and Buying History on the Drawing of Pragmatic Inferences from Advertising Claims;" Gita Johar, "Consumer Involvement and Deception from Implied Advertising Claims," *Journal of Marketing Research*, August 1995, pp. 267–279.
113. Michael Barone and Paul W. Miniard, "How and When Factual Ad Claims Mislead Consumers: Examining the Deceptive Consequences of Copy x Copy Interactions for Partial Comparative Advertisements," *Journal of Marketing Research*, February 1999, pp. 58–74.

CHAPTER 6

2. Richard E. Petty, H. Rao Unnava, and Alan J. Strathman, "Theories of Attitude Change," in eds. Thomas S. Robertson and Harold H. Kassarjian, *Handbook of Consumer Behavior* (Englewood Cliffs, N.J.: Prentice-Hall, 1991), pp. 241–280.
3. Ida E. Berger and Andrew A. Mitchell, "The Effect of Advertising on Attitude Accessibility, Attitude Confidence, and the Attitude-Behavior Relationship," *Journal of Consumer Research*, December 1989, pp. 269–279.
4. Rohini Ahluwalia, "Examination of Psychological Processes Underlying Resistance to Persuasion," *Journal of Consumer Research*, September 2000, pp. 217–232.
5. Martin Fishbein and Icek Ajzen, *Belief, Attitude, Intention, and Behavior: An Introduction to Theory and Research* (Reading, Mass.: Addison-Wesley, 1975).
6. Lizbieta Lepkowska-White, Thomas G. Brashear, and Marc G. Weinberger, "A Test of Ad Appeal Effectiveness in Poland and the United States," *Journal of Advertising*, Fall 2003, pp. 57–67.
7. Kevin E. Voss, Eric R. Spangenburg, and Bianca Grohmann, "Measuring the Hedonic and Utilitarian Dimensions of Consumer Attitude," *Journal of Marketing Research*, August 2003, pp. 310–320.
8. Petty, Unnava, and Strathman, "Theories of Attitude Change"; Richard Petty and John T. Cacioppo, *Communication and Persuasion* (New York: Springer, 1986).
9. Peter L. Wright, "Message-Evoked Thoughts: Persuasion Research Using Thought Verbalizations," *Journal of Consumer Research*, September 1980, pp. 151–175.
10. Jerry C. Olson, Daniel R. Toy, and Philip A. Dover, "Do Cognitive Responses Mediate the Effects of Advertising Content on Cognitive Structure?" *Journal of Consumer Research*, December 1982, pp. 245–262.
11. Marian Friestad and Peter Wright, "The Persuasion Knowledge Model: How People Cope with Persuasion Attempts," *Journal of Consumer Research*, June 1994, pp. 1–31.
12. Peter Wright, "Marketplace Metacognition and Social Intelligence," *Journal of Consumer Research*, March 2002, pp. 677+.
13. Daniel R. Toy, "Monitoring Communication Effects: Cognitive Structure/Cognitive Response Approach," *Journal of Consumer Research*, June 1982, pp. 66–76.

14. Petty, Unnava, and Strathman, "Theories of Attitude Change."

15. Punam Anand and Brian Sternthal, "The Effects of Program Involvement and Ease of Message Counterarguing on Advertising Persuasiveness," *Journal of Consumer Psychology*, vol. 1, no. 3, 1992, pp. 225–238; Kenneth R. Lord and Robert E. Burnkrant, "Attention versus Distraction: The Interactive Effect of Program Involvement and Attentional Devices on Commercial Processing," *Journal of Advertising*, March 1993, pp. 47–60.

16. Deborah J. MacInnis and C. Whan Park, "The Differential Role of Characteristics of Music on High- and Low-Involvement Consumers' Processing of Ads," *Journal of Consumer Research*, September 1991, pp. 161–173; Rajeev Batra and Douglas M. Stayman, "The Role of Mood in Advertising Effectiveness," *Journal of Consumer Research*, September 1990, pp. 203–214.

17. William L. Wilkie and Edgar A. Pessemier, "Issues in Marketing's Use of Multi-Attribute Models," *Journal of Marketing Research*, November 1973, pp. 428–441.

18. Richard P. Bagozzi, Nancy Wong, Shuzo Abe, and Massimo Bergami, "Cultural and Situational Contingencies and the Theory of Reasoned Action: Application to Fast Food Restaurant Consumption," *Journal of Consumer Psychology*, vol. 9, no. 2, 2000, pp. 97–106.

19. Icek Ajzen and Martin Fishbein, "Prediction of Goal-Directed Behavior: Attitudes, Intentions, and Perceived Behavioral Control," *Journal of Experimental Social Psychology*, September 1980, pp. 453–474; Blair H. Sheppard, Jon Hartwick, and Paul R. Warshaw, "The Theory of Reasoned Action: A Meta-Analysis of Past Research with Recommendations for Modifications and Future Research," *Journal of Consumer Research*, December 1988, pp. 325–342.

20. Arti Sahni Notani, "Moderators of Perceived Behavioral Control's Predictiveness in the Theory of Planned Behavior: A Meta-Analysis," *Journal of Consumer Psychology*, vol. 7, no. 3, 1998, pp. 247–271.

25. Stephen M. Nowlis and Itamar Simonson, "The Effect of New Product Features on Brand Choice," *Journal of Marketing Research*, February 1996, pp. 36–46.

26. Ashesh Mukherjee and Wayne D. Hoyer, "The Effect of Novel Attributes on Product Evaluation," *Journal of Consumer Research*, December 2001, pp. 462+.

28. Laura Bird, "Condom Campaign Fails to Increase Sales," *Wall Street Journal*, June 23, 1994, p. B7

29. Barbara Mueller, "Reflections of Culture: An Analysis of Japanese and American Advertising Appeals," *Journal of Advertising Research*, June–July 1987, pp. 51–59.

30. Ronald E. Goldsmith, Barbara A. Lafferty, and Stephen J. Newell, "The Impact of Corporate Credibility and Celebrity Credibility on Consumer Reaction to Advertisements and Brands," *Journal of Advertising*, vol. 29, no. 3, Fall 2000, pp. 43–54; also see Brian Sternthal, Ruby R. Dholakia, and Clark Leavitt, "The Persuasive Effect of Source Credibility: A Situational Analysis," *Public Opinion Quarterly*, Fall 1978, pp. 285–314.

31. Joseph R. Priester, "The Influence of Spokesperson Trustworthiness on Message Elaboration, Attitude Strength, and Advertising Effectiveness," *Journal of Consumer Psychology*, 2003, pp. 408–421.

34. Ignacio Galceran and Jon Berry, "A New World of Consumers," *American Demographics*, March 1995, pp. 26+; "Pepsi Signs Multi-Year Pact with Colombian Pop Star," *Brandweek*, June 11, 2001, p. 10.

35. Amna Kirmani and Baba Shiv, "Effects of Source Congruity on Brand Attitudes and Beliefs: The Moderating Role of Issue-Relevant Elaboration," *Journal of Consumer Psychology*, vol. 7, no. 1, 1998, pp. 25–48; "Adidas Targets Kids with Animated Beckham Ads," *Marketing*, September 29, 2004, p. 1.

36. Pablo Briñol, Richard E. Petty, and Zakary L. Tormala, "Self-Validation of Cognitive Responses to Advertisements," *Journal of Consumer Research*, March 2004, pp. 559+.

37. Chenghuan Wu and David R. Schaffer, "Susceptibility to Persuasive Appeals as a Function of Source Credibility and Prior Experience with the Attitude Object," *Journal of Personality and Social Psychology*, April 1987, pp. 677–688.

38. Carolyn Tripp, Thomas D. Jensen, and Les Carlson, "The Effects of Multiple Endorsements by Celebrities on Consumers' Attitudes and Intentions," *Journal of Consumer Research*, March 1994, pp. 535–547.

40. William Power, "Some Brokers Promise That You Will Make Money; Not This One," *Wall Street Journal*, February 23, 1994, p. B1.

42. Ignacio Galceran and Jon Berry, "A New World of Consumers," *American Demographics*, March 1995, pp. 26–33.

44. Kevin Goldman, "Women Endorsers More Credible Than Men, a Survey Suggests," *Wall Street Journal*, October 22, 1995, p. B1.

45. Sternthal, Dholakia, and Leavitt, "The Persuasive Effect of Source Credibility."

46. Darlene B. Hannah and Brian Sternthal, "Detecting and Explaining the Sleeper Effect," *Journal of Consumer Research*, September 1984, pp. 632–642.

47. Marvin E. Goldberg and Jon Hartwick, "The Effects of Advertiser Reputation and Extremity of Advertising Claim on Advertising Effectiveness," *Journal of Consumer Research*, September 1990, pp. 172–179.

48. Karen L. Becker-Olsen, "And Now, a Word from Our Sponsor," *Journal of Advertising*, Summer 2003, pp. 17–32.

49. Tülin Erdem and Joffre Swait, "Brand Credibility, Brand Consideration, and Choice," *Journal of Consumer Research*, June 2004, pp. 191+.

50. Petty, Unnava, and Strathman, "Theories of Attitude Change"; Charles S. Areni and Richard J. Lutz, "The Role of Argument Quality in the Elaboration Likelihood Model," in ed. Michael J. Houston, *Advances in Consumer Research*, vol. 15 (Provo, Utah: Association for Consumer Research, 1987), pp. 197–203.

51. Parthasarathy Krishnamurthy and Anuradha Sivararman, "Counterfactual Thinking and Advertising Responses," *Journal of Consumer Research*, March 2002, pp. 650+.

52. Jennifer Edson Escalas and Mary Frances Luce, "Process versus Outcome Thought Focus and Advertising," *Journal of Consumer Psychology,* 2003, pp. 246–254; Jennifer Edson Escalas and Mary Frances Luce, "Understanding the Effects of Process-Focused versus Outcome-Focused Thought in Response to Advertising," *Journal of Consumer Research,* September 2004, pp. 274–285.

53. Brett A. S. Martin, Bodo Lang, and Stephanie Wong, "Conclusion Explicitness in Advertising," *Journal of Advertising,* Winter 2003–2004, pp. 57–65.

57. Timothy B. Heath, Michael S. McCarthy, and David L. Mothersbaugh, "Spokesperson Fame and Vividness Effects in the Context of Issue-Relevant Thinking: The Moderating Role of Competitive Setting," *Journal of Consumer Research,* March 1994, pp. 520–534.

58. Laura A. Peracchio, "Evaluating Persuasion-Enhancing Techniques from a Resource Matching Perspective," *Journal of Consumer Research,* September 1997, pp. 178–191.

59. Joel A. Baglole, "Cough Syrup Touts 'Awful' Taste in U.S.," *Wall Street Journal,* December 15, 1999, p. B10.

60. See Gerd Bohner, Sabine Einwiller, Hans-Peter Erb, and Frank Siebler, "When Small Means Comfortable: Relations Between Product Attributes in Two-Sided Advertising," *Journal of Consumer Psychology,* 2003, pp. 454–463.

61. Michael A. Kamins and Henry Assael, "Two-Sided versus One-Sided Appeals: A Cognitive Perspective on Argumentation, Source Derogation, and the Effect of Disconfirming Trial on Belief Change," *Journal of Marketing Research,* February 1984, pp. 29–39.

62. Stephanie Kang, "Hardee's Fesses Up to Shortcomings," *Wall Street Journal,* June 24, 2003, p. B4.

63. Cornelia Pechmann and David W. Stewart, "The Effects of Comparative Advertising on Attention, Memory, and Purchase Intentions," *Journal of Consumer Research,* September 1990, pp. 180–191.

64. Theresa Howard, "Suzuki Packs Humor into Ads for SUV Spots That Poke Fun at Huge Vehicles, Appeal to Women and Men," *USA Today,* May 21, 2001, p. B4.

65. Pechmann and Stewart, "The Effects of Comparative Advertising on Attention, Memory, and Purchase Intentions"; Rita Snyder, "Comparative Advertising and Brand Evaluation: Toward Developing a Categorization Approach," *Journal of Consumer Psychology,* vol. 1, no. 1, 1992, pp. 15–30.

66. Ken Belson, "Cingular Defends Itself Against a Verizon Ad Campaign with Some Tough Talk of Its Own," *New York Times,* November 18, 2004, p. C12.

67. Patrick Meirick, "Cognitive Responses to Negative and Comparative Political Advertising," *Journal of Advertising,* Spring 2002, pp. 49–62.

68. Bruce E. Pinkleton, Nam-Hyun Um, and Erica Weintraub Austin, "An Exploration of the Effects of Negative Political Advertising on Political Decision Making," *Journal of Advertising,* Spring 2002, pp. 13–25.

69. Dhruv Grewal, Sukumar Kavanoor, Edward F. Fern, Carolyn Costley, and James Barnes, "Comparative versus Noncomparative Advertising: A Meta-Analysis," *Journal of Marketing,* October 1997, pp. 1–15.

70. Pechmann and Stewart, "The Effects of Comparative Advertising on Attention, Memory, and Purchase Intentions."

71. Kenneth C. Manning, Paul W. Miniard, Michael J. Barone, and Randall L. Rose, "Understanding the Mental Representations Created by Comparative Advertising," *Journal of Advertising,* vol. 3, no. 2, Summer 2001, pp. 27+.

72. Joseph R. Priester, John Godek, DJ Nayankuppum, and Kiwan Park, "Brand Congruity and Comparative Advertising: When and Why Comparative Advertisements Lead to Greater Elaboration," *Journal of Consumer Psychology,* 2004, pp. 115–123.

73. Jerry B. Gotlieb and Dan Sarel, "Comparative Advertising Effectiveness: The Role of Involvement and Source Credibility," *Journal of Advertising,* vol. 20, no. 1, 1991, pp. 38–45; Koprowski, "Theories of Negativity."

74. Cornelia Pechmann and S. Ratneshwar, "The Use of Comparative Advertising for Brand Positioning: Association versus Differentiation," *Journal of Consumer Research,* September 1991, pp. 145–160.

75. A. V. Muthukrishnan and S. Ramaswami, "Contextual Effects on the Revision of Evaluative Judgments: An Extension of the Omission-Detection Framework," *Journal of Consumer Research,* June 1999, pp. 70–84.

76. Pechmann and Stewart, "The Effects of Comparative Advertising on Attention, Memory, and Purchase Intentions."

77. John Tylee, "New 'Honesty' Laws Could Render Many Campaigns Illegal," *Campaign,* March 17, 2000, p. 16.

78. Barbara Mueller, "Reflections of Culture: An Analysis of Japanese and American Advertising Appeals," *Journal of Advertising Research,* June–July 1987, pp. 51–59.

79. Paschalina (Lilia) Ziamou and S. Ratneshwar, "Innovations in Product Functionality: When and Why Are Explicit Comparisons Effective?" *Journal of Marketing,* April 2003, pp. 49–61.

80. H. Onur Bodur, David Brinberg, and Eloïse Coupey, "Belief, Affect, and Attitude: Alternative Models of the Determinants of Attitude," *Journal of Consumer Psychology,* vol. 9, no. 1, 2000, pp. 17–28.

81. Michel Tuan Pham, "Representativeness, Relevance, and the Use of Feelings in Decision Making," *Journal of Consumer Research,* September 1998, pp. 144–159.

82. MacInnis and Park, "The Differential Role of Characteristics of Music on High- and Low-Involvement Consumers' Processing of Ads."

83. Deborah J. MacInnis and Douglas M. Stayman, "Focal and Emotional Integration: Constructs, Measures and Preliminary Evidence," *Journal of Advertising,* December 1993, pp. 51–66; Chris T. Allen, Karen A. Machleit, and Susan Schultz Kleine, "A Comparison of Attitudes and Emotions as Predictors of Behavior at Diverse Levels of Behavioral Experience," *Journal of Consumer Research,* March 1992, pp. 493–504.

84. Deborah J. MacInnis and Bernard J. Jaworski, "Two Routes to Persuasion in Advertising: Review, Critique, and Research Directions," *Review of Marketing,* vol. 10, 1990, pp. 1–25.

86. C. Whan Park and S. Mark Young, "Consumer Response to Television Commercials: The Impact of Involvement and Background Music on Brand Attitude Formation," *Journal of Marketing Research*, February 1986, pp. 11–24.
87. Rajeev Batra and Michael L. Ray, "Affective Responses Mediating Acceptance of Advertising," *Journal of Consumer Research*, September 1986, pp. 234–249.
88. Hans Baumgartner, Mita Sujan, and Dan Padgett, "Patterns of Affective Reactions to Advertisements: The Integration of Moment-to-Moment Responses into Overall Judgments," *Journal of Marketing Research*, May 1997, pp. 219–232.
89. Deborah J. MacInnis and Bernard J. Jaworski, "Information Processing from Advertisements: Toward an Integrative Framework," *Journal of Marketing*, October 1989, pp. 1–23.
90. "Kodak Debuts New 'Share Moments, Share Life' Advertising Campaign Which Builds on Kodak's Rich Legacy as It Extends Brand Leadership to Digital Imaging," *Business Wire*, March 19, 2001, *www.businesswire.com*.
91. Michel Tuan Pham and Tamar Avnet, "Ideals and Oughts and the Reliance on Affect versus Substance in Persuasion," *Journal of Consumer Research*, March 2004, pp. 503–518.
92. Jennifer L. Aaker and Patti Williams, "Empathy versus Pride: The Influence of Emotional Appeals across Cultures,' *Journal of Consumer Research*, December 1998, pp. 241–261.
93. Richard P. Bagozzi and David J. Moore, "Public Service Announcements: Emotions and Empathy Guide Prosocial Behavior," *Journal of Marketing*, January 1994, pp. 56–57.
94. May Frances Luce, "Choosing to Avoid: Coping with Negatively Emotion-Laden Consumer Decisions," *Journal of Consumer Research*, March 1998, pp. 409–433.
95. Joel B. Cohen and Charles S. Areni, "Affect and Consumer Behavior," in eds. Thomas S. Robertson and Harold H. Kassarjian, *Handbook of Consumer Behavior* (Englewood Cliffs, N.J.: Prentice-Hall, 1991), pp. 188–240.
96. Robert D. Jewell and H. Rao Unnava, "Exploring Differences in Attitudes Between Light and Heavy Brand Users," *Journal of Consumer Psychology*, 2004, pp. 75–80.
98. Petty, Unnava, and Strathman, "Theories of Attitude Change."
99. Harry C. Triandis, *Attitudes and Attitude Change* (New York: Wiley, 1971).
100. Stephen E. Frank, "Can Tiger Woods Sell Financial Services?" *Wall Street Journal*, May 20, 1997, pp. B1, B14.
101. Brian D. Till and Michael Busler, "The Match-Up Hypothesis: Physical Attractiveness, Expertise, and the Role of Fit on Brand Attitude, Purchase Intent, and Brand Beliefs," *Journal of Advertising*, vol. 29, no. 3, Fall 2000, pp. 1–13.
102. "Analysis: Brands Stake Their Name on Celebrity," *Marketing*, April 15, 2004, pp. 14+ David Benady, "Celebrity Scares," *Marketing Week*, August 7, 2003, pp. 22+.
103. Peter H. Reingen and Jerome B. Kernan, "Social Perception and Interpersonal Influence: Some Consequences of the Physical Attractiveness Stereotype in a Personal Selling Situation," *Journal of Consumer Psychology*, vol. 2, no. 1, 1993, pp. 25–38.
104. Scott Ward and Frederick E. Webster Jr., "Organizational Buying Behavior," in eds. Thomas S. Robertson and Harold H. Kassarjian, *Handbook of Consumer Behavior* (Englewood Cliffs, N.J.: Prentice-Hall, 1991), pp. 419–458.
105. Herbert Simon, Nancy Berkowitz, and John Moyer, "Similarity, Credibility, and Attitude Change," *Psychological Bulletin*, January 1970, pp. 1–16.
106. Kahn, "Yo, Yao."
107. Terence A. Shimp and Elnora W. Stuart, "The Role of Disgust as an Emotional Mediator of Advertising Effects," *Journal of Advertising*, Spring 2004, pp. 43–53.
108. Sally Goll Beatty, "Just What Goes in a Viagra Ad? Dancing Couples," *Wall Street Journal*, June 17, 1998, pp. B1, B8.
109. Betsy Spethmann, "Value Ads," *Promo*, March 1, 2001, pp. 74+.
110. Patti Williams and Jennifer L. Aaker, "Can Mixed Emotions Peacefully Coexist?" *Journal of Consumer Research*, March 2002, pp. 636+.
111. Batra and Stayman, "The Role of Mood in Advertising Effectiveness."
112. "'Enjoy Life'? Hey, We're Trying!" *Automotive News*, September 10, 2001, p. 4; Kevin Goldman, "Volvo Seeks to Soft-Pedal Safety Image," *Wall Street Journal*, March 16, 1993, p. B7.
113. Rajesh K. Chandy, Gerard J. Tellis, Deborah J. MacInnis, and Pattana Thaivanich, "'What to Say When' Advertising Appeals in Evolving Markets," *Journal of Marketing Research*, November 2001, pp. 399–414.
115. Valerie S. Folkes and Tina Kiesler, "Social Cognition: Consumers' Inferences about the Self and Others," in eds. Thomas S. Robertson and Harold H. Kassarjian, *Handbook of Consumer Behavior* (Englewood Cliffs, N.J.: Prentice-Hall, 1991), pp. 281–315.
116. John F. Tanner, James B. Hunt, and David R. Eppright, "The Protection Motivation Model: A Normative Model of Fear Appeals," *Journal of Marketing*, July 1991, pp. 36–45.
118. Michael L. Ray and William L. Wilkie, "Fear: The Potential of an Appeal Neglected by Marketing," *Journal of Marketing*, January 1970, pp. 54–62.
119. Ibid.
120. Ibid; Herbert J. Rotfeld, "Fear Appeals and Persuasion: Assumptions and Errors in Advertising Research," in eds. James H. Leigh and Claude R. Martin, *Current Issues and Research in Advertising* (Ann Arbor, Mich.: Graduate School of Business Administration, University of Michigan, 1990), pp. 155–175.
121. John J. Wheatley, "Marketing and the Use of Fear- or Anxiety-Arousing Appeals," *Journal of Marketing*, April 1971, pp. 62–64; Peter L. Wright, "Concrete Action Plans in TV Messages to Increase Reading of Drug Warnings," *Journal of Consumer Research*, December 1979, pp. 256–269.

122. John J. Burette and Richard L. Oliver, "Fear Appeal Effects in the Field: A Segmentation Approach," *Journal of Marketing Research*, May 1979, pp. 181–190.

123. MacInnis and Jaworski, "Two Routes to Persuasion in Advertising."

124. Thomas J. Olney, Morris B. Holbrook, and Rajeev Batra, "Consumer Responses to Advertising: The Effects of Ad Content, Emotions, and Attitude toward the Ad on Viewing Time," *Journal of Consumer Research*, March 1991, pp. 440–453.

125. Paul W. Miniard, Sunil Bhatla, and Randall L. Rose, "On the Formation and Relationship of Ad and Brand Attitudes: An Experimental and Causal Analysis," *Journal of Marketing Research*, August 1990, pp. 290–303.

126. Sally Goll Beatty, "Executive Fears Effects of Political Ads," *Wall Street Journal*, April 29, 1996, p. B6.

127. Julie A. Edell and Richard E. Staelin, "The Information Processing of Pictures in Print Advertisements," *Journal of Consumer Research*, June 1983, pp. 45–60.

128. Scott B. MacKenzie, Richard J. Lutz, and George E. Belch, "The Role of Attitude toward the Ad as a Mediator of Advertising Effectiveness: A Test of Competing Explanations," *Journal of Marketing Research*, May 1986, pp. 130–143; Pamela M. Homer, "The Mediating Role of Attitude toward the Ad: Some Additional Evidence," *Journal of Marketing Research*, February 1990, pp. 78–86.

131. Richard E. Petty, John T. Cacioppo, and David W. Schumann, "Central and Peripheral Routes to Advertising Persuasion," *Journal of Consumer Research*, September 1983, pp. 134–148.

132. Jaideep Sengupta and Gita Venkataramani Johar, "Effects of Inconsistent Attribute Information on the Predictive Value of Product Attitudes: Toward a Resolution of Opposing Perspectives," *Journal of Consumer Research*, June 2002, pp. 39+.

133. Smith and Swinyard, "Attitude-Behavior Consistency"; Russell H. Fazio and Mark P. Zanna, "Direct Experience and Attitude-Behavior Consistency," in ed. Leonard Berkowitz, *Advances in Experimental Social Psychology* (New York: Academic Press, 1981), pp. 162–202.

134. Jaideep Sengupta and Gavan J. Fitzsimons, "The Effects of Analyzing Reasons for Brand Preferences: Disruption or Reinforcement?" *Journal of Marketing Research*, vol. 37, August 2000, pp. 318–330.

135. Russell H. Fazio, Martha C. Powell, and Carol J. Williams, "The Role of Attitude Accessibility in the Attitude-to-Behavior Process," *Journal of Consumer Research*, December 1989, pp. 280–288; Berger and Mitchell, "The Effect of Advertising on Attitude Accessibility, Attitude Confidence, and the Attitude-Behavior Relationship."

136. Smith and Swinyard, "Attitude-Behavior Consistency"; Alice A. Wright and John G. Lynch, "Communication Effects of Advertising vs. Direct Experience When Both Search and Experience Attributes Are Present," *Journal of Consumer Research*, March 1995, pp. 708–718.

137. Vicki G. Morwitz and Gavan J. Fitzsimons, "The Mere-Measurement Effect: Why Does Measuring Intentions Change Actual Behavior?" *Journal of Consumer Psychology*, 2004, pp. 64–74.

138. Berger, "The Nature of Attitude Accessibility and Attitude Confidence."

139. Joseph R. Priester, Dhananhjay Nayakankuppam, Monique A. Fleming, and John Godek, "The A^2SC^2 Model: The Influence of Attitudes and Attitude Strength on Consideration and Choice," *Journal of Consumer Research*, March 2004, pp. 574+.

140. Fishbein and Ajzen, *Belief, Attitude, Intention, and Behavior.*

141. H. Shanker Krishnan and Robert E. Smith, "The Relative Endurance of Attitudes, Confidence, and Attitude-Behavior Consistency: The Role of Information Source and Delay," *Journal of Consumer Psychology*, vol. 7, no. 3, 1998, pp. 273–298.

142. Ibid.

143. John T. Cacioppo, Richard E. Petty, Chuan Fang Kao, and Regina Rodriguez, "Central and Peripheral Routes to Persuasion: An Individual Difference Perspective," *Journal of Personality and Social Psychology*, vol. 51, 1986, pp. 1032–1043.

144. Mark Snyder and William B. Swan Jr., "When Actions Reflect Attitudes: The Politics of Impression Management," *Journal of Personality and Social Psychology*, vol. 34, 1976, pp. 1034–1042.

CHAPTER 7

2. Richard E. Petty and John T. Cacioppo, *Attitudes and Persuasion: Classic and Contemporary Approaches* (Dubuque, Iowa: William C. Brown, 1981); Richard E. Petty, John T. Cacioppo, and David Schumann, "Central and Peripheral Routes to Advertising Effectiveness: The Moderating Role of Involvement," *Journal of Consumer Research*, September 1983, pp. 135–146.

3. Jaideep Sengupta, Ronald C. Goodstein, and David S. Boninger, "All Cues Are Not Created Equal: Obtaining Attitude Persistence under Low Involvement Conditions," *Journal of Consumer Research*, March 1997, pp. 315–361.

4. Ronald C. Goodstein, "Category-Based Applications and Extensions in Advertising: Motivating More Extensive Ad Processing," *Journal of Consumer Research*, June 1993, pp. 87–99.

5. Valerie S. Folkes, "Recent Attribution Research in Consumer Behavior: A Review and New Directions," *Journal of Consumer Research*, March 1988, pp. 548–656.

7. Shelly Chaiken, "Heuristic versus Systematic Information Processing and the Use of Source versus Message Cues in Persuasion," *Journal of Personality and Social Psychology*, vol. 39, 1980, pp. 752–766; also, "The Heuristic Model of Persuasion," in eds. Mark P. Zanna, J. M. Olson, and C. P. Herman, *Social Influence: The Ontario Symposium*, vol. 5 (Hillsdale, N.J.: Lawrence Erlbaum, 1987), pp. 3–49.

8. Amna Kirmani, "Advertising Repetition as a Signal of Quality: If It's Advertised So Much, Something Must Be Wrong," *Journal of Advertising*, Fall 1997, pp. 77–86.

9. Joseph W. Alba and Howard Marmorstein, "The Effects of Frequency Knowledge on Consumer Decision Making," *Journal of Consumer Research*, June 1987, pp. 14–25.

10. Scott A. Hawkins and Stephen J. Hoch, "Low-Involvement Learning: Memory without Evaluation," *Journal of Consumer Research,* September 1992, pp. 212–225; Lynn Hasher, David Goldstein, and Thomas Toppino, "Frequency and the Conference of Referential Validity," *Journal of Verbal Learning and Verbal Behavior,* February 1977, pp. 107–112.
11. S. Ratneshwar and Shelly Chaiken, "Comprehension's Role in Persuasion: The Case of Its Moderating Effect on the Persuasive Impact of Source Cues," *Journal of Consumer Research,* June 1991, pp. 52–62.
13. Charles Forelle, "Battery Makers Go 'Heavy Duty' in Price Scuffle," *Wall Street Journal,* January 25, 2005, pp. B1, B9.
15. Robert E. Burnkrant and H. Rao Unnava, "Effects of Self-Referencing on Persuasion," *Journal of Consumer Research,* June 1995, pp. 17–26; Sharon Shavitt and Timothy C. Brock," Self-Relevant Responses in Commercial Persuasion," in eds. Jerry C. Olson and Keith Sentis, *Advertising and Consumer Psychology* (New York: Praeger, 1986), pp. 149–171; Kathleen Debevec and Jean B. Romeo, "Self-Referent Processing in Perceptions of Verbal and Visual Commercial Information," *Journal of Consumer Psychology,* vol. 1, no. 1, 1992, pp. 83–102; Joan Myers-Levy and Laura A. Peracchio, "Moderators of the Impact of Self-Reference on Persuasion," *Journal of Consumer Research,* March 1996, pp. 408–423.
16. Daniel J. Howard, Charles Gengler, and Ambuj Jain, "What's in a Name? A Complimentary Means of Persuasion," *Journal of Consumer Research,* September 1995, pp. 200–211.
17. Jennifer L. Aaker, "The Malleable Self: The Role of Self-Expression in Persuasion," *Journal of Marketing Research,* vol. 36, February 1999, pp. 45–57.
18. Anne M. Brumbaugh, "Source and Nonsource Cues in Advertising and Their Effects on the Activation of Cultural and Subcultural Knowledge on the Route to Persuasion," *Journal of Consumer Research,* September 2002, pp. 258+.
19. Robert E. Burnkrant and Daniel J. Howard, "Effects of the Use of Introductory Rhetorical Questions versus Statements on Information Processing," *Journal of Personality and Social Psychology,* December 1984, pp. 1218–1230; James M. Munch, Gregory W. Boller, and John L. Swazy, "The Effects of Argument Structure and Affective Tagging on Product Attitude Formation," *Journal of Consumer Research,* September 1993, pp. 294–302.
20. Rohini Ahluwalia and Robert E. Burnkrant, "Answering Questions About Questions: A Persuasion Knowledge Perspective for Understanding the Effects of Rhetorical Questions," *Journal of Consumer Research,* June 2004, pp. 26+.
21. Chris Lee, "Trojan Horse Is Movies' New Ride," *Los Angeles Times,* April 28, 2004, p. E1.
22. Russell H. Fazio, Paul M. Herr, and Martha C. Powell, "On the Development and Strength of Category-Brand Associations in Memory: The Case of Mystery Ads," *Journal of Consumer Psychology,* vol. 1, no. 1, 1992, pp. 1–14.
23. David A. Griffin and Qimei Chen, "The Influence of Virtual Direct Experience (VDE) on On-Line Ad Message Effectiveness," *Journal of Advertising,* Spring 2004, pp. 55–68.
24. Hiawatha Bray, "'Advergames' Spark Concerns of Kids Being Targeted," *Boston Globe,* July 30, 2004, *www.boston.com/globe.*
25. Mark A. Stein, "Openers: Had Enough?" *New York Times,* October 31, 2004, sec. 3, p. 2; Jeff Manning and Kevin Lane Keller, "Got Advertising That Works?" *Marketing Management,* January–February 2004, pp. 16+.
26. Joseph W. Alba, J. Wesley Hutchinson, and John G. Lynch, "Memory and Decision Making," in eds. Thomas S. Robertson and Harold H. Kassarjian, *Handbook of Consumer Behavior* (Englewood Cliffs, N.J.: Prentice-Hall, 1991).
27. Chris Janiszewski and Tom Meyvis, "Effects of Brand Logo Complexity, Repetition, and Spacing on Processing Fluency and Judgment," *Journal of Consumer Research,* June 2001, pp. 18–32; H. Rao Unnava and Robert E. Burnkrant, "Effects of Repeating Varied Ad Executions on Brand Name Memory," *Journal of Marketing Research,* November 1991, pp. 406–416.
28. Ida E. Berger and Andrew A. Mitchell, "The Effect of Attitude Accessibility, Attitude Confidence, and the Attitude-Behavior Relationship," *Journal of Consumer Research,* December 1989, pp. 269–279.
30. Prashant Malaviya and Brian Sternthal, "The Persuasive Impact of Message Spacing," *Journal of Consumer Psychology,* vol. 6, no. 3, 1997, pp. 233–256.
31. Patrick De Pelsmacker, Maggie Geuens, and Pascal Anckaert, "Media Context and Advertising Effectiveness: The Role of Context Appreciation and Context/Ad Similarity," *Journal of Advertising,* September 2002, pp. 49–61.
32. Marjolein Moorman, Peter C. Neijens, and Edith G. Smit, "The Effects of Magazine-Induced Psychological Responses and Thematic Congruence on Memory and Attitude Toward the Life in a Real-Life Setting," *Journal of Advertising,* Winter 2002, pp. 27–40.
33. Carl Obermiller, "Varieties of Mere Exposure: The Effects of Processing Style and Repetition in Affective Response," *Journal of Consumer Research,* June 1985, pp. 17–30.
34. Arno Rethans, John L. Swazy, and Lawrence J. Marks, "The Effects of Television Commercial Repetition, Receiver Knowledge, and Commercial Length: A Test of a Two Factor Model," *Journal of Marketing Research,* February 1986, pp. 50–61.
35. William E. Baker, "When Can Affective Conditioning and Mere Exposure Directly Influence Brand Choice?" *Journal of Advertising,* vol. 28, no. 4, Winter 1999, pp. 31–46.
36. Chris Janiszewski and Tom Meyvis, "Effects of Brand Logo Complexity, Repetition, and Spacing on Processing Fluency and Judgment," *Journal of Consumer Research,* vol. 28, June 2001, pp. 18- 32.
37. Leo Bogart, *Strategy in Advertising: Matching Media and Messages of Markets and Motivation* (Lincoln, Ill.: NTC Business, 1986), p. 208.

38. Norihiko Shirouzu, "Whoppers Face Entrenched Foes in Japan: Big Macs," *Wall Street Journal*, February 4, 1997, pp. B1, B5.
39. Herbert Krugman, "Why Three Exposures May Be Enough," *Journal of Advertising Research*, December 1972, pp. 11–14.
40. George E. Belch, "The Effects of Television Commercial Repetition on Cognitive Response and Message Acceptance," *Journal of Consumer Research*, June 1982, pp. 56–65.
41. Margaret Henderson Blair, "An Empirical Investigation of Advertising Wearin and Wearout," *Journal of Advertising Research*, vol. 40, November 2000, p. 95.
42. Margaret C. Campbell and Kevin Lane Keller, "Brand Familiarity and Advertising Repetition Effects," *Journal of Consumer Research*, September 2003, pp. 292+.
43. Deborah J. MacInnis, Ambar G. Rao, and Allen M. Weiss, "Assessing When Increased Media Weight of Real-World Advertisements Helps Sales," *Journal of Marketing Research*, November 2002, pp. 391–407.
44. Christie L. Nordhielm, "The Influence of Level of Processing on Advertising Repetition Effects," *Journal of Consumer Research*, December 2002, pp. 371+.
45. Marian Burke and Julie A. Edell, "Ad Reactions over Time: Capturing Changes in the Real World," *Journal of Consumer Research*, June 1986, pp. 114–118; Curtis P. Haugtvedt, David W. Schumann, Wendy L. Schneier, and Wendy L. Warren, "Advertising Repetition and Variation Strategies: Implications for Understanding Attitude Strength," *Journal of Consumer Research*, June 1994, pp. 176–189.
46. Gerald J. Gorn, "The Effects of Music in Advertising on Choice Behavior: A Classical Conditioning Approach," *Journal of Marketing*, Winter 1982, pp. 94–101.
47. Calvin Bierley, Frances K. McSweeny, and Renee Vannieuwkerk, "Classical Conditioning of Preferences for Stimuli," *Journal of Consumer Research*, December 1985, pp. 316–323; James J. Kellaris and Anthony D. Cox, "The Effects of Background Music in Advertising: A Reassessment," *Journal of Consumer Research*, June 1989, pp. 113–118: Chris T. Allen and Thomas J. Madden, "A Closer Look at Classical Conditioning," *Journal of Consumer Research*, December 1985, pp. 301–315.
48. Bierley, McSweeny, and Vannieuwkerk, "Classical Conditioning of Preferences for Stimuli"; Elnora W. Stuart, Terence A. Shimp, and Randall W. Engle, "Classical Conditioning of Consumer Attitudes: Four Experiments in an Advertising Context," *Journal of Consumer Research*, December 1987, pp. 334–349; Terence A. Shimp, Elnora W. Stuart, and Randall W. Engle, "A Program of Classical Conditioning Experiments Testing Variations in the Conditioned Stimulus and Context," *Journal of Consumer Research*, June 1991, pp. 1–12; Chris T. Allen and Chris A. Janiszewski, "Assessing the Role of Contingency Awareness in Attitudinal Conditioning with Implications for Advertising Research," *Journal of Marketing Research*, February 1989, pp. 30–43.
49. Randi Priluck Grossman and Brian D. Till, "The Persistence of Classically Conditioned Brand Attitudes," *Journal of Advertising*, Spring 1998.
50. Terence A. Shimp, "Neo-Pavlovian Conditioning and Its Implications for Consumer Theory and Research," in eds. Thomas S. Robertson and Harold H. Kassarjian, *Handbook of Consumer Behavior* (Englewood Cliffs, N.J.: Prentice-Hall, 1991), pp. 162–187; Kurt Badenhausen, "King of the Court," *Forbes Global*, July 5, 2004, pp. 48+.
52. Steven P. Brown and Douglas M. Stayman, "Antecedents and Consequences of Attitude toward the Ad: A Meta-analysis," *Journal of Consumer Research*, June 1993, pp. 34–51; Andrew A. Mitchell and Jerry C. Olson, "Are Product Attributes Beliefs the Only Mediator of Advertising Effects on Brand Attitudes?" *Journal of Marketing Research*, August 1981, pp. 318–322; Terence A. Shimp, "Attitude toward the Ad as a Mediator of Consumer Brand Choice," *Journal of Advertising*, vol. 10, no. 2, 1981, pp. 9–15; Christian M. Derbaix, "The Impact of Affective Reactions on Attitudes toward the Advertisement and the Brand: A Step toward Ecological Validity," *Journal of Marketing Research*, November 1995, pp. 470–479.
53. Mitchell and Olson, "Are Product Attributes Beliefs the Only Mediator of Advertising Effects on Brand Attitudes?"
54. Srinivas Durvasula, J. Craig Andrews, Steven Lysonski, and Richard G. Netemeyer, "Assessing the Cross-National Applicability of Consumer Behavior Models: A Model of Attitude toward Advertising in General," *Journal of Consumer Research*, March 1993, pp. 626–636.
55. Russell I. Haley and Allan L. Baldinger, "The ARF Copy Research Validity Project," *Journal of Advertising Research*, April–May 1991, pp. 11–32.
56. Elizabeth S. Moore and Richard J. Lutz, "Children, Advertising, and Product Experiences: A Multimethod Inquiry," *Journal of Consumer Research*, vol. 27, June 2000, pp. 31–48; Scott B. MacKenzie, Richard J. Lutz, and George E. Belch, "The Role of Attitude toward the Ad as a Mediator of Advertising Effectiveness: A Test of Competing Explanations," *Journal of Marketing Research*, May 1986, pp. 130–143; Pamela M. Homer, "The Mediating Role of Attitude toward the Ad: Some Additional Evidence," *Journal of Marketing Research*, February 1990, pp. 78–86; Brown and Stayman, "Antecedents and Consequences of Attitude toward the Ad."
58. Brown and Stayman, "Antecedents and Consequences of Attitude toward the Ad."
59. Marian Chapman Burke and Julie A. Edell, "Ad Reactions over Time: Capturing Changes in the Real World," *Journal of Consumer Research*, June 1986, pp. 114–118; Amitava Chattopadhyay and Prakash Nedungadi, "Does Attitude toward the Ad Endure? The Moderating Effects of Attention and Delay," *Journal of Consumer Research*, June 1992, pp. 26–33.
60. Margaret G. Meloy, "Mood Driven Distortion of Product Information," *Journal of Consumer Research*, vol. 27, December 2000, pp. 345–359.
61. Michael J. Barone, Paul W. Miniard, and Jean B. Romeo, "The Influence of Positive Mood on Brand Extension Evaluations," *Journal of Consumer Research*, vol. 26, March 2000, pp. 386–400.
62. Rashmi Adaval, "Sometimes It Just Feels Right: The Differential Weighting of Affect-Consistent and Affect-

Inconsistent Product Information," *Journal of Consumer Research,* vol. 28, June 2001, pp. 1–17.

63. Charles S. Areni and David Kim, "The Influence of In-Store Lighting on Consumers' Examination of Merchandise in a Wine Store," *International Journal of Research in Marketing,* March 1994, pp. 117–125.
64. Ayn E. Crowley, "The Two-Dimension Impact of Color on Shopping," *Marketing Letters,* vol. 4, no. 1, 1993, pp. 59–69.
65. Julie A. Edell and Marian Chapman Burke, "The Power of Feelings in Understanding Advertising Effects," *Journal of Consumer Research,* December 1987, pp. 421–433; Douglas M. Stayman and David A. Aaker, "Are All Effects of Ad-Induced Feelings Mediated by Aad?" *Journal of Consumer Research,* December 1988, pp. 368–373; Morris B. Holbrook and Rajeev Batra, "Assessing the Role of Emotions as Mediators of Consumer Responses to Advertising," *Journal of Consumer Research,* December 1987, pp. 404–420.
66. Rajeev Batra and Michael L. Ray, "Affective Responses Mediating Acceptance of Advertising," *Journal of Consumer Research,* September 1986, pp. 234–249.
67. David A. Aaker, Douglas M. Stayman, and Michael R. Hagerty, "Warmth in Advertising: Measurement, Impact, and Sequence Effects," *Journal of Consumer Research,* March 1986, pp. 365–381.
68. Joseph A. Bellizzi, Ayn E. Crowley, and Ronald W. Hasty, "The Effects of Color in Store Design," *Journal of Retailing,* Spring 1983, pp. 21–45.
69. Jennifer Ordoñez, "Shop Till You're Cool," *Newsweek,* November 22, 2004, p. 58.
71. Curt Haugtvedt, Richard E. Petty, John T. Cacioppo, and T. Steidley, "Personality and Ad Effectiveness: Exploring the Utility of Need for Cognition," in ed. Michael J. Houston, *Advances in Consumer Research,* vol. 15 (Provo, Utah: Association for Consumer Research, 1988), pp. 209–212.
72. Susan M. Petroshius and Kenneth E. Crocker, "An Empirical Analysis of Spokesperson Characteristics on Advertisement and Product Evaluations," *Journal of the Academy of Marketing Science,* Summer 1989, pp. 217–225; Lynn R. Kahle and Pamela M. Homer, "Physical Attractiveness of the Celebrity Endorser: A Social Adaptation Perspective," *Journal of Consumer Research,* March 1985, pp. 954–961.
73. Michael A. Kamins, "An Investigation into the 'Match-Up' Hypothesis in Celebrity Advertising: When Beauty May Be Only Skin Deep," *Journal of Advertising,* vol. 19, no. 1, 1990, pp. 4–13: Marjorie J. Caballero and Paul J. Solomon, "Effects of Model Attractiveness on Sales Response," *Journal of Advertising,* vol. 13, no. 1, 1984, pp. 17–23.
74. Kahle and Homer, "Physical Attractiveness of the Celebrity Endorser"; Kathleen Debevec and Jerome B. Kernan, "More Evidence on the Effects of a Presenter's Physical Attractiveness: Some Cognitive, Affective, and Behavioral Consequences," in ed. Thomas C. Kinnear, *Advances in Consumer Research,* vol. 11 (Provo, Utah: Association for Consumer Research, 1984), pp. 127–132.; Caballero and Solomon, "Effects of Model Attractiveness on Sales Response"; Marjorie J. Caballero and William M. Pride, "Selected Effects of Salesperson Sex and Attractiveness in Direct Mail Advertising," *Journal of Marketing,* January 1984, pp. 94–100; Shelly Chaiken, "Communicator Physical Attractiveness and Persuasion," *Journal of Personality and Social Psychology,* August 1979, pp. 1387–1397; Peter H. Reingen and Jerome B. Kernan, "Social Perception and Interpersonal Influence: Some Consequences of the Physical Attractiveness Stereotype in a Personal Selling Situation," *Journal of Consumer Psychology,* vol. 2, no. 1, 1993, pp. 25–38.
75. Tommy E. Whittler and Joan Scattone Spira, "Model's Race: A Peripheral Cue in Advertising Messages?" *Journal of Consumer Psychology,* 2002, pp. 291–301.
76. Richard E. Petty, H. Rao Unnava, and Alan J. Strathman, "Theories of Attitude Change," in eds. Thomas S. Robertson and Harold H. Kassarjian, *Handbook of Consumer Behavior* (Englewood Cliffs, N.J.: Prentice-Hall, 1991), pp. 241–280; Kahle and Homer, "Physical Attractiveness of the Celebrity Endorser."
77. Ann M. Mack, "Buddy Movies," *Brandweek,* November 22, 2004, pp. 18+.
81. Sengupta, Goodstein, and Boninger, "All Cues Are Not Created Equal."
83. Claire Atkinson, "Brawny Man Now a Metrosexual," *Advertising Age,* February 16, 2004, p. 8.
84. Judith A. Garretson and Ronald W. Niedrich, "Spokes-Characters," *Journal of Advertising,* Summer 2004, pp. 25–36.
85. Marla Royne Stafford, Thomas F. Stafford, and Ellen Day, "A Contingency Approach: The Effects of Spokesperson Type and Service Type on Service Advertising Perceptions," *Journal of Advertising,* Summer 2002, pp. 17–34.
86. Greg Sandoval, "James's Value Shows in Numbers," *Washington Post,* April 16, 2004, p. D8.
87. Alan J. Bush, Craig A. Martin, and Victoria D. Bush, "Sports Celebrity Influence on the Behavioral Intentions of Generation Y," *Journal of Advertising Research,* March 2004, pp. 108+.
88. Peter Ford and Gloria Goodale, "Why Stars and Charities Need Each Other," *Christian Science Monitor,* January 13, 2005, p. 1.
89. Therese A. Louie and Carl Obermiller, "Consumer Response to a Firm's Endorser (Dis)Association Decisions," *Journal of Advertising,* Winter 2002, pp. 41–52.
90. Mitchell and Olson, "Are Product Attributes Beliefs the Only Mediator of Advertising Effects on Brand Attitudes?"; Andrew A. Mitchell, "The Effect of Verbal and Visual Components of Advertisements on Brand Attitudes and Attitude toward the Advertisement," *Journal of Consumer Research,* March 1986, pp. 12–24; Paul W. Miniard, Sunil Bhatla, Kenneth R. Lord, Peter R. Dickson, and H. Rao Unnava, "Picture-Based Persuasion Processes and the Moderating Role of Involvement," *Journal of Consumer Research,* June 1991, pp. 92–107.
91. Paul W. Miniard, Deepak Sirdeshmukh, and Daniel E. Innis, "Peripheral Persuasion and Brand Choice," *Journal of Consumer Research,* September 1992, pp. 226–239.

92. Andrea Petersen, "The Quest to Make URL's Look Cool in Ads," *Wall Street Journal*, February 26, 1997, pp. B1, B3.

95. Gordon C. Bruner, "Music, Mood, and Marketing," *Journal of Marketing*, October 1990, pp. 94–104; Gorn, "The Effects of Music in Advertising on Choice Behavior"; Judy I. Alpert and Mark I. Alpert, "Background Music as an Influence in Consumer Mood and Advertising Responses," in ed. Thomas K. Srull, *Advances in Consumer Research*, vol. 16 (Provo, Utah: Association for Consumer Research, 1989), pp. 485–491; Meryl Paula Gardner, "Mood States and Consumer Behavior: A Critical Review," *Journal of Consumer Research*, December 1985, pp. 281–300; C. Whan Park and S. Mark Young, "Consumer Response to Television Commercials: The Impact of Involvement and Background Music on Brand Attitude Formation," *Journal of Marketing Research*, February 1986, pp. 11–24.

96. Mark Alpert and Judy Alpert, "Background Music as an Influence in Consumer Mood and Advertising Responses;" *Advances in Consumer Research*, vol. 16 (Fall 1989) 485–491; Stout and Leckenby, "Let the Music Play."

97. Noel M. Murray and Sandra B. Murray, "Music and Lyrics in Commercials: A Cross-Cultural Comparison between Commercials Run in the Dominican Republic and the United States," *Journal of Advertising*, Summer 1996, pp. 51–64.

98. Marc G. Weinberger and Harlan E. Spotts, "Humor in U.S. vs. U.K. TV Advertising," *Journal of Advertising*, vol. 18, no. 2, 1989, pp. 39–44; Paul Surgi Speck, "The Humorous Message Taxonomy: A Framework for the Study of Humorous Ads," in eds. James H. Leigh and Claude R. Martin, *Current Research and Issues in Advertising* (Ann Arbor, Mich.: University of Michigan, 1991), pp. 1–44.

99. Thomas J. Madden and Marc G. Weinberger, "Humor in Advertising: A Practitioner View," *Journal of Advertising Research*, August–September 1984, pp. 23–29; Stewart and Furse, *Effective Television Advertising*; Thomas J. Madden and Marc C. Weinberger, "The Effects of Humor on Attention in Magazine Advertising," *Journal of Advertising*, vol. 1, no. 3, 1982, pp. 8–14; Marc C. Weinberger and Leland Campbell, "The Use and Impact of Humor in Radio Advertising," *Journal of Advertising Research*, December–January 1991, pp. 44–52.

100. George E. Belch and Michael A. Belch, "An Investigation of the Effects of Repetition on Cognitive and Affective Reactions to Humorous and Serious Television Commercials," in ed. Thomas C. Kinnear, *Advances in Consumer Research*, vol. 11 (Provo, Utah: Association for Consumer Research, 1984), pp. 4–10; Calvin P. Duncan and James E. Nelson, "Effects of Humor in a Radio Advertising Experiment," *Journal of Advertising*, vol. 14, no. 2, 1985, pp. 33–40, 64; Betsy D. Gelb and Charles M. Pickett, "Attitude-toward-the-Ad: Links to Humor and to Advertising Effectiveness," *Journal of Advertising*, vol. 12, no. 2, 1983, pp. 34–42; Betsy D. Gelb and George M. Zinkhan, "The Effect of Repetition on Humor in a Radio Advertising Study," *Journal of Advertising*, vol. 15, no. 2, 1986, pp. 15–20, 34.

101. Nortihiko Shirouzu, "P&G's Joy Makes an Unlikely Splash in Japan," *Wall Street Journal*, December 10, 1997, pp. B1, B8.

102. Harlan E. Spotts, Marc. G. Weinberger, and Amy L. Parsons, "Assessing the Use and Impact of Humor on Advertising Effectiveness; A Contingency Approach," *Journal of Advertising*, Fall 1997, pp. 17–32.

103. Brian Sternthal and Samuel Craig, "Humor in Advertising," *Journal of Marketing*, vol. 37, no. 4, 1973, pp. 12–18; Calvin P. Duncan, "Humor in Advertising: A Behavioral Perspective," *Journal of the Academy of Marketing Science*, vol. 7, no. 4, 1979, pp. 285–306; Weinberger and Campbell, "The Use and Impact of Humor in Radio Advertising."

104. Thomas W. Cline, Moses B. Altsech, and James J. Kellaris, "When Does Humor Enhance or Inhibit Ad Responses?" *Journal of Advertising*, Fall 2003, pp. 31–45.

105. Josephine L.C.M. Woltman Elpers, Ashesh Mukherjee, and Wayne D. Hoyer, "Humor in Television Advertising: A Moment-to-Moment Analysis," *Journal of Consumer Research*, December 2004, pp. 592–598.

106. Madden and Weinberger, "Humor in Advertising"; Weinberger and Campbell, "The Use and Impact of Humor in Radio Advertising"; Weinberger and Spotts, "Humor in U.S. vs. U.K. TV Advertising."

108. Madden and Weinberger, "Humor in Advertising"; Thomas W. Whipple and Alice E. Courtney, "How Men and Women Judge Humor: Advertising Guidelines for Action and Research," in eds. James H. Leigh and Claude R. Martin, *Current Research and Issues in Advertising* (Ann Arbor, Mich.: University of Michigan, 1981), pp. 43–56.

109. Yong Zhang, "Responses to Humorous Advertising: The Moderating Effect of Need for Cognition," *Journal of Advertising*, Spring 1996: Amitava Chattopadhyay and Kunal Basu, "Prior Brand Evaluation as a Moderator of the Effects of Humor in Advertising," *Journal of Marketing Research*, November 1989, pp. 466–476.

110. Dana L. Alden, Wayne D. Hoyer, and Chol Lee, "Identifying Global and Culture-Specific Dimensions of Humor in Advertising: A Multi-national Analysis," *Journal of Marketing*, April 1993, pp. 64–75; Dana L. Alden, Wayne D. Hoyer, Chol Lee, and Guntalee Wechasara, "The Use of Humor in Asian and Western Advertising: A Four-Country Comparison," *Journal of Asian-Pacific Business*, vol, 1, no. 2, 1995, pp. 3–23.

111. Weinberger and Spotts, "Humor in U.S. vs. U.K. TV Advertising."

114. "Godiva Launches Style Campaign," *Duty-Free International*, November 15, 2004, p. 19.

115. Nigel K. Ll. Pope, Kevin E. Voges, and Mark R. Brown, "The Effect of Provocation in the Form of Mild Erotica on Attitude to the Ad and Corporate Image," *Journal of Advertising*, Spring 2004, pp. 69–82.

116. Lawrence Soley and Gary Kurzbard, "Sex in Advertising: A Comparison of 1964 and 1984 Magazine Advertisements," *Journal of Advertising*, vol. 15, no. 3, 1986, pp. 46–54.

117. Cyndee Miller, "We've Been 'Cosbyized,'" *Marketing News*, April 16, 1990, pp. 1–2; Joshua Levine, "Marketing: Fantasy, Not Flesh," *Forbes*, January 22, 1990, pp. 118–120.
118. Vranica, "Anheuser-Busch Kicks Edgy Super Bowl Ad to Curb."
119. Robert S. Baron, "Sexual Content and Advertising Effectiveness: Comments on Belch et al. (1981) and Caccavale et al. (1981)," in ed. Andrew A. Mitchell, *Advances in Consumer Research*, vol. 9 (Ann Arbor, Mich.: Association for Consumer Research, 1982), pp. 428–430.
120. Michael S. LaTour, Robert E. Pitts, and David C. Snook-Luther, "Female Nudity, Arousal, and Ad Response: An Experimental Investigation," *Journal of Advertising*, vol. 19, no. 4, 1990, pp. 51–62.
121. Marilyn Y. Jones, Andrea J. S. Stanaland, and Betsy D. Gelb, "Beefcake and Cheesecake: Insights for Advertisers," *Journal of Advertising*, Summer 1998, pp. 33–52.
122. Rebecca Piirto, "The Romantic Sell," *American Demographics*, August 1989, pp. 38–41.
123. John Fetto, "Where's the Lovin'?" *American Demographics*, February 28, 2001.
124. Miller, "We've Been 'Cosbyized.'"
125. "Poll on Ads: Too Sexy," *Wall Street Journal*, March 8, 1993, p. B5.
126. Robert A. Peterson and Roger A. Kerin, "The Female Role in Advertisements: Some Experimental Evidence," *Journal of Marketing*, October 1977, pp. 59–63.
127. Sak Onkvisit and John J. Shaw, "A View of Marketing and Advertising Practices in Asia and Its Meaning for Marketing Managers," *Journal of Consumer Marketing*, Spring 1985, pp. 5–17.
128. Sarah Ellison, "Sex-Themed Ads Often Don't Travel Well," *Wall Street Journal*, March 31, 2000, p. B7.
129. M. Friestad and Esther Thorson, "Emotion-Eliciting Advertising: Effect on Long Term Memory and Judgment," in ed. R. J. Lutz, *Advances in Consumer Research*, vol. 13 (Provo, Utah: Association for Consumer Research, 1986), pp. 111–116.
130. Christina Cheddar Berk, "Coke to Debut 'Real' Ad on 'Idol,'" *Wall Street Journal*, January 17, 2005, p. B3; Betsy McKay, "Coke Aims to Revive 'Feel Good' Factor," *Wall Street Journal*, April 20, 2001, p. B8.
131. Barbara B. Stern, "Classical and Vignette Television Advertising Dramas: Structural Models, Formal Analysis, and Consumer Effects," *Journal of Consumer Research*, March 1994, pp. 601–615; William D. Wells, "Lectures and Dramas," in eds. Pat Cafferata and Alice M. Tybout, *Cognitive and Affective Responses to Advertising* (Lexington, Mass.: D.C. Heath, 1988); John Deighton, Daniel Romer, and Josh McQueen, "Using Dramas to Persuade," *Journal of Consumer Research*, December 1989, pp. 335–343.
132. Jennifer Edson Escalas and Barbara B. Stern, "Sympathy and Empathy: Emotional Responses to Advertising Dramas," *Journal of Consumer Research*, March 2003, pp. 566+.
133. Eleftheria Parpis, "American Theater," *Adweek*, November 29, 2004, pp. 14+.
134. Marvin E. Goldberg and Gerald J. Gorn, "Happy and Sad TV Programs: How They Affect Reactions to Commercials," *Journal of Consumer Research*, December 1987, pp. 387–403; John P. Murray Jr. and Peter A. Dacin, "Cognitive Moderators of Negative-Emotion Effects: Implications for Understanding Media Context," *Journal of Consumer Research*, March 1996, pp. 439–447.
135. John P. Murray, John L. Lastovicka, and Surendra Singh, "Feeling and Liking Responses to Television Programs: An Examination of Two Explanations for Media-Context Effects," *Journal of Consumer Research*, March 1992, pp. 441–451.
136. S. N. Singh and Gilbert A. Churchill, "Arousal and Advertising Effectiveness," *Journal of Advertising*, vol. 16, no. 1, 1987, pp. 4–10.
137. Mark A. Pavelchak, John H. Antil, and James M. Munch, "The Super Bowl: An Investigation into the Relationship among Program Context, Emotional Experience, and Ad Recall," *Journal of Consumer Research*, December 1988, pp. 360–367.
138. Sally Beatty, "Madison Avenue Should Rethink Television Violence, Study Finds," *Wall Street Journal*, December 1, 1998, p. B8.

CHAPTER 8

3. G. Sperling, "The Information Available in Brief Visual Presentations," *Psychological Monographs*, vol. 74, 1960, pp. 1–25; U. Neisser, *Cognitive Psychology* (New York: Appleton-Century-Crofts, 1967).
4. R. N. Haber, "The Impending Demise of the Icon: A Critique of the Concept of Iconic Storage in Visual Information Processing," *The Behavioral and Brain Sciences*, March 1983, pp. 1–54.
5. William James (1890) as described in Henry C. Ellis and R. Reed Hunt, *Fundamentals of Human Memory and Cognition* (Dubuque, Iowa: William C. Brown, 1989), pp. 65–66.
6. Nader T. Tavassoli and Jin Ki. Han, "Scripted Thought: Processing Korean Hancha and Hangul in a Multimedia Context," *Journal of Consumer Research*, December 2001, pp. 482–493.
7. Deborah J. MacInnis and Linda L. Price, "The Role of Imagery in Information Processing: Review and Extensions," *Journal of Consumer Research*, March 1987, pp. 473–491.
8. Allan Paivio, "Perceptual Comparisons through the Mind's Eye," *Memory and Cognition*, November 1975, pp. 635–647; Stephen M. Kosslyn, "The Medium and the Message in Mental Imagery: A Theory," *Psychological Review*, January 1981, pp. 46–66; MacInnis and Price, "The Role of Imagery in Information Processing."
9. Morris B. Holbrook and Elizabeth C. Hirschman, "The Experiential Aspects of Consumption: Consumer Fantasies, Feelings, and Fun," *Journal of Consumer Research*, September 1982, pp. 132–140; MacInnis and Price, "The Role of Imagery in Information Processing"; Alan Richardson, "Imagery: Definitions and Types," in ed. Aness Sheikh, *Imagery: Current Theory, Research, and Application* (New York: Wiley, 1983), pp. 3–42.

10. Martin S. Lindauer, "Imagery and the Arts," in ed. Aness Sheikh, *Imagery: Current Theory, Research, and Application* (New York: Wiley, 1983), pp. 468–506.

12. E. Tulving, "Episodic and Semantic Memory," in eds. E. Tulving and W. Donaldson, *Organization and Memory* (New York: Academic Press, 1972), pp. 381–403.

13. Hans Baumgartner, Mita Sujan, and James R. Bettman, "Autobiographical Memories, Affect, and Consumer Information Processing," *Journal of Consumer Psychology*, vol. 1, no. 1, 1992, pp. 53–82.

14. Morris B. Holbrook, "Nostalgia and Consumer Preferences: Some Emerging Patterns of Consumer Tastes," *Journal of Consumer Research*, September 1993, pp. 245–256; Morris B. Holbrook and Robert M. Schindler, "Echoes of the Dear Departed Past: Some Work in Progress on Nostalgia," in eds. Rebecca H. Holman and Michael R. Solomon, *Advances in Consumer Research*, vol. 18 (Provo, Utah: Association for Consumer Research, 1991), pp. 330–333.

15. Jack Neff, "Grandma's Hobby Now a Sizzling Trend," *Advertising Age*, July 14, 2003, pp. 3, 25.

16. Annamma Joy and Ruby Roy Dholakia, "Remembrances of Things Past: The Meaning of Home and Possessions of Indian Professionals in Canada," in ed. Floyd W. Rudmin, *To Have Possessions: A Handbook on Ownership and Property, Journal of Social Behavior and Personality* [Special Issue], November 1991, pp. 385–402; Melanie Wallendorf and Eric J. Arnould, "My Favorite Things: A Cross-Cultural Inquiry into Object Attachment, Possessiveness, and Social Linkage," *Journal of Consumer Research*, March 1988, pp. 531–547.

17. Kathryn A. Braun, "Postexperience Advertising Effects on Consumer Memory," *Journal of Consumer Research*, March 1999, pp. 319–334.

18. R. C. Atkinson and R. M. Shiffrin, "Human Memory: A Proposed System and Its Control Processes," in eds. K. W. Spence and J. T. Spence, *The Psychology of Learning and Motivation: Advances in Theory and Research*, vol. 2 (New York: Academic Press, 1968), pp. 89–195.

19. George A. Miller, "The Magical Number Seven, Plus or Minus Two: Some Limits on Our Capacity for Processing Information," *Psychological Review*, March 1956, pp. 81–97; James N. McGregor, "Short-Term Memory Capacity: Limitations or Optimization?" *Psychological Review*, January 1987, pp. 107–108.

20. F. I. M. Craik and R. S. Lockhart, "Levels of Processing: A Framework for Memory Research," *Verbal Learning and Verbal Behavior*, December 1972, pp. 671–684.

21. Dilip Soman, "Effects of Payment Mechanism on Spending Behavior: The Role of Rehearsal and Immediacy of Payments," *Journal of Consumer Research*, vol. 27, March 2001, pp. 460–474.

22. Alan G. Sawyer, "The Effects of Repetition: Conclusions and Suggestions about Experimental Laboratory Research," in eds. G. David Hughes and Michael L. Ray, *Buyer/Consumer Information Processing* (Chapel Hill, N.C.: University of North Carolina Press, 1974), pp. 190–219; George E. Belch, "The Effects of Television Commercial Repetition on Cognitive Response and Message Acceptance," *Journal of Consumer Research*, June 1982, pp. 56–66; H. Rao Unnava and Robert E. Burnkrant, "Effects of Repeating Varied Ad Executions on Brand Name Memory," *Journal of Marketing Research*, November 1991, pp. 406–416; Murphy S. Sewall and Dan Sarel, "Characteristics of Radio Commercials and Their Recall Effectiveness," *Journal of Marketing*, January 1986, pp. 52–60.

23. Pui-Wing Tam, "PalmOne's Ads to Plaster Airports," *Wall Street Journal*, June 9, 2004, p. B6.

25. Chris Janiszewski, Hayden Noel, and Alan G. Sawyer, "Re-Inquiries: A Meta-Analysis of the Spacing Effect in Verbal Learning: Implications for Research on Advertising Repetition and Consumer Memory," *Journal of Consumer Research*, June 2003, pp. 138+.

26. Sharmistha Law, "Can Repeating a Brand Claim Lead to Memory Confusion? The Effects of Claim Similarity and Concurrent Repetition," *Journal of Marketing Research*, August 2002, pp. 366–378.

27. Susan E. Heckler and Terry L. Childers, "The Role of Expectancy and Relevancy in Memory for Verbal and Visual Information: What Is Incongruency?" *Journal of Consumer Research*, March 1992, pp. 475–492.

28. Sally Beatty, "Ogilvy's TV-Ad Study Stresses 'Holding Power' Instead of Ratings," *Wall Street Journal*, June 4, 1999, p. B2.

29. Catherine A. Cole and Michael J. Houston, "Encoding and Media Effects on Consumer Learning Deficiencies in the Elderly," *Journal of Marketing Research*, February 1987, pp. 55–64; Deborah Roedder John and John C. Whitney Jr., "The Development of Consumer Knowledge in Children: A Cognitive Structure Approach," *Journal of Consumer Research*, March 1986, pp. 406–418.

30. H. Shanker Krishnan, "A Process Analysis of the Effects of Humorous Advertising Executions on Brand Claims Memory," *Journal of Consumer Psychology*, 2003, pp. 230–245.

31. Gabriel Biehal and Dipankar Chakravarti, "Consumers' Use of Memory and External Information in Choice: Macro and Micro Perspectives," *Journal of Consumer Research*, March 1986, pp. 382–405; John G. Lynch, Howard Marmorstein, and Michael F. Weigold, "Choices from Sets Including Remembered Brands: Use of Recalled Attributes and Prior Overall Evaluations," *Journal of Consumer Research*, September 1988, pp. 225–233; Valerie S. Folkes, "The Availability Heuristic and Perceived Risk," *Journal of Consumer Research*, June 1988, pp. 13–23.

32. A. M. Collins and E. F. Loftus, "A Spreading Activation Theory of Semantic Processing," *Psychological Review*, November 1975, pp. 407–428; Lawrence W. Barsalou, *Cognitive Psychology: An Overview for Cognitive Scientists* (Hillsdale, N.J.: Lawrence Erlbaum, 1991); John R. Anderson, *Cognitive Psychology and Its Implications* (New York: W. H. Freeman, 1990); Michael Pham and Gita Venkataramani Johar, "Contingent Processes of Source Identification," *Journal of Consumer Research*, December 1997, pp. 249–265.

34. Joseph W. Alba and J. Wesley Hutchinson, "Dimensions of Consumer Expertise," *Journal of Consumer Research*, March 1987, pp. 411–454.

35. David C. Riccio, Vita C. Rabinowitz, and Shari Axelrod, "Memory: When Less Is More," *American Psychologist*, November 1994, pp. 917–926.

36. Anthony Pratkanis, Anthony G. Greenwald, M. R. Leipe, and M. Hans Baumgartner, "In Search of Reliable Persuasion Effects: III. The Sleeper Effect Is Dead: Long Live the Sleeper Effect," *Journal of Personality and Social Psychology*, February 1988, pp. 203–218.

37. Raymond Burke and Thomas K. Srull, "Competitive Interference and Consumer Memory for Advertisements," *Journal of Consumer Research*, June 1988, pp. 55–68; Kevin Keller, "Memory and Evaluation Effects in Competitive Advertising Environments," *Journal of Consumer Research*, March 1991, pp. 463–476; Rik G. M. Pieters and Tammo H. A. Bijmolt, "Consumer Memory for Television Advertising: A Field Study of Duration, Serial Position and Competition Effects," *Journal of Consumer Research*, March 1997, pp. 362–372; Tom J. Brown and Michael L. Rothschild, "Reassessing the Impact of Television Advertising Clutter," *Journal of Consumer Research*, June 1993, pp. 138–147; Robert J. Kent and Chris T. Allen, "Competitive Interference Effects in Consumer Memory for Advertising: The Role of Brand Familiarity," *Journal of Marketing*, July 1994, pp. 97–105; H. Rao Unnava and Deepak Sirdeshmukh, "Reducing Competitive Ad Interference," *Journal of Marketing Research*, August 1994, pp. 403–411.

38. Anand Kumar and Shanker Krishnan, "Memory Interference in Advertising: A Replication and Extension," *Journal of Consumer Research*, March 2004, pp. 602–61; Anand Kumar, "Interference Effects of Contextual Cues in Advertisements on Memory for Ad Content," *Journal of Consumer Psychology*, vol. 9, no. 3, 2000, pp. 155–166.

39. Robert D. Jewell and H. Rao Unnava, "When Competitive Interference Can Be Beneficial," *Journal of Consumer Research*, September 2003, pp. 283–291.

40. David Luna and Laura A. Peracchio, "Moderators of Language Effects in Advertising to Bilinguals: A Psycholinguistic Approach," *Journal of Consumer Research*, September 2001, pp. 284+.

41. Joseph W. Alba and Amitava Chattopadhyay, "Effects of Context and Part-Category Cues on Recall of Competing Brands," *Journal of Marketing Research*, August 1985, pp. 340–349; Joseph W. Alba and Amitava Chattopadhyay, "Salience Effects in Brand Recall," *Journal of Marketing Research*, November 1986, pp. 363–369; Manoj Hastak and Anusre Mitra, "Facilitating and Inhibiting Effects of Brand Cues on Recall, Consideration Set, and Choice," *Journal of Business Research*, October 1996, pp. 121–126.

42. Burke and Srull, "Competitive Interference and Consumer Memory for Advertising;" Rik Pieters and Tammo H.A. Bijmolt, "Consumer Memory for Television Advertising: A Field Study of Duration, Serial Position, and Competition Effects," *Journal of Consumer Research*, March 1997, pp. 362–372.

43. Elizabeth F. Loftus, "When a Lie Becomes Memory's Truth: Memory and Distortion after Exposure to Misinformation," *Current Directions in Psychological Science*, August 1992, pp. 121–123.

44. Larry Percy and John R. Rossiter, "A Model of Brand Awareness and Brand Attitude in Advertising Strategies," *Psychology and Marketing*, July–August 1992, pp. 263–274.

46. John Furniss, "Rating American Banks in Japan: Survey Shows Importance of Image," *International Advertiser*, April 1986, pp. 22–23.

47. Bonnie Tsui, "Bowl Poll: Ads Don't Mean Sales," *Advertising Age*, February 5, 2001, p. 33.

48. Marc Vanhuele and Xavier Drèze, "Measuring the Price Knowledge Shoppers Bring to the Store," *Journal of Marketing*, October 2002, pp. 72–85.

49. H. Shanker Krishnan and Dipankar Chakravarti, "Memory Measures for Pretesting Advertisements: An Integrative Conceptual Framework and a Diagnostic Template," *Journal of Consumer Psychology*, vol. 8, no. 1, 1999, pp. 1–37.

50. Angela Y. Lee, "Effects of Implicit Memory on Memory-Based versus Stimulus-Based Brand Choice," *Journal of Marketing Research*, November 2002, pp. 440–454.

51. Susan T. Fiske and Shelley E. Taylor, *Social Cognition* (New York: McGraw-Hill, 1991).

52. Stewart Shapiro and Mark T. Spence, "Factors Affecting Encoding, Retrieval, and Alignment of Sensory Attributes in a Memory-Based Brand Choice Task," *Journal of Consumer Research*, March 2002, pp. 603–617.

53. Joseph W. Alba, J. Wesley Hutchinson, and John G. Lynch Jr., "Memory and Decision Making," in eds. Thomas S. Robertson and Harold Kassarjian, *Handbook of Consumer Behavior* (Englewood Cliffs, N.J.: Prentice-Hall, 1991), pp. 1–49.

54. Rik G. M. Pieters and Tammo H. A. Bijmolt, "Consumer Memory for Television Advertising: A Field Study of Duration, Serial Position and Competition Effects," *Journal of Consumer Research*, March 1997, pp. 362–372; David W. Stewart and David H. Furse, *Effective Television Advertising: A Study of 1000 Commercials* (Cambridge, Mass.: Marketing Science Institute, 1986); Pamela Homer, "Ad Size as an Indicator of Perceived Advertising Costs and Effort: The Effects on Memory and Perceptions," *Journal of Advertising*, Winter 1995, pp. 1–12.

55. Frank R. Kardes and Gurumurthy Kalyanaram, "Order of Entry Effects on Consumer Memory and Judgment: An Information Integration Perspective," *Journal of Marketing Research*, August 1992, pp. 343–357; Frank Kardes, Murali Chandrashekaran, and Ronald Dornoff, "Brand Retrieval, Consideration Set Composition, Consumer Choice, and the Pioneering Advantage," *Journal of Consumer Research*, June 1993, pp. 62–75; Frank H. Alpert and Michael A. Kamins, "An Empirical Investigation of Consumer Memory, Attitude, and Perceptions toward Pioneer and Follower Brands," *Journal of Marketing*, October 1995, pp. 34–44.

56. Jennifer Galloway, "The Franchise Fernandez Built," *Latin Finance*, September 2003, pp. 23+; Claudia Penteado, "Coca-Cola Expects to Grow by 7% in Brazil," *Advertising Age*, May 16, 2001, *www.adage.com*; Hillary Chura and Richard Linnett, "Coca-Cola Readies Massive Global Campaign," *Advertising Age*, April 2, 2001, *www.adage.com*.

57. Sridar Samu, H. Shankar Krishnan, and Robert E. Smith, "Using Advertising Alliances for New Product Introduction: Interactions between Product Complementarity and Promotional Strategies," *Journal of Marketing*, January 1999, pp. 57–74.
58. Gita Venkatatarmani Johar and Michel Tuan Pham, "Relatedness, Prominence, and Constructive Sponsor Identification," *Journal of Marketing Research*, vol. 36, August 1999, pp. 299–312.
59. Rex Briggs and Nigel Hollis, "Advertising on the Web: Is There Response before Click-Through," *Journal of Advertising Research*, March–April 1997, pp. 33–45.
60. Michael Pham and Gita Venkataramani Johar, "Contingent Processes of Source Identification," *Journal of Consumer Research*, December 1997, pp. 249–265.
61. Deborah D. Heisley and Sidney J. Levy, "Autodriving: A Photoelicitation Technique," *Journal of Consumer Research*, December 1991, pp. 257–272.
62. Nader T. Tavassoli and Yih Hwai Lee, "The Differential Interaction of Auditory and Visual Advertising Elements with Chinese and English," *Journal of Marketing Research*, November 2003, pp. 468–480.
63. Joan Meyers-Levy, "The Influence of a Brand Name's Association Set Size and Word Frequency on Brand Memory," *Journal of Consumer Research*, September 1989, pp. 197–207; Alba and Hutchinson, "Dimensions of Consumer Expertise."
64. Tina M. Lowrey, L. J. Shrum, and Tony M. Dubitsky, "The Relation Between Brand-Name Linguistic Characteristics and Brand-Name Memory," *Journal of Advertising*, Fall 2003, pp. 7–17.
65. Jaideep Sengupta and Gerald J. Gorn, "Absence Makes the Mind Grow Sharper: Effects of Element Omission on Subsequent Recall," *Journal of Marketing Research*, May 2002, pp. 186–201.
66. Terry L. Childers and Jeffrey Jass, "All Dressed Up with Something to Say: Effects of Typeface Semantic Associations on Brand Perceptions and Consumer Memory," *Journal of Consumer Psychology*, 2002, pp. 93–106.
67. Cathy J. Cobb and Wayne D. Hoyer, "The Influence of Advertising at Moment of Brand Choice," *Journal of Advertising*, December 1986, pp. 5–27.
68. Keller, "Memory Factors in Advertising," *Journal of Consumer Research*, December 1987, pp. 316–333. J. Wesley Hutchinson and Daniel L. Moore, "Issues Surrounding the Examination of Delay Effects of Advertising," in ed. Thomas C. Kinnear, *Advances in Consumer Research*, vol. 11 (Provo, Utah: Association for Consumer Research, 1984), pp. 650–655.
69. Carolyn Costley, Samar Das, and Merrie Brucks, "Presentation Medium and Spontaneous Imaging Effects on Consumer Memory," *Journal of Consumer Psychology*, vol. 6, no. 3, 1997, pp. 211–231; David W. Sewart and Girish N. Punj, "Effects of Using a Nonverbal (Musical) Cue on Recall and Playback of Television Advertising: Implications for Advertising Tracking," *Journal of Business Research*, May 1998, pp. 39–51.
70. Cole and Houston, "Encoding and Media Effects on Consumer Learning Deficiencies in the Elderly"; Sharmistha Law, Scott A. Hawkins, and Fergus I. M. Craik, "Repetition-Induced Belief in the Elderly: Rehabilitating Age-Related Memory Deficits," *Journal of Consumer Research*, September 1998, pp. 91–107.
71. H Rao Unnava and Robert E. Burnkrant, "An Imagery-Processing View of the Role of Pictures in Print Advertisements," *Journal of Marketing Research*, May 1991, pp. 226–231.
72. Alice M. Isen, "Some Ways in Which Affect Influences Cognitive Processes: Implications for Advertising and Consumer Behavior," in eds. Alice M. Tybout and P. Cafferata, *Advertising and Consumer Psychology* (Lexington, Mass.: Lexington Books, 1989), pp. 91–117; see also Patricia A. Knowles, Stephen J. Grove, and W. Jeffrey Burroughs, "An Experimental Examination of Mood Effects on Retrieval and Evaluation of Advertisement and Brand Information," *Journal of the Academy of Marketing Science*, Spring 1993, pp. 135–143; Gordon H. Bower, "Mood and Memory," *American Psychologist*, February 1981, pp. 129–148; Gordon H. Bower, Stephen Gilligan, and Kenneth Montiero, "Selectivity of Learning Caused by Affective States," *Journal of Experimental Psychology: General*, December 1981, pp. 451–473; Alice M. Isen, Thomas Shalker, Margaret Clark, and Lynn Karp, "Affect, Accessibility of Material in Memory and Behavior: A Cognitive Loop?" *Journal of Personality and Social Psychology*, 1978, pp. 1–12.
73. Alice M. Isen, "Toward Understanding the Role of Affect in Cognition," in eds. Robert S. Wyer and Thomas K. Srull, *Handbook of Social Cognition* (Hillsdale, N J.: Lawrence Erlbaum, 1984), pp. 179–236.
74. Alice M. Isen, "Some Ways in Which Affect Influences Cognitive Processes: Implications for Advertising and Consumer Behavior," in eds. Patricia Cafferata and Alice M. Tybout, *Cognitive and Affective Responses to Advertising* (Lexington, Mass.: Lexington Books, 1989), pp. 91–118.
75. Angela Y. Lee and Brian Sternthal, "The Effects of Positive Mood on Memory," *Journal of Consumer Research*, vol. 26, September 1999, pp. 115–127.
76. Alba and Hutchinson, "Dimensions of Consumer Expertise."
77. Sally Goll Beatty, "Networks Nix Ads Featuring Rival TV Stars," *Wall Street Journal*, February 21, 1997, pp. B1, B6.

CHAPTER 9

5. Nat Ives, "Selling Caution or Hedonism in a World of No Smoking," *New York Times*, July 7, 2004, p. C1; Bob Garfield, "Softly Lit or Blunt, 'Less Toxic' Cigarette Ads Hint At Health," *Advertising Age*, November 12, 2001, p. 58.
7. Joseph W. Alba, J. Wesley Hutchinson, and John G. Lynch, "Memory and Decision Making," in eds. Thomas C. Roberton and Harold H. Kassarjian, *Handbook of Consumer Behavior* (Englewood Cliffs, N.J.: Prentice Hall, 1991).
8. John R. Hauser and Birger Wernerfelt, "An Evaluation Cost Model of Consideration Sets," *Journal of Consumer Research*, March 1990, pp. 393–408.
9. "Multinationals Tap Into the Bottled Water Market," *Marketing Week*, June 7, 2001, *www.mad.co.uk/mw*.

12. Kalpesh Kaushik Desai and Wayne D. Hoyer, "Descriptive Characteristics of Memory-Based Consideration Sets: Influence of Usage Occasion Frequency and Usage Location Familiarity," *Journal of Consumer Research*, vol. 27, December 2000, pp. 309–323.

13. Prakash Nedungadi and J. Wesley Hutchinson, "The Prototypicality of Brands: Relationships with Brand Awareness, Preference, and Usage," in eds. Elizabeth C. Hirschman and Morris B. Holbrook, *Advances in Consumer Research*, vol. 12 (Provo, Utah: Association for Consumer Research, 1985), pp. 498–503; Prakash Nedungadi, "Recall and Consumer Consideration Sets: Influencing Choice without Altering Brand Evaluations," *Journal of Consumer Research*, December 1990, pp. 263–276.

14. Alba, Hutchinson, and Lynch, "Memory and Decision Making."

15. Nedungadi and Hutchinson, "The Prototypicality of Brands"; James Ward and Barbara Loken, "The Quintessential Snack Food: Measurement of Product Prototypes," in ed. Richard J. Lutz, *Advances in Consumer Research*, vol. 13 (Provo, Utah: Association for Consumer Research, 1986), pp. 126–131.

17. Siew Meng Leong, Swee Hoon Ang, and Lai Leng Tham, "Increasing Brand Name Recall in Print Advertising among Asian Consumers," *Journal of Advertising*, Summer 1996, pp. 65–82.

18. Stewart Shapiro, Deborah J. MacInnis, and Susan E. Heckler, "The Effects of Incidental Ad Exposure on the Formation of Consideration Sets," *Journal of Consumer Research*, June 1997, pp. 94–104.

19. Alba, Hutchinson, and Lynch, "Memory and Decision Making."

20. S. Ratneshwar and Allan D. Shocker, "Substitution in Use and the Role of Usage Context in Product Category Structures," *Journal of Marketing Research*, August 1991, pp. 281–295.

22. Nedungadi and Hutchinson, "The Prototypicality of Brands"; Ward and Loken, "The Quintessential Snack Food."

23. Julian E. Barnes, "The Making (Or Possible Breaking) of a Megabrand," *New York Times*, July 22, 2001, sec. 3, pp. 1, 7.

24. Olga Kharif, "Getting a Grip on Consumer Tastes," *Business Week*, July 16, 2001, p. 12.

25. Gabriel Biehal and Dipankar Chakravarti, "Consumers' Use of Memory and External Information in Choice: Macro and Micro Perspectives," *Journal of Consumer Research*, March 1986, pp. 382–405.

26. Gabriel Biehal and Dipankar Chakravarti, "Information Accessibility as a Moderator of Consumer Choice," *Journal of Consumer Research*, June 1983, pp. 1–14.

27. Michaela Waenke, Gerd Bohner, and Andreas Jurkowitsch, "There Are Many Reasons to Drive a BMW: Does Imagined Ease of Argument Generation Influence Attitudes?" *Journal of Consumer Research*, September 1997, pp. 170–177.

28. Meryl Paula Gardner, "Advertising Effects on Attributes Recalled and Criteria Used for Brand Evaluations," *Journal of Consumer Research*, December 1983, pp. 310–318; Scott B. MacKenzie, "The Role of Attention in Mediating the Effect of Advertising on Attribute Importance," *Journal of Consumer Research*, September 1986, pp. 174–195; Priya Raghubir and Geeta Menon, "AIDS and Me, Never the Twain Shall Meet: The Effects of Information Accessibility on Judgments of Risk and Advertising Effectiveness," *Journal of Consumer Research*, June 1998, pp. 52–63.

29. Fellman and Lynch, "Self-Generated Validity and Other Effects of Measurement;" John G. Lynch, Howard Marmorstein, and Michael F. Weigold, "Choices from Sets Including Remembered Brands: Use of Recalled Attributes and Prior Overall Evaluations," *Journal of Consumer Research*, September 1988, pp. 169–184.

30. Carolyn L. Costley and Merrie Brucks, "Selective Recall and Information Use in Consumer Preferences," *Journal of Consumer Research*, March 1992, pp. 464–474; Geeta Menon, Priya Raghubit, and Norbert Schwarz, "Behavioral Frequency Judgments: An Accessibility-Diagnosticity Framework," *Journal of Consumer Research*, September 1995, pp. 212–228.

31. Paul M. Herr, Frank R. Kardes, and John Kim, "Effects of Word-of-Mouth and Product-Attribute Information on Persuasion: An Accessibility-Diagnosticity Perspective," *Journal of Consumer Research*, March 1991, pp. 454–462.

32. Yumiko Ono, "Anheuser Plays on Tipsiness to Sell Japan Strong Brew," *Wall Street Journal*, November 17, 1998, pp. B1, B4.

33. Walter Kintsch and .Tuen A. Van Dyk, "Toward a Model of Text Comprehension and Production," *Psychological Review*, September 1978, pp. 363–394; S. Ratneshwar, David G. Mick, and Gail Reitinger, "Selective Attention in Consumer Information Processing: The Role of Chronically Accessible Attributes," in eds. Marvin E. Goldberg, Gerald Gorn, and Richard W. Pollay, *Advances in Consumer Research*, vol. 17 (Provo, Utah: Association for Consumer Research, 1990), pp. 547–553.

34. Jacob Jacoby, Tracy Troutman, Alfred Kuss, and David Mazursky, "Experience and Expertise in Complex Decision Making," in ed. Richard J. Lutz, *Advances in Consumer Research*, vol. 13 (Provo, Utah: Association for Consumer Research, 1986), pp. 469–475.

35. Stewart Shapiro and Mark T. Spence, "Factors Affecting Encoding, Retrieval, and Alignment of Sensory Attributes in a Memory-Based Brand Choice Task," *Journal of Consumer Research*, March 2002, pp. 603+.

36. Gardner, "Advertising Effects on Attributes Recalled"; Mackenzie, "The Role of Attention in Mediating the Effect of Advertising."

37. Vanessa O'Connell, "Labels Suggesting the Benefits of Drinking Wine Look Likely," *Wall Street Journal*, October 26, 1998, pp. B1, B3.

38. Mark I. Alpert, "Identification of Determinant Attributes: A Comparison of Methods," *Journal of Marketing Research*, May 1971, pp. 184–191.

40. "Canon PowerShot SD20 Digital Elph," *PC Magazine*, December 20, 2004, *www.pcmagazine.com;* Emily Nelson, "Camera Makers Focus on Tiny and Cute," *Wall Street Journal*, March 14, 1997, pp. B1, B2.

41. Jolita Kiselius and Brian Sternthal, "Examining the Vividness Controversy: An Availability-Valence Interpretation," *Journal of Consumer Research*, March 1986, pp. 418–431; Herr, Kardes, and Kim, "Effects of Word-of-Mouth and Product-Attribute Information."
42. Punam Anand Keller and Lauren G. Block, "Vividness Effects: A Resource-Matching Perspective," *Journal of Consumer Research*, December 1997, pp. 295–304.
43. Diane Brady, "Cult Brands," *Business Week*, August 2, 2004, pp. 64–67.
44. Reid Hastie and Bernadette Park, "The Relationship between Memory and Judgment Depends on Whether the Judgment Task Is Memory-Based or On-Line," *Psychological Review*, June 1986, pp. 258–268; Barbara Loken and Ronald Hoverstad, "Relationships between Information Recall and Subsequent Attitudes: Some Exploratory Findings," *Journal of Consumer Research*, September 1985, pp. 155–168.
45. Biehal and Chakravarti, "Consumers' Use of Memory and External Information in Choice"; Jong-Won Park and Manoj Hastak, "Memory-Based Product Judgments: Effects of Involvement at Encoding and Retrieval," *Journal of Consumer Research*, December 1994, pp. 534–547.
46. Zeynep Gürhan-Canli, "The Effect of Expected Variability of Product Quality and Attribute Uniqueness on Family Brand Evaluations," *Journal of Consumer Research*, June 2003, pp. 105–114.
47. Hans Baumgartner, Mita Sujan, and James R. Bettman, "Autobiographical Memories, Affect, and Consumer Information Processing," *Journal of Consumer Psychology*, vol. 1, no. 1, 1992, pp. 53–82.
48. Rodney Ho, "Bowling for Dollars, Alleys Try Updating," *Wall Street Journal*, January 24, 1997, pp. B1, B2.
49. Elizabeth Cowley and Eunika Janus, "Not Necessarily Better, But Certainly Different: A Limit to the Advertising Misinformation Effect on Memory," *Journal of Consumer Research*, June 2004, pp. 229–235.
50. Dave Barrager, "Retro Power," *Brandweek*, March 15, 1993, pp. 14–17.
51. Fara Warner, "The Place to Be This Year," *Brandweek*, November 30, 1992, p. 24.
52. Michael J. Houston, Terry L. Childers, and Susan E. Heckler, "Picture-Word Consistency and the Elaborative Processing of Advertisements," *Journal of Marketing Research*, November 1987, pp. 359–369.
53. Joseph W. Alba and Amitava Chattopadhyay, "Salience Effects in Brand Recall," *Journal of Marketing Research*, November 1986, pp. 363–369; Kiselius and Sternthal, "Examining the Vividness Controversy."
54. Alba and Chattopadhyay, "Salience Effects in Brand Recall"; Kiselius and Sternthal, "Examining the Vividness Controversy."
55. Gordon H. Bower, "Mood and Memory," *American Psychologist*, February 1981, pp. 129–148; Gordon H. Bower, Stephen Gilligan, and Kenneth Montiero, "Selectivity of Learning Caused by Affective States," *Journal of Experimental Psychology: General*, December 1981, pp. 451–473; Alice M. Isen, Thomas Shalker, Margaret Clark, and Lynn Karp, "Affect, Accessibility of Material in Memory and Behavior: A Cognitive Loop?" *Journal of Personality and Social Psychology*, January 1978, pp. 1–12.
56. "Microsoft Dismisses British Objections to Anti-Linux Ads," *eWeek*, August 24, 2004, *www.week.com*.
59. Peter H. Bloch, Daniel L. Sherrell, and Nancy M. Ridgway, "Consumer Search: An Extended Framework," *Journal of Consumer Research*, June 1986, pp. 119–126.
60. Sharon E. Beatty and Scott M. Smith, "External Search Effort: An Investigation across Several Product Categories," *Journal of Consumer Research*, June 1987, pp. 83–95.
61. Beatty and Smith, "External Search Effort."
62. Lorraine Mirabella, "As Shoppers Change Ways, Retailers Lag," *Baltimore Sun*, January 21, 2001, p. 1D.
63. David F. Midgley, "Patterns of Interpersonal Information Seeking for the Purchase of a Symbolic Product," *Journal of Marketing Research*, February 1983, pp. 74–83.
65. Denver D'Rozario and Susan P. Douglas, "Effect of Assimilation on Prepurchase External Information-Search Tendencies," *Journal of Consumer Psychology*, vol. 8, no. 2, 1999, pp. 187–209.
66. Niranjan J. Raman, "A Qualitative Investigation of Web-Browsing Behavior," in eds. Merrie Brucks and Deborah J. MacInnis, *Advances in Consumer Research*, vol. 24 (Provo, Utah: Association for Consumer Research, 1997), pp. 511–516.
67. Sally J. McMillan and Jang-Sun Hwang, "Measures of Perceived Interactivity: An Exploration of the Role of Direction of Communication, User Control, and Time in Shaping Perceptions of Interactivity," *Journal of Advertising*, Fall 2002, pp. 29–42; Yuping Liu and L.J. Shrum, "What Is Interactivity and Is It Always Such a Good Thing? Implications of Definition, Person, and Situation for the Influence of Interactivity on Advertising Effectiveness," *Journal of Advertising*, Winter 2002, pp. 53–64.
68. Abeer Y. Hoque and Gerald L. Lohse, "An Information Search Cost Perspective for Designing Interfaces for Electronic Commerce," *Journal of Marketing Research*, vol. 36, August 1999, pp. 387–394.
69. Charla Mathwick and Edward Rigdon, "Play, Flow, and the Online Search Experience," *Journal of Consumer Research*, September 2004, pp. 324–332.
70. Andrew D. Gershoff, Susan M. Broniarczyk, and Patricia M. West, "Recommendation or Evaluation? Task Sensitivity in Information Source Selection," *Journal of Consumer Research*, December 2001, pp. 418+.
71. Alan D.J. Cooke, Harish Sujan, Mita Sujan, and Barton A. Weitz, "Marketing the Unfamiliar: The Role of Context and Item-Specific Information in Electronic Agent Recommendations," *Journal of Marketing Research*, November 2002, pp. 499+.
72. Nicholas H. Lurie, "Decision Making in Information-Rich Environments: The Role of Information Structure," *Journal of Consumer Research*, March 2004, pp. 473–486.
73. Ross Kerber, "Direct Hit Uses Popularity to Narrow Internet Searches," *Wall Street Journal*, July 2, 1998, p. B4.

74. Michelle Slatalla, "Price-Comparison Sites Do the Legwork," *New York Times*, February 3, 2005, p. G3.

75. Robyn Weisman, "Technologies That Changed 2001," *Newsfactor.com*, January 3, 2002, *www.newsfactor.com/perl/story/?id=15569;* Sally Beatty, "IBM HotMedia Aims to Speed Online Ads," *Wall Street Journal*, October 27, 1998, p. B8.

76. Hairong Li, Terry Daugherty, and Frank Biocca, "Impact of 3-D Advertising on Product Knowledge, Brand Attitude, and Purchase Intention: The Mediating Role of Presence," *Journal of Advertising*, Fall 2002, pp. 43–57.

78. Eileen Fischer, Julia Bristor, and Brenda Gainer, "Creating or Escaping Community? An Exploratory Study of Internet Consumers' Behaviors," in eds. Kim P. Corfman and John G. Lynch, *Advances in Consumer Research*, vol. 23 (Provo, Utah: Association for Consumer Research, 1996), pp. 178–182; John Buskin, "Tales from the Front," *Wall Street Journal*, December 7, 1998, p. R6.

79. Neil A. Granitz and James C. Ward, "Virtual Community: A Sociocognitive Analysis," in eds. Kim P. Corfman and John G. Lynch, *Advances in Consumer Research*, vol. 23 (Provo, Utah: Association for Consumer Research, 1996), pp. 161–166.

80. Brady, "Cult Brands."

82. John C. Ryan, "Dipping into Books Online," *Christian Science Monitor*, November 13, 2003, p. 12.

83. Fletcher, "The Home Front: Blind Date with a Bungalow."

84. Stacy L. Wood, "Remote Purchase Environments: The Influence of Return Policy Leniency on Two-Stage Decision Process," *Journal of Marketing Research*, vol. 38, May 2001, pp. 157–169.

85. Jennifer Rewick, "Clinching the Holiday E-Sale," *Wall Street Journal*, October 9, 2000, pp. B1, B22.

86. Marcelo Prince, "Online Retailers Try to Streamline Checkout Process," *Wall Street Journal*, November 11, 2004, p. D2.

87. Prince, "Online Retailers Try to Streamline Checkout Process."

88. Michael Totty, "So Much Information . . . ," *Wall Street Journal*, December 9, 2002, p. R4; Subodh Bhat, Michael Bevans, and Sanjit Sengupta, "Measuring Users' Web Activity to Evaluate and Enhance Advertising Effectiveness," *Journal of Advertising*, Fall 2002, pp. 97–106.

90. Jacob Jacoby, Robert W. Chestnut, Karl Weigl, and William A. Fisher, "Prepurchase Information Acquisition: Description of a Process Methodology, Research Paradigm, and Pilot Investigation," in ed. Beverlee B. Anderson, *Advances in Consumer Research*, vol. 3 (Cincinnati: Association for Consumer Research, 1976), pp. 306–314; Jacob Jacoby, Robert W. Chestnut, and William Silberman, "Consumer Use and Comprehension of Nutrition Information," *Journal of Consumer Research*, September 1977, pp. 119–128.

91. Geoffrey C. Kiel and Roger A. Layton, "Dimensions of Consumer Information Seeking," *Journal of Marketing Research*, May 1981, pp. 233–239.

92. John O. Claxton, Joseph N. Fry, and Bernard Portis, "A Taxonomy of Prepurchase Information Gathering Patterns," *Journal of Consumer Research*, December 1974, pp. 35–42.

93. Bloch, Sherrell, and Ridgway, "Consumer Search."

94. R. A. Bauer, "Consumer Behavior as Risk Taking," in ed. Robert S. Hancock, *Dynamic Marketing for a Changing World* (Chicago: American Marketing Association, 1960), pp. 389–398; Rohit Deshpande and Wayne D. Hoyer, "Consumer Decision Making: Strategies, Cognitive Effort, and Perceived Risk," in *1983 Educators' Conference Proceedings* (Chicago: American Marketing Association, 1983), pp. 88–91.

95. Keith B. Murray, "A Test of Services Marketing Theory: Consumer Information Acquisition Activities," *Journal of Marketing*, January 1991, pp. 10–25; Joel E. Urbany, Peter R. Dickson, and William L. Wilkie, "Buyer Uncertainty and Information Search," *Journal of Consumer Research*, September 1989, pp. 208–215.

96. David J. Furse, Girish N. Punj, and David W. Stewart, "A Typology of Individual Search Strategies among Purchasers of New Automobiles," *Journal of Consumer Research*, March 1984, pp. 417–431; Narasimhan Srinivasan and Brian T. Ratchford, "An Empirical Test of a Model of External Search for Automobiles," *Journal of Consumer Research*, September 1991, pp. 233–242; Jacob Jacoby, James J. Jaccard, Imran Currim, Alfred Kuss, Asim Ansari, and Tracy Troutman, "Tracing the Impact of Item-by-Item Information Accessing on Uncertainty Reduction," *Journal of Consumer Research*, September 1994, pp. 291–303.

97. Calmetta Y. Coleman, "Selling Jewelry, Dolls, and TVs Next to Corn Flakes," *Wall Street Journal*, November 19, 1997, pp. B1, B8.

98. Gal Zauberman, "The Intertemporal Dynamics of Consumer Lock-In," *Journal of Consumer Research*, December 2003, pp. 405–419.

99. Sridhar Moorthy, Brian T. Ratchford, and Debabrata Talukdar, "Consumer Information Search Revisited: Theory and Empirical Analysis," *Journal of Consumer Research*, March 1997, pp. 263–277.

100. Calvin P. Duncan and Richard W. Olshavsky, "External Search: The Role of Consumer Beliefs," *Journal of Marketing Research*, February 1982, pp. 32–43; Girish N. Punj and Richard Staelin, "A Model of Information Search Behavior for New Automobiles," *Journal of Consumer Research*, September 1983, pp. 181–196.

101. Duncan and Olshavsky, "External Search."

102. Kathy Hammond, Gil McWilliam, and Andrea Narholz Diaz, "Fun and Work on the Web: Differences in Attitudes between Novices and Experienced Users," in eds. Joseph W. Alba and J. Wesley Hutchinson, *Advances in Consumer Research*, vol. 25 (Provo, Utah: Association for Consumer Research, 1998), pp. 372–378.

103. Joan E. Rigdon, "Advertisers Give Surfers Games to Play," *Wall Street Journal*, October 28, 1996, pp. B1, B6.

104. Laura A. Peracchio and Alice M. Tybout, "The Moderating Role of Prior Knowledge in Schema-Based Product Evaluation," *Journal of Consumer Research*, December 1996, pp. 177–192.

105. Joan Meyers-Levy and Alice Tybout, "Schema-Congruity as Basis for Product Evaluation," *Journal of Consumer Research,* June 1989, pp. 39–54.
107. Julie L. Ozanne, Merrie Brucks, and Dhruv Grewal, "A Study of Information Search Behavior during Categorization of New Products," *Journal of Consumer Research,* March 1992, pp. 452–463.
108. Punj and Staelin, "A Model of Consumer Information Search Behavior for New Automobiles"; Kiel and Layton, "Dimensions of Consumer Information Seeking."
109. Christine Moorman, Kristin Diehl, David Brinberg, and Blair Kidwell, "Subjective Knowledge, Search Locations, and Consumer Choice," *Journal of Consumer Research,* December 2004, pp. 673+.
110. Merrie Brucks, "The Effects of Product Class Knowledge on Information Search Behavior," *Journal of Consumer Research,* June 1985, pp. 1–16; James R. Bettman and C. Whan Park, "Effects of Prior Knowledge and Experience and Phase of the Choice Process on Consumer Decision Processes: A Protocol Analysis," *Journal of Consumer Research,* December 1980, pp. 234–248; Eric J. Johnson and J. Edward Russo, "Product Familiarity and Learning New Information," *Journal of Consumer Research,* June 1984, pp. 542–550; P. S. Raju, Subhas C. Lonial, and W. Glyn Mangold, "Differential Effects of Subjective Knowledge, Objective Knowledge, and Usage Experience on Decision Making; An Exploratory Investigation," *Journal of Consumer Psychology,* vol. 4, no. 2, 1995, pp. 153–180; Joseph W. Alba and J. Wesley Hutchinson, "Dimensions of Consumer Expertise," *Journal of Consumer Research,* March 1987, pp. 411–454.
111. Noel Capon and Roger Davis, "Basic Cognitive Ability Measures as Predictors of Consumer Information Processing Strategies," *Journal of Consumer Research,* June 1984, pp. 551–563.
112. For a summary of a number of studies, see Joseph W. Newman, "Consumer External Search: Amount and Determinants," in eds. Arch Woodside, Jagdish Sheth, and Peter Bennett, *Consumer and Industrial Buying Behavior* (New York: North-Holland, 1977), pp. 79–94; Charles M. Schaninger and Donald Sciglimpaglia, "The Influences of Cognitive Personality Traits and Demographics on Consumer Information Acquisition," *Journal of Consumer Research,* September 1981, pp. 208–216.
113. Scott Painton and James W. Gentry, "Another Look at the Impact of Information Presentation Format," *Journal of Consumer Research,* September 1985, pp. 240–244.
114. J. Edward Russo, Richard Staelin, Catherine A. Nolan, Gary J. Russell, and Barbara L. Metcalf, "Nutrition Information in the Supermarket," *Journal of Consumer Research,* June 1986, pp. 48–70.
115. Christine Moorman, "The Effects of Stimulus and Consumer Utilization of Nutrition Information," *Journal of Consumer Research,* December 1990, pp. 362–374.
116. Chris Janiszewski, "The Influence of Display Characteristics on Visual Exploratory Search Behavior," *Journal of Consumer Research,* December 1998, pp. 290–301.
117. William L. Moore and Donald L. Lehman, "Validity of Information Display Boards: An Assessment Using Longitudinal Data," *Journal of Marketing Research,* November 1980, pp. 296–307; C. Whan Park, Easwar S. Iyer, and Daniel C. Smith, "The Effects of Situational Factors on In-Store Grocery Shopping Behavior: The Role of Store Environment and Time Available for Shopping," *Journal of Consumer Research,* March 1989, pp. 422–433.
118. John R. Hauser, Glen L. Urban, and Bruce D. Weinberg, "How Consumers Allocate Their Time When Searching for Information," *Journal of Marketing Research,* November 1993, pp. 452–466.
119. Randolph E. Bucklin and Catarina Sismeiro, "A Model of Web Site Browsing Behavior Estimated on Clickstream Data," *Journal of Marketing Research,* August 2003, pp. 249–267.
120. Alhassan G. Abdul-Muhmin, "Contingent Decision Behavior: Effect of Number of Alternatives to Be Selected on Consumers' Decision Processes," *Journal of Consumer Psychology,* vol. 8, no. 1, 1999, pp. 91–111.
121. Adam L. Penenberg, "Googling the Bottom Line," *Wired News,* February 3, 2005, *www.wired.com.*
122. Naomi Mandel and Eric J. Johnson, "When Web Pages Influence Choice: Effects of Visual Primes on Experts and Novices," *Journal of Consumer Research,* September 2002, pp. 235+.
123. Furse, Punj, and Stewart, "A Typology of Individual Search Strategies Among Purchasers of New Automobiles."
124. Brian T. Ratchford, Myung-Soo Lee, and Debabrata Talukdar, "The Impact of the Internet on Information Search for Automobiles," *Journal of Marketing Research,* May 2003, pp. 193–209.
125. Judi Strebel, Tülin Erdem, and Joffre Swait, "Consumer Search in High Technology Markets: Exploring the Use of Traditional Information Channels," *Journal of Consumer Psychology,* 2004, pp. 96–104.
127. Troy Wolverton and Greg Sandoval, "Net Shoppers Wooed by In-Store Deals," *CNET News.com,* December 12, 2001, *http://news.cnet.com/news/0-1007-200-8156745.html.*
128. Jacob Jacoby, Robert W. Chestnut, and William A. Fisher, "A Behavioral Process Approach to Information Acquisition in Nondurable Purchasing," *Journal of Marketing Research,* November 1978, pp. 532–544.
129. Kent B. Monroe, "The Influence of Price Differences and Brand Familiarity on Brand Preferences," *Journal of Consumer Research,* June 1976, pp. 42–49.
130. Kristin Diehl, Laura J. Kornish, and John G. Lynch, Jr., "Smart Agents: When Lower Search Costs for Quality Information Increase Price Sensitivity," *Journal of Consumer Research,* June 2003, pp. 56–71.
131. Dhruv Grewal and Howard Marmorstein, "Market Price Variation, Perceived Price Variation, and Consumers' Price Search Decision for Durable Goods," *Journal of Consumer Research,* December 1994, pp. 453–460.
132. Sebastian Moffett and Martin Fackler, "Looking Up: As Economy Brightens, Japan May Escape Deflation's Shadow," *Wall Street Journal,* November 29, 2004, pp. A1+; Ann Zimmerman and Martin Fackler, "Pacific Aisles: Wal-Mart's Foray into Japan Spurs a Retail Upheaval," Wall Street Journal, September 19, 2003, p. A1.

134. Cynthia Huffman, "Goal Change, Information Acquisition, and Transfer," *Journal of Consumer Psychology,* vol. 5, no. 1, 1996, pp. 1–26.
135. Deborah Roedder John, Carol A. Scott, and James R. Bettman, "Sampling Data for Covariation Assessment," *Journal of Consumer Research,* March 1986, pp. 406–417.
136. Joydeep Srivastava and Nicholas Lurie, "A Consumer Perspective on Price-Matching Refund Policies; Effect on Price Perceptions and Search Behavior," *Journal of Consumer Research,* September 2001, pp. 296+.
138. J. Edward Russo and France Leclerc, "An Eye-Fixation Analysis of Choice for Consumer Nondurables," *Journal of Consumer Research,* September 1994, pp. 274–290.
139. Jacoby et al., "Prepurchase Information Acquisition."
140. J. Edward Russo, Margaret G. Meloy, and Husted Medvec, "Predecisional Distortion of Product Information," *Journal of Marketing Research,* November 1998, pp. 438–452.
141. Carol A. Berning and Jacob Jacoby, "Patterns of Information Acquisition in New Product Purchases," *Journal of Consumer Research,* September 1974, pp. 18–22.
142. Itamar Simonson, Joel Huber, and John Payne, "The Relationship between Prior Brand Knowledge and Information Acquisition Order," *Journal of Consumer Research,* March 1988, pp. 566–578.
143. Carrie M. Heilman, Douglas Bowman, and Gordon P. Wright, "The Evolution of Brand Preference and Choice Behaviors of Consumers New to a Market," *Journal of Marketing Research,* vol. 37, May 2000, pp. 139–155.
144. Jacoby et al., "Prepurchase Information Acquisition"; James R. Bettman, *An Information Processing Theory of Consumer Choice* (Reading, Mass.: Addison-Wesley, 1979).
145. Eric J. Johnson and J. Edward Russo, "Product Familiarity and Learning New Information," *Journal of Consumer Research,* June 1984, pp. 542–550; James R. Bettman and P. Kakkar, "Effects of Information Presentation Format on Consumer Information Acquisition Strategies," *Journal of Consumer Research,* March 1977, pp. 233–240.
146. Raj Sethuraman, Catherine Cole, and Dipak Jain, "Analyzing the Effect of Information Format and Task on Cutoff Search Strategies," *Journal of Consumer Psychology,* vol. 3, 1994, pp. 103–136.
147. Jacoby et al., "Tracing the Impact of Item-by-Item Information Accessing on Uncertainty Reduction."

CHAPTER 10

2. Michael D. Johnson and Christopher P. Puto, "A Review of Consumer Judgment and Choice," in ed. Michael J. Houston, *Review of Marketing* (Chicago: American Marketing Association, 1987), pp. 236–292.
3. Itamar Simonson, Joel Huber, and John Payne, "The Relationship between Prior Brand Knowledge and Information Acquisition Order," *Journal of Consumer Research,* March 1988, pp. 566–578.
4. Eric J. Johnson and J. Edward Russo, "Product Familiarity and Learning New Information," *Journal of Consumer Research,* June 1984, pp. 528–541.
5. Eloise Coupey, Julie R. Irwin, and John W. Payne, "Product Category Familiarity and Preference Construction," *Journal of Consumer Research,* March 1998, pp. 459–468.
6. Michel Tuan Pham, Joel B. Cohen, John W. Pracejus, and G. David Hughes, "Affect Monitoring and the Primacy of Feelings in Judgment," *Journal of Consumer Research,* September 2001, pp. 167+.
7. Daniel Kahneman and Amos Tversky, "On the Psychology of Prediction," *Psychology Review,* July 1973, pp. 251–275.
8. Joan Meyers-Levy and Alice M. Tybout, "Context Effects at Encoding and Judgment in Consumption Settings: The Role of Cognitive Resources," *Journal of Consumer Research,* June 1997, pp. 1–14.
9. "Starbucks Coffee Company," *Food Engineering & Ingredients,* June 2004, p. 7.
10. Irwin Levin, "Associative Effects of Information Framing," *Bulletin of the Psychonomic Society,* March 1987, pp. 85–86.
11. Manjit S. Yadav, "How Buyers Evaluate Product Bundles: A Model of Anchoring and Adjustment," *Journal of Consumer Research,* September 1994, pp. 342–353.
12. Gita Venkataramani Johar, Kamel Jedidi, and Jacob Jacoby, "A Varying-Parameter Averaging Model of On-line Brand Evaluations," *Journal of Consumer Research,* September 1997, pp. 232–247.
13. John Carroll, "The Effect of Imagining an Event on Expectations for the Event," *Journal of Experimental Social Psychology,* January 1978, pp. 88–96.
14. Deborah J. MacInnis and Linda L. Price, "The Role of Imagery in Information Processing: Review and Extensions," *Journal of Consumer Research,* March 1987, pp. 473–491.
15. Baba Shiv and Joel Huber, "The Impact of Anticipating Satisfaction on Consumer Choice," *Journal of Consumer Research,* vol. 27, September 2000, pp. 202–216.
16. Calvin P. Duncan and Richard W. Olshavsky, "External Search: The Role of Consumer Beliefs," *Journal of Marketing Research,* February 1982, pp. 32–43.
17. Raghubir and Menon, "AIDS and Me, Never the Twain Shall Meet."
18. Geeta Menon, Lauren G. Block, and Suresh Ramanathan, "We're at as Much Risk as We Are Led to Believe: Effects of Message Cues on Judgments of Health Risk," *Journal of Consumer Research,* March 2002, pp. 533+.
19. Rohini Ahluwalia, "Re-Inquiries: How Prevalent Is the Negativity Effect in Consumer Environments?" *Journal of Consumer Research,* September 2002, pp. 270–279.
20. Rohini Ahluwalia, H. Rao Unnava, and Robert E. Burnkrant, "The Moderating Effect of Commitment on the Spillover Effect of Marketing Communications," *Journal of Marketing Research,* November 2001, pp. 458–470.
21. Meryl Paula Gardner, "Mood States and Consumer Behavior: A Critical Review," *Journal of Consumer Research,* December 1985, pp. 281–300.

22. Stijn M. J. Van Osselaer and Joseph W. Alba, "Consumer Learning and Brand Equity," *Journal of Consumer Research*, vol. 27, June 2000, pp. 1–16.
23. Paul M. Herr, "Priming Price: Prior Knowledge and Context Effects," *Journal of Consumer Research*, June 1989, pp. 67–75.
24. "Conspicuous Non-consumption," *The Economist*, January 8, 2005, pp. 56–57.
26. Sung-Tai Hong and Robert S. Wyer Jr., "Effects of Country-of-Origin and Product-Attribute Information: An Information Processing Perspective," *Journal of Consumer Research*, September 1989, pp. 175–187.
27. Normandy Madden, "Study: Chinese Youth Aren't Patriotic Purchasers," *Advertising Age*, January 5, 2004, p. 6; Craig S. Smith, "Chinese Government Struggles to Rejuvenate National Brands," *Wall Street Journal*, June 24, 1996, pp. B1, B6.
28. James R. Bettman and Mita Sujan, "Effects of Framing on Evaluation of Comparable and Noncomparable Alternatives by Expert and Novice Consumers," *Journal of Consumer Research*, September 1987, pp. 141–151.
29. Lauren Gard, "We're Good Guys, Buy from Us," *Business Week*, November 22, 2004, p. 72.
30. Naomi Mandel, "Shifting Selves and Decision Making: The Effects of Self-Construal Priming on Consumer Risk-Taking," *Journal of Consumer Research*, June 2003, pp. 30+.
31. Hans Baumgartner, "On the Utility of Consumers' Theories in Judgments of Covariation," *Journal of Consumer Research*, March 1995, pp. 634–643; James R. Bettman, Deborah Roedder John, and Carol A. Scott, "Covariation Assessment by Consumers," *Journal of Consumer Research*, December 1986, pp. 316–326; Susan M. Broniarczyk and Joseph W. Alba, "Theory versus Data in Prediction and Correlation Tasks," *Organizational Behavior and Human Decision Processes*, January 1994, pp. 117–139.
32. Durairaj Maheswaran, "Country of Origin as a Stereotype: Effects of Consumer Expertise and Attribute Strength on Product Evaluations," *Journal of Consumer Research*, September 1994, pp. 354–365.
33. Amos Tversky and Daniel Kahneman, "Extensional versus Intuitive Reasoning: The Conjunction Fallacy," *Psychological Review*, October 1983, pp. 293–315.
34. Bob Garfield, "Softly Lit or Blunt, 'Less Toxic' Cigarette Ads Hint at Health," *Advertising Age*, November 12, 2001, p. 58; Gordon Fairclough, "Tobacco Titans Bid for 'Organic' Cigarette Maker," *Wall Street Journal*, December 10, 2001, pp. B1, B4; Suein Hwang, "Smokers May Mistake 'Clean' Cigarette for Safe," *Wall Street Journal*, September 30, 1995, pp. B1, B2.
35. "Hyundai in £10m 'Quality' Drive to Shed Budget Tag," *Marketing*, January 5, 2005, p. 3; Moon Ihlwan, "Hyundai Gets Hot," *Business Week*, December 17, 2001, pp. 84–86; "The Hyundai Syndrome," *Adweek's Marketing Week*, April 20, 1992, pp. 20–21.
36. F. May and R. Homans, "Evoked Set Size and the Level of Information Processing in Product Comprehension and Choice Criteria," in ed. William D. Perrault, *Advances in Consumer Research*, vol. 4 (Chicago: Association for Consumer Research, 1977), pp. 172–175.
37. Amitav Chakravarti and Chris Janiszewski, "The Influence of Macro-Level Motives on Consideration Set Composition in Novel Purchase Situations," *Journal of Consumer Research*, September 2003, pp. 244+.
38. Ravi Dhar and Itamar Simonson, 'The Effect of Forced Choice on Choice," *Journal of Marketing Research*, May 2004, pp. 146–160; Ravi Dhar, "Consumer Preference for a No-Choice Option," *Journal of Consumer Research*, September 1997, pp. 215–231.
39. John W. Payne, James R. Bettman, and Eric J. Johnson, "The Adaptive Decision-Maker," in ed. Robin M. Hogarth, *Insights in Decision Making: A Tribute to Hillel Einhorn* (Chicago: University of Chicago Press, 1990).
40. Mariele K. De Mooij and Warren Keegan, *Worldwide Advertising* (London: Prentice-Hall International, 1991).
41. Itamar Simonson, "Get Closer to Your Consumers by Understanding How They Make Choices," *California Management Review*, Summer 1993, pp. 68–84.
42. Aimee Drolet, "Inherent Rule Variability in Consumer Choice: Changing Rules for Change's Sake," *Journal of Consumer Research*, December 2002, pp. 293+.
43. Gerald Häubl and Kyle B. Murray, "Preference Construction and Persistence in Digital Marketplaces: The Role of Electronic Recommendation Agents," *Journal of Consumer Psychology*, 2003, pp. 75–91.
44. Dan Horsky, Paul Nelson, and Steven S. Posavac, "Stating Preferences for the Ethereal but Choosing the Concrete: How the Tangibility of Attributes Affects Attribute Weighting in Value Elicitation and Choice," *Journal of Consumer Psychology*, 2004, pp. 132–140.
45. Alexander Chernev, "Goal-Attribute Compatibility in Consumer Choice," *Journal of Consumer Psychology*, 2004, pp. 141–150.
46. For a good review of multiattribute models, see William L. Wilkie and Edgar A. Pessemier, "Issues in Marketing's Use of Multiattribute Models," *Journal of Marketing Research*, November 1983, pp. 428–441; Blair H. Sheppard, Jon Hartwick, and Paul R. Warshaw, "The Theory of Reasoned Action: A Meta-analysis of Past Research with Recommendations for Modifications and Future Research," *Journal of Consumer Research*, December 1988, pp. 325–342.
47. "JC Decaux Has Created a New Outdoor Format for DaimlerChrysler's Diminutive Smart City Car," *Marketing Week*, February 5, 2004, p. 10; Will Pinkston and Scott Miller, "DaimlerChrysler Clears Way for U.S. Debut of 'Smart,'" *Wall Street Journal*, August 20, 2001, pp. B1, B4.
48. "Additional Guarantee for Volkswagen Customers," *Europe Intelligence Wire*, December 30, 2004, n.p.; Chris Reiter, "VW, Opel Recoup Some Market Share from Japan Rivals," *Wall Street Journal*, December 15, 2004, p. A18.
49. Timothy B. Heath, Gangseog Ryu, Subimal Chatterjee, Michael S. McCarthy, David L. Mothersbaugh, Sandra Milberg, and Gary J. Gaeth, "Asymmetric Competition in Choice and the Leveraging of Competitive Disadvantages," *Journal of Consumer Research*, vol. 27, December 2000, pp. 291–308.

50. Rohini Ahluwalia, Robert E. Burnkrant, and H. Rao Unnava, "Consumer Response to Negative Publicity: The Moderating Role of Commitment," *Journal of Marketing Research*, vol. 37, May 2000, pp. 203–214.

52. Amos Tversky, "Intransitivity of Preferences," *Psychological Review*, January 1969, pp. 31–48.

54. Peter Wright, "Consumer Choice Strategies: Simplifying vs. Optimizing," *Journal of Marketing Research*, February 1975, pp. 60–67; Noreen Klein and Stewart W. Bither, "An Investigation of Utility-Directed Cutoff Selection," *Journal of Consumer Research*, September 1987, pp. 240–256.

55. "Why the Future Is Hybrid," *The Economist*, December 4, 2004, pp. 26+.

56. David Grether and Louis Wilde, "An Analysis of Conjunctive Choice: Theory and Experiments," *Journal of Consumer Research*, March 1984, pp. 373–385.

57. Evan Perez, "Cruising on Credit: Carnival Introduces Vacation Financing to Get More Aboard," *Wall Street Journal*, April 12, 2001, p. B12.

58. Joseph B. White, "China's SUV Surge," *Wall Street Journal*, June 10, 2004, pp. B1, B3.

59. Simonson, "Get Closer to Your Consumers by Understanding How They Make Choices."

60. Itamar Simonson, Ziv Carmon, and Suzanne O'Curry, "Experimental Evidence on the Negative Effect of Product Features and Sales Promotions on Brand Choice," *Marketing Science*, Winter 1994, pp. 23–40.

61. Amos Tversky, "Elimination by Aspects: A Theory of Choice," *Psychological Review*, July 1972, pp. 281–299.

62. Chester Dawson, "Will Plasma Revive Pioneer?" *Business Week*, December 13, 2004, p. 62; Jonathan Takiff, "Plasma TV Prices Drop in Time for Holidays," *Philadelphia Daily News*, October 26, 2004, *www.philly.com*.

63. Denis A. Lussier and Richard W. Olshavsky, "Task Complexity and Contingent Processing in Brand Choice," *Journal of Consumer Research*, September 1979, pp. 154–165; Eric J. Johnson and Robert J. Meyer, "Compensatory Choice Models of Noncompensatory Processes: The Effect of Varying Context," *Journal of Consumer Research*, June 1984, pp. 542–551.

64. James R. Bettman, Mary Frances Luce, and John W. Payne, "Constructive Consumer Choice Processes," *Journal of Consumer Research*, December 1998, pp.187–217.

65. Sanjay Sood, Yuval Rottenstreich, and Lyle Brenner, "On Decisions That Lead to Decisions: Direct and Derived Evaluations of Preference," *Journal of Consumer Research*, June 2004, pp. 17+.

66. Steve Hoeffler and Dan Ariely, "Constructing Stable Preferences: A Look into Dimensions of Experience and Their Impact on Preference Stability," *Journal of Consumer Psychology*, vol. 8, no. 2, 1999, pp. 113–139.

67. Payne, Bettman, and Johnson, "The Adaptive Decision-Maker."

69. Sid Price, "Men Fill Waiting Lists for MC Lady Brand Golf Balls," *St. Louis Business Journal*, September 7, 2001, p. 36.

70. Seymour Epstein, "Integration of the Cognitive and the Psychodynamic Unconscious," *American Psychologist*, August 1994, pp. 709–724.

71. Douglas E. Allen, "Toward a Theory of Consumer Choice as Sociohistorically Shaped Practical Experience: The Fits-Like-a-Glove (FLAG) Framework," *Journal of Consumer Research*, March 2002, pp. 515+.

72. Stephen J. Hoch and George F. Lowenstein, "Time-Inconsistent Preferences and Consumer Self-Control," *Journal of Consumer Research*, March 1991, pp. 492–507.

73. Michel Tuan Pham, "Representativeness, Relevance, and the Use of Feelings in Decision Making," *Journal of Consumer Research*, September 1998, pp. 144–159.

74. Epstein, "Integration of the Cognitive and the Psychodynamic Unconscious."

75. Pham, "Representativeness, Relevance, and the Use of Feelings in Decision Making"; Morris B. Holbrook and Elizabeth C. Hirschman, "The Experiential Aspects of Consumption: Consumer Fantasies, Feelings, and Fun," *Journal of Consumer Research*, September 1982, pp. 132–140.

76. Ran Kivetz and Itamar Simonson, "Self-Control for the Righteous: Toward a Theory of Precommitment to Indulgence," *Journal of Consumer Research*, September 2002, pp. 199+.

77. Peter H. Bloch, Frédéric F. Brunel, and Todd J. Arnold, "Individual Differences in the Centrality of Visual Product Aesthetics: Concept and Measurement," *Journal of Consumer Research*, March 2003, pp. 551–565.

78. Kathleen T. Lacher and Richard W. Mizerski, "An Exploratory Study of the Responses and Relationships Involved in the Evaluation of, and in the Intention to Purchase New Rock Music," *Journal of Consumer Research*, September 1994, pp. 366–380.

80. Morris B. Holbrook and Meryl P. Gardner, "An Approach to Investigating the Emotional Determinants of Consumption Durations: Why Do People Consume What They Consume for as Long as They Consume It?" *Journal of Consumer Psychology*, vol. 2, no. 2, 1993, pp. 123–142.

81. Nathan Novemsky and Rebecca K. Ratner, "The Time Course and Impact of Consumers' Erroneous Beliefs About Hedonic Contrast Effects," *Journal of Consumer Research*, March 2003, pp. 507+.

82. Mary Frances Luce, "Choosing to Avoid: Coping with Negatively Emotion-Laden Consumer Decisions," *Journal of Consumer Research*, March 1998, pp. 409–433.

83. Mary Frances Luce, John W. Payne, and James R. Bettman, "Emotional Trade-off Difficulty and Choice," *Journal of Marketing Research*, vol. 36, May 1999, pp. 143–159.

84. Aimee Drolet and Mary Frances Luce, "The Rationalizing Effects of Cognitive Load on Emotion-Based Trade-off Avoidance," *Journal of Consumer Research*, June 2004, pp. 63+.

85. Ellen C. Garbarino and Julie A. Edell, "Cognitive Effort, Affect, and Choice," *Journal of Consumer Research*, September 1997, pp. 147–158.

86. Michael Tsiros and Vikas Mittal, "Regret: A Model of Its Antecedents and Consequences in Consumer Decision Making," *Journal of Consumer Research*, vol. 26, March 2000, pp. 401–417.

87. Ann L. McGill and Punam Anand Keller, "Differences in the Relative Influence of Product Attributes under Alternative Processing Conditions: Attribute Importance versus Ease of Imaginability," *Journal of Consumer Psychology*, vol. 3, no. 1, 1994, pp. 29–50; MacInnis and Price, "The Role of Imagery in Information Processing."

88. Russell W. Belk, Güliz Ger, and Søren Askegaard, "The Fire of Desire: A Multisited Inquiry into Consumer Passion," *Journal of Consumer Research*, December 2003, pp. 326+.

89. Ann E. Schlosser, "Experiencing Products in the Virtual World: The Role of Goal and Imagery in Influencing Attitudes versus Purchase Intentions," *Journal of Consumer Research*, September 2003, pp. 184+.

90. Darren W. Dahl, Amitava Chattopadhyay, and Gerald J. Gorn, "The Use of Visual Mental Imagery in New Product Design," *Journal of Marketing Research*, vol. 36, February 1999, pp. 18–28.

91. Joel B. Cohen, "The Role of Affect in Categorization: Toward a Reconceptualization of the Concept of Attitude," in ed. Andrew A. Mitchell, *Advances in Consumer Research*, vol. 9 (Ann Arbor, Mich.: Association for Consumer Research, 1982), pp. 94–100; C. Whan Park and Banwari Mittal, "A Theory of Involvement in Consumer Behavior: Problems and Issues," in ed. Jagdish N. Sheth, *Research in Consumer Behavior* (Greenwich, Conn.: JAI Press, 1985), pp. 201–231.

92. "Shoprite: Africa's Wal-Mart Heads East," *The Economist*, January 15, 2005, p. 62.

93. Michael D. Johnson, "Consumer Choice Strategies for Comparing Noncomparable Alternatives," *Journal of Consumer Research*, December 1984, pp. 741–753; Michael D. Johnson, "Comparability and Hierarchical Processing in Multialternative Choice," *Journal of Consumer Research*, December 1988, pp. 303–314.

94. Kim P. Corfman, "Comparability and Comparison Levels Used in Choices among Consumer Products," *Journal of Marketing Research*, August 1991, pp. 368–374.

95. C. Whan Park and Daniel Smith, "Product-Level Choice: A Top-Down or Bottom-Up Process?" *Journal of Consumer Research*, December 1989, pp. 289–299.

96. Girish N. Punj and David W. Stewart, "An Interaction Framework of Consumer Decision Making," *Journal of Consumer Research*, September 1983, pp. 181–196.

97. Payne, Bettman, and Johnson, "The Adaptive Decision-Maker."

98. Dennis H. Gensch and Rajshelhar G. Javalgi, "The Influence of Involvement on Disaggregate Attribute Choice Models," *Journal of Consumer Research*, June 1987, pp. 71–82.

99. Eric A. Greenleaf and Donald R. Lehmann, "Reasons for Substantial Delay in Consumer Decision Making," *Journal of Consumer Research*, September 1995, pp. 186–199.

100. Elaine Sherman and Ruth Belk Smith, "Mood States of Shoppers and Store Image: Promising Interactions and Possible Behavioral Effects," in eds. Paul Anderson and Melanie Wallendorf, *Advances in Consumer Research*, vol. 14 (Provo, Utah: Association for Consumer Research, 1987), pp. 251–254.

101. Rashmi Adaval, "How Good Gets Better and Bad Gets Worse: Understanding the Impact of Affect on Evaluations of Known Brands," *Journal of Consumer Research*, December 2003, pp. 352+.

102. Stewart Shapiro, Deborah J. MacInnis, and C. Whan Park, "Understanding Program-Induced Mood Effects: Decoupling Arousal from Valence," *Journal of Advertising*, Winter 2002, pp. 15–26.

103. Gerald J. Gorn, Marvin E. Goldberg, and Kunal Basu, "Mood, Awareness, and Product Evaluation," *Journal of Consumer Psychology*, vol. 2, no. 3, 1993, pp. 237–256.

104. Catherine W.M. Yeung and Robert S. Wyer, Jr., "Affect, Appraisal, and Consumer Judgment," *Journal of Consumer Research*, September 2004, pp. 412+.

105. Joel B. Cohen and Eduardo B. Andrade, "Affective Intuition and Task-Contingent Affect Regulation," *Journal of Consumer Research*, September 2004, pp. 358–367.

106. Patricia M. West, Christina L. Brown, and Stephen J. Hoch, "Consumption Vocabulary and Preference Formation," *Journal of Consumer Research*, September 1996, pp. 120–135.

107. Johnson and Russo, "Product Familiarity and Learning New Information"; James R. Bettman and C. Whan Park, "Effects of Prior Knowledge and Experience and Phase of the Choice Process on Consumer Decision Processes, A Protocol Analysis," *Journal of Consumer Research*, December 1980, pp. 234–248.

108. Joffre Swait and Wiktor Adamowicz, "The Influence of Task Complexity on Consumer Choice: A Latent Choice Model of Decision Strategy Switching," *Journal of Consumer Research*, June 2001, pp. 135–148.

109. Jennifer L. Aaker and Jaideep Sengupta, "Additivity versus Attenuation: The Role of Culture in the Resolution of Information Incongruity," *Journal of Consumer Psychology*, vol. 9, no. 2, 2000, pp. 67–82.

110. Payne, Bettman, and Johnson, "The Adaptive Decision-Maker."

111. C. Whan Park, Easwar S. Iyer, and Daniel C. Smith, "The Effects of Situational Factors on In-Store Grocery Shopping Behavior: The Role of Store Environment and Time Available for Shopping," *Journal of Consumer Research*, March 1989, pp. 422–433.

112. Greenleaf and Lehmann, "Reasons for Substantial Delay in Consumer Decision Making."

113. Ravi Dhar and Stephen M. Nowlis, "The Effect of Time Pressure on Consumer Choice Deferral," *Journal of Consumer Research*, vol. 25, March 1999, pp. 369–384.

114. Michelle M. Bergadaa, "The Role of Time in the Action of the Consumer," *Journal of Consumer Research*, December 1990, pp. 289–302.

117. Lussier and Olshavsky, "Task Complexity and Contingent Processing in Brand Choice"; Johnson and Meyer,

"Compensatory Choice Models of Noncompensatory Processes."

118. Itamar Simonson and Amos Tversky, "Choice in Context: Tradeoff Contrast and Extremeness Aversion," *Journal of Marketing Research*, August 1992, pp. 281–295.

119. Joel Huber, John W. Payne, and Christopher Puto, "Adding Asymmetrically Dominated Alternatives: Violations of Regularity and the Similarity Hypothesis," *Journal of Consumer Research*, June 1982, pp. 90–98; Srinivasan Ratneshwar, Allan D. Shocker, and David W. Stewart, "Toward Understanding the Attraction Effect: The Implications of Product Stimulus Meaningfulness and Familiarity," *Journal of Consumer Research*, March 1987, pp. 520–533; Sanjay Mishra, U. N. Umesh, and Donald E. Stem, "Antecedents of the Attraction Effect: An Information Processing Approach," *Journal of Marketing Research*, August 1993, pp. 331–349; Yigang Pan, Sue O'Curry, and Robert Pitts, "The Attraction Effect and Political Choice in Two Elections," *Journal of Consumer Psychology*, vol. 4, no. 1, 1995, pp. 85–101.

120. Sankar Sen, "Knowledge, Information Mode, and the Attraction Effect," *Journal of Consumer Research*, June 1998, 64–77.

121. Timothy B. Heath and Subimal Chatterjee, "Asymmetric Decoy Effects on Lower-Quality versus Higher-Quality Brands: Meta-analytic and Experimental Evidence," *Journal of Consumer Research*, December 1995, pp. 268–84.

122. Frank R. Kardes, David M. Sanbonmatsu, Maria L. Cronley, and David C. Houghton, "Consideration Set Overvaluation: When Impossibly Favorable Ratings of a Set of Brands Are Observed," *Journal of Consumer Psychology*, 2002, pp. 353–361.

123. Steven S. Posavac, David M. Sanbonmatsu, and Edward A. Ho, "The Effects of Selective Consideration of Alternatives on Consumer Choice and Attitude-Decision Consistency," *Journal of Consumer Psychology*, 2002, pp. 203–213.

124. Steven S. Posavac, David M. Sanbonmatsu, Frank R. Kardes, and Gavan J. Fitzsimons, "The Brand Positivity Effect: When Evaluation Confers Preference," *Journal of Consumer Research*, December 2004, pp. 643–651.

125. Mukesh Bhargava, John Kim, and Rajendra K. Srivastava, "Explaining Context Effects on Choice Using a Model of Comparative Judgment," *Journal of Consumer Psychology*, vol. 9, no. 3, 2000, pp. 167–177; Noreen M. Klein and Manjit S. Yadav, "Context Effects on Effort and Accuracy: An Enquiry into Adaptive Decision Making," *Journal of Consumer Research*, March 1989, pp. 411–421; Payne, Bettman, and Johnson, "The Adaptive Decision-Maker."

126. Simonson, "Get Closer to Your Consumers by Understanding How They Make Choices."

127. Stephen M. Nowlis, Barbara E. Kahn, and Ravi Dhar, "Coping with Ambivalence: The Effect of Removing a Neutral Option on Consumer Attitude and Preference Judgments," *Journal of Consumer Research*, December 2002, pp. 319+.

128. Alexander Chernev, "When More Is Less and Less Is More: The Role of Ideal Point Availability and Assortment in Consumer Choice," *Journal of Consumer Research*, September 2003, pp. 170+.

129. Christina L. Brown and Gregory S. Carpenter, "Why Is the Trivial Important? A Reasons-Based Account for the Effects of Trivial Attributes on Choice," *Journal of Consumer Research*, March 2000, pp. 372+.

130. Jim Wang and Robert S. Wyer, Jr., "Comparative Judgment Processes: The Effects of Task Objectives and Time Delay on Product Evaluations," *Journal of Consumer Psychology*, 2002, pp. 327–340.

131. Rebecca W. Hamilton, "Why Do People Suggest What They Do Not Want? Using Context Effects to Influence Others' Choices," *Journal of Consumer Research*, March 2003, pp. 492–506.

133. Alexander Chernev, "Extremeness Aversion and Attribute-Balance Effects in Choice," *Journal of Consumer Research*, September 2004, pp. 249+.

134. Alan D.J. Cooke, Christ Janiszewski, Marcus Cunha, Jr., Suzanne A. Nasco, and Els De Wilde, "Stimulus Context and the Formation of Consumer Ideals," *Journal of Consumer Research*, June 2004, pp. 112+.

135. Margaret C. Campbell and Ronald C. Goodstein, "The Moderating Effect of Perceived Risk on Consumers' Evaluations of Product Incongruity: Preference for the Norm," *Journal of Consumer Research*, December 2001, pp. 439+.

136. Simonson, "Get Closer to Your Consumers by Understanding How They Make Choices."

137. Jacob Jacoby, "Perspectives on Information Overload," *Journal of Consumer Research*, March 1984, pp. 569–573; Kevin Lane Keller and Richard Staelin, "Effects of Quality and Quantity of Information on Decision Effectiveness," *Journal of Consumer Research*, September 1987, pp. 200–213.

138. Ger, "Problems of Marketization in Romania and Turkey," in eds. Clifford Schultz, Russell Belk, and Guliz Ger, *Consumption in Marketizing Economies* (Greenwich, Conn.: JAI Press, 1995).

139. Sabrina Tavernise, "In Russia, Capitalism of a Certain Size," *New York Times*, July 29, 2001, sec. 3, p. 6; Guliz Ger, Russell Belk, and Dana-Nicoleta Lascu, "The Development of Consumer Desire in Marketing and Developing Economies: The Cases of Romania and Turkey," in eds. Leigh McAlister and Michael L. Rothschild, *Advances in Consumer Research*, vol. 20 (Provo, Utah: Association for Consumer Research, 1993), pp. 102–107.

140. Keller and Staelin, "Effects of Quality and Quantity of Information on Decision Effectiveness."

141. Ran Kivetz and Itamar Simonson, "The Effects of Incomplete Information on Consumer Choice," *Journal of Marketing Research*, vol. 37, November 2000, pp. 427–448.

142. A. V. Muthukrishnan, "Decision Ambiguity and Incumbent Brand Advantage," *Journal of Consumer Research*, June 1995, pp. 98–109.

143. Madhubalan Viswanathan and Sunder Narayanan, "Comparative Judgments of Numerical and Verbal Attribute Labels," *Journal of Consumer Psychology*, vol. 3, no. 1, 1994, pp. 79–100.

144. Itamar Simonson, Stephen Nowlis, and Katherine Lemon, "The Effect of Local Consideration Sets on Global Choice between Lower Price and Higher Quality," *Marketing Science*, Fall 1993.

145. Johnson and Russo, "Product Familiarity and Learning New Information"; J. Edward Russo, "The Value of Unit Price Information," *Journal of Marketing Research*, May 1977, pp. 193–201.

146. Rashmi Adaval and Robert S. Wyer Jr., "The Role of Narratives in Consumer Information Processing," *Journal of Consumer Psychology*, vol. 7, no. 3, 1998, pp. 207–245.

147. Itamar Simonson and Russell S. Winer, "The Influence of Purchase Quantity and Display Format on Consumer Preference for Variety," *Journal of Consumer Research*, June 1992, pp. 133–138.

148. Eloise Coupey, "Restructuring: Constructive Processing of Information Displays in Consumer Choice," *Journal of Consumer Research*, June 1994, pp. 83–99.

149. Daniel Kahneman and Amos Tversky, "Prospect Theory: An Analysis of Decisions under Risk," *Econometrica*, March 1979, pp. 263–291.

150. William B. Diamond and Abhijit Sanyal, "The Effect of Framing on the Choice of Supermarket Coupons," in eds. Marvin E. Goldberg and Gerald Gorn, *Advances in Consumer Research*, vol. 17 (Provo, Utah: Association for Consumer Research, 1990), pp. 488–493.

151. Punan Anand Keller, Isaac M. Lipkus, and Barbara K. Rimer, "Affect, Framing, and Persuasion," *Journal of Marketing Research*, February 2003, pp. 54–64.

152. Christopher P. Puto, "The Framing of Buying Decisions," *Journal of Consumer Research*, December 1987, pp. 301–316.

153. Rajendra K. Srivastava, Allan D. Shocker, and George S. Day, "An Exploratory Study of the Influences of Usage Situations on Perceptions of Product Markets," in ed. H. Keith Hunt, *Advances in Consumer Research*, vol. 5 (Ann Arbor, Mich.: Association for Consumer Research, 1978), pp. 32–38.

154. Kenneth E. Miller and James L. Ginter, "An Investigation of Situational Variation in Brand Choice Behavior and Attitude," *Journal of Marketing Research*, February 1979, pp. 111–123.

155. Robert Berner, "Welcome to Procter & Gamble," *Business Week*, February 7, 2005, pp. 76–77.

157. Sucharita Chandran and Geeta Menon, "When a Day Means More Than a Year: Effects of Temporal Framing on Judgments of Health Risk," *Journal of Consumer Research*, September 2004, pp. 375–389.

158. Christopher P. Puto, W. E. Patton, and Ronald H. King, "Risk Handling Strategies in Industrial Vendor Selection Decisions," *Journal of Marketing*, January 1987, pp. 89–98.

159. John T. Gourville, "Pennies-a-Day: The Effect of Temporal Reframing on Transaction Evaluation," *Journal of Consumer Research*, March 1998, pp. 395–408.

160. Rashmi Adaval and Kent B. Monroe, "Automatic Construct and Use of Contextual Information for Product and Price Evaluations," *Journal of Consumer Research*, March 2002, pp. 572+.

161. Yaacov Schul and Yoav Ganzach, "The Effects of Accessibility of Standards and Decision Framing on Product Evaluations," *Journal of Consumer Psychology*, vol. 4, no. 1, 1995, pp. 61–83.

162. Baba Shiv, Julie A. Edell, and John W. Payne, "Factors Affecting the Impact of Negatively and Positively Framed Ad Messages," *Journal of Consumer Research*, December 1997, pp. 285–294.

163. Baba Shiv, Julie A. Edell Britton, and John W. Payne, "Re-Inquiries: Does Elaboration Increase or Decrease the Effectiveness of Negatively versus Positively Framed Messages?" *Journal of Consumer Research*, June 2004, pp. 199+.

164. Yong Zhang and Richard Buda, "Moderating Effects of Need for Cognition on Responses to Positively versus Negatively Framed Advertising Messages," *Journal of Advertising*, vol. 28, no. 2, Summer 1999, pp. 1–15.

165. C. Whan Park, Sung Youl Jun, and Deborah J. MacInnis, "Choosing What I Want versus Rejecting What I Do Not Want: An Application of Decision Framing to Product Option Choice Decisions," *Journal of Marketing Research*, vol. 37, May 2000, pp. 187–202.

166. Bettman and Sujan, "Effects of Framing on Evaluation of Comparable and Noncomparable Alternatives by Expert and Novice Consumers."

167. Cynthia Fraser, Robert E. Hite, and Paul L. Sauer, "Increasing Contributions in Solicitation Campaigns: The Use of Large and Small Anchor-Points," *Journal of Consumer Research*, September 1988, pp. 284–287.

168. Donald P. Green and Irene V. Blair, "Framing and Price Elasticity of Private and Public Goods," *Journal of Consumer Psychology*, vol. 4, no. 1, 1995, pp. 1–32.

169. Paul M. Herr and Christine M. Page, "Asymmetric Association of Liking and Disliking Judgments: So What's Not to Like?" *Journal of Consumer Research*, March 2004, pp. 588+.

170. Dan Ariely and Jonathan Levav, "Sequential Choice in Group Settings: Taking the Road Less Traveled and Less Enjoyed," *Journal of Consumer Research*, vol. 27, December 2000, pp. 279–290.

171. Brian Steinberg, "Western Union to Court Immigrants," *Wall Street Journal*, May 2, 2003, p. B2.

CHAPTER 11

3. Alan Newell and Herbert A. Simon, *Human Problem Solving* (Englewood Cliffs, N.J.: Prentice-Hall, 1972); Daniel Kahneman and Amos Tversky, "On the Psychology of Prediction," *Psychological Review*, July 1973, pp. 237–251.

4. Daniel Kahneman and Amos Tversky, "Subjective Probability: A Judgment of Representativeness," *Cognitive Psychology*, July 1972, pp. 430–454.

6. "The Hyundai Syndrome," *Adweek's Marketing Week*, April 20, 1992, pp. 20–21.

7. "Samsung: As Good As It Gets?" *The Economist*, March 10, 2005; Claudia Deutsch, "To Change Its Image and Attract New Customers, Samsung Electronics Is Putting on a Show," *New York Times*, September 20, 2004, p. C11.

8. Valerie S. Folkes, "The Availability Heuristic and Perceived Risk," *Journal of Consumer Research*, June 1988, pp. 13–23; Johnson and Puto, "A Review of Consumer Judgment and Choice," in ed. Michael J. Houston, *Review of Marketing* (Chicago: American Marketing Association, 1987), pp. 236–292.

9. Geeta Menon and Priya Raghubir, "Ease-of-Retrieval as an Automatic Input in Judgments: A Mere-Accessibility Framework?" *Journal of Consumer Research*, September 2003, pp. 230–243.

10. Peter R. Dickson, "The Impact of Enriching Case and Statistical Information on Consumer Judgments," *Journal of Consumer Research*, March 1982, pp. 398–408.

11. Chezy Ofir and John G. Lynch Jr., "Context Effects on Judgment under Uncertainty," *Journal of Consumer Research*, September 1984, pp. 668–679.

12. Amos Tversky and Daniel Kahneman, "Belief in the Law of Small Numbers," *Psychological Bulletin*, August 1971, pp. 105–110; Amos Tversky and Daniel Kahneman, "Judgment under Uncertainty: Heuristics and Biases," *Science*, September 1974, pp. 1124–1131.

15. Hanjoon Lee, Acito Acito, and Ralph Day, "Evaluation and Use of Marketing Research by Decision Makers: A Behavioral Simulation," *Journal of Marketing Research*, May 1987, pp. 187–196.

16. Hoyer, "An Examination of Consumer Decision Making for a Common Repeat Purchase Product."

17. Herbert E. Krugman, "The Impact of Television Advertising: Learning without Involvement," *Public Opinion Quarterly*, Fall 1965, pp. 349–356.

18. Michael L. Ray, *Marketing Communications and the Hierarchy of Effects* (Cambridge, Mass.: Marketing Science Institute, 1973).

19. Robert B. Zajonc, "Feeling and Thinking: Preferences Need No Inferences," *American Psychologist*, February 1980, pp. 151–175; Robert B. Zajonc and Hazel B. Markus, "Affective and Cognitive Factors in Preferences," *Journal of Consumer Research*, September 1982, pp. 122–131.

20. Hoyer, "An Examination of Consumer Decision Making for a Common Repeat Purchase Product."

21. Cathy J. Cobb and Wayne D. Hoyer, "Direct Observation of Search Behavior in the Purchase of Two Nondurable Products," *Psychology and Marketing*, Fall 1983, pp. 161–179.

22. Alain d'Astous, Idriss Bensouda, and Jean Guindon, "A Reexamination of Consumer Decision Making for a Repeat Purchase Product: Variations in Product Importance and Purchase Frequency," in ed. Thomas K. Srull, *Advances in Consumer Research*, vol. 16 (Provo, Utah: Association for Consumer Research, 1989), pp. 433–438.

23. Richard W. Olshavsky and Donald H. Granbois, "Consumer Decision Making: Fact or Fiction?" *Journal of Consumer Research*, September 1979, pp. 93–100.

24. William E. Baker and Richard J. Lutz, "An Empirical Test of an Updated Relevance-Accessibility Model of Advertising Effectiveness," *Journal of Advertising*, vol. 29, no. 1, Spring 2000, pp. 1–13.

25. Deshpande, Hoyer, and Jeffries, "Low Involvement Decision Processes."

26. Hoyer, "An Examination of Consumer Decision Making for a Common Repeat Purchase Product."

27. Siew Meng Leong, "Consumer Decision Making for Common, Repeat-Purchase Products: A Dual Replication," *Journal of Consumer Psychology*, vol. 2, no. 2, 1993, pp. 193–208.

28. Dana L. Alden, Wayne D. Hoyer, and Guntalee Wechasara, "Choice Strategies and Involvement, A Cross-Cultural Analysis," in ed. Thomas K. Srull, *Advances in Consumer Research*, vol. 16 (Provo, Utah: Association for Consumer Research, 1989), pp. 119–126.

29. Walter A. Nord and J. Paul Peter, "A Behavior Modification Perspective on Marketing," *Journal of Marketing*, Spring 1980, pp. 36–47; Michael Rothschild and William C. Gaidis, "Behavioral Learning Theory: Its Relevance to Marketing and Promotions," *Journal of Marketing*, Spring 1981, pp. 70–78.

30. Holly Heline, "Brand Loyalty Isn't Dead—But You're Not off the Hook," *Brandweek*, June 7, 1994, p. 14.

31. Robert E. Smith and William R. Swinyard, "Information Response Models: An Integrated Approach," *Journal of Marketing*, Winter 1982, pp. 81–93; Robert E. Smith and William R. Swinyard, "Attitude-Behavior Consistency: The Impact of Product Trial vs. Advertising," *Journal of Marketing Research*, August 1983, pp. 257–267.

32. Deanna S. Kempf and Robert E. Smith, "Consumer Processing of Product Trial and the Influence of Prior Advertising: A Structural Modeling Approach," *Journal of Marketing Research*, August 1998, pp. 325–338.

33. Michael L. Rothschild and Michael J. Houston, "The Consumer Involvement Matrix: Some Preliminary Findings," in eds. Barnett A. Greenberg and Danny N. Bellenger, *Proceedings of the American Marketing Association Educators' Conference*, Series no. 41, 1977, pp. 95–98.

34. Wayne D. Hoyer, "Variations in Choice Strategies across Decision Contexts: An Examination of Contingent Factors," in ed. Richard J. Lutz, *Advances in Consumer Research*, vol. 13 (Provo, Utah: Association for Consumer Research, 1986), pp. 32–36.

35. Wayne D. Hoyer and Cathy J. Cobb-Walgren, "Consumer Decision Making across Product Categories: The Influence of Task Environment," *Psychology and Marketing*, Spring 1988, pp. 45–69.

36. Leong, "Consumer Decision Making for Common, Repeat-Purchase Products."

37. Yumiko Ono, "Campbell's New Ads Heat Up Soup Sales," *Wall Street Journal*, March 17, 1994, p. B5.

38. Paulo Prada, "European Inns Take the Hilton Route," *Wall Street Journal*, April 23, 2001, pp. B1, B6.

39. Robert E. Smith, "Integrating Information from Advertising and Trial: Processes and Effects on Consumer Response to Product Information," *Journal of Marketing Research*, May 1993, pp. 204–219.

40. Charles Forelle, "Schick Seeks Edge with Four-Blade Razor," *Wall Street Journal*, August 12, 2003, pp. B1, B9.

41. Norihiko Shirouzu, "Snapple in Japan: How a Splash Dried Up," *Wall Street Journal,* April 15, 1996, pp. B1, B3.

42. Priya Raghubir and Kim Corfman, "When Do Price Promotions Affect Pretrial Brand Evaluations?" *Journal of Marketing Research,* vol. 36, May 1999, pp. 211–222.

43. Jacob Jacoby and David B. Kyner, "Brand Loyalty vs. Repeat Purchasing Behavior," *Journal of Marketing Research,* February 1973, pp. 1–9.

44. Ted Roselius, "Consumer Rankings of Risk Reduction Methods," *Journal of Marketing,* January 1971, pp. 56–61.

45. P. B. Seetharaman, Andrew Ainslie, and Pradeep K. Chintagunta, "Investigating Household State Dependence Effects across Categories," *Journal of Marketing Research,* vol. 36, November 1999, pp. 488–500.

46. Rothschild and Gaidis, "Behavioral Learning Theory."

50. Amy Johannes, "Pepsi, iTunes Double Music Promotion in New Offer," *Promo,* January 20, 2005, *www.promomagazine.com;* Brian Steinberg, "Pepsi Is Planning Promotions to Put Some Fizz into Summer," *Wall Street Journal,* May 1, 2003, p. B5.

53. Gary F. McKinnon, J. Patrick Kelly, and E. Doyle Robinson, "Sales Effects of Point-of-Purchase In-Store Signing," *Journal of Retailing,* Summer 1981, pp. 49–63.

54. Kathleen Deveny, "Displays Pay Off for Grocery Marketers," *Wall Street Journal,* October 15, 1992, pp. B1, B5.

55. "Study Claims Effectiveness of Point-of-Purchase," *Advertising Age,* July 24, 2001, *www.adage.com.*

56. "Brand Loyalty in the Food Industry," *The Food Institute Report,* November 5, 2001, p. 3.

57. "Advanced Vending: A Coke, I-mode, Tickets, and a Smile," *Global Telephony,* October 1, 2001, p. 10; Norihiko Shirouzu, "For Coca-Cola in Japan, Things Go Better with Milk," *Wall Street Journal,* January 20, 1997, pp. B1, B2.

58. George S. Day, "A Two-Dimensional Concept of Brand Loyalty," *Journal of Advertising Research,* August–September 1969, pp. 29–36; Jacoby and Kyner, "Brand Loyalty vs. Repeat Purchasing Behavior"; Jacob Jacoby and Robert W. Chestnut, *Brand Loyalty: Measurement and Management* (New York: Wiley, 1978).

59. Jacob Jacoby, "A Model of Multi-Brand Loyalty," *Journal of Advertising Research,* June–July 1971, p. 26.

60. Ronald E. Frank, William F. Massy, and Thomas L. Lodahl, "Purchasing Behavior and Personal Attributes," *Journal of Advertising Research,* December 1969–January 1970, pp. 15–24.

61. R. M. Cunningham, "Brand Loyalty—What, Where, How Much," *Harvard Business Review,* January–February 1956, pp. 116–128; "Customer Loyalty to Store and Brand," *Harvard Business Review,* November–December 1961, pp. 127–137.

62. Day, "A Two-Dimensional Concept of Brand Loyalty."

63. Eric Bellman and Deborah Bell, "Unilever, P&G Wage Price War for Edge in India," *Wall Street Journal,* August 11, 2004, pp. B1, B3.

64. Marnik G. Dekimpe, Martin Mellens, Jan-Benedict E.M. Steenkamp, and Piet Vanden Abeele, "Erosion and Variability in Brand Loyalty," Marketing Science Institute Report No. 96–114, August 1996, pp. 1–25.

66. Heline, "Brand Loyalty Isn't Dead."

68. Michelle L. Roehm, Ellen Bolman Pullins, and Harper A. Roehm, Jr., "Designing Loyalty-Building Programs for Packaged Goods Brands," *Journal of Marketing Research,* May 2002, pp. 202–213.

69. Ran Kivetz and Itamar Simonson, "The Idiosyncratic Fit Heuristic: Effort Advantage as a Determinant of Consumer Response to Loyalty Programs," *Journal of Marketing Research,* November 2003, pp. 454–467.

70. Ran Kivetz and Itamar Simonson, "Earning the Right to Indulge: Effort as a Determinant of Customer Preferences Toward Frequency Program Rewards," *Journal of Marketing Research,* May 2002, pp. 155–170.

71. "Supercharging the Digital Shoebox," *Fast Company,* March 2005, p. 56.

72. Laurie Petersen, "The Strategic Shopper," *Adweek's Marketing Week,* March 30, 1992, pp. 18–20.

73. Peter D. Dickson and Alan G. Sawyer, "Methods to Research Shoppers' Knowledge of Supermarket Prices," in ed. Richard J. Lutz, *Advances in Consumer Research,* vol. 12 (Provo, Utah: Association for Consumer Research, 1986), pp. 584–587.

74. Tulin Erdem, Glenn Mayhew, and Baohung Sun, "Understanding Reference-Price Shoppers: A Within- and Cross-Category Analysis," *Journal of Marketing Research,* November 2001, pp. 445–457.

75. Chris Janiszewski and Donald R. Lichtenstein, "A Range Theory Account of Price Perception," *Journal of Consumer Research,* vol. 25, March 1999, pp. 353–368; Kent B. Monroe and Susan M. Petroshius, "Buyers' Perception of Price: An Update of the Evidence," in eds. Harold H. Kassarjian and Thomas S. Robertson, *Perspectives in Consumer Behavior,* 3rd ed. (Dallas: Scott-Foresman, 1981), pp. 43–55.

76. Fowler, "Towels, Soap, Sponges and Mops, Look Out: Here Come the Wipes."

77. Ian Rowley, "Japan's Answer to Wal-Mart?" *Business Week Online,* February 24, 2005, *www.businessweek.com.*

78. Baba Shiv, Julie A. Edell Britton, and John W. Payne, "Re-Inquiries: Does Elaboration Increase or Decrease the Effectiveness of Negatively versus Positively Framed Messages?" *Journal of Consumer Research,* June 2004, pp. 199+.

79. Julie Baker, A. Parasuraman, Dhruv Grewal, and Glenn B. Voss, "The Influence of Multiple Store Environment Cues on Perceived Merchandise Value and Patronage Intentions," *Journal of Marketing,* April 2002, pp. 120–141.

80. Lisa E. Bolton, Luk Warlop, and Joseph W. Alba, "Consumer Perceptions of Price (Un)Fairness," *Journal of Consumer Research,* March 2003, pp. 474+.

81. Chris Janiszewski and Marcus Cunha, Jr., "The Influence of Price Discount Framing on the Evaluation of a Product Bundle," *Journal of Consumer Research,* March 2004, pp. 534+.

83. Kent B. Monroe, "The Influence of Price Differences and Brand Familiarity on Brand Preferences," *Journal of Consumer Research,* June 1976, pp. 42–49.

84. Joseph W. Alba, Carl F. Mela, Terence A. Shimp, and Joel E. Urbany, "The Effect of Discount Frequency and Depth on Consumer Price Judgments," *Journal of Consumer Research,* vol. 26, September 1999, pp. 99–114.

85. J. Jeffrey Inman, Anil C. Peter, and Priya Raghubir, "Framing the Deal: The Role of Restrictions in Accentuating Deal Value," *Journal of Consumer Research,* June 1997, pp. 68–79.

86. Dhruv Grewal, Howard Marmorstein, and Arun Sharma, "Communicating Price Information through Semantic Cues: The Moderating Effects of Situation and Discount Size," *Journal of Consumer Research,* September 1996, pp. 148–155.

87. Priya Raghubir and Joydeep Srivastava, "Effect of Face Value on Product Valuation in Foreign Currencies," *Journal of Consumer Research,* December 2002, pp. 335+.

88. *Supermarket Shoppers in a Period of Economic Uncertainty* (New York: Yankelovich, Skelly, & White, 1982), p. 53; Robert Blattberg, Thomas Buesing, Peter Peacock, and Subrata K. Sen, "Who Is the Deal Prone Consumer?" in ed. H. Keith Hunt, *Advances in Consumer Research,* vol. 5 (Ann Arbor, Mich.: Association for Consumer Research, 1978), pp. 57–62.

89. Donald R. Lichtenstein, Richard G. Netemeyer, and Scot Burton, "Assessing the Domain Specificity of Deal Proneness: A Field Study," *Journal of Consumer Research,* December 1995, pp. 314–326.

90. "More and More Shoppers Enter World of Private Label," *MMR,* November 15, 2004, p. 13.

91. Eleena de Lisser and Kevin Helliker, "Private Labels Reign in British Groceries," *Wall Street Journal,* March 3, 1994, pp. B1, B9.

92. "Vox Pop: What Does the Future Hold for Price Comparison on the Web?" *Revolution,* May 18, 2004, p. 22.

93. Betsy Spethmann, "Re-Engineering the Price-Value Equation," *Brandweek,* September 20, 1993, pp. 44–47.

94. Christine Bittar, "Tablets, Scents, and Sensibility," *Brandweek,* June 4, 2001, p. S59.

95. Nelson Schwartz, "Colgate Cleans Up," *Fortune,* April 2000, *www.adage.com;* Tara Parker-Pope, "Colgate Places a Huge Bet on a Germ-Fighter," *Wall Street Journal,* December 29, 1997, pp. B1, B2.

96. Dianne Solis, "Cost No Object for Mexico's Makeup Junkies," *Wall Street Journal,* June 7, 1994, pp. B1, B6.

97. Kathleen Deveny, "How Country's Biggest Brands Are Faring at the Supermarket," *Wall Street Journal,* March 24, 1994, p. B1.

98. "Manufacturers Offered More Than $250 Billion in Coupons in 2003 at a Cost of $7 Billion, According to the Promotion Marketing Association," *Incentive,* January 2005, p. 14.

99. "Penny-Pinchers' Paradise," *Business Week,* January 22, 2001, p. EB12.

100. "International Coupon Trends," *Direct Marketing,* August 1993, pp. 47–49, 83.

101. Bussey, "Japan's Wary Shoppers Worry Two Capitals," *Wall Street Journal,* April 29, 1993, p. A1; Yumiko Ono, "Cosmetics Industry May Get Make-Over," *Wall Street Journal,* August 17, 1993, p. B1.

102. Leslie Chang, "Western Stores Woo Chinese Wallets," *Wall Street Journal,* November 26, 2002, pp. B1, B6.

103. Daniel J. Howard and Charles Gengler, "Emotional Contagion Effects on Product Attitudes," *Journal of Consumer Research,* September 2001, pp. 189–201.

104. Susan T. Fiske, "Schema Triggered Affect: Applications to Social Perception," in eds. Margaret S. Clark and Susan T. Fiske, *Affect and Cognition: The 17th Annual Carnegie Symposium on Cognition* (Hillsdale, N.J.: Lawrence Erlbaum, 1982), pp. 55–77; Mita Sujan, James R. Bettman, and Harish Sujan, "Effects of Consumer Expectations on Information Processing and Selling Encounters," *Journal of Marketing Research,* November 1986, pp. 346–353.

105. Peter L. Wright, "An Adaptive Consumer's View of Attitudes and Choice Mechanisms as Viewed by an Equally Adaptive Advertiser," in ed. William D. Wells, *Attitude Research at Bay* (Chicago: American Marketing Association, 1976) pp. 113–131.

106. Baba Shiv and Alexander Fedorikhin, "Heart and Mind in Conflict: The Interplay of Affect and Cognition in Consumer Decision Making," *Journal of Consumer Research,* vol. 26, December 1999, pp. 278–292.

107. Susan T. Fiske and Mark A. Pavelchak, "Category-Based versus Piecemeal-Based Affective Responses: Developments in Schema-Triggered Affect," in eds. R. M. Sorrentino and E. T. Higgins, *The Handbook of Motivation and Cognition: Foundations of Social Behavior* (New York: Guilford, 1986), pp. 167–203; David M. Boush and Barbara Loken, "A Process-Tracing Study of Brand Extension Evaluation," *Journal of Marketing Research,* February 1991, pp. 16–28.

108. Fiske, "Schema Triggered Affect"; Mita Sujan, "Consumer Knowledge: Effects on Evaluation Strategies Mediating Consumer Judgments," *Journal of Consumer Research,* June 1985, pp. 31–46.

109. Stephanie Thompson, "Jell-O Sales Jiggle Downward; X-Treme Products Readied," *Advertising Age,* November 19, 2001, *www.adage.com/news.cms?newsid=33449.*

110. Ralph I. Allison and Kenneth P. Uhl, "Influence of Beer Brand Identification on Taste Perception," *Journal of Marketing Research,* August 1964, pp. 36–39.

111. Wayne D. Hoyer and Stephen P. Brown, "Effects of Brand Awareness on Choice for a Common, Repeat-Purchase Product," *Journal of Consumer Research,* September 1990, pp. 141–148.

112. M. Carole Macklin, "Preschoolers' Learning of Brand Names from Visual Cues," *Journal of Consumer Research,* December 1996, pp. 251–261.

113. Leong, "Consumer Decision Making for Common, Repeat-Purchase Products."

114. Jim Stafford, "Fame of Brand Names Has Changed with Time," *Daily Oklahoman,* February 2, 2005, *www.newsok.com;* Richard W. Stevenson, "The Brands with Billion Dollar Names," *New York Times* October 28, 1988, p. A1.

115. Gerry Khermouch, "The Best Global Brands," *Business Week,* August 6, 2001, pp. 50–57; Betsy McKay, "Siberian

Soft-Drink Queen Outmarkets Coke and Pepsi," *Wall Street Journal*, August 23, 1999, pp. B1, B4.

116. Karen V. Fernandez and Dennis L. Rosen, "The Effectiveness of Information and Color in Yellow Pages Advertising," *Journal of Advertising*, vol. 29, no. 2, Summer 2000, pp. 61–73.
117. Robert W. Veryzer and J. Wesley Hutchinson, "The Influence of Unity and Prototypicality on Aesthetic Responses to New Product Designs," *Journal of Consumer Research*, March 1998, pp. 374–394.
118. Guliz Ger, "Problems of Marketization in Romania and Turkey," in eds. Clifford Schultz, Russell Belk, and Guliz Ger, *Consumption in Marketizing Economies* (Greenwich, Conn.: JAI Press, 1995).
119. Eric Yang, "Co-brand or Be Damned," *Brandweek*, November 21, 1994, pp. 21–24.
125. Karen Benezra, "Brock Party," *Brandweek*, March 27, 1995, pp. 25–30.
126. M. Venkatesan, "Cognitive Consistency and Novelty Seeking," in eds. Scott Ward and Thomas S. Robertson, *Consumer Behavior: Theoretical Sources* (Englewood Cliffs, N.J.: Prentice-Hall, 1973), pp. 354–384; Leigh McAlister, "A Dynamic Attribute Satiation Model of Variety Seeking Behavior," *Journal of Consumer Research*, September 1982, pp. 141–150.
127. Rebecca K. Ratner, Barbara E. Kahn, and Daniel Kahneman, "Choosing Less-Preferred Experiences for the Sake of Variety," *Journal of Consumer Research*, vol. 26, June 1999, pp. 1–15.
128. Rebecca K. Ratner and Barbara E. Kahn, "The Impact of Private versus Public Consumption on Variety-Seeking Behavior," *Journal of Consumer Research*, September 2002, pp. 246+.
129. Hans C.M. Van Trijp, Wayne D. Hoyer, and J. Jeffrey Inman, "Why Switch? Product Category-Level Explanations for True Variety Seeking," *Journal of Marketing Research*, August 1996, pp. 281–292; Wayne D. Hoyer and Nancy M. Ridgway, "Variety Seeking as an Explanation for Exploratory Purchase Behavior: A Theoretical Model," in ed. Thomas C. Kinnear, *Advances in Consumer Research*, vol. 11 (Ann Arbor, Mich.: Association for Consumer Research, 1984), pp. 114–119.
130. J. Jeffrey Inman, "The Role of Sensory-Specific Satiety in Attribute-Level Variety Seeking," *Journal of Consumer Research*, vol. 28, June 2001, pp. 105–120.
131. Saatya Menon and Barbara E. Kahn, "The Impact of Context on Variety Seeking in Product Choices," *Journal of Consumer Research*, December 1995, pp. 285–295.
132. Erich A. Joachimsthaler and John L. Lastovicka, "Optimal Stimulation Level-Exploratory Behavior Models," *Journal of Consumer Research*, December 1984, pp. 830–835.
133. Albert Mehrabian and James Russell, *An Approach to Environmental Psychology* (Cambridge, Mass.: MIT Press, 1974).
134. Linda L. Price and Nancy M. Ridgway, "Use Innovativeness, Vicarious Exploration and Purchase Exploration: Three Facets of Consumer Varied Behavior," in ed. Bruce Walker, *American Marketing Association Educators' Conference Proceedings* (Chicago: American Marketing Association, 1982), pp. 56–60.
136. Hollis Ashman and Jacqueline Beckley, "The Spin on Sprite Remix: Is There Enough Novelty to Go Around?" *Food Processing*, September 2003, pp. 18+.
138. Michael Selz, "As Fast Food Menus Add Items, Dyspeptic Diners Cry, 'No More,' *Wall Street Journal*, July 25, 1995, pp. B1, B2.
139. Barbara E. Kahn and Brian Wansink, "The Influence of Assortment Structure on Perceived Variety and Consumption Quantities," *Journal of Consumer Research*, March 2004, pp. 519–533.
140. Dennis W. Rook, "The Buying Impulse," *Journal of Consumer Research*, September 1987, pp. 189–199; Craig J. Thompson, William B. Locander, and Howard R. Pollio, "The Lived Meaning of Free Choice: Existential-Phenomenological Description of Everyday Consumer Experiences of Contemporary Married Women," *Journal of Consumer Research*, December 1990, pp. 346–361.
141. Jacqueline J. Kacen and Julie Anne Lee, "The Influence of Culture on Consumer Impulsive Buying Behavior," *Journal of Consumer Psychology*, 2002, pp. 163–176.
142. Roy F. Baumeister, "Yielding to Temptation: Self-Control Failure, Impulsive Behavior, and Consumer Behavior," *Journal of Consumer Research*, March 2002, pp. 670+.
143. J. Jeffrey Inman and Russell S. Winer, "Where the Rubber Meets the Road: A Model of In-store Consumer Decision Making," *Marketing Science Institute Report Summary*, December 1998, pp. 98–122; "How We Shop . . . From Mass to Market," *Brandweek*, January 9, 1995, p. 17; Danny Bellenger, D. H. Robertson, and Elizabeth C. Hirschman, "Impulse Buying Varies by Product," *Journal of Advertising Research*, December 1978–January 1979, pp. 15–18.
144. Cathy J. Cobb and Wayne D. Hoyer, "Planned vs. Impulse Purchase Behavior," *Journal of Retailing*, Winter 1986, pp. 384–409.
145. Rook, "The Buying Impulse."
146. Russell W. Belk, "Materialism: Trait Aspects of Living in a Material World," *Journal of Consumer Research*, December 1985, pp. 265–280; P. S. Raju, "Optimum Stimulation Level: Its Relationship to Personality, Demographics, and Exploratory Behavior," *Journal of Consumer Research*, December 1980, pp. 272–282; Danny Bellenger and P. K. Korgaonkar, "Profiling the Recreational Shopper," *Journal of Retailing*, Fall 1980, pp. 77–92.
147. Dennis W. Rook and Robert J. Fisher, "Normative Influences on Impulsive Buying Behavior," *Journal of Consumer Research*, December 1995, pp. 305–313; Radhika Puri, "Measuring and Modifying Consumer Impulsiveness: A Cost-Benefit Accessibility Framework," *Journal of Consumer Psychology*, vol. 5, no. 2, 1996, pp. 87–114.
148. Inman and Winer, "Where the Rubber Meets the Road."
149. Nancy Millman, "Horn of Plenty Has Its Price," *Austin American Statesman*, August 8, 1996, pp. D1, D2.
150. "Brand News," *Global Cosmetic Industry*, February 2005, p. 17.
151. Bussey, "Japan's Wary Shoppers Worry Two Capitals."

CHAPTER 12

2. For a review, see William H. Cummings and M. Venkatesan, "Cognitive Dissonance and Consumer Behavior: A Review of the Evidence," *Journal of Marketing Research,* August 1976, pp. 303–308; also see Dieter Frey and Marita Rosch, "Information Seeking after Decisions: The Roles of Novelty of Information and Decision Reversibility," *Personality and Social Psychology Bulletin,* March 1984, pp. 91–98.
3. Michael Tsiros and Vikas Mittal, "Regret: A Model of Its Antecedents and Consequences in Consumer Decision Making," *Journal of Consumer Research,* vol. 26, March 2000, pp. 401–417.
4. Alan D. J. Cooke, Tom Meyvis, and Alan Schwartz, "Avoiding Future Regret in Purchase-Timing Decisions," *Journal of Consumer Research,* vol. 27, March 2001, pp. 447–459.
5. J. Jeffrey Inman and Marcel Zeelenberg, "Regret in Repeat Purchase versus Switching Decisions: The Attenuating Role of Decision Justifiability," *Journal of Consumer Research,* June 2002, pp. 116+.
6. Stephen J. Hoch and John Deighton, "Managing What Consumers Learn from Experience," *Journal of Marketing,* April 1989, pp. 1–20.
7. Ziv Carmon, Klaus Wertenbroch, and Marcel Zeelenberg, "Option Attachment: When Deliberating Makes Choosing Feel Like Losing," *Journal of Consumer Research,* June 2003, pp. 15+.
8. Allan Pavio, *Imagery and Verbal Processes* (New York: Holt, Rinehart, & Winston, 1981).
9. Robert E. Smith and William R. Swinyard, "Information Response Models: An Integrated Approach," *Journal of Marketing,* Winter 1982, pp. 81–93; Deanna S. Kempf and Robert E. Smith, "Consumer Processing of Product Trial and the Influence of Prior Advertising: A Structural Modeling Approach," *Journal of Marketing Research,* August 1998, pp. 325–338.
10. Ida E. Berger and Andrew A. Mitchell, "The Effect of Advertising on Attitude Accessibility, Attitude Confidence, and the Attitude-Behavior Relationship," *Journal of Consumer Research,* December 1989, pp. 269–279; Alice A. Wright and John G. Lynch Jr., "Communication Effects of Advertising vs. Direct Experience When Both Search and Experience Attributes Are Present," *Journal of Consumer Research,* March 1995, pp. 708–718.
11. Patricia M. West, "Predicting Preferences: An Examination of Agent Learning," *Journal of Consumer Research,* June 1996, pp. 68–80.
12. Jennifer Aaker, Susan Fournier, and S. Adam Brasel, "When Good Brands Do Bad," *Journal of Consumer Research,* June 2004, pp. 1–16.
13. Merrie Brucks, "The Effects of Product Class Knowledge on Information Search Behavior," *Journal of Consumer Research,* June 1985, pp. 1–16.
14. Joseph W. Alba and J. Wesley Hutchinson, "Dimensions of Consumer Expertise," *Journal of Consumer Research,* March 1987, pp. 411–454.
15. Eric J. Johnson and J. Edward Russo, "Product Familiarity and Learning New Information," *Journal of Consumer Research,* June 1984, pp. 542–551.
16. Stephen J. Hoch and Young-Won Ha, "Consumer Learning: Advertising and the Ambiguity of Product Experience," *Journal of Consumer Research,* October 1986, pp. 221–233.
17. A. V. Muthukrishnan and Frank R. Kardes, "Persistent Preferences for Product Attributes: The Effects of the Initial Choice Context and Uninformative Experience," *Journal of Consumer Research,* June 2001, pp. 89+.
18. Paul Herr, Steven J. Sherman, and Russell H. Fazio, "On the Consequences of Priming: Assimilation and Contrast Effects," *Journal of Experimental Social Psychology,* July 1983, pp. 323–340; Hoch and Ha, "Consumer Learning."
19. Reid Hastie, "Causes and Effects of Causal Attributions," *Journal of Personality and Social Psychology,* July 1984, pp. 44–56; Thomas K. Srull, Meryl Lichtenstein, and Myron Rothbart, "Associative Storage and Retrieval Processes in Person Memory," *Journal of Experimental Psychology: General,* vol. 11, no. 6, 1985, pp. 316–435.
20. Durairaj Maheswaran, "Country of Origin as a Stereotype: Effects of Consumer Expertise and Attribute Strength on Product Evaluations," *Journal of Consumer Research,* September 1994, pp. 354–365.
21. John Deighton, "The Interaction of Advertising and Evidence," *Journal of Consumer Research,* December 1984, pp. 763–770; Hoch and Ha, "Consumer Learning."
22. Bernard Weiner, "Spontaneous Causal Thinking," *Psychological Bulletin,* January 1985, pp. 74–84.
23. Hoch and Deighton, "Managing What Consumers Learn from Experience."
24. Rekha Balu, "Heinz Places Ketchup in Global Account," *Wall Street Journal,* September 9, 1998, p. B8.
25. Kate MacArthur, "KFC Hopes Seinfeld Star Will Convert Bored Burger Eaters," *Advertising Age,* July 27, 2001, *www.adage.com/news.cms?newsID=30246j;* Kathryn Chen, "KFC Rules Fast-Food Roost in Shanghai," *Wall Street Journal,* December 2, 1997, pp. B1, B12; *www.kfc.com.*
29. Youjae Yi, "A Critical Review of Consumer Satisfaction," *Review of Marketing* (Chicago: American Marketing Association, 1992), pp. 68–123.
30. Richard L. Oliver, "Processing of the Satisfaction Response in Consumption: A Suggested Framework and Research Propositions," *Journal of Consumer Satisfaction, Dissatisfaction, and Complaining Behavior,* vol. 2, 1989, pp. 1–16; Haim Mano and Richard L. Oliver, "Assessing the Dimensionality and Structure of the Consumption Experience: Evaluation, Feeling, and Satisfaction, *Journal of Consumer Research,* December 1993, pp. 451– 466.
31. Haim Mano and Richard L. Oliver, "Assessing the Dimensionality and Structure of the Consumption Experience: Evaluation, Feeling, and Satisfaction," *Journal of Consumer Research,* December 1993, pp. 451–466.
32. Michael D. Johnson, Eugene W. Anderson, and Claes Fornell, "Rational and Adaptive Performance Expectations in a Customer Satisfaction Framework," *Journal of Consumer Research,* March 1995, pp. 695–707.

33. Richard L. Oliver, "Measurement and Evaluation of Satisfaction Processes in Retail Settings," *Journal of Retailing,* Fall 1981, pp. 25–48.
34. Sarah Fisher Gardial, D. Scott Clemons, Robert B. Woodruff, David W. Schumann, and Mary Jane Burns, "Comparing Consumers' Recall of Prepurchase and Postpurchase Evaluation Experiences," *Journal of Consumer Research,* March 1994, pp. 548–560.
35. Marsha L. Richins and Peter H. Bloch, "Post-purchase Satisfaction: Incorporating the Effects of Involvement and Time," *Journal of Business Research,* September 1991, pp. 145–158; Vikas Mittal and Wagner A. Kamakura, "Satisfaction, Repurchase Intent, and Repurchase Behavior: Investigating the Moderating Effect of Customer Characteristics," *Journal of Marketing Research,* February 2001, pp. 131–142.
36. Mary C. Gilly and Betsy D. Gelb, "Post-purchase Consumer Processes and the Complaining Consumer," *Journal of Consumer Research,* December 1982, pp. 323–328.
37. Vikas Mattal and Wagner A. Kamakura, "Satisfaction, Repurchase Intent, and Repurchase Behavior: Investigating the Moderating Effect of Customer Characteristics," *Journal of Marketing Research,* vol. 38, February 2001, pp. 131–142.
38. Claes Fornell, "A National Customer Satisfaction Barometer: The Swedish Experience," *Journal of Marketing,* January 1992, pp. 6–21.
39. Robert D. Hof, "How Amazon Cleared That Hurdle," *BusinessWeek,* February 4, 2002, pp. 60–61; George Anders, "Amazon.com Sales More Than Quadruple," *Wall Street Journal,* July 23, 1998, p. B5.
40. Douglas Bowman and Das Narayandas, "Managing Customer-Initiated Contacts with Manufacturers: The Impact of Share of Category Requirements and Word-of-Mouth Behavior," *Journal of Marketing Research,* August 2001, pp. 281–297.
41. Libby Estell, "This Call Center Accelerates Sales," *Sales & Marketing Management,* February 1999, p. 72.
42. Tom Edmonds, "Speakers Examine Caring, Loyalty Issues," *Furniture Today,* February 25, 2005, *www.furnituretoday.com.*
43. Tim Triplett, "Product Recall Spurs Company to Improve Customer Satisfaction," *Marketing News,* April 11, 1994, p. 6.
44. Sharon Silke Carty, "Car Dealers Lose Service Business," *Wall Street Journal,* November 3, 2004, p. D11.
47. Randy Brandt, "Satisfaction Studies Must Measure What the Customer Wants and Expects," *Marketing News,* October 27, 1997, p. 17.
48. Chezy Ofir and Itamar Simonson, "In Search of Negative Customer Feedback: The Effect of Expecting to Evaluate on Satisfaction Evaluations," *Journal of Marketing Research,* vol. 38, May 2001, pp. 170–182.
49. Robert A. Westbrook, "Product/Consumption-Based Affective Responses and Postpurchase Processes," *Journal of Marketing Research,* August 1987, pp. 258–270.
50. Charlotte Klopp and John Sterlickhi, "Customer Satisfaction Just Catching On in Europe," *Marketing News,* May 28, 1990, p. 5.
51. Brad Gale, "Satisfaction Is Not Enough," *Marketing News,* October 27, 1997, p. 18.
52. Vavra, "Learning from Your Losses."
53. Klopp and Sterlickhi, "Customer Satisfaction Just Catching On in Europe."
54. Guliz Ger, Russell Belk, and Dana-Nicoleta Lascu, "The Development of Consumer Desire in Marketing and Developing Economies: The Cases of Romania and Turkey," in eds. Leigh McAlister and Michael L. Rothschild, *Advances in Consumer Research,* vol. 20 (Provo, Utah: Association for Consumer Research, 1993), pp. 102–107.
55. Richard L. Oliver, "A Cognitive Model of the Antecedents and Consequences of Satisfaction Decisions," *Journal of Marketing Research,* November 1980, pp. 460–469; Yu, "A Critical Review of Consumer Satisfaction," p. 92; see also Douglas M. Stayman, Dana L. Alden, and Karen H. Smith, "Some Effects of Schematic Processing on Consumer Expectations and Disconfirmation Judgments," *Journal of Consumer Research,* September 1992, pp. 240–255.
56. Yi, "A Critical Review of Consumer Satisfaction," p. 92; see also Douglas M. Stayman, Dana L. Alden, and Karen H. Smith, "Some Effects of Schematic Processing on Consumer Expectations and Disconfirmation Judgments," *Journal of Consumer Research,* September 1992, pp. 240–255.
57. Praveen K. Kopalle and Donald R. Lehman, "The Effects of Advertised and Observed Quality on Expectations about New Product Quality," *Journal of Marketing Research,* August 1995, pp. 280–291; Stephen A. LaTour and Nancy C. Peat, "The Role of Situationally-Produced Expectations, Others' Experiences, and Prior Experiences in Determining Satisfaction," in ed. Jerry C. Olson, *Advances in Consumer Research* (Ann Arbor, Mich.: Association for Consumer Research, 1980), pp. 588–592; Ernest R. Cadotte, Robert B. Woodruff, and Roger L. Jenkins, "Expectations and Norms in Models of Consumer Satisfaction," *Journal of Marketing Research,* August 1987, pp. 305–314.
58. David K. Tse and Peter C. Wilson, "Models of Consumer Satisfaction Formation: An Extension," *Journal of Marketing Research,* May 1988, pp. 204–212.
59. Ruth N. Bolton and James H. Drew, "A Multistage Model of Customers' Assessments of Service Quality and Value," *Journal of Consumer Research,* March 1991, pp. 375–384; Michael D. Johnson, Eugene W. Anderson, and Claes Fornell, "Rational and Adaptive Performance Expectations in a Customer Satisfaction Framework," *Journal of Consumer Research,* March 1995, pp. 695–707.
60. Glenn B. Voss, A. Parasuraman, and Dhruv Grewal, "The Roles of Price, Performance, and Expectations in Determining Satisfaction in Service Exchanges," *Journal of Marketing,* October 1998, pp. 46–61; A. Parasuraman, Valerie A. Zeithaml, and Leonard L. Berry, "SERVQUAL: A Multiple-Item Scale for Measuring Consumer Perceptions of Service Quality," *Journal of Retailing,* Spring 1988, pp. 12–36.

61. "Cellular Service: Best Carriers," *Consumer Reports,* February 2005, pp. 18–20.
62. Johnson, Anderson, and Fornell, "Rational and Adaptive Performance Expectations in a Customer Satisfaction Framework."
63. Martha Slud, "Properly Packed Sacks Keep Customers Coming Back," *Marketing News,* May 20, 1996, p. 5.
64. Bob Tedeschi, "Online Retailers Say They Are Ready to Deliver Goods to Christmas Shoppers Who Waited Until the Last Minute," *New York Times,* December 20, 2004, p. C4.
65. Stephanie Dellande, Mary C. Gilly, and John L. Graham, "Gaining Compliance and Losing Weight: The Role of the Service Provider in Health Care Services," *Journal of Marketing,* July 2004, pp. 78–91.
66. Tse and Wilson, "Models of Consumer Satisfaction Formation"; Richard L. Oliver, "Cognitive, Affective, and Attribute-Bases of the Satisfaction Response," *Journal of Consumer Research,* December 1993, pp. 418–430; Richard L. Oliver and Wayne S. DeSarbo, "Response Determinants in Satisfaction Judgments," *Journal of Consumer Research,* March 1988, pp. 495–507.
67. Gilbert A. Churchill and Carol Supranant, "An Investigation into the Determinants of Customer Satisfaction," *Journal of Marketing Research,* November 1982, pp. 491–504; Richard L. Oliver and William O. Bearden, "The Role of Involvement in Satisfaction Processes," in eds. Richard P. Bagozzi and Alice M. Tybout, *Advances in Consumer Research,* vol. 10 (Ann Arbor, Mich.: Association for Consumer Research, 1983), pp. 250–255; Paul G. Patterson, "Expectations and Product Performance as Determinants of Satisfaction for a High Involvement Purchase," *Psychology and Marketing,* September–October 1993, pp. 449–465.
68. Robert A. Westbrook and Michael D. Reilly, "Value-Percept Disparity: An Alternative to the Disconfirmation of Expectations Theory of Consumer Satisfaction," in eds. Richard P. Bagozzi and Alice M. Tybout, *Advances in Consumer Research,* vol. 10 (Ann Arbor, Mich.: Association for Consumer Research, 1983), pp. 256–261.
69. William O. Bearden and Jesse E. Teel, "Selected Determinants of Consumer Satisfaction and Complaint Reports," *Journal of Marketing Research,* February 1983, pp. 21–28; John E. Swan and I. Frederick Trawick, "Disconfirmation of Expectations and Satisfaction with a Retail Service," *Journal of Retailing,* Fall 1981, pp. 49–67; Westbrook and Reilly, "Value-Percept Disparity."
70. Westbrook, "Product/Consumption-Based Affective Responses and Postpurchase Processes"; Robert A. Westbrook and Richard L. Oliver, "The Dimensionality of Consumption Emotion Patterns and Consumer Satisfaction," *Journal of Consumer Research,* June 1991, pp. 84–91; Mano and Oliver, "Assessing the Dimensionality and Structure of the Consumption Experience."
71. Westbrook and Oliver, "The Dimensionality of Consumption Emotion Patterns."
72. Diane M. Phillips and Hans Baumgartner, 'The Role of Consumption Emotions in the Satisfaction Response," *Journal of Consumer Psychology,* 2002, pp. 243–252.
73. Paul W. Miniard, Sunil Bhatla, and Deepak Sirdeshmukh, "Mood as a Determinant of Postconsumption Product Evaluations: Mood Effects and Their Dependency on the Affective Intensity of the Consumption Experience," *Journal of Consumer Psychology,* 1992, pp. 173–195.
74. Susan Fournier and David Glen Mick, "Rediscovering Satisfaction," *Journal of Marketing,* vol. 63, October 1999, pp. 5–23.
75. "Customer Satisfaction Key to Success," *The Yomiuri Shimbun,* February 16, 2005, *www.yomiuri.co.jp.*
76. Richard W. Olshavsky and John A. Miller, "Consumer Expectations, Product Performance, and Perceived Product Quality," *Journal of Marketing Research,* February 1972, pp. 469–499.
77. Goll, "Pizza Hut Tosses Its Pies into the Ring."
78. Diane Halstead, Cornelia Droge, and M. Bixby Cooper, "Product Warranties and Post-purchase Service," *Journal of Services Marketing,* vol. 7, no. 1, 1993, pp. 33–40; Joshua Lyle Wiener, "Are Warranties Accurate Signals of Product Reliability?" *Journal of Consumer Research,* September 1985, pp. 245–250.
80. Ger, "Problems of Marketization in Romania and Turkey."
81. Jesse Drucker, "Hotel Rage: Losing It in the Lobby," *Wall Street Journal,* February 16, 2001, pp. W1, W7.
82. Susan Greco, "Saints Alive!" *Inc.,* August 2001, pp. 44–45.
83. Joanne Lee-Young, "In Hong Kong, Tobacco Promotes Away," *Wall Street Journal,* June 30, 1998, pp. B8.
84. C. B. Bhattacharya and Sankar Sen, "Consumer-Company Identification" A Framework for Understanding Consumers' Relationships with Companies," *Journal of Marketing,* April 2003, pp. 76–88; Dennis B. Arnett, Steve D. German, and Shelby D. Hunt, "The Identify Salience Model of Relationship Marketing Success: The Case of Nonprofit Marketing," *Journal of Marketing,* April 2003, pp. 89–105.
85. Bernard Weiner, "Reflections and Reviews: Attributional Thoughts about Consumer Behavior," *Journal of Consumer Research,* vol. 27, December 2000, pp. 382–287; Valerie S. Folkes, "Consumer Reactions to Product Failure: An Attributional Approach," *Journal of Consumer Research,* March 1984, pp. 398–409; Valerie S. Folkes, "Recent Attribution Research in Consumer Behavior: A Review and New Directions," *Journal of Consumer Research,* March 1988, pp. 548–565; Richard W. Mizerski, Linda L. Golden, and Jerome B. Kernan, "The Attribution Process in Consumer Decision Making," *Journal of Consumer Research,* September 1979, pp. 123–140.
86. Mary Jo Bitner, "Evaluating Service Encounters: The Effects of Physical Surrounding and Employee Responses," *Journal of Marketing,* April 1990, pp. 69–82.
87. Valerie S. Folkes, Susan Koletsky, and John L. Graham, "A Field Study of Causal Inferences and Consumer Reaction: The View from the Airport," *Journal of Consumer Research,* March 1987, pp. 534–539.

88. Neeli Bendapudi and Robert P. Leone, "Psychological Implications of Customer Participation in Co-Production," *Journal of Marketing*, January 2003, pp. 14–28.

89. Michael Tsiros, Vikas Mittal, and William T. Ross, Jr., "The Role of Attributions in Customer Satisfaction: A Reexamination," *Journal of Consumer Research*, September 2004, pp. 476–483.

90. David L. Margulius, "Going to the A.T.M. for More Than a Fistful of Twenties," *New York Times*, January 17, 2002, p. D7; Eleena de Lisser, "Banks Court Disenchanted Customers," *Wall Street Journal*, August 30, 1993, p. B1.

91. Amy K. Smith, Ruth N. Bolton, and Janet Wagner, "A Model of Customer Satisfaction with Service Encounters Involving Failure and Recovery," *Journal of Marketing Research*, vol. 36, August 1999, pp. 356–372.

92. Bitner, "Evaluating Service Encounters."

93. Richard L. Oliver and John E. Swan, "Equity and Disconfirmation Paradigms as Influences on Merchant and Product Satisfaction," *Journal of Consumer Research*, December 1989, pp. 372–383; Elaine G. Walster, G. William Walster, and Ellen Berscheid, *Equity: Theory and Research* (Boston: Allyn & Bacon, 1978).

94. Peter R. Darke and Darren W. Dahl, "Fairness and Discounts; The Subjective Value of a Bargain," *Journal of Consumer Psychology*, 2003, pp. 328–338.

95. Richard L. Oliver and John L. Swan, "Consumer Perceptions of Interpersonal Equity and Satisfaction in Transactions, A Field Survey Approach," *Journal of Marketing*, April 1989, pp. 21–35.

96. Ruth N. Bolton and Katherine N. Lemon, "A Dynamic Model of Customers' Usage of Services: Usage as an Antecedent and Consequence of Satisfaction," *Journal of Marketing Research*, vol. 36, May 1999, pp. 171–186.

97. James G. Maxhamm III and Richard G. Netemeyer, "Firms Reap What They Sow: The Effects of Shared Values and Perceived Organizational Justice on Customers' Evaluations of Complaint Handling," *Journal of Marketing*, January 2003, pp. 46–62.

98. Catherine Valenti, "Order with Care: Internet Sees Rapid Growth in Consumer Complaints," *ABC News.com*, November 11, 2001.

99. Ger, "Problems of Marketization in Romania and Turkey."

100. Day, "Modeling Choices among Alternative Responses to Dissatisfaction"; Marsha L. Richins, "Word-of-Mouth Communication as Negative Information," *Journal of Marketing*, Winter 1983, pp. 68–78.

101. Day, "Modeling Choices among Alternative Responses to Dissatisfaction"; Arthur Best and Alan R. Andreasen, "Consumer Response to Unsatisfactory Purchases," *Law and Society*, Spring 1977, pp. 701–742.

102. Caroline E. Mayer, "Griping about Cellular Bills," *Washington Post*, February 28, 2001, p. G17.

103. Bearden and Teel, "Selected Determinants of Consumer Satisfaction and Complaint Reports."

104. Cathy Goodwin and Ivan Ross, "Consumer Evaluations of Responses to Complaints: What's Fair and Why," *Journal of Services Marketing*, Summer 1990, pp. 53–61.

105. Day, "Modeling Choices among Alternative Responses to Dissatisfaction"; Jagdip Singh and Roy D. Howell, "Consumer Complaining Behavior: A Review," in eds. H. Keith Hunt and Ralph L. Day, *Consumer Satisfaction, Dissatisfaction, and Complaining Behavior* (Bloomington, Ind.: Indiana University Press, 1985).

106. S. Krishnan and S. A. Valle, "Dissatisfaction Attributions and Consumer Complaint Behavior," in ed. William L. Wilkie, *Advances in Consumer Research* (Miami: Association for Consumer Research, 1979), pp. 445–449.

107. Folkes, "Consumer Reactions to Product Failure."

108. Nada Nasr Bechwati and Maureen Morrin, "Outraged Customers: Getting Even at the Expense of Getting a Good Deal," *Journal of Consumer Psychology*, 2003, pp. 440–453.

109. Kjell Gronhaug and Gerald R. Zaltman, "Complainers and Noncomplainers Revisited: Another Look at the Data," in ed. Kent B. Monroe, *Advances in Consumer Research* (Ann Arbor, Mich.: Association for Consumer Research, 1981), pp. 159–165.

110. Ger, "Problems of Marketization in Romania and Turkey."

111. Larry M. Robinson and Robert L. Berl, "What about Compliments? A Follow-up Study on Consumer Complaints and Compliments," in eds. H. Keith Hunt and Ralph L. Day, *Refining Concepts and Measures of Consumer Satisfaction and Complaining Behavior* (Bloomington, Ind.: Indiana University Press, 1980), pp. 144–148.

112. T. Bettina Cornwell, Alan David Bligh, and Emin Babakus, "Complaint Behaviors of Mexican-American Consumers to a Third Party Agency," *Journal of Consumer Affairs*, Summer 1991, pp. 1–18.

113. Sigfredo A. Hernandez, William Strahle, Hector Garcia, and Robert C. Sorenson, "A Cross-Cultural Study of Consumer Complaining Behavior: VCR Owners in the U.S. and Puerto Rico," *Journal of Consumer Policy*, June 1991, pp. 35–62.

114. Jagdip Singh, "A Typology of Consumer Dissatisfaction Response Styles," *Journal of Retailing*, Spring 1990, pp. 57–99.

115. Thomas Petzinger Jr., "Customer from Hell Can Be a Blessing in Disguise for Sales," *Wall Street Journal*, March 1, 1996, p. B1.

116. Emily Nelson, "Shower or Bath? It's a Hotel's Tough Call," *Wall Street Journal*, May 14, 1998, pp. B1, B11.

117. Alan J. Resnick and Robert R. Harmon, "Consumer Complaints and Managerial Response: A Holistic Approach," *Journal of Marketing*, Winter 1983, pp. 86–97.

118. Denise T. Smart and Charles L. Martin, "Manufacturer Responsiveness to Consumer Correspondence: An Empirical Investigation of Consumer Perceptions," *Journal of Consumer Affairs*, Summer 1992, pp. 104–128; Mary Gilly and Betsy Gelb, "Post-purchase Consumer Processes and the Complaining Consumer Behavior," *Journal of Consumer Research*, December 1982, pp. 323–328.

119. Tiffany Kary, "Online Retailers Fumble on Customer Care," *CNET News.com*, January 3, 2002, *http://news.com.com/2100-1017-801668.html.*

120. Marlon A. Walker, "Online Service Lags at Big Firms," *Wall Street Journal*, July 1, 2004, p. B4.

121. Chow-Hou Wee and Celine Chong, "Determinants of Consumer Satisfaction/Dissatisfaction towards Dispute Settlements in Singapore," *European Journal of Marketing*, vol. 25, no. 10, 1991, pp. 6–16.

122. Lou Hirsh, "Consumer Gripe Sites—Hidden Treasure?" *CRM Daily.com*, January 2, 2002, *www.crmdaily.com/perl/story/?id=15555.*

123. James G. Maxham III and Richard G. Netemeyer, "A Longitudinal Study of Complaining Customers' Evaluations of Multiple Service Failures and Recovery Efforts," *Journal of Marketing*, October 2002, pp. 57–71.

124. Halstead, Droge, and Cooper, "Product Warranties and Post-purchase Service."

126. Ger, "Problems of Marketization in Romania and Turkey."

127. Claes Fornell and Nicholas M. Didow, "Economic Constraints on Consumer Complaining Behavior," in ed. Jerry C. Olson, *Advances in Consumer Research*, vol. 7 (Ann Arbor, Mich.: Association for Consumer Research, 1980), pp. 318–323; Claes Fornell and Birger Wernerfelt, "Defensive Marketing Strategy by Customer Complaint Management," *Journal of Marketing Research*, November 1987, pp. 337–346.

128. Claes Fornell and Robert A. Westbrook, "The Vicious Cycle of Consumer Complaints," *Journal of Marketing*, Summer 1984, pp. 68–78.

129. Richins, "Word-of-Mouth Communication as Negative Information."

130. Yi, "A Critical Review of Consumer Satisfaction"; Johan Arndt, "Word-of-Mouth Advertising and Perceived Risk," in eds. Harold H. Kassarjian and Thomas R. Robertson, *Perspectives in Consumer Behavior* (Glenview, Ill.: Scott-Foresman, 1968).

133. Frederick F. Reichheld, *The Loyalty Effect: The Hidden Force behind Growth* (Boston: Harvard Business School Press, 1996).

134. Priscilla La Barbera and David W. Mazursky, "A Longitudinal Assessment of Consumer Satisfaction/Dissatisfaction: The Dynamic Aspect of Cognitive Processes," *Journal of Marketing Research*, November 1983, pp. 393–404; Ruth Bolton, "A Dynamic Model of the Duration of the Customer's Relationship with a Continuous Service Provider," *Marketing Science*, vol. 17, no. 1, 1998, pp. 45–65.

135. Thomas O. Jones and W. Earl Sasser, "Why Customers Defect," *Harvard Business Review*, November–December 1995, pp. 88–99.

136. Richard L. Oliver, "Whence Consumer Loyalty?" *Journal of Marketing*, vol. 63, 1999, pp. 33–44.

137. Frederick F. Reichheld and W. Earl Sasser, "Zero Defections: Quality Comes to Services," *Harvard Business Review*, September 1990, pp. 105–111; Eugene Anderson, Claes Fornell, and Donald H. Lehman, "Customer Satisfaction, Market Share, and Profitability: Findings from Sweden," *Journal of Marketing*, July 1994, pp. 53–66; Rajendra K. Srivastava, Tassadduq A. Shervani, and Liam Fahey, "Market-Based Assets and Shareholder Value: A Framework for Analysis," *Journal of Marketing*, vol. 62, no. 1, 1998, pp. 2–18.

138. Becky Ebenkamp, "The Complaint Department," *Brandweek*, June 18, 2001, p. 21; Reichheld, *The Loyalty Effect.*

143. Dan Zehr, "Dell Opening High-Tech Service Center in China," *Austin American-Statesman*, September 8, 2004, pp. B1, C3.

144. Melissa Martin Young and Melanie Wallendorf, "Ashes to Ashes, Dust to Dust: Conceptualizing Consumer Disposition of Possessions," in *Proceedings, Marketing Educators' Conference* (Chicago: American Marketing Association, 1989), pp. 33–39.

145. Young and Wallendorf, "Ashes to Ashes, Dust to Dust: Conceptualizing Consumer Disposition of Possessions;" see also Erica Mina Okada, "Trade-Ins, Mental Accounting, and Product Replacement Decisions," *Journal of Consumer Research*, March 2001, pp. 433–446; Jacob Jacoby, Carol K. Berning, and Thomas F. Dietvorst, "What about Disposition?" *Journal of Marketing*, April 1977, pp. 22–28; Gilbert D. Harrell and Diane M. McConocha, "Personal Factors Related to Consumer Product Disposal," *Journal of Consumer Affairs*, Winter 1992, pp. 397–417.

146. Jacoby, Berning, and Dietvorst, "What about Disposition?"; Young and Wallendorf, "Ashes to Ashes, Dust to Dust."

147. Harrell and McConocha, "Personal Factors Related to Consumer Product Disposal Tendencies."

148. Jacoby, Berning, and Dietvorst, "What about Disposition?"

149. John B. Sherry, Mary Ann McGrath, and Sidney J. Levy, "The Disposition of the Gift and Many Unhappy Returns," *Journal of Retailing*, Spring 1992, pp. 40–65.

150. Young and Wallendorf, "Ashes to Ashes, Dust to Dust."

151. Russell W. Belk, "Possessions and the Extended Self," *Journal of Consumer Research*, September 1988, pp. 139–168.

152. Young and Wallendorf, "Ashes to Ashes, Dust to Dust."

154. Melissa Martin Young, "Disposition of Possessions During Role Transitions," in eds. Rebecca H. Holman and Michael R. Solomon, *Advances in Consumer Research*, vol. 18 (Provo, Utah: Association for Consumer Research, 1991), pp. 33–39.

155. James H. Alexander, "Divorce, the Disposition of the Relationship, and Everything," in eds. Rebecca H. Holman and Michael R. Solomon, *Advances in Consumer Research*, vol. 18 (Provo, Utah: Association for Consumer Research, 1991), pp. 43–48.

156. James H. Alexander, John W. Shouten, and Scott D. Roberts, "Consumer Behavior and Divorce," in eds. Janeen Costa and Russell W. Belk, *Research in Consumer Behavior*, vol. 6 (Greenwich, Conn.: JAI Press, 1993), pp. 153–184.

157. For more information on this topic, see David J. Cheal, "Intergenerational Family Transfers," *Journal of Marriage and the Family*, November 1983, pp. 805–813; Jeffrey P. Rosenfeld, "Bequests from Resident to Resident: Inheritance in a Retirement Community," *The Gerontologist*, vol. 19, no. 6, 1979, pp. 594–600.

158. John F. Sherry Jr., "A Sociocultural Analysis of a Midwestern Flea Market," *Journal of Consumer Research*, June 1990, pp. 13–30.
159. Ibid; Russell W. Belk, John F. Sherry, and Melanie Wallendorf, "A Naturalistic Inquiry into Buyer and Seller Behavior at a Swap Meet," *Journal of Consumer Research*, March 1988, pp. 449–470.
160. Michael D. Reilly and Melanie Wallendorf, "A Comparison of Group Differences in Food Consumption Using Household Refuse," *Journal of Consumer Research*, September 1987, pp. 289–294.
161. Jacoby, Berning, and Dietvorst, "What about Disposition?"
162. For a review, see L. J. Shrum, Tina M. Lowrey, and John A. McCarty, "Recycling as a Marketing Problem: A Framework for Strategy Development," *Psychology and Marketing*, July–August 1994, pp. 393–416.
163. J. M. Hines, H. R. Hungerford, and A. N. Tomera, "Analysis and Synthesis of Research on Responsible Environmental Behavior: A Meta-Analysis," *Journal of Environmental Education*, Winter 1987, pp. 1–8.
164. Abhijit Biswas, Jane W. Licata, Daryl McKee, Chris Pullig, and Christopher Daughtridge, "The Recycling Cycle: Waste Recycling and Recycling Shopping Behaviors," *Journal of Public Policy & Marketing*, vol. 19, Spring 2000, pp. 93–105.
165. Rik G. M. Pieters, "Changing Garbage Disposal Patterns of Consumers: Motivation, Ability, and Performance," *Journal of Public Policy and Marketing*, Fall 1991, pp. 59–76.
166. Richard P. Bagozzi and Pratibha Dabholkar, "Consumer Recycling Goals and Their Effect on Decisions to Recycle," *Psychology and Marketing*, July–August 1994, pp. 313–340.
167. E. Howenstein, "Marketing Segmentation for Recycling," *Environment and Behavior*, March 1993, pp. 86–102.
168. Shrum, Lowrey, and McCarty, "Recycling as a Marketing Problem."
170. Susan E. Heckler, "The Role of Memory in Understanding and Encouraging Recycling Behavior," *Psychology and Marketing*, July–August 1994, pp. 375–392.
171. Pieters, "Changing Garbage Disposal Patterns of Consumers."
172. Susan Warren, "Recycler's Nightmare: Beer in Plastic," *Wall Street Journal*, November 16, 1999, pp. B1, B4.
174. Kenneth R. Lord, "Motivating Recycling Behavior: A Quasi-Experimental Investigation of Message and Source Strategies," *Psychology and Marketing*, July–August 1994, pp. 341–358.
176. Heckler, "The Role of Memory in Understanding and Encouraging Recycling Behavior."

CHAPTER 13

2. Michael M. Phillips, "Selling by Evoking What Defines a Generation," *Wall Street Journal*, August 13, 1996, pp. B1, B7.
3. Peter Francese, "Trend Spotting," *American Demographics*, July–August 2002, pp. 50+; Vickery, Greene, Branch, and Nelson, "Marketers Tweak Strategies as Age Groups Realign."
4. Laura Zinn, "Teens: Here Comes the Biggest Wave Yet," *BusinessWeek*, April 11, 1994, pp. 76–86; Lisa Marie Petersen, "I Bought What Was on Sale," *Brandweek*, February 22, 1993, pp. 12–13.
5. Dennis H. Tootelian and Ralph M. Gaedecke, "The Teen Market: An Exploratory Analysis of Income, Spending, and Shopping Patterns," *Journal of Consumer Marketing*, Fall 1994, pp. 35–44; George P. Moschis and Roy L. Moore, "Decision Making among the Young: A Socialization Perspective," *Journal of Consumer Research*, September 1979, pp. 101–112.
6. "The Six Value Segments of Global Youth," *Brandweek*, May 22, 2000, pp. 38+.
7. David Murphy, "Connecting with Online Teenagers," *Marketing*, September 27, 2001, pp. 31+.
8. Noah Rubin Brier, "Coming of Age," *American Demographics*, November 2004, pp. 16+;
9. Peter Francese, "Ahead of the Next Wave," *American Demographics*, September 2003, pp. 42–43; Robert Guy Matthews, "Spirits Makers Aim to Shake Up Stodgy Brands with Youth Push," *Wall Street Journal*, November 11, 2004, p. B5.
10. "To Reach the Unreachable Teen," *BusinessWeek*, September 18, 2000, pp. 78+.
11. "Teen Clout Grows; Chains React," *MMR*, August 20, 2001, pp. 29+.
12. Kerry Capell, "MTV's World," *BusinessWeek*, February 18, 2001, pp. 81–84; Sally Beatty and Carol Hymowitz, "How MTV Stays Tuned In to Teens," *Wall Street Journal*, March 21, 2000, pp. B1, B4.
13. Paula Dwyer, "The Euroteens (and How to Sell to Them)," *BusinessWeek*, April 11, 1994, p. 84.
14. Bob Tedeschi, "Online Retailers Pursue Teenagers," *New York Times*, February 28, 2005, *www.nytimes.com*.
15. Emily Nelson, "Beauty Makers Now Go Where the Boys Are," *Wall Street Journal*, August 10, 2000, pp. B1, B4.
16. Murphy, "Connecting with Online Teenagers"; Fara Warner, "Booming Asia Lures Credit-Card Firms," *Wall Street Journal*, November 24, 1995, p. B10.
17. Beatty and Hymowitz, "How MTV Stays Tuned In to Teens."
18. Norihiko Shirouzu, "Japan's High-School Girls Excel in the Art of Setting Trends," *Wall Street Journal*, April 24, 1998, pp. B1, B7.
19. Maureen Tkacik, "Fast Times for Retail Chain Behind the 'Euro' Shoe Trend," *Wall Street Journal*, November 21, 2002, p. B1.
20. Matthew Grimm, "Irvington, 10533," *Brandweek*, August 17, 1993, pp. 11–13.
21. Helene Cooper, "Once Again, Ads Woo Teens with Slang," *Wall Street Journal*, March 29, 1993, pp. B1, B6; Adrienne Ward Fawcett, "When Using Slang in Advertising: BVC," *Advertising Age*, August 23, 1993, p. S-6.
22. Barbara Martinez, "Antismoking Ads Aim to Gross Out Teens," *Wall Street Journal*, March 21, 1997, pp. B1, B8.
23. Jennie L. Phipps, "Networks Drill Deeper into Teen Market," *Electronic Media*, March 12, 2001, p. 20; Erin

White, "Teen Mags for Guys, Not Dolls," *Wall Street Journal*, August 10, 2000, pp. B1, B4; Wendy Bounds, "Teen-Magazine Boom: Beauty, Fashion, Stars, and Sex," *Wall Street Journal*, December 7, 1998, pp. B1, B10.

24. "To Reach the Unreachable Teen."
25. Cristina Merrill, "Keeping Up with Teens," *American Demographics*, October 1999, pp. 27–31.
26. Tedeschi, "Online Retailers Pursue Teenagers."
27. Leigh Muzslay, "Shoes That Morph from Sneakers to Skates Are Flying out of Stores," *Wall Street Journal*, July 26, 2001, p. B1.
28. Jeffrey A. Trachtenberg, "Targeting Young Adults," *Wall Street Journal*, October 4, 2004, pp. B1, B5.
29. Christina Duff, "It's Sad but True: Good Times Are Bad for Real Slackers," *Wall Street Journal*, August 6, 1998, pp. A1, A5; Carol Angrisani, "X Marks the Spot," *Brandmarketing*, April 2001, pp. 18+.
30. "Farther Along the Axis," *American Demographics*, May 2004, pp. 21+.
31. Pamela Paul, "Echo Boomerang," *American Demographics*, June 2001, pp. 45–49.
32. Debra O'Connor, "Home Stretch: Families Remodel Houses to Accommodate Parents or 'Boomerang' Children," *Pioneer Press*, March 18, 2003, *www.twincities.com/mld/pioneerpress*.
33. Angrisani, "X Marks the Spot."
34. Cyndee Miller, "X Marks the Lucrative Spot, But Some Advertisers Can't Hit Target," *Marketing News*, August 2, 1993, pp. 1, 14; Pat Sloan, "Xers Brush Off Cosmetics Marketers," *Advertising Age*, September 27, 1993, p. 4.
35. Alfred Schreiber, "Generation X the Next Big Event Target," *Advertising Age*, June 21, 1993, p. S-3; Robert Gustafson, "Marketing to Generation X? Better Practice Safe Sex," *Advertising Age*, March 7, 1994, p. 26.
36. Gerry Khermouch, "Would You Buy a Heineken from This Dude?" *Brandweek*, February 20, 1995, pp. 1, 6.
37. Joseph B. White, "Toyota, Seeking Younger Drivers, Uses Hip Hop, Web, Low Prices," *Wall Street Journal*, September 22, 1999, p. B10.
38. Horst Stipp, "Xers Are Not Created Equal," *Mediaweek*, March 21, 1994, p. 20; Lisa Marie Petersen, "Previews of Coming Attractions," *Brandweek*, March 1993, pp. 22–23.
39. Angrisani, "X Marks the Spot."
40. Laura Koss-Feder, "Want to Catch GenX? Try Looking on the Web," *Marketing News*, June 8, 1998, p. 20.
41. Andrea Petersen, "Charities Bet Young Will Come for the Music, Stay for the Pitch," *Wall Street Journal*, September 7, 1996, p. B1.
42. "Insurance Gets Hip," *American Demographics*, January 1, 2002, p. 48.
43. Cheryl Russell, "The Power of One," *Brandweek*, October 4, 1993, pp. 27–28, 30, 32.
44. Pamela Paul, "Targeting Boomers," *American Demographics*, March 2003, pp. 24+.
45. Alison Stein Wellner, "Generational Divide," *American Demographics*, October 2000, pp. 52–58.
46. Heather Graulich, "Do You Fall into the Gap?" *Austin American Statesman*, July 28, 1997, pp. E1, E8.
47. Pamela Paul, "Global Generation Gap," *American Demographics*, March 2002, pp. 18–19.
48. Carol M. Morgan, "The Psychographic Landscape of 50-Plus," *Brandweek*, July 19, 1993, pp. 28–32; Phil Goodman, "Marketing to Age Groups Is All in the Mind Set," *Marketing News*, December 6, 1993, p. 4.
49. Catherine A. Cole and Gary J. Gaeth, "Cognitive and Age-Related Differences in the Ability to Use Nutritional Information in a Complex Environment," *Journal of Marketing Research*, May 1990, pp. 175–184; Catherine A. Cole and Siva K. Balasubramanian, "Age Differences in Consumers' Search for Information: Public Policy Implications," *Journal of Consumer Research*, June 1993, pp. 157–169; Deborah Roedder John and Catherine A. Cole, "Age Differences in Information Processing: Understanding Deficits in Young and Elderly Consumers," *Journal of Consumer Research*, December 1986, pp. 297–315.
50. Carolyn Yoon, "Age Differences in Consumers' Processing Strategies: An Investigation of Moderating Differences," *Journal of Consumer Research*, December 1997, pp. 329–342.
51. Sharmistha Law, Scott A Hawkins, and Fergus I.M. Craik, "Repetition-Induced Belief in the Elderly: Rehabilitating Age-Related Memory Deficits," *Journal of Consumer Research*, September 1998, pp. 91–107.
52. Catherine A. Cole and Gary J. Gaeth, "Cognitive and Age-Related Differences in the Ability to Use Nutritional Information in a Complex Environment," *Journal of Marketing Research*, May 1990, pp. 175–184; Catherine A. Cole and Siva K. Balasubramanian, "Age Differences in Consumers' Search for Information: Public Policy Implications," *Journal of Consumer Research*, June 1993, pp. 157–169; Deborah Roedder John and Catherine A. Cole, "Age Differences in Information Processing: Understanding Deficits in Young and Elderly Consumers," *Journal of Consumer Research*, December 1986, pp. 297–315.
53. "More at Home on the Road," *American Demographics*, June 2003, pp. 26–27.
54. Becca Mader, "Boomer Town," *Business Journal-Milwaukee*, July 20, 2001, p. 21.
55. Ken Brown, "After Roaring through the '90s, Harley's Engine Could Sputter," *Wall Street Journal*, February 12, 2002, *www.wsj.com;* Joseph Weber, "Harley Investors May Get a Wobbly Ride," *BusinessWeek*, February 11, 2002, p. 65.
56. Peter Francese, "Trend Ticker: Big Spenders," *American Demographics*, September 2001, pp. 30–31; Susan Mitchell, "How Boomers Save," *American Demographics*, September 1994, pp. 22–29; "Baby Boomers Are Top Dinner Consumers," *Frozen Food Age*, February 1994, p. 33.
57. Shirley Leung, "Fast-Food Chains Upgrade Menus, and Profits, with Pricey Sandwiches," *Wall Street Journal*, February 5, 2002, pp. 1+.
58. Cyndee Miller, "Jeans Marketers Loosen Up, Adjust to Expanding Market," *Marketing News*, August 31, 1992, pp. 6–7.

59. John Finotti, "Back in Fashion: After a Strong Start and Then a Stumble, Specialty Retailer Chico's FAS Is Riding the Baby Boomer Wave," *Florida Trend*, January 2002, pp. 16+.
60. Emily Chasan, "When the Shoes Don't Fit," *Wall Street Journal*, July 27, 2004, pp. B1, B3.
61. Michael J. Weiss, "Chasing Youth," *American Demographics*, October 2002, pp. 35+; John Fetto, "Queen for a Day," *American Demographics*, March 2000, pp. 31–32.
62. Cris Prystay and Sarah Ellison, "Time for Marketers to Grow Up?" *Wall Street Journal*, February 27, 2003, pp. B1, B4.
63. Michael Moss, "Leon Black Bets Big on the Elderly," *Wall Street Journal*, July 24, 1998, pp. B1, B8.
64. Stephanie Mehta, "Retailer with Vision Aims to Make Fading Eyesight Chic," *Wall Street Journal*, October 23, 1996, pp. B1, B2.
65. Yumiko Ono, "An Army of 'Home Helpers' Is Ready to Descend on Japan's Seniors," *Wall Street Journal*, October 7, 1999, pp. B1, B4.
66. Patrick M. Reilly, "What a Long Strange Trip It's Been," *Wall Street Journal*, April 7, 1999, pp. B1, B4.
67. John and Cole, "Age Differences in Information Processing"; John J. Burnett, "Examining the Media Habits of the Affluent Elderly," *Journal of Advertising Research*, October–November 1991, pp. 33–41.
68. Ronald E. Milliman and Robert C. Erffmeyer, "Improving Advertising Aimed at Seniors," *Journal of Advertising Research*, December 1989–January 1990, pp. 31–36.
69. Robin T. Peterson, "The Depiction of Senior Citizens in Magazine Advertisements: A Content Analysis," *Journal of Business Ethics*, September 1992, pp. 701–706; Anthony C. Ursic, Michael L. Ursic, and Virginia L. Ursic, "A Longitudinal Study of the Use of the Elderly in Magazine Advertising," *Journal of Consumer Research*, June 1986, pp. 131–133; John J. Burnett, "Examining the Media Habits of the Affluent Elderly," *Journal of Advertising Research*, October–November 1991, pp. 33–41.
70. "America's Aging Consumers," *Discount Merchandiser*, September 1993, pp. 16–28; John and Cole, "Age Differences in Information Processing."
71. Amy Merrick, "Gap's Greatest Generation?" *Wall Street Journal*, September 15, 2004, pp. B1, B3.
72. Lisa D. Spiller and Richard A. Hamilton, "Senior Citizen Discount Programs: Which Seniors to Target and Why," *Journal of Consumer Marketing*, Summer 1993, pp. 42–51; Kelly Tepper, "The Role of Labeling Processes in Elderly Consumers' Responses to Age Segmentation Cues," *Journal of Consumer Research*, March 1994, pp. 503–519.
73. Jinkook Lee and Loren V. Geistfeld, "Elderly Consumers' Receptiveness to Telemarketing Fraud," *Journal of Public Policy & Marketing*, vol. 18, no. 2, Fall 1999, pp. 208–217; John R. Emshwiller, "Having Lost Thousands to Con Artists, Elderly Widow Tells Cautionary Tale," *Wall Street Journal*, August 9, 1996, pp. B1, B5.
74. Joan Meyers-Levy, "The Influence of Sex Roles on Judgment," *Journal of Consumer Research*, March 1988, pp. 522–530.
75. Charles S. Areni and Pamela Kiecker, "Gender Differences in Motivation: Some Implications for Manipulating Task-Related Involvement," in ed. Janeen Arnold Costa, *Gender and Consumer Behavior* (Salt Lake City, Utah: University of Utah Printing Service, 1993), pp. 30–43; Brenda Giner and Eileen Fischer, "Women and Arts, Men and Sports: Two Phenomena or One?" in ed. Janeen Arnold Costa, *Gender and Consumer Behavior* (Salt Lake City, Utah: University of Utah Printing Service, 1993), p. 149.
76. Douglas B. Holt and Craig J. Thompson, "Man-of-Action Heroes: The Pursuit of Heroic Masculinity in Everyday Consumption," *Journal of Consumer Research*, September 2004, pp. 425+.
78. Chen May Yee, "High-Tech Lift for India's Women," *Wall Street Journal*, November 1, 2000, pp. B1, B4; Aladi Venkatesh, "Gender Identity in the Indian Context, a Socio-Cultural Construction of the Female Consumer," in ed. Costa, *Gender and Consumer Behavior*, pp. 119–129.
79. Lynn J. Jaffe and Paul D. Berger, "Impact on Purchase Intent of Sex-Role Identity and Product Positioning," *Psychology and Marketing*, Fall 1988, pp. 259–271.
84. Joan Meyers-Levy and Durairaj Maheswaran, "Exploring Differences in Males' and Females' Processing Strategies," *Journal of Consumer Research*, June 1991, pp. 63–70; William K. Darley and Robert E. Smith, "Gender Differences in Information Processing Strategies: An Empirical Test of the Selectivity Model in Advertising Response," *Journal of Advertising*, Spring 1995, pp. 41–56; Barbara B. Stern, "Feminist Literary Criticism and the Deconstruction of Ads: A Postmodern View of Advertising and Consumer Responses," *Journal of Consumer Research*, March 1993, pp. 556–566.
85. Meyers-Levy, "The Influence of Sex Roles on Judgment," Joan Meyers-Levy, "Priming Effects on Product Judgments: A Hemispheric Interpretation," *Journal of Consumer Research*, June 1989, pp. 76–86.
86. Laurette Dube and Michael S. Morgan, "Trend Effects and Gender Differences in Retrospective Judgments of Consumption Emotions," *Journal of Consumer Research*, September 1996, pp. 156–162.
87. Richard Elliot, "Gender and the Psychological Meaning of Fashion Brands," in ed. Janeen Arnold Costa, *Gender and Consumer Behavior* (Salt Lake City, Utah: University of Utah Printing Service, 1993), pp. 99–105.
89. Pallavi Gogoi, "I Am Woman, Hear Me Shop," *Business Week*, February 14, 2005, *www.businessweek.com*; Margaret Popper, "Why Women Should Surf to Siebert," *BusinessWeek Online*, October 24, 2001, *www.businessweek.com*.
105. Sandra Yin, "Home and Away," *American Demographics*, March 2004, p. 15.
106. Ignacio Vazquez, "Mexicans Are Buying 'Made in USA' Food," *Marketing News*, August 31,1998, p. 14.
107. Susan Mitchell, "Birds of a Feather," *American Demographics*, February 1995, pp. 40–48.
108. Michael Weiss, "Parallel Universe," *American Demographics*, October 1999, pp. 58–63.
109. Michael J. Weiss, *The Clustering of America* (New York: Harper & Row, 1988); Mitchell, "Birds of a Feather."

110. Greg Johnson, "Beyond Burgers: New McDonald's Menu Makes Run for the Border," *Los Angeles Times*, August 13, 2000, pp. C1+.
111. Chad Terhune, "Snack Giant's Boats Sting Regional Rivals," *Wall Street Journal*, July 29, 2004, pp. B1–B2.
112. Mitchell, "Birds of a Feather."
113. Amy Merrick, "New Data Will Let Starbucks Plan Store Openings, Help Blockbuster Stock Its Videos," *Wall Street Journal*, February 14, 2001, pp. B1, B4.
114. Mike Freeman, "Clusters of Customers," *San Diego Union-Tribune*, December 19, 2004, *www.signo sandiego.com.*
115. Weiss, "Parallel Universe."
116. Robert Frank, "Thai Food for the World?" *Wall Street Journal*, February 16, 2001, pp. B1, B4.
117. Sak Onkvisit and John J. Shaw, *International Marketing: Analysis and Strategy* (Columbus, Ohio: Merrill, 1989).
118. Steven M. Kates and Charlene Goh, "Brand Morphing," *Journal of Advertising*, Spring 2003, pp. 59–68.
119. Geoffrey A. Fowler, "McDonald's Asian Marketing Takes on a Regional Approach," *Wall Street Journal*, January 26, 2005, p. 1.
120. J. R. Whitaker Penteado, "Fast Food Franchises Fight for the Brazilian Aficionados," *Brandweek*, June 7, 1993, pp. 20–24.
121. Yumiko Ono, "U.S. Superstores Find Japanese Are a Hard Sell," *Wall Street Journal*, February 14, 2000, pp. B1, B4.
122. Thomas M. Burton, "Makers of Drugs for Mentally Ill Find East Asia Is Resistant Market," *Wall Street Journal*, January 10, 2001, pp. B1, B4.
123. Normandy Madden, "Inside the Asian Colossus," *Advertising Age*, August 16, 2004, *www.adage.com.*
124. George P. Moschis, *Consumer Socialization* (Lexington, Mass.: D.C. Heath, 1987); Lisa Penaloza, "Atravesando Fronteras/Border Crossings: A Critical Ethnographic Exploration of the Consumer Acculturation of Mexican Immigrants," *Journal of Consumer Research*, June 1994, pp. 32–54.
125. "Profiles of General Demographic Characteristics: 2000 Census of Population and Housing," *U.S. Department of Commerce*, May 2001, p. 3.
126. Rebecca Gardyn, "Habla English?" *American Demographics*, April 2001, pp. 54–57.
127. Rebecca Gardyn and John Fetto, "Race, Ethnicity, and the Way We Shop," *American Demographics*, February 2003, pp. 30+; Joan Raymond, "The Multicultural Report," *American Demographics*, November 2001, pp. S3–S6; Rebecca Gardyn, "True Colors," *American Demographics*, April 2001, pp. 14–17.
128. Kimberly Palmer, "Ads for Ethnic Hair Care Show a New Face," *Wall Street Journal*, July 21, 2003, pp. B1, B3.
129. Marlene Rossman, "Inclusive Marketing Shows Sensitivity," *Marketing News*, October 10, 1994, p. 4.
130. Pamela Paul, "Hispanic Heterogenity," *Forecast*, June 4, 2001, pp. 1+; Geoffrey Paulin, "A Growing Market: Expenditures by Hispanics," *Monthly Labor Review*, March 1998, pp. 3–21.
131. Carrie Goerne, "Go the Extra Mile to Catch Up with Hispanics," *Marketing News*, December 24, 1990, p. 13; Marlene Rossman, *Multicultural Marketing* (New York: American Management Association, 1994).
132. Penaloza, "Atravesando Fronteras/Border Crossings."
133. Patricia Braus, "What Does Hispanic Mean?" *American Demographics*, June 1993, pp. 46–49.
134. Paul, "Hispanic Heterogeneity."
135. Jerry Dryer, "'Más Queso, Por Favor!'" *Dairy Foods*, November 2001, pp. 16+; Lafayette Jones, "Translating for the Hispanic Market," *Promo*, September 1, 2001, pp. 30+.
136. Joe Schwartz, "Rising Status," *American Demographics*, January 10, 1989, p. 10.
137. Humberto Valencia, "Developing an Index to Measure Hispanicness," in eds. Elizabeth C. Hirschman and Morris B. Holbrook, *Advances in Consumer Research*, vol. 12 (Provo, Utah: Association for Consumer Research, 1981), pp. 18–21; Rohit Deshpande, Wayne D. Hoyer, and Naveen Donthu, "The Intensity of Ethnic Affiliation: A Study of the Sociology of Hispanic Consumption," *Journal of Consumer Research*, September 1986, pp. 214–220.
138. Cynthia Webster, "Effects of Hispanic Ethnic Identification on Marital Roles in the Purchase Decision Process," *Journal of Consumer Research*, September 1994, pp. 319–331.
139. Cynthia Webster, "The Effects of Hispanic Subcultural Identification on Information Search Behavior," *Journal of Advertising Research*, September–October 1992, pp. 54–62; Naveen Donthu and Joseph Cherian, "Hispanic Coupon Usage: The Impact of Strong and Weak Ethnic Identification," *Psychology and Marketing*, November–December 1992, pp. 501–510.
140. Cyndee Miller, "Cosmetics Firms Finally Discover the Ethnic Market," *Marketing News*, August 30, 1993, p. 2.
141. Hillary Chura, "Sweet Spot," *Advertising Age*, November 12, 2001, pp. 1, 16; Roberta Bernstein, "Food For Thought," *American Demographics*, May 2000, pp. 39–42.
142. Johnson, "Beyond Burgers."
143. Steve McClellan, "Hispanic Television," *Broadcasting & Cable*, October 1, 2001, pp. 22+; Eduardo Porter, "Hispanic TV Takes Off in the U.S.," *Wall Street Journal*, September 7, 2000, p. B1; Thomas C. O'Guinn and Thomas P. Meyer, "Segmenting the Hispanic Market: The Use of Spanish Language Radio," *Journal of Advertising Research*, December 1981, pp. 9–16.
144. Suzanne Vranica, "Miller Turns Eye Toward Hispanics," *Wall Street Journal*, October 8, 2004, p. B3.
145. "10 Largest Advertisers to the Hispanic Market, 1999 vs. 2000," *Marketing News*, July 2, 2001, p. 17.
146. Jones, "Translating for the Hispanic Market."
147. Joel Millman, "U.S. Marketers Adopt Cinco de Mayo as National Fiesta," *Wall Street Journal*, May 1, 2001, pp. B1, B4; Suein L. Hwang, "Corona, of the Lime Wedge, Makes Unlikely Comeback," *Wall Street Journal*, November 20, 1997, pp. B1, B13.

148. Jacqueline Sanchez, "Some Approaches Better than Others When Targeting Hispanics," *Marketing News*, May 25, 1992, pp. 8, 11.
149. Rossman, *Multicultural Marketing*.
150. Rohit Deshpande and Douglas M. Stayman, "A Tale of Two Cities: Distinctiveness Theory and Advertising Effectiveness," *Journal of Marketing Research*, February 1994, pp. 57–64.
151. See Claudiu V. Dimofte, Mark R. Forehand, and Rohit Deshpandé, "Ad Schema Incongruity as Elicitor of Ethnic Self-Awareness and Differential Advertising Response," *Journal of Advertising*, Winter 2003–4, pp. 7–17; Mark R. Forehand and Rohit Deshpandé, "What We See Makes Us Who We Are: Priming Ethnic Self-Awareness and Advertising Response," *Journal of Marketing Research*, August 2001, pp. 336–348.
152. Anne M. Brumbaugh, 'Source and Nonsource Cues in Advertising and Their Effects on the Activation of Cultural and Subcultural Knowledge on the Route to Persuasion," *Journal of Consumer Research*, September 2002, pp. 258+.
153. Robert E. Wilkes and Humberto Valencia, "Hispanics and Blacks in Television Commercials," *Journal of Advertising*, March 1989, pp. 19–25.
154. Joe Schwartz, "Hispanic Opportunities," *American Demographics*, May 1987, pp. 56–59; Rossman, *Multicultural Marketing*.
155. Scott Koslow, Prem N. Shamdasani, and Ellen E. Touchstone, "Exploring Language Effects in Ethnic Advertising: A Sociolinguistic Perspective," *Journal of Consumer Research*, March 1994, pp. 575–585.
156. Laurel Wentz, "Cultural Cross Over," *Advertising Age*, July 7, 2003, pp. S-4+.
157. Lee Zion, "Retail Centers Must Reflect State's Changing Face," *San Diego Business Journal*, July 30, 2001, pp. 6+; Alexia Vargas, "Harvard MBA's Chain Riles Chicago's Hispanic Grocers," *Wall Street Journal*, November 6, 1997, pp. B1, B2.; Mary Ann Linsen, "Store of the Month: Making It in Miami," *Progressive Grocer*, April 1991, pp. 128–136.
158. "The DNR List: Latino Logistics," *Daily News Record*, August 23, 2004, p. 136.
159. Jim Emerson, "African Americans," *Direct*, September 1, 2001, p. 50; "Profiles of General Demographic Characteristics."
160. William H. Frey, "Revival," *American Demographics*, October 2003, pp. 27+; "Black Population Surged During '90s: U.S. Census," *Jet*, August 27, 2001, p. 18.
161. "Where Blacks, Whites Diverge," *Brandweek*, May 3, 1993, p. 22.
162. Howard Schlossberg, "Many Marketers Still Consider Blacks 'Dark-Skinned Whites,'" *Marketing News*, January 18, 1993, pp. 1, 13.
163. Alan J. Bush, Rachel Smith, and Craig Martin, "The Influence of Consumer Socialization Variables on Attitude toward Advertising: A Comparison of African-Americans and Caucasians," *Journal of Advertising*, vol. 28, no. 3, Fall 1999, pp. 13–24.
164. Debra Goldman, "Black Like Me," *Adweek*, August 24, 1992, p. 25.
165. "Minority Buying Power," *Marketing News*, July 2, 2001, p. 17.
166. Corliss L. Green, "Ethnic Evaluations of Advertising: Interaction Effects of Strength of Ethnic Identification, Media Placement, and Degree of Racial Composition," *Journal of Advertising*, vol. 28, no. 1, Spring 1999, pp. 49–64; Pepper Miller and Ronald Miller, "Trends Are Opportunities for Targeting African-Americans," *Marketing News*, January 20, 1992, p. 9.
167. "African-Americans Go Natural," *MMR*, December 17, 2001, p. 43.
168. "L'eggs Joins New Approach in Marketing to African American Women," *Supermarket Business*, June 1998, p. 81; Cyndee Miller, "Cosmetics Firms Finally Discover the Ethnic Market," *Marketing News*, August 30, 1993, p. 2.
169. Alan J. Bush, Rachel Smith, and Craig Martin, "The Influence of Consumer Socialization Variables on Attitude toward Advertising: A Comparison of African-Americans and Caucasians," *Journal of Advertising*, vol. 28, no. 3, Fall 1999, pp. 13–24.
170. Green, "Ethnic Evaluations of Advertising."
171. Jake Holden, "The Ring of Truth, *American Demographics*, October 1998, p. 14.
172. Louise Witt, "Color Code Red," *American Demographics*, February 2004, pp. 23+.
173. Matthew S. Scott, "Can Black Radio Stations Survive an Industry Shakedown?" *Black Enterprise*, June 1993, pp. 254–260.
174. Frank S. Washington, "Mercedes' New Ad Campaign Targets Affluent Blacks," *Ward's Dealer Business*, October 2001, p. 39.
175. Helen Gregory, "Positive Discrimination," *Grocer*, July 21, 2001, pp. 45+.
176. "10 Largest Advertisers to the African American Market, 2000," *Marketing News*, July 2, 2001, p. 17.
177. Jennifer L. Aaker, Anne M. Brumbaugh, and Sonya A. Grier, "Nontarget Markets and Viewer Distinctiveness: The Impact of Target Marketing on Advertising Attitudes," *Journal of Consumer Psychology*, vol. 9, no. 3, 2000, pp. 127–140.
178. Schlossberg, "Many Marketers Still Consider Blacks 'Dark-Skinned Whites'"; William J. Qualls and David J. Moore, "Stereotyping Effects on Consumers' Evaluation of Advertising: Impact of Racial Difference Between Actors and Viewers," *Psychology and Marketing*, Summer 1990, pp. 135–151.
179. Sonia Alleyne, "The Magic Touch," *Black Enterprise*, June 2004, p. 188+.
180. Ann Cooper, "Cosmetics: Changing Looks for Changing Attitudes," *Adweek*, February 22, 1993, pp. 30–36.
181. Alleyne, "The Magic Touch."
182. Tommy E. Whittler and Joan DiMeo, "Viewers' Reactions to Racial Cues in Advertising Stimuli," *Journal of Advertising Research*, December 1991, pp. 37–46.
183. Tommy E. Whittler, "Viewers' Processing of Source and Message Cues in Advertising Stimuli," *Psychology & Marketing*, July–August 1989, pp. 287–309.

184. John P. Cortez, "KFC Stores Boast Flavor of Neighborhood," *Advertising Age*, May 31, 1993, pp. 3, 46.
185. Nicholas Kulish, "U.S. Asian Population Grew and Diversified, Census Shows," *Wall Street Journal*, May 15, 2001, p. B4; "Profiles of General Demographic Characteristics"; Gregory Spencer and Frederick W. Hollman, "U.S. Census Bureau, the Official Statistics," September 21, 1998, pp. 8–9.
186. "Diversity in America: Asians," *American Demographics*, November 2002, p. S14; Frey, " Micro Melting Pots."
187. "Diversity in America: Asians."
188. Jonathan Burton, "Advertising Targeting Asians," *Far Eastern Economic Review*, January 21, 1993, pp. 40–41.
189. Saul Gitlin, "An Optional Data Base," *Brandweek*, January 5, 1998, p. 16.
190. Bill Kossen, "Japanese-Language Ads Demonstrate Novel Marketing Approach," *Seattle Times*, July 3, 2001, *www.seattletimes.com*.
191. Gardyn and Fetto, "The Way We Shop."
192. "Asian Americans Lead the Way Online," *Min's New Media Report*, December 31, 2001.
193. Rebecca Gardyn and John Fetto, "The Way We Shop," *American Demographics*, February 2003, pp. 31+.
194. U.S. Census Bureau, "Income 2002," *Current Population Survey, 2002, www.census.gov;* "Diversity in America: Asians."
195. Chui Li, "The Asian Market for Personal Products," *Drug & Cosmetic Industry*, November 1992, pp. 32–36; William Dunn, "The Move Toward Ethnic Marketing," *Nation's Business*, July 1992, pp. 39–41; Rossman, *Multicultural Marketing*.
196. Marty Bernstein, "Auto Advertisers Shift Some Attention to Asian-Americans," *Automotive News*, October 13, 2003, p. 4M; Julie Cantwell, "Zero Gives New Life to Big 3 in the West; New Plans Include More Dealer Ad Money and Multicultural Marketing," *Automotive News*, November 12, 2001, p. 35.
197. Levey, "Home Market."
198. "HSBC Banks on World Cup Soccer Web Site, in Chinese," *Brandweek*, April 1, 2002, p. 30.
199. Dawn Cornitcher, "The Explosive Growth of Ethnic Media in the United States," *Adweek*, May 17, 1999, p. 18.
200. Wayne Karrfalt, "Case Study: Cruising to New Customers," *Cable TV: The Multicultural Connection*, n.d., p. S10.
201. "NBA Drops Chinese Insert to Salute Yao, Wang, and Bateer," *People's Daily Online*, October 30, 2003, *www.english.people.com.cn*.
202. Jonathan Burton, "Advertising Targeting Asians," *Far Eastern Economic Review*, January 21, 1993, pp. 40–41; Maria Shao, "Suddenly Asian-Americans Are a Marketer's Dream," *BusinessWeek*, June 17, 1991, pp. 54–55.
203. Charles R. Taylor and Barbara B. Stern, "Asian-Americans: Television Advertising and the 'Model Minority' Stereotype," *Journal of Advertising*, Summer 1997, pp. 47–62.
204. "Banking on Asian-Americans," *Sales & Marketing Management*, September 1993, p. 88.
205. Onkvisit and Shaw, *International Marketing;* Charles M. Schaninger, Jacques C. Bourgeois, and W. Christian Buss, "French-English Canadian Subcultural Consumption Differences," *Journal of Marketing*, Spring 1985, pp. 82–92.
206. Brian Dunn, "Nationalism in Advertising: Dead or Alive?" *Adweek*, November 22, 1993.
207. Hans Hoefer, *Thailand* (Boston: Houghton Mifflin, 1993).
208. Saritha Rai, "India's Boom Spreads to Smaller Cities," *New York Times*, January 4, 2005, p. C5.
209. Pamela Paul, "Religious Identity and Mobility," *American Demographics*, March 2003, pp. 20–21; Pamela Paul, "One Nation, Under God?" *American Demographics*, January 2002, pp. 16–17.
210. Elizabeth C. Hirschman, "American Jewish Ethnicity: Its Relationship to Some Selected Aspects of Consumer Behavior," *Journal of Marketing*, Summer 1981, pp. 102–110; Elizabeth C. Hirschman, "Religious Affiliation and Consumption Processes: An Initial Paradigm," *Research in Marketing* (Greenwich, Conn.: JAI Press, 1983), pp. 131–170.
211. Hirschman, "Religious Affiliation and Consumption Processes."
212. Priscilla L. Barbera, "Consumer Behavior and Born Again Christianity," in eds. Jagdish N. Sheth and Elizabeth C. Hirschman, *Research in Consumer Behavior* (Greenwich, Conn.: JAI Press, 1988), pp. 193–222.
213. Rodney Ho, "Rappin' and Rockin' for the Lord," *Wall Street Journal*, February 28, 2001, pp. B1, B4.
214. Michael Fielding, "The Halo Effect," *Marketing News*, February 1, 2005, pp. 18+.
215. Lisa Miller, "Registers Ring in Sanctuary Stores," *Wall Street Journal*, December 17, 1999, pp. B1, B4; Elizabeth Bernstein, "Holy Frappuccino!" *Wall Street Journal*, August 3, 2001, pp. W1, W8.
216. Stephanie Kang, "Pop Culture Gets Religion," *Wall Street Journal*, May 5, 2004, pp. B1, B2.

CHAPTER 14

2. Pierre Bourdieu, *Language and Symbolic Power* (Cambridge, Mass.: Harvard University Press, 1991).
4. Edward W. Cundiff and Marye T. Hilger, *Marketing in the International Environment* (New York: Prentice-Hall, 1988) as cited in Mariele K. DeMooij and Warren Keegan, *Advertising Worldwide* (New York: Prentice-Hall, 1991), p. 96.
5. Onkvisit and Shaw, *International Marketing*.
6. "The Great Indian Middle Class and Its Consumption Levels," *Asia Africa Intelligence Wire*, January 22, 2005, n.p.; "Clash on Definition of China's Middle Class.
7. Russell W. Belk, "Daily Life in Romania," in Consumption in Marketizing Economies, eds. Cliford Shultz II and Güliz (Greenwich, Conn.: JAI Press, 1994).
8. Ernest Dichter, "The World Consumer," *Harvard Business Review*, July–August 1962, pp. 113–123 as cited in Cundiff and Hilger, *Marketing in the International Environment*, p. 135.

9. Richard P. Coleman, "The Significance of Social Stratification in Selling," in ed. Martin L. Bell, *Marketing: A Maturing Discipline* (Chicago: American Marketing Association, 1960), pp. 171–184.
10. Douglas E. Allen and Paul F. Anderson, "Consumption and Social Stratification: Bourdieu's Distinction," in eds. Chris T. Allan and Deborah Roedder John, *Advances in Consumer Research,* vol. 21 (Provo, Utah: Association for Consumer Research, 1994), pp. 70–73.
11. Pierre Bourdieu, *Distinction: A Social Critique of the Judgment of Taste* (Cambridge, Mass.: Harvard University Press, 1984).
12. Michael R. Solomon, "Deep Seated Materialism: The Case of Levi's 501 Jeans," in ed. Richard J. Lutz, *Advances in Consumer Research,* vol. 13 (Provo, Utah: Association for Consumer Research, 1986), pp. 619–622.
13. Coleman, "The Continuing Significance of Social Class to Marketing."
14. See Joan M. Ostrove and Elizabeth R. Cole, "Privileging Class: Toward a Critical Psychology of Social Class in the Context of Education," *Journal of Social Issues,* Winter 2003, pp. 677+; and Charles M. Schaninger, "Social Class versus Income Revisited: An Empirical Investigation," *Journal of Marketing Research,* May 1981, pp. 192–208.
15. Gillian Stevens and Joo Hyun Cho, "Socioeconomic Indexes and the New 1980 Census Occupational Classification Scheme," *Social Science Research,* March 1985, pp. 142–168; Charles B. Nam and Mary G. Powers, *The Socioeconomic Approach to Status Measurement* (Houston: Cap and Gown Press, 1983).
16. Diane Crispell, "The Real Middle Americans," *American Demographics,* October 1994, pp. 28–35; Michael Hout, "More Universalism, Less Structural Mobility: The American Occupational Structure in the 1980s," *American Journal of Sociology,* May 1988, pp. 1358–1400.
18. William L. Wilkie, *Consumer Behavior,* 2nd ed. (New York: Wiley, 1990).
19. Güliz Ger, Russell W. Belk, and Dana-Nicoleta Lascu, "The Development of Consumer Desire in Marketizing and Developing Economies: The Cases of Romania and Turkey," in eds. Leigh McAlister and Michael L. Rothschild, *Advances in Consumer Research,* vol. 20 (Provo, Utah: Association for Consumer Research, 1992), pp. 102–107.
20. M. R. Haque, "Marketing Opportunities in the Middle East," in ed. V. H. Manek Kirpalani, *International Business Handbook* (New York: Haworth Press, 1990), pp. 375–416.
21. W. Lloyd Warner, Marchia Meeker, and Kenneth Eells, *Social Class in America* (Chicago: Science Research Associates, 1949); August B. Hollingshead and Fredrick C. Redlich, *Social Class and Mental Illness, A Community Study* (New York: Wiley, 1958).
22. Gerhard Lenski, "Status Crystallization: A Non-Vertical Dimension of Social Status," *American Sociological Review,* August 1956, pp. 458–464.
23. Alison Stein Wellner, "The Money in the Middle," *American Demographics,* April 2000, pp. 56–64.
26. Allen and Anderson, "Consumption and Social Stratification."
27. Jake Ryan and Charles Sackrey, *Strangers in Paradise: Academics from the Working Class* (Boston: South End Press, 1984).
32. David Wessel, "Barbell Effect: The Future of Jobs," *Wall Street Journal,* April 2, 2004, p. A1; Matt Murray, "Settling for Less," *Wall Street Journal,* August 13, 2003, p. A1; Greg J. Duncan, Martha Hill, and Willard Rogers, "The Changing Fortunes of Young and Old," *American Demographics,* August 1986, pp. 26–33; Katherine S. Newman, *Falling from Grace: The Experience of Downward Mobility in the American Middle Class* (New York: Free Press, 1988); Kenneth Labich, "Class in America," *Fortune,* February 7, 1994, pp. 114–126.
33. Newman, *Falling from Grace*; Eisler, *Class Act.*
34. Michael J. Weiss, "Great Expectations," *American Demographics,* May 2003, pp. 27+.
35. Scott D. Roberts, "Consumer Responses to Involuntary Job Loss," in eds. Rebecca H. Holman and Michael R. Solomon, *Advances in Consumer Research,* vol. 18 (Provo, Utah: Association for Consumer Research, 1988), pp. 40–42.
36. Deborah Ball, "Despite Downturn, Japanese Are Still Having Fits for Luxury Goods," *Wall Street Journal,* April 24, 2001, pp. B1, B4.
37. Labich, "Class in America."
39. John Brooks, *Showing Off in America: From Conspicuous Consumption to Parody Display* (Boston: Little, Brown, 1981); for those interested in reading more about the theory of conspicuous consumption, see Thorstein Veblen, *The Theory of the Leisure Class* (New York: Macmillan, 1899).
40. Christine Page, "A History of Conspicuous Consumption," in eds. Floyd Rudmin and Marsha Richins, *Meaning, Measure, and Morality of Materialism* (Provo, Utah: Association for Consumer Research, 1993), pp. 82–87.
41. Ger, Belk, and Lascu, "The Development of Consumer Desire in Marketizing and Developing Economies."
42. Janeen Arnold Costa and Russell W. Belk, "Nouveaux Riches as Quintessential Americans: Case Studies of Consumption in the Extended Family," in ed. Russell W. Belk, *Advances in Nonprofit Marketing,* vol. 3 (Greenwich, Conn.: JAI Press, 1990), pp. 83–140.
43. Christina Duff, "Indulging in Inconspicuous Consumption," *Wall Street Journal,* April 14, 1997, pp. B1, B4.
44. Peter Francese, "The Exotic Travel Boom," *American Demographics,* June 2002, pp. 48–49.
45. Rebecca H. Holman, "Product Use as Communication: A Fresh Appraisal of a Venerable Topic," in eds. Ben M. Enis and Kenneth J. Roering, *Review of Marketing* (Chicago: American Marketing Association, 1981), pp. 106–119.
47. Rebecca Gardyn, "Oh, the Good Life," *American Demographics,* November 2002, pp. 32+.
48. Brooks, *Showing Off in America.*

49. Stephen Buckley, "Brazil Rediscovers Its Culture; Poor Man's Cocktail, Martial Art Hip Among Middle Class," *Washington Post*, April 15, 2001, p. A16.
50. Teri Agins, "Now, Subliminal Logos," *Wall Street Journal*, July 20, 2001, p. B1.
51. Sigmund Gronmo, "Compensatory Consumer Behavior: Theoretical Perspectives, Empirical Examples and Methodological Challenges," in eds. Paul F. Anderson and Michael J. Ryan, *1984 American Marketing Association Winter Educators' Conference* (Chicago: American Marketing Association, 1984), pp. 184–188.
52. Russell W. Belk, "Yuppies as Arbiters of the Emerging Consumption Style," in ed. Richard J. Lutz, *Advances in Consumer Research*, vol. 13 (Provo, Utah: Association for Consumer Research, 1986), pp. 514–519.
54. Russell W. Belk and Melanie Wallendorf, "The Sacred Meanings of Money," *Journal of Economic Psychology*, March 1990, pp. 35–67.
55. Abraham McLaughlin, "Africans' New Motto: 'Charge It,'" *Christian Science Monitor*, February 14, 2005, p. 6.
56. "Rabobank Deploys Siebel CRM OnDemand," *Canadian Corporate News*, November 17, 2004, *www.comtextnews.com*.
57. C. Rubenstein, "Your Money or Your Life," *Psychology Today*, vol. 12, 1980, pp. 47–58.
58. Adrian Furnham and Alan Lewis, *The Economic Mind: The Social Psychology of Economic Behavior* (Brighton, Sussex: Harvester Press, 1986); Belk and Wallendorf, "The Sacred Meanings of Money."
59. H. Goldberg and R. Lewis, *Money Madness: The Psychology of Saving, Spending, Loving, and Hating Money* (London: Springwood, 1979).
60. Rebecca Gardyn, "Generosity and Income," *American Demographics*, December 2002–January 2003, pp. 46–47.
61. C. W. Young, "Bijan Designs a Very Exclusive Image," *Advertising Age*, March 13, 1986, pp. 18, 19, 21, as cited in LaBarbera, "The Nouveaux Riches"; V. Kanti Prasad, "Socioeconomic Product Risk and Patronage Preferences of Retail Shoppers," *Journal of Marketing*, July 1975, pp. 42–47.
62. Mercedes M. Cardona, "Affluent Shoppers Like Their Luxe Goods Cheap," *Advertising Age*, December 1, 2003, p. 6.
63. John Fetto, "Sensible Santas," *American Demographics*, December 2000, pp. 10–11.
64. See "Old Money," *American Demographics*, June 2003, pp. 34+.
65. Jean Halliday, "Ultra-luxury Car Marketers Roll Out Red Carpet for Buyers," *Advertising Age*, February 2, 2004, p. 6.
66. Dagmar Aalund, "'Your Penthouse Is *Prefab*-ulous!'" *Wall Street Journal*, May 8, 2000, pp. B1, B6.
67. Kathryn Kranhold, "Marketing to the New Millionaire," *Wall Street Journal*, October 11, 2000, pp. B1, B6.
68. Carole Ann King, "The New Wealthy: Younger, Richer, More Proactive," *National Underwriter Life & Health-Financial Services Edition*, February 12, 2001, p. 4.
69. "Who Are the Millionaires?" *Greater Baton Rouge Business Report*, July 31, 2001, p. 9.
70. Trevor Thomas, "'Decamillionaires' Thriving," *National Underwriter Life & Health-Financial Services Edition*, February 12, 2001, p. 10.
71. John Fetto, "I Want My MTV," *American Demographics*, March 2003, p. 8.
72. Elisabeth Malkin, "Mexico's Working Poor Become Homeowners," *New York Times*, December 17, 2004, p. W1.
73. Dave Montgomery, "Ten Years After Russia's Failed Coup, Middle Class Is Small but Growing," *Knight Ridder*, August 11, 2001.
74. Jacob, "The Big Rise."
75. Rebecca Piirto Heath, "The New Working Class," *American Demographics*, vol. 20, no. 1, January 1998, pp. 51–55.
76. Coleman, "The Continuing Significance of Social Class to Marketing."
77. Prasad, "Socioeconomic Product Risk and Patronage Preferences of Retail Shoppers"; Stuart Rich and Subhish Jain, "Social Class and Life Cycle as Predictors of Shopping Behavior," *Journal of Marketing Research*, June–July 1987, pp. 51–59.
78. John Fetto, "Watering Holes," *American Demographics*, June 2003, p. 8.
79. Ronald Paul Hill and Mark Stamey, "The Homeless in America: An Examination of Possessions and Consumption Behaviors," *Journal of Consumer Research*, December 1990, pp. 303–321; Frank Caro, *Estimating the Numbers of Homeless Families* (New York: Community Service Society of New York, 1981).
80. National Coalition for the Homeless, "How Many People Experience Homelessness?" February 1999, *http://nch.ari.net/numbers.html*.
81. Lakshmi Bhargave, "Homeless Help Themselves With 'Advocate,'" *Daily Texan (Austin)*, February 16, 2000, pp. 1, 8.
82. Richard B. Freeman and Brian Hall, "Permanent Homelessness in America?" *Population Research and Policy Review*, vol. 6, 1987, pp. 3–27.
83. Ronald Paul Hill, "Homeless Women, Special Possessions, and the Meaning of 'Home': An Ethnographic Case Study," *Journal of Consumer Research*, December 1991, pp. 298–310.
84. David A. Snow and Leon Anderson, "Identity Work among the Homeless: The Verbal Construction and Avowal of Personal Identities," *American Journal of Sociology*, May 1987, pp. 1336–1371.
85. Peter Katel, "Petro Padillo Longoria: A Retailer Focused on Working-Class Needs," *Time International*, October 15, 2001, p. 49.
86. Kjell Gronhaug and Paul S. Trapp, "Perceived Social Class Appeals of Branded Goods and Services," *Journal of Consumer Marketing*, Winter 1989, pp. 13–18.
87. Jack Neff, "Value Positioning Becomes a Priority," *Advertising Age*, February 23, 2004, pp. 24, 30.
88. Teri Agins, "New Kors Line Stars Luxury Look-Alikes: 'Carpool Couture,'" *Wall Street Journal*, August 20, 2004, pp. B1, B3.

89. Sonya A. Grier and Rohit Deshpandé, "Social Dimensions of Consumer Distinctiveness: The Influence of Social Status on Group Identity and Advertising Persuasion," *Journal of Marketing Research,* vol. 38, May 2001, pp. 216–224.
90. Anita Sharpe, "Magazines for the Rich Rake in Readers," *Wall Street Journal,* February 16, 1996, pp. B1, B2.
91. Kelly Shermach, "Study Identifies Types of Interactive Shoppers," *Marketing News,* September 25, 1995, p. 22; *eMarketer,* February 3, 2000 (online reference).
92. Rich and Jain, "Social Class and Life Cycle as Predictors of Shopping Behavior."
93. Teri Agins and Deborah Ball, "Designer Stores, in Extra Large," *Wall Street Journal,* June 6, 2001, pp. B1, B12.
94. Page, "A History of Conspicuous Consumption."
95. Matthew Grimm, "Target Hits Its Mark," *American Demographics,* November 2002, pp. 42+.
96. Labich, "Class in America."
97. "Multigenerational Households Number 4 Million According to Census 2000," *U.S. Department of Commerce News,* September 7, 2001, *www.census.gov/pressrelease/ www/2001/cb01cn182.html.*
98. Sak Onkvisit and John J. Shaw, *International Marketing: Analysis and Strategy* (Columbus, Ohio: Merrill, 1989).
99. Patrick Barta, "Looming Need for Housing a Big Surprise," *Wall Street Journal,* May 15, 2001, pp. B1, B4.
100. "The Future of Households," *American Demographics,* December 1993, pp. 27–40.
101. "Nation's Median Age Highest Ever, But 65-and-Over Population's Growth Lags, Census 2000 Shows." United States Department of Commerce News (soundbite), May 15, 2001. Webpage news release.
102. Pamela Paul, "Childless by Choice," *American Demographics,* November 2001, pp. 45–50.
103. Mary C. Gilly and Ben M. Enis, "Recycling the Family Life Cycle," in ed. Andrew A. Mitchell, *Advances in Consumer Research,* vol. 9 (Ann Arbor, Mich.: Association for Consumer Research, 1982), pp. 271–276; William D. Danko and Charles M. Schaninger, "An Empirical Evaluation of the Gilly-Enis Updated Household Life Cycle Model," *Journal of Business Research,* August 1990, pp. 39–57.
104. Robert E. Wilkes, "Household Life-Cycle Stages, Transitions, and Product Expenditures," *Journal of Consumer Research,* June 1995, pp. 27–42.
105. John Fetto, "The Baby Business," *American Demographics,* May 2003, p. 40.
106. Alan R. Andreasen, "Life Status Changes and Changes in Consumer Preferences and Satisfaction," *Journal of Consumer Research,* December 1984, pp. 784–794.
107. Rebecca Gardyn, "A Market Kept in the Closet," *American Demographics,* November 2001, pp. 37–43.
108. "The Mommies, in Numbers," *Brandweek,* November 13, 1993, p. 17; Lee Smith, "The New Wave of Illegitimacy," *Fortune,* April 18, 1994, pp. 81–94.
109. John Palmer, "Animal Instincts," *Promo,* May 2001, pp. 25–33; "Pets Can Drive," *American Demographics,* March 2000, pp. 10–12; Elizabeth C. Hirschman, "Consumers and Their Animal Companions," *Journal of Consumer Research,* March 1994, pp. 616–632; Clinton R. Sanders, "The Animal 'Other': Self-Definition, Social Identity, and Companion Animals," in eds. Marvin E. Goldberg, Gerald Gorn, and Richard W. Pollay, *Advances in Consumer Research,* vol. 17 (Provo, Utah: Association for Consumer Research, 1990), pp. 662–668; Alan Beck and Aaron Katcher, *Between Pets and People: The Importance of Animal Companionship* (New York: Putnam, 1983).
110. Rebecca Gardyn, "VIPs (Very Important Pets)," *American Demographics,* March 2001, pp. 16–18; "Pets Can Drive"; Ellen Graham, "Santa Has Lavish Plans for Cats, Dogs, Birds, Iguanas," *Wall Street Journal,* December 9, 1996, pp. B1, B2; Kathie Jenkins, "It's Dining Cats and Dogs," *Los Angeles Times,* June 22, 1995, pp. H14.
111. Peter Francese, "Marriage Drain's Big Cost," *American Demographics,* April 2004, pp. 40+; Matthew Grimm, "Hitch Switch," *American Demographics,* November 2003, pp. 34+.
112. James Morrow, "A Place for One," *American Demographics,* November 2003, pp. 25+; "Multigenerational Households Number 4 Million According to Census 2000," U.S. Department of Commerce news release, September 7, 2001.
113. Patricia Braus, "Sex and the Single Spender," *American Demographics,* November 1993, pp. 28–34.
114. Morrow, "A Place for One."
115. Peter Francese, "Well Enough Alone," *American Demographics,* November 2003, pp. 32–33.
116. Barbara Carton, "It's a Niche! Twins, Triplets and Beyond," *Wall Street Journal,* February 2, 1999, pp. B1, B4.
117. Rebecca Gardyn, "Unmarried Bliss," *American Demographics,* December 2000, pp. 56–61.
118. Clark D. Olson, "Materialism in the Home: The Impact of Artifacts on Dyadic Communication," in eds. Elizabeth C. Hirschman and Morris B. Holbrook, *Advances in Consumer Research,* vol. 12 (Provo, Utah: Association for Consumer Research, 1985), pp. 388–393.
119. Jeanne L. Hafstrom and Marilyn M. Dunsing, "Socioeconomic and Social-Psychological Influences on Reasons Wives Work," *Journal of Consumer Research,* December 1978, pp. 169–175; Rena Bartos, *The Moving Target: What Every Marketer Should Know about Women* (New York: Free Press, 1982).
120. Rose M. Rubin, Bobye J. Riney, and David J. Molina, "Expenditure Pattern Differentials Between One-Earner and Dual-Earner Households: 1972–1973 and 1984," *Journal of Consumer Research,* June 1990, pp. 43–52; Horacio Soberon-Ferrer and Rachel Dardis, "Determinants of Household Expenditures for Services," *Journal of Consumer Research,* March 1991, pp. 385–397; Don Bellante and Ann C. Foster, "Working Wives and Expenditure on Services," *Journal of Consumer Research,* September 1984, pp. 700–707.
121. Michael D. Reilly, "Working Wives and Convenience Consumption," *Journal of Consumer Research,* March 1982, pp. 407–418; Ralph W. Jackson, Stephen W. McDaniel, and C. P. Rao, "Food Shopping and Preparation:

Psychographic Differences of Working Wives and Housewives," *Journal of Consumer Research,* June 1985, pp. 110–113; Janet C. Hunt and B. F. Kiker, "The Effect of Fertility on the Time Use of Working Wives," *Journal of Consumer Research,* March 1981, pp. 380–387; Keith W. Bryant, "Durables and Wives' Employment Yet Again," *Journal of Consumer Research,* June 1988, pp. 37–47.

122. See John Fetto, "Does Father Really Know Best?" *American Demographics,* June 2002, pp. 10+; Pamela Paul, "Meet the Parents," *American Demographics,* January 2002, pp. 43+; Linda Thompson and Alexis Walker, "Gender in Families: Women and Men in Marriage, Work, and Parenthood," *Journal of Marriage and the Family,* November 1989, pp. 845–871.
123. Joan Raymond, "The Ex-Files," *American Demographics,* February 2001, pp. 60–64.
124. "Do Us Part," *American Demographics,* September 2002, p. 9.
125. James H. Alexander, John W. Shouten, and Scott D. Roberts, "Consumer Behavior and Divorce," in eds. Janeen Costa and Russell W. Belk, *Research in Consumer Behavior,* vol. 6 (Greenwich, Conn.: JAI Press, 1993), pp. 153–184.
126. Kalpana Srinivasan, "More Single Fathers Raising Kids, Though Moms Far More Common," *Austin American Statesman,* December 11, 1998, p. A23.
127. Raymond, "The Ex-Files."
128. Barbara Rosewicz, "Here Comes the Bride .º.º. and for the Umpteenth Time," *Wall Street Journal,* September 10, 1996, pp. B1, B10.
129. Jan Larson, "Understanding Stepfamilies," *American Demographics,* July 1992, pp. 36–40.
130. "Profiles of General Demographic Characteristics: 2000 Census of Population and Housing," United States Department of Commerce News.
131. Hideo Takayama, "Spending More on Fewer Kids," *Journal of Japanese Trade and Industry,* May 1991, pp. 24–27.
132. Paul, "Childless by Choice."
133. Lyle V. Harris, "Shopping by Male," *Austin American Statesman,* April 27, 1999, pp. E1, E2.
134. Gardyn, "Unmarried Bliss."
135. Ann Zimmerman, "Wal-Marts in Germany Redefine the Term 'Checkout Aisle,'" *Wall Street Journal,* November 9, 2004, pp. B1, B4.
136. Harry L. Davis, "Dimensions of Marital Roles in Consumer Decision Making," *Journal of Marketing Research,* May 1970, pp. 168–177; Conway Lackman and John M. Lanasa, "Family Decision Making Theory: An Overview and Assessment," *Psychology and Marketing,* March–April 1993, pp. 81–93.
137. "Gender Bender," *American Demographics,* April 2001, p. 25.
138. P. Doyle and P. Hutchinson, "Individual Differences in Family Decision Making," *Journal of the Market Research Society,* October 1973, pp. 193–206; Jagdish N. Sheth, "A Theory of Family Buying Decisions," in ed. J. N. Sheth, *Models of Buyer Behavior* (New York: Harper & Row, 1974), pp. 17–33; Daniel Seymour and Greg Lessne, "Spousal Conflict Arousal: Scale Development," *Journal of Consumer Research,* December 1984, pp. 810–821.
139. Neal Templin, "The PC Wars: Who Gets to Use the Family Computer?" *Wall Street Journal,* October 5, 1996, pp. B1, B2.
140. Sheth, "A Theory of Family Buying Decisions"; Michael A. Belch, George E. Belch, and Donald Sciglimpaglia, "Conflict in Family Decision Making: An Exploratory Investigation," in ed. Jerry C. Olson, *Advances in Consumer Research,* vol. 7 (Chicago: Association for Consumer Research, 1980), pp. 475–479.
141. W. Christian Buss and Charles M. Schaninger, "The Influence of Family Decision Processes and Outcomes," in eds. Richard P. Bagozzi and Alice M. Tybout, *Advances in Consumer Research,* vol. 10 (Ann Arbor, Mich.: Association for Consumer Research, 1983), pp. 439–444.
142. Terry L. Childers and Akshay R. Rao, "The Influence of Familial and Peer-Based Reference Groups on Consumer Decisions," *Journal of Consumer Research,* September 1992, pp. 198–211.
143. Harry L. Davis and Benny P. Rigaux, "Perception of Marital Roles in Decision Processes," *Journal of Consumer Research,* June 1974, pp. 5–14; Mandy Putnam and William R. Davidson, *Family Purchasing Behavior: 11 Family Roles by Product Category* (Columbus, Ohio: Management Horizons, Inc., a Division of Price Waterhouse, 1987).
144. Rosann Spiro, "Persuasion in Family Decision Making," *Journal of Consumer Research,* March 1983, pp. 393–402; Alvin Burns and Donald Granbois, "Factors Moderating the Resolution of Preference Conflict," *Journal of Marketing Research,* February 1977, pp. 68–77.
145. Pierre Filiarault and J. R. Brent Ritchie, "Joint Purchasing Decisions: A Comparison of Influence Structure in Family and Couple Decision Making Units," *Journal of Consumer Research,* September 1980, pp. 131–140; Dennis Rosen and Donald Granbois, "Determinants of Role Structure in Financial Management," *Journal of Consumer Research,* September 1983, pp. 253–258; Spiro, "Persuasion in Family Decision Making"; Kim P. Corfman and Donald R. Lehmann, "Models of Cooperative Group Decision-Making and Relative Influence: An Experimental Investigation of Family Purchase Decisions," *Journal of Consumer Research,* June 1987, pp. 1–13.
146. William J. Qualls, "Household Decision Behavior: The Impact of Husbands' and Wives' Sex Role Orientation," *Journal of Consumer Research,* September 1987, pp. 264–279; Giovanna Imperia, Thomas O'Guinn, and Elizabeth MacAdams, "Family Decision Making Role Perceptions among Mexican-American and Anglo Wives: A Cross-Cultural Comparison," in eds. Elizabeth C. Hirschman and Morris B. Holbrook, *Advances in Consumer Research,* vol. 12 (Provo, Utah: Association for Consumer Research, 1985), pp. 71–74.
147. Michael Flagg, "Asian Marketing," Asian *Wall Street Journal,* March 19, 2001, p. A12.
148. Robert T. Green, Jean-Paul Leonardi, Jean-Louis Chandon, Isabella C. M. Cunningham, Bronis Verhage, and Alain Strazzieri, "Societal Development and Family Purchasing Roles: A Cross-National Study," *Journal of Consumer Research,* March 1983, pp. 436–442; Leonidas C. Leonidou, "Understanding the Russian Consumer,"

Marketing and Research Today, March 1992, pp. 75–83; Sak Onkvisit and John J. Shaw, *International Marketing: Analysis and Strategy* (Columbus, Ohio: Merrill, 1989).

149. Michael B. Menasco and David J. Curry, "Utility and Choice: An Empirical Study of Wife/Husband Decision Making," *Journal of Consumer Research,* June 1989, pp. 87–97; Qualls, "Household Decision Behavior."
150. C. Whan Park, "Joint Decisions in Home Purchasing: A Muddling-Through Process," *Journal of Consumer Research,* September 1982, pp. 151–162; Harry L. Davis, Stephen J. Hoch, and E. K. Easton Ragsdale, "An Anchoring and Adjustment Model of Spousal Predictions," *Journal of Consumer Research,* June 1986, pp. 25–37; Gary M. Munsinger, Jean E. Weber, and Richard W. Hansen, "Joint Home Purchasing by Husbands and Wives," *Journal of Consumer Research,* March 1975, pp. 60–66; Lakshman Krisnamurthi, "The Salience of Relevant Others and Its Effect on Individual and Joint Preferences: An Experimental Investigation," *Journal of Consumer Research,* June 1983, pp. 62–72; Robert F. Krampf, David J. Burns, and Dale M. Rayman, "Consumer Decision Making and the Nature of the Product: A Comparison of Husband and Wife Adoption Process Location," *Psychology and Marketing,* March–April 1993, pp. 95–109.
151. Chenting Su, Edward F. Fern, and Keying Ye, "A Temporal Dynamic Model of Spousal Family Purchase-Decision Behavior," *Journal of Marketing Research,* August 2003, pp. 268–281.
152. Tamara F. Mangleburg, "Children's Influence in Purchase Decisions: A Review and Critique," in eds. Marvin E. Goldberg, Gerald Gorn, and Richard W. Pollay, *Advances in Consumer Research,* vol. 17 (Provo, Utah: Association for Consumer Research, 1990), pp. 813–825; Ellen R. Foxman, Patriya S. Tansuhaj, and Karin M. Ekstrom, "Family Members' Perceptions of Adolescents' Influence in Family Decision Making," *Journal of Consumer Research,* March 1989, pp. 481–490; George Belch, Michael A. Belch, and Gayle Ceresino, "Parental and Teenage Influences in Family Decision Making," *Journal of Business Research,* April 1985, pp. 163–176; Lackman and Lanasa, "Family Decision Making Theory."
153. Selina S. Guber and Jon Berry, "War Stories from the Sandbox: What Kids Say," *Brandweek,* July 5, 1993, pp.vol. 21, 26–30; Andre Caron and Scott Ward, "Gift Decisions by Kids and Parents," *Journal of Advertising Research,* August–September 1975, pp. 15–20.
154. Mary Lou Roberts, Lawrence H. Wortzel, and Robert L. Berkeley, "Mothers' Attitudes and Perceptions of Children's Influence and Their Effect on Family Consumption," in ed. Jerry C. Olson, *Advances in Consumer Research,* vol. 8 (Ann Arbor, Mich.: Association for Consumer Research, 1981), pp. 730–735; Ellen Foxman and Patriya Tansuhaj, "Adolescents' and Mothers' Perceptions of Relative Influence in Family Purchase Decisions: Patterns of Agreement and Disagreement," in ed. Michael J. Houston, *Advances in Consumer Research,* vol. 15 (Provo, Utah: Association for Consumer Research, 1988), pp. 449–453.
155. Sharon E. Beatty and Salil Talpade, "Adolescent Influence in Family Decision Making: A Replication with Extension," *Journal of Consumer Research,* September 1994, pp. 332–341; Christopher Power, "Getting 'Em While They're Young," *BusinessWeek,* September 9, 1991, pp. 94–95; Scott Ward and Daniel B. Wackman, "Children's Purchase Influence Attempts and Parental Yielding," *Journal of Marketing Research,* November 1972, pp. 316–319.
156. William K. Darley and Jeen-Su Lim, "Family Decision Making in Leisure Time Activities: An Exploratory Analysis of the Impact of Locus of Control, Child Age Influence Factor and Parental Type on Perceived Child Influence," in ed. Richard J. Lutz, *Advances in Consumer Research,* vol. 13 (Ann Arbor, Mich.: Association for Consumer Research, 1986), pp. 370–374; George P. Moschis and Linda G. Mitchell, "Television Advertising and Interpersonal Influences on Teenagers' Participation in Family Consumer Decisions," in ed. Lutz, *Advances in Consumer Research,* vol. 13, pp. 181–186; James E. Nelson, "Children as Information Sources in Family Decisions to Eat Out," in ed. William L. Wilkie, *Advances in Consumer Research,* vol. 6 (Ann Arbor, Mich.: Association for Consumer Research, 1978), pp. 419–423; Beatty and Talpade, "Adolescent Influence in Family Decision Making."
157. Jeff Brazil, "Play Dough," *American Demographics,* December 1999, pp. 57–61.
158. June Cotte and Stacy L. Wood, "Families and Innovative Consumer Behavior: A Triadic Analysis of Sibling and Parental Influence," *Journal of Consumer Research,* June 2004, pp. 78+.
159. Kay M. Palan and Robert E. Wilkes, "Adolescent-Parent Interaction in Family Decision Making," *Journal of Consumer Research,* September 1997, pp. 159–169.
160. Les Carlson and Sanford Grossbart, "Parental Style and Consumer Socialization of Children," *Journal of Consumer Research,* June 1988, pp. 77–94.
161. Belch, Belch, and Ceresino, "Parental and Teenage Influences in Family Decision Making."
162. Vauhini Vara, "Cellphone Makers Are Creating Designs for 8- to 13-Year-Olds," *Wall Street Journal,* March 15, 2005, p. A4B.
163. Rebecca Gardyn, "Born To Be Wired," *American Demographics,* April 2003, pp. 14–15.
164. Janae Lepir, "Targeting Online Youth," *Global Cosmetic Industry,* September 2001, p. 56.
165. Rebecca Quick, "New Web Sites Let Kids Shop, Like, without Credit Cards," *Wall Street Journal,* June 14, 1999, pp. B1, B4.
166. Dobrow, "How Old Is Old Enough?"
167. Nat Ives, "Nickelodeon Is Moving Beyond the Confines of a TV Screen to Try to Draw Fans to a Hotel," *New York Times,* October 5, 2004, p. C3; Joe Flint, "Testing Limits of Licensing: SpongeBob-Motif Holiday Inn," *Wall Street Journal,* October 9, 2003, pp. B1, B4.
168. Thomas C. O'Guinn and Timothy P. Meyer, "The Family VCR: Ordinary Family Life with a Common Textual Product," Working paper, University of Illinois, 1994.

CHAPTER 15

2. Milton Rokeach, *The Nature of Human Values* (New York: Free Press, 1973), p. 5.
3. Wagner A. Kamakura and Jose Alfonso Mazzon, "Value Segmentation: A Model for the Measurement of Values and Value Systems," *Journal of Consumer Research*, September 1991, pp. 208–218; see also Milton Rokeach and Sandra J. Ball-Rokeach, "Stability and Change in American Value Priorities, 1968–1981," *American Psychologist*, May 1989, pp. 775–784; Milton Rokeach, *Understanding Human Values* (New York: Free Press, 1979); Shalom H. Schwartz and Wolfgang Bilsky, "Toward a Universal Psychological Structure of Human Values," *Journal of Personality and Social Psychology*, September 1987, pp. 550–562.
4. Francesco M. Nicosia and Robert N. Mayer, "Toward a Sociology of Consumption," *Journal of Consumer Research*, September 1976, pp. 65–75; Hugh E. Kramer, "The Value of Higher Education and Its Impact on Value Formation," in eds. Robert E. Pitts and Arch G. Woodside, *Personal Values and Consumer Psychology* (Lexington, Mass.: Lexington Books, 1984), pp. 239–251.
5. Sally Beatty, "Kids Are Glued to a Violent Japanese Cartoon Show," *Wall Street Journal*, December 3, 1999, pp. B1, B4.
6. Mary Gilly and Lisa Penaloza, "Barriers and Incentives in Consumer Acculturation," in eds. W. Fred van Raaij and Gary J. Bamossy, *European Advances in Consumer Research*, vol. 1 (Provo, Utah: Association for Consumer Research, 1993), pp. 278–286.
7. Rokeach, *The Nature of Human Values;* Schwartz and Bilsky, "Toward a Universal Psychological Structure of Human Values."
8. Russell W. Belk, "Materialism: Trait Aspects of Living in the Material World," *Journal of Consumer Research*, December 1985, pp. 265–280; Russell W. Belk, "Three Scales to Measure Constructs Related to Materialism: Reliability, Validity, and Relationships to Happiness," in ed. Thomas P. Kinnear, *Advances in Consumer Research*, vol. 11 (Provo, Utah: Association for Consumer Research, 1984), pp. 291–297.
9. Marsha L. Richins, "Special Possessions and the Expression of Material Values," *Journal of Consumer Research*, December 1994, pp. 522–533.
10. Marsha L. Richins and Scott Dawson, "A Consumer Values Orientation for Materialism and Its Measurement: Scale Development and Validation," *Journal of Consumer Research*, December 1992, pp. 303–316.
11. James E. Burroughs and Aric Rindfleisch, "Materialism and Well-Being: A Conflicting Values Perspective," *Journal of Consumer Research*, December 2002, pp. 348+.
12. Mary Yoko Brannen, "Cross Cultural Materialism: Commodifying Culture in Japan," in eds. Floyd Rudmin and Marsha Richins, *Meaning, Measure, and Morality of Materialism* (Provo, Utah: The Association for Consumer Research, 1992), pp. 167–180; Dorothy E. Jones, Dorinda Elliott, Edith Terry, Carla A. Robbins, Charles Gaffney, and Bruce Nussbaum, "Capitalism in China," *BusinessWeek*, January 1985, pp. 53–59; see also Tse, Belk, and Zhou, "Becoming a Consumer Society."
13. Ger, "Problems of Marketization in Romania and Turkey," in eds. Schultz, Belk, and Ger, *Consumption in Marketizing Economies;* Güliz Ger, Russell Belk, and Dana–Nicoleta Lascu, "The Development of Consumer Desire in Marketizing and Developing Economies: The Cases of Romania and Turkey," in eds. Leigh McAlister and Michael L. Rothschild, *Advances in Consumer Research*, vol. 20 (Provo, Utah: Association for Consumer Research, 1992), pp. 102–107.
14. P. H. Ferguson, "Shoppers Leave Ivory Towers for Bargain Basements in Japan," *Austin American Statesman*, December 26, 1993, p. A26.
15. Meg Dupont, "Cocooning Morphs into Hiving," *Hartford Courant*, October 29, 2004, p. H2.
16. "Fastest-Growing Internet Activity Is Online Banking," *InternetWeek*, February 10, 2005, *www.internetweek.com*.
17. John Fetto, "Nowhere to Hide," *American Demographics*, July–August 2002, pp. 12+.
19. Craig J. Thompson, "Caring Consumers: Gendered Consumption Meanings and the Juggling Lifestyle," *Journal of Consumer Research*, March 1996, pp. 388–407.
20. Marleis Welms Floet, "Youth in Holland," *Industry Report*.
21. Elizabeth C. Hirschman, "Men, Dogs, Guns, and Cars," *Journal of Advertising*, Spring 2003, pp. 9–22.
22. Mohan J Dutta-Bergman and William D. Wells, "The Values and Lifestyles of Idiocentrics and Allocentrics in an Individualist Culture: A Descriptive Approach," *Journal of Consumer Psychology*, 2002, pp. 232–242.
23. Christopher T. Linen, "Marketing and the Global Economy," *Direct Marketing*, January 1991, pp. 54–56.
26. Joanne Lipman, "Marketers of Luxury Goods Are Turning from Self-Indulgence to Family Values," *Wall Street Journal*, October 22, 1992, pp. B1, B10.
27. Shelly Branch and Ernest Beck, "For Unilever, It's Sweetness and Light," *Wall Street Journal*, April 13, 2000, pp. B1, B4.
28. Chad Terhune, "Gatorade Works on Endurance," *Wall Street Journal*, March 21, 2005, p. B6.
29. Jay Krall, "Big-Brand Logos Pop Up in Organic Aisle," *Wall Street Journal*, July 29, 2003, p. B1.
30. Matthew Grimm, "Veggie Delight," *American Demographics*, August 2000, pp. 66–67.
31. Scott Kilman, "Monsanto Brings 'Genetic' Ads to Europe," *Wall Street Journal*, June 16, 1998, p. B3.
32. John Fetto, "Quackery No More," *American Demographics*, January 2001, pp. 10–11; Matt Murray, "GNC Makes Ginseng, Shark Pills Its Potion for Growth," *Wall Street Journal*, March 15, 1996, pp. B1, B3.
33. Tara Parker-Pope, "Antismoking Sentiment Flares in Europe's Smoke-Filled Cafes," *Wall Street Journal*, August 28, 1996, pp. B1, B8.
36. Chad Terhune, "Market Shares Drop at Coca-Cola, PepsiCo," *Wall Street Journal*, March 7, 2005, p. B6.
37. Sarah McBride, "Entrepreneurs Cater to a Growing Nation," *Wall Street Journal*, April 10, 1997, pp. B1, B15.

40. Valerie Reitman, "For Frozen Yogurt, a Chill Wind Blows," *Wall Street Journal*, June 3, 1992, p. B1; Curry, "Skip the Tofu."

43. Michael J. Weiss, "To Be About to Be," *American Demographics*, September 1, 2003.

49. Stephen Baker and Adam Aston, "The Business of Nanotech," *Business Week*, February 14, 2005, pp. 64+.

50. Paul Schweitzer, "The Third Millennium: Riding the Waves of Turbulence," *News Tribune*, December 1993, pp. 5–27.

51. Sak Onkvisit and John J. Shaw, *International Marketing: Analysis and Strategy* (Columbus, Ohio: Merrill, 1989), p. 243.

52. Robert Wilk, "INFOPLAN: The New Rich: A Psychographic Approach to Marketing to the Wealthy Japanese Consumer," ESOMAR Conference, Venice, Italy, June 1990, reported in de Mooij and Keegan, *Advertising Worldwide*, pp. 122–129.

53. K. S. Yang, "Expressed Values of Chinese College Students," in eds. K. S. Yang and Y. Y. Li, *Symposium on the Character of the Chinese: An Interdisciplinary Approach* (Taipei, Taiwan: Institute of Ethnology Academic Sinica, 1972), pp. 257–312; see also Oliver H. M. Yau, *Consumer Behavior in China: Customer Satisfaction and Cultural Values* (New York: Rutledge, 1994).

54. Alfred S. Boote, cited in Rebecca Piirto, *Beyond Mind Games* (Ithaca, N.Y.: American Demographic Books, 1991).

55. Geert Hofstede, "National Cultures in Four Dimensions," *International Studies of Management and Organization*, Spring–Summer 1983, pp. 46–74.

56. Michael Lynn, George M. Zinkhan, and Judy Harris, "Consumer Tipping: A Cross-Country Study," *Journal of Consumer Research*, December 1993, pp. 478–488.

57. Dana L. Alden, Wayne D. Hoyer, and Chol Lee, "Identifying Global and Culture-Specific Dimensions of Humor in Advertising: A Multinational Analysis," *Journal of Marketing*, April 1993, pp. 64–75.

58. Van R. Wood and Roy Howell, "A Note on Hispanic Values and Subcultural Research: An Alternative View," *Journal of the Academy of Marketing Science*, Winter 1991, pp. 61–67; see also Humberto Valencia, "Hispanic Values and Subcultural Research," *Journal of the Academy of Marketing Science*, Winter 1989, pp. 23–28; Thomas E. Ness and Melvin T. Smith, "Middle-Class Values in Blacks and Whites," in eds. Pitts and Woodside, *Personal Values and Consumer Psychology*, pp. 231–237.

59. "China's Golden Oldies," *The Economist*, February 26, 2005, p. 65.

60. Richard P. Coleman, "The Continuing Significance of Social Class to Marketing," *Journal of Consumer Research*, December 1983, pp. 265–280.

61. William Strauss and Neil Howe, "The Cycle of Generations, *American Demographics*, April 1991, pp. 25–33, 52; see also William Strauss and Neil Howe, *Generations: The History of America's Future, 1584 to 2069* (New York: William Morrow, 1992); Lawrence A. Crosby, James D. Gill, and Robert E. Lee, "Life Status and Age as Predictors of Value Orientation," in eds. Pitts and Woodside, *Personal Values and Consumer Psychology*, pp. 201–218.

62. Sharon Beatty, Lynn R. Kahle, Pamela Homer, and Shekhar Misra, "Alternative Measurement Approaches to Consumer Values: The List of Values and the Rokeach Value Survey," *Psychology and Marketing*, Fall 1985, pp. 181–200.

63. Lynn R. Kahle, *Social Values and Social Change: Adaptation to Life in America* (New York: Praeger, 1983).

64. Judith Valente, "Body Shop Has a Few Aches and Pains," *Wall Street Journal*, August 6, 1993, pp. B1, B12.

65. Yoram Wind, "The Myth of Globalization," *Journal of Consumer Marketing*, Spring 1986, pp. 23–26.

66. Buss, "Green Cars."

67. David K. Tse, John K. Wong, and Chin Tiong Tan, "Towards Some Standardized Cross-Cultural Consumption Values," in ed. Michael J. Houston, *Advances in Consumer Research*, vol. 15 (Provo, Utah: Association for Consumer Research, 1988), pp. 387–393; Ved Prakash, "Segmentation of Women's Market Based on Personal Values and the Means-End Chain Model: A Framework for Advertising Strategy," in ed. Richard J. Lutz, *Advances in Consumer Research*, vol. 13 (Provo, Utah: Association for Consumer Research 1986), pp. 215–220.

68. Rebecca Piirto, *Beyond Mind Games* (Ithaca, N.Y.: American Demographic Books, 1991).

69. Edward F. McQuarrie and Daniel Langmeyer, "Using Values to Measure Attitudes Toward Discontinuous Innovations," *Psychology and Marketing*, Winter 1985, pp. 239–252.

71. Patricia F. Kennedy, Roger J. Best, and Lynn R. Kahle, "An Alternative Method for Measuring Value-Based Segmentation and Advertisement Positioning," in eds. James H. Leigh and Claude R. Martin Jr., *Current Issues and Research in Advertising*, vol. 11 (Ann Arbor, Mich.: Division of Research, School of Business Administration, University of Michigan, 1988), pp. 139–156; Daniel L. Sherrell, Joseph F. Hair Jr., and Robert P. Bush, "The Influence of Personal Values on Measures of Advertising Effectiveness: Interactions with Audience Involvement," in eds. Pitts and Woodside, *Personal Values and Consumer Psychology*, pp. 169–185.

73. Lisa Bannon and Margaret Studer, "For 2 Revealing European Ads, Overexposure Can Have Benefits," *Wall Street Journal*, June 17, 1993, p. B8.

74. Pichayaporn Utumporn, "Ad with Hitler Brings Outcry in Thailand," *Wall Street Journal*, June 5, 1995, p. C1.

75. Robert E. Pitts, John K. Wong, and D. Joel Whalen, "Consumers' Evaluative Structures in Two Ethical Situations: A Means-End Approach," *Journal of Business Research*, March 1991, pp. 119–130.

76. Scott Hensley, "In Switch, J&J Gives Straight Talk on Drug Risks on New Ads," *Wall Street Journal*, March 21, 2005, pp. B1+.

77. Russell W. Belk and Richard W. Pollay, "Materialism and Status Appeals in Japanese and U.S. Print Advertising," *International Marketing Review*, Winter 1985, pp. 38–47; see also Russell W. Belk, Wendy J. Bryce, and

Richard W. Pollay, "Advertising Themes and Cultural Values: A Comparison of U.S. and Japanese Advertising," in eds. K. C. Mun and T. S. Chan, *Proceedings of the Inaugural Meeting of the Southeast Asia Region Academy of International Business* (Hong Kong: The Chinese University of Hong Kong, 1985), pp. 11–20.

78. David K. Tse, Russell W. Belk, and Nan Zhou, "Becoming a Consumer Society: A Longitudinal and Cross-Cultural Content Analysis of Print Ads from Hong Kong, the People's Republic of China, and Taiwan," *Journal of Consumer Research*, March 1989, pp. 457–472.

79. Tse, Belk, and Zhou, "Becoming a Consumer Society."

80. Russell W. Belk, "Material Values in the Comics: A Content Analysis of Comic Books Featuring Themes of Wealth," *Journal of Consumer Research*, June 1987, pp. 26–42.

81. For more on means-end chain analysis, see Beth A. Walker and Jerry C. Olson, "Means-End Chains: Connecting Products with Self," *Journal of Business Research*, March 1991, pp. 111–118; Thomas J. Reynolds and John P. Richon, "Means-End Based Advertising Research: Copy Testing Is Not Strategy Assessment," *Journal of Business Research*, March 1991, pp. 131–142; Jonathan Gutman, "Exploring the Nature of Linkages between Consequences and Values," *Journal of Business Research*, March 1991, pp. 143–148; Thomas J. Reynolds and Jonathan Gutman, "Laddering Theory, Method, Analysis and Interpretation," *Journal of Advertising Research*, February/March 1988, pp. 11–31; Thomas J. Reynolds and Jonathan Gutman, "Laddering: Extending the Repertory Grid Methodology to Construct Attribute-Consequence-Value Hierarchies," in eds. Pitts and Woodside, *Personal Values and Consumer Psychology*, pp. 155–167.

82. Thomas J. Reynolds and J. P. Jolly, "Measuring Personal Values: An Evaluation of Alternative Methods," *Journal of Marketing Research*, November 1980, pp. 531–536; Reynolds and Gutman, "Laddering"; Jonathan Gutman, "A Means-End Model Based on Consumer Categorization Processes," *Journal of Marketing*, Spring 1982, pp. 60–72.

83. T. L. Stanley, "Death of the Sports Car?" *Brandweek*, January 2, 1995, p. 38.

84. Frenkel Ter Hofstede, Jan-Benedict E. M. Steenkamp, and Michel Wedel, "International Market Segmentation Based on Consumer-Product Relations," *Journal of Marketing Research*, vol. 36, February 1999, pp. 1–17.

85. Marsha L. Richins, "The Material Values Scale: Measurement Properties and Development of a Short Form," *Journal of Consumer Research*, June 2004, pp. 209+.

86. J. Michael Munson and Edward F. McQuarrie, "Shortening the Rokeach Value Survey for Use in Consumer Research," in ed. Michael J. Houston, *Advances in Consumer Research*, vol. 15 (Provo, Utah: Association for Consumer Research, 1988), pp. 381–386.

87. Lynn R. Kahle, Sharon Beatty, and Pamela Homer, "Alternative Measurement Approaches to Consumer Values: The List of Values (LOV) and Values and Life Style (VALS)," *Journal of Consumer Research*, December 1986, pp. 405–409; Kahle, *Social Values and Social Change.*

88. Wagner Kamakura and Thomas P. Novak, "Value-System Segmentation: Exploring the Meaning of LOV," *Journal of Consumer Research*, June 1992, pp. 119–132.

89. Sigmund Freud, *Collected Papers*, vols. I–V (New York: Basic Books, 1959); Erik Erickson, *Childhood and Society* (New York: Norton, 1963); Erik Erickson, *Identity: Youth and Crisis* (New York: Norton, 1968).

90. Yumiko Ono, "Marketers Seek the 'Naked' Truth," *Wall Street Journal*, May 30, 1997, pp. B1, B13.

91. Gordon Allport, *Personality: A Psychological Interpretation* (New York: Holt, Rinehart, & Winston, 1937); Raymond B. Cattell, *The Scientific Analysis of Personality* (Baltimore: Penguin, 1965).

92. Carl G. Jung, *Man and His Symbols* (Garden City, N.Y.: Doubleday, 1964); see also Hans J. Eysenck, "Personality, Stress and Disease: An Interactionistic Perspective," *Psychological Inquiry*, vol. 2, 1991, pp. 221–232.

93. Carl R. Rogers, "Some Observations on the Organization of Personality," *American Psychologist*, September 1947, pp. 358–368; George A. Kelly, *The Psychology of Personal Constructs*, vols. 1 and 2 (New York: Norton, 1955).

94. Bernard Weiner, "Attribution in Personality Psychology," in ed. Lawrence A. Pervin, *Handbook of Personality: Theory and Research* (New York: Guilford, 1990), pp. 465–484; Harold H. Kelly, "The Processes of Causal Attribution," *American Psychologist*, February 1973, pp. 107–128.

95. David Glen Mick and Claus Buhl, "A Meaning-Based Model of Advertising Experiences," *Journal of Consumer Research*, December 1992, pp. 317–338.

96. Karen B. Horney, *Our Inner Conflicts* (New York: Norton, 1945).

97. Joel B. Cohen, "An Interpersonal Orientation to the Study of Consumer Behavior," *Journal of Marketing Research*, August 1967, pp. 270–277; Jon P. Noerager, "An Assessment of CAD—A Personality Instrument Developed Specifically for Marketing Research," *Journal of Marketing Research*, February 1979, pp. 53–59.

98. Marsha L. Richins, "An Analysis of Consumer Interaction Styles in the Marketplace," *Journal of Consumer Research*, June 1983, pp. 73–82.

99. Richard P. Bagozzi, Hans Baumgartner, and Youjae Yi, "State versus Action Orientation and the Theory of Reasoned Action, An Application to Coupon Usage," *Journal of Consumer Research*, March 1992, pp. 505–518; William O. Bearden and Randall L. Rose, "Attention to Social Comparison Information: An Individual Difference Factor Affecting Consumer Conformity," *Journal of Consumer Research*, March 1990, pp. 461–471; Bobby J. Calder and Robert E. Burnkrant, "Interpersonal Influence on Consumer Behavior: An Attribution Theory Approach," *Journal of Consumer Research*, December 1979, pp. 29–38.

100. B. F. Skinner, *About Behaviorism* (New York: Knopf, 1974); B. F. Skinner, *Beyond Freedom and Dignity* (New York: Knopf, 1971).

101. Jacob Jacoby, "Multiple Indicant Approaches for Studying New Product Adopters," *Journal of Applied Psychology*, August 1971, pp. 384–388; Harold H. Kassarjian, "Personality and Consumer Behavior: A Review," *Journal of Marketing Research*, November 1971, pp. 409–418; see also Harold H. Kassarjian, "Personality: The Longest Fad," in ed. William L. Wilkie, *Advances in Consumer Research*, vol. 6 (Ann Arbor, Mich.: Association for Consumer Research, 1979), pp. 122–124.
102. Franklin B. Evans, "Psychological and Objective Factors in the Prediction of Brand Choice," *Journal of Business*, October 1959, pp. 340–369.
103. John L. Lastovicka and Erich A. Joachimsthaler, "Improving the Detection of Personality-Behavior Relationships in Consumer Research," *Journal of Consumer Research*, March 1988, pp. 583–587; Kathryn E. A. Villani and Yoram Wind, "On the Usage of 'Modified' Personality Trait Measures in Consumer Research," *Journal of Consumer Research*, December 1975, pp. 223–228.
104. William O. Bearden, David M. Hardesty, and Randall L. Rose, "Consumer Self-Confidence: Refinements in Conceptualization and Measurement," *Journal of Consumer Research*, vol. 28, June 2001, pp. 121–134.
105. D. E. Berlyne, *Conflict, Arousal and Curiosity*, (New York: McGraw-Hill, 1960); D. E. Berlyne, "Novelty, Complexity, and Hedonic Value," *Perception and Psychophysics*, November 1970, pp. 279–286.
106. Marvin Zuckerman, *Sensation Seeking: Beyond the Optimal Level of Arousal* (Hillsdale, N.J.: Lawrence Erlbaum, 1979); Elizabeth C. Hirschman, "Innovativeness, Novelty Seeking, and Consumer Creativity," *Journal of Consumer Research*, December 1980, pp. 283–295.
107. R. A. Mittelstadt, S. L. Grossbart, W. W. Curtis, and S. P. DeVere, "Optimal Stimulation Level and the Adoption Decision Process," *Journal of Consumer Research*, September 1976, pp. 84–94; P. S. Raju, "Optimum Stimulation Level: Its Relationship to Personality, Demographics, and Exploratory Behavior," *Journal of Consumer Research*, December 1980, pp. 272–282; Jan-Benedict E. M. Steenkamp and Hans Baumgartner, "The Role of Optimum Stimulation Level in Exploratory Consumer Behavior," *Journal of Consumer Research*, December 1992, pp. 434–448; Erich A. Joachimsthaler and John Lastovicka, "Optimal Stimulation Level—Exploratory Behavior Models," *Journal of Consumer Research*, December 1984, pp. 830–835.
108. Leon G. Schiffman, William R. Dillon, and Festus E. Ngumah, "The Influence of Subcultural and Personality Factors on Consumer Acculturation," *Journal of International Business Studies*, Fall 1981, pp. 137–143.
109. Kelly Tepper Tian, William O. Bearden, and Gary L. Hunter, "Consumers' Need for Uniqueness: Scale Development and Validation," *Journal of Consumer Research*, vol. 28, June 2001, pp. 50–66.
110. Itamar Simonson and Stephen M. Nowlis, "The Role of Explanations and Need for Uniqueness in Consumer Decision Making: Unconventional Choices Based on Reasons," *Journal of Consumer Research*, vol. 27, June 2000, pp. 49–68.
111. James E. Burroughs and David Glen Mick, "Exploring Antecedents and Consequences of Consumer Creativity in a Problem-Solving Context," *Journal of Consumer Research*, September 2004, pp. 402+.
112. Ibid., and Alice M. Isen, "Positive Effect," *Handbook of Cognition and Emotion*, Tim Dageleisch and Mick Power (eds.), New York: Wiley, 1999, pp. 521–539.
113. John T. Cacioppo, Richard E. Petty, and Chuan F. Kao, "The Efficient Assessment of Need for Cognition," *Journal of Personality Assessment*, June 1984, pp. 306–307; Curtis R. Haugtvedt, Richard E. Petty, and John T. Cacioppo, "Need for Cognition and Advertising: Understanding the Role of Personality Variables in Consumer Behavior," *Journal of Consumer Psychology*, vol. 1, no. 3, 1992, pp. 239–260; Rajeev Batra and Douglas M. Stayman, "The Role of Mood in Advertising Effectiveness," *Journal of Consumer Research*, September 1990, pp. 203–214; John T. Cacioppo, Richard E. Petty, and K. Morris, "Effects of Need for Cognition on Message Evaluation, Recall and Persuasion," *Journal of Personality and Social Psychology*, October 1983, pp. 805–818.
114. Susan Powell Mantel and Frank R. Kardes, "The Role of Direction of Comparison, Attribute-Based Processing, and Attitude-Based Processing in Consumer Preference," *Journal of Consumer Research*, vol. 25, March 1999, pp. 335–352.
115. William O. Bearden, Richard G. Netemeyer, and Jesse H. Teel, "Measurement of Consumer Susceptibility to Interpersonal Influence," *Journal of Consumer Research*, March 1989, pp. 472–480; Peter Wright, "Factors Affecting Cognitive Resistance to Ads," *Journal of Marketing Research*, June 1975, pp. 1–9.
116. John L. Lastovicka, Lance A. Bettencourt, Renée Shaw Hughner, and Ronald J. Kuntze, "Lifestyle of the Tight and Frugal: Theory and Measurement," *Journal of Consumer Research*, vol. 26, June 1999, pp. 85–98.
117. Terrence H. Witkowski, "World War II Poster Campaigns," *Journal of Advertising*, Spring 2003, pp. 69–82.
118. "Free Magazines Popping Up All Over Japan," *Japan Close-Up*, March 2005, p. 7.
119. Richard C. Becherer and Lawrence C. Richard, "Self-Monitoring as a Moderating Variable in Consumer Behavior," *Journal of Consumer Research*, December 1978, pp. 159–162; Mark Snyder and Kenneth G. DeBono, "Appeals to Image and Claims about Quality: Understanding the Psychology of Advertising," *Journal of Personality and Social Psychology*, September 1985, pp. 586–597.
120. Dean Peabody, *National Characteristics* (Cambridge, England: Cambridge University Press, 1985); Allan B. Yates, "Americans, Canadians Similar but Vive La Difference," *Direct Marketing*, October 1985, p. 152.
121. Terry Clark, "International Marketing and National Character: A Review and Proposal for an Integrative Theory," *Journal of Marketing*, October 1990, pp. 66–79.
122. Greg Sandoval, "China Bans LeBron James Nike Ad," *Washington Post*, December 7, 2004, p. E2.
123. "Getting Burned by Expansion Plans," *Marketing Week*, June 14, 2001, *www.marketingweek.com*.
124. Rob Walker, "For Kicks," *New York Times Magazine*, March 20, 2005, p. 38.

125. John L. Lastovicka, John P. Murray, Erich A. Joachimsthaler, Gaurav Bhalla, and Jim Scheurich, "A Lifestyle Typology to Model Young Male Drinking and Driving," *Journal of Consumer Research*, September 1987, pp. 257–263.
126. Morris B. Holbrook, "Nostalgia and Consumption Preferences: Some Emerging Patterns of Consumer Tastes," *Journal of Consumer Research*, September 1993, pp. 245–256.
127. Sandra Yin, "Going to Extremes," *American Demographics*, June 1, 2001, p. 26.
128. Michelle Moran, "Category Analysis: Small Electrics & Consumer Lifestyles Dictate Trends," *Gourmet Retailer*, June 2001, pp. 34+.
130. Leonidas C. Leonidou, "Understanding the Russian Consumer," *Marketing and Research Today*, March 1992, pp. 75–83.
135. ACE Brochure 1989; published by RISC, Paris, France; see also de Mooij and Keegan, *Advertising Worldwide.*
136. Elisabeth Rubinfien, "Travel Alert: Luxury Arrives in Moscow," *Wall Street Journal*, June 29, 1992, p. B7.
137. Yumiko Ono, "Off-Road Vehicles Leave Others in the Dust," *Wall Street Journal*, July 17, 1993, p. B1.
138. Tara Parker-Pope, "Nonalcoholic Beer Hits the Spot in Mideast," *Wall Street Journal*, December 6, 1996, pp. B1, B2.
139. Jennifer Saranow, "Forget About Bankers' Hours, As More Branches Extend Days," *Wall Street Journal*, March 17, 2005, p. D2.
140. Basil G. Englis and Michael R. Solomon, "To Be and Not to Be: Life Style Imagery, Reference Groups, and the Clustering of America," *Journal of Advertising*, Spring 1995, pp. 13–28.
143. Chad Rubel, "Parents Magazines Make Room for Daddy," *Marketing News*, February 27, 1995, pp. 1, 5.
147. Jacob Hornik and Mary Jane Schlinger, "Allocation of Time to the Mass Media," *Journal of Consumer Research*, March 1981, pp. 343–355.
148. Eben Shapiro, "Web Lovers Love TV, Often Watch Both," *Wall Street Journal*, June 12, 1998, p. B9.
149. Michael J. Weiss, Morris B. Holbrook, and John Habich, "Death of the Arts Snob," *American Demographics*, June 2001, pp. 40–42.
150. James Prichard, "Gerber Food to Be Packaged in Plastic Containers Instead of Glass Jars," *Associated Press Newswires*, June 19, 2001.
151. Bernard Wysocki Jr., "Are Profits in Sickness, Or in Health?" *Wall Street Journal*, August 10, 2001, pp. B1, B3.
152. SRI Consulting Business Intelligence, *VALS Framework and Segment Descriptions, www.sricbi.com/VALS/types.shtml.*
153. Pamela Paul, "Sell It to the Psyche," *Time*, September 15, 2003, pp. A2+.
154. Louise Witt, "Inside Intent," *American Demographics*, March 1, 2004.
155. David J. Lipke, "Head Trips," *American Demographics*, October 2000, pp. 38–39; Yankelovich Web site, *http://www.yankelovich.com.*
156. Douglas B. Holt, "Poststructuralist Lifestyle Analysis: Conceptualizing the Social Patterning of Consumption in Postmodernity," *Journal of Consumer Research*, March 1997, pp. 326–350.
157. Marvin Shoenwald, "Psychographic Segmentation: Used or Abused?" *Brandweek*, January 22, 2001, p. 34.
158. Piirto, *Beyond Mind Games.*
159. Pamela Paul, "Sell It to the Psyche."
160. Antoinette Alexander, "Tech-Savvy Young Shoppers May Be Untapped Market," *Drug Store News*, June 21, 2004, pp. 97+.

CHAPTER 16

3. Amna Kirmani and Margaret C. Campbell, "Goal Seeker and Persuasion Sentry: How Consumer Targets Respond to Interpersonal Marketing Persuasion," *Journal of Consumer Research*, December 2004, pp. 573+.
4. Claire Atkinson, "Marketers Weigh Efficacy and Ethics of Guerilla Efforts," *Advertising Age*, February 16, 2004, p. 88.
5. Robert L. Simison and Joseph B. White, "Reputation for Poor Quality Still Plagues Detroit," *Wall Street Journal*, May 4, 2000, pp. B1, B4.
6. Dana James, "Skoda Is Taken from Trash to Treasure," *Marketing News*, February 18, 2002, pp. 4–5.
7. Rebecca Gardyn, "How Does This Work?" *American Demographics*, December 2002/January 2003, pp. 18–19.
10. Frederick Koenig, *Rumor in the Marketplace: The Social Psychology of Commercial Hearsay* (Dover, Mass.: Auburn House, 1985); Paul M. Herr, Frank R. Kardes, and John Kim, "Effects of Word-of-Mouth and Product-Attribute Information on Persuasion: An Accessibility-Diagnosticity Perspective," *Journal of Consumer Research*, March 1991, pp. 454–462.
11. Paul F. Lazarsfeld, Bernard Berelson, and Hazel Gaudet, *The People's Choice; How the Voter Makes Up His Mind in a Presidential Campaign* (New York: Columbia University Press, 1948); see also Herr, Kardes, and Kim, "Effects of Word-of-Mouth and Product-Attribute Information on Persuasion."
13. Dale Duhan, Scott Johnson, James Wilcox, and Gilbert Harrell, "Influences on Consumer Use of Word-of-Mouth Recommendation Sources," *Journal of the Academy of Marketing Science*, vol. 25, Fall 1997, pp. 283–295.
14. Vicki Clift, "Systematically Solicit Testimonial Letters," *Marketing News*, June 6, 1994, p. 7.
18. See Robert V. Kozinets, "E-Tribalized Marketing? The Strategic Implications of Virtual Communities of Consumption," *European Management Journal*, 1999, pp. 252–264.
20. David Kirkpatrick and Daniel Roth, "Why There's No Escaping the Blog," *Fortune*, January 10, 2005, p. 44.
21. John W. Milligan, "Choosing Mediums for the Message," *US Banker*, February 1995, pp. 42–45.
22. Keiron Culligan, "Word-of-Mouth to Become True Measure of Ads," *Marketing*, February 9, 1995, p. 7.

23. Cris Prystay, "Companies Market to India's Have-Littles," *Wall Street Journal*, June 5, 2003, pp. B1, B12.
24. "Wave of Internet Surfers Has Chinese Censors Nervous," *Los Angeles Times*, June 26, 1995, p. D6; Jeffrey A. Trachtenberg, "Time Warner Unit Sets Joint Venture to Market TV Programming in China," *Wall Street Journal*, March 8, 1995, p. B2; Fred D. Reynolds and William R. Darden, "Mutually Adaptive Effects of Interpersonal Communication," *Journal of Marketing Research*, November 1971, pp. 449–454.
25. Kara Swisher, "The Gatekeeper," *Wall Street Journal*, December 8, 1997, pp. R18, R27.
26. Jacob Jacoby and Wayne D. Hoyer, "What If Opinion Leaders Didn't Really Know More: A Question of Nomological Validity," in ed. Kent B. Monroe, *Advances in Consumer Research*, vol. 8 (Chicago: Association for Consumer Research, 1980), pp. 299–302; Robin M. Higie, Lawrence F. Feick, and Linda L. Price, "Types and Amount of Word-of-Mouth Communications about Retailers," *Journal of Retailing*, Fall 1987, pp. 260–277; regarding innovativeness, Terry L. Childers ("Assessment of the Psychometric Properties of an Opinion Leadership Scale," *Journal of Marketing Research*, May 1986, pp. 184–187) found opinion leadership was related to consumer creativity/curiosity and to using products in multiple ways.
27. Morris B. Holbrook, "Popular Appeal versus Expert Judgments of Motion Pictures," *Journal of Consumer Research*, vol. 26, September 1999, pp. 144–155.
28. Marsha L. Richins and Teri Root-Shafer, "The Role of Involvement and Opinion Leadership in Consumer Word of Mouth: An Implicit Model Made Explicit," in ed. Michael J. Houston, *Advances in Consumer Research*, vol. 15 (Provo, Utah: Association for Consumer Research, 1988), pp. 32–36.
29. Audrey Guskey-Federouch and Robert L. Heckman, "The Good Samaritan in the Marketplace: Motives for Helpful Behavior," Paper presented at the Society for Consumer Psychology Conference, St. Petersburg, Fla., February 1994.
30. Lawrence F. Feick, Linda L. Price, and Robin Higie, "People Who Use People: The Opposite Side of Opinion Leadership," in ed. Richard J. Lutz, *Advances in Consumer Research*, vol. 13 (Provo, Utah: Association for Consumer Research, 1986), pp. 301–305; see also Jagdish N. Sheth, "Word-of-Mouth in Low-Risk Innovations," *Journal of Advertising Research*, June–July 1971, pp. 15–18.
31. Lawrence F. Feick and Linda L. Price, "The Market Maven: A Diffuser of Marketplace Information," *Journal of Marketing*, January 1987, pp. 83–97.
32. See, for example, Dorothy Leonard-Barton, "Experts as Negative Opinion Leaders in the Diffusion of a Technological Innovation," *Journal of Consumer Research*, March 1985, pp. 914–926.
33. Everett M. Rogers, *Diffusion of Innovations* (New York: Free Press, 1983).
34. Laura Bird, "Consumers Smile on Unilever's Mentadent," *Wall Street Journal*, May 31, 1994, p. B9; Joseph R. Mancuso, "Why Not Create Opinion Leaders for New Product Introduction?" *Journal of Marketing*, July 1969, pp. 20–25.
35. "Smoking Cessation: GSK Strikes a Chord with Reality Ads," *Chemist and Druggist*, March 5, 2005, p. 40.
36. Gabriel Bar-Haim, "The Meaning of Western Commercial Artifacts for Eastern European Youth," *Journal of Contemporary Ethnography*, July 1987, pp. 205–226.
37. Christopher Reynolds, "Up on the Envy Meter," *American Demographics*, June 2004, pp. 6–7.
38. Jim Patterson, "Branding Campaign Meant to Take Stigma off Country Music," *Associated Press Newswires*, May 1, 2001.
39. Robert V. Kozinets, "Can Consumers Escape the Market? Emancipatory Illuminations from Burning Man," *Journal of Consumer Research*, June 2002, pp. 201.
40. T. L. Stanley, "Heavies of Hip-Hop Lend Phat to Nokia," *Advertising Age*, December 15, 2003, p. 6.
41. Basil G. Englis and Michael R. Solomon, "To Be and Not to Be: Lifestyle Imagery, Reference Groups, and the Clustering of America," *Journal of Advertising*, March 1995, pp. 13–28.
42. Stefan Fatsis, "'Rad' Sports Give Sponsors Cheap Thrills," *Wall Street Journal*, May 12, 1995, p. B8.
43. John Gaffney, "Shoe Fetish," *Business 2.0*, March 2002, pp. 98–99.
44. Albert M. Muniz Jr. and Thomas C. O'Guinn, "Brand Community," *Journal of Consumer Research*, vol. 27, March 2001, pp. 412–432; James H. McAlexander, John W. Schouten, and Harold F. Koenig, "Building Brand Community," *Journal of Marketing*, January 2002, pp. 38–54.
45. Jonathan Fahey, "Love Into Money," *Forbes*, January 7, 2002, pp. 60–65.
46. Todd Nissen, "McDonald's Sees Good Results in Middle East," *ClariNet Electronic News Service*, February 20, 1994.
47. A. Benton Cocanougher and Grady D. Bruce, "Socially Distant Referent Groups and Consumer Aspiration," *Journal of Marketing Research*, August 1971, pp. 379–383.
48. Linda L. Price, Lawrence Feick, and Robin Higie, "Preference Heterogeneity and Coorientation as Determinants of Perceived Informational Influence," *Journal of Business Research*, November 1989, pp. 227–242; Jacqueline J. Brown and Peter Reingen, "Social Ties and Word-of-Mouth Referral Behavior," *Journal of Consumer Research*, December 1987, pp. 350–362; Mary C. Gilly, John L. Graham, Mary Wolfinbarger, and Laura Yale, "A Dyadic Study of Interpersonal Information Search," *Journal of the Academy of Marketing Science*, vol. 26, no. 2, pp. 83–100; George Moschis, "Social Comparison and Informal Group Influence," *Journal of Marketing Research*, August 1976, pp. 237–244.
49. Randall L. Rose, William O. Bearden, and Kenneth C. Manning, "Attributions and Conformity in Illicit Consumption: The Mediating Role of Group Attractiveness," *Journal of Public Policy & Marketing*, vol. 20, no. 1, Spring 2001, pp. 84–92.
50. Rohit Desphande, Wayne D. Hoyer, and Naveen Donthu, "The Intensity of Ethnic Affiliation: A Study of the Sociology of Hispanic Consumption," *Journal of Con-*

sumer Research, September 1986, pp. 214–220; Douglas M. Stayman and Rohit Deshpande, "Situational Ethnicity and Consumer Behavior," *Journal of Consumer Research,* December 1989, pp. 361–371.

51. Robert Madrigal, "The Influence of Social Alliances with Sports Teams on Intentions to Purchase Corporate Sponsors' Products," *Journal of Advertising,* vol. 29, no. 4, Winter 2000, pp. 13–24.
52. Americus Reed II, "Activating the Self-Importance of Consumer Selves: Exploring Identity Salience Effects on Judgments," *Journal of Consumer Research,* September 2004, pp. 2861.
53. Jonathan K. Frenzen and Harry L. Davis, "Purchasing Behavior in Embedded Markets," *Journal of Consumer Research,* June 1990, pp. 1–12; see also Mark S. Granovetter, "The Strength of Weak Ties," *American Journal of Sociology,* May 1973, pp. 1360–1380; Brown and Reingen, "Social Ties and Word-of-Mouth Referral Behavior"; Jonathan K. Frenzen and Kent Nakamoto, "Structure, Cooperation, and the Flow of Market Information," *Journal of Consumer Research,* December 1993, pp. 360–375.
55. David Orenstein, "A Family Affair for Mobile Phones," *Business 2.0,* December 26, 2001, *www.business2.com/articles/web/0,1653,36561,FF.html?ref=cnet.*
56. Reingen and Kernan, "Analysis of Referral Networks in Marketing"; Brown and Reingen, "Social Ties and Word-of-Mouth Referral Behavior"; see also Frenzen and Nakamoto, "Structure, Cooperation, and the Flow of Market Information."
58. Nicole Woolsey Biggart, *Charismatic Capitalism* (Chicago: University of Chicago Press, 1989); see also Jonathan K. Frenzen and Harry L. Davis, "Purchasing Behavior in Embedded Markets," *Journal of Consumer Research,* June 1990, pp. 1–12.
59. Barbara Carton, "PCs Replace Lettuce Tubs at Sales Parties," *Wall Street Journal,* March 31, 1997, pp. B1, B10.
60. Frenzen and Davis, "Purchasing Behavior in Embedded Markets."
61. Scott Ward, "Consumer Socialization," *Journal of Consumer Research,* September 1974, pp. 1–16; George P. Moschis, "The Role of Family Communication in Consumer Socialization of Children and Adolescents," *Journal of Consumer Research,* March 1985, pp. 898–913; George P. Moschis, *Consumer Socialization: A Life Cycle Perspective* (Lexington, Mass.: Lexington Books, 1987); Scott Ward, "Consumer Socialization," in eds. Harold H. Kassarjian and Thomas S. Robertson, *Perspectives in Consumer Behavior* (Glenview, Ill.: Scott-Foresman, 1980), pp. 380–396; Les Carlson and Sanford Grossbart, "Parental Style and Consumer Socialization of Children," *Journal of Consumer Research,* June 1988, pp. 77–92.
62. Deborah Roedder John, "Consumer Socialization of Children: A Retrospective Look at Twenty-Five Years of Research," *Journal of Consumer Research,* vol. 26, December 1999, pp. 183–213.
63. Moschis, "The Role of Family Communication in Consumer Socialization of Children and Adolescents"; Harriet L. Rheingold and Kaye V. Cook, "The Contents of Boys' and Girls' Rooms as an Index of Parents' Behavior," *Child Development,* June 1975, pp. 459–463; Scott Ward, Daniel B. Wackman, and Ellen Wartella, *How Children Learn to Buy: The Development of Consumer Information Processing Skills* (Beverly Hills, Calif.: Sage, 1979).
64. Elizabeth S. Moore, William L. Wilkie, and Richard J. Lutz, "Passing the Torch: Intergenerational Influences as a Source of Brand Equity," *Journal of Marketing,* April 2002, pp. 17–37.
65. Gwen Bachmann Achenreiner and Deborah Roedder John, "The Meaning of Brand Names to Children: A Developmental Investigation," *Journal of Consumer Psychology,* 2003, pp. 205–219.
66. Gregory M. Rose, Vassilis Dalakas, and Fredric Kropp, "Consumer Socialization and Parental Style Across Cultures: Findings from Australia, Greece, and India," *Journal of Consumer Psychology,* 2003, pp. 366–376.
67. Ann Walsh, Russell Laczniak, and Les Carlson, "Mothers' Preferences for Regulating Children's Television," *Journal of Advertising,* Fall 1998, pp. 23–36.
69. Moschis, "The Role of Family Communication in Consumer Socialization of Children and Adolescents"; Conway Lackman and John M. Lanasa, "Family Decision Making Theory: An Overview and Assessment," *Psychology and Marketing,* March–April 1993, pp. 81–93; George P. Moschis, *Acquisition of the Consumer Role by Adolescents* (Atlanta: Georgia State University, 1978).
70. Beverly A. Browne, "Gender Stereotypes in Advertising on Children's Television in the 1990s: A Cross-National Analysis," *Journal of Advertising,* Spring 1998, pp. 83–96.
71. See, for example, Greta Fein, David Johnson, Nancy Kosson, Linda Stork, and Lisa Wasserman, "Sex Stereotypes and Preferences in the Toy Choices of 20-Month-Old Boys and Girls," *Developmental Psychology,* July 1975, pp. 527–528; Lenore A. DeLucia, "The Toy Preference Test: A Measure of Sex-Role Identification," *Child Development,* March 1963, pp. 107–117; Judith E. O. Blackmore and Asenath A. LaRue, "Sex-Appropriate Toy Preference and the Ability to Conceptualize Toys as Sex-Role Related," *Developmental Psychology,* May 1979, pp. 339–340; Nancy Eisenberg-Berg, Rita Boothby, and Tom Matson, "Correlates of Preschool Girls' Feminine and Masculine Toy Preferences," *Developmental Psychology,* May 1979, pp. 354–355.
72. Donna Rouner, "Rock Music Use as a Socializing Function," *Popular Music and Society,* Spring 1990, pp. 97–108; Thomas L. Eugene, "Clothing and Counterculture: An Empirical Study," *Adolescence,* Spring 1973, pp. 93–112.
73. Fein et al., "Sex Stereotypes and Preferences in the Toy Choices of 20-Month-Old Boys and Girls"; Eisenberg-Berg, Boothby, and Matson, "Correlates of Preschool Girls' Feminine and Masculine Toy Preferences"; Sheila Fling and Main Manosevitz, "Sex Typing in Nursery School Children's Play," *Developmental Psychology,* vol. 7, September 1972, pp. 146–152.
74. Tamara Mangleburg and Terry Bristol, "Socialization and Adolescents' Skepticism toward Advertising," *Journal of Advertising,* Fall 1998, pp. 11–21.

75. Robert E. Burnkrant and Alain Cousineau, "Informational and Normative Social Influence in Buyer Behavior," *Journal of Consumer Research,* December 1975, pp. 206–215; Morton Deutsch and Harold B. Gerard, "A Study of Normative and Informational Influence upon Individual Judgment," *Journal of Abnormal and Social Psychology,* November 1955, pp. 629–636.
76. Dennis Rook and Robert Fisher, "Normative Influences on Impulsive Buying Behavior," *Journal of Consumer Research,*" December 1995, pp. 305–313.
77. Paul Rozin and Leher Singh, "The Moralization of Cigarette Smoking in the United States," *Journal of Consumer Psychology,* vol. 8, no. 3, 1999, pp. 321–337.
78. Margaret Talbot, "Girls Just Want to Be Mean," *New York Times Magazine,* February 24, 2002, pp. 241.
79. Ernest Beck, "Let Labor Lean to Leisurewear: The Harrods Shopper Stays Proper," *Wall Street Journal,* May 27, 1997, p. B1.
80. Peter Reingen, Brian Foster, Jacqueline Brown, and Stephen B. Seidman, "Brand Congruence in Interpersonal Relations: A Social Network Analysis," *Journal of Consumer Research,* December 1984, pp. 771–783.
81. Tina M. Lowrey, Cele C. Otnes, and Julie A. Ruth, "Social Influences on Dyadic Giving over Time: A Taxonomy from the Giver's Perspective," *Journal of Consumer Research,* March 2004, pp 5471.
82. Ann E. Schlosser and Sharon Shavitt, "Anticipating Discussion About a Product: Rehearsing What to Say Can Affect Your Judgments," *Journal of Consumer Research,* June 2002, pp. 1011.
83. James E. Stafford, "Effects of Group Influence on Consumer Brand Preferences," *Journal of Marketing Research,* February 1966, pp. 68–75.
84. Pankaj Aggarwal, "The Effects of Brand Relationship Norms on Consumer Attitudes and Behavior," *Journal of Consumer Research,* June 2004, pp. 871.
85. Randall L. Rose, William O. Bearden, and Jesse E. Teel, "An Attributional Analysis of Resistance to Group Pressure Regarding Illicit Drug and Alcohol Consumption," *Journal of Consumer Research,* June 1992, pp. 1–13; see also Bobby J. Calder and Robert E. Burnkrant, "Interpersonal Influences on Consumer Behavior: An Attribution Theory Approach," *Journal of Consumer Research,* June 1977, pp. 29–38, 71; Solomon E. Asch, "Effects of Group Pressure upon the Modification and Distortion of Judgment," in ed. H. Guetzkow, *Groups, Leadership and Men* (Pittsburgh, Pa.: Carnegie Press, 1951); Sak Onkvisit and John J. Shaw, *International Marketing: Analysis and Strategy* (Columbus, Ohio: Merrill, 1989); see also Chin Tiong Tan and John U. Farley, "The Impact of Cultural Patterns on Cognition and Intention in Singapore," *Journal of Consumer Research,* March 1987, pp. 540–544.
86. For a general discussion of reactance behavior, see Mona A. Clee and Robert A. Wicklund, "Consumer Behavior and Psychological Reactance," *Journal of Consumer Research,* March 1980, pp. 389–405.
87. William O. Bearden and Michael J. Etzel, "Reference Group Influence on Product and Brand Purchase Decisions," *Journal of Consumer Research,* vol. 9, no. 2, 1982, pp. 183–194.
88. Robert E. Witt and Grady D. Bruce, "Group Influence and Brand Choice Congruence," *Journal of Marketing Research,* November 1972, pp. 440–443.
89. Darren W. Dahl, Rajesh V. Manchanda, and Jennifer J. Argo, "Embarrassment in Consumer Purchase: The Roles of Social Presence and Purchase Familiarity," *Journal of Consumer Research,* December 2001, pp. 4731.
90. Bobby J. Calder and Robert E. Burnkrant, "Interpersonal Influences on Consumer Behavior: An Attribution Theory Approach," *Journal of Consumer Research,* June 1977, pp. 29–38; William O. Bearden, Richard G. Netemeyer, and Jesse E. Teel, "Measurement of Consumer Susceptibility to Interpersonal Influence," *Journal of Consumer Research,* March 1989, pp. 473–481; William O. Bearden and Randall L. Rose, "Attention to Social Comparison Information: An Individual Difference Factor Affecting Conformity," *Journal of Consumer Research,* March 1990, pp. 461–471.
91. John C. Mowen, "Exploring the Trait of Competitiveness and Its Consumer Behavior Consequences," *Journal of Consumer Psychology,* 2004, pp. 52–63.
93. Charles S. Gulas and Kim McKeage, "Extending Social Comparison: An Examination of the Unintended Consequences of Idealized Advertising Imagery," *Journal of Advertising,* vol. 29, no. 2, Summer 2000, pp. 17–28.
94. David B. Wooten and Americus Reed II, "Playing It Safe: Susceptibility to Normative Influence and Protective Self-Presentation," *Journal of Consumer Research,* December 2004, pp. 551–556.
95. C. Whan Park and Parker Lessig, "Students and Housewives: Differences in Susceptibility to Reference Group Influence," *Journal of Consumer Research,* September 1977, pp. 102–110.
96. Robert Fisher and Kirk Wakefield, "Factors Leading to Group Identification: A Field Study of Winners and Losers," *Psychology and Marketing,* January 1998, pp. 23–40.
97. John R. French and Bertram Raven, "The Bases of Social Power," in ed. D. Cartwright, *Studies in Social Power* (Ann Arbor, Mich.: Institute for Social Research, 1969), pp. 150–167.
98. Reingen et al., "Brand Congruence in Interpersonal Relations"; Park and Lessig, "Students and Housewives."
99. Donnel A. Briley and Robert S. Wyer, Jr., "The Effect of Group Membership Salience on the Avoidance of Negative Outcomes: Implications for Social and Consumer Decisions," *Journal of Consumer Research,* December 2002, pp. 4001.
100. Dana-Nicoleta Lascu, William O. Bearden, and Randall L. Rose, "Norm Extremity and Interpersonal Influences on Consumer Conformity," *Journal of Business Research,* March 1995, pp. 200–212.
101. Social influence, attitudes toward the ads, and prior trial behavior all affect antismoking beliefs, as discussed in J. Craig Andrews, Richard G. Netemeyer, Scot Burton, D. Paul Moberg, and Ann Christiansen, "Understanding Adolescent Intentions to Smoke: An Examination of Relationships Among Social Influence, Prior

Trial Behavior, and Antitobacco Campaign Advertising," *Journal of Marketing,* July 2004, pp. 110–123.

102. J. L. Freeman and S. Fraser, "Compliance without Pressure: The Foot-in-the-Door Technique," *Journal of Personality and Social Psychology,* August 1966, pp. 195–202.

103. Robert A. Hansen and Larry M. Robinson, "Testing the Effectiveness of Alternative Foot-in-the-Door Manipulations," *Journal of Marketing Research,* August 1980, pp. 359–364; Jacob Hornik, Tamar Zaig, and Diro Shadmon, "Reducing Refusals in Telephone Surveys on Sensitive Topics," *Journal of Advertising Research,* June–July 1991, pp. 48–57; Michael Kamins, "The Enhancement of Response Rates to a Mail Survey through a Labeled Foot-in-the-Door Approach," *Journal of the Market Research Society,* April 1989, pp. 273–284.

104. Robert B. Cialdini, J. E. Vincent, S. K. Lewis, J. Caalan, D. Wheeler, and B. L. Darby, "Reciprocal Concessions Procedure for Inducing Compliance: The Door-in-the-Face Effect," *Journal of Personality and Social Psychology,* February 1975, pp. 200–215; John C. Mowen and Robert Cialdini, "On Implementing the Door-in-the-Face Compliance Strategy in a Marketing Context," *Journal of Marketing Research,* May 1980, pp. 253–258; see also Edward Fern, Kent Monroe, and Ramon Avila, "Effectiveness of Multiple Request Strategies: A Synthesis of Research Results," *Journal of Marketing Research,* May 1986, pp. 144–152.

105. Alice Tybout, Brian Sternthal, and Bobby J. Calder, "Information Availability as a Determinant of Multiple Request Effectiveness," *Journal of Marketing Research,* August 1983, pp. 279–290; John T. Gourville, "Pennies-a-Day: The Effect of Temporal Reframing on Transaction Evaluation," *Journal of Consumer Research,* March 1998, pp. 395–408.

106. Eric R. Spangenberg and Anthony G. Greenwald, "Social Influence by Requesting Self-Prophecy," *Journal of Consumer Psychology,* vol. 8, no. 1, 1999, pp. 61–89.

107. For more about self-prophecy, see Eric R. Spangenberg, David E. Sprott, Bianca Grohmann, and Ronn J. Smith, "Mass-Communicated Prediction Requests: Practical Application and a Cognitive Dissonance Explanation for Self-Prophecy," *Journal of Marketing,* July 2003, pp. 47–62.

108. Deutsch and Gerard, "A Study of Normative and Informational Influence upon Individual Judgment"; C. Whan Park and Parker Lessig, "Students and Housewives: Differences in Susceptibility to Reference Group Influences" *Journal of Consumer Research,* vol. 4, September 1977, 102–110. Dennis L. Rosen and Richard W. Olshavsky, "The Dual Role of Informational Social Influence: Implications for Marketing Management," *Journal of Business Research,* April 1987, pp. 123–144.

109. Jeffrey D. Ford and Elwood A. Ellis, "A Re-examination of Group Influence on Member Brand Preference," *Journal of Marketing Research,* vol. 17, no. 1, 1980, pp. 125–133; Linda L. Price and Lawrence F. Feick, "The Role of Interpersonal Sources in External Search: An Informational Perspective," in ed. Thomas Kinnear, *Advances in Consumer Research,* vol. 11 (Ann Arbor, Mich.: Association for Consumer Research, 1984), pp. 250–255.

110. Arch G. Woodside and M. Wayne DeLosier, "Effects of Word-of-Mouth Advertising on Consumer Risk Taking," *Journal of Advertising,* September 1976, pp. 17–26.

111. Henry Assael, *Consumer Behavior and Marketing Action,* 4th ed. (Boston: PWS-Kent, 1992).

112. John R. French and Bertram Raven, "The Bases of Social Power," in ed. D. Cartwright, *Studies in Social Power* (Ann Arbor, Mich.: Institute for Social Research, 1959), pp. 150–167; Dana-Nicoleta Lascu, William Bearden, and Randall Rose, "Norm Extremity and Interpersonal Influences on Consumer Conformity," *Journal of Business Research,* March 1995, pp. 200–212; David B, Wooten and Americus Reed II, "Informational Influence and the Ambiguity of Product Experience: Order Effects on the Weighting of Evidence," *Journal of Consumer Psychology,* vol. 7, no. 1, 1998, pp. 79–99.

113. Bearden, Netemeyer, and Teel, "Measurement of Consumer Susceptibility to Interpersonal Influence"; Bearden and Rose, "Attention to Social Comparison Information."

114. Gerald Zaltman and Melanie Wallendorf, *Consumer Behavior: Basic Findings and Management Implications,* 2d ed. (New York: Wiley, 1983); Reingen et al., "Brand Congruence in Interpersonal Relations."

115. Charles R. Taylor, Gordon E. Miracle, and R. Dale Wilson, "The Impact of Information Level on the Effectiveness of U.S. and Korean Television Commercials," *Journal of Advertising,* Spring 1997, pp. 1–18.

116. For more about Web-based chatting, see George M. Zinkhan, Hyokjin Kwak, Michelle Morrison, and Cara Okleshen Peters, "Web-Based Chatting: Consumer Communications in Cyberspace," *Journal of Consumer Psychology,* 2003, pp. 17–27.

117. Stephen A. LaTour and Ajay Manrai, "Interactive Impact of Informational and Normative Influence on Donations," *Journal of Marketing Research,* August 1989, pp. 327–335.

118. Asim Ansari, Skander Essegaier, and Rajeev Kohli, "Internet Recommendation Systems," *Journal of Marketing Research,* vol. 37, August 2000, pp. 363–375.

119. Johan Arndt, "Role of Product-Related Conversations in the Diffusion of a New Product," *Journal of Marketing Research,* August 1967, pp. 291–295.

120. Marsha L. Richins, "Negative Word of Mouth by Dissatisfied Consumers: A Pilot Study," *Journal of Marketing,* January 1983, pp. 68–78.

121. Laurence C. Harmon and Kathleen M. McKenna-Harmon, "The Hidden Costs of Resident Dissatisfaction," *Journal of Property Management,* May–June 1994, pp. 52–55.

122. Herr, Kardes, and Kim, "Effects of Word-of-Mouth and Product-Attribute Information on Persuasion"; Richard W. Mizerski, "An Attribution Explanation of the Disproportionate Influence of Unfavorable Information," *Journal of Consumer Research,* December 1982, pp. 301–310.

123. Suman Basuroy, Subimal Chatterjee, and S. Abraham Ravid, "How Critical Are Critical Reviews? The Box Office Effects of Film Critics, Star Power, and Budgets," *Journal of Marketing,* October 2003, pp. 103–117.

124. Brown and Reingen, "Social Ties and Word-of-Mouth Referral Behavior"; Arndt, "Role of Product-Related Conversations in the Diffusion of a New Product"; Laura Yale and Mary C. Gilly, "Dyadic Perceptions in Personal Source Information Search," *Journal of Business Research,* March 1995, pp. 225–238.

125. Chip Walker, "Word of Mouth," *American Demographics,* July 1995, pp. 39–46.

126. Herr, Kardes, and Kim, "Effects of Word-of-Mouth and Product-Attribute Information on Persuasion."

127. Elihu Katz and Paul F. Lazarsfeld, *Personal Influence* (Glencoe, Ill.: Free Press, 1955).

128. Bob Donath, "Shed Some Light: Handling Online Threats to Firm's Image," *Marketing News,* February 16, 1998, p. 12.

129. David Orenstein, "Hidden Treasure," *Business 2.0,* July 10, 2001, pp. 41, 43.

130. Jennifer Netherby, "Studios Embracing Online, E-Mail Marketing Campaigns," *Video Business,* January 17, 2005, pp. 61.

131. A. Coskun and Cheryl J. Frohlich, "Service: The Competitive Edge in Banking," *Journal of Services Marketing,* Winter 1992, pp. 15–23; Jeffrey G. Blodgett, Donald H. Granbois, and Rockney Waters, "The Effects of Perceived Justice on Complainants' Negative Word-of-Mouth Behavior and Repatronage Intentions," *Journal of Retailing,* Winter 1993, pp. 399–429; Karen Maru File, Ben B. Judd, and Russ A. Prince, "Interactive Marketing: The Influence of Participation on Positive Word-of-Mouth Referrals," *Journal of Services Marketing,* Fall 1992, pp. 5–15; Gary L. Clark, Peter F. Kaminski, and David R. Rink, "Consumer Complaints: Advice on How Companies Should Respond Based on an Empirical Study," *Journal of Services Marketing,* Winter 1992, pp. 41–51.

132. Nat Ives, "Wal-Mart Turns to Ads to Address Its Critics," *New York Times,* January 14, 2005, *www.nytimes.com.*

133. Kathryn Kranhold and Erin White, "The Perils and Potential Rewards of Crisis Managing for Firestone," *Wall Street Journal,* September 8, 2000, pp. B1, B4.

134. Mara Adelman, "Social Support in the Service Sector: The Antecedents, Processes, and Outcomes of Social Support in an Introductory Service," *Journal of Business Research,* March 1995, pp. 273–283; Jerry D. Rogers, Kenneth E. Clow, and Toby J. Kash, "Increasing Job Satisfaction of Service Personnel," *Journal of Services Marketing,* Winter 1994, pp. 14–27.

136. Michael Kamins, Valerie Folkes, and Lars Perner, "Consumer Responses to Rumors: Good News, Bad News," *Journal of Consumer Psychology,* vol. 6, no. 2, 1997, 165–187.

137. Koenig, *Rumor in the Marketplace;* see also Alice M. Tybout, Bobby J. Calder, and Brian Sternthal, "Using Information Processing Theory to Design Marketing Strategies," *Journal of Marketing Research,* February 1981, pp. 73–79.

138. Samantha Marshall, "Labor Problems in Asia Hurt Nike's Image," *Wall Street Journal,* September 26, 1997, p. B18.

139. Reingen and Kernan, "Analysis of Referral Networks in Marketing."

140. Vicki Clift, "Word-of-Mouth Can Be Easily Engineered," *Marketing News,* June 17, 1994, p. 11.

CHAPTER 17

1. Steve Rosenbush, "Broadband Ads' Speedy Progress," *Business Week,* April 4, 2005, *www.businessweek.com;* Peter Lewis, "Broadband Wonderland," *Fortune,* September 20, 2004, pp. 191+; "Netherlands: Survey Shows Dutch Lead Europe in Broadband Penetration," *Asia Africa Intelligence Wire,* March 22, 2005, n.p.

2. Lori Dahm, "Secrets of Success: The Strategies Driving New Product Development at Kraft," *Stagnito's New Products Magazine,* January 2002, pp. 17a–19.

3. Hubert Gatignon and Thomas S. Robertson, "Innovative Decision Processes," in eds. Thomas S. Robertson and Harold H. Kassarjian, *Handbook of Consumer Behavior* (New York: Prentice-Hall, 1991), pp. 316–317; see also Everett M. Rogers, *The Diffusion of Innovations* (New York: Free Press, 1983).

4. Miriam Jordan, "Selling Birth Control to India's Poor," *New York Times,* September 21, 1999, pp. B1, B4.

7. Robert Langreth, "From a Prostate Drug Comes a Pill for Baldness," *Wall Street Journal,* March 20, 1997, pp. B1, B4.

8. Characteristics of employees involved in new product development can also affect innovativeness; see, for example: Rajesh Sethi, Daniel C. Smith, and C. Whan Park, "Cross-Functional Product Development Teams, Creativity, and the Innovativeness of New Consumer Products," *Journal of Marketing Research,* February 2001, pp. 73–85.

9. Yumiko Ono, "Overcoming the Stigma of Dishwashers in Japan," *Wall Street Journal,* May 19, 2000, pp. B1, B4.

10. Lewis, "Broadband Wonderland."

11. Tara Parker-Pope, "New Devices Add Up Bill, Measure Shoppers' Honesty," *Wall Street Journal,* June 6, 1995, pp. B1, B13.

12. Thomas S. Robertson, "The Process of Innovation and the Diffusion of Innovation," *Journal of Marketing,* January 1967, pp. 14–19; Thomas S. Robertson, *Innovative Behavior and Communication* (New York: Holt, Reinhart, & Winston, 1971).

13. Cris Prystay, "When Being First Doesn't Make You No. 1," *Wall Street Journal,* August 12, 2004, pp. B1, B2.

14. C. Page Moreau, Arthur B. Markman, and Donald R. Lehmann, "'What Is It?' Categorization Flexibility and Consumers' Responses to Really New Products," *Journal of Consumer Research,* vol. 27, March 2001, pp. 489–498.

15. Alfred R. Petrosky, "Extending Innovation Characteristic Perception to Diffusion Channel Intermediaries and Aesthetic Products," in eds. Rebecca Holman and Michael Solomon, *Advances in Consumer Research,* vol. 17a (Provo, Utah: Association for Consumer Research, 1991), pp. 627–634.

18. Wilton Woods, "Dressed to Spill," *Fortune,* October 17, 1995, p. 209.

19. S. Ram, "A Model of Innovation Resistance," in eds. Melanie Wallendorf and Paul Anderson, *Advances in Consumer Research,* vol. 14 (Provo, Utah: Association

for Consumer Research, 1987), pp. 208–212; Jagdish N. Sheth, "Psychology of Innovation Resistance: The Less Developed Concept (LDC) in Diffusion Research," in *Research in Marketing* (Greenwich, Conn.: JAI Press, 1981), pp. 273–282.

20. Don Clark, "Upgrade Fatigue Threatens PC Profits," *Wall Street Journal*, May 14, 1998, pp. B1, B8.
21. David Glen Mick and Susan Fournier, "Paradoxes of Technology: Consumer Cognizance, Emotions, and Coping Strategies," *Journal of Consumer Research*, September 1998, pp. 123–143.
22. Stacy L. Wood and Joffre Swait, "Psychological Indicators of Innovation Adoption: Cross-Classification Based on Need for Cognition and Need for Change," *Journal of Consumer Psychology*, 2002, pp. 1–13.
23. C. Page Moreau, Donald R. Lehmann, and Arthur B. Markman, "Entrenched Knowledge Structures and Consumer Response to New Products," *Journal of Marketing Research*, February 2001, pp. 14–29.
24. Glen Urban and Gilbert A. Churchill, "Five Dimensions of the Industrial Adoption Process," *Journal of Marketing Research*, August 1971, pp. 322–327; Charles R. O'Neal, Hans B. Thorelli, and James M. Utterback, "Adoption of Innovation by Industrial Organizations," *Industrial Marketing Management*, March 1973, pp. 235–250; Gerald Zaltman, Robert Duncan, and Jonny Holbek, *Innovations and Organizations* (New York: Wiley, 1973).
25. Tim Parry, "Teaching Tools," *Promo*, April 1, 2005, n.p.
26. Rachel Metz, "Oft-Scorned Segway Finds Friends Among the Disabled," *New York Times*, October 14, 2004, p. G5; Walter S. Mossberg, "Segway Gives an Easy Ride, But It's Best on City Sidewalks," *Wall Street Journal*, April 10, 2003, pp. B1, B3.
27. Rogers, *The Diffusion of Innovations*.
28. Geoffrey A. Moore, *Crossing the Chasm* (New York: HarperBusiness, 1991).
29. Adam Lashinsky, "Early Adopters' Paradise," *Fortune*, January 10, 2005, p. 52.
33. Moore, *Crossing the Chasm*.
34. Robert A. Peterson, "A Note on Optimal Adopter Category Determination," *Journal of Marketing Research*, August 1973, pp. 325–329; see also William R. Darden and Fred D. Reynolds, "Backward Profiling of Male Innovators," *Journal of Marketing Research*, February 1974, pp. 79–85; Steven A. Baumgarten, "The Innovative Communicator in the Diffusion Process," *Journal of Marketing Research*, February 1975, pp. 12–17a. Schemes based on consumers' involvement in the new product development process, for example, might be utilized by managers (see Jerry Wind and Vijay Mahajan, "Issues and Opportunities in New Product Development: An Introduction to the Special Issue," *Journal of Marketing Research*, February 1997, pp.1–12).
35. David F. Midgley and Grahame R. Dowling, "Innovativeness: The Concept and Its Measurement," *Journal of Consumer Research*, March 1978, pp. 229–242; Mary Dee Dickerson and James W. Gentry, "Characteristics of Adopters and Non Adopters of Home Computers," *Journal of Consumer Research*, September 1983, pp. 225–235; see also Vijay Mahajan, Eitan Muller, and Rajendra Srivastava, "Determination of Adopter Categories by Using Innovation Diffusion Models," *Journal of Marketing Research*, February 1990, pp. 37–50; Kenneth C. Manning, William O. Bearden, and Thomas J. Madden, "Consumer Innovativeness and the Adoption Process," *Journal of Consumer Psychology*, vol. 4, no. 4, 1995, pp. 329–345.
36. Chuan-Fong Shih and Alladi Venkatesh, "Beyond Adoption: Development and Application of a Use-Diffusion Model," *Journal of Marketing*, January 2004, pp. 59–72.
37. See review in Thomas S. Robertson, Joan Zielinski, and Scott Ward, *Consumer Behavior* (Glenview, Ill.: Scott, Foresman, 1984); see also Dickerson and Gentry, "Characteristics of Adopters and Non Adopters of Home Computers"; Duncan G. Labay and Thomas C. Kinnear, "Exploring the Consumer Decision Process in the Adoption of Solar Energy Systems," *Journal of Consumer Research*, December 1981, pp. 271–277; Kenneth Uhl, Roman Andrus, and Lance Poulsen, "How Are Laggards Different? An Empirical Inquiry," *Journal of Marketing Research*, February 1970, pp. 51–54; Rogers, *The Diffusion of Innovations*, pp. 383–384.
38. Robert A. Guth, "Can Your Cell Phone Shop, Play or Fish?" *Wall Street Journal*, August 3, 2000, p. B1; S. Karene Witcher, "Credit-Card Issuers Find Australia Fertile Ground for Launching Products," *Wall Street Journal*, March 31, 1995, p. B6; Lewis, "Broadband Wonderland."
39. Rogers, *The Diffusion of Innovations;* see also Mark S. Granovetter, "The Strength of Weak Ties," *American Journal of Sociology*, May 1973, pp. 1360–1380; John A. Czepiel, "Word-of-Mouth Processes in the Diffusion of a Major Technological Innovation," *Journal of Marketing Research*, May 1974, pp. 172–17a0.
40. Manning, Bearden, and Madden, "Consumer Innovativeness and the Adoption Process"; Jan-Benedict E.M. Steenkamp and Hans Baumgartner, "The Role of Optimum Stimulation Level in Exploratory Consumer Behavior," *Journal of Consumer Research*, December 1992, pp. 434–448; P. S. Raju, "Optimum Stimulation Level: Its Relationship to Personality, Demographics, and Exploratory Behavior," *Journal of Consumer Research*, December 1980, pp. 272–282.
41. Thomas S. Robertson and James H. Myers, "Personality Correlates of Opinion Leadership and Innovative Buying Behavior," *Journal of Marketing Research*, May 1969, pp. 164–167.
42. Gordon R. Foxall and Christopher G. Haskins, "Cognitive Style and Consumer Innovativeness," *Marketing Intelligence and Planning*, January 1986, pp. 26–46; Gordon R. Foxall, "Consumer Innovativeness: Novelty Seeking, Creativity and Cognitive Style," in eds. Elizabeth C. Hirschman and Jagdish N. Sheth, *Research in Consumer Behavior*, vol. 3 (Greenwich, Conn.: JAI Press, 1988), pp. 79–114.
43. Ronald E. Goldsmith and Charles F. Hofacker, "Measuring Consumer Innovativeness," *Journal of the Academy of Marketing Science*, Summer 1991, pp. 209–221.
44. Jan-Benedict E.M. Steenkamp, Frenkel ter Hofstede, and Michael Wedel, "A Cross-National Investigation

into the Individual and National Cultural Antecedents of Consumer Innovativeness," *Journal of Marketing*, April 1999, pp. 55–69.

45. Hubert Gatignon and Thomas S. Robertson, "A Propositional Inventory for New Diffusion Research," *Journal of Consumer Research*, March 1985, pp. 849–867; see also John O. Summers, "Media Exposure Patterns of Consumer Innovators," *Journal of Marketing*, January 1972, pp. 43–49.
46. James J. Engel, Robert J. Kegerreis, and Roger D. Blackwell, "Word-of-Mouth Communication by the Innovator," *Journal of Marketing*, July 1969, pp. 15–19.
47. Dickerson and Gentry, "Characteristics of Adopters and Non Adopters of Home Computers"; Robertson, *Innovative Behavior and Communication;* James W. Taylor, "A Striking Characteristic of Innovators," *Journal of Marketing Research*, February 1977, pp. 104–107; see also Gatignon and Robertson, "A Propositional Inventory for New Diffusion Research"; Elizabeth C. Hirschman, "Innovativeness, Novelty Seeking and Consumer Creativity," *Journal of Consumer Research*, December 1980, pp. 283–295; Engel, Kegerreis, and Blackwell, "Word-of-Mouth Communication by the Innovator."
48. Alex Frew McMillan, "China Cell-Phone Use Hits 140 Million," *CNN.com*, December 21, 2001, *www.cnn.com/2001/BUSINESS/asia/12/21/china.cellphone*; Miriam Jordan, "It Takes a Cell Phone: A New Nokia Transforms a Village in Bangladesh," *Wall Street Journal*, June 25, 1999, pp. B1, B4.
49. Frank M. Bass, "New Product Growth Models for Consumer Durables," *Management Science*, September 1969, pp. 215–227; Wellesley Dodds, "An Application of the Bass Model in Long-Term New Product Forecasting," *Journal of Marketing Research*, August 1973, pp. 308–311; Roger M. Heeler and Thomas P. Hustad, "Problems in Predicting New Product Growth for Consumer Durables," *Management Science*, October 1980, pp. 1007–1020; Douglas Tigart and Behrooz Farivar, "The Bass New Product Growth Model: A Sensitivity Analysis for a High Technology Product," *Journal of Marketing*, Fall 1981, pp. 81–90.
50. William E. Cox Jr., "Product Life Cycles as Marketing Models," *Journal of Business*, October 1967, pp. 375–384; Rolando Polli and Victor Cook, "Validity of the Product Life Cycle," *Journal of Business*, October 1969, pp. 385–400; D. R. Rink and J. E. Swan, "Product Life Cycle Research: A Literature Review," *Journal of Business Research*, September 1979, pp. 219–242; Robertson, *Innovative Behavior and Communication.*
55. David H. Henard and David M. Szymanski, "Why Some New Products Are More Successful Than Others," *Journal of Marketing Research*, August 2001, pp. 362–375.
57. Elliot Spagat, "At $70 a Pop, Consumers Put Discount DVD Players on Holiday List," *Wall Street Journal*, December 13, 2001, pp. B1, B4.
60. Gwendolyn Mariano, "Companies Fear Costly MPEG-4 Licenses," *CnetNews.com*, February 8, 2002, *www.cnetnews.com.*
61. Victoria Shannon, "Online Music Catches On, But Profit Is Hard to Find," *International Herald Tribune*, January 24, 2005, *www.technewsworld.com/story/39953. html.*
62. Jan-Benedict E. M. Steenkamp and Katrijn Gielens, "Consumer and Market Drivers of the Trial Probability of New Consumer Packaged Goods," *Journal of Consumer Research*, December 2003, pp. 368–384.
63. Steve Hoeffler, "Measuring Preferences for Really New Products," *Journal of Marketing Research*, November 2003, pp. 406–420.
64. Paschalina Ziamou and S. Ratneshwar, "Promoting Consumer Adoption of High-Technology Products: Is More Information Always Better?" *Journal of Consumer Psychology*, 2002, pp. 341–351.
65. Gatignon and Robertson, "A Propositional Inventory for New Diffusion Research"; Vijay Mahajan, Eitan Muller, and Frank M. Bass, "New Product Diffusion Models in Marketing: A Review and Directions for Research," *Journal of Marketing*, April 1990, pp. 1–27.
68. Rogers, *The Diffusion of Innovations.*
69. Rogers, *The Diffusion of Innovations.*
70. Ashesh Mukherjee and Wayne D. Hoyer, "The Effect of Novel Attributes on Product Evaluation," *Journal of Consumer Research*, December 2001, pp. 462–472.
71. Al Doyle, "Getting the Perfect Picture," *Technology & Learning*, January 2002, pp. 9–11.
72. Jagdish N. Sheth and S. Ram, *Bringing Innovation to Market*, 1987 (New York: Wiley).
73. David P. Hamilton, "Japanese Firms Focus on Simpler Camcorders," *Wall Street Journal*, May 5, 1993, p. B1.
74. Sheth and Ram, *Bringing Innovation to Market.*
75. Sheth and Ram, *Bringing Innovation to Market.*
77. Kranhold, "Toyota Makes a Bet on New Hybrid Prius."
79. Robert J. Fisher and Linda L. Price, "An Investigation into the Social Context of Early Adoption Behavior," *Journal of Consumer Research*, December 1992, pp. 477–486.
80. Sandra D. Atchison, "Lifting the Golf Bag Burden," *BusinessWeek*, July 25, 1994, p. 84.
81. June Fletcher, "New Machines Measure That Holiday Flab at Home," *Wall Street Journal*, December 26, 1997, p. B8.
82. Rogers, *The Diffusion of Innovations*, p. 99.
83. C. Whan Park, Bernard J. Jaworski, and Deborah J. MacInnis, "Strategic Brand Concept-Image Management," *Journal of Marketing*, October 1986, pp. 135–145.
84. Fisher and Price, "An Investigation into the Social Context of Early Adoption Behavior."
85. Petrosky, "Extending Innovation Characteristic Perception to Diffusion Channel Intermediaries and Aesthetic Products."
86. Alfred Petrosky labels this factor *genrefication* and discusses it in the context of aesthetic innovations in: "Extending Innovation Characteristic Perception to Diffusion Channel Intermediaries and Aesthetic Products."
89. Everett M. Rogers and F. Floyd. Shoemaker, *Communication of Innovations* (New York: Free Press, 1971); Elizabeth C. Hirschman, "Consumer Modernity, Cognitive Complexity, Creativity and Innovativeness," in ed. Richard P. Bagozzi, *Marketing in the 80s: Changes and Challenges* (Chicago: American Marketing Association, 1980), pp. 152–161.

90. Jaishankar Ganesh, V. Kumar, and Velavan Subramaniam, "Learning Effect in Multinational Diffusion of Consumer Durables: An Exploratory Investigation," *Journal of the Academy of Marketing Science*, vol. 25, Summer 1997, pp. 214–228; Gatignon and Robertson, "A Propositional Inventory for New Diffusion Research."

91. Seth Stevenson, "I'd Like to Buy the World a Shelf-Stable Children's Lactic Drink," *New York Times Magazine*, March 10, 2002, pp. 38+; John C. Jay, "The Valley of the New," *American Demographics*, March 2000, pp. 58–59; Norihiko Shirouzu, "Japan's High-School Girls Excel in Art of Setting Trends, *Wall Street Journal*, April 24, 1998, pp. B1, B7.

92. Gatignon and Robertson, "A Propositional Inventory for New Diffusion Research"; Lawrence A. Brown, Edward J. Malecki, and Aron N. Spector, "Adopter Categories in a Spatial Context: Alternative Explanations for an Empirical Regularity," *Rural Sociology*, Spring 1976, pp. 99–117a.

93. Dorothy Leonard-Barton, "Experts as Negative Opinion Leaders in the Diffusion of a Technological Innovation," *Journal of Consumer Research*, March 1985, pp. 914–926.

94. Everett Rogers and D. Lawrence Kincaid, *Communication Networks: Toward a New Paradigm for Research* (New York: Free Press, 1981).

95. Rogers and Kincaid, *Communication Networks.*

96. Frank M. Bass, "The Relationship between Diffusion Curves, Experience Curves, and Demand Elasticities for Consumer Durable Technological Innovations," *Journal of Business*, July 1980, pp. s51–s57; Dan Horskey and Leonard S. Simon, "Advertising and the Diffusion of New Products," *Marketing Science*, Winter 1983, pp. 1–17; Vijay Mahajan and Eitan Muller, "Innovation Diffusion and New Product Growth Models in Marketing," *Journal of Marketing*, Fall 1979, pp. 55–68; Mahajan, Muller, and Bass, "New Product Diffusion Models in Marketing."

97. Lauriston Sharp, "Steel Axes for Stone Age Australians," in ed. Edward H. Spicer, *Human Problems in Technological Change* (New York: Russell Sage Foundation, 1952).

98. H. David Banta, "The Diffusion of the Computer Tomography (CT) Scanner in the United States," *International Journal of Health Services*, 10, 1980, pp. 251–269, as reported in Rogers, *The Diffusion of Innovations*, pp. 231–237.

CHAPTER 18

1. "Britney's Gum Is Hot eBay Item," *UPI NewsTrack*, September 2, 2004, n.p.; Michele Himmelberg, "Disney Fan Pays $37,400 to Have Name Placed on Haunted Mansion Tombstone," *Orange County Register*, October 23, 2004, *www.ocregister.com;* Daniel P. Finney, "Happy 25 for the Happy Meal!" *St. Louis Post-Dispatch*, June 14, 2004, *www.stltoday.com;* Meredith Schwartz, "The Accidental Collector: eBay Offers Insights into Two Types of Collectors," *Gifts & Decorative Accessories*, June 2004, p. 100+; *ebay.com.*

2. Grant McCracken, "Culture and Consumption: A Theoretical Account of the Structure and Movement of the Cultural Meaning of Consumer Goods," *Journal of Consumer Research*, June 1986, pp. 71–84; Grant McCracken, *Culture and Consumption* (Indianapolis, Ind.: Indiana University Press, 1990).

7. Jennifer Edson Escalas and James R. Bettman, "You Are What They Eat: The Influence of Reference Groups on Consumers' Connections to Brands," *Journal of Consumer Psychology*, 2003, pp. 339–348.

8. For a discussion of how consumers use fashion to both characterize their identity and infer aspects of others' identities, see Craig J. Thompson and Diana L. Haytko, "Speaking of Fashion: Consumers' Use of Fashion Discourses and the Appropriation of Countervailing Cultural Meanings," *Journal of Consumer Research*, June 1997, pp. 15–42.

10. Maureen Tkacik, "Why This Season's Hot Sneaker Is Nowhere to Be Found, *Wall Street Journal*, December 10, 2002, p. B1; Goldstein, "Urban Wear Goes Suburban."

18. For more on the use of clothing as symbols, see Rebecca H. Holman, "Apparel as Communication," in eds. Elizabeth C. Hirschman and Morris B. Holbrook, *Symbolic Consumer Behavior* (Ann Arbor, Mich.: Association for Consumer Research, 1981), pp. 7–15.

19. Pierre Bourdieu, *Distinction: A Social Critique of the Judgment of Taste* (Cambridge, Mass.: Harvard University Press, 1984), for other research on gender associations with food, see Deborah Heisley, "Gender Symbolism in Food," doctoral dissertation, Northwestern University, 1991.

20. Sidney Levy, "Interpreting Consumer Mythology: A Structural Approach to Consumer Behavior," *Journal of Marketing*, vol. 45, no. 3, 1982, pp. 49–62.

21. Karen Lundegaard, "Macho Lite: Latest Crop of SUVs to Hit the Streets," *Wall Street Journal*, February 10, 2005, pp. D1, D4.

22. Michelle Krebs, "To Complete the Pregnancy Experience, Just Add Some Pickles and Ice," *New York Times*, September 28, 2003, sec. 12, p. 1.

23. Jeffrey Ball, "Detroit Worries Some Consumers Are Souring on Big SUVs," *Wall Street Journal*, January 8, 2003, pp. B1, B4.

25. Jean Bond Rafferty, "Surpassing the Test of Time: Patek Philippe," *Town & Country*, January 2002, pp. 98+; Deborah Weisgall, "Buying Time," *Fortune*, September 8, 1997, p. 192.

26. James B. Arndorfer, "Miller Lite: Bob Mikulay," *Advertising Age*, November 1, 2004, p. S12; "Miller Lite," *Beverage Dynamics*, January–February 2002, p. 40.

27. Michael R. Solomon, "Building Up and Breaking Down: The Impact of Cultural Sorting on Symbolic Consumption," in eds. Elizabeth C. Hirschman and Jagdish N. Sheth, *Research in Consumer Behavior* (Greenwich, Conn.: JAI Press, 1988), pp. 325–351; McCracken, "Culture and Consumption"; McCracken, *Culture and Consumption.*

28. Solomon, "Building Up and Breaking Down"; C. Whan Park, Bernard J. Jaworski, and Deborah J. MacInnis, "Strategic Brand Concept-Image Management," *Journal of Marketing*, October 1986, pp. 135–145; James H. Leigh and Terrace G. Gabel, "Symbolic Interactionism:

Its Effects on Consumer Behavior and Implications for Marketing Strategy," *Journal of Consumer Marketing*, Winter 1992, pp. 27–39.

29. Myrna L. Armstrong and Donata C. Gabriel, "Motivation for Tattoo Removal," *Archives of Dermatology*, April 1996, pp. 412–416.
30. John W. Schouten, "Personal Rites of Passage and the Reconstruction of Self," in eds. Rebecca H. Holman and Michael R. Solomon, *Advances in Consumer Research*, vol. 18 (Provo, Utah: Association for Consumer Research, 1991), pp. 49–51.
31. Melissa Martin Young, "Dispositions of Possessions During Role Transitions," in eds. Rebecca H. Holman and Michael R. Solomon, *Advances in Consumer Research*, vol. 18 (Provo, Utah: Association for Consumer Research, 1991), pp. 33–39.
32. Robert A. Wicklund and Peter M. Gollwitzer, *Symbolic Self-Completion* (Hillsdale, N.J.: Lawrence Erlbaum, 1982).
33. Diane Ackerman, *A Natural History of Love* (New York: Random House, 1994).
34. See, for example, Samuel K. Bonsu and Russell W. Belk, "Do Not Go Cheaply into That Good Night: Death-Ritual Consumption in Asante, Ghana," *Journal of Consumer Research*, June 2003, pp. 41–55.
35. James H. McAlexander, John W. Schouten, and Scott D. Roberts, "Consumer Behavior and Divorce," in eds. Janeen Arnold Costa and Russell W. Belk, *Research in Consumer Behavior*, vol. 6 (Greenwich, Conn.: JAI Press, 1993), pp. 162; see also Rita Fullerman and Kathleen Debevec, "Till Death Do We Part: Family Dissolution, Transition, and Consumer Behavior," in eds. John F. Sherry and Brian Sternthal, *Advances in Consumer Research*, vol. 19 (Provo, Utah: Association for Consumer Research, 1992), pp. 514–521.
36. Penaloza, "Atravesando Fronteras/Border Crossings"; Melanie Wallendorf and Michael D. Reilly, "Ethnic Migration, Assimilation, and Consumption," *Journal of Consumer Research*, December 1983, pp. 292–302; Rohit Deshpande, Wayne Hoyer, and Naveen Donthu, "The Intensity of Ethnic Affiliation: A Study of the Sociology of Hispanic Consumption," *Journal of Consumer Research*, September 1986, pp. 214–220; for a discussion of acculturation of Chinese Americans, see Wei-Na Lee, "Acculturation and Advertising Communication Strategies: A Cross-Cultural Study of Chinese Americans," *Psychology and Marketing*, September–October 1993, pp. 381–397; for an interesting study on the immigration of Haitian consumers, see Laura R. Oswald, "Culture Swapping: Consumption and the Ethnogenesis of Middle-Class Haitian Immigrants," *Journal of Consumer Research*, March 1999, pp. 303–318; for a discussion of Turkish consumers immigrating to Denmark, see Güliz Gur and Per Ostergaard, "Constructing Immigrant Identities in Consumption: Appearance Among the Turko-Danes," in eds. Joseph W. Alba and Wesley Hutchinson, *Advances in Consumer Research*, vol. 25, (Provo, Utah: Association for Consumer Research, 1998), pp. 48–52.
37. Annamma Joy and Ruby Roy Dholakia, "Remembrances of Things Past: The Meaning of Home and Possessions of Indian Professionals in Canada," in ed., Floyd W. Rudmin, *To Have Possessions: A Handbook of Ownership and Property, Journal of Social Behavior and Personality*, Special Issue, vol. 6, no. 6, 1991, 385–402; see also Raj Mehta and Russell W. Belk, "Artifacts, Identity, and Transition: Favorite Possessions of Indians and Indian Immigrants to the United States," *Journal of Consumer Research*, March 1991, pp. 398–411.
38. Craig J. Thompson and Siok Kuan Tambyah, "Trying to Be Cosmopolitan," *Journal of Consumer Research*, vol. 26, December 1999, pp. 214–241.
39. Priscilla A. LaBarbera, "The Nouveaux Riches: Conspicuous Consumption and the Issue of Self-Fulfillment," in eds. Elizabeth C. Hirschman and Jagdish N. Sheth, *Research in Consumer Behavior* (Greenwich, Conn.: JAI Press, 1988), pp. 181–182.
40. Sarah Ellison and Carlos Tejada, "Mr., Mrs., Meet Mr. Clean," *Wall Street Journal*, January 30, 2003, pp. B1, B3.
41. Blythe Yee, "Ads Remind Women They Have Two Hands," *Wall Street Journal*, August 14, 2003, pp. B1, B5; for an extensive discussion of consumer life transitions and related products, see Paula Mergenhagen, *Targeting Transitions* (Ithaca, N.Y.: American Demographics Books, 1995).
44. Otnes and Scott, "Something Old, Something New."
45. In line with our notion that the meaning of the symbol may derive from the culture as opposed to the individual and that symbols may have public or private meaning, see Marsha L. Richins, "Valuing Things: The Public and Private Meaning of Possessions," *Journal of Consumer Research*, December 1994, pp. 504–521.
46. Mihaly Csikzentmihalyi and Eugene Rochberg-Halton, *The Meaning of Things: Domestic Symbols and the Self* (Cambridge, England: Cambridge University Press, 1981); N. Laura Kamptner, "Personal Possessions and Their Meanings: A Life Span Perspective," *Journal of Social Behavior and Personality*, vol 6, no. 6, 1991, pp. 209–228; see also Richins, "Valuing Things."
47. Wallendorf and Arnould, "We Gather Together."
48. Adam Kuper, "The English Christmas and the Family: Time Out and Alternative Realities," in ed. Daniel Miller, *Unwrapping Christmas* (Oxford, England: Oxford University Press, 1993), pp. 157–175; Barbara Bodenhorn, "Christmas Present: Christmas Public," in ed. Miller, *Unwrapping Christmas*, pp. 193–216.
49. Carolyn Folkman Curasi, Linda L. Price, and Eric J. Arnould, "How Individuals' Cherished Possessions Become Families' Inalienable Wealth," *Journal of Consumer Research*, December 2004, pp. 609–622.
50. See, for example, Russell W. Belk, "Possessions and the Sense of Past" in ed. Russell Belk, *Highways* and *Buyways* (Provo, Utah: Association for Consumer Research, 1988).
51. Kelly Tepper Tian, William O. Bearden, and Gary L. Hunter, "Consumers' Need for Uniqueness: Scale Development and Validation," *Journal of Consumer Research*, vol. 28, June 2001, pp. 50–66; Howard L. Fromkin and C. R. Snyder, "The Search for Uniqueness and Valuation of Scarcity," in eds. Kenneth Gergen,

Martin S. Greenberg, and Richard H. Willis, *Social Exchanges: Advances in Theory and Research* (New York: Plenum, 1980), pp. 57–75; Csikszentmihalyi and Rochberg-Halton, *The Meaning of Things*; see also Richins, "Valuing Things."

52. Gabriel Bar-Haim, "The Meaning of Western Commercial Artifacts for Eastern European Youth," *Journal of Contemporary Ethnography*, July 1987, pp. 205–226.
53. Robert P. Libbon, "Datadog," *American Demographics*, September 2000, p. 26.
56. Russell W. Belk, "Possessions and the Extended Self," *Journal of Consumer Research*, September 1988, pp. 139–168; A. Dwayne Ball and Lori H. Tasaki, "The Role and Measurement of Attachment in Consumer Behavior," *Journal of Consumer Psychology*, vol. 1, no. 2, 1992, pp. 155–172; M. Joseph Sirgy, "Self-Concept and Consumer Behavior: A Critical Review," *Journal of Consumer Research*, December 1982, pp. 287–300; Robert E. Kleine, Susan Schultz Kleine, and Jerome B. Kernan, "Mundane Consumption and the Self: A Social Identity Perspective," *Journal of Consumer Psychology*, vol. 2, no. 3, 1993, pp. 209–235.
57. Kleine, Kleine, and Kernan, "Mundane Consumption and the Self"; see also Sirgy, "Self-Concept and Consumer Behavior"; M. Joseph Sirgy, *Social Cognition and Consumer Behavior* (New York: Praeger, 1983); George M. Zinkhan and J. W. Hong, "Self-Concept and Advertising Effectiveness: A Conceptual Model of Congruence, Conspicuousness, and Response Mode," in eds. Rebecca Holman and Michael Solomon, *Advances in Consumer Research*, vol. 18 (Provo, Utah: Association for Consumer Research, 1991), pp. 348–354; Morris B. Holbrook, "Patterns, Personalities, and Complex Relationships in the Effects of Self on Mundane Everyday Consumption: These Are 495 of My Most and Least Favorite Things," in eds. John F. Sherry and Brian Sternthal, *Advances in Consumer Research*, vol. 19 (Provo, Utah: Association for Consumer Research, 1992), pp. 417–423.
58. For example, see Robert V. Kozinets, "Utopian Enterprise: Articulating the Meanings of *Star Trek*'s Culture of Consumption," *Journal of Consumer Research*, June 2001, pp. 67–88; Douglas B. Holt, "Why Do Brands Cause Trouble? A Dialectical Theory of Consumer Culture and Branding," *Journal of Consumer Research*, June 2002, pp. 70+.
59. Kleine, Kleine, and Kernan, "Mundane Consumption and the Self."
60. C. R. Snyder and Howard L. Fromkin, *Uniqueness: Human Pursuit of Difference* (New York: Plenum, 1981).
61. Hope Jensen Schau and Mary C. Gilly, "We Are What We Post? Self-Presentation in Personal Web Space," *Journal of Consumer Research*, December 2003, pp. 385–404.
64. Sirgy, "Self-Concept and Consumer Behavior"; Sirgy, *Social Cognition and Consumer Behavior.*
65. Cheng Lu Wang, Terry Bristol, John C. Mowen, and Goutam Chakraborty, "Alternative Modes of Self-Construal: Dimensions of Connectedness-Separateness and Advertising Appeals to the Cultural and Gender-Specific Self," *Journal of Consumer Psychology*, vol. 9, no. 2, 2000, pp. 107–115.
66. Susan E. Schultz, Robert E. Kleine, and Jerome B. Kernan, "These Are a Few of My Favorite Things, Toward an Explication of Attachment as a Consumer Behavior Construct," in ed. Thomas K. Srull, *Advances in Consumer Research*, vol. 16 (Provo, Utah: Association for Consumer Research, 1989), pp. 359–366; Richins, "Valuing Things"; Marsha L. Richins, "Special Possessions and the Expression of Material Values," *Journal of Consumer Research*, December 1994, pp. 522–533.
67. Richins, "Valuing Things."
68. Richins, "Valuing Things."
69. Richard C. Morais, "Dog Days," *Forbes Global*, June 21, 2004, p. 30; Rebecca Gardyn, "VIPs (Very Important Pets)," *American Demographics*, March 2001, pp. 16–18; Belk, "Possessions and the Extended Self"; Elizabeth C. Hirschman, "Consumers and Their Animal Companions," *Journal of Consumer Research*, March 1994, pp. 616–632; see also Clinton R. Sanders, "The Animal 'Other': Self Definition, Social Identity and Companion Animals," in eds. Marvin Goldberg, Jerry Gorn, and Richard Pollay, *Advances in Consumer Research*, vol. 17 (Provo, Utah: Association for Consumer Research, 1990), pp. 662–668.
70. John Fetto, "In the Doghouse," *American Demographics*, January 2002, p. 7; John Fetto, "Pets Can Drive," *American Demographics*, March 2000, pp. 10–12.
71. Morais, "Dog Days;" Fetto, "In the Doghouse."
72. Belk, "Possessions and the Sense of Past"; Susan Schultz Kleine, Robert E. Kleine III, and Chris T. Allen, "How Is a Possession 'Me' or 'Not Me'? Characterizing Types and an Antecedent of Material Possession Attachment," *Journal of Consumer Research*, December 1995, pp. 327–343; McAlexander, Schouten, and Roberts, "Consumer Behavior and Divorce"; Lisa L. Love and Peter S. Sheldon, "Souvenirs: Messengers of Meaning," in eds. Joseph W. Alba and Wesley Hutchinson, *Advances in Consumer Research*, vol. 25 (Provo, Utah: Association for Consumer Research, 1998), pp. 170–175.
73. Belk, "Possessions and the Sense of Past."
74. Russell W. Belk, "Moving Possessions: An Analysis Based on Personal Documents from the 1847–1869 Mormon Migration," *Journal of Consumer Research*, December 1992, pp. 339–361.
75. Schwartz, "The Accidental Collector;" Temma Ehrenfeld, "Why Executives Collect," *Fortune*, January 11, 1993, pp. 94–97.
76. Russell W. Belk, Melanie Wallendorf, John F. Sherry Jr., and Morris B. Holbrook, "Collecting in a Consumer Culture," in ed. Belk, *Highways and Buyways.*
77. Alexandra Peers, "Baseball's Card of Cards Is Up for Grabs," *Wall Street Journal*, September 20, 1996, pp. B1–B9.
78. Russell W. Belk, Melanie Wallendorf, John F. Sherry Jr., Morris Holbrook, and Scott Roberts, "Collectors and Collecting," in ed. Michael J. Houston, *Advances in Consumer Research*, vol. 15 (Provo, Utah: Association for Consumer Research, 1988), pp. 548–553.
79. Belk, Wallendorf, Sherry, Holbrook, and Roberts, "Collectors and Collecting."

80. Russell W. Belk, "The Ineluctable Mysteries of Possessions," in ed. Floyd W. Rudmin, *To Have Possessions: A Handbook on Ownership and Property, Journal of Social Behavior and Personality*, Special Issue, vol. 6, no. 6, 1991, pp. 17–55.
81. Kent Grayson and David Shulman, "Indexicality and the Verification Function of Irreplaceable Possessions: A Semiotic Analysis," *Journal of Consumer Research*, vol. 27, June 2000, pp. 17–30.
82. Daniel Terdiman, "Curiously High-Tech Hacks for a Classic Tin," *New York Times*, February 3, 2005, *www.nytimes.com*.
83. Belk et al., "Collecting in a Consumer Culture."
84. Susan Fournier, "The Development of Intense Consumer-Product Relationships," Paper presented at the AMA Winter Educator's Conference, St. Petersburg, Fla., February 20, 1994.
85. Fournier, "The Development of Intense Consumer-Product Relationships."
86. Csikszentmihalyi and Rochberg-Halton, *The Meaning of Things;* Wallendorf and Arnould, "My Favorite Things"; Belk, "Moving Possessions."
87. A. Peter McGraw, Philip E. Tetlock, and Orie V. Kristel, "The Limits of Fungibility: Relational Schemata and the Value of Things," *Journal of Consumer Research*, September 2003, pp. 219–228.
88. Csikszentmihalyi and Rochberg-Halton, *The Meaning of Things.*
89. Csikszentmihalyi and Rochberg-Halton, *The Meaning of Things.*
90. Helga Dittmar, "Meaning of Material Possessions as Reflections of Identity: Gender and Social-Material Position in Society," in ed. Rudmin, *To Have Possessions*, pp. 165–186; see also Helga Dittmar, *The Social Psychology of Material Possessions* (New York: St. Martin's, 1992).
91. Jaideep Sengupta, Darren W. Dahl, and Gerald J. Gorn, "Misrepresentation in the Consumer Context," *Journal of Consumer Psychology*, 2002, pp. 69–79.
92. Dittmar, "Meaning of Material Possessions as Reflections of Identity"; Kamptner, "Personal Possessions and Their Meanings."
93. Wallendorf and Arnould, "My Favorite Things."
94. Russell W. Belk and Melanie Wallendorf, "Of Mice and Men: Gender Identity in Collecting," in eds. K. Ames and K. Martinez, *The Gender of Material Culture* (Ann Arbor, Mich.: University of Michigan Press), reprinted in ed. Susan M. Pearce, *Objects and Collections* (London: Routledge, 1994), pp. 240–253; Belk et al., "Collectors and Collecting."
95. Elizabeth Myers, "Phenomenological Analysis of the Importance of Special Possessions: An Exploratory Study," in eds. Elizabeth C. Hirschman and Morris B. Holbrook, *Advances in Consumer Research*, vol. 12 (Provo, Utah: Association for Consumer Research, 1985), pp. 560–565.
96. McCracken, "Culture and Consumption"; McCracken, *Culture and Consumption.*
97. McCracken, "Culture and Consumption"; McCracken, *Culture and Consumption.*
98. McCracken, "Culture and Consumption"; McCracken, *Culture and Consumption.*
99. Mark Gimein, "Little Better Yellow Different in Gumbo America," *New York*, October 4, 2004, pp. 32+.
100. Linda L. Price, Eric J. Arnold, and Carolyn Folkman Curasi, "Older Consumers' Disposition of Special Possessions," *Journal of Consumer Research*, vol. 27, September 2000, pp. 179–201.
101. Russell W. Belk, Melanie Wallendorf, and John F. Sherry Jr., "The Sacred and the Profane in Consumer Behavior: Theodicy on the Odyssey," *Journal of Consumer Research*, June 1989, pp. 1–38.
102. "Buddha Finger Relic Draws 600,000," *UPI NewsTrack*, May 30, 2004, n.p.
103. Maya Kaneko, "Seattle Tries to Extend Appeal to Japanese Visitors Beyond Baseball Superstar," *Kyodo News International*, January 9, 2005, *www.kyodonews.com.*
104. Belk, "Possessions and the Sense of Past."
105. Belk, Wallendorf, and Sherry, "The Sacred and the Profane in Consumer Behavior."
106. Amitai Etzioni, "The Socio-Economics of Property," in ed. Rudmin, *To Have Possessions*, pp. 465–468.
107. McAlexander, Schouten, and Roberts, "Consumer Behavior and Divorce."
108. Robert V. Kozinets, "Utopian Enterprise: Articulating the Meanings of *Star Trek*'s Culture of Consumption," *Journal of Consumer Research*, vol. 28, June 2001, pp. 67–88.
110. See, for example, Leigh Schmidt, "The Commercialization of the Calendar," *Journal of American History*, December 1991, pp. 887–916.
111. For fascinating historical and sociological accounts of Christmas, see Daniel Miller, "A Theory of Christmas," in ed. Miller, *Unwrapping Christmas*, pp. 3–37; Claude Levi-Strauss, "Father Christmas Executed," in ed. Miller, *Unwrapping Christmas*, pp. 38–54; Belk, "Materialism and the Making of the Modern American Christmas"; Daniel Miller, "Christmas against Materialism in Trinidad," in ed. Miller, *Unwrapping Christmas*, pp. 134–153; Barbara Bodenhorn, "Christmas Present: Christmas Public," in ed. Miller, *Unwrapping Christmas*, pp. 193–216; William B. Waits, *The Modern Christmas in America* (New York: New York University Press, 1993); and Stephen Nissenbaum, *The Battle for Christmas* (New York: Vantage Books, 1997).
112. John F. Sherry Jr., "Gift Giving in Anthropological Perspective," *Journal of Consumer Research*, September 1983, pp. 157–168.
113. For a discussion of several of these motives, see Sherry, "Gift Giving in Anthropological Perspective"; for research on gender differences in motives, see Mary Ann McGrath, "Gender Differences in Gift Exchanges: New Directions from Projections," *Psychology and Marketing*, August 1995, pp. 229–234; Cele Otnes, Julie A. Ruth, and Constance Milbourne, "The Pleasure and Pain of Being Close: Men's Mixed Feelings about Participation in Valentine's Day Gift Exchange," in eds. Chris Allen and Debbie Roedder-John, *Advances in Consumer Research*, vol. 21 (Provo, Utah: Association for Consumer Research, 1994), pp. 159–164; Cele Otnes, Kyle Zolner,

and Tina M. Lowry, "In-Laws and Outlaws: The Impact of Divorce and Remarriage upon Christmas Gift Exchange," in eds. Chris Allen and Debbie Roedder-John, *Advances in Consumer Research*, vol. 21 (Provo, Utah: Association for Consumer Research, 1994), pp. 25–29; for other gift-giving motives, see Russell W. Belk, "Gift Giving Behavior," in ed. Jagdish N. Sheth, *Research in Marketing* (Greenwich, Conn.: JAI Press, 1979), pp. 95–126; Russell W. Belk, "The Perfect Gift," in eds. Cele Otnes and Richard Beltrami, *Gift Giving Behavior: An Interdisciplinary Anthology* (Bowling Green, Ohio: Bowling Green University Popular Press, 1996); for a discussion of the roles played by gift givers (the pleaser, the provider, the compensator, the socializer, and the acknowledger), see Cele Otnes, Tina M. Lowrey, and Young Chan Kim, "Gift Selection for Easy and Difficult Recipients," *Journal of Consumer Research*, September 1993, pp. 229–244; Kleine, Kleine, and Allen, "How Is a Possession 'Me' or 'Not Me'?"

114. McAlexander, Schouten, and Roberts, "Consumer Behavior and Divorce."
115. David B. Wooten, "Qualitative Steps toward an Expanded Model of Anxiety in Gift-Giving," *Journal of Consumer Research*, vol. 27, June 2000, pp. 84–95.
116. Russell W. Belk and Gregory S. Coon, "Gift Giving as Agapic Love: An Alternative to the Exchange Paradigm Based on Dating Experiences," *Journal of Consumer Research*, December 1993, pp. 393–417.
117. Sherry, "Gift Giving in Anthropological Perspective"; Mary Searle-Chatterjee, "Christmas Cards and the Construction of Social Relations in Britain Today," in ed. Miller, *Unwrapping Christmas*, pp. 176–192.
118. Belk and Coon, "Gift Giving as Agapic Love"; see also Sherry, "Gift Giving in Anthropological Perspective."
120. Sak Onkvisit and John J. Shaw, *International Marketing: Analysis and Strategy* (Columbus, Ohio: Merrill, 1989), pp. 241–242.
121. "The Efficiency of Gift Giving: Is It Really Better to Give than to Receive?" *Marketing: Knowledge at Wharton*, December 15, 2004, *knowledge.wharton.upenn.edu.*
122. Sandra Yin, "Give and Take," *American Demographics*, November 2003, pp. 12–13; Eileen Fischer and Stephen J. Arnold, "More Than a Labor of Love: Gender Roles and Christmas Shopping," *Journal of Consumer Research*, December 1990, pp. 333–345.
123. John F. Sherry Jr. and Mary Ann McGrath, "Unpacking the Holiday Presence: A Comparative Ethnography of Two Gift Stores," in ed. Elizabeth C. Hirschman, *Interpretive Consumer Research* (Provo, Utah: Association for Consumer Research, 1989), pp. 148–167; see also David Cheal, "Showing Them You Love Them: Gift Giving and the Dialectic of Intimacy," *Sociological Review*, January 1987, pp. 151–169; Lewis Hyde, *The Gift* (New York: Vintage, 1979).
124. See, for example, Theodore Caplow, "Rule Enforcement without Visible Means: Christmas Gift Giving in Middletown," *American Journal of Sociology*, March 1984, pp. 1306–1323.
125. James G. Carrier, "The Rituals of Christmas Giving," in ed. Miller, *Unwrapping Christmas*, pp. 55–74.
126. Mary Ann McGrath, "An Ethnography of a Gift Store: Trappings, Wrappings, and Rapture," *Journal of Retailing*, Winter 1989, p. 434.
127. Wooten, "Qualitative Steps toward an Expanded Model of Anxiety in Gift-Giving."
128. Julie A. Ruth, Cele C. Otnes, and Frederic F. Brunel, "Gift Receipt and the Reformulation of Interpersonal Relationships," *Journal of Consumer Research*, March 1999, pp. 385–402; Ming-Hui Huang and Shihti Yu, "Gifts in a Romantic Relationship: A Survival Analysis," *Journal of Consumer Psychology*, vol. 9, no. 3, 2000, pp. 179–188.
129. Belk, "Gift Giving Behavior"; see also Sherry, "Gift Giving in Anthropological Perspective"; for research on this factor and others discussed above, see Rick G. M. Pieters, and Henry S. J. Robben, "Beyond the Horse's Mouth: Exploring Acquisition and Exchange Utility in Gift Evaluation," in eds. Joseph W. Alba and Wesley Hutchinson, *Advances in Consumer Research*, vol. 25, (Provo, Utah: Association for Consumer Research 1998), pp. 160–163.
130. Belk and Coon, "Gift Giving as Agapic Love."
131. Annamma Joy, "Gift Giving in Hong Kong and the Continuum of Social Ties," *Journal of Consumer Research*, September 2001, pp. 239–256.
133. Michal Strahilevitz, "The Effects of Product Type and Donation Magnitude on Willingness to Pay More for a Charity-Linked Brand," *Journal of Consumer Psychology*, vol. 8, no. 3, 1999, pp. 215–241.
135. "More Marketers Wish You a Merry Winter," *Wall Street Journal*, December 5, 1996, pp. B1, B12.
136. Susan Carey, "Over the River, through the Woods, to a Posh Resort We Go," *Wall Street Journal*, November 21, 1997, pp. B1, B4.

CHAPTER 19

2. Louis Harris and Associates, *Consumerism in the Eighties*, Study No. 822047, 1983, as referenced in John C. Mowen, *Consumer Behavior*, 3rd ed. (New York: Macmillan, 1993), p. 751.
3. Executive Office of the President, *Consumer Advisory Council*, First Report (Washington, D.C.: U.S. Government Printing Office, October 1963).
4. Rachel Dardis, "Risk Regulation and Consumer Welfare," *Journal of Consumer Affairs*, Summer 1988, pp. 303–317.
5. For more on the implications of FCC policy regarding broadband and other marketing information technology, see David E. M. Sappington and Donald K. Stockdale, Jr., "The Federal Communications Commission's Competition Policy and Marketing's Information Technology Revolution," *Journal of Public Policy & Marketing*, Spring 2003, pp. 26–34.
6. For more on the benefits of direct-to-consumer advertising, see John E. Calfee, "Public Policy Issues in Direct-to-Consumer Advertising of Prescription Drugs," *Journal of Public Policy & Marketing*, Fall 2002, pp. 174–193.
7. Kim Bartel Sheehan, "Balancing Acts: An Analysis of Food and Drug Administration Letters About Direct-to-

Consumer Advertising Violations," *Journal of Public Policy & Marketing,* Fall 2003, pp. 159–169; Barbara Obstoj, "Editor's Views on DTC Advertising," *Pharma Marketletter,* March 28, 2005, n.p.; Michael S. Rosenwald, "Digene's Ads Take Their Case to Women," *Washington Post,* March 21, 2005, p. E1.

8. See Ross D. Petty, "Wireless Advertising Messaging: Legal Analysis and Public Policy Issues," *Journal of Public Policy & Marketing,* Spring 2003, pp. 71–82.
13. Joanne Jacobs, "Hollywood Gets the Message on Violence," *Denver Post,* January 2, 2001, p. B07.
14. Stuart Elliott, "A Marketing Barrier Poised to Fall: CNN Is Set to Be the First Cable News Network to Run Liquor Ads," *New York Times,* March 1, 2005, p. C5; David Kiley, "A Green Flag for Booze," *Business Week,* March 7, 2005, p. 95.
15. Daniel Rosenberg, "Animal-Rights Ad, Toned Down, Still Hits a Wall at the Networks," *Wall Street Journal,* December 29, 1998, p. B5.
16. Sarah Ellison, "Rivals Take P&G To Court To Challenge Ads," *Advertising Age,* June 17, 2003, pp. B1, B11.
17. Melissa Healy, "Those Sugary Saturday Mornings," *Los Angeles Times,* January 25, 2005, p. F1.
18. Daniel Rosenberg, "Veal Industry Focuses on Chefs in Countering Animal-Rights Ads," *Wall Street Journal,* March 18, 1998, p. B3.
19. Kathryn Kranhold, "New Groups Seek Remedy to Drug Ads," *Wall Street Journal,* June 22, 2000, p. B16.
20. "Advertising and Marketing," *Factiva Advertising and Media Digest,* February 26, 2001.
21. Jacob Jacoby and Constance Small, "The FDA Approach to Defining Misleading Advertising," *Journal of Marketing,* October 1975, pp. 65–68.
22. Federal Trade Commission, "Policy Statement on Deception," 45 ATRR 689, October 27, 1983, as cited in Gary T. Ford and John E. Calfee, "Recent Developments in FTC Policy on Deception," *Journal of Marketing,* July 1986, pp. 82–103; also see Jef I. Richards and Ivan L. Preston, "Proving and Disproving Materiality of Deceptive Advertising Claims," *Journal of Public Policy and Marketing,* Fall 1992, pp. 45–56.
23. Jacob Jacoby, Wayne D. Hoyer, and David A. Sheluga, *Miscomprehension of Televised Communication* (New York: American Association of Advertising Agencies, 1980); Jacob Jacoby and Wayne D. Hoyer, *The Comprehension and Miscomprehension of Print Communications: An Investigation of Mass Media Magazines* (New York: The Advertising Education Foundation, 1987).
24. Lee D. Dahringer and Denise R. Johnson, "The Federal Trade Commission Redefinition of Deception and Public Policy Implications: Let the Buyer Beware," *Journal of Consumer Affairs,* vol. 18, 1984, pp. 326–342.
25. Gary Armstrong, Metin Gurol, and Frederick Russ, "Detecting and Correcting Deceptive Advertising," *Journal of Consumer Research,* December 1979, pp. 237–246; Dorothy Cohen, "Unfairness in Advertising Revisited," *Journal of Marketing,* Winter 1982, pp. 73–80; Michael R. Hyman, "Deception in Advertising: A Proposed Complex of Definitions for Researchers, Lawyers, and Regulators," *International Journal of Advertising,* vol. 9, no. 3, 1990, pp. 259–270; Richards and Preston, "Proving and Disproving Materiality of Deceptive Advertising Claims."
26. Bruce Ingersoll, "Home Shopping and iMall to Pay Millions in FTC Ad-Claim Cases," *Wall Street Journal,* April 16, 1999, p. B2.
27. Gary J. Gaeth and Timothy B. Heath, "The Cognitive Processing of Misleading Advertising in Young and Old Adults: Assessment and Training," *Journal of Consumer Research,* June 1987, pp. 43–54.
28. Michael J. Barone, Kay M. Palan, and Paul W. Miniard, "Brand Usage and Gender as Moderators of the Potential Deception Associated with Partial Comparative Advertising," *Journal of Advertising,* Spring 2004, pp. 19–28.
29. David M. Gardner, "Deception in Advertising: A Conceptual Approach," *Journal of Marketing,* January 1975, pp. 40–46.
30. "Pfizer Deploys $2m Effort to Change Listerine Ads," *Brandweek,* January 17, 2005, p. 5.
31. Joel E. Urbany, William O. Bearden, and Dan C. Weilbaker, "The Effect of Plausible and Exaggerated Reference Prices on Consumer Perceptions and Price Search," *Journal of Consumer Research,* June 1988, pp. 95–110; John Liefield and Louise A. Heslop, "Reference Prices and Deception in Newspaper Advertising," *Journal of Consumer Research,* March 1985, pp. 868–876.
32. Bonnie B. Reece and Robert H. Ducoffe, "Deception in Brand Names," *Journal of Public Policy and Marketing,* vol. 6, 1987, pp. 93–103.
33. Vanessa O'Connell, "A Wine Label with a Bouquet of Controversy,' *Wall Street Journal,* December 8, 1998, pp. B1, B4.
34. Aaron Lucchetti, "Produce Sleuths Search for Label Scams," *Wall Street Journal,* June 17, 1997, pp. B1, B6.
35. Ivan L. Preston, "The FTC's Handling of Puffery and Other Selling Claims Made 'By Implication,'" *Journal of Business Research,* June 1977, pp. 155–181.
36. Richard L. Oliver, "An Interpretation of the Attitudinal and Behavioral Effects of Puffery," *Journal of Consumer Affairs,* Summer 1979, pp. 8–27; Terence A. Shimp and Ivan L. Preston, "Deceptive and Nondeceptive Consequences of Evaluative Advertising," *Journal of Marketing,* Winter 1981, pp. 22–32.
37. Gardner, "Deception in Advertising"; Raymond R. Burke, Wayne S. De Sarbo, Richard L. Oliver, and Thomas S. Robertson, "Deception by Implication: An Empirical Investigation," *Journal of Consumer Research,* March 1988, pp. 483–494.
38. Gita Venkataramani Johar, "Consumer Involvement and Deception from Implied Advertising Claims," *Journal of Marketing Research,* August 1995, pp. 267–279.
39. John E. Calfee, "FTC's Hidden Weight Loss Ad Agenda," *Advertising Age,* October 25, 1993, p. 29.
40. Burke et al., "Deception by Implication."
41. Gordon Fairclough, "Tobacco Titans Bid for 'Organic' Cigarette Maker," *Wall Street Journal,* December 10, 2001, pp. B1, B4; Bob Garfield, "Softly Lit or Blunt, 'Less Toxic' Cigarette Ads Hint at Health," *Advertising Age,*

November 12, 2001, p. 58; Gordon Fairclough, "Philip Morris Tells Smokers 'Light' Cigarettes Aren't Safer," *Wall Street Journal,* November 20, 2002, p. B1.

42. Sandra J. Burke, Sandra J. Milberg, and Wendy W. Moe, "Displaying Common but Previously Neglected Health Claims on Product Labels: Understanding Competitive Advantages, Deception, and Education," *Journal of Public Policy and Marketing,* Fall 1997, pp. 242–255.

43. J. Craig Andrews, Richard G. Netemeyer, and Scot Burton, "Consumer Generalization of Nutrient Content Claims in Advertising," *Journal of Marketing,* October 1998, pp. 62–75.

44. J. Edward Russo, Barbara L. Metcalf, and Debra Stephens, "Identifying Misleading Advertising," *Journal of Consumer Research,* September 1981, pp. 119–131; Gardner, "Deception in Advertising"; Armstrong, Gurol, and Russ, "Detecting and Correcting Deceptive Advertising."

45. "Feds Charge Shopping Network," *Austin American Statesman,* March 4, 1995, p. A7.

46. Laurie McGinley, "FTC Probes Fat-Content Claims Made by Some Restaurant Chains," *Wall Street Journal,* April 30, 1996, p. B8; Lauran Neergaard, "FDA Requires That Health Claims on Dietary Supplements Be Verifiable," *Austin American Statesman,* December 30, 1993, p. A3.

47. Phil Wallace, "FTC Still Exempting Media from Ad Claims Enforcement," *Food Chemical News,* November 15, 2004, p. 16.

48. Betty J. Parker, "Food for Health," *Journal of Advertising,* Fall 2003, pp. 47–55; Julie A. Caswell, Yumei Ning, Fang Liu, and Eliza M. Mojduszka, "The Impact of New Labeling Regulations on the Use of Voluntary Nutrient-Content and Health Claims by Food Manufacturers," *Journal of Public Policy & Marketing,* Fall 2003, pp. 147–158.

49. Thomas Lee, "Yoplait Becomes General Mills' Star Brand," *Star Tribune (Minneapolis),* March 24, 2005, *www.startribune.com.*

50. Elyse Tanouye, "Heartburn Drug Makers Feel Judge's Heat," *Wall Street Journal,* October 16, 1995, p. B8.

51. Calfee, "FTC's Hidden Weight Loss Ad Agenda."

52. David C. Vladeck, "Truth and Consequences: The Perils of Half-Truths and Unsubstantiated Health Claims for Dietary Supplements," *Journal of Public Policy and Marketing,* vol.19, no. 1, Spring 2000, pp. 132–138; Jacob Jacoby, Margaret C. Nelson, and Wayne D. Hoyer, "Corrective Advertising and Affirmative Disclosure Statements: Their Potential for Confusing and Misleading the Consumer," *Journal of Marketing,* Winter 1982, pp. 61–72; G. Ray Funkhouser, "An Empirical Study of Consumers' Sensitivity to the Wording of Affirmative Disclosure Messages," *Journal of Public Policy and Marketing,* vol. 3, 1984, pp. 26–37; Ellen R. Foxman, Darrel D. Muehling, and Patrick A. Moore, "Disclaimer Footnotes in Ads: Discrepancies between Purpose and Performance," *Journal of Public Policy and Marketing,* vol. 7, 1988, pp. 127–137.

53. Gita Venkataramani Johar and Carolyn J. Simmons, "The Use of Concurrent Disclosures to Correct Invalid Inferences," *Journal of Consumer Research,* vol. 26, March 2000, pp. 307–322.

54. William L. Wilkie, Dennis L. McNeil, and Michael B. Mazis, "Marketing's 'Scarlet Letter': The Theory and Practice of Corrective Advertising," *Journal of Marketing,* Spring 1984, pp. 11–31; Gary M. Armstrong, Metin N. Gurol, and Frederick A. Russ, "A Longitudinal Evaluation of the Listerine Corrective Advertising Campaign," *Journal of Public Policy and Marketing,* vol. 2, 1983, pp. 16–28.

55. Armstrong, Gurol, and Russ, "Detecting and Correcting Deceptive Advertising"; Richard W. Mizerski, Neil K. Allison, and Stephen Calvert, "A Controlled Field Study of Corrective Advertising Using Multiple Exposures and a Commercial Medium," *Journal of Marketing Research,* August 1979, pp. 341–348; Michael B. Mazis and Janice E. Atkinson, "An Experimental Evaluation of a Proposed Corrective Advertising Remedy," *Journal of Marketing Research,* May 1986, pp. 178–183; Tyzoon T. Tyebjee, "The Role of Publicity in FTC Corrective Advertising Remedies," *Journal of Public Policy and Marketing,* vol. 1, 1982, pp. 111–121.

56. Gita Venkataramani Johar, "Intended and Unintended Effects of Corrective Advertising on Beliefs and Evaluations: An Exploratory Analysis," *Journal of Consumer Psychology,* vol. 5, no. 3, 1996, pp. 209–230.

57. "FTC Invites Self-Policing," *Advertising Age,* December 15, 2003, p. 18.

58. "Chain to Pay $250,000 in Bait-and-Switch Case," *New York Times,* July 14, 1999, p. B6; "Nationwide Computers and Electronics Settles with State," *New Jersey Division of Consumer Affairs news release,* July 13, 1999, *www.state.nj.us;* "Troubled Company Reporter," IBL, June 25, 2001, *www.bankrupt.com.*

59. William L. Wilkie, *Consumer Behavior,* 2nd ed. (New York: Wiley, 1990).

60. Christopher Scanian, "Postcards Offering 'Free Prizes' Can Prove Costly, Experts Warn," *Austin American Statesman,* November 18, 1992, pp. A1, A17.

61. Pratibha A. Dabholkar and James J. Kellaris, "Toward Understanding Marketing Students' Ethical Judgment of Controversial Selling Practices," *Journal of Business Research,* June 1992, pp. 313–329.

62. Karl A. Boedecker, Fred W. Morgan, and Jeffrey J. Stoltman, "Legal Dimensions of Salespersons' Statements: A Review and Managerial Suggestions," *Journal of Marketing,* January 1991, pp. 70–80.

63. Stephanie N. Mehta, "Visions of Wealth and Independence Lead Professionals to Try Multilevel Marketing," *Wall Street Journal,* June 23, 1995, pp. B1, B2.

64. Leslie Chang, "Amway in China: Once Barred, Now Booming," *Wall Street Journal,* March 12, 2004, pp. B1, B5.

65. Jinkook Lee and Loren V. Geistfeld, "Elderly Consumers' Receptiveness to Telemarketing Fraud," *Journal of Public Policy and Marketing,* vol. 18, no. 2, Fall 1999, pp. 208–217.

66. "Senior Citizens Warned about Fraud Schemes," *Austin American Statesman,* July 13, 1999, p. B2; John R. Emshwiller, "Having Lost Thousands to Con Artists, Elderly Widow Tells Cautionary Tale," *Wall Street Journal,* August 20, 1995, pp. B1, B5.

67. Samantha Levine, "AARP Educating Elderly on Telemarketing Dangers," *Austin American Statesman*, August 7, 1996, p. A3.

68. A. C. Nielsen Company, *1990 Nielsen Report on Television* (New York: Nielsen Media Research); J. Condry, P. Bence, and C. Scheibe, "Nonprogram Content of Children's Television," *Journal of Broadcasting and Electronic Media*, Summer 1988, pp. 255–270; Carol Lawson, "Guarding the Children's Hour on TV," *New York Times*, January 24, 1991, pp. C1, C13.

69. W. Melody, *Children's Television: The Economics of Exploitation* (New Haven, Conn.: Yale University Press, 1973); Ellen Notar, "Children and TV Commercials: Wave after Wave of Exploitation," *Childhood Education*, Winter 1989, pp. 66–67.

70. Scott Ward, "Consumer Socialization," *Journal of Consumer Research*, September 1974, pp. 1–13; Laurene Krasney Meringoff and Gerald S. Lesser, "Children's Ability to Distinguish Television Commercials from Program Material," in ed. R. P. Adler, *The Effect of Television Advertising on Children* (Lexington, Mass.: Lexington Books, 1980), pp. 29–42; S. Levin, T. Petros, and F. Petrella, "Preschoolers' Awareness of Television Advertising," *Child Development*, August 1982, pp. 933–937.

71. M. Carole Macklin, "Preschoolers' Understanding of the Informational Function of Advertising," *Journal of Consumer Research*, September 1987, pp. 229–239; Merrie Brucks, Gary M. Armstrong, and Marvin E. Goldberg, "Children's Use of Cognitive Defenses against Television Advertising: A Cognitive Response Approach," *Journal of Consumer Research*, March 1988, pp. 471–482.

72. Mary C. Martin, "Children's Understanding of the Intent of Advertising: A Meta-Analysis," *Journal of Public Policy and Marketing*, Fall 1997, pp. 205–216.

73. Deborah L. Roedder, "Age Differences in Children's Responses to Television Advertising: An Information Processing Approach," *Journal of Consumer Research*, September 1981, pp. 144–153.

74. Jon Berry, "The New Generation of Kids and Ads," *Adweek's Marketing Week*, April 15, 1991, pp. 25–28; Marvin E. Goldberg and Gerald J. Gorn, "Some Unintended Consequences of TV Advertising to Children," *Journal of Consumer Research*, June 1978, pp. 22–29; Gary M. Armstrong and Merrie Brucks, "Dealing with Children's Advertising: Public Policy Issues and Alternatives," *Journal of Public Policy and Marketing*, vol. 7, 1988, pp. 98–113.

75. Bonnie B. Reece, "Children and Shopping: Some Public Policy Questions," *Journal of Public Policy and Marketing*, vol. 5, 1986, pp. 185–194; Armstrong and Brucks, "Dealing with Children's Advertising."

76. Scott Ward and Daniel B. Wackman, "Children's Information Processing of Television Advertising," in ed. Peter Clarke, *New Models for Mass Communication Research* (Beverly Hills, Calif.: Sage, 1973), pp. 119–146; Thomas S. Robertson and John R. Rossiter, "Children and Commercial Persuasion: Testing the Defenses," *Journal of Consumer Research*, June 1974, pp. 13–20; Deborah L. Roedder, Brian B. Sternthal, and Bobby J. Calder, "Attitude-Behavior Consistency in Children's Responses to Television Advertising," *Journal of Marketing Research*, November 1983, pp. 337–349; Scott Ward, Daniel B. Wackman, and Ellen Wartella, *How Children Learn to Buy* (Beverly Hills, Calif.: Sage, 1977).

77. Jeffrey E. Brand and Bradley S. Greenberg, "Commercials in the Classroom: The Impact of Channel One Advertising," *Journal of Advertising Research*, January–February 1994, pp. 18–27.

78. Scott Ward and Daniel Wackman, "Children's Purchase Influence Attempts and Parental Yielding," *Journal of Marketing Research*, August 1972, pp. 316–319; Goldberg and Gorn, "Some Unintended Consequences of TV Advertising to Children"; Tamara F. Mangleburg, "Children's Influence in Purchase Decisions: A Review and Critique," in eds. Marvin E. Goldberg, Gerald Gorn, and Richard W. Pollay, *Advances in Consumer Research*, vol. 17 (Provo, Utah: Association for Consumer Research, 1990), pp. 813–825.

79. Joe Flint, "Proposed 900-Number and Rules Worry Advertisers," *Broadcasting and Cable*, April 5, 1993, p. 44.

80. Russell N. Laczniak, Darrel D. Muehling, and Les Carlson, "Mothers' Attitudes toward 900-Number Advertising Directed at Children," *Journal of Public Policy and Marketing*, Spring 1995, pp. 108–116.

81. Gerald J. Gorn and Renee Florsheim, "The Effects of Commercials for Adult Products on Children," *Journal of Consumer Research*, March 1985, pp. 962–967.

82. Judann Dagnoli, "Consumers Union Hits Kids Advertising," *Advertising Age*, July 23, 1990, p. 4.

83. Mary Lu Carnevale, "Parents Say PBS Stations Exploit Barney in Fund Drives," *Wall Street Journal*, March 19, 1993, pp. B1, B8; Maria Grubbs Hoy, Clifford Young, and John C. Mowen, "Animated Host-Selling Advertisements: Their Impact on Young Children's Recognition, Attitudes, and Behavior," *Journal of Public Policy and Marketing*, vol. 5, 1986, pp. 171–184.

84. Marvin E. Goldberg, Gerald Gorn, and Wendy Gibson, "TV Messages for Snack and Breakfast Foods: Do They Influence Children's Preferences?" *Journal of Consumer Research*, September 1978, pp. 73–81; Debra L. Scammon and Carole L. Christopher, "Nutrition Education with Children via Television," *Journal of Advertising*, vol. 10, 1981, pp. 26–36; Thomas S. Robertson and John R. Rossiter, "Children and Commercial Persuasion: An Attributional Approach," *Journal of Consumer Research*, June 1974, pp. 12–20.

85. David Kiley, "SpongeBob: For Obesity or Health?" *Business Week*, February 17, 2005, *www.businessweek.com*.

86. "For Kids on the Web, It's an Ad, Ad, Ad, Ad World," *BusinessWeek*, August 13, 2001, pp. 108+.

87. Joan Blatt, Lyle Spencer, and Scott Ward, "A Cognitive-Developmental Study of Children's Reaction to Television Advertising," in eds. E. A. Rubenstein, G. A. Constock, and J. P. Murray, *Television and Social Behavior* (Washington, D.C.: U.S. Government Printing Office, 1972), pp. 452–467.

88. Meringoff and Lesser, "Children's Ability to Distinguish Television Commercials from Program Material."

89. Doug Halonen, "FCC Urged to Monitor Total Hours of Kids TV," *Electronic Media*, September 24, 2002, p. 2; Jon Berry, "Kids' Advocates to TV: 'We've Only Begun to Fight,'" *Adweek's Marketing Week*, April 15, 1991, p. 25.

90. Gerald J. Gorn and Marvin E. Goldberg, "Behavioral Evidence of the Effects of Televised Food Messages on Children," *Journal of Consumer Research*, September 1982, pp. 200–205; Cyndee Miller, "Marketers Find a Seat in the Classroom," *Marketing News*, June 20, 1994, p. 2.
91. Dale Kunkel and Walter Granz, "Assessing Compliance with Industry Self-Regulation of Television Advertising to Children," *Journal of Applied Communication Research*, May 1993, pp. 148–162.
92. "Try to Keep It Simple," *Advertising Age*, February 4, 2002, p. S4.
93. Daniel Golden, "'Media Literacy' Sparks a New Debate Over Commercialism in Schools," *Wall Street Journal*, December 17, 1999, pp. B1, B4.
94. Armstrong and Brucks, "Dealing with Children's Advertising."
95. Eve M. Caudill and Patrick E. Murphy, "Consumer Online Privacy: Legal and Ethical Issues," *Journal of Public Policy and Marketing*, vol. 19, no. 1, Spring 2000, pp. 7–19.
96. Kim Bartel Sheehan and Mariea Grubbs Hoy, "Dimensions of Privacy Concern among Online Consumers," *Journal of Public Policy and Marketing*, vol. 19, no. 1, Spring 2000, pp. 62–73.
97. Ross D. Petty, "Marketing without Consent: Consumer Choice and Costs, Privacy, and Public Policy," *Journal of Public Policy and Marketing*, vol. 19, no. 1, Spring 2000, pp. 42–53.
98. Pamela Paul, "Mixed Signals," *American Demographics*, July 2001, pp.45–49; Joseph Phelps, Glen Nowak, and Elizabeth Ferrell, "Privacy Concerns and Consumer Willingness to Provide Personal Information," *Journal of Public Policy and Marketing*, vol. 19, no. 1, Spring 2000, pp. 27–41.
99. George R. Milne, "Privacy and Ethical Issues in Database/Interactive Marketing and Public Policy: A Research Framework and Overview of the Special Issue," *Journal of Public Policy and Marketing*, vol. 19, no. 1, Spring 2000, pp. 1–6.
100. Mary J. Culnan, "Protecting Privacy Online: Is Self-Regulation Working?" *Journal of Public Policy and Marketing*, vol. 19, no. 1, Spring 2000, pp. 20–26.
101. Anthony D. Miyazaki and Ana Fernandez, "Internet Privacy and Security: An Examination of Online Retailer Disclosures," *Journal of Public Policy and Marketing*, vol. 19, no. 1, Spring 2000, pp. 54–61.
102. "FTC Receives Largest COPPA Civil Penalties to Date in Settlements with Mrs. Fields Cookies and Hershey Foods," *Federal Trade Commission news release*, February 27, 2003, *www.ftc.gov/opa/2003/02/hersheyfield.htm.*
103. Larry Dobrow, "How Old Is Old Enough?" *Advertising Age*, February 4, 2002, p. S4.
104. Kimberly Bonvissuto, "Net Latest Snare for Senior Scams," *Crain's Cleveland Business*, July 30, 2001, p. 17.
105. Bob Tedeschi, "Poll Says Identity Theft Concerns Rose After High-Profile Breaches," *New York Times*, March 10, 2005, p. G5.
106. Rebecca Gardyn, "Full Speed Ahead?" *American Demographics*, October 2001, pp. 12–13.
107. Don Clark, "Safety First," *Wall Street Journal*, December 7, 1998, p. R14.
108. Steve Hill, "Safe Hands," *Internet Magazine*, March 2002, pp. 28+.
109. Peter Barton Hutt, "FDA Regulation of Product Claims in Food Labeling," *Journal of Public Policy and Marketing*, Spring 1993, pp. 132–134; Gabriella Stern, "In a Turnabout, Fast-Food Fare Becomes Fattier," *Wall Street Journal*, August 23, 1993, pp. B1, B6; Richard Gibson, "Restaurant Menus' Health Claims May Be Regulated," *Wall Street Journal*, June 2, 1993, p. B1.
110. Jacob Jacoby, Robert W. Chestnut, and William Silberman, "Consumer Use and Comprehension of Nutrition Information," *Journal of Consumer Research*, March 1977, pp. 119–128.
111. Catherine A. Cole and Gary J. Gaeth, "Cognitive and Age-Related Differences in the Ability to Use Nutritional Information in a Complex Environment," *Journal of Marketing Research*, May 1990, pp. 175–184; Catherine A. Cole and Siva K. Balasubramanian, "Age Differences in Consumers' Search for Information: Public Policy Implications," *Journal of Consumer Research*, June 1993, pp. 157–169.
112. Jinkook Lee and Jeanne M. Hogarth, "The Price of Money: Consumers' Understanding of APRs and Contract Interest Rates," *Journal of Public Policy and Marketing*, Spring 1999, pp. 66–76.
113. Ivonne M. Torres, Betsy D. Gelb, and Jaime L. Noriega, "Warning and Informing the Domestic International Market," *Journal of Public Policy and Marketing*, Fall 2003, pp. 216–222.
114. Jacoby, Chestnut, and Silberman, "Consumer Use and Comprehension of Nutrition Information."
115. Brian Roe, Alan S. Levy, and Brenda M. Derby, "The Impact of Health Claims on Consumer Search and Product Evaluation Outcomes: Results from FDA Experimental Data," *Journal of Public Policy and Marketing*, Spring 1999, pp. 89–105.
116. Stern, "In a Turnabout, Fast-Food Fare Becomes Fattier."
117. Judith A. Garretson and Scot Burton, "Effects of Nutrition Facts Panel Values, Nutrition Claims, and Health Claims on Consumer Attitudes, Perceptions of Disease-Related Risks, and Trust," *Journal of Public Policy and Marketing*, vol. 19, no. 2, Fall 2000, pp. 213–227; Anu Mitra, Manoj Hastak, Gary T. Ford, and Debra Jones Ringold, "Can the Educationally Disadvantaged Interpret the FDA-Mandated Nutrition Facts Panel in the Presence of an Implied Health Claim?" *Journal of Public Policy and Marketing*, vol. 18, no. 1, Spring 1999, pp. 106–117.
118. Siva K. Balasubramanian and Catherine Cole, "Consumers' Search and Use of Nutrition Information: The Challenge and Promise of the Nutrition Labeling and Education Act," *Journal of Marketing Research*, July 2002, pp. 112–127.
119. Lisa R. Szykman, Paul N. Bloom, and Alan S. Levy, "A Proposed Model of the Use of Package Claims and Nutrition Labels," *Journal of Public Policy and Marketing*, Fall 1997, pp. 228–241.

120. David Brimberg and Marta L. Axelson, "Improving the Dietary Status of Low-Income Pregnant Women at Nutritional Risk," *Journal of Public Policy and Marketing*, Spring 2002, pp. 100–104.

121. For example, see Jacob Jacoby, Donald E. Speller, and Carol A. Kohn, "Brand Choice Behavior as a Function of Information Load," *Journal of Marketing Research*, February 1974, pp. 63–69; Jacob Jacoby, "Perspectives on Information Overload," *Journal of Consumer Research*, March 1984, pp. 432–435; Naresh K. Malhotra, "Reflections on the Information Overload Paradigm in Consumer Decision Making," *Journal of Consumer Research*, March 1984, pp. 436–440; Kevin Lane Keller and Richard Staelin, "Effects of Quality and Quantity of Information on Decision Effectiveness," *Journal of Consumer Research*, September 1987, pp. 200–213.

122. Yumiko Ono, "Fine Print in Drug Ads Sparks a Debate," *Wall Street Journal*, April 1, 1997, pp. B1, B8.

123. Ajit M. Menon, Aparna D. Deshpande, Matthew Perri III, and George M. Zinkan, "Consumers' Attention to the Brief Summary in Print Direct-to-Consumer Advertisements: Perceived Usefulness in Patient-Physician Discussions," *Journal of Public Policy & Marketing*, Fall 2003, pp. 181–191.

124. J. Edward Russo, Richard Staelin, Catherine A. Nolan, Gary J. Russell, and Barbara L. Metcalf, "Nutrition Information in the Supermarket," *Journal of Consumer Research*, June 1986, pp. 48–70; James R. Bettman and Pradeep Kakkar, "Effects of Information Presentation Format on Consumer Information Acquisition Strategies," *Journal of Consumer Research*, March 1977, pp. 233–240; Cole and Gaeth, "Cognitive and Age-Related Differences in the Ability to Use Nutritional Information"; Christine Moorman, "The Effects of Stimulus and Consumer Characteristics on the Utilization of Nutrition Information," *Journal of Consumer Research*, December 1990, pp. 362–374.

125. Pauline M. Ippolito and Alan D. Mathios, "New Food Labeling Regulations and the Flow of Nutrition Information to Consumers," *Journal of Public Policy and Marketing*, Fall 1993, pp. 118–205; John Sinisi, "New Rules Exact a Heavy Price as Labels Are Recast," *Brandweek*, December 7, 1992, p. 3; Nita Lelyveid, "What's in the Food You Eat," *Austin American Statesman*, May 3, 1994, pp. A7, A13.

126. See John C. Kozup, Elizabeth H. Creyer, and Scot Burton, "Making Healthful Food Choices," *Journal of Marketing Research*, April 2003, pp. 19–34; Scot Burton and Abhijit Biswas, "Preliminary Assessment of Changes in Labels Required by the Nutrition Labeling and Education Act of 1990," *Journal of Consumer Affairs*, Summer 1993, pp. 127–144; Scot Burton, Abhijit Biswas, and Richard Netermeyer, "Effects of Alternative Nutrition Label Formats and Nutrition Reference Information on Consumer Perceptions, Comprehension, and Product Evaluations," *Journal of Public Policy and Marketing*, Spring 1994, pp. 36–47.

127. Christine Moorman, "A Quasi Experiment to Assess the Consumer and Information Determinants of Nutrition Information Processing Activities: The Case of the Nutrition Labeling and Education Act," *Journal of Public Policy and Marketing*, Spring 1996, pp. 28–44.

128. Mitra, Hastak, Ford, and Ringold, "Can the Educationally Disadvantaged Interpret the FDA-Mandated Nutrition Facts Panel"; Gary T. Ford, Manoj Hastak, Anu Mitra, and Debra Jones Ringold, "Can Consumers Interpret Nutrition Information in the Presence of a Health Claim? A Laboratory Investigation," *Journal of Public Policy and Marketing*, Spring 1996, pp. 16–27.

129. Scott B. Keller, Mike Landry, Jeanne Olson, Anne M. Velliquette, Scot Burton, and J. Craig Andrews, "The Effects of Nutrition Package Claims, Nutrition Facts Panels, and Motivation to Process Information on Consumer Product Evaluations," *Journal of Public Policy and Marketing*, Fall 1997, pp. 256–269.

130. Madhubalan Viswanathan, "The Influence of Summary Information on the Usage of Nutrition Information," *Journal of Public Policy and Marketing*, Spring 1994, pp. 48–60: Alan S. Levey, Sara B. Fein, and Raymond E. Schucker, "Performance Characteristics of Seven Nutrition Label Formats," *Journal of Public Policy and Marketing*, Spring 1996, pp. 1–15.

131. See Madhubalan Viswanathan and Manoj Hastak, "The Role of Summary Information in Facilitating Consumers' Comprehension of Nutrition Information," *Journal of Public Policy & Marketing*, Fall 2002, pp. 305–318; and Michael J. Barone, Randall L. Rose, Kenneth C. Manning, and Paul W. Miniard, "Another Look at the Impact of Reference Information on Consumer Impressions of Nutrition Information," *Journal of Public Policy and Marketing*, Spring 1996, pp. 55–62.

132. Anna Wilde Mathews and Sarah Ellison, "The FDA Eases Its Stance on Old Nutritional Nemesis; 'It Didn't Seem to Work,'" *Wall Street Journal*, August 11, 2004, pp. B1, B10.

133. Dennis L. McNeill and William L. Wilkie, "Public Policy and Consumer Information: Impacts of the New Energy Labels," *Journal of Consumer Research*, June 1979, pp. 1–11; R. Bruce Hutton and William L. Wilkie, "Life Cycle Cost: A New Form of Consumer Information," *Journal of Consumer Research*, March 1980, pp. 349–360.

134. Fred W. Morgan and Dana I. Avrunin, "Consumer Conduct in Product Liability Litigation," *Journal of Consumer Research*, June 1982, pp. 47–55.

135. Judith S. Riddle, "New Alcohol-Reduced Remedies Put P&G in Re-Marketing Hotseat," *Brandweek*, April 12, 1993, pp. 1, 6.

136. Michael J. McCarthy, "A Design with Twists and Turns," *Wall Street Journal*, February 3, 2000, pp. B1, B4.

137. "Answers Still Elusive in Tire Crisis," *Wall Street Journal*, September 15, 2000, pp. B1, B4.

138. Joseph Pereira, "Toy Story: Industry Strikes Back against Safety Sleuth," *Wall Street Journal*, November 17, 1997, pp. B1, B15.

139. Rob Norton, "Why Airbags Are Killing Kids," *Fortune*, August 19, 1996, p. 40.

140. Asra Q. Nomani, "Regulators Plan Safety Rules for Child Seats," *Wall Street Journal*, February 13, 1997, pp. B1, B12.

141. E. Scott Geller, "Seat Belt Psychology," *Psychology Today*, May 1985, pp. 12–13.

142. Banwari Mittal, "Achieving Higher Seat Belt Usage: The Role of Habit in Bridging the Attitude-Behavior Gap," *Journal of Applied Social Psychology*, September 1988, pp. 993–1016; David L. Ryan and Guy A. Bridgeman, "Judging the Roles of Legislation, Education, and Offsetting Behavior in Seat Belt Use: A Survey and New Evidence from Alberta," *Canadian Public Policy*, March 1992, pp. 27–46.
143. Oscar Suris, "General Motors Plans to Recall Million Vehicles," *Wall Street Journal*, February 5, 1996; Asra Q. Nomani, "Chrysler Effort to Fix Minivans Has Slow Start," *Wall Street Journal*, February 12, 1996, p. B2; Nichole M. Christain and Asra Q. Nomani, "Ford Recalls 8.7 Million Cars to Fix Ignitions," *Wall Street Journal*, April 26, 1996, pp. B1, B2.
144. George C. Jackson and Fred W. Morgan, "Responding to Recall Requests: A Strategy for Managing Goods Withdrawals," *Journal of Public Policy and Marketing*, vol. 7, 1988, pp. 152–165.
145. Laura Johannes and Steve Stecklow, "Withdrawal of Redux Spotlights Predicament FDA Faces on Obesity," *Wall Street Journal*, September 16, 1997, pp. A1, A10; Bruce Ingersoll, "FDA Proposes to Force Seldane off the Market," *Wall Street Journal*, January 14, 1997, pp. B1, B8.
146. Walter Guzzardi, "The Mindless Pursuit of Safety," *Fortune*, April 9, 1979, pp. 54–64; Mowen, *Consumer Behavior.*
147. James F. Engel, Roger D. Blackwell, and Paul W. Miniard, *Consumer Behavior*, 8th ed. (Fort Worth, Tex.: Dryden Press, 1995).
148. Mark R. Lehto and James M. Miller, "The Effectiveness of Warning Labels," *Journal of Product Liability*, vol. 11, no. 3, 1988, pp. 225–270.
149. James R. Bettman, John W. Payne, and Richard Staelin, "Cognitive Considerations in Designing Labels for Presenting Risk Information," *Journal of Public Policy and Marketing*, vol. 5, 1986, pp. 1–28.
150. Kenneth C. Schneider, "Prevention of Accidental Poisoning through Package and Label Design," *Journal of Consumer Research*, September 1977, pp. 67–75.
151. Richard Staelin, "The Effects of Consumer Education on Consumer Product Safety Behavior," *Journal of Consumer Research*, June 1978, pp. 30–40.
152. Vanessa O'Connell, "Gun Makers to Push Use of Gun Locks," *Wall Street Journal*, May 9, 2001, p. B12.
153. Miriam Jordan, "Electric Buses Put to Test in Nepal," *Wall Street Journal*, May 31, 2000, pp. B1, B4.
154. Stacy Kravetz, "Dry Cleaners' New Wrinkle: Going Green," *Wall Street Journal*, June 3, 1998, pp. B1, B15.
155. Jacquelyn Ottman, "Use Less, Make It More Durable, and Then Take It Back," *Marketing News*, December 7, 1992, p. 13.
156. Seema Nayyar, "Refillable Pouch a Lotions First," *Brandweek*, October 26, 1992, p. 3; Seema Nayyar, "L&F Cleaner Refills Greener," *Brandweek*, September 14, 1992, p. 5; Belk, "Daily Life in Romania."
157. "Retailers Set to Trial Greener Packaging," *Marketing*, March 23, 2005, p. 13.
158. Howard Schlossberg, "'Project Clean Mail' Would Fine Tune Direct Marketing," *Marketing News*, September 14, 1992, pp. 18–19.
159. Shirley Taylor and Peter Todd, "Understanding Household Garbage Reduction: A Test of an Integrated Model," *Journal of Public Policy and Marketing*, Fall 1995, pp. 192–204.
160. Anna Peltola, "Finland: Nokia Hopes for Biodegradable Phones in Few Years," *Reuters English News Service*, June 14, 2001, *www.reuters.com*.
161. Kathleen Deveny, "For Growing Band of Shoppers, Clean Means Green," *Wall Street Journal*, April 6, 1993, pp. B1, B7.
162. Charles H. Schwepker and T. Bettina Cornwell, "An Examination of Ecologically Concerned Consumers and Their Intention to Purchase Ecologically Packaged Products," *Journal of Public Policy and Marketing*, Fall 1991, pp. 77–101.
163. Linda F. Alwitt and Robert E. Pitts, "Predicting Purchase Intentions for an Environmentally Sensitive Product," *Journal of Consumer Psychology*, vol. 5, no. 1, 1996, pp. 49–64.
164. John A. McCarty and L. J. Shrum, "The Influence of Individualism, Collectivism, and Locus of Control on Environmental Beliefs and Behavior," *Journal of Public Policy and Marketing*, vol. 20, no. 1, Spring 2001, pp. 93–104.
165. Allan Glass, "Does a Green Message Still Belong on Your Package?" *Brandweek*, October 19, 1992, pp. 26, 28.
166. Pam Scholder Ellen, Joshua Lyle Wiener, and Cathy Cobb-Walgren, "The Role of Perceived Consumer Effectiveness in Motivating Environmentally Conscious Behaviors," *Journal of Public Policy and Marketing*, Fall 1991, pp. 102–117; Thomas C. Kinnear, James R. Taylor, and Sadrudin A. Ahmed, "Ecologically Concerned Consumers: Who Are They?" *Journal of Marketing*, April 1972, pp. 46–57.
167. Jacquelyn Ottman, "Environmentalism Will Be the Trend of the 90s," *Marketing News*, December 7, 1992, p. 13.
168. Cheryl Powell, "The Green Movement Sows Demand for Ecofurniture," *Wall Street Journal*, August 2, 1994, pp. B1, B2.
169. Russell Belk, John Painter, and Richard Semenik, "Preferred Solutions to the Energy Crisis as a Function of Causal Attributions," *Journal of Consumer Research*, December 1981, pp. 306–312.
170. C. Dennis Anderson and John D. Claxton, "Barriers to Consumer Choice of Energy-Efficient Products," *Journal of Consumer Research*, September 1982, pp. 163–170.
171. Rik Peters, Tammo Bijmo, H. Fred van Raaij, and Mark de Kruijk, "Consumers' Attributions of Proenvironmental Behavior, Motivation, and Ability to Self and Others," *Journal of Public Policy and Marketing*, Fall 1998, pp. 215–225.
172. Dorothy Leonard-Barton, "Voluntary Simplicity Lifestyles and Energy Conservation," *Journal of Consumer Research*, December 1981, pp. 243–252.
173. Louise A. Helsop, Lori Moran, and Amy Cousineau, "'Consciousness' in Energy Conservation Behavior:

An Exploratory Study," *Journal of Consumer Research*, December 1981, pp. 299–305; Gregory M. Pickett, Norman Kangun, and Stephen J. Grove, "Is There a General Conserving Consumer?" *Journal of Public Policy and Marketing*, Fall 1993, pp. 234–243.

174. Marta Tienda and Osei-Mensah Aborampah, "Energy-Related Adaptations in Low-Income Nonmetropolitan Wisconsin Counties," *Journal of Consumer Research*, December 1981, pp. 265–270.
175. Theo M. M. Verhallen and W. Fred van Raaij, "Household Behavior and the Use of Natural Gas for Heating," *Journal of Consumer Research*, December 1981, pp. 253–257.
176. Gordon H. G. McDougall, John D. Claxton, J. R. Brent Ritchie, and C. Dennis Anderson, "Consumer Energy Research: A Review," *Journal of Consumer Research*, December 1981, pp. 343–354.
177. Ibid; Dennis L. McNeill and William L. Wilkie, "Public Policy and Consumer Information: Impact of the New Energy Labels," *Journal of Consumer Research*, June 1979, pp. 1–11.
178. R. Bruce Hutton and Dennis L. McNeill, "The Value of Incentives in Stimulating Energy Conservation," *Journal of Consumer Research*, December 1981, pp. 291–298; Peter D. Bennett and Noreen Klein Moore, "Consumers' Preferences for Alternative Energy Conservation Policies: A Trade-off Analysis," *Journal of Consumer Research*, December 1981, pp. 313–321; Robert E. Pitts and James L. Wittenbach, "Tax Credits as a Means of Influencing Consumer Behavior," *Journal of Consumer Research*, December 1981, pp. 335–338; Bruce R. Hutton, Gary A. Mauser, Pierre Filiatrault, and Olli T. Ahtola, "Effects of Cost Related Feedback on Consumer Knowledge and Consumption Behavior: A Field Experiment," *Journal of Consumer Research*, December 1986, pp. 327–336; Jeannet H. van Houwelingen and W. Fred van Raaij, "The Effect of Goal-Setting and Daily Electronic Feedback on In-Home Energy Use," *Journal of Consumer Research*, June 1989, pp. 98–105.
179. Edward Cundiff and Marye Hilger Tharpe, *Marketing in the International Environment*, 2nd ed. (Englewood Cliffs, N.J.: Prentice-Hall, 1988).
180. For more on such international organizations, see Paula Fitzgerald Bone and Karen Russo France, "International Harmonization of Food and Nutrition Regulation: The Good and the Bad," *Journal of Public Policy & Marketing*, Spring 2003, pp. 102–110.
181. "French Government Announces Crackdown on Racy Ads; DDB Ad Pulled," *Advertising Age*, May 2, 2001, *www.adage.com.*
182. Gary M. Armstrong and Merrie Brucks, "Dealing with Children's Advertising: Public Policy Issues and Alternatives," *Journal of Public Policy and Marketing*, vol. 7, 1988, pp. 98–113.
183. Marian Burros, "It'd Be Easier if SpongeBob Were Hawking Broccoli," *New York Times*, January 12, 2005, p. F5.
184. Ross D. Petty, "Advertising Law in the United States and European Union," *Journal of Public Policy and Marketing*, Spring 1997, pp. 2–13.
185. Matthew Rose, "French Court Blocks Philip Morris Ads That Liken Passive Smoke to Cookies," *Wall Street Journal*, June 27, 1996, B1.
186. "Nielsen in Dutch over Ad," *Austin American Statesman*, April 3, 1999, p. B8.
187. Jean-Pierre Jeannet and Hubert D. Hennessey, *Global Marketing Strategies* (Boston: Houghton Mifflin, 1992); Vern Terpstra and Ravi Sarathy, *International Marketing*, 5th ed. (Chicago: Dryden Press, 1991).
188. Joan Stephenson, "Global Antismoking Measures," *Journal of the American Medical Association*, March 13, 2002, p. 1255; Conor Dignam and Mike Leidig, "Big Tobacco Riding High," *Advertising Age Global*, April 2001, p. 4; Julie Wolf and Ernest Beck, "European Union Seems Set to Ban Most Kinds of Tobacco Advertising," *Wall Street Journal*, December 3, 1997, p. B13.
189. Marcia Kunstel and Joseph Albright, "Russia Mourns Assassination of Famous Television Journalist," *Austin American Statesman*, March 4, 1995, p. A16.
190. Laurel Wentz, "Playing by the Same Rules," *Advertising Age*, December 2, 1991, p. S2.
191. Sally D. Goll, "Chinese Officials Attempt to Ban False Ad Claims," *Wall Street Journal*, February 28, 1995, pp. B1, B9.
192. Terpstra and Sarathy, *International Marketing.*
193. Ron Scherer, "Global Effort to Curtail Smoking Hits Milestone," *Christian Science Monitor*, December 2, 2004, p. 3.

CHAPTER 20

1. Peter Lewis, "Taking a Bite Out of Identity Theft," *Fortune*, May 2, 2005, p. 36; David Myron, "Stolen Names, Big Numbers," *American Demographics*, September 2004, pp. 36+; Matt Richtel, "Comcast Says It Will Stop Storing Data on Customers," *New York Times*, February 14, 2002, p. C5; Cliff Saran, "Eli Lilly Case Raises Privacy Fears," *Computer Weekly*, January 31, 2002, p. 6; Pamela Paul, "Mixed Signals," *American Demographics*, July 2001, pp. 45–49; Rebecca Gardyn, "Swap Meet," *American Demographics*, July 2001, pp. 51–55; John Fetto, "Candy for Cookies," *American Demographics*, August 2000, p. 10.
2. Thomas C. O'Guinn and Ronald J. Faber, "Compulsive Buying: A Phenomenological Exploration," *Journal of Consumer Research*, September 1989, pp. 147–157.
3. Ronald Faber, Gary Christenson, Martina DeZwaan, and James Mitchell, "Two Forms of Compulsive Consumption: Comorbidity of Compulsive Buying and Binge Eating," *Journal of Consumer Research*, December 1995, pp. 296–304; O'Guinn and Faber, "Compulsive Buying"; Ronald J. Faber and Thomas C. O'Guinn, "Compulsive Consumption and Credit Abuse," *Journal of Consumer Policy*, March 1988, pp. 97–109; Gilles Valence, Alain D'Astous, and Louis Fortier, "Compulsive Buying: Concept and Measurement," *Journal of Consumer Policy*, December 1988, pp. 419–433; Rajan Nataraajan and Brent G. Goff, "Compulsive Buying: Toward a Reconceptualization," in ed. Floyd W. Rudman, *To Have Possessions: A Handbook on Ownership and*

Property (Corte Madera, Calif.: Select Press, 1991), pp. 307–328; "Compulsive Shopping Could Be Hereditary," *Marketing News*, September 14, 1998, pp. 31; Wayne S. DeSarbo and Elizabeth A. Edwards, "Typologies of Compulsive Buying Behavior: A Constrained Clusterwise Regression Approach," *Journal of Consumer Psychology*, vol. 5, no. 3, 1996, pp. 231–262.

4. Faber and O'Guinn, "Compulsive Consumption and Credit Abuse"; Ronald J. Faber and Thomas C. O'Guinn, "A Clinical Screener for Compulsive Buying," *Journal of Consumer Research*, December 1992, pp. 459–469; O'Guinn and Faber, "Compulsive Buying"; James A. Roberts, "Compulsive Buying among College Students: An Investigation of Its Antecedents, Consequences, and Implications for Public Policy," *Journal of Consumer Affairs*, Winter 1998, pp. 295–319.
5. Hyokjin Kwak, George M. Zinkhan, and Melvin R. Crask, "Diagnostic Screener for Compulsive Buying: Applications to the USA and South Korea," *Journal of Consumer Affairs*, Summer 2003, pp. 161+.
6. "Study Puts Retail Shrinkage at $31 Billion," *Chain Drug Review*, December 16, 2002, p. 3.
7. Daniel McGinn, "Shoplifting: The Five-Finger Fix?" *Newsweek*, December 20, 2004, p. 13; Steven Gray, "Return This (Beeping) Shopping Cart, or Else . . ." *Wall Street Journal*, June 30, 2004, pp. B1–B2.
8. Julia Angwin, "Credit-Card Scams Bedevil E-Stores," *Wall Street Journal*, September 19, 2000, pp. B1, B4; Ronald A. Fullerton and Girish Punj, "Choosing to Misbehave: A Structural Model of Aberrant Consumer Behavior," in eds. Leigh McAlister and Michael Rothschild, *Advances in Consumer Research*, vol. 20 (Provo, Utah: Association for Consumer Research, 1993), pp. 570–574; Ronald A. Fullerton and Girish Punj, "The Unintended Consequences of the Culture of Consumption: A Theory of Consumer Misbehavior," Working paper, University of Hartford, Department of Marketing, 1994; John J. Keller, "Call-Sell Rings Steal Cellular Service," *Wall Street Journal*, March 13, 1992, pp. A5, B3; Jacqueline Simmons, "Hotels Snoop to Stop Guests' Thievery of Everything That Isn't Nailed Down," *Wall Street Journal*, March 17, 1995, pp. B1, B7; Steven Stecklow, "Student Applications for Financial Aid Give Lots of False Answers," *Wall Street Journal*, March 11, 1997, pp. A1, A15; Ronald A. Fullerton and Girish Punj, "The Unintended Consequences of the Culture of Consumption: An Historical-Theoretical Analysis of Consumer Misbehavior," *Consumption, Markets and Culture*, vol. 1, no. 4, 1998, pp. 393–423.
9. Cynthia Ramsaran, "ID Theft Hits Paper Harder," *Bank Systems & Technology*, March 2005, p. 14; Robert P. Libbon, "Datadog," *American Demographics*, July 2001, p. 26.
10. David Myron, "What Uncle Sam Doesn't Know," *American Demographics*, November 2004, pp. 10–11; Dena Cox, Anthony P. Cox, and George P. Moschis, "When Consumer Behavior Goes Bad: An Investigation of Adolescent Shoplifting," *Journal of Consumer Research*, September 1990, pp. 149–159; Fullerton and Punj, "The Unintended Consequences of the Culture of Consumption"; George P. Moschis, Dena S. Cox, and James J. Kellaris, "An Exploratory Study of Adolescent Shoplifting Behavior," in eds. Melanie Wallendorf and Paul Anderson, *Advances in Consumer Research*, vol. 14 (Provo, Utah: Association for Consumer Research, 1987), pp. 526–530.
11. Fullerton and Punj, "The Unintended Consequences of the Culture of Consumption."
12. Cox, Cox, and Moschis, "When Consumer Behavior Goes Bad."
13. Paul Bernstein, "Cheating—The New National Pastime?" *Business*, October–December 1985, pp. 24–33; Fullerton and Punj, "Some Unintended Consequences of the Culture of Consumption."
14. The behavior of consumers using file-sharing technology recalls the behavior of consumers using VCRs to copy movies or TV shows; see similar Hal R. Varian, "In the Clash of Technology and Copyright, File Sharing Is Only the Latest Battleground," *New York Times*, April 7, 2005, p. C2.
15. Fullerton and Punj, "Choosing to Misbehave"; Donald R. Katz, *The Big Store* (New York: Penguin, 1988).
16. Cox, Cox, and Moschis, "When Consumer Behavior Goes Bad"; Moschis, Cox, and Kellaris, "An Exploratory Study of Adolescent Shoplifting Behavior"; Fullerton and Punj, "Some Unintended Consequences of the Culture of Consumption."
17. Katz, *The Big Store.*
18. Cox, Cox, and Moschis, "When Consumer Behavior Goes Bad"; Moschis, Cox, and Kellaris, "An Exploratory Study of Adolescent Shoplifting Behavior."
19. Anthony D. Cox, Dena Cox, Ronald D. Anderson, and George P. Moschis, "Social Influences on Adolescent Shoplifting—Theory, Evidence, and Implications for the Retail Industry," *Journal of Retailing*, Summer 1993, p. 234.
20. John Fetto, "Penny for Your Thoughts," *American Demographics*, September 2000, pp. 8–9.
21. Chok C. Hiew, "Prevention of Shoplifting: A Community Action Approach," *Canadian Journal of Criminology*, January 1981, pp. 57–68.
22. Cox, Cox, and Moschis, "When Consumer Behavior Goes Bad"; Fullerton and Punj, "The Unintended Consequences of the Culture of Consumption"; Fullerton and Punj, "Choosing to Misbehave"; Cox, Cox, Anderson, and Moschis, "Social Influences on Adolescent Shoplifting."
23. Janine Latus Musick, "Keeping Would-Be Thieves at Bay," *Nation's Business*, October 1998, pp. 41–43; Marc Millstein, "Cutting Losses," *Supermarket News*, March 20, 1995, pp. 13–16.
24. McGinn, "Shoplifting: The Five-Finger Fix?"
25. Mark McLaughlin, "Subliminal Tapes Urge Shoppers to Heed the Warning Sounds of Silence: 'Don't Steal,'" *New England Business*, February 1987, pp. 36–38.
26. "Retailers to Tighten up Security," *Retail World*, February 22–26, 1999; Charles Goldsmith, "Less Honor, More Case at Europe Minibars," *Wall Street Journal*, March 22, 1996, pp. B6; Simmons, "Hotels Snoop to Stop Guests' Thievery of Everything That Isn't Nailed Down"; Steve Weinstein, "The Enemy Within," *Progressive Grocer*, May 1994, pp. 175–179.

27. Elizabeth Parks, "Let Fragrance Sales Break out of Their Glass Prison," *Drug Store News*, April 3, 1989, p. 28.

28. William Echikson, "Ticket Madness at the World Cup," *BusinessWeek*, July 13, 1998, p. 126; Joel Engardio, "L.A. Air Bag Thieves May Be Popping up in East County," *Los Angeles Times*, July 1, 1998, p. 1; Ann Marie O'Connon, "Where There's Smoke," *Los Angeles Times*, September 7, 1997, p. A3R.

29. Lisa R. Szykman and Ronald P. Hill, "A Consumer-Behavior Investigation of a Prison Economy," in eds. Janeen Costa Arnold and Russell W. Belk, *Research in Consumer Behavior*, vol. 6 (Greenwich, Conn.: JAI Press, 1993), pp. 231–260; David Bevan, Paul Collier, and Jan Willem Gunning, "Black Markets: Illegality, Information, and Rents," *World Development*, December 1989, pp. 1955–1963.

30. Harvey D. Shapiro, "Buying Miles Is Thrifty—But Iffy," *Los Angeles Times*, March 9, 1995, p. D5.

31. "Hey, Anybody Want a Gun," *The Economist*, May 16, 1998, pp. 47–48; Mark Hosenball and Daniel Klaidman, "A Deadly Mix of Drugs and Firepower," *Newsweek*, April 19, 1999, p. 27.

32. Jonathan Karp, "Awaiting Knockoffs, Indians Buy Black-Market Viagra," *Wall Street Journal*, July 10, 1998, pp. B1, B2; M. B. Sheridan, "Men Around the Globe Lust after Viagra," *Los Angeles Times*, May 26, 1998, p. 1.

33. Ken Bensinger, "Can You Spot the Fake?" *Wall Street Journal*, February 16, 2001, pp. W1, W14.

34. Gordon Fairclough, "Pssst! Wanna Cheap Smoke?" *Wall Street Journal*, December 27, 2002, pp. B1, B4.

35. Elizabeth C. Hirschman, "The Consciousness of Addiction: Toward a General Theory of Compulsive Consumption," *Journal of Consumer Research*, September 1992, pp. 155–179.

36. Christine Gorman, Barbara Dolan, and Glenn Garelik, "Why It's So Hard to Quit Smoking," *Time*, May 30, 1988, p. 131; Gilbert J. Botvin, Catherine J. Goldberg, Elizabeth M. Botvin, and Linda Dusenbury, "Smoking Behavior of Adolescents Exposed to Cigarette Advertising," *Public Health Reports*, March–April 1993, pp. 217–223; James Ryan, Craig Zwerling, and Endel John Orav, "Occupational Risks Associated with Cigarette Smoking: A Prospective Study," *American Journal of Public Health*, January 1992, pp. 29–33; John R. Nelson and Jeanne E. Lukas, "Target: Minorities," *Marketing and Media Decisions*, October 1990, pp. 70–71; Clara Manfreid, Loretta Lacey, Richard Warnecke, and Marianne Buis, "Smoking-Related Behavior, Beliefs, and Social Environment of Young Black Women in Subsidized Public Housing in Chicago," *American Journal of Public Health*, February 1992, pp. 267–272; Tara Parker-Pope, "Health Activists Light into Cigars' Glamorous Image," *Wall Street Journal*, July 8, 1997, pp. B1, B6.

37. Hannah Karp, "The Senior Trip to the Strip," *Wall Street Journal*, April 8, 2005, p. W4.

38. Ronald Gaudia, "Effects of Compulsive Gambling on the Family," *Social Work*, May–June 1987, pp. 254–256.

39. Richard G. Netemeyer, Scot Burton, Leslie K. Cole, Donald A. Williamson, Nancy Zucker, Lisa Bertman, and Gretchen Diefenbach, "Characteristics and Beliefs Associated with Probably Pathological Gambling: A Pilot Study with Implications for the National Gambling Impact and Policy Commission," *Journal of Public Policy and Marketing*, vol. 17, no. 2, Fall 1998, pp. 147–160.

40. Laurence Arnold, "Link to Other Addictions Raises New Questions about Gambling," *Associate Press*, June 12, 2001.

41. Jeffrey N. Weatherly, John M. Sauter, and Brent M. King, "The 'Big Win' and Resistance to Extinction When Gambling," *Journal of Psychology*, November 2004, pp. 495+.

42. United Press International, "High Correlation Found between Gambling Addiction and Crime," *ClariNet Electronic News Service*, December 1, 1992.

43. "High Correlation Found between Gambling Addiction and Crime"; Ricardo Chavira, "The Rise of Teenage Gambling," *Time*, February 25, 1991, p. 78.

44. Patricia B. Sutker and Albert N. Allain Jr., "Issues in Personality Conceptualizations of Addictive Behavior," *Journal of Consulting and Clinical Psychology*, April 1988, pp. 172–182; Alex Blaszczynski, Neil McConaghy, and Anna Frankova, "Boredom Proneness in Pathological Gambling," *Psychological Reports*, August 1990, pp. 35–42; John R. Graham and Virginia E. Strenger, "MMPI Characteristics of Alcoholics: A Review," *Journal of Consulting and Clinical Psychology*, April 1988, pp. 197–205; Robert C. McMahon, David Gersh, and Robert S. Davidson, "Personality and Symptom Characteristics of Continuous vs. Episodic Drinkers," *Journal of Clinical Psychology*, January 1989, pp. 161–168; Robert K. Brooner, Chester W. Schmidt, Linda Felch, and George E. Bigelow, "Antisocial Behavior of Intravenous Drug Abusers: Implications for Diagnosis of Antisocial Personality Disorder," *American Journal of Psychiatry*, April 1992, pp. 482–487; Ralph E. Tarter, "Are There Inherited Behavioral Traits That Predispose to Substance Abuse?" *Journal of Consulting and Clinical Psychology*, February 1988, pp. 189–196; Hirschman, "The Consciousness of Addiction."

45. Kevin Heubusch, "Taking Chances on Casinos," *American Demographics*, May 1997, pp. 35–40; Tom Gorman, "Indian Casinos in Middle of Battle over Slots," *Los Angeles Times*, May 9, 1995, pp. A3, A24; Max Vanzi, "Gambling Industry Studies the Odds," *Los Angeles Times*, May 9, 1995, pp. A3, A24; James Popkin, "America's Gambling Craze," *US News and World Report*, March 14, 1994, pp. 42–45; Iris Cohen Selinger, "The Big Lottery Gamble," *Advertising Age*, May 10, 1993, pp. 22–26; Tony Horwitz, "In a Bible Belt State, Video Poker Mutates into an Unholy Mess," *Wall Street Journal*, December 2, 1997, pp. A1, A13; Rebecca Quick, "For Sports Fans, The Internet Is a Whole New Ball Game," *Wall Street Journal*, September 3, 1998, p. B9; Stephen Braun, "Lives Lost in a River of Debt," *Los Angeles Times*, June 22, 1997, pp. A1, A14–A15.

46. Dan Seligman, "In Defense of Gambling," *Forbes*, June 23, 2003, p. 86.

47. "World Watch," *Wall Street Journal*, April 19, 2005, p. A18.

48. Jeff Harrington, "Booming Online-Gambling Industry Alarms Law-Enforcement, Addiction Experts," *St. Petersburg Times*, April 23, 2001.
49. Joe Ashbrook Nickell, "Datamining: Welcome to Harrah's," *Business 2.0*, April 2002, pp. 48–54.
50. Justin Supon, "Gambling Hotline Braces for Post–Super Bowl Calls," *ClariNet Electronic News Service*, January 27, 1993; Donald Janson, "Two Casinos Post Compulsive Gambler Hot Line," *New York Times*, August 9, 1987, pp. 14, 36.
51. Ron Winslow and Peter Landers, "Obesity: A World-Wide Woe," *Wall Street Journal*, July 1, 2002, pp. B1, B4.
52. Betsy McKay, "The Children's Menu: Do Ads Make Kids Fat?" *Wall Street Journal*, January 27, 2005, pp. B1, B7.
53. Caroline E. Mayer, "Group Takes Aim at Junk-Food Marketing," *Washington Post*, January 7, 2005, p. E3.
54. Nat Ives, "McDonald's Says It's Time to Turn Off the TV," *New York Times*, March 9, 2005, p. C6.
55. Claudia Kalb and Karen Springen, "Pump Up the Family," *Newsweek*, April 25, 2005, pp. 62+.
56. George A. Hacker, "Liquor Advertisements on Television: Just Say No," *Journal of Public Policy and Marketing*, Spring 1998, pp. 139–142; William K. Eaton, "College Binge Drinking Soars, Study Finds," *Los Angeles Times*, June 8, 1994, p. A21; Mike Fuer and Rita Walters, "Mixed Message Hurts Kids: Ban Tobacco, Alcohol Billboards: The Targeting of Children Is Indisputable and Intolerable," *Los Angeles Times*, June 8, 1997, p. M5; Joseph Coleman, "Big Tobacco Still Calls the Shots in Japan," *Marketing News*, August 4, 1997, p. 12.
57. Richard J. Bonnie, "Reducing Underage Drinking: the Role of Law," *Journal of Law, Medicine, and Ethics*, Winter 2004, pp. S38+.
58. "Underage Drinking in the United States: A Status Report, 2004," *Georgetown University Center on Alcohol Marketing and Youth*, February 2005, p. 2; Mindy Sink, "Drinking Deaths Draw Attention to Old Campus Problem," *New York Times*, November 9, 2004, p. A16.
59. "Tobacco Use, Access, and Exposure to Tobacco in Media Among Middle and High School Students, United States, 2004," *Morbidity and Mortality Weekly Report, Centers for Disease Control and Prevention*, April 1, 2005, *www.cdc.gov/mmwr.*
60. Charles S. Clark, "Underage Drinking," *The CQ Researcher*, vol. 2, no. 10, 1992, pp. 219–244; Courtney Leatherman, "College Officials Are Split on Alcohol Policies: Some Seek to End Underage Drinking; Others Try to Encourage 'Responsible Use,'" *Chronicle of Higher Education*, January 31, 1990, pp. A33–A35.
61. Antonia C. Novello, "Alcohol and Tobacco Advertising," *Vital Speeches of the Day*, May 15, 1993, pp. 454–459.
62. Ibid; K. M. Cummings, E. Sciandra, T. F. Pechacek, J. P. Pierce, L. Wallack, S. L. Mills, W. R. Lynn, and S. E. Marcus, "Comparison of the Cigarette Brand Preferences of Adult and Teenaged Smokers—United States, 1989, and 10 U.S. Communities, 1988 and 1990," *Journal of the American Medical Association*, April 8, 1992, p. 1893.
63. "Tobacco Use, Access, and Exposure to Tobacco in Media Among Middle and High School Students."
64. Clark, "Underage Drinking;" Erica H. van Roosmalen and Susan A. McDaniel, "Peer Group Influence as a Factor in Smoking Behavior of Adolescents," *Adolescence*, Winter 1989, pp. 801–816; Nancy Twitchell Murphy and Cynthia J. Price, "The Influence of Self-Esteem, Parental Smoking, and Living in a Tobacco Production Region on Adolescent Smoking Behaviors," *Journal of School Health*, December 1988, pp. 401–450; Botvin et al., "Smoking Behavior of Adolescents Exposed to Cigarette Advertising"; Sarah A. McGraw, Kevin W. Smith, Jean J. Schensul, and J. Emilio Carrillo, "Sociocultural Factors Associated with Smoking Behavior by Puerto Rican Adolescents in Boston," *Social Science Medicine*, December 1991, pp. 1355–1364.
65. Cornelia Pechmann and Susan J. Knight, "An Experimental Investigation of the Joint Effects of Advertising and Peers on Adolescents' Beliefs and Intentions About Cigarette Consumption," *Journal of Consumer Research*, June 2002, pp. 5+.
66. Joan Ryan, "Steroids? Alcohol Is the Real Problem," *San Francisco Chronicle*, March 17, 2005, *www.sfgate.com;* Vanessa O'Connell and Christopher Lawton, "Alcohol TV Ads Ignite Bid to Curb," *Wall Street Journal*, December 18, 2002, p. B2; Associated Press, "Study: Kids Remember Beer Ads," *ClariNet Electronic News Service*, February 11, 1994; Fara Warner, "Cheers! It's Happy Hour in Cyberspace," *Wall Street Journal*, March 15, 1995, pp. B1, B4; Kirk Davidson, "Looking for Abundance of Opposition to TV Liquor Ads," *Marketing News*, January 6, 1997, pp. 4, 30; Rosanna Tamburri, "Dodging Bans on Cigarette Ads in Canada," *Wall Street Journal*, December 27, 1994, p. B5.
67. See Alyse R. Lancaster and Kent M. Lancaster, "Teenage Exposure to Cigarette Advertising in Popular Consumer Magazines," *Journal of Advertising*, Fall 2003, pp. 69–76; Dean M. Krugman and Karen Whitehill King, "Teenage Exposure to Cigarette Advertising in Popular Consumer Magazines," *Journal of Public Policy and Marketing*, vol. 19, no. 2, Fall 2000, pp. 183–188; Gordon Fairclough, "Are Cigarette Ads in Magazines Angling for Teens?" *Wall Street Journal*, May 17, 2000, pp. B1, B4.
68. "RJR Must Reduce Profile in Teen Pubs," *Adweek Online*, December 23, 2004, n.p.
69. Fara Warner, "Tobacco Brands Outmaneuver Asian Ad Bans," *Wall Street Journal*, August 6, 1996, pp. B1, B3; Eben Shapiro, "Cigarette Makers Outfit Smokers in Icons Eluding Warning and Enraging Activists," *Wall Street Journal*, August 27, 1993, p. B1; Botvin et al., "Smoking Behavior of Adolescents Exposed to Cigarette Advertising"; Novello, "Alcohol and Tobacco Advertising"; Bruce Horovitz, "Most Advertised Cigarettes Are Teens' Choice, Study Says," *Los Angeles Times*, March 13, 1992, p. D4; Cummings et al., "Comparison of the Cigarette Brand Preferences of Adult and Teenaged Smokers."
70. Betsy Spethmann, "Five States Sue RJR," *Promo*, May 2001, p. 22.
71. Vanessa O'Connell, "U.S. Liquor Sellers Want to Run TV Ads," *Wall Street Journal*, May 7, 2001, p. B6; Vanessa O'Connell, "Bacardi Brings Out Bottle in Cable TV Ad for Amaretto," *Wall Street Journal*, April 30, 2001, p. B8.

72. Arch G. Woodside, "Advertising and Consumption of Alcoholic Beverages," *Journal of Consumer Psychology,* vol. 8, no. 2, 1999, pp. 167–186.

73. Elizabeth M. Botvin, Gilbert J. Botvin, John L. Michela, Eli Baker, and Anne D. Filazolla, "Adolescent Smoking Behavior and the Recognition of Cigarette Advertisements," *Journal of Applied Social Psychology,* November 1991, pp. 919–932; Botvin et al., "Smoking Behavior of Adolescents Exposed to Cigarette Advertising"; Richard W. Pollay, S. Siddarth, Michael Siegel, Anne Hadix, Robert K. Merritt, Gary A. Giovino, and Michael P. Eriksen, "The Last Straw? Cigarette Advertising and Realized Market Shares among Youths and Adults, 1979–1993," *Journal of Marketing,* April 1996, pp. 1–16; Joseph DiFranza, John W. Richards, Paul M. Paulman, Nancy Wolf-Gillespie, Christopher Fletcher, Robert D. Jaffe, and David Murray, "RJR Nabisco's Cartoon Camel Promotes Camel Cigarettes to Children," *Journal of the American Medical Association,* December 11, 1991, p. 3149; Cummings et al., "Comparison of the Cigarette Brand Preferences of Adult and Teenaged Smokers."

74. Kathleen J. Kelly, Michael D. Slater, and David Karan, "Image Advertisements' Influence on Adolescents' Perceptions of the Desirability of Beer and Cigarettes," *Journal of Public Policy & Marketing,* Fall 2002, pp. 295–304.

75. Richard W. Pollay and Ann M. Lavack, "The Targeting of Youths by Cigarette Marketers: Archival Evidence on Trial," in eds. Leigh McAlister and Michael Rothschild, *Advances in Consumer Research,* vol. 20 (Provo, Utah: Association for Consumer Research, 1993), pp. 266–271.

76. See Kathleen J. Kelly, Michael D. Slater, David Karan, and Liza Hunn, "The Use of Human Models and Cartoon Characters in Magazine Advertisements for Cigarettes, Beer, and Nonalcoholic Beverages," *Journal of Public Policy and Marketing,* vol. 19, no. 2, Fall 2000, pp. 189–200.

77. Richard Morgan, "Is Old Joe Taking Too Much Heat?" *Adweek,* March 16, 1992, p. 44.

78. Reuters, "Joe Camel Doesn't Make Kids Smoke—RJR Funded Survey," *ClariNet Electronic News Service,* February 21, 1994.

79. Clark, "Underage Drinking."

80. Stuart Elliott, "Film's Beer Ads Anger Alcohol Policy Group," *New York Times,* June 23, 2004, p. C5.

81. Stuart Elliott, "Hoping to Show It Can Police Itself, the Liquor Industry Takes the Wraps Off Its Review Board," *New York Times,* March 8, 2005, p. C3.

82. Vanessa O'Connell, "Tobacco Makers Want Cigarettes Cut From Films," *Wall Street Journal,* June 13, 2004, pp. B1, B4.

83. Debra L. Scammon, Robert N. Mayer, and Ken R. Smith, "Alcohol Warnings: How Do You Know When You've Had One Too Many?" *Journal of Public Policy and Marketing,* Spring 1991, pp. 214–228; Michael B. Mazis, Louis A. Morris, and John L. Swasy, "An Evaluation of the Alcohol Warning Label: Initial Survey Results," *Journal of Public Policy and Marketing,* Spring 1991, pp. 229–241; Novello, "Alcohol and Tobacco Advertising"; Richard Gibson and Marj Charlier, "Anheuser Leads the Way in Listing Alcohol Levels," *Wall Street Journal,* March 11, 1993, pp. B1, B2; Richard J. Fox, Dean M. Krugman, James E. Fletcher, and Paul M. Fischer, "Adolescents' Attention to Beer and Cigarette Print Ads and Associated Product Warnings," *Journal of Advertising,* Fall 1998, pp. 57–68.

84. David P. MacKinnon, Rhonda M. Williams-Avery, Kathryn L. Wilcox, and Andrea M. Fenaughty, "Effects of the Arizona Alcohol Warning Poster," *Journal of Public Policy and Marketing,* vol. 18, no. 1, Spring 1999, pp. 77–88.

85. Cornelia Pechmann and Chuan-Fong Shih, "Smoking Scenes in Movies and Antismoking Advertisements Before Movies: Effects on Youth," *Journal of Marketing,* vol. 63, July 1999, pp. 1–13.

86. Debbie Treise, Joyce M. Wolburg, and Cele C. Otnes, "Understanding the 'Social Gifts' of Drinking Rituals: an Alternative Framework for PSA Developers," *Journal of Advertising,* vol. 28, no. 2, Summer 1999, pp. 17–31.

87. U.S. Department of Health and Human Services, as cited in Lague et al., "How Thin Is Too Thin?" *People,* September 20, 1993, pp. 74–80.

88. Michael Fay and Christopher Price, "Female Body-Shape in Print Advertisements and the Increase in Anorexia Nervosa," *European Journal of Marketing,* December 1994, pp. 5–19.

89. Isabel Reynolds, "Japan: Feature—Eating Disorders Plague Young Japanese," *Reuters,* June 20, 2001, *www.reuters.com.*

90. Catherine Fitzpatrick, "How Buff Is Enough? Reality Check Is In the Male," *Milwaukee Journal Sentinel,* June 24, 2001, p. 1-L.

91. Laura Landro, "The Informed Patient: Amid Focus on Obesity and Diet, Anorexia, Bulimia Are on the Rise," *Wall Street Journal,* March 30, 2004, p. D1.

92. R. Freedman, *Beauty Bound* (Lexington, Mass.: D.C. Heath, 1986).

93. P. S. Powers, *Obesity: The Regulation of Weight* (Baltimore, Md.: Williams and Wilkins, 1980); A. Furnham and N. Alibhai, "Cross-Cultural Differences in the Perception of Female Body Shapes," *Psychological Medicine,* November 1983, pp. 829–837.

94. See also Debra Lynn Stephens, Ronald P. Hill, and Cynthia Hanson, "The Beauty Myth and Female Consumers: The Controversial Role of Advertising," *Journal of Consumer Affairs,* Summer 1994, pp. 137–154.

95. Leon Festinger, "A Theory of Social Comparison Processes," *Human Relations,* May 1954, pp. 117–140.

96. Mary C. Martin and James W. Gentry, "Stuck in the Model Trap: The Effects of Beautiful Models in Ads on Female Pre-Adolescents and Adolescents," *Journal of Advertising,* Summer 1997, pp. 19–33.
Richins, "Social Comparison and the Idealized Images of Advertising," *Journal of Consumer Research,* June 1991, pp. 71–83; Richard W. Pollay, "The Distorted Mirror: Reflections on the Unintended Consequences of Advertising," *Journal of Marketing,* April 1986, pp. 18–36; Lague et al., "How Thin Is Too Thin?"

97. Christy Karras, "Study Shows Link Between Fitness Magazines and Eating Disorders," *Associated Press Newswires*, June 20, 2001.

98. Marilyn Gardner, "Slim But Curvy: The Pursuit of Ideal Beauty," *Christian Science Monitor*, January 24, 2001, p. 16.

99. Charles S. Gulas and Kim McKeage, "Extending Social Comparison: An Examination of the Unintended Consequences of Idealized Advertising Imagery," *Journal of Advertising*, vol. 29, no. 2, Summer 2000, pp. 17–28.

100. Calmetta Y. Coleman, "Can't Be Too Thin, but Plus-Size Models Get More Work Now," *Wall Street Journal*, May 3, 1999, pp. A1, A10.

101. "Fashion Scoops: I'm a Barbie Girl . . . Plus-Size Parade," *WWD*, March 11, 2005, p. 23.

102. Sally Goll Beatty, "Women's Views of Their Lives Aren't Reflected by Advertisers," *Wall Street Journal*, December 19, 1995, p. B2.

103. For more about the role of hope, see Deborah J. MacInnis and Gustavo E. de Mello, "The Concept of Hope and Its Relevance to Product Evaluation and Choice," *Journal of Marketing Research*, January 2005, pp. 1–14.

104. M. Joseph Sirgy, Dong-Jin Lee, Rustan Kosenko, H. Lee Meadow, Don Rahtz, et al., "Does Television Viewership Play a Role in the Perception of Quality of Life?" *Journal of Advertising*, Spring 1998, pp. 125–143; Pollay, "The Distorted Mirror: Reflections on the Unintended Consequences of Advertising," Russell W. Belk and Richard W. Pollay, "Images of Ourselves: The Good Life in Twentieth Century Advertising," *Journal of Consumer Research*, March 1985, pp. 887–897; Russell W. Belk, "Materialism: Trait Aspects of Living in a Material World," *Journal of Consumer Research*, December 1985, pp. 265–280; Mary Yoko Brannen, "Cross-Cultural Materialism: Commodifying Culture in Japan," in eds. Floyd Rudmin and Marsha L. Richins, *Meaning, Measure, and Morality of Materialism* (Provo, Utah: Association for Consumer Research, 1992), pp. 167–180; Güliz Ger and Russell W. Belk, "Cross-Cultural Differences in Materialism," *Journal of Economic Psychology*, February 1996, pp. 55–77; Marsha L. Richins, "Media, Materialism, and Human Happiness," in eds. Melanie Wallendorf and Paul Anderson, *Advances in Consumer Research*, vol. 14 (Provo, Utah: Association for Consumer Research, 1986), pp. 352–356; Thomas C. O'Guinn and Ronald J. Faber, "Mass Mediated Consumer Socialization: Non-Utilitarian and Dysfunctional Outcomes," in eds. Melanie Wallendorf and Paul Anderson, *Advances in Consumer Research*, vol. 14 (Provo, Utah; Association for Consumer Research, 1987), pp. 473–477; Ronald J. Faber and Thomas C. O'Guinn, "Expanding the View of Consumer Socialization: A Non-Utilitarian Mass Mediated Perspective," in eds. Elizabeth C. Hirschman and Jagdish N. Sheth, *Research in Consumer Behavior*, vol. 3 (Greenwich, Conn.: JAI Press, 1988), pp. 49–78.

105. Richins, "Media, Materialism and Human Happiness," in eds. Melanie Wallendorf and Paul Anderson, *Advances in Consumer Research*, vol. 14 (Provo, Utah: Association for Consumer Research, 1987), 352–356.

106. Aaron C. Ahuvia and Nancy Y. Wong, "Personality and Values Based Materialism: Their Relationship and Origins," *Journal of Consumer Psychology*, 2002, pp. 389–402; Marvin E. Goldberg, Gerald J. Gorn, Laura A. Peracchio, and Gary Bamossy, "Understanding Materialism Among Youth," *Journal of Consumer Psychology*, 2003, pp. 278–288.

107. Goldberg, Gorn, Peracchio, and Bamossy, "Understanding Materialism Among Youth."

108. Noel C. Paul, *"Branded for Life?" Christian Science Monitor, April 1, 2002, www.csmonitor.com/2002/0401/p15s02-wmcn.html.*

109. Tracie Rozhon, "Born with a Silver Spoon? No, That's So Ordinary," *New York Times*, April 17, 2005, sec. 3, p. 7.

110. Richins, "Media, Materialism, and Human Happiness."

111. See for example James M. Hunt, Jerome B. Kernan, and Deborah J. Mitchell, "Materialism as Social Cognition: People, Possessions, and Perception," *Journal of Consumer Psychology*, vol. 5, no. 1, 1996, pp. 65–83.

112. Russell W. Belk, "The Third World Consumer Culture," in ed. Jagdish N. Sheth, *Research in Marketing* (Greenwich, Conn.: JAI Press, 1988), pp. 103–127.

113. Liesl Schillinger, "Barbski," *New Republic*, September 20 and 27, 1993, pp. 10–11.

114. Lynn T. Lovdal, "Sex Role Messages in Television Commercials: An Update," *Sex Roles*, November/December 1989, pp. 715–724; A. E. Courtney and T. Whipple, *Sex Stereotyping in Advertising: An Annotated Bibliography* (Cambridge, Mass.: Marketing Science Institute, 1984).

115. Mary C. Gilly, "Sex Roles in Advertising: A Comparison of Television Advertisements in Australia, Mexico, and the United States," *Journal of Marketing*, April 1988, pp. 75–85.

116. Sandra Yin, "Color Bind," *American Demographics*, September 2003, pp. 22+.

117. Robert E. Wilkes and Humberto Valencia, "Hispanics and Blacks in Television Commercials," *Journal of Advertising*, December 1989, pp. 19–26; Helena Czepiec and J. Steven Kelly, "Analyzing Hispanic Roles in Advertising: A Portrait of an Emerging Subculture," in eds. James H. Leigh and Claude R. Martin, *Current Issues and Research in Advertising* (Ann Arbor, Mich.: University of Michigan Press, 1983), pp. 219–240.

118. Yuri Radzievsky, "Untapped Markets: Ethnics in the US," *Advertising Age*, June 21, 1993, p. 26.

119. Tara Parker-Pope, "Ford Puts Blacks in Whiteface, Turns Red," *Wall Street Journal*, February 22, 1996, p. B5.

120. Linda E. Swayne and Alan J. Greco, "The Portrayal of Older Americans in Television Commercials," *Journal of Advertising*, Winter 1987, pp. 47–56; Anthony C. Ursic, Michael L. Ursic, and Virginia L. Ursic, "A Longitudinal Study of the Use of the Elderly in Magazine Advertising," *Journal of Consumer Research*, June 1986, pp. 131–134; Walter Gantz, Howard M. Garenberg, and Cindy K. Rainbow, "Approaching Invisibility: The Portrayal of the Elderly in Magazine Advertisements," *Journal of Communication*, January 1980, pp. 56–60.

121. Michael L. Klassen, Cynthia R. Jasper, and Anne M. Schwartz, "Men and Women: Images of Their Relationships in Magazine Advertisements," *Journal of Advertising Research*, March–April 1993, pp. 30–39; Sally Goll Beatty, "Critics Rail at Racy TV Programs but Ads Are Often the Sexiest Fare," *Wall Street Journal*, May 28, 1996, p. A25; Courtney and Whipple, *Sex Stereotyping in Advertising: An Annotated Bibliography;* Beverly A. Browne, "Gender Stereotypes in Advertising on Children's Television in the 1990s: A Cross National Analysis," *Journal of Advertising*, Spring 1998, pp. 83–96; John B. Ford, Patricia Kramer Voli, Earl D. Honeycutt Jr., and Susan L. Casey, "Gender Role Portrayals in Japanese Advertising: A Magazine Content Analysis," *Journal of Advertising*, Spring 1998, pp. 113–124; Gilly, "Sex Roles in Advertising"; F. L. Geis, V. Brown, J. J. Walstedt, and N. Porter, "TV Commercials as Achievement Scripts for Women," *Sex Roles*, April 1984, pp. 513–525; Sally D. Goll, "Beer Ads in Hong Kong Criticized as Sexist," *Wall Street Journal*, June 19, 1995, p. B4; Cyndee Miller, "Babe-Based Beer Ads Likely to Flourish," *Marketing News*, January 6, 1992, p. 1; Jill Hicks Ferguson, Peggy J. Kreshel, and Spencer F. Tinkham, "In the Pages of *Ms:* Sex Role Portrayals of Women in Advertising," *Journal of Advertising*, December 1990, pp. 40–52; see also Michael Klassen, Cynthia R. Jasper, and Anne M. Schwartz, "Men and Women: Images of Their Relationships in Magazine Advertisements," *Journal of Advertising Research*, March–April 1993, pp. 30–40; Kathy Brown, "The Fine Line between Good Taste and Bad Taste Should Be Thicker Than a String Bikini," *Adweek*, April 27, 1992, p. 52.

122. Michael L. Maynard and Charles R. Taylor, "Girlish Images Across Cultures: Analyzing Japanese versus U.S. *Seventeen* Magazine Ads," *Journal of Advertising*, vol. 28, no. 1, Spring 1999, pp. 39–48.

123. Charles R. Taylor and Barbara B. Stern, "Asian-Americans: Television Advertising and the 'Model Minority' Stereotype," *Journal of Advertising*, Summer 1997, pp. 47–61.

124. Alan Greco, "The Elderly as Communicators," *Journal of Advertising Research*, June–July 1988, pp. 39–45; Kevin Goldman, "Seniors Get Little Respect on Madison Avenue," *Wall Street Journal*, September 20, 1993, p. B4; David B. Wolfe, "The Ageless Market," *American Demographics*, July 1987, pp. 26–29, 55–56; Warren A. French and Richard Fox, "Segmenting the Senior Citizen Market," *Journal of Consumer Marketing*, Winter 1985, pp. 61–74.

125. Thomas Stevenson, "How Are Blacks Portrayed in Business Ads?" *Industrial Marketing Management*, August 1991, pp. 193–200; Susan DeYoung, and F. G. Crane, "Females' Attitudes toward the Portrayal of Women in Advertising: A Canadian Study," *International Journal of Advertising*, Summer 1992, pp. 249–256; Leon Wynter, "Global Marketers Learn to Say No to Bad Ads," *Wall Street Journal*, April 1, 1998, p. B1.

126. Wilkes and Valencia, "Hispanics and Blacks in Television Commercials"; Ursic, Ursic, and Ursic, "A Longitudinal Study of the Use of the Elderly in Magazine Advertising"; Phyllis Furman, "The New Wrinkle in Casting," *Madison Avenue*, October 1985, pp. 66–70.

127. Bruce Horovitz, "Color Them Beautiful—and Visible," *USA Today*, May 2, 2001, p. B1.

128. For a discussion of consumers collecting marketing artifacts featuring African American stereotypes as a tangible way of remembering the cultural or historic context, see Carol M. Motley, Geraldine R. Henderson, and Stacey Menzel Baker, "Exploring Collective Memories Associated with African-American Advertising Memorabilia," *Journal of Advertising*, Spring 2003, pp. 47–57.

129. Nancy A. Reese, Thomas W. Whipple, and Alice E. Courtney, "Is Industrial Advertising Sexist?" *Industrial Marketing Management*, November 1987, pp. 231–241; Cyndee Miller, "Liberation for Women in Ads: Nymphettes, June Cleaver Are Out: Middle Ground Is In," *Marketing News*, August 17, 1992, pp. 1, 3; Cyndee Miller, "Michelob Ads Feature Women—And They're Not Wearing Bikinis," *Marketing News*, March 2, 1992, p. 2.

130. Gary Levin, "Shops Make the Most of Ethnic Niches," *Advertising Age*, September 17, 1990, p. 29.

131. Ruth Simon, "Stop Them from Selling Your Financial Secrets," *Money*, March 1992, pp. 99–110.

132. Ellen Foxman and Paula Kilcoyne, "Information Technology, Marketing Practice, and Consumer Privacy: Ethical Issues," *Journal of Public Policy & Marketing*, Spring 1993, p. 106.

133. Carol Krol, "Consumers Reach the Boiling Point Over Privacy Issues," *Advertising Age*, March 29, 1999, p. 22; "Survey Results Show Consumers Want Privacy," *Direct Marketing*, March 1999, p. 10.

134. Kevin Heubusch, "Big Brother and the Internet," *American Demographics*," February 1997, p. 22.

135. Michael Moss, "A Web CEO's Elusive Goal: Privacy," *Wall Street Journal*, February 7, 2000, p. B1, B6.

136. Kim Bartel Sheehan and Mariea Grubbs Hoy, "Flaming, Complaining, Abstaining: How Online Users Respond to Privacy Concerns," *Journal of Advertising*, vol. 28, no. 3, Fall 1999, pp. 37–51; G. Bruce Knecht, "Junk Mail Hater Seeks Profits from Sale of His Name," *Wall Street Journal*, October 13, 1995, pp. B1, B8.

137. Mag Gottlieb, "If Trends Continue, Legislative Nightmare Will Become Reality," *Marketing News*, August 16, 1993, pp. A9–A16; H. Jeff Smith, Sandra J. Milberg, and Sandra J. Burke, "Information Privacy: Measuring Individuals' Concerns about Organizational Practices," *MIS Quarterly*, June 1996, pp. 167–196.

138. "Personal Data on Over 120,000 Tokyo Disney Resort Customers Leaked," *Japan Today*, March 17, 2005, *www.japantoday.com*.

139. Foxman and Kilcoyne, "Information Technology, Marketing Practice, and Consumer Privacy."

140. Gottleib, "If Trends Continue, Legislative Nightmare Will Become Reality."

141. Simon, "Stop Them from Selling Your Financial Secrets."

142. Paula Nichols, "Canadian Privacy Code Shows U.S. the Way," *American Demographics*, September 1993, p. 15.

143. Ann Reilly Dowd, "Protect Your Privacy," *Money*, August 1997, pp. 104–115.

144. Ira Teinowitz, "Do-Not-Call? Few Were to Start With," *Advertising Age,* October 27, 2003, p. 8.

145. "Invasion of Privacy: When Is Access to Information Foul—or Fair?" *Harvard Business Review,* September–October 1993, pp. 154–155.

146. Rebecca Quick, "On-line Groups Are Offering Up Privacy Plans," *Wall Street Journal,* June 22, 1998, pp. B1, B12.

147. Moss, "A Web CEO's Elusive Goal."

148. Robin Sidel and Christopher Conkey, "Security Breach Hits Credit Cards," *Wall Street Journal,* April 14, 2005, pp. D1–D2.

149. N. Craig Smith and Elizabeth Cooper-Martin, "Ethics and Target Marketing: The Role of Product Harm and Consumer Vulnerability," *Journal of Marketing,* July 1997, pp. 1–20; Robert O. Hermann, "The Tactics of Consumer Resistance: Group Action and Marketplace Exit," in eds. Leigh McAlister and Michael Rothschild, *Advances in Consumer Research,* vol. 20 (Provo, Utah: Association for Consumer Research, 1993), pp. 130–134; Lisa Penaloza and Linda L. Price, "Consumer Resistance: A Conceptual Overview," in eds. Leigh McAlister and Michael L. Rothschild, *Advances in Consumer Research,* vol. 20 (Provo, Utah: Association for Consumer Research, 1993), pp. 123–128.

150. Cyndee Miller, "Sexy Sizzle Backfires," *Marketing News,* September 25, 1995, p. 1.

151. Richard W. Pollay, "Media Resistance to Consumer Resistance: On the Stonewalling of 'Adbusters' and Advocates," in eds. Leigh McAlister and Michael Rothschild, *Advances in Consumer Research,* vol. 20 (Provo, Utah: Association for Consumer Research, 1993), p. 129.

152. Scott Kilman, "Campbell Soup Is a Target of Protests Over Biotechnology," *Wall Street Journal,* July 20, 2000, B18.

153. H.J. Cummins, "Judging a Book Cover," *Star-Tribune of the Twin Cities,* January 17, 2001, p. 1E.

154. Jill Gabrielle Klein, N. Craig Smith, and Andrew John, "Why We Boycott: Consumer Motivations for Boycott Participation," *Journal of Marketing Research,* July 2004, pp. 92–109; Sakar Sen, Zeynep Gürhan-Canli, and Vicki Morwitz, "Withholding Consumption: A Social Dilemma Perspective on Consumer Boycotts," *Journal of Consumer Research,* December 2001, pp. 399+.

155. Jonathan Baron, "Consumer Attitudes about Personal and Political Action," *Journal of Consumer Psychology,* vol. 8, no. 3, 1999, pp. 261–275.

156. Stephanie Kang, "Just Do It: Nike Gets Revelatory," *Wall Street Journal,* April 13, 2005, p. 11.

157. "PETA Drops Anti-Petco Campaign," *UPI Newstrack,* April 13, 2005, n.p.

158. Tony Spleen, "OJ Sales Off 6%, Limbaugh Effect?" *Supermarket News,* May 9, 1994, p. 3; Armando Duron, "Boycott Based on 30 Years of Waiting," *Los Angeles Times,* June 19, 1995, p. F3; Cyndee Miller, "Marketers Weigh Effects of Sweatshop Crackdown," *Marketing News, May 12,* 1997, pp. 1, 19.

159. Dennis Rodkin, "Boycott Power," *Mother Jones,* July–August 1991, pp. 18–19; see also Monroe Friedman, "Consumer Boycotts in the United States, 1970–1980: Contemporary Events in Historical Perspective," *Journal of Consumer Affairs,* Summer 1985, pp. 96–117.

160. Todd Putnam and Timothy Muck, "Wielding the Boycott Weapon for Social Change," *Business and Society Review,* Summer 1991, pp. 5–8.

161. David Greenberg, "Boycott Hurts Hotels, But Fails to Advance Negotiations," *Los Angeles Business Journal,* March 21, 2005, p. 6.

162. Rodkin, "Boycott Power."

Glossary

A

Ability The extent to which consumers have the resources (knowledge, intelligence, and money) necessary to make an outcome happen. (3)

Absolute threshold The minimal level of stimulus intensity needed to detect a stimulus. (4)

Accessibility The likelihood that an item will be retrieved from long-term memory. (8, 9)

Accommodation theory The more effort one puts forth in trying to communicate with an ethnic group, the more positive the reaction. (13)

Acculturation Learning how to adapt to a new culture. (13)

Acquisition The process by which a consumer comes to own an offering. (1)

Activities, interests, and opinions (AIOs) The three components of lifestyles. (15)

Actual identity schemas The set of multiple, salient identities that reflect our self-concept. (18)

Actual state The way things actually are. (9)

Adaptability The extent to which the innovation can foster new styles. (17)

Addiction Excessive behavior typically brought on by a chemical dependence. (20)

Additive difference model Compensatory model in which brands are compared by attribute, two brands at a time. (10)

Adoption A purchase of an innovation by an individual consumer or household. (17)

Aesthetic or **hedonic innovation** An innovation tat appeals to our aesthetic pleasure seeking, and/or sensory needs. (17)

Affect Low-level feelings. (11)

Affect referral A simple type of affective tactic where we simply remember our feelings for the product or service. (11)

Affective decision making Decisions based on feelings and emotions. (10)

Affective function How attitudes influence our feelings. (6)

Affective involvement Expending emotional energy and heightened feelings regarding an offering or activity. (3, 6)

Affective responses When consumers generate feelings and images in response to a message. (6)

Affect-related tactics Tactics based on feelings. (11)

Affirmative disclosure Messages that must be altered to provide correct information. (19)

Agentic goals Goals that stress mastery, self-assertiveness, self-efficacy, strength, assertiveness, and no emotion. (13)

Alternative-based strategy Developing an overall liking or disliking for each option in order to make a noncomparable decision. (10)

Ambiguity of information A condition whereby decision options are hard to differentiate. (12)

Anchoring and adjustment process Starting with an initial evaluation and adjusting it with additional information. (10)

Approach-approach conflict A conflict that occurs when a consumer must choose between two or more equally desirable options that fulfill different needs. (3)

Approach-avoidance conflict A conflict that occurs when a given behavior or outcome is seen as both desirable and undesirable because it satisfies some needs but fails to satisfy others. (3)

Aspirational reference group Group that we admire and desire to be like. (16)

Associative reference group Group to which we currently belong. (16)

Attention The process by which an individual allocates part of his or her mental activity to a stimulus. (4)

Attitude A relatively global and enduring evaluation of an object, issue, person, or action. (6)

Attitude accessibility How easily an attitude can be remembered. (6)

Attitude confidence How strongly we hold an attitude. (6)

Attitude persistence How long our attitude lasts. (6)

Attitude resistance How difficult it is to change an attitude. (6)

Attitude specificity How specific the attitude is to the behavior being predicted. (6)

Attitude toward the act (A_{act}) How we feel about doing something. (6)

Attitude toward the ad (A_{ad}) Whether the consumer likes or dislikes an ad. (6)

Attraction effect The adding of an inferior brand to a consideration, which increases the attractiveness of the dominant brand. (10)

Attractiveness A source characteristic that evokes favorable attitudes if a source is physically attractive, likable, familiar, or similar to ourselves. (6)

Attribute determinance Attributes that are both salient and diagnostic. (9)

Attribute-based strategy Making noncomparable choices by making abstract representations of comparable attributes. (10)

Attribute processing Comparing brands, one attribute at a time. (10)

Attribution theory A theory of how individuals find explanations for events. (12)

Autobiographical (or episodic) memory Knowledge we have about ourselves and our personal experiences. (8)

Autonomic decision Decision equally likely to be made by the husband or wife, but not by both. (14)

Availability heuristic Basing judgments on events that are easier to recall. (11)

Avoidance-avoidance conflict A conflict that occurs when the consumer must choose between two equally undesirable options. (3)

B

Baby boomers Individuals born between 1946 and 1964. (13)

Bait-and-switch A technique whereby consumers are attracted by a low price and then enticed to trade up to a more expensive item. (19)

Bargaining A fair exchange of preferences. (14)

Base-rate information How often an event really occurs for all consumers. (11)

Basic level A level of categorization below the superordinate category that contains objects in more refined categories. (5)

Behavior (B) What we do. (6)

Behavioral intention (BI) What we intend to do. (6)

Belief discrepancy When a message is different from what consumers believe. (6)

Black market An illegal market in which consumers pay (often exorbitant amounts) for items not readily available. (20)

Boycott An organized activity in which consumers avoid purchasing products or services from a company whose policies or practices are seen as unfair or unjust. (20)

Brand alliance A marketing strategy in which two companies' brand names are presented together on a single product. (5)

Brand-choice congruence The likelihood that consumers will buy what others in their group buy. (16)

Brand community A specialized group of consumers with a structured set of relationships involving a particular brand, fellow customers of that brand, and the product in use. (16)

Brand extension A marketing strategy in which a firm that markets a product with a well-developed image uses the same brand name but in a different product category. (5, 10)

Brand familiarity Easy recognition of a well-known brand. (11)

Brand image A subset of salient and feeling-related associations stored in a brand schema. (5)

Brand loyalty Buying the same brand repeatedly because of a strong preference. (11)

Brand personality The set of associations that reflect the personification of the brand. (5)

Brand processing Evaluating one brand at a time. (10)

C

Categorization The process of labeling or identifying an object. Involves relating what we perceive in our external environment to what we already know. (5)

Cease-and-desist order An order whereby a company must immediately discontinue all advertising that contains an offending claim. (19)

Central-route processing The attitude formation and change process when effort is high. (6)

Choice tactics Simple rules of thumb used to make low effort decisions. (11)

Chunk A group of items that can be processed as a unit. (8)

Class average Families with an average income in a particular class. (14)

Classic A successful innovation that has a lengthy product life cycle. (17)

Classical conditioning Producing a response to a stimulus by repeatedly pairing it with another stimulus that automatically produces this response. (7)

Closure According to this principle, individuals have a need to organize perceptions so that they form a meaningful whole. (4)

Clustering The grouping of consumers according to common characteristics using statistical techniques. (13)

Co-branding An arrangement by which two brands form a partnership to benefit from the power of two. (11)

Coercive power The extent to which the group has the capacity to deliver rewards and sanctions. (16)

Confirmation bias Tendency to recall information that reinforces or confirms our overall beliefs rather than contradicting them, thereby making our judgment or decision more positive than it should be. (9)

Cognitive complexity The extent to which consumers prefer information to be presented in a simple or complex manner. (3)

Cognitive function How attitudes influence our thoughts. (6)

Cognitive involvement Interest in thinking about and processing information related to one's goal. (3)

Cognitive models The process by which consumers combine items of information about attributes to reach a decision. (10)

Cognitive responses Thoughts we have in response to a communication. (6)

Cognitive style Preferences for how information is received (e.g., visually or verbally). (3)

Communal goals Goals that stress affiliation and fostering harmonious relations with others, submissiveness, emotionality, and home oriented. (13)

Comparative messages Messages that make direct comparisons to competitors. (6)

Compatible The extent to which an innovation fits with existing needs, values, norms, or behaviors. (17)

Compensatory consumption The comsumer behavior of buying products or services to offset frustrations or difficulties in life. (14)

Compensatory eating Making up for lack of social contact or depression by eating. (13)

Compensatory model A mental cost-benefit analysis model to make a decision. (10)

Compliance Doing what the group or social influencer asks. (16)

Comprehension The process of deepening understanding. Involves using prior knowledge to understand more about what we have categorized. (5)

Compulsive consumption An irresistible urge to perform an irrational consumption act. (20)

Computerized Status Index (CSI) A modern index used to determine social class through education, occupation, residence, and income. (14)

Concession Giving in on some points to get what one wants in other areas. (14)

Concreteness The extent to which a stimulus is capable of being imagined. (4)

Confirmation bias The greater likelihood of being able to recall things consistent with our beliefs. (9)

Conformity Doing what others in the group do. (16)

Conjoint analysis A research technique to determine the relative importance and appeal of different levels of an offering's attributes. (2)

Conjunctive model A noncompensatory model that sets minimum cutoffs to reject "bad" options. (10)

Conjunctive probability assessment Estimating the extent two events will occur together. (10)

Connative function How attitudes influence our behavior. (6)

Connectedness function The use of products as symbols of our personal connections to significant people, events, or experiences. (18)

Conservation behavior Consumer preservation of natural resources. (19)

Consideration or **evoked set** The subset of brands evaluated when making a choice. (9, 10)

Conspicuous consumption The acquisition and display of goods and services to show off one's status. (14)

Conspicuous waste Visibly buying products and services that one never uses. (14)

Consumer behavior The totality of consumers' decisions with respect to the acquisition, consumption, and disposition of goods, services, time, and ideas by (human) decision-making units [over time]. (1)

Consumer memory A personal storehouse of knowledge about products and services, shopping, and consumption experiences. (8)

Consumer rights Protection and access to information in certain consumer-related areas that are guaranteed to consumers. (19)

Consumer socialization The process by which we learn to become consumers. (16)

Consumerism Activities of government, business, independent organizations, and consumers designed to protect the rights of consumers. (19)

Contextual effects The influence of the decision situation on the decision-making process. (10)

Continuous innovation An innovation that has a limited effect on existing consumption patterns. (17)

Corrective advertising The formal statement a company must make to correct false beliefs. (19)

Correlated associations The extent to which two or more associations linked to a schema go together. (5)

Counterarguments (CAs) Thoughts that disagree with the message. (6)

Credibility Extent to which the source is trustworthy, expert, or has status. (6)

Curtailment behaviors Activities that result in using less energy. (19)

Culture The typical or expected behaviors, norms, and ideas that characterize a group of people. (1)

Cultural categories The natural grouping of objects that reflect our culture. (18)

Cultural principles Ideas or values that specify how aspects of our culture are organized and/or how they should be perceived or evaluated. (18)

Customer retention The practice of keeping customers by building long-term relationships. (12)

Cutoff levels For each attribute, the point at which a brand is rejected with a noncompensatory model. (10)

D

Data mining Searching for patterns in the company database that offer clues to customer needs, preferences, and behaviors. (2)

Deal-prone consumers Consumers who are more likely to be influenced by price. (11)

Decay The weakening of nodes or links over time. (8)

Deception Marketing communications that leave consumers with information or beliefs that are incorrect or cannot be substantiated. (19)

Decision framing The initial reference point or anchor in the decision process. (10)

Decision making Making a selection between options or courses of action. (10)

Demand-shift behaviors Activities that use more efficient energy sources. (19)

Diagnostic information That which helps us discriminate among objects. (9)

Differential threshold/just noticeable difference (j.n.d.) The intensity difference needed between two stimuli before they are perceived to be different. (4)

Diffusion The percentage of the population that has adopted an innovation at a specific point in time. (17)

Disconfirmation The existence of a discrepancy between expectations and performance. (12)

Discontinuous innovation An offering that is so new that we have never known anything like it before. (17)

Discursive processing The processing of information as words. (8)

Disjunctive model A noncompensatory model that sets acceptable cutoffs to find options that are "good." (10)

Disposition The process by which a consumer parts with or gets rid of a possession / offering. (1, 12)

Dissatisfaction The feeling that results when consumers make a negative evaluation or are unhappy with a decision. (12)

Dissociative reference group Group we do not want to emulate. (16)

Divestment rituals Rituals enacted at the disposition stage that are designed to wipe away all traces of our personal meaning in a product. (18)

Doctrine of foreseeability The expectation that companies should be able to anticipate normal risky uses of a product/service. (19)

Dogmatism A tendency to be resistant to change or new ideas. (15)

Domain-specific values Values that may apply to only a particular area of activities. (15)

Door-in-the-face technique A technique designed to induce compliance by first asking an individual to comply with a very large and possibly outrageous request, followed by a smaller and more reasonable request. (16)

Downward mobility Losing one's social standing. (14)

Dramas Ads with characters, a plot, and a story. (7)

Dual coding The representation of a stimulus in two modalities (e.g., pictures and words) in memory. (8)

Dual-mediation hypothesis Explains how attitudes toward the ad influence brand attitudes. (7)

Dynamically continuous innovation An innovation that has a pronounced effect on consumption practices and often involves a new technology. (17)

E

Earned status Status acquired later in life through achievements. (14)

Echoic memory Very brief memory for things we hear. (8)

Efficiency behaviors Activities that result in more efficient energy usage. (19)

Elaboration Transferring information into long-term memory by processing it at deeper levels. (8)

Elimination-by-aspects model Similar to the lexicographic model but adds the notion of acceptable cutoffs. (10)

Embedded markets Markets in which the social relationships among buyers and sellers change the way the market operates. (16)

Emblematic function The use of products to symbolize membership in social groups. (18)

Emotional appeals Messages that elicit an emotional response. (6)

Emotional detachment Emotionally disposing of a possession. (12)

Encoding the evidence Processing the information experienced. (12)

Enduring involvement Interest in an offering or activity over an extended period of time. (3)

Equity theory A theory that focuses on the fairness of exchanges between individuals, which helps in understanding consumer satisfaction and dissatisfaction. (12)

Estimation of likelihood Judging how likely it is something will occur. (10)

Ethnic groups Subcultures with a similar heritage and values. (13)

Ethnographic research A technique in which researchers observe how consumers behave in real-world surroundings. (2)

Even-a-penny-will-help technique A technique designed to induce compliance by asking individuals to do a very small favor—one that is so small it almost does not qualify as a favor. (16)

Expectancy-value model A widely used model that explains how attitudes form and change. (6)

Expectations Beliefs about how a product/service will perform. (12)

Explicit memory Memory for some prior episode achieved by active attempts to remember. (8)

Exponential diffusion curve A diffusion curve characterized by rapid initial growth. (17)

Exposure The process by which the consumer comes in physical contact with a stimulus. (4)

Exposure to evidence Actually experiencing the product or service. (12)

Expressive roles Roles that involve an indication of family norms. (14)

Expressiveness function The use of products as symbols to demonstrate our uniqueness—how we stand out as different from others. (18)

Extended family The nuclear family plus relatives such as grandparents, aunts, uncles, and cousins. (14)

External search The process of collecting information from outside sources (e.g., magazines, dealers, ads). (9)

Extremeness aversion Options that are extreme on some attributes are less attractive than those with a moderate level of those attributes. (10)

F

Fad A successful innovation that has a very short product life cycle. (17)

Fairness of exchange The perception that people's inputs are equal to their outputs in an exchange. (12)

False objective claim A claim made by a company that has no validity. (19)

Family life cycle Different stages of family life depending on the age of the parents and how many children are living at home. (14)

Fashion A successful innovation that has a moderately long and potentially cyclical product life cycle. (17)

Favorability The degree to which we like or dislike something. (6)

Fear appeals Messages that stress negative consequences. (6)

Felt involvement The psychological experience of the motivated consumer. Includes psychological states such as interest, excitement, anxiety, passion, and engagement. (3)

Figure and ground According to this principle, people interpret stimuli in the context of a background. (4)

Financial risk Risk associated with monetary investment in an offering. (3)

Focus group A form of in-depth interview involving 8 to 12 people; a moderator leads the group and asks participants to discuss a product, concept, or other marketing stimulus. (2)

Foot-in-the-door technique A technique designed to induce compliance by getting an individual to agree first to a small favor, then to a larger one, and then to an even larger one. (16)

Fraudulent symbols Symbols that become so widely adopted that they lose their status. (14)

Frequency heuristic Beliefs based simply on the number of supporting arguments or amount of repetition. (7)

Functional innovation A new product, service, attribute, or idea that proved utilitarian benefits different from or better than existing alternatives. (17)

Functional needs Needs that motivate the search for products to solve consumption related problems. (3)

G

Gatekeepers Sources that control the flow of information. (16)

Gender Biological state of male or female. (13)

Generation X Individuals born between 1965 and 1976. (13)

Generation Y Mini-population explosion from the children of baby boomers. (13)

Gestation stage The first stage of gift giving, when we consider what to give someone. (18)

Global values A person's most enduring, strongly held, and abstract values that hold in many situations. (15)

Goal-derived category Things that are viewed as belonging in the same category because they serve the same goals. (5)

Goals Objectives that we would like to achieve. (3)

Graded structure The fact that category members vary in how well they represent a category. (5)

Gray market Individuals over 65. (13)

Grooming rituals Rituals we engage in to bring out or maintain the best in special products. (18)

Grouping A tendency to group stimuli to form a unified picture or impression. (4)

H

Habit Doing the same thing time after time. (11)

Habituation The process in which a stimulus loses its attention-getting abilities by virtue of its familiarity. (4)

Hedonic dimension An ad that creates positive or negative feelings. (6)

Hedonic needs Needs that relate to sensory pleasure. (3)

Hedonism The principle of pleasure seeking. (15)

Heuristic A simple rule of thumb used to make judgments or decisions. (7, 11)

Hierarchy of effects Sequential steps used in decision making involving thinking, then feeling, then behavior. (11)

High-effort hierarchy of effects A purchase of an innovation based on considerable decision-making effort. (17)

Homeless People at the low end of the status hierarchy. (14)

Homophily The overall similarity among members in the social system. (16)

Host selling A technique that features a character in a TV show in ads. (19)

Household A single person living alone or a group of individuals who live together in a common dwelling, regardless of whether they are related. (14)

Household decision roles Roles that different members play in a household decision. (14)

Husband-dominant decision Decision made primarily by the male head-of-household. (14)

Hypothesis generation Forming expectations about the product or service. (12)

Hypothesis testing Testing out expectations through experience. (12)

I

Iconic memory Very brief memory for things we see. (8)

Ideal identity schema A set of ideas about how the identity would be indicated in its ideal form. (18)

Ideal state The way we want things to be. (9)

Illusory correlation When consumers think two things occur together when they actually do not. (10)

Imagery Imagining an event in order to make a judgment. (10)

Imagery processing The processing of information in sensory form. (8)

Implicit memory Memory for things without any conscious attempt at remembering them. (8)

Impulse purchase An unexpected purchase based on a strong feeling. (11)

Incidental learning Learning that occurs from repetition rather than from conscious processing. (7)

Independent variable The "treatment" or the entity that researchers vary in a research project. (2)

Inept set Options that are unacceptable when making a decision. (10)

Inert set Options toward which consumers are indifferent. (10)

Information overload The negative effect on a decision caused by having too much information. (10)

Informational influence The extent to which sources influence consumers simply by providing information. (16)

Inherited status Status that derives from parents at birth. (14)

Inhibition The recall of one attribute inhibiting the recall of another. (9)

Innovation An offering that is perceived as new by consumers within a market segment and that has an effect on existing consumption patterns. (17)

Instrumental roles Roles that relate to tasks affecting the buying decision. (14)

Instrumental values The values needed to achieve the desired end states such as ambition and cheerfulness. (15)

Integration of evidence Combining new information with stored knowledge. (12)

Intensity of ethnic affiliation How strongly people identify with their ethnic group. (13)

Interference That which causes us not to remember which features go with which brand or concept due to semantic networks being too closely aligned. (8)

Internal search The process of recalling stored information from memory. (9)

J

Judgments Estimating or evaluating the likelihood of an event. (10)

Judgments of goodness/badness Evaluating the desirability of something. (10)

K

Knowledge content Information we already have in memory. (5)

Knowledge structure The way in which knowledge is organized. (5)

L

Law of small numbers The expectation that information obtained from a small number of people represents the larger population. (11)

Legitimacy The extent to which the innovation follows established guidelines for what seems appropriate in the category. (17)

Lexicographic model A noncompensatory model that compares brands by attributes, one at a time. (10)

Licensing A marketing strategy in which a firm sells the rights to the brand name to another company who will use the name on its product. (5)

Lifestyles People's patterns of behavior. (15)

List of Values (LOV) A survey that measures nine principal values in consumer behavior. (15)

Locus of control How people interpret why things happen (internal vs. external). (15)

Long-term memory (LTM) The part of memory where information is placed for later use; permanently stored knowledge. (8)

Low-effort hierarchy of effects A purchase of an innovation based on limited decision-making effort. (17)

M

Market maven A consumer who has and communicates considerable marketplace information to others. (16)

Market test A study in which the effectiveness of one or more elements of the marketing mix is examined by evaluating sales of the product in an actual market (e.g., a specific city). (2)

Marketer-dominated source Influence delivered from a marketing agent (e.g., advertising, personal selling). (16)

Marketing A social and managerial process by which individuals and groups obtain what they need and want through creating and exchanging products and value with others. (1)

Marketing stimuli Information about products or brands communicated by either the marketer (via ads, salespeople, brand symbols, packages, signs, prices, and so on) or nonmarketing sources (e.g., the media, word of mouth). (4)

Match-up hypothesis The idea that the source must be appropriate for the product/service. (6)

Materialism Placing importance on money and material goods. (15)

Means-ends chain analysis A technique that helps us understand how values link to attributes in products and services. (15)

Mere exposure effect When familiarity leads to liking an object. (7)

Middle class Primarily white-collar workers. (14)

Miscomprehension Inaccurate understanding of a message. (5)

Modernity The extent to which consumers in the social system have positive attitudes toward change. (17)

Motivated reasoning. Consumers process information in a way that allows them to reach a particular conclusion they want to reach. (3)

Motivation An inner state of arousal that denotes energy to achieve a goal. (3)

Multiattribute (expectancy-value) model A type of brand-based compensatory model. (10)

Multibrand loyalty Buying two or more brands repeatedly because of a strong preference. (11)

Multicultural marketing Strategies used to appeal to a variety of cultures at the same time. (13)

Mystery ad An ad in which the brand is not identified until the end of the message. (7)

N

NAD/NARB system A system set up by the National Advertising Division to self-regulate advertising messages. (19)

National character The personality of a country. (15)

Need for cognition (NFC) A trait that describes how much people like to think. (15)

Need for uniqueness (NFU) The desire for novelty through the purchase, use, and disposition of products and services. (15)

Needs An internal state of tension caused by disequilibrium from an ideal/desired physical or psychological state. (3)

Negative word-of-mouth communication The act of consumers saying negative things about a product or service to other consumers. (12)

Noncomparable decisions The process of making decisions from products or services from different categories. (10)

Noncompensatory model Simple decision model in which negative information leads to rejection of the option. (10)

Non-marketer-dominated source Influence delivered from an entity outside a marketing organization (e.g., friends, family, the media). (16)

Normative choice tactics Low elaboration decision making that is based on others' opinions. (11)

Normative influences How other people influence our behavior through social pressure. (6)

Norms Collective decisions about what constitutes appropriate behavior. (16)

Nuclear family Father, mother, and children. (14)

O

Objective comprehension The extent to which the receiver accurately understands the message a sender intended to communicate. (5)

Offering A product, service, activity, or idea offered by a marketing organization to consumers. (1)

One-sided message A marketing message that presents only positive information. (6)

Ongoing search A search that occurs regularly, regardless of whether the consumer is making a choice. (9)

Online processing The ability of consumers to process an ad as they are viewing it. (9)

Operant conditioning The view that behavior is a function of the reinforcements and punishments received in the past. (11)

Opinion leader An individual who acts as an information broker between the mass media and the opinions and behaviors of an individual or group. (16)

Optimal stimulation level (OSL) The level of arousal that is most comfortable for an individual in any given situation. (11)

Overprivileged Families with an income higher than the average in their class. (14)

P

Parody display Status symbols that start in the lower classes and move upward. (14)

Passive (incidental) learning Low-level learning that occurs through repetition. (11)

Perceived risk The extent to which the consumer is uncertain about the consequences of an action (e.g., buying, using, or disposing of an offering). (3)

Perception The process by which incoming stimuli activate our sensory receptors (eyes, ears, taste buds, skin, and so on). (4)

Perceptual organization The process by which stimuli are organized into meaningful units. (4)

Performance risk Uncertainty about whether the offering will perform as expected. (3)

Performance The measurement of whether the product/service actually fulfills consumers' needs. (12)

Performance-related tactics Tactics based on benefits, features, or evaluations of the brand. (11)

Peripheral cues Easily processed aspects of a message such as music, an attractive source or picture, or humor. (7)

Peripheral route to persuasion Aspects other than key message arguments that are used to influence attitudes. (7)

Peripheral-route processing The attitude formation and change process when effort is low. (6)

Personal relevance Something that has a direct bearing on the self and has potentially significant consequences or implications for our lives. (3)

Personality An internal characteristic that determines how individuals behave in various situations. (15)

Physical (or safety) risk The potential harm that an offering might pose to one's safety. (3)

Physical detachment Physically disposing of an item. (12)

Possession rituals Rituals we engage in when we first acquire a product that help to make it "ours." (18)

Postcard scheme A deceptive practice in which a consumer receives a postcard that claims he or she has won a valuable prize but that is really a front for intensive selling pressure. (19)

Post-decision dissonance A feeling of anxiety over whether the correct decision was made. (12)

Post-decision feelings Positive or negative emotions experienced while using the products or services. (12)

Post-decision regret A feeling that one has made the wrong purchase decision. (12)

Preattentive processing The nonconscious processing of stimuli in peripheral vision. (4)

Prepurchase search A search that occurs to aid a specific decision. (9)

Presentation stage The second stage of gift giving, when we actually give the gift. (18)

Price-related tactics Tactics based on price or cost. (11)

Primacy effect The tendency to show greater memory for information that comes first in a sequence. (8)

Primary data Data originating from a researcher and collected to provide information relevant to a specific research project. (2)

Primary reference group Group with whom we have physical (face-to-face) interaction. (16)

Priming Activation of a node in memory, often without conscious awareness. (8)

Problem recognition The perceived difference between an actual and an ideal state. (9)

Product life cycle A concept that suggests that products go through an initial introductory period followed by periods of sales growth, maturity, and decline. (17)

Profane things Things that are ordinary and hence have no special power. (18)

Prominence The intensity of stimuli that causes them to stand out relative to the environment. (4)

Prototype The best example of the category. (5)

Psychographics A description of consumers on the basis of their psychological and behavioral characteristics. (15)

Psychological risk Risk associated with the extent to which the offering fits with the way consumers perceive themselves. (3)

Puffery The exaggerated claims made by companies that are not generally believed by consumers. (19)

R

Reactance Doing the opposite of what the individual or group wants us to do. (16)

Recall The ability to retrieve information from memory. (8)

Recency effect The tendency to show greater memory for information that comes last in a sequence. (8)

Recirculation The process by which information is remembered via simple repetition without active rehearsal. (8)

Recognition The process of determining whether a stimulus has or has not been encountered before. (8)

Reference group A group of people we compare ourselves to for information regarding behavior, attitudes, or values. (1)

Reflexive evaluation Feedback from others that tells us whether we are fulfilling the role correctly. (18)

Reformulation stage The final stage of gift giving, when we reevaluate the relationship based on the gift-giving experience. (18)

Rehearsal The process of actively reviewing material in an attempt to remember it. (8)

Relative advantage Benefits in an innovation superior to those found in existing products. (17)

Representativeness heuristic Making a judgment by simply comparing a stimulus to the category prototype or exemplar. (11)

Research foundation A nonprofit organization that sponsors research on topics relevant to the foundation's goals. (2)

Resistance A desire not to buy the innovation, even in the face of pressure to do so. (17)

Response involvement Interest in certain decisions and behaviors. (3)

Retrieval cue Stimulus that facilitates a node's activation in memory. (8)

Retrieval The process of remembering. (8)

Rokeach Value Survey (RVS) A survey that measures instrumental and terminal values. (15)

Role acquisition function The use of products as symbols to help us feel more comfortable in a new role. (18)

S

Sacred entities People, things, and places that are set apart, revered, worshiped, and treated with great respect. (18)

Salient attributes Attributes that are "top of mind" or more important. (9)

Satisfaction The feeling that results when consumers make a positive evaluation or feel happy with their decision. (12)

Satisfice Finding a brand that satisfies a need even though the brand may not be the best brand. (11)

Schema The set of associations linked to a concept. (5, 7)

Script A special type of schema that represents knowledge of a sequence of events. (5)

Searching by attribute Comparing brands on attributes, one at a time. (9)

Searching by brand Collecting information on one brand before moving to another. (9)

Secondary data Data collected for some other purpose that is subsequently used in a research project. (2)

Secondary reference group Group with whom we do not have direct contact. (16)

Self-concept Our mental view of who we are. (3)

Self-referencing Relating a message to one's own experience or self-image. (7)

Semantic (or associative) network A set of associations in memory that are linked to a concept. (8)

Semantic memory Knowledge about an entity that is detached from specific episodes. (8)

Sensation seekers Those who actively look for variety. (11)

Sensory memory Sensory experiences stored temporarily in memory. (8)

Sexual orientation A person's preference toward certain behaviors. (13)

Shaping Leading consumers through a series of steps to create a desired response. (11)

Short-term memory (STM) The portion of memory where incoming information is encoded or interpreted in light of existing knowledge. (8)

Simple inferences Beliefs based on peripheral cues. (7)

Situational involvement Temporary interest in an offering or activity, often caused by situational circumstances. (3)

Sleeper effect Consumers forget the source of a message more quickly than they forget the message. (6)

Social class fragmentation The disappearance of class distinctions. (14)

Social class hierarchy The grouping of members of society according to status (high to low). (14)

Social comparison theory A theory that proposes that individuals have a drive to compare themselves to other people. (20)

Social influences Information by and pressures from individuals, groups, and the mass media that affect how a person behaves. (16)

Social relevance The extent to which an innovation can be observed or the extent to which having others observe it has social cachet. (17)

Social risk Potential harm to one's social standing that may arise from buying, using, or disposing of an offering. (3)

Source derogations (SDs) Thoughts that discount or attack the source of the message. (6)

Spreading of activation Strong semantic links between concepts. (8)

S-shaped diffusion curve A diffusion curve characterized by slow initial growth followed by a rapid increase in diffusion. (17)

Status crystallization When consumers are consistent across indicators of social class (income, education, occupation, etc.). (14)

Status float Trends that start in the lower and middle classes and move upward. (14)

Status panic The inability of children to reach their parents' level of social status. (14)

Status symbols Products or services that tell others about someone's social class standing. (14)

Storytelling A research method by which consumers are asked to tell stories about product acquisition, usage, or disposition experiences. These stories help marketers gain insights into consumer needs and identify the product attributes that meet these needs. (2)

Strong argument A presentation that features the best or central merits of an offering in a convincing manner. (6)

Subjective comprehension Reflects what we think we know, whether or not it is -accurate. (5)

Subjective norms (SN) How others feel about us doing something. (6)

Subliminal perception The activation of sensory receptors by stimuli presented below the perceptual threshold. (4)

Subordinate level A level of categorization below the basic level that contains objects in very finely differentiated categories. (5)

Substantiation Having to prove questionable claims. (19)

Superordinate level The broadest level of category organization containing different objects that share few associations but are still members of the category. (5)

Support arguments (SAs) Thoughts that agree with the message. (6)

Survey A written instrument that asks consumers to respond to a predetermined set of research questions. (2)

Symbolic innovations A product, service, attribute, or idea that has new social meaning. (17)

Symbolic needs Needs that relate to how we perceive ourselves, how we are perceived by others, how we relate to others, and the esteem in which we are held by others. (3)

Symbols External signs that we use to express our identity. (1)

Syncratic decision Decision made jointly by the husband and wife. (14)

T

Taxonomic category An orderly classification of objects, with similar objects in the same category. (5)

Terminal values A highly desired end states such as social recognition and pleasure. (15)

Theory of reasoned action (TORA) A model that provides an explanation of how, when, and why attitudes predict behavior. (6)

Tie-strength The extent to which a close, intimate relationship connects people. (16)

Time risk Uncertainties over the length of time consumers must invest in buying, using, or disposing of the offering. (3)

Trace strength The extent to which an association (or link) is strongly or weakly linked to a concept in memory. (8)

Trade group A professional organization made up of marketers in the same industry. (2)

Transformational advertising Ads that try to increase emotional involvement with the product or service. (7)

Trialability The extent to which an innovation can be tried on a limited basis before it is adopted. (17)

Trickle-down effect Trends that start in the upper classes and then are copied by lower classes. (14)

Truth effect When consumers believe a statement simply because it has been repeated a number of times. (7)

Two-sided message A marketing message that presents both positive and negative information. (6)

U

Underprivileged Families below the average income in their class. (14)

Upper class The aristocracy, new social elite, and the upper-middle class. (14)

Upward mobility Raising one's status level. (14)

Usage The process by which a consumer uses an offering. (1)

Use innovativeness Using products in new ways. (11)

Utilitarian (functional) dimension An ad that is informative. (6)

V

Valence Whether information about something is good (positive valence) or bad (negative valence). (16)

Value segmentation The grouping of consumers by common values. (15)

Value system Our total set of values and their relative importance. (15)

VALS (Values and Lifestyle Survey) A psychographic tool that measures demographic, value, attitude, and lifestyle variables. (15)

Values Enduring beliefs about what is good or appropriate. (3, 15)

Variable The entity that is studied or that varies in a research project. In a study on how humor in ads influences attitudes toward a brand, one variable might be the level of humor in the ads. (2)

Variety seeking Trying something different. (11)

Vicarious exploration Seeking information simply for stimulation. (11)

Viral marketing Online consumer-to-consumer communication that supports a particular offering. (16)

W

Wearout Becoming bored with a stimulus. (7)

Weber's Law The stronger the initial stimulus, the greater the additional intensity needed for the second stimulus to be perceived as different. (4)

Wife-dominant decision Decision made primarily by the female head-of-household. (14)

Word of mouth Information about products or services that is communicated verbally. (12, 16)

Working class Primarily blue-collar workers. (14)

Y

Young again Individuals age 50 to around 65. (13)

Z

Zapping Use of a remote control to switch channels during commercial breaks. (4)

Zipping Fast-forwarding through the commercials recorded on a VCR. (4)

Zone of acceptance The acceptable range of prices for any purchase decision. (11)